Oxford German Mini Dictionary

FIFTH EDITION

German–English
English–German

Deutsch–Englisch
Englisch–Deutsch

OXFORD
UNIVERSITY PRESS

Great Clarendon Street, Oxford OX2 6DP

Oxford University Press is a department of the University of Oxford.
It furthers the University's objective of excellence in research, scholarship, and education by publishing worldwide in

Oxford New York

Auckland Cape Town Dar es Salaam Hong Kong Karachi Kuala Lumpur Madrid Melbourne Mexico City Nairobi New Delhi Shanghai Taipei Toronto

With offices in
Argentina Austria Brazil Chile Czech Republic France Greece Guatemala Hungary Italy Japan South Korea Poland Portugal Singapore Switzerland Thailand Turkey Ukraine Vietnam

Oxford is a registered trade mark of Oxford University Press in the UK and in certain other countries

First edition published 1993
Second edition published 1997
Third edition published 2002
Fourth edition published 2005
This edition published 2008. Reissued in new binding 2011

British Library Cataloguing in Publication Data
Data available

Library of Congress Cataloging in Publication Data
Data available

ISBN 978-0-19-969266-8

10 9 8 7 6 5 4 3 2 1

Typeset by Interactive Sciences Ltd, Gloucester
Printed and bound in Italy by Legoprint S.p.A.

6365529163036014

Contents

Preface

This new edition of the Oxford German Mini Dictionary provides a handy and up-to-date reference work for tourists, students, and business people. It fully reflects recent changes to the spelling of German.

The dictionary also includes an easy-to-use Phrasefinder, which groups together essential phrases you will need for everyday conversation. The section is thematically arranged and covers key topics including: going places, keeping in touch, food and drink, places to stay, shopping and money, sports and leisure, time and dates, and conversion charts.

Proprietary terms

This dictionary includes some words which are, or are asserted to be, proprietary names or trademarks. Their inclusion does not imply that they have acquired for legal purposes a non-proprietary or general significance, nor is any other judgement implied concerning their legal status. In cases where the editor has some evidence that a word is used as a proprietary name or trademark this is indicated by the symbol ®, but no judgement concerning the legal status of such words is made or implied thereby.

Symbols used in this dictionary

familiar	[!]	familiär
slang	[x]	Slang
old spelling	*	alte Schreibung
proprietary term	®	Markenzeichen

List of contributors

Fifth Edition

Editors
Joanna Rubery
Nicholas Rollin

Supplementary Material
Eva Vennebusch
Inge Milfull

Fourth Edition

Editors
Nicholas Rollin
Roswitha Morris
Eva Vennebusch

Data Capture
Susan Wilkin
Anne McConnell

Proof-reading
Katrin Thier
Stephen Curtis

Third Edition

Editors
Gunhild Prowe
Jill Schneider

Second Edition

Editors
Roswitha Morris
Robin Sawers

Supplementary Material
Robin Sawers
Neil and Roswitha Morris
Valerie Grundy
Eva Vennebusch

First Edition

Editors
Gunhild Prowe
Jill Schneider

Introduction

The text of this dictionary reflects changes to the spelling of German ratified in July 1996. The symbol * has been introduced to refer from the old spelling to the new, preferred one:

As* *nt* **-ses, -se** *s.* **Ass**
dasein* *vi sep (sein)* **da-sein**, *s.* **da**
Schiffahrt* *f s.* **Schifffahrt**

Where both the old and new forms are valid, an equals sign = is used to refer to the preferred form:

aufwändig *adj* = **aufwendig**
Tunfisch *m* = **Thunfisch**

When such forms follow each other alphabetically, they are given with commas, with the preferred form in first place:

Panther, Panter *m* **-s, -** panther

In phrases, od (oder) is used:

...deine(r,s) *poss pron* yours;
die D~en *od* **d~en** *pl* your family *sg*

On the English–German side, only the preferred German form is given.

- A swung dash ~ represents the headword or that part of the headword preceding a vertical bar |. The initial letter of a German headword is given to show whether or not it is a capital.
- The vertical bar | precedes the part of the headword which is not repeated in compounds or derivatives.
- Square brackets [ ] are used for optional material.
- Parentheses are used after a verb translation to indicate the object; before a verb translation to indicate the subject; before an adjective to indicate a typical noun which it qualifies.

- Parentheses are also used for field or style labels (see the inside covers), and for explanatory matter.
- A bold bullet indicates a new part of speech within an entry.
- *od* (oder) and *or* denote that words or portions of a phrase are synonymous. An oblique stroke / is used where there is a difference in usage or meaning.
- ≈ is used where no exact equivalent exists in the other language.
- A dagger † indicates that a German verb is irregular and that the parts can be found in the verb table on pages 604–608. Compound verbs are not listed there as they follow the pattern of the basic verb.
- The stressed vowel is marked in a German headword by _ (long) or . (short). A phonetic transcription is only given for words which do not follow the normal rules of pronunciation. A guide to German pronunciation rules can be found on pages ix–x.
- Phonetics are given for all English headwords. In blocks of compounds, if no stress is shown, it falls on the first element.
- A change in pronunciation or stress shown within a block of compounds applies only to that particular word (subsequent entries revert to the pronunciation and stress of the headword).
- German headword nouns are followed by the gender and, with the exception of compound nouns, by the genitive and plural. These are only given at compound nouns if they present some difficulty. Otherwise the user should refer to the final element.
- Nouns that decline like adjectives are entered as follows: **-e(r)** *m/f*, **-e(s)** *nt*.
- Adjectives which have no undeclined form are entered in the feminine form with the masculine and neuter in brackets **-e(r,s)**.
- The reflexive pronoun sich is accusative unless marked (*dat*).

Phonetic symbols used for German words

a	Hand	hant	ŋ	lang	laŋ
a:	Bahn	ba:n	o	Moral	mo'ra:l
ɐ	Ober	'o:bɐ	o:	Boot	bo:t
ɐ̯	Uhr	u:ɐ̯	o̯	loyal	lo̯a'ja:l
ã	Conférencier	kõferã'si̯e:	õ	Konkurs	kõ'kʊrs
ã:	Abonnement	abɔnə'mã:	õ:	Ballon	ba'lõ:
a͜i	weit	va͜it	ɔ	Post	pɔst
a͜u	Haut	ha͜ut	ø	Ökonom	øko'no:m
b	Ball	bal	ø:	Öl	ø:l
ç	ich	ɪç	œ	göttlich	'gœtlɪç
d	dann	dan	ɔ͜y	heute	'hɔ͜ytə
d͜ʒ	Gin	d͜ʒɪn	p	Pakt	pakt
e	Metall	me'tal	r	Rast	rast
e:	Beet	be:t	s	Hast	hast
ɛ	mästen	'mɛstən	ʃ	Schal	ʃa:l
ɛ:	wählen	'vɛ:lən	t	Tal	ta:l
ɛ̃	Cousin	ku'zɛ̃:	t͜s	Zahl	t͜sa:l
ə	Nase	'na:zə	tʃ	Couch	ka͜utʃ
f	Faß	fas	u	Kupon	ku'põ:
g	Gast	gast	u:	Hut	hu:t
h	haben	'ha:bən	u̯	aktuell	ak'tu̯ɛl
i	Rivale	ri'va:lə	ʊ	Pult	pʊlt
i:	viel	fi:l	v	was	vas
i̯	Aktion	ak't͜si̯o:n	x	Bach	bax
ɪ	Birke	'bɪrkə	y	Physik	fy'zi:k
j	ja	ja:	y:	Rübe	'ry:bə
k	kalt	kalt	y̌	Nuance	'ny̌ã:sə
l	Last	last	ʏ	Fülle	'fʏlə
m	Mast	mast	z	Nase	'na:zə
n	Naht	na:t	ʒ	Regime	re'ʒi:m

ʔ Glottal stop, e.g. Koordination /koʔɔrdina't͜si̯on/.
: length sign after a vowel, e.g. Chrom /kro:m/.
' Stress mark before stressed syllable, e.g. Balkon/bal'kõ:/.

Guide to German pronunciation

Consonants

Pronounced as in English with the following exceptions:

b	as	p	*at the end of a word or syllable*
d	as	t	
g	as	k	
ch	as in Scottish lo<u>ch</u>		*after a, o, u, au*
	like an exaggerated h as in <u>h</u>uge		*after i, e, ä, ö, ü, eu, ei*
-chs	as	x	(as in bo<u>x</u>)
-ig	as	-ich / ıç /	*when a suffix*
j	as	y	(as in <u>y</u>es)
ps			the p is pronounced
pn			
qu	as	k + v	
s	as	z	(as in <u>z</u>ero) *at the beginning of a word*
	as	s	(as in bu<u>s</u>) *at the end of a word or syllable, before a consonant (except p and t), or when doubled*
sch	as	sh	
sp	as	shp	*at the beginning of a word or syllable*
st	as	sht	*at the beginning of a word or syllable*
v	as	f	(as in <u>f</u>or)
	as	v	(as in <u>v</u>ery) *within a word*
w	as	v	(as in <u>v</u>ery)
z	as	ts	

Vowels

Approximately as follows:

a	short	as	u	(as in but)
	long	as	a	(as in car)
e	short	as	e	(as in pen)
	long	as	a	(as in paper)
i	short	as	i	(as in bit)
	long	as	ee	(as in queen)
o	short	as	o	(as in hot)
	long	as	o	(as in pope)
u	short	as	oo	(as in foot)
	long	as	oo	(as in boot)

Vowels are always short before a double consonant, and long when followed by an h or when double

ie	is pronounced	ee	(as in keep)

Diphthongs

au	as	ow	(as in how)
ei ai	as	y	(as in my)
eu äu	as	oy	(as in boy)

Die für das Englische verwendeten Zeichen der Lautschrift

ɑ:	barn	bɑ:n	l	lot	lɒt
ɑ̃	nuance	'nju:ɑ̃s	m	mat	mæt
æ	fat	fæt	n	not	nɒt
æ̃	lingerie	'læ̃ʒərɪ	ŋ	sing	sɪŋ
aɪ	fine	faɪn	ɒ	got	gɒt
aʊ	now	naʊ	ɔ:	paw	pɔ:
b	bat	bæt	ɔɪ	boil	bɔɪl
d	dog	dɒg	p	pet	pet
dʒ	jam	dʒæm	r	rat	ræt
e	met	met	s	sip	sɪp
eɪ	fate	feɪt	ʃ	ship	ʃɪp
eə	fairy	'feərɪ	t	tip	tɪp
əʊ	goat	gəʊt	tʃ	chin	tʃɪn
ə	ago	ə'gəʊ	θ	thin	θɪn
ɜ:	fur	fɜ:(r)	ð	the	ðə
f	fat	fæt	u:	boot	bu:t
g	good	gʊd	ʊ	book	bʊk
h	hat	hæt	ʊə	tourism	'tʊərɪzm
ɪ	bit, happy	bɪt, 'hæpɪ	ʌ	dug	dʌg
ɪə	near	nɪə(r)	v	van	væn
i:	meet	mi:t	w	win	wɪn
j	yet	jet	z	zip	zɪp
k	kit	kɪt	ʒ	vision	'vɪʒn

: bezeichnet Länge des vorhergehenden Vokals, z. B. boot /bu:t/.

' Betonung, steht unmittelbar vor einer betonten Silbe, z. B. ago /ə'gəʊ/.

(r) Ein „r" in runden Klammern wird nur gesprochen, wenn im Textzusammenhang ein Vokal unmittelbar folgt, z. B. fire /'faɪə(r)/; fire at /'faɪər æt/.

Pronunciation of the alphabet/ Aussprache des Alphabets

English/Englisch		*German/Deutsch*
eɪ	**a**	a:
bi:	**b**	be:
si:	**c**	t͜se:
di:	**d**	de:
i:	**e**	e:
ef	**f**	ɛf
dʒi:	**g**	ge:
eɪtʃ	**h**	ha:
aɪ	**i**	i:
dʒeɪ	**j**	jɔt
keɪ	**k**	ka:
el	**l**	ɛl
em	**m**	ɛm
en	**n**	ɛn
əʊ	**o**	o:
pi:	**p**	pe:
kju:	**q**	ku:
a:(r)	**r**	ɛr
es	**s**	ɛs
ti:	**t**	te:
ju:	**u**	u:
vi:	**v**	fau
'dʌblju:	**w**	ve:
eks	**x**	ɪks
waɪ	**y**	'ʏpsilɔn
zed	**z**	tsɛt
eɪ umlaut	**ä**	ɛ:
əʊ umlaut	**ö**	ø:
ju: umlaut	**ü**	y:
es'zed	**ß**	ɛs'tsɛt

Aa

Aal *m* **-[e]s,-e** eel
Aas *nt* **-es** carrion; ☒ swine
ab *prep* (+ *dat*) from ● *adv* off; (*weg*) away; (*auf Fahrplan*) departs; **ab und zu** now and then; **auf und ab** up and down
abändern *vt sep* alter; (*abwandeln*) modify
Abbau *m* dismantling; (*Kohlen-*) mining. **a~en** *vt sep* dismantle; mine (*Kohle*)
abbeißen† *vt sep* bite off
abbeizen *vt sep* strip
abberufen† *vt sep* recall
abbestellen *vt sep* cancel; **jdn a~** put s.o. off
abbiegen† *vi sep* (*sein*) turn off; **[nach] links a~** turn left
Abbildung *f* **-,-en** illustration
abblättern *vi sep* (*sein*) flake off
abblend|en *vt/i sep* (*haben*) **[die Scheinwerfer] a~en** dip one's headlights. **A~licht** *nt* dipped headlights *pl*
abbrechen† *v sep* ● *vt* break off; (*abreißen*) demolish; (*Computer*) cancel ● *vi* (*sein/haben*) break off
abbrennen† *v sep* ● *vt* burn off; (*niederbrennen*) burn down ● *vi* (*sein*) burn down
abbringen† *vt sep* dissuade (**von** from)
Abbruch *m* demolition; (*Beenden*) breaking off
abbuchen *vt sep* debit
abbürsten *vt sep* brush down; (*entfernen*) brush off
abdanken *vi sep* (*haben*) resign; (*Herrscher:*) abdicate
abdecken *vt sep* uncover; (*abnehmen*) take off; (*zudecken*) cover; **den Tisch a~** clear the table
abdichten *vt sep* seal
abdrehen *vt sep* turn off
Abdruck *m* (*pl* **⸚e**) impression. **a~en** *vt sep* print
abdrücken *vt/i sep* (*haben*) fire; **sich a~** leave an impression
Abend *m* **-s,-e** evening; **am A~** in the evening; **heute A~** this evening, tonight; **gestern A~** yesterday evening, last night. **A~brot** *nt* supper. **A~essen** *nt* dinner; (*einfacher*) supper. **A~mahl** *nt* (*Relig*) [Holy] Communion. **a~s** *adv* in the evening
Abenteuer *nt* **-s,-** adventure; (*Liebes-*) affair. **a~lich** *adj* fantastic
aber *conj* but; **oder a~** or else ● *adv* (*wirklich*) really
Aber|glaube *m* superstition. **a~gläubisch** *adj* superstitious
abfahr|en† *v sep* ● *vi* (*sein*) leave; (*Auto:*) drive off ● *vt* take away; (*entlangfahren*) drive along; use (*Fahrkarte*); **abgefahrene Reifen** worn tyres. **A~t** *f* departure; (*Talfahrt*) descent; (*Piste*) run; (*Ausfahrt*) exit
Abfall *m* refuse, rubbish; (*auf der Straße*) litter; (*Industrie-*) waste
abfallen† *vi sep* (*sein*) drop, fall; (*übrig bleiben*) be left (**für** for); (*sich neigen*) slope away. **a~d** *adj* sloping
Abfallhaufen *m* rubbish-dump
abfällig *adj* disparaging
abfangen† *vt sep* intercept
abfärben *vi sep* (*haben*) (*Farbe:*)

run; (*Stoff:*) not be colour-fast

abfassen *vt sep* draft

abfertigen *vt sep* attend to; (*zollamtlich*) clear; **jdn kurz a~** [!] give s.o. short shrift

abfeuern *vt sep* fire

abfind|en† *vt sep* pay off; (*entschädigen*) compensate; **sich a~en mit** come to terms with. **A~ung** *f* **-,-en** compensation

abfliegen† *vi sep* (*sein*) fly off; (*Aviat*) take off

abfließen† *vi sep* (*sein*) drain *or* run away

Abflug *m* (*Aviat*) departure

Abfluss *m* drainage; (*Öffnung*) drain. **A~rohr** *nt* drain-pipe

abfragen *vt sep* **jdn** *od* **jdm Vokabeln a~** test s.o. on vocabulary

Abfuhr *f* - removal; (*fig*) rebuff

abführ|en *vt sep* take *or* lead away. **A~mittel** *nt* laxative

abfüllen *vt sep* **auf** *od* **in Flaschen a~** bottle

Abgase *ntpl* exhaust fumes

abgeben† *vt sep* hand in; (*abliefern*) deliver; (*verkaufen*) sell; (*zur Aufbewahrung*) leave; (*Fußball*) pass; (*ausströmen*) give off; (*abfeuern*) fire; (*verlauten lassen*) give; cast (*Stimme*); **jdm etw a~** give s.o. a share of sth

abgehen† *v sep* ● *vi* (*sein*) leave; (*Theat*) exit; (*sich lösen*) come off; (*abgezogen werden*) be deducted ● *vt* walk along

abgehetzt *adj* harassed. **abgelegen** *adj* remote. **abgeneigt** *adj* **etw** (*dat*) **nicht abgeneigt sein** not be averse to sth. **abgenutzt** *adj* worn. **Abgeordnete(r)** *m/f* deputy; (*Pol*) Member of Parliament. **abgepackt** *adj* pre-packed

abgeschieden *adj* secluded

abgeschlossen *adj* (*fig*) complete; (*Wohnung*) self-contained.

abgesehen *prep* apart (from **von**).

abgespannt *adj* exhausted. **abgestanden** *adj* stale. **abgestorben** *adj* dead; (*Glied*) numb. **abgetragen** *adj* worn. **abgewetzt** *adj* threadbare

abgewinnen† *vt sep* win (**jdm** from s.o.); **etw** (*dat*) **Geschmack a~** get a taste for sth

abgewöhnen *vt sep* **jdm/sich das Rauchen a~** cure s.o. of/give up smoking

abgießen† *vt sep* pour off; drain (*Gemüse*)

Abgott *m* idol

abgöttisch *adv* **a~ lieben** idolize

abgrenz|en *vt sep* divide off; (*fig*) define. **A~ung** *f* - demarcation

Abgrund *m* abyss; (*fig*) depths *pl*

abgucken *vt sep* [!] copy

Abguss *m* cast

abhacken *vt sep* chop off

abhaken *vt sep* tick off

abhalten† *vt sep* keep off; (*hindern*) keep, prevent (**von** from); (*veranstalten*) hold

abhanden *adv* **a~ kommen** get lost

Abhandlung *f* treatise

Abhang *m* slope

abhängen[1] *vt sep* (*reg*) take down; (*abkuppeln*) uncouple

abhäng|en[2]† *vi sep* (*haben*) depend (**von** on). **a~ig** *adj* dependent (**von** on). **A~igkeit** *f* - dependence

abhärten *vt sep* toughen up

abheben† *v sep* ● *vt* take off; (*vom Konto*) withdraw; **sich a~** stand out (**gegen** against) ● *vi* (*haben*) (*Cards*) cut [the cards]; (*Aviat*) take off; (*Rakete:*) lift off

abheften *vt sep* file

Abhilfe *f* remedy

abholen *vt sep* collect

abhör|en *vt sep* listen to; (*überwachen*) tap; **jdn** *od* **jdm Vokabeln a~en** test s.o. on vocabulary. **A~gerät** *nt* bugging device

Abitur *nt* **-s** ≈ A levels *pl*

> **Abitur** The *Abitur*, or *Matura* in Austria, is the final exam taken by pupils at a ▷**GYMNASIUM** or comprehensive school. The result is based on continuous assessment during the last two years before the *Abitur*, plus examinations in four subjects. The *Abitur* is an obligatory qualification for university entrance.

abkaufen *vt sep* buy (*dat* from)

abklingen† *vi sep* (*sein*) die away; (*nachlassen*) subside

abkochen *vt sep* boil

abkommen† *vi sep* (*sein*) **a~ von** stray from; (*aufgeben*) give up. **A~** *nt* **-s,-** agreement

Abkömmling *m* **-s,-e** descendant

abkratzen *vt sep* scrape off

abkühlen *vt/i sep* (*sein*) cool; **sich a~** cool [down]

Abkunft *f* **-** origin

abkuppeln *vt sep* uncouple

abkürz|en *vt sep* shorten; abbreviate (*Wort*). **A~ung** *f* short cut; (*Wort*) abbreviation

abladen† *vt sep* unload

Ablage *f* shelf; (*für Akten*) tray

ablager|n *vt sep* deposit. **A~ung** *f* **-,-en** deposit

ablassen† *vt sep* drain [off]; let off (*Dampf*)

Ablauf *m* drain; (*Verlauf*) course; (*Ende*) end; (*einer Frist*) expiry. **a~en**† *v sep* ● *vi* (*sein*) run *or* drain off; (*verlaufen*) go off; (*enden*) expire; (*Zeit:*) run out; (*Uhrwerk:*) run down ● *vt* walk along; (*absuchen*) scour (**nach** for)

ableg|en *v sep* ● *vt* put down; discard (*Karte*); (*abheften*) file; (*ausziehen*) take off; sit, take (*Prüfung*); **abgelegte Kleidung** cast-offs *pl* ● *vi* (*haben*) take off one's coat; (*Naut*) cast off. **A~er** *m* **-s,-** (*Bot*) cutting; (*Schössling*) shoot

ablehn|en *vt sep* refuse; (*missbilligen*) reject. **A~ung** *f* **-,-en** refusal; rejection

ableit|en *vt sep* divert; **sich a~en** be derived (**von**/**aus** from). **A~ung** *f* derivation; (*Wort*) derivative

ablenk|en *vt sep* deflect; divert (*Aufmerksamkeit*). **A~ung** *f* **-,-en** distraction

ablesen† *vt sep* read

ablicht|en *vt sep* photocopy. **A~ung** *f* photocopy

abliefern *vt sep* deliver

ablös|en *vt sep* detach; (*abwechseln*) relieve; **sich a~en** come off; (*sich abwechseln*) take turns. **A~ung** *f* relief

abmach|en *vt sep* remove; (*ausmachen*) arrange; (*vereinbaren*) agree. **A~ung** *f* **-,-en** agreement

abmager|n *vi sep* (*sein*) lose weight. **A~ungskur** *f* slimming diet

abmelden *vt sep* cancel; **sich a~** (*im Hotel*) check out; (*Computer*) log off

abmessen† *vt sep* measure

abmühen (sich) *vr sep* struggle

Abnäher *m* **-s,-** dart

abnehm|en† *v sep* ● *vt* take off, remove; pick up (*Hörer*); **jdm etw a~en** take/(*kaufen*) buy sth from s.o. ● *vi* (*haben*) decrease; (*nachlassen*) decline; (*Person:*) lose weight; (*Mond:*) wane. **A~er** *m* **-s,-** buyer

a

Abneigung *f* dislike (**gegen** of)
abnorm *adj* abnormal
abnutz|en *vt sep* wear out. **A~ung** *f* - wear [and tear]
Abon|nement /abɔnəˈmã:/ *nt* **-s,-s** subscription. **A~nent** *m* **-en, -en** subscriber. **a~nieren** *vt* take out a subscription to
Abordnung *f* **-,-en** deputation
abpassen *vt sep* wait for; **gut a~** time well
abraten† *vi sep* (*haben*) **jdm von etw a~** advise s.o. against sth
abräumen *vt/i* (*haben*) clear away
abrechn|en *v sep* ●*vt* deduct ●*vi* (*haben*) settle up. **A~ung** *f* settlement; (*Rechnung*) account
Abreise *f* departure. **a~n** *vi sep* (*sein*) leave
abreißen† *v sep* ●*vt* tear off; (*demolieren*) pull down ●*vi* (*sein*) come off
abrichten *vt sep* train
Abriss *m* demolition; (*Übersicht*) summary
abrufen† *vt sep* call away; (*Computer*) retrieve
abrunden *vt sep* round off
abrüst|en *vi sep* (*haben*) disarm. **A~ung** *f* disarmament
abrutschen *vi sep* (*sein*) slip
Absage *f* **-,-n** cancellation; (*Ablehnung*) refusal. **a~n** *v sep* ●*vt* cancel ●*vi* (*haben*) **[jdm] a~n** cancel an appointment [with s.o.]; (*auf Einladung*) refuse [s.o.'s invitation]
Absatz *m* heel; (*Abschnitt*) paragraph; (*Verkauf*) sale
abschaff|en *vt sep* abolish; get rid of (*Auto, Hund*)
abschalten *vt/i sep* (*haben*) switch off
Abscheu *m* - revulsion
abscheulich *adj* revolting
abschicken *vt sep* send off
Abschied *m* **-[e]s,-e** farewell; (*Trennung*) parting; **A~ nehmen** say goodbye (**von** to)
abschießen† *vt sep* shoot down; (*abfeuern*) fire; launch (*Rakete*)
abschirmen *vt sep* shield
abschlagen† *vt sep* knock off; (*verweigern*) refuse
Abschlepp|dienst *m* breakdown service. **a~en** *vt sep* tow away. **A~seil** *nt* tow-rope
abschließen† *v sep* ●*vt* lock; (*beenden, abmachen*) conclude; make (*Wette*); balance (*Bücher*) ●*vi* (*haben*) lock up; (*enden*) end. **a~d** *adv* in conclusion
Abschluss *m* conclusion. **A~zeugnis** *nt* diploma
abschmecken *vt sep* season
abschmieren *vt sep* lubricate
abschneiden† *v sep* ●*vt* cut off ●*vi* (*haben*) **gut/schlecht a~** do well/badly
Abschnitt *m* section; (*Stadium*) stage; (*Absatz*) paragraph
abschöpfen *vt sep* skim off
abschrauben *vt sep* unscrew
abschreck|en *vt sep* deter; (*Culin*) put in cold water (*Ei*). **a~end** *adj* repulsive. **A~ungsmittel** *nt* deterrent
abschreib|en† *v sep* ●*vt* copy; (*Comm & fig*) write off ●*vi* (*haben*) copy. **A~ung** *f* (*Comm*) depreciation
Abschrift *f* copy
Abschuss *m* shooting down; (*Abfeuern*) firing; (*Raketen-*) launch
abschüssig *adj* sloping; (*steil*) steep
abschwellen† *vi sep* (*sein*) go down
abseh|bar *adj* **in a~barer Zeit** in

the foreseeable future. **a∼en**† *vt/i sep* (*haben*) copy; (*voraussehen*) foresee; **a∼en von** disregard; (*aufgeben*) refrain from

abseits *adv* apart; (*Sport*) offside ● *prep* (+ *gen*) away from. **A∼** *nt* - (*Sport*) offside

absend|en† *vt sep* send off. **A∼er** *m* sender

absetzen *v sep* ● *vt* put *or* set down; (*ablagern*) deposit; (*abnehmen*) take off; (*abbrechen*) stop; (*entlassen*) dismiss; (*verkaufen*) sell; (*abziehen*) deduct ● *vi* (*haben*) pause

Absicht *f* **-,-en** intention; **mit A∼** intentionally, on purpose

absichtlich *adj* intentional

absitzen† *v sep* ● *vi* (*sein*) dismount ● *vt* ⊡ serve (*Strafe*)

absolut *adj* absolute

absolvieren *vt* complete; (*bestehen*) pass

absonder|n *vt sep* separate; (*ausscheiden*) secrete. **A∼ung** *f* **-,-en** secretion

absorbieren *vt* absorb

abspeisen *vt sep* fob off (**mit** with)

absperr|en *vt sep* cordon off; (*abstellen*) turn off; (*SGer*) lock. **A∼ung** *f* **-,-en** barrier

abspielen *vt sep* play; (*Fußball*) pass; **sich a∼** take place

Absprache *f* agreement

absprechen† *vt sep* arrange; **sich a∼** agree

abspringen† *vi sep* (*sein*) jump off; (*mit Fallschirm*) parachute; (*abgehen*) come off

Absprung *m* jump

abspülen *vt sep* rinse

abstamm|en *vi sep* (*haben*) be descended (**von** from). **A∼ung** *f* - descent

Abstand *m* distance; (*zeitlich*) interval; **A∼ halten** keep one's distance

abstatten *vt sep* **jdm einen Besuch a∼** pay s.o. a visit

Abstecher *m* **-s,-** detour

abstehen† *vi sep* (*haben*) stick out

absteigen† *vi sep* (*sein*) dismount; (*niedersteigen*) descend; (*Fußball*) be relegated

abstell|en *vt sep* put down; (*lagern*) store; (*parken*) park; (*abschalten*) turn off. **A∼gleis** *nt* siding. **A∼raum** *m* box-room

absterben† *vi sep* (*sein*) die; (*gefühllos werden*) go numb

Abstieg *m* **-[e]s,-e** descent; (*Fußball*) relegation

abstimm|en *v sep* ● *vi* (*haben*) vote (**über** + *acc* on) ● *vt* coordinate (**auf** + *acc* with). **A∼ung** *f* vote

Abstinenzler *m* **-s, -** teetotaller

abstoßen† *vt sep* knock off; (*verkaufen*) sell; (*fig: ekeln*) repel. **a∼d** *adj* repulsive

abstreiten† *vt sep* deny

Abstrich *m* (*Med*) smear

abstufen *vt sep* grade

Absturz *m* fall; (*Aviat*) crash

abstürzen *vi sep* (*sein*) fall; (*Aviat*) crash

absuchen *vt sep* search

absurd *adj* absurd

Abszess *m* **-es,-e** abscess

Abt *m* **-[e]s,¨e** abbot

abtasten *vt sep* feel; (*Techn*) scan

abtauen *vt/i sep* (*sein*) thaw; (*entfrosten*) defrost

Abtei *f* **-,-en** abbey

Abteil *nt* compartment

Abteilung *f* **-,-en** section; (*Admin, Comm*) department

abtragen† *vt sep* clear; (*einebnen*)

a

level; (*abnutzen*) wear out

abträglich *adj* detrimental (*dat* to)

abtreib|en† *vt sep* (*Naut*) drive off course; **ein Kind a∼en lassen** have an abortion. **A∼ung** *f* **-,-en** abortion

abtrennen *vt sep* detach; (*abteilen*) divide off

Abtreter *m* **-s,-** doormat

abtrocknen *vt/i sep* (*haben*) dry; **sich a∼** dry oneself

abtropfen *vi sep* (*sein*) drain

abtun† *vt sep* (*fig*) dismiss

abwägen† *vt sep* (*fig*) weigh

abwandeln *vt sep* modify

abwarten *v sep* ●*vt* wait for ●*vi* (*haben*) wait [and see]

abwärts *adv* down[wards]

Abwasch *m* **-[e]s** washing-up; (*Geschirr*) dirty dishes *pl*. **a∼en**† *v sep* ●*vt* wash; wash up (*Geschirr*); (*entfernen*) wash off ●*vi* (*haben*) wash up. **A∼lappen** *m* dishcloth

Abwasser *nt* **-s,⸚** sewage. **A∼kanal** *m* sewer

abwechseln *vi/r sep* (*haben*) **[sich] a∼** alternate; (*Personen:*) take turns. **a∼d** *adj* alternate

Abwechslung *f* **-,-en** change; **zur A∼** for a change

abwegig *adj* absurd

Abwehr *f* **-** defence; (*Widerstand*) resistance; (*Pol*) counter-espionage. **a∼en** *vt sep* ward off. **A∼system** *nt* immune system

abweich|en† *vi sep* (*sein*) deviate/(*von Regel*) depart (**von** from); (*sich unterscheiden*) differ (**von** from). **a∼end** *adj* divergent; (*verschieden*) different. **A∼ung** *f* **-,-en** deviation

abweis|en† *vt sep* turn down; turn away (*Person*). **a∼end** *adj* unfriendly. **A∼ung** *f* rejection

abwenden† *vt sep* turn away; (*verhindern*) avert

abwerfen† *vt sep* throw off; throw (*Reiter*); (*Aviat*) drop; (*Kartenspiel*) discard; shed (*Haut, Blätter*); yield (*Gewinn*)

abwert|en *vt sep* devalue. **A∼ung** *f* **-,-en** devaluation

Abwesenheit *f* **-** absence; absent-mindedness

abwickeln *vt sep* unwind; (*erledigen*) settle

abwischen *vt sep* wipe

abzahlen *vt sep* pay off

abzählen *vt sep* count

Abzahlung *f* instalment

Abzeichen *nt* badge

abzeichnen *vt sep* copy

Abzieh|bild *nt* transfer. **a∼en**† *v sep* ●*vt* pull off; take off (*Laken*); strip (*Bett*); (*häuten*) skin; (*Phot*) print; run off (*Kopien*); (*zurückziehen*) withdraw; (*abrechnen*) deduct ●*vi* (*sein*) go away, (*Rauch:*) escape

Abzug *m* withdrawal; (*Abrechnung*) deduction; (*Phot*) print (*Korrektur-*) proof; (*am Gewehr*) trigger; (*A∼söffnung*) vent; **A⸚e** *pl* deductions

abzüglich *prep* (+ *gen*) less

Abzugshaube *f* [cooker] hood

abzweig|en *v sep* ●*vi* (*sein*) branch off ●*vt* divert. **A∼ung** *f* **-,-en** junction; (*Gabelung*) fork

ach *int* oh; **a∼ je!** oh dear! **a∼ so** I see

Achse *f* **-,-n** axis; (*Rad-*) axle

Achsel *f* **-,-n** shoulder. **A∼höhle** *f* armpit. **A∼zucken** *nt* **-s** shrug

acht *inv adj*, **A∼**[1] *f* **-,-en** eight

Acht *f* **A∼ geben** be careful; **A∼ geben auf** (+ *acc*) look after; **außer A∼ lassen** disregard; **sich in A∼ nehmen** be careful

acht|e(r,s) *adj* eighth. **a~eckig** *adj* octagonal. **A~el** *nt* **-s,-** eighth
achten *vt* respect ● *vi* (*haben*) **a~ auf** (+ *acc*) pay attention to; (*aufpassen*) look after
Achterbahn *f* roller-coaster
achtlos *adj* careless
achtsam *adj* careful
Achtung *f* **-** respect (**vor** + *dat* for); A~! look out!
acht|zehn *inv adj* eighteen. **a~zehnte(r,s)** *adj* eighteenth. **a~zig** *a inv* eighty. **a~zigste(r,s)** *adj* eightieth
Acker *m* **-s,¨** field. **A~bau** *m* agriculture. **A~land** *nt* arable land
addieren *vt/i* (*haben*) add
Addition /-'tsi̯o:n/ *f* **-,-en** addition
ade *int* goodbye
Adel *m* **-s** nobility
Ader *f* **-,-n** vein
Adjektiv *nt* **-s,-e** adjective
Adler *m* **-s,-** eagle
adlig *adj* noble. **A~e(r)** *m* nobleman
Administration /-'tsi̯o:n/ *f* **-** administration
Admiral *m* **-s,¨e** admiral
adop|tieren *vt* adopt. **A~tion** *f* **-,-en** adoption. **A~tiveltern** *pl* adoptive parents. **A~tivkind** *nt* adopted child
Adrenalin *nt* **-s** adrenalin
Adres|se *f* **-,-n** address. **a~sieren** *vt* address
Adria *f* **-** Adriatic
Adverb *nt* **-s,-ien** adverb
Affäre *f* **-,-n** affair
Affe *m* **-n,-n** monkey; (*Menschen-*) ape
affektiert *adj* affected
affig *adj* affected; (*eitel*) vain
Afrika *nt* **-s** Africa
Afrikan|er(in) *m* **-s,-** (*f* **-,-nen**) African. **a~isch** *adj* African
After *m* **-s,-** anus
Agen|t(in) *m* **-en,-en** (*f* **-,-nen**) agent. **A~tur** *f* **-,-en** agency
Aggres|sion *f* **-,-en** aggression. **a~siv** *adj* aggressive
Agnostiker *m* **-s,-** agnostic
Ägypt|en /ɛ'gʏptən/ *nt* **-s** Egypt. **Ä~er(in)** *m* **-s,-** (*f* **-,-nen**) Egyptian. **ä~isch** *adj* Egyptian
ähneln *vi* (*haben*) (+ *dat*) resemble; **sich ä~** be alike
ahnen *vt* have a presentiment of; (*vermuten*) suspect
Ahnen *mpl* ancestors. **A~forschung** *f* genealogy
ähnlich *adj* similar; **jdm ä~ sehen** resemble s.o. **Ä~keit** *f* **-,-en** similarity; resemblance
Ahnung *f* **-,-en** premonition; (*Vermutung*) idea, hunch
Ahorn *m* **-s,-e** maple
Ähre *f* **-,-n** ear [of corn]
Aids /e:ts/ *nt* **-** Aids
Airbag /'ɛ:ɐ̯bɛk/ *m* **-s, -s** (*Auto*) air bag
Akademie *f* **-,-n** academy
Akadem|iker(in) *m* **-s,-** (*f* **-,-nen**) university graduate. **a~isch** *adj* academic
akklimatisieren (sich) *vr* become acclimatized
Akkord *m* **-[e]s,-e** (*Mus*) chord. **A~arbeit** *f* piecework
Akkordeon *nt* **-s,-s** accordion
Akkumulator *m* **-s,-en** (*Electr*) accumulator
Akkusativ *m* **-s,-e** accusative. **A~objekt** *nt* direct object
Akrobat|(in) *m* **-en,-en** (*f* **-,-nen**) acrobat. **a~isch** *adj* acrobatic
Akt *m* **-[e]s,-e** act; (*Kunst*) nude

a

Akte *f* -,-n file; **A~n** documents. **A~ntasche** *f* briefcase

Aktie /'aktsiə/ *f* -,-n (*Comm*) share. **A~ngesellschaft** *f* joint-stock company

Aktion /ak'tsio:n/ *f* -,-en action. **A~är** *m* -s,-e shareholder

aktiv *adj* active

aktuell *adj* topical; (*gegenwärtig*) current

Akupunktur *f* - acupuncture

Akustik *f* - acoustics *pl.*

akut *adj* acute

Akzent *m* -[e]s,-e accent

akzept|abel *adj* acceptable. **a~ieren** *vt* accept

Alarm *m* -s alarm; (*Mil*) alert. **a~ieren** *vt* alert; (*beunruhigen*) alarm

Albdruck *m* nightmare

albern *adj* silly ● *vi* (*haben*) play the fool

Albtraum *m* nightmare

Al|bum *nt* -s,-ben album

Algebra *f* - algebra

Algen *fpl* algae

Algerien /-iən/ *nt* -s Algeria

Alibi *nt* -s,-s alibi

Alimente *pl* maintenance *sg*

Alkohol *m* -s alcohol. **a~frei** *adj* non-alcoholic

Alkohol|iker(in) *m* -s,- (*f* -,-nen) alcoholic. **a~isch** *adj* alcoholic

Alkopop *nt* -(s), -s alcopop

all *inv pron* **all das/mein Geld** all the/my money; **all dies** all this

All *nt* -s universe

alle *pred adj* finished

all|e(r,s) *pron* all; (*jeder*) every; **a~es** everything, all; (*alle Leute*) everyone; **a~e** *pl* all; **a~es Geld** all the money; **a~e beide** both [of them/us]; **a~e Tage** every day; **a~e drei Jahre** every three years; **ohne a~en Grund** without any reason; **vor a~em** above all; **a~es in a~em** all in all; **a~es aussteigen!** all change!

Allee *f* -,-n avenue

allein *adv* alone; (*nur*) only; **a~stehend** single; **a~ der Gedanke** the mere thought; **von a~[e]** of its/(*Person*) one's own accord; (*automatisch*) automatically ● *conj* but. **A~erziehende(r)** *m/f* single parent. **a~ig** *adj* sole. **A~stehende** *pl* single people

allemal *adv* every time; (*gewiss*) certainly

allenfalls *adv* at most; (*eventuell*) possibly

aller|beste(r,s) *adj* very best; **am a~besten** best of all. **a~dings** *adv* indeed; (*zwar*) admittedly. **a~erste(r,s)** *adj* very first

Allergie *f* -,-n allergy

allergisch *adj* allergic (**gegen** to)

Aller|heiligen *nt* -s All Saints Day. **a~höchstens** *adv* at the very most. **a~lei** *inv adj* all sorts of ● *pron* all sorts of things. **a~letzte(r,s)** *adj* very last. **a~liebste(r,s)** *adj* favourite ● *adv* **am a~liebsten** for preference; **am a~liebsten haben** like best of all. **a~meiste(r,s)** *adj* most ● *adv* **am a~meisten** most of all. **A~seelen** *nt* -s All Souls Day. **a~wenigste(r,s)** *adj* very least ● *adv* **am a~wenigsten** least of all

allgemein *adj* general; **im A~en** (**a~en**) in general. **A~heit** *f* - community; (*Öffentlichkeit*) general public

Allianz *f* -,-en alliance

Alligator *m* -s,-en alligator

alliiert *adj* allied; **die A~en** *pl*

the Allies

all|jährlich *adj* annual. **a∼mählich** *adj* gradual

Alltag *m* working day; **der A∼** (*fig*) everyday life

alltäglich *adj* daily; (*gewöhnlich*) everyday; (*Mensch*) ordinary

alltags *adv* on weekdays

allzu *adv* [far] too; **a∼ oft** all too often; **a∼ vorsichtig** over-cautious

Alm *f* **-,-en** alpine pasture

Almosen *ntpl* alms

Alpdruck* *m* = **Albdruck**

Alpen *pl* Alps

Alphabet *nt* **-[e]s,-e** alphabet. **a∼isch** *adj* alphabetical

Alptraum* *m* = **Albtraum**

als *conj* as; (*zeitlich*) when; (*mit Komparativ*) than; **nichts als** nothing but; **als ob** as if *or* though

also *adv & conj* so; **a∼ gut** all right then; **na a∼!** there you are!

alt *adj* old; (*gebraucht*) second-hand; (*ehemalig*) former; **alt werden** grow old

Alt *m* **-s, -e** (*Mus*) contralto

Altar *m* **-s,⸚e** altar

Alt|e(r) *m/f* old man/woman; **die A∼en** old people. **A∼eisen** *nt* scrap iron. **A∼enheim** *nt* old people's home

Alter *nt* **-s,-** age; (*Bejahrtheit*) old age; **im A∼ von** at the age of

älter *adj* older; **mein ä∼er Bruder** my elder brother

altern *vi* (*sein*) age

Alternative *f* **-,-n** alternative

Alters|grenze *f* age limit. **A∼heim** *nt* old people's home. **A∼rente** *f* old-age pension. **a∼schwach** *adj* old and infirm. **A∼vorsorge** *f* provision for old age

Alter|tum *nt* **-s,⸚er** antiquity. **a∼tümlich** *adj* old; (*altmodisch*) old-fashioned

altklug *adj* precocious

alt|modisch *adj* old-fashioned. **A∼papier** *nt* waste paper. **A∼warenhändler** *m* second-hand dealer

Alufolie *f* [aluminium] foil

Aluminium *nt* **-s** aluminium, (*Amer*) aluminum

am *prep* = **an dem; am Montag** on Monday; **am Morgen** in the morning; **am besten** [the] best

Amateur /-ˈtøːɐ̯/ *m* **-s,-e** amateur

Ambition /-ˈtsi̯oːn/ *f* **-,-en** ambition

Amboss *m* **-es,-e** anvil

ambulan|t *adj* out-patient ● *adv* **a∼t behandeln** treat as an out-patient. **A∼z** *f* **-,-en** out-patients' department

Ameise *f* **-,-n** ant

amen *int*, **A∼** *nt* **-s** amen

Amerika *nt* **-s** America

Amerikan|er(in) *m* **-s,-** (*f* **-,-nen**) American. **a∼isch** *adj* American

Ammoniak *nt* **-s** ammonia

Amnestie *f* **-,-n** amnesty

amoralisch *adj* amoral

Ampel *f* **-,-n** traffic lights *pl*

Amphitheater *nt* amphitheatre

Amput|ation /-ˈtsi̯oːn/ *f* **-,-en** amputation. **a∼ieren** *vt* amputate

Amsel *f* **-,-n** blackbird

Amt *nt* **-[e]s,⸚er** office; (*Aufgabe*) task; (*Teleph*) exchange. **a∼lich** *adj* official. **A∼szeichen** *nt* dialling tone

Amulett *nt* **-[e]s,-e** [lucky] charm

amüs|ant *adj* amusing. **a∼ieren** *vt* amuse; **sich a∼ieren** be amused (**über** + *acc* at); (*sich vergnügen*) enjoy oneself

a

an

● *preposition (+ dative)*

! Note that **an** plus **dem** can become **am**

····➤ (*räumlich*) on; (*Gebäude, Ort*) at. **an der Wand** on the wall. **Frankfurt an der Oder** Frankfurt on [the] Oder. **an der Ecke** at the corner. **am Bahnhof** at the station. **an vorbei** past. **am 24. Mai** on May 24th

····➤ (*zeitlich*) on. **am Montag** on Monday. **an jedem Sonntag** every Sunday

····➤ (*sonstige Verwendungen*) **arm/reich an Vitaminen** low/rich in vitamins. **jdn an etw erkennen** recognize s.o. by sth. **an etw leiden** suffer from sth. **an einer Krankheit sterben** die of a disease. **an [und für] sich** actually

● *preposition (+ accusative)*

! Note that **an** plus **das** can become **ans**

····➤ to. **schicke es an deinen Bruder** send it to your brother. **er ging ans Fenster** he went to the window

····➤ (*auf, gegen*) on. **etw an die Wand hängen** to hang sth on the wall. **lehne es an den Baum** lean it on *or* against the tree

····➤ (*sonstige Verwendungen*) **an etw/jdn glauben** believe in sth/s.o. **an etw denken** think of sth. **sich an etw erinnern** remember sth

● *adverb*

····➤ (*auf Fahrplan*) **Köln an: 9.15** arriving Cologne 09.15

····➤ (*angeschaltet*) on. **die Waschmaschine/der Fernseher/das Licht/das Gas ist an** the washing machine/television/light/gas is on

····➤ (*ungefähr*) around; about. **an [die] 20000 DM** around *or* about 20,000 DM

····➤ (*in die Zukunft*) **von heute an** from today (onwards)

analog *adj* analogous; (*Computer*) analog. **A~ie** *f* **-,-n** analogy

Analphabet *m* **-en,-en** illiterate person. **A~entum** *nt* **-s** illiteracy

Analy|se *f* **-,-n** analysis. **a~sieren** *vt* analyse. **A~tiker** *m* **-s,-** analyst. **a~tisch** *adj* analytical

Anämie *f* **-** anaemia

Ananas *f* **-,-[se]** pineapple

Anatomie *f* **-** anatomy

Anbau *m* cultivation; (*Gebäude*) extension. **a~en** *vt sep* build on; (*anpflanzen*) cultivate, grow

anbei *adv* enclosed

anbeißen† *v sep* ● *vt* take a bite of ● *vi* (*haben*) (*Fisch:*) bite

anbeten *vt sep* worship

Anbetracht *m* **in A~** (+ *gen*) in view of

anbieten† *vt sep* offer; **sich a~** offer (**zu** to)

anbinden† *vt sep* tie up

Anblick *m* sight. **a~en** *vt sep* look at

anbrechen† *v sep* ● *vt* start on; break into (*Vorräte*) ● *vi* (*sein*) begin; (*Tag:*) break; (*Nacht:*) fall

anbrennen† *v sep* ● *vt* light ● *vi* (*sein*) burn

anbringen† *vt sep* bring [along]; (*befestigen*) fix

Anbruch *m* (*fig*) dawn; **bei A~ des Tages/der Nacht** at daybreak/nightfall

Andacht *f* **-,-en** reverence; (*Gottesdienst*) prayers *pl*

andächtig *adj* reverent; (*fig*) rapt

andauern *vi sep* (*haben*) last; (*anhalten*) continue. **a~d** *adj* persistent; (*ständig*) constant

Andenken *nt* **-s,-** memory; (*Souvenir*) souvenir

ander|e(r,s) *adj* other; (*verschieden*) different; (*nächste*) next; **ein a~er, eine a~e** another ● *pron* **der a~e/die a~en** the other/others; **ein a~er** another [one]; (*Person*) someone else; **kein a~er** no one else; **einer nach dem a~en** one after the other; **alles a~e/nichts a~es** everything/nothing else; **unter a~em** among other things. **a~enfalls** *adv* otherwise. **a~erseits** *adv* on the other hand. **a~mal** *adv* **ein a~mal** another time

ändern *vt* alter; (*wechseln*) change; **sich ä~** change

anders *pred adj* different; **a~ werden** change ● *adv* differently; (*riechen, schmecken*) different; (*sonst*) else; **jemand a~** someone else

andersherum *adv* the other way round

anderthalb *inv adj* one and a half; **a~ Stunden** an hour and a half

Änderung *f* **-,-en** alteration; (*Wechsel*) change

andeut|en *vt sep* indicate; (*anspielen*) hint at. **A~ung** *f* **-,-en** indication; hint

Andrang *m* rush (**nach** for); (*Gedränge*) crush

androhen *vt sep* **jdm etw a~** threaten s.o. with sth

aneignen *vt sep* **sich** (*dat*) **a~** appropriate; (*lernen*) learn

aneinander *adv & prefix* together; (*denken*) of one another; **a~ vorbei** past one another; **a~ geraten** quarrel

Anekdote *f* **-,-n** anecdote

anerkannt *adj* acknowledged

anerkenn|en† *vt sep* acknowledge, recognize; (*würdigen*) appreciate. **a~end** *adj* approving. **A~ung** *f* - acknowledgement, recognition; appreciation

anfahren† *v sep* ● *vt* deliver; (*streifen*) hit ● *vi* (*sein*) start

Anfall *m* fit, attack. **a~en**† *v sep* ● *vt* attack ● *vi* (*sein*) arise; (*Zinsen:*) accrue

anfällig *adj* susceptible (**für** to); (*zart*) delicate

Anfang *m* **-s,⸚e** beginning, start; **zu** *od* **am A~** at the beginning; (*anfangs*) at first. **a~en**† *vt/i sep* (*haben*) begin, start; (*tun*) do

Anfänger(in) *m* **-s,-** (*f* **-,-nen**) beginner

anfangs *adv* at first. **A~buchstabe** *m* initial letter. **A~gehalt** *nt* starting salary

anfassen *vt sep* touch; (*behandeln*) treat; tackle (*Arbeit*); **sich a~** hold hands

anfechten† *vt sep* contest

anfertigen *vt sep* make

anfeuchten *vt sep* moisten

anflehen *vt sep* implore, beg

Anflug *m* (*Avia*) approach

anforder|n *vt sep* demand; (*Comm*) order. **A~ung** *f* demand

Anfrage *f* enquiry. **a~n** *vi sep* (*haben*) enquire, ask

anfreunden (sich) *vr sep* make friends (**mit** with)

anfügen *vt sep* add

anfühlen *vt sep* feel; **sich weich a~** feel soft

a

anführ|en *vt sep* lead; (*zitieren*) quote; (*angeben*) give. **A~er** *m* leader. **A~ungszeichen** *ntpl* quotation marks

Angabe *f* statement; (*Anweisung*) instruction; (*Tennis*) service; **nähere A~n** particulars

angeb|en† *v sep* ●*vt* state; give (*Namen, Grund*); (*anzeigen*) indicate; set (*Tempo*) ●*vi* (*haben*) (*Tennis*) serve; (🅘: *protzen*) show off. **A~er(in)** *m* **-s,-** (*f* **-,-nen**) 🅘 show-off. **A~erei** *f* **-** 🅘 showing-off

angeblich *adj* alleged

angeboren *adj* innate; (*Med*) congenital

Angebot *nt* offer; (*Auswahl*) range; **A~ und Nachfrage** supply and demand

angebracht *adj* appropriate

angeheiratet *adj* (*Onkel, Tante*) by marriage

angeheitert *adj* 🅘 tipsy

angehen† *v sep* ●*vi* (*sein*) begin, start; (*Licht, Radio:*) come on; (*anwachsen*) take root; **a~ gegen** fight ●*vt* attack; tackle (*Arbeit*); (*bitten*) ask (**um** for); (*betreffen*) concern

angehör|en *vi sep* (*haben*) (+ *dat*) belong to. **A~ige(r)** *m/f* relative

Angeklagte(r) *m/f* accused

Angel *f* **-,-n** fishing-rod; (*Tür-*) hinge

Angelegenheit *f* matter

Angel|haken *m* fish-hook. **a~n** *vi* (*haben*) fish (**nach** for); **a~n gehen** go fishing ●*vt* (*fangen*) catch. **A~rute** *f* fishing-rod

angelsächsisch *adj* Anglo-Saxon

angemessen *adj* commensurate (*dat* with); (*passend*) appropriate

angenehm *adj* pleasant; (*bei Vorstellung*) **a~!** delighted to meet you!

angeregt *adj* animated

angesehen *adj* respected; (*Firma*) reputable

angesichts *prep* (+ *gen*) in view of

angespannt *adj* intent; (*Lage*) tense

Angestellte(r) *m/f* employee

angewandt *adj* applied

angewiesen *adj* dependent (**auf** + *acc* on); **auf sich selbst a~** on one's own

angewöhnen *vt sep* **jdm etw a~** get s.o. used to sth; **sich** (*dat*) **etw a~** get into the habit of doing sth

Angewohnheit *f* habit

Angina *f* **-** tonsillitis

angleichen† *vt sep* adjust (*dat* to)

anglikanisch *adj* Anglican

Anglistik *f* **-** English [language and literature]

Angorakatze *f* Persian cat

angreif|en† *vt sep* attack; tackle (*Arbeit*); (*schädigen*) damage. **A~er** *m* **-s,-** attacker; (*Pol*) aggressor

angrenzen *vi sep* (*haben*) adjoin (**an etw** *acc* sth). **a~d** *adj* adjoining

Angriff *m* attack; **in A~ nehmen** tackle. **a~slustig** *adj* aggressive

Angst *f* **-,¨e** fear; (*Psychology*) anxiety; (*Sorge*) worry (**um** about); **A~ haben** be afraid (**vor** + *dat* of); (*sich sorgen*) be worried (**um** about); **jdm A~ machen** frighten s.o.

ängstigen *vt* frighten; (*Sorge machen*) worry; **sich ä~** be frightened; be worried (**um** about)

ängstlich *adj* nervous; (*scheu*) timid; (*verängstigt*) frightened, scared; (*besorgt*) anxious

angucken *vt sep* 🅘 look at

angurten (sich) *vr sep* fasten one's seat belt

anhaben† *vt sep* have on; **er/es kann mir nichts a~** (*fig*) he/it cannot hurt me

anhalt|en† *v sep* ● *vt* stop; hold (*Atem*); **jdn zur Arbeit a~en** urge s.o. to work ● *vi* (*haben*) stop; (*andauern*) continue. **a~end** *adj* persistent. **A~er(in)** *m* **-s,-** (*f* **-,-nen**) hitchhiker; **per A~er fahren** hitchhike. **A~spunkt** *m* clue

anhand *prep* (+ *gen*) with the aid of

Anhang *m* (*zu Buch*) appendix; (*zu E-mail*) attachment

anhängen[1] *vt sep* (*reg*) hang up; (*befestigen*) attach

anhäng|en[2]† *vi* (*haben*) be a follower of. **A~er** *m* **-s,-** follower; (*Auto*) trailer; (*Schild*) [tie-on] label; (*Schmuck*) pendant. **A~erin** *f* **-,-nen** follower. **a~lich** *adj* affectionate

anhäufen *vt sep* pile up

Anhieb *m* **auf A~** straight away

Anhöhe *f* hill

anhören *vt sep* listen to; **sich gut a~** sound good

animieren *vt* encourage (**zu** to)

Anis *m* **-es** aniseed

Anker *m* **-s,-** anchor; **vor A~ gehen** drop anchor. **a~n** *vi* (*haben*) anchor; (*liegen*) be anchored

anketten *vt sep* chain up

Anklage *f* accusation; (*Jur*) charge; (*Ankläger*) prosecution. **A~bank** *f* dock. **a~n** *vt sep* accuse (*gen* of); (*Jur*) charge (*gen* with)

Ankläger *m* accuser; (*Jur*) prosecutor

anklammern *vt sep* clip on; **sich a~** cling (**an** + *acc* to)

ankleben *v sep* ● *vt* stick on ● *vi* (*sein*) stick (**an** + *dat* to)

anklicken *vt sep* click on

anklopfen *vi sep* (*haben*) knock

anknipsen *vt sep* ⊡ switch on

ankommen† *vi sep* (*sein*) arrive; (*sich nähern*) approach; **gut a~** arrive safely; (*fig*) go down well (**bei** with); **nicht a~ gegen** (*fig*) be no match for; **a~ auf** (+ *acc*) depend on; **das kommt darauf an** it [all] depends

ankreuzen *vt sep* mark with a cross

ankündig|en *vt sep* announce. **A~ung** *f* announcement

Ankunft *f* - arrival

ankurbeln *vt sep* (*fig*) boost

anlächeln *vt sep* smile at

anlachen *vt sep* smile at

Anlage *f* **-,-n** installation; (*Industrie-*) plant; (*Komplex*) complex; (*Geld-*) investment; (*Plan*) layout; (*Beilage*) enclosure; (*Veranlagung*) aptitude; (*Neigung*) predisposition; **[öffentliche] A~n** [public] gardens; **als A~** enclosed

Anlass *m* **-es,¨e** reason; (*Gelegenheit*) occasion; **A~ geben zu** give cause for

anlass|en† *vt sep* (*Auto*) start; ⊡ leave on (*Licht*); keep on (*Mantel*). **A~er** *m* **-s,-** starter

anlässlich *prep* (+ *gen*) on the occasion of

Anlauf *m* (*Sport*) run-up; (*fig*) attempt. **a~en**† *v sep* ● *vi* (*sein*) start; (*beschlagen*) mist up; (*Metall:*) tarnish; **rot a~en** blush ● *vt* (*Naut*) call at

anlegen *v sep* ● *vt* put (**an** + *acc* against); put on (*Kleidung, Verband*); lay back (*Ohren*); aim (*Gewehr*); (*investieren*) invest; (*ausgeben*) spend (**für** on); draw up (*Liste*); **es darauf a~** (*fig*) aim (**zu** to) ● *vi* (*haben*) (*Schiff:*) moor; **a~ auf** (+ *acc*) aim at

anlehnen *vt sep* lean (**an** + *acc* against); **sich a~** lean (**an** + *acc* on)

Anleihe *f* **-,-n** loan

anleit|en *vt sep* instruct. **A~ung** *f* instructions *pl*
anlernen *vt sep* train
Anliegen *nt* **-s,-** request; (*Wunsch*) desire
anlieg|en† *vi sep* (*haben*) **[eng] a~en** fit closely; **[eng] a~end** close-fitting. **A~er** *mpl* residents; **'A~er frei'** 'access for residents only'
anlügen† *vt sep* lie to
anmachen *vt sep* ⊡ fix; (*anschalten*) turn on; dress (*Salat*)
anmalen *vt sep* paint
Anmarsch *m* (*Mil*) approach
anmeld|en *vt sep* announce; (*Admin*) register; **sich a~en** say that one is coming; (*Admin*) register; (*Sch*) enrol; (*im Hotel*) check in; (*beim Arzt*) make an appointment; (*Computer*) log on. **A~ung** *f* announcement; (*Admin*) registration; (*Sch*) enrolment; (*Termin*) appointment
anmerk|en *vt sep* mark; **sich** (*dat*) **etw a~en lassen** show sth. **A~ung** *f* **-,-en** note
Anmut *f* **-** grace; (*Charme*) charm
anmutig *adj* graceful
annähen *vt sep* sew on
annäher|nd *adj* approximate. **A~ungsversuche** *mpl* advances
Annahme *f* **-,-n** acceptance; (*Adoption*) adoption; (*Vermutung*) assumption
annehm|bar *adj* acceptable. **a~en**† *vt sep* accept; (*adoptieren*) adopt; acquire (*Gewohnheit*); (*sich zulegen, vermuten*) assume; **angenommen, dass** assuming that. **A~lichkeiten** *fpl* comforts
Anno *adv* **A~ 1920** in the year 1920
Annon|ce /a'nõ:sə/ *f* **-,-n** advertisement. **a~cieren** *vt/i* (*haben*) advertise
annullieren *vt* annul; cancel
Anomalie *f* **-,-n** anomaly
anonym *adj* anonymous
Anorak *m* **-s,-s** anorak
anordn|en *vt sep* arrange; (*befehlen*) order. **A~ung** *f* arrangement; order
anorganisch *adj* inorganic
anormal *adj* abnormal
anpass|en *vt sep* try on; (*angleichen*) adapt (*dat* to); **sich a~** adapt (*dat* to). **A~ung** *f* **-** adaptation. **a~ungsfähig** *adj* adaptable. **A~ungsfähigkeit** *f* adaptability
Anpfiff *m* (*Sport*) kick-off
Anprall *m* **-[e]s** impact. **a~en** *vi sep* (*sein*) strike (**an etw** *acc* sth)
anpreisen† *vt sep* commend
Anprob|e *f* fitting. **a~ieren** *vt sep* try on
anrechnen *vt sep* count (**als** as); (*berechnen*) charge for; (*verrechnen*) allow (*Summe*)
Anrecht *nt* right (**auf** + *acc* to)
Anrede *f* [form of] address. **a~n** *vt sep* address; speak to
anreg|en *vt sep* stimulate; (*ermuntern*) encourage (**zu** to); (*vorschlagen*) suggest. **a~end** *adj* stimulating. **A~ung** *f* stimulation; (*Vorschlag*) suggestion
Anreise *f* journey; (*Ankunft*) arrival. **a~n** *vi sep* (*sein*) arrive
Anreiz *m* incentive
Anrichte *f* **-,-n** sideboard. **a~n** *vt sep* (*Culin*) prepare; (*garnieren*) garnish (**mit** with); (*verursachen*) cause
anrüchig *adj* disreputable
Anruf *m* call. **A~beantworter** *m* **-s,-** answering machine. **a~en**† *v sep* ●*vt* call to; (*bitten*) call on (**um** for); (*Teleph*) ring ●*vi* (*haben*) ring (**bei jdm** s.o.)

anrühren *vt sep* touch; (*verrühren*) mix

ans *prep* = **an das**

Ansage *f* announcement. **a~n** *vt sep* announce

ansamm|eln *vt sep* collect; (*anhäufen*) accumulate; **sich a~eln** collect; (*sich häufen*) accumulate; (*Leute:*) gather. **A~lung** *f* collection; (*Menschen-*) crowd

ansässig *adj* resident

Ansatz *m* beginning; (*Versuch*) attempt

anschaffen *vt sep* [**sich** *dat*] **etw a~en** acquire/(*kaufen*) buy sth

anschalten *vt sep* switch on

anschau|en *vt sep* look at. **a~lich** *adj* vivid. **A~ung** *f* -,-en (*fig*) view

Anschein *m* appearance. **a~end** *adv* apparently

anschirren *vt sep* harness

Anschlag *m* notice; (*Vor-*) estimate; (*Überfall*) attack (**auf** + *acc* on); (*Mus*) touch; (*Techn*) stop. **a~en**† *v sep* ●*vt* put up (*Aushang*), strike (*Note, Taste*); cast on (*Masche*); (*beschädigen*) chip ●*vi* (*haben*) strike/(*stoßen*) knock (**an** + *acc* against); (*wirken*) be effective ●*vi* (*sein*) knock (**an** + *acc* against)

anschließen† *v sep* ●*vt* connect (**an** + *acc* to); (*zufügen*) add; **sich a~ an** (+ *acc*) (*anstoßen*) adjoin; (*folgen*) follow; (*sich anfreunden*) become friendly with; **sich jdm a~** join s.o. ●*vi* (*haben*) **a~ an** (+ *acc*) adjoin; (*folgen*) follow. **a~d** *adj* adjoining; (*zeitlich*) following ●*adv* afterwards

Anschluss *m* connection; (*Kontakt*) contact; **A~ finden** make friends; **im A~ an** (+ *acc*) after

anschmiegsam *adj* affectionate

anschmieren *vt sep* smear

anschnallen *vt sep* strap on; **sich a~** fasten one's seat-belt

anschneiden† *vt sep* cut into; broach (*Thema*)

anschreiben† *vt sep* write (**an** + *acc* on); (*Comm*) put on s.o.'s account; (*sich wenden*) write to

Anschrift *f* address

anschuldig|en *vt sep* accuse. **A~ung** *f* -,-en accusation

anschwellen† *vi sep* (*sein*) swell

ansehen† *vt sep* look at; (*einschätzen*) regard (**als** as); [**sich** *dat*] **etw a~** look at sth; (*TV*) watch sth. **A~** *nt* **-s** respect; (*Ruf*) reputation

ansehnlich *adj* considerable

ansetzen *v sep* ●*vt* join (**an** + *acc* to); (*veranschlagen*) estimate ●*vi* (*haben*) (*anbrennen*) burn; **zum Sprung a~** get ready to jump

Ansicht *f* view; **meiner A~ nach** in my view; **zur A~** (*Comm*) on approval. **A~s[post]karte** *f* picture postcard. **A~ssache** *f* matter of opinion

ansiedeln (sich) *vr sep* settle

ansonsten *adv* apart from that

anspannen *vt sep* hitch up; (*anstrengen*) strain; tense (*Muskel*)

Anspielung *f* -,-en allusion; hint

Anspitzer *m* **-s,-** pencil-sharpener

Ansprache *f* address

ansprechen† *v sep* ●*vt* speak to; (*fig*) appeal to ●*vi* (*haben*) respond (**auf** + *acc* to)

anspringen† *v sep* ●*vt* jump at ●*vi* (*sein*) (*Auto*) start

Anspruch *m* claim/(*Recht*) right (**auf** + *acc* to); **A~ haben** be entitled (**auf** + *acc* to); **in A~ nehmen** make use of; (*erfordern*) demand; take up (*Zeit*); occupy (*Person*); **hohe A~̈e stellen** be very demanding. **a~slos** *adj* undemanding. **a~svoll** *adj* demanding; (*kri-*

a

tisch) discriminating; (*vornehm*) up-market

anstacheln *vt sep* (*fig*) spur on

Anstalt *f* **-,-en** institution

Anstand *m* decency; (*Benehmen*) [good] manners *pl*

anständig *adj* decent; (*ehrbar*) respectable; (*richtig*) proper

anstandslos *adv* without any trouble

anstarren *vt sep* stare at

anstatt *conj & prep* (+ *gen*) instead of

ansteck|en *v sep* ● *vt* pin (**an** + *acc* to/on); put on (*Ring*); (*anzünden*) light; (*in Brand stecken*) set fire to; (*Med*) infect; **sich a~en** catch an infection (**bei** from) ● *vi* (*haben*) be infectious. **a~end** *adj* infectious. **A~ung** *f* **-,-en** infection

anstehen† *vi sep* (*haben*) queue

anstelle *prep* (+ *gen*) instead of

anstell|en *vt sep* put, stand (**an** + *acc* against); (*einstellen*) employ; (*anschalten*) turn on; (*tun*) do; **sich a~en** queue [up]. **A~ung** *f* employment; (*Stelle*) job

Anstieg *m* **-[e]s,-e** climb; (*fig*) rise

anstifte|n *vt sep* cause; (*anzetteln*) instigate

Anstoß *m* (*Anregung*) impetus; (*Stoß*) knock; (*Fußball*) kick-off; **A~ erregen** give offence. **a~en**† *v sep* ● *vt* knock; (*mit dem Ellbogen*) nudge ● *vi* (*sein*) knock (**an** + *acc* against) ● *vi* (*haben*) adjoin (**an etw** *acc* sth); **a~en auf** (+ *acc*) drink to; **mit der Zunge a~en** lisp

anstößig *adj* offensive

anstrahlen *vt sep* floodlight

anstreichen† *vt sep* paint; (*anmerken*) mark

anstreng|en *vt sep* strain; (*ermüden*) tire; **sich a~en** exert oneself; (*sich bemühen*) make an effort (**zu** to). **a~end** *adj* strenuous; (*ermüdend*) tiring. **A~ung** *f* **-,-en** strain; (*Mühe*) effort

Anstrich *m* coat [of paint]

Ansturm *m* rush; (*Mil*) assault

Ansuchen *nt* **-s,-** request

Antarktis *f* **-** Antarctic

Anteil *m* share; **A~ nehmen** take an interest (**an** + *dat* in). **A~nahme** *f* **-** interest (**an** + *dat* in); (*Mitgefühl*) sympathy

Antenne *f* **-,-n** aerial

Anthologie *f* **-,-n** anthology

Anthrax *m* **-** anthrax

Anthropologie *f* **-** anthropology

Anti|alkoholiker *m* teetotaller. **A~biotikum** *nt* **-s,-ka** antibiotic

antik *adj* antique. **A~e** *f* **-** [classical] antiquity

Antikörper *m* antibody

Antilope *f* **-,-n** antelope

Antipathie *f* **-** antipathy

Antiquariat *nt* **-[e]s,-e** antiquarian bookshop

Antiquitäten *fpl* antiques. **A~händler** *m* antique dealer

Antrag *m* **-[e]s,⸚e** proposal; (*Pol*) motion; (*Gesuch*) application. **A~steller** *m* **-s,-** applicant

antreffen† *vt sep* find

antreten† *v sep* ● *vt* start; take up (*Amt*) ● *vi* (*sein*) line up

Antrieb *m* urge; (*Techn*) drive; **aus eigenem A~** of one's own accord

Antritt *m* start; **bei A~ eines Amtes** when taking office

antun† *vt sep* **jdm etw a~** do sth to s.o.; **sich** (*dat*) **etwas a~** take one's own life

Antwort *f* **-,-en** answer, reply (**auf** + *acc* to). **a~en** *vt/i* (*haben*) answer (**jdm** s.o.)

anvertrauen *vt sep* entrust/(*mitteilen*) confide (**jdm** to s.o.)

Anwalt *m* **-[e]s,⸚e, Anwältin** *f* **-,-nen** lawyer; (*vor Gericht*) counsel

Anwandlung *f* **-,-en** fit (**von** of)

Anwärter(in) *m(f)* candidate

anweis|en† *vt sep* assign (*dat* to); (*beauftragen*) instruct. **A~ung** *f* instruction; (*Geld-*) money order

anwend|en *vt sep* apply (**auf** + *acc* to); (*gebrauchen*) use. **A~ung** *f* application; use

anwerben† *vt sep* recruit

Anwesen *nt* **-s,-** property

anwesen|d *adj* present (**bei** at); **die A~den** those present. **A~heit** *f* **-** presence

anwidern *vt sep* disgust

Anwohner *mpl* residents

Anzahl *f* number

anzahl|en *vt sep* pay a deposit on. **A~ung** *f* deposit

anzapfen *vt sep* tap

Anzeichen *nt* sign

Anzeige *f* **-,-n** announcement; (*Inserat*) advertisement; **A~ erstatten gegen jdn** report s.o. to the police. **a~n** *vt sep* announce; (*inserieren*) advertise; (*melden*) report [to the police]; (*angeben*) indicate

anzieh|en† *vt sep* ●*vt* attract; (*festziehen*) tighten; put on (*Kleider, Bremse*); (*ankleiden*) dress; **sich a~en** get dressed. **a~end** *adj* attractive. **A~ungskraft** *f* attraction; (*Phys*) gravity

Anzug *m* suit

anzüglich *adj* suggestive

anzünden *vt sep* light; (*in Brand stecken*) set fire to

anzweifeln *vt sep* question

apart *adj* striking

Apathie *f* **-** apathy

apathisch *adj* apathetic

Aperitif *m* **-s,-s** aperitif

Apfel *m* **-s,⸚** apple

Apfelsine *f* **-,-n** orange

Apostel *m* **-s,-** apostle

Apostroph *m* **-s,-e** apostrophe

Apothek|e *f* **-,-n** pharmacy. **A~er(in)** *m* **-s,-** (*f* **-,-nen**) pharmacist, [dispensing] chemist

Apparat *m* **-[e]s,-e** device; (*Phot*) camera; (*Radio, TV*) set; (*Teleph*) telephone; **am A~!** speaking!

Appell *m* **-s,-e** appeal; (*Mil*) roll-call. **a~ieren** *vi* (*haben*) appeal (**an** + *acc* to)

Appetit *m* **-s** appetite; **guten A~!** enjoy your meal! **a~lich** *adj* appetizing

Applaus *m* **-es** applause

Aprikose *f* **-,-n** apricot

April *m* **-[s]** April

Aquarell *nt* **-s,-e** water-colour

Aquarium *nt* **-s,-ien** aquarium

Äquator *m* **-s** equator

Ära *f* **-** era

Araber(in) *m* **-s,-** (*f* **-,-nen**) Arab

arabisch *adj* Arab; (*Geog*) Arabian; (*Ziffer*) Arabic

Arbeit *f* **-,-en** work; (*Anstellung*) employment, job; (*Aufgabe*) task; (*Sch*) [written] test; (*Abhandlung*) treatise; (*Qualität*) workmanship; **sich an die A~ machen** set to work; **sich** (*dat*) **viel A~ machen** go to a lot of trouble. **a~en** *v sep* ●*vi* (*haben*) work (**an** + *dat* on) ●*vt* make. **A~er(in)** *m* **-s,-** (*f* **-,-nen**) worker; (*Land-, Hilfs-*) labourer. **A~erklasse** *f* working class

Arbeit|geber *m* **-s,-** employer. **A~nehmer** *m* **-s,-** employee

Arbeits|amt *nt* employment exchange. **A~erlaubnis, A~genehmigung** *f* work permit. **A~kraft** *f* worker. **a~los** *adj* unemployed;

a

~**los sein** be out of work. **A~lose(r)** *m/f* unemployed person; **die A~losen** the unemployed *pl*. **A~losenunterstützung** *f* unemployment benefit. **A~losigkeit** *f* - unemployment

arbeitsparend *adj* labour-saving

Arbeitsplatz *m* job

Archäo|loge *m* **-n,-n** archaeologist. **A~logie** *f* - archaeology

Arche *f* - **die A~ Noah** Noah's Ark

Architek|t(in) *m* **-en,-en** (*f* **-,-nen**) architect. **a~tonisch** *adj* architectural. **A~tur** *f* - architecture

Archiv *nt* **-s,-e** archives *pl*

Arena *f* **-,-nen** arena

arg *adj* bad; (*groß*) terrible

Argentin|ien /-i̯ən/ *nt* **-s** Argentina. **a~isch** *adj* Argentinian

Ärger *m* **-s** annoyance; (*Unannehmlichkeit*) trouble. **ä~lich** *adj* annoyed; (*leidig*) annoying; **ä~lich sein** be annoyed. **ä~n** *vt* annoy; (*necken*) tease; **sich ä~n** get annoyed (**über jdn/etw** with s.o./about sth). **Ä~nis** *nt* **-ses, -se** annoyance; **öffentliches Ä~nis** public nuisance

Arglist *f* - malice

arglos *adj* unsuspecting

Argument *nt* **-[e]s,-e** argument. **a~ieren** *vi* (*haben*) argue (**dass** that)

Arie /ˈaːri̯ə/ *f* **-,-n** aria

Aristo|krat *m* **-en,-en** aristocrat. **A~kratie** *f* - aristocracy. **a~kratisch** *adj* aristocratic

Arkt|is *f* - Arctic. **a~isch** *adj* Arctic

arm *adj* poor

Arm *m* **-[e]s,-e** arm; **jdn auf den Arm nehmen** 🄸 pull s.o.'s leg

Armaturenbrett *nt* instrument panel; (*Auto*) dashboard

Armband *nt* (*pl* **-bänder**) bracelet; (*Uhr-*) watch-strap. **A~uhr** *f* wrist-watch

Arm|e(r) *m/f* poor man/woman; **die A~en** the poor *pl*

Armee *f* **-,-n** army

Ärmel *m* **-s,-** sleeve. **Ä~kanal** *m* [English] Channel. **ä~los** *adj* sleeveless

Arm|lehne *f* arm. **A~leuchter** *m* candelabra

ärmlich *adj* poor; (*elend*) miserable

armselig *adj* miserable

Armut *f* - poverty

Arran|gement /arãʒəˈmãː/ *nt* **-s,-s** arrangement. **a~gieren** *vt* arrange

arrogant *adj* arrogant

Arsch *m* **-[e]s,¨e** (*vulgar*) arse

Arsen *nt* **-s** arsenic

Art *f* **-,-en** manner; (*Weise*) way; (*Natur*) nature; (*Sorte*) kind; (*Biology*) species; **auf diese Art** in this way

Arterie /-i̯ə/ *f* **-,-n** artery

Arthritis *f* - arthritis

artig *adj* well-behaved

Artikel *m* **-s,-** article

Artillerie *f* - artillery

Artischocke *f* **-,-n** artichoke

Arznei *f* **-,-en** medicine

Arzt *m* **-[e]s,¨e** doctor

Ärzt|in *f* **-,-nen** [woman] doctor. **ä~lich** *adj* medical

As* *nt* **-ses,-se** = **Ass**

Asbest *m* **-[e]s** asbestos

Asche *f* - ash. **A~nbecher** *m* ashtray. **A~rmittwoch** *m* Ash Wednesday

Asiat|(in) *m* **-en,-en** (*f* **-,-nen**) Asian. **a~isch** *adj* Asian

Asien /ˈaːzi̯ən/ *nt* **-s** Asia

asozial *adj* antisocial

Aspekt *m* **-[e]s,-e** aspect
Asphalt *m* **-[e]s** asphalt. **a~ieren** *vt* asphalt
Ass *nt* **-es,-e** ace
Assistent(in) *m* **-en,-en** (*f* **-,-nen**) assistant
Ast *m* **-[e]s,¨-e** branch
ästhetisch *adj* aesthetic
Asth|ma *nt* **-s** asthma. **a~matisch** *adj* asthmatic
Astro|loge *m* **-n,-n** astrologer. **A~logie** *f* **-** astrology. **A~naut** *m* **-en,-en** astronaut. **A~nomie** *f* **-** astronomy
Asyl *nt* **-s,-e** home; (*Pol*) asylum. **A~bewerber(in)** *m* **-e, -** (*f* **-en, -en**) asylum seeker
Atelier /-'li̯e:/ *nt* **-s,-s** studio
Atem *m* **-s** breath. **a~los** *adj* breathless. **A~zug** *m* breath
Atheist *m* **-en,-en** atheist
Äther *m* **-s** ether
Äthiopien /-i̯ən/ *nt* **-s** Ethiopia
Athlet|(in) *m* **-en,-en** (*f* **-,-nen**) athlete. **a~isch** *adj* athletic
Atlant|ik *m* **-s** Atlantic. **a~isch** *adj* Atlantic; **der A~ische Ozean** the Atlantic Ocean
Atlas *m* **-lasses,-lanten** atlas
atmen *vt/i* (*haben*) breathe
Atmosphäre *f* **-,-n** atmosphere
Atmung *f* **-** breathing
Atom *nt* **-s,-e** atom. **A~bombe** *f* atom bomb. **A~krieg** *m* nuclear war
Atten|tat *nt* **-[e]s,-e** assassination attempt. **A~täter** *m* assassin
Attest *nt* **-[e]s,-e** certificate
Attrak|tion /-'tsi̯o:n/ *f* **-,-en** attraction. **a~tiv** *adj* attractive
Attribut *nt* **-[e]s,-e** attribute
ätzen *vt* corrode; (*Med*) cauterize; (*Kunst*) etch. **ä~d** *adj* corrosive; (*Spott*) caustic

au *int* ouch; **au fein!** oh good!
Aubergine /obɛr'ʒi:nə/ *f* **-,-n** aubergine
auch *adv & conj* also, too; (*außerdem*) what's more; (*selbst*) even; **a~ wenn** even if; **sie weiß es a~ nicht** she doesn't know either; **wer/wie/was a~ immer** whoever/however/whatever
Audienz *f* **-,-en** audience
audiovisuell *adj* audio-visual
Auditorium *nt* **-s,-ien** (*Univ*) lecture hall

auf

● *preposition (+ dative)*
····➤ (*nicht unter*) on. **auf dem Tisch** on the table. **auf Deck** on deck. **auf der Erde** on earth. **auf der Welt** in the world. **auf der Straße** in the street
····➤ (*bei Institution, Veranstaltung usw.*) at; (*bei Gebäude, Zimmer*) in. **auf der Schule/Uni** at school/university. **auf einer Party/Hochzeit** at a party/wedding. **Geld auf der Bank haben** have money in the bank. **sie ist auf ihrem Zimmer** she's in her room. **auf einem Lehrgang** on a course. **auf Urlaub** on holiday
● *preposition (+ accusative)*
····➤ (*nicht unter*) on[to]. **er legte das Buch auf den Tisch** he laid the book on the table. **auf eine Mauer steigen** climb onto a wall. **auf die Straße gehen** go [out] into the street
····➤ (*bei Institution, Veranstaltung usw.*) to. **auf eine Party/die Toilette gehen** go to a party/the toilet. **auf die Schule/Uni gehen** go to school/university. **auf einen Lehrgang/auf Urlaub**

a

gehen go on a course/on holiday

····➤(*bei Entfernung*) **auf 10 km [Entfernung] zu sehen/hören** visible/audible for [a distance of] 10 km

····➤(*zeitlich*) (*wie lange*) for; (*bis*) until; (*wann*) on. **auf Jahre [hinaus]** for years [to come]. **auf ein paar Tage** for a few days. **etw auf nächsten Mittwoch verschieben** postpone sth until next Wednesday. **das fällt auf einen Montag** it falls on a Monday

····➤(*Art und Weise*) in. **auf diese [Art und] Weise** in this way. **auf Deutsch/Englisch** in German/English

····➤(*aufgrund*) **auf Wunsch** on request. **auf meine Bitte** on or at my request. **auf Befehl** on command

····➤(*Proportion*) to. **ein Teelöffel auf einen Liter Wasser** one teaspoon to one litre of water. **auf die Sekunde/den Millimeter [genau]** [precise] to the nearest second/millimetre

····➤ (*Toast*) to. **auf deine Gesundheit!** your health!

●*adverb*

····➤(*aufgerichtet, aufgestanden*) up. **auf!** (*steh auf!*) up you get! **auf und ab** (*hin und her*) up and down

····➤(*aufsetzen*) **Helm/Hut/Brille auf!** helmet/hat/glasses on!

····➤(*geöffnet, offen*) open. **Fenster/Mund auf!** open the window/your mouth!

aufatmen *vi sep* (*haben*) heave a sigh of relief

aufbahren *vt sep* lay out

Aufbau *m* construction; (*Struktur*) structure. **a~en** *v sep* ●*vt* construct, build; (*errichten*) erect; (*schaffen*) build up; (*arrangieren*) arrange; **sich a~en** (*fig*) be based (**auf** + *dat* on) ●*vi* (*haben*) be based (**auf** + *dat* on)

aufbauschen *vt sep* puff out; (*fig*) exaggerate

aufbekommen† *vt sep* get open; (*Sch*) be given [as homework]

aufbessern *vt sep* improve; (*erhöhen*) increase

aufbewahr|en *vt sep* keep; (*lagern*) store. **A~ung** *f* - safe keeping; storage; (*Gepäck-*) left-luggage office

aufblas|bar *adj* inflatable. **a~en**† *vt sep* inflate

aufbleiben† *vi sep* (*sein*) stay open; (*Person:*) stay up

aufblenden *vt/i sep* (*haben*) (*Auto*) switch to full beam

aufblühen *vi sep* (*sein*) flower

aufbocken *vt sep* jack up

aufbrauchen *vt sep* use up

aufbrechen† *v sep* ●*vt* break open ●*vi* (*sein*) (*Knospe:*) open; (*sich aufmachen*) set out, start

aufbringen† *vt sep* raise (*Geld*); find (*Kraft*)

Aufbruch *m* start, departure

aufbrühen *vt sep* make (*Tee*)

aufbürden *vt sep* **jdm etw a~** (*fig*) burden s.o. with sth

aufdecken *vt sep* (*auflegen*) put on; (*abdecken*) uncover; (*fig*) expose

aufdrehen *vt sep* turn on

aufdringlich *adj* persistent

aufeinander *adv* one on top of the other; (*schießen*) at each other; (*warten*) for each other; **a~ folgend** successive; (*Tage*) consecutive.

Aufenthalt *m* stay; **10 Minuten A~ haben** (*Zug:*) stop for 10 minutes. **A~serlaubnis, A~sgenehmigung** *f* residence permit. **A~sraum** *m* recreation room; (*im Hotel*) lounge

Auferstehung *f* - resurrection

aufessen† *vt sep* eat up

auffahr|en† *vi sep* (*sein*) drive up; (*aufprallen*) crash, run (**auf** + *acc* into). **A~t** *f* drive; (*Autobahn-*) access road, slip road; (*Bergfahrt*) ascent

auffallen† *vi sep* (*sein*) be conspicuous; **unangenehm a~** make a bad impression

auffällig *adj* conspicuous

auffangen† *vt sep* catch; pick up

auffass|en *vt sep* understand; (*deuten*) take. **A~ung** *f* understanding; (*Ansicht*) view

aufforder|n *vt sep* ask; (*einladen*) invite. **A~ung** *f* request; invitation

auffrischen *v sep* ● *vt* freshen up; revive (*Erinnerung*); **seine Englischkenntnisse a~** brush up one's English

aufführ|en *vt sep* perform; (*angeben*) list; **sich a~en** behave. **A~ung** *f* performance

auffüllen *vt sep* fill up

Aufgabe *f* task; (*Rechen-*) problem; (*Verzicht*) giving up; **A~n** (*Sch*) homework *sg*

Aufgang *m* way up; (*Treppe*) stairs *pl*; (*der Sonne*) rise

aufgeben† *v sep* ● *vt* give up; post (*Brief*); send (*Telegramm*); place (*Bestellung*); register (*Gepäck*); put in the paper (*Annonce*); **jdm eine Aufgabe a~** set s.o. a task; **jdm Suppe a~** serve s.o. with soup ● *vi* (*haben*) give up

Aufgebot *nt* contingent (**an** + *dat* of); (*Relig*) banns *pl*

aufgedunsen *adj* bloated

aufgehen† *vi sep* (*sein*) open; (*sich lösen*) come undone; (*Teig, Sonne:*) rise; (*Saat:*) come up; (*Math*) come out exactly; **in Flammen a~** go up in flames

aufgelegt *adj* **gut/schlecht a~ sein** be in a good/bad mood

aufgeregt *adj* excited; (*erregt*) agitated

aufgeschlossen *adj* (*fig*) open-minded

aufgeweckt *adj* (*fig*) bright

aufgießen† *vt sep* pour on; (*aufbrühen*) make (*Tee*)

aufgreifen† *vt sep* pick up; take up (*Vorschlag, Thema*)

aufgrund *prep* (+ *gen*) on the strength of

Aufguss *m* infusion

aufhaben† *v sep* ● *vt* have on; **den Mund a~** have one's mouth open; **viel a~** (*Sch*) have a lot of homework ● *vi* (*haben*) be open

aufhalten† *vt sep* hold up; (*anhalten*) stop; (*abhalten*) keep; (*offenhalten*) hold open; hold out (*Hand*); **sich a~** stay; (*sich befassen*) spend one's time (**mit** on)

aufhäng|en *vt/i sep* (*haben*) hang up; (*henken*) hang; **sich a~en** hang oneself. **A~er** *m* **-s,-** loop

aufheben† *vt sep* pick up; (*hochheben*) raise; (*aufbewahren*) keep; (*beenden*) end; (*rückgängig machen*) lift; (*abschaffen*) abolish; (*Jur*) quash (*Urteil*); repeal (*Gesetz*); (*ausgleichen*) cancel out; **gut aufgehoben sein** be well looked after

aufheitern *vt sep* cheer up; **sich a~** (*Wetter:*) brighten up

aufhellen *vt sep* lighten; **sich a~** (*Himmel:*) brighten

aufhetzen *vt sep* incite

aufholen *v sep* ● *vt* make up ● *vi* (*haben*) catch up; (*zeitlich*) make up time

aufhören *vi sep (haben)* stop

aufklappen *vt/i sep (sein)* open

aufklär|en *vt sep* solve; **jdn a~en** enlighten s.o.; **sich a~en** be solved; *(Wetter:)* clear up. **A~ung** *f* solution; enlightenment; *(Mil)* reconnaissance; **sexuelle A~ung** sex education

aufkleb|en *vt sep* stick on. **A~er** *m* **-s,-** sticker

aufknöpfen *vt sep* unbutton

aufkochen *v sep* ●*vt* bring to the boil ●*vi (sein)* come to the boil

aufkommen† *vi sep (sein)* start; *(Wind:)* spring up; *(Mode:)* come in

aufkrempeln *vt sep* roll up

aufladen† *vt sep* load; *(Electr)* charge

Auflage *f* impression; *(Ausgabe)* edition; *(Zeitungs-)* circulation

auflassen† *vt sep* leave open; leave on *(Hut)*

Auflauf *m* crowd; *(Culin)* ≈ soufflé

auflegen *v sep* ●*vt* apply **(auf +** *acc* to); put down *(Hörer)*; **neu a~** reprint ●*vi (haben)* ring off

auflehn|en (sich) *vr sep (fig)* rebel. **A~ung** *f* - rebellion

auflesen† *vt sep* pick up

aufleuchten *vi sep (haben)* light up

auflös|en *vt sep* dissolve; close *(Konto)*; **sich a~en** dissolve; *(Nebel:)* clear. **A~ung** dissolution; *(Lösung)* solution

aufmach|en *v sep* ●*vt* open; *(lösen)* undo; **sich a~en** set out **(nach** for) ●*vi (haben)* open; **jdm a~en** open the door to s.o. **A~ung** *f* **-,-en** get-up

aufmerksam *adj* attentive; **a~ werden auf** (+ *acc*) notice; **jdn a~ machen auf** (+ *acc*) draw s.o.'s attention to. **A~keit** *f* **-,-en** attention; *(Höflichkeit)* courtesy

aufmuntern *vt sep* cheer up

Aufnahme *f* **-,-n** acceptance; *(Empfang)* reception; *(in Klub, Krankenhaus)* admission; *(Einbeziehung)* inclusion; *(Beginn)* start; *(Foto)* photograph; *(Film-)* shot; *(Mus)* recording; *(Band-)* tape recording. **a~fähig** *adj* receptive. **A~prüfung** *f* entrance examination

aufnehmen† *vt sep* pick up; *(absorbieren)* absorb; take *(Nahrung, Foto)*; *(fassen)* hold; *(annehmen)* accept; *(leihen)* borrow; *(empfangen)* receive; *(in Klub, Krankenhaus)* admit; *(beherbergen, geistig erfassen)* take in; *(einbeziehen)* include; *(beginnen)* take up; *(niederschreiben)* take down; *(filmen)* film, shoot; *(Mus)* record; **auf Band a~** tape[-record]

aufopfer|n *vt sep* sacrifice; **sich a~n** sacrifice oneself. **A~ung** *f* self-sacrifice

aufpassen *vi sep (haben)* pay attention; *(sich vorsehen)* take care; **a~ auf** (+ *acc*) look after

Aufprall *m* **-[e]s** impact. **a~en** *vi sep (sein)* **a~en auf** (+ *acc*) hit

aufpumpen *vt sep* pump up, inflate

aufputsch|en *vt sep* incite. **A~mittel** *nt* stimulant

aufquellen† *vi sep (sein)* swell

aufraffen *vt sep* pick up; **sich a~** pick oneself up; *(fig)* pull oneself together

aufragen *vi sep (sein)* rise [up]

aufräumen *vt/i sep (haben)* tidy up; *(wegräumen)* put away

aufrecht *adj & adv* upright. **a~erhalten**† *vt sep (fig)* maintain

aufreg|en *vt* excite; *(beunruhigen)* upset; *(ärgern)* annoy; **sich a~en** get excited; *(sich erregen)* get worked up. **a~end** *adj* exciting. **A~ung** *f* excitement

aufreiben† *vt sep* chafe; (*fig*) wear down. **a~d** *adj* trying

aufreißen† *v sep* ●*vt* tear open; dig up (*Straße*); open wide (*Augen, Mund*) ●*vi* (*sein*) split open

aufrichtig *adj* sincere. **A~keit** *f* - sincerity

aufrollen *vt sep* roll up; (*entrollen*) unroll

aufrücken *vi sep* (*sein*) move up; (*fig*) be promoted

Aufruf *m* appeal (**an** + *dat* to); **a~en**† *vt sep* call out (*Namen*); **jdn a~en** call s.o.'s name

Aufruhr *m* **-s,-e** turmoil; (*Empörung*) revolt

aufrühr|en *vt sep* stir up. **A~er** *m* **-s,-** rebel. **a~erisch** *adj* inflammatory; (*rebellisch*) rebellious

aufrunden *vt sep* round up

aufrüsten *vi sep* (*haben*) arm

aufsagen *vt sep* recite

aufsässig *adj* rebellious

Aufsatz *m* top; (*Sch*) essay

aufsaugen† *vt sep* soak up

aufschauen *vi sep* (*haben*) look up (**zu** at/(*fig*) to)

aufschichten *vt sep* stack up

aufschieben† *vt sep* slide open; (*verschieben*) put off, postpone

Aufschlag *m* impact; (*Tennis*) service; (*Hosen-*) turn-up; (*Ärmel-*) upturned cuff; (*Revers*) lapel; (*Comm*) surcharge. **a~en**† *v sep* ●*vt* open; crack (*Ei*); (*hochschlagen*) turn up; (*errichten*) put up; (*erhöhen*) increase; cast on (*Masche*); **sich** (*dat*) **das Knie a~en** cut [open] one's knee ●*vi* (*haben*) hit (**auf etw** *acc/dat* sth); (*Tennis*) serve; (*teurer werden*) go up

aufschließen† *v sep* ●*vt* unlock ●*vi* (*haben*) unlock the door

aufschlussreich *adj* revealing; (*lehrreich*) informative

aufschneiden† *v sep* ●*vt* cut open; (*in Scheiben*) slice ●*vi* (*haben*) ⓘ exaggerate

Aufschnitt *m* sliced sausage, cold meat [and cheese]

aufschrauben *vt sep* screw on; (*abschrauben*) unscrew

Aufschrei *m* [sudden] cry

aufschreiben† *vt sep* write down; **jdn a~** (*Polizist:*) book s.o.

Aufschrift *f* inscription; (*Etikett*) label

Aufschub *m* delay; (*Frist*) grace

aufschürfen *vt sep* **sich** (*dat*) **das Knie a~** graze one's knee

aufschwingen† **(sich)** *vr sep* find the energy (**zu** for)

Aufschwung *m* (*fig*) upturn

aufsehen† *vi sep* (*haben*) look up (**zu** at/(*fig*) to). **A~** *nt* **-s A~ erregen** cause a sensation; **A~ erregend** sensational

Aufseher(in) *m* **-s,-** (*f* **-,-nen**) supervisor; (*Gefängnis-*) warder

aufsetzen *vt sep* put on; (*verfassen*) draw up; (*entwerfen*) draft; **sich a~** sit up

Aufsicht *f* supervision; (*Person*) supervisor. **A~srat** *m* board of directors

aufsperren *vt sep* open wide

aufspielen *v sep* ●*vi* (*haben*) play ●*vr* **sich a~** show off

aufspießen *vt sep* spear

aufspringen† *vi sep* (*sein*) jump up; (*aufprallen*) bounce; (*sich öffnen*) burst open

aufspüren *vt sep* track down

aufstacheln *vt sep* incite

Aufstand *m* uprising, rebellion

aufständisch *adj* rebellious

aufstehen† *vi sep* (*sein*) get up; (*offen sein*) be open; (*fig*) rise up

a

aufsteigen† *vi sep* (*sein*) get on; (*Reiter:*) mount; (*Bergsteiger:*) climb up; (*hochsteigen*) rise [up]; (*fig: befördert werden*) rise (**zu** to); (*Sport*) be promoted

aufstell|en *vt sep* put up; (*Culin*) put on; (*postieren*) post; (*in einer Reihe*) line up; (*nominieren*) nominate; (*Sport*) select (*Mannschaft*); make out (*Liste*); lay down (*Regel*); make (*Behauptung*); set up (*Rekord*). **A~ung** *f* nomination; (*Liste*) list

Aufstieg *m* **-[e]s, -e** ascent; (*fig*) rise; (*Sport*) promotion

Aufstoßen *nt* **-s** burping

aufstrebend *adj* (*fig*) ambitious

Aufstrich *m* [sandwich] spread

aufstützen *vt sep* rest (**auf** + *acc* on); **sich a~** lean (**auf** + *acc* on)

Auftakt *m* (*fig*) start

auftauchen *vi sep* (*sein*) emerge; (*fig*) turn up; (*Frage:*) crop up

auftauen *vt/i sep* (*sein*) thaw

aufteil|en *vt sep* divide [up]. **A~ung** *f* division

auftischen *vt sep* serve [up]

Auftrag *m* **-[e]s,⸗e** task; (*Kunst*) commission; (*Comm*) order; **im A~** (+ *gen*) on behalf of. **a~en**† *vt sep* apply; (*servieren*) serve; (*abtragen*) wear out; **jdm a~en** instruct s.o. (**zu** to). **A~geber** *m* **-s,-** client

auftrennen *vt sep* unpick, undo

auftreten† *vi sep* (*sein*) tread; (*sich benehmen*) behave, act; (*Theat*) appear; (*die Bühne betreten*) enter; (*vorkommen*) occur

Auftrieb *m* buoyancy; (*fig*) boost

Auftritt *m* (*Theat*) appearance; (*auf die Bühne*) entrance; (*Szene*) scene

aufwachen *vi sep* (*sein*) wake up

aufwachsen† *vi sep* (*sein*) grow up

Aufwand *m* **-[e]s** expenditure; (*Luxus*) extravagance; (*Mühe*) trouble; **A~ treiben** be extravagant

aufwändig *adj* = **aufwendig**

aufwärmen *vt sep* heat up; (*fig*) rake up; **sich a~** warm oneself; (*Sport*) warm up

Aufwartefrau *f* cleaner

aufwärts *adv* upwards; (*bergauf*) uphill; **es geht a~ mit jdm/etw** someone/something is improving

Aufwartung *f* - cleaner

aufwecken *vt sep* wake up

aufweichen *v sep* ●*vt* soften ●*vi* (*sein*) become soft

aufweisen† *vt sep* have, show

aufwend|en† *vt sep* spend; **Mühe a~en** take pains. **a~ig** *adj* lavish; (*teuer*) expensive

aufwert|en *vt sep* revalue. **A~ung** *f* revaluation

aufwickeln *vt sep* roll up; (*auswickeln*) unwrap

Aufwiegler *m* **-s,-** agitator

aufwisch|en *vt sep* wipe up; wash (*Fußboden*). **A~lappen** *m* floorcloth

aufwühlen *vt sep* churn up

aufzähl|en *vt sep* enumerate, list. **A~ung** *f* list

aufzeichn|en *vt sep* record; (*zeichnen*) draw. **A~ung** *f* recording; **A~ungen** notes

aufziehen† *v sep* ●*vt* pull up; hoist (*Segel*); (*öffnen*) open; draw (*Vorhang*); (*großziehen*) bring up; rear (*Tier*); mount (*Bild*); thread (*Perlen*); wind up (*Uhr*); (🅸: *necken*) tease ●*vi* (*sein*) approach

Aufzug *m* hoist; (*Fahrstuhl*) lift, (*Amer*) elevator; (*Prozession*) procession; (*Theat*) act

Augapfel *m* eyeball

Auge *nt* **-s,-n** eye; (*Punkt*) spot;

vier A~n werfen throw a four; **gute A~n** good eyesight; **unter vier A~n** in private; **im A~ behalten** keep in sight; (*fig*) bear in mind

Augenblick *m* moment; **A~!** just a moment! **a~lich** *adj* immediate; (*derzeitig*) present ● *adv* immediately; (*derzeit*) at present

Augen|braue *f* eyebrow. **A~höhle** *f* eye socket. **A~licht** *nt* sight. **A~lid** *nt* eyelid

August *m* **-[s]** August

Auktion /ˈtsi̯oːn/ *f* **-,-en** auction

Aula *f* **-,-len** (*Sch*) [assembly] hall

Au-pair-Mädchen /oˈpɛːr-/ *nt* aupair

aus *prep* (+ *dat*) out of; (*von*) from; (*bestehend*) [made] of; **aus Angst** from *or* out of fear; **aus Spaß** for fun ● *adv* out; (*Licht, Radio*) off; **aus sein auf** (+ *acc*) be after; **aus und ein** in and out; **von sich aus** of one's own accord; **von mir aus** as far as I'm concerned

ausarbeiten *vt sep* work out

ausarten *vi sep* (*sein*) degenerate (**in** + *acc* into)

ausatmen *vt/i sep* (*haben*) breathe out

ausbauen *vt sep* remove; (*vergrößern*) extend; (*fig*) expand

ausbedingen† *vt sep* **sich** (*dat*) **a~** insist on; (*zur Bedingung machen*) stipulate

ausbesser|n *vt sep* mend, repair. **A~ung** *f* repair

ausbeulen *vt sep* remove the dents from; (*dehnen*) make baggy

ausbild|en *vt sep* train; (*formen*) form; (*entwickeln*) develop; **sich a~en** train (**als/zu** as); (*entstehen*) develop. **A~ung** *f* training; (*Sch*) education

ausbitten† *vt sep* **sich** (*dat*) **a~** ask for; (*verlangen*) insist on

ausblasen† *vt sep* blow out

ausbleiben† *vi sep* (*sein*) fail to appear/ (*Erfolg:*) materialize; (*nicht heimkommen*) stay out

Ausblick *m* view

ausbrech|en† *vi sep* (*sein*) break out; (*Vulkan:*) erupt; (*fliehen*) escape; **in Tränen a~en** burst into tears. **A~er** *m* runaway

ausbreit|en *vt sep* spread [out]. **A~ung** *f* spread

Ausbruch *m* outbreak; (*Vulkan-*) eruption; (*Wut-*) outburst; (*Flucht*) escape, break-out

ausbrüten *vt sep* hatch

Ausdauer *f* perseverance; (*körperlich*) stamina. **a~nd** *adj* persevering; (*unermüdlich*) untiring

ausdehnen *vt sep* stretch; (*fig*) extend; **sich a~** stretch; (*Phys & fig*) expand; (*dauern*) last

ausdenken† *vt sep* **sich** (*dat*) **a~** think up; (*sich vorstellen*) imagine

Ausdruck *m* expression; (*Fach-*) term; (*Computer*) printout. **a~en** *vt sep* print

ausdrücken *vt sep* squeeze out; squeeze (*Zitrone*); stub out (*Zigarette*); (*äußern*) express

ausdrucks|los *adj* expressionless. **a~voll** *adj* expressive

auseinander *adv* apart; (*entzwei*) in pieces; **a~ falten** unfold; **a~ gehen** part; (*Linien, Meinungen:*) diverge; (*Ehe:*) break up; **a~ halten** tell apart; **a~ nehmen** take apart *or* to pieces; **a~ setzen** explain (**jdm** to s.o.); **sich a~ setzen** sit apart; (*sich aussprechen*) have it out (**mit jdm** with s.o.); come to grips (**mit einem Problem** with a problem). **A~setzung** *f* **-,-en** discussion; (*Streit*) argument

auserlesen *adj* select, choice

Ausfahrt *f* drive; (*Autobahn-,*

Garagen-) exit

Ausfall *m* failure; (*Absage*) cancellation; (*Comm*) loss. **a~en**† *vi sep* (*sein*) fall out; (*versagen*) fail; (*abgesagt werden*) be cancelled; **gut/schlecht a~en** turn out to be good/poor

ausfallend, **ausfällig** *adj* abusive

ausfertig|en *vt sep* make out. **A~ung** *f* **-,-en in doppelter A~ung** in duplicate

ausfindig *adj* **a~ machen** find

Ausflug *m* excursion, outing

Ausflügler *m* **-s,-** [day-]tripper

Ausfluss *m* outlet; (*Abfluss*) drain; (*Med*) discharge

ausfragen *vt sep* question

Ausfuhr *f* **-,-en** (*Comm*) export

ausführ|en *vt sep* take out; (*Comm*) export; (*erklären*) explain. **a~lich** *adj* detailed ● *adv* in detail. **A~ung** *f* execution; (*Comm*) version; (*äußere*) finish; (*Qualität*) workmanship; (*Erklärung*) explanation

Ausgabe *f* issue; (*Buch-*) edition; (*Comm*) version

Ausgang *m* way out, exit; (*Flugsteig*) gate; (*Ende*) end; (*Ergebnis*) outcome. **A~spunkt** *m* starting point. **A~ssperre** *f* curfew

ausgeben† *vt sep* hand out; issue (*Fahrkarten*); spend (*Geld*); **sich a~ als** pretend to be

ausgebildet *adj* trained

ausgebucht *adj* fully booked; (*Vorstellung*) sold out

ausgefallen *adj* unusual

ausgefranst *adj* frayed

ausgeglichen *adj* [well-]balanced

ausgeh|en† *vi sep* (*sein*) go out; (*Haare:*) fall out; (*Vorräte, Geld:*) run out; (*verblassen*) fade; **gut/schlecht a~en** end well/badly; **davon a~en, dass** assume that. **A~verbot** *nt* curfew

ausgelassen *adj* high-spirited

ausgemacht *adj* agreed

ausgenommen *conj* except; **a~ wenn** unless

ausgeprägt *adj* marked

ausgeschlossen *pred adj* out of the question

ausgeschnitten *adj* low-cut

ausgesprochen *adj* marked ● *adv* decidedly

ausgestorben *adj* extinct; **[wie] a~** (*Straße:*) deserted

Ausgestoßene(r) *m/f* outcast

ausgezeichnet *adj* excellent

ausgiebig *adj* extensive; (*ausgedehnt*) long; **a~ Gebrauch machen von** make full use of

ausgießen† *vt sep* pour out

Ausgleich *m* **-[e]s** balance; (*Entschädigung*) compensation. **a~en**† *v sep* ● *vt* balance; even out (*Höhe*); (*wettmachen*) compensate for; **sich a~en** balance out ● *vi* (*haben*) (*Sport*) equalize. **A~streffer** *m* equalizer

ausgrab|en† *vt sep* dig up; (*Archaeology*) excavate. **A~ung** *f* **-,-en** excavation

Ausguss *m* [kitchen] sink

aushaben† *vt sep* have finished (*Buch*)

aushalten† *vt sep* bear, stand; hold (*Note*); (*Unterhalt zahlen für*) keep; **nicht auszuhalten, nicht zum A~** unbearable

aushändigen *vt sep* hand over

aushängen[1] *vt sep* (*reg*) display; take off its hinges (*Tür*)

aushäng|en[2]† *vi sep* (*haben*) be displayed. **A~eschild** *nt* sign

ausheben† *vt sep* excavate

aushecken *vt sep* (*fig*) hatch

aushelfen† *vi sep* (*haben*)

help out (**jdm** s.o.)

Aushilf|e *f* [temporary] assistant; **zur A~e** to help out. **A~skraft** *f* temporary worker. **a~sweise** *adv* temporarily

aushöhlen *vt sep* hollow out

auskennen† **(sich)** *vr sep* know one's way around; **sich mit/in etw** (*dat*) **a~** know all about sth

auskommen† *vi sep* (*sein*) manage (**mit/ohne** with/without); (*sich vertragen*) get on (**gut** well)

auskugeln *vt sep* **sich** (*dat*) **den Arm a~** dislocate one's shoulder

auskühlen *vt/i sep* (*sein*) cool

auskundschaften *vt sep* spy out

Auskunft *f* **-,¨e** information; (*A~sstelle*) information desk/ (*Büro*) bureau; (*Teleph*) enquiries *pl*; **eine A~** a piece of information

auslachen *vt sep* laugh at

Auslage *f* [window] display; **A~n** expenses

Ausland *nt* **im/ins A~** abroad

Ausländ|er(in) *m* **-s,-** (*f* **-,-nen**) foreigner. **a~isch** *adj* foreign

Auslandsgespräch *nt* international call

auslass|en† *vt sep* let out; let down (*Saum*); (*weglassen*) leave out; (*versäumen*) miss; (*Culin*) melt; (*fig*) vent (*Ärger*) (**an** + *dat* on). **A~ungszeichen** *nt* apostrophe

Auslauf *m* run. **a~en**† *vi sep* (*sein*) run out; (*Farbe:*) run; (*Naut*) put to sea; (*Modell:*) be discontinued

ausleeren *vt sep* empty [out]

ausleg|en *vt sep* lay out; display (*Waren*); (*auskleiden*) line (**mit** with); (*bezahlen*) pay; (*deuten*) interpret. **A~ung** *f* **-,-en** interpretation

ausleihen† *vt sep* lend; **sich** (*dat*) **a~** borrow

Auslese *f* **-** selection; (*fig*) pick; (*Elite*) elite

ausliefer|n *vt sep* hand over; (*Jur*) extradite. **A~ung** *f* handing over; (*Jur*) extradition; (*Comm*) distribution

ausloggen *vi sep* log off *or* out

auslosen *vt sep* draw lots for

auslös|en *vt sep* set off, trigger; (*fig*) cause; arouse (*Begeisterung*); (*einlösen*) redeem; pay a ransom for (*Gefangene*). **A~er** *m* **-s,-** trigger; (*Phot*) shutter release

Auslosung *f* draw

auslüften *vt/i sep* (*haben*) air

ausmachen *vt sep* put out; (*abschalten*) turn off; (*abmachen*) arrange; (*erkennen*) make out; (*betragen*) amount to; (*wichtig sein*) matter

Ausmaß *nt* extent; **A~e** dimensions

Ausnahm|e *f* **-,-n** exception. **A~ezustand** *m* state of emergency. **a~slos** *adv* without exception. **a~sweise** *adv* as an exception

ausnehmen† *vt sep* take out; gut (*Fisch*); **sich gut a~** look good. **a~d** *adv* exceptionally

ausnutz|en, **ausnütz|en** *vt sep* exploit. **A~ung** *f* exploitation

auspacken *vt sep* unpack; (*auswickeln*) unwrap

ausplaudern *vt sep* let out, blab

ausprobieren *vt sep* try out

Auspuff *m* **-s** exhaust [system]. **A~gase** *ntpl* exhaust fumes. **A~rohr** *nt* exhaust pipe

auspusten *vt sep* blow out

ausradieren *vt sep* rub out

ausrauben *vt sep* rob

ausräuchern *vt sep* smoke out; fumigate (*Zimmer*)

ausräumen *vt sep* clear out

a

ausrechnen *vt sep* work out

Ausrede *f* excuse. **a~n** *v sep* ●*vi* (*haben*) finish speaking ●*vt* **jdm etw a~n** talk s.o. out of sth

ausreichen *vi sep* (*haben*) be enough. **a~d** *adj* adequate

Ausreise *f* departure. **a~n** *vi sep* (*sein*) leave the country. **A~visum** *nt* exit visa

ausreißen† *v sep* ●*vt* pull *or* tear out ●*vi* (*sein*) [!] run away

ausrenken *vt sep* dislocate

ausrichten *vt sep* align; (*bestellen*) deliver; (*erreichen*) achieve; **jdm a~** tell s.o. (**dass** that); **ich soll Ihnen Grüße von X a~** X sends [you] his regards

ausrotten *vt sep* exterminate; (*fig*) eradicate

Ausruf *m* exclamation. **a~en**† *vt sep* exclaim; call out (*Namen*); (*verkünden*) proclaim; **jdn a~en lassen** put out a call for s.o. **A~ezeichen** *nt* exclamation mark

ausruhen *vt/i sep* (*haben*) rest; **sich a~** have a rest

ausrüst|en *vt sep* equip. **A~ung** *f* equipment; (*Mil*) kit

ausrutschen *vi sep* (*sein*) slip

Aussage *f* **-,-n** statement; (*Jur*) testimony, evidence; (*Gram*) predicate. **a~n** *vt/i sep* (*haben*) state; (*Jur*) give evidence, testify

ausschalten *vt sep* switch off

Ausschank *m* sale of alcoholic drinks; (*Bar*) bar

Ausschau *f* - **A~ halten nach** look out for

ausscheiden† *vi sep* (*sein*) leave; (*Sport*) drop out; (*nicht in Frage kommen*) be excluded

ausschenken *vt sep* pour out

ausscheren *vi sep* (*sein*) (*Auto*) pull out

ausschildern *vt sep* signpost

ausschimpfen *vt sep* tell off

ausschlafen† *vi/r sep* (*haben*) **[sich] a~** get enough sleep; (*morgens*) sleep late

Ausschlag *m* (*Med*) rash; **den A~ geben** (*fig*) tip the balance. **a~gebend** *adj* decisive

ausschließ|en† *vt sep* lock out; (*fig*) exclude; (*entfernen*) expel. **a~lich** *adj* exclusive

ausschlüpfen *vi sep* (*sein*) hatch

Ausschluss *m* exclusion; expulsion; **unter A~ der Öffentlichkeit** in camera

ausschneiden† *vt sep* cut out

Ausschnitt *m* excerpt, extract; (*Zeitungs-*) cutting; (*Hals-*) neckline

ausschöpfen *vt sep* ladle out; (*Naut*) bail out; exhaust (*Möglichkeiten*)

ausschreiben† *vt sep* write out; (*ausstellen*) make out; (*bekanntgeben*) announce; put out to tender (*Auftrag*)

Ausschreitungen *fpl* riots; (*Exzesse*) excesses

Ausschuss *m* committee; (*Comm*) rejects *pl*

ausschütten *vt sep* tip out; (*verschütten*) spill; (*leeren*) empty

aussehen† *vi sep* (*haben*) look; **wie sieht er/es aus?** what does he/it look like? **A~** *nt* **-s** appearance

außen *adv* [on the] outside; **nach a~** outwards. **A~bordmotor** *m* outboard motor. **A~handel** *m* foreign trade. **A~minister** *m* Foreign Minister. **A~politik** *f* foreign policy. **A~seite** *f* outside. **A~seiter** *m* **-s,-** outsider; (*fig*) misfit. **A~stände** *mpl* outstanding debts

außer *prep* (+ *dat*) except [for], apart from; (*außerhalb*) out of; **a~**

sich (*fig*) beside oneself •*conj* except; **a~ wenn** unless. **a~dem** *adv* in addition, as well •*conj* moreover

äußer|e(r,s) *adj* external; (*Teil, Schicht*) outer. **Ä~e(s)** *nt* exterior; (*Aussehen*) appearance

außer|ehelich *adj* extramarital. **a~gewöhnlich** *adj* exceptional. **a~halb** *prep* (+ *gen*) outside •*adv* **a~halb wohnen** live outside town

äußer|lich *adj* external; (*fig*) outward. **ä~n** *vt* express; **sich ä~n** comment; (*sich zeigen*) manifest itself

außerordentlich *adj* extraordinary

äußerst *adv* extremely

äußerste|(r,s) *adj* outermost; (*weiteste*) furthest; (*höchste*) utmost, extreme; (*letzte*) last; (*schlimmste*) worst. **Ä~(s)** *nt* **das Ä~** the limit; (*Schlimmste*) the worst; **sein Ä~s tun** do one's utmost; **aufs Ä~** extremely

Äußerung *f* **-,-en** comment; (*Bemerkung*) remark

aussetzen *v sep* •*vt* expose (*dat* to); abandon (*Kind*); launch (*Boot*); offer (*Belohnung*); **etwas auszusetzen haben an** (+ *dat*) find fault with •*vi* (*haben*) stop; (*Motor:*) cut out

Aussicht *f* **-,-en** view/(*fig*) prospect (**auf** + *acc* of); **weitere A~en** (*Meteorology*) further outlook *sg*. **a~slos** *adj* hopeless

ausspannen *v sep* •*vt* spread out; unhitch (*Pferd*) •*vi* (*haben*) rest

aussperren *vt sep* lock out

ausspielen *v sep* •*vt* play (*Karte*); (*fig*) play off (**gegen** against) •*vi* (*haben*) (*Kartenspiel*) lead

Aussprache *f* pronunciation; (*Gespräch*) talk

aussprechen† *vt sep* pronounce; (*äußern*) express; **sich a~** talk; come out (**für**/**gegen** in favour of/against)

Ausspruch *m* saying

ausspucken *v sep* •*vt* spit out •*vi* (*haben*) spit

ausspülen *vt sep* rinse out

ausstatt|en *vt sep* equip. **A~ung** *f* **-,-en** equipment; (*Innen-*) furnishings *pl*; (*Theat*) scenery and costumes *pl*

ausstehen† *v sep* •*vt* suffer; **Angst a~** be frightened; **ich kann sie nicht a~** I can't stand her •*vi* (*haben*) be outstanding

aussteigen† *vi sep* (*sein*) get out; (*aus Bus, Zug*) get off; **alles a~!** all change!

ausstell|en *vt sep* exhibit; (*Comm*) display; (*ausfertigen*) make out; issue (*Pass*). **A~ung** *f* exhibition; (*Comm*) display

aussterben† *vi sep* (*sein*) die out; (*Biology*) become extinct

Aussteuer *f* trousseau

Ausstieg *m* **-[e]s,-e** exit

ausstopfen *vt sep* stuff

ausstoßen† *vt sep* emit; utter (*Fluch*); heave (*Seufzer*); (*ausschließen*) expel

ausstrahl|en *vt/i sep* (*sein*) radiate, emit; (*Radio, TV*) broadcast. **A~ung** *f* radiation

ausstrecken *vt sep* stretch out; put out (*Hand*)

ausstreichen† *vt sep* cross out

ausströmen *v sep* •*vi* (*sein*) pour out; (*entweichen*) escape •*vt* emit; (*ausstrahlen*) radiate

aussuchen *vt sep* pick, choose

Austausch *m* exchange. **a~bar** *adj* interchangeable. **a~en** *vt sep* exchange; (*auswechseln*) replace

austeilen *vt sep* distribute

Auster *f* **-,-n** oyster

a

austragen† *vt sep* deliver; hold (*Wettkampf*); play (*Spiel*)

Austral|ien /-i̯ən/ *nt* **-s** Australia. **A~ier(in)** *m* **-s,-** (*f* **-,-nen**) Australian. **a~isch** *adj* Australian

austreiben† *vt sep* drive out; (*Relig*) exorcize

austreten† *v sep* ● *vt* stamp out; (*abnutzen*) wear down ● *vi* (*sein*) come out; (*ausscheiden*) leave (**aus etw** sth); **[mal] a~** ⓘ go to the loo

austrinken† *vt/i sep* (*haben*) drink up; (*leeren*) drain

Austritt *m* resignation

austrocknen *vt/i sep* (*sein*) dry out

ausüben *vt sep* practise; carry on (*Handwerk*); exercise (*Recht*); exert (*Druck, Einfluss*)

Ausverkauf *m* [clearance] sale. **a~t** *adj* sold out

Auswahl *f* choice, selection; (*Comm*) range; (*Sport*) team

auswählen *vt sep* choose, select

Auswander|er *m* emigrant. **a~n** *vi sep* (*sein*) emigrate. **A~ung** *f* emigration

auswärt|ig *adj* non-local; (*ausländisch*) foreign. **a~s** *adv* outwards; (*Sport*) away. **A~sspiel** *nt* away game

auswaschen† *vt sep* wash out

auswechseln *vt sep* change; (*ersetzen*) replace; (*Sport*) substitute

Ausweg *m* (*fig*) way out

ausweichen† *vi sep* (*sein*) get out of the way; **jdm/etw a~en** avoid/ (*sich entziehen*) evade someone/ something

Ausweis *m* **-es,-e** pass; (*Mitglieds-, Studenten-*) card. **a~en**† *vt sep* deport; **sich a~en** prove one's identity. **A~papiere** *ntpl* identification papers. **A~ung** *f* deportation

auswendig *adv* by heart

auswerten *vt sep* evaluate

auswickeln *vt sep* unwrap

auswirk|en (sich) *vr sep* have an effect (**auf** + *acc* on). **A~ung** *f* effect; (*Folge*) consequence

auswringen *vt sep* wring out

auszahlen *vt sep* pay out; (*entlohnen*) pay off; (*abfinden*) buy out; **sich a~** (*fig*) pay off

auszählen *vt sep* count; (*Boxen*) count out

Auszahlung *f* payment

auszeichn|en *vt sep* (*Comm*) price; (*ehren*) honour; (*mit einem Preis*) award a prize to; (*Mil*) decorate; **sich a~en** distinguish oneself. **A~ung** *f* honour; (*Preis*) award; (*Mil*) decoration; (*Sch*) distinction

ausziehen† *v sep* ● *vt* pull out; (*auskleiden*) undress; take off (*Mantel, Schuhe*) ● *vi* (*sein*) move out; (*sich aufmachen*) set out

Auszug *m* departure; (*Umzug*) move; (*Ausschnitt*) extract; (*Bank-*) statement

Auto *nt* **-s,-s** car; **A~ fahren** drive; (*mitfahren*) go in the car. **A~bahn** *f* motorway

Autobiographie *f* autobiography

Auto|bus *m* bus. **A~fahrer(in)** *m(f)* driver, motorist. **A~fahrt** *f* drive

Autogramm *nt* **-s,-e** autograph

Automat *m* **-en,-en** automatic device; (*Münz-*) slot-machine; (*Verkaufs-*) vending-machine; (*Fahrkarten-*) machine; (*Techn*) robot. **A~ik** *f* - automatic mechanism; (*Auto*) automatic transmission

automatisch *adj* automatic

Autonummer *f* registration number

Autopsie *f* **-,-n** autopsy

Autor *m* **-s,-en** author
Auto|reisezug *m* Motorail. **A~rennen** *nt* motor race
Autorin *f* **-,-nen** author[ess]
Autori|sation /-'tsi̯o:n/ *f* **-** authorization. **A~tät** *f* **-,-en** authority
Auto|schlosser *m* motor mechanic. **A~skooter** *m* **-s,-** dodgem. **A~stopp** *m* **-s per A~stopp fahren** hitch-hike. **A~verleih** *m* car hire [firm]. **A~waschanlage** *f* car wash
autsch *int* ouch
Axt *f* **-,¨e** axe

Bb

B, b /be:/ *nt* **-** (*Mus*) B flat
Baby /'be:bi/ *nt* **-s,-s** baby. **B~ausstattung** *f* layette. **B~sitter** *m* **-s,-** babysitter
Bach *m* **-[e]s,¨e** stream
Backbord *nt* **-[e]s** port [side]
Backe *f* **-,-n** cheek
backen *vt/i*† (*haben*) bake; (*braten*) fry
Backenzahn *m* molar
Bäcker *m* **-s,-** baker. **B~ei** *f* **-,-en, B~laden** *m* baker's shop
Back|obst *nt* dried fruit. **B~ofen** *m* oven. **B~pfeife** *f* [F] slap in the face. **B~pflaume** *f* prune. **B~pulver** *nt* baking-powder. **B~stein** *m* brick
Bad *nt* **-[e]s,¨er** bath; (*Zimmer*) bathroom; (*Schwimm-*) pool; (*Ort*) spa
Bade|anstalt *f* swimming baths *pl*. **B~anzug** *m* swim-suit. **B~hose** *f* swimming trunks *pl*. **B~kappe** *f* bathing-cap. **B~mantel** *m* bathrobe. **b~n** *vi* (*haben*) have a bath; (*im Meer*) bathe ● *vt* bath; (*waschen*) bathe. **B~ort** *m* seaside resort. **B~wanne** *f* bath. **B~zimmer** *nt* bathroom
Bagger *m* **-s,-** excavator; (*Nass-*) dredger. **B~see** *m* flooded gravel-pit
Bahn *f* **-,-en** path; (*Astronomy*) orbit; (*Sport*) track; (*einzelne*) lane; (*Rodel-*) run; (*Stoff-*) width; (*Eisen-*) railway; (*Zug*) train; (*Straßen-*) tram. **b~brechend** *adj* (*fig*) pioneering. **B~hof** *m* [railway] station. **B~steig** *m* **-[e]s,-e** platform. **B~übergang** *m* level crossing
Bahre *f* **-,-n** stretcher
Baiser /bɛ'ze:/ *nt* **-s,-s** meringue
Bake *f* **-,-n** (*Naut, Aviat*) beacon
Bakterien /-i̯ən/ *fpl* bacteria
Balanc|e /ba'lã:sə/ *f* **-** balance. **b~ieren** *vt/i* (*haben/sein*) balance
bald *adv* soon; (*fast*) almost
Baldachin /-xi:n/ *m* **-s,-e** canopy
bald|ig *adj* early; (*Besserung*) speedy. **b~möglichst** *adv* as soon as possible
Balg *nt & m* **-[e]s,¨er** [F] brat
Balkan *m* **-s** Balkans *pl*
Balken *m* **-s,-** beam
Balkon /bal'kõ:/ *m* **-s,-s** balcony; (*Theat*) circle
Ball[1] *m* **-[e]s,¨e** ball
Ball[2] *m* **-[e]s,¨e** (*Tanz*) ball
Ballade *f* **-,-n** ballad
Ballast *m* **-[e]s** ballast. **B~stoffe** *mpl* roughage *sg*
Ballen *m* **-s,-** bale; (*Anat*) ball of the hand/(*Fuß-*) foot; (*Med*) bunion
Ballerina *f* **-,-nen** ballerina
Ballett *nt* **-s,-e** ballet
Ballon /ba'lõ:/ *m* **-s,-s** balloon
Balsam *m* **-s** balm

b

Balt|ikum *nt* **-s** Baltic States *pl*. **b~isch** *adj* Baltic

Bambus *m* **-ses,-se** bamboo

banal *adj* banal

Banane *f* **-,-n** banana

Banause *m* **-n,-n** philistine

Band[1] *nt* **-[e]s,¨er** ribbon; (*Naht-, Ton-, Ziel-*) tape; **am laufenden B~** [!] non-stop

Band[2] *m* **-[e]s,¨e** volume

Band[3] *nt* **-[e]s,-e** (*fig*) bond

Band[4] /bɛnt/ *f* **-,-s** [jazz] band

Bandag|e /ban'daːʒə/ *f* **-,-n** bandage. **b~ieren** *vt* bandage

Bande *f* **-,-n** gang

bändigen *vt* control, restrain; (*zähmen*) tame

Bandit *m* **-en,-en** bandit

Band|maß *nt* tape-measure. **B~scheibe** *f* (*Anat*) disc. **B~wurm** *m* tapeworm

Bang|e *f* **B~e haben** be afraid; **jdm B~e machen** frighten s.o. **b~en** *vi* (*haben*) fear (**um** for)

Banjo *nt* **-s,-s** banjo

Bank[1] *f* **-,¨e** bench

Bank[2] *f* **-,-en** (*Comm*) bank. **B~einzug** *m* direct debit

Bankett *nt* **-s,-e** banquet

Bankier /baŋ'kieː/ *m* **-s,-s** banker

Bankkonto *nt* bank account

Bankrott *m* **-s,-s** bankruptcy. **b~** *adj* bankrupt

Bankwesen *nt* banking

Bann *m* **-[e]s,-e** (*fig*) spell. **b~en** *vt* exorcize; (*abwenden*) avert; **[wie] gebannt** spellbound

Banner *nt* **-s,-** banner

bar *adj* (*rein*) sheer; (*Gold*) pure; **b~es Geld** cash; **[in] bar bezahlen** pay cash

Bar *f* **-,-s** bar

Bär *m* **-en,-en** bear

Baracke *f* **-,-n** (*Mil*) hut

Barb|ar *m* **-en,-en** barbarian. **b~arisch** *adj* barbaric

bar|fuß *adv* barefoot. **B~geld** *nt* cash

barmherzig *adj* merciful

barock *adj* baroque. **B~** *nt* & *m* **-[s]** baroque

Barometer *nt* **-s,-** barometer

Baron *m* **-s,-e** baron. **B~in** *f* **-,-nen** baroness

Barren *m* **-s,-** (*Gold-*) bar, ingot; (*Sport*) parallel bars *pl*. **B~gold** *nt* gold bullion

Barriere *f* **-,-n** barrier

Barrikade *f* **-,-n** barricade

barsch *adj* gruff

Barsch *m* **-[e]s,-e** (*Zool*) perch

Bart *m* **-[e]s,¨e** beard; (*der Katze*) whiskers *pl*

bärtig *adj* bearded

Barzahlung *f* cash payment

Basar *m* **-s,-e** bazaar

Base[1] *f* **-,-n** [female] cousin

Base[2] *f* **-,-n** (*Chemistry*) alkali, base

Basel *nt* **-s** Basle

basieren *vi* (*haben*) be based (**auf** + *dat* on)

Basilikum *nt* **-s** basil

Basis *f* **-,Basen** base; (*fig*) basis

basisch *adj* (*Chemistry*) alkaline

Bask|enmütze *f* beret. **b~isch** *adj* Basque

Bass *m* **-es,¨e** bass

Bassin /ba'sɛ̃ː/ *nt* **-s,-s** pond; (*Brunnen-*) basin; (*Schwimm-*) pool

Bassist *m* **-en,-en** bass player; (*Sänger*) bass

Bast *m* **-[e]s** raffia

basteln *vt* make ● *vi* (*haben*) do handicrafts

Batterie *f* **-,-n** battery

Bau¹ *m* **-[e]s,-e** burrow; (*Fuchs-*) earth

Bau² *m* **-[e]s,-ten** construction; (*Gebäude*) building; (*Auf-*) structure; (*Körper-*) build; (*B~stelle*) building site. **B~arbeiten** *fpl* building work *sg*; (*Straßen-*) roadworks

Bauch *m* **-[e]s, Bäuche** abdomen, belly; (*Magen*) stomach; (*Bauchung*) bulge. **b~ig** *adj* bulbous. **B~nabel** *m* navel. **B~redner** *m* ventriloquist. **B~schmerzen** *mpl* stomach-ache *sg*. **B~speicheldrüse** *f* pancreas

bauen *vt* build; (*konstruieren*) construct ● *vi* (*haben*) build (**an etw** *dat* sth); **b~ auf** (+ *acc*) (*fig*) rely on

Bauer¹ *m* **-n,-n** farmer; (*Schach*) pawn

Bauer² *nt* **-s,-** [bird]cage

bäuerlich *adj* rustic

Bauern|haus *nt* farmhouse. **B~hof** *m* farm

bau|fällig *adj* dilapidated. **B~genehmigung** *f* planning permission. **B~gerüst** *nt* scaffolding. **B~jahr** *nt* year of construction. **B~kunst** *f* architecture. **b~lich** *adj* structural

Baum *m* **-[e]s, Bäume** tree

baumeln *vi* (*haben*) dangle

bäumen (sich) *vr* rear [up]

Baum|schule *f* [tree] nursery. **B~wolle** *f* cotton

Bausch *m* **-[e]s, Bäusche** wad; **in B~ und Bogen** (*fig*) wholesale. **b~en** *vt* puff out

Bau|sparkasse *f* building society. **B~stein** *m* building brick. **B~stelle** *f* building site; (*Straßen-*) roadworks *pl*. **B~unternehmer** *m* building contractor

Bayer|(in) *m* **-n,-n** (*f* **-,-nen**) Bavarian. **B~n** *nt* **-s** Bavaria

bay[e]risch *adj* Bavarian

> *i*
>
> **Bayreuth** The Bavarian city of Bayreuth is a magnet for opera fans. The German composer Richard Wagner (1813-83) lived there, and since 1876 the Richard Wagner Festival has been staged annually. The Bayreuth festival theatre was built by Ludwig II, King of Bavaria, who was Wagner's greatest admirer.

Bazillus *m* **-,-len** bacillus

beabsichtig|en *vt* intend. **b~t** *adj* intended; intentional

beacht|en *vt* take notice of; (*einhalten*) observe; (*folgen*) follow; **nicht b~en** ignore. **b~lich** *adj* considerable. **B~ung** *f* **-** observance; **etw** (*dat*) **keine B~ung schenken** take no notice of sth

Beamte(r) *m*, **Beamtin** *f* **-,-nen** official; (*Staats-*) civil servant; (*Schalter-*) clerk

beanspruchen *vt* claim; (*erfordern*) demand

beanstand|en *vt* find fault with; (*Comm*) make a complaint about. **B~ung** *f* **-,-en** complaint

beantragen *vt* apply for

beantworten *vt* answer

bearbeiten *vt* work; (*weiter-*) process; (*behandeln*) treat (**mit** with); (*Admin*) deal with; (*redigieren*) edit; (*Theat*) adapt; (*Mus*) arrange

Beatmungsgerät *nt* ventilator

beaufsichtig|en *vt* supervise. **B~ung** *f* **-** supervision

beauftragen *vt* instruct; commission (*Künstler*)

bebauen *vt* build on; (*bestellen*) cultivate

beben *vi* (*haben*) tremble

Becher *m* **-s,-** beaker; (*Henkel-*) mug; (*Joghurt-, Sahne-*) carton

Becken *nt* **-s,-** basin; pool; (*Mus*)

cymbals *pl*; (*Anat*) pelvis

bedacht *adj* careful; **darauf b~** anxious (**zu** to)

bedächtig *adj* careful; slow

bedanken (sich) *vr* thank (**bei jdm** s.o.)

Bedarf *m* **-s** need/(*Comm*) demand (**an** + *dat* for); **bei B~** if required. **B~shaltestelle** *f* request stop

bedauer|lich *adj* regrettable. **b~licherweise** *adv* unfortunately. **b~n** *vt* regret; (*bemitleiden*) feel sorry for; **bedaure**! sorry! **b~nswert** *adj* pitiful; (*bedauerlich*) regrettable

bedeckt *adj* covered; (*Himmel*) overcast

bedenken† *vt* consider; (*überlegen*) think over. **B~** *pl* misgivings; **ohne B~** without hesitation

bedenklich *adj* doubtful; (*verdächtig*) dubious; (*ernst*) serious

bedeut|en *vi* (*haben*) mean. **b~end** *adj* important; (*beträchtlich*) considerable. **B~ung** *f* **-,-en** meaning; (*Wichtigkeit*) importance. **b~ungslos** *adj* meaningless; (*unwichtig*) unimportant. **b~ungsvoll** *adj* significant; (*vielsagend*) meaningful

bedien|en *vt* serve; (*betätigen*) operate; **sich [selbst] b~en** help oneself. **B~ung** *f* **-,-en** service; (*Betätigung*) operation; (*Kellner*) waiter; (*Kellnerin*) *f* waitress. **B~ungsgeld** *nt* service charge

Bedingung *f* **-,-en** condition; B~en conditions; (*Comm*) terms. **b~slos** *adj* unconditional

bedroh|en *vt* threaten. **b~lich** *adj* threatening. **B~ung** *f* threat

bedrücken *vt* depress

bedruckt *adj* printed

bedürf|en† *vi* (*haben*) (+ *gen*) need. **B~nis** *nt* **-ses,-se** need

Beefsteak /'bi:fste:k/ *nt* **-s,-s** steak; **deutsches B~** hamburger

beeilen (sich) *vr* hurry; hasten (**zu** to)

beeindrucken *vt* impress

beeinflussen *vt* influence

beeinträchtigen *vt* mar; (*schädigen*) impair

beengen *vt* restrict

beerdig|en *vt* bury. **B~ung** *f* **-,-en** funeral

Beere *f* **-,-n** berry

Beet *nt* **-[e]s,-e** (*Horticulture*) bed

Beete *f* **-,-n Rote B~** beetroot

befähig|en *vt* enable; (*qualifizieren*) qualify. **B~ung** *f* **-** qualification; (*Fähigkeit*) ability

befahrbar *adj* passable

befallen† *vt* attack; (*Angst:*) seize

befangen *adj* shy; (*gehemmt*) self-conscious; (*Jur*) biased. **B~heit** *f* **-** shyness; self-consciousness; bias

befassen (sich) *vr* concern oneself/(*behandeln*) deal (**mit** with)

Befehl *m* **-[e]s,-e** order; (*Leitung*) command (**über** + *acc* of). **b~en** † *vt* **jdm etw b~en** order s.o. to do sth ●*vi* (*haben*) give the orders. **B~sform** *f* (*Gram*) imperative. **B~shaber** *m* **-s,-** commander

befestigen *vt* fasten (**an** + *dat* to); (*Mil*) fortify

befeuchten *vt* moisten

befinden† **(sich)** *vr* be. **B~** *nt* **-s** [state of] health

beflecken *vt* stain

befolgen *vt* follow

beförder|n *vt* transport; (*im Rang*) promote. **B~ung** *f* **-,-en** transport; promotion

befragen *vt* question

befrei|en *vt* free; (*räumen*) clear (**von** of); (*freistellen*) exempt (**von** from); **sich b~en** free oneself.

B~er *m* **-s,-** liberator. **B~ung** *f* **-** liberation; exemption

befreunden (sich) *vr* make friends; **befreundet sein** be friends

befriedig|en *vt* satisfy. **b~end** *adj* satisfying; (*zufrieden stellend*) satisfactory. **B~ung** *f* **-** satisfaction

befrucht|en *vt* fertilize. **B~ung** *f* **-** fertilization; **künstliche B~ung** artificial insemination

Befugnis *f* **-,-se** authority

Befund *m* result

befürcht|en *vt* fear. **B~ung** *f* **-,-en** fear

befürworten *vt* support

begab|t *adj* gifted. **B~ung** *f* **-,-en** gift, talent

begeben† **(sich)** *vr* go; **sich in Gefahr b~** expose oneself to danger

begegn|en *vi* (*sein*) **jdm/etw b~en** meet someone/something. **B~ung** *f* **-,-en** meeting

begehr|en *vt* desire. **b~t** *adj* sought-after

begeister|n *vt* **jdn b~n** arouse someone's enthusiasm. **b~t** *adj* enthusiastic; (*eifrig*) keen. **B~ung** *f* **-** enthusiasm

Begierde *f* **-,-n** desire

Beginn *m* **-s** beginning. **b~en**† *vt/i* (*haben*) start, begin

beglaubigen *vt* authenticate

begleichen† *vt* settle

begleit|en *vt* accompany. **B~er** *m* **-s,-** companion; (*Mus*) accompanist. **B~ung** *f* **-,-en** company; (*Mus*) accompaniment

beglück|en *vt* make happy. **b~wünschen** *vt* congratulate (**zu** on)

begnadig|en *vt* (*Jur*) pardon. **B~ung** *f* **-,-en** (*Jur*) pardon

begraben† *vt* bury

Begräbnis *n* **-ses,-se** burial; (*Feier*) funeral

begreif|en† *vt* understand; **nicht zu b~en** incomprehensible. **b~lich** *adj* understandable

begrenz|en *vt* form the boundary of; (*beschränken*) restrict. **b~t** *adj* limited. **B~ung** *f* **-,-en** restriction; (*Grenze*) boundary

Begriff *m* **-[e]s,-e** concept; (*Ausdruck*) term; (*Vorstellung*) idea

begründ|en *vt* give one's reason for. **b~et** *adj* justified. **B~ung** *f* **-,-en** reason

begrüß|en *vt* greet; (*billigen*) welcome. **b~enswert** *adj* welcome. **B~ung** *f* **-** greeting; welcome

begünstigen *vt* favour

begütert *adj* wealthy

behaart *adj* hairy

behäbig *adj* portly

behag|en *vi* (*haben*) please (**jdm** s.o.). **B~en** *nt* **-s** contentment; (*Genuss*) enjoyment. **b~lich** *adj* comfortable. **B~lichkeit** *f* **-** comfort

behalten† *vt* keep; (*sich merken*) remember

Behälter *m* **-s,-** container

behand|eln *vt* treat; (*sich befassen*) deal with. **B~lung** *f* treatment

beharr|en *vi* (*haben*) persist (**auf** + *dat* in). **b~lich** *adj* persistent

behaupt|en *vt* maintain; (*vorgeben*) claim; (*sagen*) say; (*bewahren*) retain; **sich b~en** hold one's own. **B~ung** *f* **-,-en** assertion; claim; (*Äußerung*) statement

beheben† *vt* remedy

behelf|en† **(sich)** *vr* make do (**mit** with). **b~smäßig** *adj* makeshift ● *adv* provisionally

beherbergen *vt* put up

beherrsch|en *vt* rule over; (*dominieren*) dominate; (*meistern, zügeln*) control; (*können*) know. **b~t** *adj* self-controlled. **B~ung** *f* - control

b

beherzigen *vt* heed

behilflich *adj* **jdm b~ sein** help s.o.

behinder|n *vt* hinder; (*blockieren*) obstruct. **b~t** *adj* handicapped; (*schwer*) disabled. **B~te(r)** *m/f* handicapped/disabled person. **B~ung** *f* -,-**en** obstruction; (*Med*) handicap; disability

Behörde *f* -,-**n** [public] authority

behüte|n *vt* protect. **b~t** *adj* sheltered

behutsam *adj* careful; (*zart*) gentle

bei

● *preposition* (+ *dative*)

! Note that **bei** plus **dem** can become **beim**

····➤ (*nahe*) near; (*dicht an, neben*) by; (*als Begleitung*) with. **wer steht da bei ihm?** who is standing there next to *or* with him? **etw bei sich haben** have sth with *or* on one. **bleiben Sie beim Gepäck/bei den Kindern** stay with the luggage/the children. **war heute ein Brief für mich bei der Post?** was there a letter for me in the post today?

····➤ (*an*) by. **jdn bei der Hand nehmen** take s.o. by the hand

····➤ (*in der Wohnung von*) at ... 's home *or* house/flat. **bei mir [zu Hause]** at my home *or* [!] place. **bei seinen Eltern leben** live with one's parents. **wir sind bei Ulrike eingeladen** we have been invited to Ulrike's. **bei Schmidt** at the Schmidts'; (*Geschäft*) at Schmidts'; (*auf Briefen*) c/o Schmidt. **bei jdm/einer Firma arbeiten** work for s.o./a firm. **bei uns tut man das nicht** we don't do that where I come from.

····➤ (*gegenwärtig*) at; (*verwickelt*) in. **bei einer Hochzeit/einem Empfang** at a wedding/reception. **bei einem Unfall** in an accident

····➤ (*im Falle von*) in the case of, with; (*bei Wetter*) in. **wie bei den Römern** as with the Romans. **bei Nebel** in fog, if there is fog. **bei dieser Hitze** in this heat

····➤ (*angesichts*) with; (*trotz*) in spite of. **bei deinen guten Augen** with your good eyesight. **bei all seinen Bemühungen** in spite of *or* despite all his efforts

····➤ (*Zeitpunkt*) at, on. **bei diesen Worten errötete er** he blushed at this *or* on hearing this. **bei seiner Ankunft** on his arrival. **bei Tag/Nacht** by day/night.

····➤ (*Gleichzeitigkeit, mit Verbalsubstantiv*) **beim ... en** while *or* when ... ing. **beim Spazierengehen im Walde** while walking in the woods. **beim Überqueren der Straße** when crossing the road. **sie war beim Lesen** she was reading. **wir waren beim Frühstück** we were having breakfast

beibehalten† *vt sep* keep

beibringen† *vt sep* **jdm etw b~** teach s.o. sth; (*mitteilen*) break sth to s.o.; (*zufügen*) inflict sth on s.o.

Beicht|e *f* -,-**n** confession. **b~en** *vt/i* (*haben*) confess. **B~stuhl** *m* confessional

beide *adj & pron* both; **b~s** both; **dreißig b~** (*Tennis*) thirty all.

b~rseitig *adj* mutual. **b~rseits** *adv & prep* (+ *gen*) on both sides (of)
beieinander *adv* together
Beifahrer(in) *m*(*f*) [front-seat] passenger; (*Motorrad*) pillion passenger
Beifall *m* **-[e]s** applause; (*Billigung*) approval; **B~ klatschen** applaud
beifügen *vt sep* add; (*beilegen*) enclose
beige /bɛ:ʒ/ *inv adj* beige
beigeben† *vt sep* add
Beihilfe *f* financial aid; (*Studien-*) grant; (*Jur*) aiding and abetting
Beil *nt* **-[e]s,-e** hatchet, axe
Beilage *f* supplement; (*Gemüse*) vegetable
beiläufig *adj* casual
beilegen *vt sep* enclose; (*schlichten*) settle
Beileid *nt* condolences *pl*. **B~sbrief** *m* letter of condolence
beiliegend *adj* enclosed
beim *prep* = **bei dem; b~ Militär** in the army; **b~ Frühstück** at breakfast
beimessen† *vt sep* (*fig*) attach (*dat* to)
Bein *nt* **-[e]s,-e** leg; **jdm ein B~ stellen** trip s.o. up
beinah[e] *adv* nearly, almost
Beiname *m* epithet
beipflichten *vi sep* (*haben*) agree (*dat* with)
Beirat *m* advisory committee
beisammen *adv* together; **b~ sein** be together
Beisein *nt* presence
beiseite *adv* aside; (*abseits*) apart; **b~ legen** put aside; (*sparen*) put by
beisetz|en *vt sep* bury. **B~ung** *f* **-,-en** funeral
Beispiel *nt* example; **zum B~** for example. **b~sweise** *adv* for example
beißen† *vt/i* (*haben*) bite; (*brennen*) sting; **sich b~** (*Farben*:) clash
Bei|stand *m* **-[e]s** help. **b~stehen**† *vi sep* (*haben*) **jdm b~stehen** help s.o.
beistimmen *vi sep* (*haben*) agree
Beistrich *m* comma
Beitrag *m* **-[e]s,⸚e** contribution; (*Mitglieds-*) subscription; (*Versicherungs-*) premium; (*Zeitungs-*) article. **b~en**† *vt/i sep* (*haben*) contribute
bei|treten† *vi sep* (*sein*) (+ *dat*) join. **B~tritt** *m* joining
Beize *f* **-,-n** (*Holz-*) stain
beizeiten *adv* in good time
beizen *vt* stain (*Holz*)
bejahen *vt* answer in the affirmative; (*billigen*) approve of
bejahrt *adj* aged, old
bekämpf|en *vt* fight. **B~ung** *f* fight (*gen* against)
bekannt *adj* well-known; (*vertraut*) familiar; **jdn b~ machen** introduce s.o.; **etw b~ machen** *od* **geben** announce sth; **b~ werden** become known. **B~e(r)** *m/f* acquaintance; (*Freund*) friend. **B~gabe** *f* announcement. **b~lich** *adv* as is well known. **B~machung** *f* **-,-en** announcement; (*Anschlag*) notice. **B~schaft** *f* **-** acquaintance; (*Leute*) acquaintances *pl*; (*Freunde*) friends *pl*
bekehr|en *vt* convert. **B~ung** *f* **-,-en** conversion
bekenn|en† *vt* confess, profess (*Glauben*); **sich [für] schuldig b~en** admit one's guilt. **B~tnis** *nt* **-ses,-se** confession; (*Konfession*) denomination
beklag|en *vt* lament; (*bedauern*) deplore; **sich b~en** complain. **b~enswert** *adj* unfortunate.

b

B~te(r) *m/f* (*Jur*) defendant

bekleid|en *vt* hold (*Amt*). **B~ung** *f* clothing

Beklemmung *f* **-,-en** feeling of oppression

bekommen† *vt* get; have (*Baby*); catch (*Erkältung*) ● *vi* (*sein*) **jdm gut b~** do s.o. good; (*Essen:*) agree with s.o.

beköstig|en *vt* feed. **B~ung** *f* - board; (*Essen*) food

bekräftigen *vt* reaffirm

bekreuzigen (sich) *vr* cross oneself

bekümmert *adj* troubled; (*besorgt*) worried

bekunden *vt* show

Belag *m* **-[e]s,¨e** coating; (*Fußboden-*) covering; (*Brot-*) topping; (*Zahn-*) tartar; (*Brems-*) lining

belager|n *vt* besiege. **B~ung** *f* **-,-en** siege

Belang *m* **von B~** of importance; **B~e** *pl* interests. **b~los** *adj* irrelevant; (*unwichtig*) trivial

belassen† *vt* leave; **es dabei b~** leave it at that

belasten *vt* load; (*fig*) burden; (*beanspruchen*) put a strain on; (*Comm*) debit; (*Jur*) incriminate

belästigen *vt* bother; (*bedrängen*) pester; (*unsittlich*) molest

Belastung *f* **-,-en** load; (*fig*) strain; (*Comm*) debit. **B~smaterial** *nt* incriminating evidence. **B~szeuge** *m* prosecution witness

belaufen† **(sich)** *vr* amount (**auf** + *acc* to)

belauschen *vt* eavesdrop on

beleb|en *vt* (*fig*) revive; (*lebhaft machen*) enliven. **b~t** *adj* lively; (*Straße*) busy

Beleg *m* **-[e]s,-e** evidence; (*Beispiel*) instance (**für** of); (*Quittung*) receipt. **b~en** *vt* cover/(*garnieren*) garnish (**mit** with); (*besetzen*) reserve; (*Univ*) enrol for; (*nachweisen*) provide evidence for; **den ersten Platz b~en** (*Sport*) take first place. **B~schaft** *f* **-,-en** workforce. **b~t** *adj* occupied; (*Zunge*) coated; (*Stimme*) husky; **b~te Brote** open sandwiches

belehren *vt* instruct

beleidig|en *vt* offend; (*absichtlich*) insult. **B~ung** *f* **-,-en** insult

belesen *adj* well-read

beleucht|en *vt* light; (*anleuchten*) illuminate. **B~ung** *f* **-,-en** illumination

Belg|ien /-i̯ən/ *nt* **-s** Belgium. **B~ier(in)** *m* **-s,-** (*f* **-,-nen**) Belgian. **b~isch** *adj* Belgian

belicht|en *vt* (*Phot*) expose. **B~ung** *f* - exposure

Belieb|en *nt* **-s nach B~en** [just] as one likes. **b~ig** *adj* **eine b~ige Zahl** any number you like ● *adv* **b~ig oft** as often as one likes. **b~t** *adj* popular

bellen *vi* (*haben*) bark

belohn|en *vt* reward. **B~ung** *f* **-,-en** reward

belustig|en *vt* amuse. **B~ung** *f* **-,-en** amusement

bemalen *vt* paint

bemängeln *vt* criticize

bemannt *adj* manned

bemerk|bar *adj* **sich b~bar machen** attract attention. **b~en** *vt* notice; (*äußern*) remark. **b~enswert** *adj* remarkable. **B~ung** *f* **-,-en** remark

bemitleiden *vt* pity

bemüh|en *vt* trouble; **sich b~en** try (**zu** to; **um etw** to get sth); (*sich kümmern*) attend (**um** to); **b~t sein** endeavour (**zu** to). **B~ung** *f* **-,-en** effort

benachbart *adj* neighbouring

benachrichtig|en *vt* inform; (*amtlich*) notify. **B~ung** *f* -,-en notification

benachteiligen *vt* discriminate against; (*ungerecht sein*) treat unfairly

benehmen† **(sich)** *vr* behave. **B~** *nt* -s behaviour

beneiden *vt* envy (**um etw** sth)

Bengel *m* -s,- boy; (*Rüpel*) lout

benötigen *vt* need

benutz|en, (*SGer*) **benütz|en** *vt* use; take (*Bahn*) **B~ung** *f* use

Benzin *nt* -s petrol

beobacht|en *vt* observe. **B~er** *m* -s,- observer. **B~ung** *f* -,-en observation

bequem *adj* comfortable; (*mühelos*) easy; (*faul*) lazy. **b~en (sich)** *vr* deign (**zu** to). **B~lichkeit** *f* -,-en comfort; (*Faulheit*) laziness

berat|en† *vt* advise; (*überlegen*) discuss; **sich b~en** confer ● *vi* (*haben*) discuss (**über etw** *acc* sth); (*beratschlagen*) confer. **B~er(in)** *m* -s,-, (*f* -,-nen) adviser. **B~ung** *f* -,-en guidance; (*Rat*) advice; (*Besprechung*) discussion; (*Med, Jur*) consultation

berechn|en *vt* calculate; (*anrechnen*) charge for; (*abfordern*) charge. **B~ung** *f* calculation

berechtig|en *vt* entitle; (*befugen*) authorize; (*fig*) justify. **b~t** *adj* justified, justifiable. **B~ung** *f* -,-en authorization; (*Recht*) right; (*Rechtmäßigkeit*) justification

bered|en *vt* talk about; **sich b~en** talk. **B~samkeit** *f* - eloquence

beredt *adj* eloquent

Bereich *m* -[e]s,-e area; (*fig*) realm; (*Fach-*) field

bereichern *vi* enrich

bereit *adj* ready. **b~en** *vt* prepare; (*verursachen*) cause; give (*Überraschung*). **b~halten**† *vt sep* have/(*ständig*) keep ready. **b~legen** *vt sep* put out [ready]. **b~machen** *vt sep* get ready. **b~s** *adv* already

Bereitschaft *f* -,-en readiness; (*Einheit*) squad. **B~sdienst** *m* **B~sdienst haben** (*Mil*) be on stand-by; (*Arzt:*) be on call. **B~spolizei** *f* riot police

bereit|stehen† *vi sep* (*haben*) be ready. **b~stellen** *vt sep* put out ready; (*verfügbar machen*) make available. **B~ung** *f* - preparation. **b~willig** *adj* willing

bereuen *vt* regret

Berg *m* -[e]s,-e mountain; (*Anhöhe*) hill; **in den B~en** in the mountains. **b~ab** *adv* downhill. **B~arbeiter** *m* miner. **b~auf** *adv* uphill. **B~bau** *m* -[e]s mining

bergen† *vt* recover; (*Naut*) salvage; (*retten*) rescue

Berg|führer *m* mountain guide. **b~ig** *adj* mountainous. **B~kette** *f* mountain range. **B~mann** *m* (*pl* -leute) miner. **B~steiger(in)** *m* -s,- (*f* -,-nen) mountaineer, climber

Bergung *f* - recovery; (*Naut*) salvage; (*Rettung*) rescue

Berg|wacht *f* mountain rescue service. **B~werk** *nt* mine

Bericht *m* -[e]s,-e report; (*Reise-*) account. **b~en** *vt/i* (*haben*) report; (*erzählen*) tell (**von** of). **B~erstatter(in)** *m* -s,- (*f* -,-nen) reporter

berichtigen *vt* correct

beriesel|n *vt* irrigate. **B~ungsanlage** *f* sprinkler system

Berlin *nt* -s Berlin. **B~er** *m* -s,- Berliner

Bernhardiner *m* -s,- St Bernard

Bernstein *m* amber

berüchtigt *adj* notorious

berücksichtig|en *vt* take into

consideration. **B~ung** *f* - consideration

b **Beruf** *m* profession; (*Tätigkeit*) occupation; (*Handwerk*) trade. **b~en**† *vt* appoint; **sich b~en** refer (**auf** + *acc* to); (*vorgeben*) plead (**auf etw** *acc* sth); ● *adj* competent; **b~en sein** be destined (**zu** to). **b~lich** *adj* professional; (*Ausbildung*) vocational ● *adv* professionally; **b~lich tätig sein** work, have a job. **B~sberatung** *f* vocational guidance. **B~sausbildung** *f* professional training. **b~smäßig** *adv* professionally. **B~sschule** *f* vocational school. **B~ssoldat** *m* regular soldier. **b~stätig** *adj* working; **b~stätig sein** work, have a job. **B~stätige(r)** *m/f* working man/woman. **B~ung** *f* -,-en appointment; (*Bestimmung*) vocation; (*Jur*) appeal; **B~ung einlegen** appeal. **B~ungsgericht** *nt* appeal court

beruhen *vi* (*haben*) be based (**auf** + *dat* on)

beruhig|en *vt* calm [down]; (*zuversichtlich machen*) reassure. **b~end** *adj* calming; (*tröstend*) reassuring; (*Med*) sedative. **B~ung** *f* - calming; reassurance; (*Med*) sedation. **B~ungsmittel** *nt* sedative; (*bei Psychosen*) tranquillizer

berühmt *adj* famous. **B~heit** *f* -,-en fame; (*Person*) celebrity

berühr|en *vt* touch; (*erwähnen*) touch on. **B~ung** *f* -,-en touch; (*Kontakt*) contact

besänftigen *vt* soothe

Besatz *m* -es,⸚e trimming

Besatzung *f* -,-en crew; (*Mil*) occupying force

beschädig|en *vt* damage. **B~ung** *f* -,-en damage

beschaffen *vt* obtain, get ● *adj* **so b~ sein, dass** be such that. **B~heit** *f* - consistency

beschäftig|en *vt* occupy; (*Arbeitgeber:*) employ; **sich b~en** occupy oneself. **b~t** *adj* busy; (*angestellt*) employed (**bei** at). **B~ung** *f* -,-en occupation; (*Anstellung*) employment

beschämt *adj* ashamed; (*verlegen*) embarrassed

beschatten *vt* shade; (*überwachen*) shadow

Bescheid *m* -[e]s information; **jdm B~ sagen** *od* **geben** let s.o. know; **B~ wissen** know

bescheiden *adj* modest. **B~heit** *f* - modesty

bescheinen† *vt* shine on; **von der Sonne beschienen** sunlit

bescheinig|en *vt* certify. **B~ung** *f* -,-en [written] confirmation; (*Schein*) certificate

beschenken *vt* give a present/presents to

Bescherung *f* -,-en distribution of Christmas presents

beschildern *vt* signpost

beschimpf|en *vt* abuse, swear at. **B~ung** *f* -,-en abuse

beschirmen *vt* protect

Beschlag *m* **in B~ nehmen** monopolize. **b~en**† *vt* shoe ● *vi* (*sein*) steam *or* mist up ● *adj* steamed *or* misted up. **B~nahme** *f* -,-n confiscation; (*Jur*) seizure. **b~nahmen** *vt* confiscate; (*Jur*) seize

beschleunig|en *vt* hasten; (*schneller machen*) speed up (*Schritt*) ● *vi* (*haben*) accelerate. **B~ung** *f* - acceleration

beschließen† *vt* decide; (*beenden*) end ● *vi* (*haben*) decide (**über** + *acc* about)

Beschluss *m* decision

beschmutzen *vt* make dirty

beschneid|en† *vt* trim; (*Horticulture*) prune; (*Relig*) circumcise.

B~ung *f* - circumcision

beschnüffeln *vt* sniff at

beschönigen *vt* (*fig*) gloss over

beschränken *vt* limit, restrict; **sich b~ auf** (+ *acc*) confine oneself to

beschrankt *adj* (*Bahnübergang*) with barrier[s]

beschränk|t *adj* limited; (*geistig*) dull-witted. **B~ung** *f* **-,-en** limitation, restriction

beschreib|en† *vt* describe. **B~ung** *f* -,-en description

beschuldig|en *vt* accuse. **B~ung** *f* -,-en accusation

beschummeln *vt* ▣ cheat

Beschuss *m* (*Mil*) fire; (*Artillerie-*) shelling

beschütz|en *vt* protect. **B~er** *m* **-s,-** protector

Beschwer|de *f* **-,-n** complaint; **B~den** (*Med*) trouble *sg*. **b~en** *vt* weight down; **sich b~en** complain. **b~lich** *adj* difficult

beschwindeln *vt* cheat (**um** out of); (*belügen*) lie to

beschwipst *adj* ▣ tipsy

beseitig|en *vt* remove. **B~ung** *f* - removal

Besen *m* **-s,-** broom

> **Besenwirtschaft** An inn set up by a local wine-grower for a few weeks after the new wine has been made. An inflated pig's bladder is hung up outside the door to show that the new vintage may be sampled there. This is mainly found in Southern Germany. ▸**HEURIGE**.

besessen *adj* obsessed (**von** by)

besetz|en *vt* occupy; fill (*Posten*); (*Theat*) cast (*Rolle*); (*verzieren*) trim (**mit** with). **b~t** *adj* occupied; (*Toilette, Leitung*) engaged; (*Zug, Bus*) full up; **der Platz ist b~t** this seat is taken. **B~tzeichen** *nt* engaged tone. **B~ung** *f* **-,-en** occupation; (*Theat*) cast

besichtig|en *vt* look round (*Stadt*); (*prüfen*) inspect; (*besuchen*) visit. **B~ung** *f* **-,-en** visit; (*Prüfung*) inspection; (*Stadt-*) sightseeing

besiedelt *adj* **dünn/dicht b~** sparsely/densely populated

besiegen *vt* defeat

besinn|en† **(sich)** *vr* think, reflect; (*sich erinnern*) remember (**auf jdn/etw** someone/something). **B~ung** *f* - reflection; (*Bewusstsein*) consciousness; **bei/ohne B~ung** conscious/unconscious. **b~ungslos** *adj* unconscious

Besitz *m* possession; (*Eigentum, Land-*) property; (*Gut*) estate. **b~en**† *vt* own, possess; (*haben*) have. **B~er(in)** *m* **-s,-** (*f* **-,-nen**) owner; (*Comm*) proprietor

besoffen *adj* ⊠ drunken; **b~ sein** be drunk

besonder|e(r,s) *adj* special; (*bestimmt*) particular; (*gesondert*) separate. **b~s** *adv* [e]specially, particularly; (*gesondert*) separately

besonnen *adj* calm

besorg|en *vt* get; (*kaufen*) buy; (*erledigen*) attend to; (*versorgen*) look after. **b~t** *adj* worried/(*bedacht*) concerned (**um** about). **B~ung** *f* **-,-en** errand; **B~ungen machen** do shopping

bespitzeln *vt* spy on

besprech|en† *vt* discuss; (*rezensieren*) review. **B~ung** *f* **-,-en** discussion; review; (*Konferenz*) meeting

besser *adj & adv* better. **b~n** *vt* improve; **sich b~n** get better. **B~ung** *f* - improvement; **gute B~ung!** get well soon!

b

Bestand *m* **-[e]s,⸚e** existence; (*Vorrat*) stock (**an** + *dat* of)

beständig *adj* constant; (*Wetter*) settled; **b~ gegen** resistant to

Bestand|saufnahme *f* stocktaking. **B~teil** *m* part

bestätig|en *vt* confirm; acknowledge (*Empfang*); **sich b~en** prove to be true. **B~ung** *f* **-,-en** confirmation

bestatt|en *vt* bury. **B~ung** *f* **-,-en** funeral

Bestäubung *f* **-** pollination

bestaunen *vt* gaze at in amazement; (*bewundern*) admire

best|e(r,s) *adj* best; **b~en Dank!** many thanks! **B~e(r,s)** *m/f/nt* best; **sein B~es tun** do one's best

bestech|en† *vt* bribe; (*bezaubern*) captivate. **b~end** *adj* captivating. **b~lich** *adj* corruptible. **B~ung** *f* **-** bribery. **B~ungsgeld** *nt* bribe

Besteck *nt* **-[e]s,-e** [set of] knife, fork and spoon; (*coll*) cutlery

bestehen† *vi* (*haben*) exist; (*fortdauern*) last; (*bei Prüfung*) pass; **~ aus** consist/(*gemacht sein*) be made of; **~ auf** (+ *dat*) insist on ●*vt* pass (*Prüfung*)

besteig|en† *vt* climb; (*aufsteigen*) mount; ascend (*Thron*). **B~ung** *f* ascent

bestell|en *vt* order; (*vor-*) book; (*ernennen*) appoint; (*bebauen*) cultivate; (*ausrichten*) tell; **zu sich b~en** send for; **b~t sein** have an appointment; **kann ich etwas b~en?** can I take a message? **B~schein** *m* order form. **B~ung** *f* order; (*Botschaft*) message; (*Bebauung*) cultivation

besteuer|n *vt* tax. **B~ung** *f* **-** taxation

Bestie /ˈbɛstiə/ *f* **-,-n** beast

bestimm|en *vt* fix; (*entscheiden*) decide; (*vorsehen*) intend; (*ernennen*) appoint; (*ermitteln*) determine; (*definieren*) define; (*Gram*) qualify ●*vi* (*haben*) be in charge (**über** + *acc* of). **~t** *adj* definite; (*gewiss*) certain; (*fest*) firm. **B~ung** *f* fixing; (*Vorschrift*) regulation; (*Ermittlung*) determination; (*Definition*) definition; (*Zweck*) purpose; (*Schicksal*) destiny. **B~ungsort** *m* destination

Bestleistung *f* (*Sport*) record

bestraf|en *vt* punish. **B~ung** *f* **-,-en** punishment

Bestrahlung *f* radiotherapy

Bestreb|en *nt* **-s** endeavour; (*Absicht*) aim. **B~ung** *f* **-,-en** effort

bestreiten† *vt* dispute; (*leugnen*) deny; (*bezahlen*) pay for

bestürz|t *adj* dismayed; (*erschüttert*) stunned. **B~ung** *f* **-** dismay, consternation

Bestzeit *f* (*Sport*) record [time]

Besuch *m* **-[e]s,-e** visit; (*kurz*) call; (*Schul-*) attendance; (*Gast*) visitor; (*Gäste*) visitors *pl*; **B~ haben** have a visitor/visitors; **bei jdm zu** *od* **auf B~ sein** be staying with s.o. **~en** *vt* visit; (*kurz*) call on; (*teilnehmen*) attend; go to (*Schule, Ausstellung*). **B~er(in)** *m* **-s,-** (*f* **-,-nen**) visitor; caller. **B~szeit** *f* visiting hours *pl*

betagt *adj* aged, old

betätig|en *vt* operate; **sich b~en** work (**als** as). **B~ung** *f* **-,-en** operation; (*Tätigkeit*) activity

betäub|en *vt* stun; (*Lärm:*) deafen; (*Med*) anaesthetize; (*lindern*) ease; deaden (*Schmerz*); **wie b~t** dazed. **B~ung** *f* **-** daze; (*Med*) anaesthesia. **B~ungsmittel** *nt* anaesthetic

Bete *f* **-,-n Rote B~** beetroot

beteilig|en *vt* give a share to; **sich b~en** take part (**an** + *dat* in); (*beitragen*) contribute (**an** + *dat* to). **b~t** *adj* **b~t sein** take part/(*an Un-*

fall) be involved/(*Comm*) have a share (**an** + *dat* in); **alle B∼ten** all those involved. **B∼ung** *f* **-,-en** participation; involvement; (*Anteil*) share

beten *vi* (*haben*) pray

Beton /be'tɔŋ/ *m* **-s** concrete

betonen *vt* stressed, emphasize

beton|t *adj* stressed; (*fig*) pointed. **B∼ung** *f* **-,-en** stress

Betracht *m* **in B∼ ziehen** consider; **außer B∼ lassen** disregard; **nicht in B∼ kommen** be out of the question. **b∼en** *vt* look at; (*fig*) regard (**als** as)

beträchtlich *adj* considerable

Betrachtung *f* **-,-en** contemplation; (*Überlegung*) reflection

Betrag *m* **-[e]s,¨e** amount. **b∼en**† *vt* amount to; **sich b∼en** behave. **B∼en** *nt* **-s** behaviour; (*Sch*) conduct

betreff|en† *vt* affect; (*angehen*) concern. **b∼end** *adj* relevant. **b∼s** *prep* (+ *gen*) concerning

betreiben† *vt* (*leiten*) run; (*ausüben*) carry on

betreten† *vt* step on; (*eintreten*) enter; '**B∼ verboten**' 'no entry'; (*bei Rasen*) 'keep off [the grass]'

betreu|en *vt* look after. **B∼er(in)** *m* **-s,-** (*f* **-,-nen**) helper; (*Kranken-*) nurse. **B∼ung** *f* **-** care

Betrieb *m* business; (*Firma*) firm; (*Treiben*) activity; (*Verkehr*) traffic; **außer B∼** not in use; (*defekt*) out of order

Betriebs|anleitung, **B∼anweisung** *f* operating instructions *pl*. **B∼ferien** *pl* firm's holiday. **B∼leitung** *f* management. **B∼rat** *m* works committee. **B∼störung** *f* breakdown

betrinken† **(sich)** *vr* get drunk

betroffen *adj* disconcerted; **b∼ sein** be affected (**von** by)

betrüb|en *vt* sadden. **b∼t** *adj* sad

Betrug *m* **-[e]s** deception; (*Jur*) fraud

betrüg|en† *vt* cheat, swindle; (*Jur*) defraud; (*in der Ehe*) be unfaithful to. **B∼er(in)** *m* **-s,-** (*f* **-,-nen**) swindler. **B∼erei** *f* **-,-en** fraud

betrunken *adj* drunken; **b∼ sein** be drunk. **B∼e(r)** *m* drunk

Bett *nt* **-[e]s,-en** bed. **B∼couch** *f* sofa-bed. **B∼decke** *f* blanket; (*Tages-*) bedspread

Bettel|ei *f* **-** begging. **b∼n** *vi* (*haben*) beg

Bettler(in) *m* **-s,-** (*f* **-,-nen**) beggar

Bettpfanne *f* bedpan

Betttuch (**Bettuch**) *nt* sheet

Bett|wäsche *f* bed linen. **B∼zeug** *nt* bedding

betupfen *vt* dab (**mit** with)

beug|en *vt* bend; (*Gram*) decline; conjugate (*Verb*); **sich b∼en** bend; (*lehnen*) lean; (*sich fügen*) submit (*dat* to). **B∼ung** *f* **-,-en** (*Gram*) declension; conjugation

Beule *f* **-,-n** bump; (*Delle*) dent

beunruhig|en *vt* worry; **sich b∼en** worry. **B∼ung** *f* **-** worry

beurlauben *vt* give leave to

beurteil|en *vt* judge. **B∼ung** *f* **-,-en** judgement; (*Ansicht*) opinion

Beute *f* **-** booty, haul; (*Jagd-*) bag; (*eines Raubtiers*) prey

Beutel *m* **-s,-** bag; (*Tabak- & Zool*) pouch. **B∼tier** *nt* marsupial

Bevölkerung *f* **-,-en** population

bevollmächtigen *vt* authorize

bevor *conj* before; **b∼ nicht** until

bevormunden *vt* treat like a child

bevorstehen† *vi sep* (*haben*) approach; (*unmittelbar*) be imminent.

b

b~d *adj* approaching, forthcoming; **unmittelbar b~d** imminent

bevorzug|en *vt* prefer; (*begünstigen*) favour. **b~t** *adj* privileged; (*Behandlung*) preferential

bewachen *vt* guard

Bewachung *f* - guard; **unter B~** under guard

bewaffn|en *vt* arm. **b~et** *adj* armed. **B~ung** *f* - armament; (*Waffen*) arms *pl*

bewahren *vt* protect (**vor** + *dat* from); (*behalten*) keep; **die Ruhe b~** keep calm

bewähren (sich) *vr* prove one's/(*Ding:*) its worth; (*erfolgreich sein*) prove a success

bewähr|t *adj* reliable; (*erprobt*) proven. **B~ung** *f* - (*Jur*) probation. **B~ungsfrist** *f* [period of] probation. **B~ungsprobe** *f* (*fig*) test

bewältigen *vt* cope with; (*überwinden*) overcome

bewässer|n *vt* irrigate. **B~ung** *f* - irrigation

bewegen[1] *vt* (*reg*) move; **sich b~** move; (*körperlich*) take exercise

bewegen[2]† *vt* **jdn dazu b~, etw zu tun** induce s.o. to do sth

Beweg|grund *m* motive. **b~lich** *adj* movable, mobile; (*wendig*) agile. **B~lichkeit** *f* - mobility; agility. **B~ung** *f* -,-**en** movement; (*Phys*) motion; (*Rührung*) emotion; (*Gruppe*) movement; **körperliche B~ung** physical exercise. **b~ungslos** *adj* motionless

Beweis *m* **-es,-e** proof; (*Zeichen*) token; **B~e** evidence *sg*. **b~en**† *vt* prove; (*zeigen*) show; **sich b~en** prove oneself/(*Ding:*) itself. **B~material** *nt* evidence

bewerb|en† **(sich)** *vr* apply (**um** for; **bei** to). **B~er(in)** *m* **-s,-** (*f* **-,-nen**) applicant. **B~ung** *f* -,-**en** application

bewerten *vt* value; (*einschätzen*) rate; (*Sch*) mark, grade

bewilligen *vt* grant

bewirken *vt* cause; (*herbeiführen*) bring about

bewirt|en *vt* entertain. **B~ung** *f* - hospitality

bewohn|bar *adj* habitable. **b~en** *vt* inhabit, live in. **B~er(in)** *m* **-s,-** (*f* **-,-nen**) resident, occupant; (*Einwohner*) inhabitant

bewölk|en (sich) *vr* cloud over; **b~t** cloudy. **B~ung** *f* - clouds *pl*

bewunder|n *vt* admire. **b~nswert** *adj* admirable. **B~ung** *f* - admiration

bewusst *adj* conscious (*gen* of); (*absichtlich*) deliberate. **b~los** *adj* unconscious. **B~losigkeit** *f* - unconsciousness; **B~sein** *nt* **-s** consciousness; (*Gewissheit*) awareness; **bei B~sein** conscious

bezahl|en *vt/i* (*haben*) pay; pay for (*Ware, Essen*). **B~ung** *f* - payment; (*Lohn*) pay. **B~fernsehen** *nt* pay television; pay TV

bezaubern *vt* enchant

bezeichn|en *vt* mark; (*bedeuten*) denote; (*beschreiben, nennen*) describe (**als** as). **b~end** *adj* typical. **B~ung** *f* marking; (*Beschreibung*) description (**als** as); (*Ausdruck*) term; (*Name*) name

bezeugen *vt* testify to

bezichtigen *vt* accuse (*gen* of)

bezieh|en† *vt* cover; (*einziehen*) move into; (*beschaffen*) obtain; (*erhalten*) get; (*in Verbindung bringen*) relate (**auf** + *acc* to); **sich b~en** (*bewölken*) cloud over; **sich b~en auf** (+ *acc*) refer to; **das Bett frisch b~en** put clean sheets on the bed. **B~ung** *f* -,-**en** relation; (*Verhältnis*) relationship; (*Bezug*) respect; **B~un-**

gen **haben** have connections. **b~ungsweise** *adv* respectively; (*vielmehr*) or rather

Bezirk *m* **-[e]s,-e** district

Bezug *m* cover; (*Kissen-*) case; (*Beschaffung*) obtaining; (*Kauf*) purchase; (*Zusammenhang*) reference; **B~e** *pl* earnings; **B~ nehmen** refer (**auf** + *acc* to); **in B~ auf** (+ *acc*) regarding

bezüglich *prep* (+ *gen*) regarding ●*adj* relating (**auf** + *acc* to)

bezwecken *vt* (*fig*) aim at

bezweifeln *vt* doubt

BH /beːˈhaː/ *m* **-[s],-[s]** bra

Bibel *f* **-,-n** Bible

Biber *m* **-s,-** beaver

Biblio|thek *f* **-,-en** library. **B~thekar(in)** *m* **-s,-** (*f* **-,-nen**) librarian

biblisch *adj* biblical

bieg|en† *vt* bend; **sich b~en** bend ●*vi* (*sein*) curve (**nach** to); **um die Ecke b~en** turn the corner. **b~sam** *adj* flexible, supple. **B~ung** *f* **-,-en** bend

Biene *f* **-,-n** bee. **B~nstock** *m* beehive. **B~nwabe** *f* honey-comb

Bier *nt* **-s,-e** beer. **B~deckel** *m* beer-mat. **B~krug** *m* beer-mug

> *i* **Bier** Germany and Austria rank among the world's top beer consumers. Germans brew more than 5000 varieties, and each beer tastes different. German beer is brewed according to the *Reinheitsgebot* (brewing regulations) of 1516, which stipulate that no ingredients other than hops, malted barley, yeast and water may be used. The standard pale ale or lager is a *Helles*, a dark beer is a *Dunkles*, and a wheat beer is a *Weißbier* (south), *Weizenbier* (north-west) and *Weiße* (Berlin). A *Biergarten* is a rustic open-air pub, or beer garden, which is traditional in Bavaria and Austria.

bieten† *vt* offer; (*bei Auktion*) bid

Bifokalbrille *f* bifocals *pl*

Bigamie *f* **-** bigamy

bigott *adj* over-pious

Bikini *m* **-s,-s** bikini

Bilanz *f* **-,-en** balance sheet; (*fig*) result; **die B~ ziehen** (*fig*) draw conclusions (**aus** from)

Bild *nt* **-[e]s,-er** picture; (*Theat*) scene

bilden *vt* form; (*sein*) be; (*erziehen*) educate

Bild|erbuch *nt* picture-book. **B~fläche** *f* screen. **B~hauer** *m* **-s,-** sculptor. **b~lich** *adj* pictorial; (*figurativ*) figurative. **B~nis** *nt* **-ses,-se** portrait. **B~punkt** *m* pixel. **B~schirm** *m* (*TV*) screen. **B~schirmgerät** *nt* visual display unit, VDU. **b~schön** *adj* very beautiful

Bildung *f* **-** formation; (*Erziehung*) education; (*Kultur*) culture

Billard /ˈbɪljart/ *nt* **-s** billiards *sg*. **B~tisch** *m* billiard table

Billett /bɪlˈjɛt/ *nt* **-[e]s,-e & -s** ticket

Billiarde *f* **-,-n** thousand million million

billig *adj* cheap; (*dürftig*) poor; **recht und b~** right and proper. **b~en** *vt* approve. **B~flieger** *m* low-cost airline. **B~ung** *f* **-** approval

Billion /bɪljoːn/ *f* **-,-en** million million, billion

Bimsstein *m* pumice stone

Binde *f* **-,-n** band; (*Verband*) bandage; (*Damen-*) sanitary towel. **B~hautentzündung** *f* conjunctivitis. **b~n†** *vt* tie (**an** + *acc* to); make (*Strauß*); bind (*Buch*); (*fesseln*) tie up; (*Culin*) thicken; **sich b~n** commit oneself. **B~strich** *m* hyphen. **B~wort** *nt* (*pl* **-wörter**) (*Gram*) conjunction

Bind|faden *m* string. **B~ung** *f* **-,-en** (*fig*) tie; (*Beziehung*) relationship; (*Verpflichtung*) commitment; (*Ski-*) binding; (*Textiles*) weave

binnen *prep* (+ *dat*) within. **B~handel** *m* home trade

Bio- *prefix* organic

Bio|chemie *f* biochemistry. **b~dynamisch** *m* organic. **B~graphie**, **B~grafie** *f* **-,-n** biography

Bio|hof *m* organic farm. **B~laden** *m* health-food store

Biokraftstoff *m* biofuel

Biolog|e *m* **-n,-n** biologist. **B~ie** *f* **-** biology. **b~isch** *adj* biological; **b~ischer Anbau** organic farming; **b~isch angebaut** organically grown

Bioterrorismus *m* bioterrorism

Birke *f* **-,-n** birch [tree]

Birm|a *nt* **-s** Burma. **b~anisch** *adj* Burmese

Birn|baum *m* pear-tree. **B~e** *f* **-,-n** pear; (*Electr*) bulb

bis *prep* (+ *acc*) as far as, [up] to; (*zeitlich*) until, till; (*spätestens*) by; **bis zu** up to; **bis auf** (+ *acc*) (*einschließlich*) [down] to; (*ausgenommen*) except [for]; **drei bis vier Minuten** three to four minutes; **bis morgen!** see you tomorrow! ● *conj* until

Bischof *m* **-s,¨e** bishop

bisher *adv* so far, up to now

Biskuit|rolle /bɪsˈkviːt-/ *f* Swiss roll. **B~teig** *m* sponge mixture

Biss *m* **-es,-e** bite

bisschen *inv pron* **ein b~** a bit, a little; **kein b~** not a bit

Biss|en *m* **-s,-** bite, mouthful. **b~ig** *adj* vicious; (*fig*) caustic

bisweilen *adv* from time to time

bitt|e *adv* please; (*nach Klopfen*) come in; (*als Antwort auf 'danke'*) don't mention it, you're welcome; **wie b~e?** pardon? **B~e** *f* **-,-n** request/(*dringend*) plea (**um** for). **b~en†** *vt/i* (*haben*) ask/(*dringend*) beg (**um** for); (*einladen*) invite, ask. **b~end** *adj* pleading

bitter *adj* bitter. **B~keit** *f* **-** bitterness. **b~lich** *adv* bitterly

Bittschrift *f* petition

bizarr *adj* bizarre

bläh|en *vt* swell; (*Vorhang, Segel:*) billow ● *vi* (*haben*) cause flatulence. **B~ungen** *fpl* flatulence *sg*, [!] wind *sg*

Blamage /blaˈmaːʒə/ *f* **-,-n** humiliation; (*Schande*) disgrace

blamieren *vt* disgrace; **sich b~** disgrace oneself; (*sich lächerlich machen*) make a fool of oneself

blanchieren /blãˈʃiːrən/ *vt* (*Culin*) blanch

blank *adj* shiny. **B~oscheck** *m* blank cheque

Blase *f* **-,-n** bubble; (*Med*) blister; (*Anat*) bladder. **b~n†** *vt/i* (*haben*) blow; play (*Flöte*). **B~nentzündung** *f* cystitis

Blas|instrument *nt* wind instrument. **B~kapelle** *f* brass band

blass *adj* pale; (*schwach*) faint

Blässe *f* **-** pallor

Blatt *nt* **-[e]s,¨er** (*Bot*) leaf; (*Papier*) sheet; (*Zeitung*) paper

Blattlaus *f* greenfly

blau *adj*, **B~** *nt* **-s,-** blue; **b~er Fleck** bruise; **b~es Auge** black eye; **b~ sein** [!] be tight; **Fahrt ins B~e** mystery tour. **B~beere** *f* bilberry. **B~licht** *nt* blue flashing light

Blech *nt* **-[e]s,-e** sheet metal; (*Weiß-*) tin; (*Platte*) metal sheet;

(*Back-*) baking sheet; (*Mus*) brass; (**!**: *Unsinn*) rubbish. **B~schaden** *m* (*Auto*) damage to the bodywork

Blei *nt* **-[e]s** lead

Bleibe *f* **-** place to stay. **b~n†** *vi* (*sein*) remain, stay; (*übrig-*) be left; **ruhig b~n** keep calm; **bei etw b~n** (*fig*) stick to sth; **b~n Sie am Apparat** hold the line; **etw b~n lassen** not do sth. **b~nd** *adj* permanent; (*anhaltend*) lasting

bleich *adj* pale. **b~en†** *vi* (*sein*) bleach; (*ver-*) fade ● *vt* (*reg*) bleach. **B~mittel** *nt* bleach

blei|ern *adj* leaden. **~frei** *adj* unleaded. **B~stift** *m* pencil. **B~stiftabsatz** *m* stiletto heel. **B~stiftspitzer** *m* **-s,-** pencil sharpener

Blende *f* **-,-n** shade, shield; (*Sonnen-*) [sun] visor; (*Phot*) diaphragm; (*Öffnung*) aperture; (*an Kleid*) facing. **b~n** *vt* dazzle, blind

Blick *m* **-[e]s,-e** look; (*kurz*) glance; (*Aussicht*) view; **auf den ersten B~** at first sight. **b~en** *vi* (*haben*) look/(*kurz*) glance (**auf** + *acc* at). **B~punkt** *m* (*fig*) point of view

blind *adj* blind; (*trübe*) dull; **b~er Alarm** false alarm; **b~er Passagier** stowaway. **B~darm** *m* appendix. **B~darmentzündung** *f* appendicitis. **B~e(r)** *m/f* blind man/woman; **die B~en** the blind *pl*. **B~enhund** *m* guidedog. **B~enschrift** *f* braille. **B~gänger** *m* **-s,-** (*Mil*) dud. **B~heit** *f* **-** blindness

blink|en *vi* (*haben*) flash; (*funkeln*) gleam; (*Auto*) indicate. **B~er** *m* **-s,-** (*Auto*) indicator. **B~licht** *nt* flashing light

blinzeln *vi* (*haben*) blink

Blitz *m* **-es,-e** [flash of] lightning; (*Phot*) flash. **B~ableiter** *m* lightning-conductor. **b~artig** *adj* lightning ● *adv* like lightning. **b~en** *vi* (*haben*) flash; (*funkeln*) sparkle; **es hat geblitzt** there was a flash of lightning. **B~eis** *nt* sheet ice. **B~licht** *nt* (*Phot*) flash. **b~sauber** *adj* spick and span. **b~schnell** *adj* lightning ● *adv* like lightning

Block *m* **-[e]s,⸚e** block ● **-[e]s,-s** & **⸚e** pad; (*Häuser-*) block

Blockade *f* **-,-n** blockade

Blockflöte *f* recorder

blockieren *vt* block; (*Mil*) blockade

Blockschrift *f* block letters *pl*

blöd[e] *adj* feeble-minded; (*dumm*) stupid

Blödsinn *m* **-[e]s** idiocy; (*Unsinn*) nonsense

Blog *nt/m* blog

blöken *vi* (*haben*) bleat

blond *adj* fair-haired; (*Haar*) fair

bloß *adj* bare; (*alleinig*) mere ● *adv* only, just

bloß|legen *vt sep* uncover. **b~stellen** *vt sep* compromise

Bluff *m* **-s,-s** bluff. **b~en** *vt/i* (*haben*) bluff

blühen *vi* (*haben*) flower; (*fig*) flourish. **b~d** *adj* flowering; (*fig*) flourishing, thriving

Blume *f* **-,-n** flower; (*vom Wein*) bouquet. **B~nbeet** *nt* flower-bed. **B~ngeschäft** *nt* flower-shop, florist's. **B~nkohl** *m* cauliflower. **B~nmuster** *nt* floral design. **B~nstrauß** *m* bunch of flowers. **B~ntopf** *m* flowerpot; (*Pflanze*) pot plant. **B~nzwiebel** *f* bulb

blumig *adj* (*fig*) flowery

Bluse *f* **-,-n** blouse

Blut *nt* **-[e]s** blood. **b~arm** *adj* anaemic. **B~bahn** *f* blood-stream. **B~bild** *nt* blood count. **B~druck** *m* blood pressure. **b~dürstig** *adj* bloodthirsty

Blüte *f* **-,-n** flower, bloom; (*vom Baum*) blossom; (*B~zeit*) flowering period; (*Baum-*) blossom time;

(*Höhepunkt*) peak, prime

Blut|egel *m* **-s,-** leech. **b~en** *vi* (*haben*) bleed

Blüten|blatt *nt* petal. **B~staub** *m* pollen

Blut|er *m* **-s,-** haemophiliac. **B~erguss** *m* bruise. **B~gefäß** *nt* blood-vessel. **B~gruppe** *f* blood group. **b~ig** *adj* bloody. **B~körperchen** *nt* **-s,-** corpuscle. **B~probe** *f* blood test. **b~rünstig** *adj* (*fig*) bloody, gory. **B~schande** *f* incest. **B~spender** *m* blood donor. **B~sturz** *m* haemorrhage. **B~transfusion, B~übertragung** *f* blood transfusion. **B~ung** *f* **-,-en** bleeding; (*Med*) haemorrhage; (*Regel-*) period. **b~unterlaufen** *adj* bruised; (*Auge*) bloodshot. **B~vergiftung** *f* blood-poisoning. **B~wurst** *f* black pudding

Bö *f* **-,-en** gust; (*Regen-*) squall

Bob *m* **-s,-s** bob[-sleigh]

Bock *m* **-[e]s,¨e** buck; (*Ziege*) billy goat; (*Schaf*) ram; (*Gestell*) support. **b~ig** *adj* [!] stubborn. **B~springen** *nt* leap-frog

Boden *m* **-s,¨** ground; (*Erde*) soil; (*Fuß-*) floor; (*Grundfläche*) bottom; (*Dach-*) loft, attic. **B~satz** *m* sediment. **B~schätze** *mpl* mineral deposits. **B~see (der)** Lake Constance

Bogen *m* **-s,- & ¨** curve; (*Geometry*) arc; (*beim Skilauf*) turn; (*Architecture*) arch; (*Waffe, Geigen-*) bow; (*Papier*) sheet; **einen großen B~ um jdn/etw machen** [!] give s.o./sth a wide berth. **B~schießen** *nt* archery

Bohle *f* **-,-n** [thick] plank

Böhm|en *nt* **-s** Bohemia. **b~isch** *adj* Bohemian

Bohne *f* **-,-n** bean; **grüne B~n** French beans

bohner|n *vt* polish. **B~wachs** *nt* floor-polish

bohr|en *vt/i* (*haben*) drill (**nach** for); drive (*Tunnel*); sink (*Brunnen*); (*Insekt:*) bore. **B~er** *m* **-s,-** drill. **B~insel** *f* [offshore] drilling rig. **B~turm** *m* derrick

Boje *f* **-,-n** buoy

Böllerschuss *m* gun salute

Bolzen *m* **-s,-** bolt; (*Stift*) pin

bombardieren *vt* bomb; (*fig*) bombard (**mit** with)

Bombe *f* **-,-n** bomb. **B~nangriff** *m* bombing raid. **B~nerfolg** *m* huge success

Bon /bɔŋ/ *m* **-s,-s** voucher; (*Kassen-*) receipt

Bonbon /bɔŋˈbɔŋ/ *m & nt* **-s,-s** sweet

Bonus *m* **-[ses],-[se]** bonus

Boot *nt* **-[e]s,-e** boat. **B~ssteg** *m* landing-stage

Bord[1] *nt* **-[e]s,-e** shelf

Bord[2] *m* (*Naut*) **an B~** aboard, on board; **über B~** overboard. **B~buch** *nt* log[-book]

Bordell *nt* **-s,-e** brothel

Bordkarte *f* boarding-pass

borgen *vt* borrow; **jdm etw b~** lend s.o. sth

Borke *f* **-,-n** bark

Börse *f* **-,-n** purse; (*Comm*) stock exchange. **B~nmakler** *m* stockbroker

Borst|e *f* **-,-n** bristle. **b~ig** *adj* bristly

Borte *f* **-,-n** braid

Böschung *f* **-,-en** embankment

böse *adj* wicked, evil; (*unartig*) naughty; (*schlimm*) bad; (*zornig*) cross; **jdm** *od* **auf jdn b~ sein** be cross with s.o.

bos|haft *adj* malicious, spiteful. **B~heit** *f* **-,-en** malice; spite; (*Handlung*) spiteful act/(*Bemerkung*) remark

böswillig *adj* malicious

Botani|k *f* - botany. **B~ker(in)** *m* **-s,-** (*f* **-,-nen**) botanist

Bot|e *m* **-n,-n** messenger. **B~engang** *m* errand. **B~schaft** *f* **-,-en** message; (*Pol*) embassy. **B~schafter** *m* **-s,-** ambassador

Bouillon /bʊlˈjɔŋ/ *f* **-,-s** clear soup. **B~würfel** *m* stock cube

Bowle /ˈboːlə/ *f* **-,-n** punch

Box *f* **-,-en** box; (*Pferde-*) loose box; (*Lautsprecher-*) speaker; (*Autorennen*) pit

box|en *vi* (*haben*) box ● *vt* punch. **B~en** *nt* **-s** boxing. **B~enluder** *nt* pit babe. **B~er** *m* **-s,-** boxer. **B~stopp** *m* pit stop

brachliegen† *vi sep* (*haben*) lie fallow

Branche /ˈbrãːʃə/ *f* **-,-n** [line of] business. **B~nverzeichnis** *nt* (*Teleph*) classified directory

Brand *m* **-[e]s,⸚e** fire; (*Med*) gangrene; (*Bot*) blight; **in B~ geraten** catch fire; **in B~ setzen** *od* **stecken** set on fire. **B~bombe** *f* incendiary bomb

Brand|stifter *m* arsonist. **B~stiftung** *f* arson

Brandung *f* - surf

Brand|wunde *f* burn. **B~zeichen** *nt* brand

Branntwein *m* spirit; (*coll*) spirits *pl*. **B~brennerei** *f* distillery

bras|ilianisch *adj* Brazilian. **B~ilien** *nt* **-s** Brazil

Brat|apfel *m* baked apple. **b~en**† *vt/i* (*haben*) roast; (*in der Pfanne*) fry. **B~en** *m* **-s,-** roast; (*B~stück*) joint. **b~fertig** *adj* oven-ready. **B~hähnchen** roasting chicken. **B~kartoffeln** *fpl* fried potatoes. **B~pfanne** *f* frying-pan

Bratsche *f* **-,-n** (*Mus*) viola

Bratspieß *m* spit

Brauch *m* **-[e]s,Bräuche** custom. **b~bar** *adj* usable; (*nützlich*) useful. **b~en** *vt* need; (*ge-, verbrauchen*) use; take (*Zeit*); **er b~t es nur zu sagen** he only has to say

Braue *f* **-,-n** eyebrow

brau|en *vt* brew. **B~er** *m* **-s,-** brewer. **B~erei** *f* **-,-en** brewery

braun *adj*, **B~** *nt* **-s,-** brown; **b~ werden** (*Person:*) get a tan; **b~ [gebrannt] sein** be [sun-]tanned

Bräune *f* - [sun-]tan. **b~n** *vt/i* (*haben*) brown; (*in der Sonne*) tan

Braunschweig *nt* **-s** Brunswick

Brause *f* **-,-n** (*Dusche*) shower; (*an Gießkanne*) rose; (*B~limonade*) fizzy drink

Braut *f* **-,⸚e** bride; (*Verlobte*) fiancée

Bräutigam *m* **-s,-e** bridegroom; (*Verlobter*) fiancé

Brautkleid *nt* wedding dress

Brautpaar *nt* bridal couple; (*Verlobte*) engaged couple

brav *adj* good; (*redlich*) honest ● *adv* dutifully; (*redlich*) honestly

bravo *int* bravo!

BRD *abbr* (**Bundesrepublik Deutschland**) FRG

Brech|eisen *nt* jemmy; (*B~stange*) crowbar. **b~en**† *vt* break; (*Phys*) refract (*Licht*); (*erbrechen*) vomit; **sich b~en** (*Wellen:*) break; (*Licht:*) be refracted; **sich** (*dat*) **den Arm b~en** break one's arm ● *vi* (*sein*) break ● *vi* (*haben*) vomit, be sick. **B~reiz** *m* nausea. **B~stange** *f* crowbar

Brei *m* **-[e]s,-e** paste; (*Culin*) purée; (*Hafer-*) porridge

breit *adj* wide; (*Schultern, Grinsen*) broad. **B~band** *nt* broadband. **B~e** *f* **-,-n** width; breadth; (*Geog*) latitude. **b~en** *vt* spread (**über** + *acc* over). **B~engrad** *m* [degree of] latitude. **B~enkreis** *m* parallel

Bremse¹ *f* **-,-n** horsefly

Bremse² *f* **-,-n** brake. **b~n** *vt* slow down; (*fig*) restrain ● *vi* (*haben*) brake

Bremslicht *nt* brake-light

brenn|bar *adj* combustible; **leicht b~bar** highly [in]flammable. **b~en**† *vi* (*haben*) burn; (*Licht:*) be on; (*Zigarette:*) be alight; (*weh tun*) smart, sting ● *vt* burn; (*rösten*) roast; (*im Brennofen*) fire; (*destillieren*) distil. **b~end** *adj* burning; (*angezündet*) lighted; (*fig*) fervent. **B~er** *m* **-s, -** burner. **B~erei** *f* **-,-en** distillery

Brennessel* *f* = **Brennnessel**

Brenn|holz *nt* firewood. **B~ofen** *m* kiln. **B~nessel** *f* stinging nettle. **B~punkt** *m* (*Phys*) focus. **B~spiritus** *m* methylated spirits. **B~stoff** *m* fuel. **B~stoffzelle** *f* fuel cell

Bretagne /bre'tanjə/ **(die) -** Brittany

Brett *nt* **-[e]s,-er** board; (*im Regal*) shelf; **schwarzes B~** notice board. **B~spiel** *nt* board game

Brezel *f* **-,-n** pretzel

Bridge /brɪtʃ/ *nt* **-** (*Spiel*) bridge

Brief *m* **-[e]s,-e** letter. **B~beschwerer** *m* **-s,-** paperweight. **B~freund(in)** *m*(*f*) pen-friend. **B~kasten** *m* letter-box. **B~kopf** *m* letter-head. **b~lich** *adj & adv* by letter. **B~marke** *f* [postage] stamp. **B~öffner** *m* paper-knife. **B~papier** *nt* notepaper. **B~tasche** *f* wallet. **B~träger** *m* postman. **B~umschlag** *m* envelope. **B~wahl** *f* postal vote. **B~wechsel** *m* correspondence

Brikett *nt* **-s,-s** briquette

Brillant *m* **-en,-en** [cut] diamond

Brille *f* **-,-n** glasses *pl*, spectacles *pl*; (*Schutz-*) goggles *pl*; (*Klosett-*) toilet seat

bringen† *vt* bring; (*fort-*) take; (*ein-*) yield; (*veröffentlichen*) publish; (*im Radio*) broadcast; show (*Film*); **ins Bett b~** put to bed; **jdn nach Hause b~** take/(*begleiten*) see s.o. home; **um etw b~** deprive of sth; **jdn dazu b~, etw zu tun** get s.o. to do sth; **es weit b~** (*fig*) go far

Brise *f* **-,-n** breeze

Brit|e *m* **-n,-n, B~in** *f* **-,-nen** Briton. **b~isch** *adj* British

Bröck|chen *nt* **-s,-** (*Culin*) crouton. **b~elig** *adj* crumbly; (*Gestein*) friable. **b~eln** *vt/i* (*haben/sein*) crumble

Brocken *m* **-s,-** chunk; (*Erde, Kohle*) lump

Brokat *m* **-[e]s,-e** brocade

Brokkoli *pl* broccoli *sg*

Brombeere *f* blackberry

Bronchitis *f* **-** bronchitis

Bronze /'brõ:sə/ *f* **-,-n** bronze

Brosch|e *f* **-,-n** brooch. **b~iert** *adj* paperback. **B~üre** *f* **-,-n** brochure; (*Heft*) booklet

Brösel *mpl* (*Culin*) breadcrumbs

Brot *nt* **-[e]s,-e** bread; **ein B~** a loaf [of bread]; (*Scheibe*) a slice of bread

Brötchen *nt* **-s,-** [bread] roll

Brotkrümel *m* breadcrumb

Bruch *m* **-[e]s,⸚e** break; (*Brechen*) breaking; (*Rohr-*) burst; (*Med*) fracture; (*Eingeweide-*) rupture, hernia; (*Math*) fraction; (*fig*) breach; (*in Beziehung*) break-up

brüchig *adj* brittle

Bruch|landung *f* crash-landing. **B~rechnung** *f* fractions *pl*. **B~stück** *nt* fragment. **B~teil** *m* fraction

Brücke *f* **-,-n** bridge; (*Teppich*) rug

Bruder *m* **-s,⸚** brother

brüderlich *adj* brotherly, fraternal
Brügge *nt* **-s** Bruges
Brüh|e *f* **-,-n** broth, stock. **B~würfel** *m* stock cube
brüllen *vt/i* (*haben*) roar
brumm|eln *vt/i* (*haben*) mumble. **b~en** *vi* (*haben*) (*Insekt:*) buzz; (*Bär:*) growl; (*Motor:*) hum; (*murren*) grumble. **B~er** *m* **-s,-** 🅸 bluebottle. **b~ig** *adj* 🅸 grumpy
brünett *adj* dark-haired
Brunnen *m* **-s,-** well; (*Spring-*) fountain; (*Heil-*) spa water
brüsk *adj* brusque
Brüssel *nt* **-s** Brussels
Brust *f* **-,⸚e** chest; (*weibliche, Culin: B~stück*) breast. **B~bein** *nt* breastbone
brüsten (sich) *vr* boast
Brust|fellentzündung *f* pleurisy. **B~schwimmen** *nt* breaststroke
Brüstung *f* **-,-en** parapet
Brustwarze *f* nipple
Brut *f* **-,-en** incubation
brutal *adj* brutal
brüten *vi* (*haben*) sit (*on eggs*); (*fig*) ponder (**über** + *dat* over)
Brutkasten *m* (*Med*) incubator
brutto *adv*, **B~-** *prefix* gross
BSE *f* **-** BSE
Bub *m* **-en,-en** (*SGer*) boy. **B~e** *m* **-n,-n** (*Karte*) jack, knave
Buch *nt* **-[e]s,⸚er** book; **B~ führen** keep a record (**über** + *acc* of); **die B⸚er führen** keep the accounts
Buche *f* **-,-n** beech
buchen *vt* book; (*Comm*) enter
Bücher|ei *f* **-,-en** library. **B~regal** *nt* bookcase, bookshelves *pl*. **B~schrank** *m* bookcase
Buchfink *m* chaffinch
Buch|führung *f* bookkeeping. **B~halter(in)** *m* **-s,-** (*f* **-,-nen**) bookkeeper, accountant. **B~haltung** *f* bookkeeping, accountancy; (*Abteilung*) accounts department. **B~handlung** *f* bookshop
Büchse *f* **-,-n** box; (*Konserven-*) tin, can
Buch|stabe *m* **-n,-n** letter. **b~stabieren** *vt* spell [out]. **b~stäblich** *adv* literally
Bucht *f* **-,-en** (*Geog*) bay
Buchung *f* **-,-en** booking, reservation; (*Comm*) entry
Buckel *m* **-s,-** hump; (*Beule*) bump; (*Hügel*) hillock
bücken (sich) *vr* bend down
bucklig *adj* hunchbacked
Bückling *m* **-s,-e** smoked herring
Buddhis|mus *m* **-** Buddhism. **B~t(in)** *m* **-en,-en** (*f* **-,-nen**) Buddhist. **b~tisch** *adj* Buddhist
Bude *f* **-,-n** hut; (*Kiosk*) kiosk; (*Markt-*) stall; (🅸: *Zimmer*) room
Budget /bʏˈdʒeː/ *nt* **-s,-s** budget
Büfett *nt* **-[e]s,-e** sideboard; (*Theke*) bar; **kaltes B~** cold buffet
Büffel *m* **-s,-** buffalo
Bügel *m* **-s,-** frame; (*Kleider-*) coathanger; (*Steig-*) stirrup; (*Brillen-*) sidepiece. **B~brett** *nt* ironing-board. **B~eisen** *nt* iron. **B~falte** *f* crease. **b~frei** *adj* non-iron. **b~n** *vt/i* (*haben*) iron
Bühne *f* **-,-n** stage. **B~nbild** *nt* set. **B~neingang** *m* stage door
Buhrufe *mpl* boos
Bukett *nt* **-[e]s,-e** bouquet
Bulgarien /-i̯ən/ *nt* **-s** Bulgaria
Bull|auge *nt* (*Naut*) porthole. **B~dogge** *f* bulldog. **B~dozer** *m* **-s,-** bulldozer. **B~e** *m* **-n,-n** bull; (*sl: Polizist*) cop
Bumme|l *m* **-s,-** 🅸 stroll. **B~lei** *f* **-** 🅸 dawdling
bummel|ig *adj* 🅸 slow; (*nachläs-*

sig) careless. **b~n** *vi* (*sein*) [!] stroll • *vi* (*haben*) [!] dawdle. **B~streik** *m* go-slow. **B~zug** *m* [!] slow train

Bums *m* **-es,-e** [!] bump, thump

Bund[1] *nt* **-[e]s,-e** bunch

Bund[2] *m* **-[e]s,¨e** association; (*Bündnis*) alliance; (*Pol*) federation; (*Rock-, Hosen-*) waistband; **der B~** the Federal Government

Bündel *nt* **-s,-** bundle. **b~n** *vt* bundle [up]

Bundes|- *prefix* Federal. **B~genosse** *m* ally. **B~kanzler** *m* Federal Chancellor. **B~land** *nt* [federal] state; (*Aust*) province. **B~liga** *f* German national league. **B~rat** *m* Upper House of Parliament. **B~regierung** *f* Federal Government. **B~republik** *f* **die B~republik Deutschland** the Federal Republic of Germany. **B~tag** *m* Lower House of Parliament. **B~wehr** *f* [Federal German] Army

> *i* **Bundestag** The lower house of the German parliament, which is elected every four years. The *Bundestag* is responsible for federal legislation, the federal budget, and electing the *Bundeskanzler*, or Federal Chancellor, (equivalent of prime minister). Half the MPs are elected directly and half by proportional representation. Every citizen has two votes.

> *i* **Bundeswappen**
> ▷WAPPEN

bünd|ig *adj & adv* **kurz und b~ig** short and to the point. **B~nis** *nt* **-ses,-se** alliance

Bunker *m* **-s,-** bunker; (*Luftschutz-*) shelter

bunt *adj* coloured; (*farbenfroh*) colourful; (*grell*) gaudy; (*gemischt*) varied; (*wirr*) confused; **b~e Platte** assorted cold meats. **B~stift** *m* crayon

Bürde *f* **-,-n** (*fig*) burden

Burg *f* **-,-en** castle

Bürge *m* **-n,-n** guarantor. **b~n** *vi* (*haben*) **b~n für** vouch for; (*fig*) guarantee

Bürger|(in) *m* **-s,-** (*f* **-,-nen**) citizen. **B~krieg** *m* civil war. **b~lich** *adj* civil; (*Pflicht*) civic; (*mittelständisch*) middle-class. **B~liche(r)** *m/f* commoner. **B~meister** *m* mayor. **B~rechte** *npl* civil rights. **B~steig** *m* **-[e]s,-e** pavement

Bürgschaft *f* **-,-en** surety

Burgunder *m* **-s,-** (*Wein*) Burgundy

Büro *nt* **-s,-s** office. **B~angestellte(r)** *m/f* office worker. **B~klammer** *f* paper clip. **B~kratie** *f* **-,-n** bureaucracy. **b~kratisch** *adj* bureaucratic

Bursche *m* **-n,-n** lad, youth

Bürste *f* **-,-n** brush. **b~n** *vt* brush. **B~nschnitt** *m* crew cut

Bus *m* **-ses,-se** bus; (*Reise-*) coach

Busch *m* **-[e]s,¨e** bush

Büschel *nt* **-s,-** tuft

buschig *adj* bushy

Busen *m* **-s,-** bosom

Bussard *m* **-s,-e** buzzard

Buße *f* **-,-n** penance; (*Jur*) fine

Bußgeld *nt* (*Jur*) fine

Büste *f* **-,-n** bust; (*Schneider-*) dummy. **B~nhalter** *m* **-s,-** bra

Butter *f* **-** butter. **B~blume** *f* buttercup. **B~brot** *nt* slice of bread and butter. **B~milch** *f* buttermilk. **b~n** *vt* butter

b.w. *abbr* (**bitte wenden**) P.T.O.

Cc

ca. *abbr* (**circa**) about
Café /ka'fe:/ *nt* **-s,-s** café
Camcorder /'kamkɔrdɐ/ *m* **-s, -** camcorder
camp|en /'kɛmpən/ *vi* (*haben*) go camping. **C~ing** *nt* **-s** camping. **C~ingplatz** *m* campsite
Caravan /'ka[:]ravan/ *m* **-s,-s** (*Auto*) caravan; (*Kombi*) estate car
CD /tse:'de:/ *f* **-,-s** compact disc, CD. **CD-ROM** *f* **-,-(s)** CD-ROM
Cell|ist(in) /tʃɛ'lɪst(ɪn)/ *m* **-en,-en** (*f* **-,-nen**) cellist. **C~o** *nt* **-,-los & -li** cello
Celsius /'tsɛlzi̯ʊs/ *inv* Celsius, centigrade
Cent/tsɛnt/ *m* **-[s], -[s]** cent
Champagner /ʃam'panjɐ/ *m* **-s** champagne
Champignon /'ʃampɪnjɔŋ/ *m* **-s,-s** [field] mushroom
Chance /'ʃã:s[ə]/ *f* **-,-n** chance
Chaos /'ka:ɔs/ *nt* **-** chaos
Charakter /ka'raktɐ/ *m* **-s,-e** character. **c~isieren** *vt* characterize. **c~istisch** *adj* characteristic (für of)
charm|ant /ʃar'mant/ *adj* charming. **C~e** *m* **-s** charm
Charter|flug /'tʃ-, 'ʃartɐ-/ *m* charter flight. **c~n** *vt* charter
Chassis /ʃa'si:/ *nt* **-,-** chassis
Chauffeur /ʃɔ'fø:ɐ̯/ *m* **-s,-e** chauffeur; (*Taxi-*) driver
Chauvinist /ʃovi'nɪst/ *m* **-en,-en** chauvinist
Chef /ʃɛf/ *m* **-s,-s** head; **[!]** boss
Chemie /çe'mi:/ *f* **-** chemistry
Chem|iker(in) /'çe:-/ *m* **-s,-** (*f* **-,-nen**) chemist. **c~isch** *adj* chemical; **c~ische Reinigung** dry-cleaning; (*Geschäft*) dry-cleaner's
Chicorée /'ʃɪkore:/ *m* **-s** chicory
Chiffre /'ʃɪfɐ, 'ʃɪfrə/ *f* **-,-n** cipher
Chile /'çi:le/ *nt* **-s** Chile
Chin|a /'çi:na/ *nt* **-s** China. **C~ese** *m* **-n,-n, C~esin** *f* **-,-nen** Chinese. **c~esisch** *adj* Chinese. **C~esisch** *nt* **-[s]** (*Lang*) Chinese
Chip /tʃɪp/ *m* **-s,-s** [micro]chip. **C~s** *pl* crisps
Chirurg /çi'rʊrk/ *m* **-en,-en** surgeon. **C~ie** *f* **-** surgery
Chlor /klo:ɐ̯/ *nt* **-s** chlorine
Choke /tʃo:k/ *m* **-s,-s** (*Auto*) choke
Cholera /'ko:lera/ *f* **-** cholera
cholerisch /ko'le:rɪʃ/ *adj* irascible
Cholesterin /ço-, kolɛste'ri:n/ *nt* **-s** cholesterol
Chor /ko:ɐ̯/ *m* **-[e]s,⸚e** choir
Choreographie, Choreografie /koreogra'fi:/ *f* **-,-n** choreography
Christ /krɪst/ *m* **-en,-en** Christian. **C~baum** *m* Christmas tree. **C~entum** *nt* **-s** Christianity **c~lich** *adj* Christian
Christus /'krɪstʊs/ *m* **-ti** Christ
Chrom /kro:m/ *nt* **-s** chromium
Chromosom /kromo'zo:m/ *nt* **-s,-en** chromosome
Chronik /'kro:nɪk/ *f* **-,-en** chronicle
chronisch /'kro:nɪʃ/ *adj* chronic
Chrysantheme /krʏzan'te:mə/ *f* **-,-n** chrysanthemum
circa /'tsɪrka/ *adv* about
Clique /'klɪkə/ *f* **-,-n** clique
Clou /klu:/ *m* **-s,-s** highlight, **[!]** high spot
Clown /kla̯un/ *m* **-s,-s** clown
Club /klʊp/ *m* **-s,-s** club
Co_2-Fußabdruck *m* carbon footprint
Cocktail /'kɔkte:l/ *m* **-s,-s** cocktail
Code /'ko:t/ *m* **-s,-s** code

c d

Comic-Heft /'kɔmɪk-/ *nt* comic
Computer /kɔm'pju:tɐ/ *m* **-s,-** computer. **c~isieren** *vt* computerize. **C~spiel** *nt* computer game
Conférencier /kõ'ferã'si̯e:/ *m* **-s,-** compère
Cord /kɔrt/ *m* **-s, C~samt** *m* corduroy
Couch /kau̯tʃ/ *f* **-,-s** settee
Cousin /ku'zɛ̃:/ *m* **-s,-s** [male] cousin. **C~e** *f* **-,-n** [female] cousin
Creme /kre:m/ *f* **-s,-s** cream; (*Speise*) cream dessert
Curry /'kari, 'kœri/ *nt* & *m* **-s** curry powder ● *nt* **-s,-s** (*Gericht*) curry
Cursor /'kø:ɐ̯sɐ/ *m* **-s, -** cursor
Cyberspace /'sai̯bɐspe:s/ *m* **-** cyberspace

Dd

da *adv* there; (*hier*) here; (*zeitlich*) then; (*in dem Fall*) in that case; **von da an** from then on; **da sein** be there/(*hier*) here; (*existieren*) exist; **wieder da sein** be back ● *conj* as, since
dabei (*emphatic:* **dabei**) *adv* nearby; (*daran*) with it; (*eingeschlossen*) included; (*hinsichtlich*) about it; (*währenddem*) during this; (*gleichzeitig*) at the same time; (*doch*) and yet; **dicht d~** close by; **d~ sein** be present; (*mitmachen*) be involved; **d~ sein, etw zu tun** be just doing sth
Dach *nt* **-[e]s,¨er** roof. **D~boden** *m* loft. **D~luke** *f* skylight. **D~rinne** *f* gutter
Dachs *m* **-es,-e** badger
Dachsparren *m* **-s,-** rafter
Dackel *m* **-s,-** dachshund
dadurch (*emphatic:* **dadurch**) *adv* through it/them; (*Ursache*) by it; (*deshalb*) because of that; **d~, dass** because
dafür (*emphatic:* **dafür**) *adv* for it/them; (*anstatt*) instead; (*als Ausgleich*) but [on the other hand]; **d~, dass** considering that; **ich kann nichts dafür** it's not my fault
dagegen (*emphatic:* **dagegen**) *adv* against it/them; (*Mittel, Tausch*) for it; (*verglichen damit*) by comparison; (*jedoch*) however; **hast du was d~?** do you mind?
daheim *adv* at home
daher (*emphatic:* **daher**) *adv* from there; (*deshalb*) for that reason; **das kommt d~, weil** that's because ● *conj* that is why
dahin (*emphatic:* **dahin**) *adv* there; **bis d~** up to there; (*bis dann*) until/(*Zukunft*) by then; **jdn d~ bringen, dass er etw tut** get s.o. to do sth
dahinten *adv* back there
dahinter (*emphatic:* **dahinter**) *adv* behind it/them; **d~ kommen** (*fig*) get to the bottom of it
Dahlie /-i̯ə/ *f* **-,-n** dahlia
dalassen† *vt sep* leave there
daliegen† *vi sep* (*haben*) lie there
damalig *adj* at that time; **der d~e Minister** the then minister
damals *adv* at that time
Damast *m* **-es,-e** damask
Dame *f* **-,-n** lady; (*Karte, Schach*) queen; (*D~spiel*) draughts *sg*. **d~nhaft** *adj* ladylike
damit (*emphatic:* **damit**) *adv* with it/them; (*dadurch*) by it; **hör auf d~!** stop it! ● *conj* so that
Damm *m* **-[e]s,¨e** dam
dämmer|ig *adj* dim. **D~licht** *nt* twilight. **d~n** *vi* (*haben*) (*Morgen:*)

dawn; **es d~t** it is getting light/(*abends*) dark. **D~ung** *f* dawn; (*Abend-*) dusk

Dämon *m* **-s,-en** demon

Dampf *m* **-es,¨-e** steam; (*Chemistry*) vapour. **d~en** *vi* (*haben*) steam

dämpfen *vt* (*Culin*) steam; (*fig*) muffle (*Ton*); lower (*Stimme*)

Dampf|er *m* **-s,-** steamer. **D~kochtopf** *m* pressure-cooker. **D~maschine** *f* steam engine. **D~walze** *f* steamroller

danach (*emphatic:* **danach**) *adv* after it/them; (*suchen*) for it/them; (*riechen*) of it; (*später*) afterwards; (*entsprechend*) accordingly; **es sieht d~ aus** it looks like it

Däne *m* **-n,-n** Dane

daneben (*emphatic:* **daneben**) *adv* beside it/them; (*außerdem*) in addition; (*verglichen damit*) by comparison

Dän|emark *nt* **-s** Denmark. **D~in** *f* **-,-nen** Dane. **d~isch** *adj* Danish

Dank *m* **-es** thanks *pl*; **vielen D~!** thank you very much! **d~** *prep* (+ *dat or gen*) thanks to. **d~bar** *adj* grateful; (*erleichtert*) thankful; (*lohnend*) rewarding. **D~barkeit** *f* - gratitude. **d~e** *adv* **d~e [schön** *od* **sehr]!** thank you [very much]! **d~en** *vi* (*haben*) thank (**jdm** s.o.); (*ablehnen*) decline; **nichts zu d~en!** don't mention it!

dann *adv* then; **selbst d~, wenn** even if

daran (*emphatic:* **daran**) *adv* on it/them; at it/them; (*denken*) of it; **nahe d~** on the point (**etw zu tun** of doing sth). **d~setzen** *vt sep* **alles d~setzen** do one's utmost (**zu** to)

darauf (*emphatic:* **darauf**) *adv* on it/them; (*warten*) for it; (*antworten*) to it; (*danach*) after that; (*d~hin*) as a result. **d~hin** *adv* as a result

daraus (*emphatic:* **daraus**) *adv* out of *or* from it/them; **er macht sich nichts d~** he doesn't care for it

darlegen *vt sep* expound; (*erklären*) explain

Darlehen *nt* **-s,-** loan

Darm *m* **-[e]s,¨-e** intestine

darstell|en *vt sep* represent; (*bildlich*) portray; (*Theat*) interpret; (*spielen*) play; (*schildern*) describe. **D~er** *m* **-s,-** actor. **D~erin** *f* **-,-nen** actress. **D~ung** *f* representation; interpretation; description

darüber (*emphatic:* **darüber**) *adv* over it/them; (*höher*) above it/them; (*sprechen, lachen, sich freuen*) about it; (*mehr*) more; **d~ hinaus** beyond [it]; (*dazu*) on top of that

darum (*emphatic:* **darum**) *adv* round it/them; (*bitten, kämpfen*) for it; (*deshalb*) that is why; **d~, weil** because

darunter (*emphatic:* **darunter**) *adv* under it/them; (*tiefer*) below it/them; (*weniger*) less; (*dazwischen*) among them

das *def art & pron s.* **der**

dasein* *vi sep* (*sein*) = **da sein**, *s.* **da. D~** *nt* **-s** existence

dass *conj* that

dasselbe *pron s.* **derselbe**

Daten|sichtgerät *nt* visual display unit, VDU. **D~verarbeitung** *f* data processing

datieren *vt/i* (*haben*) date

Dativ *m* **-s,-e** dative. **D~objekt** *nt* indirect object

Dattel *f* **-,-n** date

Datum *nt* **-s,-ten** date; **Daten** dates; (*Angaben*) data

Dauer *f* - duration, length; (*Jur*) term; **auf die D~** in the long run. **D~auftrag** *m* standing order. **d~haft** *adj* lasting, enduring; (*fest*)

durable. **D~karte** *f* season ticket. **d~n** *vi* (*haben*) last; **lange d~n** take a long time. **d~nd** *adj* lasting; (*ständig*) constant. **D~welle** *f* perm

Daumen *m* **-s,-** thumb; **jdm den D~ drücken** *od* **halten** keep one's fingers crossed for s.o.

Daunen *fpl* down *sg*. **D~decke** *f* [down-filled] duvet

davon (*emphatic:* **davon**) *adv* from it/them; (*dadurch*) by it; (*damit*) with it/them; (*darüber*) about it; (*Menge*) of it/them; **das kommt d~!** it serves you right! **d~kommen†** *vi sep* (*sein*) escape (**mit dem Leben** with one's life). **d~laufen†** *vi sep* (*sein*) run away. **d~machen (sich)** *vr sep* [!] make off. **d~tragen†** *vt sep* carry off; (*erleiden*) suffer; (*gewinnen*) win

davor (*emphatic:* **davor**) *adv* in front of it/them; (*sich fürchten*) of it; (*zeitlich*) before it/them

dazu (*emphatic:* **dazu**) *adv* to it/them; (*damit*) with it/them; (*dafür*) for it; **noch d~** in addition to that; **jdn d~ bringen, etw zu tun** get s.o. to do sth; **ich kam nicht d~** I didn't get round to [doing] it. **d~kommen†** *vi sep* (*sein*) arrive [on the scene]; (*hinzukommen*) be added. **d~rechnen** *vt sep* add to it/them

dazwischen (*emphatic:* **dazwischen**) *adv* between them; in between; (*darunter*) among them. **d~kommen†** *vi sep* (*sein*) (*fig*) crop up; **wenn nichts d~kommt** if all goes well

Debat|te *f* **-,-n** debate; **zur D~te stehen** be at issue. **d~tieren** *vt/i* (*haben*) debate

Debüt /de'by:/ *nt* **-s,-s** début

Deck *nt* **-[e]s,-s** (*Naut*) deck; **an D~** on deck. **D~bett** *nt* duvet

Decke *f* **-,-n** cover; (*Tisch-*) tablecloth; (*Bett-*) blanket; (*Reise-*) rug; (*Zimmer-*) ceiling; **unter einer D~ stecken** [!] be in league

Deckel *m* **-s,-** lid; (*Flaschen-*) top; (*Buch-*) cover

decken *vt* cover; tile (*Dach*); lay (*Tisch*); (*schützen*) shield; (*Sport*) mark; meet (*Bedarf*); **jdn d~** (*fig*) cover up for s.o.; **sich d~** (*fig*) cover oneself (**gegen** against); (*übereinstimmen*) coincide

Deckname *m* pseudonym

Deckung *f* **-** (*Mil*) cover; (*Sport*) defence; (*Mann-*) marking; (*Boxen*) guard; (*Sicherheit*) security; **in D~ gehen** take cover

defin|ieren *vt* define. **D~ition** *f* **-,-en** definition

Defizit *nt* **-s,-e** deficit

deformiert *adj* deformed

deftig *adj* [!] (*Mahlzeit*) hearty; (*Witz*) coarse

Degen *m* **-s,-** sword; (*Fecht-*) épée

degeneriert *adj* (*fig*) degenerate

degradieren *vt* (*Mil*) demote; (*fig*) degrade

dehn|bar *adj* elastic. **d~en** *vt* stretch; lengthen (*Vokal*); **sich d~en** stretch

Deich *m* **-[e]s,-e** dike

dein *poss pron* your. **d~e(r,s)** *poss pron* yours; **die D~en** *od* **d~en** *pl* your family *sg*. **d~erseits** *adv* for your part. **d~etwegen** *adv* for your sake; (*wegen dir*) because of you, on your account. **d~etwillen** *adv* **um d~etwillen** for your sake. **d~ige** *poss pron* **der/die/das d~ige** yours. **d~s** *poss pron* yours

Dekan *m* **-s,-e** dean

Deklin|ation /-'tsi̯o:n/ *f* **-,-en** declension. **d~ieren** *vt* decline

Dekolleté, Dekolletee /dekɔl'te:/ *nt* **-s,-s** low neckline

Dekor *m* & *nt* **-s** decoration. **D~**

ateur *m* **-s,-e** interior decorator; (*Schaufenster-*) window-dresser. **D~ation** *f* **-,-en** decoration; (*Schaufenster-*) window-dressing; (*Auslage*) display. **d~ativ** *adj* decorative. **d~ieren** *vt* decorate; dress (*Schaufenster*)

Deleg|ation /-'tsi̯o:n/ *f* **-,-en** delegation. **D~ierte(r)** *m/f* delegate

delikat *adj* delicate; (*lecker*) delicious; (*taktvoll*) tactful. **D~essengeschäft** *nt* delicatessen

Delikt *nt* **-[e]s,-e** offence

Delinquent *m* **-en,-en** offender

Delle *f* **-,-n** dent

Delphin *m* **-s,-e** dolphin

Delta *nt* **-s,-s** delta

dem *def art & pron s.* **der**

dementieren *vt* deny

dem|entsprechend *adj* corresponding; (*passend*) appropriate ● *adv* accordingly; (*passend*) appropriately. **d~nächst** *adv* soon; (*in Kürze*) shortly

Demokrat *m* **-en,-en** democrat. **D~ie** *f* **-,-n** democracy. **d~isch** *adj* democratic

demolieren *vt* wreck

Demonstr|ant *m* **-en,-en** demonstrator. **D~ation** *f* **-,-en** demonstration. **d~ieren** *vt/i* (*haben*) demonstrate

demontieren *vt* dismantle

Demoskopie *f* **-** opinion research

Demut *f* **-** humility

den *def art & pron s.* **der. d~en** *pron s.* **der**

denk|bar *adj* conceivable. **d~en**† *vt/i* (*haben*) think (**an** + *acc* of); (*sich erinnern*) remember (**an etw** *acc* sth); **das kann ich mir d~en** I can imagine [that]; **ich d~e nicht daran** I have no intention of doing it. **D~mal** *nt* memorial; (*Monument*) monument. **d~würdig** *adj* memorable

denn *conj* for; **besser/mehr d~ je** better/more than ever ● *adv* **wie/wo d~?** but how/where? **warum d~ nicht?** why ever not? **es sei d~ [, dass]** unless

dennoch *adv* nevertheless

Denunz|iant *m* **-en,-en** informer. **d~ieren** *vt* denounce

Deodorant *nt* **-s,-s** deodorant

deplaciert, **deplatziert** /-'tsi:ɐ̯t/ *adj* (*fig*) out of place

Deponie *f* **-,-n** dump. **d~ren** *vt* deposit

deportieren *vt* deport

Depot /de'po:/ *nt* **-s,-s** depot; (*Lager*) warehouse; (*Bank-*) safe deposit

Depression *f* **-,-en** depression

deprimieren *vt* depress

der, **die, das,** *pl* **die**

● *definite article*

acc **den, die, das,** *pl* **die**; *gen* **des, der, des,** *pl* **der**; *dat* **dem, der, dem,** *pl* **den**

····➤ the. **der Mensch** the person; (*als abstrakter Begriff*) man. **die Natur** nature. **das Leben** life. **das Lesen/Tanzen** reading/dancing. **sich** (*dat*) **das Gesicht/die Hände waschen** wash one's face/hands. **3 Euro das Pfund** 3 euros a pound

● *pronoun*

acc **den, die, das,** *pl* **die**; *gen* **dessen, deren, dessen,** *pl* **deren**; *dat* **dem, der, dem,** *pl* **denen**

● *demonstrative pronoun*

····➤ that; (*pl*) those

d

····➤ (*attributiv*) **der Mann war es** it was 'that man
····➤ (*substantivisch*) he, she, it; (*pl*) they. **der war es** it was 'him. **die da** (*person*) that woman/girl; (*thing*) that one
● *relative pronoun*
····➤ (*Person*) who. **der Mann, der/dessen Sohn hier arbeitet** the man who/whose son works here. **die Frau, mit der ich Tennis spiele** the woman with whom I play tennis, the woman I play tennis with. **das Mädchen, das ich gestern sah** the girl I saw yesterday
····➤ (*Ding*) which, that. **ich sah ein Buch, das mich interessierte** I saw a book that interested me. **die CD, die ich mir anhöre** the CD I am listening to. **das Auto, mit dem wir nach Deutschland fahren** the car we are going to Germany in *or* in which we are going to Germany

derb *adj* tough; (*kräftig*) strong; (*grob*) coarse; (*unsanft*) rough
deren *pron s.* **der**
dergleichen *inv adj* such ● *pron* such a thing/such things
der-/die-/dasselbe, *pl* **dieselben** *pron* the same; **ein- und dasselbe** one and the same thing
derzeit *adv* at present
des *def art s.* **der**
Desert|eur /-'tøːɐ̯/ *m* **-s,-e** deserter. **d~ieren** *vi* (*sein/haben*) desert
desgleichen *adv* likewise ● *pron* the like
deshalb *adv* for this reason; (*also*) therefore
Design *nt* **-s, -s** design
Designer(in) /di'zainɐ, -nərɪn/ *m* **-s,-** (*f* **-,-nen**) designer
Desin|fektion /dɛs?ɪnfɛk'tsi̯oːn/ *f* disinfecting. **D~fektionsmittel** *nt* disinfectant. **d~fizieren** *vt* disinfect
dessen *pron s.* **der**
Destill|ation /-'tsi̯oːn/ *f* - distillation. **d~ieren** *vt* distil
desto *adv* **je mehr d~besser** the more the better
deswegen *adv* = **deshalb**
Detektiv *m* **-s,-e** detective
Deton|ation /-'tsi̯oːn/ *f* **-,-en** explosion. **d~ieren** *vi* (*sein*) explode
deut|en *vt* interpret; predict (*Zukunft*) ● *vi* (*haben*) point (**auf** + *acc* at/(*fig*) to). **d~lich** *adj* clear; (*eindeutig*) plain
deutsch *adj* German. **D~** *nt* **-[s]** (*Lang*) German; **auf D~** in German. **D~e(r)** *m/f* German. **D~land** *nt* **-s** Germany
Deutung *f* **-,-en** interpretation
Devise *f* **-,-n** motto. **D~n** *pl* foreign currency *or* exchange *sg*
Dezember *m* **-s,-** December
dezent *adj* unobtrusive; (*diskret*) discreet
Dezernat *nt* **-[e]s,-e** department
Dezimalzahl *f* decimal
d.h. *abbr* (*das heißt*) i.e.
Dia *nt* **-s,-s** (*Phot*) slide
Diabet|es *m* - diabetes. **D~iker** *m* **-s,-** diabetic
Diadem *nt* **-s,-e** tiara
Diagnose *f* **-,-n** diagnosis
diagonal *adj* diagonal. **D~e** *f* **-,-n** diagonal
Diagramm *nt* **-s,-e** diagram; (*Kurven-*) graph
Diakon *m* **-s,-e** deacon
Dialekt *m* **-[e]s,-e** dialect
Dialog *m* **-[e]s,-e** dialogue
Diamant *m* **-en,-en** diamond

Diapositiv *nt* **-s,-e** (*Phot*) slide
Diaprojektor *m* slide projector
Diät *f* **-,-en** (*Med*) diet; **D~ leben** be on a diet
dich *pron* (*acc of* **du**) you; (*reflexive*) yourself
dicht *adj* dense; (*dick*) thick; (*undurchlässig*) airtight; (*wasser-*) watertight ●*adv* densely; (*nahe*) close (**bei** to). **D~e** density. **d~en**[1] *vt* make watertight
dicht|en[2] *vi* (*haben*) write poetry. ●*vt* write. **D~er(in)** *m* **-s,-** (*f* **-,-nen**) poet. **d~erisch** *adj* poetic. **D~ung**[1] *f* **-,-en** poetry; (*Gedicht*) poem
Dichtung[2] *f* **-,-en** seal; (*Ring*) washer; (*Auto*) gasket
dick *adj* thick; (*beleibt*) fat; (*geschwollen*) swollen; (*fam: eng*) close; **d~ machen** be fattening. **d~flüssig** *adj* thick; (*Phys*) viscous. **D~kopf** *m* ▣ stubborn person; **einen D~kopf haben** be stubborn
die *def art & pron s.* **der**
Dieb|(in) *m* **-[e]s,-e** (*f* **-,-nen**) thief. **d~isch** *adj* thieving; (*Freude*) malicious. **D~stahl** *m* **-[e]s,⸚e** theft
Diele *f* **-,-n** floorboard; (*Flur*) hall
dien|en *vi* (*haben*) serve. **D~er** *m* **-s,-** servant; (*Verbeugung*) bow. **D~erin** *f* **-,-nen** maid, servant
Dienst *m* **-[e]s,-e** service; (*Arbeit*) work; (*Amtsausübung*) duty; **außer D~** off duty; (*pensioniert*) retired; **D~ haben** work; (*Soldat, Arzt:*) be on duty
Dienstag *m* Tuesday. **d~s** *adv* on Tuesdays
Dienst|bote *m* servant. **d~frei** *adj* **d~freier Tag** day off; **d~frei haben** have time off; (*Soldat, Arzt:*) be off duty. **D~grad** *m* rank. **D~leistung** *f* service. **d~lich** *adj* official ●*adv* **d~lich verreist** away on business. **D~mädchen** *nt* maid. **D~reise** *f* business trip. **D~stelle** *f* office. **D~stunden** *fpl* office hours
dies *inv pron* this. **d~bezüglich** *adj* relevant ●*adv* regarding this matter. **d~e(r,s)** *pron* this; (*pl*) these; (*substantivisch*) this [one]; (*pl*) these; **d~e Nacht** tonight; (*letzte*) last night
dieselbe *pron s.* **derselbe**
Dieselkraftstoff *m* diesel [oil]
diesmal *adv* this time
Dietrich *m* **-s,-e** skeleton key
Diffamation /-ˈtsi̯o:n/ *f* **-** defamation
Differential* /-ˈtsi̯a:l/ *nt* **-s,-e** = **Differenzial**
Differenz *f* **-,-en** difference. **D~ial** *nt* **-s,-e** differential. **d~ieren** *vt/i* (*haben*) differentiate (**zwischen** + *dat* between)
digital *adj* digital
Digital- *prefix* digital. **D~kamera** *f* digital camera. **D~uhr** *f* digital clock/watch
digitalisieren *vt* digitize
Dikt|at *nt* **-[e]s,-e** dictation. **D~ator** *m* **-s,-en** dictator. **D~atur** *f* **-,-en** dictatorship. **d~ieren** *vt/i* (*haben*) dictate
Dill *m* **-s** dill
Dimension *f* **-,-en** dimension
Ding *nt* **-[e]s,-e** & ▣ **-er** thing; **guter D~e sein** be cheerful; **vor allen D~en** above all
Dinosaurier /-i̯ɐ/ *m* **-s,-** dinosaur
Diözese *f* **-,-n** diocese
Diphtherie *f* **-** diphtheria
Diplom *nt* **-s,-e** diploma; (*Univ*) degree
Diplomat *m* **-en,-en** diplomat
dir *pron* (*dat of* **du**) [to] you; (*reflexive*) yourself; **ein Freund von dir** a

d

friend of yours

direkt *adj* direct ● *adv* directly; (*wirklich*) really. **D~ion** *f* - management; (*Vorstand*) board of directors. **D~or** *m* **-s,-en**, **D~orin** *f* **-,-nen** director; (*Bank-, Theater-*) manager; (*Sch*) head; (*Gefängnis*) governor. **D~übertragung** *f* live transmission

Dirig|ent *m* **-en,-en** (*Mus*) conductor. **d~ieren** *vt* direct; (*Mus*) conduct

Dirndl *nt* **-s,-** dirndl [dress]

Discounter *m* **-s, -** discount supermarket

Diskette *f* **-,-n** floppy disc

Disko *f* **-,-s** 🄵 disco. **D~thek** *f* **-,-en** discothèque

diskret *adj* discreet

Diskus *m* **-,-se & Disken** discus

Disku|ssion *f* **-,-en** discussion. **d~tieren** *vt/i* (*haben*) discuss

disponieren *vi* (*haben*) make arrangements; **d~ [können] über** (+ *acc*) have at one's disposal

Disqualifi|kation /-'tsi̯o:n/ *f* disqualification. **d~zieren** *vt* disqualify

Dissertation /-'tsi̯o:n/ *f* **-,-en** dissertation

Dissident *m* **-en,-en** dissident

Distanz *f* **-,-en** distance. **d~ieren (sich)** *vr* dissociate oneself (**von** from). **d~iert** *adj* aloof

Distel *f* **-,-n** thistle

Disziplin *f* **-,-en** discipline. **d~arisch** *adj* disciplinary. **d~iert** *adj* disciplined

dito *adv* ditto

diverse *attrib a pl* various

Divid|ende *f* **-,-en** dividend. **d~ieren** *vt* divide (**durch** by)

Division *f* **-,-en** division

DJH *abbr* (**Deutsche Jugendherberge**) [German] youth hostel

DM *abbr* (**Deutsche Mark**) DM

doch *conj & adv* but; (*dennoch*) yet; (*trotzdem*) after all; **wenn d~ ... !** if only ... ! **nicht d~!** don't!

Docht *m* **-[e]s,-e** wick

Dock *nt* **-s,-s** dock. **d~en** *vt/i* (*haben*) dock

> *i* **documenta** This international contemporary arts exhibition takes place in Kassel every four to five years. It includes drama, music and film events. *documenta 12* will take place in 2007. The events are subsidized by state and private sponsors.

Dogge *f* **-,-n** Great Dane

Dogm|a *nt* **-s,-men** dogma. **d~atisch** *adj* dogmatic

Dohle *f* **-,-n** jackdaw

Doktor *m* **-s,-en** doctor. **D~arbeit** *f* [doctoral] thesis

Dokument *nt* **-[e]s,-e** document. **D~arbericht** *m* documentary. **D~arfilm** *m* documentary film

Dolch *m* **-[e]s,-e** dagger

Dollar *m* **-s,-** dollar

dolmetsch|en *vt/i* (*haben*) interpret. **D~er(in)** *m* **-s,-** (*f* **-,-nen**) interpreter

Dom *m* **-[e]s,-e** cathedral

Domino *nt* **-s,-s** dominoes *sg*. **D~stein** *m* domino

Dompfaff *m* **-en,-en** bullfinch

Donau *f* - Danube

Donner *m* **-s** thunder. **d~n** *vi* (*haben*) thunder

Donnerstag *m* Thursday. **d~s** *adv* on Thursdays

doof *adj* 🄵 stupid

Doppel *nt* **-s,-** duplicate; (*Tennis*) doubles *pl*. **D~bett** *nt* double bed. **D~decker** *m* **-s,-** doubledecker [bus]. **d~deutig** *adj* ambiguous.

D∼gänger *m* **-s,-** double. **D∼kinn** *nt* double chin. **d∼klicken** *vi* (*haben*) double-click (**auf** + *acc* on). **D∼name** *m* double-barrelled name. **D∼punkt** *m* (*Gram*) colon. **D∼stecker** *m* two-way adaptor. **d∼t** *adj* double; (*Boden*) false; **in d∼ter Ausfertigung** in duplicate; **die d∼te Menge** twice the amount ●*adv* doubly; (*zweimal*) twice; **d∼t so viel** twice as much. **D∼zimmer** *nt* double room

Dorf *nt* **-[e]s,¨er** village. **D∼bewohner** *m* villager

dörflich *adj* rural

Dorn *m* **-[e]s,-en** thorn. **d∼ig** *adj* thorny

Dorsch *m* **-[e]s,-e** cod

dort *adv* there. **d∼ig** *adj* local

Dose *f* **-,-n** tin, can

dösen *vi* (*haben*) doze

Dosen|milch *f* evaporated milk. **D∼öffner** *m* tin *or* can opener. **D∼pfand** *nt* deposit (*on beer cans etc*)

dosieren *vt* measure out

Dosis *f* **-, Dosen** dose

Dotter *m & nt* **-s,-** [egg] yolk

Dozent(in) *m* **-en,-en** (*f* **-,-nen**) (*Univ*) lecturer

Dr. *abbr* (**Doktor**) Dr

Drache *m* **-n,-n** dragon. **D∼n** *m* **-s,-** kite. **D∼nfliegen** *nt* hang-gliding

Draht *m* **-[e]s,¨e** wire; **auf D∼** 🅃 on the ball. **D∼seilbahn** *f* cable railway

Dram|a *nt* **-s,-men** drama. **D∼atik** *f* **-** drama. **D∼atiker** *m* **-s,-** dramatist. **d∼atisch** *adj* dramatic

dran *adv* 🅃 = **daran; gut/schlecht d∼ sein** be well off/in a bad way; **ich bin d∼** it's my turn

Drang *m* **-[e]s** urge; (*Druck*) pressure

dräng|eln *vt/i* (*haben*) push; (*bedrängen*) pester. **d∼en** *vt* push; (*bedrängen*) urge; **sich d∼en** crowd (**um** round) ●*vi* (*haben*) push; (*eilen*) be urgent; **d∼en auf** (+ *acc*) press for

dran|halten† **(sich)** *vr sep* hurry. **d∼kommen**† *vi sep* (*sein*) have one's turn

drauf *adv* 🅃 = **darauf**; **d∼ und dran sein** be on the point (**etw zu tun** of doing sth). **D∼gänger** *m* **-s,-** daredevil

draußen *adv* outside; (*im Freien*) out of doors

drechseln *vt* (*Techn*) turn

Dreck *m* **-s** dirt; (*Morast*) mud

Dreh *m* **-s** 🅃 knack; **den D∼ heraushaben** have got the hang of it. **D∼bank** *f* lathe. **D∼bleistift** *m* propelling pencil. **D∼buch** *nt* screenplay, script. **d∼en** *vt* turn; (*im Kreis*) rotate; (*verschlingen*) twist; roll (*Zigarette*); shoot (*Film*); **lauter/leiser d∼en** turn up/down; **sich d∼en** turn; (*im Kreis*) rotate; (*schnell*) spin; (*Wind:*) change; **sich d∼en um** revolve around; (*sich handeln*) be about ●*vi* (*haben*) turn; (*Wind:*) change; **an etw** (*dat*) **d∼en** turn sth. **D∼stuhl** *m* swivel chair. **D∼tür** *f* revolving door. **D∼ung** *f* **-,-en** turn; (*im Kreis*) rotation. **D∼zahl** *f* number of revolutions

drei *inv adj*, **D∼** *f* **-,-en** three; (*Sch*) ≈ pass. **D∼eck** *nt* **-[e]s,-e** triangle. **d∼eckig** *adj* triangular. **d∼erlei** *inv adj* three kinds of ●*pron* three things. **d∼fach** *adj* triple. **d∼mal** *adv* three times. **D∼rad** *nt* tricycle

dreißig *inv adj* thirty. **d∼ste(r,s)** *adj* thirtieth

dreiviertel* *inv adj* = **drei viertel**, *s.* **viertel**. **D∼stunde** *f* three-quarters of an hour

dreizehn *inv adj* thirteen

d∼te(r,s) *adj* thirteenth

dreschen† *vt* thresh

dress|ieren *vt* train. **D∼ur** *f* - training

dribbeln *vi* (*haben*) dribble

d

Drill *m* **-[e]s** (*Mil*) drill. **d∼en** *vt* drill

Drillinge *mpl* triplets

dringlich *adj* urgent

Drink *m* **-[s],-s** [alcoholic] drink

drinnen *adv* inside

dritt *adv* **zu d∼** in threes; **wir waren zu d∼** there were three of us. **d∼e(r,s)** *adj* third; **ein D∼er** a third person. **d∼el** *inv adj* third. **D∼el** *nt* **-s,-** third. **d∼ens** *adv* thirdly. **d∼rangig** *adj* third-rate

Drog|e *f* **-,-n** drug. **D∼enabhängige(r)** *m/f* drug addict. **D∼erie** *f* **-,-n** chemist's shop. **D∼ist** *m* **-en, -en** chemist

drohen *vi* (*haben*) threaten (**jdm** s.o.)

dröhnen *vi* (*haben*) resound; (*tönen*) boom

Drohung *f* **-,-en** threat

drollig *adj* funny; (*seltsam*) odd

Drops *m* **-,-** [fruit] drop

Drossel *f* **-,-n** thrush

drosseln *vt* (*Techn*) throttle; (*fig*) cut back

drüben *adv* over there

Druck[1] *m* **-[e]s,⸚e** pressure; **unter D∼ setzen** (*fig*) pressurize

Druck[2] *m* **-[e]s,-e** printing; (*Schrift, Reproduktion*) print. **D∼buchstabe** *m* block letter

drucken *vt* print

drücken *vt/i* (*haben*) press; (*aus-*) squeeze; (*Schuh:*) pinch; (*umarmen*) hug; **Preise d∼** force down prices; (*an Tür*) **d∼** push; **sich d∼** 🄸 make oneself scarce; **sich d∼ vor** (+ *dat*) 🄸 shirk. **d∼d** *adj* heavy; (*schwül*) oppressive

Drucker *m* **-s,-** printer

Druckerei *f* **-,-en** printing works

Druck|fehler *m* misprint. **D∼knopf** *m* press-stud. **D∼luft** *f* compressed air. **D∼sache** *f* printed matter. **D∼schrift** *f* type; (*Veröffentlichung*) publication; **in D∼schrift** in block letters *pl*

Druckstelle *f* bruise

Drüse *f* **-,-n** (*Anat*) gland

Dschungel *m* **-s,-** jungle

du *pron* (*familiar address*) you; **auf Du und Du** on familiar terms

Dübel *m* **-s,-** plug

Dudelsack *m* bagpipes *pl*

Duell *nt* **-s,-e** duel

Duett *nt* **-s,-e** [vocal] duet

Duft *m* **-[e]s,⸚e** fragrance, scent; (*Aroma*) aroma. **d∼en** *vi* (*haben*) smell (**nach** of)

dulden *vt* tolerate; (*erleiden*) suffer ● *vi* (*haben*) suffer

dumm *adj* stupid; (*unklug*) foolish; (🄸: *lästig*) awkward; **wie d∼!**. **d∼erweise** *adv* stupidly; (*leider*) unfortunately. **D∼heit** *f* **-,-en** stupidity; (*Torheit*) foolishness; (*Handlung*) folly. **D∼kopf** *m* 🄸 fool.

dumpf *adj* dull

Düne *f* **-,-n** dune

Dung *m* **-s** manure

Düng|emittel *nt* fertilizer. **d∼en** *vt* fertilize. **D∼er** *m* **-s,-** fertilizer

dunk|el *adj* dark; (*vage*) vague; (*fragwürdig*) shady; **d∼les Bier** brown ale; **im D∼eln** in the dark

Dunkel|heit *f* - darkness. **D∼kammer** *f* dark-room. **d∼n** *vi* (*haben*) get dark

dünn *adj* thin; (*Buch*) slim; (*spärlich*) sparse; (*schwach*) weak

Dunst *m* **-es,⸚e** mist, haze; (*Dampf*) vapour

dünsten *vt* steam
dunstig *adj* misty, hazy
Duo *nt* **-s,-s** [instrumental] duet
Duplikat *nt* **-[e]s,-e** duplicate
Dur *nt* **-** (*Mus*) major [key]
durch *prep* (+ *acc*) through; (*mittels*) by; **[geteilt] d~** (*Math*) divided by ● *adv* **die Nacht d~** throughout the night; **d~ und d~ nass** wet through
durchaus *adv* absolutely; **d~nicht** by no means
durchblättern *vt sep* leaf through
durchblicken *vi sep* (*haben*) look through; **d~ lassen** (*fig*) hint at
Durchblutung *f* circulation
durchbohren *vt insep* pierce
durchbrechen[1]† *vt/i sep* (*haben*) break [in two]
durchbrechen[2]† *vt insep* break through; break (*Schallmauer*)
durchbrennen† *vi sep* (*sein*) burn through; (*Sicherung:*) blow
Durchbruch *m* breakthrough
durchdrehen *v sep* ● *vt* mince ● *vi* (*haben/sein*) [F] go crazy
durchdringen† *vi sep* (*sein*) penetrate; (*sich durchsetzen*) get one's way. **d~d** *adj* penetrating; (*Schrei*) piercing
durcheinander *adv* in a muddle; (*Person*) confused; **d~ bringen** muddle [up]; confuse (*Person*); **d~ geraten** get mixed up; **d~ reden** all talk at once. **D~** *nt* **-s** muddle
durchfahren *vi sep* (*sein*) drive through; (*Zug:*) go through
Durchfahrt *f* journey/drive through; **auf der D~** passing through; **'D~ verboten'** 'no thoroughfare'
Durchfall *m* diarrhoea. **d~en**/*vi sep* (*sein*) fall through; ([F]: *versagen*) flop; (*bei Prüfung*) fail
Durchfuhr *f* **-** (*Comm*) transit
durchführ|bar *adj* feasible. **d~en** *vt sep* carry out
Durchgang *m* passage; (*Sport*) round; **'D~ verboten'** 'no entry'. **D~sverkehr** *m* through traffic
durchgeben† *vt sep* pass through; (*übermitteln*) transmit; (*Radio, TV*) broadcast
durchgebraten *adj* **gut d~** well done
durchgehen† *vi sep* (*sein*) go through; (*davonlaufen*) run away; (*Pferd:*) bolt; **jdm etw d~ lassen** let s.o. get away with sth. **d~d** *adj* continuous; **d~d geöffnet** open all day; **d~der Zug** through train
durchgreifen† *vi sep* (*haben*) reach through; (*vorgehen*) take drastic action. **d~d** *adj* drastic
durchhalte|n† *v sep* (*fig*) ● *vi* (*haben*) hold out ● *vt* keep up. **D~vermögen** *nt* stamina
durchkommen† *vi sep* (*sein*) come through; (*gelangen, am Telefon*) get through
durchlassen† *vt sep* let through
durchlässig *adj* permeable; (*undicht*) leaky
Durchlauferhitzer *m* **-s,-** geyser
durchlesen† *vt sep* read through
durchleuchten *vt insep* X-ray
durchlöchert *adj* riddled with holes
durchmachen *vt sep* go through; (*erleiden*) undergo
Durchmesser *m* **-s,-** diameter
durchnässt *adj* wet through
durchnehmen† *vt sep* (*Sch*) do
durchnummeriert *adj* numbered consecutively
durchpausen *vt sep* trace

durchqueren *vt insep* cross
Durchreiche *f* **-,-n** hatch
Durchreise *f* journey through; **auf der D~** passing through. **d~n** *vi sep* (*sein*) pass through
durchreißen† *vt/i sep* (*sein*) tear
Durchsage *f* **-,-n** announcement. **d~n** *vt sep* announce
Durchschlag *m* carbon copy; (*Culin*) colander. **d~en**† *v sep* ● *vt* (*Culin*) rub through a sieve; **sich d~en** (*fig*) struggle through ● *vi* (*sein*) (*Sicherung:*) blow
durchschlagend *adj* (*fig*) effective; (*Erfolg*) resounding
durchschneiden† *vt sep* cut
Durchschnitt *m* average; **im D~** on average. **d~lich** *adj* average ● *adv* on average. **D~s-** *prefix* average
Durchschrift *f* carbon copy
durchsehen† *v sep* ● *vi* (*haben*) see through ● *vt* look through
durchseihen *vt sep* strain
durchsetzen *vt sep* force through; **sich d~** assert oneself; (*Mode:*) catch on
Durchsicht *f* check
durchsichtig *adj* transparent
durchsickern *vi sep* (*sein*) seep through; (*Neuigkeit:*) leak out
durchstehen† *vt sep* (*fig*) come through
durchstreichen† *vt sep* cross out
durchsuch|en *vt insep* search. **D~ung** *f* -,-en search
durchwachsen *adj* (*Speck*) streaky; (⊡: *gemischt*) mixed
durchwählen *vi sep* (*haben*) (*Teleph*) dial direct
durchweg *adv* without exception
durchwühlen *vt insep* rummage through; ransack (*Haus*)
Durchzug *m* through draught

dürfen†

● *transitive & auxiliary verb*

····➤ (*Erlaubnis haben zu*) be allowed; may, can. **etw [tun] dürfen** be allowed to do sth. **darf ich das tun?** may *or* can I do that? **nein, das darfst du nicht** no you may not *or* cannot [do that]. **er sagte mir, ich dürfte sofort gehen** he told me I could go at once. **hier darf man nicht rauchen** smoking is prohibited here. **sie darf/durfte es nicht sehen** she must not/was not allowed to see it.

····➤ (*in Höflichkeitsformeln*) may. **darf ich rauchen?** may I smoke? **darf/dürfte ich um diesen Tanz bitten?** may/might I have the pleasure of this dance?

····➤ **dürfte** (*sollte*) should, ought. **jetzt dürften sie dort angekommen sein** they should *or* ought to be there by now. **das dürfte nicht allzu schwer sein** that should not be too difficult. **ich hätte es nicht tun/sagen dürfen** I ought not to have done/said it

● *intransitive verb*

····➤ (*irgendwohin gehen dürfen*) be allowed to go; may go; can go. **darf ich nach Hause?** may *or* can I go home? **sie durfte nicht ins Theater** she was not allowed to go the theatre

dürftig *adj* poor; (*Mahlzeit*) scanty
dürr *adj* dry; (*Boden*) arid; (*mager*) skinny. **D~e** *f* **-,-n** drought
Durst *m* **-[e]s** thirst; **D~ haben** be thirsty. **d~ig** *adj* thirsty
Dusche *f* **-,-n** shower. **d~n** *vi/r* (*haben*) **[sich] d~n** have a shower

Düse *f* **-,-n** nozzle. **D∼nflugzeug** *nt* jet

Dutzend *nt* **-s,-e** dozen. **d∼weise** *adv* by the dozen

duzen *vt* **jdn d∼** call s.o. 'du'

DVD *f* **-, -s** DVD

Dynam|ik *f* **-** dynamics *sg*; (*fig*) dynamism. **d∼isch** *adj* dynamic; (*Rente*) index-linked

Dynamit *nt* **-es** dynamite

Dynamo *m* **-s,-s** dynamo

Dynastie *f* **-,-n** dynasty

D-Zug /'de:-/ *m* express [train]

Ee

Ebbe *f* **-,-n** low tide

eben *adj* level; (*glatt*) smooth; **zu e∼er Erde** on the ground floor ● *adv* just; (*genau*) exactly; **e∼ noch** only just; (*gerade vorhin*) just now; **das ist es e∼!** that's just it! **E∼bild** *nt* image

Ebene *f* **-,-n** (*Geog*) plain; (*Geometry*) plane; (*fig: Niveau*) level

eben|falls *adv* also; **danke, e∼falls** thank you, [the] same to you. **E∼holz** *nt* ebony. **e∼so** *adv* just the same; (*ebenso sehr*) just as much; **e∼so gut** just as good; *adv* just as well; **e∼so sehr** just as much; **e∼so viel** just as much/many; **e∼so wenig** just as little/few; (*noch*) no more

Eber *m* **-s,-** boar

ebnen *vt* level; (*fig*) smooth

Echo *nt* **-s,-s** echo

echt *adj* genuine, real; authentic ● *adv* 🅸 really; typically. **E∼heit** *f* **-** authenticity

Eck|ball *m* (*Sport*) corner. **E∼e** *f* **-,-n** corner; **um die E∼e bringen** 🅸 bump off. **e∼ig** *adj* angular; (*Klammern*) square; (*unbeholfen*) awkward. **E∼zahn** *m* canine tooth

Ecu, **ECU** /e'ky:/ *m* **-[s],-[s]** ecu

edel *adj* noble; (*wertvoll*) precious; (*fein*) fine. **e∼mütig** *adj* magnanimous. **E∼stahl** *m* stainless steel. **E∼stein** *m* precious stone

Efeu *m* **-s** ivy

Effekt *m* **-[e]s,-e** effect. **E∼en** *pl* securities. **e∼iv** *adj* actual; (*wirksam*) effective

EG *f* **-** *abbr* (**Europäische Gemeinschaft**) EC

egal *adj* **das ist mir e∼** 🅸 it's all the same to me ● *adv* **e∼ wie/wo** no matter how/where

Egge *f* **-,-n** harrow

Ego|ismus *m* **-** selfishness. **E∼ist(in)** *m* **-en,-en** (*f* **-,-nen**) egoist. **e∼istisch** *adj* selfish

eh *adv* (*Aust*, 🅸) anyway

ehe *conj* before; **ehe nicht** until

Ehe *f* **-,-n** marriage. **E∼bett** *nt* double bed. **E∼bruch** *m* adultery. **E∼frau** *f* wife. **e∼lich** *adj* marital; (*Recht*) conjugal; (*Kind*) legitimate

ehemalig *adj* former. **e∼s** *adv* formerly

Ehe|mann *m* (*pl* **-männer**) husband. **E∼paar** *nt* married couple

eher *adv* earlier, sooner; (*lieber, vielmehr*) rather; (*mehr*) more

Ehering *m* wedding ring

Ehr|e *f* **-,-n** honour. **e∼en** *vt* honour. **e∼enamtlich** *adj* honorary ● *adv* in an honorary capacity. **E∼engast** *m* guest of honour. **e∼enhaft** a honourable. **E∼ensache** *f* point of honour. **E∼enwort** *nt* word of honour. **e∼erbietig** *adj* deferential. **E∼furcht** *f* reverence; (*Scheu*) awe. **e∼fürchtig** *adj* reverent. **E~gefühl** *nt* sense of honour. **E~geiz** *m* ambition. **e~geizig** *adj* ambitious. **e~lich** *adj* honest; **e~lich gesagt** to be honest. **E~lichkeit** *f* - honesty. **e~los** *adj* dishonourable. **e~würdig** *adj* venerable; (*als Anrede*) Reverend

Ei *nt* **-[e]s,-er** egg

Eibe *f* **-,-n** yew

Eiche *f* **-,-n** oak. **E~l** *f* **-,-n** acorn

eichen *vt* standardize

Eichhörnchen *nt* **-s,-** squirrel

Eid *m* **-[e]s,-e** oath

Eidechse *f* **-,-n** lizard

eidlich *adj* sworn ● *adv* on oath

Eidotter *m* & *nt* egg yolk

Eier|becher *m* egg-cup. **E~kuchen** *m* pancake; (*Omelett*) omelette. **E~schale** *f* eggshell. **E~schnee** *m* beaten egg-white. **E~stock** *m* ovary

Eifer *m* **-s** eagerness. **E~sucht** *f* jealousy. **e~süchtig** *adj* jealous

eifrig *adj* eager

Eigelb *nt* **-[e]s,-e** [egg] yolk

eigen *adj* own; (*typisch*) characteristic (*dat* of); (*seltsam*) odd; (*genau*) particular. **E~art** *f* peculiarity. **e~artig** *adj* peculiar. **e~händig** *adj* personal; (*Unterschrift*) own. **E~heit** *f* **-,-en** peculiarity. **E~name** *m* proper name. **e~nützig** *adj* selfish. **e~s** *adv* specially. **E~schaft** *f* **-,-en** quality; (*Phys*) property; (*Merkmal*) characteristic; (*Funktion*) capacity. **E~schaftswort** *nt* (*pl* **-wörter**) adjective. **E~sinn** *m* obstinacy. **e~sinnig** *adj* obstinate

eigentlich *adj* actual, real; (*wahr*) true ● *adv* actually, really; (*streng genommen*) strictly speaking

Eigen|tor *nt* own goal. **E~tum** *nt* **-s** property. **E~tümer(in)** *m* **-s,-** (*f* **-,-nen**) owner. **E~tumswohnung** *f* freehold flat. **e~willig** *adj* self-willed; (*Stil*) highly individual

eignen (sich) *vr* be suitable

Eil|brief *m* express letter. **E~e** *f* - hurry; **E~e haben** be in a hurry; (*Sache:*) be urgent. **e~en** *vi* (*sein*) hurry ● (*haben*) (*drängen*) be urgent. **e~ig** *adj* hurried; (*dringend*) urgent; **es e~ig haben** be in a hurry. **E~zug** *m* semi-fast train

Eimer *m* **-s,-** bucket; (*Abfall-*) bin

ein

● *indefinite article*

····➤ a, (*vor Vokal*) an. **ein Kleid/Apfel/Hotel/Mensch** a dress/an apple/a[n] hotel/a human being. **so ein** such a. **was für ein ...** (*Frage*) what kind of a ... ? (*Ausruf*) what a ... !

● *adjective*

····➤ (*Ziffer*) one. **eine Minute** one minute. **wir haben nur eine Stunde** we only have an/(*betont*) one hour. **eines Tages/Abends** one day/evening

····➤ (*derselbe*) the same. **einer Meinung sein** be of the same opinion. **mit jdm in einem Zimmer schlafen** sleep in the same room as s.o.

einander *pron* one another

Einäscherung *f* **-,-en** cremation

einatmen *vt/i sep* (*haben*) inhale, breathe in

Einbahnstraße *f* one-way street

einbalsamieren *vt sep* embalm

Einband *m* binding

Einbau *m* installation; (*Montage*) fitting. **e~en** *vt sep* install; (*montieren*) fit. **E~küche** *f* fitted kitchen

einbegriffen *pred* adj included

Einberufung *f* call-up

Einbettzimmer *nt* single room

einbeulen *vt sep* dent

einbeziehen† *vt sep* **[mit] e∼** include; (*berücksichtigen*) take into account

einbiegen† *vi sep* (*sein*) turn

einbild|en *vt sep* **sich** (*dat*) **etw e∼en** imagine sth; **sich** (*dat*) **viel e∼en** be conceited. **E∼ung** *f* imagination; (*Dünkel*) conceit. **E∼ungskraft** *f* imagination

einblenden *vt sep* fade in

Einblick *m* insight

einbrech|en† *vi sep* (*haben/sein*) break in; **bei uns ist eingebrochen worden** we have been burgled. **E∼er** *m* burglar

einbringen† *vt sep* get in; bring in (*Geld*)

Einbruch *m* burglary; **bei E∼ der Nacht** at nightfall

einbürger|n *vt sep* naturalize. **E∼ung** *f* - naturalization

einchecken /-tʃɛkən/ *vt/i sep* (*haben*) check in

eindecken (sich) *vr sep* stock up

eindeutig *adj* unambiguous; (*deutlich*) clear

eindicken *vt sep* (*Culin*) thicken

eindringen† *vi sep* (*sein*) **e∼en in** (+ *acc*) penetrate into; (*mit Gewalt*) force one's/(*Wasser:*) its way into; (*Mil*) invade

Eindruck *m* impression

eindrücken *vt sep* crush

eindrucksvoll *adj* impressive

ein|e(r,s) *pron* one; (*jemand*) someone; (*man*) one, you

einebnen *vt sep* level

eineiig *adj* (*Zwillinge*) identical

eineinhalb *inv adj* one and a half; **e∼ Stunden** an hour and a half

Einelternfamilie *f* one-parent family

einengen *vt sep* restrict

Einer *m* **-s,-** (*Math*) unit. **e∼** *pron s.* **eine(r,s). e∼lei** *inv adj* ●*attrib adj* one kind of; (*eintönig, einheitlich*) the same ●*pred adj* ⓘ immaterial; **es ist mir e∼lei** it's all the same to me. **e∼seits** *adv* on the one hand

einfach *adj* simple; (*Essen*) plain; (*Faden, Fahrt*) single; **e∼er Soldat** private. **E∼heit** *f* - simplicity

einfädeln *vt sep* thread; (*fig; arrangieren*) arrange

einfahr|en† *v sep* ●*vi* (*sein*) arrive; (*Zug:*) pull in ●*vt* (*Auto*) run in. **E∼t** *f* arrival; (*Eingang*) entrance, way in; (*Auffahrt*) drive; (*Autobahn-*) access road; **keine E∼t** no entry

Einfall *m* idea; (*Mil*) invasion. **e∼en**† *vi sep* (*sein*) collapse; (*eindringen*) invade; **jdm e∼en** occur to s.o.; **was fällt ihm ein!** what does he think he is doing!

Einfalt *f* - naïvety

einfarbig *adj* of one colour; (*Stoff, Kleid*) plain

einfass|en *vt sep* edge; set (*Edelstein*). **E∼ung** *f* border, edging

einfetten *vt sep* grease

Einfluss *m* influence. **e∼reich** *adj* influential

einförmig *adj* monotonous. **E∼keit** *f* - monotony

einfrieren† *vt/i sep* (*sein*) freeze

einfügen *vt sep* insert; (*einschieben*) interpolate; **sich e∼** fit in

einfühlsam *adj* sensitive

Einfuhr *f* **-,-en** import

einführ|en *vt sep* introduce; (*einstecken*) insert; (*einweisen*) initiate; (*Comm*) import. **e∼end** *adj* introductory. **E∼ung** *f* introduction; (*Einweisung*) initiation

Eingabe *f* petition; (*Computer*) input

Eingang *m* entrance, way in; (*Ankunft*) arrival

e

eingebaut *adj* built-in; (*Schrank*) fitted
eingeben† *vt sep* hand in; (*Computer*) feed in
eingebildet *adj* imaginary; (*überheblich*) conceited
Eingeborene(r) *m/f* native
e
eingehen† *v sep* ● *vi* (*sein*) come in; (*ankommen*) arrive; (*einlaufen*) shrink; (*sterben*) die; (*Zeitung, Firma:*) fold; **auf etw** (*acc*) **e~** go into sth; (*annehmen*) agree to sth ● *vt* enter into; contract (*Ehe*); make (*Wette*); take (*Risiko*)
eingemacht *adj* (*Culin*) bottled
eingenommen *pred adj* (*fig*) taken (**von** with); prejudiced (**gegen** against)
eingeschneit *adj* snowbound
eingeschrieben *adj* registered
Einge|ständnis *nt* admission. **e~stehen**† *vt sep* admit
eingetragen *adj* registered
Eingeweide *pl* bowels, entrails
eingewöhnen (sich) *vr sep* settle in
eingießen† *vt sep* pour in; (*einschenken*) pour
eingleisig *adj* single-track
einglieder|n *vt sep* integrate. **E~ung** *f* integration
eingravieren *vt sep* engrave
eingreifen† *vi sep* (*haben*) intervene. **E~** *nt* **-s** intervention
Eingriff *m* intervention; (*Med*) operation
einhaken *vt/r sep* **jdn e~** *od* **sich bei jdm e~** take someone's arm
einhalten† *v sep* ● *vt* keep; (*befolgen*) observe ● *vi* (*haben*) stop
einhändigen *vt sep* hand in
einhängen *vt sep* hang; put down (*Hörer*)
einheimisch *adj* local; (*eines Landes*) native; (*Comm*) homeproduced. **E~e(r)** *m/f* local, native
Einheit *f* **-,-en** unity; (*Maß-, Mil*) unit. **e~lich** *adj* uniform. **E~spreis** *m* standard price; (*Fahrpreis*) flat fare
einholen *vt sep* catch up with; (*aufholen*) make up for; (*erbitten*) seek; (*einkaufen*) buy
einhüllen *vt sep* wrap
einhundert *inv adj* one hundred
einig *adj* united; [**sich** (*dat*)] **e~ sein** be in agreement
einig|e(r,s) *pron* some; (*ziemlich viel*) quite a lot of; (*substantivisch*) **e~e** *pl* some; (*mehrere*) several; (*ziemlich viele*) quite a lot; **e~es** *sg* some things; **vor e~er Zeit** some time ago
einigen *vt* unite; unify (*Land*); **sich e~** come to an agreement
einigermaßen *adv* to some extent; (*ziemlich*) fairly; (*ziemlich gut*) fairly well
Einigkeit *f* **-** unity; (*Übereinstimmung*) agreement
einjährig *adj* one-year-old; **e~e Pflanze** annual
einkalkulieren *vt sep* take into account
einkassieren *vt sep* collect
Einkauf *m* purchase; (*Einkaufen*) shopping; **Einkäufe machen** do some shopping. **e~en** *vt sep* buy; **e~en gehen** go shopping. **E~swagen** *m* shopping trolley
einklammern *vt sep* bracket
Einklang *m* harmony; **in E~ stehen** be in accord (**mit** with)
einkleben *vt sep* stick in
einkleiden *vt sep* fit out
einklemmen *vt sep* clamp
einkochen *v sep* ● *vi* (*sein*) boil down ● *vt* preserve, bottle

Einkommen *nt* **-s** income. **E~[s]steuer** *f* income tax

Einkünfte *pl* income *sg*; (*Einnahmen*) revenue *sg*

einlad|en† *vt sep* load; (*auffordern*) invite; (*bezahlen für*) treat. **E~ung** *f* invitation

Einlage *f* enclosure; (*Schuh-*) arch support; (*Programm-*) interlude; (*Comm*) investment; (*Bank-*) deposit; **Suppe mit E~** soup with noodles/dumplings

Ein|lass *m* **-es** admittance. **e~lassen**† *vt sep* let in; run (*Bad, Wasser*); **sich auf etw** (*acc*) **e~lassen** get involved in sth

einleben (sich) *vr sep* settle in

Einlege|arbeit *f* inlaid work. **e~n** *vt sep* put in; lay in (*Vorrat*); lodge (*Protest*); (*einfügen*) insert; (*Auto*) engage (*Gang*); (*Culin*) pickle; (*marinieren*) marinade; **eine Pause e~n** have a break. **E~sohle** *f* insole

einleit|en *vt sep* initiate; (*eröffnen*) begin. **E~ung** *f* introduction

einleuchten *vi sep* (*haben*) be clear (*dat* to). **e~d** *adj* convincing

einliefer|n *vt sep* take (**ins Krankenhaus** to hospital). **E~ung** *f* admission

einlösen *vt sep* cash (*Scheck*); redeem (*Pfand*); (*fig*) keep

einmachen *vt sep* preserve

einmal *adv* once; (*eines Tages*) one or some day; **noch/schon e~** again/before; **noch e~ so teuer** twice as expensive; **auf e~** at the same time; (*plötzlich*) suddenly; **nicht e~** not even. **E~eins** *nt* - [multiplication] tables *pl*. **e~ig** *adj* (*einzigartig*) unique; (🄸: *großartig*) fantastic

einmarschieren *vi sep* (*sein*) march in

einmisch|en (sich) *vr sep* interfere. **E~ung** *f* interference

Einnahme *f* **-,-n** taking; (*Mil*) capture; **E~n** *pl* income *sg*; (*Einkünfte*) revenue *sg*; (*Comm*) receipts; (*eines Ladens*) takings

einnehmen† *vt sep* take; have (*Mahlzeit*); (*Mil*) capture; take up (*Platz*)

einordnen *vt sep* put in its proper place; (*klassifizieren*) classify; **sich e~** fit in; (*Auto*) get in lane

einpacken *vt sep* pack

einparken *vt sep* park

einpflanzen *vt sep* plant; implant (*Organ*)

einplanen *vt sep* allow for

einprägen *vt sep* impress (**jdm** [up]on s.o.); **sich** (*dat*) **etw e~en** memorize sth

einrahmen *vt sep* frame

einrasten *vi sep* (*sein*) engage

einräumen *vt sep* put away; (*zugeben*) admit; (*zugestehen*) grant

einrechnen *vt sep* include

einreden *v sep* ● *vt* **jdm/sich** (*dat*) **etw e~** persuade s.o./oneself of sth

einreiben† *vt sep* rub (**mit** with)

einreichen *vt sep* submit; **die Scheidung e~** file for divorce

Einreih|er *m* **-s,-** single-breasted suit. **e~ig** *adj* single-breasted

Einreise *f* entry. **e~n** *vi sep* (*sein*) enter (**nach Irland** Ireland)

einrenken *vt sep* (*Med*) set

einricht|en *vt sep* fit out; (*möblieren*) furnish; (*anordnen*) arrange; (*Med*) set (*Bruch*); (*eröffnen*) set up; **sich e~en** furnish one's home; (*sich einschränken*) economize; (*sich vorbereiten*) prepare (**auf** + *acc* for). **E~ung** *f* furnishing; (*Möbel*) furnishings *pl*; (*Techn*) equipment; (*Vor-*

e

richtung) device; (*Eröffnung*) setting up; (*Institution*) institution; (*Gewohnheit*) practice

einrosten *vi sep* (*sein*) rust; (*fig*) get rusty

eins *inv adj & pron* one; **noch e~** one other thing; **mir ist alles e~** [!] it's all the same to me. **E~** *f* **-,-en** one; (*Sch*) ≈ A

einsam *adj* lonely; (*allein*) solitary; (*abgelegen*) isolated. **E~keit** *f* **-** loneliness; solitude; isolation

einsammeln *vt sep* collect

Einsatz *m* use; (*Mil*) mission; (*Wett-*) stake; (*E~teil*) insert; **im E~** in action

einschalt|en *vt sep* switch on; (*einschieben*) interpolate; (*fig: beteiligen*) call in; **sich e~en** (*fig*) intervene. **E~quote** *f* (*TV*) viewing figures *pl*; ≈ ratings *pl*

einschätzen *vt sep* assess; (*bewerten*) rate

einschenken *vt sep* pour

einscheren *vi sep* (*sein*) pull in

einschicken *vt sep* send in

einschieben† *vt sep* push in; (*einfügen*) insert

einschiff|en (sich) *vr sep* embark. **E~ung** *f* **-** embarkation

einschlafen† *vi sep* (*sein*) go to sleep; (*aufhören*) peter out

einschläfern *vt sep* lull to sleep; (*betäuben*) put out; (*töten*) put to sleep. **e~d** *adj* soporific

Einschlag *m* impact. **e~en**† *v sep* ● *vt* knock in; (*zerschlagen*) smash; (*drehen*) turn; take (*Weg*); take up (*Laufbahn*) ● *vi* (*haben*) hit/(*Blitz:*) strike (**in etw** *acc* sth); (*Erfolg haben*) be a hit

einschleusen *vt sep* infiltrate

einschließ|en† *vt sep* lock in; (*umgeben*) enclose; (*einkreisen*) surround; (*einbeziehen*) include; **sich e~en** lock oneself in; **Bedienung eingeschlossen** service included. **e~lich** *adv* inclusive ● *prep* (+ *gen*) including

einschneiden† *vt/i sep* (*haben*) **[in] etw** *acc* **e~** cut into sth. **e~d** *adj* (*fig*) drastic

Einschnitt *m* cut; (*Med*) incision; (*Lücke*) gap; (*fig*) decisive event

einschränk|en *vt sep* restrict; (*reduzieren*) cut back; **sich e~en** economize. **E~ung** *f* **-,-en** restriction; (*Reduzierung*) reduction; (*Vorbehalt*) reservation

Einschreib|[e]brief *m* registered letter. **e~en**† *vt sep* enter; register (*Brief*); **sich e~en** put one's name down; (*sich anmelden*) enrol. **E~en** *nt* registered letter/packet; **als od per E~en** by registered post

einschüchtern *vt sep* intimidate

Einsegnung *f* **-,-en** confirmation

einsehen† *vt sep* inspect; (*lesen*) consult; (*begreifen*) see

einseitig *adj* one-sided; (*Pol*) unilateral ● *adv* on one side; (*fig*) one-sidedly; (*Pol*) unilaterally

einsenden† *vt sep* send in

einsetzen *v sep* ● *vt* put in; (*einfügen*) insert; (*verwenden*) use; put on (*Zug*); call out (*Truppen*); (*Mil*) deploy; (*ernennen*) appoint; (*wetten*) stake; (*riskieren*) risk ● *vi* (*haben*) start; (*Winter, Regen:*) set in

Einsicht *f* insight; (*Verständnis*) understanding; (*Vernunft*) reason. **e~ig** *adj* understanding

Einsiedler *m* hermit

einsinken† *vi sep* (*sein*) sink in

einspannen *vt sep* harness; **jdn e~** [!] rope s.o. in

einsparen *vt sep* save

einsperren *vt sep* shut/(*im Gefängnis*) lock up

einsprachig *adj* monolingual

einspritzen *vt sep* inject

Einspruch *m* objection; **E~ erheben** object; (*Jur*) appeal

einspurig *adj* single-track; (*Auto*) single-lane

einst *adv* once; (*Zukunft*) one day

Einstand *m* (*Tennis*) deuce

einstecken *vt sep* put in; post (*Brief*); (*Electr*) plug in; (Ⓕ: *behalten*) pocket; (Ⓕ: *hinnehmen*) take; suffer (*Niederlage*); **etw e~** put sth in one's pocket

einsteigen† *vi sep* (*sein*) get in; (*in Bus/Zug*) get on

einstell|en *vt sep* put in; (*anstellen*) employ; (*aufhören*) stop; (*regulieren*) adjust, set; (*Optik*) focus; tune (*Motor, Zündung*); tune to (*Sender*); **sich e~en** turn up; (*Schwierigkeiten:*) arise; **sich e~en auf** (+ *acc*) adjust to; (*sich vorbereiten*) prepare for. **E~ung** *f* employment; (*Regulierung*) adjustment; (*TV, Auto*) tuning; (*Haltung*) attitude

einstig *adj* former

einstimmig *adj* unanimous. **E~keit** *f* - unanimity

einstöckig *adj* single-storey

einstudieren *vt sep* rehearse

einstufen *vt sep* classify

Ein|sturz *m* collapse. **e~stürzen** *vi sep* (*sein*) collapse

einstweilen *adv* for the time being; (*inzwischen*) meanwhile

eintasten *vt sep* key in

eintauchen *vt/i sep* (*sein*) dip in

eintauschen *vt sep* exchange

eintausend *inv adj* one thousand

einteil|en *vt sep* divide (**in** + *acc* into); (*Biology*) classify; **sich** (*dat*) **seine Zeit gut e~en** organize one's time well. **e~ig** *adj* one-piece. **E~ung** *f* division

eintönig *adj* monotonous. **E~keit** *f* - monotony

Eintopf *m*, **E~gericht** *nt* stew

Eintracht *f* - harmony

Eintrag *m* -[e]s,⸚e entry. **e~en**† *vt sep* enter; (*Admin*) register; **sich e~en** put one's name down

einträglich *adj* profitable

Eintragung *f* -,-en registration

eintreffen† *vi sep* (*sein*) arrive; (*fig*) come true

eintreiben† *vt sep* drive in; (*einziehen*) collect

eintreten† *v sep* ● *vi* (*sein*) enter; (*geschehen*) occur; **in einen Klub e~** join a club; **e~ für** (*fig*) stand up for ● *vt* kick in

Eintritt *m* entrance; (*zu Veranstaltung*) admission; (*Beitritt*) joining; (*Beginn*) beginning. **E~skarte** *f* [admission] ticket

einüben *vt sep* practise

einundachtzig *inv adj* eighty-one

Einvernehmen *nt* -s understanding; (*Übereinstimmung*) agreement

einverstanden *adj* **e~ sein** agree

Einverständnis *nt* agreement; (*Zustimmung*) consent

Einwand *m* -[e]s,⸚e objection

Einwander|er *m* immigrant. **e~n** *vi sep* (*sein*) immigrate. **E~ung** *f* immigration

einwandfrei *adj* perfect

einwärts *adv* inwards

einwechseln *vt sep* change

einwecken *vt sep* preserve, bottle

Einweg- *prefix* non-returnable

einweichen *vt sep* soak

einweih|en *vt sep* inaugurate; (*Relig*) consecrate; (*einführen*) initiate; **in ein Geheimnis e~en** let into a secret. **E~ung** *f* **-,-en** inauguration; consecration; initiation

einweisen† *vt sep* direct; (*einführen*) initiate; **ins Krankenhaus e~** send to hospital

einwerfen† *vt sep* insert; post (*Brief*); (*Sport*) throw in

einwickeln *vt sep* wrap [up]

einwillig|en *vi sep* (*haben*) consent, agree (**in** + *acc* to). **E~ung** *f* - consent

Einwohner|(in) *m* **-s,-** (*f* **-,-nen**) inhabitant. **E~zahl** *f* population

Einwurf *m* interjection; (*Einwand*) objection; (*Sport*) throw-in; (*Münz-*) slot

Einzahl *f* (*Gram*) singular

einzahl|en *vt sep* pay in. **E~ung** *f* payment; (*Einlage*) deposit

einzäunen *vt sep* fence in

Einzel *nt* **-s,-** (*Tennis*) singles *pl*. **E~bett** *nt* single bed. **E~gänger** *m* **-s,-** loner. **E~haft** *f* solitary confinement. **E~handel** *m* retail trade. **E~händler** *m* retailer. **E~haus** *nt* detached house. **E~heit** *f* **-,-en** detail. **E~karte** *f* single ticket. **E~kind** *nt* only child

einzeln *adj* single; (*individuell*) individual; (*gesondert*) separate; odd (*Handschuh, Socken*); **e~e Fälle** some cases. **E~e(r,s)** *pron* **der**/**die** **E~e** the individual; **E~e** *pl* some; **im E~en** in detail

Einzel|teil *nt* [component] part. **E~zimmer** *nt* single room

einziehen† *v sep* ● *vt* pull in; draw in (*Atem, Krallen*); (*Zool, Techn*) retract; indent (*Zeile*); (*aus dem Verkehr ziehen*) withdraw; (*beschlagnahmen*) confiscate; (*eintreiben*) collect; make (*Erkundigungen*); (*Mil*) call up ● *vi* (*sein*) enter; (*umziehen*) move in; (*eindringen*) penetrate

einzig *adj* only; (*einmalig*) unique; **eine e~e Frage** a a single question ● *adv* only; **e~ und allein** solely. **E~e(r,s)** *pron* **der**/**die**/**das E~e** the only one; **ein**/**kein E~er** a/not a single one; **das E~e, was mich stört** the only thing that bothers me

Eis *nt* **-es** ice; (*Speise-*) ice-cream; **Eis am Stiel** ice lolly; **Eis laufen** skate. **E~bahn** *f* ice rink. **E~bär** *m* polar bear. **E~becher** *m* ice-cream sundae. **E~berg** *m* iceberg. **E~diele** *f* ice-cream parlour

Eisen *nt* **-s,-** iron. **E~bahn** *f* railway

eisern *adj* iron; (*fest*) resolute; **e~er Vorhang** (*Theat*) safety curtain; (*Pol*) Iron Curtain

Eis|fach *nt* freezer compartment. **e~gekühlt** *adj* chilled. **e~ig** *adj* icy. **E~kaffee** *m* iced coffee. **E~lauf** *m* skating. **E~läufer(in)** *m*(*f*) skater. **E~pickel** *m* ice-axe. **E~scholle** *f* ice-floe. **E~vogel** *m* kingfisher. **E~würfel** *m* icecube. **E~zapfen** *m* icicle. **E~zeit** *f* ice age

eitel *adj* vain; (*rein*) pure. **E~keit** *f* - vanity

Eiter *m* **-s** pus. **e~n** *vi* (*haben*) discharge pus

Eiweiß *nt* **-es,-e** egg-white

Ekel *m* **-s** disgust; (*Widerwille*) revulsion. **e~haft** *adj* nauseating; (*widerlich*) repulsive. **e~n** *vt*/*i* (*haben*) **mich** *od* **mir e~t [es] davor** it makes me feel sick ● *vr* **sich e~n vor** (+ *dat*) find repulsive

eklig *adj* disgusting, repulsive

Ekzem *nt* **-s,-e** eczema

elastisch *adj* elastic; (*federnd*) springy; (*fig*) flexible

Elch *m* **-[e]s,-e** elk

Elefant *m* **-en,-en** elephant

elegan|t *adj* elegant.

E~z *f* - elegance

Elektri|ker *m* **-s,-** electrician. **e~sch** *adj* electric

Elektrizität *f* - electricity. **E~swerk** *nt* power station

Elektr|oartikel *mpl* electrical appliances. **E~ode** *f* **-,-n** electrode. **E~onik** *f* - electronics *sg*. **e~onisch** *adj* electronic

Elend *nt* **-s** misery; (*Armut*) poverty. **e~** *adj* miserable; (*krank*) poorly; (*gemein*) contemptible. **E~sviertel** *nt* slum

elf *inv adj*, **E~** *f* **-,-en** eleven

Elfe *f* **-,-n** fairy

Elfenbein *nt* ivory

Elfmeter *m* (*Fußball*) penalty

elfte(r,s) *adj* eleventh

Ell[en]bogen *m* elbow

Ellip|se *f* **-,-n** ellipse. **e~tisch** *adj* elliptical

Elsass *nt* - Alsace

elsässisch *adj* Alsatian

Elster *f* **-,-n** magpie

elter|lich *adj* parental. **E~n** *pl* parents. **e~nlos** *adj* orphaned. **E~nteil** *m* parent

Email /e'mai/ *nt* **-s,-s**, **E~le** *f* **-,-n** enamel

E-Mail /'i:me:l/ *f* **-,-s** e-mail

Emanzi|pation /-'tsi̯o:n/ *f* - emancipation. **e~piert** *adj* emancipated

Embargo *nt* **-s,-s** embargo

Embryo *m* **-s,-s** embryo

Emigr|ant(in) *m* **-en,-en** (*f* **-,-nen**) emigrant. **E~ation** *f* - emigration. **e~ieren** *vi* (*sein*) emigrate

Empfang *m* **-[e]s,¨e** reception; (*Erhalt*) receipt; **in E~ nehmen** receive; (*annehmen*) accept. **e~en†** *vt* receive; (*Biology*) conceive

Empfäng|er *m* **-s,-** recipient; (*Post-*) addressee; (*Zahlungs-*) payee; (*Radio, TV*) receiver. **E~nis** *f* - (*Biology*) conception

Empfängnisverhütung *f* contraception. **E~smittel** *nt* contraceptive

Empfangs|bestätigung *f* receipt. **E~dame** *f* receptionist. **E~halle** *f* [hotel] foyer

empfehl|en† *vt* recommend. **E~ung** *f* **-,-en** recommendation; (*Gruß*) regards *pl*

empfind|en† *vt* feel. **e~lich** *adj* sensitive (**gegen** to); (*zart*) delicate. **E~lichkeit** *f* - sensitivity; delicacy; tenderness; touchiness. **E~ung** *f* **-,-en** sensation; (*Regung*) feeling

empor *adv* (*literarisch*) up[wards]

empören *vt* incense; **sich e~** be indignant; (*sich auflehnen*) rebel

Emporkömmling *m* **-s,-e** upstart

empör|t *adj* indignant. **E~ung** *f* - indignation; (*Auflehnung*) rebellion

Ende *nt* **-s,-n** end; (*eines Films, Romans*) ending; (🅃: *Stück*) bit; **zu E~ sein** be finished; **etw zu E~ schreiben** finish writing sth; **am E~** at the end; (*schließlich*) in the end; (🅃: *vielleicht*) perhaps; (🅃: *erschöpft*) at the end of one's tether

end|en *vi* (*haben*) end. **e~gültig** *adj* final; (*bestimmt*) definite

Endivie /-i̯ə/ *f* **-,-n** endive

end|lich *adv* at last, finally; (*schließlich*) in the end. **e~los** *adj* endless. **E~station** *f* terminus. **E~ung** *f* **-,-en** (*Gram*) ending

Energie *f* - energy

energieeffizient *adj* energy-efficient

energisch *adj* resolute; (*nachdrücklich*) vigorous

eng *adj* narrow; (*beengt*) cramped; (*anliegend*) tight; (*nah*) close; **e~ anliegend** tight-fitting

e

Engagement /ãgaʒəˈmã:/ *nt* **-s,-s** (*Theat*) engagement; (*fig*) commitment

Engel *m* **-s,-** angel

England *nt* **-s** England

Engländer *m* **-s,-** Englishman; (*Techn*) monkey-wrench; **die E~** the English *pl*. **E~in** *f* **-,-nen** Englishwoman

e

englisch *adj* English. **E~** *nt* **-[s]** (*Lang*) English; **auf E~** in English

Engpass *m* (*fig*) bottleneck

en gros /ãˈgro:/ *adv* wholesale

Enkel *m* **-s,-** grandson; **E~** *pl* grandchildren. **E~in** *f* **-,-nen** granddaughter. **E~kind** *nt* grandchild. **E~sohn** *m* grandson. **E~tochter** *f* granddaughter

Ensemble /ãˈsã:bəl/ *nt* **-s,-s** ensemble; (*Theat*) company

entart|en *vi* (*sein*) degenerate. **e~et** *adj* degenerate

entbehren *vt* do without; (*vermissen*) miss

entbind|en† *vt* release (**von** from); (*Med*) deliver (**von** of) ● *vi* (*haben*) give birth. **E~ung** *f* delivery. **E~ungsstation** *f* maternity ward

entdeck|en *vt* discover. **E~er** *m* **-s,-** discoverer; (*Forscher*) explorer. **E~ung** *f* **-,-en** discovery

Ente *f* **-,-n** duck

entehren *vt* dishonour

enteignen *vt* dispossess; expropriate (*Eigentum*)

enterben *vt* disinherit

Enterich *m* **-s,-e** drake

entfallen† *vi* (*sein*) not apply; **auf jdn e~** be s.o.'s share

entfern|en *vt* remove; **sich e~en** leave. **e~t** *adj* distant; (*schwach*) vague; **2 Kilometer e~t** 2 kilometres away; **e~t verwandt** distantly related. **E~ung** *f* **-,-en** removal; (*Abstand*) distance; (*Reichweite*) range

entfliehen† *vi* (*sein*) escape

entfremden *vt* alienate

entfrosten *vt* defrost

entführ|en *vt* abduct, kidnap; hijack (*Flugzeug*). **E~er** *m* abductor, kidnapper; hijacker. **E~ung** *f* abduction, kidnapping; hijacking

entgegen *adv* towards ● *prep* (+ *dat*) contrary to. **e~gehen**† *vi sep* (*sein*) (+ *dat*) go to meet; (*fig*) be heading for. **e~gesetzt** *adj* opposite; (*gegensätzlich*) opposing. **e~kommen**† *vi sep* (*sein*) (+ *dat*) come to meet; (*zukommen auf*) come towards; (*fig*) oblige. **E~kommen** *nt* **-s** helpfulness; (*Zugeständnis*) concession. **e~kommend** *adj* approaching; (*Verkehr*) oncoming; (*fig*) obliging. **e~nehmen**† *vt sep* accept. **e~wirken** *vi sep* (*haben*) (+ *dat*) counteract; (*fig*) oppose

entgegn|en *vt* reply (**auf** + *acc* to). **E~ung** *f* **-,-en** reply

entgehen† *vi sep* (*sein*) (+ *dat*) escape; **jdm e~** (*unbemerkt bleiben*) escape s.o.'s notice; **sich** (*dat*) **etw e~ lassen** miss sth

Entgelt *nt* **-[e]s** payment; **gegen E~** for money

entgleis|en *vi* (*sein*) be derailed; (*fig*) make a gaffe. **E~ung** *f* **-,-en** derailment; (*fig*) gaffe

entgräten *vt* fillet, bone

Enthaarungsmittel *nt* depilatory

enthalt|en† *vt* contain; **in etw** (*dat*) **e~en sein** be contained/ (*eingeschlossen*) included in sth; **sich der Stimme e~en** (*Pol*) abstain. **e~sam** *adj* abstemious. **E~ung** *f* (*Pol*) abstention

enthaupten *vt* behead

entheben† *vt* **jdn seines Amtes e~** relieve s.o. of his post
Enthüllung *f* **-,-en** revelation
Enthusias|mus *m* **-** enthusiasm. **E~t** *m* **-en,-en** enthusiast
entkernen *vt* stone; core (*Apfel*)
entkleiden *vt* undress; **sich e~en** undress
entkommen† *vi* (*sein*) escape
entkorken *vt* uncork
entladen† *vt* unload; (*Electr*) discharge; **sich e~** discharge; (*Gewitter:*) break; (*Zorn:*) explode
entlang *adv & prep* (*+ preceding acc or following dat*) along; **die Straße e~** along the road; **an etw** (*dat*) **e~** along sth. **e~fahren**† *vi sep* (*sein*) drive along. **e~gehen**† *vi sep* (*sein*) walk along
entlarven *vt* unmask
entlass|en† *vt* dismiss; (*aus Krankenhaus*) discharge; (*aus der Haft*) release. **E~ung** *f* **-,-en** dismissal; discharge; release
entlast|en *vt* relieve the strain on; ease (*Gewissen, Verkehr*); relieve (**von** of); (*Jur*) exonerate. **E~ung** *f* **-** relief; exoneration
entlaufen† *vi* (*sein*) run away
entleeren *vt* empty
entlegen *adj* remote
entlohnen *vt* pay
entlüft|en *vt* ventilate. **E~er** *m* **-s,-** extractor fan. **E~ung** *f* ventilation
entmündigen *vt* declare incapable of managing his own affairs
entmutigen *vt* discourage
entnehmen† *vt* take (*dat* from); (*schließen*) gather (*dat* from)
entpuppen (sich) *vr* (*fig*) turn out (**als etw** to be sth)
entrahmt *adj* skimmed
entrichten *vt* pay
entrinnen† *vi* (*sein*) escape
entrüst|en *vt* fill with indignation; **sich e~en** be indignant (**über** + *acc* at). **e~et** *adj* indignant. **E~ung** *f* **-** indignation
entsaft|en *vt* extract the juice from. **E~er** *m* **-s,-** juice extractor
entsagen *vi* (*haben*) (+ *dat*) renounce
entschädig|en *vt* compensate. **E~ung** *f* **-,-en** compensation
entschärfen *vt* defuse
entscheid|en† *vt/i* (*haben*) decide; **sich e~en** decide; (*Sache:*) be decided. **e~end** *adj* decisive; (*kritisch*) crucial. **E~ung** *f* decision
entschließen† **(sich)** *vr* decide, make up one's mind; **sich anders e~** change one's mind
entschlossen *adj* determined; (*energisch*) resolute; **kurz e~** without hesitation. **E~heit** *f* **-** determination
Entschluss *m* decision
entschlüsseln *vt* decode
entschuld|bar *adj* excusable. **e~igen** *vt* excuse; **sich e~igen** apologize (**bei** to); **e~igen Sie [bitte]!** sorry! (*bei Frage*) excuse me. **E~igung** *f* **-,-en** apology; (*Ausrede*) excuse; **um E~igung bitten** apologize
entsetz|en *vt* horrify. **E~en** *nt* **-s** horror. **e~lich** *adj* horrible; (*schrecklich*) terrible
Entsorgung *f* **-** waste disposal
entspann|en *vt* relax; **sich e~en** relax; (*Lage:*) ease. **E~ung** *f* **-** relaxation; easing; (*Pol*) détente
entsprech|en† *vi* (*haben*) (+ *dat*) correspond to; (*übereinstimmen*) agree with. **e~end** *adj* corresponding; (*angemessen*) appropriate; (*zuständig*) relevant ● *adv* correspondingly; appropriately; (*demgemäß*)

accordingly ●*prep* (+ *dat*) in accordance with
entspringen† *vi* (*sein*) (*Fluss:*) rise; (*fig*) arise, spring (*dat* from)
entstammen *vi* (*sein*) come/(*abstammen*) be descended (*dat* from)
entsteh|en† *vi* (*sein*) come into being; (*sich bilden*) form; (*sich entwickeln*) develop; (*Brand:*) start; (*stammen*) originate. **E~ung** *f* - origin; formation; development
entstell|en *vt* disfigure; (*verzerren*) distort. **E~ung** *f* disfigurement; distortion
entstört *adj* (*Electr*) suppressed
enttäusch|en *vt* disappoint. **E~ung** *f* disappointment
entwaffnen *vt* disarm
entwässer|n *vt* drain. **E~ung** *f* - drainage
entweder *conj & adv* either
entwerfen† *vt* design; (*aufsetzen*) draft; (*skizzieren*) sketch
entwert|en *vt* devalue; (*ungültig machen*) cancel. **E~er** *m* **-s,-** ticket-cancelling machine. **E~ung** *f* devaluation; cancelling
entwick|eln *vt* develop; **sich e~eln** develop. **E~lung** *f* **-,-en** development; (*Biology*) evolution. **E~lungsland** *nt* developing country
entwöhnen *vt* wean (*gen* from); cure (*Süchtige*)
entwürdigend *adj* degrading
Entwurf *m* design; (*Konzept*) draft; (*Skizze*) sketch
entwurzeln *vt* uproot
entzie|hen† *vt* take away (*dat* from); **jdm den Führerschein e~hen** disqualify s.o. from driving; **sich e~hen** (+ *dat*) withdraw from. **E~hungskur** *f* treatment for drug/alcohol addiction
entziffern *vt* decipher
Entzug *m* withdrawal; (*Vorenthaltung*) deprivation
entzünd|en *vt* ignite; (*anstecken*) light; (*fig: erregen*) inflame; **sich e~en** ignite; (*Med*) become inflamed. **e~et** *adj* (*Med*) inflamed. **e~lich** *adj* inflammable. **E~ung** *f* (*Med*) inflammation
entzwei *adj* broken
Enzian *m* **-s,-e** gentian
Enzyklo|pädie *f* **-,-en** encyclopaedia. **e~pädisch** *adj* encyclopaedic
Enzym *nt* **-s,-e** enzyme
Epidemie *f* **-,-n** epidemic
Epi|lepsie *f* - epilepsy. **E~leptiker(in)** *m* **-s,-** (*f* **-,-nen**) epileptic. **e~leptisch** *adj* epileptic
Epilog *m* **-s,-e** epilogue
Episode *f* **-,-n** episode
Epoche *f* **-,-n** epoch
Epos *nt* **-, Epen** epic
er *pron* he; (*Ding, Tier*) it
erachten *vt* consider (**für nötig** necessary). **E~** *nt* **-s meines E~s** in my opinion
erbarmen (sich) *vr* have pity/(*Gott:*) mercy (*gen* on). **E~** *nt* **-s** pity; mercy
erbärmlich *adj* wretched
erbauen *vt* build; (*fig*) edify; **nicht e~t von** 🅱 not pleased about
Erbe[1] *m* **-n,-n** heir
Erbe[2] *nt* **-s** inheritance; (*fig*) heritage. **e~n** *vt* inherit
erbeuten *vt* get; (*Mil*) capture
Erbfolge *f* (*Jur*) succession
erbieten† **(sich)** *vr* offer (**zu** to)
Erbin *f* **-,-nen** heiress
erbitten† *vt* ask for
erbittert *adj* bitter; (*heftig*) fierce
erblassen *vi* (*sein*) turn pale

erblich *adj* hereditary
erblicken *vt* catch sight of
erblinden *vi* (*sein*) go blind
erbrechen† *vt* vomit ● *vi/r* **[sich]** e~ vomit. **E~** *nt* **-s** vomiting
Erbschaft *f* **-,-en** inheritance
Erbse *f* **-,-n** pea
Erb|stück *nt* heirloom. **E~teil** *nt* inheritance
Erd|apfel *m* (*Aust*) potato. **E~beben** *nt* **-s,-** earthquake. **E~beere** *f* strawberry
Erde *f* **-,-n** earth; (*Erdboden*) ground; (*Fußboden*) floor. **e~n** *vt* (*Electr*) earth
erdenklich *adj* imaginable
Erd|gas *nt* natural gas. **E~geschoss** *nt* ground floor. **E~kugel** *f* globe. **E~kunde** *f* geography. **E~nuss** *f* peanut. **E~öl** *nt* [mineral] oil
erdrosseln *vt* strangle
erdrücken *vt* crush to death
Erd|rutsch *m* landslide. **E~teil** *m* continent
erdulden *vt* endure
ereignen (sich) *vr* happen
Ereignis *nt* **-ses,-se** event. **e~los** *adj* uneventful. **e~reich** *adj* eventful
Eremit *m* **-en,-en** hermit
erfahr|en† *vt* learn, hear; (*erleben*) experience ● *adj* experienced. **E~ung** *f* **-,-en** experience; **in E~ung bringen** find out
erfassen *vt* seize; (*begreifen*) grasp; (*einbeziehen*) include; (*aufzeichnen*) record
erfind|en† *vt* invent. **E~er** *m* **-s,-** inventor. **e~erisch** *adj* inventive. **E~ung** *f* **-,-en** invention
Erfolg *m* **-[e]s,-e** success; (*Folge*) result; E~ **haben** be successful. **e~en** *vi* (*sein*) take place; (*geschehen*) happen. **e~los** *adj* unsuccessful. **e~reich** *adj* successful
erforder|lich *adj* required, necessary. **e~n** *vt* require, demand
erforsch|en *vt* explore; (*untersuchen*) investigate. **E~ung** *f* exploration; investigation
erfreu|en *vt* please. **e~lich** *adj* pleasing. **e~licherweise** *adv* happily. **e~t** *adj* pleased
erfrier|en† *vi* (*sein*) freeze to death; (*Glied:*) become frostbitten; (*Pflanze:*) be killed by the frost. **E~ung** *f* **-,-en** frostbite
erfrisch|en *vt* refresh. **E~ung** *f* **-,-en** refreshment
erfüll|en *vt* fill; (*nachkommen*) fulfil; serve (*Zweck*); discharge (*Pflicht:*) **sich e~en** come true. **E~ung** *f* fulfilment
erfunden invented
ergänz|en *vt* complement; (*hinzufügen*) add. **E~ung** *f* complement; supplement; (*Zusatz*) addition
ergeben† *vt* produce, (*zeigen*) show, establish; **sich e~en** result; (*Schwierigkeit:*) arise; (*kapitulieren*) surrender; (*sich fügen*) submit ● *adj* devoted; (*resigniert*) resigned
Ergebnis *nt* **-ses,-se** result. **e~los** *adj* fruitless
ergiebig *adj* productive; (*fig*) rich
ergreifen† *vt* seize; take (*Maßnahme, Gelegenheit*); take up (*Beruf*); (*rühren*) move; **die Flucht e~** flee. **e~d** *adj* moving
ergriffen *adj* deeply moved. **E~heit** *f* **-** emotion
ergründen *vt* (*fig*) get to the bottom of
erhaben *adj* raised; (*fig*) sublime
Erhalt *m* **-[e]s** receipt. **e~en**† *vt* receive, get; (*gewinnen*) obtain; (*bewahren*) preserve, keep; (*instand halten*) maintain; (*unterhalten*) support;

am Leben e~en keep alive ● *adj* gut/schlecht e~en in good/bad condition; e~en bleiben survive

erhältlich *adj* obtainable

Erhaltung *f* - preservation; maintenance

erhängen (sich) *vr* hang oneself

e

erheb|en† *vt* raise; levy (*Steuer*); charge (*Gebühr*); **Anspruch e~en** lay claim (**auf** + *acc* to); **Protest e~en** protest; **sich e~en** rise; (*Frage:*) arise. **e~lich** *adj* considerable. **E~ung** *f* **-,-en** elevation; (*Anhöhe*) rise; (*Aufstand*) uprising; (*Ermittlung*) survey

erheiter|n *vt* amuse. **E~ung** *f* - amusement

erhitzen *vt* heat

erhöh|en *vt* raise; (*fig*) increase; **sich e~en** rise, increase. **E~ung** *f* **-,-en** increase

erhol|en (sich) *vr* recover (**von** from); (*nach Krankheit*) convalesce; (*sich ausruhen*) have a rest. **e~sam** *adj* restful. **E~ung** *f* - recovery; (*Ruhe*) rest

erinner|n *vt* remind (**an** + *acc* of); **sich e~n** remember (**an jdn/etw** s.o./sth). **E~ung** *f* **-,-en** memory; (*Andenken*) souvenir

erkält|en (sich) *vr* catch a cold; **e~et sein** have a cold. **E~ung** *f* **-,-en** cold

erkenn|bar *adj* recognizable; (*sichtbar*) visible. **e~en**† *vt* recognize; (*wahrnehmen*) distinguish. **E~tnis** *f* **-,-se** recognition; realization; (*Wissen*) knowledge; **die neuesten E~tnisse** the latest findings

Erker *m* **-s,-** bay

erklär|en *vt* declare; (*erläutern*) explain; **sich bereit e~en** agree (**zu** to). **e~end** *adj* explanatory. **e~lich** *adj* explicable; (*verständlich*) understandable. **e~licherweise** *adv* understandably. **E~ung** *f* **-,-en** declaration; explanation; **öffentliche E~ung** public statement

erkrank|en *vi* (*sein*) fall ill; be taken ill (**an** + *dat* with). **E~ung** *f* **-,-en** illness

erkundig|en (sich) *vr* enquire (**nach jdm/etw** after s.o./about sth). **E~ung** *f* **-,-en** enquiry

erlangen *vt* attain, get

Erlass *m* **-es,⸚e** (*Admin*) decree; (*Befreiung*) exemption; (*Straf-*) remission

erlassen† *vt* (*Admin*) issue; **jdm etw e~** exempt s.o. from sth; let s.o. off (*Strafe*)

erlauben *vt* allow, permit; **ich kann es mir nicht e~** I can't afford it

Erlaubnis *f* - permission. **E~schein** *m* permit

erläutern *vt* explain

Erle *f* **-,-n** alder

erleb|en *vt* experience; (*mit-*) see; have (*Überraschung*). **E~nis** *nt* **-ses,-se** experience

erledigen *vt* do; (*sich befassen mit*) deal with; (*beenden*) finish; (*entscheiden*) settle; (*töten*) kill

erleichter|n *vt* lighten; (*vereinfachen*) make easier; (*befreien*) relieve; (*lindern*) ease. **e~t** *adj* relieved. **E~ung** *f* - relief

erleiden† *vt* suffer

erleuchten *vt* illuminate; **hell e~et** brightly lit

erlogen *adj* untrue, false

Erlös *m* **-es** proceeds *pl*

erlöschen† *vi* (*sein*) go out; (*vergehen*) die; (*aussterben*) die out; (*ungültig werden*) expire; **erloschener Vulkan** extinct volcano

erlös|en *vt* save; (*befreien*) release (**von** from); (*Relig*) redeem. **e~t** *adj* relieved. **E~ung** *f* release; (*Erleichte-*

rung) relief; (*Relig*) redemption
ermächtig|en *vt* authorize. **E~ung** *f* **-,-en** authorization
Ermahnung *f* exhortation; admonition
ermäßig|en *vt* reduce. **E~ung** *f* **-,-en** reduction
ermessen† *vt* judge; (*begreifen*) appreciate. **E~** *nt* **-s** discretion; (*Urteil*) judgement; **nach eigenem E~** at one's own discretion
ermitt|eln *vt* establish; (*herausfinden*) find out ● *vi* (*haben*) investigate (**gegen jdn** s.o.). **E~lungen** *fpl* investigations. **E~lungsverfahren** *nt* (*Jur*) preliminary inquiry
ermöglichen *vt* make possible
ermord|en *vt* murder. **E~ung** *f* **-,-en** murder
ermüd|en *vt* tire ● *vi* (*sein*) get tired. **E~ung** *f* **-** tiredness
ermutigen *vt* encourage. **e~d** *adj* encouraging
ernähr|en *vt* feed; (*unterhalten*) support, keep; **sich e~en von** live/(*Tier:*) feed on. **E~er** *m* **-s,-** breadwinner. **E~ung** *f* **-** nourishment; nutrition; (*Kost*) diet
ernenn|en† *vt* appoint. **E~ung** *f* **-,-en** appointment
erneu|ern *vt* renew; (*auswechseln*) replace; change (*Verband*); (*renovieren*) renovate. **E~erung** *f* renewal; replacement; renovation. **e~t** *adj* renewed; (*neu*) new ● *adv* again
ernst *adj* serious; **e~ nehmen** take seriously. **E~** *m* **-es** seriousness; **im E~** seriously; **mit einer Drohung E~ machen** carry out a threat; **ist das dein E~?** are you serious? **e~haft** *adj* serious. **e~lich** *adj* serious
Ernte *f* **-,-n** harvest; (*Ertrag*) crop. **E~dankfest** *nt* harvest festival. **e~n** *vt* harvest; (*fig*) reap, win
ernüchter|n *vt* sober up; (*fig*) bring down to earth. **e~nd** *adj* (*fig*) sobering
Erober|er *m* **-s,-** conqueror. **e~n** *vt* conquer. **E~ung** *f* **-,-en** conquest
eröffn|en *vt* open; **jdm etw e~en** announce sth to s.o. **E~ung** *f* opening; (*Mitteilung*) announcement
erörter|n *vt* discuss. **E~ung** *f* **-,-en** discussion
Erot|ik *f* **-** eroticism. **e~isch** *adj* erotic
Erpel *m* **-s,-** drake
erpicht *adj* **e~ auf** (+ *acc*) keen on
erpress|en *vt* extort; blackmail (*Person*). **E~er** *m* **-s,-** blackmailer. **E~ung** *f* **-** extortion; blackmail
erprob|en *vt* test. **e~t** *adj* proven
erraten† *vt* guess
erreg|bar *adj* excitable. **e~en** *vt* excite; (*hervorrufen*) arouse; **sich e~en** get worked up. **e~end** *adj* exciting. **E~er** *m* **-s,-** (*Med*) germ. **e~t** *adj* agitated; (*hitzig*) heated. **E~ung** *f* **-** excitement
erreich|bar *adj* within reach; (*Ziel*) attainable; (*Person*) available. **e~en** *vt* reach; catch (*Zug*); live to (*Alter*); (*durchsetzen*) achieve
errichten *vt* erect
erringen† *vt* gain, win
erröten *vi* (*sein*) blush
Errungenschaft *f* **-,-en** achievement; (🄸: *Anschaffung*) acquisition
Ersatz *m* **-es** replacement, substitute; (*Entschädigung*) compensation. **E~reifen** *m* spare tyre. **E~teil** *nt* spare part
erschaffen† *vt* create
erschein|en† *vi* (*sein*) appear; (*Buch:*) be published. **E~ung** *f* **-,-en** appearance; (*Person*) figure; (*Phänomen*) phenomenon; (*Symptom*) symptom; (*Geist*) apparition

e

erschießen† *vt* shoot [dead]. **E~ungskommando** *nt* firing squad
erschlaffen *vi* (*sein*) go limp
erschlagen† *vt* beat to death; (*tödlich treffen*) strike dead; **vom Blitz e~ werden** be killed by lightning
erschließen† *vt* develop
erschöpf|en *vt* exhaust. **e~t** *adj* exhausted. **E~ung** *f* - exhaustion
erschrecken† *vi* (*sein*) get a fright ● *vt* (*reg*) startle; (*beunruhigen*) alarm; **du hast mich e~t** you gave me a fright
erschrocken *adj* frightened; (*erschreckt*) startled
erschütter|n *vt* shake; (*ergreifen*) upset deeply. **E~ung** *f* -,-**en** shock
erschwinglich *adj* affordable
ersehen† *vt* (*fig*) see (**aus** from)
ersetzen *vt* replace; make good (*Schaden*); refund (*Kosten*); **jdm etw e~** compensate s.o. for sth
ersichtlich *adj* obvious, apparent
erspar|en *vt* save. **E~nis** *f* -,-**se** saving; **E~nisse** savings
erst *adv* (*zuerst*) first; (*noch nicht mehr als*) only; (*nicht vor*) not until; **e~ dann** only then; **eben e~** [only] just
erstarren *vi* (*sein*) solidify; (*gefrieren*) freeze; (*steif werden*) go stiff; (*vor Schreck*) be paralysed
erstatten *vt* (*zurück-*) refund; **Bericht e~** report (**jdm** to s.o.)
Erstaufführung *f* first performance, première
erstaun|en *vt* amaze, astonish. **E~en** *nt* amazement, astonishment. **e~lich** *adj* amazing
Erst|ausgabe *f* first edition. **e~e(r,s)** *adj* first; (*beste*) best; **e~e Hilfe** first aid. **E~e(r)** *m/f* first; (*Beste*) best; **fürs E~e** for the time being; **als E~es** first of all; **er kam als E~er** he arrived first
erstechen† *vt* stab to death
ersteigern *vt* buy at an auction
erst|ens *adv* firstly, in the first place. **e~ere(r,s)** *adj* the former; **der/die/das E~ere** the former
ersticken *vt* suffocate; smother (*Flammen*) ● *vi* (*sein*) suffocate. **E~** *nt* **-s** suffocation; **zum E~** stifling
erstklassig *adj* first-class
ersuchen *vt* ask, request. **E~** *nt* **-s** request
ertappen *vt* [I] catch
erteilen *vt* give (**jdm** s.o.)
ertönen *vi* (*sein*) sound; (*erschallen*) ring out
Ertrag *m* -[e]s,⸗e yield. **e~en**† *vt* bear
erträglich *adj* bearable; (*leidlich*) tolerable
ertränken *vt* drown
ertrinken† *vi* (*sein*) drown
erübrigen (sich) *vr* be unnecessary
erwachsen *adj* grown-up. **E~e(r)** *m/f* adult, grown-up
erwäg|en† *vt* consider. **E~ung** *f* -,-**en** consideration; **in E~ung ziehen** consider
erwähn|en *vt* mention. **E~ung** *f* -,-**en** mention
erwärmen *vt* warm; **sich e~** warm up; (*fig*) warm (**für** to)
erwart|en *vt* expect; (*warten auf*) wait for. **E~ung** *f* -,-**en** expectation
erweisen† *vt* prove; (*bezeigen*) do (*Gefallen, Dienst, Ehre*); **sich e~ als** prove to be
erweitern *vt* widen; dilate (*Pupille*); (*fig*) extend, expand
Erwerb *m* -[e]s acquisition; (*Kauf*) purchase; (*Brot-*) livelihood; (*Verdienst*) earnings *pl.* **e~en**† *vt* acquire; (*kaufen*) purchase. **e~slos** *adj*

unemployed. **e∼stätig** *adj* employed

erwider|n *vt* reply; return (*Besuch, Gruß*). **E∼ung** *f* -,-en reply

erwirken *vt* obtain

erwürgen *vt* strangle

Erz *nt* -es,-e ore

erzähl|en *vt* tell (**jdm** s.o.) ●*vi* (*haben*) talk (**von** about). **E∼er** *m* -s,- narrator. **E∼ung** *f* -,-en story, tale

Erzbischof *m* archbishop

erzeug|en *vt* produce; (*Electr*) generate. **E∼er** *m* -s,- producer. **E∼nis** *nt* -ses,-se product; **landwirtschaftliche E∼nisse** farm produce *sg*.

erzieh|en† *vt* bring up; (*Sch*) educate. **E∼er** *m* -s,- [private] tutor. **E∼erin** *f* -,-nen governess. **E∼ung** *f* - upbringing; education

erzielen *vt* achieve; score (*Tor*)

erzogen *adj* **gut/schlecht e∼** well/badly brought up

es

● *pronoun*

····➤ (*Sache*) it; (*weibliche Person*) she/her; (*männliche Person*) he/him. **ich bin es** it's me. **wir sind traurig, ihr seid es auch** we are sad, and so are you. **er ist es, der ...** he is the one who ... **es sind Studenten** they are students

····➤ (*impers*) it. **es hat geklopft** there was a knock. **es klingelt** someone is ringing. **es wird schöner** the weather is improving. **es geht ihm gut/schlecht** he is well/unwell. **es lässt sich aushalten** it is bearable. **es gibt** there is *or* (*pl*) are

····➤ (*als formales Objekt*) **er hat es gut** he has it made; he's well off. **er meinte es gut** he meant well. **ich hoffe/glaube es** I hope/think so

Esche *f* -,-n ash

Esel *m* -s,- donkey; (**!**: *Person*) ass

Eskimo *m* -[s],-[s] Eskimo

Eskort|e *f* -,-n (*Mil*) escort. **e∼ieren** *vt* escort

essbar *adj* edible

essen† *vt/i* (*haben*) eat; **zu Mittag/Abend e∼** have lunch/supper; **e∼ gehen** eat out. **E∼** *nt* -s,- food; (*Mahl*) meal; (*festlich*) dinner

Esser(in) *m* -s,- (*f* -,-nen) eater

Essig *m* -s vinegar. **E∼gurke** *f* [pickled] gherkin

Esslöffel *m* ≈ dessertspoon. **Essstäbchen** *ntpl* chopsticks. **Esstisch** *m* dining-table. **Esswaren** *fpl* food *sg*; (*Vorräte*) provisions. **Esszimmer** *nt* dining-room

Estland *nt* -s Estonia

Estragon *m* -s tarragon

etablieren (sich) *vr* establish oneself/(*Geschäft:*) itself

Etage /e'ta:ʒə/ *f* -,-n storey. **E∼nbett** *nt* bunk-beds *pl*. **E∼nwohnung** *f* flat

Etappe *f* -,-n stage

Etat /e'ta:/ *m* -s,-s budget

Eth|ik *f* - ethic; (*Sittenlehre*) ethics *sg*. **e∼isch** *adj* ethical

ethnisch *adj* ethnic; **e∼e Säuberung** ethnic cleansing

Etikett *nt* -[e]s,-e[n] label; (*Preis-*) tag. **e∼ieren** *vt* label

Etui /e'tvi:/ *nt* -s,-s case

etwa *adv* (*ungefähr*) about; (*zum Beispiel*) for instance; (*womöglich*) perhaps; **nicht e∼, dass ...** not that ... ; **denkt nicht e∼ ...** don't imagine ...

etwas *pron* something; (*fragend/*

e

verneint) anything; (*ein bisschen*) some, a little; **sonst noch e~?** anything else? **so e~ Ärgerliches!** what a nuisance! ● *adv* a bit

Etymologie *f* - etymology

euch *pron* (*acc of* **ihr** *pl*) you; (*dat*) [to] you; (*reflexive*) yourselves; (*einander*) each other

euer *poss pron pl* your. **e~e, e~t-** *s.* **eure, euret-**

Eule *f* **-,-n** owl

Euphorie *f* - euphoria

eur|e *poss pron pl* your. **e~e(r,s)** *poss pron* yours. **e~etwegen** *adv* for your sake; (*wegen euch*) because of you, on your account. **e~etwillen** *adv* **um e~etwillen** for your sake. **e~ige** *poss pron* **der/die/das e~ige** yours

Euro *m* **-[s],[-s]** euro. **E~-** *prefix* Euro-

Europa *nt* **-s** Europe. **E~-** *prefix* European

Europä|er(in) *m* **-s,-** (*f* **-,-nen**) European. **e~isch** *adj* European

Euter *nt* **-s,-** udder

evakuier|en *vt* evacuate. **E~ung** *f* - evacuation

evan|gelisch *adj* Protestant. **E~gelium** *nt* **-s,-ien** gospel

eventuell *adj* possible ● *adv* possibly; (*vielleicht*) perhaps

Evolution /-ˈtsi̯o:n/ *f* - evolution

ewig *adj* eternal; (*endlos*) never-ending; **e~ dauern** [!] take ages. **E~keit** *f* - eternity

Examen *nt* **-s,-** & **-mina** (*Sch*) examination

Exemplar *nt* **-s,-e** specimen; (*Buch*) copy. **e~isch** *adj* exemplary

exerzieren *vt/i* (*haben*) (*Mil*) drill; (*üben*) practise

exhumieren *vt* exhume

Exil *nt* **-s** exile

Existenz *f* **-,-en** existence; (*Lebensgrundlage*) livelihood

existieren *vi* (*haben*) exist

exklusiv *adj* exclusive. **e~e** *prep* (+ *gen*) excluding

exkommunizieren *vt* excommunicate

Exkremente *npl* excrement *sg*

Expedition /-ˈtsi̯o:n/ *f* **-,-en** expedition

Experiment *nt* **-[e]s,-e** experiment. **e~ieren** *vi* (*haben*) experiment

Experte *m* **-n,-n** expert

explo|dieren *vi* (*sein*) explode. **E~sion** *f* **-,-en** explosion

Expor|t *m* **-[e]s,-e** export. **E~teur** *m* **-s,-e** exporter. **e~tieren** *vt* export

extra *adv* separately; (*zusätzlich*) extra; (*eigens*) specially; ([!]: *absichtlich*) on purpose

extravagan|t *adj* flamboyant; (*übertrieben*) extravagant

extravertiert *adj* extrovert

extrem *adj* extreme. **E~ist** *m* **-en,-en** extremist

Exzellenz *f* - (*title*) Excellency

Exzentr|iker *m* **-s,-** eccentric. **e~isch** *adj* eccentric

Fabel *f* **-,-n** fable. **f~haft** *adj* [!] fantastic

Fabrik *f* **-,-en** factory. **F~ant** *m* **-en,-en** manufacturer. **F~at** *nt* **-[e]s,-e** product; (*Marke*) make. **F~ation** *f* - manufacture

Fach *nt* **-[e]s,⸚er** compartment;

(*Schub-*) drawer; (*Gebiet*) field; (*Sch*) subject. **F~arbeiter** *m* skilled worker. **F~arzt** *m*, **F~ärztin** *f* specialist. **F~ausdruck** *m* technical term

Fächer *m* **-s,-** fan

Fach|gebiet *nt* field. **f~kundig** *adj* expert. **f~lich** *adj* technical; (*beruflich*) professional. **F~mann** *m* (*pl* **-leute**) expert. **f~männisch** *adj* expert. **F~schule** *f* technical college. **F~werkhaus** *nt* half-timbered house. **F~wort** *nt* (*pl* **-wörter**) technical term

Fackel *f* **-,-n** torch

fade *adj* insipid; (*langweilig*) dull

Faden *m* **-s,⁼** thread; (*Bohnen-*) string; (*Naut*) fathom

Fagott *nt* **-[e]s,-e** bassoon

fähig *adj* capable (**zu**/*gen* of); (*tüchtig*) able, competent. **F~keit** *f* **-,-en** ability; competence

fahl *adj* pale

fahnd|en *vi* (*haben*) search (**nach** for). **F~ung** *f* **-,-en** search

Fahne *f* **-,-n** flag; (*Druck-*) galley [proof]; **eine F~ haben** ⊡ reek of alcohol. **F~nflucht** *f* desertion

Fahr|ausweis *m* ticket. **F~bahn** *f* carriageway; (*Straße*) road. **f~bar** *adj* mobile

Fähre *f* **-,-n** ferry

fahr|en† *vi* (*sein*) go, travel; (*Fahrer:*) drive; (*Radfahrer:*) ride; (*verkehren*) run, (*ab-*) leave; (*Schiff:*) sail; **mit dem Auto/Zug f~en** go by car/train; **was ist in ihn gefahren?** ⊡ what has got into him? ● *vt* drive; ride (*Fahrrad*); take (*Kurve*). **f~end** *adj* moving; (*f~bar*) mobile; (*nicht sesshaft*) travelling. **F~er** *m* **-s,-** driver. **F~erflucht** *f* failure to stop after an accident. **F~erhaus** *nt* driver's cab. **F~erin** *f* **-,-nen** woman driver. **F~gast** *m* passenger. **F~geld** *nt* fare. **F~gestell** *nt* chassis; (*Aviat*) undercarriage. **F~karte** *f* ticket. **F~kartenschalter** *m* ticket office. **f~lässig** *adj* negligent. **F~lässigkeit** *f* **-** negligence. **F~lehrer** *m* driving instructor. **F~plan** *m* timetable. **f~planmäßig** *adj* scheduled ● *adv* according to/(*pünktlich*) on schedule. **F~preis** *m* fare. **F~prüfung** *f* driving test. **F~rad** *nt* bicycle. **F~schein** *m* ticket. **F~schule** *f* driving school. **F~schüler(in)** *m*(*f*) learner driver. **F~stuhl** *m* lift

Fahrt *f* **-,-en** journey; (*Auto*) drive; (*Ausflug*) trip; (*Tempo*) speed

Fährte *f* **-,-n** track; (*Witterung*) scent

Fahr|tkosten *pl* travelling expenses. **F~werk** *nt* undercarriage. **F~zeug** *nt* **-[e]s,-e** vehicle; (*Wasser-*) craft, vessel

fair /fɛːɐ̯/ *adj* fair

Fakultät *f* **-,-en** faculty

Falke *m* **-n,-n** falcon

Fall *m* **-[e]s,⁼e** fall; (*Jur, Med, Gram*) case; **im F~[e]** in case (*gen* of); **auf jeden F~** in any case; (*bestimmt*) definitely; **für alle F⁼~e** just in case; **auf keinen F~** on no account

Falle *f* **-,-n** trap

fallen† *vi* (*sein*) fall; (*sinken*) go down; **[im Krieg] f~** be killed in the war; **f~ lassen** drop (*etw, fig: Plan, jdn*); make (*Bemerkung*)

fällen *vt* fell; (*fig*) pass (*Urteil*)

fällig *adj* due; (*Wechsel*) mature; **längst f~** long overdue. **F~keit** *f* **-** (*Comm*) maturity

falls *conj* in case; (*wenn*) if

Fallschirm *m* parachute. **F~jäger** *m* paratrooper. **F~springer** *m* parachutist

Falltür *f* trapdoor

falsch *adj* wrong; (*nicht echt, unauf-*

richtig) false; (*gefälscht*) forged; (*Geld*) counterfeit; (*Schmuck*) fake ● *adv* wrongly; falsely; (*singen*) out of tune; **f~ gehen** (*Uhr:*) be wrong

fälschen *vt* forge, fake

Falschgeld *nt* counterfeit money

fälschlich *adj* wrong; (*irrtümlich*) mistaken

Falsch|meldung *f* false report; (*absichtlich*) hoax report. **F~münzer** *m* **-s,-** counterfeiter

Fälschung *f* **-,-en** forgery, fake

Falte *f* **-,-n** fold; (*Rock-*) pleat; (*Knitter-*) crease; (*im Gesicht*) line; wrinkle

falten *vt* fold

Falter *m* **-s,-** butterfly; moth

faltig *adj* creased; (*Gesicht*) lined; wrinkled

familiär *adj* family ; (*vertraut, zudringlich*) familiar; (*zwanglos*) informal

Familie /-iə/ *f* **-,-n** family. **F~nforschung** *f* genealogy. **F~nname** *m* surname. **F~nplanung** *f* family planning. **F~nstand** *m* marital status

Fan /fɛn/ *m* **-s,-s** fan

Fana|tiker *m* **-s,-** fanatic. **f~tisch** *adj* fanatical

Fanfare *f* **-,-n** trumpet; (*Signal*) fanfare

Fang *m* **-[e]s,⸚e** capture; (*Beute*) catch; **F~̈e** (*Krallen*) talons; (*Zähne*) fangs. **F~arm** *m* tentacle. **f~en†** *vt* catch; (*ein-*) capture; **gefangen nehmen** take prisoner. **F~en** *nt* **-s F~en spielen** play tag. **F~frage** *f* catch question

Fantasie *f* **-,-n** = **Phantasie**

Farb|aufnahme *f* colour photograph. **F~band** *nt* (*pl* **-bänder**) typewriter ribbon. **F~e** *f* **-,-n** colour; (*Maler-*) paint; (*zum Färben*) dye; (*Karten*) suit. **f~echt** *adj* colour-fast

färben *vt* colour; dye (*Textilien, Haare*) ● *vi* (*haben*) not be colour-fast

farb|enblind *adj* colour-blind. **f~enfroh** *adj* colourful. **F~film** *m* colour film. **f~ig** *adj* coloured ● *adv* in colour. **F~ige(r)** *m/f* coloured man/woman. **F~kasten** *m* box of paints. **f~los** *adj* colourless. **F~stift** *m* crayon. **F~stoff** *m* dye; (*Lebensmittel-*) colouring. **F~ton** *m* shade

Färbung *f* **-,-en** colouring

Farn *m* **-[e]s,-e** fern

Färse *f* **-,-n** heifer

Fasan *m* **-[e]s,-e[n]** pheasant

Faschierte(s) *nt* (*Aust*) mince

Fasching *m* **-s** (*SGer*) carnival

> **Fasching, Fastnachtszeit** *i*
> The carnival season begins at Epiphany and ends on *Aschermittwoch* (Ash Wednesday) for Lent. Depending on the region, it is also called *Karneval* or *Fasnet*, and is celebrated in Germany, Austria and Switzerland. Celebrations reach a climax on *Faschingsdienstag*, or *Rosenmontag* in the Rhineland, when there are street processions.

Faschis|mus *m* **-** fascism. **F~t** *m* **-en,-en** fascist. **f~tisch** *adj* fascist

Faser *f* **-,-n** fibre

Fass *nt* **-es,⸚er** barrel, cask; **Bier vom F~** draught beer

Fassade *f* **-,-n** façade

fassbar *adj* comprehensible; (*greifbar*) tangible

fassen *vt* take [hold of], grasp; (*ergreifen*) seize; (*fangen*) catch; (*ein-*) set; (*enthalten*) hold; (*fig: begreifen*) take in, grasp; conceive (*Plan*); make (*Entschluss*); **sich f~** compose oneself; **sich kurz f~** be brief; **nicht zu f~** (*fig*) unbelievable ● *vi* (*haben*) **f~ an** (+ *acc*) touch

Fassung *f* -,-en mount; (*Edelstein-*) setting; (*Electr*) socket; (*Version*) version; (*Beherrschung*) composure; **aus der F~ bringen** disconcert. **f~slos** *adj* shaken; (*erstaunt*) flabbergasted. **F~svermögen** *nt* capacity

fast *adv* almost, nearly; **f~ nie** hardly ever

fast|en *vi* (*haben*) fast. **F~enzeit** *f* Lent. **F~nacht** *f* Shrovetide; (*Karneval*) carnival. **F~nachtsdienstag** *m* Shrove Tuesday

fatal *adj* fatal; (*peinlich*) embarrassing

Fata Morgana *f* - -,- -nen mirage

fauchen *vi* (*haben*) spit, hiss ● *vt* snarl

faul *adj* lazy; (*verdorben*) rotten, bad; (*Ausrede*) lame

faul|en *vi* (*sein*) rot; (*Zahn:*) decay; (*verwesen*) putrefy. **f~enzen** *vi* (*haben*) be lazy. **F~enzer** *m* -s,- lazy-bones *sg*. **F~heit** *f* - laziness

Fäulnis *f* - decay

Fauna *f* - fauna

Faust *f* -,Fäuste fist; **auf eigene F~** (*fig*) off one's own bat. **F~handschuh** *m* mitten. **F~schlag** *m* punch

Fauxpas /fo'pa/ *m* -,- gaffe

Favorit(in) /favo'ri:t(ɪn)/ *m* -en, -en (*f* -,-nen) (*Sport*) favourite

Fax *nt* -,-[e] fax. **f~en** *vt* fax

Faxen *fpl* ⊡ antics; **F~ machen** fool about

Faxgerät *nt* fax machine

Februar *m* -s,-e February

fecht|en† *vi* (*haben*) fence. **F~er** *m* -s,- fencer

Feder *f* -,-n feather; (*Schreib-*) pen; (*Spitze*) nib; (*Techn*) spring. **F~ball** *m* shuttlecock; (*Spiel*) badminton. **F~busch** *m* plume. **f~leicht** *adj* as light as a feather. **f~n** *vi* (*haben*) be springy; (*nachgeben*) give; (*hoch-*) bounce. **f~nd** *adj* springy; (*elastisch*) elastic. **F~ung** *f* - (*Techn*) springs *pl*; (*Auto*) suspension

Fee *f* -,-n fairy

Fegefeuer *nt* purgatory

fegen *vt* sweep

Fehde *f* -,-n feud

fehl *adj* **f~ am Platze** out of place. **F~betrag** *m* deficit. **f~en** *vi* (*haben*) be missing/(*Sch*) absent; (*mangeln*) be lacking; **mir f~t die Zeit** I haven't got the time; **was f~t ihm?** what's the matter with him? **das hat uns noch gefehlt!** that's all we need! **f~end** *adj* missing; (*Sch*) absent

Fehler *m* -s,- mistake, error; (*Sport* & *fig*) fault; (*Makel*) flaw. **f~frei** *adj* faultless. **f~haft** *adj* faulty. **f~los** *adj* flawless

Fehl|geburt *f* miscarriage. **F~griff** *m* mistake. **F~kalkulation** *f* miscalculation. **F~schlag** *m* failure. **f~schlagen**† *vi sep* (*sein*) fail. **F~start** *m* (*Sport*) false start. **F~zündung** *f* (*Auto*) misfire

Feier *f* -,-n celebration; (*Zeremonie*) ceremony; (*Party*) party. **F~abend** *m* end of the working day; **F~abend machen** stop work. **f~lich** *adj* solemn; (*fömlich*) formal. **f~n** *vt* celebrate; hold (*Fest*) ● *vi* (*haben*) celebrate. **F~tag** *m* [public] holiday; (*kirchlicher*) feast-day; **erster/zweiter F~tag** Christmas Day / Boxing Day. **f~tags** *adv* on public holidays

feige *adj* cowardly; **f~ sein** be a coward ● *adv* in a cowardly way

Feige *f* -,-n fig

f

Feig|heit *f* **-** cowardice. **F∼ling** *m* **-s,-e** coward

Feile *f* **-,-n** file. **f∼n** *vt/i* (*haben*) file

feilschen *vi* (*haben*) haggle

fein *adj* fine; (*zart*) delicate; (*Strümpfe*) sheer; (*Unterschied*) subtle; (*scharf*) keen; (*vornehm*) refined; (*prima*) great; **sich f∼ machen** dress up. **F∼arbeit** *f* precision work

f

Feind(in) *m* **-es,-e** (*f* **-,-nen**) enemy. **f∼lich** *adj* enemy; (*f∼selig*) hostile. **F∼schaft** *f* **-,-en** enmity

fein|fühlig *adj* sensitive. **F∼gefühl** *nt* sensitivity; (*Takt*) delicacy. **F∼heit** *f* **-,-en** fineness; delicacy; subtlety; refinement; **F∼heiten** subtleties. **F∼kostgeschäft** *nt* delicatessen [shop]

feist *adj* fat

Feld *nt* **-[e]s,-er** field; (*Fläche*) ground; (*Sport*) pitch; (*Schach-*) square; (*auf Formular*) box. **F∼bett** *nt* camp-bed. **F∼forschung** *f* fieldwork. **F∼herr** *m* commander. **F∼stecher** *m* **-s,-** field-glasses *pl*. **F∼webel** *m* **-s,-** (*Mil*) sergeant. **F∼zug** *m* campaign

Felge *f* **-,-n** [wheel] rim

Fell *nt* **-[e]s,-e** (*Zool*) coat; (*Pelz*) fur; (*abgezogen*) skin, pelt

Fels *m* **-en,-en** rock. **F∼block** *m* boulder. **F∼en** *m* **-s,-** rock

Femininum *nt* **-s,-na** (*Gram*) feminine

Feminist|(in) *m* **-en,-en** (*f* **-,-nen**) feminist. **f∼isch** *adj* feminist

Fenchel *m* **-s** fennel

Fenster *nt* **-s,-** window. **F∼brett** *nt* window sill. **F∼scheibe** *f* [window-]pane

Ferien /ˈfeːri̯ən/ *pl* holidays; (*Univ*) vacation *sg*; **F∼ haben** be on holiday. **F∼ort** *m* holiday resort

Ferkel *nt* **-s,-** piglet

fern *adj* distant; **der F∼e Osten** the Far East; **sich f∼ halten** keep away ●*adv* far away; **von f∼** from a distance ●*prep* (+ *dat*) far [away] from. **F∼bedienung** *f* remote control. **F∼e** *f* **-** distance; **in weiter F∼e** far away; (*zeitlich*) in the distant future. **f∼er** *adj* further ●*adv* (*außerdem*) furthermore; (*in Zukunft*) in future. **f∼gelenkt** *adj* remote-controlled; (*Rakete*) guided. **F∼gespräch** *nt* long-distance call. **F∼glas** *nt* binoculars *pl*. **F∼kurs[us]** *m* correspondence course. **F∼licht** *nt* (*Auto*) full beam. **F∼meldewesen** *nt* telecommunications *pl*. **F∼rohr** *nt* telescope. **F∼schreiben** *nt* telex

Fernseh|apparat *m* television set. **f∼en†** *vi sep* (*haben*) watch television. **F∼en** *nt* **-s** television. **F∼er** *m* **-s,-** [television] viewer; (*Gerät*) television set

Fernsprech|amt *nt* telephone exchange. **F∼er** *m* telephone

Fern|steuerung *f* remote control. **F∼studium** *nt* distance learning

Ferse *f* **-,-n** heel

fertig *adj* finished; (*bereit*) ready; (*Comm*) ready-made; (*Gericht*) ready-to-serve; **f∼ werden mit** finish; (*bewältigen*) cope with; **f∼ sein** have finished; (*fig*) be through (**mit jdm** with s.o.); (🅸: *erschöpft*) be all in/(*seelisch*) shattered; **etw f∼ bringen** manage to do sth; (*beenden*) finish sth; **etw/jdn f∼ machen** finish sth; (*bereitmachen*) get sth/s.o. ready; (🅸: *erschöpfen*) wear s.o. out; (*seelisch*) shatter s.o.; **sich f∼ machen** get ready; **etw f∼ stellen** complete sth ●*adv* **f∼ essen/lesen** finish eating/reading. **F∼bau** *m* (*pl* **-bauten**) prefabricated building. **f∼en** *vt* make. **F∼gericht** *nt* ready-to-serve meal. **F~haus** *nt* prefabricated house. **F~keit** *f* **-,-en** skill. **F~stellung** *f* completion. **F~ung** *f* - manufacture

fesch *adj* [!] attractive

Fessel *f* **-,-n** ankle

fesseln *vt* tie up; tie (**an** + *acc* to); (*fig*) fascinate

fest *adj* firm; (*nicht flüssig*) solid; (*erstarrt*) set; (*haltbar*) strong; (*nicht locker*) tight; (*feststehend*) fixed; (*ständig*) steady; (*Anstellung*) permanent; (*Schlaf*) sound; (*Blick, Stimme*) steady; **f~ werden** harden; (*Gelee:*) set; **f~e Nahrung** solids *pl* ●*adv* firmly; tightly; steadily; soundly; (*kräftig, tüchtig*) hard; **f~ schlafen** be fast asleep; **f~ angestellt** permanent

Fest *nt* **-[e]s,-e** celebration; (*Party*) party; (*Relig*) festival; **frohes F~!** happy Christmas!

fest|binden† *vt sep* tie (**an** + *dat* to). **f~bleiben**† *vi sep* (*sein*) (*fig*) remain firm. **f~halten**† *v sep* ●*vt* hold on to; (*aufzeichnen*) record; **sich f~halten** hold on ●*vi* (*haben*) **f~halten an** (+ *dat*) (*fig*) stick to; cling to (*Tradition*). **f~igen** *vt* strengthen. **F~iger** *m* **-s,-** styling lotion/(*Schaum-*) mousse. **F~igkeit** *f* - (*s.* **fest**) firmness; solidity; strength; steadiness. **F~land** *nt* mainland; (*Kontinent*) continent. **f~legen** *vt sep* (*fig*) fix, settle; lay down (*Regeln*); tie up (*Geld*); **sich f~legen** commit oneself

festlich *adj* festive. **F~keiten** *fpl* festivities

fest|liegen† *vi sep* (*haben*) be fixed, settled. **f~machen** *v sep* ●*vt* fasten/(*binden*) tie (**an** + *dat* to); (*f~legen*) fix, settle ●*vi* (*haben*) (*Naut*) moor. **F~mahl** *nt* feast. **F~nahme** *f* **-,-n** arrest. **f~nehmen**† *vt sep* arrest. **F~netz** *nt* land-line network. **F~platte** *f* hard disk. **f~setzen** *vt sep* fix, settle; (*inhaftieren*) gaol; **sich f~setzen** collect. **f~sitzen**† *vi sep* (*haben*) be firm/(*Schraube:*) tight; (*haften*) stick; (*nicht weiterkommen*) be stuck. **F~spiele** *npl* festival *sg.* **f~stehen**† *vi sep* (*haben*) be certain. **f~stellen** *vt sep* fix; (*ermitteln*) establish; (*bemerken*) notice; (*sagen*) state. **F~tag** *m* special day

Festung *f* **-,-en** fortress

Festzug *m* [grand] procession

Fete /ˈfe:tə, ˈfɛ:tə/ *f* **-,-n** party

fett *adj* fat; fatty; (*fettig*) greasy; (*üppig*) rich; (*Druck*) bold. **F~** *nt* **-[e]s,-e** fat; (*flüssig*) grease. **f~arm** *adj* low-fat. **f~en** *vt* grease ●*vi* (*haben*) be greasy. **F~fleck** *m* grease mark. **f~ig** *adj* greasy

Fetzen *m* **-s,-** scrap; (*Stoff*) rag

feucht *adj* damp, moist; (*Luft*) humid. **F~igkeit** *f* - dampness; (*Nässe*) moisture; (*Luft-*) humidity. **F~igkeitscreme** *f* moisturizer

Feuer *nt* **-s,-** fire; (*für Zigarette*) light; (*Begeisterung*) passion; **F~ machen** light a fire. **F~alarm** *m* fire alarm. **f~gefährlich** *adj* [in]-flammable. **F~leiter** *f* fire escape. **F~löscher** *m* **-s,-** fire extinguisher. **F~melder** *m* **-s,-** fire alarm. **f~n** *vi* (*haben*) fire (**auf** + *acc* on). **F~probe** *f* (*fig*) test. **f~rot** *adj* crimson. **F~stein** *m* flint. **F~stelle** *f* hearth. **F~treppe** *f* fire escape. **F~wache** *f* fire station. **F~waffe** *f* firearm. **F~wehr** *f* **-,-en** fire brigade. **F~wehrauto** *nt* fire engine. **F~wehrmann** *m* (*pl* **-männer** & **-leute**) fireman. **F~werk** *nt* firework display, fireworks *pl.* **F~zeug** *nt* lighter

feurig *adj* fiery; (*fig*) passionate

Fiaker *m* **-s,-** (*Aust*) horse-drawn cab

Fichte *f* **-,-n** spruce
Fieber *nt* **-s** [raised] temperature; **F~ haben** have a temperature. **f~n** *vi* (*haben*) be feverish. **F~thermometer** *nt* thermometer
fiebrig *adj* feverish
Figur *f* **-,-en** figure; (*Roman-, Film-*) character; (*Schach-*) piece
Filet /fi'le:/ *nt* **-s,-s** fillet
f
Filiale *f* **-,-n** (*Comm*) branch
Filigran *nt* **-s** filigree
Film *m* **-[e]s,-e** film; (*Kino-*) film; (*Schicht*) coating. **f~en** *vt/i* (*haben*) film. **F~kamera** *f* cine/(*für Kinofilm*) film camera
Filt|er *m* & (*Techn*) *nt* **-s,-** filter; (*Zigaretten-*) filter-tip. **f~ern** *vt* filter. **F~erzigarette** *f* filter-tipped cigarette. **f~rieren** *vt* filter
Filz *m* **-es** felt. **F~stift** *m* felt-tipped pen
Fimmel *m* **-s,-** 🅘 obsession
Finale *nt* **-s,-** (*Mus*) finale; (*Sport*) final
Finanz *f* **-,-en** finance. **F~amt** *nt* tax office. **f~iell** *adj* financial. **f~ieren** *vt* finance. **F~minister** *m* minister of finance
find|en† *vt* find; (*meinen*) think; **den Tod f~en** meet one's death; **wie f~est du das?** what do you think of that? **es wird sich f~en** it'll turn up; (*fig*) it'll be all right ● *vi* (*haben*) find one's way. **F~er** *m* **-s,-** finder. **F~erlohn** *m* reward. **f~ig** *adj* resourceful
Finesse *f* **-,-n** (*Kniff*) trick; **F~n** (*Techn*) refinements
Finger *m* **-s,-** finger; **die F~ lassen von** 🅘 leave alone. **F~abdruck** *m* finger mark; (*Admin*) fingerprint. **F~hut** *m* thimble. **F~nagel** *m* fingernail. **F~spitze** *f* fingertip. **F~zeig** *m* **-[e]s,-e** hint
Fink *m* **-en,-en** finch
Finn|e *m* **-n,-n, F~in** *f* **-,-nen** Finn. **f~isch** *adj* Finnish. **F~land** *nt* **-s** Finland
finster *adj* dark; (*düster*) gloomy; (*unheildrohend*) sinister. **F~nis** *f* **-** darkness; (*Astronomy*) eclipse
Firm|a *f* **-,-men** firm, company
Firmen|wagen *m* company car. **F~zeichen** *nt* trade mark, logo
Firmung *f* **-,-en** (*Relig*) confirmation
Firnis *m* **-ses,-se** varnish. **f~sen** *vt* varnish
First *m* **-[e]s,-e** [roof] ridge
Fisch *m* **-[e]s,-e** fish; **F~e** (*Astrology*) Pisces. **F~dampfer** *m* trawler. **f~en** *vt/i* (*haben*) fish. **F~er** *m* **-s,-** fisherman. **F~erei** *f* **-** fishing. **F~händler** *m* fishmonger. **F~reiher** *m* heron
Fiskus *m* **- der F~** the Treasury
fit *adj* fit. **Fitness** *f* **-** fitness
fix *adj* 🅘 quick; (*geistig*) bright; **f~e Idee** obsession; **fix und fertig** all finished; (*bereit*) all ready; (🅘*: erschöpft*) shattered. **F~er** *m* **-s,-** ☒ junkie
fixieren *vt* stare at; (*Phot*) fix
Fjord *m* **-[e]s,-e** fiord
flach *adj* flat; (*eben*) level; (*niedrig*) low; (*nicht tief*) shallow
Flachbildschirm *m* flat screen
Fläche *f* **-,-n** area; (*Ober-*) surface; (*Seite*) face. **F~nmaß** *nt* square measure
Flachs *m* **-es** flax. **f~blond** *adj* flaxen-haired; (*Haar*) flaxen
flackern *vi* (*haben*) flicker
Flagge *f* **-,-n** flag
Flair /flɛ:ɐ̯/ *nt* **-s** air, aura
Flak *f* **-,-[s]** anti-aircraft artillery/(*Geschütz*) gun
flämisch *adj* Flemish
Flamme *f* **-,-n** flame;

(*Koch-*) burner
Flanell *m* **-s** (*Textiles*) flannel
Flank|e *f* **-,-n** flank. **f~ieren** *vt* flank
Flasche *f* **-,-n** bottle. **F~nbier** *nt* bottled beer. **F~nöffner** *m* bottle-opener. **F~npfand** *nt* deposit (*on bottle*)
flatter|haft *adj* fickle. **f~n** *vi* (*sein/haben*) flutter; (*Segel:*) flap
flau *adj* (*schwach*) faint; (*Comm*) slack
Flaum *m* **-[e]s** down. **f~ig** *adj* downy; **f~ig rühren** (*Aust Culin*) cream
flauschig *adj* fleecy; (*Spielzeug*) fluffy
Flausen *fpl* [!] silly ideas
Flaute *f* **-,-n** (*Naut*) calm; (*Comm*) slack period; (*Schwäche*) low
fläzen (sich) *vr* [!] sprawl
Flechte *f* **-,-n** (*Med*) eczema; (*Bot*) lichen; (*Zopf*) plait. **f~n†** *vt* plait; weave (*Korb*)
Fleck *m* **-[e]s,-e[n]** spot; (*größer*) patch; (*Schmutz-*) stain, mark; **blauer F~** bruise. **f~en** *vi* (*haben*) stain. **f~enlos** *adj* spotless. **F~entferner** *m* **-s,-** stain remover. **f~ig** *adj* stained
Fledermaus *f* bat
Flegel *m* **-s,-** lout. **f~haft** *adj* loutish
flehen *vi* (*haben*) beg (**um** for)
Fleisch *nt* **-[e]s** flesh; (*Culin*) meat; (*Frucht-*) pulp; **F~ fressend** carnivorous. **F~er** *m* **-s,-** butcher. **F~fresser** *m* **-s,-** carnivore. **f~ig** *adj* fleshy. **f~lich** *adj* carnal. **F~wolf** *m* mincer
Fleiß *m* **-es** diligence; **mit F~** diligently; (*absichtlich*) on purpose. **f~ig** *adj* diligent; (*arbeitsam*) industrious
fletschen *vt* **die Zähne f~** (*Tier:*) bare its teeth
flex|ibel *adj* flexible; (*Einband*) limp. **F~ibilität** *f* **-** flexibility
flicken *vt* mend; (*mit Flicken*) patch. **F~** *m* **-s,-** patch
Flieder *m* **-s** lilac
Fliege *f* **-,-n** fly; (*Schleife*) bow-tie. **f~n†** *vi* (*sein*) fly; (*geworfen werden*) be thrown; ([!]: *fallen*) fall; ([!]: *entlassen werden*) be fired/(*von der Schule*) expelled; **in die Luft f~n** blow up ● *vt* fly. **f~nd** *adj* flying. **F~r** *m* **-s,-** airman; (*Pilot*); pilot; ([!]: *Flugzeug*) plane. **F~rangriff** *m* air raid
flieh|en† *vi* (*sein*) flee (**vor** + *dat* from); (*entweichen*) escape ● *vt* shun. **f~end** *adj* fleeing; (*Kinn, Stirn*) receding
Fliese *f* **-,-n** tile
Fließ|band *nt* assembly line. **f~en†** *vi* (*sein*) flow; (*aus Wasserhahn*) run. **f~end** *adj* flowing; (*Wasser*) running; (*Verkehr*) moving; (*geläufig*) fluent
flimmern *vi* (*haben*) shimmer; (*TV*) flicker
flink *adj* nimble; (*schnell*) quick
Flinte *f* **-,-n** shotgun
Flirt /flœɐ̯t/ *m* **-s,-s** flirtation. **f~en** *vi* (*haben*) flirt
Flitter *m* **-s** sequins *pl*. **F~wochen** *fpl* honeymoon *sg*
flitzen *vi* (*sein*) [!] dash
Flock|e *f* **-,-n** flake; (*Wolle*) tuft. **f~ig** *adj* fluffy
Floh *m* **-[e]s,⸚e** flea. **F~spiel** *nt* tiddly-winks *sg*
Flora *f* **-** flora
Florett *nt* **-[e]s,-e** foil
florieren *vi* (*haben*) flourish
Floskel *f* **-,-n** [empty] phrase
Floß *nt* **-es,⸚e** raft
Flosse *f* **-,-n** fin; (*Seehund-, Gum-*

mi-) flipper; (*sl: Hand*) paw

Flöt|e *f* **-,-n** flute; (*Block-*) recorder. **f~en** *vi* (*haben*) play the flute/recorder; (*⊡: pfeifen*) whistle ● *vt* play on the flute/recorder. **F~ist(in)** *m* **-en,-en** (*f* **-,-nen**) flautist

flott *adj* quick; (*lebhaft*) lively; (*schick*) smart

Flotte *f* **-,-n** fleet

flottmachen *vt sep* **wieder f~** (*Naut*) refloat; get going again (*Auto*); put back on its feet (*Unternehmen*)

Flöz *nt* **-es,-e** [coal] seam

Fluch *m* **-[e]s,¨e** curse. **f~en** *vi* (*haben*) curse, swear

Flucht *f* **-** flight; (*Entweichen*) escape; **die F~ ergreifen** take flight. **f~artig** *adj* hasty

flücht|en *vi* (*sein*) flee (**vor** + *dat* from); (*entweichen*) escape ● *vr* **sich f~en** take refuge. **f~ig** *adj* fugitive; (*kurz*) brief; (*Blick*) fleeting; (*Bekanntschaft*) passing; (*oberflächlich*) cursory; (*nicht sorgfältig*) careless. **f~ig kennen** know slightly. **F~igkeitsfehler** *m* slip. **F~ling** *m* **-s,-e** fugitive; (*Pol*) refugee

Fluchwort *nt* (*pl* **-wörter**) swear word

Flug *m* **-[e]s,¨e** flight. **F~abwehr** *f* anti-aircraft defence

Flügel *m* **-s,-** wing; (*Fenster-*) casement; (*Mus*) grand piano

Fluggast *m* [air] passenger

flügge *adj* fully-fledged

Flug|gesellschaft *f* airline. **F~hafen** *m* airport. **F~lotse** *m* air-traffic controller. **F~platz** *m* airport; (*klein*) airfield. **F~preis** *m* air fare. **F~schein** *m* air ticket. **F~schneise** *f* flight path. **F~schreiber** *m* **-s,-** flight recorder. **F~schrift** *f* pamphlet. **F~steig** *m* **-[e]s,-e** gate. **F~zeug** *nt* **-[e]s,-e** aircraft, plane

Flunder *f* **-,-n** flounder

flunkern *vi* (*haben*) ⊡ tell fibs

Flur *m* **-[e]s,-e** [entrance] hall; (*Gang*) corridor

Fluss *m* **-es,¨e** river; (*Fließen*) flow; **im F~** (*fig*) in a state of flux. **f~abwärts** *adv* downstream. **f~aufwärts** *adv* upstream

flüssig *adj* liquid; (*Lava*) molten; (*fließend*) fluent; (*Verkehr*) freely moving. **F~keit** *f* **-,-en** liquid; (*Anat*) fluid

Flusspferd *nt* hippopotamus

flüstern *vt/i* (*haben*) whisper

Flut *f* **-,-en** high tide; (*fig*) flood

Föderation /-ˈtsi̯oːn/ *f* **-,-en** federation

Fohlen *nt* **-s,-** foal

Föhn *m* **-s** föhn [wind]; (*Haartrockner*) hairdrier. **f~en** *vt* [blow-]dry

Folg|e *f* **-,-n** consequence; (*Reihe*) succession; (*Fortsetzung*) instalment; (*Teil*) part. **f~en** *vi* (*sein*) follow (**jdm/etw** s.o./sth); (*zuhören*) listen (*dat* to); **wie f~t** as follows ● (*haben*) (*gehorchen*) obey (**jdm** s.o.). **f~end** *adj* following; **F~endes** the following

folger|n *vt* conclude (**aus** from). **F~ung** *f* **-,-en** conclusion

folg|lich *adv* consequently. **f~sam** *adj* obedient

Folie /ˈfoːli̯ə/ *f* **-,-n** foil; (*Plastik-*) film

Folklore *f* **-** folklore

Folter *f* **-,-n** torture. **f~n** *vt* torture

Fön ® *m* **-s,-e** hairdrier

Fonds /fõː/ *m* **-,-** fund

fönen* *vt* = **föhnen**

Förder|band *nt* (*pl* **-bänder**) conveyor belt. **f~lich** *adj* beneficial

fordern *vt* demand; (*beanspruchen*) claim; (*zum Kampf*) challenge

fördern *vt* promote; (*unterstützen*) encourage; (*finanziell*) sponsor; (*gewinnen*) extract

Forderung *f* **-,-en** demand; (*Anspruch*) claim

Förderung *f* **-** promotion; encouragement; (*Techn*) production

Forelle *f* **-,-n** trout

Form *f* **-,-en** form; (*Gestalt*) shape; (*Culin, Techn*) mould; (*Back-*) tin; **[gut] in F~** in good form

Formalität *f* **-,-en** formality

Format *nt* **-[e]s,-e** format; (*Größe*) size; (*fig: Bedeutung*) stature

formatieren *vt* format

Formel *f* **-,-n** formula

formen *vt* shape, mould; (*bilden*) form; **sich f~** take shape

förmlich *adj* formal

form|los *adj* shapeless; (*zwanglos*) informal. **F~sache** *f* formality

Formular *nt* **-s,-e** [printed] form

formulier|en *vt* formulate, word. **F~ung** *f* **-,-en** wording

forsch|en *vi* (*haben*) search (**nach** for). **f~end** *adj* searching. **F~er** *m* **-s,-** research scientist; (*Reisender*) explorer. **F~ung** *f* **-,-en** research

Forst *m* **-[e]s,-e** forest

Förster *m* **-s,-** forester

Forstwirtschaft *f* forestry

Fort *nt* **-s,-s** (*Mil*) fort

fort *adv* away; **f~ sein** be away; (*gegangen/verschwunden*) have gone; **und so f~** and so on; **in einem f~** continuously. **F~bewegung** *f* locomotion. **F~bildung** *f* further education/training. **f~bleiben**† *vi sep* (*sein*) stay away. **f~bringen**† *vt sep* take away. **f~fahren**† *vi sep* (*sein*) go away ● (*haben/sein*) continue (**zu** to). **f~fallen**† *vi sep* (*sein*) be dropped/(*ausgelassen*) omitted; (*entfallen*) no longer apply; (*aufhören*) cease. **f~führen** *vt sep* continue. **f~gehen**† *vi sep* (*sein*) leave, go away; (*ausgehen*) go out; (*andauern*) go on. **f~geschritten** *adj* advanced; (*spät*) late. **F~geschrittene(r)** *m/f* advanced student. **f~lassen**† *vt sep* let go; (*auslassen*) omit. **f~laufen**† *vi sep* (*sein*) run away; (*sich f~setzen*) continue. **f~laufend** *adj* consecutive. **f~pflanzen (sich)** *vr sep* reproduce; (*Ton, Licht:*) travel. **F~pflanzung** *f* **-** reproduction. **F~pflanzungsorgan** *nt* reproductive organ. **f~schicken** *vt sep* send away; (*abschicken*) send off. **f~schreiten**† *vi sep* (*sein*) continue; (*Fortschritte machen*) progress, advance. **f~schreitend** *adj* progressive; (*Alter*) advancing. **F~schritt** *m* progress; **F~schritte machen** make progress. **f~schrittlich** *adj* progressive. **f~setzen** *vt sep* continue; **sich f~setzen** continue. **F~setzung** *f* **-,-en** continuation; (*Folge*) instalment; **F~setzung folgt** to be continued. **F~setzungsroman** *m* serialized novel, serial. **f~während** *adj* constant. **f~ziehen**† *v sep* ● *vt* pull away ● *vi* (*sein*) move away

Fossil *nt* **-s,-ien** fossil

Foto *nt* **-s,-s** photo. **F~apparat** *m* camera. **f~gen** *adj* photogenic

Fotograf|(in) *m* **-en,-en** (*f* **-,-nen**) photographer. **F~ie** *f* **-,-n** photography; (*Bild*) photograph. **f~ieren** *vt* take a photo[graph] of ● *vi* (*haben*) take photographs. **f~isch** *adj* photographic

Fotohandy *nt* camera phone

Fotokopie *f* photocopy. **f~ren** *vt* photocopy. **F~rgerät** *nt* photocopier

Föt|us *m* **-,-ten** foetus

Foul /faul/ *nt* **-s,-s** (*Sport*) foul.

f~en *vt* foul

Fracht *f* -,-en freight. **F~er** *m* -s,- freighter. **F~gut** *nt* freight. **F~schiff** *nt* cargo boat

Frack *m* -[e]s,⸚e & -s tailcoat

Frage *f* -,-n question; **nicht in F~ kommen** *s.* **infrage. F~bogen** *m* questionnaire. **f~n** *vt* (*haben*) ask; **sich f~n** wonder (**ob** whether). **f~nd** *adj* questioning. **F~zeichen** *nt* question mark

f

frag|lich *adj* doubtful; (*Person, Sache*) in question. **f~los** *adv* undoubtedly

Fragment *nt* -[e]s,-e fragment

fragwürdig *adj* questionable; (*verdächtig*) dubious

Fraktion /-ˈtsi̯o:n/ *f* -,-en parliamentary party

Franken[1] *m* -s,- (*Swiss*) franc

Franken[2] *nt* -s Franconia

frankieren *vt* stamp, frank

Frankreich *nt* -s France

Fransen *fpl* fringe *sg*

Franz|ose *m* -n,-n Frenchman; **die F~osen** the French *pl*. **F~ösin** *f* -,-nen Frenchwoman. **f~ösisch** *adj* French. **F~ösisch** *nt* -[s] (*Lang*) French

Fraß *m* -es feed; (*pej: Essen*) muck

Fratze *f* -,-n grotesque face; (*Grimasse*) grimace

Frau *f* -,-en woman; (*Ehe-*) wife; **F~ Thomas** Mrs Thomas; **Unsere Liebe F~** (*Relig*) Our Lady

Frauen|arzt *m*, **F~ärztin** *f* gynaecologist. **F~rechtlerin** *f* -,-nen feminist

Fräulein *nt* -s,- single woman; (*jung*) young lady; (*Anrede*) Miss

frech *adj* cheeky; (*unverschämt*) impudent. **F~heit** *f* -,-en cheekiness; impudence; (*Äußerung*) impertinence

frei *adj* free; (*freischaffend*) freelance; (*Künstler*) independent; (*nicht besetzt*) vacant; (*offen*) open; (*bloß*) bare; **f~er Tag** day off; **sich** (*dat*) **f~ nehmen** take time off; **f~ machen** (*räumen*) clear; vacate (*Platz*); (*befreien*) liberate; **f~ lassen** leave free; **ist dieser Platz f~?** is this seat taken? **'Zimmer f~'** 'vacancies' ●*adv* freely; (*ohne Notizen*) without notes; (*umsonst*) free

Frei|bad *nt* open-air swimming pool. **f~beruflich** *adj & adv* freelance. **F~e** *nt* **im F~en** in the open air, out of doors. **F~gabe** *f* release. **f~geben**† *v sep* ●*vt* release; (*eröffnen*) open; **jdm einen Tag f~geben** give s.o. a day off ●*vi* (*haben*) **jdm f~geben** give s.o. time off. **f~gebig** *adj* generous. **F~gebigkeit** *f* - generosity. **f~haben**† *v sep* ●*vt* **eine Stunde f~haben** have an hour off; (*Sch*) have a free period ●*vi* (*haben*) be off work/(*Sch*) school; (*beurlaubt sein*) have time off. **f~händig** *adv* without holding on

Freiheit *f* -,-en freedom, liberty. **F~sstrafe** *f* prison sentence

Frei|herr *m* baron. **F~körperkultur** *f* naturism. **F~lassung** *f* - release. **F~lauf** *m* free-wheel. **f~legen** *vt sep* expose. **f~lich** *adv* admittedly; (*natürlich*) of course. **F~lichttheater** *nt* open-air theatre. **f~machen** *vt sep* (*frankieren*) frank; (*entkleiden*) bare; **einen Tag f~machen** take a day off. **F~maurer** *m* Freemason. **f~schaffend** *adj* freelance. **f~schwimmen**† **(sich)** *v sep* pass one's swimming test. **f~sprechen**† *vt sep* acquit. **F~spruch** *m* acquittal. **f~stehen**† *vi sep* (*haben*) stand empty; **es steht ihm f~** (*fig*) he is free (**zu** to). **f~stellen** *vt sep* exempt (**von** from); **jdm etw f~stellen** leave sth up to s.o. **F~stil** *m* freestyle. **F~stoß** *m* free kick

Freitag *m* Friday. **f~s** *adv* on Fridays

Frei|tod *m* suicide. **F~umschlag** *m* stamped envelope. **f~weg** *adv* freely; (*offen*) openly. **f~willig** *adj* voluntary. **F~willige(r)** *m/f* volunteer. **F~zeichen** *nt* ringing tone; (*Rufzeichen*) dialling tone. **F~zeit** *f* free *or* spare time; (*Muße*) leisure. **F~zeit-** *prefix* leisure; **F~zeitbekleidung** *f* casual wear. **f~zügig** *adj* unrestricted; (*großzügig*) liberal

fremd *adj* foreign; (*unbekannt*) strange; (*nicht das eigene*) other people's; **ein f~er Mann** a stranger; **f~e Leute** strangers; **unter f~em Namen** under an assumed name; **ich bin hier f~** I'm a stranger here. **F~e** *f* - **in der F~e** away from home; (*im Ausland*) in a foreign country. **F~e(r)** *m/f* stranger; (*Ausländer*) foreigner; (*Tourist*) tourist. **F~enführer** *m* [tourist] guide. **F~enverkehr** *m* tourism. **F~enzimmer** *nt* room [to let]; (*Gäste-*) guest room. **f~gehen**† *vi sep* (*sein*) [!] be unfaithful. **F~sprache** *f* foreign language. **F~wort** *nt* (*pl* **-wörter**) foreign word

Freske *f* **-,-n, Fresko** *nt* **-s,-ken** fresco

Fresse *f* **-,-n** [x] (*Mund*) gob; (*Gesicht*) mug. **f~n**† *vt/i* (*haben*) eat. **F~n** *nt* **-s** feed; (*sl: Essen*) grub

Fressnapf *m* feeding bowl

Freud|e *f* **-,-n** pleasure; (*innere*) joy; **mit F~en** with pleasure; **jdm eine F~e machen** please s.o. **f~ig** *adj* joyful

freuen *vt* please; **sich f~** be pleased (**über** + *acc* about); **sich f~ auf** (+ *acc*) look forward to; **es freut mich** I'm glad (**dass** that)

Freund *m* **-es,-e** friend; (*Verehrer*) boyfriend. **F~in** *f* **-,-nen** friend; (*Liebste*) girlfriend. **f~lich** *adj* kind; (*umgänglich*) friendly; (*angenehm*) pleasant. **f~licherweise** *adv* kindly. **F~lichkeit** *f* **-,-en** kindness; friendliness; pleasantness

Freundschaft *f* **-,-en** friendship; **F~ schließen** become friends. **f~lich** *adj* friendly

Frieden *m* **-s** peace; **F~ schließen** make peace; **im F~** in peacetime; **lass mich in F~!** leave me alone! **F~svertrag** *m* peace treaty

Fried|hof *m* cemetery. **f~lich** *adj* peaceful

frieren† *vi* (*haben*) (*Person:*) be cold; *impers* **es friert/hat gefroren** it is freezing/there has been a frost; **frierst du?** are you cold? ● (*sein*) (*gefrieren*) freeze

Fries *m* **-es,-e** frieze

frisch *adj* fresh; (*sauber*) clean; (*leuchtend*) bright; (*munter*) lively; (*rüstig*) fit; **sich f~ machen** freshen up ● *adv* freshly, newly; **ein Bett f~ beziehen** put clean sheets on a bed; **f~ gestrichen!** wet paint! **F~e** *f* - freshness; brightness; liveliness; fitness. **F~haltepackung** *f* vacuum pack

Fri|seur /friˈzøːɐ̯/ *m* **-s,-e** hairdresser; (*Herren-*) barber. **F~seursalon** *m* hairdressing salon. **F~seuse** *f* **-,-n** hairdresser

frisier|en *vt* **jdn/sich f~en** do someone's/one's hair; **die Bilanz/einen Motor f~en** [!] fiddle the accounts/soup up an engine

Frisör *m* **-s,-e** = **Friseur**

Frist *f* **-,-en** period; (*Termin*) deadline; (*Aufschub*) time; **drei Tage F~** three days' grace. **f~los** *adj* instant

Frisur *f* **-,-en** hairstyle

frittieren *vt* deep-fry

frivol /friˈvoːl/ *adj* frivolous

froh *adj* happy; (*freudig*) joyful; (*erleichtert*) glad

fröhlich *adj* cheerful; (*vergnügt*) merry. **F~keit** *f* - cheerfulness; merriment

fromm *adj* devout; (*gutartig*) docile

Frömmigkeit *f* - devoutness

Fronleichnam *m* Corpus Christi

f

Front *f* **-,-en** front. **f~al** *adj* frontal; (*Zusammenstoß*) head-on ● *adv* from the front; (*zusammenstoßen*) head-on. **F~alzusammenstoß** *m* head-on collision

Frosch *m* **-[e]s,¨e** frog. **F~laich** *m* frog-spawn. **F~mann** *m* (*pl* **-männer**) frogman

Frost *m* **-[e]s,¨e** frost. **F~beule** *f* chilblain

frösteln *vi* (*haben*) shiver

frost|ig *adj* frosty. **F~schutzmittel** *nt* antifreeze

Frottee *nt & m* **-s** towelling; **F~[hand]tuch** *nt* terry towel

frottieren *vt* rub down

Frucht *f* **-,¨e** fruit; **F~ tragen** bear fruit. **f~bar** *adj* fertile; (*fig*) fruitful. **F~barkeit** *f* - fertility

früh *adj* early ● *adv* early; (*morgens*) in the morning; **heute f~** this morning; **von f~ an** *od* **auf** from an early age. **F~aufsteher** *m* **-s,-** early riser. **F~e** *f* - **in aller F~e** bright and early; **in der F~e** (*SGer*) in the morning. **f~er** *adv* earlier; (*eher*) sooner; (*ehemals*) formerly; (*vor langer Zeit*) in the old days; **f~er oder später** sooner or later; **ich wohnte f~er in X** I used to live in X. **f~ere(r,s)** *adj* earlier; (*ehemalig*) former; (*vorige*) previous; **in f~eren Zeiten** in former times. **f~estens** *adv* at the earliest. **F~geburt** *f* premature birth/(*Kind*) baby. **F~jahr** *nt* spring. **F~ling** *m* **-s,-e** spring. **f~morgens** *adv* early in the morning. **f~reif** *adj* precocious

Frühstück *nt* breakfast. **f~en** *vi* (*haben*) have breakfast

frühzeitig *adj & adv* early; (*vorzeitig*) premature

Frustr|ation /-ˈtsi̯oːn/ *f* **-,-en** frustration. **f~ieren** *vt* frustrate

Fuchs *m* **-es,¨e** fox; (*Pferd*) chestnut. **f~en** *vt* [!] annoy

Füchsin *f* **-,-nen** vixen

Fuge[1] *f* **-,-n** joint

Fuge[2] *f* **-,-n** (*Mus*) fugue

füg|en *vt* fit (**in** + *acc* into); (*an-*) join (**an** + *acc* on to); (*dazu-*) add (**zu** to); **sich f~en** fit (**in** + *acc* into); adjoin/(*folgen*) follow (**an etw** *acc* sth); (*fig: gehorchen*) submit (*dat* to). **f~sam** *adj* obedient. **F~ung** *f* **-,-en eine F~ung des Schicksals** a stroke of fate

fühl|bar *adj* noticeable. **f~en** *vt/i* (*haben*) feel; **sich f~en** feel (**krank/einsam** ill/lonely); ([!]: *stolz sein*) fancy oneself. **F~er** *m* **-s,-** feeler. **F~ung** *f* - contact

Fuhre *f* **-,-n** load

führ|en *vt* lead; guide (*Tourist*); (*geleiten*) take; (*leiten*) run; (*befehligen*) command; (*verkaufen*) stock; bear (*Namen*); keep (*Liste, Bücher*); **bei** *od* **mit sich f~en** carry ● *vi* (*haben*) lead; (*verlaufen*) go, run; **zu etw f~en** lead to sth. **f~end** *adj* leading. **F~er** *m* **-s,-** leader; (*Fremden-*) guide; (*Buch*) guide[book]. **F~erhaus** *nt* driver's cab. **F~erschein** *m* driving licence; **den F~erschein machen** take one's driving test. **F~erscheinentzug** *m* disqualification from driving. **F~ung** *f* **-,-en** leadership; (*Leitung*) management; (*Mil*) command; (*Betragen*) conduct; (*Besichtigung*) guided tour; (*Vorsprung*) lead; **in F~ung gehen** go into the lead

Fuhr|unternehmer *m* haulage contractor. **F~werk** *nt* cart
Fülle *f* **-,-n** abundance, wealth (**an** + *dat* of); (*Körper-*) plumpness. **f~n** *vt* fill; (*Culin*) stuff
Füllen *nt* **-s,-** foal
Füll|er *m* **-s,-** [!], **F~federhalter** *m* fountain pen. **F~ung** *f* **-,-en** filling; (*Braten-*) stuffing
fummeln *vi* (*haben*) fumble (**an** + *dat* with)
Fund *m* **-[e]s,-e** find
Fundament *nt* **-[e]s,-e** foundations *pl*. **f~al** *adj* fundamental
Fundbüro *nt* lost-property office
fünf *inv adj*, **F~** *f* **-,-en** five; (*Sch*) ≈ fail mark. **F~linge** *mpl* quintuplets. **f~te(r,s)** *adj* fifth. **f~zehn** *inv adj* fifteen. **f~zehnte(r,s)** *adj* fifteenth. **f~zig** *inv adj* fifty. **f~zigste(r,s)** *adj* fiftieth
fungieren *vi* (*haben*) act (**als** as)
Funk *m* **-s** radio. **F~e** *m* **-n,-n** spark. **f~eln** *vi* (*haben*) sparkle; (*Stern:*) twinkle. **F~en** *m* **-s,-** spark. **f~en** *vt* radio. **F~sprechgerät** *nt* walkie-talkie. **F~spruch** *m* radio message. **F~streife** *f* [police] radio patrol
Funktion /-'tsio:n/ *f* **-,-en** function; (*Stellung*) position; (*Funktionieren*) working; **außer F~** out of action. **F~är** *m* **-s,-e** official. **f~ieren** *vi* (*haben*) work
für *prep* (+ *acc*) for; **Schritt für Schritt** step by step; **was für [ein]** what [a]! (*fragend*) what sort of [a]? **Für** *nt* **das Für und Wider** the pros and cons *pl*
Furche *f* **-,-n** furrow
Furcht *f* **-** fear (**vor** + *dat* of); **F~erregend** terrifying. **f~bar** *adj* terrible
fürcht|en *vt/i* (*haben*) fear; **sich f~en** be afraid (**vor** + *dat* of). **f~erlich** *adj* dreadful
füreinander *adv* for each other
Furnier *nt* **-s,-e** veneer. **f~t** *adj* veneered
Fürsorg|e *f* care; (*Admin*) welfare; ([!]: *Geld*) ≈ social security. **F~er(in)** *m* **-s,-** (*f* **-,-nen**) social worker. **f~lich** *adj* solicitous
Fürst *m* **-en,-en** prince. **F~entum** *nt* **-s,¨-er** principality. **F~in** *f* **-,-nen** princess
Furt *f* **-,-en** ford
Furunkel *m* **-s,-** (*Med*) boil
Fürwort *nt* (*pl* **-wörter**) pronoun
Furz *m* **-es,-e** (*vulgar*) fart
Fusion *f* **-,-en** fusion; (*Comm*) merger
Fuß *m* **-es,¨-e** foot; (*Aust: Bein*) leg; (*Lampen-*) base; (*von Weinglas*) stem; **zu Fuß** on foot; **zu Fuß gehen** walk; **auf freiem Fuß** free. **F~abdruck** *m* footprint. **F~abtreter** *m* **-s,-** doormat. **F~ball** *m* football. **F~ballspieler** *m* footballer. **F~balltoto** *nt* football pools *pl*. **F~bank** *f* footstool. **F~boden** *m* floor
Fussel *f* **-,-n** & *m* **-s,-[n]** piece of fluff; F~n fluff *sg*. **f~n** *vi* (*haben*) shed fluff
fußen *vi* (*haben*) be based (**auf** + *dat* on)
Fußgänger|(in) *m* **-s,-** (*f* **-,-nen**) pedestrian. **F~brücke** *f* footbridge. **F~zone** *f* pedestrian precinct
Fuß|geher *m* **-s,-** (*Aust*) = **F~gänger. F~gelenk** *nt* ankle. **F~hebel** *m* pedal. **F~nagel** *m* toenail. **F~note** *f* footnote. **F~pflege** *f* chiropody. **F~rücken** *m* instep. **F~sohle** *f* sole of the foot. **F~tritt** *m* kick. **F~weg** *m* footpath; **eine Stunde F~weg** an hour's walk
futsch *pred adj* [!] gone
Futter[1] *nt* **-s** feed; (*Trocken-*)

fodder
Futter² *nt* **-s,-** (*Kleider-*) lining
Futteral *nt* **-s,-e** case
füttern¹ *vt* feed
füttern² *vt* line
Futur *nt* **-s** (*Gram*) future

Gg

Gabe *f* **-,-n** gift; (*Dosis*) dose
Gabel *f* **-,-n** fork. **g~n (sich)** *vr* fork. **G~stapler** *m* **-s,-** fork-lift truck. **G~ung** *f* **-,-en** fork
gackern *vi* (*haben*) cackle
gaffen *vi* (*haben*) gape, stare
Gage /'ga:ʒə/ *f* **-,-n** (*Theat*) fee
gähnen *vi* (*haben*) yawn
Gala *f* **-** ceremonial dress
Galavorstellung *f* gala performance
Galerie *f* **-,-n** gallery
Galgen *m* **-s,-** gallows *sg*. **G~frist** *f* [F] reprieve
Galionsfigur *f* figurehead
Galle *f* **-** bile; (*G~nblase*) gall-bladder. **G~nblase** *f* gall-bladder. **G~nstein** *m* gallstone
Galopp *m* **-s** gallop; **im G~** at a gallop. **g~ieren** *vi* (*sein*) gallop
gamm|eln *vi* (*haben*) [F] loaf around. **G~ler(in)** *m* **-s,-** (*f* **-,-nen**) drop-out
Gams *f* **-,-en** (*Aust*) chamois
Gämse *f* **-,-n** chamois
Gang *m* **-[e]s,⁼e** walk; (*G~art*) gait; (*Boten-*) errand; (*Funktionieren*) running; (*Verlauf, Culin*) course; (*Durch-*) passage; (*Korridor*) corridor; (*zwischen Sitzreihen*) aisle, gangway; (*Anat*) duct; (*Auto*) gear; **in G~ bringen** get going; **im G~e sein** be in progress; **Essen mit vier G⁼en** four-course meal
gängig *adj* common; (*Comm*) popular
Gangschaltung *f* gear change
Gangster /'gɛŋstɐ/ *m* **-s,-** gangster
Ganove *m* **-n,-n** [F] crook
Gans *f* **-,⁼e** goose
Gänse|blümchen *nt* **-s,-** daisy. **G~füßchen** *ntpl* inverted commas. **G~haut** *f* goose-pimples *pl*. **G~rich** *m* **-s,-e** gander
ganz *adj* whole, entire; (*vollständig*) complete; ([F]: *heil*) undamaged, intact; **die g~e Zeit** all the time, the whole time; **eine g~e Weile/Menge** quite a while/lot; *inv* **g~ Deutschland** the whole of Germany; **wieder g~ machen** [F] mend; **im Großen und G~en** on the whole ● *adv* quite; (*völlig*) completely, entirely; (*sehr*) very; **nicht g~** not quite; **g~ allein** all on one's own; **g~ und gar** completely, totally; **g~ und gar nicht** not at all. **G~e(s)** *nt* whole. **g~jährig** *adv* all the year round. **g~tägig** *adj & adv* full-time; (*geöffnet*) all day. **g~tags** *adv* all day; (*arbeiten*) full-time
gar¹ *adj* done, cooked
gar² *adv* **gar nicht/nichts/niemand** not/nothing/no one at all
Garage /ga'ra:ʒə/ *f* **-,-n** garage
Garantie *f* **-,-n** guarantee. **g~ren** *vt/i* (*haben*) **[für] etw g~ren** guarantee sth. **G~schein** *m* guarantee
Garderobe *f* **-,-n** (*Kleider*) wardrobe; (*Ablage*) cloakroom; (*Künstler-*) dressing-room. **G~nfrau** *f* cloakroom attendant
Gardine *f* **-,-n** curtain

garen *vt/i* (*haben*) cook
gären† *vi* (*haben*) ferment; (*fig*) seethe
Garn *nt* **-[e]s,-e** yarn; (*Näh-*) cotton
Garnele *f* **-,-n** shrimp; prawn
garnieren *vt* decorate; (*Culin*) garnish
Garnison *f* **-,-en** garrison
Garnitur *f* **-,-en** set; (*Möbel-*) suite
Garten *m* **-s,⸚** garden. **G~arbeit** *f* gardening. **G~bau** *m* horticulture. **G~haus** *nt*, **G~laube** *f* summerhouse. **G~schere** *f* secateurs *pl*
Gärtner|(in) *m* **-s,-** (*f* **-,-nen**) gardener. **G~ei** *f* **-,-en** nursery
Gärung *f* **-** fermentation
Gas *nt* **-es,-e** gas; **Gas geben** 🅸 accelerate. **G~maske** *f* gas mask. **G~pedal** *nt* (*Auto*) accelerator
Gasse *f* **-,-n** alley; (*Aust*) street
Gast *m* **-[e]s,⸚e** guest; (*Hotel-*) visitor; (*im Lokal*) patron; **zum Mittag G⸚e haben** have people to lunch; **bei jdm zu G~ sein** be staying with s.o. **G~arbeiter** *m* foreign worker. **G~bett** *nt* spare bed
Gäste|bett *nt* spare bed. **G~buch** *nt* visitors' book. **G~zimmer** *nt* [hotel] room; (*privat*) spare room
gast|freundlich *adj* hospitable. **G~freundschaft** *f* hospitality. **G~geber** *m* **-s,-** host. **G~geberin** *f* **-,-nen** hostess. **G~haus** *nt*, **G~hof** *m* inn, hotel
gastlich *adj* hospitable
Gastronomie *f* **-** gastronomy
Gast|spiel *nt* guest performance. **G~spielreise** *f* (*Theat*) tour. **G~stätte** *f* restaurant. **G~wirt** *m* landlord. **G~wirtin** *f* landlady. **G~wirtschaft** *f* restaurant
Gas|werk *nt* gasworks *sg*. **G~zähler** *m* gas meter

Gatte *m* **-n,-n** husband
Gattin *f* **-,-nen** wife
Gattung *f* **-,-en** kind; (*Biology*) genus; (*Kunst*) genre
Gaudi *f* **-** (*Aust*, 🅸) fun
Gaumen *m* **-s,-** palate
Gauner *m* **-s,-** crook, swindler. **G~ei** *f* **-,-en** swindle
Gaze /ˈgaːzə/ *f* **-** gauze
Gazelle *f* **-,-n** gazelle
Gebäck *nt* **-s** [cakes and] pastries *pl*; (*Kekse*) biscuits *pl*
Gebälk *nt* **-s** timbers *pl*
geballt *adj* (*Faust*) clenched
Gebärde *f* **-,-n** gesture
gebär|en† *vt* give birth to, bear; **geboren werden** be born. **G~mutter** *f* womb, uterus
Gebäude *nt* **-s,-** building
Gebeine *ntpl* [mortal] remains
Gebell *nt* **-s** barking
geben† *vt* give; (*tun, bringen*) put; (*Karten*) deal; (*aufführen*) perform; (*unterrichten*) teach; **etw verloren g~** give sth up as lost; **viel/wenig g~ auf** (+ *acc*) set great/little store by; **sich g~** (*nachlassen*) wear off; (*besser werden*) get better; (*sich verhalten*) behave ● *impers* **es gibt** there is/are; **was gibt es Neues/zum Mittag/im Kino?** what's the news/for lunch/on at the cinema? **es wird Regen g~** it's going to rain ● *vi* (*haben*) (*Karten*) deal
Gebet *nt* **-[e]s,-e** prayer
Gebiet *nt* **-[e]s,-e** area; (*Hoheits-*) territory; (*Sach-*) field
gebieten† *vt* command; (*erfordern*) demand ● *vi* (*haben*) rule
Gebilde *nt* **-s,-** structure
gebildet *adj* educated; (*kultiviert*) cultured
Gebirg|e *nt* **-s,-** mountains *pl*. **g~ig** *adj* mountainous

g

Gebiss *nt* **-es,-e** teeth *pl*; (*künstliches*) false teeth *pl*; dentures *pl*, (*des Zaumes*) bit

geblümt *adj* floral, flowered

gebogen *adj* curved

geboren *adj* born; **g~er Deutscher** German by birth; **Frau X, g~e Y** Mrs X, née Y

Gebot *nt* **-[e]s,-e** rule

gebraten *adj* fried

Gebrauch *m* use; (*Sprach-*) usage; Gebräuche customs; **in G~** in use; **G~ machen von** make use of. **g~en** *vt* use; **zu nichts zu g~en** useless

gebräuchlich *adj* common; (*Wort*) in common use

Gebrauch|sanleitung, G~sanweisung *f* directions *pl* for use. **g~t** *adj* used; (*Comm*) secondhand. **G~twagen** *m* used car

gebrechlich *adj* frail, infirm

gebrochen *adj* broken ● *adv* **g~Englisch sprechen** speak broken English

Gebrüll *nt* **-s** roaring

Gebühr *f* **-,-en** charge, fee; **über G~** excessively. **g~end** *adj* due; (*geziemend*) proper. **g~enfrei** *adj* free ● *adv* free of charge. **g~enpflichtig** *adj & adv* subject to a charge; **g~enpflichtige Straße** toll road

Geburt *f* **-,-en** birth; **von G~** by birth. **G~enkontrolle, G~enregelung** *f* birth control. **G~enziffer** *f* birth rate

gebürtig *adj* native (**aus** of); **g~er Deutscher** German by birth

Geburts|datum *nt* date of birth. **G~helfer** *m* obstetrician. **G~hilfe** *f* obstetrics *sg*. **G~ort** *m* place of birth. **G~tag** *m* birthday. **G~urkunde** *f* birth certificate

Gebüsch *nt* **-[e]s,-e** bushes *pl*

Gedächtnis *nt* **-ses** memory; **aus dem G~** from memory

Gedanke *m* **-ns,-n** thought (**an** + *acc* of); (*Idee*) idea; **sich** (*dat*) **G~n machen** worry (**über** + *acc* about). **g~nlos** *adj* thoughtless; (*zerstreut*) absent-minded. **G~nstrich** *m* dash

Gedärme *ntpl* intestines; (*Tier-*) entrails

Gedeck *nt* **-[e]s,-e** place setting; (*auf Speisekarte*) set meal

gedeihen† *vi* (*sein*) thrive, flourish

gedenken† *vi* (*haben*) propose (**etw zu tun** to do sth); **jds g~** remember s.o. **G~** *nt* **-s** memory

Gedenk|feier *f* commemoration. **G~gottesdienst** *m* memorial service

Gedicht *nt* **-[e]s,-e** poem

Gedräng|e *nt* **-s** crush, crowd. **g~t** *adj* (*knapp*) concise ● *adv* **g~t voll** packed

Geduld *f* **-** patience; **G~ haben** be patient. **g~en (sich)** *vr* be patient. **g~ig** *adj* patient. **G~[s]spiel** *nt* puzzle

gedunsen *adj* bloated

geehrt *adj* honoured; **Sehr g~er Herr X** Dear Mr X

geeignet *adj* suitable; **im g~en Moment** at the right moment

Gefahr *f* **-,-en** danger; **in G~** in danger; **auf eigene G~** at one's own risk; **G~ laufen** run the risk (**etw zu tun** of doing sth)

gefähr|den *vt* endanger; (*fig*) jeopardize. **g~lich** *adj* dangerous

gefahrlos *adj* safe

Gefährt *nt* **-[e]s,-e** vehicle

Gefährte *m* **-n,-n, Gefährtin** *f* **-,-nen** companion

gefahrvoll *adj* dangerous, perilous

Gefälle *nt* **-s,-** slope;

(*Straßen-*) gradient

gefallen† *vi* (*haben*) **jdm g~** please s.o.; **er/es gefällt mir** I like him/it; **sich** (*dat*) **etw g~ lassen** put up with sth

Gefallen[1] *m* **-s,-** favour

Gefallen[2] *nt* **-s** pleasure (**an** + *dat* in); **dir zu G~** to please you

Gefallene(r) *m* soldier killed in the war

gefällig *adj* pleasing; (*hübsch*) attractive; (*hilfsbereit*) obliging; **noch etwas g~?** will there be anything else? **G~keit** *f* **-,-en** favour; (*Freundlichkeit*) kindness

Gefangen|e(r) *m/f* prisoner. **G~nahme** *f* **-** capture. **g~nehmen*** *vt sep* = **g~ nehmen**, *s.* **fangen. G~schaft** *f* **-** captivity

Gefängnis *nt* **-ses,-se** prison; (*Strafe*) imprisonment. **G~strafe** *f* imprisonment; (*Urteil*) prison sentence. **G~wärter** *m* [prison] warder

Gefäß *nt* **-es,-e** container; (*Blut-*) vessel

gefasst *adj* composed; (*ruhig*) calm; **g~ sein auf** (+ *acc*) be prepared for

gefedert *adj* sprung

gefeiert *adj* celebrated

Gefieder *nt* **-s** plumage

gefleckt *adj* spotted

Geflügel *nt* **-s** poultry. **G~klein** *nt* **-s** giblets *pl*. **g~t** *adj* winged

Geflüster *nt* **-s** whispering

Gefolge *nt* **-s** retinue, entourage

gefragt *adj* popular

Gefreite(r) *m* lance corporal

gefrier|en† *vi* (*sein*) freeze. **G~fach** *nt* freezer compartment. **G~punkt** *m* freezing point. **G~schrank** *m* upright freezer. **G~truhe** *f* chest freezer

gefroren *adj* frozen

gefügig *adj* compliant; (*gehorsam*) obedient

Gefühl *nt* **-[e]s,-e** feeling; (*Empfindung*) sensation; (*G~sregung*) emotion; **im G~ haben** know instinctively. **g~los** *adj* insensitive; (*herzlos*) unfeeling; (*taub*) numb. **g~smäßig** *adj* emotional; (*instinktiv*) instinctive. **G~sregung** *f* emotion. **g~voll** *adj* sensitive; (*sentimental*) sentimental

gefüllt *adj* filled; (*voll*) full

gefürchtet *adj* feared, dreaded

gefüttert *adj* lined

gegeben *adj* given; (*bestehend*) present; (*passend*) appropriate. **g~enfalls** *adv* if need be

gegen *prep* (+ *acc*) against; (*Sport*) versus; (*g~über*) to[-wards]; (*Vergleich*) compared with; (*Richtung, Zeit*) towards; (*ungefähr*) around; **ein Mittel g~** a remedy for ● *adv* **g~ 100 Leute** about 100 people. **G~angriff** *m* counter-attack

Gegend *f* **-,-en** area, region; (*Umgebung*) neighbourhood

gegeneinander *adv* against/(*gegenüber*) towards one another

Gegen|fahrbahn *f* opposite carriageway. **G~gift** *nt* antidote. **G~maßnahme** *f* countermeasure. **G~satz** *m* contrast; (*Widerspruch*) contradiction; (*G~teil*) opposite; **im G~satz zu** unlike. **g~seitig** *adj* mutual; **sich g~seitig hassen** hate one another. **G~stand** *m* object; (*Gram, Gesprächs-*) subject. **G~stück** *nt* counterpart; (*G~teil*) opposite. **G~teil** *nt* opposite, contrary; **im G~teil** on the contrary. **g~teilig** *adj* opposite

gegenüber *prep* (+ *dat*) opposite; (*Vergleich*) compared with; **jdm g~ höflich sein** be polite to s.o. ● *adv* opposite. **G~** *nt* **-s** person opposite.

g

g~liegend *adj* opposite. **g~stehen†** *vi sep (haben)* (+ *dat*) face; **feindlich g~stehen** (+ *dat*) be hostile to. **g~stellen** *vt sep* confront; (*vergleichen*) compare

Gegen|verkehr *m* oncoming traffic. **G~vorschlag** *m* counter-proposal. **G~wart** *f* - present; (*Anwesenheit*) presence. **g~wärtig** *adj* present ● *adv* at present. **G~wehr** *f* - resistance. **G~wert** *m* equivalent. **G~wind** *m* head wind. **g~zeichnen** *vt sep* countersign

g

geglückt *adj* successful

Gegner|(in) *m* **-s,-** (*f* **-,-nen**) opponent. **g~isch** *adj* opposing

Gehabe *nt* **-s** affected behaviour

Gehackte(s) *nt* mince

Gehalt *nt* **-[e]s,⸚er** salary. **G~serhöhung** *f* rise

gehässig *adj* spiteful

gehäuft *adj* heaped

Gehäuse *nt* **-s,-** case; (*TV, Radio*) cabinet; (*Schnecken-*) shell

Gehege *nt* **-s,-** enclosure

geheim *adj* secret; **g~ halten** keep secret; **im g~en** secretly. **G~dienst** *m* Secret Service. **G~nis** *nt* **-ses,-se** secret. **g~nisvoll** *adj* mysterious. **G~nummer** *f* PIN

gehemmt *adj* (*fig*) inhibited

gehen†

● *intransitive verb (sein)*

····➤ (*sich irgendwohin begeben*) go; (*zu Fuß*) walk. **tanzen/schwimmen/einkaufen gehen** go dancing/swimming/shopping. **schlafen gehen** go to bed. **zum Arzt gehen** go to the doctor's. **in die Schule gehen** go to school. **auf und ab gehen** walk up and down. **über die Straße gehen** cross the street

····➤ (*weggehen; fam: abfahren*) go; leave. **ich muss bald gehen** I must go soon. **Sie können gehen** you may go. **der Zug geht um zehn Uhr** 🅸 the train leaves *or* goes at ten o'clock

····➤ (*funktionieren*) work. **der Computer geht wieder/nicht mehr** the computer is working again/has stopped working. **meine Uhr geht falsch/richtig** my watch is wrong/right

····➤ (*möglich sein*) be possible. **ja, das geht** yes, I *or* we can manage that. **das geht nicht** that can't be done; (🅸: *ist nicht akzeptabel*) it's not good enough, it's not on 🅸. **es geht einfach nicht, dass du so spät nach Hause kommst** it simply won't do for you to come home so late

····➤ (🅸: *gerade noch angehen*) **es geht [so]** it is all right. **Wie war die Party? — Es ging so** How was the party? — Not bad *or* So-so

····➤ (*sich entwickeln*) do; go. **der Laden geht gut** the shop is doing well. **es geht alles nach Wunsch** everything is going to plan

····➤ (*impers*) **wie geht es Ihnen?** how are you? **jdm geht es gut/schlecht** (*gesundheitlich*) s.o. is doing well/badly

····➤ (*impers; sich um etw handeln*) **es geht um** it concerns. **worum geht es hier?** what is this all about? **es geht ihr nur ums Geld** she is only interested in money

Geheul *nt* **-s** howling

Gehilfe *m* **-n,-n, Gehilfin** *f* **-,-nen** trainee; (*Helfer*) assistant

Gehirn *nt* **-s** brain; (*Verstand*) brains *pl* **G~erschütterung** *f* concussion. **G~hautentzündung** *f* meningitis. **G~wäsche** *f* brainwashing

gehoben *adj* (*fig*) superior

Gehöft *nt* **-[e]s,-e** farm

Gehör *nt* **-s** hearing

gehorchen *vi* (*haben*) (+ *dat*) obey

gehören *vi* (*haben*) belong (*dat* to); **dazu gehört Mut** that takes courage; **es gehört sich nicht** it isn't done

gehörlos *adj* deaf

Gehörn *nt* **-s,-e** horns *pl*; (*Geweih*) antlers *pl*

gehorsam *adj* obedient. **G~** *m* **-s** obedience

Geh|steig *m* **-[e]s,-e** pavement. **G~weg** *m* = **Gehsteig**; (*Fußweg*) footpath

Geier *m* **-s,-** vulture

Geig|e *f* **-,-n** violin. **g~en** *vi* (*haben*) play the violin ● *vt* play on the violin. **G~er(in)** *m* **-s,-** (*f* **-,-nen**) violinist

geil *adj* lecherous; randy; (**!**: *toll*) great

Geisel *f* **-,-n** hostage

Geiß *f* **-,-en** (*SGer*) [nanny-]goat. **G~blatt** *nt* honeysuckle

Geist *m* **-[e]s,-er** mind; (*Witz*) wit; (*Gesinnung*) spirit; (*Gespenst*) ghost; **der Heilige G~** the Holy Ghost *or* Spirit

geistes|abwesend *adj* absent-minded. **G~blitz** *m* brainwave. **g~gegenwärtig** *adv* with great presence of mind. **g~gestört** *adj* [mentally] deranged. **g~krank** *adj* mentally ill. **G~krankheit** *f* mental illness. **G~wissenschaften** *fpl* arts. **G~zustand** *m* mental state

geist|ig *adj* mental; (*intellektuell*) intellectual. **g~lich** *adj* spiritual; (*religiös*) religious; (*Musik*) sacred; (*Tracht*) clerical. **G~liche(r)** *m* clergyman. **G~lichkeit** *f* **-** clergy. **g~reich** *adj* clever; (*witzig*) witty

Geiz *m* **-es** meanness. **g~en** *vi* (*haben*) be mean (**mit** with). **G~hals** *m* **!** miser. **g~ig** *adj* mean, miserly. **G~kragen** *m* **!** miser

Gekicher *nt* **-s** giggling

geknickt *adj* **!** dejected

gekonnt *adj* accomplished ● *adv* expertly

gekränkt *adj* offended, hurt

Gekritzel *nt* **-s** scribble

Gelächter *nt* **-s** laughter

geladen *adj* loaded

gelähmt *adj* paralysed

Geländer *nt* **-s,-** railings *pl*; (*Treppen-*) banisters

gelangen *vi* (*sein*) reach/(*fig*) attain (**zu etw/an etw** *acc* sth)

gelassen *adj* composed; (*ruhig*) calm. **G~heit** *f* **-** equanimity; (*Fassung*) composure

Gelatine /ʒela-/ *f* **-** gelatine

geläufig *adj* common, current; (*fließend*) fluent; **jdm g~ sein** be familiar to s.o.

gelaunt *adj* **gut/schlecht g~ sein** be in a good/bad mood

gelb *adj* yellow; (*bei Ampel*) amber; **das G~e vom Ei** the yolk of the egg. **G~** *nt* **-s,-** yellow. **g~lich** *adj* yellowish. **G~sucht** *f* jaundice

Geld *nt* **-es,-er** money; **öffentliche G~er** public funds. **G~automat** *m* cashpoint machine. **G~beutel** *m*, **G~börse** *f* purse. **G~geber** *m* **-s,-** backer. **g~lich** *adj* financial. **G~mittel** *ntpl* funds. **G~schein** *m* banknote. **G~schrank** *m* safe. **G~strafe** *f* fine. **G~stück** *nt* coin

Gelee /ʒeˈleː/ *nt* **-s,-s** jelly

g

gelegen *adj* situated; (*passend*) convenient

Gelegenheit *f* **-,-en** opportunity, chance; (*Anlass*) occasion; (*Comm*) bargain; **bei G~** some time. **G~sarbeit** *f* casual work. **G~skauf** *m* bargain

gelegentlich *adj* occasional ● *adv* occasionally; (*bei Gelegenheit*) some time

Gelehrte(r) *m/f* scholar

Geleit *nt* **-[e]s** escort; **freies G~** safe conduct. **g~en** *vt* escort

Gelenk *nt* **-[e]s,-e** joint. **g~ig** *adj* supple; (*Techn*) flexible

gelernt *adj* skilled

Geliebte(r) *m/f* lover

gelingen† *vi* (*sein*) succeed, be successful. **G~** *nt* **-s** success

gellend *adj* shrill

geloben *vt* promise [solemnly]; **das Gelobte Land** the Promised Land

Gelöbnis *nt* **-ses,-se** vow

gelöst *adj* (*fig*) relaxed

gelten† *vi* (*haben*) be valid; (*Regel:*) apply; **g~ als** be regarded as; **etw nicht g~ lassen** not accept sth; **wenig/viel g~** be worth/(*fig*) count for little/a lot; **jdm g~** be meant for s.o.; **das gilt nicht** that doesn't count. **g~d** *adj* valid; (*Preise*) current; (*Meinung*) prevailing; **g~d machen** assert (*Recht, Forderung*); bring to bear (*Einfluss*)

Geltung *f* **-** validity; (*Ansehen*) prestige; **zur G~ bringen** set off

Gelübde *nt* **-s,-** vow

gelungen *adj* successful

Gelüst *nt* **-[e]s,-e** desire

gemächlich *adj* leisurely ● *adv* in a leisurely manner

Gemahl *m* **-s,-e** husband. **G~in** *f* **-,-nen** wife

Gemälde *nt* **-s,-** painting. **G~galerie** *f* picture gallery

gemäß *prep* (+ *dat*) in accordance with

gemäßigt *adj* moderate; (*Klima*) temperate

gemein *adj* common; (*unanständig*) vulgar; (*niederträchtig*) mean; **g~er Soldat** private

Gemeinde *f* **-,-n** [local] community; (*Admin*) borough; (*Pfarr-*) parish; (*bei Gottesdienst*) congregation. **G~rat** *m* local council/(*Person*) councillor. **G~wahlen** *fpl* local elections

gemein|gefährlich *adj* dangerous. **G~heit** *f* **-,-en** commonness; vulgarity; meanness; (*Bemerkung, Handlung*) mean thing [to say/do]; **so eine G~heit!** how mean! **G~kosten** *pl* overheads. **g~nützig** *adj* charitable. **g~sam** *adj* common ● *adv* together

Gemeinschaft *f* **-,-en** community. **g~lich** *adj* joint; (*Besitz*) communal ● *adv* jointly; (*zusammen*) together. **G~sarbeit** *f* team work

Gemenge *nt* **-s,-** mixture

Gemisch *nt* **-[e]s,-e** mixture. **g~t** *adj* mixed

Gemme *f* **-,-n** engraved gem

Gemse* *f* **-,-n** = **Gämse**

Gemurmel *nt* **-s** murmuring

Gemüse *nt* **-s,-** vegetable; (*coll*) vegetables *pl*. **G~händler** *m* greengrocer

gemustert *adj* patterned

Gemüt *nt* **-[e]s,-er** nature, disposition; (*Gefühl*) feelings *pl*

gemütlich *adj* cosy; (*gemächlich*) leisurely; (*zwanglos*) informal; (*Person*) genial; **es sich** (*dat*) **g~ machen** make oneself comfortable. **G~keit** *f* **-** cosiness

Gen *nt* **-s,-e** gene

genau *adj* exact, precise; (*Waage, Messung*) accurate; (*sorgfältig*) meticulous; (*ausführlich*) detailed; **nichts G~es wissen** not know any details; **g~ genommen** strictly speaking; **g~!** exactly! **G~igkeit** *f* - exactitude; precision; accuracy; meticulousness

genauso *adv* just the same; (*g~sehr*) just as much; **g~ teuer** just as expensive; **g~ gut** just as good; *adv* just as well; **g~ sehr** just as much; **g~ viel** just as much/many; **g~ wenig** just as little/few; (*noch*) no more

Gendarm /ʒã'darm/ *m* **-en,-en** (*Aust*) policeman

Genealogie *f* - genealogy

genehmig|en *vt* grant; approve (*Plan*). **G~ung** *f* **-,-en** permission; (*Schein*) permit

geneigt *adj* sloping, inclined; (*fig*) well-disposed (*dat* towards)

General *m* **-s,⸚e** general. **G~direktor** *m* managing director. **G~probe** *f* dress rehearsal. **G~streik** *m* general strike

Generation /-'tsi̯o:n/ *f* **-,-en** generation

Generator *m* **-s,-en** generator

generell *adj* general

genes|en† *vi* (*sein*) recover. **G~ung** *f* - recovery; (*Erholung*) convalescence

Genetik *f* - genetics *sg*

genetisch *adj* genetic

Genf *nt* **-s** Geneva. **G~er** *adj* Geneva ; **G~er See** Lake Geneva

genial *adj* brilliant. **G~ität** *f* genius

Genick *nt* **-s,-e** [back of the] neck; **sich** (*dat*) **das G~ brechen** break one's neck

Genie /ʒe'ni:/ *nt* **-s,-s** genius

genieren /ʒe'ni:rən/ *vt* embarrass; **sich g~** feel *or* be embarrassed

genieß|bar *adj* fit to eat/drink. **g~en**† *vt* enjoy; (*verzehren*) eat/drink

Genitiv *m* **-s,-e** genitive

genmanipuliert *adj* genetically modified

Genom *nt* **-s, -e** genome

Genosse *m* **-n,-n** (*Pol*) comrade. **G~nschaft** *f* **-,-en** cooperative

Gentechnologie *f* genetic engineering

genug *inv adj & adv* enough

Genüge *f* **zur G~** sufficiently. **g~n** *vi* (*haben*) be enough. **g~nd** *inv adj* sufficient, enough; (*Sch*) fair ● *adv* sufficiently, enough

Genuss *m* **-es,⸚e** enjoyment; (*Vergnügen*) pleasure; (*Verzehr*) consumption

geöffnet *adj* open

Geo|graphie, G~grafie *f* - geography. **g~graphisch, g~grafisch** *adj* geographical. **G~logie** *f* - geology. **g~logisch** *adj* geological. **G~meter** *m* **-s,-** surveyor. **G~metrie** *f* - geometry. **g~metrisch** *adj* geometric[al]

geordnet *adj* well-ordered; (*stabil*) stable; **alphabetisch g~** in alphabetical order

Gepäck *nt* **-s** luggage, baggage. **G~ablage** *f* luggage-rack. **G~aufbewahrung** *f* left-luggage office. **G~schein** *m* left-luggage ticket; (*Aviat*) baggage check. **G~träger** *m* porter; (*Fahrrad-*) luggage carrier; (*Dach-*) roof-rack

Gepard *m* **-s,-e** cheetah

gepflegt *adj* well-kept; (*Person*) well-groomed; (*Hotel*) first-class

gepunktet *adj* spotted

gerade *adj* straight; (*direkt*) direct; (*aufrecht*) upright; (*aufrichtig*) straightforward; (*Zahl*) even ● *adv* straight; directly; (*eben*) just;

(*genau*) exactly; (*besonders*) especially; **g~ sitzen/stehen** sit/stand [up] straight; **g~ erst** only just. **G~** *f* **-,-n** straight line. **g~aus** *adv* straight ahead/on. **g~heraus** *adv* (*fig*) straight out. **g~so** *adv* just the same; **g~so gut** just as good; *adv* just as well. **g~stehen**† *vi sep* (*haben*) (*fig*) accept responsibility (**für** for). **g~zu** *adv* virtually; (*wirklich*) absolutely

g

Geranie /-i̯ə/ *f* **-,-n** geranium

Gerät *nt* **-[e]s,-e** tool; (*Acker-*) implement; (*Küchen-*) utensil; (*Elektro-*) appliance; (*Radio-, Fernseh-*) set; (*Turn-*) piece of apparatus; (*coll*) equipment

geraten† *vi* (*sein*) get; **in Brand g~** catch fire; **in Wut g~** get angry; **gut g~** turn out well

Geratewohl *nt* **aufs G~** at random

geräuchert *adj* smoked

geräumig *adj* spacious, roomy

Geräusch *nt* **-[e]s,-e** noise. **g~los** *adj* noiseless

gerben *vt* tan

gerecht *adj* just; (*fair*) fair. **g~fertigt** *adj* justified. **G~igkeit** *f* - justice; fairness

Gerede *nt* **-s** talk

geregelt *adj* regular

gereizt *adj* irritable

Geriatrie *f* - geriatrics *sg*

Gericht[1] *nt* **-[e]s,-e** (*Culin*) dish

Gericht[2] *nt* **-[e]s,-e** court [of law]; **vor G~** in court; **das Jüngste G~** the Last Judgement. **g~lich** *adj* judicial; (*Verfahren*) legal ● *adv* **g~lich vorgehen** take legal action. **G~shof** *m* court of justice. **G~smedizin** *f* forensic medicine. **G~ssaal** *m* court room. **G~svollzieher** *m* **-s,-** bailiff

gerieben *adj* grated; (🄸: *schlau*) crafty

gering *adj* small; (*niedrig*) low; (*g~fügig*) slight. **g~fügig** *adj* slight. **g~schätzig** *adj* contemptuous; (*Bemerkung*) disparaging. **g~ste(r,s)** *adj* least; **nicht im G~sten** not in the least

gerinnen† *vi* (*sein*) curdle; (*Blut:*) clot

Gerippe *nt* **-s,-** skeleton; (*fig*) framework

gerissen *adj* 🄸 crafty

Germ *m* **-[e]s** & (*Aust*) *f* - yeast

German|e *m* **-n,-n** [ancient] German. **g~isch** *adj* Germanic. **G~istik** *f* - German [language and literature]

gern[e] *adv* gladly; **g~ haben** like; (*lieben*) be fond of; **ich tanze g~** I like dancing; **willst du mit?—g~!** do you want to come?—I'd love to!

Gerste *f* - barley. **G~nkorn** *nt* (*Med*) stye

Geruch *m* **-[e]s,¨e** smell (**von/nach** of). **g~los** *adj* odourless. **G~ssinn** *m* sense of smell

Gerücht *nt* **-[e]s,-e** rumour

gerührt *adj* (*fig*) moved, touched

Gerümpel *nt* **-s** lumber, junk

Gerüst *nt* **-[e]s,-e** scaffolding; (*fig*) framework

gesammelt *adj* collected; (*gefasst*) composed

gesamt *adj* entire, whole. **G~ausgabe** *f* complete edition. **G~eindruck** *m* overall impression. **G~heit** *f* - whole. **G~schule** *f* comprehensive school. **G~summe** *f* total

Gesandte(r) *m/f* envoy

Gesang *m* **-[e]s,¨e** singing; (*Lied*) song; (*Kirchen-*) hymn. **G~verein** *m* choral society

Gesäß *nt* **-es** buttocks *pl*

Geschäft *nt* **-[e]s,-e** business; (*Laden*) shop, store; (*Transaktion*) deal; **schmutzige G~e** shady dealings; **ein gutes G~ machen** do very well (**mit** out of). **g~ig** *adj* busy; (*Treiben*) bustling. **G~igkeit** *f* **-** activity. **g~lich** *adj* business ● *adv* on business

Geschäfts|brief *m* business letter. **G~führer** *m* manager; (*Vereins-*) secretary. **G~mann** *m* (*pl* **-leute**) businessman. **G~stelle** *f* office; (*Zweigstelle*) branch. **g~tüchtig** *adj* **g~tüchtig sein** be a good businessman/-woman. **G~zeiten** *fpl* hours of business

geschehen† *vi* (*sein*) happen (*dat* to); **das geschieht dir recht!** it serves you right! **gern g~!** you're welcome! **G~** *nt* **-s** events *pl*

gescheit *adj* clever

Geschenk *nt* **-[e]s,-e** present, gift

Geschicht|e *f* **-,-n** history; (*Erzählung*) story; (**!**: *Sache*) business. **g~lich** *adj* historical

Geschick *nt* **-[e]s** fate; (*Talent*) skill. **G~lichkeit** *f* **-** skilfulness, skill. **g~t** *adj* skilful; (*klug*) clever

geschieden *adj* divorced

Geschirr *nt* **-s,-e** (*coll*) crockery; (*Porzellan*) china; (*Service*) service; (*Pferde-*) harness; **schmutziges G~** dirty dishes *pl*. **G~spülmaschine** *f* dishwasher. **G~tuch** *nt* tea towel

Geschlecht *nt* **-[e]s,-er** sex; (*Gram*) gender; (*Generation*) generation. **g~lich** *adj* sexual. **G~skrankheit** *f* venereal disease. **G~steile** *ntpl* genitals. **G~sverkehr** *m* sexual intercourse. **G~swort** *nt* (*pl* **-wörter**) article

geschliffen *adj* (*fig*) polished

Geschmack *m* **-[e]s,¨e** taste; (*Aroma*) flavour; (*G~ssinn*) sense of taste; **einen guten G~ haben** (*fig*) have good taste. **g~los** *adj* tasteless; **g~los sein** (*fig*) be in bad taste. **g~voll** *adj* (*fig*) tasteful

Geschoss *nt* **-es,-e** missile; (*Stockwerk*) storey, floor

Geschrei *nt* **-s** screaming; (*fig*) fuss

Geschütz *nt* **-es,-e** gun, cannon

geschützt *adj* protected; (*Stelle*) sheltered

Geschwader *nt* **-s,-** squadron

Geschwätz *nt* **-es** talk

geschweige *conj* **g~ denn** let alone

Geschwindigkeit *f* **-,-en** speed; (*Phys*) velocity. **G~sbegrenzung, G~sbeschränkung** *f* speed limit

Geschwister *pl* brother[s] and sister[s]; siblings

geschwollen *adj* swollen; (*fig*) pompous

Geschworene|(r) *m/f* juror; **die G~n** the jury *sg*

Geschwulst *f* **-,¨e** swelling; (*Tumor*) tumour

geschwungen *adj* curved

Geschwür *nt* **-s,-e** ulcer

gesellig *adj* sociable; (*Zool*) gregarious; (*unterhaltsam*) convivial; **g~er Abend** social evening

Gesellschaft *f* **-,-en** company; (*Veranstaltung*) party; **die G~** society; **jdm G~ leisten** keep s.o. company. **g~lich** *adj* social. **G~sspiel** *nt* party game

Gesetz *nt* **-es,-e** law. **G~entwurf** *m* bill. **g~gebend** *adj* legislative. **G~gebung** *f* **-** legislation. **g~lich** *adj* legal. **g~mäßig** *adj* lawful; (*gesetzlich*) legal. **g~widrig** *adj* illegal

gesichert *adj* secure

Gesicht *nt* **-[e]s,-er** face; (*Aussehen*) appearance. **G~sfarbe** *f* complexion. **G~spunkt** *m* point of view. **G~szüge** *mpl* features

Gesindel *nt* **-s** riff-raff
Gesinnung *f* **-,-en** mind; (*Einstellung*) attitude
gesondert *adj* separate
Gespann *nt* **-[e]s,-e** team; (*Wagen*) horse and cart/carriage
gespannt *adj* taut; (*fig*) tense; (*Beziehungen*) strained; (*neugierig*) eager; (*erwartungsvoll*) expectant; **g~ sein, ob** wonder whether; **auf etw g~ sein** look forward eagerly to sth
Gespenst *nt* **-[e]s,-er** ghost. **g~isch** *adj* ghostly; (*unheimlich*) eerie
Gespött *nt* **-[e]s** mockery; **zum G~ werden** become a laughing stock
Gespräch *nt* **-[e]s-e** conversation; (*Telefon-*) call; **ins G~ kommen** get talking; **im G~ sein** be under discussion. **g~ig** *adj* talkative **G~sthema** *nt* topic of conversation
Gestalt *f* **-,-en** figure; (*Form*) shape, form; **G~ annehmen** (*fig*) take shape. **g~en** *vt* shape; (*organisieren*) arrange; (*schaffen*) create; (*entwerfen*) design; **sich g~en** turn out
Geständnis *nt* **-ses,-se** confession
Gestank *m* **-s** stench, [bad] smell
gestatten *vt* allow, permit; **nicht gestattet** prohibited; **g~ Sie?** may I?
Geste /ˈgɛ-, ˈgeːstə/ *f* **-,-n** gesture
Gesteck *nt* **-[e]s,-e** flower arrangement
gestehen† *vt/i* (*haben*) confess; confess to (*Verbrechen*)
Gestein *nt* **-[e]s,-e** rock
Gestell *nt* **-[e]s,-e** stand; (*Flaschen-*) rack; (*Rahmen*) frame
gesteppt *adj* quilted
gestern *adv* yesterday; **g~ Nacht** last night
gestrandet *adj* stranded
gestreift *adj* striped
gestrichelt *adj* (*Linie*) dotted
gestrichen *adj* **g~er Teelöffel** level teaspoon[ful]
gestrig /ˈgɛstrɪç/ *adj* yesterday's; **am g~en Tag** yesterday
Gestrüpp *nt* **-s,-e** undergrowth
Gestüt *nt* **-[e]s,-e** stud [farm]
Gesuch *nt* **-[e]s,-e** request; (*Admin*) application. **g~t** *adj* sought-after
gesund *adj* healthy; **g~ sein** be in good health; (*Sport, Getränk:*) be good for one; **wieder g~ werden** get well again
Gesundheit *f* **-** health; **G~!** (*bei Niesen*) bless you! **g~lich** *adj* health ; **g~licher Zustand** state of health ● *adv* **es geht ihm g~lich gut/schlecht** he is in good/poor health. **g~sschädlich** *adj* harmful
getäfelt *adj* panelled
Getöse *nt* **-s** racket, din
Getränk *nt* **-[e]s,-e** drink. **G~ekarte** *f* wine-list
getrauen *vt* **sich** (*dat*) **etw g~** dare [to] do sth; **sich g~** dare
Getreide *nt* **-s** (*coll*) grain
getrennt *adj* separate; **g~ leben** live apart; **g~ schreiben** write as two words
getreu *adj* faithful ● *prep* (+ *dat*) true to. **g~lich** *adv* faithfully
Getriebe *nt* **-s,-** bustle; (*Techn*) gear; (*Auto*) transmission; (*Gehäuse*) gearbox
getrost *adv* with confidence
Getto *nt* **-s,-s** ghetto
Getue *nt* **-s** 🄸 fuss
Getümmel *nt* **-s** tumult
geübt *adj* skilled
Gewächs *nt* **-es,-e** plant
gewachsen *adj* **jdm g~ sein** be

a match for s.o.

Gewächshaus *nt* greenhouse

gewagt *adj* daring

gewählt *adj* refined

gewahr *adj* **g~ werden** become aware (*acc/gen* of)

Gewähr *f* - guarantee

gewähr|en *vt* grant; (*geben*) offer. **g~leisten** *vt* guarantee

Gewahrsam *m* **-s** safekeeping; (*Haft*) custody

Gewalt *f* **-,-en** power; (*Kraft*) force; (*Brutalität*) violence; **mit G~** by force. **G~herrschaft** *f* tyranny. **g~ig** *adj* powerful; (🄸: *groß*) enormous; (*stark*) tremendous. **g~sam** *adj* forcible; (*Tod*) violent. **g~tätig** *adj* violent. **G~tätigkeit** *f* **-,-en** violence; (*Handlung*) act of violence

Gewand *nt* **-[e]s,¨er** robe

gewandt *adj* skilful. **G~heit** *f* - skill

Gewebe *nt* **-s,-** fabric; (*Anat*) tissue

Gewehr *nt* **-s,-e** rifle, gun

Geweih *nt* **-[e]s,-e** antlers *pl*

Gewerb|e *nt* **-s,-** trade. **g~lich** *adj* commercial. **g~smäßig** *adj* professional

Gewerkschaft *f* **-,-en** trade union. **G~ler(in)** *m* **-s,-** (*f* **-,-nen**) trade unionist

Gewicht *nt* **-[e]s,-e** weight; (*Bedeutung*) importance. **G~heben** *nt* **-s** weight lifting

Gewinde *nt* **-s,-** [screw] thread

Gewinn *m* **-[e]s,-e** profit; (*fig*) gain, benefit; (*beim Spiel*) winnings *pl*; (*Preis*) prize; (*Los*) winning ticket. **G~beteiligung** *f* profit-sharing. **g~en**† *vt* win; (*erlangen*) gain; (*fördern*) extract ● *vi* (*haben*) win; **g~en an** (+ *dat*) gain in. **g~end** *adj* engaging. **G~er(in)** *m* **-s,-** (*f* **-,-nen**) winner

Gewirr *nt* **-s,-e** tangle; (*Straßen-*) maze

gewiss *adj* certain

Gewissen *nt* **-s,-** conscience. **g~haft** *adj* conscientious. **g~los** *adj* unscrupulous. **G~sbisse** *mpl* pangs of conscience

gewissermaßen *adv* to a certain extent; (*sozusagen*) as it were

Gewissheit *f* - certainty

Gewitt|er *nt* **-s,-** thunderstorm. **g~rig** *adj* thundery

gewogen *adj* (*fig*) well-disposed (*dat* towards)

gewöhnen *vt* **jdn/sich g~ an** (+ *acc*) get s.o. used to/get used to; **[an] jdn/etw gewöhnt sein** be used to s.o./sth

Gewohnheit *f* **-,-en** habit. **G~srecht** *nt* common law

gewöhnlich *adj* ordinary; (*üblich*) usual; (*ordinär*) common

gewohnt *adj* customary; (*vertraut*) familiar; (*üblich*) usual; **etw** (*acc*) **g~ sein** be used to sth

Gewölbe *nt* **-s,-** vault

Gewühl *nt* **-[e]s** crush

gewunden *adj* winding

Gewürz *nt* **-es,-e** spice. **G~nelke** *f* clove

gezackt *adj* serrated

gezähnt *adj* serrated; (*Säge*) toothed

Gezeiten *fpl* tides

gezielt *adj* specific; (*Frage*) pointed

geziert *adj* affected

gezwungen *adj* forced. **g~ermaßen** *adv* of necessity

Gicht *f* - gout

Giebel *m* **-s,-** gable

Gier *f* - greed (**nach** for). **g~ig** *adj* greedy

gieß|en† *vt* pour; water (*Blumen, Garten*); (*Techn*) cast ● *v impers* **es**

g~t it is pouring [with rain]. **G~kanne** *f* watering can

Gift *nt* **-[e]s,-e** poison; (*Schlangen-*) venom; (*Med*) toxin. **g~ig** *adj* poisonous; (*Schlange*) venomous; (*Med, Chemistry*) toxic; (*fig*) spiteful. **G~müll** *m* toxic waste. **G~pilz** *m* toadstool

Gilde *f* **-,-n** guild

Gin /dʒɪn/ *m* **-s** gin

g

Ginster *m* **-s** (*Bot*) broom

Gipfel *m* **-s,-** summit, top; (*fig*) peak. **G~konferenz** *f* summit conference. **g~n** *vi* (*haben*) culminate (**in** + *dat* in)

Gips *m* **-es** plaster. **G~verband** *m* (*Med*) plaster cast

Giraffe *f* **-,-n** giraffe

Girlande *f* **-,-n** garland

Girokonto /ˈʒiːro-/ *nt* current account

Gischt *m* **-[e]s** & *f* **-** spray

Gitar|re *f* **-,-n** guitar. **G~rist(in)** *m* **-en,-en** (*f* **-,-nen**) guitarist

Gitter *nt* **-s,-** bars *pl*; (*Rost*) grating, grid; (*Geländer, Zaun*) railings *pl*; (*Fenster-*) grille; (*Draht-*) wire screen

Glanz *m* **-es** shine; (*von Farbe, Papier*) gloss; (*Seiden-*) sheen; (*Politur*) polish; (*fig*) brilliance; (*Pracht*) splendour

glänzen *vi* (*haben*) shine. **g~d** *adj* shining, bright; (*Papier*) glossy; (*fig*) brilliant

glanz|los *adj* dull. **G~stück** *nt* masterpiece

Glas *nt* **-es,⸚er** glass; (*Brillen-*) lens; (*Fern-*) binoculars *pl*; (*Marmeladen-*) [glass] jar. **G~er** *m* **-s,-** glazier

glasieren *vt* glaze; ice (*Kuchen*)

glas|ig *adj* glassy; (*durchsichtig*) transparent. **G~scheibe** *f* pane

Glasur *f* **-,-en** glaze; (*Culin*) icing

glatt *adj* smooth; (*eben*) even; (*Haar*) straight; (*rutschig*) slippery; (*einfach*) straightforward; (*Absage*) flat; **g~ streichen** smooth out; **g~ rasiert** clean-shaven; **g~ gehen** go off smoothly; **das ist g~ gelogen** it's a downright lie

Glätte *f* **-** smoothness; (*Rutschigkeit*) slipperiness

Glatt|eis *nt* [black] ice. **g~weg** *adv* 🅸 outright

Glatz|e *f* **-,-n** bald patch; (*Voll-*) bald head; **eine G~e bekommen** go bald. **g~köpfig** *adj* bald

Glaube *m* **-ns** belief (**an** + *acc* in); (*Relig*) faith; **G~n schenken** (+ *dat*) believe. **g~n** *vt/i* (*haben*) believe (**an** + *acc* in); (*vermuten*) think; **jdm g~n** believe s.o.; **nicht zu g~n** unbelievable, incredible. **G~nsbekenntnis** *nt* creed

gläubig *adj* religious; (*vertrauend*) trusting. **G~e(r)** *m/f* (*Relig*) believer; **die G~en** the faithful. **G~er** *m* **-s,-** (*Comm*) creditor

glaub|lich *adj* **kaum g~lich** scarcely believable. **g~würdig** *adj* credible; (*Person*) reliable

gleich *adj* same; (*identisch*) identical; (*g~wertig*) equal; **g~ bleibend** constant; **2 mal 5 [ist] g~ 10** two times 5 equals 10; **das ist mir g~** it's all the same to me; **ganz g~, wo/wer** no matter where/who ● *adv* equally; (*übereinstimmend*) identically, the same; (*sofort*) immediately; (*in Kürze*) in a minute; (*fast*) nearly; (*direkt*) right. **g~altrig** *adj* [of] the same age. **g~bedeutend** *adj* synonymous. **g~berechtigt** *adj* equal. **G~berechtigung** *f* equality

gleichen† *vi* (*haben*) **jdm/etw g~** be like *or* resemble s.o./something

gleich|ermaßen *adv* equally. **g~falls** *adv* also, likewise; **danke g~falls** thank you, the same to you. **G~gewicht** *nt* balance; (*Phys* & *fig*) equilibrium. **g~gültig** *adj* indifferent; (*unwichtig*) unimportant. **G~gültigkeit** *f* indifference. **g~machen** *vt sep* make equal; **dem Erdboden g~machen** raze to the ground. **g~mäßig** *adj* even, regular; (*beständig*) constant. **G~mäßigkeit** *f* - regularity

Gleichnis *nt* **-ses,-se** parable

Gleich|schritt *m* **im G~schritt** in step. **g~setzen** *vt sep* equate/(*g~stellen*) place on a par (*dat*/**mit** with). **g~stellen** *vt sep* place on a par (*dat* with). **G~strom** *m* direct current

Gleichung *f* **-,-en** equation

gleichwertig *adv adj* of equal value. **g~zeitig** *adj* simultaneous

Gleis *nt* **-es,-e** track; (*Bahnsteig*) platform; **G~ 5** platform 5

gleiten† *vi* (*sein*) glide; (*rutschen*) slide. **g~d** *adj* sliding; **g~de Arbeitszeit** flexitime

Gleitzeit *f* flexitime

Gletscher *m* **-s,-** glacier

Glied *nt* **-[e]s,-er** limb; (*Teil*) part; (*Ketten-*) link; (*Mitglied*) member; (*Mil*) rank. **g~ern** *vt* arrange; (*einteilen*) divide. **G~maßen** *fpl* limbs

glitschig *adj* slippery

glitzern *vi* (*haben*) glitter

global *adj* global

globalisier|en *vt* globalize. **G~ung** *f* **-,-en** globalization

Globus *m* **-** & **-busses,-ben** & **-busse** globe

Glocke *f* **-,-n** bell. **G~nturm** *m* bell tower, belfry

glorreich *adj* glorious

Glossar *nt* **-s,-e** glossary

Glosse *f* **-,-n** comment

glotzen *vi* (*haben*) stare

Glück *nt* **-[e]s** [good] luck; (*Zufriedenheit*) happiness; **G~ bringend** lucky; **G~/kein G~ haben** be lucky/unlucky; **zum G~** luckily, fortunately; **auf gut G~** on the off chance; (*wahllos*) at random. **g~en** *vi* (*sein*) succeed

glücklich *adj* lucky, fortunate; (*zufrieden*) happy; (*sicher*) safe ●*adv* happily; safely. **g~erweise** *adv* luckily, fortunately

Glücksspiel *nt* game of chance; (*Spielen*) gambling

g

Glückwunsch *m* good wishes *pl*; (*Gratulation*) congratulations *pl*; **herzlichen G~!** congratulations! (*zum Geburtstag*) happy birthday! **G~karte** *f* greetings card

Glüh|birne *f* light bulb. **g~en** *vi* (*haben*) glow. **g~end** *adj* glowing; (*rot-*) red-hot; (*Hitze*) scorching; (*leidenschaftlich*) fervent. **G~faden** *m* filament. **G~wein** *m* mulled wine. **G~würmchen** *nt* **-s,-** glow-worm

Glukose *f* **-** glucose

Glut *f* **-** embers *pl*; (*Röte*) glow; (*Hitze*) heat; (*fig*) ardour

Glyzinie /-i̯ə/ *f* **-,-n** wisteria

GmbH *abbr* (**Gesellschaft mit beschränkter Haftung**) ≈ plc

Gnade *f* **-** mercy; (*Gunst*) favour; (*Relig*) grace. **G~nfrist** *f* reprieve

gnädig *adj* gracious; (*mild*) lenient; **g~e Frau** Madam

Gnom *m* **-en,-en** gnome

Gobelin /gobəˈlɛ̃ː/ *m* **-s,-s** tapestry

Gold *nt* **-[e]s** gold. **g~en** *adj* gold; (*g~farben*) golden. **G~fisch** *m* goldfish. **g~ig** *adj* sweet, lovely. **G~lack** *m* wallflower. **G~regen** *m* laburnum. **G~schmied** *m* goldsmith

Golf[1] *m* **-[e]s,-e** (*Geog*) gulf

Golf[2] *nt* **-s** golf. **G~platz** *m* golf course. **G~schläger** *m* golf club. **G~spieler(in)** *m*(*f*) golfer

Gondel *f* **-,-n** gondola; (*Kabine*) cabin
gönnen *vt* **jdm etw g~** not begrudge s.o. sth; **jdm etw nicht g~** begrudge s.o. sth
googeln *vt/i* ® google
Gör *nt* **-s,-en, Göre** *f* **-,-n** [!] kid
Gorilla *m* **-s,-s** gorilla
Gosse *f* **-,-n** gutter
Got|ik *f* **-** Gothic. **g~isch** *adj* Gothic
Gott *m* **-[e]s,¨er** God; (*Myth*) god
Götterspeise *f* jelly
Gottes|dienst *m* service. **G~lästerung** *f* blasphemy
Gottheit *f* **-,-en** deity
Göttin *f* **-,-nen** goddess
göttlich *adj* divine
gottlos *adj* ungodly; (*atheistisch*) godless
Grab *nt* **-[e]s,¨er** grave
graben† *vi* (*haben*) dig
Graben *m* **-s,¨** ditch; (*Mil*) trench
Grab|mal *nt* tomb. **G~stein** *m* gravestone, tombstone
Grad *m* **-[e]s,-e** degree
Graf *m* **-en,-en** count
Grafik *f* **-,-en** graphics *sg*; (*Kunst*) graphic arts *pl*; (*Druck*) print
Gräfin *f* **-,-nen** countess
grafisch *adj* graphic; **g~e Darstellung** diagram
Grafschaft *f* **-,-en** county
Gram *m* **-s** grief
grämen (sich) *vr* grieve
Gramm *nt* **-s,-e** gram
Gram|matik *f* **-,-en** grammar. **g~matikalisch** *adj* grammatical
Granat *m* **-[e]s,-e** garnet. **G~e** *f* **-,-n** shell; (*Hand-*) grenade
Granit *m* **-s,-e** granite
Gras *nt* **-es,¨er** grass. **g~en** *vi* (*haben*) graze. **G~hüpfer** *m* **-s,-** grasshopper
grässlich *adj* dreadful
Grat *m* **-[e]s,-e** [mountain] ridge
Gräte *f* **-,-n** fishbone
Gratifikation /-ˈtsi̯oːn/ *f* **-,-en** bonus
gratis *adv* free [of charge]. **G~probe** *f* free sample
Gratu|lant(in) *m* **-en,-en** (*f* **-,-nen**) well-wisher. **G~lation** *f* **-,-en** congratulations *pl*; (*Glückwünsche*) best wishes *pl*. **g~lieren** *vi* (*haben*) **jdm g~lieren** congratulate s.o. (**zu** on); (*zum Geburtstag*) wish s.o. happy birthday
grau *adj*, **G~** *nt* **-s,-** grey
Gräuel *m* **-s,-** horror
grauen *v impers* **mir graut [es] davor** I dread it. **G~** *nt* **-s** dread. **g~haft** *adj* gruesome; (*grässlich*) horrible
gräulich *adj* horrible
grausam *adj* cruel. **G~keit** *f* **-,-en** cruelty
graus|en *v impers* **mir graust davor** I dread it. **G~en** *nt* **-s** horror, dread. **g~ig** *adj* gruesome
gravieren *vt* engrave. **g~d** *adj* (*fig*) serious
graziös *adj* graceful
greifen† *vt* take hold of; (*fangen*) catch ● *vi* (*haben*) reach (**nach** for); **um sich g~** (*fig*) spread
Greis *m* **-es,-e** old man. **G~in** *f* **-,-nen** old woman
grell *adj* glaring; (*Farbe*) garish; (*schrill*) shrill
Gremium *nt* **-s,-ien** committee
Grenz|e *f* **-,-n** border; (*Staats-*) frontier; (*Grundstücks-*) boundary; (*fig*) limit. **g~en** *vi* (*haben*) border (**an** + *acc* on). **g~enlos** *adj* boundless; (*maßlos*) infinite
Griech|e *m* **-n,-n** Greek. **G~en-**

land *nt* **-s** Greece. **G~in** *f* **-,-nen** Greek woman. **g~isch** *adj* Greek. **G~isch** *nt* **-[s]** (*Lang*) Greek

Grieß *m* **-es** semolina

Griff *m* **-[e]s,-e** grasp, hold; (*Hand-*) movement of the hand; (*Tür-, Messer-*) handle; (*Schwert-*) hilt. **g~bereit** *adj* handy

Grill *m* **-s,-s** grill; (*Garten-*) barbecue

Grille *f* **-,-n** (*Zool*) cricket

grill|en *vt* grill; (*im Freien*) barbecue ● *vi* (*haben*) have a barbecue. **G~fest** *nt* barbecue

Grimasse *f* **-,-n** grimace; **G~n schneiden** pull faces

grimmig *adj* furious; (*Kälte*) bitter

grinsen *vi* (*haben*) grin

Grippe *f* **-,-n** influenza, [!] flu

grob *adj* coarse; (*unsanft, ungefähr*) rough; (*unhöflich*) rude; (*schwer*) gross; (*Fehler*) bad; **g~ geschätzt** roughly. **G~ian** *m* **-s,-e** brute

Groll *m* **-[e]s** resentment. **g~en** *vi* (*haben*) be angry (*dat* with); (*Donner:*) rumble

Grönland *nt* **-s** Greenland

Gros *nt* **-es,-** (*Maß*) gross

Groschen *m* **-s,-** (*Aust*) groschen; [!] ten-pfennig piece

groß *adj* big; (*Anzahl, Summe*) large; (*bedeutend, stark*) great; (*g~artig*) grand; (*Buchstabe*) capital; **g~e Ferien** summer holidays; **der größte Teil** the majority *or* bulk; **g~ werden** (*Person:*) grow up; **g~ in etw** (*dat*) **sein** be good at sth; **G~ und Klein** young and old; **im G~en und Ganzen** on the whole ● *adv* (*feiern*) in style; ([!]: *viel*) much

groß|artig *adj* magnificent. **G~aufnahme** *f* close-up. **G~britannien** *nt* **-s** Great Britain. **G~buchstabe** *m* capital letter. **G~e(r)** *m/f* **unser G~er** our eldest; **die G~en** the grown-ups; (*fig*) the great *pl*

Größe *f* **-,-n** size; (*Ausmaß*) extent; (*Körper-*) height; (*Bedeutsamkeit*) greatness; (*Math*) quantity; (*Person*) great figure

Großeltern *pl* grandparents

Groß|handel *m* wholesale trade. **G~händler** *m* wholesaler. **G~macht** *f* superpower. **g~mütig** *adj* magnanimous. **G~mutter** *f* grandmother. **G~schreibung** *f* capitalization. **g~spurig** *adj* pompous; (*überheblich*) arrogant. **G~stadt** *f* [large] city. **g~städtisch** *adj* city; **G~teil** *m* large proportion; (*Hauptteil*) bulk

größtenteils *adv* for the most part

groß|tun† **(sich)** *vr sep* brag. **G~vater** *m* grandfather. **g~ziehen**† *vt sep* bring up; rear (*Tier*). **g~zügig** *adj* generous. **G~zügigkeit** *f* **-** generosity

Grotte *f* **-,-n** grotto

Grübchen *nt* **-s,-** dimple

Grube *f* **-,-n** pit

grübeln *vi* (*haben*) brood

Gruft *f* **-,¨e** [burial] vault

grün *adj* green; **im G~en** out in the country; **die G~en** the Greens

Grund *m* **-[e]s,¨e** ground; (*Boden*) bottom; (*Hinter-*) background; (*Ursache*) reason; **aus diesem G~e** for this reason; **im G~e [genommen]** basically; **auf G~ laufen** (*Naut*) run aground; **zu G~e richten/gehen** *s.* **zugrunde**. **G~begriffe** *mpl* basics. **G~besitzer** *m* landowner

gründ|en *vt* found, set up; start (*Familie*); (*fig*) base (**auf** + *acc* on); **sich g~en** be based (**auf** + *acc* on). **G~er(in)** *m* **-s,-** (*f* **-,-nen**) founder

Grund|farbe *f* primary colour. **G~form** *f* (*Gram*) infinitive. **G~**

gesetz *nt* (*Pol*) constitution. **G~lage** *f* basis, foundation

> **Grundgesetz** The written German constitution, or "basic law", which came into force in May 1949. It lays down the basic rights of German citizens and the legal framework of the German state.

gründlich *adj* thorough. **G~keit** *f* - thoroughness

Gründonnerstag *m* Maundy Thursday

Grund|regel *f* basic rule. **G~riss** *m* ground plan; (*fig*) outline. **G~satz** *m* principle. **g~sätzlich** *adj* fundamental; (*im Allgemeinen*) in principle; (*prinzipiell*) on principle. **G~schule** *f* primary school. **G~stück** *nt* plot [of land]

Gründung *f* -,-en foundation

Grün|span *m* verdigris. **G~streifen** *m* grass verge; (*Mittel-*) central reservation

grunzen *vi* (*haben*) grunt

Gruppe *f* -,-n group; (*Reise-*) party

gruppieren *vt* group

Grusel|geschichte *f* horror story. **g~ig** *adj* creepy

Gruß *m* -es,¨e greeting; (*Mil*) salute; **einen schönen G~ an X** give my regards to X; **viele/herzliche G~e** regards; **Mit freundlichen G~en** Yours sincerely/faithfully

grüßen *vt/i* (*haben*) say hallo (**jdn** to s.o.); (*Mil*) salute; **g~ Sie X von mir** give my regards to X; **grüß Gott!** (*SGer, Aust*) good morning/afternoon/evening!

gucken *vi* (*haben*) [!] look

Guerilla /ge'rɪlja/ *f* - guerrilla warfare. **G~kämpfer** *m* guerrilla

Gulasch *nt* & *m* -[e]s goulash

gültig *adj* valid

Gummi *m* & *nt* -s,-[s] rubber; (*Harz*) gum. **G~band** *nt* (*pl* -bänder) elastic *or* rubber band

gummiert *adj* gummed

Gummi|knüppel *m* truncheon. **G~stiefel** *m* gumboot, wellington. **G~zug** *m* elastic

Gunst *f* - favour

günstig *adj* favourable; (*passend*) convenient

Gurgel *f* -,-n throat. **g~n** *vi* (*haben*) gargle

Gurke *f* -,-n cucumber; (*Essig-*) gherkin

Gurt *m* -[e]s,-e strap; (*Gürtel*) belt; (*Auto*) safety belt. **G~band** *nt* (*pl* -bänder) waistband

Gürtel *m* -s,- belt. **G~linie** *f* waistline. **G~rose** *f* shingles *sg*

Guss *m* -es,¨e (*Techn*) casting; (*Strom*) stream; (*Regen-*) downpour; (*Torten-*) icing. **G~eisen** *nt* cast iron

gut *adj* good; (*Gewissen*) clear; (*gütig*) kind (**zu** to); **jdm gut sein** be fond of s.o.; **im G~en** amicably; **schon gut** that's all right ● *adv* well; (*schmecken, riechen*) good; (*leicht*) easily; **gut zu sehen** clearly visible; **gut drei Stunden** a good three hours

Gut *nt* -[e]s,¨er possession, property; (*Land-*) estate; **Gut und Böse** good and evil; **Güter** (*Comm*) goods

Gutacht|en *nt* -s,- expert's report. **G~er** *m* -s,- expert

gutartig *adj* good-natured; (*Med*) benign

Gute|(s) *nt* **etwas/nichts G~s** something/nothing good; **G~s tun** do good; **alles G~!** all the best!

Güte *f* -,-n goodness, kindness; (*Qualität*) quality

Güterzug *m* goods train

gut|gehen* *vi sep* (*sein*) **gut**

gehen, *s.* **gehen. g~gehend*** *adj* **gut gehend**, *s.* **gehen. g~gläubig** *adj* trusting. **g~haben†** *vt sep* **fünfzig Euro g~haben** have fifty euros credit (**bei** with). **G~haben** *nt* **-s,-** [credit] balance; (*Kredit*) credit

gut|machen *vt sep* make up for; make good (*Schaden*). **g~mütig** *adj* good-natured. **G~mütigkeit** *f* **-** good nature. **G~schein** *m* credit note; (*Bon*) voucher; (*Geschenk-*) gift token. **g~schreiben†** *vt sep* credit. **G~schrift** *f* credit

Guts|haus *nt* manor house

gut|tun* *vi sep* (*haben*) **gut tun**, *s.* **tun. g~willig** *adj* willing

Gymnasium *nt* **-s,-ien** ≈ grammar school

> i
>
> **Gymnasium** The secondary school that prepares pupils for the Abitur. After primary school the most academically gifted pupils go to a *Gymnasium*, or grammar school, for nine years. In their last three years they have some choice as to which subjects they study.

Gymnastik *f* **-** [keep-fit] exercises *pl*; (*Turnen*) gymnastics *sg*

Gynäko|loge *m* **-n,-n** gynaecologist. **G~logie** *f* **-** gynaecology

H, h /ha:/ *nt* **-,-** (*Mus*) B, b

Haar *nt* **-[e]s,-e** hair; **sich** (*dat*) **die Haare** *od* **das H~ waschen** wash one's hair; **um ein H~** [!] very nearly. **H~bürste** *f* hairbrush. **h~en** *vi* (*haben*) shed hairs; (*Tier:*) moult ● *vr* **sich h~en** moult. **h~ig** *adj* hairy; [!] tricky. **H~klemme** *f* hair grip. **H~nadelkurve** *f* hairpin bend. **H~schnitt** *m* haircut. **H~spange** *f* slide. **H~waschmittel** *nt* shampoo

Habe *f* **-** possessions *pl*

haben†

● *transitive verb*

····➤ have; (*im Präsens*) have got [!]. **er hat kein Geld** he has no money *or* [!] he hasn't got any money. **ich habe/hatte die Grippe** I've got flu/had flu. **was haben Sie da?** what have you got there? **wenn ich die Zeit hätte** if I had the time

····➤ (*empfinden*) **Angst/Hunger/Durst haben** be frightened/hungry/thirsty. **was hat er?** what's wrong with him?

····➤ (+ *Adj., es*) **es gut/schlecht haben** be well/badly off. **es schwer haben** be having a difficult time

····➤ (+ *zu*) (*müssen*) **du hast zu gehorchen** you must obey

● *auxiliary verb*

····➤ have. **ich habe/hatte ihn eben gesehen** I have *or* I've/I had *or* I'd just seen him. **er hat es gewusst** he knew it. **er hätte ihr geholfen** he would have helped her

● *reflexive verb*

····➤ ([!]: *sich aufregen*) make a fuss. **hab dich nicht so!** don't make such a fuss!

Habgier *f* greed. **h~ig** *adj* greedy

Habicht *m* **-[e]s,-e** hawk

Hachse *f* **-,-n** (*Culin*) knuckle

Hackbraten *m* meat loaf

Hacke[1] *f* **-,-n** hoe; (*Spitz-*) pick

Hacke[2] *f* **-,-n**, **Hacken** *m* **-s,-** heel
hack|en *vt* hoe; (*schlagen, zerkleinern*) chop; (*Vogel:*) peck. **H~fleisch** *nt* mince
Hafen *m* **-s,⸚** harbour; (*See-*) port. **H~arbeiter** *m* docker. **H~stadt** *f* port
Hafer *m* **-s** oats *pl*. **H~flocken** *fpl* [rolled] oats
Haft *f* **-** (*Jur*) custody; (*H~strafe*) imprisonment. **h~bar** *adj* (*Jur*) liable. **H~befehl** *m* warrant
h
haften *vi* (*haben*) cling; (*kleben*) stick; (*bürgen*) vouch/(*Jur*) be liable (**für** for)
Häftling *m* **-s,-e** detainee
Haftpflicht *f* (*Jur*) liability. **H~versicherung** *f* (*Auto*) third-party insurance
Haftung *f* **-** (*Jur*) liability
Hagebutte *f* **-,-n** rose hip
Hagel *m* **-s** hail. **h~n** *vi* (*haben*) hail
hager *adj* gaunt
Hahn *m* **-[e]s,⸚e** cock; (*Techn*) tap
Hähnchen *nt* **-s,-** (*Culin*) chicken
Hai[fisch] *m* **-[e]s,-e** shark
Häkchen *nt* **-s,-** tick
häkel|n *vt/i* (*haben*) crochet. **H~nadel** *f* crochet hook
Haken *m* **-s,-** hook; (*Häkchen*) tick; (☐*: Schwierigkeit*) snag. **h~** *vt* hook (**an** + *acc* to). **H~kreuz** *nt* swastika
halb *adj* half; **auf h~em Weg** halfway ●*adv* half; **h~ drei** half past two; **fünf [Minuten] vor/nach h~ vier** twenty-five [minutes] past three/to four. **H~e(r,s)** *f/m/nt* half [a litre]
halber *prep* (+ *gen*) for the sake of; **Geschäfte h~** on business
Halbfinale *nt* semifinal
halbieren *vt* halve, divide in half; (*Geometry*) bisect
Halb|insel *f* peninsula. **H~kreis** *m* semicircle. **H~kugel** *f* hemisphere. **h~laut** *adj* low ●*adv* in an undertone. **h~mast** *adv* at half-mast. **H~mond** *m* half moon. **H~pension** *f* half board. **h~rund** *adj* semicircular. **H~schuh** *m* [flat] shoe. **h~tags** *adv* [for] half a day; **h~tags arbeiten** ≈ work part-time. **H~ton** *m* semitone. **h~wegs** *adv* half-way; (*ziemlich*) more or less. **h~wüchsig** *adj* adolescent. **H~zeit** *f* (*Sport*) half-time; (*Spielzeit*) half
Halde *f* **-,-n** dump, tip
Hälfte *f* **-,-n** half; **zur H~** half
Halfter *f* **-,-n** & *nt* **-s,-** holster
Halle *f* **-,-n** hall; (*Hotel-*) lobby; (*Bahnhofs-*) station concourse
hallen *vi* (*haben*) resound; (*wider-*) echo
Hallen- *prefix* indoor
hallo *int* hallo
Halluzination /-ˈtsi̯oːn/ *f* **-,-en** hallucination
Halm *m* **-[e]s,-e** stalk; (*Gras-*) blade
Hals *m* **-es,⸚e** neck; (*Kehle*) throat; **aus vollem H~e** at the top of one's voice; (*lachen*) out loud. **H~band** *nt* (*pl* **-bänder**) collar. **H~schmerzen** *mpl* sore throat *sg*
halt *int* stop! (*Mil*) halt!; ☐ wait a minute!
Halt *m* **-[e]s,-e** hold; (*Stütze*) support; (*innerer*) stability; (*Anhalten*) stop; **H~ machen** stop. **h~bar** *adj* durable; (*Textiles*) hard-wearing; (*fig*) tenable; **h~bar bis** (*Comm*) use by
halten† *vt* hold; make (*Rede*); give (*Vortrag*); (*einhalten, bewahren*) keep; **[sich** (*dat*)**] etw h~** keep (*Hund*); take (*Zeitung*); **h~ für** regard as; **viel h~ von** think highly of; **sich links h~** keep left; **sich**

h~ an (+ *acc*) (*fig*) keep to ●*vi* (*haben*) hold; (*haltbar sein, bestehen bleiben*) keep; (*Freundschaft, Blumen:*) last; (*Halt machen*) stop; **auf sich** (*acc*) **h~** take pride in oneself; **zu jdm h~** be loyal to s.o.

Halte|stelle *f* stop. **H~verbot** *nt* waiting restriction; **'H~verbot'** 'no waiting'

Haltung *f* -,-en (*Körper-*) posture; (*Verhalten*) manner; (*Einstellung*) attitude; (*Fassung*) composure; (*Halten*) keeping

Hammel *m* -s,- ram; (*Culin*) mutton. **H~fleisch** *nt* mutton

Hammer *m* -s,¨ hammer

hämmern *vt/i* (*haben*) hammer

Hamster *m* -s,- hamster. **h~n** *vt/i* [!] hoard

Hand *f* -,¨e hand; **jdm die H~ geben** shake hands with s.o.; **rechter/linker H~** on the right/left; **zweiter H~** second-hand; **unter der H~** unofficially; (*geheim*) secretly; **H~ und Fuß haben** (*fig*) be sound. **H~arbeit** *f* manual work; (*handwerklich*) handicraft; (*Nadelarbeit*) needlework; (*Gegenstand*) hand-made article. **H~ball** *m* [German] handball. **H~bewegung** *f* gesture. **H~bremse** *f* handbrake. **H~buch** *nt* handbook, manual

Händedruck *m* handshake

Handel *m* -s trade, commerce; (*Unternehmen*) business; (*Geschäft*) deal; **H~ treiben** trade. **h~n** *vi* (*haben*) act; (*Handel treiben*) trade (**mit** in); **von etw** *od* **über etw** (*acc*) **h~n** deal with sth; **sich h~n um** be about, concern. **H~smarine** *f* merchant navy. **H~sschiff** *nt* merchant vessel. **H~sschule** *f* commercial college. **H~sware** *f* merchandise

Hand|feger *m* -s,- brush. **H~fläche** *f* palm. **H~gelenk** *nt* wrist. **H~gemenge** *nt* -s,- scuffle. **H~gepäck** *nt* hand luggage. **h~geschrieben** *adj* hand-written. **h~greiflich** *adj* tangible; **h~greiflich werden** become violent. **H~griff** *m* handle

handhaben *vt insep* (*reg*) handle

Handikap /'hɛndikɛp/ *nt* -s,-s handicap

Handkuss *m* kiss on the hand

Händler *m* -s,- dealer, trader

handlich *adj* handy

Handlung *f* -,-en act; (*Handeln*) action; (*Roman-*) plot; (*Geschäft*) shop. **H~sweise** *f* conduct

Hand|schellen *fpl* handcuffs. **H~schlag** *m* handshake. **H~schrift** *f* handwriting; (*Text*) manuscript. **H~schuh** *m* glove. **H~stand** *m* handstand. **H~tasche** *f* handbag. **H~tuch** *nt* towel

Handwerk *nt* craft, trade. **H~er** *m* -s,- craftsman; (*Arbeiter*) workman

Handy /'hɛndi/ *nt* -s,-s mobile phone, cell phone *Amer*

Hanf *m* -[e]s hemp

Hang *m* -[e]s,¨e slope; (*fig*) inclination

Hänge|brücke *f* suspension bridge. **H~matte** *f* hammock

hängen[1] *vt* (*reg*) hang

hängen[2]† *vi* (*haben*) hang; **h~ an** (+ *dat*) (*fig*) be attached to; **h~ lassen** leave

Hannover *nt* -s Hanover

hänseln *vt* tease

hantieren *vi* (*haben*) busy oneself

Happen *m* -s,- mouthful; **einen H~ essen** have a bite to eat

Harfe *f* -,-n harp

Harke *f* -,-n rake. **h~n** *vt/i* (*haben*) rake

harmlos *adj* harmless;

h

(*arglos*) innocent
Harmonie *f* -,-n harmony
Harmonika *f* -,-s accordion; (*Mund-*) mouth organ
harmonisch *adj* harmonious
Harn *m* -[e]s urine. **H~blase** *f* bladder
Harpune *f* -,-n harpoon
hart *adj* hard; (*heftig*) violent; (*streng*) harsh
Härte *f* -,-n hardness; (*Strenge*) harshness; (*Not*) hardship. **h~n** *vt* harden

h

Hart|faserplatte *f* hardboard. **h~näckig** *adj* stubborn; (*ausdauernd*) persistent. **H~näckigkeit** *f* - stubbornness; persistence
Harz *nt* -es,-e resin
Haschee *nt* -s,-s (*Culin*) hash
Haschisch *nt* & *m* -[s] hashish
Hase *m* -n,-n hare
Hasel *f* -,-n hazel. **H~maus** *f* dormouse. **H~nuss** *f* hazel nut
Hass *m* -es hatred
hassen *vt* hate
hässlich *adj* ugly; (*unfreundlich*) nasty. **H~keit** *f* - ugliness; nastiness
Hast *f* - haste. **h~ig** *adj* hasty, *adv* -ily, hurried
hast, hat, hatte, hätte *s.* **haben**
Haube *f* -,-n cap; (*Trocken-*) drier; (*Kühler-*) bonnet
Hauch *m* -[e]s breath; (*Luft-*) breeze; (*Duft*) whiff; (*Spur*) tinge. **h~dünn** *adj* very thin
Haue *f* -,-n pick; (🄸: *Prügel*) beating. **h~n†** *vt* beat; (*hämmern*) knock; (*meißeln*) hew; **sich h~n** fight; **übers Ohr h~n** 🄸 cheat ● *vi* (*haben*) bang (**auf** + *acc* on); **jdm ins Gesicht h~n** hit s.o. in the face
Haufen *m* -s,- heap, pile; (*Leute*) crowd
häufen *vt* heap *or* pile [up]; **sich h~** pile up; (*zunehmen*) increase
häufig *adj* frequent
Haupt *nt* -[e]s, **Häupter** head. **H~bahnhof** *m* main station. **H~fach** *nt* main subject. **H~gericht** *nt* main course
Häuptling *m* -s,-e chief
Haupt|mahlzeit *f* main meal. **H~mann** *m* (*pl* **-leute**) captain. **H~post** *f* main post office. **H~quartier** *nt* headquarters *pl.* **H~rolle** *f* lead; (*fig*) leading role. **H~sache** *f* main thing; **in der H~sache** in the main. **h~sächlich** *adj* main. **H~satz** *m* main clause. **H~stadt** *f* capital. **H~verkehrsstraße** *f* main road. **H~verkehrszeit** *f* rush hour. **H~wort** *nt* (*pl* **-wörter**) noun
Haus *nt* **-es, Häuser** house; (*Gebäude*) building; (*Schnecken-*) shell; **zu H~e** at home; **nach H~e** home. **H~arbeit** *f* housework; (*Sch*) homework. **H~arzt** *m* family doctor. **H~aufgaben** *fpl* homework *sg*. **H~besetzer** *m* -s,- squatter
hausen *vi* (*haben*) live; (*wüten*) wreak havoc
Haus|frau *f* housewife. **h~gemacht** *adj* home-made. **H~halt** *m* -[e]s,-e household; (*Pol*) budget. **h~halten†** *vi sep* (*haben*) **h~halten mit** manage carefully; conserve (*Kraft*). **H~hälterin** *f* -,-nen housekeeper. **H~haltsgeld** *nt* housekeeping [money]. **H~haltsplan** *m* budget. **H~herr** *m* head of the household; (*Gastgeber*) host
Hausierer *m* -s,- hawker
Haus|lehrer *m* [private] tutor. **H~in** *f* governess
häuslich *adj* domestic, (*Person*) domesticated
Haus|meister *m* caretaker. **H~ordnung** *f* house rules *pl.*

H~putz *m* cleaning. **H~rat** *m* -[e]s household effects *pl.* **H~schlüssel** *m* front-door key. **H~schuh** *m* slipper. **H~suchung** *f* [police] search. **H~suchungsbefehl** *m* search warrant. **H~tier** *nt* domestic animal; (*Hund, Katze*) pet. **H~tür** *f* front door. **H~wirt** *m* landlord. **H~wirtin** *f* landlady

Haut *f* -,Häute skin; (*Tier-*) hide. **H~arzt** *m* dermatologist

häuten *vt* skin; **sich h~** moult

haut|eng *adj* skin-tight. **H~farbe** *f* colour; (*Teint*) complexion

Hebamme *f* -,-n midwife

Hebel *m* -s,- lever

heben† *vt* lift; (*hoch-, steigern*) raise; **sich h~** rise; (*Nebel:*) lift; (*sich verbessern*) improve

hebräisch *adj* Hebrew

hecheln *vi* (*haben*) pant

Hecht *m* -[e]s,-e pike

Heck *nt* -s,-s (*Naut*) stern; (*Aviat*) tail; (*Auto*) rear

Hecke *f* -,-n hedge

Heck|fenster *nt* rear window. **H~tür** *f* hatchback

Heer *nt* -[e]s,-e army

Hefe *f* - yeast

Heft *nt* -[e]s,-e booklet; (*Sch*) exercise book; (*Zeitschrift*) issue. **h~en** *vt* (*nähen*) tack; (*stecken*) pin/(*klammern*) clip/(*mit Heftmaschine*) staple (**an** + *acc* to). **H~er** *m* -s,- file

heftig *adj* fierce, violent; (*Regen*) heavy; (*Schmerz, Gefühl*) intense

Heft|klammer *f* staple; (*Büro-*) paper clip. **H~maschine** *f* stapler. **H~zwecke** *f* -,-n drawing pin

Heide[1] *m* -n,-n heathen

Heide[2] *f* -,-n heath; (*Bot*) heather. **H~kraut** *nt* heather

Heidelbeere *f* bilberry

Heidin *f* -,-nen heathen

heikel *adj* difficult, tricky

heil *adj* undamaged, intact; (*Person*) unhurt; **mit h~er Haut** [!] unscathed

Heil *nt* -s salvation

Heiland *m* -s (*Relig*) Saviour

Heil|anstalt *f* sanatorium; (*Nerven-*) mental hospital. **H~bad** *nt* spa. **h~bar** *adj* curable

Heilbutt *m* -[e]s,-e halibut

heilen *vt* cure; heal (*Wunde*) ●*vi* (*sein*) heal

Heilgymnastik *f* physiotherapy

heilig *adj* holy; (*geweiht*) sacred; **der H~e Abend** Christmas Eve; **die h~e Anna** Saint Anne; (*Feiertag*); **h~ sprechen** canonize. **H~abend** *m* Christmas Eve. **H~e(r)** *m/f* saint. **H~enschein** *m* halo. **H~keit** *f* - sanctity, holiness. **H~tum** *nt* -s,⸚er shrine

heil|kräftig *adj* medicinal. **H~kräuter** *ntpl* medicinal herbs. **H~mittel** *nt* remedy. **H~praktiker** *m* -s,- practitioner of alternative medicine. **H~sarmee** *f* Salvation Army. **H~ung** *f* - cure

Heim *nt* -[e]s,-e home; (*Studenten-*) hostel. **h~** *adv* home

Heimat *f* -,-en home; (*Land*) native land. **H~stadt** *f* home town

heim|begleiten *vt sep* see home. **H~computer** *m* home computer. **h~fahren**† *v sep* ●*vi* (*sein*) go/drive home ●*vt* take/drive home. **H~fahrt** *f* way home. **h~gehen**† *vi sep* (*sein*) go home

heimisch *adj* native, indigenous; (*Pol*) domestic

Heim|kehr *f* - return [home]. **h~kehren** *vi sep* (*sein*) return home. **h~kommen**† *vi sep* (*sein*) come home

heimlich *adj* secret; **etw h~ tun**

do sth secretly. **H~keit** *f* -,-en secrecy; **H~keiten** secrets

Heim|reise *f* journey home. **H~spiel** *nt* home game. **h~suchen** *vt sep* afflict. **h~tückisch** *adj* treacherous; (*Krankheit*) insidious. **h~wärts** *adv* home. **H~weg** *m* way home. **H~weh** *nt* **-s** homesickness; **H~weh haben** be homesick. **H~werker** *m* **-s,-** [home] handyman. **h~zahlen** *vt sep* **jdm etw h~zahlen** (*fig*) pay s.o. back for sth

h

Heirat *f* -,-en marriage. **h~en** *vt/i* (*haben*) marry. **H~santrag** *m* proposal; **jdm einen H~santrag machen** propose to s.o.

heiser *adj* hoarse. **H~keit** *f* - hoarseness

heiß *adj* hot; (*hitzig*) heated; (*leidenschaftlich*) fervent

heißen† *vi* (*haben*) be called; (*bedeuten*) mean; **ich heiße** ... my name is ...; **wie h~Sie?** what is your name? **wie heißt ... auf Englisch?** what's the English for ...? ● *vt* call; **jdn etw tun h~** tell s.o. to do sth

heiter *adj* cheerful; (*Wetter*) bright; (*amüsant*) amusing; **aus h~em Himmel** (*fig*) out of the blue

Heiz|anlage *f* heating; (*Auto*) heater. **H~decke** *f* electric blanket. **h~en** *vt* heat; light (*Ofen*) ● *vi* (*haben*) put the heating on; (*Ofen:*) give out heat. **H~gerät** *nt* heater. **H~kessel** *m* boiler. **H~körper** *m* radiator. **H~lüfter** *m* **-s,-** fan heater. **H~material** *nt* fuel. **H~ung** *f* -,-en heating; (*Heizkörper*) radiator

Hektar *nt* & *m* **-s,-** hectare

Held *m* **-en,-en** hero. **h~enhaft** *adj* heroic. **H~entum** *nt* **-s** heroism. **H~in** *f* -,-nen heroine

helf|en† *vi* (*haben*) help (**jdm** s.o.); (*nützen*) be effective; **sich** (*dat*) **nicht zu h~en wissen** not know what to do; **es hilft nichts** it's no use. **H~er(in)** *m* **-s,-** (*f* -,-nen) helper, assistant

hell *adj* light; (*Licht ausstrahlend, klug*) bright; (*Stimme*) clear; (!: *völlig*) utter; **h~es Bier** ≈ lager ● *adv* brightly

Hell|igkeit *f* - brightness. **H~seher(in)** *m* **-s,-** (*f* -,-nen) clairvoyant

Helm *m* **-[e]s,-e** helmet

Hemd *nt* **-[e]s,-en** vest; (*Ober-*) shirt

Hemisphäre *f* -,-n hemisphere

hemm|en *vt* check; (*verzögern*) impede; (*fig*) inhibit. **H~ung** *f* -,-en (*fig*) inhibition; (*Skrupel*) scruple; **H~ungen haben** be inhibited. **h~ungslos** *adj* unrestrained

Hendl *nt* **-s,-[n]** (*Aust*) chicken

Hengst *m* **-[e]s,-e** stallion

Henkel *m* **-s,-** handle

Henne *f* -,-n hen

her *adv* here; (*zeitlich*) ago; **her mit** ... ! give me ... ! **von Norden/weit her** from the north/far away; **vom Thema her** as far as the subject is concerned; **her sein** come (**von** from); **es ist schon lange her** it was a long time ago

herab *adv* down [here]; **von oben h~** from above; (*fig*) condescending

herablassen† *vt sep* let down; **sich h~** condescend (**zu** to)

herab|sehen† *vi sep* (*haben*) look down (**auf** + *acc* on). **h~setzen** *vt sep* reduce, cut; (*fig*) belittle

Heraldik *f* - heraldry

heran *adv* near; **[bis] h~ an** (+ *acc*) up to. **h~kommen**† *vi sep* (*sein*) approach; **h~kommen an** (+ *acc*) come up to; (*erreichen*) get at; (*fig*) measure up to. **h~machen**

(sich) *vr sep* **sich h~machen an** (+ *acc*) approach; get down to (*Arbeit*). **h~wachsen**† *vi sep* (*sein*) grow up. **h~ziehen**† *v sep* ● *vt* pull up (**an** + *acc* to); (*züchten*) raise; (*h~bilden*) train; (*hinzuziehen*) call in ● *vi* (*sein*) approach

herauf *adv* up [here]; **die Treppe h~** up the stairs. **h~setzen** *vt sep* raise, increase

heraus *adv* out (**aus** of); **h~ damit** *od* **mit der Sprache!** out with it! **h~bekommen**† *vt sep* get out; (*ausfindig machen*) find out; (*lösen*) solve; **Geld h~bekommen** get change. **h~finden**† *v sep* ● *vt* find out ● *vi* (*haben*) find one's way out. **h~fordern** *vt sep* provoke; challenge (*Person*). **H~forderung** *f* provocation; challenge. **H~gabe** *f* handing over; (*Admin*) issue; (*Veröffentlichung*) publication. **h~geben**† *vt sep* hand over; (*Admin*) issue; (*veröffentlichen*) publish; edit (*Zeitschrift*); **jdm Geld h~geben** give s.o. change ● *vi* (*haben*) give change (**auf** + *acc* for). **H~geber** *m* **-s,-** publisher; editor. **h~halten**† **(sich)** *vr sep* (*fig*) keep out (**aus** of). **h~kommen**† *vi sep* (*sein*) come out; (*aus Schwierigkeit, Takt*) get out; **auf eins** *od* **dasselbe h~kommen** 🄸 come to the same thing. **h~lassen**† *vt sep* let out. **h~nehmen**† *vt sep* take out; **sich zu viel h~nehmen** (*fig*) take liberties. **h~reden (sich)** *vr sep* make excuses. **h~rücken** *v sep* ● *vt* move out; (*hergeben*) hand over ● *vi* (*sein*) **h~rücken mit** hand over; (*fig: sagen*) come out with. **h~schlagen**† *vt sep* knock out; (*fig*) gain. **h~stellen** *vt sep* put out; **sich h~stellen** turn out (**als** to be; **dass** that). **h~ziehen**† *vt sep* pull out

herb *adj* sharp; (*Wein*) dry; (*fig*) harsh

herbei *adv* here. **h~führen** *vt sep* (*fig*) bring about. **h~schaffen** *vt sep* get. **h~sehnen** *vt sep* long for

Herberg|e *f* **-,-n** [youth] hostel; (*Unterkunft*) lodging. **H~svater** *m* warden

herbestellen *vt sep* summon

herbitten† *vt sep* ask to come

herbringen† *vt sep* bring [here]

Herbst *m* **-[e]s,-e** autumn. **h~lich** *adj* autumnal

Herd *m* **-[e]s,-e** stove, cooker

Herde *f* **-,-n** herd; (*Schaf-*) flock

herein *adv* in [here]; **h~!** come in! **h~bitten**† *vt sep* ask in. **h~fallen**† *vi sep* (*sein*) 🄸 be taken in (**auf** + *acc* by). **h~kommen**† *vi sep* (*sein*) come in. **h~lassen**† *vt sep* let in. **h~legen** *vt sep* 🄸 take for a ride

Herfahrt *f* journey/drive here

herfallen† *vi sep* (*sein*) **~ über** (+ *acc*) attack; fall upon (*Essen*)

hergeben† *vt sep* hand over; (*fig*) give up

hergehen† *vi sep* (*sein*) **h~ vor** (+ *dat*) walk along in front of; **es ging lustig her** 🄸 there was a lot of merriment

herholen *vt sep* fetch; **weit hergeholt** (*fig*) far-fetched

Hering *m* **-s,-e** herring; (*Zeltpflock*) tent peg

her|kommen† *vi sep* (*sein*) come here; **wo kommt das her?** where does it come from? **h~kömmlich** *adj* traditional. **H~kunft** *f* **-** origin

herleiten *vt sep* derive

hermachen *vt sep* **viel/wenig h~** be impressive/unimpressive; (*wichtig nehmen*) make a lot of/little fuss (**von** of); **sich h~ über** (+ *acc*) fall upon; tackle (*Arbeit*)

Hermelin[1] *nt* **-s,-e** (*Zool*) stoat

Hermelin[2] *m* **-s,-e** (*Pelz*) ermine

h

Hernie /ˈhɛrnɪ̯ə/ *f* **-,-n** hernia
Heroin *nt* **-s** heroin
heroisch *adj* heroic
Herr *m* **-n,-en** gentleman; (*Gebieter*) master (**über** + *acc* of); **[Gott,] der H~** the Lord [God]; **H~ Meier** Mr Meier; **Sehr geehrte H~en** Dear Sirs. **H~enhaus** *nt* manor [house]. **h~enlos** *adj* ownerless; (*Tier*) stray
Herrgott *m* **der H~** the Lord
herrichten *vt sep* prepare; **wieder h~** renovate

h

Herrin *f* **-,-nen** mistress
herrlich *adj* marvellous; (*großartig*) magnificent
Herrschaft *f* **-,-en** rule; (*Macht*) power; (*Kontrolle*) control; **meine H~en!** ladies and gentlemen!
herrsch|en *vi* (*haben*) rule; (*verbreitet sein*) prevail; **es h~te Stille** there was silence. **H~er(in)** *m* **-s,-** (*f* **-,-nen**) ruler
herrühren *vi sep* (*haben*) stem (**von** from)
herstammen *vi sep* (*haben*) come (**aus**/**von** from)
herstell|en *vt sep* establish; (*Comm*) manufacture, make. **H~er** *m* **-s,-** manufacturer, maker. **H~ung** *f* **-** establishment; manufacture
herüber *adv* over [here]
herum *adv* **im Kreis h~** [round] in a circle; **falsch h~** the wrong way round; **um ... h~** round ... ; (*ungefähr*) [round] about ; **h~ sein** be over. **h~drehen** *vt sep* turn round/ (*wenden*) over; turn (*Schlüssel*). **h~gehen**† *vi sep* (*sein*) walk around; (*Zeit:*) pass; **h~gehen um** go round. **h~kommen**† *vi sep* (*sein*) get about; **h~kommen um** get round; come round (*Ecke*); **um etw [nicht] h~kommen** (*fig*) [not] get out of sth. **h~sitzen**† *vi sep* (*haben*) sit around; **h~sitzen um** sit round. **h~sprechen**† **(sich)** *vr sep* (*Gerücht:*) get about. **h~treiben**† **(sich)** *vr sep* hang around. **h~ziehen**† *vi sep* (*sein*) move around; (*ziellos*) wander about
herunter *adv* down [here]; **die Treppe h~** down the stairs. **h~fallen**† *vi* fall off. **h~gekommen** *adj* (*fig*) run-down; (*Gebäude*) dilapidated; (*Person*) down-at-heel. **h~kommen**† *vi sep* (*sein*) come down; (*fig*) go to rack and ruin; (*Firma, Person:*) go downhill; (*gesundheitlich*) get run down. **h~laden** *sep vt* † download. **h~lassen**† *vt sep* let down, lower. **h~machen** *vt sep* [!] reprimand; (*herabsetzen*) run down. **h~spielen** *vt sep* (*fig*) play down
hervor *adv* out (**aus** of). **h~bringen**† *vt sep* produce; utter (*Wort*). **h~gehen**† *vi sep* (*sein*) come/(*sich ergeben*) emerge/(*folgen*) follow (**aus** from). **h~heben**† *vt sep* (*fig*) stress, emphasize. **h~ragen** *vi sep* (*haben*) jut out; (*fig*) stand out. **h~ragend** *adj* (*fig*) outstanding. **h~rufen**† *vt sep* (*fig*) cause. **h~stehen**† *vi sep* (*haben*) protrude. **h~treten**† *vi sep* (*sein*) protrude, bulge; (*fig*) stand out. **h~tun**† **(sich)** *vr sep* (*fig*) distinguish oneself; (*angeben*) show off
Herweg *m* way here
Herz *nt* **-ens,-en** heart; (*Kartenspiel*) hearts *pl*; **sich** (*dat*) **ein H~ fassen** pluck up courage. **H~anfall** *m* heart attack
herzhaft *adj* hearty; (*würzig*) savoury
herziehen† *v sep* ● *vt* **hinter sich** (*dat*) **h~** pull along [behind one] ● *vi* (*sein*) **hinter jdm h~** follow along behind s.o.; **über jdn h~** [!] run s.o. down

herz|ig *adj* sweet, adorable. **H~infarkt** *m* heart attack. **H~klopfen** *nt* **-s** palpitations *pl*

herzlich *adj* cordial; (*warm*) warm; (*aufrichtig*) sincere; **h~en Dank!** many thanks! **h~e Grüße** kind regards

herzlos *adj* heartless

Herzog *m* **-s,⁼e** duke. **H~in** *f* **-,-nen** duchess. **H~tum** *nt* **-s,⁼er** duchy

Herzschlag *m* heartbeat; (*Med*) heart failure

Hessen *nt* **-s** Hesse

heterosexuell *adj* heterosexual

Hetze *f* **-** rush; (*Kampagne*) virulent campaign (**gegen** against). **h~n** *vt* chase; **sich h~n** hurry

Heu *nt* **-s** hay

Heuchelei *f* **-** hypocrisy

heuch|eln *vt* feign ● *vi* (*haben*) pretend. **H~ler(in)** *m* **-s,-** (*f* **-,-nen**) hypocrite. **h~lerisch** *adj* hypocritical

heuer *adv* (*Aust*) this year

heulen *vi* (*haben*) howl; (**!**: *weinen*) cry

> **Heurige** This is an Austrian term for both a new wine and an inn with new wine on tap, especially an inn with its own vineyard in the Vienna region. A garland of pine twigs outside the gates of the *Heurige* shows that the new barrel has been tapped.

Heu|schnupfen *m* hay fever. **H~schober** *m* **-s,-** haystack. **H~schrecke** *f* **-,-n** grasshopper

heut|e *adv* today; (*heutzutage*) nowadays; **h~e früh** *od* **Morgen** this morning; **von h~e auf morgen** from one day to the next. **h~ig** *adj* today's; (*gegenwärtig*) present; **der h~ige Tag** today. **h~zutage** *adv* nowadays

Hexe *f* **-,-n** witch. **h~n** *vi* (*haben*) work magic. **H~nschuss** *m* lumbago

Hieb *m* **-[e]s,-e** blow; (*Peitschen-*) lash; **H~e** hiding *sg*

hier *adv* here; **h~ sein/bleiben/lassen/behalten** be/stay/leave/keep here; **h~ und da** here and there; (*zeitlich*) now and again

hier|auf *adv* on this/these; (*antworten*) to this; (*zeitlich*) after this. **h~aus** *adv* out of *or* from this/these. **h~durch** *adv* through this/these; (*Ursache*) as a result of this. **h~her** *adv* here. **h~hin** *adv* here. **h~in** *adv* in this/these. **h~mit** *adv* with this/these; (*Comm*) herewith; (*Admin*) hereby. **h~nach** *adv* after this/these; (*demgemäß*) according to this/these. **h~über** *adv* over/(*höher*) above this/these; (*sprechen, streiten*) about this/these. **h~von** *adv* from this/these; (*h~über*) about this/these; (*Menge*) of this/these. **h~zu** *adv* to this/these; (*h~für*) for this/these. **h~zulande** *adv* here

hiesig *adj* local. **H~e(r)** *m/f* local

Hilf|e *f* **-,-n** help, aid; **um H~e rufen** call for help. **h~los** *adj* helpless. **H~losigkeit** *f* **-** helplessness. **h~reich** *adj* helpful

Hilfs|arbeiter *m* unskilled labourer. **h~bedürftig** *adj* needy; **h~bedürftig sein** be in need of help. **h~bereit** *adj* helpful. **H~kraft** *f* helper. **H~mittel** *nt* aid. **H~verb** *nt* auxiliary verb

Himbeere *f* raspberry

Himmel *m* **-s,-** sky; (*Relig & fig*) heaven; (*Bett-*) canopy; **unter freiem H~** in the open air. **H~bett** *nt* four-poster [bed].

H~fahrt *f* Ascension

himmlisch *adj* heavenly

hin *adv* there; **hin und her** to and fro; **hin und zurück** there and back; (*Rail*) return; **hin und wieder** now and again; **an** (+ *dat*) ... **hin** along; **auf** (+ *acc*) ... **hin** in reply to (*Brief, Anzeige*); on (*jds Rat*); **zu** *od* **nach** ... **hin** towards; **hin sein** 🗉 be gone; **es ist noch lange hin** it's a long time yet

hinauf *adv* up [there]. **h~gehen**† *vi sep* (*sein*) go up. **h~setzen** *vt sep* raise

hinaus *adv* out [there]; (*nach draußen*) outside; **zur Tür h~** out of the door; **auf Jahre h~** for years to come; **über etw** (*acc*) **h~** beyond sth; (*Menge*) [over and] above sth; **über etw** (*acc*) **h~ sein** (*fig*) be past sth. **h~gehen**† *vi sep* (*sein*) go out; (*Zimmer:*) face (**nach Norden** north); **h~gehen über** (+ *acc*) go beyond, exceed. **h~laufen**† *vi sep* (*sein*) run out; **h~laufen auf** (+ *acc*) (*fig*) amount to. **h~lehnen (sich)** *vr sep* lean out. **h~schieben**† *vt sep* push out; (*fig*) put off. **h~werfen**† *vt sep* throw out; (🗉: *entlassen*) fire. **h~wollen**† *vi sep* (*haben*) want to go out; **h~wollen auf** (+ *acc*) (*fig*) aim at. **h~ziehen**† *v sep* ●*vt* pull out; (*in die Länge ziehen*) drag out; (*verzögern*) delay; **sich h~ziehen** drag on; be delayed ●*vi* (*sein*) move out. **h~zögern** *vt* delay; **sich h~zögern** be delayed

Hinblick *m* **im H~ auf** (+ *acc*) in view of; (*hinsichtlich*) regarding

hinder|lich *adj* awkward; **jdm h~lich sein** hamper s.o. **h~n** *vt* hamper; (*verhindern*) prevent. **H~nis** *nt* **-ses,-se** obstacle. **H~nisrennen** *nt* steeplechase

Hindu *m* **-s,-s** Hindu.

hindurch *adv* through it/them

hinein *adv* in [there]; (*nach drinnen*) inside; **h~ in** (+ *acc*) into. **h~fallen**† *vi sep* (*sein*) fall in. **h~gehen**† *vi sep* (*sein*) go in; **h~gehen in** (+ *acc*) go into. **h~reden** *vi sep* (*haben*) **jdm h~reden** interrupt s.o.; (*sich einmischen*) interfere in s.o.'s affairs. **h~versetzen (sich)** *vr sep* **sich in jds Lage h~versetzen** put oneself in s.o.'s position. **h~ziehen**† *vt sep* pull in; **h~ziehen in** (+ *acc*) pull into; **in etw** (*acc*) **h~gezogen werden** (*fig*) become involved in sth

hin|fahren† *v sep* ●*vi* (*sein*) go/drive there ●*vt* take/drive there. **H~fahrt** *f* journey/drive there; (*Rail*) outward journey. **h~fallen**† *vi sep* (*sein*) fall. **h~fliegen**† *v sep* ●*vi* (*sein*) fly there; 🗉 fall ●*vt* fly there. **H~flug** *m* flight there; (*Aviat*) outward flight

Hingeb|ung *f* - devotion. **h~ungsvoll** *adj* devoted

hingehen† *vi sep* (*sein*) go/(*zu Fuß*) walk there; (*vergehen*) pass; **h~ zu** go up to; **wo gehst du hin?** where are you going?

hingerissen *adj* rapt; **h~ sein** be carried away (**von** by)

hinhalten† *vt sep* hold out; (*warten lassen*) keep waiting

hinken *vi* (*haben/sein*) limp

hin|knien (sich) *vr sep* kneel down. **h~kommen**† *vi sep* (*sein*) get there; (*h~gehören*) belong, go; (🗉: *auskommen*) manage (**mit** with); (🗉: *stimmen*) be right. **h~laufen**† *vi sep* (*sein*) run/(*gehen*) walk there. **h~legen** *vt sep* lay or put down; **sich h~legen** lie down. **h~nehmen**† *vt sep* (*fig*) accept

hinreichen *v sep* ●*vt* hand (*dat* to) ●*vi* (*haben*) extend (**bis** to); (*ausreichen*) be adequate. **h~d** *adj* adequate

Hinreise *f* journey there; (*Rail*) outward journey

hinreißen† *vt sep* (*fig*) carry away; **sich h~ lassen** get carried away. **h~d** *adj* ravishing

hinricht|en *vt sep* execute. **H~ung** *f* execution

hinschreiben† *vt sep* write there; (*aufschreiben*) write down

hinsehen† *vi sep* (*haben*) look

hinsetzen *vt sep* put down; **sich h~** sit down

Hinsicht *f* - **in dieser H~** in this respect; **in finanzieller H~** financially. **h~lich** *prep* (+ *gen*) regarding

hinstellen *vt sep* put *or* set down; park (*Auto*)

hinstrecken *vt sep* hold out; **sich h~** extend

hinten *adv* at the back; **dort h~** back there; **nach/von h~** to the back/from behind. **h~herum** *adv* round the back; ! by devious means

hinter *prep* (+ *dat/acc*) behind; (*nach*) after; **h~ jdm/etw herlaufen** run after s.o./something; **h~ etw** (*dat*) **stecken** (*fig*) be behind sth; **h~ etw** (*acc*) **kommen** (*fig*) get to the bottom of sth; **etw h~ sich** (*acc*) **bringen** get sth over [and done] with

Hinterbliebene *pl* (*Admin*) surviving dependants; **die H~n** the bereaved family *sg*

hintere|(r,s) *adj* back, rear; **h~s Ende** far end

hintereinander *adv* one behind/(*zeitlich*) after the other; **dreimal h~** three times in succession

Hintergedanke *m* ulterior motive

hintergehen† *vt* deceive

Hinter|grund *m* background. **H~halt** *m* **-[e]s,-e** ambush. **h~hältig** *adj* underhand

hinterher *adv* behind, after; (*zeitlich*) afterwards

Hinter|hof *m* back yard. **H~kopf** *m* back of the head

hinterlassen† *vt* leave [behind]; (*Jur*) leave, bequeath (*dat* to). **H~schaft** *f* **-,-en** (*Jur*) estate

hinterlegen *vt* deposit

Hinter|leib *m* (*Zool*) abdomen. **H~list** *f* deceit. **h~listig** *adj* deceitful. **H~n** *m* **-s,-** ! bottom, backside. **H~rad** *nt* rear *or* back wheel. **h~rücks** *adv* from behind. **h~ste(r,s)** *adj* last; **h~ste Reihe** back row. **H~teil** *nt* ! behind. **H~treppe** *f* back stairs *pl*

hinterziehen† *vt* (*Admin*) evade

hinüber *adv* over *or* across [there]; **h~ sein** (!: *unbrauchbar, tot*) have had it. **h~gehen**† *vi sep* (*sein*) go over *or* across; **h~gehen über** (+ *acc*) cross

hinunter *adv* down [there]. **h~gehen**† *vi sep* (*sein*) go down. **h~schlucken** *vt sep* swallow

Hinweg *m* way there

hinweg *adv* away, off; **h~ über** (+ *acc*) over; **über eine Zeit h~** over a period. **h~kommen**† *vt sep* (*sein*) **h~kommen über** (+ *acc*) (*fig*) get over. **h~sehen**† *vi sep* (*haben*) **h~sehen über** (+ *acc*) see over; (*fig*) overlook. **h~setzen** (sich) *vr sep* **sich h~setzen über** (+ *acc*) ignore

Hinweis *m* **-es,-e** reference; (*Andeutung*) hint; (*Anzeichen*) indication; **unter H~ auf** (+ *acc*) with reference to. **h~en**† *v sep* ●*vi* (*haben*) point (**auf** + *acc* to) ●*vt* **jdn auf etw** (*acc*) **h~en** point sth out to s.o.

hinwieder *adv* on the other hand

hin|zeigen *vi sep (haben)* point (**auf** + *acc* to). **h~ziehen**† *vt sep* pull; (*fig: in die Länge ziehen*) drag out; (*verzögern*) delay; **sich h~ziehen** drag on

hinzu *adv* in addition. **h~fügen** *vt sep* add. **h~kommen**† *vt sep (sein)* be added; (*ankommen*) arrive [on the scene]; join (**zu jdm** s.o.). **h~ziehen**† *vt sep* call in

Hiobsbotschaft *f* bad news *sg*

Hirn *nt* **-s** brain; (*Culin*) brains *pl*. **H~hautentzündung** *f* meningitis

h

Hirsch *m* **-[e]s,-e** deer; (*männlich*) stag; (*Culin*) venison

Hirse *f* **-** millet

Hirt *m* **-en,-en**, **Hirte** *m* **-n,-n** shepherd

hissen *vt* hoist

Histor|iker *m* **-s,-** historian. **h~isch** *adj* historical; (*bedeutend*) historic

Hitz|e *f* **-** heat. **h~ig** *adj* (*fig*) heated; (*Person*) hot-headed; (*jähzornig*) hot-tempered. **H~schlag** *m* heat-stroke

H-Milch /'ha:-/ *f* long-life milk

Hobby *nt* **-s,-s** hobby

Hobel *m* **-s,-** (*Techn*) plane; (*Culin*) slicer. **h~n** *vt/i (haben)* plane. **H~späne** *mpl* shavings

hoch *adj* (*attrib* **hohe(r,s)**) high; (*Baum, Mast*) tall; (*Offizier*) high-ranking; (*Alter*) great; (*Summe*) large; (*Strafe*) heavy; **hohe Schuhe** ankle boots ● *adv* high; (*sehr*) highly; **h~ gewachsen** tall; **h~ begabt** highly gifted; **h~ gestellte Persönlichkeit** important person; **die Treppe h~** up the stairs; **sechs Mann h~** six of us/them. **H~** *nt* **-s,-s** cheer; (*Meteorology*) high

Hoch|achtung *f* high esteem. **H~achtungsvoll** *adv* Yours faithfully. **H~betrieb** *m* great activity; **in den Geschäften herrscht H~betrieb** the shops are terribly busy. **H~deutsch** *nt* High German. **H~druck** *m* high pressure. **H~ebene** *f* plateau. **h~fahren**† *vi sep (sein)* go up; (*auffahren*) start up; (*aufbrausen*) flare up. **h~gehen**† *vi sep (sein)* go up; (*explodieren*) blow up; (*aufbrausen*) flare up. **h~gestellt** *attrib adj* (*Zahl*) superior; (*fig*) ***h~ gestellt**, *s.* **hoch**. **H~glanz** *m* high gloss. **h~gradig** *adj* extreme. **h~hackig** *adj* high-heeled. **h~halten**† *vt sep* hold up; (*fig*) uphold. **H~haus** *nt* high-rise building. **h~heben**† *vt sep* lift up; raise (*Hand*). **h~kant** *adv* on end. **h~kommen**† *vi sep (sein)* come up; (*aufstehen*) get up; (*fig*) get on [in the world]. **H~konjunktur** *f* boom. **h~krempeln** *vt sep* roll up. **h~leben** *vi sep (haben)* **h~leben lassen** give three cheers for; **H~mut** *m* pride, arrogance. **h~näsig** *adj* [!] snooty. **H~ofen** *m* blast-furnace. **h~ragen** *vi sep* rise [up]; (*Turm:*) soar. **H~ruf** *m* cheer. **H~saison** *f* high season. **h~schlagen**† *vt sep* turn up (*Kragen*). **H~schule** *f* university; (*Musik-, Kunst-*) academy. **H~sommer** *m* midsummer. **H~spannung** *f* high/(*fig*) great tension. **h~spielen** *vt sep* (*fig*) magnify. **H~sprung** *m* high jump

> i
>
> **Hochdeutsch** There are many regional dialects in Germany, Austria and Switzerland. *Hochdeutsch* (High German) is the standard language that can be understood by all German speakers. Newspapers and books are generally printed in *Hochdeutsch*.

höchst *adv* extremely, most

Hochstapler *m* **-s,-** confidence trickster

höchst|e(r,s) *adj* highest; (*Baum, Turm*) tallest; (*oberste, größte*) top; **es ist h~e Zeit** it is high time. **h~ens** *adv* at most; (*es sei denn*) except perhaps. **H~geschwindigkeit** *f* top or maximum speed. **H~maß** *nt* maximum. **h~persönlich** *adv* in person. **H~preis** *m* top price. **H~temperatur** *f* maximum temperature

Hoch|verrat *m* high treason. **H~wasser** *nt* high tide; (*Überschwemmung*) floods *pl.* **H~würden** *m* **-s** Reverend; (*Anrede*) Father

Hochzeit *f* **-,-en** wedding. **H~skleid** *nt* wedding dress. **H~sreise** *f* honeymoon [trip]. **H~stag** *m* wedding day/(*Jahrestag*) anniversary

Hocke *f* **- in der H~ sitzen** squat. **h~n** *vi* (*haben*) squat ●*vr* **sich h~n** squat down

Hocker *m* **-s,-** stool

Höcker *m* **-s,-** bump; (*Kamel-*) hump

Hockey /hɔki/ *nt* **-s** hockey

Hode *f* **-,-n, Hoden** *m* **-s,-** testicle

Hof *m* **-[e]s,⸚e** [court]yard; (*Bauern-*) farm; (*Königs-*) court; (*Schul-*) playground; (*Astronomy*) halo

hoffen *vt/i* (*haben*) hope (**auf** + *acc* for). **h~tlich** *adv* I hope so, hopefully

Hoffnung *f* **-,-en** hope. **h~slos** *adj* hopeless. **h~svoll** *adj* hopeful

höflich *adj* polite. **H~keit** *f* **-,-en** politeness, courtesy

hohe(r,s) *adj s.* **hoch**

Höhe *f* **-,-n** height; (*Aviat, Geog*) altitude; (*Niveau*) level; (*einer Summe*) size; (*An-*) hill

Hoheit *f* **-,-en** (*Staats-*) sovereignty; (*Titel*) Highness. **H~sgebiet** *nt* [sovereign] territory. **H~szeichen** *nt* national emblem

Höhe|nlinie *f* contour line. **H~nsonne** *f* sun lamp. **H~punkt** *m* (*fig*) climax, peak. **h~r** *adj & adv* higher; **h~re Schule** secondary school

hohl *adj* hollow; (*leer*) empty

Höhle *f* **-,-n** cave; (*Tier-*) den; (*Hohlraum*) cavity; (*Augen-*) socket

Hohl|maß *nt* measure of capacity. **H~raum** *m* cavity

Hohn *m* **-s** scorn, derision

höhnen *vt* deride

holen *vt* fetch, get; (*kaufen*) buy; (*nehmen*) take (**aus** from)

Holland *nt* **-s** Holland

Holländ|er *m* **-s,-** Dutchman; **die H~er** the Dutch *pl.* **H~erin** *f* **-,-nen** Dutchwoman. **h~isch** *adj* Dutch

Höll|e *f* **-** hell. **h~isch** *adj* infernal; (*schrecklich*) terrible

Holunder *m* **-s** (*Bot*) elder

Holz *nt* **-es,⸚er** wood; (*Nutz-*) timber. **H~blasinstrument** *nt* woodwind instrument

hölzern *adj* wooden

Holz|hammer *m* mallet. **~ig** *adj* woody. **H~kohle** *f* charcoal. **H~schnitt** *m* woodcut. **H~wolle** *f* wood shavings *pl*

Homöopathie *f* **-** homoeopathy

homöopathisch *adj* homoeopathic

homosexuell *adj* homosexual. **H~e(r)** *m/f* homosexual

Honig *m* **-s** honey. **H~wabe** *f* honeycomb

Hono|rar *nt* **-s,-e** fee. **h~rieren** *vt* remunerate; (*fig*) reward

Hopfen *m* **-s** hops *pl*; (*Bot*) hop

hopsen *vi* (*sein*) jump

horchen *vi* (*haben*) listen (**auf** +

acc to); (*heimlich*) eavesdrop

hören *vt* hear; (*an-*) listen to ● *vi* (*haben*) hear; (*horchen*) listen; (*gehorchen*) obey; **h~ auf** (+ *acc*) listen to

Hör|er *m* **-s,-** listener; (*Teleph*) receiver. **H~funk** *m* radio. **H~gerät** *nt* hearing aid

Horizon|t *m* **-[e]s** horizon. **h~tal** *adj* horizontal

Hormon *nt* **-s,-e** hormone

Horn *nt* **-s,¨er** horn. **H~haut** *f* hard skin; (*Augen-*) cornea

Hornisse *f* **-,-n** hornet

Horoskop *nt* **-[e]s,-e** horoscope

Horrorfilm *m* horror film

Hör|saal *m* (*Univ*) lecture hall. **H~spiel** *nt* radio play

Hort *m* **-[e]s,-e** (*Schatz*) hoard; (*fig*) refuge. **h~en** *vt* hoard

Hortensie /-i̯ə/ *f* **-,-n** hydrangea

Hose *f* **-,-n**, **Hosen** *pl* trousers *pl.* **H~nrock** *m* culottes *pl.* **H~nschlitz** *m* fly, flies *pl.* **H~nträger** *mpl* braces

Hostess *f* **-,-tessen** hostess; (*Aviat*) air hostess

Hostie /ˈhɔsti̯ə/ *f* **-,-n** (*Relig*) host

Hotel *nt* **-s,-s** hotel

hübsch *adj* pretty; (*nett*) nice

Hubschrauber *m* **-s,-** helicopter

Huf *m* **-[e]s,-e** hoof. **H~eisen** *nt* horseshoe

Hüft|e *f* **-,-n** hip. **H~gürtel** *m* **-s,-** girdle

Hügel *m* **-s,-** hill. **h~ig** *adj* hilly

Huhn *nt* **-s,¨er** chicken; (*Henne*) hen

Hühn|chen *nt* **-s,-** chicken. **H~erauge** *nt* corn **H~erstall** *m* henhouse

Hülle *f* **-,-n** cover; (*Verpackung*) wrapping; (*Platten-*) sleeve. **h~n** *vt* wrap

Hülse *f* **-,-n** (*Bot*) pod; (*Etui*) case. **H~nfrüchte** *fpl* pulses

human *adj* humane. **H~ität** *f* **-** humanity

Hummel *f* **-,-n** bumble bee

Hummer *m* **-s,-** lobster

Hum|or *m* **-s** humour; **H~or haben** have a sense of humour. **h~orvoll** *adj* humorous

humpeln *vi* (*sein/haben*) hobble

Humpen *m* **-s,-** tankard

Hund *m* **-[e]s,-e** dog; (*Jagd-*) hound. **H~ehütte** *f* kennel

hundert *inv adj* one/a hundred. **H~** *nt* **-s,-e** hundred; **H~e** *od* **h~e von** hundreds of. **H~jahrfeier** *f* centenary. **h~prozentig** *adj & adv* one hundred per cent. **h~ste(r,s)** *adj* hundredth. **H~stel** *nt* **-s,-** hundredth

Hündin *f* **-,-nen** bitch

Hüne *m* **-n,-n** giant

Hunger *m* **-s** hunger; **H~ haben** be hungry. **h~n** *vi* (*haben*) starve. **H~snot** *f* famine

hungrig *adj* hungry

Hupe *f* **-,-n** (*Auto*) horn. **h~n** *vi* (*haben*) sound one's horn

hüpfen *vi* (*sein*) skip; (*Frosch:*) hop; (*Grashüpfer:*) jump

Hürde *f* **-,-n** (*Sport & fig*) hurdle; (*Schaf-*) pen, fold

Hure *f* **-,-n** whore

hurra *int* hurray

husten *vi* (*haben*) cough. **H~** *m* **-s** cough. **H~saft** *m* cough mixture

Hut[1] *m* **-[e]s,¨e** hat; (*Pilz-*) cap

Hut[2] *f* **-** **auf der H~ sein** be on one's guard (**vor** + *dat* against)

hüten *vt* watch over; tend (*Tiere*); (*aufpassen*) look after; **das Bett h~ müssen** be confined to bed; **sich h~** be on one's guard (**vor** + *dat* against); **sich h~, etw zu tun** take care not to do sth

Hütte *f* **-,-n** hut; (*Hunde-*) kennel; (*Techn*) iron and steel works. **H~nkäse** *m* cottage cheese. **H~nkunde** *f* metallurgy

Hyäne *f* **-,-n** hyena

hydraulisch *adj* hydraulic

Hygien|e /hy'gje:nə/ *f* - hygiene. **h~isch** *adj* hygienic

Hypno|se *f* - hypnosis. **h~tisch** *adj* hypnotic. **H~tiseur** *m* **-s,-e** hypnotist. **h~tisieren** *vt* hypnotize

Hypochonder /hypo'xɔndɐ/ *m* **-s,-** hypochondriac

Hypothek *f* **-,-en** mortgage

Hypothese *f* **-,-n** hypothesis

Hys|terie *f* - hysteria. **h~terisch** *adj* hysterical

Ii

ich *pron* I; **ich bins** it's me. **Ich** *nt* **-[s],-[s]** self; (*Psychology*) ego

IC-Zug /i'tse:-/ *m* inter-city train

ideal *adj* ideal. **I~** *nt* **-s,-e** ideal. **I~ismus** *m* - idealism. **I~ist(in)** *m* **-en,-en** (*f* **-,-nen**) idealist. **i~istisch** *adj* idealistic

Idee *f* **-,-n** idea; **fixe I~** obsession

identifizieren *vt* identify

identisch *adj* identical

Identität *f* **-, -en** identity

Ideo|logie *f* **-,-n** ideology. **i~logisch** *adj* ideological

idiomatisch *adj* idiomatic

Idiot *m* **-en,-en** idiot. **i~isch** *adj* idiotic

idyllisch /i'dʏlɪʃ/ *adj* idyllic

Igel *m* **-s,-** hedgehog

ihm *pron* (*dat of* **er, es**) [to] him; (*Ding, Tier*) [to] it

ihn *pron* (*acc of* **er**) him; (*Ding, Tier*) it. **i~en** *pron* (*dat of* **sie** *pl*) [to] them. **I~en** *pron* (*dat of* **Sie**) [to] you

ihr *pron* (*2nd pers pl*) you ● (*dat of* **sie** *sg*) [to] her; (*Ding, Tier*) [to] it ● *poss pron* her; (*Ding, Tier*) its; (*pl*) their. **Ihr** *poss pron* your. **i~e(r,s)** *poss pron* hers; (*pl*) theirs. **I~e(r,s)** *poss pron* yours. **i~erseits** *adv* for her/(*pl*) their part. **I~erseits** *adv* on your part. **i~etwegen** *adv* for her/(*Ding, Tier*) its/(*pl*) their sake; (*wegen*) because of her/it/them, on her/its/their account. **I~etwegen** *adv* for your sake; (*wegen*) because of you, on your account. **i~ige** *poss pron* **der/die/das i~ige** hers; (*pl*) theirs. **I~ige** *poss pron* **der/die/das I~ige** yours. **i~s** *poss pron* hers; (*pl*) theirs. **I~s** *poss pron* yours

Ikone *f* **-,-n** icon

illegal *adj* illegal

Illus|ion *f* **-,-en** illusion. **i~orisch** *adj* illusory

Illustr|ation /-'tsjo:n/ *f* **-,-en** illustration. **i~ieren** *vt* illustrate. **I~ierte** *f* **-n,-[n]** [illustrated] magazine

Iltis *m* **-ses,-se** polecat

im *prep* = **in dem**

Imbiss *m* snack. **I~stube** *f* snack bar

Imit|ation /-'tsjo:n/ *f* **-,-en** imitation. **i~ieren** *vt* imitate

Imker *m* **-s,-** bee-keeper

Immatrikul|ation /-'tsjo:n/ *f* - (*Univ*) enrolment. **i~ieren** *vt* (*Univ*) enrol; **sich i~ieren** enrol

immer *adv* always; **für i~** for ever;

(*endgültig*) for good; **i~ noch** still; **i~ mehr** more and more; **was i~** whatever. **i~hin** *adv* (*wenigstens*) at least; (*trotzdem*) all the same; (*schließlich*) after all. **i~zu** *adv* all the time

Immobilien /-i̯ən/ *pl* real estate *sg*. **I~makler** *m* estate agent

immun *adj* immune (**gegen** to)

Imperialismus *m* - imperialism

impf|en *vt* vaccinate, inoculate. **I~stoff** *m* vaccine. **I~ung** *f* -,-en vaccination, inoculation

imponieren *vi* (*haben*) impress (**jdm** s.o.)

Impor|t *m* -[e]s,-e import. **I~teur** *m* -s,-e importer. **i~tieren** *vt* import

impoten|t *adj* (*Med*) impotent. **I~z** *f* - (*Med*) impotence

imprägnieren *vt* waterproof

Impressionismus *m* - impressionism

improvisieren *vt/i* (*haben*) improvise

imstande *pred adj* able (**zu** to); capable (**etw zu tun** of doing sth)

in *prep* (+ *dat*) in; (+ *acc*) into, in; (*bei Bus, Zug*) on; **in der Schule** at school; **in die Schule** to school ● *adj* **in sein** be in

Inbegriff *m* embodiment

indem *conj* (*während*) while; (*dadurch*) by (+ -ing)

Inder(in) *m* -s,- (*f* -,-nen) Indian

indessen *conj* while ● *adv* (*unterdessen*) meanwhile

Indian|er(in) *m* -s,- (*f* -,-nen) (American) Indian. **i~isch** *adj* Indian

Indien /ˈɪndi̯ən/ *nt* -s India

indirekt *adj* indirect

indisch *adj* Indian

indiskret *adj* indiscreet

indiskutabel *adj* out of the question

Individu|alist *m* -en,-en individualist. **I~alität** *f* - individuality. **i~ell** *adj* individual

Indizienbeweis /ɪnˈdiːtsi̯ən-/ *m* circumstantial evidence

industr|ialisiert *adj* industrialized. **I~ie** *f* -,-n industry. **i~iell** *adj* industrial

ineinander *adv* in/into one another

Infanterie *f* - infantry

Infektion /-ˈtsi̯oːn/ *f* -,-en infection. **I~skrankheit** *f* infectious disease

infizieren *vt* infect; **sich i~** become/ (*Person:*) be infected

Inflation /-ˈtsi̯oːn/ *f* - inflation. **i~är** *adj* inflationary

infolge *prep* (+ *gen*) as a result of. **i~dessen** *adv* consequently

Inform|atik *f* - information science. **I~ation** *f* -,-en information; **I~ationen** information *sg*. **i~ieren** *vt* inform; **sich i~ieren** find out (**über** + *acc* about)

infrage *adv* **etw i~ stellen** question sth; (*ungewiss machen*) make sth doubtful; **nicht i~ kommen** be out of the question

infrarot *adj* infra-red

Ingenieur /ɪnʒeˈni̯øːɐ̯/ *m* -s,-e engineer

Ingwer *m* -s ginger

Inhaber(in) *m* -s,- (*f* -,-nen) holder; (*Besitzer*) proprietor; (*Scheck-*) bearer

inhaftieren *vt* take into custody

inhalieren *vt/i* (*haben*) inhale

Inhalt *m* -[e]s,-e contents *pl*; (*Bedeutung, Gehalt*) content; (*Ge-*

schichte) story. **I~sangabe** *f* summary. **I~sverzeichnis** *nt* list/(*in Buch*) table of contents

Initiative /initsi̯a'ti:və/ *f* -,-**n** initiative

inklusive *prep* (+ *gen*) including ● *adv* inclusive

inkonsequent *adj* inconsistent

inkorrekt *adj* incorrect

Inkubationszeit /-'tsi̯o:ns-/ *f* (*Med*) incubation period

Inland *nt* -**[e]s** home country; (*Binnenland*) interior. **I~sgespräch** *nt* inland call

inmitten *prep* (+ *gen*) in the middle of; (*unter*) amongst

innen *adv* inside; **nach i~** inwards. **I~architekt(in)** *m*(*f*) interior designer. **I~minister** *m* Minister of the Interior; (*in UK*) Home Secretary. **I~politik** *f* domestic policy. **I~stadt** *f* town centre

inner|e(r,s) *adj* inner; (*Med, Pol*) internal. **I~e(s)** *nt* interior; (*Mitte*) centre; (*fig: Seele*) inner being. **I~eien** *fpl* (*Culin*) offal *sg*. **i~halb** *prep* (+ *gen*) inside; (*zeitlich & fig*) within; (*während*) during ● *adv* **i~halb von** within. **i~lich** *adj* internal

innig *adj* sincere

innovativ *adj* innovative

Innung *f* -,-**en** guild

ins *prep* = **in das**

Insasse *m* -**n**,-**n** inmate; (*im Auto*) occupant; (*Passagier*) passenger

insbesondere *adv* especially

Inschrift *f* inscription

Insekt *nt* -[e]s,-**en** insect. **I~envertilgungsmittel** *nt* insecticide

Insel *f* -,-**n** island

Inser|at *nt* -[e]s,-**e** [newspaper] advertisement. **i~ieren** *vt/i* (*haben*) advertise

insge|heim *adv* secretly. **i~samt** *adv* [all] in all

insofern, **insoweit** *adv* in this respect; **i~ als** in as much as

Insp|ektion /ɪnspɛk'tsi̯o:n/ *f* -,-**en** inspection. **I~ektor** *m* -**en**,-**en** inspector

Install|ateur /ɪnstala'tø:ɐ̯/ *m* -**s**,-**e** fitter; (*Klempner*) plumber. **i~ieren** *vt* install

instand *adv* **i~ halten** maintain; (*pflegen*) look after. **I~haltung** *f* - maintenance, upkeep

Instandsetzung *f* - repair

Instanz /-st-/ *f* -,-**en** authority

Instinkt /-st-/ *m* -**[e]s**,-**e** instinct. **i~iv** *adj* instinctive

Institut /-st-/ *nt* -**[e]s**,-**e** institute

Instrument /-st-/ *nt* -**[e]s**,-**e** instrument. **I~almusik** *f* instrumental music

Insulin *nt* -**s** insulin

inszenier|en *vt* (*Theat*) produce. **I~ung** *f* -,-**en** production

Integr|ation /-'tsi̯o:n/ *f* - integration. **i~ieren** *vt* integrate; **sich i~ieren** integrate

Intellekt *m* -**[e]s** intellect. **i~uell** *adj* intellectual

intelligen|t *adj* intelligent. **I~z** *f* - intelligence

Intendant *m* -**en**,-**en** director

Intensivstation *f* intensive-care unit

interaktiv *adj* interactive

inter|essant *adj* interesting. **I~esse** *nt* -**s**,-**n** interest; **I~esse haben** be interested (**an** + *dat* in). **I~essengruppe** *f* pressure group. **I~essent** *m* -**en**,-**en** interested party; (*Käufer*) prospective buyer. **i~essieren** *vt* interest; **sich i~es-**

sieren be interested (**für** in)

Inter|nat *nt* **-[e]s,-e** boarding school. **i~national** *adj* international. **I~nist** *m* **-en,-en** specialist in internal diseases. **I~pretation** /-'ts:iʃo:n/ *f* **-,-en** interpretation. **i~pretieren** *vt* interpret. **I~vall** *nt* **-s,-e** interval. **I~vention** /-'ts:iʃo:n/ *f* **-,-en** intervention

Internet *nt* **-s,-s** Internet; **im I~** on the Internet

Interview /'ɪntɐvju:/ *nt* **-s,-s** interview. **i~en** *vt* interview

intim *adj* intimate

i

intoleran|t *adj* intolerant. **I~z** *f* **-** intolerance

intravenös *adj* intravenous

Intrige *f* **-,-n** intrigue

introvertiert *adj* introverted

Invalidenrente *f* disability pension

Invasion *f* **-,-en** invasion

Inven|tar *nt* **-s,-e** furnishings and fittings *pl*; (*Techn*) equipment; (*Bestand*) stock; (*Liste*) inventory. **I~tur** *f* **-,-en** stock-taking

investieren *vt* invest

inwie|fern *adv* in what way. **i~weit** *adv* how far, to what extent

Inzest *m* **-[e]s** incest

inzwischen *adv* in the meantime

Irak (der) -[s] Iraq. **i~isch** *adj* Iraqi

Iran (der) -[s] Iran. **i~isch** *adj* Iranian

irdisch *adj* earthly

Ire *m* **-n,-n** Irishman; **die I~n** the Irish *pl*

irgend *adv* **wenn i~ möglich** if at all possible. **i~ein** *indefinite article* some/any; **i~ein anderer** someone/anyone else. **i~eine(r,s)** *pron* any one; (*jemand*) someone/anyone. **i~etwas** *pron* something; anything. **i~jemand** *pron* someone; anyone. **i~wann** *pron* at some time [or other]/at any time. **i~was** *pron* [!] something [or other]/anything. **i~welche(r,s)** *pron* any. **i~wer** *pron* someone/anyone. **i~wie** *adv* somehow [or other]. **i~wo** *adv* somewhere

Irin *f* **-,-nen** Irishwoman

irisch *adj* Irish

Irland *nt* **-s** Ireland

Ironie *f* **-** irony

ironisch *adj* ironic

irre *adj* mad, crazy; ([!]: *gewaltig*) incredible. **I~(r)** *m*/*f* lunatic. **i~führen** *vt sep* (*fig*) mislead

irre|machen *vt sep* confuse. **i~n** *vi*/*r* (*haben*) **[sich] i~n** be mistaken ● *vi* (*sein*) wander. **I~nanstalt** *f*, **I~nhaus** *nt* lunatic asylum. **i~werden**† *vi sep* (*sein*) get confused

Irrgarten *m* maze

irritieren *vt* irritate

Irr|sinn *m* madness, lunacy. **i~sinnig** *adj* mad; ([!]: *gewaltig*) incredible. **I~tum** *m* **-s,¨er** mistake

Ischias *m* & *nt* **-** sciatica

Islam (der) -[s] Islam. **islamisch** *adj* Islamic

Island *nt* **-s** Iceland

Isolier|band *nt* insulating tape. **i~en** *vt* isolate; (*Phys, Electr*) insulate; (*gegen Schall*) soundproof. **I~ung** *f* **-** isolation; insulation; soundproofing

Isra|el /'ɪsrae:l/ *nt* **-s** Israel. **I~eli** *m* **-[s],-s** & *f* **-,-[s]** Israeli. **i~elisch** *adj* Israeli

ist *s.* **sein; er ist** he is

Ital|ien /-i̯ən/ *nt* **-s** Italy. **I~iener(in)** *m* **-s,-** (*f* **-,-nen**) Italian. **i~ienisch** *adj* Italian. **I~ienisch** *nt* **-[s]** (*Lang*) Italian

Jj

ja *adv*, **Ja** *nt* **-[s]** yes; **ich glaube ja** I think so; **ja nicht!** not on any account! **da seid ihr ja!** there you are!

Jacht *f* **-,-en** yacht

Jacke *f* **-,-n** jacket; (*Strick-*) cardigan

Jackett /ʒa'kɛt/ *nt* **-s,-s** jacket

Jade *m* **-[s]** & *f* **-** jade

Jagd *f* **-,-en** hunt; (*Schießen*) shoot; (*Jagen*) hunting; shooting; (*fig*) pursuit (**nach** of); **auf die J∼ gehen** go hunting/shooting. **J∼gewehr** *nt* sporting gun. **J∼hund** *m* gun-dog: (*Hetzhund*) hound

jagen *vt* hunt; (*schießen*) shoot; (*verfolgen, wegjagen*) chase; (*treiben*) drive; **sich j∼** chase each other; **in die Luft j∼** blow up ●*vi* (*haben*) hunt, go hunting/shooting; (*fig*) chase (**nach** after) ●*vi* (*sein*) race, dash

Jäger *m* **-s,-** hunter

Jahr *nt* **-[e]s,-e** year. **j∼elang** *adv* for years. **J∼eszahl** *f* year. **J∼eszeit** *f* season. **J∼gang** *m* year; (*Wein*) vintage. **J∼hundert** *nt* century

jährlich *adj* annual, yearly

Jahr|markt *m* fair. **J∼tausend** *nt* millennium. **J∼zehnt** *nt* **-[e]s,-e** decade

Jähzorn *m* violent temper. **j∼ig** *adj* hot-tempered

Jalousie /ʒalu'zi:/ *f* **-,-n** venetian blind

Jammer *m* **-s** misery

jämmerlich *adj* miserable; (*Mitleid erregend*) pitiful

jammern *vi* (*haben*) lament ●*vt* **jdn j∼n** arouse s.o.'s pity

Jänner *m* **-s,-** (*Aust*) January

Januar *m* **-s,-e** January

Jap|an *nt* **-s** Japan. **J∼aner(in)** *m* **-s,-** (*f* **-,-nen**) Japanese. **j∼anisch** *adj* Japanese. **J∼anisch** *nt* **-[s]** (*Lang*) Japanese

jäten *vt/i* (*haben*) **weed**

jaulen *vi* (*haben*) yelp

Jause *f* **-,-n** (*Aust*) snack

jawohl *adv* yes

Jazz /jats, dʒɛs/ *m* **-** jazz

je *adv* (*jemals*) ever; (*jeweils*) each; (*pro*) per; **je nach** according to; **seit eh und je** always ●*conj* **je mehr, desto besser** the more the better ●*prep* (+ *acc*) per

Jeans /dʒi:ns/ *pl* jeans

jed|e(r,s) *pron* every; (*j∼er Einzelne*) each; (*j∼er Beliebige*) any; (*substantivisch*) everyone; each one; anyone; **ohne j∼en Grund** without any reason. **j∼enfalls** *adv* in any case; (*wenigstens*) at least. **j∼ermann** *pron* everyone. **j∼erzeit** *adv* at any time. **j∼esmal** *adv* every time

jedoch *adv* & *conj* however

jemals *adv* ever

jemand *pron* someone, somebody; (*fragend, verneint*) anyone, anybody

jen|e(r,s) *pron* that; (*pl*) those; (*substantivisch*) that one; (*pl*) those. **j∼seits** *prep* (+ *gen*) [on] the other side of

jetzt *adv* now

jiddisch *adj*, **J∼** *nt* **-[s]** Yiddish

Job /dʒɔp/ *m* **-s,-s** job. **j∼ben** *vi* (*haben*) [!] work

Joch *nt* **-[e]s,-e** yoke

Jockei, **Jockey** /'dʒɔki/ *m* **-s,-s** jockey

Jod *nt* **-[e]s** iodine

jodeln *vi* (*haben*) yodel

Joga *m* & *nt* **-[s]** yoga

joggen /'dʒɔgən/ *vi* (*haben*/

sein) jog
Joghurt, **Jogurt** *m* & *nt* -[s] yoghurt
Johannisbeere *f* redcurrant
Joker *m* -s,- (*Karte*) joker
Jolle *f* -,-n dinghy
Jongleur /ʒõ'glø:ɐ̯/ *m* -s,-e juggler
Jordanien /-i̯ən/ *nt* -s Jordan
Journalis|mus /ʒʊrna'lɪsmʊs/ *m* - journalism. **J~t(in)** *m* -en,-en (*f* -,-nen) journalist
Jubel *m* -s rejoicing, jubilation. **j~n** *vi* (*haben*) rejoice
Jubiläum *nt* -s,-äen jubilee; (*Jahrestag*) anniversary
jucken *vi* (*haben*) itch; **sich j~en** scratch; **es j~t mich** I have an itch
Jude *m* -n,-n Jew. **J~ntum** *nt* -s Judaism; (*Juden*) Jewry
Jüd|in *f* -,-nen Jewess. **j~isch** *adj* Jewish
Judo *nt* -[s] judo
Jugend *f* - youth; (*junge Leute*) young people *pl*. **J~herberge** *f* youth hostel. **J~kriminalität** *f* juvenile delinquency. **j~lich** *adj* youthful. **J~liche(r)** *m/f* young man/woman. **J~liche** *pl* young people. **J~stil** *m* art nouveau
Jugoslaw|ien /-i̯ən/ *nt* -s Yugoslavia. **j~isch** *adj* Yugoslav
Juli *m* -[s],-s July
jung *adj* young; (*Wein*) new ● *pron* **J~ und Alt** young and old. **J~e** *m* -n,-n boy. **J~e(s)** *nt* young animal/bird; (*Katzen-*) kitten; (*Bären-*) cub; (*Hunde-*) pup; **die J~en** the young *pl*
Jünger *m* -s,- disciple
Jung|frau *f* virgin; (*Astrology*) Virgo. **J~geselle** *m* bachelor
Jüngling *m* -s,-e youth
jüngst|e(r,s) *adj* youngest; (*neueste*) latest; **in j~er Zeit** recently
Juni *m* -[s],-s June
Jura *pl* law *sg*
Jurist|(in) *m* -en,-en (*f* -,-nen) lawyer. **j~isch** *adj* legal
Jury /ʒy'ri:/ *f* -,-s jury; (*Sport*) judges *pl*
Justiz *f* - die **J~** justice
Juwel *nt* -s,-en & (*fig*) -e jewel. **J~ier** *m* -s,-e jeweller
Jux *m* -es,-e ⊡ joke; **aus Jux** for fun

Kk

Kabarett *nt* -s,-s & -e cabaret
Kabel *nt* -s,- cable. **K~fernsehen** *nt* cable television
Kabeljau *m* -s,-e & -s cod
Kabine *f* -,-n cabin; (*Umkleide-*) cubicle; (*Telefon-*) booth; (*einer K~nbahn*) car. **K~nbahn** *f* cable-car
Kabinett *nt* -s,-e (*Pol*) Cabinet
Kabriolett *nt* -s,-s convertible
Kachel *f* -,-n tile. **k~n** *vt* tile
Kadenz *f* -,-en (*Mus*) cadence
Käfer *m* -s,- beetle
Kaffee /'kafe:, ka'fe:/ *m* -s,-s coffee. **K~kanne** *f* coffee pot. **K~maschine** *f* coffee maker. **K~mühle** *f* coffee grinder
Käfig *m* -s,-e cage
kahl *adj* bare; (*haarlos*) bald; **k~geschoren** shaven
Kahn *m* -s,⸚e boat; (*Last-*) barge
Kai *m* -s,-s quay
Kaiser *m* -s,- emperor. **K~in** *f* -,-nen empress. **k~lich** *adj* imperial. **K~reich** *nt* empire. **K~schnitt**

m Caesarean [section]
Kajüte *f* **-,-n** (*Naut*) cabin
Kakao /ka'kau/ *m* **-s** cocoa
Kakerlak *m* **-s & -en,-en** cockroach
Kaktus *m* **-,-teen** cactus
Kalb *nt* **-[e]s,⸚er** calf. **K~fleisch** *nt* veal
Kalender *m* **-s,-** calendar; (*Termin-*) diary
Kaliber *nt* **-s,-** calibre; (*Gewehr-*) bore
Kalium *nt* **-s** potassium
Kalk *m* **-[e]s,-e** lime; (*Kalzium*) calcium. **k~en** *vt* whitewash. **K~stein** *m* limestone
Kalkul|ation /-'tsi̯o:n/ *f* **-,-en** calculation. **k~ieren** *vt/i* (*haben*) calculate
Kalorie *f* **-,-n** calorie
kalt *adj* cold; **mir ist k~** I am cold
Kälte *f* **-** cold; (*Gefühls-*) coldness; **10 Grad K~** 10 degrees below zero
Kalzium *nt* **-s** calcium
Kamel *nt* **-s,-e** camel
Kamera *f* **-,-s** camera
Kamerad(in) *m* **-en,-en** (*f* **-,-nen**) companion; (*Freund*) mate; (*Mil, Pol*) comrade
Kameramann *m* (*pl* **-männer & -leute**) cameraman
Kamille *f* **-** chamomile
Kamin *m* **-s,-e** fireplace; (*SGer: Schornstein*) chimney
Kamm *m* **-[e]s,⸚e** comb; (*Berg-*) ridge; (*Zool, Wellen-*) crest
kämmen *vt* comb; **jdn/sich k~** comb someone's/one's hair
Kammer *f* **-,-n** small room; (*Techn, Biology, Pol*) chamber. **K~musik** *f* chamber music
Kammgarn *nt* (*Textiles*) worsted
Kampagne /kam'panjə/ *f* **-,-n** (*Pol, Comm*) campaign
Kampf *m* **-es,⸚e** fight; (*Schlacht*) battle; (*Wett-*) contest; (*fig*) struggle
kämpf|en *vi* (*haben*) fight; **sich k~en durch** fight one's way through. **K~er(in)** *m* **-s,-** (*f* **-,-nen**) fighter
Kampfrichter *m* (*Sport*) judge
Kanada *nt* **-s** Canada
Kanad|ier(in) /-i̯ɐ, -i̯ərɪn/ *m* **-s,-** (*f* **-,-nen**) Canadian. **k~isch** *adj* Canadian
Kanal *m* **-s,⸚e** canal; (*Abfluss-*) drain, sewer; (*Radio, TV*) channel; **der K~** the [English] Channel
Kanalisation /-'tsi̯o:n/ *f* **-** sewerage system, drains *pl*
Kanarienvogel /-i̯ən-/ *m* canary
Kanarisch *adj* **K~e Inseln** Canaries
Kandidat(in) *m* **-en,-en** (*f* **-,-nen**) candidate
kandiert *adj* candied
Känguru *nt* **-s,-s** kangaroo
Kaninchen *nt* **-s,-** rabbit
Kanister *m* **-s,-** canister; (*Benzin-*) can
Kännchen *nt* **-s,-** [small] jug; (*Kaffee-*) pot
Kanne *f* **-,-n** jug; (*Tee-*) pot; (*Öl-*) can; (*große Milch-*) churn
Kannibal|e *m* **-n,-n** cannibal. **K~ismus** *m* **-** cannibalism
Kanon *m* **-s,-s** canon; (*Lied*) round
Kanone *f* **-,-n** cannon, gun
kanonisieren *vt* canonize
Kantate *f* **-,-n** cantata
Kante *f* **-,-n** edge
Kanten *m* **-s,-** crust [of bread]
Kanter *m* **-s,-** canter
kantig *adj* angular
Kantine *f* **-,-n** canteen
Kanton *m* **-s,-e** (*Swiss*) canton

> **Kanton** The name for the individual autonomous states that make up Switzerland. There are 26 cantons, each with its own government and constitution.

Kanu *nt* **-s,-s** canoe
Kanzel *f* **-,-n** pulpit; (*Aviat*) cockpit
Kanzler *m* **-s,-** chancellor
Kap *nt* **-s,-s** (*Geog*) cape
Kapazität *f* **-,-en** capacity
Kapelle *f* **-,-n** chapel; (*Mus*) band
kapern *vt* (*Naut*) seize
kapieren *vt* ⊡ understand
Kapital *nt* **-s** capital. **K~ismus** *m* **-** capitalism. **K~ist** *m* **-en,-en** capitalist. **k~istisch** *adj* capitalist
Kapitän *m* **-s,-e** captain
Kapitel *nt* **-s,-** chapter
Kaplan *m* **-s,⸚e** curate
Kappe *f* **-,-n** cap
Kapsel *f* **-,-n** capsule; (*Flaschen-*) top
kaputt *adj* ⊡ broken; (*zerrissen*) torn; (*defekt*) out of order; (*ruiniert*) ruined; (*erschöpft*) worn out. **k~gehen**† *vi sep* (*sein*) ⊡ break; (*zerreißen*) tear; (*defekt werden*) pack up; (*Ehe, Freundschaft:*) break up. **k~lachen (sich)** *vr sep* ⊡ be in stitches. **k~machen** *vt sep* ⊡ break; (*zerreißen*) tear; (*defekt machen*) put out of order; (*erschöpfen*) wear out; **sich k~machen** wear oneself out
Kapuze *f* **-,-n** hood
Kapuzinerkresse *f* nasturtium
Karaffe *f* **-,-n** carafe; (*mit Stöpsel*) decanter
Karamell *m* **-s** caramel. **K~bonbon** *m* & *nt* ≈ toffee
Karat *nt* **-[e]s,-e** carat
Karawane *f* **-,-n** caravan
Kardinal *m* **-s,⸚e** **cardinal.** **K~zahl** *f* cardinal number
Karfreitag *m* Good Friday
karg *adj* meagre; (*frugal*) frugal; (*spärlich*) sparse; (*unfruchtbar*) barren; (*gering*) scant
Karibik *f* **-** Caribbean
kariert *adj* check[ed]; (*Papier*) squared; **schottisch k~** tartan
Karik|atur *f* **-,-en** caricature; (*Journalism*) cartoon. **k~ieren** *vt* caricature
Karneval *m* **-s,-e** & **-s** carnival
Kärnten *nt* **-s** Carinthia
Karo *nt* **-s,-s** (*Raute*) diamond; (*Viereck*) square; (*Muster*) check (*Kartenspiel*) diamonds *pl*
Karosserie *f* **-,-n** bodywork
Karotte *f* **-,-n** carrot
Karpfen *m* **-s,-** carp
Karren *m* **-s,-** cart; (*Hand-*) barrow. **k~** *vt* cart
Karriere /ka'ri̯eːrə/ *f* **-,-n** career; **K~ machen** get to the top
Karte *f* **-,-n** card; (*Eintritts-, Fahr-*) ticket; (*Speise-*) menu; (*Land-*) map
Kartei *f* **-,-en** card index
Karten|spiel *nt* card game; (*Spielkarten*) pack of cards. **K~vorverkauf** *m* advance booking
Kartoffel *f* **-,-n** potato. **K~brei** *m* mashed potatoes
Karton /kar'tɔŋ/ *m* **-s,-s** cardboard; (**Schachtel**) carton
Karussell *nt* **-s,-s** & **-e** roundabout
Käse *m* **-s,-** cheese
Kaserne *f* **-,-n** barracks *pl*
Kasino *nt* **-s,-s** casino
Kasperle *nt* & *m* **-s,-** Punch. **K~theater** *nt* Punch and Judy show
Kasse *f* **-,-n** till; (*Registrier-*) cash register; (*Zahlstelle*) cash desk; (*im Supermarkt*) check out; (*Theater-*)

box office; (*Geld*) pool [of money], [!] kitty; (*Kranken-*) health insurance scheme; **knapp bei K~ sein** [!] be short of cash. **K~nwart** *m* **-[e]s,-e** treasurer. **K~nzettel** *m* receipt

Kasserolle *f* **-,-n** saucepan

Kassette *f* **-,-n** cassette; (*Film-, Farbband-*) cartridge. **K~nrekorder** *m* **-s,-** cassette recorder

kassier|en *vi* (*haben*) collect the money/(*im Bus*) the fares ● *vt* collect. **K~er(in)** *m* **-s,-** (*f* **-,-nen**) cashier

Kastanie /kas'taːni̯ə/ *f* **-,-n** [horse] chestnut, [!] conker

Kasten *m* **-s,⁼** box; (*Brot-*) bin; (*Flaschen-*) crate; (*Brief-*) letter box; (*Aust: Schrank*) cupboard

kastrieren *vt* castrate; neuter

Katalog *m* **-[e]s,-e** catalogue

Katalysator *m* **-s,-en** catalyst; (*Auto*) catalytic converter

Katapult *nt* **-[e]s,-e** catapult

Katarrh, **Katarr** *m* **-s,-e** catarrh

Katastrophe *f* **-,-n** catastrophe

Katechismus *m* **-** catechism

Kategorie *f* **-,-n** category

Kater *m* **-s,-** tom cat; ([!]: *Katzenjammer*) hangover

Kathedrale *f* **-,-n** cathedral

Kath|olik(in) *m* **-en,-en** (*f* **-,-nen**) Catholic. **k~olisch** *adj* Catholic. **K~olizismus** *m* **-** Catholicism

Kätzchen *nt* **-s,-** kitten; (*Bot*) catkin

Katze *f* **-,-n** cat. **K~njammer** *m* [!] hangover. **K~nsprung** *m* **ein K~nsprung** [!] a stone's throw

Kauderwelsch *nt* **-[s]** gibberish

kauen *vt/i* (*haben*) chew; bite (*Nägel*)

Kauf *m* **-[e]s, Käufe** purchase; **guter K~** bargain; **in K~ nehmen** (*fig*) put up with. **k~en** *vt/i* (*haben*) buy; **k~en bei** shop at

Käufer(in) *m* **-s,-** (*f* **-,-nen**) buyer; (*im Geschäft*) shopper

Kauf|haus *nt* department store. **K~laden** *m* shop

käuflich *adj* saleable; (*bestechlich*) corruptible; **k~ erwerben** buy

Kauf|mann *m* (*pl* **-leute**) businessman; (*Händler*) dealer; (*Dialekt*) grocer. **K~preis** *m* purchase price

Kaugummi *m* chewing gum

Kaulquappe *f* **-,-n** tadpole

kaum *adv* hardly

Kaution /-'tsi̯oːn/ *f* **-,-en** surety; (*Jur*) bail; (*Miet-*) deposit

Kautschuk *m* **-s** rubber

Kauz *m* **-es, Käuze** owl

Kavalier *m* **-s,-e** gentleman

Kavallerie *f* **-** cavalry

Kaviar *m* **-s** caviare

keck *adj* bold; cheeky

Kegel *m* **-s,-** skittle; (*Geometry*) cone. **K~bahn** *f* skittle-alley. **k~n** *vi* (*haben*) play skittles

Kehl|e *f* **-,-n** throat; **aus voller K~e** at the top of one's voice. **K~kopf** *m* larynx. **K~kopfentzündung** *f* laryngitis

Kehr|e *f* **-,-n** [hairpin] bend. **k~en** *vi* (*haben*) (*fegen*) sweep ● *vt* sweep; (*wenden*) turn; **sich nicht k~en an** (+ *acc*) not care about. **K~icht** *m* **-[e]s** sweepings *pl*. **K~reim** *m* refrain. **K~seite** *f* (*fig*) drawback. **k~tmachen** *vi sep* (*haben*) turn back; (*sich umdrehen*) turn round

Keil *m* **-[e]s,-e** wedge

Keilriemen *m* fan belt

Keim *m* **-[e]s,-e** (*Bot*) sprout; (*Med*) germ. **k~en** *vi* (*haben*) germinate; (*austreiben*) sprout. **k~frei** *adj* sterile

k

kein *pron* no; not a; **k~e fünf Minuten** less than five minutes. **k~e(r,s)** *pron* no one, nobody; (*Ding*) none, not one. **k~esfalls** *adv* on no account. **k~eswegs** *adv* by no means. **k~mal** *adv* not once. **k~s** *pron* none, not one

Keks *m* -[es],-[e] biscuit

Kelch *m* -[e]s,-e goblet, cup; (*Relig*) chalice; (*Bot*) calyx

Kelle *f* -,-n ladle; (*Maurer*) trowel

Keller *m* -s,- cellar. **K~ei** *f* -,-en winery. **K~wohnung** *f* basement flat

Kellner *m* -s,- waiter. **K~in** *f* -,-nen waitress

keltern *vt* press

k

keltisch *adj* Celtic

Kenia *nt* -s Kenya

kenn|en† *vt* know; **k~en lernen** get to know; (*treffen*) meet; **sich k~en lernen** meet; (*näher*) get to know one another. **K~er** *m* -s,-, **K~erin** *f* -,-nen connoisseur; (*Experte*) expert. **k~tlich** *adj* recognizable; **k~tlich machen** mark. **K~tnis** *f* -,-se knowledge; **zur K~tnis nehmen** take note of; **in K~tnis setzen** inform (**von** of). **K~wort** *nt* (*pl* **-wörter**) reference; (*geheimes*) password. **K~zeichen** *nt* distinguishing mark *or* feature; (*Merkmal*) characteristic, (*Markierung*) marking; (*Auto*) registration. **k~zeichnen** *vt* distinguish; (*markieren*) mark

kentern *vi* (*sein*) capsize

Keramik *f* -,-en pottery

Kerbe *f* -,-n notch

Kerker *m* -s,- dungeon; (*Gefängnis*) prison

Kerl *m* -s,-e & -s [!] fellow, bloke

Kern *m* -s,-e pip; (*Kirsch-*) stone; (*Nuss-*) kernel; (*Techn*) core; (*Atom-, Zell- & fig*) nucleus; (*Stadt-*) centre; (*einer Sache*) heart. **K~energie** *f* nuclear energy. **K~gehäuse** *nt* core. **k~los** *adj* seedless. **K~physik** *f* nuclear physics *sg*

Kerze *f* -,-n candle. **K~nhalter** *m* -s,- candlestick

kess *adj* pert

Kessel *m* -s,- kettle

Kette *f* -,-n chain; (*Hals-*) necklace. **k~n** *vt* chain (**an** + *acc* to). **K~nladen** *m* chain store

Ketze|r(in) *m* -s,- (*f* -,-nen) heretic. **K~rei** *f* - heresy

keuch|en *vi* (*haben*) pant. **K~husten** *m* whooping cough

Keule *f* -,-n club; (*Culin*) leg; (*Hühner-*) drumstick

keusch *adj* chaste

Khaki *nt* - khaki

kichern *vi* (*haben*) giggle

Kiefer[1] *f* -,-n pine[-tree]

Kiefer[2] *m* -s,- jaw

Kiel *m* -s,-e (*Naut*) keel

Kiemen *fpl* gills

Kies *m* -es gravel. **K~el** *m* -s,-. **K~elstein** *m* pebble

Kilo *nt* -s,-[s] kilo. **K~gramm** *nt* kilogram. **K~hertz** *nt* kilohertz. **K~meter** *m* kilometre. **K~meterstand** *m* ≈ mileage. **K~watt** *nt* kilowatt

Kind *nt* -es,-er child; **von K~ auf** from childhood

Kinder|arzt *m*, **K~ärztin** *f* paediatrician. **K~bett** *nt* child's cot. **K~garten** *m* nursery school. **K~geld** *nt* child benefit. **K~lähmung** *f* polio. **k~leicht** *adj* very easy. **k~los** *adj* childless. **K~mädchen** *nt* nanny. **K~reim** *m* nursery rhyme. **K~spiel** *nt* children's game. **K~tagesstätte** *f* day nursery. **K~teller** *m* children's menu. **K~wagen** *m* pram. **K~zimmer** *nt* child's/children's room; (*für*

Baby) nursery

Kind|heit *f* - childhood. **k~isch** *adj* childish. **k~lich** *adj* childlike

kinetisch *adj* kinetic

Kinn *nt* **-[e]s,-e** chin. **K~lade** *f* jaw

Kino *nt* **-s,-s** cinema

Kiosk *m* **-[e]s,-e** kiosk

Kippe *f* **-,-n** (*Müll-*) dump; (🄸*: Zigaretten-*) fag end. **k~n** *vt* tilt; (*schütten*) tip (**in** + *acc* into) ● *vi* (*sein*) topple

Kirch|e *f* **-,-n** church. **K~enbank** *f* pew. **K~endiener** *m* verger. **K~enlied** *nt* hymn. **K~enschiff** *nt* nave. **K~hof** *m* churchyard. **k~lich** *adj* church ● *adv* **k~lich getraut werden** be married in church. **K~turm** *m* church tower, steeple. **K~weih** *f* **-,-en** [village] fair

Kirmes *f* **-,-sen** = **Kirchweih**

Kirsche *f* **-,-n** cherry

Kissen *nt* **-s,-** cushion; (*Kopf-*) pillow

Kiste *f* **-,-n** crate; (*Zigarren-*) box

Kitsch *m* **-es** sentimental rubbish; (*Kunst*) kitsch

Kitt *m* **-s** [adhesive] cement; (*Fenster-*) putty

Kittel *m* **-s,-** overall, smock

Kitz *nt* **-es,-e** (*Zool*) kid

Kitz|el *m* **-s,-** tickle; (*Nerven-*) thrill. **k~eln** *vt/i* (*haben*) tickle. **k~lig** *adj* ticklish

kläffen *vi* (*haben*) yap

Klage *f* **-,-n** lament; (*Beschwerde*) complaint; (*Jur*) action. **k~n** *vi* (*haben*) lament; (*sich beklagen*) complaint; (*Jur*) sue

Kläger(in) *m* **-s,-** (*f* **-,-nen**) (*Jur*) plaintiff

klamm *adj* cold and damp; (*steif*) stiff. **K~** *f* **-,-en** (*Geog*) gorge

Klammer *f* **-,-n** (*Wäsche-*) peg; (*Büro-*) paper clip; (*Heft-*) staple; (*Haar-*) grip; (*für Zähne*) brace; (*Techn*) clamp; (*Typography*) bracket. **k~n (sich)** *vr* cling (**an** + *acc* to)

Klang *m* **-[e]s,¨-e** sound; (*K~farbe*) tone

Klapp|e *f* **-,-n** flap; (🄸*: Mund*) trap. **k~en** *vt* fold; (*hoch-*) tip up ● *vi* (*haben*) 🄸 work out. **Klapphandy** *nt* folding mobile phone

Klapper *f* **-,-n** rattle. **k~n** *vi* (*haben*) rattle. **K~schlange** rattlesnake

klapp|rig *adj* rickety; (*schwach*) decrepit. **K~stuhl** *m* folding chair

Klaps *m* **-es,-e** pat, smack

klar *adj* clear; **sich** (*dat*) **k~ werden** make up one's mind; (*erkennen*) realize (**dass** that); **sich** (*dat*) **k~** *od* **im K~en sein** realize (**dass** that) ● *adv* clearly; (🄸*: natürlich*) of course

klären *vt* clarify; **sich k~** clear; (*fig: sich lösen*) resolve itself

Klarheit *f* **-,-** clarity

Klarinette *f* **-,-n** clarinet

klar|machen *vt sep* make clear (*dat* to); **sich** (*dat*) **etw k~machen** understand sth. **k~stellen** *vt sep* clarify

Klärung *f* - clarification

Klasse *f* **-,-n** class; (*Sch*) class, form; (*Zimmer*) classroom. **k~** *inv adj* 🄸 super. **K~narbeit** *f* [written] test. **K~nzimmer** *nt* classroom

Klass|ik *f* - classicism; (*Epoche*) classical period. **K~iker** *m* **-s,-** classical author/(*Mus*) composer. **k~isch** *adj* classical; (*typisch*) classic

Klatsch *m* **-[e]s** gossip. **K~base** *f* 🄸 gossip. **k~en** *vt* slap; **Beifall k~en** applaud ● *vi* (*haben*) make a slapping sound; (*im Wasser*) splash; (*tratschen*) gossip; (*applaudieren*) clap. **k~nass** *adj* 🄸 soaking wet

klauen *vt/i* (*haben*) 🄸 steal

Klausel *f* **-,-n** clause

Klaustrophobie *f* **-** claustrophobia

Klausur *f* **-,-en** (*Univ*) paper

Klavier *nt* **-s,-e** piano. **K~spieler(in)** *m(f)* pianist

kleb|en *vt* stick/(*mit Klebstoff*) glue (**an** + *acc* to) ● *vi* (*haben*) stick (**an** + *dat* to). **k~rig** *adj* sticky. **K~stoff** *m* adhesive, glue. **K~streifen** *m* adhesive tape

Klecks *m* **-es,-e** stain; (*Tinten-*) blot; (*kleine Menge*) dab. **k~en** *vi* (*haben*) make a mess

Klee *m* **-s** clover

Kleid *nt* **-[e]s,-er** dress; **K~er** dresses; (*Kleidung*) clothes. **k~en** *vt* dress; (*gut stehen*) suit. **K~erbügel** *m* coat hanger. **K~erbürste** *f* clothes brush. **K~erhaken** *m* coathook. **K~erschrank** *m* wardrobe. **k~sam** *adj* becoming. **K~ung** *f* **-** clothes *pl*, clothing. **K~ungsstück** *nt* garment

Kleie *f* **-** bran

klein *adj* small, little; (*von kleinem Wuchs*) short; **k~ schneiden** cut up small. **von k~ auf** from childhood. **K~arbeit** *f* painstaking work. **K~e(r,s)** *m/f/nt* little one. **K~geld** *nt* [small] change. **K~handel** *m* retail trade. **K~heit** *f* **-** smallness; (*Wuchs*) short stature. **K~holz** *nt* firewood. **K~igkeit** *f* **-,-en** trifle; (*Mahl*) snack. **K~kind** *nt* infant. **k~laut** *adj* subdued. **k~lich** *adj* petty

klein|schreiben† *vt sep* write with a small [initial] letter. **K~stadt** *f* small town. **k~städtisch** *adj* provincial

Kleister *m* **-s** paste. **k~n** *vt* paste

Klemme *f* **-,-n** [hair-]grip. **k~n** *vt* jam; **sich** (*dat*) **den Finger k~n** get one's finger caught ● *vi* (*haben*) jam

Klempner *m* **-s,-** plumber

Klerus **(der)** **-** the clergy

Klette *f* **-,-n** burr

kletter|n *vi* (*sein*) climb. **K~pflanze** *f* climber

Klettverschluss *m* Velcro ® fastening

klicken *vi* (*haben*) click

Klient(in) /kli'ɛnt(ɪn)/ *m* **-en,-en** (*f* **-,-nen**) (*Jur*) client

Kliff *nt* **-[e]s,-e** cliff

Klima *nt* **-s** climate. **K~anlage** *f* air conditioning. **K~wandel** *m* climate change

klimat|isch *adj* climatic. **k~isiert** *adj* air-conditioned

klimpern *vi* (*haben*) jingle; **k~ auf** (+ *dat*) tinkle on (*Klavier*); strum (*Gitarre*)

Klinge *f* **-,-n** blade

Klingel *f* **-,-n** bell. **k~n** *vi* (*haben*) ring; **es k~t** there's a ring at the door

klingen† *vi* (*haben*) sound

Klinik *f* **-,-en** clinic

Klinke *f* **-,-n** [door] handle

Klippe *f* **-,-n** [submerged] rock

Klips *m* **-es,-e** clip; (*Ohr-*) clip-on ear ring

klirren *vi* (*haben*) rattle; (*Glas:*) chink

Klo *nt* **-s,-s** 🄵 loo

Klon *m* **-s, -e** clone. **k~en** *vt* clone

klopfen *vi* (*haben*) knock; (*leicht*) tap; (*Herz:*) pound; **es k~te** there was a knock at the door

Klops *m* **-es,-e** meatball

Klosett *nt* **-s,-s** lavatory

Kloß *m* **-es,⸚e** dumpling

Kloster *nt* **-s,⸚** monastery; (*Nonnen-*) convent

klösterlich *adj* monastic

Klotz *m* **-es,⸚e** block

Klub *m* **-s,-s** club
Kluft *f* **-,⸚e** cleft; (*fig: Gegensatz*) gulf
klug *adj* intelligent; (*schlau*) clever. **K∼heit** *f* **-** cleverness
Klump|en *m* **-s,-** lump
knabbern *vt/i* (*haben*) nibble
Knabe *m* **-n,-n** boy. **k∼nhaft** *adj* boyish
Knäckebrot *nt* crispbread
knack|en *vt/i* (*haben*) crack. **K∼s** *m* **-es,-e** crack
Knall *m* **-[e]s,-e** bang. **K∼bonbon** *m* cracker. **k∼en** *vi* (*haben*) go bang; (*Peitsche:*) crack ●*vt* ([!]: *werfen*) chuck; **jdm eine k∼en** [!] clout s.o. **k∼ig** *adj* [!] gaudy
knapp *adj* (*gering*) scant; (*kurz*) short; (*mangelnd*) scarce; (*gerade ausreichend*) bare; (*eng*) tight. **K∼heit** *f* **-** scarcity
knarren *vi* (*haben*) creak
Knast *m* **-[e]s** [!] prison
knattern *vi* (*haben*) crackle; (*Gewehr:*) stutter
Knäuel *m & nt* **-s,-** ball
Knauf *m* **-[e]s, Knäufe** knob
knauserig *adj* [!] stingy
knautschen *vt* [!] crumple ●*vi* (*haben*) crease
Knebel *m* **-s,-** gag. **k∼n** *vt* gag
Knecht *m* **-[e]s,-e** farm-hand; (*fig*) slave
kneif|en† *vt* pinch ●*vi* (*haben*) pinch; ([!]: *sich drücken*) chicken out. **K∼zange** *f* pincers *pl*
Kneipe *f* **-,-n** [!] pub
knet|en *vt* knead; (*formen*) mould. **K∼masse** *f* Plasticine®
Knick *m* **-[e]s,-e** bend; (*Kniff*) crease. **k∼en** *vt* bend; (*kniffen*) fold; **geknickt sein** [!] be dejected
Knicks *m* **-es,-e** curtsy. **k∼en** *vi* (*haben*) curtsy
Knie *nt* **-s,-** knee
knien /ˈkniːən/ *vi* (*haben*) kneel ●*vr* **sich k∼** kneel [down]
Kniescheibe *f* kneecap
Kniff *m* **-[e]s,-e** pinch; (*Falte*) crease; ([!]: *Trick*) trick. **k∼en** *vt* fold
knipsen *vt* (*lochen*) punch; (*Phot*) photograph ●*vi* (*haben*) take a photograph/photographs
Knirps *m* **-es,-e** [!] little chap; ® (*Schirm*) telescopic umbrella
knirschen *vi* (*haben*) grate; (*Schnee, Kies:*) crunch
knistern *vi* (*haben*) crackle; (*Papier:*) rustle
Knitter|falte *f* crease. **k∼frei** *adj* crease-resistant. **k∼n** *vi* (*haben*) crease
knobeln *vi* (*haben*) toss (**um** for)
Knoblauch *m* **-s** garlic
Knöchel *m* **-s,-** ankle; (*Finger-*) knuckle
Knochen *m* **-s,-** bone. **K∼mark** *nt* bone marrow
knochig *adj* bony
Knödel *m* **-s,-** (*SGer*) dumpling
Knoll|e *f* **-,-n** tuber
Knopf *m* **-[e]s,⸚e** button; (*Griff*) knob
knöpfen *vt* button
Knopfloch *nt* buttonhole
Knorpel *m* **-s** gristle; (*Anat*) cartilage
Knospe *f* bud
Knoten *m* **-s,-** knot; (*Med*) lump; (*Haar-*) bun, chignon. **k∼** *vt* knot. **K∼punkt** *m* junction
knüll|en *vt* crumple ●*vi* (*haben*) crease. **K∼er** *m* **-s,-** [!] sensation
knüpfen *vt* knot; (*verbinden*) attach (**an** + *acc* to)
Knüppel *m* **-s,-** club; (*Gummi-*) truncheon

knurren *vi* (*haben*) growl; (*Magen:*) rumble
knusprig *adj* crunchy, crisp
knutschen *vi* (*haben*) [!] smooch
k.o. /ka'ʔo:/ *adj* **k.o. schlagen** knock out; **k.o. sein** [!] be worn out
Koalition /koali'tsio:n/ *f* **-,-en** coalition
Kobold *m* **-[e]s,-e** goblin, imp
Koch *m* **-[e]s,¨e** cook; (*im Restaurant*) chef. **K~buch** *nt* cookery book. **k~en** *vt* cook; (*sieden*) boil; make (*Kaffee, Tee*); **hart gekochtes Ei** hard-boiled egg ● *vi* (*haben*) cook; (*sieden*) boil; [!] seethe (**vor** + *dat* with). **K~en** *nt* **-s** cooking; (*Sieden*) boiling. **k~end** *adj* boiling. **K~herd** *m* cooker, stove
Köchin *f* **-,-nen** [woman] cook
Koch|löffel *m* wooden spoon. **K~nische** *f* kitchenette. **K~platte** *f* hotplate. **K~topf** *m* saucepan
Köder *m* **-s,-** bait
Koffein /kɔfe'i:n/ *nt* **-s** caffeine. **k~frei** *adj* decaffeinated
Koffer *m* **-s,-** suitcase. **K~kuli** *m* luggage trolley. **K~raum** *m* (*Auto*) boot
Kognak /'kɔnjak/ *m* **-s,-s** brandy
Kohl *m* **-[e]s** cabbage
Kohle *f* **-,-n** coal. **K~[n]hydrat** *nt* **-[e]s,-e** carbohydrate. **K~nbergwerk** *nt* coal mine, colliery. **K~ndioxid** *nt* carbon dioxide. **K~nsäure** *f* carbon dioxide. **K~nstoff** *m* carbon
Koje *f* **-,-n** (*Naut*) bunk
Kokain /koka'i:n/ *nt* **-s** cocaine
kokett *adj* flirtatious. **k~ieren** *vi* (*haben*) flirt
Kokon /ko'kõ:/ *m* **-s,-s** cocoon
Kokosnuss *f* coconut
Koks *m* **-es** coke
Kolben *m* **-s,-** (*Gewehr-*) butt; (*Mais-*) cob; (*Techn*) piston; (*Chemistry*) flask
Kolibri *m* **-s,-s** humming bird
Kolik *f* **-,-en** colic
Kollaborateur /-'tø:ɐ̯/ *m* **-s,-e** collaborator
Kolleg *nt* **-s,-s & -ien** (*Univ*) course of lectures
Kolleg|e *m* **-n,-n**, **K~in** *f* **-,-nen** colleague. **K~ium** *nt* **-s,-ien** staff
Kollek|te *f* **-,-n** (*Relig*) collection. **K~tion** /-'tsi̯o:n/ *f* **-,-en** collection
Köln *nt* **-s** Cologne. **K~ischwasser, K~isch Wasser** *nt* eau-de-Cologne
Kolonie *f* **-,-n** colony
Kolonne *f* **-,-n** column; (*Mil*) convoy
Koloss *m* **-es,-e** giant
Koma *nt* **-s,-s** coma
Kombi *m* **-s,-s** = **K~wagen**. **K~nation** /-'tsi̯o:n/ *f* **-,-en** combination; (*Folgerung*) deduction; (*Kleidung*) co-ordinating outfit. **k~nieren** *vt* combine; (*fig*) reason; (*folgern*) deduce. **K~wagen** *m* estate car
Kombüse *f* **-,-n** (*Naut*) galley
Komet *m* **-en,-en** comet
Komfort /kɔm'fo:ɐ̯/ *m* **-s** comfort; (*Luxus*) luxury
Komik *f* **-** humour. **K~er** *m* **-s,-** comic, comedian
komisch *adj* funny; (*Oper*) comic; (*sonderbar*) odd, funny. **k~erweise** *adv* funnily enough
Komitee *nt* **-s,-s** committee
Komma *nt* **-s,-s & -ta** comma; (*Dezimal-*) decimal point; **drei K~ fünf** three point five
Kommando *nt* **-s,-s** order; (*Befehlsgewalt*) command; (*Einheit*) detachment. **K~brücke** *f* bridge
kommen† *vi* (*sein*) come; (*eintref-*

fen) arrive; (*gelangen*) get (**nach** to); **k~ lassen** send for; **auf/hinter etw** (*acc*) **k~** think of/find out about sth; **um/zu etw k~** lose/acquire sth; **wieder zu sich k~** come round; **wie kommt das?** why is that? **k~d** *adj* coming; **k~den Montag** next Monday

Kommen|tar *m* **-s,-e** commentary; (*Bemerkung*) comment. **k~tieren** *vt* comment on

kommerziell *adj* commercial

Kommissar *m* **-s,-e** commissioner; (*Polizei-*) superintendent

Kommission *f* **-,-en** commission; (*Gremium*) committee

Kommode *f* **-,-n** chest of drawers

Kommunalwahlen *fpl* local elections

Kommunion *f* **-,-en** [Holy] Communion

Kommun|ismus *m* **-** Communism. **K~ist(in)** *m* **-en,-en** (*f* **-,-nen**) Communist. **k~istisch** *adj* Communist

kommunizieren *vi* (*haben*) receive [Holy] Communion

Komödie /ko'mø:di̯ə/ *f* **-,-n** comedy

Kompagnon /'kɔmpanjõ:/ *m* **-s,-s** (*Comm*) partner

Kompanie *f* **-,-n** (*Mil*) company

Komparse *m* **-n,-n** (*Theat*) extra

Kompass *m* **-es,-e** compass

komplett *adj* complete

Komplex *m* **-es,-e** complex

Komplikation /-'tsi̯o:n/ *f* **-,-en** complication

Kompliment *nt* **-[e]s,-e** compliment

Komplize *m* **-n,-n** accomplice

komplizier|en *vt* complicate. **k~t** *adj* complicated

Komplott *nt* **-[e]s,-e** plot

kompo|nieren *vt/i* (*haben*) compose. **K~nist** *m* **-en,-en** composer

Kompost *m* **-[e]s** compost

Kompott *nt* **-[e]s,-e** stewed fruit

Kompromiss *m* **-es,-e** compromise; **einen K~ schließen** compromise. **k~los** *adj* uncompromising

Konden|sation /-'tsi̯o:n/ *f* **-** condensation. **k~sieren** *vt* condense

Kondensmilch *f* evaporated/(*gesüßt*) condensed milk

Kondition /-'tsi̯o:n/ *f* **-** (*Sport*) fitness; **in K~** in form

Konditor *m* **-s,-en** confectioner. **K~ei** *f* **-,-en** patisserie

Kondo|lenzbrief *m* letter of condolence. **k~lieren** *vi* (*haben*) express one's condolences

Kondom *nt & m* **-s,-e** condom

Konfekt *nt* **-[e]s** confectionery; (*Pralinen*) chocolates *pl*

Konfektion /-'tsi̯o:n/ *f* **-** ready-to-wear clothes *pl*

Konferenz *f* **-,-en** conference; (*Besprechung*) meeting

Konfession *f* **-,-en** [religious] denomination. **k~ell** *adj* denominational

Konfetti *nt* **-s** confetti

Konfirm|and(in) *m* **-en,-en** (*f* **-,-nen**) candidate for confirmation. **K~ation** *f* **-,-en** (*Relig*) confirmation. **k~ieren** *vt* (*Relig*) confirm

Konfitüre *f* **-,-n** jam

Konflikt *m* **-[e]s,-e** conflict

Konföderation /-'tsi̯o:n/ *f* confederation

konfus *adj* confused

Kongress *m* **-es,-e** congress

König *m* **-s,-e** king. **K~in** *f* **-,-nen** queen. **k~lich** *adj* royal; (*hoheitsvoll*) regal; (*großzügig*) handsome. **K~reich** *nt* kingdom

Konjunktiv *m* **-s,-e** subjunctive

Konjunktur *f* - economic situation; (*Hoch-*) boom

konkret *adj* concrete

Konkurren|t(in) *m* -en,-en (*f* -,-nen) competitor, rival. **K~z** *f* - competition; **jdm K~z machen** compete with s.o. **K~zkampf** *m* competition, rivalry

konkurrieren *vi* (*haben*) compete

Konkurs *m* -es,-e bankruptcy

können†

● *auxiliary verb*

····➤ (*vermögen*) be able to; (*Präsens*) can; (*Vergangenheit, Konditional*) could. **ich kann nicht schlafen** I cannot *or* can't sleep. **kann ich Ihnen helfen?** can I help you? **kann/könnte das explodieren?** can/could it explode? **es kann sein, dass er kommt** he may come

> ! Distinguish **konnte** and **könnte** (both can be 'could'): **er konnte sie nicht retten** he couldn't *or* was unable to rescue them. **er konnte sie noch retten** he was able to rescue them. **er könnte sie noch retten, wenn** ... he could still rescue them if ...

····➤ (*dürfen*) can, may. **kann ich gehen?** can *or* may I go? **können wir mit[kommen]?** can *or* may we come too?

● *transitive verb*

····➤ (*beherrschen*) know (language); be able to play (game). **können Sie Deutsch?** do you know any German? **sie kann das [gut]** she can do that [well]. **ich kann nichts dafür** I can't help that, I'm not to blame

● *intransitive verb*

····➤ (*fähig sein*) **ich kann [heute] nicht** I can't [today]. **er kann nicht anders** there's nothing else he can do; (*es ist seine Art*) he can't help it. **er kann nicht mehr** [!] he can't go on; (*nicht mehr essen*) he can't eat any more

····➤ (*irgendwohin gehen können*) be able to go; can go. **ich kann nicht ins Kino** I can't go to the cinema. **er konnte endlich nach Florenz** at last he was able to go to Florence

konsequen|t *adj* consistent; (*logisch*) logical. **K~z** *f* -,-en consequence

konservativ *adj* conservative

Konserv|en *fpl* tinned or canned food *sg*. **K~endose** *f* tin, can. **K~ierungsmittel** *nt* preservative

Konsonant *m* -en,-en consonant

Konstitution /-'ts̮io:n/ *f* -,-en constitution. **k~ell** *adj* constitutional

konstruieren *vt* construct; (*entwerfen*) design

Konstruk|tion /-'ts̮io:n/ *f* -,-en construction; (*Entwurf*) design. **k~tiv** *adj* constructive

Konsul *m* -s,-n consul. **K~at** *nt* -[e]s,-e consulate

Konsum *m* -s consumption. **K~güter** *npl* consumer goods

Kontakt *m* -[e]s,-e contact. **K~linsen** *fpl* contact lenses. **K~person** *f* contact

kontern *vt/i* (*haben*) counter

Kontinent /'kɔn-, kɔnti'nɛnt/ *m* -[e]s,-e continent

Konto *nt* -s,-s account. **K~auszug**

m [bank] statement. **K~nummer** *f* account number. **K~stand** *m* [bank] balance

Kontrabass *m* double bass

Kontroll|abschnitt *m* counterfoil. **K~e** *f* **-,-n** control; (*Prüfung*) check. **K~eur** *m* **-s,-e** [ticket] inspector. **k~ieren** *vt* check; inspect (*Fahrkarten*); (*beherrschen*) control

Kontroverse *f* **-,-n** controversy

Kontur *f* **-,-en** contour

konventionell *adj* conventional

Konversationslexikon *nt* encyclopaedia

konvert|ieren *vi* (*haben*) (*Relig*) convert. **K~it** *m* **-en,-en** convert

Konzentration /-'tsio:n/ *f* **-,-en** concentration. **K~slager** *nt* concentration camp

konzentrieren *vt* concentrate; **sich k~** concentrate (**auf** + *acc* on)

Konzept *nt* **-[e]s,-e** [rough] draft; **jdn aus dem K~bringen** put s.o. off his stroke

Konzern *m* **-s,-e** (*Comm*) group [of companies]

Konzert *nt* **-[e]s,-e** concert; (*Klavier-*) concerto

Konzession *f* **-,-en** licence; (*Zugeständnis*) concession

Konzil *nt* **-s,-e** (*Relig*) council

Kooperation /koʔopera'tsio:n/ *f* co-operation

Koordin|ation /koʔɔrdina'tsio:n/ *f* **-** co-ordination. **k~ieren** *vt* co-ordinate

Kopf *m* **-[e]s,¨e** head; **ein K~ Kohl/Salat** a cabbage/lettuce; **aus dem K~** from memory; (*auswendig*) by heart; **auf dem K~** (*verkehrt*) upside down; **K~ stehen** stand on one's head; **sich** (*dat*) **den K~ waschen** wash one's hair; **sich** (*dat*) **den K~ zerbrechen** rack one's brains. **K~ball** *m* header

köpfen *vt* behead; (*Fußball*) head

Kopf|ende *nt* head. **K~haut** *f* scalp. **K~hörer** *m* headphones *pl*. **K~kissen** *nt* pillow. **k~los** *adj* panic-stricken. **K~rechnen** *nt* mental arithmetic. **K~salat** *m* lettuce. **K~schmerzen** *mpl* headache *sg*. **K~sprung** *m* header, dive. **K~stand** *m* headstand. **K~steinpflaster** *nt* cobblestones *pl*. **K~tuch** *nt* headscarf. **k~über** *adv* head first; (*fig*) headlong. **K~wäsche** *f* shampoo. **K~weh** *nt* headache

Kopie *f* **-,-n** copy. **k~ren** *vt* copy. **K~rschutz** *m* copy protection

Koppel¹ *f* **-,-n** enclosure; (*Pferde-*) paddock

Koppel² *nt* **-s,-** (*Mil*) belt. **k~n** *vt* couple

Koralle *f* **-,-n** coral

Korb *m* **-[e]s,¨e** basket; **jdm einen K~ geben** (*fig*) turn s.o. down. **K~ball** *m* [kind of] netball

Kord *m* **-s** (*Textiles*) corduroy

Kordel *f* **-,-n** cord

Korinthe *f* **-,-n** currant

Kork *m* **-s,-e** cork. **K~en** *m* **-s,-** cork. **K~enzieher** *m* **-s,-** corkscrew

Korn *nt* **-[e]s,¨er** grain, (*Samen-*) seed; (*am Visier*) front sight

Körn|chen *nt* **-s,-** granule. **k~ig** *adj* granular

Körper *m* **-s,-** body; (*Geometry*) solid. **K~bau** *m* build, physique. **k~behindert** *adj* physically disabled. **k~lich** *adj* physical; (*Strafe*) corporal. **K~pflege** *f* personal hygiene. **K~schaft** *f* **-,-en** corporation, body

korrekt *adj* correct. **K~or** *m* **-s,-en** proof reader. **K~ur** *f* **-,-en** correction. **K~urabzug** *m* proof

Korrespon|dent(in) *m* **-en,-en** (*f* **-,-nen**) correspondent. **K~denz** *f*

k

-,-en correspondence
Korridor *m* **-s,-e** corridor
korrigieren *vt* correct
Korrosion *f* **-** corrosion
korrup|t *adj* corrupt. **K~tion** *f* **-** corruption
Korsett *nt* **-[e]s,-e** corset
koscher *adj* kosher
Kosename *m* pet name
Kosmet|ik *f* **-** beauty culture. **K~ika** *ntpl* cosmetics. **K~ikerin** *f* **-,-nen** beautician. **k~isch** *adj* cosmetic; (*Chirurgie*) plastic
kosm|isch *adj* cosmic. **K~onaut(in)** *m* **-en,-en** (*f* **-,-nen**) cosmonaut
Kosmos *m* **-** cosmos
Kost *f* **-** food; (*Ernährung*) diet; (*Verpflegung*) board
kostbar *adj* precious. **K~keit** *f* **-,-en** treasure
kosten[1] *vt/i* (*haben*) **[von] etw k~** taste sth
kosten[2] *vt* cost; (*brauchen*) take; **wie viel kostet es?** how much is it? **K~** *pl* expense *sg*, cost *sg*; (*Jur*) costs; **auf meine K~** at my expense. **K~[vor]anschlag** *m* estimate. **k~los** *adj* free ● *adv* free [of charge]
köstlich *adj* delicious; (*entzückend*) delightful
Kostprobe *f* taste; (*fig*) sample
Kostüm *nt* **-s,-e** (*Theat*) costume; (*Verkleidung*) fancy dress; (*Schneider-*) suit. **k~iert** *adj* **k~iert sein** be in fancy dress
Kot *m* **-[e]s** excrement
Kotelett /kɔtˈlɛt/ *nt* **-s,-s** chop, cutlet. **K~en** *pl* sideburns
Köter *m* **-s,-** (*pej*) dog
Kotflügel *m* (*Auto*) wing
kotzen *vi* (*haben*) ☒ throw up
Krabbe *f* **-,-n** crab, shrimp
krabbeln *vi* (*sein*) crawl
Krach *m* **-[e]s,¨e** din, racket; (*Knall*) crash; (🅸: *Streit*) row; (🅸: *Ruin*) crash. **k~en** *vi* (*haben*) crash; **es hat gekracht** there was a bang/(🅸: *Unfall*) a crash ● (*sein*) break, crack; (*auftreffen*) crash (**gegen** into)
krächzen *vi* (*haben*) croak
Kraft *f* **-,¨e** strength; (*Gewalt*) force; (*Arbeits-*) worker; **in/außer K~** in/no longer in force. **K~fahrer** *m* driver. **K~fahrzeug** *nt* motor vehicle. **K~fahrzeugbrief** *m* [vehicle] registration document
kräftig *adj* strong; (*gut entwickelt*) sturdy; (*nahrhaft*) nutritious; (*heftig*) hard
kraft|los *adj* weak. **K~probe** *f* trial of strength. **K~stoff** *m* (*Auto*) fuel. **K~wagen** *m* motor car. **K~werk** *nt* power station
Kragen *m* **-s,-** collar
Krähe *f* **-,-n** crow
krähen *vi* (*haben*) crow
Kralle *f* **-,-n** claw
Kram *m* **-s** 🅸 things *pl*, 🅸 stuff; (*Angelegenheiten*) business. **k~en** *vi* (*haben*) rummage about (**in** + *dat* in; **nach** for)
Krampf *m* **-[e]s,¨e** cramp. **K~adern** *fpl* varicose veins. **k~haft** *adj* convulsive; (*verbissen*) desperate
Kran *m* **-[e]s,¨e** (*Techn*) crane
Kranich *m* **-s,-e** (*Zool*) crane
krank *adj* sick; (*Knie, Herz*) bad; **k~ sein/werden** be/fall ill. **K~e(r)** *m/f* sick man/woman, invalid; **die K~en** the sick *pl*
kränken *vt* offend, hurt
Kranken|bett *nt* sick bed. **K~geld** *nt* sickness benefit. **K~gymnast(in)** *m* **-en,-en** (*f* **-,-nen**) physiotherapist. **K~gymnastik** *f* physiotherapy. **K~haus** *nt*

hospital. **K~kasse** *f* health insurance scheme/(*Amt*) office. **K~pflege** *f* nursing. **K~saal** *m* [hospital] ward. **K~schein** *m* certificate of entitlement to medical treatment. **K~schwester** *f* nurse. **K~versicherung** *f* health insurance. **K~wagen** *m* ambulance

Krankheit *f* **-,-en** illness, disease

kränklich *adj* sickly

krank|melden *vt sep* **jdn k~melden** report s.o. sick; **sich k~melden** report sick

Kranz *m* **-es,⸚e** wreath

Krapfen *m* **-s,-** doughnut

Krater *m* **-s,-** crater

kratzen *vt/i* (*haben*) scratch. **K~er** *m* **-s,-** scratch

Kraul *nt* **-s** (*Sport*) crawl. **k~en**[1] *vi* (*haben/sein*) (*Sport*) do the crawl

kraulen[2] *vt* tickle; **sich am Kopf k~** scratch one's head

kraus *adj* wrinkled; (*Haar*) frizzy; (*verworren*) muddled. **K~e** *f* **-,-n** frill

kräuseln *vt* wrinkle; frizz (*Haar-*); gather (*Stoff*); **sich k~** wrinkle; (*sich kringeln*) curl; (*Haar:*) go frizzy

Kraut *nt* **-[e]s, Kräuter** herb; (*SGer*) cabbage; (*Sauer-*) sauerkraut

Krawall *m* **-s,-e** riot; (*Lärm*) row

Krawatte *f* **-,-n** [neck]tie

krea|tiv /krea'ti:f/ *adj* creative. **K~tur** *f* **-,-en** creature

Krebs *m* **-es,-e** crayfish; (*Med*) cancer; (*Astrology*) Cancer

Kredit *m* **-s,-e** credit; (*Darlehen*) loan; **auf K~** on credit. **K~karte** *f* credit card

Kreid|e *f* **-** chalk. **k~ig** *adj* chalky

kreieren /kre'i:rən/ *vt* create

Kreis *m* **-es,-e** circle; (*Admin*) district

kreischen *vt/i* (*haben*) screech; (*schreien*) shriek

Kreisel *m* **-s,-** [spinning] top

kreis|en *vi* (*haben*) circle; revolve (**um** around). **k~förmig** *adj* circular. **K~lauf** *m* cycle; (*Med*) circulation. **K~säge** *f* circular saw. **K~verkehr** *m* [traffic] roundabout

Krem *f* **-,-s** & *m* **-s,-e** cream

Krematorium *nt* **-s,-ien** crematorium

Krempe *f* **-,-n** [hat] brim

krempeln *vt* turn (**nach oben** up)

Krepp *m* **-s,-s** & **-e** crêpe

Krepppapier *nt* crêpe paper

Kresse *f* **-,-n** cress; (*Kapuziner-*) nasturtium

Kreta *nt* **-s** Crete

Kreuz *nt* **-es,-e** cross; (*Kreuzung*) intersection; (*Mus*) sharp; (*Kartenspiel*) clubs *pl*; (*Anat*) small of the back; **über K~** crosswise; **das K~ schlagen** cross oneself. **k~en** *vt* cross; **sich k~en** cross; (*Straßen:*) intersect; (*Meinungen:*) clash ● *vi* (*haben/sein*) cruise. **K~fahrt** *f* (*Naut*) cruise. **K~gang** *m* cloister

kreuzig|en *vt* crucify. **K~ung** *f* **-,-en** crucifixion

Kreuz|otter *f* adder, common viper. **K~ung** *f* **-,-en** intersection; (*Straßen-*) crossroads *sg*. **K~verhör** *nt* cross-examination. **k~weise** *adv* crosswise. **K~worträtsel** *nt* crossword [puzzle]. **K~zug** *m* crusade

kribbel|ig *adj* 🅃 edgy. **k~n** *vi* (*haben*) tingle; (*kitzeln*) tickle

kriech|en† *vi* (*sein*) crawl; (*fig*) grovel (**vor** + *dat* to). **K~spur** *f* (*Auto*) crawler lane. **K~tier** *nt* reptile

Krieg *m* **-[e]s,-e** war

kriegen *vt* 🅃 get; **ein Kind k~** have a baby

kriegs|beschädigt *adj* war-disabled. **K~dienstverweigerer** *m*

-s,- conscientious objector. **K~gefangene(r)** *m* prisoner of war. **K~gefangenschaft** *f* captivity. **K~gericht** *nt* court martial. **K~list** *f* stratagem. **K~rat** *m* council of war. **K~recht** *nt* martial law

Krimi *m* **-s,-s** ☐ crime story/film. **K~nalität** *f* - crime; (*Vorkommen*) crime rate. **K~nalpolizei** *f* criminal investigation department. **K~nalroman** *m* crime novel. **k~nell** *adj* criminal

Krippe *f* **-,-n** manger; (*Weihnachts-*) crib; (*Kinder-*) crèche. **K~nspiel** *nt* Nativity play

Krise *f* **-,-n** crisis

Kristall *nt* **-s** crystal; (*geschliffen*) cut glass

k

Kritik *f* **-,-en** criticism; (*Rezension*) review; **unter aller K~** ☐ abysmal

Kriti|ker *m* **-s,-** critic; (*Rezensent*) reviewer. **k~sch** *adj* critical. **k~sieren** *vt* criticize; review

kritzeln *vt/i* (*haben*) scribble

Krokodil *nt* **-s,-e** crocodile

Krokus *m* **-,-[se]** crocus

Krone *f* **-,-n** crown; (*Baum-*) top

krönen *vt* crown

Kronleuchter *m* chandelier

Krönung *f* **-,-en** coronation; (*fig: Höhepunkt*) crowning event

Kropf *m* **-[e]s,¨e** (*Zool*) crop; (*Med*) goitre

Kröte *f* **-,-n** toad

Krücke *f* **-,-n** crutch

Krug *m* **-[e]s,¨e** jug; (*Bier-*) tankard

Krümel *m* **-s,-** crumb. **k~ig** *adj* crumbly. **k~n** *vt* crumble ● *vi* (*haben*) be crumbly

krumm *adj* crooked; (*gebogen*) curved; (*verbogen*) bent

krümmen *vt* bend; crook (*Finger*); **sich k~** bend; (*sich winden*) writhe; (*vor Lachen*) double up

Krümmung *f* **-,-en** bend, curve

Krüppel *m* **-s,-** cripple

Kruste *f* **-,-n** crust; (*Schorf*) scab

Kruzifix *nt* **-es,-e** crucifix

Kub|a *nt* **-s** Cuba. **k~anisch** *adj* Cuban

Kübel *m* **-s,-** tub; (*Eimer*) bucket; (*Techn*) skip

Küche *f* **-,-n** kitchen; (*Kochkunst*) cooking; **kalte/warme K~** cold/hot food

Kuchen *m* **-s,-** cake

Küchen|herd *m* cooker, stove. **K~maschine** *f* food processor, mixer. **K~schabe** *f* **-,-n** cockroach

Kuckuck *m* **-s,-e** cuckoo

Kufe *f* **-,-n** [sledge] runner

Kugel *f* **-,-n** ball; (*Geometry*) sphere; (*Gewehr-*) bullet; (*Sport*) shot. **k~förmig** *adj* spherical. **K~lager** *nt* ball-bearing. **k~n** *vt/i* (*haben*) roll; **sich k~n** (*vor Lachen*) fall about. **K~schreiber** *m* **-s,-** ballpoint [pen]. **k~sicher** *adj* bulletproof. **K~stoßen** *nt* **-s** shot-putting

Kuh *f* **-,¨e** cow

kühl *adj* cool; (*kalt*) chilly. **K~box** *f* **-,-en** cool box. **K~e** *f* - coolness; chilliness. **k~en** *vt* cool; refrigerate (*Lebensmittel*); chill (*Wein*). **K~er** *m* **-s,-** (*Auto*) radiator. **K~erhaube** *f* bonnet. **K~fach** *nt* frozen-food compartment. **K~raum** *m* cold store. **K~schrank** *m* refrigerator. **K~truhe** *f* freezer. **K~wasser** *nt* [radiator] water

kühn *adj* bold

Kuhstall *m* cowshed

Küken *nt* **-s,-** chick; (*Enten-*) duckling

Kulissen *fpl* (*Theat*) scenery *sg*; (*seitlich*) wings; **hinter den K~** (*fig*) behind the scenes

Kult *m* **-[e]s,-e** cult

kultivier|en *vt* cultivate. **k~t** *adj* cultured

Kultur *f* **-,-en** culture. **K~beutel** *m* toilet bag. **k~ell** *adj* cultural. **K~film** *m* documentary film. **K~tourismus** *m* cultural tourism

Kultusminister *m* Minister of Education and Arts

Kümmel *m* **-s** caraway; (*Getränk*) kümmel

Kummer *m* **-s** sorrow, grief; (*Sorge*) worry; (*Ärger*) trouble

kümmer|lich *adj* puny; (*dürftig*) meagre; (*armselig*) wretched. **k~n** *vt* concern; **sich k~n um** look after; (*sich befassen*) concern oneself with; (*beachten*) take notice of

kummervoll *adj* sorrowful

Kumpel *m* **-s,-** [F] mate

Kunde *m* **-n,-n** customer. **K~ndienst** *m* [after-sales] service

Kundgebung *f* **-,-en** (*Pol*) rally

kündig|en *vt* cancel (*Vertrag*); give notice of withdrawal for (*Geld*); give notice to quit (*Wohnung*); **seine Stellung k~en** give [in one's] notice ● *vi* (*haben*) give [in one's] notice; **jdm k~en** give s.o. notice. **K~ung** *f* **-,-en** cancellation; notice [of withdrawal/dismissal/to quit]; (*Entlassung*) dismissal. **K~ungsfrist** *f* period of notice

Kund|in *f* **-,-nen** [woman] customer. **K~schaft** *f* **-** clientele, customers *pl*

künftig *adj* future ● *adv* in future

Kunst *f* **-,⸚e** art; (*Können*) skill. **K~faser** *f* synthetic fibre. **K~galerie** *f* art gallery. **K~geschichte** *f* history of art. **K~gewerbe** *nt* arts and crafts *pl*. **K~griff** *m* trick

Künstler *m* **-s,-** artist; (*Könner*) master. **K~in** *f* **-,-nen** [woman] artist. **k~isch** *adj* artistic

künstlich *adj* artificial

Kunst|stoff *m* plastic. **K~stück** *nt* trick; (*große Leistung*) feat. **k~voll** *adj* artistic; (*geschickt*) skilful

kunterbunt *adj* multicoloured; (*gemischt*) mixed

Kupfer *nt* **-s** copper

Kupon /ku'põ:/ *m* **-s,-s** voucher; (*Zins-*) coupon; (*Stoff-*) length

Kuppe *f* **-,-n** [rounded] top

Kuppel *f* **-,-n** dome

kupp|eln *vt* couple (**an** + *acc* to) ● *vi* (*haben*) (*Auto*) operate the clutch. **K~lung** *f* **-,-en** coupling; (*Auto*) clutch

Kur *f* **-,-en** course of treatment, cure

> *i* **Kur** A health cure in a spa town may last up to 6 weeks and usually involves a special diet, exercise programmes, physiotherapy and massage. The cure is intended for people with minor complaints or who are recovering from illness, and it plays an important role in preventative medicine in Germany.

Kür *f* **-,-en** (*Sport*) free exercise; (*Eislauf*) free programme

Kurbel *f* **-,-n** crank. **K~welle** *f* crankshaft

Kürbis *m* **-ses,-se** pumpkin

Kurier *m* **-s,-e** courier

kurieren *vt* cure

kurios *adj* curious, odd. **K~ität** *f* **-,-en** oddness; (*Objekt*) curiosity

Kurort *m* health resort; (*Badeort*) spa

Kurs *m* **-es,-e** course; (*Aktien-*) price. **K~buch** *nt* timetable

kursieren *vi* (*haben*) circulate

kursiv *adj* italic ● *adv* in italics. **K~schrift** *f* italics *pl*

Kursus *m* -,Kurse course
Kurswagen *m* through carriage
Kurtaxe *f* visitors' tax
Kurve *f* -,-n curve; (*Straßen-*) bend
kurz *adj* short; (*knapp*) brief; (*rasch*) quick; (*schroff*) curt; **k~e Hosen** shorts; **vor k~em** a short time ago; **seit k~em** lately; **den Kürzeren ziehen** get the worst of it; **k~ vor** shortly before; **sich k~ fassen** be brief; **k~ und gut** in short; **zu k~ kommen** get less than one's fair share. **k~ärmelig** *adj* short-sleeved. **k~atmig** *adj* **k~atmig sein** be short of breath
Kürze *f* - shortness; (*Knappheit*) brevity; **in K~** shortly. **k~n** *vt* shorten; (*verringern*) cut
kurzfristig *adj* short-term ● *adv* at short notice
kürzlich *adv* recently
Kurz|meldung *f* newsflash. **K~schluss** *m* short circuit. **K~schrift** *f* shorthand. **k~sichtig** *adj* short-sighted. **K~sichtigkeit** *f* - short-sightedness. **K~streckenrakete** *f* short-range missile
Kürzung *f* -,-en shortening; (*Verringerung*) cut (*gen* in)
Kurz|waren *fpl* haberdashery *sg*. **K~welle** *f* short wave
kuscheln (sich) *vr* snuggle (**an** + *acc* up to)
Kusine *f* -,-n [female] cousin
Kuss *m* -es,⸚e kiss
küssen *vt/i* (*haben*) kiss; **sich k~** kiss
Küste *f* -,-n coast
Küster *m* -s,- verger
Kutsch|e *f* -,-n [horse-drawn] carriage/(*geschlossen*) coach. **K~er** *m* -s,- coachman, driver
Kutte *f* -,-n (*Relig*) habit
Kutter *m* -s,- (*Naut*) cutter
Kuvert /ku'veːɐ̯/ *nt* -s,-s envelope

L l

Labor *nt* -s,-s & -e laboratory. **L~ant(in)** *m* -en,-en (*f* -,-nen) laboratory assistant
Labyrinth *nt* -[e]s,-e maze, labyrinth
Lache *f* -,-n puddle; (*Blut-*) pool
lächeln *vi* (*haben*) smile. **L~** *nt* -s smile. **l~d** *adj* smiling
lachen *vi* (*haben*) laugh. **L~** *nt* -s laugh; (*Gelächter*) laughter
lächerlich *adj* ridiculous; **sich l~ machen** make a fool of oneself. **L~keit** *f* -,-en ridiculousness; (*Kleinigkeit*) triviality
Lachs *m* -es,-e salmon
Lack *m* -[e]s,-e varnish; (*Japan-*) lacquer; (*Auto*) paint. **l~en** *vt* varnish. **l~ieren** *vt* varnish; (*spritzen*) spray. **L~schuhe** *mpl* patent-leather shoes
laden† *vt* load; (*Electr*) charge; (*Jur: vor-*) summon
Laden *m* -s,⸚ shop; (*Fenster-*) shutter. **L~dieb** *m* shoplifter. **L~schluss** *m* [shop] closing time. **L~tisch** *m* counter
Laderaum *m* (*Naut*) hold
lädieren *vt* damage
Ladung *f* -,-en load; (*Naut, Aviat*) cargo; (*elektrische*) charge
Lage *f* -,-n position, situation; (*Schicht*) layer; **nicht in der L~ sein** not be in a position (**zu** to)
Lager *nt* -s,- camp; (*L~haus*) warehouse; (*Vorrat*) stock; (*Techn*) bearing; (*Erz-, Ruhe-*) bed; (*eines Tieres*)

lair; **[nicht] auf L~** [not] in stock. **L~haus** *nt* warehouse. **l~n** *vt* store; (*legen*) lay; **sich l~n** settle. **L~raum** *m* store-room. **L~ung** *f* - storage

Lagune *f* -,-n lagoon

lahm *adj* lame. **l~en** *vi* (*haben*) be lame

lähmen *vt* paralyse

Lähmung *f* -,-en paralysis

Laib *m* -[e]s,-e loaf

Laich *m* -[e]s (*Zool*) spawn

Laie *m* -n,-n layman; (*Theat*) amateur. **l~nhaft** *adj* amateurish

Laken *nt* -s,- sheet

Lakritze *f* - liquorice

lallen *vt/i* (*haben*) mumble; (*Baby:*) babble

Lametta *nt* -s tinsel

Lamm *nt* -[e]s,¨er lamb

Lampe *f* -,-n lamp; (*Decken-, Wand-*) light; (*Glüh-*) bulb. **L~nfieber** *nt* stage fright

Lampion /lam'pi̯ɔŋ/ *m* -s,-s Chinese lantern

Land *nt* -[e]s,¨er country; (*Fest-*) land; (*Bundes-*) state, Land; (*Aust*) province; **auf dem L~e** in the country; **an L~ gehen** (*Naut*) go ashore. **L~arbeiter** *m* agricultural worker. **L~ebahn** *f* runway. **l~en** *vt/i* (*sein*) land; (🄵: *gelangen*) end up

> **Land** Germany is a federal republic consisting of 16 member states called *Länder* or *Bundesländer*. Each *Land* is responsible for local government, educational and cultural affairs, police and the environment. Austria has 9 *Länder*, while the Swiss equivalent is the ▷KANTON.

Ländereien *pl* estates

Länderspiel *nt* international

Landesverrat *m* treason

Landkarte *f* map

ländlich *adj* rural

Land|schaft *f* -,-en scenery; (*Geog, Kunst*) landscape; (*Gegend*) country[side]. **l~schaftlich** *adj* scenic; (*regional*) regional. **L~streicher** *m* -s,- tramp. **L~tag** *m* state/(*Aust*) provincial parliament

Landung *f* -,-en landing

Land|vermesser *m* -s,- surveyor. **L~weg** *m* country lane; **auf dem L~weg** overland. **L~wirt** *m* farmer. **L~wirtschaft** *f* agriculture; (*Hof*) farm. **l~wirtschaftlich** *adj* agricultural

lang[1] *adv & prep* (+ *preceding acc or preceding* **an** + *dat*) along; **den** *od* **am Fluss l~** along the river

lang[2] *adj* long; (*groß*) tall; **seit l~em** for a long time ● *adv* **eine Stunde l~** for an hour; **mein Leben l~** all my life. **l~ärmelig** *adj* long-sleeved. **l~atmig** *adj* long-winded. **l~e** *adv* a long time; (*schlafen*) late; **schon l~e** [for] a long time; (*zurückliegend*) a long time ago; **l~e nicht** not for a long time; (*bei weitem nicht*) nowhere near

Länge *f* -,-n length; (*Geog*) longitude; **der L~ nach** lengthways

Läng|engrad *m* degree of longitude. **l~er** *adj & adv* longer; (*längere Zeit*) [for] some time

Langeweile *f* - boredom; **L~ haben** be bored

lang|fristig *adj* long-term; (*Vorhersage*) long-range. **l~jährig** *adj* long-standing; (*Erfahrung*) long

länglich *adj* oblong; **l~ rund** oval

längs *adv & prep* (+ *gen/dat*) along; (*der Länge nach*) lengthways

lang|sam *adj* slow. **L~samkeit** *f* -

slowness

längst *adv* **[schon] l~** for a long time; (*zurückliegend*) a long time ago; **l~ nicht** nowhere near

Lang|strecken- *prefix* long-distance; (*Mil, Aviat*) long-range. **l~weilen** *vt* bore; **sich l~weilen** be bored. **l~weilig** *adj* boring

Lanze *f* **-,-n** lance

Lappalie /la'pa:li̯ə/ *f* **-,-n** trifle

Lappen *m* **-s,-** cloth; (*Anat*) lobe

Laptop *m* **-s,-s** laptop

Lärche *f* **-,-n** larch

Lärm *m* **-s** noise. **l~end** *adj* noisy

Larve /'larfə/ *f* **-,-n** larva; (*Maske*) mask

lasch *adj* listless; (*schlaff*) limp

Lasche *f* **-,-n** tab, flap

Laser /'le:-, 'la:zɐ/ *m* **-s,-** laser

lassen†

● *transitive verb*

····➤ (*+ infinitive; veranlassen*) **etw tun lassen** have *or* get sth done. **jdn etw tun lassen** make s.o. do sth; get s.o. to do sth **sich** *dat* **die Haare schneiden lassen** have *or* get one's hair cut. **jdn warten lassen** make *or* let s.o. wait; keep s.o. waiting. **jdn grüßen lassen** send one's regards to s.o. **jdn kommen/rufen lassen** send for s.o.

····➤ (*+ infinitive; erlauben*) let; allow; (*hineinlassen/herauslassen*) let *or* allow (**in** + *acc* into, **aus** + *dat* out of). **jdn etw tun lassen** let s.o. do sth; allow s.o. to do sth. **er ließ mich nicht ausreden** he didn't let me finish [what I was saying]

····➤ (*belassen, bleiben lassen*) leave. **jdn in Frieden lassen** leave s.o. in peace. **etw ungesagt lassen** leave sth unsaid

····➤ (*unterlassen*) stop. **das Rauchen lassen** stop smoking. **er kann es nicht lassen, sie zu quälen** he can't stop *or* he is forever tormenting her

····➤ (*überlassen*) **jdm etw lassen** let s.o. have sth

····➤ (*als Aufforderung*) **lass/lasst uns gehen/fahren!** let's go!

● *reflexive verb*

····➤ **das lässt sich machen** that can be done. **das lässt sich nicht beweisen** it can't be proved. **die Tür lässt sich leicht öffnen** the door opens easily

● *intransitive verb*

····➤ [!] **Lass mal. Ich mache das schon** Leave it. I'll do it

lässig *adj* casual. **L~keit** *f* - casualness

Lasso *nt* **-s,-s** lasso

Last *f* **-,-en** load; (*Gewicht*) weight; (*fig*) burden; **L~en** charges; (*Steuern*) taxes. **L~auto** *nt* lorry. **l~en** *vi* (*haben*) weigh heavily/(*liegen*) rest (**auf** + *dat* on)

Laster[1] *m* **-s,-** [!] lorry

Laster[2] *nt* **-s,-** vice

läster|n *vt* blaspheme ● *vi* (*haben*) make disparaging remarks (**über** + *acc* about). **L~ung** *f* **-,-en** blasphemy

lästig *adj* troublesome; **l~ sein/werden** be/become a nuisance

Last|kahn *m* barge. **L~[kraft]wagen** *m* lorry

Latein *nt* **-[s]** Latin. **L~amerika** *nt* Latin America. **l~isch** *adj* Latin

Laterne *f* **-,-n** lantern; (*Straßen-*) street lamp. **L~npfahl** *m* lamp-post

latschen *vi* (*sein*) [!] traipse

Latte *f* **-,-n** slat; (*Tor-, Hochsprung-*) bar

Latz *m* **-es,⸚e** bib
Lätzchen *nt* **-s,-** [baby's] bib
Latzhose *f* dungarees *pl*
Laub *nt* **-[e]s** leaves *pl*; (*L~werk*) foliage. **L~baum** *m* deciduous tree
Laube *f* **-,-n** summer-house
Laub|säge *f* fretsaw. **L~wald** *m* deciduous forest
Lauch *m* **-[e]s** leeks *pl*
Lauer *f* **auf der L~ liegen** lie in wait. **l~n** *vi* (*haben*) lurk; **l~n auf** (+ *acc*) lie in wait for
Lauf *m* **-[e]s, Läufe** run; (*Laufen*) running; (*Verlauf*) course; (*Wett-*) race; (*Sport: Durchgang*) heat; (*Gewehr-*) barrel; **im L~[e]** (+ *gen*) in the course of. **L~bahn** *f* career. **l~en**† *vi* (*sein*) run; (*zu Fuß gehen*) walk; (*gelten*) be valid; **Ski/Schlittschuh l~en** ski/skate. **l~end** *adj* running; (*gegenwärtig*) current; (*regelmäßig*) regular; **auf dem L~enden sein** be up to date ● *adv* continually
Läufer *m* **-s,-** (*Person, Teppich*) runner; (*Schach*) bishop
Lauf|gitter *nt* play-pen. **L~masche** *f* ladder. **L~text** *m* marquee text. **L~zettel** *m* circular
Lauge *f* **-,-n** soapy water
Laun|e *f* **-,-n** mood; (*Einfall*) whim; **guter L~e sein, gute L~e haben** be in a good mood. **l~isch** *adj* moody
Laus *f* **-,Läuse** louse; (*Blatt-*) greenfly
lauschen *vi* (*haben*) listen
laut *adj* loud; (*geräuschvoll*) noisy; **l~ lesen** read aloud; **l~er stellen** turn up ● *prep* (+ *gen*/*dat*) according to. **L~** *m* **-es,-e** sound
Laute *f* **-,-n** (*Mus*) lute
lauten *vi* (*haben*) (*Text:*) run, read
läuten *vt*/*i* (*haben*) ring
lauter *adj* pure; (*ehrlich*) honest; (*Wahrheit*) plain ● *adj inv* sheer; (*nichts als*) nothing but
laut|hals *adv* at the top of one's voice, (*lachen*) out loud. **l~los** *adj* silent, (*Stille*) hushed. **L~schrift** *f* phonetics *pl*. **L~sprecher** *m* loudspeaker. **L~stärke** *f* volume
lauwarm *adj* lukewarm
Lava *f* **-,-ven** lava
Lavendel *m* **-s** lavender
lavieren *vi* (*haben*) manœuvre
Lawine *f* **-,-n** avalanche
Lazarett *nt* **-[e]s,-e** military hospital
leasen /'li:sən/ *vt* rent
Lebehoch *nt* cheer
leben *vt*/*i* (*haben*) live (**von** on); **leb wohl!** farewell! **L~** *nt* **-s,-** life, (*Treiben*) bustle; **am L~** alive. **l~d** *adj* living
lebendig *adj* live; (*lebhaft*) lively; (*anschaulich*) vivid; **l~ sein** be alive. **L~keit** *f* **-** liveliness; vividness
Lebens|abend *m* old age. **L~alter** *nt* age. **l~fähig** *adj* viable. **L~gefahr** *f* mortal danger; **in L~gefahr** in mortal danger; (*Patient*) critically ill. **l~gefährlich** *adj* extremely dangerous; (*Verletzung*) critical. **L~haltungskosten** *pl* cost of living *sg*. **l~länglich** *adj* life-long ● *adv* for life. **L~lauf** *m* curriculum vitae. **L~mittel** *ntpl* food *sg*. **L~mittelgeschäft** *nt* food shop. **L~mittelhändler** *m* grocer. **L~partnerschaft** *f* civil partnership. **L~retter** *m* rescuer; (*beim Schwimmen*) life-guard. **L~unterhalt** *m* livelihood; **seinen L~unterhalt verdienen** earn one's living. **L~versicherung** *f* life assurance. **L~wandel** *m* conduct. **l~wichtig** *adj* vital. **L~zeit** *f* **auf L~zeit** for life
Leber *f* **-,-n** liver. **L~fleck** *m* mole
Lebe|wesen *nt* living being.

L~wohl *nt* **-s,-s** & **-e** farewell

leb|haft *adj* lively; (*Farbe*) vivid. **L~kuchen** *m* gingerbread. **l~los** *adj* lifeless. **L~zeiten** *fpl* **zu jds L~zeiten** in s.o.'s lifetime

leck *adj* leaking. **L~** *nt* **-s,-s** leak. **l~en**[1] *vi* (*haben*) leak

lecken[2] *vi* (*haben*) lick

lecker *adj* tasty. **L~bissen** *m* delicacy

Leder *nt* **-s,-** leather

ledig *adj* single, unmarried

leer *adj* empty; (*unbesetzt*) vacant; **l~ laufen** (*Auto*) idle. **l~en** *vt* empty; **sich l~en** empty. **L~lauf** *m* (*Auto*) neutral. **L~ung** *f* **-,-en** (*Post*) collection

legal *adj* legal. **l~isieren** *vt* legalize. **L~ität** *f* **-** legality

Legas|thenie *f* **-** dyslexia **L~theniker** *m* **-s,-** dyslexic

legen *vt* put; (*hin-, ver-*) lay; set (*Haare*); **sich l~** lie down; (*nachlassen*) subside

Legende *f* **-,-n** legend

leger /le'ʒeːɐ̯/ *adj* casual

Legierung *f* **-,-en** alloy

Legion *f* **-,-en** legion

Legislative *f* **-** legislature

legitim *adj* legitimate. **L~ität** *f* **-** legitimacy

Lehm *m* **-s** clay

Lehn|e *f* **-,-n** (*Rücken-*) back; (*Arm-*) arm. **l~en** *vt* lean (**an** + *acc* against); **sich l~en** lean (**an** + *acc* against) ● *vi* (*haben*) be leaning (**an** + *acc* against)

Lehr|buch *nt* textbook. **L~e** *f* **-,-n** apprenticeship; (*Anschauung*) doctrine; (*Theorie*) theory; (*Wissenschaft*) science; (*Erfahrung*) lesson. **l~en** *vt/i* (*haben*) teach. **L~er** *m* **-s,-** teacher; (*Fahr-*) instructor. **L~erin** *f* **-,-nen** teacher. **L~erzimmer** *nt* staff-room. **L~fach** *nt* (*Sch*) subject. **L~gang** *m* course. **L~kraft** *f* teacher. **L~ling** *m* **-s,-e** apprentice; (*Auszubildender*) trainee. **L~plan** *m* syllabus. **l~reich** *adj* instructive. **L~stelle** *f* apprenticeship. **L~stuhl** *m* (*Univ*) chair. **L~zeit** *f* apprenticeship

Leib *m* **-es,-er** body; (*Bauch*) belly. **L~eserziehung** *f* (*Sch*) physical education. **L~gericht** *nt* favourite dish. **l~lich** *adj* physical; (*blutsverwandt*) real, natural. **L~wächter** *m* bodyguard

Leiche *f* **-,-n** [dead] body; corpse. **L~nbestatter** *m* **-s,-** undertaker. **L~nhalle** *f* mortuary. **L~nwagen** *m* hearse. **L~nzug** *m* funeral procession, cortège

Leichnam *m* **-s,-e** [dead] body

leicht *adj* light; (*Stoff*) lightweight; (*gering*) slight; (*mühelos*) easy; **jdm l~ fallen** be easy for s.o.; **etw l~ machen** make sth easy (**dat** for); **es sich** (*dat*) **l~ machen** take the easy way out; **etw l~ nehmen** (*fig*) take sth lightly. **L~athletik** *f* [track and field] athletics *sg*. **L~gewicht** *nt* (*Boxen*) lightweight. **l~gläubig** *adj* gullible. **l~hin** *adv* casually. **L~igkeit** *f* **-** lightness; (*Mühelosigkeit*) ease; (*L~sein*) easiness; **mit L~igkeit** with ease. **L~sinn** *m* carelessness; recklessness; (*Frivolität*) frivolity. **l~sinnig** *adj* careless; (*unvorsichtig*) reckless

Leid *nt* **-[e]s** sorrow, grief; (*Böses*) harm; **es tut mir L~** I am sorry; **er tut mir L~** I feel sorry for him. **l~** *adj* **jdn/etw l~ sein/werden** be/get tired of s.o./something

Leide|form *f* passive. **l~n**† *vt/i* (*haben*) suffer (**an** + *dat* from); **jdn/etw nicht l~n können** dislike s.o./something. **L~n** *nt* **-s,-** suffering; (*Med*) complaint; (*Krankheit*) disease. **l~nd** *adj* suffering. **L~nschaft** *f* **-,-en** passion. **l~nschaftlich** *adj* passionate

leider *adv* unfortunately; **l~er ja-/nicht** I'm afraid so/not

Leier|kasten *m* barrel-organ. **l~n** *vt/i* (*haben*) wind; (*herunter-*) drone out

Leih|e *f* **-,-n** loan. **l~en†** *vt* lend; **sich** (*dat*) **etw l~en** borrow sth. **L~gabe** *f* loan. **L~gebühr** *f* rental; lending charge. **L~haus** *nt* pawnshop. **L~wagen** *m* hire-car. **l~weise** *adv* on loan

Leim *m* **-s** glue. **l~en** *vt* glue

Leine *f* **-,-n** rope; (*Wäsche-*) line; (*Hunde-*) lead, leash

Lein|en *nt* **-s** linen. **L~wand** *f* linen; (*Kunst*) canvas; (*Film-*) screen

leise *adj* quiet; (*Stimme, Berührung*) soft; (*schwach*) faint; (*leicht*) light; **l~r stellen** turn down

Leiste *f* **-,-n** strip; (*Holz-*) batten; (*Anat*) groin

leist|en *vt* achieve, accomplish; **sich** (*dat*) **etw l~en** treat oneself to sth; (*[!]: anstellen*) get up to sth; **ich kann es mir nicht l~en** I can't afford it. **L~ung** *f* **-,-en** achievement; (*Sport, Techn*) performance; (*Produktion*) output; (*Zahlung*) payment

Leit|artikel *m* leader, editorial. **l~en** *vt* run, manage; (*an-/hinführen*) lead; (*Mus, Techn, Phys*) conduct; (*lenken, schicken*) direct. **l~end** *adj* leading; (*Posten*) executive

Leiter[1] *f* **-,-n** ladder

Leit|er[2] *m* **-s,-** director; (*Comm*) manager; (*Führer*) leader; (*Mus, Phys*) conductor. **L~erin** *f* **-,-nen** director; manageress; leader. **L~planke** *f* crash barrier. **L~spruch** *m* motto. **L~ung** *f* **-,-en** (*Führung*) direction; (*Comm*) management; (*Aufsicht*) control; (*Electr: Schnur*) lead, flex; (*Kabel*) cable; (*Telefon-*) line; (*Rohr-*) pipe; (*Haupt-*) main. **L~ungswasser** *nt* tap water

Lektion /-'tsio:n/ *f* **-,-en** lesson

Lekt|or *m* **-s,-en**, **L~orin** *f* **-,-nen** (*Univ*) assistant lecturer; (*Verlags-*) editor. **L~üre** *f* **-,-n** reading matter

Lende *f* **-,-n** loin

lenk|en *vt* guide; (*steuern*) steer; (*regeln*) control; **jds Aufmerksamkeit auf sich** (*acc*) **l~en** attract s.o.'s attention. **L~rad** *nt* steering-wheel. **L~stange** *f* handlebars *pl*. **L~ung** *f* **-** steering

Leopard *m* **-en,-en** leopard

Lepra *f* **-** leprosy

Lerche *f* **-,-n** lark

lernen *vt/i* (*haben*) learn; (*für die Schule*) study

Lernkurve *f* learning curve

Lesb|ierin /'lɛsbiərɪn/ *f* **-,-nen** lesbian. **l~isch** *adj* lesbian

les|en† *vt/i* (*haben*) read; (*Univ*) lecture ● *vt* pick, gather. **L~en** *nt* **-s** reading. **L~er(in)** *m* **-s,-** (*f* **-,-nen**) reader. **l~erlich** *adj* legible. **L~ezeichen** *nt* bookmark

lethargisch *adj* lethargic

Lettland *nt* **-s** Latvia

letzt|e(r,s) *adj* last; (*neueste*) latest; **in l~er Zeit** recently; **l~en Endes** in the end. **l~ens** *adv* recently; (*zuletzt*) lastly. **l~ere(r,s)** *adj* the latter; **der/die/das L~ere** (**l~ere**) the latter

Leucht|e *f* **-,-n** light. **l~en** *vi* (*haben*) shine. **l~end** *adj* shining. **L~er** *m* **-s,-** candlestick. **L~feuer** *nt* beacon. **L~rakete** *f* flare. **L~reklame** *f* neon sign. **L~röhre** *f* fluorescent tube. **L~turm** *m* lighthouse

leugnen *vt* deny

Leukämie *f* - leukaemia
Leumund *m* **-s** reputation
Leute *pl* people; (*Mil*) men; (*Arbeiter*) workers
Leutnant *m* **-s,-s** second lieutenant
Lexikon *nt* **-s,-ka** encyclopaedia; (*Wörterbuch*) dictionary
Libanon (der) -s Lebanon
Libelle *f* **-,-n** dragonfly
liberal *adj* (*Pol*) liberal
Libyen *nt* **-s** Libya
Licht *nt* **-[e]s,-er** light; (*Kerze*) candle; **L~ machen** turn on the light. **l~** *adj* bright; (*Med*) lucid; (*spärlich*) sparse. **L~bild** *nt* [passport] photograph; (*Dia*) slide. **L~blick** *m* (*fig*) ray of hope. **l~en** *vt* thin out; **den Anker l~en** (*Naut*) weigh anchor; **sich l~en** become less dense; thin. **L~hupe** *f* headlight flasher; **die L~hupe betätigen** flash one's headlights. **L~maschine** *f* dynamo. **L~ung** *f* **-,-en** clearing
Lid *nt* **-[e]s,-er** [eye]lid. **L~schatten** *m* eye-shadow
lieb *adj* dear; (*nett*) nice; (*artig*) good; **jdn l~ haben** be fond of s.o.; (*lieben*) love s.o.; **es wäre mir l~er** I should prefer it (**wenn** if)
Liebe *f* **-,-n** love. **l~n** *vt* love; (*mögen*) like; **sich l~n** love each other; (*körperlich*) make love. **l~nd** *adj* loving. **l~nswert** a lovable. **l~nswürdig** *adj* kind. **l~nswürdigerweise** *adv* very kindly
lieber *adv* rather; (*besser*) better; **l~ mögen** like better; **ich trinke l~ Tee** I prefer tea
Liebes|brief *m* love letter. **L~dienst** *m* favour. **L~kummer** *m* heartache. **L~paar** *nt* [pair of] lovers *pl*
lieb|evoll *adj* loving, affectionate. **L~haber** *m* **-s,-** lover; (*Sammler*) collector. **L~haberei** *f* **-,-en** hobby. **L~kosung** *f* **-,-en** caress. **l~lich** *adj* lovely; (*sanft*) gentle; (*süß*) sweet. **L~ling** *m* **-s,-e** darling; (*Bevorzugte*) favourite. **L~lings-** *prefix* favourite. **l~los** *adj* loveless; (*Eltern*) uncaring; (*unfreundlich*) unkind. **L~schaft** *f* **-,-en** [love] affair. **l~ste(r,s)** *adj* dearest; (*bevorzugt*) favourite ● *adv* **am l~sten** best [of all]; **jdn/etw am l~sten mögen** like s.o./something best [of all]. **L~ste(r)** *m/f* beloved; (*Schatz*) sweetheart
Lied *nt* **-[e]s,-er** song
liederlich *adj* slovenly; (*unordentlich*) untidy. **L~keit** *f* - slovenliness; untidiness
Lieferant *m* **-en,-en** supplier
liefer|bar *adj* (*Comm*) available. **l~n** *vt* supply; (*zustellen*) deliver; (*hervorbringen*) yield. **L~ung** *f* **-,-en** delivery; (*Sendung*) consignment
Liege *f* **-,-n** couch. **l~n**† *vi* (*haben*) lie; (*gelegen sein*) be situated; **l~n bleiben** remain lying [there]; (*im Bett*) stay in bed; (*Ding:*) be left; (*Schnee:*) settle; (*Arbeit:*) remain undone; (*zurückgelassen werden*) be left behind; **l~n lassen** leave; (*zurücklassen*) leave behind; (*nicht fortführen*) leave undone; **l~n an** (+ *dat*) (*fig*) be due to; (*abhängen*) depend on; **jdm [nicht] l~n** [not] suit s.o.; **mir liegt viel daran** it is very important to me. **L~stuhl** *m* deckchair. **L~stütz** *m* **-es,-e** press-up, (*Amer*) push-up. **L~wagen** *m* couchette car
Lift *m* **-[e]s,-e & -s** lift
Liga *f* **-,-gen** league
Likör *m* **-s,-e** liqueur
lila *inv adj* mauve; (*dunkel*) purple
Lilie /ˈliːli̯ə/ *f* **-,-n** lily
Liliputaner(in) *m* **-s,-** (*f* **-,-nen**) dwarf

Limo *f* -,-[s] [!], **L∼nade** *f* -,-n fizzy drink; lemonade

Limousine /limu'ziːnə/ *f* -,-n saloon

lind *adj* mild

Linde *f* -,-n lime tree

linder|n *vt* relieve, ease. **L∼ung** *f* - relief

Lineal *nt* -s,-e ruler

Linie /-i̯ə/ *f* -,-n line; (*Zweig*) branch; (*Bus-*) route; **L∼ 4** number 4 [bus/tram]; **in erster L∼** primarily. **L∼nflug** *m* scheduled flight. **L∼nrichter** *m* linesman

lin[i]iert *adj* lined, ruled

Link|e *f* -n,-n left side; (*Hand*) left hand; (*Boxen*) left; **die L∼e** (*Pol*) the left. **l∼e(r,s)** *adj* left; (*Pol*) left-wing; **l∼e Masche** purl

links *adv* on the left; (*bei Stoff*) on the wrong side; (*verkehrt*) inside out; **l∼stricken** purl. **L∼händer(in)** *m* -s,- (*f* -,-nen) lefthander. **l∼händig** *adj & adv* lefthanded

Linoleum /-leʊm/ *nt* -s lino, linoleum

Linse *f* -,-n lens; (*Bot*) lentil

Lippe *f* -,-n lip. **L∼nstift** *m* lipstick

Liquid|ation /-'tsi̯oːn/ *f* -,-en liquidation. **l∼ieren** *vt* liquidate

lispeln *vt/i* (*haben*) lisp

List *f* -,-en trick, ruse

Liste *f* -,-n list

listig *adj* cunning, crafty

Litanei *f* -,-en litany

Litauen *nt* -s Lithuania

Liter *m & nt* -s,- litre

Literatur *f* - literature

Liturgie *f* -,-n liturgy

Litze *f* -,-n braid

Lizenz *f* -,-en licence

Lob *nt* -[e]s praise

Lobby /'lɔbi/ *f* - (*Pol*) lobby

loben *vt* praise

löblich *adj* praiseworthy

Lobrede *f* eulogy

Loch *nt* -[e]s,⸚er hole. **l∼en** *vt* punch a hole/holes in; punch (*Fahrkarte*). **L∼er** *m* -s,- punch

löcherig *adj* full of holes

Locke *f* -,-n curl. **l∼n**[1] *vt* curl; **sich l∼n** curl

locken[2] *vt* lure, entice; (*reizen*) tempt. **l∼d** *adj* tempting

Lockenwickler *m* -s,- curler; (*Rolle*) roller

locker *adj* loose; (*Seil*) slack; (*Erde*) light; (*zwanglos*) casual; (*zu frei*) lax. **l∼n** *vt* loosen; slacken (*Seil*); break up (*Boden*); relax (*Griff*); **sich l∼n** become loose; (*Seil:*) slacken; (*sich entspannen*) relax

lockig *adj* curly

Lockmittel *nt* bait

Loden *m* -s (*Textiles*) loden

Löffel *m* -s,- spoon; (*L∼ voll*) spoonful. **l∼n** *vt* spoon up

Logarithmus *m* -,-men logarithm

Logbuch *nt* (*Naut*) log-book

Loge /'loːʒə/ *f* -,-n lodge; (*Theat*) box

Log|ik *f* - logic. **l∼isch** *adj* logical

Logo *nt* -s,-s logo

Lohn *m* -[e]s,⸚e wages *pl*, pay; (*fig*) reward. **L∼empfänger** *m* wage-earner. **l∼en** *vi|r* (*haben*) **[sich] l∼en** be worth it *or* worth while ● *vt* be worth. **l∼end** *adj* worthwhile; (*befriedigend*) rewarding. **L∼erhöhung** *f* [pay] rise. **L∼steuer** *f* income tax

Lok *f* -,-s [!] = **Lokomotive**

Lokal *nt* -s,-e restaurant; (*Trink-*) bar

Lokomotiv|e *f* -,-n engine, locomotive. **L∼führer** *m* engine driver

London *nt* **-s** London. **L~er** *adj* London ● *m* **-s,-** Londoner

Lorbeer *m* **-s,-en** laurel. **L~blatt** *nt* (*Culin*) bay-leaf

Lore *f* **-,-n** (*Rail*) truck

Los *nt* **-es,-e** lot; (*Lotterie-*) ticket; (*Schicksal*) fate

los *pred adj* **los sein** be loose; **jdn/etw los sein** be rid of s.o./something; **was ist [mit ihm] los?** what's the matter [with him]? ● *adv* **los!** go on! **Achtung, fertig, los!** ready, steady, go!

lösbar *adj* soluble

losbinden† *vt sep* untie

Lösch|blatt *nt* sheet of blotting-paper. **l~en** *vt* put out, extinguish; quench (*Durst*); blot (*Tinte*); (*tilgen*) cancel; (*streichen*) delete

Löschfahrzeug *nt* fire-engine

lose *adj* loose

Lösegeld *nt* ransom

losen *vt* (*haben*) draw lots (**um** for)

lösen *vt* undo; (*lockern*) loosen; (*entfernen*) detach; (*klären*) solve; (*auflösen*) dissolve; cancel (*Vertrag*); break off (*Beziehung*); (*kaufen*) buy; **sich l~** come off; (*sich trennen*) detach oneself/itself; (*lose werden*) come undone; (*sich klären*) resolve itself; (*sich auflösen*) dissolve

los|fahren† *vi sep* (*sein*) start; (*Auto:*) drive off; **l~fahren nach** (+ *dat*) head for. **l~gehen**† *vi sep* (*sein*) set off; (🅃: *anfangen*) start; (*Bombe:*) go off; **l~gehen nach** (+ *dat*) head for; (*fig: angreifen*) go for. **l~kommen**† *vi sep* (*sein*) get away (**von** from). **l~lassen**† *vt sep* let go of; (*freilassen*) release

löslich *adj* soluble

los|lösen *vt sep* detach; **sich l~lösen** become detached; (*fig*) break away (**von** from). **l~machen** *vt sep* detach; untie. **l~reißen**† *vt sep* tear off; **sich l~reißen** break free; (*fig*) tear oneself away. **l~schicken** *vt sep* send off. **l~sprechen**† *vt sep* absolve (**von** from)

Losung *f* **-,-en** (*Pol*) slogan; (*Mil*) password

Lösung *f* **-,-en** solution. **L~smittel** *nt* solvent

loswerden† *vt sep* get rid of

Lot *nt* **-[e]s,-e** perpendicular; (*Blei-*) plumb[-bob]. **l~en** *vt* plumb

löt|en *vt* solder. **L~lampe** *f* blow-lamp

lotrecht *adj* perpendicular

Lotse *m* **-n,-n** (*Naut*) pilot. **l~n** *vt* (*Naut*) pilot; (*fig*) guide

Lotterie *f* **-,-n** lottery

Lotto *nt* **-s,-s** lotto; (*Lotterie*) lottery

> *i* **Love Parade** A techno music and dance festival, which takes place in Berlin every summer. Originally a celebration of youth culture and very popular with young people, this festival has become a major tourist attraction.

Löw|e *m* **-n,-n** lion; (*Astrology*) Leo. **L~enzahn** *m* (*Bot*) dandelion. **L~in** *f* **-,-nen** lioness

loyal /lo̩a'ja:l/ *adj* loyal. **L~ität** *f* - loyalty

Luchs *m* **-es,-e** lynx

Lücke *f* **-,-n** gap. **l~nhaft** *adj* incomplete; (*Wissen*) patchy. **l~nlos** *adj* complete; (*Folge*) unbroken

Luder *nt* **-s,-** ✖ (*Frau*) bitch

Luft *f* **-,⸚e** air; **tief L~ holen** take a deep breath; **in die L~ gehen** explode. **L~angriff** *m* air raid. **L~aufnahme** *f* aerial photograph. **L~ballon** *m* balloon. **L~blase** *f* air bubble. **L~druck** *m* atmospheric pressure

lüften *vt* air; raise (*Hut*); reveal (*Geheimnis*)
Luft|fahrt *f* aviation. **L~fahrtgesellschaft** *f* airline. **L~gewehr** *nt* airgun. **l~ig** *adj* airy; (*Kleid*) light. **L~kissenfahrzeug** *nt* hovercraft. **L~krieg** *m* aerial warfare. **l~leer** *adj* **l~leerer Raum** vacuum. **L~linie** *f* 100 km **L~linie** 100 km as the crow flies. **L~matratze** *f* airbed, inflatable mattress. **L~pirat** *m* hijacker. **L~post** *f* airmail. **L~röhre** *f* windpipe. **L~schiff** *nt* airship. **L~schlange** *f* [paper] streamer. **L~schutzbunker** *m* air-raid shelter
Lüftung *f* - ventilation
Luft|veränderung *f* change of air. **L~waffe** *f* air force. **L~zug** *m* draught
Lüg|e *f* -,-n lie. **l~en†** *vt/i* (*haben*) lie. **L~ner(in)** *m* -s,- (*f* -,-nen) liar. **l~nerisch** *adj* untrue; (*Person*) untruthful
Luke *f* -,-n hatch; (*Dach-*) skylight
Lümmel *m* -s,- lout
Lump *m* -en,-en scoundrel. **L~en** *m* -s,- rag; **in L~en** in rags. **L~enpack** *nt* riff-raff. **L~ensammler** *m* rag-and-bone man. **l~ig** *adj* mean, shabby
Lunge *f* -,-n lungs *pl*; (*L~nflügel*) lung. **L~nentzündung** *f* pneumonia
Lupe *f* -,-n magnifying glass
Lurch *m* -[e]s,-e amphibian
Lust *f* -,¨e pleasure; (*Verlangen*) desire; (*sinnliche Begierde*) lust; **L~ haben** feel like (**auf etw** *acc* sth); **ich habe keine L~** I don't feel like it; (*will nicht*) I don't want to
lustig *adj* jolly; (*komisch*) funny; **sich l~ machen über** (+ *acc*) make fun of
Lüstling *m* -s,-e lecher
lust|los *adj* listless. **L~mörder** *m* sex killer. **L~spiel** *nt* comedy
lutsch|en *vt/i* (*haben*) suck. **L~er** *m* -s,- lollipop
Lüttich *nt* -s Liège
Luv *f* & *nt* - **nach Luv** (*Naut*) to windward
luxuriös *adj* luxurious
Luxus *m* - luxury
Lymph|drüse /ˈlʏmf-/ *f*, **L~knoten** *m* lymph gland
lynchen /ˈlʏnçən/ *vt* lynch
Lyr|ik *f* - lyric poetry. **L~iker** *m* -s,- lyric poet. **l~isch** *adj* lyrical

Mm

Machart *f* style

machen
● *transitive verb*
····➤ (*herstellen, zubereiten*) make (*money, beds, music, exception, etc*). **aus Plastik/Holz gemacht** made of plastic/wood. **sich** (*dat*) **etw machen lassen** have sth made. **etw aus jdm machen** make s.o. into sth. **jdn zum Präsidenten machen** make s.o. president. **er machte sich** (*dat*) **viele Freunde/Feinde** he made a lot of friends/enemies. **jdm/sich** (*dat*) **[einen] Kaffee machen** make [some] coffee for s.o./oneself. **ein Foto machen** take a photo
····➤ (*verursachen*) make, cause (*difficulties*); cause (*pain, anxiety*). **jdm Arbeit machen** make [extra] work for s.o., cause s.o. extra work. **jdm Mut/Hoffnung machen** give s.o. courage/hope.

das macht Hunger/Durst this makes you hungry/thirsty. **das macht das Wetter** that's [because of] the weather

····➤ (*ausführen, ordnen*) do (*job, repair, fam: room, washing, etc.*).; take (*walk, trip, exam, course*). **sie machte mir die Haare** [!] she did my hair for me. **einen Besuch [bei jdm] machen** pay [s.o.] a visit

····➤ (*tun*) do (*nothing, everything*). **was machst du [da]?** what are you doing? **so etwas macht man nicht** that [just] isn't done

····➤ **was macht ... ?** (*wie ist es um bestellt?*) how is ...? **was macht die Gesundheit/Arbeit?** how are you keeping/how is the job [getting on]?

····➤ (*Math: ergeben*) be. **zwei mal zwei macht vier** two times two is four. **das macht 6 Euro [zusammen]** that's *or* that comes to six euros [altogether]

····➤ (*schaden*) **was macht das schon?** what does it matter? **[das] macht nichts!** [!] it doesn't matter

····➤ **mach's gut!** [!] look after yourself!; (*auf Wiedersehen*) so long!

● *reflexive verb*

····➤ **sich machen** [!] do well

····➤ **sich an etw** (*acc*) **machen** get down to sth. **sie machte sich an die Arbeit** she got down to work

● *intransitive verb*

····➤ **das macht hungrig/durstig** it makes you hungry/thirsty. **das macht dick** it's fattening

Macht *f* **-,⸚e** power. **M~haber** *m* **-s,-** ruler

mächtig *adj* powerful ● *adv* [!] terribly

machtlos *adj* powerless

Mädchen *nt* **-s,-** girl; (*Dienst-*) maid. **m~haft** *adj* girlish. **M~name** *m* girl's name; (*vor der Ehe*) maiden name

Made *f* **-,-n** maggot

madig *adj* maggoty

Madonna *f* **-,-nen** madonna

Magazin *nt* **-s,-e** magazine; (*Lager*) warehouse; store-room

Magd *f* **-,⸚e** maid

Magen *m* **-s,⸚** stomach. **M~verstimmung** *f* stomach upset

mager *adj* thin; (*Fleisch*) lean; (*Boden*) poor; (*dürftig*) meagre. **M~keit** *f* **-** thinness; leanness. **M~sucht** *f* anorexia

Magie *f* **-** magic

Mag|ier /ˈma:gi̯ɐ/ *m* **-s,-** magician. **m~isch** *adj* magic

Magistrat *m* **-s,-e** city council

Magnet *m* **-en** & **-[e]s,-e** magnet. **m~isch** *adj* magnetic

Mahagoni *nt* **-s** mahogany

Mäh|drescher *m* **-s,-** combine harvester. **m~en** *vt/i* (*haben*) mow

Mahl *nt* **-[e]s,⸚er** & **-e** meal

mahlen† *vt* grind

Mahlzeit *f* meal; **M~!** enjoy your meal!

Mähne *f* **-,-n** mane

mahn|en *vt/i* (*haben*) remind (**wegen** about); (*ermahnen*) admonish; (*auffordern*) urge (**zu** to). **M~ung** *f* **-,-en** reminder; admonition

Mai *m* **-[e]s,-e** May; **der Erste Mai** May Day. **M~glöckchen** *nt* **-s,-** lily of the valley

Mailand *nt* **-s** Milan

Mais *m* **-es** maize; (*Culin*) sweet corn

Majestät *f* **-,-en** majesty.

m~isch *adj* majestic
Major *m* **-s,-e** major
Majoran *m* **-s** marjoram
makaber *adj* macabre
Makel *m* **-s,-** blemish; (*Defekt*) flaw
Makkaroni *pl* macaroni *sg*
Makler *m* **-s,-** (*Comm*) broker
Makrele *f* **-,-n** mackerel
Makrone *f* **-,-n** macaroon
mal *adv* (*Math*) times; (*bei Maßen*) by; (🅘: *einmal*) once; (*eines Tages*) one day; **nicht mal** not even
Mal *nt* **-[e]s,-e** time; **zum ersten/letzten Mal** for the first/last time; **ein für alle Mal** once and for all; **jedes Mal** every time; **jedes Mal, wenn** whenever
Mal|buch *nt* colouring book. **m~en** *vt/i* (*haben*) paint. **M~er** *m* **-s,-** painter. **M~erei** *f* **-,-en** painting. **M~erin** *f* **-,-nen** painter. **m~erisch** *adj* picturesque
Mallorca /ma'lɔrka, -'jɔrka/ *nt* **-s** Majorca
mal|nehmen† *vt sep* multiply (**mit** by)
Malz *nt* **-es** malt
Mama /'mama, ma'ma:/ *f* **-s** mummy
Mammut *nt* **-s,-e** & **-s** mammoth
mampfen *vt* 🅘 munch
man *pron* one, you; (*die Leute*) people, they; **man sagt** they say, it is said
manch|e(r,s) *pron* many a; **[so] m~es Mal** many a time; **m~e Leute** some people ●(*substantivisch*) **m~er/m~e** many a man/woman; **m~e** *pl* some; (*Leute*) some people; (*viele*) many [people]; **m~es** some things; (*vieles*) many things. **m~erlei** *inv adj* various ●*pron* various things
manchmal *adv* sometimes
Mandant(in) *m* **-en,-en** (*f* **-,-nen**) (*Jur*) client
Mandarine *f* **-,-n** mandarin
Mandat *nt* **-[e]s,-e** mandate; (*Jur*) brief; (*Pol*) seat
Mandel *f* **-,-n** almond; (*Anat*) tonsil. **M~entzündung** *f* tonsillitis
Manege /ma'ne:ʒə/ *f* **-,-n** ring; (*Reit-*) arena
Mangel[1] *m* **-s,¨** lack; (*Knappheit*) shortage; (*Med*) deficiency; (*Fehler*) defect
Mangel[2] *f* **-,-n** mangle
mangel|haft *adj* faulty, defective; (*Sch*) unsatisfactory. **m~n**[1] *vi* (*haben*) **es m~t an** (+ *dat*) there is a lack/(*Knappheit*) shortage of
mangeln[2] *vt* put through the mangle
Manie *f* **-,-n** mania
Manier *f* **-,-en** manner; **M~en** manners. **m~lich** *adj* well-mannered ●*adv* properly
Manifest *nt* **-[e]s,-e** manifesto
Maniküre *f* **-,-n** manicure; (*Person*) manicurist. **m~n** *vt* manicure
Manko *nt* **-s,-s** disadvantage; (*Fehlbetrag*) deficit
Mann *m* **-[e]s,¨er** man; (*Ehe-*) husband
Männchen *nt* **-s,-** little man; (*Zool*) male
Mannequin /'manəkɛ̃/ *nt* **-s,-s** model
männlich *adj* male; (*Gram & fig*) masculine; (*mannhaft*) manly; (*Frau*) mannish. **M~keit** *f* **-** masculinity; (*fig*) manhood
Mannschaft *f* **-,-en** team; (*Naut*) crew
Manöv|er *nt* **-s,-** manœuvre; (*Winkelzug*) trick. **m~rieren** *vt/i* (*haben*) manœuvre
Mansarde *f* **-,-n** attic room;

(*Wohnung*) attic flat
Manschette *f* -,-n cuff. **M~knopf** *m* cuff-link
Mantel *m* -s,¨ coat; overcoat
Manuskript *nt* -[e]s,-e manuscript
Mappe *f* -,-n folder; (*Akten-*) briefcase; (*Schul-*) bag
Märchen *nt* -s,- fairy-tales
Margarine *f* - margarine
Marienkäfer /ma'ri:ən-/ *m* lady-bird
Marihuana *nt* -s marijuana
Marine *f* marine; (*Kriegs-*) navy. **m~blau** *adj* navy [blue]
marinieren *vt* marinade
Marionette *f* -,-n puppet, marionette
Mark[1] *f* -,- (*alte Währung*) mark; drei M~ three marks
m
Mark[2] *nt* -[e]s (*Knochen-*) marrow (*Bot*)pith; (*Frucht-*) pulp
markant *adj* striking
Marke *f* -,-n token; (*rund*) disc; (*Erkennungs-*) tag; (*Brief-*) stamp; (*Lebensmittel-*) coupon; (*Spiel-*) counter; (*Markierung*) mark; (*Fabrikat*) make; (*Tabak-*) brand. **M~nartikel** *m* branded article
markieren *vt* mark; (▯: *vortäuschen*) fake
Markise *f* -,-n awning
Markstück *nt* one-mark piece
Markt *m* -[e]s,¨e market; (*M~-platz*) market-place. **M~forschung** *f* market research
Marmelade *f* -,-n jam; (*Orangen-*) marmalade
Marmor *m* -s marble
Marokko *nt* -s Morocco
Marone *f* -,-n [sweet] chestnut
Marsch *m* -[e]s,¨e march. **m~** *int* (*Mil*) march!
Marschall *m* -s,¨e marshal
marschieren *vi* (*sein*) march
Marter *f* -,-n torture. **m~n** *vt* torture
Märtyrer(in) *m* -s,- (*f* -,-nen) martyr
Marxismus *m* - Marxism
März *m* -,-e March
Marzipan *nt* -s marzipan
Masche *f* -,-n stitch; (*im Netz*) mesh; (▯: *Trick*) dodge. **M~ndraht** *m* wire netting
Maschin|e *f* -,-n machine; (*Flugzeug*) plane; (*Schreib-*) typewriter; **M~e schreiben** type. **m~egeschrieben** *adj* typewritten, typed. **m~ell** *adj* machine ● *adv* by machine. **M~enbau** *m* mechanical engineering. **M~engewehr** *nt* machine-gun. **M~ist** *m* -en,-en machinist; (*Naut*) engineer
Masern *pl* measles *sg*
Maserung *f* -,-en [wood] grain
Maske *f* -,-n mask; (*Theat*) make-up
maskieren *vt* mask; **sich m~** dress up (**als** as)
maskulin *adj* masculine
Masochist *m* -en,-en masochist
Maß[1] *nt* -es,-e measure; (*Abmessung*) measurement; (*Grad*) degree; (*Mäßigung*) moderation; **in hohem Maße** to a high degree
Maß[2] *f* -,- (*SGer*) litre [of beer]
Massage /ma'sa:ʒə/ *f* -,-n massage
Massaker *nt* -s,- massacre
Maßband *nt* (*pl* -**bänder**) tape-measure
Masse *f* -,-n mass; (*Culin*) mixture; (*Menschen-*) crowd; **eine M~ Arbeit** ▯ masses of work. **m~nhaft** *adv* in huge quantities. **M~nproduktion** *f* mass production. **M~nvernichtungswaffen** *fpl* weapons of

mass destruction. **m~nweise** *adv* in huge numbers

Masseu|r /ma'søːɐ̯/ *m* **-s,-e** masseur. **M~se** *f* **-,-n** masseuse

maß|gebend *adj* authoritative; (*einflussreich*) influential. **m~geblich** *adj* decisive. **m~geschneidert** *adj* made-to-measure

massieren *vt* massage

massig *adj* massive

mäßig *adj* moderate; (*mittelmäßig*) indifferent. **m~en** *vt* moderate; **sich m~en** moderate; (*sich beherrschen*) restrain oneself. **M~ung** *f* - moderation

massiv *adj* solid; (*stark*) heavy

Maß|krug *m* beer mug. **m~los** *adj* excessive; (*grenzenlos*) boundless; (*äußerst*) extreme. **M~nahme** *f* **-,-n** measure

Maßstab *m* scale; (*Norm & fig*) standard. **m~sgerecht, m~sgetreu** *adj* scale ● *adv* to scale

Mast[1] *m* **-[e]s,-en** pole; (*Überland-*) pylon; (*Naut*) mast

Mast[2] *f* - fattening

mästen *vt* fatten

masturbieren *vi* (*haben*) masturbate

Material *nt* **-s,-ien** material; (*coll*) materials *pl*. **M~ismus** *m* - materialism. **m~istisch** *adj* materialistic

Mathe *f* - ⓘ maths *sg*

Mathe|matik *f* - mathematics *sg*. **M~matiker** *m* **-s,-** mathematician. **m~matisch** *adj* mathematical

Matinee *f* **-,-n** (*Theat*) morning performance

Matratze *f* **-,-n** mattress

Matrose *m* **-n,-n** sailor

Matsch *m* **-[e]s** mud; (*Schnee-*) slush

matt *adj* weak; (*gedämpft*) dim; (*glanzlos*) dull; (*Politur, Farbe*) matt. **M~** *nt* **-s** (*Schach*) mate

Matte *f* **-,-n** mat

Mattglas *nt* frosted glass

Matura *f* - (*Aust*) ≈ A levels *pl*

Matura ▷**ABITUR**

Mauer *f* **-,-n** wall. **M~werk** *nt* masonry

Maul *nt* **-[e]s, Mäuler** (*Zool*) mouth; **halts M~!** ⓘ shut up! **M~- und Klauenseuche** *f* foot-and-mouth disease. **M~korb** *m* muzzle. **M~tier** *nt* mule. **M~wurf** *m* mole

Maurer *m* **-s,-** bricklayer

Maus *f* **-,Mäuse** mouse

Maut *f* **-,-en** (*Aust*) toll. **M~straße** *f* toll road

maximal *adj* maximum

Maximum *nt* **-s,-ma** maximum

Mayonnaise /majɔ'nɛːzə/ *f* **-,-n** mayonnaise

Mechan|ik /me'çaːnɪk/ *f* - mechanics *sg*; (*Mechanismus*) mechanism. **M~iker** *m* **-s,-** mechanic. **m~isch** *adj* mechanical. **m~isieren** *vt* mechanize. **M~ismus** *m* **-,-men** mechanism

meckern *vi* (*haben*) bleat; (ⓘ: *nörgeln*) grumble

Medaill|e /me'daljə/ *f* **-,-n** medal. **M~on** *nt* **-s,-s** medallion (*Schmuck*) locket

Medikament *nt* **-[e]s,-e** medicine

Medit|ation /-'tsi̯oːn/ *f* **-,-en** meditation. **m~ieren** *vi* (*haben*) meditate

Medium *nt* **-s,-ien** medium; **die Medien** the media

Medizin *f* **-,-en** medicine. **M~er** *m* **-s,-** doctor; (*Student*) medical student. **m~isch** *adj* medical;

m

(*heilkräftig*) medicinal

Meer *nt* **-[e]s,-e** sea. **M~busen** *m* gulf. **M~enge** *f* strait. **M~esspiegel** *m* sea-level. **M~jungfrau** *f* mermaid. **M~rettich** *m* horseradish. **M~schweinchen** *nt* **-s,-** guinea-pig

Mehl *nt* **-[e]s** flour. **M~schwitze** *f* (*Culin*) roux

mehr *pron & adv* more; **nicht m~** no more; (*zeitlich*) no longer; **nichts m~** no more; (*nichtsweiter*) nothing else; **nie m~** never again. **m~eres** *pron* several things *pl*. **m~fach** *adj* multiple; (*mehrmalig*) repeated ● *adv* several times. **M~fahrtenkarte** *f* book of tickets. **M~heit** *f* **-,-en** majority. **m~malig** *adj* repeated. **m~mals** *adv* several times. **m~sprachig** *adj* multilingual. **M~wertsteuer** *f* value-added tax, VAT. **M~zahl** *f* majority; (*Gram*) plural. **M~zweck-** *prefix* multipurpose

m

meiden† *vt* avoid, shun

Meile *f* **-,-n** mile. **m~nweit** *adv* [for] miles

mein *poss pron* my. **m~e(r,s)** *poss pron* mine; **die M~en** *od* **m~en** *pl* my family *sg*

Meineid *m* perjury

meinen *vt* mean; (*glauben*) think; (*sagen*) say

mein|erseits *adv* for my part. **m~etwegen** *adv* for my sake; (*wegen mir*) because of me; ([!]: *von mir aus*) as far as I'm concerned

Meinung *f* **-,-en** opinion; **jdm die M~ sagen** give s.o. a piece of one's mind. **M~sumfrage** *f* opinion poll

Meise *f* **-,-n** (*Zool*) tit

Meißel *m* **-s,-** chisel. **m~n** *vt/i* (*haben*) chisel

meist *adv* mostly; (*gewöhnlich*) usually. **m~e** *adj* **der/die/das m~e** most; **die m~en Leute** most people; **am m~en** [the] most ● *pron* **das m~e** most [of it]; **die m~en** most. **m~ens** *adv* mostly; (*gewöhnlich*) usually

Meister *m* **-s,-** master craftsman; (*Könner*) master; (*Sport*) champion. **m~n** *vt* master. **M~schaft** *f* **-,-en** mastery; (*Sport*) championship

meld|en *vt* report; (*anmelden*) register; (*ankündigen*) announce; **sich m~en** report (**bei** to); (*zum Militär*) enlist; (*freiwillig*) volunteer; (*Teleph*) answer; (*Sch*) put up one's hand; (*von sich hören lassen*) get in touch (**bei** with). **M~ung** *f* **-,-en** report; (*Anmeldung*) registration

melken† *vt* milk

Melodie *f* **-,-n** tune, melody

melodisch *adj* melodic

Melone *f* **-,-n** melon

Memoiren /me'mo̯a:rən/ *pl* memoirs

Memorystick *m* memory stick

Menge *f* **-,-n** amount, quantity; (*Menschen-*) crowd; (*Math*) set; **eine M~ Geld** a lot of money. **m~n** *vt* mix

Mensa *f* **-,-sen** (*Univ*) refectory

Mensch *m* **-en,-en** human being; **der M~** man; **die M~en** people; **jeder/kein M~** everybody/nobody. **M~enaffe** *m* ape. **m~enfeindlich** *adj* antisocial. **M~enfresser** *m* **-s,-** cannibal; (*Zool*) man-eater. **m~enfreundlich** *adj* philanthropic. **M~enleben** *nt* human life; (*Lebenszeit*) lifetime. **m~enleer** *adj* deserted. **M~enmenge** *f* crowd. **M~enraub** *m* kidnapping. **M~enrechte** *ntpl* human rights. **m~enscheu** *adj* unsociable. **m~enwürdig** *adj* humane. **M~heit** *f* **-** **die M~heit** mankind, humanity. **m~lich** *adj* human; (*human*) humane. **M~lichkeit** *f* - humanity

Menstru|ation /-'tsio:n/ *f* - menstruation. **m~ieren** *vi* (*haben*) menstruate

Mentalität *f* -,-en mentality

Menü *nt* -s,-s menu; (*festes M~*) set meal

Meridian *m* -s,-e meridian

merk|bar *adj* noticeable. **M~blatt** *nt* [explanatory] leaflet. **m~en** *vt* notice; **sich** (*dat*) **etw m~en** remember sth. **M~mal** *nt* feature

merkwürdig *adj* odd, strange

Messe[1] *f* -,-n (*Relig*) mass; (*Comm*) [trade] fair

Messe[2] *f* -,-n (*Mil*) mess

messen† *vt/i* (*haben*) measure; (*ansehen*) look at; **[bei jdm] Fieber m~** take s.o.'s temperature; **sich mit jdm m~ können** be a match for s.o.

Messer *nt* -s,- knife

Messias *m* - Messiah

Messing *nt* -s brass

Messung *f* -,-en measurement

Metabolismus *m* - metabolism

Metall *nt* -s,-e metal. **m~isch** *adj* metallic

Metamorphose *f* -,-n metamorphosis

metaphorisch *adj* metaphorical

Meteor *m* -s,-e meteor. **M~ologie** *f* - meteorology

Meter *m* & *nt* -s,- metre. **M~maß** *nt* tape-measure

Method|e *f* -,-n method. **m~isch** *adj* methodical

Metropole *f* -,-n metropolis

Metzger *m* -s,- butcher. **M~ei** *f* -,-en butcher's shop

Meuterei *f* -,-en mutiny

meutern *vi* (*haben*) mutiny; (**[!]**: *schimpfen*) grumble

Mexikan|er(in) *m* -s,- (*f* -,-nen) Mexican. **m~isch** *adj* Mexican

Mexiko *nt* -s Mexico

miauen *vi* (*haben*) mew, miaow

mich *pron* (*acc of* **ich**) me; (*reflexive*) myself

Mieder *nt* -s,- bodice

Miene *f* -,-n expression

mies *adj* **[!]** lousy

Miet|e *f* -,-n rent; (*Mietgebühr*) hire charge; **zur M~e wohnen** live in rented accommodation. **m~en** *vt* rent (*Haus, Zimmer*); hire (*Auto, Boot*). **M~er(in)** *m* -s,- (*f* -,-nen) tenant. **m~frei** *adj* & *adv* rent-free. **M~shaus** *nt* block of rented flats. **M~vertrag** *m* lease. **M~wagen** *m* hire-car. **M~wohnung** *f* rented flat; (*zu vermieten*) flat to let

Migräne *f* -,-n migraine

Mikro|chip *m* microchip. **M~computer** *m* microcomputer. **M~film** *m* microfilm

Mikro|fon, **M~phon** *nt* -s,-e microphone. **M~skop** *nt* -s,-e microscope. **m~skopisch** *adj* microscopic

Mikrowelle *f* microwave. **M~nherd** *m* microwave oven

Milbe *f* -,-n mite

Milch *f* - milk. **M~glas** *nt* opal glass. **m~ig** *adj* milky. **M~mann** *m* (*pl* -männer) milkman. **M~straße** *f* Milky Way

mild *adj* mild; (*nachsichtig*) lenient. **M~e** *f* - mildness; leniency. **m~ern** *vt* make milder; (*mäßigen*) moderate; (*lindern*) ease; **sich m~ern** become milder; (*sich mäßigen*) moderate; (*Schmerz:*) ease; **m~ernde Umstände** mitigating circumstances

Milieu /mi'liø:/ *nt* -s,-s [social] environment

Militär *nt* -s army; (*Soldaten*)

m

troops *pl*; **beim M~** in the army. **m~isch** *adj* military

Miliz *f* -,-en militia

Milliarde /mɪˈli̯ardə/ *f* -,-n thousand million, billion

Milli|gramm *nt* milligram. **M~meter** *m & nt* millimetre. **M~meterpapier** *nt* graph paper

Million /mɪˈli̯oːn/ *f* -,-en million. **M~är** *m* -s,-e millionaire

Milz *f* - (*Anat*) spleen. **~brand** *m* anthrax

mimen *vt* (!: *vortäuschen*) act

Mimose *f* -,-n mimosa

Minderheit *f* -,-en minority

minderjährig *adj* (*Jur*) underage. **M~e(r)** *m/f* (*Jur*) minor

mindern *vt* diminish; decrease

minderwertig *adj* inferior. **M~keit** *f* - inferiority. **M~keitskomplex** *m* inferiority complex

Mindest- *prefix* minimum. **m~e** *adj & pron* **der/die/das M~e** *od* **m~e** the least; **nicht im M~en** not in the least. **m~ens** *adv* at least. **M~lohn** *m* minimum wage. **M~maß** *nt* minimum

Mine *f* -,-n mine; (*Bleistift-*) lead; (*Kugelschreiber-*) refill. **M~nräumboot** *nt* minesweeper

Mineral *nt* -s,-e & -ien mineral. **m~isch** *adj* mineral. **M~wasser** *nt* mineral water

Miniatur *f* -,-en miniature

Minigolf *nt* miniature golf

minimal *adj* minimal

Minimum *nt* -s,-ma minimum

Mini|ster *m*, -s,- minister. **m~steriell** *adj* ministerial. **M~sterium** *nt* -s,-ien ministry

minus *conj, adv & prep* (+ *gen*) minus. **M~** *nt* - deficit; (*Nachteil*) disadvantage. **M~zeichen** *nt* minus [sign]

Minute *f* -,-n minute

mir *pron* (*dat of* **ich**) [to] me; (*reflexive*) myself

Misch|ehe *f* mixed marriage. **m~en** *vt* mix; blend (*Tee, Kaffee*); toss (*Salat*); shuffle (*Karten*); **sich m~en** mix; (*Person*;) mingle (**unter** + *acc* with); **sich m~en in** (+ *acc*) join in (*Gespräch*); meddle in (*Angelegenheit*) ● *vi* (*haben*) shuffle the cards. **M~ling** *m* -s,-e half-caste. **M~ung** *f* -,-en mixture; blend

miserabel *adj* abominable

missachten *vt* disregard

Miss|achtung *f* disregard. **M~bildung** *f* deformity

missbilligen *vt* disapprove of

Miss|billigung *f* disapproval. **M~brauch** *m* abuse

missbrauchen *vt* abuse; (*vergewaltigen*) rape

Misserfolg *m* failure

Misse|tat *f* misdeed. **M~täter** *m* ! culprit

missfallen† *vi* (*haben*) displease (jdm s.o.)

Miss|fallen *nt* -s displeasure; (*Missbilligung*) disapproval. **M~geburt** *f* freak; (*fig*) monstrosity. **M~geschick** *nt* mishap; (*Unglück*) misfortune

miss|glücken *vi* (*sein*) fail. **m~gönnen** *vt* begrudge

misshandeln *vt* ill-treat

Misshandlung *f* ill-treatment

Mission *f* -,-en mission

Missionar(in) *m* -s,-e (*f* -,-nen) missionary

Missklang *m* discord

misslingen† *vi* (*sein*) fail; **es misslang ihr** she failed. **M~** *nt* -s failure

Missmut *m* ill humour. **m~ig** *adj* morose

missraten† *vi* (*sein*) turn

out badly

Miss|stand *m* abuse; (*Zustand*) undesirable state of affairs. **M~stimmung** *f* discord; (*Laune*) bad mood

misstrauen *vi* (*haben*) **jdm/etw m~** mistrust s.o./sth; (*Argwohn hegen*) distrust s.o./sth

Misstrau|en *nt* **-s** mistrust; (*Argwohn*) distrust. **M~ensvotum** *nt* vote of no confidence. **m~isch** *adj* distrustful; (*argwöhnisch*) suspicious

Miss|verständnis *nt* misunderstanding. **m~verstehen**† *vt* misunderstand. **M~wirtschaft** *f* mismanagement

Mist *m* **-[e]s** manure; 🄸 rubbish

Mistel *f* **-,-n** mistletoe

Misthaufen *m* dungheap

mit *prep* (+ *dat*) with; (*sprechen*) to; (*mittels*) by; (*inklusive*) including; (*bei*) at; **mit Bleistift** in pencil; **mit lauter Stimme** in a loud voice; **mit drei Jahren** at the age of three ● *adv* (*auch*) as well; **mit anfassen** (*fig*) lend a hand

Mitarbeit *f* collaboration. **m~en** *vi sep* collaborate (**an** + *dat* on). **M~er(in)** *m*(*f*) collaborator; (*Kollege*) colleague; employee

Mitbestimmung *f* co-determination

mitbringen† *vt sep* bring [along]

miteinander *adv* with each other

Mitesser *m* (*Med*) blackhead

mitfahren† *vi sep* (*sein*) go/come along; **mit jdm m~** go with s.o.; (*mitgenommen werden*) be given a lift by s.o.

mitfühlen *vi sep* (*haben*) sympathize

mitgeben† *vt sep* **jdm etw m~** give s.o. sth to take with him

Mitgefühl *nt* sympathy

mitgehen† *vi sep* (*sein*) **mit jdm m~** go with s.o.

Mitgift *f* **-,-en** dowry

Mitglied *nt* member. **M~schaft** *f* **-** membership

mithilfe *prep* (+ *gen*) with the aid of

Mithilfe *f* assistance

mitkommen† *vi sep* (*sein*) come [along] too; (*fig: folgen können*) keep up; (*verstehen*) follow

Mitlaut *m* consonant

Mitleid *nt* pity, compassion; **M~erregend** pitiful. **m~ig** *adj* pitying; (*mitfühlend*) compassionate. **m~slos** *adj* pitiless

mitmachen *v sep* ● *vt* take part in; (*erleben*) go through ● *vi* (*haben*) join in

Mitmensch *m* fellow man

mitnehmen† *vt sep* take along; (*mitfahren lassen*) give a lift to; (*fig: schädigen*) affect badly; (*erschöpfen*) exhaust; **'zum M~'** 'to take away'

mitreden *vi sep* (*haben*) join in [the conversation]; (*mit entscheiden*) have a say (**bei** in)

mitreißen† *vt sep* sweep along; (*fig: begeistern*) carry away; **m~d** rousing

mitsamt *prep* (+ *dat*) together with

mitschreiben† *vt sep* (*haben*) take down

Mitschuld *f partial blame*. **m~ig** *adj* **m~ig sein** be partly to blame

Mitschüler(in) *m*(*f*) fellow pupil

mitspielen *vi sep* (*haben*) join in; (*Theat*) be in the cast; (*beitragen*) play a part

Mittag *m* midday, noon; (*Mahlzeit*) lunch; (*Pause*) lunch-break; **heute/gestern M~** at lunch-time today/yesterday; **[zu] M~ essen** have lunch. **M∼essen** *nt* lunch. **m∼s** *adv* at noon; (*als Mahlzeit*) for lunch; **um 12 Uhr m∼s** at noon. **M∼spause** *f* lunch-hour; (*Pause*) lunch-break. **M∼sschlaf** *m* after-lunch nap

Mittäter|(in) *m*(*f*) accomplice. **M∼schaft** *f* - complicity

Mitte *f* -,-n middle; (*Zentrum*) centre; **die goldene M∼** the golden mean; **M∼ Mai** in mid-May; **in unserer M∼** in our midst

mitteil|en *vt sep* **jdm etw m∼en** tell s.o. sth; (*amtlich*) inform s.o. of sth. **M∼ung** *f* **-,-en** communication; (*Nachricht*) piece of news

Mittel *nt* **-s,-** means *sg*; (*Heil-*) remedy; (*Medikament*) medicine; (*M∼wert*) mean; (*Durchschnitt*) average; **M∼** *pl* (*Geld-*) funds, resources. **m∼** *pred adj* medium; (*m∼mäßig*) middling. **M∼alter** *nt* Middle Ages *pl*. **m∼alterlich** *adj* medieval. **M∼ding** *nt* (*fig*) cross. **m∼europäisch** *adj* Central European. **M∼finger** *m* middle finger. **m∼los** *adj* destitute. **m∼mäßig** *adj* middling; **[nur] m∼mäßig** mediocre. **M∼meer** *nt* Mediterranean. **M∼punkt** *m* centre; (*fig*) centre of attention

mittels *prep* (+ *gen*) by means of

Mittel|schule *f* = **Realschule**. **M∼smann** *m* (*pl* **-männer**) intermediary, go-between. **M∼stand** *m* middle class. **m∼ste(r,s)** *adj* middle. **M∼streifen** *m* (*Auto*) central reservation. **M∼stürmer** *m* centre-forward. **M∼welle** *f* medium wave. **M∼wort** *nt* (*pl* **-wörter**) participle

mitten *adv* **m∼ in/auf** (*dat/acc*) in the middle of. **m∼durch** *adv* [right] through the middle

Mitternacht *f* midnight

mittler|e(r,s) *adj* middle; (*Größe, Qualität*) medium; (*durchschnittlich*) mean, average. **m∼weile** *adv* meanwhile; (*seitdem*) by now

Mittwoch *m* **-s,-e** Wednesday. **m∼s** *adv* on Wednesdays

mitunter *adv* now and again

mitwirk|en *vi sep* (*haben*) take part; (*helfen*) contribute. **M∼ung** *f* participation

mix|en *vt* mix. **M∼er** *m* **-s,-** (*Culin*) liquidizer, blender

mobb|en *vt* bully, harass. **M∼ing** *nt* **-s** bullying, harassment

Möbel *pl* furniture *sg*. **M∼stück** *nt* piece of furniture. **M∼wagen** *m* removal van

Mobiliar *nt* **-s** furniture

mobilisier|en *vt* mobilize. **M∼ung** *f* - mobilization

Mobil|machung *f* **-** mobilization. **M∼telefon** *nt* mobile phone

möblier|en *vt* furnish; **m∼tes Zimmer** furnished room

mochte, **möchte** *s.* **mögen**

Mode *f* **-,-n** fashion; **M∼ sein** be fashionable

Modell *nt* **-s,-e** model. **m∼ieren** *vt* model

Modenschau *f* fashion show

Modera|tor *m* **-s,-en**, **M∼torin** *f* **-,-nen** (*TV*) presenter

modern *adj* modern; (*modisch*) fashionable. **m∼isieren** *vt* modernize

Mode|schmuck *m* costume jewellery. **M∼schöpfer** *m* fashion designer

modisch *adj* fashionable

Modistin *f* **-,-nen** milliner

modrig *adj* musty

modulieren *vt* modulate

Mofa *nt* **-s,-s** moped

mogeln *vi* (*haben*) [!] cheat

mögen†

- *transitive verb*

····➤ like. **sie mag ihn sehr [gern]** she likes him very much. **möchten Sie ein Glas Wein?** would you like a glass of wine? **lieber mögen** prefer. **ich möchte lieber Tee** I would prefer tea

- *auxiliary verb*

····➤ (*wollen*) want to. **sie mochte nicht länger bleiben** she didn't want to stay any longer. **ich möchte ihn [gerne] sprechen** I'd like to speak to him. **möchtest du nach Hause?** do you want to go home? *or* would you like to go home?

····➤ (*Vermutung, Möglichkeit*) may. **ich mag mich irren** I may be wrong. **wer/was mag das sein?** whoever/whatever can it be? **[das] mag sein** that may well be. **mag kommen, was da will** come what may

möglich *adj* possible; **alle m~en** all sorts of; **über alles M~e sprechen** talk about all sorts of things. **m~erweise** *adv* possibly. **M~keit** *f* **-,-en** possibility. **M~keitsform** *f* subjunctive. **m~st** *adv* if possible; **m~st viel** as much as possible

Mohammedan|er(in) *m* **-s,-** (*f* **-,-nen**) Muslim. **m~isch** *adj* Muslim

Mohn *m* **-s** poppy

Möhre, **Mohrrübe** *f* **-,-n** carrot

Mokka *m* **-s** mocha; (*Geschmack*) coffee

Molch *m* **-[e]s,-e** newt

Mole *f* **-,-n** (*Naut*) mole

Molekül *nt* **-s,-e** molecule

Molkerei *f* **-,-en** dairy

Moll *nt* **-** (*Mus*) minor

mollig *adj* cosy; (*warm*) warm; (*rundlich*) plump

Moment *m* **-s,-e** moment; **M~[mal]!** just a moment! **m~an** *adj* momentary; (*gegenwärtig*) at the moment

Monarch *m* **-en,-en** monarch. **M~ie** *f* **-,-n** monarchy

Monat *m* **-s,-e** month. **m~elang** *adv* for months. **m~lich** *adj & adv* monthly

Mönch *m* **-[e]s,-e** monk

Mond *m* **-[e]s,-e** moon

mondän *adj* fashionable

Mond|finsternis *f* lunar eclipse. **m~hell** *adj* moonlit. **M~sichel** *f* crescent moon. **M~schein** *m* moonlight

monieren *vt* criticize

Monitor *m* **-s,-en** (*Techn*) monitor

Monogramm *nt* **-s,-e** monogram

Mono|log *m* **-s,-e** monologue. **M~pol** *nt* **-s,-e** monopoly. **m~ton** *adj* monotonous

Monster *nt* **-s,-** monster

Monstrum *nt* **-s,-stren** monster

Monsun *m* **-s,-e** monsoon

Montag *m* Monday

Montage /mɔn'ta:ʒə/ *f* **-,-n** fitting; (*Zusammenbau*) assembly; (*Film-*) editing; (*Kunst*) montage

montags *adv* on Mondays

Montanindustrie *f* coal and steel industry

Monteur /mɔn'tø:ɐ̯/ *m* **-s,-e** fitter. **M~anzug** *m* overalls *pl*

montieren *vt* fit; (*zusammenbauen*) assemble

Monument *nt* **-[e]s,-e** monument. **m~al** a monumental

Moor *nt* **-[e]s,-e** bog; (*Heide-*) moor

Moos *nt* **es,-e** moss **m~ig** *adj* mossy

Moped *nt* **-s,-s** moped

Mopp *m* **-s,-s** mop

Moral *f* - morals *pl*, (*Selbstvertrauen*) morale; (*Lehre*) moral. **m~isch** *adj* moral
Mord *m* -[e]s,-e murder, (*Pol*) assassination. **M~anschlag** *m* murder/assassination attempt. **m~en** *vt/i* (*haben*) murder, kill
Mörder *m* -s,- murderer, (*Pol*) assassin. **M~in** *f* -,-nen murderess. **m~isch** *adj* murderous; (Ⅱ: *schlimm*) dreadful
morgen *adv* tomorrow; **m~ Abend** tomorrow evening
Morgen *m* -s,- morning; (*Maß*) ≈ acre; **am M~** in the morning; **heute/Montag M~** this/Monday morning. **M~dämmerung** *f* dawn. **M~rock** *m* dressing-gown. **M~rot** *nt* red sky in the morning. **m~s** *adj* in the morning
morgig *adj* tomorrow's; **der m~e Tag** tomorrow

m

Morphium *nt* -s morphine
morsch *adj* rotten
Morsealphabet *nt* Morse code
Mörtel *m* -s mortar
Mosaik /moza'i:k/ *nt* -s,-e[n] mosaic
Moschee *f* -,-n mosque
Mosel *f* - Moselle
Moskau *nt* -s Moscow
Moskito *m* -s,-s mosquito
Moslem *m* -s,-s Muslim
Motiv *nt* -s,-e motive; (*Kunst*) motif
Motor /'mo:tɔr, mo'to:ɐ̯/ *m* -s,-en engine; (*Elektro-*) motor. **M~boot** *nt* motor boat
motorisieren *vt* motorize
Motor|rad *nt* motor cycle. **M~roller** *m* motor scooter
Motte *f* -,-n moth. **M~nkugel** *f* mothball
Motto *nt* -s,-s motto
Möwe *f* -,-n gull
Mücke *f* -,-n gnat; (*kleine*) midge; (*Stech-*) mosquito
müd|e *adj* tired; **es m~e sein** be tired (**etw zu tun** of doing sth). **M~igkeit** *f* - tiredness
muffig *adj* musty; (Ⅱ: *mürrisch*) grumpy
Mühe *f* -,-n effort; (*Aufwand*) trouble; **sich** (*dat*) **M~ geben** make an effort; (*sich bemühen*) try; **nicht der M~ wert** not worth while; **mit M~ und Not** with great difficulty; (*gerade noch*) only just. **m~los** *adj* effortless
muhen *vi* (*haben*) moo
Mühl|e *f* -,-n mill; (*Kaffee-*) grinder. **M~stein** *m* millstone
Müh|sal *f* -,-e (*literarisch*) toil; (*Mühe*) trouble. **m~sam** *adj* laborious; (*beschwerlich*) difficult
Mulde *f* -,-n hollow
Müll *m* -s refuse. **M~abfuhr** *f* refuse collection
Mullbinde *f* gauze bandage
Mülleimer *m* waste bin; (*Mülltonne*) dustbin
Müller *m* -s,- miller
Müll|halde *f* [rubbish] dump. **M~schlucker** *m* refuse chute. **M~tonne** *f* dustbin
multi|national *adj* multinational. **M~plikation** *f* -,-en multiplication. **m~plizieren** *vt* multiply
Mumie /'mu:mi̯ə/ *f* -,-n mummy
Mumm *m* -s Ⅱ energy
Mumps *m* - mumps
Mund *m* -[e]s,⸚er mouth; **ein M~ voll Suppe** a mouthful of soup; **halt den M~!** ⊠ shut up! **M~art** *f* dialect. **m~artlich** *adj* dialect
Mündel *nt* & *m* -s,- (*Jur*) ward. **m~sicher** *adj* gilt-edged
münden *vi* (*sein*) flow/(*Straße:*) lead (**in** + *acc* into)

Mundharmonika *f* mouth-organ
mündig *adj* **m∼ sein/werden** (*Jur*) be/come of age. **M∼keit** *f* - (*Jur*) majority
mündlich *adj* verbal; **m∼e Prüfung** oral
Mündung *f* **-,-en** (*Fluss-*) mouth; (*Gewehr-*) muzzle
Mundwinkel *m* corner of the mouth
Munition /-'tsi̯o:n/ *f* - ammunition
munkeln *vt/i* (*haben*) talk (**von** of); **es wird gemunkelt** rumour has it (**dass** that)
Münster *nt* **-s,-** cathedral
munter *adj* lively; (*heiter*) merry; **m∼ sein** (*wach*) be wide awake ; **gesund und m∼** fit and well
Münz|e *f* **-,-n** coin; (*M∼stätte*) mint. **M∼fernsprecher** *m* payphone
mürbe *adj* crumbly; (*Obst*) mellow; (*Fleisch*) tender. **M∼teig** *m* short pastry
Murmel *f* **-,-n** marble
murmeln *vt/i* (*haben*) murmur; (*undeutlich*) mumble
Murmeltier *nt* marmot
murren *vt/i* (*haben*) grumble
mürrisch *adj* surly
Mus *nt* **-es** purée
Muschel *f* **-,-n** mussel; [sea] shell
Museum /mu'ze:ʊm/ *nt* **-s,-seen** museum
Musik *f* - music. **m∼alisch** *adj* musical
Musiker(in) *m* **-s,-** (*f* **-,-nen**) musician
Musik|instrument *nt* musical instrument. **M∼kapelle** *f* band. **M∼pavillon** *m* bandstand
musisch *adj* artistic
musizieren *vi* (*haben*) make music
Muskat *m* **-[e]s** nutmeg
Muskel *m* **-s,-n** muscle. **M∼kater** *m* stiff and aching muscles *pl*
muskulös *adj* muscular
muss *s.* **müssen**
Muße *f* - leisure

müssen†

● *auxiliary verb*

····➤ (*gezwungen/verpflichtet/notwendig sein*) have to; must. **er muss es tun** he must *or* has to do it; 🄸 he's got to do it. **ich musste schnell fahren** I had to drive fast. **das muss 1968 gewesen sein** it must have been in 1968. **er muss gleich hier sein** he must be here at any moment

····➤ (*in negativen Sätzen; ungezwungen*) **sie muss es nicht tun** she does not have to *or* 🄸 she hasn't got to do it. **es musste nicht so sein** it didn't have to be like that

····➤ **es müsste** (*sollte*) **doch möglich sein** it ought to *or* should be possible. **du müsstest es mal versuchen** you ought to *or* should try it

● *intransitive verb*

····➤ (*irgendwohin gehen müssen*) have to *or* must go. **ich muss nach Hause/zum Arzt** I have to *or* must go home/to the doctor. **ich musste mal [aufs Klo]** I had to go [to the loo]

müßig *adj* idle
musste, müsste *s.* **müssen**
Muster *nt* **-s,-** pattern; (*Probe*) sample; (*Vorbild*) model. **M∼beispiel** *nt* typical example; (*Vorbild*) perfect example. **m∼gültig, m∼haft** *adj* exemplary. **m∼n** *vt* eye; (*inspizieren*) inspect. **M∼ung** *f*

-,-en inspection; (*Mil*) medical; (*Muster*) pattern

Mut *m* **-[e]s** courage; **jdm Mut machen** encourage s.o.; **zu M~e sein** feel like it; *s.* **zumute**

mut|ig *adj* courageous. **m~los** *adj* despondent

mutmaßen *vt* presume; (*Vermutungen anstellen*) speculate

Mutprobe *f* test of courage

Mutter[1] *f* **-,⸚** mother

Mutter[2] *f* **-,-n** (*Techn*) nut

Muttergottes *f* **-** madonna

Mutterland *nt* motherland

mütterlich *adj* maternal; (*fürsorglich*) motherly. **m~erseits** *adv* on one's/the mother's side

Mutter|mal *nt* birthmark; (*dunkel*) mole. **M~schaft** *f* **-** motherhood. **m~seelenallein** *adj & adv* all alone. **M~sprache** *f* mother tongue. **M~tag** *m* Mother's Day

Mütze *f* **-,-n** cap; **wollene M~** woolly hat

MwSt. *abbr* (**Mehrwertsteuer**) VAT

mysteriös *adj* mysterious

Mystik /ˈmʏstɪk/ *f* **-** mysticism

myth|isch *adj* mythical. **M~ologie** *f* **-** mythology

Nn

na *int* well; **na gut** all right then

Nabel *m* **-s,-** navel. **N~schnur** *f* umbilical cord

nach

● *preposition* (+ *dative*)

····➤ (*räumlich*) to. **nach London fahren** go to London. **der Zug nach München** the train to Munich; (*noch nicht abgefahren*) the train for Munich; the Munich train. **nach Hause gehen** go home. **nach Osten [zu]** eastwards; towards the east

····➤ (*zeitlich*) after; (*Uhrzeit*) past. **nach fünf Minuten/dem Frühstück** after five minutes/breakfast. **zehn [Minuten] nach zwei** ten [minutes] past two

····➤ ([*räumliche und zeitliche*] *Reihenfolge*) after. **nach Ihnen/dir!** after you!

····➤ (*mit bestimmten Verben*) for. **greifen/streben/schicken nach** grasp/strive/send for

····➤ (*gemäß*) according to. **nach der neuesten Mode gekleidet** dressed in [accordance with] the latest fashion. **dem Gesetz nach** in accordance with the law; by law. **nach meiner Ansicht** *od* **Meinung, meiner Ansicht** *od* **Meinung nach** in my view *or* opinion. **nach etwas schmecken/riechen** taste/smell of sth

● *adverb*

····➤ (*zeitlich*) **nach und nach** little by little; gradually. **nach wie vor** still

nachahm|en *vt sep* imitate. **N~ung** *f* **-,-en** imitation

Nachbar|(in) *m* **-n,-n** (*f* **-,-nen**) neighbour. **N~haus** *nt* house next door. **n~lich** *adj* neighbourly; (*Nachbar-*) neighbouring. **N~schaft** *f* **-** neighbourhood

nachbestell|en *vt sep* reorder. **N~ung** *f* repeat order

nachbild|en *vt sep* copy, reproduce. **N~ung** *f* copy, reproduction

nachdatieren *vt sep* backdate

nachdem *conj* after; **je n~** it depends

nachdenk|en† *vi sep* (*haben*) think (**über** + *acc* about). **n~lich** *adj* thoughtful

nachdrücklich *adj* emphatic

nacheinander *adv* one after the other

Nachfahre *m* **-n,-n** descendant

Nachfolg|e *f* succession. **N~er(in)** *m* **-s,-** (*f* **-,-nen**) successor

nachforsch|en *vi sep* (*haben*) make enquiries. **N~ung** *f* enquiry

Nachfrage *f* (*Comm*) demand. **n~n** *vi sep* (*haben*) enquire

nachfüllen *vt sep* refill

nachgeben† *v sep* ● *vi* (*haben*) give way: (*sich fügen*) give in, yield ● *vt* **jdm Suppe n~** give s.o. more soup

Nachgebühr *f* surcharge

nachgehen† *vi sep* (*sein*) (*Uhr:*) be slow; **jdm/etw n~** follow s.o./something; follow up (*Spur, Angelegenheit*); pursue (*Angelegenheit*)

Nachgeschmack *m* after-taste

nachgiebig *adj* indulgent; (*gefällig*) compliant. **N~keit** *f* **-** indulgence; compliance

nachgrübeln *vi sep* (*haben*) ponder (**über** + *acc* on)

nachhaltig *adj* lasting

nachhelfen† *vi sep* (*haben*) help

nachher *adv* later; (*danach*) afterwards; **bis n~!** see you later!

Nachhilfeunterricht *m* coaching

Nachhinein *adv* **im N~** afterwards

nachhinken *vi sep* (*sein*) (*fig*) lag behind

nachholen *vt sep* (*später holen*) fetch later; (*mehr holen*) get more; (*später machen*) do later; (*aufholen*) catch up on

Nachkomme *m* **-n,-n** descendant. **n~n**† *vi sep* (*sein*) follow [later], come later; **etw** (*dat*) **n~n** (*fig*) comply with (*Bitte*); carry out (*Pflicht*). **N~nschaft** *f* **-** descendants *pl*, progeny

Nachkriegszeit *f* post-war period

Nachlass *m* **-es,¨e** discount; (*Jur*) [deceased's] estate

nachlassen† *v sep* ● *vi* (*haben*) decrease; (*Regen, Hitze:*) let up; (*Schmerz:*) ease; (*Sturm:*) abate; (*Augen, Leistungen:*) deteriorate ● *vt* **etw vom Preis n~** take sth off the price

nachlässig *adj* careless; (*leger*) casual; (*unordentlich*) sloppy. **N~keit** *f* **-** carelessness; sloppiness

nachlesen† *vt sep* look up

nachlöse|n *vi sep* (*haben*) pay one's fare on the train/on arrival. **N~schalter** *m* excess-fare office

nachmachen *vt sep* (*später machen*) do later; (*imitieren*) imitate, copy; (*fälschen*) forge

Nachmittag *m* afternoon; **heute/gestern N~** this/yesterday afternoon. **n~s** *adv* in the afternoon

Nachnahme *f* **etw per N~ schicken** send sth cash on delivery *or* COD

Nachname *m* surname

Nachporto *nt* excess postage

nachprüfen *vt sep* check, verify

Nachricht *f* **-,-en** [piece of] news *sg*; **N~en** news *sg*; **eine N~ hinterlassen** leave a message; **jdm N~ geben** inform s.o. **N~endienst** *m* (*Mil*) intelligence service

nachrücken *vi sep* (*sein*) move up

Nachruf *m* obituary

nachsagen *vt sep* repeat (**jdm** after s.o.); **jdm Schlechtes/Gutes n~** speak ill/well of s.o.

Nachsaison *f* late season
nachschicken *vt sep* (*später schicken*) send later; (*hinterher-*) send after (**jdm** s.o.); send on (*Post*) (**jdm** to s.o.)
nachschlagen† *v sep* ● *vt* look up ● *vi* (*haben*) **in einem Wörterbuch n∼en** consult a dictionary; **jdm n∼en** take after s.o.
Nachschrift *f* transcript; (*Nachsatz*) postscript
Nachschub *m* (*Mil*) supplies *pl*
nachsehen† *v sep* ● *vt* (*prüfen*) check; (*nachschlagen*) look up; (*hinwegsehen über*) overlook ● *vi* (*haben*) have a look; (*prüfen*) check; **im Wörterbuch n∼** consult a dictionary
nachsenden† *vt sep* forward (*Post*) (**jdm** to s.o.); **'bitte n∼'** 'please forward'
nachsichtig *adj* forbearing; lenient; indulgent
n
Nachsilbe *f* suffix
nachsitzen† *vi sep* (*haben*) **n∼ müssen** be kept in [after school]; **jdn n∼ lassen** give s.o. detention. **N∼** *nt* **-s** (*Sch*) detention
Nachspeise *f* dessert, sweet
nachsprechen† *vt sep* repeat (**jdm** after s.o.)
nachspülen *vt sep* rinse
nächst /-çst/ *prep* (+ *dat*) next to. **n∼beste(r,s)** *adj* first [available]; (*zweitbeste*) next best. **n∼e(r,s)** *adj* next; (*nächstgelegene*) nearest; (*Verwandte*) closest; **in n∼er Nähe** close by; **am n∼en sein** be nearest *or* closest ● *pron* **der/die/das N∼e (n∼e)** the next; **der N∼e (n∼e) bitte** next please; **als N∼es (n∼es)** next; **fürs N∼e (n∼e)** for the time being. **N∼e(r)** *m* fellow man
nachstehend *adj* following ● *adv* below
Nächst|enliebe *f* charity. **n∼ens** *adv* shortly. **n∼gelegen** *adj* nearest
nachsuchen *vi sep* (*haben*) search; **n∼ um** request
Nacht *f* **-,¨e** night; **über/bei N∼** overnight/at night; **morgen N∼** tomorrow night; **heute N∼** tonight; (*letzte Nacht*) last night; **gestern N∼** last night; (*vorletzte Nacht*) the night before last. **N∼dienst** *m* night duty
Nachteil *m* disadvantage; **zum N∼** to the detriment (*gen* of)
Nacht|falter *m* moth. **N∼hemd** *nt* night-dress; (*Männer-*) night-shirt
Nachtigall *f* **-,-en** nightingale
Nachtisch *m* dessert
Nachtklub *m* night-club
nächtlich *adj* nocturnal, night
Nacht|lokal *nt* night-club. **N∼mahl** *nt* (*Aust*) supper
Nachtrag *m* postscript; (*Ergänzung*) supplement. **n∼en**† *vt sep* add; **jdm etw n∼en** (*fig*) bear a grudge against s.o. for sth. **n∼end** *adj* vindictive; **n∼end sein** bear grudges
nachträglich *adj* subsequent, later; (*verspätet*) belated ● *adv* later; (*nachher*) afterwards; (*verspätet*) belatedly
Nacht|ruhe *f* night's rest; **angenehme N∼ruhe!** sleep well! **n∼s** *adv* at night; **2 Uhr n∼s** 2 o'clock in the morning. **N∼schicht** *f* night-shift. **N∼tisch** *m* bedside table. **N∼tischlampe** *f* bedside lamp. **N∼topf** *m* chamber-pot. **N∼wächter** *m* night-watchman. **N∼zeit** *f* night-time
Nachuntersuchung *f* check-up
Nachwahl *f* by-election
Nachweis *m* **-es,-e** proof. **n∼bar** *adj* demonstrable. **n∼en**† *vt sep* prove; (*aufzeigen*) show; (*vermitteln*)

give details of; **jdm nichts n∼en können** have no proof against s.o.
Nachwelt *f* posterity
Nachwirkung *f* after-effect
Nachwuchs *m* new generation; (☐: *Kinder*) offspring. **N∼spieler** *m* young player
nachzahlen *vt/i sep* (*haben*) pay extra; (*später zahlen*) pay later; **Steuern n∼** pay tax arrears
nachzählen *vt/i sep* (*haben*) count again; (*prüfen*) check
Nachzahlung *f* extra/later payment; (*Gehalts-*) back-payment
nachzeichnen *vt sep* copy
Nachzügler *m* **-s,-** late-comer; (*Zurückgebliebener*) straggler
Nacken *m* **-s,-** nape *or* back of the neck
nackt *adj* naked; (*bloß, kahl*) bare; (*Wahrheit*) plain. **N∼heit** *f* **-** nakedness, nudity. **N∼kultur** *f* nudism. **N∼schnecke** *f* slug
Nadel *f* **-,-n** needle; (*Häkel-*) hook; (*Schmuck-, Hut-*) pin. **N∼arbeit** *f* needlework. **N∼baum** *m* conifer. **N∼stich** *m* stitch; (*fig*) pinprick. **N∼wald** *m* coniferous forest
Nagel *m* **-s,⁼** nail. **N∼haut** *f* cuticle. **N∼lack** *m* nail varnish. **n∼n** *vt* nail. **n∼neu** *adj* brand-new
nagen *vt/i* (*haben*) gnaw (**an** + *dat* at); **n∼d** (*fig*) nagging
Nagetier *nt* rodent
nah *adj, adv & prep* = **nahe**
Näharbeit *f* sewing
Nahaufnahme *f* close-up
nahe *adj* nearby; (*zeitlich*) imminent; (*eng*) close; **der N∼ Osten** the Middle East; **in n∼r Zukunft** in the near future; **von n∼m** [from] close to; **n∼ sein** be close (*dat* to) ● *adv* near, close; (*verwandt*) closely; **n∼ an** (+ *acc*/*dat*) near [to], close to; **n∼ daran sein, etw zu tun** nearly do sth; **n∼ liegen** be close; (*fig*) be highly likely; **n∼ legen** (*fig*) recommend (**dat** to); **jdm n∼ legen, etw zu tun** urge s.o. to do sth; **jdm n∼ gehen** (*fig*) affect s.o. deeply; **jdm zu n∼ treten** (*fig*) offend s.o. ● *prep* (+ *dat*) near [to], close to
Nähe *f* **-** nearness, proximity; **aus der N∼** [from] close to; **in der N∼** near *or* close by
nahe|gehen* *vi sep* (*sein*) **n∼ gehen**, *s.* **nahe**. **n∼legen*** *vt sep* **n∼ legen**, *s.* **nahe**. **n∼liegen*** *vi sep* (*haben*) **n∼ liegen**, *s.* **nahe**
nähen *vt/i* (*haben*) sew; (*anfertigen*) make; (*Med*) stitch [up]
näher *adj* closer; (*Weg*) shorter; (*Einzelheiten*) further ● *adv* closer; (*genauer*) more closely; **n∼ kommen** come closer; (*fig*) get closer (**dat** to); **sich n∼ erkundigen** make further enquiries; **n∼an** (+ *acc*/*dat*) nearer [to], closer to ● *prep* (+ *dat*) nearer [to], closer to. **N∼e[s]** *nt* [further] details *pl*. **n∼n (sich)** *vr* approach
nahezu *adv* almost
Nähgarn *nt* [sewing] cotton
Nahkampf *m* close combat
Näh|maschine *f* sewing machine. **N∼nadel** *f* sewing-needle
nähren *vt* feed; (*fig*) nurture
nahrhaft *adj* nutritious
Nährstoff *m* nutrient
Nahrung *f* **-** food, nourishment. **N∼smittel** *nt* food
Nährwert *m* nutritional value
Naht *f* **-,⁼e** seam; (*Med*) suture. **n∼los** *adj* seamless
Nahverkehr *m* local service
Nähzeug *nt* sewing; (*Zubehör*) sewing kit
naiv /na'i:f/ *adj* naïve. **N∼ität** *f* **-** naïvety

Name *m* **-ns,-n** name; **im N~n** (+ *gen*) in the name of; (*handeln*) on behalf of. **n~nlos** *adj* nameless; (*unbekannt*) unknown, anonymous. **N~nstag** *m* name-day. **N~nsvetter** *m* namesake. **N~nszug** *m* signature. **n~ntlich** *adv* by name; (*besonders*) especially

namhaft *adj* noted; (*ansehnlich*) considerable; **n~ machen** name

nämlich *adv* (*und zwar*) namely; (*denn*) because

Nanotechnologie *f* nanotechnology

nanu *int* hallo

Napf *m* **-[e]s,⸚e** bowl

Narbe *f* **-,-n** scar

Narkose *f* **-,-n** general anaesthetic. **N~arzt** *m* anaesthetist. **N~mittel** *nt* anaesthetic

Narr *m* **-en,-en** fool; **zum N~en halten** make a fool of. **n~en** *vt* fool

Närr|in *f* **-,-nen** fool. **n~isch** *adj* foolish; (🄸: *verrückt*) crazy (**auf** + *acc* about)

Narzisse *f* **-,-n** narcissus

naschen *vt/i* (*haben*) nibble (**an** + *dat* at)

Nase *f* **-,-n** nose

näseln *vi* (*haben*) speak through one's nose; **n~d** nasal

Nasen|bluten *nt* **-s** nosebleed. **N~loch** *nt* nostril

Nashorn *nt* rhinoceros

nass *adj* wet

Nässe *f* **-** wet; wetness. **n~n** *vt* wet

Nation /na'tsio:n/ *f* **-,-en** nation. **n~al** *adj* national. **N~alhymne** *f* national anthem. **N~alismus** *m* **-** nationalism. **N~alität** *f* **-,-en** nationality. **N~alspieler** *m* international

> **Nationalrat** In Austria the *Nationalrat* is the Federal Assembly's lower house, whose 183 members are elected for four years under a system of proportional representation. In Switzerland, the *Nationalrat* is made up of 200 representatives.

Natrium *nt* **-s** sodium

Natron *nt* **-s doppeltkohlensaures N~** bicarbonate of soda

Natter *f* **-,-n** snake; (*Gift-*) viper

Natur *f* **-,-en** nature; **von N~ aus** by nature. **n~alisieren** *vt* naturalize. **N~alisierung** *f* **-,-en** naturalization

Naturell *nt* **-s,-e** disposition

Natur|erscheinung *f* natural phenomenon. **N~forscher** *m* naturalist. **N~heilkunde** *f* natural medicine. **N~kunde** *f* natural history

natürlich *adj* natural ● *adv* naturally; (*selbstverständlich*) of course. **N~keit** *f* **-** naturalness

natur|rein *adj* pure. **N~schutz** *m* nature conservation; **unter N~schutz stehen** be protected. **N~schutzgebiet** *nt* nature reserve. **N~wissenschaft** *f* [natural] science. **N~wissenschaftler** *m* scientist

nautisch *adj* nautical

Navigation /-'tsio:n/ *f* **-** navigation

Nazi *m* **-s,-s** Nazi

n.Chr. *abbr* (**nach Christus**) AD

Nebel *m* **-s,-** fog; (*leicht*) mist

neben *prep* (+ *dat/acc*) next to, beside; (+ *dat*) (*außer*) apart from. **n~an** *adv* next door

Neben|anschluss *m* (*Teleph*) extension. **N~ausgaben** *fpl* incidental expenses

nebenbei *adv* in addition; (*beiläufig*) casually
Neben|bemerkung *f* passing remark. **N~beruf** *m* second job
nebeneinander *adv* next to each other, side by side
Neben|eingang *m* side entrance. **N~fach** *nt* (*Univ*) subsidiary subject. **N~fluss** *m* tributary
nebenher *adv* in addition
nebenhin *adv* casually
Neben|höhle *f* sinus. **N~kosten** *pl* additional costs. **N~produkt** *nt* by-product. **N~rolle** *f* supporting role; (*Kleine*) minor role. **N~sache** *f* unimportant matter. **n~sächlich** *adj* unimportant. **N~satz** *m* subordinate clause. **N~straße** *f* minor road; (*Seiten-*) side street. **N~wirkung** *f* side-effect. **N~zimmer** *nt* room next door
neblig *adj* foggy; (*leicht*) misty
neck|en *vt* tease. **N~erei** *f* - teasing. **n~isch** *adj* teasing
Neffe *m* **-n,-n** nephew
negativ *adj* negative. **N~** *nt* **-s,-e** (*Phot*) negative
Neger *m* **-s,-** Negro
nehmen† *vt* take (*dat* from); **sich** (*dat*) **etw n~** take sth; help oneself to (*Essen*)
Neid *m* **-[e]s** envy, jealousy. **n~isch** *adj* envious, jealous (**auf** + *acc* of); **auf jdn n~isch sein** envy s.o.
neig|en *vt* incline; (*zur Seite*) tilt; (*beugen*) bend; **sich n~en** incline; (*Boden:*) slope; (*Person:*) bend (**über** + *acc* over) ● *vi* (*haben*) **n~en zu** (*fig*) have a tendency towards; be prone to (*Krankheit*); incline towards (*Ansicht*); **dazu n~en, etw zu tun** tend to do sth. **N~ung** *f* **-,-en** inclination; (*Gefälle*) slope; (*fig*) tendency
nein *adv*, **N~** *nt* **-s** no
Nektar *m* **-s** nectar
Nelke *f* **-,-n** carnation; (*Culin*) clove
nenn|en† *vt* call; (*taufen*) name; (*angeben*) give; (*erwähnen*) mention; **sich n~en** call oneself. **n~enswert** *adj* significant
Neon *nt* **-s** neon. **N~beleuchtung** *f* fluorescent lighting
Nerv *m* **-s,-en** nerve; **die N~en verlieren** lose control of oneself. **n~en** *vt* **jdn n~en** ☒ get on s.o.'s nerves. **N~enarzt** *m* neurologist. **n~enaufreibend** *adj* nerve-racking. **N~enkitzel** *m* [I] thrill. **N~ensystem** *nt* nervous system. **N~enzusammenbruch** *m* nervous breakdown
nervös *adj* nervy, edgy; (*Med*) nervous; **n~ sein** be on edge
Nervosität *f* - nerviness, edginess
Nerz *m* **-es,-e** mink
Nessel *f* **-,-n** nettle
Nest *nt* **-[e]s,-er** nest; ([I]: *Ort*) small place
nett *adj* nice; (*freundlich*) kind
netto *adv* net
Netz *nt* **-es,-e** net; (*Einkaufs-*) string bag; (*Spinnen-*) web; (*auf Landkarte*) grid; (*System*) network; (*Electr*) mains *pl*. **N~haut** *f* retina. **N~karte** *f* area season ticket. **N~werk** *nt* network
neu *adj* new; (*modern*) modern; **wie neu** as good as new; **das ist mir neu** it's news to me; **von n~em** all over again ● *adv* newly; (*gerade erst*) only just; (*erneut*) again; **etw neu schreiben** rewrite sth; **neu vermähltes Paar** newly-weds *pl*. **N~auflage** *f* new edition; (*unverändert*) reprint. **N~bau** *m* (*pl* **-ten**) new house/building
Neu|e(r) *m/f* new person, newcomer; (*Schüler*) new boy/girl.

N∼e(s) *nt* **das N∼e** the new; **etwas N∼es** something new; (*Neuigkeit*) a piece of news; **was gibt's N∼es?** what's the news?

neuerdings *adv* [just] recently

neuest|e(r,s) *adj* newest; (*letzte*) latest; **seit n∼em** just recently. **N∼e** *nt* **das N∼e** the latest thing: (*Neuigkeit*) the latest news *sg*

neugeboren *adj* newborn

Neugier, **Neugierde** *f* - curiosity; (*Wissbegierde*) inquisitiveness

neugierig *adj* curious (**auf** + *acc* about); (*wissbegierig*) inquisitive

Neuheit *f* -,-**en** novelty; newness

Neuigkeit *f* -,-**en** piece of news; **N∼en** news *sg*

Neujahr *nt* New Year's Day; **über N∼** over the New Year

neulich *adv* the other day

Neumond *m* new moon

neun *inv adj*, **N∼** *f* -,-**en** nine. **n∼te(r,s)** *adj* ninth. **n∼zehn** *inv adj* nineteen. **n∼zehnte(r,s)** *adj* nineteenth. **n∼zig** *inv adj* ninety. **n∼zigste(r,s)** *adj* ninetieth

n

Neuralgie *f* -,-**n** neuralgia

neureich *adj* nouveau riche

Neurologe *m* -**n**,-**n** neurologist

Neurose *f* -,-**n** neurosis

Neuschnee *m* fresh snow

Neuseeland *nt* -**s** New Zealand

neuste(r,s) *adj* = **neueste(r,s)**

neutral *adj* neutral. **N∼ität** *f* - neutrality

Neutrum *nt* -**s**,-**tra** neuter noun

neu|vermählt* *adj* **n∼ vermählt**, *s.* **neu**. **N∼zeit** *f* modern times *pl*

nicht *adv* not; **ich kann n∼** I cannot *or* can't; **er ist n∼ gekommen** he hasn't come; **bitte n∼!** please don't! **n∼ berühren!** do not touch! **du kennst ihn doch, n∼?** you do know him, don't you?

Nichte *f* -,-**n** niece

Nichtraucher *m* non-smoker

nichts *pron & a* nothing; **n∼ mehr** no more; **n∼ ahnend** unsuspecting; **n∼ sagend** meaningless; (*uninteressant*) nondescript. **N∼** *nt* - nothingness; (*fig: Leere*) void

Nichtschwimmer *m* non-swimmer

nichts|nutzig *adj* good-for-nothing; (!: *unartig*) naughty. **n∼sagend*** *adj* **n∼ sagend**, *s.* **nichts**. **N∼tun** *nt* -**s** idleness

Nickel *nt* -**s** nickel

nicken *vi* (*haben*) nod

Nickerchen *nt* -**s**,-, ! nap

nie *adv* never

nieder *adj* low ● *adv* down. **n∼brennen**† *vt/i sep* (*sein*) burn down. **N∼deutsch** *nt* Low German. **N∼gang** *m* (*fig*) decline. **n∼gedrückt** *adj* (*fig*) depressed. **n∼geschlagen** *adj* dejected, despondent. **N∼kunft** *f* -,**¨e** confinement. **N∼lage** *f* defeat

Niederlande (die) *pl* the Netherlands

Niederländ|er *m* -**s**,- Dutchman; **die N∼er** the Dutch *pl*. **N∼erin** *f* -,-**nen** Dutchwoman. **n∼isch** *adj* Dutch

nieder|lassen† *vt sep* let down; **sich n∼lassen** settle; (*sich setzen*) sit down. **N∼lassung** *f* -,-**en** settlement; (*Zweigstelle*) branch. **n∼legen** *vt sep* put *or* lay down; resign (*Amt*); **die Arbeit n∼legen** go on strike. **n∼metzeln** *vt sep* massacre. **N∼sachsen** *nt* Lower Saxony. **N∼schlag** *m* precipitation; (*Regen*) rainfall; (*radioaktiver*) fallout. **n∼schlagen**† *vt sep* knock down; lower (*Augen*); (*unterdrücken*) crush. **n∼schmettern** *vt sep* (*fig*) shatter.

n~setzen *vt sep* put *or* set down; sich n~setzen sit down. **n~strecken** *vt sep* fell; (*durch Schuss*) gun down. **n~trächtig** *adj* base, vile. **n~walzen** *vt sep* flatten

niedlich *adj* pretty; sweet

niedrig *adj* low; (*fig: gemein*) base ● *adv* low

niemals *adv* never

niemand *pron* nobody, no one

Niere *f* **-,-n** kidney; **künstliche N~** kidney machine

niesel|n *vi* (*haben*) drizzle. **N~regen** *m* drizzle

niesen *vi* (*haben*) sneeze. **N~** *nt* **-s** sneezing; (*Nieser*) sneeze

Niete[1] *f* **-,-n** rivet; (*an Jeans*) stud

Niete[2] *f* **-,-n** blank; [!] failure

nieten *vt* rivet

Nikotin *nt* **-s** nicotine

Nil *m* **-[s]** Nile. **N~pferd** *nt* hippopotamus

nimmer *adv* (*SGer*) not any more; nie und n~ never

nirgend|s, n~wo *adv* nowhere

Nische *f* **-,-n** recess, niche

nisten *vi* (*haben*) nest

Nitrat *nt* **-[e]s,-e** nitrate

Niveau /ni'vo:/ *nt* **-s,-s** level; (*geistig, künstlerisch*) standard

nix *adv* [!] nothing

Nixe *f* **-,-n** mermaid

nobel *adj* noble; ([!]: *luxuriös*) luxurious; ([!]: *großzügig*) generous

noch *adv* still; (*zusätzlich*) as well; (*mit Komparativ*) even; **n~ nicht** not yet; **gerade n~** only just; **n~ immer** *od* **immer n~** still; **n~ letzte Woche** only last week; **wer n~?** who else? **n~ etwas** something else; (*Frage*) anything else? **n~ einmal** again; **n~ ein Bier** another beer; **n~ größer** even bigger; **n~ so sehr** however much ● *conj* **weder n~** ... neither nor ...

nochmals *adv* again

Nomad|e *m* **-n,-n** nomad. **n~isch** *adj* nomadic

nominier|en *vt* nominate. **N~ung** *f* **-,-en** nomination

Nonne *f* **-,-n** nun. **N~nkloster** *nt* convent

Nonstopflug *m* direct flight

Nord *m* **-[e]s** north. **N~amerika** *nt* North America

Norden *m* **-s** north

nordisch *adj* Nordic

nördlich *adj* northern; (*Richtung*) northerly ● *adv & prep* (+ *gen*) **n~ [von] der Stadt** [to the] north of the town

Nordosten *m* north-east

Nord|pol *m* North Pole. **N~see** *f* **-** North Sea. **N~westen** *m* north-west

Nörgelei *f* **-,-en** grumbling

nörgeln *vi* (*haben*) grumble

Norm *f* **-,-en** norm; (*Techn*) standard; (*Soll*) quota

normal *adj* normal. **n~erweise** *adv* normally

normen *vt* standardize

Norwe|gen *nt* **-s** Norway. **N~ger(in)** *m* **-s,-** (*f* **-,-nen**) Norwegian. **n~gisch** *adj* Norwegian

Nost|algie *f* **-** nostalgia. **n~algisch** *adj* nostalgic

Not *f* **-,¨e** need; (*Notwendigkeit*) necessity; (*Entbehrung*) hardship; (*seelisch*) trouble; **Not leiden** be in need, suffer hardship; **Not leidende Menschen** needy people; **zur Not** if need be; (*äußerstenfalls*) at a pinch

Notar *m* **-s,-e** notary public

Not|arzt *m* emergency doctor. **N~ausgang** *m* emergency exit. **N~behelf** *m* **-[e]s,-e** makeshift. **N~bremse** *f* emergency brake.

n

N~dienst *m* **N~dienst haben** be on call

Note *f* **-,-n** note; (*Zensur*) mark; **ganze/halbe N~** (*Mus*) semi-breve/minim; **N~n lesen** read music; **persönliche N~** personal touch. **N~nblatt** *nt* sheet of music. **N~nschlüssel** *m* clef

Notfall *m* emergency; **für den N~** just in case. **n~s** *adv* if need be

notieren *vt* note down; (*Comm*) quote; **sich** (*dat*) **etw n~** make a note of sth

nötig *adj* necessary; **n~ haben** need; **das N~ste** the essentials *pl* ● *adv* urgently. **n~enfalls** *adv* if need be. **N~ung** *f* **-** coercion

Notiz *f* **-,-en** note; (*Zeitungs-*) item; **[keine] N~ nehmen von** take [no] notice of. **N~buch** *nt* notebook. **N~kalender** *m* diary

Not|lage *f* plight. **n~landen** *vi* (*sein*) make a forced landing. **N~landung** *f* forced landing. **n~leidend*** *adj* **Not leidend**, *s.* **Not. N~lösung** *f* stopgap

Not|ruf *m* emergency call; (*Naut, Aviat*) distress call; (*Nummer*) emergency services number. **N~signal** *nt* distress signal. **N~stand** *m* state of emergency. **N~unterkunft** *f* emergency accommodation. **N~wehr** *f* **-** (*Jur*) self-defence

notwendig *adj* necessary; essential ● *adv* urgently. **N~keit** *f* **-,-en** necessity

Notzucht *f* **-** (*Jur*) rape

Nougat /'nu:gat/ *m & nt* **-s** nougat

Novelle *f* **-,-n** novella; (*Pol*) amendment

November *m* **-s,-** November

Novize *m* **-n,-n, Novizin** *f* **-,-nen** (*Relig*) novice

Nu *m* **im Nu** [!] in a flash

nüchtern *adj* sober; (*sachlich*) matter-of-fact; (*schmucklos*) bare; (*ohne Würze*) bland; **auf n~en Magen** on an empty stomach

Nudel *f* **-,-n** piece of pasta; **N~n** pasta *sg*; (*Band-*) noodles. **N~holz** *nt* rolling-pin

Nudist *m* **-en,-en** nudist

nuklear *adj* nuclear

null *inv adj* zero, nought; (*Teleph*) O; (*Sport*) nil; (*Tennis*) love; **n~ Fehler** no mistakes; **n~ und nichtig** (*Jur*) null and void. **N~** *f* **-,-en** nought, zero; (*fig: Person*) nonentity. **N~punkt** *m* zero

numerieren* *vt* = **nummerieren**

Nummer *f* **-,-n** number; (*Ausgabe*) issue; (*Darbietung*) item; (*Zirkus-*) act; (*Größe*) size. **n~ieren** *vt* number. **N~nschild** *nt* number-plate

nun *adv* now; (*na*) well; (*halt*) just; **nun gut!** very well then!

nur *adv* only, just; **wo kann sie nur sein?** wherever can she be? **er soll es nur versuchen!** just let him try!

Nürnberg *nt* **-s** Nuremberg

nuscheln *vt/i* (*haben*) mumble

Nuss *f* **-,⸚e** nut. **N~knacker** *m* **-s,-** nutcrackers *pl*

Nüstern *fpl* nostrils

Nut *f* **-,-en**, **Nute** *f* **-,-n** groove

Nutte *f* **-,-n** [x] tart [x]

nutz|bar *adj* usable; **n~bar machen** utilize; cultivate (*Boden*). **n~bringend** *adj* profitable

nutzen *vt* use, utilize; (*aus-*) take advantage of ● *vi* (*haben*) = **nützen. N~** *m* **-s** benefit; (*Comm*) profit; **N~ ziehen aus** benefit from; **von N~ sein** be useful

nützen *vi* (*haben*) be useful *or* of use (*dat* to); (*Mittel:*) be effective; **nichts n~** be useless *or* no use; **was nützt mir das?** what good is that to me? ● *vt* = **nutzen**

nützlich *adj* useful. **N~keit** *f* **-**

usefulness
nutz|los *adj* useless; (*vergeblich*) vain. **N~losigkeit** *f* - uselessness. **N~ung** *f* - use, utilization
Nylon /'nailɔn/ *nt* **-s** nylon
Nymphe /'nʏmfə/ *f* **-,-n** nymph

Oo

o *int* **o ja/nein!** oh yes/no!
Oase *f* **-,-n** oasis
ob *conj* whether; **ob reich, ob arm** rich or poor; **und ob!** ⓘ you bet!
Obacht *f* **O~ geben** pay attention; **O~!** look out!
Obdach *nt* **-[e]s** shelter. **o~los** *adj* homeless. **O~lose(r)** *m/f* homeless person; **die O~losen** the homeless *pl*
Obduktion /-'tsio:n/ *f* **-,-en** postmortem
O-Beine *ntpl* ⓘ bow-legs, bandy legs
oben *adv* at the top; (*auf der Oberseite*) on top; (*eine Treppe hoch*) upstairs; (*im Text*) above; **da o~** up there; **o~ im Norden** up in the north; **siehe o~** see above; **o~ auf** (+ *acc/dat*) on top of; **nach o~** up[wards]; (*die Treppe hinauf*) upstairs; **von o~** from above/upstairs; **von o~ bis unten** from top to bottom/(*Person*) to toe; **jdn von o~ bis unten mustern** look s.o. up and down; **o~ erwähnt** *od* **genannt** above-mentioned. **o~drein** *adv* on top of that
Ober *m* **-s,-** waiter
Ober|arm *m* upper arm. **O~arzt** *m* ≈ senior registrar. **O~deck** *nt* upper deck. **o~e(r,s)** *adj* upper; (*höhere*) higher. **O~fläche** *f* surface. **o~flächlich** *adj* superficial. **O~geschoss** *nt* upper storey. **o~halb** *adv & prep* (+ *gen*) above. **O~haupt** *nt* (*fig*) head. **O~haus** *nt* (*Pol*) upper house; (*in UK*) House of Lords. **O~hemd** *nt* [man's] shirt. **o~irdisch** *adj* surface ● *adv* above ground. **O~kiefer** *m* upper jaw. **O~körper** *m* upper part of the body. **O~leutnant** *m* lieutenant. **O~lippe** *f* upper lip
Obers *nt* - (*Aust*) cream
Ober|schenkel *m* thigh. **O~schule** *f* grammar school. **O~seite** *f* upper/(*rechte Seite*) right side
Oberst *m* **-en** & **-s,-en** colonel
oberste(r,s) *adj* top; (*höchste*) highest; (*Befehlshaber, Gerichtshof*) supreme; (*wichtigste*) first
Ober|stimme *f* treble. **O~teil** *nt* top. **O~weite** *f* chest/(*der Frau*) bust size
obgleich *conj* although
Obhut *f* - care
obig *adj* above
Objekt *nt* **-[e]s,-e** object; (*Haus, Grundstück*) property
Objektiv *nt* **-s,-e** lens. **o~** *adj* objective. **O~ität** *f* - objectivity
Oblate *f* **-,-n** (*Relig*) wafer
Obmann *m* (*pl* **-männer**) [jury] foreman; (*Sport*) referee
Oboe /o'bo:ə/ *f* **-,-n** oboe
Obrigkeit *f* - authorities *pl*
obschon *conj* although
Observatorium *nt* **-s,-ien** observatory
obskur *adj* obscure; dubious
Obst *nt* **-es** (*coll*) fruit. **O~baum** *m* fruit-tree. **O~garten** *m* orchard. **O~händler** *m* fruiterer

obszön *adj* obscene
O-Bus *m* trolley bus
obwohl *conj* although
Ochse *m* **-n,-n** ox
öde *adj* desolate; (*unfruchtbar*) barren; (*langweilig*) dull. **Öde** *f* - desolation; barrenness; dullness
oder *conj* or; **du kennst ihn doch, o~?** you know him, don't you?
Ofen *m* **-s,⁼** stove; (*Heiz-*) heater; (*Back-*) oven; (*Techn*) furnace
offen *adj* open; (*Haar*) loose; (*Flamme*) naked; (*o~herzig*) frank; (*o~ gezeigt*) overt; (*unentschieden*) unsettled; **o~e Stelle** vacancy; **Wein o~ verkaufen** sell wine by the glass; **o~ bleiben** remain open; **o~ halten** hold open (*Tür*); keep open (*Mund, Augen*); **o~ lassen** leave open; leave vacant (*Stelle*); **o~ stehen** be open; (*Rechnung:*) be outstanding; **jdm o~ stehen** (*fig*) be open to s.o.; *adv* **o~ gesagt** *od* **gestanden** to be honest. **o~bar** *adj* obvious ● *adv* apparently. **o~baren** *vt* reveal. **O~barung** *f* **-,-en** revelation. **O~heit** *f* - frankness, openness. **o~sichtlich** *adj* obvious
offenstehen* *vi sep* (*haben*) **offen stehen**, *s.* **offen**
öffentlich *adj* public. **Ö~keit** *f* - public; **in aller Ö~keit** in public, publicly
Offerte *f* **-,-n** (*Comm*) offer
offiziell *adj* official
Offizier *m* **-s,-e** (*Mil*) officer
öffn|en *vt/i* (*haben*) open; **sich ö~en** open. **Ö~er** *m* **-s,-** opener. **Ö~ung** *f* **-,-en** opening. **Ö~ungszeiten** *fpl* opening hours
oft *adv* often
öfter *adv* quite often. **ö~e(r,s)** *adj* frequent; **des Ö~en (ö~en)** frequently. **ö~s** *adv* [T] quite often
oh *int* oh!

O

ohne *prep* (+ *acc*) without; **o~ mich!** count me out! **oben o~** topless ● *conj* **o~ zu überlegen** without thinking; **o~ dass ich es merkte** without my noticing it. **o~dies** *adv* anyway. **o~gleichen** *pred adj* unparalleled. **o~hin** *adv* anyway
Ohn|macht *f* **-,-en** faint; (*fig*) powerlessness; **in O~macht fallen** faint. **o~mächtig** *adj* unconscious; (*fig*) powerless; **o~mächtig werden** faint
Ohr *nt* **-[e]s,-en** ear
Öhr *nt* **-[e]s,-e** eye (*of needle*)
Ohrenschmalz *nt* ear-wax. **O~schmerzen** *mpl* earache *sg*
Ohrfeige *f* slap in the face. **o~n** *vt* **jdn o~n** slap s.o.'s face
Ohr|läppchen *nt* **-s,-** ear-lobe. **O~ring** *m* ear-ring. **O~wurm** *m* earwig
oje *int* oh dear!
okay /o'ke:/ *adj & adv* [T] OK
Öko|logie *f* - ecology. **ö~logisch** *adj* ecological. **Ö~nomie** *f* - economy; (*Wissenschaft*) economics *sg*. **ö~nomisch** *adj* economic; (*sparsam*) economical
Oktave *f* **-,-n** octave
Oktober *m* **-s,-** October

> *i*
> **Oktoberfest** Germany's biggest beer festival and funfair, which takes place every year in Munich. Over 16 days more than 5 million litres of beer are drunk in marquees erected by the major breweries. The festival goes back to 1810, when a horse race was held to celebrate the wedding of Ludwig, Crown Prince of Bavaria.

ökumenisch *adj* ecumenical
Öl *nt* **-[e]s,-e** oil; **in Öl malen** paint

in oils. **Ölbaum** *m* olivetree. **ölen** *vt* oil. **Ölfarbe** *f* oil-paint. **Ölfeld** *nt* oilfield. **Ölgemälde** *nt* oil-painting. **ölig** *adj* oily

Oliv|e *f* **-,-n** olive. **O~enöl** *nt* olive oil

Ölmessstab *m* dip-stick. **Ölsardinen** *fpl* sardines in oil. **Ölstand** *m* oil-level. **Öltanker** *m* oil-tanker. **Ölteppich** *m* oil-slick

Olympiade *f* **-,-n** Olympic Games *pl*

Olymp|iasieger(in) /o'lympi̯a-/ *m(f)* Olympic champion. **o~isch** *adj* Olympic; **O~ische Spiele** Olympic Games

Ölzeug *nt* oilskins *pl*

Oma *f* **-,-s** 🄸 granny

Omnibus *m* bus; (*Reise-*) coach

onanieren *vi* (*haben*) masturbate

Onkel *m* **-s,-** uncle

Online-Tagebuch *nt* blog

Opa *m* **-s,-s** 🄸 grandad

Opal *m* **-s,-e** opal

Oper *f* **-,-n** opera

Operation /-'tsi̯o:n/ *f* **-,-en** operation. **O~ssaal** *m* operating theatre

Operette *f* **-,-n** operetta

operieren *vt* operate on (*Patient, Herz*); **sich o~ lassen** have an operation ● *vi* (*haben*) operate

Opernglas *nt* opera-glasses *pl*

Opfer *nt* **-s,-** sacrifice; (*eines Unglücks*) victim; **ein O~ bringen** make a sacrifice; **jdm/etw zum O~ fallen** fall victim to s.o./something. **o~n** *vt* sacrifice

Opium *nt* **-s** opium

Opposition /-'tsi̯o:n/ *f* **-** opposition. **O~spartei** *f* opposition party

Optik *f* **-** optics *sg*, (🄸: *Objektiv*) lens. **O~er** *m* **-s,-** optician

optimal *adj* optimum

Optimis|mus *m* **-** optimism. **O~t** *m* **-en,-en** optimist. **o~tisch** *adj* optimistic

optisch *adj* optical; (*Eindruck*) visual

Orakel *nt* **-s,-** oracle

Orange /o'rã:ʒə/ *f* **-,-n** orange. **o~** *inv adj* orange. **O~ade** *f* **-,-n** orangeade. **O~nmarmelade** *f* [orange] marmalade

Oratorium *nt* **-s,-ien** oratorio

Orchester /ɔr'kɛstɐ/ *nt* **-s,-** orchestra

Orchidee /ɔrçi'de:ə/ *f* **-,-n** orchid

Orden *m* **-s,-** (*Ritter-, Kloster-*) order; (*Auszeichnung*) medal, decoration

ordentlich *adj* neat. tidy; (*anständig*) respectable; (*ordnungsgemäß, fam: richtig*) proper; (*Mitglied, Versammlung*) ordinary; (🄸: *gut*) decent; (🄸: *gehörig*) good

Order *f* **-,-s & -n** order

ordinär *adj* common

Ordination /-'tsi̯o:n/ *f* **-,-en** (*Relig*) ordination; (*Aust*) surgery

ordn|en *vt* put in order; tidy; (*an-*) arrange. **O~er** *m* **-s,-** steward; (*Akten-*) file

Ordnung *f* **-** order; **O~ machen** tidy up; **in O~ bringen** put in order; (*aufräumen*) tidy; (*reparieren*) mend; (*fig*) put right; **in O~ sein** be in order; (*ordentlich sein*) be tidy; (*fig*) be all right; **[geht] in O~!** OK! **o~sgemäß** *adj* proper. **O~sstrafe** *f* (*Jur*) fine. **o~swidrig** *adj* improper

Ordonnanz, **Ordonanz** *f* **-,-en** (*Mil*) orderly

Organ *nt* **-s,-e** organ; voice

Organisation /-'tsi̯o:n/ *f* **-,-en** organization

organisch *adj* organic

organisieren *vt* organize; (🄸: *beschaffen*) get [hold of]

Organismus *m* **-,-men** organism; (*System*) system

Organspenderkarte *f* donor card

Orgasmus *m* **-,-men** orgasm

Orgel *f* **-,-n** (*Mus*) organ. **O~pfeife** *f* organ-pipe

Orgie /'ɔrgi̯ə/ *f* **-,-n** orgy

Orien|t /'o:ri̯ɛnt/ *m* **-s** Orient. **o~talisch** *adj* Oriental

orientier|en /ori̯ɛn'ti:rən/ *vt* inform (**über** + *acc* about); **sich o~en** get one's bearings, orientate oneself; (*unterrichten*) inform oneself (**über** + *acc* about). **O~ung** *f* **-** orientation; **die O~ung verlieren** lose one's bearings

original *adj* original. **O~** *nt* **-s,-e** original. **O~übertragung** *f* live transmission

originell *adj* original; (*eigenartig*) unusual

Orkan *m* **-s,-e** hurricane

Ornament *nt* **-[e]s,-e** ornament

Ort *m* **-[e]s,-e** place; (*Ortschaft*) [small] town; **am Ort** locally; **am Ort des Verbrechens** at the scene of the crime

ortho|dox *adj* orthodox. **O~graphie**, **O~grafie** *f* **-** spelling. **O~päde** *m* **-n,-n** orthopaedic specialist

örtlich *adj* local

Ortschaft *f* **-,-en** [small] town; (*Dorf*) village; **geschlossene O~** (*Auto*) built-up area

Orts|gespräch *nt* (*Teleph*) local call. **O~verkehr** *m* local traffic. **O~zeit** *f* local time

Öse *f* **-,-n** eyelet; (*Schlinge*) loop; **Haken und Öse** hook and eye

Ost *m* **-[e]s** east

Osten *m* **-s** east; **nach O~** east

ostentativ *adj* pointed

Osteopath *m* **-en,-en** osteopath

Oster|ei /'o:stɐʔai̯/ *nt* Easter egg. **O~fest** *nt* Easter. **O~glocke** *f* daffodil. **O~n** *nt* **-,-** Easter; **frohe O~n!** happy Easter!

Österreich *nt* **-s** Austria. **Ö~er** *m*, **-s,-**, **Ö~erin** *f* **-,-nen** Austrian. **ö~isch** *adj* Austrian

östlich *adj* eastern; (*Richtung*) easterly ●*adv & prep* (+ *gen*) **ö~ [von] der Stadt** [to the] east of the town

Ostsee *f* Baltic [Sea]

Otter[1] *m* **-s,-** otter

Otter[2] *f* **-,-n** adder

Ouverture /uvɛr'ty:rə/ *f* **-,-n** overture

oval *adj* oval. **O~** *nt* **-s,-e** oval

Oxid, **Oxyd** *nt* **-[e]s,-e** oxide

Ozean *m* **-s,-e** ocean

Ozon *nt* **-s** ozone. **O~loch** *nt* hole in the ozone layer. **O~schicht** *f* ozone layer

Pp

paar *pron inv* **ein p~** a few; **ein p~ Mal** a few times; **alle p~ Tage** every few days. **P~** *nt* **-[e]s,-e** pair; (*Ehe-, Liebes-*) couple. **p~en** *vt* mate; (*verbinden*) combine; **sich p~en** mate. **P~ung** *f* **-,-en** mating. **p~weise** *adv* in pairs, in twos

Pacht *f* **-,-en** lease; (*P~summe*) rent. **p~en** *vt* lease

Pächter *m* **-s,-** lessee; (*eines Hofes*) tenant

Pachtvertrag *m* lease

Päckchen *nt* **-s,-** package, small packet

pack|en *vt/i* (*haben*) pack; (*ergrei-*

fen) seize; (*fig: fesseln*) grip. **P~en** *m* **-s,-** bundle. **p~end** *adj* (*fig*) gripping. **P~papier** *nt* [strong] wrapping paper. **P~ung** *f* **-,-en** packet; (*Med*) pack

Pädagog|e *m* **-n,-n** educationalist; (*Lehrer*) teacher. **P~ik** *f* - educational science

Paddel *nt* **-s,-** paddle. **P~boot** *nt* canoe. **p~n** *vt/i* (*haben/sein*) paddle. **P~sport** *m* canoeing

Page /ˈpaːʒə/ *m* **-n,-n** page

Paillette /paiˈjɛtə/ *f* **-,-n** sequin

Paket *nt* **-[e]s,-e** packet; (*Post-*) parcel

Pakist|an *nt* **-s** Pakistan. **P~aner(in)** *m* **-s,-** (*f* **-,-nen**) Pakistani. **p~anisch** *adj* Pakistani

Palast *m* **-[e]s,⸚e** palace

Paläst|ina *nt* **-s** Palestine. **P~inenser(in)** *m* **-s,-** (*f* **-,-nen**) Palestinian. **p~inensisch** *adj* Palestinian

Palette *f* **-,-n** palette

Palme *f* **-,-n** palm[-tree]

Pampelmuse *f* **-,-n** grapefruit

Panier|mehl *nt* (*Culin*) breadcrumbs *pl*. **p~t** *adj* (*Culin*) breaded

Panik *f* - panic

Panne *f* **-,-n** breakdown; (*Reifen-*) flat tyre; (*Missgeschick*) mishap

Panter, **Panther** *m* **-s,-** panther

Pantine *f* **-,-n** [wooden] clog

Pantoffel *m* **-s,-n** slipper; mule

Pantomime[1] *f* **-,-n** mime

Pantomime[2] *m* **-n,-n** mime artist

Panzer *m* **-s,-** armour; (*Mil*) tank; (*Zool*) shell. **p~n** *vt* armourplate. **P~schrank** *m* safe

Papa /ˈpapa, paˈpaː/ *m* **-s,-s** daddy

Papagei *m* **-s** & **-en,-en** parrot

Papier *nt* **-[e]s,-e** paper. **P~korb** *m* waste-paper basket. **P~schlange** *f* streamer. **P~waren** *fpl* stationery *sg*

Pappe *f* - cardboard

Pappel *f* **-,-n** poplar

pappig *adj* 🄸 sticky

Papp|karton *m*, **P~schachtel** *f* cardboard box

Paprika *m* **-s,-[s]** [sweet] pepper; (*Gewürz*) paprika

Papst *m* **-[e]s,⸚e** pope

päpstlich *adj* papal

Parade *f* **-,-n** parade

Paradies *nt* **-es,-e** paradise

Paraffin *nt* **-s** paraffin

Paragraf, **Paragraph** *m* **-en,-en** section

parallel *adj & adv* parallel. **P~e** *f* **-,-n** parallel

Paranuss *f* Brazil nut

Parasit *m* **-en,-en** parasite

parat *adj* ready

Parcours /parˈkuːɐ̯/ *m* **-,-** /**-[s],-s**/ (*Sport*) course

Pardon /parˈdõː/ *int* sorry!

Parfüm *nt* **-s,-e** & **-s** perfume, scent. **p~iert** *adj* perfumed, scented

parieren *vi* (*haben*) 🄸 obey

Park *m* **-s,-s** park. **p~en** *vt/i* (*haben*) park. **P~en** *nt* **-s** parking; '**P~en verboten**' 'no parking'

Parkett *nt* **-[e]s, -e** parquet floor; (*Theat*) stalls *pl*

Park|haus *nt* multi-storey car park. **P~kralle** *f* wheel clamp. **P~lücke** *f* parking space. **P~platz** *m* car park; parking space. **P~scheibe** *f* parking-disc. **P~schein** *m* car-park ticket. **P~uhr** *f* parking-meter. **P~verbot** *nt* parking ban; '**P~verbot**' 'no parking'

Parlament *nt* **-[e]s,-e** parliament. **p~arisch** *adj* parliamentary

Parodie *f* **-,-n** parody

Parole *f* **-,-n** slogan; (*Mil*) password
Partei *f* **-,-en** (*Pol, Jur*) party; (*Miet-*) tenant; **für jdn P~ ergreifen** take s.o.'s part. **p~isch** *adj* biased
Parterre /par'tɛr/ *nt* **-s,-s** ground floor; (*Theat*) rear stalls *pl*
Partie *f* **-,-n** part; (*Tennis, Schach*) game; (*Golf*) round; (*Comm*) batch; **eine gute P~ machen** marry well
Partikel *nt* **-s,-** particle
Partitur *f* **-,-en** (*Mus*) full score
Partizip *nt* **-s,-ien** participle
Partner|(in) *m* **-s,-** (*f* **-,-nen**) partner. **P~schaft** *f* **-,-en** partnership. **P~stadt** *f* twin town
Party /'pa:ɐ̯ti/ *f* **-,-s** party
Parzelle *f* **-,-n** plot [of ground]
Pass *m* **-es,⸗e** passport; (*Geog, Sport*) pass
Passage /pa'sa:ʒə/ *f* **-,-n** passage; (*Einkaufs-*) shopping arcade
Passagier /pasa'ʒi:ɐ̯/ *m* **-s,-e** passenger
Passant(in) *m* **-en,-en** (*f* **-,-nen**) passer-by
P
Passe *f* **-,-n** yoke
passen *vi* (*haben*) fit; (*geeignet sein*) be right (**für** for); (*Sport*) pass the ball; (*aufgeben*) pass; **p~ zu go** [well] with; (*übereinstimmen*) match; **jdm p~** fit s.o.; (*gelegen sein*) suit s.o.; **[ich] passe** pass. **p~d** *adj* suitable; (*angemessen*) appropriate; (*günstig*) convenient; (*übereinstimmend*) matching
passier|en *vt* pass; cross (*Grenze*); (*Culin*) rub through a sieve ● *vi* (*sein*) happen (**jdm** to s.o.); **es ist ein Unglück p~t** there has been an accident. **P~schein** *m* pass
Passiv *nt* **-s,-e** (*Gram*) passive
Passstraße *f* pass
Paste *f* **-,-n** paste

Pastell *nt* **-[e]s,-e** pastel
Pastete *f* **-,-n** pie; (*Gänseleber-*) pâté
pasteurisieren /pastøri'zi:rən/ *vt* pasteurize
Pastor *m* **-s,-en** pastor
Pate *m* **-n,-n** godfather; (*fig*) sponsor; **P~n** godparents. **P~nkind** *nt* godchild
Patent *nt* **-[e]s,-e** patent; (*Offiziers-*) commission. **p~** *adj* 🅸 clever; (*Person*) resourceful. **p~ieren** *vt* patent
Pater *m* **-s,-** (*Relig*) Father
Patholog|e *m* **-n,-n** pathologist. **p~isch** *adj* pathological
Patience /pa'sjã̯:s/ *f* **-,-n** patience
Patient(in) /pa'tsi̯ɛnt(ɪn)/ *m* **-en,-en** (*f* **-,-nen**) patient
Patin *f* **-,-nen** godmother
Patriot|(in) *m* **-en,-en** (*f* **-,-nen**) patriot. **p~isch** *adj* patriotic. **P~ismus** *m* **-** patriotism
Patrone *f* **-,-n** cartridge
Patrouille /pa'trʊljə/ *f* **-,-n** patrol
Patsch|e *f* **in der P~e sitzen** 🅸 be in a jam. **p~nass** *adj* 🅸 soaking wet
Patt *nt* **-s** stalemate
Patz|er *m* **-s,-** 🅸 slip. **p~ig** *adj* 🅸 insolent
Pauk|e *f* **-,-n** kettledrum; **auf die P~e hauen** 🅸 have a good time; (*prahlen*) boast. **p~en** *vt/i* (*haben*) 🅸 swot
pauschal *adj* all-inclusive; (*einheitlich*) flat-rate; (*fig*) sweeping (*Urteil*); **p~e Summe** lump sum. **P~e** *f* **-,-n** lump sum. **P~reise** *f* package tour. **P~summe** *f* lump sum
Pause[1] *f* **-,-n** break; (*beim Sprechen*) pause; (*Theat*) interval; (*im Kino*) intermission; (*Mus*) rest; **P~ machen** have a break

Pause² *f* -,-n tracing. **p~n** *vt* trace

pausenlos *adj* incessant

pausieren *vi* (*haben*) have a break; (*ausruhen*) rest

Pauspapier *nt* tracing-paper

Pavian *m* -s,-e baboon

Pavillon /ˈpavɪljõ/ *m* -s,-s pavilion

Pazifi|k *m* -s Pacific [Ocean]. **p~sch** *adj* Pacific

Pazifist *m* -en,-en pacifist

Pech *nt* -s pitch; (*Unglück*) bad luck; **P~ haben** be unlucky

Pedal *nt* -s,-e pedal

Pedant *m* -en,-en pedant

Pediküre *f* -,-n pedicure

Pegel *m* -s,- level; (*Gerät*) water-level indicator. **P~stand** *m* [water] level

peilen *vt* take a bearing on

peinigen *vt* torment

peinlich *adj* embarrassing, awkward; (*genau*) scrupulous; **es war mir sehr p~** I was very embarrassed

Peitsche *f* -,-n whip. **p~n** *vt* whip; (*fig*) lash ● *vi* (*sein*) lash (**an** + *acc* against). **P~nhieb** *m* lash

Pelikan *m* -s,-e pelican

Pell|e *f* -,-n skin. **p~en** *vt* peel; shell (*Ei*); **sich p~en** peel

Pelz *m* -es,-e fur

Pendel *nt* -s,- pendulum. **p~n** *vi* (*haben*) swing ● *vi* (*sein*) commute. **P~verkehr** *m* shuttle-service; (*für Pendler*) commuter traffic

Pendler *m* -s,- commuter

penetrant *adj* penetrating; (*fig*) obtrusive

Penis *m* -,-se penis

Penne *f* -,-n 🅃 school

Pension /pãˈzi̯oːn/ *f* -,-en pension; (*Hotel*) guest-house; **bei voller/halber P~** with full/half board. **P~är(in)** *m* -s,-e (*f* -,-nen) pensioner. **P~at** *nt* -[e]s,-e boarding-school. **p~ieren** *vt* retire. **P~ierung** *f* - retirement

Pensum *nt* -s [allotted] work

Peperoni *f* -,- chilli

per *prep* (+ *acc*) by

Perfekt *nt* -s (*Gram*) perfect

Perfektion /-ˈtsi̯oːn/ *f* - perfection

perforiert *adj* perforated

Pergament *nt* -[e]s,-e parchment. **P~papier** *nt* greaseproof paper

Period|e *f* -,-n period. **p~isch** *adj* periodic

Perl|e *f* -,-n pearl; (*Glas-, Holz-*) bead; (*Sekt-*) bubble. **P~mutt** *nt* -s mother-of-pearl

Pers|ien /-i̯ən/ *nt* -s Persia. **p~isch** *adj* Persian

Person *f* -,-en person; (*Theat*) character; **für vier P~en** for four people

Personal *nt* -s personnel, staff. **P~ausweis** *m* identity card. **P~chef** *m* personnel manager. **P~ien** *pl* personal particulars. **P~mangel** *m* staff shortage

persönlich *adj* personal ● *adv* personally, in person. **P~keit** *f* -,-en personality

Perücke *f* -,-n wig

pervers *adj* [sexually] perverted. **P~ion** *f* -,-en perversion

Pessimis|mus *m* - pessimism. **P~t** *m* -en,-en pessimist. **p~tisch** *adj* pessimistic

Pest *f* - plague

Petersilie /-i̯ə/ *f* - parsley

Petroleum /-leʊm/ *nt* -s paraffin

Petze *f* -,-n 🅃 sneak. **p~n** *vi* (*haben*) 🅃 sneak

Pfad *m* -[e]s,-e path. **P~finder** *m* -s,- [Boy] Scout. **P~finderin** *f* -,-nen [Girl] Guide

P

Pfahl *m* **-[e]s,¨e** stake, post
Pfalz (die) - the Palatinate
Pfand *nt* **-[e]s,¨er** pledge; (*beim Spiel*) forfeit; (*Flaschen-*) deposit
pfänd|en *vt* (*Jur*) seize. **P~erspiel** *nt* game of forfeits
Pfandleiher *m* **-s,-** pawnbroker
Pfändung *f* **-,-en** (*Jur*) seizure
Pfann|e *f* **-,-n** [frying-]pan. **P~kuchen** *m* pancake
Pfarr|er *m* **-s,-** vicar, parson; (*katholischer*) priest. **P~haus** *nt* vicarage
Pfau *m* **-s,-en** peacock
Pfeffer *m* **-s** pepper. **P~kuchen** *m* gingerbread. **P~minze** *f* - (*Bot*) peppermint. **p~n** *vt* pepper; (🅸: *schmeißen*) chuck. **P~streuer** *m* **-s,-** pepperpot
Pfeif|e *f* **-,-n** whistle; (*Tabak-, Orgel-*) pipe. **p~en**† *vt/i* (*haben*) whistle; (*als Signal*) blow the whistle
Pfeil *m* **-[e]s,-e** arrow
Pfeiler *m* **-s,-** pillar; (*Brücken-*) pier
Pfennig *m* **-s,-e** pfennig
Pferch *m* **-[e]s,-e** [sheep] pen
Pferd *nt* **-es,-e** horse; **zu P~e** on horseback. **P~erennen** *nt* horse-race; (*als Sport*) [horse-]racing. **P~eschwanz** *m* horse's tail; (*Frisur*) pony-tail. **P~estall** *m* stable. **P~estärke** *f* horsepower
Pfiff *m* **-[e]s,-e** whistle
Pfifferling *m* **-s,-e** chanterelle
pfiffig *adj* 🅸 smart
Pfingst|en *nt* **-s** Whitsun. **P~rose** *f* peony
Pfirsich *m* **-s,-e** peach
Pflanz|e *f* **-,-n** plant. **p~en** *vt* plant. **P~enfett** *nt* vegetable fat. **p~lich** *adj* vegetable
Pflaster *nt* **-s,-** pavement; (*Heft-*) plaster. **p~n** *vt* pave
Pflaume *f* **-,-n** plum
Pflege *f* - care; (*Kranken-*) nursing; **in P~ nehmen** look after; (*Admin*) foster (*Kind*). **p~bedürftig** *adj* in need of care. **P~eltern** *pl* foster-parents. **P~kind** *nt* foster-child. **p~leicht** *adj* easy-care. **p~n** *vt* look after, care for; nurse (*Kranke*); cultivate (*Künste, Freundschaft*). **P~r(in)** *m* **-s,-** (*f* **-,-nen**) nurse; (*Tier-*) keeper
Pflicht *f* **-,-en** duty; (*Sport*) compulsory exercise/routine. **p~bewusst** *adj* conscientious. **P~gefühl** *nt* sense of duty
pflücken *vt* pick
Pflug *m* **-[e]s,¨e** plough
pflügen *vt/i* (*haben*) plough
Pforte *f* **-,-n** gate
Pförtner *m* **-s,-** porter
Pfosten *m* **-s,-** post
Pfote *f* **-,-n** paw
Pfropfen *m* **-s,-** stopper; (*Korken*) cork. **p~** *vt* graft (**auf** + *acc* on [to]); (🅸: *pressen*) cram (**in** + *acc* into)
pfui *int* ugh
Pfund *nt* **-[e]s,-e** & - pound
Pfusch|arbeit *f* 🅸 shoddy work. **p~en** *vi* (*haben*) 🅸 botch one's work. **P~erei** *f* **-,-en** 🅸 botch-up
Pfütze *f* **-,-n** puddle
Phantasie *f* **-,-n** imagination; **P~n** fantasies; (*Fieber-*) hallucinations. **p~los** *adj* unimaginative. **p~ren** *vi* (*haben*) fantasize; (*im Fieber*) be delirious. **p~voll** *adj* imaginative
phantastisch *adj* fantastic
pharma|zeutisch *adj* pharmaceutical. **P~zie** *f* - pharmacy
Phase *f* **-,-n** phase
Philologie *f* - [study of] language and literature
Philosoph *m* **-en,-en** philosopher.

P~ie *f* **-,-n** philosophy
philosophisch *adj* philosophical
Phobie *f* **-,-n** phobia
Phonet|ik *f* **-** phonetics *sg*. **p~isch** *adj* phonetic
Phosphor *m* **-s** phosphorus
Photo *nt*, **Photo-** = **Foto, Foto-**
Phrase *f* **-,-n** empty phrase
Physik *f* **-** physics *sg*. **p~alisch** *adj* physical
Physiker(in) *m* **-s,-** (*f* **-,-nen**) physicist
Physiologie *f* **-** physiology
physisch *adj* physical
Pianist(in) *m* **-en,-en** (*f* **-,-nen**) pianist
Pickel *m* **-s,-** pimple, spot; (*Spitzhacke*) pick. **p~ig** *adj* spotty
Picknick *nt* **-s,-s** picnic
piep[s]|en *vi* (*haben*) (*Vogel:*) cheep; (*Maus:*) squeak; (*Techn*) bleep. **P~er** *m* **-s,-** bleeper
Pier *m* **-s,-e** [harbour] pier
Pietät /pi̯e'tɛ:t/ *f* **-** reverence. **p~los** *adj* irreverent
Pigment *nt* **-[e]s,-e** pigment. **P~ierung** *f* **-** pigmentation
Pik *nt* **-s,-s** (*Karten*) spades *pl*
pikant *adj* piquant; (*gewagt*) racy
piken *vt* [!] prick
pikiert *adj* offended, hurt
Pilger|(in) *m* **-s,-** (*f* **-,-nen**) pilgrim. **P~fahrt** *f* pilgrimage. **p~n** *vi* (*sein*) make a pilgrimage
Pille *f* **-,-n** pill
Pilot *m* **-en,-en** pilot
Pilz *m* **-es,-e** fungus; (*essbarer*) mushroom
PIN *f* PIN
pingelig *adj* [!] fussy
Pinguin *m* **-s,-e** penguin
Pinie /-i̯ə/ *f* **-,-n** stone-pine
pinkeln *vi* (*haben*) [!] pee
Pinsel *m* **-s,-** [paint]brush
Pinzette *f* **-,-n** tweezers *pl*
Pionier *m* **-s,-e** (*Mil*) sapper; (*fig*) pioneer
Pirat *m* **-en,-en** pirate
Piste *f* **-,-n** (*Ski-*) run, piste; (*Renn-*) track; (*Aviat*) runway
Pistole *f* **-,-n** pistol
pitschnass *adj* [!] soaking wet
pittoresk *adj* picturesque
Pizza *f* **-,-s** pizza
Pkw /'pe:kave:/ *m* **-s,-s** car
plädieren *vi* (*haben*) plead (**für** for); **auf Freispruch p~** (*Jur*) ask for an acquittal
Plädoyer /plɛdo̯a'je:/ *nt* **-s,-s** (*Jur*) closing speech; (*fig*) plea
Plage *f* **-,-n** [hard] labour; (*Mühe*) trouble; (*Belästigung*) nuisance. **p~n** *vt* torment, plague; (*bedrängen*) pester; **sich p~n** struggle
Plakat *nt* **-[e]s,-e** poster
Plakette *f* **-,-n** badge
Plan *m* **-[e]s,⸚e** plan
Plane *f* **-,-n** tarpaulin; (*Boden-*) groundsheet
planen *vt/i* (*haben*) plan
Planet *m* **-en,-en** planet
planier|en *vt* level. **P~raupe** *f* bulldozer
Planke *f* **-,-n** plank
plan|los *adj* unsystematic. **p~mäßig** *adj* systematic; (*Ankunft*) scheduled
Plansch|becken *nt* paddling pool. **p~en** *vi* (*haben*) splash about
Plantage /plan'ta:ʒə/ *f* **-,-n** plantation
Planung *f* **-** planning
plappern *vi* (*haben*) chatter ● *vt* talk (*Unsinn*)
plärren *vi* (*haben*) bawl
Plasma *nt* **-s** plasma
Plastik[1] *f* **-,-en** sculpture

Plast|ik² *nt* -s plastic. **p~isch** *adj* three-dimensional; (*formbar*) plastic; (*anschaulich*) graphic
Plateau /pla'to:/ *nt* **-s,-s** plateau
Platin *nt* -s platinum
platonisch *adj* platonic
plätschern *vi* (*haben*) splash; (*Bach:*) babble ●*vi* (*sein*) (*Bach:*) babble along
platt *adj* & *adv* flat. **P~** *nt* **-[s]** (*Lang*) Low German
Plättbrett *nt* ironing-board
Platte *f* -,-n slab; (*Druck-*) plate; (*Metall-, Glas-*) sheet; (*Fliese*) tile; (*Koch-*) hotplate; (*Tisch-*) top; (*Schall-*) record, disc; (*zum Servieren*) [flat] dish, platter; **kalte P~** assorted cold meats and cheeses *pl*
Plätt|eisen *nt* iron. **p~en** *vt/i* (*haben*) iron
Plattenspieler *m* record-player
Platt|form *f* -,-en platform. **P~füße** *mpl* flat feet
Platz *m* **-es,⸚e** place; (*von Häusern umgeben*) square; (*Sitz-*) seat; (*Sport-*) ground; (*Fußball-*) pitch; (*Tennis-*) court; (*Golf-*) course; (*freier Raum*) room, space; **P~ nehmen** take a seat; **P~ machen** make room; **vom P~ stellen** (*Sport*) send off. **P~anweiserin** *f* **-,-nen** usherette
Plätzchen *nt* **-s,-** spot; (*Culin*) biscuit
platzen *vi* (*sein*) burst; (*auf-*) split; (🄸: *scheitern*) fall through; (*Verlobung:*) be off
Platz|karte *f* seat reservation ticket. **P~mangel** *m* lack of space. **P~patrone** *f* blank. **P~verweis** *m* (*Sport*) sending off. **P~wunde** *f* laceration
Plauderei *f* **-,-en** chat
plaudern *vi* (*haben*) chat
plausibel *adj* plausible

pleite *adj* 🄸 **p~ sein** be broke: (*Firma:*) be bankrupt. **P~** *f* **-,-n** 🄸 bankruptcy; (*Misserfolg*) flop; **P~ gehen** *od* **machen** go bankrupt
plissiert *adj* [finely] pleated
Plomb|e *f* -,-n seal; (*Zahn-*) filling. **p~ieren** *vt* seal; fill (*Zahn*)
plötzlich *adj* sudden
plump *adj* plump; clumsy
plumpsen *vi* (*sein*) 🄸 fall
plündern *vt/i* (*haben*) loot
Plunderstück *nt* Danish pastry
Plural *m* **-s,-e** plural
plus *adv, conj* & *prep* (+ *dat*) plus. **P~** *nt* - surplus; (*Gewinn*) profit (*Vorteil*) advantage, plus. **P~punkt** *m* (*Sport*) point; (*fig*) plus
Po *m* **-s,-s** 🄸 bottom
Pöbel *m* -s mob, rabble. **p~haft** *adj* loutish
pochen *vi* (*haben*) knock, (*Herz:*) pound; **p~ auf** (+ *acc*) (*fig*) insist on
pochieren /pɔ'ʃi:rən/ *vt* poach
Pocken *pl* smallpox *sg*
Podest *nt* **-[e]s,-e** rostrum
Podium *nt* **-s,-ien** platform; (*Podest*) rostrum
Poesie /poe'zi:/ *f* - poetry
poetisch *adj* poetic
Pointe /'po̯ɛ̃:tə/ *f* **-,-n** punchline (*of a joke*)
Pokal *m* **-s,-e** goblet; (*Sport*) cup
pökeln *vt* (*Culin*) salt
Poker *nt* -s poker
Pol *m* **-s,-e** pole. **p~ar** *adj* polar
Polarstern *m* pole-star
Pole *m*, **-n,-n** Pole. **P~n** *nt* **-s** Poland
Police /po'li:sə/ *f* **-,-n** policy
Polier *m* **-s,-e** foreman
polieren *vt* polish
Polin *f* **-,-nen** Pole

Politesse *f* -,-n [woman] traffic warden

Politik *f* - politics *sg*; (*Vorgehen, Maßnahme*) policy

Polit|iker(in) *m* -s,- (*f*, -,-nen) politician. **p~isch** *adj* political

Politur *f* -,-en polish

Polizei *f* - police *pl*. **p~lich** *adj* police ● *adv* by the police; (*sich anmelden*) with the police. **P~streife** *f* police patrol. **P~stunde** *f* closing time. **P~wache** *f* police station

Polizist *m* -en,-en policeman. **P~in** *f* -,-nen policewoman

Pollen *m* -s pollen

polnisch *adj* Polish

Polster *nt* -s,- pad; (*Kissen*) cushion; (*Möbel-*) upholstery. **p~n** *vt* pad; upholster (*Möbel*). **P~ung** *f* - padding; upholstery

Polter|abend *m* eve-of-wedding party. **p~n** *vi* (*haben*) thump bang

> **Polterabend** This is Germany's equivalent of pre-wedding stag and hen nights. The *Polterabend* is a party for family and friends of both bride and groom. It is held a few days before the wedding, and guests traditionally smash crockery to bring good luck to the happy couple.

Polyäthylen *nt* -s polythene

Polyester *m* -s polyester

Polyp *m* -en,-en polyp. **P~en** adenoids *pl*

Pommes frites /pɔm'fri:t/ *pl* chips; (*dünner*) French fries

Pomp *m* -s pomp

Pompon /põ'põ:/ *m* -s,-s pompon

pompös *adj* ostentatious

Pony[1] *nt* -s,-s pony

Pony[2] *m* -s,-s fringe

Pop *m* -[s] pop

Popo *m* -s,-s [I] bottom

populär *adj* popular

Pore *f* -,-n pore

Porno|grafie, **Pornographie** *f* - pornography. **p~grafisch**, **p~graphisch** *adj* pornographic

Porree *m* -s leeks *pl*

Portal *nt* -s,-e portal

Portemonnaie /pɔrtmɔ'ne:/ *nt* -s,-s purse

Portier /pɔr'tje:/ *m* -s,-s doorman, porter

Portion /-'tsjo:n/ *f* -,-en helping, portion

Portmonee *nt* -s,-s = Portemonnaie

Porto *nt* -s postage. **p~frei** *adv* post free, post paid

Porträ|t /pɔr'trɛ:/ *nt* -s,-s portrait. **p~tieren** *vt* paint a portrait of

Portugal *nt* -s Portugal

Portugies|e *m* -n,-n, **P~in** *f* -,-nen Portuguese. **p~isch** *adj* Portuguese

Portwein *m* port

Porzellan *nt* -s china, porcelain

Posaune *f* -,-n trombone

Position /-'tsjo:n/ *f* -,-en position

positiv *adj* positive. **P~** *nt* -s,-e (*Phot*) positive

Post *f* - post office; (*Briefe*) mail, post; **mit der P~** by post

postalisch *adj* postal

Post|amt *nt* post office. **P~anweisung** *f* postal money order. **P~bote** *m* postman

Posten *m* -s,- post; (*Wache*) sentry; (*Waren-*) batch; (*Rechnungs-*) item, entry

Poster *nt* & *m* -s,- poster

Postfach *nt* post-office *or* PO box

Post|karte *f* postcard. **p~lagernd** *adv* poste restante. **P~leit-**

zahl *f* postcode. **P~scheckkonto** *nt* ≈ National Girobank account. **P~stempel** *m* postmark

postum *adj* posthumous

post|wendend *adv* by return of post. **P~wertzeichen** *nt* [postage] stamp

Potenz *f* **-,-en** potency; (*Math & fig*) power

Pracht *f* **-** magnificence, splendour

prächtig *adj* magnificent; splendid

prachtvoll *adj* magnificent

Prädikat *nt* **-[e]s,-e** rating; (*Comm*) grade; (*Gram*) predicate

prägen *vt* stamp (**auf** + *acc* on); emboss (*Leder*); mint (*Münze*); coin (*Wort*); (*fig*) shape

prägnant *adj* succinct

prähistorisch *adj* prehistoric

prahl|en *vi* (*haben*) boast, brag (**mit** about)

Prakti|k *f* **-,-en** practice. **P~kant(in)** *m* **-en,-en** (*f* **-,-nen**) trainee

Prakti|kum *nt* **-s,-ka** practical training. **p~sch** *adj* practical; (*nützlich*) handy; (*tatsächlich*) virtual; **p~scher Arzt** general practitioner ● *adv* practically; virtually; (*in der Praxis*) in practice. **p~zieren** *vt/i* (*haben*) practise; (*anwenden*) put into practice; (🄸: *bekommen*) get

Praline *f* **-,-n** chocolate

prall *adj* bulging; (*dick*) plump; (*Sonne*) blazing ● *adv* **p~ gefüllt** full to bursting. **p~en** *vi* (*sein*) **p~ auf** (+ *acc*)/**gegen** collide with, hit; (*Sonne:*) blaze down on

Prämie /-i̯ə/ *f* **-,-n** premium; (*Preis*) award

präm[i]ieren *vt* award a prize to

Pranger *m* **-s,-** pillory

Pranke *f* **-,-n** paw

Präparat *nt* **-[e]s,-e** preparation

Präsens *nt* **-** (*Gram*) present

präsentieren *vt* present

Präsenz *f* **-** presence

Präservativ *nt* **-s,-e** condom

Präsident|(in) *m* **-en,-en** (*f* **-,-nen**) president. **P~schaft** *f* **-** presidency

Präsidium *nt* **-s** presidency; (*Gremium*) executive committee; (*Polizei-*) headquarters *pl*

prasseln *vi* (*haben*) (*Regen:*) beat down; (*Feuer:*) crackle

> *i* **Prater** Vienna's largest amusement park was a private game reserve for the Austrian royal family until 1766. The *Prater* is famous for its old-fashioned carousels. A *Riesenrad*, big wheel or Ferris wheel, with a diameter of 67 metres was built there for the World Exhibition of 1897.

Präteritum *nt* **-s** imperfect

Praxis *f* **-,-xen** practice; (*Erfahrung*) practical experience; (*Arzt-*) surgery; **in der P~** in practice

Präzedenzfall *m* precedent

präzis[e] *adj* precise

predig|en *vt/i* (*haben*) preach. **P~t** *f* **-,-en** sermon

Preis *m* **-es,-e** price; (*Belohnung*) prize. **P~ausschreiben** *nt* competition

Preiselbeere *f* (*Bot*) cowberry; (*Culin*) ≈ cranberry

preisen† *vt* praise

preisgeben† *vt sep* abandon (*dat* to); reveal (*Geheimnis*)

preis|gekrönt *adj* award-winning. **p~günstig** *adj* reasonably priced ● *adv* at a reasonable price. **P~lage** *f* price range. **p~lich** *adj* price ● *adv* in price. **P~richter** *m* judge. **P~schild** *nt* price-tag. **P~träger(in)** *m*(*f*) prize-winner.

P

p~wert *adj* reasonable

Prell|bock *m* buffers *pl*. **p~en** *vt* bounce; (*verletzen*) bruise; (ⓘ: *betrügen*) cheat. **P~ung** *f* **-,-en** bruise

Premiere /prəˈmi̯eːrə/ *f* **-,-n** première

Premierminister(in) /prəˈmi̯eː-/ *m*(*f*) Prime Minister

Presse *f* **-,-n** press. **p~n** *vt* press

Pressluftbohrer *m* pneumatic drill

Preuß|en *nt* **-s** Prussia. **p~isch** *adj* Prussian

prickeln *vi* (*haben*) tingle

Priester *m* **-s,-** priest

prima *inv adj* ⓘ first-class, first-rate; (*toll*) fantastic

primär *adj* primary

Primel *f* **-,-n** primula

primitiv *adj* primitive

Prinz *m* **-en,-en** prince. **P~essin** *f* **-,-nen** princess

Prinzip *nt* **-s,-ien** principle. **p~iell** *adj* (*Frage*) of principle ● *adv* on principle

Prise *f* **-,-n P~ Salz** pinch of salt

Prisma *nt* **-s,-men** prism

privat *adj* private, personal. **P~adresse** *f* home address. **p~isieren** *vt* privatize

Privileg *nt* **-[e]s,-ien** privilege. **p~iert** *adj* privileged

pro *prep* (+ *dat*) per. **Pro** *nt* **- das Pro und Kontra** the pros and cons *pl*

Probe *f* **-,-n** test, trial; (*Menge, Muster*) sample; (*Theat*) rehearsal; **auf die P~ stellen** put to the test; **ein Auto P~ fahren** test-drive a car. **p~n** *vt/i* (*haben*) (*Theat*) rehearse. **p~weise** *adv* on a trial basis. **P~zeit** *f* probationary period

probieren *vt/i* (*haben*) try; (*kosten*) taste; (*proben*) rehearse

Problem *nt* **-s,-e** problem. **p~atisch** *adj* problematic

problemlos *adj* problem-free ● *adv* without any problems

Produkt *nt* **-[e]s,-e** product

Produk|tion /-ˈtsi̯oːn/ *f* **-,-en** production. **p~tiv** *adj* productive

Produ|zent *m* **-en,-en** producer. **p~zieren** *vt* produce

Professor *m* **-s,-en** professor

Profi *m* **-s,-s** (*Sport*) professional

Profil *nt* **-s,-e** profile; (*Reifen-*) tread; (*fig*) image

Profit *m* **-[e]s,-e** profit. **p~ieren** *vi* (*haben*) profit (**von** from)

Prognose *f* **-,-n** forecast; (*Med*) prognosis

Programm *nt* **-s,-e** programme; (*Computer-*) program; (*TV*) channel; (*Comm: Sortiment*) range. **p~ieren** *vt/i* (*haben*) (*Computer*) program. **P~ierer(in)** *m* **-s,-** (*f* **-,-nen**) [computer] programmer

Projekt *nt* **-[e]s,-e** project

Projektor *m* **-s,-en** projector

Prolet *m* **-en,-en** boor. **P~ariat** *nt* **-[e]s** proletariat

Prolog *m* **-s,-e** prologue

Promenade *f* **-,-n** promenade

Promille *pl* ⓘ alcohol level *sg* in the blood; **zu viel P~ haben** ⓘ be over the limit

Prominenz *f* **-** prominent figures *pl*

Promiskuität *f* **-** promiscuity

promovieren *vi* (*haben*) obtain one's doctorate

prompt *adj* prompt

Pronomen *nt* **-s,-** pronoun

Propaganda *f* **-** propaganda; (*Reklame*) publicity

Propeller *m* **-s,-** propeller

Prophet *m* **-en,-en** prophet

prophezei|en *vt* prophesy.

P~ung *f* -,-en prophecy
Proportion /-'tsi̯o:n/ *f* -,-en proportion
Prosa *f* - prose
prosit *int* cheers!
Prospekt *m* -[e]s,-e brochure; (*Comm*) prospectus
prost *int* cheers!
Prostitu|ierte *f* -n,-n prostitute. **P~tion** *f* - prostitution
Protest *m* -[e]s,-e protest
Protestant|(in) *m* -en,-en (*f* -,-nen) (*Relig*) Protestant. **p~isch** *adj* (*Relig*) Protestant
protestieren *vi* (*haben*) protest
Prothese *f* -,-n artificial limb; (*Zahn-*) denture
Protokoll *nt* -s,-e record; (*Sitzungs-*) minutes *pl*; (*diplomatisches*) protocol
protz|en *vi* (*haben*) show off (**mit** etw sth). **p~ig** *adj* ostentatious
Proviant *m* -s provisions *pl*
Provinz *f* -,-en province
Provision *f* -,-en (*Comm*) commission
provisorisch *adj* provisional, temporary
Provokation /-'tsi̯o:n/ *f* -,-en provocation
provozieren *vt* provoke
Prozedur *f* -,-en [lengthy] business
Prozent *nt* -[e]s,-e & - per cent; 5 P~ 5 per cent. **P~satz** *m* percentage. **p~ual** *adj* percentage
Prozess *m* -es,-e process; (*Jur*) lawsuit; (*Kriminal-*) trial
Prozession *f* -,-en procession
Prozessor *m* -s,-en processor
prüde *adj* prudish
prüf|en *vt* test/(*über-*) check (**auf** + *acc* for); audit (*Bücher*); (*Sch*) examine; **p~ender Blick** searching look. **P~er** *m* -s,- inspector; (*Buch-*) auditor; (*Sch*) examiner. **P~ling** *m* -s,-e examination candidate. **P~ung** *f* -,-en examination; (*Test*) test; (*Bücher-*) audit; (*fig*) trial
Prügel *m* -s,- cudgel; **P~** *pl* hiding *sg*, beating *sg*. **P~ei** *f* -,-en brawl, fight. **p~n** *vt* beat, thrash
Prunk *m* -[e]s magnificence, splendour
Psalm *m* -s,-en psalm
Pseudonym *nt* -s,-e pseudonym
pst *int* shush!
Psychi|ater *m* -s,- psychiatrist. **P~atrie** *f* - psychiatry. **p~atrisch** *adj* psychiatric
psychisch *adj* psychological
Psycho|analyse *f* psychoanalysis. **P~loge** *m* -n,-n psychologist. **P~logie** *f* - psychology. **p~logisch** *adj* psychological
Pubertät *f* - puberty
Publi|kum *nt* -s public; (*Zuhörer*) audience; (*Zuschauer*) spectators *pl*. **p~zieren** *vt* publish
Pudding *m* -s,-s blancmange; (*im Wasserbad gekocht*) pudding
Pudel *m* -s,- poodle
Puder *m* & [T] *nt* -s,- powder. **P~dose** *f* [powder] compact. **p~n** *vt* powder. **P~zucker** *m* icing sugar
Puff *m* & *nt* -s,-s [x] brothel
Puffer *m* -s,- (*Rail*) buffer; (*Culin*) pancake. **P~zone** *f* buffer zone
Pull|i *m* -s,-s jumper. **P~over** *m* -s,- jumper; (*Herren-*) pullover
Puls *m* -es pulse. **P~ader** *f* artery
Pult *nt* -[e]s,-e desk
Pulver *nt* -s,- powder. **p~ig** *adj* powdery
Pulverkaffee *m* instant coffee
pummelig *adj* [T] chubby
Pumpe *f* -,-n pump. **p~n** *vt/i* (*haben*) pump; ([T]: *leihen*) lend;

[sich (*dat*)] **etw p~n** ([I]: *borgen*) borrow sth

Pumps /pœmps/ *pl* court shoes

Punkt *m* **-[e]s,-e** dot; (*Textiles*) spot; (*Geometry, Sport & fig*) point; (*Gram*) full stop, period; **P~ sechs Uhr** at six o'clock sharp

pünktlich *adj* punctual. **P~keit** *f* **-** punctuality

Pupille *f* **-,-n** (*Anat*) pupil

Puppe *f* **-,-n** doll; (*Marionette*) puppet; (*Schaufenster-, Schneider-*) dummy; (*Zool*) chrysalis

pur *adj* pure; ([I]: *bloß*) sheer

Püree *nt* **-s,-s** purée; (*Kartoffel-*) mashed potatoes *pl*

purpurrot *adj* crimson

Purzel|baum *m* [I] somersault. **p~n** *vi* (*sein*) [I] tumble

Puste *f* **-** [I] breath. **p~n** *vt/i* (*haben*) [I] blow

Pute *f* **-,-n** turkey

Putsch *m* **-[e]s,-e** coup

Putz *m* **-es** plaster; (*Staat*) finery. **p~en** *vt* clean; (*Aust*) dry-clean; (*zieren*) adorn; **sich p~en** dress up; **sich** (*dat*) **die Zähne/Nase p~en** clean one's teeth/blow one's nose. **P~frau** *f* cleaner, charwoman. **p~ig** *adj* [I] amusing, cute; (*seltsam*) odd

Puzzlespiel /'pazl-/ *nt* jigsaw

Pyramide *f* **-,-n** pyramid

Qq

Quacksalber *m* **-s,-** quack

Quadrat *nt* **-[e]s,-e** square. **q~isch** *adj* square

quaken *vi* (*haben*) quack; (*Frosch:*) croak

Quäker(in) *m* **-s,-** (*f* **-,-nen**) Quaker

Qual *f* **-,-en** torment; (*Schmerz*) agony

quälen *vt* torment; (*foltern*) torture; (*bedrängen*) pester; **sich q~** torment oneself; (*leiden*) suffer; (*sich mühen*) struggle

Quälerei *f* **-,-en** torture

Qualifi|kation /-'tsi̯o:n/ *f* **-,-en** qualification. **q~zieren** *vt* qualify. **q~ziert** *adj* qualified; (*fähig*) competent; (*Arbeit*) skilled

Qualität *f* **-,-en** quality

Qualle *f* **-,-n** jellyfish

Qualm *m* **-s** [thick] smoke

qualvoll *adj* agonizing

Quantum *nt* **-s,-ten** quantity; (*Anteil*) share, quota

Quarantäne *f* **-** quarantine

Quark *m* **-s** quark, ≈ curd cheese

Quartal *nt* **-s,-e** quarter

Quartett *nt* **-[e]s,-e** quartet

Quartier *nt* **-s,-e** accommodation; (*Mil*) quarters *pl*

Quarz *m* **-es** quartz

quasseln *vi* (*haben*) [I] jabber

Quaste *f* **-,-n** tassel

Quatsch *m* **-[e]s** [I] nonsense, rubbish; **Q~ machen** (*Unfug machen*) fool around; (*etw falsch machen*) do a silly thing. **q~en** [I] *vi* (*haben*) talk; (*Wasser, Schlamm:*) squelch ● *vt* talk

Quecksilber *nt* mercury

Quelle *f* **-,-n** spring; (*Fluss- & fig*) source

quengeln *vi* [I] whine

quer *adv* across, crosswise; (*schräg*) diagonally; **q~ gestreift** horizontally striped

Quere *f* **- der Q~ nach** across, crosswise; **jdm in die Q~ kommen** get in s.o.'s way

Quer|latte *f* crossbar. **Q~schiff** *nt* transept. **Q~schnitt** *m* cross-section. **q~schnittsgelähmt** *adj* paraplegic. **Q~straße** *f* side-street. **Q~verweis** *m* cross-reference
quetschen *vt* squash; (*drücken*) squeeze; (*zerdrücken*) crush; (*Culin*) mash; **sich q~ in** (+ *acc*) squeeze into
Queue /kø:/ *nt* **-s,-s** cue
quieken *vi* (*haben*) squeal; (*Maus:*) squeak
quietschen *vi* (*haben*) squeal; (*Tür, Dielen:*) creak
Quintett *nt* **-[e]s,-e** quintet
quirlen *vt* mix
Quitte *f* **-,-n** quince
quittieren *vt* receipt (*Rechnung*); sign for (*Geldsumme, Sendung*); **den Dienst q~** resign
Quittung *f* **-,-en** receipt
Quiz /kvɪs/ *nt* **-,-** quiz
Quote *f* **-,-n** proportion

Rr

Rabatt *m* **-[e]s,-e** discount
Rabatte *f* **-,-n** (*Horticulture*) border
Rabattmarke *f* trading stamp
Rabbiner *m* **-s,-** rabbi
Rabe *m* **-n,-n** raven
Rache *f* **-** revenge, vengeance
Rachen *m* **-s,-** pharynx
rächen *vt* avenge; **sich r~** take revenge (**an** + *dat* on); (*Fehler:*) cost s.o. dear
Rad *nt* **-[e]s,¨er** wheel; (*Fahr-*) bicycle, [!] bike; **Rad fahren** cycle
Radar *m* & *nt* **-s** radar
Radau *m* **-s** [!] din, racket
radeln *vi* (*sein*) [!] cycle
Rädelsführer *m* ringleader
radfahr|en* *vi sep* (*sein*) **Rad fahren**, *s.* **Rad. R~er(in)** *m*(*f*) **-s,-** (*f* **-,-nen**) cyclist
radier|en *vt/i* (*haben*) rub out; (*Kunst*) etch. **R~gummi** *m* eraser, rubber. **R~ung** *f* **-,-en** etching
Radieschen /-ˈdi:sçən/ *nt* **-s,-** radish
radikal *adj* radical, drastic
Radio *nt* **-s,-s** radio
radioaktiv *adj* radioactive. **R~ität** *f* **-** radioactivity
Radius *m* **-,-ien** radius
Rad|kappe *f* hub-cap. **R~ler** *m* **-s,-** cyclist; (*Getränk*) shandy
raffen *vt* grab; (*kräuseln*) gather; (*kürzen*) condense
Raffin|ade *f* **-** refined sugar. **R~erie** *f* **-,-n** refinery. **R~esse** *f* **-,-n** refinement; (*Schlauheit*) cunning. **r~iert** *adj* ingenious; (*durchtrieben*) crafty
ragen *vi* (*haben*) rise [up]
Rahm *m* **-s** (*SGer*) cream
rahmen *vt* frame. **R~** *m* **-s,-** frame; (*fig*) framework; (*Grenze*) limits *pl*; (*einer Feier*) setting
Rakete *f* **-,-n** rocket; (*Mil*) missile
Rallye /ˈrɛli/ *nt* **-s,-s** rally
rammen *vt* ram
Rampe *f* **-,-n** ramp; (*Theat*) front of the stage
Ramsch *m* **-[e]s** junk
ran *adv* = **heran**
Rand *m* **-[e]s,¨er** edge; (*Teller-, Gläser-, Brillen-*) rim; (*Zier-*) border, edging; (*Brief-*) margin; (*Stadt-*) outskirts *pl*; (*Ring*) ring
randalieren *vi* (*haben*) rampage
Randstreifen *m* (*Auto*) hard shoulder
Rang *m* **-[e]s,¨e** rank; (*Theat*) tier;

erster/zweiter R~ (*Theat*) dress/upper circle; **ersten R~es** first-class

rangieren /raŋ'ʒi:rən/ *vt* shunt ●*vi* (*haben*) rank (**vor** + *dat* before)

Rangordnung *f* order of importance; (*Hierarchie*) hierarchy

Ranke *f* **-,-n** tendril; (*Trieb*) shoot

ranken (sich) *vr* (*Bot*) trail; (*in die Höhe*) climb

Ranzen *m* **-s,-** (*Sch*) satchel

ranzig *adj* rancid

Rappe *m* **-n,-n** black horse

Raps *m* **-es** (*Bot*) rape

rar *adj* rare; **er macht sich rar** [!] we don't see much of him. **R~ität** *f* **-,-en** rarity

rasant *adj* fast; (*schnittig, schick*) stylish

rasch *adj* quick

rascheln *vi* (*haben*) rustle

Rasen *m* **-s,-** lawn

rasen *vi* (*sein*) tear [along]; (*Puls:*) race; (*Zeit:*) fly; **gegen eine Mauer r~** career into a wall ●*vi* (*haben*) rave; (*Sturm:*) rage. **r~d** *adj* furious; (*tobend*) raving; (*Sturm, Durst*) raging; (*Schmerz*) excruciating; (*Beifall*) tumultuous

Rasenmäher *m* lawn-mower

Rasier|apparat *m* razor. **r~en** *vt* shave; **sich r~en** shave. **R~klinge** *f* razor blade. **R~wasser** *nt* aftershave [lotion]

Raspel *f* **-,-n** rasp; (*Culin*) grater. **r~n** *vt* grate

Rasse *f* **-,-n** race. **R~hund** *m* pedigree dog

Rassel *f* **-,-n** rattle. **r~n** *vi* (*haben*) rattle; (*Schlüssel:*) jangle; (*Kette:*) clank

Rassendiskriminierung *f* racial discrimination

Rassepferd *nt* thoroughbred. **rassisch** *adj* racial

Rassis|mus *m* **-** racism. **r~tisch** *adj* racist

Rast *f* **-,-en** rest. **R~platz** *m* picnic area. **R~stätte** *f* motorway restaurant [and services]

Rasur *f* **-,-en** shave

Rat *m* **-[e]s** [piece of] advice; **sich** (*dat*) **keinen Rat wissen** not know what to do; **zu Rat[e] ziehen** = **zurate ziehen**, *s.* **zurate**

Rate *f* **-,-n** instalment

raten† *vt* guess; (*empfehlen*) advise ●*vi* (*haben*) guess; **jdm r~** advise s.o.

Ratenzahlung *f* payment by instalments

Rat|geber *m* **-s,-** adviser; (*Buch*) guide. **R~haus** *nt* town hall

ratifizier|en *vt* ratify. **R~ung** *f* **-,-en** ratification

Ration /ra'tsi̯o:n/ *f* **-,-en** ration. **r~ell** *adj* efficient. **r~ieren** *vt* ration

rat|los *adj* helpless; **r~los sein** not know what to do. **r~sam** *pred adj* advisable; prudent. **R~schlag** *m* piece of advice; **R~schläge** advice *sg*

Rätsel *nt* **-s,-** riddle; (*Kreuzwort-*) puzzle; (*Geheimnis*) mystery. **r~haft** *adj* puzzling, mysterious. **r~n** *vi* (*haben*) puzzle

Ratte *f* **-,-n** rat

rau *adj* rough; (*unfreundlich*) gruff; (*Klima*) harsh, raw; (*heiser*) husky; (*Hals*) sore

Raub *m* **-[e]s** robbery; (*Menschen-*) abduction; (*Beute*) loot, booty. **r~en** *vt* steal; abduct (*Menschen*)

Räuber *m* **-s,-** robber

Raub|mord *m* robbery with murder. **R~tier** *nt* predator. **R~vogel** *m* bird of prey

Rauch *m* **-[e]s** smoke. **r~en** *vt/i* (*haben*) smoke. **R~en** *nt* **-s** smok-

r

ing; '**R~en verboten**' 'no smoking'. **R~er** *m* **-s**,-smoker
Räucher|lachs *m* smoked salmon. **r~n** *vt* (*Culin*) smoke
rauf *adv* = **herauf, hinauf**
rauf|en *vt* pull ● *vr/i* (*haben*) **[sich] r~en** fight. **R~erei** *f* -,-en fight
rauh* *adj* = **rau**
Raum *m* **-[e]s, Räume** room; (*Gebiet*) area; (*Welt-*) space
räumen *vt* clear; vacate (*Wohnung*); evacuate (*Gebäude, Gebiet*, (*Mil*) *Stellung*); (*bringen*) put (**in**/**auf** + *acc* into/on); (*holen*) get (**aus** out of)
Raum|fahrer *m* astronaut. **R~fahrt** *f* space travel. **R~inhalt** *m* volume
räumlich *adj* spatial
Raum|pflegerin *f* cleaner. **R~schiff** *nt* spaceship
Räumung *f* - clearing; vacating; evacuation. **R~sverkauf** *m* clearance/closing-down sale
Raupe *f* -,-n caterpillar
raus *adv* = **heraus, hinaus**
Rausch *m* **-[e]s, Räusche** intoxication; (*fig*) exhilaration; **einen R~haben** be drunk
rauschen *vi* (*haben*) (*Wasser, Wind:*) rush; (*Bäume Blätter:*) rustle ● *vi* ⊡ (*sein*) rush [along]
Rauschgift *nt* [narcotic] drug; (*coll*) drugs *pl*. **R~süchtige(r)** *m/f* drug addict
räuspern (sich) *vr* clear one's throat
rausschmeißen† *vt sep* ⊡ throw out; (*entlassen*) sack
Raute *f* -,-n diamond
Razzia *f* -,-ien [police] raid
Reagenzglas *nt* test-tube
reagieren *vi* (*haben*) react (**auf** + *acc* to)
Reaktion /-'tsjo:n/ *f* -,-en reaction. **r~är** *adj* reactionary
Reaktor *m* **-s,-en** reactor
realisieren *vt* realize
Realis|mus *m* - realism. **R~t** *m* -en,-en realist. **r~tisch** *adj* realistic
Realität *f* -,-en reality
Realschule *f* ≈ secondary modern school
Rebe *f* -,-n vine
Rebell *m* **-en,-en** rebel. **r~ieren** *vi* (*haben*) rebel. **R~ion** *f* -,-en rebellion
rebellisch *adj* rebellious
Rebhuhn *nt* partridge
Rebstock *m* vine
Rechen *m* **-s,-** rake
Rechen|aufgabe *f* arithmetical problem; (*Sch*) sum. **R~maschine** *f* calculator
recherchieren /reʃɛr'ʃi:rən/ *vt/i* (*haben*) investigate; (*Journalism*) research
rechnen *vi* (*haben*) do arithmetic; (*schätzen*) reckon; (*zählen*) count (**zu** among; **auf** + *acc* on); **r~ mit** reckon with; (*erwarten*) expect ● *vt* calculate, work out; (*fig*) count (**zu** among). **R~** *nt* **-s** arithmetic
Rechner *m* **-s,-** calculator; (*Computer*) computer
Rechnung *f* -,-en bill; (*Comm*) invoice; (*Berechnung*) calculation; **R~ führen über** (+ *acc*) keep account of. **R~sjahr** *nt* financial year. **R~sprüfer** *m* auditor
Recht *nt* **-[e]s,-e** law; (*Berechtigung*) right (**auf** + *acc* to); **im R~ sein** be in the right; **R~ haben/behalten** be right; **R~ bekommen** be proved right; **jdm R~ geben** agree with s.o.; **mit** *od* **zu R~** rightly
recht *adj* right; (*wirklich*) real; **ich habe keine r~e Lust** I don't really feel like it; **es jdm r~ machen**

please s.o.; **jdm r~ sein** be all right with s.o. **r~ vielen Dank** many thanks

Recht|e *f* **-n,-[n]** right side; (*Hand*) right hand; (*Boxen*) right; **die R~e** (*Pol*) the right; **zu meiner R~en** on my right. **r~e(r,s)** *adj* right; (*Pol*) right-wing; **r~e Masche** plain stitch. **R~e(r)** *m/f* **der/die R~e** the right man/woman; **R~e(s)** *nt* **das R~e** the right thing; **etwas R~es lernen** learn something useful; **nach dem R~en sehen** see that everything is all right

Rechteck *nt* **-[e]s,-e** rectangle. **r~ig** *adj* rectangular

rechtfertigen *vt* justify; **sich r~en** justify oneself

recht|haberisch *adj* opinionated. **r~lich** *adj* legal. **r~mäßig** *adj* legitimate

rechts *adv* on the right; (*bei Stoff*) on the right side; **von/nach r~** from/to the right; **zwei r~, zwei links stricken** knit two, purl two. **R~anwalt** *m*, **R~anwältin** *f* lawyer

Rechtschreib|programm *nt* spell checker. **R~ung** *f* **-** spelling

Rechts|händer(in) *m* **-s,-** (*f* **-,-nen**) right-hander. **r~händig** *adj & adv* right-handed. **r~kräftig** *adj* legal. **R~streit** *m* law suit. **R~verkehr** *m* driving on the right. **r~widrig** *adj* illegal. **R~wissenschaft** *f* jurisprudence

rechtzeitig *adj & adv* in time

Reck *nt* **-[e]s,-e** horizontal bar

recken *vt* stretch

Redakteur /redak'tø:ɐ̯/ *m* **-s,-e** editor; (*Radio, TV*) producer

Redaktion /-'tsi̯o:n/ *f* **-,-en** editing; (*Radio, TV*) production; (*Abteilung*) editorial/production department

Rede *f* **-,-n** speech; **zur R~stellen** demand an explanation from; **nicht der R~ wert** not worth mentioning

reden *vi* (*haben*) talk (**von** about; **mit** to); (*eine Rede halten*) speak ● *vt* talk; speak (*Wahrheit*). **R~sart** *f* saying

Redewendung *f* idiom

redigieren *vt* edit

Redner *m* **-s,-** speaker

reduzieren *vt* reduce

Reeder *m* **-s,-** shipowner. **R~ei** *f* **-,-en** shipping company

Refer|at *nt* **-[e]s,-e** report; (*Abhandlung*) paper; (*Abteilung*) section. **R~ent(in)** *m* **-en,-en** (*f* **-,-nen**) speaker; (*Sachbearbeiter*) expert. **R~enz** *f* **-,-en** reference

Reflex *m* **-es,-e** reflex; (*Widerschein*) reflection. **R~ion** *f* **-,-en** reflection. **r~iv** *adj* reflexive

Reform *f* **-,-en** reform. **R~ation** *f* **-** (*Relig*) Reformation

Reform|haus *nt* health-food shop. **r~ieren** *vt* reform

Refrain /rə'frɛ̃:/ *m* **-s,-s** refrain

Regal *nt* **-s,-e** [set of] shelves *pl*

Regatta *f* **-,-ten** regatta

rege *adj* active; (*lebhaft*) lively; (*geistig*) alert; (*Handel*) brisk

Regel *f* **-,-n** rule; (*Monats-*) period. **r~mäßig** *adj* regular. **r~n** *vt* regulate; direct (*Verkehr*); (*erledigen*) settle. **r~recht** *adj* real, proper ● *adv* really. **R~ung** *f* **-,-en** regulation; settlement

regen *vt* move; **sich r~** move; (*wach werden*) stir

Regen *m* **-s,-** rain. **R~bogen** *m* rainbow. **R~bogenhaut** *f* iris

Regener|ation /-'tsi̯o:n/ *f* **-** regeneration. **r~ieren** *vt* regenerate

Regen|mantel *m* raincoat.

r

R~schirm *m* umbrella. **R~tag** *m* rainy day. **R~wetter** *nt* wet weather. **R~wurm** *m* earthworm

Regie /re'ʒi:/ *f* - direction; **R~ führen** direct

regier|en *vt/i* (*haben*) govern, rule; (*Monarch:*) reign [over]; (*Gram*) take. **R~ung** *f* -,-**en** government; (*Herrschaft*) rule; (*eines Monarchen*) reign

Regiment *nt* -**[e]s,-er** regiment

Region *f* -,-**en** region. **r~al** *adj* regional

Regisseur /reʒɪ'sø:ɐ̯/ *m* -**s,-e** director

Register *nt* -**s,-** register; (*Inhaltsverzeichnis*) index; (*Orgel-*) stop

Regler *m* -**s,-** regulator

reglos *adj & adv* motionless

regn|en *vi* (*haben*) rain; **es r~et** it is raining. **r~erisch** *adj* rainy

regul|är *adj* normal; (*rechtmäßig*) legitimate. **r~ieren** *vt* regulate

Regung *f* -,-**en** movement; (*Gefühls-*) emotion. **r~slos** *adj & adv* motionless

Reh *nt* -**[e]s,-e** roe-deer; (*Culin*) venison

Rehbock *m* roebuck

reib|en† *vt* rub; (*Culin*) grate ● *vi* (*haben*) rub. **R~ung** *f* - friction. **r~ungslos** *adj* (*fig*) smooth

reich *adj* rich (**an** + *dat* in)

Reich *nt* -**[e]s,-e** empire; (*König-*) kingdom; (*Bereich*) realm

Reiche(r) *m/f* rich man/woman; **die R~en** the rich *pl*

reichen *vt* hand; (*anbieten*) offer ● *vi* (*haben*) be enough; (*in der Länge*) be long enough; **r~ bis zu** reach [up to]; (*sich erstrecken*) extend to; **mit dem Geld r~** have enough money

reich|haltig *adj* extensive, large (*Mahlzeit*) substantial. **r~lich** *adj* ample: (*Vorrat*) abundant. **R~tum** *m* -**s,-tümer** wealth (**an** + *dat* of); **R~tümer** riches. **R~weite** *f* reach; (*Techn, Mil*) range

> *i* **Reichstag** This historic building in the centre of Berlin was Germany's parliament building until 1945. It became the seat of the enlarged ▸**BUNDESTAG** in 1999. The refurbishment of the *Reichstag* in the 1990s included the building of a glass cupola, with a walkway and viewing platform providing spectacular views over the city.

Reif *m* -**[e]s** [hoar-]frost

reif *adj* ripe; (*fig*) mature; **r~ für** ready for. **r~en** *vi* (*sein*) ripen; (*Wein, Käse & fig*) mature

Reifen *m* -**s,-** hoop; (*Arm-*) bangle; (*Auto-*) tyre. **R~druck** *m* tyre pressure. **R~panne** *f* puncture, flat tyre

reiflich *adj* careful

Reihe *f* -,-**n** row; (*Anzahl & Math*) series; **der R~ nach** in turn; **wer ist an der R~?** whose turn is it? **r~n (sich)** *vr* **sich r~n an** (+ *acc*) follow. **R~nfolge** *f* order. **R~nhaus** *nt* terraced house

Reiher *m* -**s,-** heron

Reim *m* -**[e]s,-e** rhyme. **r~en** *vt* rhyme; **sich r~en** rhyme

rein[1] *adj* pure; (*sauber*) clean; (*Unsinn, Dummheit*) sheer; **ins R~e (r~e) schreiben** make a fair copy of

rein[2] *adv* = **herein, hinein**

Reineclaude /rɛ:nə'klo:də/ *f* -,-**n** greengage

Reinfall *m* [!] let-down; (*Misserfolg*) flop

Rein|gewinn *m* net profit. **R~heit** *f* - purity

reinig|en *vt* clean; (*chemisch*) dry-clean. **R~ung** *f* **-,-en** cleaning; (*chemische*) dry-cleaning; (*Geschäft*) dry cleaner's

reinlegen *vt sep* put in; [!] dupe; (*betrügen*) take for a ride

reinlich *adj* clean. **R~keit** *f* **-** cleanliness

Reis *m* **-es** rice

Reise *f* **-,-n** journey; (*See-*) voyage; (*Urlaubs-, Geschäfts-*) trip. **R~andenken** *nt* souvenir. **R~büro** *nt* travel agency. **R~bus** *m* coach. **R~führer** *m* tourist guide; (*Buch*) guide. **R~gesellschaft** *f* tourist group. **R~leiter(in)** *m*(*f*) courier. **r~n** *vi* (*sein*) travel. **R~nde(r)** *m*/*f* traveller. **R~pass** *m* passport. **R~scheck** *m* traveller's cheque. **R~veranstalter** *m* **-s,-** tour operator. **R~ziel** *nt* destination

Reisig *nt* **-s** brushwood

Reißaus *m* **R~ nehmen** [!] run away

Reißbrett *nt* drawing-board

reißen† *vt* tear; (*weg-*) snatch; (*töten*) kill; **Witze r~** crack jokes; **an sich** (*acc*) **r~**snatch; seize (*Macht*); **sich r~ um** [!] fight for ● *vi* (*sein*) tear; (*Seil, Faden:*) break ● *vi* (*haben*) **r~ an** (+ *dat*) pull at

Reißer *m* **-s,-** [!] thriller; (*Erfolg*) big hit

Reiß|nagel *m* = **R~zwecke. R~verschluss** *m* zip [fastener]. **R~wolf** *m* shredder. **R~zwecke** *f* **-,-n** drawing-pin

reit|en† *vt/i* (*sein*) ride. **R~er(in)** *m* **-s,-** (*f* **-,-nen**) rider. **R~hose** *f* riding breeches *pl*. **R~pferd** *nt* saddle-horse. **R~weg** *m* bridle-path

Reiz *m* **-es,-e** stimulus; (*Anziehungskraft*) attraction, appeal; (*Charme*) charm. **r~bar** *adj* irritable. **R~barkeit** *f* **-** irratability. **r~en** *vt* provoke; (*Med*) irritate; (*interessieren, locken*) appeal to, attract; arouse (*Neugier*); (*beim Kartenspiel*) bid. **R~ung** *f* **-,-en** (*Med*) irritation. **r~voll** *adj* attractive

rekeln (sich) *vr* [!] stretch

Reklamation /-ˈtsi̯oːn/ *f* **-,-en** (*Comm*) complaint

Reklam|e *f* **-,-n** advertising, publicity; (*Anzeige*) advertisement; (*TV, Radio*) commercial; **R~e machen** advertise (**für etw** sth). **r~ieren** *vt* complain about; (*fordern*) claim ● *vi* (*haben*) complain

Rekord *m* **-[e]s,-e** record

Rekrut *m* **-en,-en** recruit

Rek|tor *m* **-s,-en** (*Sch*) head[master]; (*Univ*) vice-chancellor. **R~torin** *f* **-,-nen** head, headmistress; vice-chancellor

Relais /rəˈlɛː/ *nt* **-,-** /-s,-s/ (*Electr*) relay

relativ *adj* relative

Religi|on *f* **-,-en** religion; (*Sch*) religious education. **r~ös** *adj* religious

Reling *f* **-,-s** (*Naut*) rail

Reliquie /reˈliːkvi̯ə/ *f* **-,-n** relic

rempeln *vt* jostle; (*stoßen*) push

Reneklode *f* **-,-n** greengage

Rennbahn *f* race-track; (*Pferde-*) racecourse. **R~boot** *nt* speed-boat. **r~en**† *vi* (*sein*) run; **um die Wette r~en** have a race. **R~en** *nt* **-s,-** race. **R~pferd** *nt* racehorse. **R~sport** *m* racing. **R~wagen** *m* racing car

renommiert *adj* renowned; (*Hotel, Firma*) of repute

renovier|en *vt* renovate; redecorate (*Zimmer*). **R~ung** *f* **-** renovation; redecoration

rentabel *adj* profitable

Rente *f* **-,-n** pension; **in R~ gehen** [!] retire. **R~nversicherung** *f* pension scheme

Rentier *nt* reindeer
rentieren (sich) *vr* be profitable; (*sich lohnen*) be worth while
Rentner(in) *m* **-s,-** (*f* **-,-nen**) [old-age] pensioner
Reparatur *f* **-,-en** repair. **R~werkstatt** *f* repair workshop; (*Auto*) garage
reparieren *vt* repair, mend
Reportage /-'ta:ʒə/ *f* **-,-n** report
Reporter(in) *m* **-s,-** (*f* **-,-nen**) reporter
repräsentativ *adj* representative (für of); (*eindrucksvoll*) imposing
Reprodu|ktion /-'tsi̯o:n/ *f* **-,-en** reproduction. **r~zieren** *vt* reproduce
Reptil *nt* **-s,-ien** reptile
Republik *f* **-,-en** republic. **r~anisch** *adj* republican
Requisiten *pl* (*Theat*) properties, ▣ props
Reservat *nt* **-[e]s,-e** reservation
Reserve *f* **-,-n** reserve; (*Mil, Sport*) reserves *pl*. **R~rad** *nt* spare wheel
reservier|en *vt* reserve; **r~en** lassen book. **r~t** *adj* reserved. **R~ung** *f* **-,-en** reservation
Reservoir /rezɛr'vo̯a:ɐ̯/ *nt* **-s,-s** reservoir
Residenz *f* **-,-en** residence
Resign|ation /-'tsi̯o:n/ *f* **-** resignation. **r~ieren** *vi* (*haben*) (*fig*) give up. **r~iert** *adj* resigned
resolut *adj* resolute
Resonanz *f* **-,-en** resonanance
Respekt /-sp-, -ʃp-/ *m* **-[e]s** respect (vor + *dat* for). **r~ieren** *vt* respect
respektlos *adj* disrespectful
Ressort /rɛ'so:ɐ̯/ *nt* **-s,-s** department
Rest *m* **-[e]s,-e** remainder, rest; **R~e** remains; (*Essens-*) leftovers
Restaurant /rɛsto'rã:/ *nt* **-s,-s** restaurant
Restaur|ation /rɛstau̯ra'tsi̯o:n/ *f* **-** restoration. **r~ieren** *vt* restore
Rest|betrag *m* balance. **r~lich** *adj* remaining
Resultat *nt* **-[e]s,-e** result
rett|en *vt* save (**vor** + *dat* from); (*aus Gefahr befreien*) rescue; **sich r~en** save oneself; (*flüchten*) escape. **R~er** *m* **-s,-** rescuer; (*fig*) saviour
Rettich *m* **-s,-e** white radish
Rettung *f* **-,-en** rescue; (*fig*) salvation; **jds letzte R~** s.o.'s last hope. **R~sboot** *nt* lifeboat. **R~sdienst** *m* rescue service. **R~sgürtel** *m* lifebelt. **r~slos** *adv* hopelessly. **R~sring** *m* lifebelt. **R~ssanitäter(in)** *m*(*f*) paramedic. **R~swagen** *m* ambulance
retuschieren *vt* (*Phot*) retouch
Reue *f* **-** remorse; (*Relig*) repentance
Revanch|e /re'vã:ʃə/ *f* **-,-n** revenge; **R~e fordern** (*Sport*) ask for a return match. **r~ieren (sich)** *vr* take revenge; (*sich erkenntlich zeigen*) reciprocate (**mit** with)
Revers /re've:ɐ̯/ *nt* **-,-** /-[s],-s/ lapel
Revier *nt* **-s,-e** district; (*Zool & fig*) territory; (*Polizei-*) [police] station
Revision *f* **-,-en** revision; (*Prüfung*) check; (*Jur*) appeal
Revolution /-'tsi̯o:n/ *f* **-,-en** revolution. **r~är** *adj* revolutionary. **r~ieren** *vt* revolutionize
Revolver *m* **-s,-** revolver
rezen|sieren *vt* review. **R~sion** *f* **-,-en** review
Rezept *nt* **-[e]s,-e** prescription; (*Culin*) recipe
Rezession *f* **-,-en** recession
R-Gespräch *nt* reverse-charge call
Rhabarber *m* **-s** rhubarb
Rhein *m* **-s** Rhine. **R~land** *nt* **-s**

Rhineland. **R~wein** *m* hock

Rhetorik *f* - rhetoric

Rheum|a *nt* **-s** rheumatism. **r~atisch** *adj* rheumatic. **R~atismus** *m* - rheumatism

Rhinozeros *nt* **-[ses],-se** rhinoceros

rhyth|misch /ˈrʏt-/ *adj* rhythmic[al]. **R~mus** *m* **-,-men** rhythm

richten *vt* direct (**auf** + *acc* at); address (*Frage*) (**an** + *acc* to); aim (*Waffe*) (**auf** + *acc* at); (*einstellen*) set; (*vorbereiten*) prepare; (*reparieren*) mend; **in die Höhe r~** raise [up]; **sich r~** be directed (**auf** + *acc* at; **gegen** against); (*Blick:*) turn (**auf** + *acc* on); **sich r~nach** comply with (*Vorschrift*); fit in with (*jds Plänen*); (*abhängen*) depend on ● *vi* (*haben*) **r~ über** (+ *acc*) judge

Richter *m* **-s,-** judge

richtig *adj* right, correct; (*wirklich, echt*) real; **das R~e** the right thing ● *adv* correctly; really; **r~ stellen** put right (*Uhr*); (*fig*) correct (*Irrtum*); **die Uhr geht r~** the clock is right

Richtlinien *fpl* guidelines

Richtung *f* **-,-en** direction

riechen† *vt/i* (*haben*) smell (**nach** of; **an etw** *dat* sth)

Riegel *m* **-s,-** bolt; (*Seife*) bar

Riemen *m* **-s,-** strap; (*Ruder*) oar

Riese *m* **-n,-n** giant

rieseln *vi* (*sein*) trickle; (*Schnee:*) fall lightly

riesengroß *adj* huge, enormous

riesig *adj* huge; (*gewaltig*) enormous ● *adv* [!] terribly

Riff *nt* **-[e]s,-e** reef

Rille *f* **-,-n** groove

Rind *nt* **-es,-er** ox; (*Kuh*) cow; (*Stier*) bull; (*R~fleisch*) beef; **R~er** cattle *pl*

Rinde *f* **-,-n** bark; (*Käse-*) rind; (*Brot-*) crust

Rinder|braten *m* roast beef. **R~wahnsinn** *m* [!] mad cow disease

Rindfleisch *nt* beef

Ring *m* **-[e]s,-e** ring

ringeln (sich) *vr* curl

ring|en† *vi* (*haben*) wrestle; (*fig*) struggle (**um/nach** for) ● *vt* wring (*Hände*). **R~er** *m* **-s,-** wrestler. **R~kampf** *m* wrestling match; (*als Sport*) wrestling

ringsherum, **r~um** *adv* all around

Rinn|e *f* **-,-n** channel; (*Dach-*) gutter. **r~en**† *vi* (*sein*) run; (*Sand:*) trickle. **R~stein** *m* gutter

Rippe *f* **-,-n** rib. **R~nfellentzündung** *f* pleurisy

Risiko *nt* **-s,-s & -ken** risk

risk|ant *adj* risky. **r~ieren** *vt* risk

Riss *m* **-es,-e** tear; (*Mauer-*) crack; (*fig*) rift

rissig *adj* cracked; (*Haut*) chapped

Rist *m* **-[e]s,-e** instep

Ritt *m* **-[e]s,-e** ride

Ritter *m* **-s,-** knight

Ritual *nt* **-s,-e** ritual

Ritz *m* **-es,-e** scratch. **R~e** *f* **-,-n** crack; (*Fels-*) cleft; (*zwischen Betten, Vorhängen*) gap. **r~en** *vt* scratch

Rival|e *m* **-n,-n, R~in** *f* **-,-nen** rival. **R~ität** *f* **-,-en** rivalry

Robbe *f* **-,-n** seal

Robe *f* **-,-n** gown; (*Talar*) robe

Roboter *m* **-s,-** robot

robust *adj* robust

röcheln *vi* (*haben*) breathe noisily

Rochen *m* **-s,-** (*Zool*) ray

Rock[1] *m* **-[e]s,¨e** skirt; (*Jacke*) jacket

Rock[2] *m* **-[s]** (*Mus*) rock

rodel|n *vi* (*sein/haben*) toboggan. **R~schlitten** *m* toboggan
roden *vt* clear (*Land*); grub up (*Stumpf*)
Rogen *m* **-s,-** [hard] roe
Roggen *m* **-s** rye
roh *adj* rough; (*ungekocht*) raw; (*Holz*) bare; (*brutal*) brutal. **R~bau** *m* **-[e]s,-ten** shell. **R~kost** *f* raw [vegetarian] food. **R~ling** *m* **-s,-e** brute. **R~öl** *nt* crude oil
Rohr *nt* **-[e]s,-e** pipe; (*Geschütz-*) barrel; (*Bot*) reed; (*Zucker-, Bambus-*) cane
Röhre *f* **-,-n** tube; (*Radio-*) valve; (*Back-*) oven
Rohstoff *m* raw material
Rokoko *nt* **-s** rococo
Roll|bahn *f* taxiway; (*Start-/Landebahn*) runway. **R~balken** *m* scroll bar
Rolle *f* **-,-n** roll; (*Garn-*) reel; (*Draht-*) coil; (*Techn*) roller; (*Seil-*) pulley; (*Lauf-*) castor; (*Theat*) part, role; **das spielt keine R~** (*fig*) that doesn't matter. **r~n** *vt* roll; (*auf-*) roll up; (*Computer*) scroll; **sich r~n** roll ●*vi* (*sein*) roll; (*Flugzeug:*) taxi. **R~r** *m* **-s,-** scooter. **R~rblades®** /-ble:ds/ *mpl* Rollerblades®
Roll|feld *nt* airfield. **R~kragen** *m* polo-neck. **R~mops** *m* rollmop[s] *sg*
Rollo *nt* **-s,-s** [roller] blind
Roll|schuh *m* roller-skate; **R~schuh laufen** roller-skate. **R~stuhl** *m* wheelchair. **R~treppe** *f* escalator
Rom *nt* **-s** Rome
Roman *m* **-s,-e** novel. **r~isch** *adj* Romanesque; (*Sprache*) Romance
Romant|ik *f* **-** romanticism. **r~isch** *adj* romantic
Röm|er(in) *m* **-s,-** (*f* **-,-nen**) Roman. **r~isch** *adj* Roman
Rommé, Rommee /ˈrɔme:/ *nt* **-s** rummy
röntgen *vt* X-ray. **R~aufnahme** *f*, **R~bild** *nt* X-ray. **R~strahlen** *mpl* X-rays
rosa *inv adj*, **R~** *nt* **-[s],-** pink
Rose *f* **-,-n** rose. **R~nkohl** *m* [Brussels] sprouts *pl*. **R~nkranz** *m* (*Relig*) rosary
Rosine *f* **-,-n** raisin
Rosmarin *m* **-s** rosemary
Ross *nt* **-es,⸚er** horse
Rost[1] *m* **-[e]s,-e** grating; (*Kamin-*) grate; (*Brat-*) grill
Rost[2] *m* **-[e]s** rust. **r~en** *vi* (*haben*) rust
rösten *vt* roast; toast (*Brot*)
rostfrei *adj* stainless
rostig *adj* rusty
rot *adj*, **Rot** *nt* **-s,-** red; **rot werden** turn red; (*erröten*) go red, blush
Röte *f* **-** redness; (*Scham-*) blush
Röteln *pl* German measles *sg*
röten *vt* redden; **sich r~** turn red
rothaarig *adj* red-haired
rotieren *vi* (*haben*) rotate
Rot|kehlchen *nt* **-s,-** robin. **R~kohl** *m* red cabbage
rötlich *adj* reddish
Rotwein *m* red wine
Rou|lade /ruˈla:də/ *f* **-,-n** beef olive. **R~leau** *nt* **-s,-s** [roller] blind
Routin|e /ruˈti:nə/ *f* **-,-n** routine; (*Erfahrung*) experience. **r~emäßig** *adj* routine ●*adv* routinely. **r~iert** *adj* experienced
Rowdy /ˈraudi/ *m* **-s,-s** hooligan
Rübe *f* **-,-n** beet; **rote R~** beetroot
Rubin *m* **-s,-e** ruby
Rubrik *f* **-,-en** column
Ruck *m* **-[e]s,-e** jerk
ruckartig *adj* jerky
rück|bezüglich *adj* (*Gram*) re-

flexive. **R~blende** *f* flashback. **R~blick** *m* (*fig*) review (**auf** + *acc* of). **r~blickend** *adv* in retrospect. **r~datieren** *vt* (*infinitive & pp only*) backdate

Rücken *m* **-s,-** back; (*Buch-*) spine; (*Berg-*) ridge. **R~lehne** *f* back. **R~mark** *nt* spinal cord. **R~schwimmen** *nt* backstroke. **R~wind** *m* following wind; (*Aviat*) tail wind

rückerstatten *vt* (*infinitive & pp only*) refund

Rückfahr|karte *f* return ticket. **R~t** *f* return journey

Rück|fall *m* relapse. **R~flug** *m* return flight. **R~frage** *f* [further] query. **r~fragen** *vi* (*haben*) (*infinitive & pp only*) check (**bei** with). **R~gabe** *f* return. **r~gängig** *adj* **r~gängig machen** cancel; break off (*Verlobung*). **R~grat** *nt* **-[e]s,-e** spine, backbone. **R~hand** *f* backhand. **R~kehr** return. **R~lagen** *fpl* reserves. **R~licht** *nt* rear-light. **R~reise** *f* return journey

Rucksack *m* rucksack

Rück|schau *f* review. **R~schlag** *m* (*Sport*) return; (*fig*) set-back. **r~schrittlich** *adj* retrograde. **R~seite** *f* back; (*einer Münze*) reverse

Rücksicht *f* **-,-en** consideration. **R~nahme** *f* **-** consideration. **r~slos** *adj* inconsiderate; (*schonungslos*) ruthless. **r~svoll** *adj* considerate

Rück|sitz *m* back seat; (*Sozius*) pillion. **R~spiegel** *m* rear-view mirror. **R~spiel** *nt* return match. **R~stand** *m* (*Chemistry*) residue; (*Arbeits-*) backlog; **im R~stand sein** be behind. **r~ständig** *adj* (*fig*) backward. **R~stau** *m* (*Auto*) tailback. **R~strahler** *m* **-s,-** reflector. **R~tritt** *m* resignation; (*Fahrrad*) back pedalling

rückwärt|ig *adj* back, rear. **r~s** *adv* backwards. **R~sgang** *m* reverse [gear]

Rückweg *m* way back

rück|wirkend *adj* retrospective. **R~wirkung** *f* retrospective force; **mit R~wirkung vom** backdated to. **R~zahlung** *f* repayment

Rüde *m* **-n,-n** [male] dog

Rudel *nt* **-s,-** herd; (*Wolfs-*) pack; (*Löwen-*) pride

Ruder *nt* **-s,-** oar; (*Steuer-*) rudder; **am R~** (*Naut & fig*) at the helm. **R~boot** *nt* rowing boat. **r~n** *vt/i* (*haben/sein*) row

Ruf *m* **-[e]s,-e** call; (*laut*) shout; (*Telefon*) telephone number; (*Ansehen*) reputation. **r~en†** *vt/i* (*haben*) call (**nach** for); **r~en lassen** send for

Ruf|name *m* forename by which one is known. **R~nummer** *f* telephone number. **R~zeichen** *nt* dialling tone

Rüge *f* **-,-n** reprimand. **r~n** *vt* reprimand; (*kritisieren*) criticize

Ruhe *f* **-** rest; (*Stille*) quiet; (*Frieden*) peace; (*innere*) calm; (*Gelassenheit*) composure; **R~ [da]!** quiet! **r~los** *adj* restless. **r~n** *vi* (*haben*) rest (**auf** + *dat* on); (*Arbeit, Verkehr:*) have stopped. **R~pause** *f* rest, break. **R~stand** *m* retirement; **im R~stand** retired. **R~störung** *f* disturbance of the peace. **R~tag** *m* day of rest; **'Montag R~tag'** 'closed on Mondays'

ruhig *adj* quiet; (*erholsam*) restful; (*friedlich*) peaceful; (*unbewegt, gelassen*) calm; **man kann r~ darüber sprechen** there's no harm in talking about it

Ruhm *m* **-[e]s** fame; (*Ehre*) glory

rühmen *vt* praise

ruhmreich *adj* glorious

r

Ruhr *f* - (*Med*) dysentery
Rühr|ei *nt* scrambled eggs *pl*. **r∼en** *vt* move; (*Culin*) stir; **sich r∼en** move ● *vi* (*haben*) stir; **r∼en an** (+ *acc*) touch; (*fig*) touch on. **r∼end** *adj* touching
Rührung *f* - emotion
Ruin *m* **-s** ruin. **R∼e** *f* **-,-n** ruin; ruins *pl* (*gen* of). **r∼ieren** *vt* ruin
rülpsen *vi* (*haben*) ⊡ belch
Rum *m* **-s** rum
Rumän|ien /-i̯ən/ *nt* **-s** Romania. **r∼isch** *adj* Romanian
Rummel *m* **-s** ⊡ hustle and bustle; (*Jahrmarkt*) funfair
Rumpelkammer *f* junk-room
Rumpf *m* **-[e]s,⸚e** body, trunk; (*Schiffs-*) hull; (*Aviat*) fuselage
rund *adj* round ● *adv* approximately; **r∼ um** [a]round. **R∼blick** *m* panoramic view. **R∼brief** *m* circular [letter]
Runde *f* **-,-n** round; (*Kreis*) circle; (*eines Polizisten*) beat; (*beim Rennen*) lap; **eine R∼ Bier** a round of beer
Rund|fahrt *f* tour. **R∼frage** *f* poll
Rundfunk *m* radio; **im R∼** on the radio. **R∼gerät** *nt* radio [set]
Rund|gang *m* round; (*Spaziergang*) walk (**durch** round). **r∼heraus** *adv* straight out. **r∼herum** *adv* all around. **r∼lich** *adj* rounded; (*mollig*) plump. **R∼reise** *f* [circular] tour. **R∼schreiben** *nt* circular. **r∼um** *adv* all round. **R∼ung** *f* **-,-en** curve
Runzel *f* **-,-n** wrinkle
runzlig *adj* wrinkled
Rüpel *m* **-s,-** ⊡ lout
rupfen *vt* pull out; pluck (*Geflügel*)
Rüsche *f* **-,-n** frill
Ruß *m* **-es** soot
Russe *m* **-n,-n** Russian
Rüssel *m* **-s,-** (*Zool*) trunk
Russ|in *f* **-,-nen** Russian. **r∼isch** *adj* Russian. **R∼isch** *nt* **-[s]** (*Lang*) Russian
Russland *nt* **-s** Russia
rüsten *vi* (*haben*) prepare (**zu**/**für** for) ● *vr* **sich r∼** get ready
rüstig *adj* sprightly
rustikal *adj* rustic
Rüstung *f* **-,-en** armament; (*Harnisch*) armour. **R∼skontrolle** *f* arms control
Rute *f* **-,-n** twig; (*Angel-*, *Wünschel-*) rod; (*zur Züchtigung*) birch; (*Schwanz*) tail
Rutsch *m* **-[e]s,-e** slide. **R∼bahn** *f* slide. **R∼e** *f* **-,-n** chute. **r∼en** *vt* slide; (*rücken*) move ● *vi* (*sein*) slide; (*aus-*, *ab-*) slip; (*Auto*) skid. **r∼ig** *adj* slippery
rütteln *vt* shake ● *vi* (*haben*) **r∼ an** (+ *dat*) rattle

Ss

Saal *m* **-[e]s,Säle** hall; (*Theat*) auditorium; (*Kranken-*) ward
Saat *f* **-,-en** seed; (*Säen*) sowing; (*Gesätes*) crop
sabbern *vi* (*haben*) ⊡ slobber; (*Baby:*) dribble; (*reden*) jabber
Säbel *m* **-s,-** sabre
Sabo|tage /zaboˈtaːʒə/ *f* - sabotage. **S∼teur** *m* **-s,-e** saboteur. **s∼tieren** *vt* sabotage
Sach|bearbeiter *m* expert. **S∼buch** *nt* non-fiction book
Sache *f* **-,-n** matter, business; (*Ding*) thing; (*fig*) cause
Sach|gebiet *nt* (*fig*) area, field. **s∼kundig** *adj* expert. **s∼lich** *adj*

factual; (*nüchtern*) matter-of-fact

sächlich *adj* (*Gram*) neuter

Sachse *m* **-n,-n** Saxon. **S~n** *nt* **-s** Saxony

sächsisch *adj* Saxon

Sach|verhalt *m* **-[e]s** facts *pl*. **S~verständige(r)** *m/f* expert

Sack *m* **-[e]s,⸚e** sack

Sack|gasse *f* cul-de-sac; (*fig*) impasse. **S~leinen** *nt* sacking

Sadis|mus *m* **-** sadism. **S~t** *m* **-en,-en** sadist

säen *vt/i* (*haben*) sow

Safe /ze:f/ *m* **-s,-s** safe

Saft *m* **-[e]s,⸚e** juice; (*Bot*) sap. **s~ig** *adj* juicy

Sage *f* **-,-n** legend

Säge *f* **-,-n** saw. **S~mehl** *nt* sawdust

sagen *vt* say; (*mitteilen*) tell; (*bedeuten*) mean

sägen *vt/i* (*haben*) saw

sagenhaft *adj* legendary

Säge|späne *mpl* wood shavings. **S~werk** *nt* sawmill

Sahn|e *f* **-** cream. **S~ebonbon** *m* & *nt* ≈ toffee. **s~ig** *adj* creamy

Saison /zɛ'zõ:/ *f* **-,-s** season

Saite *f* **-,-n** (*Mus, Sport*) string. **S~ninstrument** *nt* stringed instrument

Sakko *m* & *nt* **-s,-s** sports jacket

Sakrament *nt* **-[e]s,-e** sacrament

Sakristei *f* **-,-en** vestry

Salat *m* **-[e]s,-e** salad. **S~soße** *f* salad-dressing

Salbe *f* **-,-n** ointment

Salbei *m* **-s** & *f* **-** sage

salben *vt* anoint

Saldo *m* **-s,-dos** & **-den** balance

Salon /za'lõ:/ *m* **-s,-s** salon

salopp *adj* casual; (*Benehmen*) informal

Salto *m* **-s,-s** somersault

Salut *m* **-[e]s,-e** salute. **s~ieren** *vi* (*haben*) salute

Salve *f* **-,-n** volley; (*Geschütz-*) salvo, (*von Gelächter*) burst

Salz *nt* **-es,-e** salt. **s~en†** *vt* salt. **S~fass** *nt* salt-cellar. **s~ig** *adj* salty. **S~kartoffeln** *fpl* boiled potatoes. **S~säure** *f* hydrochloric acid

Salzburger Festspiele
The Austrian city of Salzburg, the home of Wolfgang Amadeus Mozart (1756-91), hosts this annual festival as a tribute to the great composer. Every summer since 1920, Mozart-lovers have enjoyed his music at the Salzburg Festival.

Samen *m* **-s,-** seed; (*Anat*) semen, sperm

Sammel|becken *nt* reservoir. **s~n** *vt/i* (*haben*) collect; (*suchen, versammeln*) gather; **sich s~n** collect; (*sich versammeln*) gather; (*sich fassen*) collect oneself. **S~name** *m* collective noun

Samm|ler(in) *m* **-s,-** (*f* **-,-nen**) collector. **S~lung** *f* **-,-en** collection; (*innere*) composure

Samstag *m* **-s** Saturday. **s~s** *adv* on Saturdays

samt *prep* (+ *dat*) together with

Samt *m* **-[e]s** velvet

sämtlich *indefinite pronoun inv* all. **s~e(r,s)** *indefinite pronoun* all the; **s~e Werke** complete works

Sanatorium *nt* **-s,-ien** sanatorium

Sand *m* **-[e]s** sand

Sandale *f* **-,-n** sandal

Sand|bank *f* sandbank. **S~kasten** *m* sand-pit. **S~papier** *nt* sandpaper

S

sanft *adj* gentle
Sänger(in) *m* **-s,-** (*f* **-,-nen**) singer
sanieren *vt* clean up; redevelop (*Gebiet*); (*modernisieren*) modernize; make profitable (*Industrie, Firma*); **sich s~** become profitable
sanitär *adj* sanitary
Sanität|er *m* **-s,-** first-aid man; (*Fahrer*) ambulance man; (*Mil*) medical orderly. **S~swagen** *m* ambulance
Sanktion /zaŋk'tsi̯o:n/ *f* **-,-en** sanction. **s~ieren** *vt* sanction
Saphir *m* **-s,-e** sapphire
Sardelle *f* **-,-n** anchovy
Sardine *f* **-,-n** sardine
Sarg *m* **-[e]s,⸚e** coffin
Sarkasmus *m* **-** sarcasm
Satan *m* **-s** Satan; (🗉: *Teufel*) devil
Satellit *m* **-en,-en** satellite. **S~enfernsehen** *nt* satellite television. **S~enschüssel** *f* satellite dish. **S~entelefon** *nt* satphone
Satin /za'tɛŋ/ *m* **-s** satin
Satire *f* **-,-n** satire
satt *adj* full; (*Farbe*) rich; **s~ sein** have had enough [to eat]; **etw s~ haben** 🗉 be fed up with sth
Sattel *m* **-s,⸚** saddle. **s~n** *vt* saddle. **S~zug** *m* articulated lorry
sättigen *vt* satisfy; (*Chemistry & fig*) saturate ● *vi* (*haben*) be filling
Satz *m* **-es,⸚e** sentence; (*Teil-*) clause; (*These*) proposition; (*Math*) theorem; (*Mus*) movement; (*Tennis, Zusammengehöriges*) set; (*Boden-*) sediment; (*Kaffee-*) grounds *pl*; (*Steuer-, Zins-*) rate; (*Druck-*) setting; (*Schrift-*) type; (*Sprung*) leap, bound. **S~aussage** *f* predicate. **S~gegenstand** *m* subject. **S~zeichen** *nt* punctuation mark
Sau *f* **-,Säue** sow
sauber *adj* clean; (*ordentlich*) neat; (*anständig*) decent; **s~ machen** clean. **S~keit** *f* **-** cleanliness; neatness
säuberlich *adj* neat
Sauce /'zo:sə/ *f* **-,-n** sauce; (*Braten-*) gravy
Saudi-Arabien /-i̯ən/ *nt* **-s** Saudi Arabia
sauer *adj* sour; (*Chemistry*) acid; (*eingelegt*) pickled; (*schwer*) hard; **saurer Regen** acid rain
Sauerkraut *nt* sauerkraut
säuerlich *adj* slightly sour
Sauerstoff *m* oxygen
saufen† *vt/i* (*haben*) drink; ⊠ booze
Säufer *m* **-s,-** ⊠ boozer
saugen† *vt/i* (*haben*) suck; (*staub-*) vacuum, hoover; **sich voll Wasser s~** soak up water
säugen *vt* suckle
Säugetier *nt* mammal
saugfähig *adj* absorbent
Säugling *m* **-s,-e** infant
Säule *f* **-,-n** column
Saum *m* **-[e]s,Säume** hem; (*Rand*) edge
säumen *vt* hem; (*fig*) line
Sauna *f* **-,-nas & -nen** sauna
Säure *f* **-,-n** acidity; (*Chemistry*) acid
sausen *vi* (*haben*) rush; (*Ohren:*) buzz ● *vi* (*sein*) rush [along]
Saxophon, **Saxofon** *nt* **-s,-e** saxophone
S-Bahn *f* city and suburban railway
Scanner *m* **-s,-** scanner
sch *int* shush! (*fort*) shoo!
Schabe *f* **-,-n** cockroach
schaben *vt/i* (*haben*) scrape
schäbig *adj* shabby
Schablone *f* **-,-n** stencil; (*Muster*) pattern; (*fig*) stereotype

Schach *nt* **-s** chess; **S~!** check! **S~brett** *nt* chessboard

Schachfigur *f* chess-man

schachmatt *adj* **s~ setzen** checkmate; **s~!** checkmate!

Schachspiel *nt* game of chess

Schacht *m* **-[e]s,⸚e** shaft

Schachtel *f* **-,-n** box; (*Zigaretten-*) packet

Schachzug *m* move

schade *adj* **s~ sein** be a pity or shame: **zu s~ für** too good for

Schädel *m* **-s**, skull. **S~bruch** *m* fractured skull

schaden *vi* (*haben*) (+ *dat*) damage; (*nachteilig sein*) hurt. **S~** *m* **-s,⸚** damage; (*Defekt*) defect; (*Nachteil*) disadvantage. **S~ersatz** *m* damages *pl.* **S~freude** *f* malicious glee. **s~froh** *adj* gloating

schädig|en *vt* damage, harm. **S~ung** *f* **-,-en** damage

schädlich *adj* harmful

Schädling *m* **-s,-e** pest. **S~sbekämpfungsmittel** *nt* pesticide

Schaf *nt* **-[e]s,-e** sheep. **S~bock** *m* ram

Schäfer *m* **-s,-** shepherd. **S~hund** *m* sheepdog; **Deutscher S~hund** alsatian

schaffen[1]† *vt* create; (*herstellen*) establish; make (*Platz*)

schaffen[2] *v* (*reg*) ● *vt* manage [to do]; pass (*Prüfung*); catch (*Zug*); (*bringen*) take

Schaffner *m* **-s,-** conductor; (*Zug-*) ticket-inspector

Schaffung *f* **-** creation

Schaft *m* **-[e]s,⸚e** shaft; (*Gewehr-*) stock; (*Stiefel-*) leg

Schal *m* **-s,-s** scarf

Schale *f* **-,-n** skin; (*abgeschält*) peel; (*Eier-, Nuss-, Muschel-*) shell; (*Schüssel*) dish

schälen *vt* peel; **sich s~** peel

Schall *m* **-[e]s** sound. **S~dämpfer** *m* silencer. **s~dicht** *adj* soundproof. **s~en** *vi* (*haben*) ring out: (*nachhallen*) resound. **S~mauer** *f* sound barrier. **S~platte** *f* record, disc

schalt|en *vt* switch ● *vi* (*haben*) switch/(*Ampel:*) turn (**auf** + *acc* to); (*Auto*) change gear; (**[!]**: *begreifen*) catch on. **S~er** *m* **-s,-** switch; (*Post-, Bank-*) counter; (*Fahrkarten-*) ticket window. **S~hebel** *m* switch; (*Auto*) gear lever. **S~jahr** *nt* leap year. **S~ung** *f* **-,-en** circuit: (*Auto*) gear change

Scham *f* **-** shame; (*Anat*) private parts *pl*

schämen **(sich)** *vr* be ashamed

scham|haft *adj* modest. **s~los** *adj* shameless

Schampon *nt* **-s** shampoo. **s~ieren** *vt* shampoo

Schande *f* **-** disgrace, shame

schändlich *adj* disgraceful

Schanktisch *m* bar

Schanze *f*, **-,-n** [ski-]jump

Schar *f* **-,-en** crowd; (*Vogel-*) flock

Scharade *f* **-,-n** charade

scharen *vt* **um sich s~** gather round one; **sich s~ um** flock round. **s~weise** *adv* in droves

scharf *adj* sharp; (*stark*) strong; (*stark gewürzt*) hot; (*Geruch*) pungent; (*Wind, Augen, Verstand*) keen; (*streng*) harsh; (*Galopp*) hard; (*Munition*) live; (*Hund*) fierce; **s~ einstellen** (*Phot*) focus; **s~ sein** (*Phot*) be in focus; **s~ sein auf** (+ *acc*) **[!]** be keen on

Schärfe *f* sharpness; strength; hotness; pungency; keenness; harshness. **s~n** *vt* sharpen

Scharf|richter *m* executioner. **S~schütze** *m* marksman. **S~sinn** *m* astuteness

Scharlach *m* **-s** scarlet fever
Scharlatan *m* **-s,-e** charlatan
Scharnier *nt* **-s,-e** hinge
Schärpe *f* **-,-n** sash
scharren *vi* (*haben*) scrape; (*Huhn*) scratch ● *vt* scrape
Schaschlik *m* & *nt* **-s,-s** kebab
Schatten *m* **-s,-** shadow; (*schattige Stelle*) shade. **S~riss** *m* silhouette. **S~seite** *f* shady side; (*fig*) disadvantage
schattier|en *vt* shade. **S~ung** *f* **-,-en** shading
schattig *adj* shady
Schatz *m* **-es,⸚e** treasure; (*Freund, Freundin*) sweetheart
schätzen *vt* estimate; (*taxieren*) value; (*achten*) esteem; (*würdigen*) appreciate
Schätzung *f* **-,-en** estimate; (*Taxierung*) valuation
Schau *f* **-,-en** show. **S~ bild** *nt* diagram
Schauder *m* **-s** shiver; (*vor Abscheu*) shudder. **s~ haft** *adj* dreadful. **s~n** *vi* (*haben*) shiver; (*vor Abscheu*) shudder
schauen *vi* (*haben*) (*SGer, Aust*) look; **s~, dass** make sure that
Schauer *m* **-s,-** shower; (*Schauder*) shiver. **S~geschichte** *f* horror story. **s~lich** *adj* ghastly
Schaufel *f* **-,-n** shovel; (*Kehr-*) dustpan. **s~n** *vt* shovel; (*graben*) dig
Schaufenster *nt* shop-window. **S~puppe** *f* dummy
Schaukel *f* **-,-n** swing. **s~n** *vt* rock ● *vi* (*haben*) rock; (*auf einer Schaukel*) swing; (*schwanken*) sway. **S~pferd** *nt* rocking-horse. **S~stuhl** *m* rocking-chair
Schaum *m* **-[e]s** foam; (*Seifen-*) lather; (*auf Bier*) froth; (*als Frisier-, Rasiermittel*) mousse
schäumen *vi* (*haben*) foam, froth; (*Seife:*) lather
Schaum|gummi *m* foam rubber. **s~ig** *a* frothy; **s~ig rühren** (*Culin*) cream. **S~stoff** *m* [synthetic] foam. **S~wein** *m* sparkling wine
Schauplatz *m* scene
schaurig *adj* dreadful; (*unheimlich*) eerie
Schauspiel *nt* play; (*Anblick*) spectacle. **S~er** *m* actor. **S~erin** *f* actress
Scheck *m* **-s,-s** cheque. **S~buch, S~heft** *nt* cheque-book. **S~karte** *f* cheque card
Scheibe *f* **-,-n** disc; (*Schieß-*) target; (*Glas-*) pane; (*Brot-, Wurst-*) slice. **S~nwischer** *m* **-s,-** windscreen-wiper
Scheich *m* **-s,-e** & **-s** sheikh
Scheide *f* **-,-n** sheath; (*Anat*) vagina
scheid|en† *vt* separate; (*unterscheiden*) distinguish; dissolve (*Ehe*); **sich s~en lassen** get divorced ● *vi* (*sein*) leave; (*voneinander*) part. **S~ung** *f* **-,-en** divorce
Schein *m* **-[e]s,-e** light; (*Anschein*) appearance; (*Bescheinigung*) certificate; (*Geld-*) note. **s~bar** *adj* apparent. **s~en**† *vi* (*haben*) shine; (*den Anschein haben*) seem, appear
scheinheilig *adj* hypocritical
Scheinwerfer *m* **-s,-** floodlight; (*Such-*) searchlight; (*Auto*) headlight; (*Theat*) spotlight
Scheiße *f* **-** (*vulgar*) shit. **s~n**† *vi* (*haben*) (*vulgar*) shit
Scheit *nt* **-[e]s,-e** log
Scheitel *m* **-s,-** parting
scheitern *vi* (*sein*) fail
Schelle *f* **-,-n** bell. **s~n** *vi* (*haben*) ring

Schellfisch *m* haddock
Schelm *m* **-s,-e** rogue
Schelte *f* **-** scolding
Schema *nt* **-s,-mata** model, pattern; (*Skizze*) diagram
Schemel *m* **-s,-** stool
Schenke *f* **-,-n** tavern
Schenkel *m* **-s,-** thigh
schenken *vt* give [as a present]; **jdm Vertrauen s~** trust s.o.
Scherbe *f* **-,-n** [broken] piece
Schere *f* **-,-n** scissors *pl*; (*Techn*) shears *pl*; (*Hummer-*) claw. **s~n¹†** *vt* shear; crop (*Haar*)
scheren² *vt* (*reg*) ! bother; **sich nicht s~ um** not care about
Scherenschnitt *m* silhouette
Scherereien *fpl* ! trouble *sg*
Scherz *m* **-es,-e** joke; **im/zum S~** as a joke. **s~en** *vi* (*haben*) joke
scheu *adj* shy; (*Tier*) timid; **s~ werden** (*Pferd:*) shy
scheuchen *vt* shoo
scheuen *vt* be afraid of; (*meiden*) shun; **keine Mühe/Kosten s~** spare no effort/expense; **sich s~** be afraid (**vor** + *dat* of); shrink (**etw zu tun** from doing sth)
scheuern *vt* scrub; (*reiben*) rub; **[wund] s~n** chafe ● *vi* (*haben*) rub, chafe
Scheuklappen *fpl* blinkers
Scheune *f* **-,-n** barn
Scheusal *nt* **-s,-e** monster
scheußlich *adj* horrible
Schi *m* **-s,-er** ski; **S~ fahren** *od* **laufen** ski
Schicht *f* **-,-en** layer; (*Geology*) stratum; (*Gesellschafts-*) class; (*Arbeits-*) shift. **S~arbeit** *f* shift work. **s~en** *vt* stack [up]
schick *adj* stylish; (*Frau*) chic. **S~** *m* **-[e]s** style
schicken *vt/i* (*haben*) send; **s~ nach** send for
Schicksal *nt* **-s,-e** fate. **S~sschlag** *m* misfortune
Schieb|edach *nt* (*Auto*) sun-roof. **s~en†** *vt* push; (*gleitend*) slide; (!: *handeln mit*) traffic in; **etw s~en auf** (+ *acc*) (*fig*) put sth down to; shift (*Schuld*) on to ● *vi* (*haben*) push. **S~etür** *f* sliding door. **S~ung** *f* **-,-en** ! illicit deal; (*Betrug*) rigging, fixing
Schieds|gericht *nt* panel of judges; (*Jur*) arbitration tribunal. **S~richter** *m* referee; (*Tennis*) umpire; (*Jur*) arbitrator
schief *adj* crooked; (*unsymmetrisch*) lopsided; (*geneigt*) slanting, sloping; (*nicht senkrecht*) leaning; (*Winkel*) oblique; (*fig*) false; suspicious ● *adv* not straight; **s~ gehen** ! go wrong
Schiefer *m* **-s** slate
schielen *vi* (*haben*) squint
Schienbein *nt* shin
Schiene *f* **-,-n** rail; (*Gleit-*) runner; (*Med*) splint. **s~n** *vt* (*Med*) put in a splint
Schieß|bude *f* shooting-gallery. **s~en†** *vt* shoot; fire (*Kugel*); score (*Tor*) ● *vi* (*haben*) shoot, fire (**auf** + *acc* at). **S~scheibe** *f* target. **S~stand** *m* shooting-range
Schifahr|en *nt* skiing. **S~er(in)** *m(f)* skier
Schiff *nt* **-[e]s,-e** ship; (*Kirchen-*) nave; (*Seiten-*) aisle
Schiffahrt* *f* = **Schifffahrt**
schiff|bar *adj* navigable. **S~bruch** *m* shipwreck. **s~brüchig** *adj* shipwrecked. **S~fahrt** *f* shipping
Schikan|e *f* **-,-n** harassment; **mit allen S~en** ! with every refinement. **s~ieren** *vt* harass
Schi|laufen *nt* **-s** skiing. **S~läufer(in)** *m(f)* **-s,-** (*f* **-,-nen**) skier

Schild[1] *m* **-[e]s,-e** shield
Schild[2] *nt* **-[e]s,-er** sign; (*Nummern-*) plate; (*Mützen-*) badge; (*Etikett*) label
Schilddrüse *f* thyroid [gland]
schilder|n *vt* describe. **S~ung** *f* **-,-en** description
Schild|kröte *f* tortoise; (*See-*) turtle. **S~patt** *nt* **-[e]s** tortoiseshell
Schilf *nt* **-[e]s** reeds *pl*
schillern *vi* (*haben*) shimmer
Schimmel *m* **-s,-** mould; (*Pferd*) white horse. **s~n** *vi* (*haben/sein*) go mouldy
schimmern *vi* (*haben*) gleam
Schimpanse *m* **-n,-n** chimpanzee
schimpf|en *vi* (*haben*) grumble (**mit** at; **über** + *acc* about); scold (**mit jdm** s.o.) ● *vt* call. **S~wort** *nt* (*pl* **-wörter**) swear-word
Schinken *m* **-s,-** ham. **S~speck** *m* bacon
Schippe *f* **-,-n** shovel. **s~n** *vt* shovel
Schirm *m* **-[e]s,-e** umbrella; (*Sonnen-*) sunshade; (*Lampen-*) shade; (*Augen-*) visor; (*Mützen-*) peak; (*Ofen-, Bild-*) screen; (*fig: Schutz*) shield. **S~herrschaft** *f* patronage. **S~mütze** *f* peaked cap
schizophren *adj* schizophrenic. **S~ie** *f* **-** schizophrenia
Schlacht *f* **-,-en** battle
schlachten *vt* slaughter, kill
Schlacht|feld *nt* battlefield. **S~hof** *m* abattoir
Schlacke *f* **-,-n** slag
Schlaf *m* **-[e]s** sleep; **im S~** in one's sleep. **S~anzug** *m* pyjamas *pl*
Schläfe *f* **-,-n** (*Anat*) temple
schlafen† *vi* (*haben*) sleep; **s~ gehen** go to bed; **er schläft noch** he is still asleep
schlaff *adj* limp; (*Seil*) slack; (*Muskel*) flabby
Schlaf|lied *nt* lullaby. **s~los** *adj* sleepless. **S~losigkeit** *f* **-** insomnia. **S~mittel** *nt* sleeping drug
schläfrig *adj* sleepy
Schlaf|saal *m* dormitory. **S~sack** *m* sleeping-bag. **S~tablette** *f* sleeping-pill. **S~wagen** *m* sleeping-car, sleeper. **s~wandeln** *vi* (*haben/sein*) sleep-walk. **S~zimmer** *nt* bedroom
Schlag *m* **-[e]s,⸚e** blow; (*Faust-*) punch; (*Herz-, Puls-, Trommel-*) beat; (*einer Uhr*) chime; (*Glocken-, Gong- & Med*) stroke; (*elektrischer*) shock; (*Art*) type; **S⸚e bekommen** get a beating; **S~ auf S~** in rapid succession. **S~ader** *f* artery. **S~anfall** *m* stroke. **S~baum** *m* barrier
schlagen† *vt* hit, strike; (*fällen*) fell; knock (*Loch, Nagel*) (**in** + *acc* into); (*prügeln, besiegen*) beat; (*Culin*) whisk (*Eiweiß*); whip (*Sahne*); (*legen*) throw; (*wickeln*) wrap; **sich s~** fight ● *vi* (*haben*) beat; (*Tür:*) bang; (*Uhr:*) strike; (*melodisch*) chime; **mit den Flügeln s~** flap its wings ● *vi* (*sein*) **in etw** (*acc*) **s~** (*Blitz, Kugel:*) strike sth; **nach jdm s~** (*fig*) take after s.o.
Schlager *m* **-s,-** popular song; (*Erfolg*) hit
Schläger *m* **-s,-** racket; (*Tischtennis-*) bat; (*Golf-*) club; (*Hockey-*) stick. **S~ei** *f* **-,-en** fight, brawl
schlag|fertig *adj* quick-witted. **S~loch** *nt* pot-hole. **S~sahne** *f* whipped cream; (*ungeschlagen*) whipping cream. **S~seite** *f* (*Naut*) list. **S~stock** *m* truncheon. **S~wort** *nt* (*pl* **-worte**) slogan. **S~zeile** *f* headline. **S~zeug** *nt* (*Mus*) percussion. **S~zeuger** *m* **-s,-** percussionist; (*in Band*) drummer
Schlamm *m* **-[e]s** mud. **s~ig** *adj* muddy

Schlamp|e *f* **-,-n** 🄵 slut. **s~en** *vi* (*haben*) 🄵 be sloppy (**bei** in). **s~ig** *adj* slovenly; (*Arbeit*) sloppy

Schlange *f* **-,-n** snake; (*Menschen-, Auto-*) queue; **S~ stehen** queue

schlängeln (sich) *vr* wind; (*Person:*) weave (**durch** through)

schlank *adj* slim. **S~heitskur** *f* slimming diet

schlapp *adj* tired; (*schlaff*) limp

schlau *adj* clever; (*gerissen*) crafty; **ich werde nicht s~ daraus** I can't make head or tail of it

Schlauch *m* **-[e]s,Schläuche** tube; (*Wasser-*) hose[pipe]. **S~boot** *nt* rubber dinghy

Schlaufe *f* **-,-n** loop

schlecht *adj* bad; (*böse*) wicked; (*unzulänglich*) poor; **s~ werden** go bad; (*Wetter:*) turn bad; **mir ist s~** I feel sick; **s~ machen** 🄵 run down. **s~gehen*** *vi sep* (*sein*) **s~ gehen**, *s.* **gehen**

schlecken *vt/i* (*haben*) lick (**an etw** *dat* sth); (*auf-*) lap up

Schlegel *m* **-s,-** (*SGer: Keule*) leg; (*Hühner-*) drumstick

schleichen† *vi* (*sein*) creep; (*langsam gehen/fahren*) crawl ●*vr* **sich s~** creep. **s~d** *adj* creeping

Schleier *m* **-s,-** veil; (*fig*) haze

Schleife *f* **-,-n** bow; (*Fliege*) bowtie; (*Biegung*) loop

schleifen[1] *v* (*reg*) ●*vt* drag ●*vi* (*haben*) trail, drag

schleifen[2]† *vt* grind; (*schärfen*) sharpen; cut (*Edelstein, Glas*)

Schleim *m* **-[e]s** slime; (*Anat*) mucus; (*Med*) phlegm. **s~ig** *adj* slimy

schlendern *vi* (*sein*) stroll

schlenkern *vt/i* (*haben*) swing; **s~ mit** swing; dangle (*Beine*)

Schlepp|dampfer *m* tug. **S~e** *f* **-,-n** train. **s~en** *vt* drag; (*tragen*) carry; (*ziehen*) tow; **sich s~en** drag oneself; (*sich hinziehen*) drag on; **sich s~en mit** carry. **S~er** *m* **-s,-** tug; (*Traktor*) tractor. **S~kahn** *m* barge. **S~lift** *m* T-bar lift. **S~tau** *nt* tow-rope; **ins S~tau nehmen** take in tow

Schleuder *f* **-,-n** catapult; (*Wäsche-*) spin-drier. **s~n** *vt* hurl; spin (*Wäsche*) ●*vi* (*sein*) skid; **ins S~n geraten** skid. **S~sitz** *m* ejector seat

Schleuse *f* **-,-n** lock; (*Sperre*) sluice[-gate]. **s~n** *vt* steer

Schliche *pl* tricks

schlicht *adj* plain; simple

Schlichtung *f* **-** settlement; (*Jur*) arbitration

Schließe *f* **-,-n** clasp; buckle

schließen† *vt* close (*ab-*) lock; fasten (*Kleid, Verschluss*); (*stilllegen*) close down; (*beenden, folgern*) conclude; enter into (*Vertrag*); **sich s~** close; **etw s~ an** (+ *acc*) connect sth to; **sich s~ an** (+ *acc*) follow ●*vi* (*haben*) close, (*den Betrieb einstellen*) close down; (*den Schlüssel drehen*) turn the key; (*enden, folgern*) conclude

Schließ|fach *nt* locker. **s~lich** *adv* finally, in the end; (*immerhin*) after all. **S~ung** *f* **-,-en** closure

Schliff *m* **-[e]s** cut; (*Schleifen*) cutting; (*fig*) polish

schlimm *adj* bad

Schlinge *f* **-,-n** loop; (*Henkers-*) noose; (*Med*) sling; (*Falle*) snare

Schlingel *m* **-s,-** 🄵 rascal

schlingen† *vt* wind, wrap; tie (*Knoten*) ●*vt/i* (*haben*) bolt one's food

Schlips *m* **-es,-e** tie

Schlitten *m* **-s,-** sledge; (*Rodel-*) toboggan; (*Pferde-*) sleigh; **S~ fahren** toboggan

schlittern *vi* (*haben/ sein*) slide

Schlittschuh *m* skate; **S~ laufen** skate. **S~läufer(in)** *m*(*f*) **-s,-** (*f* **-,-nen**) skater

Schlitz *m* **-es,-e** slit; (*für Münze*) slot; (*Jacken-*) vent; (*Hosen-*) flies *pl*. **s~en** *vt* slit

Schloss *nt* **-es,¨er** lock; (*Vorhänge-*) padlock; (*Verschluss*) clasp; (*Gebäude*) castle; palace

Schlosser *m* **-s,-** locksmith; (*Auto-*) mechanic

Schlucht *f* **-,-en** ravine, gorge

schluchzen *vi* (*haben*) sob

Schluck *m* **-[e]s,-e** mouthful; (*klein*) sip

Schluckauf *m* **-s** hiccups *pl*

schlucken *vt/i* (*haben*) swallow

Schlummer *m* **-s** slumber

Schlund *m* **-[e]s** [back of the] throat; (*fig*) mouth

schlüpf|en *vi* (*sein*) slip; [**aus dem Ei**] **s~en** hatch. **S~er** *m* **-s,-** knickers *pl*. **s~rig** *adj* slippery

schlürfen *vt/i* (*haben*) slurp

Schluss *m* **-es,¨e** end; (*S~folgerung*) conclusion; **zum S~** finally; **S~ machen** stop (**mit etw** sth); finish (**mit jdm** with s.o.)

Schlüssel *m* **-s,-** key; (*Schrauben-*) spanner; (*Geheim-*) code; (*Mus*) clef. **S~bein** *nt* collar-bone. **S~bund** *m* & *nt* bunch of keys. **S~loch** *nt* keyhole

Schlussfolgerung *f* conclusion

schlüssig *adj* conclusive

Schluss|licht *nt* rear-light. **S~verkauf** *m* sale

schmächtig *adj* slight

schmackhaft *adj* tasty

schmal *adj* narrow; (*dünn*) thin; (*schlank*) slender; (*karg*) meagre

schmälern *vt* diminish; (*herabsetzen*) belittle

Schmalz[1] *nt* **-es** lard; (*Ohren-*) wax

Schmalz[2] *m* **-es** [!] schmaltz

Schmarotzer *m* **-s,-** parasite; (*Person*) sponger

schmatzen *vi* (*haben*) eat noisily

schmausen *vi* (*haben*) feast

schmecken *vi* (*haben*) taste (**nach** of); [**gut**] **s~** taste good ● *vt* taste

Schmeichelei *f* **-,-en** flattery; (*Kompliment*) compliment

schmeichel|haft *adj* complimentary, flattering. **s~n** *vi* (*haben*) (+ *dat*) flatter

schmeißen† *vt/i* (*haben*) **s~** [**mit**] [!] chuck

Schmeißfliege *f* bluebottle

schmelz|en† *vt/i* (*sein*) melt; smelt (*Erze*). **S~wasser** *nt* melted snow and ice

Schmerbauch *m* [!] paunch

Schmerz *m* **-es,-en** pain; (*Kummer*) grief; **S~en haben** be in pain. **s~en** *vt* hurt; (*fig*) grieve ● *vi* (*haben*) hurt, be painful. **S~ensgeld** *nt* compensation for pain and suffering. **s~haft** *adj* painful. **s~los** *adj* painless **s~stillend** *adj* pain-killing; **s~stillendes Mittel** analgesic, pain-killer. **S~tablette** *f* pain-killer

Schmetterball *m* (*Tennis*) smash

Schmetterling *m* **-s,-e** butterfly

schmettern *vt* hurl; (*Tennis*) smash; (*singen*) sing ● *vi* (*haben*) sound

Schmied *m* **-[e]s,-e** blacksmith

Schmiede *f* **-,-n** forge. **S~eisen** *nt* wrought iron. **s~n** *vt* forge

Schmier|e *f* **-,-n** grease; (*Schmutz*) mess. **s~en** *vt* lubricate; (*streichen*) spread; (*schlecht schreiben*) scrawl ● *vi* (*haben*) smudge; (*schreiben*) scrawl. **S~geld** *nt* [!] bribe. **s~ig** *adj* greasy; (*schmutzig*) grubby. **S~mittel** *nt* lubricant

Schminke *f* -,-n make-up. **s~n** *vt* make up; **sich s~n** put on make-up; **sich** (*dat*) **die Lippen s~n** put on lipstick

schmirgel|n *vt* sand down. **S~papier** *nt* emery-paper

schmollen *vi* (*haben*) sulk

schmor|en *vt/i* (*haben*) braise. **S~topf** *m* casserole

Schmuck *m* -[e]s jewellery; (*Verzierung*) ornament, decoration

schmücken *vt* decorate, adorn

schmuck|los *adj* plain. **S~stück** *nt* piece of jewellery

Schmuggel *m* -s smuggling. **s~n** *vt* smuggle. **S~ware** *f* contraband

Schmuggler *m* -s,- smuggler

schmunzeln *vi* (*haben*) smile

schmusen *vi* (*haben*) cuddle

Schmutz *m* -es dirt. **s~en** *vi* (*haben*) get dirty. **s~ig** *adj* dirty

Schnabel *m* -s,¨ beak, bill; (*eines Kruges*) lip; (*Tülle*) spout

Schnalle *f* -,-n buckle. **s~n** *vt* strap; (*zu-*) buckle

schnalzen *vi* (*haben*) **mit der Zunge s~** click one's tongue

schnapp|en *vi* (*haben*) **s~en nach** snap at; gasp for (*Luft*) ● *vt* snatch, grab; (ⓘ: *festnehmen*) nab. **S~schloss** *nt* spring lock. **S~schuss** *m* snapshot

Schnaps *m* -es,¨e schnapps

schnarchen *vi* (*haben*) snore

schnaufen *vi* (*haben*) puff, pant

Schnauze *f* -,-n muzzle; (*eines Kruges*) lip; (*Tülle*) spout

schnäuzen (sich) *vr* blow one's nose

Schnecke *f* -,-n snail; (*Nackt-*) slug; (*Spirale*) scroll. **S~nhaus** *nt* snail-shell

Schnee *m* -s snow; (*Eier-*) beaten egg-white. **S~besen** *m* whisk. **S~brille** *f* snow-goggles *pl*. **S~fall** *m* snow-fall. **S~flocke** *f* snowflake. **S~glöckchen** *nt* -s,- snowdrop. **S~kette** *f* snow chain. **S~mann** *m* (*pl* -männer) snowman. **S~pflug** *m* snowplough. **S~schläger** *m* whisk. **S~sturm** *m* snowstorm, blizzard. **S~wehe** *f* -,-n snowdrift

Schneide *f* -,-n [cutting] edge; (*Klinge*) blade

schneiden† *vt* cut; (*in Scheiben*) slice; (*kreuzen*) cross; (*nicht beachten*) cut dead; **Gesichter s~** pull faces; **sich s~** cut oneself; (*über-*) intersect

Schneider *m* -s,- tailor. **S~in** *f* -,-nen dressmaker. **s~n** *vt* make (*Anzug, Kostüm*)

Schneidezahn *m* incisor

schneien *vi* (*haben*) snow; es schneit it is snowing

Schneise *f* -,-n path

schnell *adj* quick; (*Auto, Tempo*) fast ● *adv* quickly; (*in s~em Tempo*) fast; (*bald*) soon; **mach s~!** hurry up! **S~igkeit** *f* - rapidity; (*Tempo*) speed. **S~kochtopf** *m* pressure-cooker. **s~stens** *adv* as quickly as possible. **S~zug** *m* express [train]

schnetzeln *vt* cut into thin strips

Schnipsel *m* & *nt* -s,- scrap

Schnitt *m* -[e]s,-e cut; (*Film-*) cutting; (*S~muster*) [paper] pattern; **im S~** (*durchschnittlich*) on average

Schnitte *f* -,-n slice [of bread]

schnittig *adj* stylish; (*stromlinienförmig*) streamlined

Schnitt|lauch *m* chives *pl*. **S~muster** *nt* [paper] pattern. **S~punkt** *m* [point of] intersection. **S~stelle** *f* interface. **S~wunde** *f* cut

Schnitzel *nt* -s,- scrap; (*Culin*) escalope. **s~n** *vt* shred

schnitzen *vt/i* (*haben*) carve

S

schnodderig *adj* [!] brash
Schnorchel *m* **-s,-** snorkel
Schnörkel *m* **-s,-** flourish; (*Kunst*) scroll. **s~ig** *adj* ornate
schnüffeln *vi* (*haben*) sniff (**an etw** *dat* sth); ([!]: *spionieren*) snoop [around]
Schnuller *m* **-s,-** [baby's] dummy
Schnupf|en *m* **-s,-** [head] cold. **S~tabak** *m* snuff
schnuppern *vt/i* (*haben*) sniff (**an etw** *dat* sth)
Schnur *f* **-,¨e** string; (*Kordel*) cord; (*Electr*) flex
schnüren *vt* tie; lace [up] (*Schuhe*)
Schnurr|bart *m* moustache. **s~en** *vi* (*haben*) hum; (*Katze:*) purr
Schnürsenkel *m* [shoe-]lace
Schock *m* **-[e]s,-s** shock. **s~en** *vt* [!] shock. **s~ieren** *vt* shock
Schöffe *m* **-n,-n** lay judge
Schokolade *f* **-** chocolate
Scholle *f* **-,-n** clod [of earth]; (*Eis-*) [ice-]floe; (*Fisch*) plaice
schon *adv* already; (*allein*) just; (*sogar*) even; (*ohnehin*) anyway; **s~ einmal** before; (*jemals*) ever; **s~ immer/oft/wieder** always/often/again; **s~ deshalb** for that reason alone; **das ist s~ möglich** that's quite possible; **ja s~, aber** well yes, but
schön *adj* beautiful; (*Wetter*) fine; (*angenehm, nett*) nice; (*gut*) good; ([!]: *beträchtlich*) pretty; **s~en Dank!** thank you very much!
schonen *vt* spare; (*gut behandeln*) look after. **s~d** *adj* gentle
Schönheit *f* **-,-en** beauty. **S~sfehler** *m* blemish. **S~skonkurrenz** *f* beauty contest
Schonung *f* **-,-en** gentle care; (*nach Krankheit*) rest; (*Baum-*) plantation. **s~slos** *adj* ruthless
Schonzeit *f* close season
schöpf|en *vt* scoop [up]; ladle (*Suppe*); **Mut s~en** take heart. **s~erisch** *adj* creative. **S~kelle** *f*. **S~löffel** *m* ladle. **S~ung** *f* **-,-en** creation
Schoppen *m* **-s,-** (*SGer*) ≈ pint
Schorf *m* **-[e]s** scab
Schornstein *m* chimney. **S~feger** *m* **-s,-** chimney sweep
Schoß *m* **-es,¨e** lap; (*Frack-*) tail
Schössling *m* **-s,-e** (*Bot*) shoot
Schote *f* **-,-n** pod; (*Erbse*) pea
Schotte *m* **-n,-n** Scot, Scotsman
Schottin *f* **-nen** Scot, Scotswoman
Schotter *m* **-s** gravel
schott|isch *adj* Scottish, Scots. **S~land** *nt* **-s** Scotland
schraffieren *vt* hatch
schräg *adj* diagonal; (*geneigt*) sloping; **s~ halten** tilt. **S~strich** *m* oblique stroke
Schramme *f* **-,-n** scratch
Schrank *m* **-[e]s,¨e** cupboard; (*Kleider-*) wardrobe; (*Akten-, Glas-*) cabinet
Schranke *f* **-,-n** barrier
Schraube *f* **-,-n** screw; (*Schiffs-*) propeller. **s~n** *vt* screw; (*ab-*) unscrew; (*drehen*) turn. **S~nschlüssel** *m* spanner. **S~nzieher** *m* **-s,-** screwdriver
Schraubstock *m* vice
Schreck *m* **-[e]s,-e** fright. **S~en** *m* **-s,-** fright; (*Entsetzen*) horror
Schreck|gespenst *nt* spectre. **s~haft** *adj* easily frightened; (*nervös*) jumpy. **s~lich** *adj* terrible.
Schrei *m* **-[e]s,-e** cry, shout; (*gellend*) scream; **der letzte S~** [!] the latest thing
schreib|en† *vt/i* (*haben*) write; (*auf der Maschine*) type; **richtig/falsch s~en** spell right/wrong; **sich**

s~en (*Wort:*) be spelt; (*korrespondieren*) correspond. **S~en** *nt* **-s,-** writing; (*Brief*) letter. **S~fehler** *m* spelling mistake. **S~heft** *nt* exercise book. **S~kraft** *f* clerical assistant; (*für Maschineschreiben*) typist. **S~maschine** *f* typewriter. **S~tisch** *m* desk. **S~ung** *f* **-,-en** spelling. **S~waren** *fpl* stationery *sg.*

schreien† *vt/i* (*haben*) cry; (*gellend*) scream; (*rufen, laut sprechen*) shout

Schreiner *m* **-s,-** joiner

schreiten† *vi* (*sein*) walk

Schrift *f* **-,-en** writing; (*Druck-*) type; (*Abhandlung*) paper; **die Heilige S~** the Scriptures *pl.* **S~führer** *m* secretary. **s~lich** *adj* written ● *adv* in writing. **S~sprache** *f* written language. **S~steller(in)** *m* **-s,-** (*f* **-,-nen**) writer. **S~stück** *nt* document. **S~zeichen** *nt* character

schrill *adj* shrill

Schritt *m* **-[e]s,-e** step; (*Entfernung*) pace; (*Gangart*) walk; (*der Hose*) crotch. **S~macher** *m* **-s,-** pace-maker. **s~weise** *adv* step by step

schroff *adj* precipitous; (*abweisend*) brusque; (*unvermittelt*) abrupt; (*Gegensatz*) stark

Schrot *m & nt* **-[e]s** coarse meal; (*Blei-*) small shot. **S~flinte** *f* shotgun

Schrott *m* **-[e]s** scrap[-metal]; **zu S~ fahren** ! write off. **S~platz** *m* scrap-yard

schrubben *vt/i* (*haben*) scrub

Schrull|e *f* **-,-n** whim; **alte S~e** ! old crone. **s~ig** *adj* cranky

schrumpfen *vi* (*sein*) shrink

schrump[e]lig *adj* wrinkled

Schub *m* **-[e]s,⸚e** (*Phys*) thrust; (*S~fach*) drawer; (*Menge*) batch. **S~fach** *nt* drawer. **S~karre** *f*, **S~karren** *m* wheelbarrow. **S~lade** *f* drawer

Schubs *m* **-es,-e** push, shove **s~en** *vt* push, shove

schüchtern *adj* shy. **S~heit** *f* **-** shyness

Schuft *m* **-[e]s,-e** (*pej*) swine

Schuh *m* **-[e]s,-e** shoe. **S~anzieher** *m* **-s,-** shoehorn. **S~band** *nt* (*pl* **-bänder**) shoe-lace. **S~creme** *f* shoe-polish. **S~löffel** *m* shoehorn. **S~macher** *m* **-s,-** shoemaker

Schul|abgänger *m* **-s,-** schoolleaver. **S~arbeiten, S~aufgaben** *fpl* homework *sg.*

Schuld *f* **-,-en** guilt; (*Verantwortung*) blame; (*Geld-*) debt; **S~en machen** get into debt; **S~ haben** be to blame (**an** + *dat* for); **jdm S~ geben** blame s.o. ● **s~ sein** be to blame (**an** + *dat* for). **s~en** *vt* owe

schuldig *adj* guilty (*gen* of); (*gebührend*) due; **jdm etw s~sein** owe s.o. sth. **S~keit** *f* **-** duty

schuld|los *adj* innocent. **S~ner** *m* **-s,-** debtor. **S~spruch** *m* guilty verdict

Schule *f* **-,-n** school; **in der/die S~** at/to school. **s~n** *vt* train

Schüler(in) *m* **-s,-** (*f* **-,-nen**) pupil

schul|frei *adj* **s~freier Tag** day without school; **wir haben morgen s~frei** there's no school tomorrow. **S~hof** *m* [school] playground. **S~jahr** *nt* school year; (*Klasse*) form. **S~kind** *nt* schoolchild. **S~stunde** *f* lesson

Schulter *f* **-,-n** shoulder. **S~blatt** *nt* shoulder-blade

Schulung *f* **-** training

schummeln *vi* (*haben*) ! cheat

Schund *m* **-[e]s** trash

Schuppe *f* **-,-n** scale; **S~n** *pl* dandruff *sg.* **s~n (sich)** *vr* flake [off]

Schuppen *m* **-s,-** shed

schürf|en *vt* mine; **sich** (*dat*) **das Knie s~en** graze one's knee ● *vi* (*haben*) **s~en nach** prospect for. **S~wunde** *f* abrasion, graze

Schürhaken *m* poker

Schurke *m* **-n,-n** villain

Schürze *f* **-,-n** apron

Schuss *m* **-es,¨e** shot; (*kleine Menge*) dash

Schüssel *f* **-,-n** bowl; (*TV*) dish

Schuss|fahrt *f* (*Ski*) schuss. **S~waffe** *f* firearm

Schuster *m* **-s,-** = **Schuhmacher**

Schutt *m* **-[e]s** rubble. **S~abladeplatz** *m* rubbish dump

Schüttel|frost *m* shivering fit. **s~n** *vt* shake; **sich s~n** shake oneself/itself; (*vor Ekel*) shudder; **jdm die Hand s~n** shake s.o.'s hand

schütten *vt* pour; (*kippen*) tip; (*ver-*) spill ● *vi* (*haben*) **es schüttet** it is pouring [with rain]

Schutz *m* **-es** protection; (*Zuflucht*) shelter; (*Techn*) guard; **S~ suchen** take refuge. **S~anzug** *m* protective suit. **S~blech** *nt* mudguard. **S~brille** goggles *pl*

Schütze *m* **-n,-n** marksman; (*Tor-*) scorer; (*Astrology*) Sagittarius

schützen *vt* protect; (*Zuflucht gewähren*) shelter (**vor** + *dat* from) ● *vi* (*haben*) give protection/shelter (**vor** + *dat* from)

Schutz|engel *m* guardian angel. **S~heilige(r)** *m/f* patron saint

Schützling *m* **-s,-e** charge

schutz|los *adj* defenceless, helpless. **S~mann** *m* (*pl* **-männer & -leute**) policeman. **S~umschlag** *m* dust-jacket

Schwaben *nt* **-s** Swabia

schwäbisch *adj* Swabian

schwach *adj* weak; (*nicht gut; gering*) poor; (*leicht*) faint

Schwäche *f* **-,-n** weakness. **s~n** *vt* weaken

schwäch|lich *adj* delicate. **S~ling** *m* **-s,-e** weakling

Schwachsinn *m* mental deficiency. **s~ig** *adj* mentally deficient; [!] idiotic

Schwager *m* **-s,¨** brother-in-law

Schwägerin *f* **-,-nen** sister-in-law

Schwalbe *f* **-,-n** swallow

Schwall *m* **-[e]s** torrent

Schwamm *m* **-[e]s,¨e** sponge; (*SGer: Pilz*) fungus; (*essbar*) mushroom. **s~ig** *adj* spongy

Schwan *m* **-[e]s,¨e** swan

schwanger *adj* pregnant

Schwangerschaft *f* **-,-en** pregnancy

Schwank *m* **-[e]s,¨e** (*Theat*) farce

schwank|en *vi* (*haben*) sway; (*Boot:*) rock; (*sich ändern*) fluctuate; (*unentschieden sein*) be undecided ● (*sein*) stagger. **S~ung** *f* **-,-en** fluctuation

Schwanz *m* **-es,¨e** tail

schwänzen *vt* [!] skip; **die Schule s~** play truant

Schwarm *m* **-[e]s,¨e** swarm; (*Fisch-*) shoal; ([!]: *Liebe*) idol

schwärmen *vi* (*haben*) swarm; **s~ für** [!] adore; (*verliebt sein*) have a crush on

Schwarte *f* **-,-n** (*Speck-*) rind

schwarz *adj* black; ([!]: *illegal*) illegal; **s~er Markt** black market; **s~ gekleidet** dressed in black; **s~ auf weiß** in black and white; **s~ sehen** (*fig*) be pessimistic; **ins S~e treffen** score a bull's-eye. **S~** *nt* **-[e]s,-** black. **S~arbeit** *f* moonlighting. **s~arbeiten** *vi sep* (*haben*) moonlight. **S~e(r)** *m/f* black

Schwärze *f* **-** blackness. **s~n** *vt* blacken

Schwarz|fahrer *m* fare-dodger. **S~handel** *m* black market (**mit** in). **S~händler** *m* black marketeer. **S~markt** *m* black market. **S~wald** *m* Black Forest. **s~weiß** *adj* black and white

schwatzen, (*SGer*) **schwätzen** *vi* (*haben*) chat; (*klatschen*) gossip; (*Sch*) talk [in class] ● *vt* talk

Schwebe *f* - **in der S~** (*fig*) undecided. **S~bahn** *f* cable railway. **s~n** *vi* (*haben*) float; (*fig*) be undecided; (*Verfahren:*) be pending; **in Gefahr s~n** be in danger ● (*sein*) float

Schwed|e *m* **-n,-n** Swede. **S~en** *nt* **-s** Sweden. **S~in** *f* **-,-nen** Swede. **s~isch** *adj* Swedish

Schwefel *m* **-s** sulphur

schweigen† *vi* (*haben*) be silent; **ganz zu s~ von** let alone. **S~** *nt* **-s** silence; **zum S~ bringen** silence

schweigsam *adj* silent; (*wortkarg*) taciturn

Schwein *nt* **-[e]s,-e** pig; (*Culin*) pork; (✖ *Schuft*) swine; **S~haben** ! be lucky. **S~ebraten** *m* roast pork. **S~efleisch** *nt* pork. **S~erei** *f* **-,-en** ✖ [dirty] mess; (*Gemeinheit*) dirty trick. **S~estall** *m* pigsty. **S~sleder** *nt* pigskin

Schweiß *m* **-es** sweat

schweißen *vt* weld

Schweiz (die) - Switzerland. **S~er** *adj* & *m* **-s,-, S~erin** *f* **-,-nen** Swiss. **s~erisch** *adj* Swiss

Schweizerische Eidgenossenschaft The Swiss Confederation is the official name for Switzerland. The confederation was established in 1291 when the cantons (▷**KANTON**) of Uri, Schwyz and Unterwalden swore to defend their traditional rights against the Habsburg Empire. The unified federal state as it is known today was formed in 1848.

Schwelle *f* **-,-n** threshold; (*Eisenbahn-*) sleeper

schwell|en† *vi* (*sein*) swell. **S~ung** *f* **-,-en** swelling

schwer *adj* heavy; (*schwierig*) difficult; (*mühsam*) hard; (*ernst*) serious; (*schlimm*) bad; **3 Pfund s~ sein** weigh 3 pounds ● *adv* heavily; with difficulty; (*mühsam*) hard; (*schlimm, sehr*) badly, seriously; **s~ krank/verletzt** seriously ill/injured; **s~ hören** be hard of hearing; **etw s~ nehmen** take sth seriously; **jdm s~ fallen** be hard for s.o.; **es jdm s~ machen** make it *or* things difficult for s.o.; **sich s~ tun** have difficulty (**mit** with); **s~ zu sagen** difficult *or* hard to say

Schwere *f* - heaviness; (*Gewicht*) weight; (*Schwierigkeit*) difficulty; (*Ernst*) gravity. **S~losigkeit** *f* - weightlessness

schwer|fällig *adj* ponderous, clumsy. **S~gewicht** *nt* heavyweight. **s~hörig** *adj* **s~hörig sein** be hard of hearing. **S~kraft** *f* (*Phys*) gravity. **s~mütig** *adj* melancholic. **S~punkt** *m* centre of gravity; (*fig*) emphasis

Schwert *nt* **-[e]s,-er** sword. **S~lilie** *f* iris

Schwer|verbrecher *m* serious offender. **s~wiegend** *adj* weighty

Schwester *f* **-,-n** sister; (*Kranken-*) nurse. **s~lich** *adj* sisterly

Schwieger|eltern *pl* parents-in-law. **S~mutter** *f* mother-in-law. **S~sohn** *m* son-in-law. **S~tochter** *f* daughter-in-law. **S~vater** *m* father-in-law

schwierig *adj* difficult. **S~keit** *f*

-,-en difficulty

Schwimm|bad *nt* swimming-baths *pl.* **S~becken** *nt* swimming-pool. **s~en†** *vt/i* (*sein/haben*) swim; (*auf dem Wasser treiben*) float. **S~weste** *f* life-jacket

Schwindel *m* **-s** dizziness, vertigo; (ⓘ: *Betrug*) fraud; (*Lüge*) lie. **S~anfall** *m* dizzy spell. **s~frei** *adj* **s~frei sein** have a good head for heights. **s~n** *vi* (*haben*) lie

Schwindl|er *m* **-s,-** liar; (*Betrüger*) fraud, con-man. **s~ig** *adj* dizzy; **mir ist** *od* **wird s~ig** I feel dizzy

schwing|en† *vi* (*haben*) swing; (*Phys*) oscillate; (*vibrieren*) vibrate ● *vt* swing; wave (*Fahne*); (*drohend*) brandish. **S~ung** *f* **-,-en** oscillation; vibration

Schwips *m* **-es,-e einen S~ haben** ⓘ be tipsy

schwitzen *vi* (*haben*) sweat; **ich s~e** I am hot

schwören† *vt/i* (*haben*) swear (**auf** + *acc* by)

schwul *adj* (ⓘ: *homosexuell*) gay

schwül *adj* close. **S~e** *f* - closeness

Schwung *m* **-[e]s,⸗e** swing; (*Bogen*) sweep; (*Schnelligkeit*) momentum; (*Kraft*) vigour. **s~los** *adj* dull. **s~voll** *adj* vigorous; (*Bogen, Linie*) sweeping; (*mitreißend*) spirited

S

Schwur *m* **-[e]s,⸗e** vow; (*Eid*) oath. **S~gericht** *nt* jury [court]

sechs *inv adj*, **S~** *f* **-,-en** six; (*Sch*) ≈ fail mark. **s~eckig** *adj* hexagonal. **s~te(r,s)** *adj* sixth

sech|zehn *inv adj* sixteen. **s~zehnte(r,s)** *adj* sixteenth. **s~zig** *inv adj* sixty. **s~zigste(r,s)** *adj* sixtieth

See[1] *m* **-s,-n** lake

See[2] *f* - sea; **an die/der See** to/at the seaside; **auf See** at sea. **S~fahrt** *f* [sea] voyage; (*Schifffahrt*) navigation. **S~gang** *m* **schwerer S~gang** rough sea. **S~hund** *m* seal. **s~krank** *adj* seasick

Seele *f* **-,-n** soul

seelisch *adj* psychological; (*geistig*) mental

See|macht *f* maritime power. **S~mann** *m* (*pl* **-leute**) seaman, sailor. **S~not** *f* **in S~not** in distress. **S~räuber** *m* pirate. **S~reise** *f* [sea] voyage. **S~rose** *f* water-lily. **S~sack** *m* kitbag. **S~stern** *m* starfish. **S~tang** *m* seaweed. **s~tüchtig** *adj* seaworthy. **S~zunge** *f* sole

Segel *nt* **-s,-** sail. **S~boot** *nt* sailing-boat. **S~flugzeug** *nt* glider. **s~n** *vt/i* (*sein/haben*) sail. **S~schiff** *nt* sailing-ship. **S~sport** *m* sailing. **S~tuch** *nt* canvas

Segen *m* **-s** blessing

Segler *m* **-s,-** yachtsman

segnen *vt* bless

sehen† *vt* see; watch (*Fernsehsendung*); **jdn/etw wieder s~** see s.o./sth again; **sich s~ lassen** show oneself ● *vi* (*haben*) see; (*blicken*) look (**auf** + *acc* at); (*ragen*) show (**aus** above); **gut/schlecht s~** have good/bad eyesight; **vom S~ kennen** know by sight; **s~ nach** keep an eye on; (*betreuen*) look after; (*suchen*) look for. **s~swert, s~swürdig** *adj* worth seeing. **S~swürdigkeit** *f* **-,-en** sight

Sehne *f* **-,-n** tendon; (*eines Bogens*) string

sehnen (sich) *vr* long (**nach** for)

Sehn|sucht *f* - longing (**nach** for). **s~süchtig** *adj* longing; (*Wunsch*) dearest

sehr *adv* very; (*mit Verb*) very much; **so s~, dass** so much that

seicht *adj* shallow

seid *s.* **sein**[1]

Seide *f* **-,-n** silk

Seidel *nt* **-s,-** beer-mug

seiden *adj* silk **S~papier** *nt* tissue paper. **S~raupe** *f* silk-worm

seidig *adj* silky

Seife *f* **-,-n** soap. **S~npulver** *nt* soap powder. **S~nschaum** *m* lather

Seil *nt* **-[e]s,-e** rope; (*Draht-*) cable. **S~bahn** *f* cable railway. **s~springen†** *vi* (*sein*) (*infinitive & pp only*) skip. **S~tänzer(in)** *m(f)* tightrope walker

sein†[1]

● *intransitive verb* (*sein*)

····➤ be. **ich bin glücklich** I am happy. **er ist Lehrer/Schwede** he is a teacher/Swedish. **bist du es?** is that you? **sei still!** be quiet! **sie waren in Paris** they were in Paris. **morgen bin ich zu Hause** I shall be at home tomorrow. **er ist aus Berlin** he is or comes from Berlin

····➤ (*impers + dat*) **mir ist kalt/besser** I am cold/better. **ihr ist schlecht** she feels sick

····➤ (*existieren*) be. **es ist/sind ...** there is/are .... **es ist keine Hoffnung mehr** there is no more hope. **es sind vier davon** there are four of them. **es war einmal ein Prinz** once upon a time there was a prince

● *auxiliary verb*

····➤ (*zur Perfektumschreibung*) have. **er ist gestorben** he has died. **sie sind angekommen** they have arrived. **sie war dort gewesen** she had been there. **ich wäre gefallen** I would have fallen

····➤ (*zur Bildung des Passivs*) be. **wir sind gerettet worden/wir waren gerettet** we were saved

····➤ (*+ zu + Infinitiv*) be to be. **es war niemand zu sehen** there was no one to be seen. **das war zu erwarten** that was to be expected. **er ist zu bemitleiden** he is to be pitied. **die Richtlinien sind strengstens zu beachten** the guidelines are to be strictly followed

sein[2] *poss pron* his; (*Ding, Tier*) its; (*nach man*) one's; **sein Glück versuchen** try one's luck. **s~e(r,s)** *poss pron* his; (*nach man*) one's own; **das S~e tun** do one's share. **s~erseits** *adv* for his part. **s~erzeit** *adv* in those days. **s~etwegen** *adv* for his sake; (*wegen ihm*) because of him, on his account. **s~ige** *poss pron* **der/die/das s~ige** his

seins *poss pron* his; (*nach man*) one's own

seit *conj & prep* (+ *dat*) since; **s~ einiger** Zeit for some time [past]; **ich wohne s~ zehn Jahren hier** I've lived here for ten years. **s~dem** *conj* since ● *adv* since then

Seite *f* **-,-n** side; (*Buch-*) page; **zur S~ treten** step aside; **auf der einen/anderen S~** (*fig*) on the one/other hand

seitens *prep* (+ *gen*) on the part of

Seiten|schiff *nt* [side] aisle. **S~sprung** *m* infidelity. **S~stechen** *nt* **-s** (*Med*) stitch. **S~straße** *f* side-street. **S~streifen** *m* verge; (*Autobahn-*) hard shoulder

seither *adv* since then

seit|lich *adj* side ● *adv* at/on the side; **s~lich von** to one side of ● *prep* (+ *gen*) to one side of. **s~wärts** *adv* on/to one side; (*zur Seite*) sideways

Sekret|är *m* **-s,-e** secretary; (*Schrank*) bureau. **S~ariat** *nt* **-[e]s,-e** secretary's office. **S~ärin** *f* **-,-nen**

secretary
Sekt *m* -[e]s [German] sparkling wine
Sekte *f* -,-n sect
Sektor *m* -s,-en sector
Sekunde *f* -,-n second
Sekundenschlaf *m* microsleep
selber *pron* [!] = selbst
selbst *pron* oneself; **ich/du/er/sie s~** I myself /you yourself/ he himself/she herself; **wir/ihr/sie s~** we ourselves/you yourselves/they themselves; **ich schneide mein Haar s~** I cut my own hair; **von s~** of one's own accord; (*automatisch*) automatically; **s~ gemacht** home-made ● *adv* even
selbständig *adj* = selbstständig. **S~keit** *f* - = Selbstständigkeit
Selbst|bedienung *f* self-service. **S~befriedigung** *f* masturbation. **s~bewusst** *adj* self-confident. **S~bewusstsein** *nt* self-confidence. **S~bildnis** *nt* self-portrait. **S~erhaltung** *f* self-preservation. **s~gemacht*** *adj* = **s~ gemacht**, s. selbst. **s~haftend** *adj* self-adhesive. **S~hilfe** *f* self-help. **s~klebend** *adj* self-adhesive. **S~kostenpreis** *m* cost price. **S~laut** *m* vowel. **s~los** *adj* selfless. **S~mord** *m* suicide. **S~mordattentat** *nt* suicide attack. **S~mörder(in)** *m(f)* suicide. **s~mörderisch** *adj* suicidal. **S~porträt** *nt* self-portrait. **s~sicher** *adj* self-assured. **s~ständig** *adj* independent; self-employed (*Handwerker*); **sich s~ständig machen** set up on one's own. **S~ständigkeit** *f* - independence. **s~süchtig** *adj* selfish. **S~tanken** *nt* self-service (*for petrol*). **s~tätig** *adj* automatic. **S~versorgung** *f* self-catering. **s~verständlich** *adj* natural; **etw für s~ halten** take sth for granted; **das ist s~** that goes without saying; **s~!** of course! **S~verteidigung** *f* self-defence. **S~vertrauen** *nt* self-confidence. **S~verwaltung** *f* self-government
selig *adj* blissfully happy; (*Relig*) blessed; (*verstorben*) late. **S~keit** *f* - bliss
Sellerie *m* -s,-s & *f* -,- celeriac; (*Stangen-*) celery
selten *adj* rare ● *adv* rarely, seldom; (*besonders*) exceptionally. **S~heit** *f* -,-en rarity
seltsam *adj* odd, strange. **s~erweise** *adv* oddly
Semester *nt* -s,- (*Univ*) semester
Semikolon *nt* -s,-s semicolon
Seminar *nt* -s,-e seminar; (*Institut*) department; (*Priester-*) seminary
Semmel *f* -,-n (*Aust, SGer*) [bread] roll. **S~brösel** *pl* breadcrumbs
Senat *m* -[e]s,-e senate. **S~or** *m* -s,-en senator
senden[1]† *vt* send
sende|n[2] *vt* (*reg*) broadcast; (*über Funk*) transmit, send. **S~r** *m* -s,- [broadcasting] station; (*Anlage*) transmitter. **S~reihe** *f* series
Sendung *f* -,-en consignment, shipment; (*TV*) programme
Senf *m* -s mustard
senil *adj* senile. **S~ität** *f* - senility
Senior *m* -s,-en senior; **S~en** senior citizens. **S~enheim** *nt* old people's home
senken *vt* lower; bring down (*Fieber, Preise*); bow (*Kopf*); **sich s~** come down, fall; (*absinken*) subside
senkrecht *adj* vertical. **S~e** *f* -n,-n perpendicular
Sensation /-ˈtsi̯oːn/ *f* -,-en sensation. **s~ell** *adj* sensational
Sense *f* -,-n scythe
sensibel *adj* sensitive
sentimental *adj* sentimental

S

September *m* **-s,-** September
Serie /'ze:ri̯ə/ *f* **-,-n** series; (*Briefmarken*) set; (*Comm*) range. **S~nnummer** *f* serial number
seriös *adj* respectable; (*zuverlässig*) reliable
Serpentine *f* **-,-n** winding road; (*Kehre*) hairpin bend
Serum *nt* **-s,Sera** serum
Server *m* **-s,-** server
Service[1] /zɛr'vi:s/ *nt* **-[s],-** service, set
Service[2] /'zø:ɐ̯vɪs/ *m & nt* **-s** (*Comm, Tennis*) service
servier|en *vt/i* (*haben*) serve. **S~erin** *f* **-,-nen** waitress
Serviette *f* **-,-n** napkin, serviette
Servus *int* (*Aust*) cheerio; (*Begrüßung*) hallo
Sessel *m* **-s,-** armchair. **S~bahn** *f*, **S~lift** *m* chairlift
sesshaft *adj* settled
Set /zɛt/ *nt & m* **-[s],-s** set; (*Deckchen*) place-mat
setz|en *vt* put; (*abstellen*) set down; (*hin-*) sit down (*Kind*); move (*Spielstein*); (*pflanzen*) plant; (*schreiben, wetten*) put; **sich s~en** sit down; (*sinken*) settle ●*vi* (*sein*) leap ●*vi* (*haben*) **s~en auf** (+ *acc*) back
Seuche *f* **-,-n** epidemic
seufz|en *vi* (*haben*) sigh. **S~er** *m* **-s,-** sigh
Sex /zɛks/ *m* **-[es]** sex
Sexu|alität *f* **-** sexuality. **s~ell** *adj* sexual
sezieren *vt* dissect
Shampoo /ʃam'pu:/, **Shampoon** /ʃam'po:n/ *nt* **-s** shampoo
siamesisch *adj* Siamese
sich *reflexive pron* oneself; (*mit er/sie/es*) himself/herself/itself; (*mit sie pl*) themselves; (*mit Sie*) yourself; (*pl*) yourselves; (*einander*) each other; **s~ kennen** know oneself/(*einander*) each other; **s~ waschen** have a wash; **s~** (*dat*) **die Haare kämmen** comb one's hair; **s~ wundern** be surprised; **s~ gut verkaufen** sell well; **von s~ aus** of one's own accord
Sichel *f* **-,-n** sickle
sicher *adj* safe; (*gesichert*) secure; (*gewiss*) certain; (*zuverlässig*) reliable; sure (*Urteil*); steady (*Hand*); (*selbstbewusst*) self-confident; **bist du s~?** are you sure? ●*adv* safely; securely; certainly; reliably; self-confidently; (*wahrscheinlich*) most probably; **s~!** certainly! **s~gehen**† *vi sep* (*sein*) (*fig*) be sure
Sicherheit *f* **-** safety; (*Pol, Psych, Comm*) security; (*Gewissheit*) certainty; (*Zuverlässigkeit*) reliability; (*des Urteils*) surety; (*Selbstbewusstsein*) self-confidence. **S~sgurt** *m* safety belt; (*Auto*) seat belt. **S~snadel** *f* safety pin
sicherlich *adv* certainly; (*wahrscheinlich*) most probably
sicher|n *vt* secure; (*garantieren*) safeguard; (*schützen*) protect; put the safety catch on (*Pistole*). **S~ung** *f* **-,-en** safeguard, protection; (*Gewehr-*) safety catch; (*Electr*) fuse
Sicht *f* **-** view; (*S~weite*) visibility; **auf lange S~** in the long term. **s~bar** *adj* visible. **S~vermerk** *m* visa. **S~weite** *f* visibility; **außer S~weite** out of sight
sie *pron* (*nom*) (*sg*) she; (*Ding, Tier*) it; (*pl*) they; (*acc*) (*sg*) her; (*Ding, Tier*) it; (*pl*) them
Sie *pron* you; **gehen/warten Sie!** go/wait!
Sieb *nt* **-[e]s,-e** sieve; (*Tee-*) strainer. **s~en**[1] *vt* sieve, sift
sieben[2] *inv adj*, **S~** *f* **-,-en** seven. **S~sachen** *fpl* [T] belongings.

S

s~te(r,s) *adj* seventh
sieb|te(r,s) *adj* seventh. **s~zehn** *inv adj* seventeen. **s~zehnte(r,s)** *adj* seventeenth. **s~zig** *inv adj* seventy. **s~zigste(r,s)** *adj* seventieth
siede|n† *vt/i* (*haben*) boil. **S~punkt** *m* boiling point
Siedlung *f* **-,-en** [housing] estate; (*Niederlassung*) settlement
Sieg *m* **-[e]s,-e** victory
Siegel *nt* **-s,-** seal. **S~ring** *m* signet-ring
sieg|en *vi* (*haben*) win. **S~er(in)** *m* **-s,-** (*f* **-,-nen**) winner. **s~reich** *adj* victorious
siezen *vt* **jdn s~** call s.o. 'Sie'
Signal *nt* **-s,-e** signal
Silbe *f* **-,-n** syllable
Silber *nt* **-s** silver. **s~n** *adj* silver
Silhouette /zi'luɛtə/ *f* **-,-n** silhouette
Silizium *nt* **-s** silicon
Silo *m & nt* **-s,-s** silo
Silvester *nt* **-s** New Year's Eve
SIM-Karte *f* SIM card
Sims *m & nt* **-es,-e** ledge
simsen *vi* send a text
simultan *adj* simultaneous
sind *s.* **sein**[1]
Sinfonie *f* **-,-n** symphony
singen† *vt/i* (*haben*) sing
Singvogel *m* songbird
sinken† *vi* (*sein*) sink; (*nieder-*) drop; (*niedriger werden*) go down, fall; **den Mut s~ lassen** lose courage
Sinn *m* **-[e]s,-e** sense; (*Denken*) mind; (*Zweck*) point; **in gewissem S~e** in a sense; **es hat keinen S~** it is pointless. **S~bild** *nt* symbol
sinnlich *adj* sensory; (*sexuell*) sensual; (*Genüsse*) sensuous. **S~keit** *f* **-** sensuality; sensuousness
sinn|los *adj* senseless; (*zwecklos*) pointless. **s~voll** *adj* meaningful; (*vernünftig*) sensible
Sintflut *f* flood
Siphon /'zi:fõ/ *m* **-s,-s** siphon
Sippe *f* **-,-n** clan
Sirene *f* **-,-n** siren
Sirup *m* **-s,-e** syrup; treacle
Sitte *f* **-,-n** custom; **S~n** manners
sittlich *adj* moral. **S~keit** *f* **-** morality. **S~keitsverbrecher** *m* sex offender
sittsam *adj* well-behaved; (*züchtig*) demure
Situ|ation /-'tsi̯o:n/ *f* **-,-en** situation. **s~iert** *adj* **gut/schlecht s~iert** well/badly off
Sitz *m* **-es,-e** seat; (*Passform*) fit
sitzen† *vi* (*haben*) sit; (*sich befinden*) be; (*passen*) fit; (**!**: *treffen*) hit home; **[im Gefängnis] s~ !** be in jail; **s~ bleiben** remain seated; **!** (*Sch*) stay *or* be kept down; (*nicht heiraten*) be left on the shelf; **s~ bleiben auf** (+ *dat*) be left with
Sitz|gelegenheit *f* seat. **S~platz** *m* seat. **S~ung** *f* **-,-en** session
Sizilien /-i̯ən/ *nt* **-s** Sicily
Skala *f* **-,-len** scale; (*Reihe*) range
Skalpell *nt* **-s,-e** scalpel
skalpieren *vt* scalp
Skandal *m* **-s,-e** scandal. **s~ös** *adj* scandalous
Skandinav|ien /-i̯ən/ *nt* **-s** Scandinavia. **s~isch** *adj* Scandinavian
Skat *m* **-s** skat
Skateboard /'ske:tbo:ɐ̯t/ *nt* **-s, -s** skateboard
Skelett *nt* **-[e]s,-e** skeleton
Skep|sis *f* **-** scepticism. **s~tisch** *adj* sceptical
Ski /ʃi:/ *m* **-s,-er** ski; **Ski fahren** *od* **laufen** ski. **S~fahrer(in), S~läufer(in)** *m(f)* **-s,-** (*f* **-,-nen**) skier.

S

S~sport *m* skiing

Skizz|e *f* **-,-n** sketch. **s~ieren** *vt* sketch

Sklav|e *m* **-n,-n** slave. **S~erei** *f* **-** slavery. **S~in** *f* **-,-nen** slave

Skorpion *m* **-s,-e** scorpion; (*Astrology*) Scorpio

Skrupel *m* **-s,-** scruple. **s~los** *adj* unscrupulous

Skulptur *f* **-,-en** sculpture

Slalom *m* **-s,-s** slalom

Slaw|e *m* **-n,-n, S~in** *f* **-,-nen** Slav. **s~isch** *adj* Slav; (*Lang*) Slavonic

Slip *m* **-s,-s** briefs *pl*

Smaragd *m* **-[e]s,-e** emerald

Smoking *m* **-s,-s** dinner jacket

SMS-Nachricht *f* text message

Snob *m* **-s,-s** snob. **S~ismus** *m* **-** snobbery **s~istisch** *adj* snobbish

so *adv* so; (*so sehr*) so much; (*auf diese Weise*) like this/that; (*solch*) such; ([F]*: sowieso*) anyway; ([F]*: umsonst*) free; ([F]*: ungefähr*) about; **so viel** so much; **so gut/bald wie** as good/soon as; **so ein Zufall!** what a coincidence! **mir ist so, als ob** I feel as if; **so oder so** in any case; **so um zehn Euro** [F] about ten euros; **so?** really? ● *conj* (*also*) so; (*dann*) then; **so dass** = **sodass**

sobald *conj* as soon as

Söckchen *nt* **-s,-** [ankle] sock

Socke *f* **-,-n** sock

Sockel *m* **-s,-** plinth, pedestal

Socken *m* **-s,-** sock

sodass *conj* so that

Sodawasser *nt* soda water

Sodbrennen *nt* **-s** heartburn

soeben *adv* just [now]

Sofa *nt* **-s,-s** settee, sofa

sofern *adv* provided [that]

sofort *adv* at once, immediately; (*auf der Stelle*) instantly

Software /'zɔftvɛːɐ̯/ *f* **-** software

sogar *adv* even

sogenannt *adj* so-called

sogleich *adv* at once

Sohle *f* **-,-n** sole; (*Tal-*) bottom

Sohn *m* **-[e]s,¨-e** son

Sojabohne *f* soya bean

solange *conj* as long as

solch *inv pron* such; **s~ ein(e)** such a; **s~ einer/eine/eins** one/(*Person*) someone like that. **s~e(r,s)** *pron* such ● (*substantivisch*) **ein s~er/ eine s~e/ein s~es** one/(*Person*) someone like that; **s~e** *pl* those; (*Leute*) people like that

Soldat *m* **-en,-en** soldier

Söldner *m* **-s,-** mercenary

Solidarität *f* **-** solidarity

solide *adj* solid; (*haltbar*) sturdy; (*sicher*) sound; (*anständig*) respectable

Solist(in) *m* **-en,-en** (*f* **-,-nen**) soloist

Soll *nt* **-s** (*Comm*) debit; (*Produktions-*) quota

sollen†

● *auxiliary verb*

····➤ (*Verpflichtung*) be [supposed *or* meant] to. **er soll morgen zum Arzt gehen** he is [supposed] to go to the doctor tomorrow. **die beiden Flächen sollen fluchten** the two surfaces are meant to be *or* should be in alignment. **du solltest ihn anrufen** you were meant to phone him *or* should have phoned him

····➤ (*Befehl*) **du sollst sofort damit aufhören** you're to stop that at once. **er soll hereinkommen** he is to come in; (*sagen Sie es ihm*) tell him to come in

····➤ **sollte** (*subjunctive*) should;

ought to. **wir sollten früher aufstehen** we ought to *or* should get up earlier. **das hätte er nicht tun/sagen sollen** he shouldn't have done/said that

····➤ (*Zukunft, Geplantes*) be to. **ich soll die Abteilung übernehmen** I am to take over the department. **du sollst dein Geld zurückbekommen** you are to *or* shall get your money back. **es soll nicht wieder vorkommen** it won't happen again. **sie sollten ihr Reiseziel nie erreichen** they were never to reach their destination

····➤ (*Ratlosigkeit*) be to; shall. **was soll man nur machen?** what is one to do?; what shall I/we do? **ich weiß nicht, was ich machen soll** I don't know what I should do *or* what to do

····➤ (*nach Bericht*) be supposed to. **er soll sehr reich sein** he is supposed *or* is said to be very rich. **sie soll geheiratet haben** they say *or* I gather she has got married

····➤ (*Absicht*) be meant *or* supposed to. **was soll dieses Bild darstellen?** what is this picture supposed to represent? **das sollte ein Witz sein** that was meant *or* supposed to be a joke

····➤ (*in Bedingungssätzen*) should. **sollte er anrufen, falls** *od* **wenn er anrufen sollte** should he *or* if he should telephone

● *intransitive verb*

····➤ (*irgendwohin gehen sollen*) be [supposed] to go. **er soll morgen zum Arzt/nach Berlin** he is [supposed] to go to the doctor/to Berlin tomorrow. **ich sollte ins Theater** I was supposed to go to the theatre

····➤ (*sonstige Wendungen*) **soll er doch!** let him! **was soll das?** what's that in aid of? 🅸

Solo *nt* **-s,-los & -li** solo

somit *adv* therefore, so

Sommer *m* **-s,-** summer. **s~lich** *adj* summery; (*Sommer-*) summer ● *adv* **s~lich warm** as warm as summer. **S~sprossen** *fpl* freckles

Sonate *f* **-,-n** sonata

Sonde *f* **-,-n** probe

Sonder|angebot *nt* special offer. **s~bar** *adj* odd. **S~fahrt** *f* special excursion. **S~fall** *m* special case. **s~gleichen** *adv* **eine Gemeinheit s~gleichen** unparalleled meanness. **S~ ling** *m* **-s,-e** crank. **S~marke** *f* special stamp

sondern *conj* but; **nicht nur ... s~ auch** not only ... but also

Sonder|preis *m* special price. **S~schule** *f* special school

Sonett *nt* **-[e]s,-e** sonnet

Sonnabend *m* **-s,-e** Saturday. **s~s** *adv* on Saturdays

Sonne *f* **-,-n** sun. **s~n (sich)** *vr* sun oneself

Sonnen|aufgang *m* sunrise. **s~baden** *vi* (*haben*) sunbathe. **S~bank** *f* sun-bed. **S~blume** *f* sunflower. **S~brand** *m* sunburn. **S~brille** *f* sunglasses *pl*. **S~energie** *f* solar energy. **S~finsternis** *f* solar eclipse. **S~milch** *f* sun-tan lotion. **S~öl** *nt* sun-tan oil. **S~schein** *m* sunshine. **S~schirm** *m* sunshade. **S~stich** *m* sunstroke. **S~uhr** *f* sundial. **S~untergang** *m* sunset. **S~wende** *f* solstice

sonnig *adj* sunny

Sonntag *m* **-s,-e** Sunday. **s~s** *adv* on Sundays

sonst *adv* (*gewöhnlich*) usually; (*im

Übrigen) apart from that; (*andernfalls*) otherwise, or [else]; **wer/was/wie/wo s~?** who/what/how/where else? **s~ niemand** no one else; **s~ noch etwas?** anything else? **s~ noch Fragen?** any more questions? **s~ jemand** *od* **wer** someone/(*fragend, verneint*) anyone else; (*irgendjemand*) [just] anyone; **s~ wo** somewhere/(*fragend, verneint*) anywhere else; (*irgendwo*) [just] anywhere. **s~ig** *adj* other

sooft *conj* whenever

Sopran *m* **-s,-e** soprano

Sorge *f* **-,-n** worry (**um** about); (*Fürsorge*) care; **sich** (*dat*) **S~n machen** worry. **s~n** *vi* (*haben*) **s~n für** look after, care for; (*vorsorgen*) provide for; (*sich kümmern*) see to; **dafür s~n, dass** see *or* make sure that ● *vr* **sich s~n** worry. **s~nfrei** *adj* carefree. **s~nvoll** *adj* worried. **S~recht** *nt* (*Jur*) custody

Sorg|falt *f* - care. **s~fältig** *adj* careful

Sorte *f* **-,-n** kind, sort; (*Comm*) brand

sort|ieren *vt* sort [out]; (*Comm*) grade. **S~iment** *nt* **-[e]s,-e** range

sosehr *conj* however much

Soße *f* **-,-n** sauce; (*Braten-*) gravy; (*Salat-*) dressing

Souvenir /zuvəˈniːɐ̯/ *nt* **-s,-s** souvenir

souverän /zuvəˈrɛːn/ *adj* sovereign

soviel *conj* however much; **s~ ich weiß** as far as I know ● *adv* ***so viel**, *s.* **viel**

soweit *conj* as far as; (*insoweit*) [in] so far as ● *adv** **so weit**, *s.* **weit**

sowenig *conj* however little ● *adv* ***so wenig**, *s.* **wenig**

sowie *conj* as well as; (*sobald*) as soon as

sowieso *adv* anyway, in any case

sowjet|isch *adj* Soviet. **S~union** *f* - Soviet Union

sowohl *adv* **s~ ... als** *od* **wie auch** as well as ...

sozial *adj* social; (*Einstellung, Beruf*) caring. **S~arbeit** *f* social work. **S~demokrat** *m* social democrat. **S~hilfe** *f* social security

Sozialis|mus *m* - socialism. **S~t** *m* **-en,-en** socialist

Sozial|versicherung *f* National Insurance. **S~wohnung** *f* ≈ council flat

Soziologie *f* - sociology

Sozius *m* **-,-se** (*Comm*) partner; (*Beifahrersitz*) pillion

Spachtel *m* **-s,-** & *f* **-,-n** spatula

Spagat *m* **-[e]s,-e** (*Aust*) string; **S~ machen** do the splits *pl*

Spaghetti, **Spagetti** *pl* spaghetti *sg*

Spalier *nt* **-s,-e** trellis

Spalt|e *f* **-,-n** crack; (*Gletscher-*) crevasse; (*Druck-*) column; (*Orangen-*) segment. **s~en†** *vt* split. **S~ung** *f* **-,-en** splitting; (*Kluft*) split; (*Phys*) fission

Span *m* **-[e]s,¨e** [wood] chip

Spange *f* **-,-n** clasp; (*Haar-*) slide; (*Zahn-*) brace

Span|ien /-i̯ən/ *nt* **-s** Spain. **S~ier** *m* **-s,-**, **S~ierin** *f* **-,-nen** Spaniard. **s~isch** *adj* Spanish. **S~isch** *nt* **-[s]** (*Lang*) Spanish

Spann *m* **-[e]s** instep

Spanne *f* **-,-n** span; (*Zeit-*) space; (*Comm*) margin

spann|en *vt* stretch; put up (*Leine*); (*straffen*) tighten; (*an-*) harness (**an** + *acc* to); **sich s~en** tighten ● *vi* (*haben*) be too tight. **s~end** *adj* exciting. **S~ung** *f* **-,-en** tension; (*Erwartung*) suspense; (*Electr*) voltage

Spar|buch *nt* savings book. **S~büchse** *f* money-box. **s~en** *vt/i* (*haben*) save; (*sparsam sein*) economize (**mit/an** + *dat* on). **S~er** *m* **-s,-** saver

Spargel *m* **-s,-** asparagus

Spar|kasse *f* savings bank. **S~konto** *nt* deposit account

sparsam *adj* economical; (*Person*) thrifty. **S~keit** *f* **-** economy; thrift

Sparschwein *nt* piggy bank

Sparte *f* **-,-n** branch; (*Zeitungs-*) section; (*Rubrik*) column

Spaß *m* **-es,⸗e** fun; (*Scherz*) joke; **im/aus/zum S~** for fun; **S~ machen** be fun; (*Person:*) be joking; **viel S~!** have a good time! **s~en** *vi* (*haben*) joke. **S~vogel** *m* joker

Spastiker *m* **-s,-** spastic

spät *adj & adv* late; **wie s~ ist es?** what time is it? **zu s~ kommen** be late

Spaten *m* **-s,-** spade

später *adj* later; (*zukünftig*) future ● *adv* later

spätestens *adv* at the latest

Spatz *m* **-en,-en** sparrow

Spätzle *pl* (*Culin*) noodles

spazieren *vi* (*sein*) stroll; **s~ gehen** go for a walk

Spazier|gang *m* walk; **einen S~gang machen** go for a walk. **S~gänger(in)** *m* **-s,-** (*f* **-,-nen**) walker. **S~stock** *m* walking-stick

Specht *m* **-[e]s,-e** woodpecker

Speck *m* **-s** bacon. **s~ig** *adj* greasy

Spedi|teur /ʃpediˈtøːɐ̯/ *m* **-s,-e** haulage/(*für Umzüge*) removals contractor. **S~tion** *f* **-,-en** carriage, haulage; (*Firma*) haulage/(*für Umzüge*) removals firm

Speer *m* **-[e]s,-e** spear; (*Sport*) javelin

Speiche *f* **-,-n** spoke

Speichel *m* **-s** saliva

Speicher *m* **-s,-** warehouse; (*Dialekt: Dachboden*) attic; (*Computer*) memory. **s~n** *vt* store

Speise *f* **-,-n** food; (*Gericht*) dish; (*Pudding*) blancmange. **S~eis** *nt* ice-cream. **S~kammer** *f* larder. **S~karte** *f* menu. **s~n** *vi* (*haben*) eat ● *vt* feed. **S~röhre** *f* oesophagus. **S~saal** *m* dining room. **S~wagen** *m* dining car

Spektrum *nt* **-s,-tra** spectrum

Spekul|ant *m* **-en,-en** speculator. **s~ieren** *vi* (*haben*) speculate; **s~ieren auf** (+ *acc*) 🄸 hope to get

Spelze *f* **-,-n** husk

spendabel *adj* generous

Spende *f* **-,-n** donation. **s~n** *vt* donate; give (*Blut, Schatten*); **Beifall s~n** applaud. **S~r** *m* **-s,-** donor; (*Behälter*) dispenser

spendieren *vt* pay for

Sperling *m* **-s,-e** sparrow

Sperre *f* **-,-n** barrier; (*Verbot*) ban; (*Comm*) embargo. **s~n** *vt* close; (*ver-*) block; (*verbieten*) ban; cut off (*Strom, Telefon*); stop (*Scheck, Kredit*); **s~n in** (+ *acc*) put in (*Gefängnis, Käfig*)

Sperr|holz *nt* plywood. **S~müll** *m* bulky refuse. **S~stunde** *f* closing time

Spesen *pl* expenses

spezial|isieren (sich) *vr* specialize (**auf** + *acc* in). **S~ist** *m* **-en,-en** specialist. **S~ität** *f* **-,-en** speciality

spicken *vt* (*Culin*) lard; **gespickt mit** (*fig*) full of ● *vi* (*haben*) 🄸 crib (**bei** from)

Spiegel *m* **-s,-** mirror; (*Wasser-, Alkohol-*) level. **S~bild** *nt* reflection. **S~ei** *nt* fried egg. **s~n** *vt* reflect; **sich s~n** be reflected ● *vi* (*haben*) reflect [the light]; (*glänzen*) gleam. **S~ung** *f* **-,-en** reflection

Spiel *nt* **-[e]s,-e** game; (*Spielen*) playing; (*Glücks-*) gambling; (*Schau-*) play; (*Satz*) set; **auf dem S~ stehen** be at stake; **aufs S~ setzen** risk. **S~automat** *m* fruit machine. **S~bank** *f* casino. **S~dose** *f* musical box. **s~en** *vt/i* (*haben*) play; (*im Glücksspiel*) gamble; (*vortäuschen*) act; (*Roman:*) be set (**in** + *dat* in); **s~en mit** (*fig*) toy with

Spieler(in) *m* **-s,-** (*f* **-,-nen**) player; (*Glücks-*) gambler

Spiel|feld *nt* field, pitch. **S~marke** *f* chip. **S~plan** *m* programme. **S~platz** *m* playground. **S~raum** *m* (*fig*) scope; (*Techn*) clearance. **S~regeln** *fpl* rules [of the game]. **S~sachen** *fpl* toys. **S~verderber** *m* **-s,-** spoilsport. **S~waren** *fpl* toys. **S~warengeschäft** *nt* toyshop. **S~zeug** *nt* toy; (*S~sachen*) toys *pl*

Spieß *m* **-es,-e** spear; (*Brat-*) spit; skewer; (*Fleisch-*) kebab. **S~er** *m* **-s,-** [petit] bourgeois. **s~ig** *adj* bourgeois

Spike[s]reifen /ˈʃpaik[s]-/ *m* studded tyre

Spinat *m* **-s** spinach

Spindel *f* **-,-n** spindle

Spinne *f* **-,-n** spider

spinn|en† *vt/i* (*haben*) spin; **er spinnt** [!] he's crazy. **S~[en]gewebe** *nt*, **S~webe** *f* **-,-n** cobweb

Spion *m* **-s,-e** spy

Spionage /ʃpioˈna:ʒə/ *f* **-** espionage, spying. **S~abwehr** *f* counter-espionage

spionieren *vi* (*haben*) spy

Spionin *f* **-,-nen** [woman] spy

Spiral|e *f* **-,-n** spiral. **s~ig** *adj* spiral

Spirituosen *pl* spirits

Spiritus *m* **-** alcohol; (*Brenn-*) methylated spirits *pl*. **S~kocher** *m* spirit stove

spitz *adj* pointed; (*scharf*) sharp; (*schrill*) shrill; (*Winkel*) acute. **S~bube** *m* scoundrel

Spitze *f* **-,-n** point; (*oberer Teil*) top; (*vorderer Teil*) front; (*Pfeil-, Finger-, Nasen-*) tip; (*Schuh-, Strumpf-*) toe; (*Zigarren-, Zigaretten-*) holder; (*Höchstleistung*) maximum; (*Textiles*) lace; ([!]: *Anspielung*) dig; **an der S~ liegen** be in the lead

Spitzel *m* **-s,-** informer

spitzen *vt* sharpen; purse (*Lippen*); prick up (*Ohren*). **S~geschwindigkeit** *f* top speed

Spitzname *m* nickname

Spleen /ʃpli:n/ *m* **-s,-e** obsession

Splitter *m* **-s,-** splinter. **s~n** *vi* (*sein*) shatter

sponsern *vt* sponsor

Spore *f* **-,-n** (*Biology*) spore

Sporn *m* **-[e]s, Sporen** spur

Sport *m* **-[e]s** sport; (*Hobby*) hobby. **S~art** *f* sport. **S~ler** *m* **-s,-** sportsman. **S~lerin** *f* **-,-nen** sportswoman. **s~lich** *adj* sports; (*fair*) sporting; (*schlank*) sporty. **S~platz** *m* sports ground. **S~verein** *m* sports club. **S~wagen** *m* sports car; (*Kinder-*) push-chair, (*Amer*) stroller

Spott *m* **-[e]s** mockery

spotten *vi* (*haben*) mock; **s~ über** (+ *acc*) make fun of; (*höhnend*) ridicule

spöttisch *adj* mocking

Sprach|e *f* **-,-n** language; (*Sprechfähigkeit*) speech; **zur S~e bringen** bring up. **S~fehler** *m* speech defect. **S~labor** *nt* language laboratory. **s~lich** *adj* linguistic. **s~los** *adj* speechless

Spray /ʃpre:/ *nt* & *m* **-s,-s** spray. **S~dose** *f* aerosol [can]

Sprechanlage *f* intercom

sprechen† *vi* (*haben*) speak/(*sich unterhalten*) talk (**über** + *acc*/**von** about/of); **Deutsch s~** speak German ● *vt* speak; (*sagen*) say; pronounce (*Urteil*); **schuldig s~** find guilty; **Herr X ist nicht zu s~** Mr X is not available

Sprecher(in) *m* **-s,-** (*f* **-,-nen**) speaker; (*Radio, TV*) announcer; (*Wortführer*) spokesman, *f* spokeswoman

Sprechstunde *f* consulting hours *pl*; (*Med*) surgery. **S~nhilfe** *f* (*Med*) receptionist

Sprechzimmer *nt* consulting room

spreizen *vt* spread

spreng|en *vt* blow up; blast (*Felsen*); (*fig*) burst; (*begießen*) water; (*mit Sprenger*) sprinkle; dampen (*Wäsche*). **S~er** *m* **-s,-** sprinkler. **S~kopf** *m* warhead. **S~körper** *m* explosive device. **S~stoff** *m* explosive

Spreu *f* **-** chaff

Sprich|wort *nt* (*pl* **-wörter**) proverb. **s~wörtlich** *adj* proverbial

Springbrunnen *m* fountain

spring|en† *vi* (*sein*) jump; (*Schwimmsport*) dive; (*Ball:*) bounce; (*spritzen*) spurt; (*zer-*) break; (*rissig werden*) crack; (*SGer: laufen*) run. **S~er** *m* **-s,-** jumper; (*Kunst-*) diver; (*Schach*) knight. **S~reiten** *nt* showjumping

Sprint *m* **-s,-s** sprint

Spritz|e *f* **-,-n** syringe; (*Injektion*) injection; (*Feuer-*) hose. **s~en** *vt* spray; (*be-, ver-*) splash; (*Culin*) pipe; (*Med*) inject ● *vi* (*haben*) splash; (*Fett:*) spit ● *vi* (*sein*) splash; (*hervor-*) spurt. **S~er** *m* **-s,-** splash; (*Schuss*) dash

spröde *adj* brittle; (*trocken*) dry

Sprosse *f* **-,-n** rung

Sprotte *f* **-,-n** sprat

Spruch *m* **-[e]s,⸚e** saying; (*Denk-*) motto; (*Zitat*) quotation. **S~band** *nt* (*pl* **-bänder**) banner

Sprudel *m* **-s,-** sparkling mineral water. **s~n** *vi* (*haben/sein*) bubble

Sprüh|dose *f* aerosol [can]. **s~en** *vt* spray ● *vi* (*sein*) (*Funken:*) fly; (*fig*) sparkle

Sprung *m* **-[e]s,⸚e** jump, leap; (*Schwimmsport*) dive; (🅸: *Katzen-*) stone's throw; (*Riss*) crack. **S~brett** *nt* springboard. **S~schanze** *f* skijump. **S~seil** *nt* skipping rope

Spucke *f* **-** spit. **s~n** *vt/i* (*haben*) spit; (*sich übergeben*) be sick

Spuk *m* **-[e]s,-e** [ghostly] apparition. **s~en** *vi* (*haben*) (*Geist:*) walk; **in diesem Haus s~t es** this house is haunted

Spülbecken *nt* sink

Spule *f* **-,-n** spool

Spüle *f* **-,-n** sink

spulen *vt* spool

spül|en *vt* rinse; (*schwemmen*) wash; **Geschirr s~en** wash up ● *vi* (*haben*) flush [the toilet]. **S~kasten** *m* cistern. **S~mittel** *nt* washing-up liquid

Spur *f* **-,-en** track; (*Fahr-*) lane; (*Fährte*) trail; (*Anzeichen*) trace; (*Hinweis*) lead

spürbar *adj* noticeable

spür|en *vt* feel; (*seelisch*) sense. **S~hund** *m* tracker dog

spurlos *adv* without trace

spurten *vi* (*sein*) put on a spurt

sputen (sich) *vr* hurry

Staat *m* **-[e]s,-en** state; (*Land*) country; (*Putz*) finery. **s~lich** *adj* state ● *adv* by the state

Staatsangehörig|e(r) *m/f* national. **S~keit** *f* **-** nationality

S

Staats|anwalt *m* state prosecutor. **S~beamte(r)** *m* civil servant. **S~besuch** *m* state visit. **S~bürger(in)** *m(f)* national. **S~mann** *m* (*pl* **-männer**) statesman. **S~streich** *m* coup

Stab *m* **-[e]s,¨e** rod; (*Gitter-*) bar (*Sport*) baton; (*Mil*) staff

Stäbchen *ntpl* chopsticks

Stabhochsprung *m* pole-vault

stabil *adj* stable; (*gesund*) robust; (*solide*) sturdy

Stachel *m* **-s,-** spine; (*Gift-*) sting; (*Spitze*) spike. **S~beere** *f* gooseberry. **S~draht** *m* barbed wire. **S~schwein** *nt* porcupine

Stadion *nt* **-s,-ien** stadium

Stadium *nt* **-s,-ien** stage

Stadt *f* **-,¨e** town; (*Groß-*) city

städtisch *adj* urban; (*kommunal*) municipal

Stadt|mitte *f* town centre. **S~plan** *m* street map. **S~teil** *m* district

Staffel *f* **-,-n** team; (*S~lauf*) relay; (*Mil*) squadron

Staffelei *f* **-,-en** easel

Staffel|lauf *m* relay race. **s~n** *vt* stagger; (*abstufen*) grade

Stahl *m* **-s** steel. **S~beton** *m* reinforced concrete

Stall *m* **-[e]s,¨e** stable; (*Kuh-*) shed; (*Schweine-*) sty; (*Hühner-*) coop; (*Kaninchen-*) hutch

Stamm *m* **-[e]s¨e** trunk; (*Sippe*) tribe; (*Wort-*) stem. **S~baum** *m* family tree; (*eines Tieres*) pedigree

stammeln *vt/i* (*haben*) stammer

stammen *vi* (*haben*) come/(*zeitlich*) date (**von/aus** from)

stämmig *adj* sturdy

Stamm|kundschaft *f* regulars *pl*. **S~lokal** *nt* favourite pub

> **Stammtisch** A large table reserved for regulars in most German *Kneipen* (pubs). The word is also used to refer to the group of people who meet around this table for a drink and lively discussion.

stampfen *vi* (*haben*) stamp; (*Maschine:*) pound ● *vi* (*sein*) tramp ● *vt* pound; mash (*Kartoffeln*)

Stand *m* **-[e]s,¨e** standing position; (*Zustand*) state; (*Spiel-*) score; (*Höhe*) level; (*gesellschaftlich*) class; (*Verkaufs-*) stall; (*Messe-*) stand; (*Taxi-*) rank; **auf den neuesten S~ bringen** up-date

Standard *m* **-s,-s** standard

Standbild *nt* statue

Ständer *m* **-s,-** stand; (*Geschirr-*) rack; (*Kerzen-*) holder

Standes|amt *nt* registry office. **S~beamte(r)** *m* registrar

standhaft *adj* steadfast

ständig *adj* constant; (*fest*) permanent

Stand|licht *nt* sidelights *pl*. **S~ort** *m* position; (*Firmen-*) location; (*Mil*) garrison. **S~punkt** *m* point of view. **S~uhr** *f* grandfather clock

Stange *f* **-,-n** bar; (*Holz-*) pole; (*Gardinen-*) rail; (*Hühner-*) perch; (*Zimt-*) stick; **von der S~** [!] off the peg

Stängel *m* **-s,-** stalk, stem

Stangenbohne *f* runner bean

Stanniol *nt* **-s** tin foil. **S~papier** *nt* silver paper

stanzen *vt* stamp; punch (*Loch*)

Stapel *m* **-s,-** stack, pile. **S~lauf** *m* launch[ing]. **s~n** *vt* stack *or* pile up

Star[1] *m* **-[e]s,-e** starling

Star[2] *m* **-[e]s** (*Med*) **[grauer] S~** cataract; **grüner S~** glaucoma

S

Star[3] *m* **-s,-s** (*Theat, Sport*) star

stark *adj* strong; (*Motor*) powerful; (*Verkehr, Regen*) heavy; (*Hitze, Kälte*) severe; (*groß*) big; (*schlimm*) bad; (*dick*) thick; (*korpulent*) stout ● *adv* (*sehr*) very much

Stärk|e *f* **-,-n** strength; power; thickness; stoutness; (*Größe*) size; (*Mais-, Wäsche-*) starch. **S~emehl** *nt* cornflour. **s~en** *vt* strengthen; starch (*Wäsche*); **sich s~en** fortify oneself. **S~ung** *f* **-,-en** strengthening; (*Erfrischung*) refreshment

starr *adj* rigid; (*steif*) stiff

starren *vi* (*haben*) stare

Starr|sinn *m* obstinacy. **s~sinnig** *adj* obstinate

Start *m* **-s,-s** start; (*Aviat*) take-off. **S~bahn** *f* runway. **s~en** *vi* (*sein*) start; (*Aviat*) take off ● *vt* start; (*fig*) launch

Station /-ˈtsi̯o:n/ *f* **-,-en** station; (*Haltestelle*) stop; (*Abschnitt*) stage; (*Med*) ward; **S~ machen** break one's journey. **s~är** *adv* as an in-patient. **s~ieren** *vt* station

statisch *adj* static

Statist(in) *m* **-en,-en** (*f* **-,-nen**) (*Theat*) extra

Statisti|k *f* **-,-en** statistics *sg*; (*Aufstellung*) statistics *pl*. **s~sch** *adj* statistical

Stativ *nt* **-s,-e** (*Phot*) tripod

statt *prep* (+ *gen*) instead of; **an seiner s~** in his place; **an Kindes s~ annehmen** adopt ● *conj* **s~ etw zu tun** instead of doing sth. **s~dessen** *adv* instead

statt|finden† *vi sep* (*haben*) take place. **s~haft** *adj* permitted

Statue /ˈʃta:tu̯ə/ *f* **-,-n** statue

Statur *f* **-** build, stature

Status *m* **-** status. **S~symbol** *nt* status symbol

Statut *nt* **-[e]s,-en** statute

Stau *m* **-[e]s,-s** congestion; (*Auto*) [traffic] jam; (*Rück-*) tailback

Staub *m* **-[e]s** dust; **S~ wischen** dust; **S~ saugen** vacuum, hoover

Staubecken *nt* reservoir

staub|ig *adj* dusty. **s~saugen** *vt/i* (*haben*) vacuum, hoover. **S~sauger** *m* vacuum cleaner, Hoover®

Staudamm *m* dam

stauen *vt* dam up; **sich s~** accumulate; (*Autos:*) form a tailback

staunen *vi* (*haben*) be amazed *or* astonished

Stau|see *m* reservoir. **S~ung** *f* **-,-en** congestion; (*Auto*) [traffic] jam

Steak /ʃte:k, ste:k/ *nt* **-s,-s** steak

stechen† *vt* stick (**in** + *acc* in); (*verletzen*) prick; (*mit Messer*) stab; (*Insekt:*) sting; (*Mücke:*) bite ● *vi* (*haben*) prick; (*Insekt:*) sting; (*Mücke:*) bite; (*mit Stechuhr*) clock in/out; **in See s~** put to sea

Stech|ginster *m* gorse. **S~kahn** *m* punt. **S~palme** *f* holly. **S~uhr** *f* time clock

Steck|brief *m* 'wanted' poster. **S~dose** *f* socket. **s~en** *vt* put; (*mit Nadel, Reißzwecke*) pin; (*pflanzen*) plant ● *vi* (*haben*) be; (*fest-*) be stuck; **s~ bleiben** get stuck; **den Schlüssel s~ lassen** leave the key in the lock

Steckenpferd *nt* hobby-horse

Steck|er *m* **-s,-** (*Electr*) plug. **S~nadel** *f* pin

Steg *m* **-[e]s,-e** foot-bridge; (*Boots-*) landing-stage; (*Brillen-*) bridge

stehen† *vi* (*haben*) stand; (*sich befinden*) be; (*still-*) be stationary; (*Maschine, Uhr:*) have stopped; **s~ bleiben** remain standing; (*gebäude:*) be left standing; (*anhalten*) stop; (*Motor:*) stall; (*Zeit:*) stand still; **vor dem Ruin s~** face ruin; **zu jdm/etw s~** (*fig*) stand by s.o./sth

jdm [gut] s~ suit s.o.; **sich gut s~** be on good terms; **es steht 3 zu 1** the score is 3–1. **s~d** *adj* standing; (*sich nicht bewegend*) stationary; (*Gewässer*) stagnant

Stehlampe *f* standard lamp

stehlen† *vt/i* (*haben*) steal; **sich s~** steal, creep

Steh|platz *m* standing place. **S~vermögen** *nt* stamina, staying-power

steif *adj* stiff

Steig|bügel *m* stirrup. **S~eisen** *nt* crampon

steigen† *vi* (*sein*) climb; (*hochgehen*) rise, go up; (*Schulden, Spannung:*) mount; **s~ auf** (+ *acc*) climb on [to] (*Stuhl*); climb (*Berg, Leiter*); get on (*Pferd, Fahrrad*); **s~ in** (+ *acc*) climb into; get in (*Auto*); get on (*Bus, Zug*); **s~ aus** climb out of; get out of (*Bett, Auto*); get off (*Bus, Zug*); **s~de Preise** rising prices

steiger|n *vt* increase; **sich s~n** increase; (*sich verbessern*) improve. **S~ung** *f* -,-en increase; improvement; (*Gram*) comparison

steil *adj* steep. **S~küste** *f* cliffs *pl*

Stein *m* **-[e]s,-e** stone; (*Ziegel-*) brick; (*Spiel-*) piece. **S~bock** *m* ibex; (*Astrology*) Capricorn. **S~bruch** *m* quarry. **S~garten** *m* rockery. **S~gut** *nt* earthenware. **s~ig** *adj* stony. **s~igen** *vt* stone. **S~kohle** *f* [hard] coal. **S~schlag** *m* rock fall

Stelle *f* **-,-n** place; (*Fleck*) spot; (*Abschnitt*) passage; (*Stellung*) job, post; (*Behörde*) authority; **auf der S~** immediately

stellen *vt* put; (*aufrecht*) stand; set (*Wecker, Aufgabe*); ask (*Frage*); make (*Antrag, Forderung, Diagnose*); **zur Verfügung s~** provide; **lauter/leiser s~** turn up/down; **kalt/warm s~** chill/keep hot; **sich s~** [go and] stand; give oneself up (**der Polizei** to the police); **sich tot s~** pretend to be dead; **gut gestellt sein** be well off

Stellen|anzeige *f* job advertisement. **S~vermittlung** *f* employment agency. **s~weise** *adv* in places

Stellung *f* **-,-en** position; (*Arbeit*) job; **S~nehmen** make a statement (**zu** on). **S~suche** *f* job-hunting

Stellvertreter *m* deputy

Stelzen *fpl* stilts. **s~** *vi* (*sein*) stalk

stemmen *vt* press; lift (*Gewicht*)

Stempel *m* **-s,-** stamp; (*Post-*) post-mark; (*Präge-*) die; (*Feingehalts-*) hallmark. **s~n** *vt* stamp; hallmark (*Silber*); cancel (*Marke*)

Stengel *m* **-s,-** * **Stängel**

Steno *f* - 🅃 shorthand

Steno|gramm *nt* **-[e]s,-e** shorthand text. **S~grafie** *f* - shorthand. **s~grafieren** *vt* take down in shorthand ● *vi* (*haben*) do shorthand

Steppdecke *f* quilt

Steppe *f* **-,-n** steppe

Stepptanz *m* tap-dance

sterben† *vi* (*sein*) die (**an** + *dat* of); **im S~ liegen** be dying

sterblich *adj* mortal. **S~keit** *f* - mortality

stereo *adv* in stereo. **S~anlage** *f* stereo [system]

steril *adj* sterile. **s~isieren** *vt* sterilize. **S~ität** *f* - sterility

Stern *m* **-[e]s,-e** star. **S~bild** *nt* constellation. **S~chen** *nt* **-s,-** asterisk. **S~kunde** *f* astronomy. **S~schnuppe** *f* **-,-n** shooting star. **S~warte** *f* **-,-n** observatory

stets *adv* always

Steuer[1] *nt* **-s,-** steering-wheel; (*Naut*) helm; **am S~** at the wheel

Steuer[2] *f* **-,-n** tax

Steuer|bord *nt* -[e]s starboard [side]. **S~erklärung** *f* tax return. **s~frei** *adj & adv* tax-free. **S~mann** *m* (*pl* **-leute**) helmsman; (*beim Rudern*) cox. **s~n** *vt* steer; (*Aviat*) pilot; (*Techn*) control ● *vi* (*haben*) be at the wheel/(*Naut*) helm. **s~pflichtig** *adj* taxable. **S~rad** *nt* steering-wheel. **S~ruder** *nt* helm. **S~ung** *f* - steering; (*Techn*) controls *pl*. **S~zahler** *m* **-s,-** taxpayer

Stewardess /'stju:ɐdɛs/ *f* **-,-en** air hostess, stewardess

Stich *m* **-[e]s,-e** prick; (*Messer-*) stab; (**S~***wunde*) stab wound; (*Bienen-*) sting; (*Mücken-*) bite; (*Schmerz*) stabbing pain; (*Näh-*) stitch; (*Kupfer-*) engraving; (*Kartenspiel*) trick

stick|en *vt/i* (*haben*) embroider. **S~erei** *f* - embroidery

Stickstoff *m* nitrogen

Stiefel *m* **-s,-** boot

Stief|kind *nt* stepchild. **S~mutter** *f* stepmother. **S~mütterchen** *nt* **-s,-** pansy. **S~sohn** *m* stepson. **S~tochter** *f* stepdaughter. **S~vater** *m* stepfather

Stiege *f* **-,-n** stairs *pl*

Stiel *m* **-[e]s,-e** handle; (*Blumen-, Gläser-*) stem; (*Blatt-*) stalk

Stier *m* **-[e]s,-e** bull; (*Astrology*) Taurus

Stierkampf *m* bullfight

Stift[1] *m* **-[e]s,-e** pin; (*Nagel*) tack; (*Blei-*) pencil; (*Farb-*) crayon

Stift[2] *nt* **-[e]s,-e** [endowed] foundation. **s~en** *vt* endow; (*spenden*) donate; create (*Unheil, Verwirrung*); bring about (*Frieden*). **S~ung** *f* **-,-en** foundation; (*Spende*) donation

Stil *m* **-[e]s,-e** style

still *adj* quiet; (*reglos, ohne Kohlensäure*) still; (*heimlich*) secret; **der S~e Ozean** the Pacific; **im S~en** secretly. **S~e** *f* - quiet; (*Schweigen*) silence

Stilleben* *nt* = **Stillleben**

stillen *vt* satisfy; quench (*Durst*); stop (*Schmerzen, Blutung*); breastfeed (*Kind*)

still|halten† *vi sep* (*haben*) keep still. **S~leben** *nt* still life. **s~legen** *vt sep* close down. **S~schweigen** *nt* silence. **S~stand** *m* standstill; **zum S~stand bringen/kommen** stop. **s~stehen**† *vi sep* (*haben*) stand still; (*anhalten*) stop; (*Verkehr:*) be at a standstill

Stimm|bänder *ntpl* vocal cords. **s~berechtigt** *adj* entitled to vote. **S~bruch** *m* **er ist im S~bruch** his voice is breaking

Stimme *f* **-,-n** voice; (*Wahl-*) vote

stimmen *vi* (*haben*) be right; (*wählen*) vote ● *vt* tune

Stimmung *f* **-,-en** mood; (*Atmosphäre*) atmosphere

Stimmzettel *m* ballot-paper

stink|en† *vi* (*haben*) smell/(*stark*) stink (**nach** of). **S~tier** *nt* skunk

Stipendium *nt* **-s,-ien** scholarship; (*Beihilfe*) grant

Stirn *f* **-,-en** forehead

stochern *vi* (*haben*) **s~ in** (+ *dat*) poke (*Feuer*); pick at (*Essen*)

Stock[1] *m* **-[e]s,⸚e** stick; (*Ski-*) pole; (*Bienen-*) hive; (*Rosen-*) bush; (*Reb-*) vine

Stock[2] *m* **-[e]s,-** storey, floor. **S~bett** *nt* bunk-beds *pl*.

stock|en *vi* (*haben*) stop; (*Verkehr:*) come to a standstill; (*Person:*) falter. **S~ung** *f* **-,-en** hold-up

Stockwerk *nt* storey, floor

Stoff *m* **-[e]s,-e** substance; (*Textiles*) fabric, material; (*Thema*) subject [matter]; (*Gesprächs-*) topic. **S~wechsel** *m* metabolism

stöhnen *vi* (*haben*) groan, moan

Stola *f* -,-len stole

Stollen *m* -s,- gallery; (*Kuchen*) stollen

stolpern *vi* (*sein*) stumble; **s~ über** (+ *acc*) trip over

stolz *adj* proud (**auf** + *acc* of). **S~** *m* -es pride

stopfen *vt* stuff; (*stecken*) put; (*ausbessern*) darn ●*vi* (*haben*) be constipating

Stopp *m* -s,-s stop. **s~** *int* stop!

stoppelig *adj* stubbly

stopp|en *vt* stop; (*Sport*) time ●*vi* (*haben*) stop. **S~uhr** *f* stop-watch

Stöpsel *m* -s,- plug; (*Flaschen-*) stopper

Storch *m* -[e]s,⸚e stork

Store /ʃtoːɐ̯/ *m* -s,-s net curtain

stören *vt* disturb; disrupt (*Rede*); jam (*Sender*); (*missfallen*) bother ●*vi* (*haben*) be a nuisance

stornieren *vt* cancel

störrisch *adj* stubborn

Störung *f* -,-en disturbance; disruption; (*Med*) trouble; (*Radio*) interference; **technische S~** technical fault

Stoß *m* -es,⸚e push, knock; (*mit Ellbogen*) dig; (*Hörner-*) butt; (*mit Waffe*) thrust; (*Schwimm-*) stroke; (*Ruck*) jolt; (*Erd-*) shock; (*Stapel*) stack, pile. **S~dämpfer** *m* -s,- shock absorber

stoßen† *vt* push, knock; (*mit Füßen*) kick; (*mit Kopf*) butt; (*an-*) poke, nudge; (*treiben*) thrust; **sich s~** knock oneself; **sich** (*dat*) **den Kopf s~** hit one's head ●*vi* (*haben*) push; **s~ an** (+ *acc*) knock against; (*angrenzen*) adjoin ●*vi* (*sein*) **s~ gegen** knock against; bump into (*Tür*); **s~ auf** (+ *acc*) bump into; (*entdecken*) come across; strike (*Öl*)

Stoß|stange *f* bumper. **S~verkehr** *m* rush-hour traffic. **S~zahn** *m* tusk. **S~zeit** *f* rush-hour

stottern *vt/i* (*haben*) stutter, stammer

Str. *abbr* (**Straße**) St

Strafanstalt *f* prison

Strafe *f* -,-n punishment; (*Jur & fig*) penalty; (*Geld-*) fine; (*Freiheits-*) sentence. **s~n** *vt* punish

straff *adj* tight, taut. **s~en** *vt* tighten

Strafgesetz *nt* criminal law

sträf|lich *adj* criminal. **S~ling** *m* -s,-e prisoner

Straf|mandat *nt* (*Auto*) [parking/speeding] ticket. **S~porto** *nt* excess postage. **S~raum** *m* penalty area. **S~stoß** *m* penalty. **S~tat** *f* crime

Strahl *m* -[e]s,-en ray; (*einer Taschenlampe*) beam; (*Wasser-*) jet. **s~en** *vi* (*haben*) shine; (*funkeln*) sparkle; (*lächeln*) beam. **S~enbehandlung** *f* radiotherapy. **S~ung** *f* - radiation

Strähne *f* -,-n strand

stramm *adj* tight

Strampel|höschen /-sç-/ *nt* -s,- rompers *pl*. **s~n** *vi* (*haben*) (*Baby:*) kick

Strand *m* -[e]s,⸚e beach. **s~en** *vi* (*sein*) run aground

Strang *m* -[e]s,⸚e rope

Strapaz|e *f* -,-n strain. **s~ieren** *vt* be hard on; tax (*Nerven*)

Strass *m* - & -es paste

Straße *f* -,-n road; (*in der Stadt auch*) street; (*Meeres-*) strait. **S~nbahn** *f* tram. **S~nkarte** *f* road-map. **S~nsperre** *f* road-block

Strat|egie *f* -,-n strategy. **s~egisch** *adj* strategic

Strauch *m* -[e]s, **Sträucher** bush

Strauß[1] *m* -es, **Sträuße** bunch [of flowers]; (*Bukett*) bouquet

Strauß[2] *m* **-es,-e** ostrich
streben *vi* (*haben*) strive (**nach** for) ● *vi* (*sein*) head (**nach/zu** for)
Streber *m* **-s,-** pushy person
Strecke *f* **-,-n** stretch, section; (*Entfernung*) distance; (*Rail*) line; (*Route*) route
strecken *vt* stretch; (*aus-*) stretch out; (*gerade machen*) straighten; (*Culin*) thin down; **den Kopf aus dem Fenster s~** put one's head out of the window
Streich *m* **-[e]s,-e** prank, trick
streicheln *vt* stroke
streichen† *vt* spread; (*weg-*) smooth; (*an-*) paint; (*aus-*) delete; (*kürzen*) cut ● *vi* (*haben*) **s~ über** (+ *acc*) stroke
Streichholz *nt* match
Streich|instrument *nt* stringed instrument. **S~käse** *m* cheese spread. **S~orchester** *nt* string orchestra. **S~ung** *f* **-,-en** deletion; (*Kürzung*) cut
Streife *f* **-,-n** patrol
streifen *vt* brush against; (*berühren*) touch; (*verletzen*) graze; (*fig*) touch on (*Thema*)
Streifen *m* **-s,-** stripe; (*Licht-*) streak; (*auf der Fahrbahn*) line; (*schmales Stück*) strip
Streifenwagen *m* patrol car
Streik *m* **-s,-s** strike; **in den S~ treten** go on strike. **S~brecher** *m* strike-breaker, (*pej*) scab. **s~en** *vi* (*haben*) strike; 🄸 refuse; (*versagen*) pack up
Streit *m* **-[e]s,-e** quarrel; (*Auseinandersetzung*) dispute. **s~en**† *vr/i* (*haben*) **[sich] s~en** quarrel. **S~igkeiten** *fpl* quarrels. **S~kräfte** *fpl* armed forces
streng *adj* strict; (*Blick, Ton*) stern; (*rau, nüchtern*) severe; (*Geschmack*) sharp; **s~ genommen** strictly speaking. **S~e** *f* **-** strictness; sternness; severity
Stress *m* **-es,-e** stress
stressig *adj* stressful
streuen *vt* spread; (*ver-*) scatter; sprinkle (*Zucker, Salz*); **die Straßen s~** grit the roads
streunen *vi* (*sein*) roam
Strich *m* **-[e]s,-e** line; (*Feder-, Pinsel-*) stroke; (*Morse-, Gedanken-*) dash. **S~kode** *m* bar code. **S~punkt** *m* semicolon
Strick *m* **-[e]s,-e** cord; (*Seil*) rope
strick|en *vt/i* (*haben*) knit. **S~jacke** *f* cardigan. **S~leiter** *f* rope ladder. **S~nadel** *f* knitting-needle. **S~waren** *fpl* knitwear *sg*. **S~zeug** *nt* knitting
striegeln *vt* groom
strittig *adj* contentious
Stroh *nt* **-[e]s** straw. **S~blumen** *fpl* everlasting flowers. **S~dach** *nt* thatched roof. **S~halm** *m* straw
Strolch *m* **-[e]s,-e** 🄸 rascal
Strom *m* **-[e]s,⸚e** river; (*Menschen-, Auto-, Blut-*) stream; (*Tränen-*) flood; (*Schwall*) torrent; (*Electr*) current, power; **gegen den S~** (*fig*) against the tide. **s~abwärts** *adv* downstream. **s~aufwärts** *adv* upstream
strömen *vi* (*sein*) flow; (*Menschen, Blut:*) stream, pour
Strom|kreis *m* circuit. **s~linienförmig** *adj* streamlined. **S~sperre** *f* power cut
Strömung *f* **-,-en** current
Strophe *f* **-,-n** verse
Strudel *m* **-s,-** whirlpool; (*SGer Culin*) strudel
Strumpf *m* **-[e]s,⸚e** stocking; (*Knie-*) sock. **S~band** *nt* (*pl* **-bänder**) suspender. **S~hose** *f* tights *pl*
Strunk *m* **-[e]s,⸚e** stalk
struppig *adj* shaggy

Stube *f* **-,-n** room. **s~nrein** *adj* house-trained

Stuck *m* **-s** stucco

Stück *nt* **-[e]s,-e** piece; (*Zucker-*) lump; (*Seife*) tablet; (*Theater-*) play; (*Gegenstand*) item; (*Exemplar*) specimen; **ein S~** (*Entfernung*) some way. **S~chen** *nt* **-s,-** [little] bit. **s~weise** *adv* bit by bit; (*einzeln*) singly

Student|(in) *m* **-en,-en** (*f* **-,-nen**) student. **s~isch** *adj* student

Studie /-i̯ə/ *f* **-,-n** study

studieren *vt/i* (*haben*) study

Studio *nt* **-s,-s** studio

Studium *nt* **-s,-ien** studies *pl*

Stufe *f* **-,-n** step; (*Treppen-*) stair; (*Raketen-*) stage; (*Niveau*) level. **s~n** *vt* terrace; (*staffeln*) grade

Stuhl *m* **-[e]s,¨e** chair; (*Med*) stools *pl*. **S~gang** *m* bowel movement

stülpen *vt* put (**über** + *acc* over)

stumm *adj* dumb; (*schweigsam*) silent

Stummel *m* **-s,-** stump; (*Zigaretten-*) butt; (*Bleistift-*) stub

Stümper *m* **-s,-** bungler

stumpf *adj* blunt; (*Winkel*) obtuse; (*glanzlos*) dull; (*fig*) apathetic. **S~** *m* **-[e]s,¨e** stump

Stumpfsinn *m* apathy; tedium

Stunde *f* **-,-n** hour; (*Sch*) lesson

stunden *vt* **jdm eine Schuld s~** give s.o. time to pay a debt

Stunden|kilometer *mpl* kilometres per hour. **s~lang** *adv* for hours. **S~lohn** *m* hourly rate. **S~plan** *m* timetable. **s~weise** *adv* by the hour

stündlich *adj & adv* hourly

stur *adj* pigheaded

Sturm *m* **-[e]s,¨e** gale; storm; (*Mil*) assault

stürm|en *vi* (*haben*) (*Wind:*) blow hard ● *vi* (*sein*) rush ● *vt* storm; (*bedrängen*) besiege. **S~er** *m* **-s,-** forward. **s~isch** *adj* stormy; (*Überfahrt*) rough

Sturz *m* **-es,¨e** [heavy] fall; (*Preis-*) sharp drop; (*Pol*) overthrow

stürzen *vi* (*sein*) fall [heavily]; (*in die Tiefe*) plunge; (*Preise:*) drop sharply; (*Regierung:*) fall; (*eilen*) rush ● *vt* throw; (*umkippen*) turn upside down; turn out (*Speise, Kuchen*); (*Pol*) overthrow, topple; **sich s~** throw oneself (**aus**/**in** + *acc* out of/into)

Sturzhelm *m* crash-helmet

Stute *f* **-,-n** mare

Stütze *f* **-,-n** support

stützen *vt* support; (*auf-*) rest; **sich s~ auf** (+ *acc*) lean on

stutzig *adj* puzzled; (*misstrauisch*) suspicious

Stützpunkt *m* (*Mil*) base

Substantiv *nt* **-s,-e** noun

Substanz *f* **-,-en** substance

Subvention /-ˈtsi̯o:n/ *f* **-,-en** subsidy. **s~ieren** *vt* subsidize

Such|e *f* **-** search; **auf der S~e nach** looking for. **s~en** *vt* look for; (*intensiv*) search for; seek (*Hilfe, Rat*); **'Zimmer gesucht'** 'room wanted' ● *vi* (*haben*) look, search (**nach** for). **S~er** *m* **-s,-** (*Phot*) viewfinder. **S~maschine** *f* search engine

Sucht *f* **-,¨e** addiction; (*fig*) mania

süchtig *adj* addicted. **S~e(r)** *m/f* addict

Süd *m* **-[e]s** south. **S~afrika** *nt* South Africa. **S~amerika** *nt* South America. **s~deutsch** *adj* South German

Süden *m* **-s** south; **nach S~** south

Süd|frucht *f* tropical fruit. **s~lich** *adj* southern; (*Richtung*) southerly ● *adv & prep* (+ *gen*) **s~lich der Stadt** south of the town. **S~pol** *m*

South Pole. **s~wärts** *adv* southwards
Sühne *f* **-,-n** atonement; (*Strafe*) penalty. **s~n** *vt* atone for
Sultanine *f* **-,-n** sultana
Sülze *f* **-,-n** [meat] jelly
Summe *f* **-,-n** sum
summen *vi* (*haben*) hum; (*Biene:*) buzz ●*vt* hum
summieren (sich) *vr* add up
Sumpf *m* **-[e]s,⸚e** marsh, swamp
Sünd|e *f* **-,-n** sin. **S~enbock** *m* scapegoat. **S~er(in)** *m* **-s,-** (*f* **-,-nen**) sinner. **s~igen** *vi* (*haben*) sin
super *inv adj* **[I]** great. **S~markt** *m* supermarket
Suppe *f* **-,-n** soup. **S~nlöffel** *m* soup-spoon. **S~nteller** *m* soup plate. **S~nwürfel** *m* stock cube
Surf|brett /'sø:ɐ̯f-/ *nt* surfboard. **s~en** *vi* (*haben*) surf. **S~en** *nt* **-s** surfing
surren *vi* (*haben*) whirr
süß *adj* sweet. **S~e** *f* **-** sweetness. **s~en** *vt* sweeten. **S~igkeit** *f* **-,-en** sweet. **s~lich** *adj* sweetish; (*fig*) sugary. **S~speise** *f* sweet. **S~stoff** *m* sweetener. **S~waren** *fpl* confectionery *sg*, sweets *pl*. **S~wasser-** *prefix* freshwater
Sylvester *nt* **-s = Silvester**
Symbol *nt* **-s,-e** symbol. **S~ik** *f* **-** symbolism. **s~isch** *adj* symbolic
Sym|metrie *f* **-** symmetry. **s~metrisch** *adj* symmetrical
Sympathie *f* **-,-n** sympathy
sympathisch *adj* agreeable; (*Person*) likeable
Symptom *nt* **-s,-e** symptom. **s~atisch** *adj* symptomatic
Synagoge *f* **-,-n** synagogue
synchronisieren /zynkroni'zi:rən/ *vt* synchronize; dub (*Film*)
Syndikat *nt* **-[e]s,-e** syndicate
Syndrom *nt* **-s,-e** syndrome
synonym *adj* synonymous
Synthese *f* **-,-n** synthesis
Syrien /-i̯ən/ *nt* **-s** Syria
System *nt* **-s,-e** system. **s~atisch** *adj* systematic
Szene *f* **-,-n** scene

Tt

Tabak *m* **-s,-e** tobacco
Tabelle *f* **-,-n** table; (*Sport*) league table
Tablett *nt* **-[e]s,-s** tray
Tablette *f* **-,-n** tablet
tabu *adj* taboo. **T~** *nt* **-s,-s** taboo
Tacho *m* **-s,-s**, **Tachometer** *m & nt* speedometer
Tadel *m* **-s,-** reprimand; (*Kritik*) censure; (*Sch*) black mark. **t~los** *adj* impeccable. **t~n** *vt* reprimand; censure
Tafel *f* **-,-n** (*Tisch*, *Tabelle*) table; (*Platte*) slab; (*Anschlag-*, *Hinweis-*) board; (*Gedenk-*) plaque; (*Schiefer-*) slate; (*Wand-*) blackboard; (*Bild-*) plate; (*Schokolade*) bar
Täfelung *f* **-** panelling
Tag *m* **-[e]s,-e** day; **unter T~e** underground; **es wird Tag** it is getting light; **guten Tag!** good morning/afternoon!
Tage|buch *nt* diary. **t~lang** *adv* for days
Tages|anbruch *m* daybreak. **T~ausflug** *m* day trip. **T~decke** *f* bedspread. **T~karte** *f* day ticket; (*Speise-*) menu of the day. **T~licht** *nt* daylight. **T~mutter** *f* child-

minder. **T~ordnung** *f* agenda. **T~rückfahrkarte** *f* day return [ticket]. **T~zeit** *f* time of the day. **T~zeitung** *f* daily [news]paper

täglich *adj & adv* daily; **zweimal t~** twice a day

tags *adv* by day; **t~ zuvor/darauf** the day before/after

tagsüber *adv* during the day

tag|täglich *adj* daily ● *adv* every single day. **T~ung** *f* **-,-en** meeting; conference

Taill|e /'taljə/ *f* **-,-n** waist. **t~iert** *adj* fitted

Takt *m* **-[e]s,-e** tact; (*Mus*) bar; (*Tempo*) time; (*Rhythmus*) rhythm; **im T~** in time

Taktik *f* **-** tactics *pl.*

takt|los *adj* tactless. **T~losigkeit** *f* **-** tactlessness. **T~stock** *m* baton. **t~voll** *adj* tactful

Tal *nt* **-[e]s,¨er** valley

Talar *m* **-s,-e** robe; (*Univ*) gown

Talent *nt* **-[e]s,-e** talent. **t~iert** *adj* talented

Talg *m* **-s** tallow; (*Culin*) suet

Talsperre *f* dam

Tampon /tam'põ:/ *m* **-s,-s** tampon

Tank *m* **-s,-s** tank. **t~en** *vt* fill up with (*Benzin*) ● *vi* (*haben*) fill up with petrol; (*Aviat*) refuel. **T~er** *m* **-s,-** tanker. **T~stelle** *f* petrol station. **T~wart** *m* **-[e]s,-e** petrol-pump attendant

Tanne *f* **-,-n** fir [tree]. **T~nbaum** *m* fir tree; (*Weihnachtsbaum*) Christmas tree. **T~nzapfen** *m* fir cone

Tante *f* **-,-n** aunt

Tantiemen /tan'tie:mən/ *pl* royalties

Tanz *m* **-es,¨e** dance. **t~en** *vt/i* (*haben*) dance

Tänzer(in) *m* **-s,-** (*f* **-,-nen**) dancer

Tapete *f* **-,-n** wallpaper

tapezieren *vt* paper

tapfer *adj* brave. **T~keit** *f* **-** bravery

Tarif *m* **-s,-e** rate; (*Verzeichnis*) tariff

tarn|en *vt* disguise; (*Mil*) camouflage. **T~ung** *f* **-** disguise; camouflage

Tasche *f* **-,-n** bag; (*Hosen-, Mantel-*) pocket. **T~nbuch** *nt* paperback. **T~ndieb** *m* pickpocket. **T~ngeld** *nt* pocket-money. **T~nlampe** *f* torch. **T~nmesser** *nt* penknife. **T~ntuch** *nt* handkerchief

Tasse *f* **-,-n** cup

Tastatur *f* **-,-en** keyboard

Tast|e *f* **-,-n** key; (*Druck-*) push button. **t~en** *vi* (*haben*) feel, grope (**nach** for) ● *vt* key in (*Daten*); **sich t~en** feel one's way (**zu** to)

Tat *f* **-,-en** action; (*Helden-*) deed; (*Straf-*) crime; **auf frischer Tat ertappt** caught in the act

Täter(in) *m* **-s,-** (*f* **-,-nen**) culprit; (*Jur*) offender

tätig *adj* active; **t~ sein** work. **T~keit** *f* **-,-en** activity; (*Arbeit*) work, job

Tatkraft *f* energy

Tatort *m* scene of the crime

tätowier|en *vt* tattoo. **T~ung** *f* **-,-en** tattooing; (*Bild*) tattoo

Tatsache *f* fact. **T~nbericht** *m* documentary

tatsächlich *adj* actual

Tatze *f* **-,-n** paw

Tau[1] *m* **-[e]s** dew

Tau[2] *nt* **-[e]s,-e** rope

taub *adj* deaf; (*gefühllos*) numb

Taube *f* **-,-n** pigeon; dove. **T~nschlag** *m* pigeon loft

Taub|heit *f* **-** deafness. **t~stumm** *adj* deaf and dumb

tauch|en *vt* dip, plunge; (*unter-*)

duck ● *vi* (*haben/sein*) dive/(*ein-*) plunge (**in** + *acc* into); (*auf-*) appear (**aus** out of). **T~er** *m* **-s,-** diver. **T~eranzug** *m* diving-suit

tauen *vi* (*sein*) melt, thaw ● *impers* **es taut** it is thawing

Tauf|becken *nt* font. **T~e** *f* **-,-n** christening, baptism. **t~en** *vt* christen, baptize. **T~pate** *m* godfather

taugen *vi* (*haben*) **etwas/nichts t~n be good**/no good

tauglich *adj* suitable; (*Mil*) fit

Tausch *m* **-[e]s,-e** exchange, ! swap. **t~en** *vt* exchange/(*handeln*) barter (*gegen* for) ● *vi* (*haben*) swap (**mit etw** sth; **mit jdm** with s.o.)

täuschen *vt* deceive, fool; betray (*Vertrauen*); **sich t~** delude oneself; (*sich irren*) be mistaken ● *vi* (*haben*) be deceptive. **t~d** *adj* deceptive; (*Ähnlichkeit*) striking

Täuschung *f* **-,-en** deception; (*Irrtum*) mistake; (*Illusion*) delusion

tausend *inv adj* one/a thousand. **T~** *nt* **-s,-e** thousand. **T~füßler** *m* **-s,-** centipede. **t~ste(r, s)** *adj* thousandth. **T~stel** *nt* **-s,-** thousandth

Tau|tropfen *m* dewdrop. **T~wetter** *nt* thaw

Taxe *f* **-,-n** charge; (*Kur-*) tax; (*Taxi*) taxi

Taxi *nt* **-s,-s** taxi, cab

Taxi|fahrer *m* taxi driver. **T~stand** *m* taxi rank

Teakholz /'ti:k-/ *nt* teak

Team /ti:m/ *nt* **-s,-s** team

Techni|k *f* **-,-en** technology; (*Methode*) technique. **T~ker** *m* **-s,-** technician. **t~sch** *adj* technical; (*technologisch*) technological; **T~sche Hochschule** Technical University

Techno|logie *f* **-,-n** technology. **t~logisch** *adj* technological

Teddybär *m* teddy bear

Tee *m* **-s,-s** tea. **T~beutel** *m* teabag. **T~kanne** *f* teapot. **T~löffel** *m* teaspoon

Teer *m* **-s** tar. **t~en** *vt* tar

Tee|sieb *nt* tea strainer. **T~wagen** *m* [tea] trolley

Teich *m* **-[e]s,-e** pond

Teig *m* **-[e]s,-e** pastry; (*Knet-*) dough; (*Rühr-*) mixture; (*Pfannkuchen-*) batter. **T~rolle** *f* rolling-pin. **T~waren** *fpl* pasta *sg*

Teil *m* **-[e]s,-e** part; (*Bestand-*) component; (*Jur*) party; **zum T~** partly; **zum großen/größten T~** for the most part ● *m & nt* **-[e]s** (*Anteil*) share; **ich für mein[en] T~** for my part ● *nt* **-[e]s,-e** part; (*Ersatz-*) spare part; (*Anbau-*) unit

teil|bar *adj* divisible. **T~chen** *nt* **-s,-** particle. **t~en** *vt* divide; (*auf-*) share out; (*gemeinsam haben*) share; (*Pol*) partition (*Land*); **sich** (*dat*) **etw t~en** share sth; **sich t~en** divide; (*sich gabeln*) fork; (*Meinungen:*) differ ● *vi* (*haben*) share

Teilhaber *m* **-s,-** (*Comm*) partner

Teilnahme *f* **-** participation; (*innere*) interest; (*Mitgefühl*) sympathy

teilnehm|en† *vi sep* (*haben*) **t~en an** (+ *dat*) take part in; (*mitfühlen*) share [in]. **T~er(in)** *m* **-s,-** (*f* **-,-nen**) participant; (*an Wettbewerb*) competitor

teil|s *adv* partly. **T~ung** *f* **-,-en** division; (*Pol*) partition. **t~weise** *adj* partial ● *adv* partially, partly. **T~zahlung** *f* part payment; (*Rate*) instalment. **T~zeitbeschäftigung** *f* part-time job

Teint /tɛ̃:/ *m* **-s,-s** complexion

Telearbeit *f* teleworking

Telefax *nt* fax

Telefon *nt* **-s,-e** [tele]phone. **T~anruf** *m*, **T~at** *nt* **-[e]s,-e**

[tele]phone call. **T~buch** *nt* [tele-] phone book. **t~ieren** *vi* (*haben*) [tele]phone

telefon|isch *adj* [tele]phone ● *adv* by [tele]phone. **T~ist(in)** *m* **-en,-en** (*f* **-,-nen**) telephonist. **T~karte** *f* phone card. **T~nummer** *f* [tele]phone number. **T~zelle** *f* [tele]phone box

Telegraf *m* **-en,-en** telegraph. **T~enmast** *m* telegraph pole. **t~ieren** *vi* (*haben*) send a telegram. **t~isch** *adj* telegraphic ● *adv* by telegram

Telegramm *nt* **-s,-e** telegram

Teleobjektiv *nt* telephoto lens

Telepathie *f* **-** telepathy

Teleskop *nt* **-s,-e** telescope

Telex *nt* **-,-[e]** telex. **t~en** *vt* telex

Teller *m* **-s,-** plate

Tempel *m* **-s,-** temple

Temperament *nt* **-s,-e** temperament; (*Lebhaftigkeit*) vivacity

Temperatur *f* **-,-en** temperature

Tempo *nt* **-s,-s** speed; **T~ [T~]!** hurry up!

Tendenz *f* **-,-en** trend; (*Neigung*) tendency

Tennis *nt* **-** tennis. **T~platz** *m* tennis-court. **T~schläger** *m* tennis-racket

Teppich *m* **-s,-e** carpet. **T~boden** *m* fitted carpet

Termin *m* **-s,-e** date; (*Arzt-*) appointment. **T~kalender** *m* [appointments] diary

Terpentin *nt* **-s** turpentine

Terrasse *f* **-,-n** terrace

Terrier /ˈtɛri̯ɐ/ *m* **-s,-** terrier

Terrine *f* **-,-n** tureen

Territorium *nt* **-s,-ien** territory

Terror *m* **-s** terror. **t~isieren** *vt* terrorize. **T~ismus** *m* **-** terrorism. **T~ist** *m* **-en,-en** terrorist

Tesafilm® *m* ≈ Sellotape®

Test *m* **-[e]s,-s & -e** test

Testament *nt* **-[e]s,-e** will; **Altes/Neues T~** Old/New Testament. **T~svollstrecker** *m* **-s,-** executor

testen *vt* test

Tetanus *m* **-** tetanus

teuer *adj* expensive; (*lieb*) dear; **wie t~?** how much?

Teufel *m* **-s,-** devil. **T~skreis** *m* vicious circle

teuflisch *adj* fiendish

Text *m* **-[e]s,-e** text; (*Passage*) passage; (*Bild-*) caption; (*Lied-*) lyrics *pl*. **T~er** *m* **-s,-** copywriter; (*Schlager-*) lyricist

Textilien /-i̯ən/ *pl* textiles; (*Textilwaren*) textile goods

Text|nachricht *f* text message. **T~verarbeitungssystem** *nt* word processor

Theater *nt* **-s,-** theatre; (🅃: *Getue*) fuss. **T~kasse** *f* box-office. **T~stück** *nt* play

Theke *f* **-,-n** bar; (*Ladentisch*) counter

Thema *nt* **-s,-men** subject

Themse *f* **-** Thames

Theolo|ge *m* **-n,-n** theologian. **T~gie** *f* **-** theology

theor|etisch *adj* theoretical. **T~ie** *f* **-,-n** theory

Therapeut(in) *m* **-en,-en** (*f* **-,-nen**) therapist

Therapie *f* **-,-n** therapy

Thermalbad *nt* thermal bath

Thermometer *nt* **-s,-** thermometer

Thermosflasche® *f* Thermos flask®

Thermostat *m* **-[e]s,-e** thermostat

These *f* **-,-n** thesis

Thrombose *f* **-,-n** thrombosis

t

Thron *m* -[e]s,-e throne. **t~en** *vi* (*haben*) sit [in state]. **T~folge** *f* succession. **T~folger** *m* -s,- heir to the throne

Thunfisch *m* tuna

Thymian *m* -s thyme

ticken *vi* (*haben*) tick

tief *adj* deep; (*t~ liegend, niedrig*) low; (*t~gründig*) profound; **t~er Teller** soup-plate ● *adv* deep; low; (*sehr*) deeply, profoundly; (*schlafen*) soundly. **T~** *nt* -s,-s (*Meteorology*) depression. **T~bau** *m* civil engineering. **T~e** *f* -,-n depth. **T~garage** *f* underground car park. **t~gekühlt** *adj* [deep-]frozen

Tiefkühl|fach *nt* freezer compartment. **T~kost** *f* frozen food. **T~truhe** *f* deep-freeze

Tiefsttemperatur *f* minimum temperature

Tier *nt* -[e]s,-e animal. **T~arzt** *m*, **T~ärztin** *f* vet, veterinary surgeon. **T~garten** *m* zoo. **T~kreis** *m* zodiac. **T~kunde** *f* zoology. **T~quälerei** *f* cruelty to animals

Tiger *m* -s,- tiger

tilgen *vt* pay off (*Schuld*); (*streichen*) delete; (*fig: auslöschen*) wipe out

Tinte *f* -,-n ink. **T~nfisch** *m* squid

Tipp (**Tip**) *m* -s,-s 🄸 tip

tipp|en *vt* 🄸 type ● *vi* (*haben*) (*berühren*) touch (**auf/an etw** *acc* sth); (🄸: *Maschine schreiben*) type; **t~en auf** (+ *acc*) (🄸: *wetten*) bet on. **T~schein** *m* pools/lottery coupon

tipptopp *adj* 🄸 immaculate

Tirol *nt* -s [the] Tyrol

Tisch *m* -[e]s,-e table; (*Schreib-*) desk; **nach T~** after the meal. **T~decke** *f* table-cloth. **T~gebet** *nt* grace. **T~ler** *m* -s,- joiner; (*Möbel-*) cabinet-maker. **T~rede** *f* after-dinner speech. **T~tennis** *nt* table tennis

Titel *m* -s,- title

Toast /to:st/ *m* -[e]s,-e toast; (*Scheibe*) piece of toast. **T~er** *m* -s,- toaster

toben *vi* (*haben*) rave; (*Sturm:*) rage; (*Kinder:*) play boisterously

Tochter *f* -,¨ daughter. **T~gesellschaft** *f* subsidiary

Tod *m* -es death

Todes|angst *f* mortal fear. **T~anzeige** *f* death announcement; (*Zeitungs-*) obituary. **T~fall** *m* death. **T~opfer** *nt* fatality, casualty. **T~strafe** *f* death penalty. **T~urteil** *nt* death sentence

todkrank *adj* dangerously ill

tödlich *adj* fatal; (*Gefahr*) mortal

Toilette /to̥a'lɛtə/ *f* -,-n toilet. **T~npapier** *nt* toilet paper

toler|ant *adj* tolerant. **T~anz** *f* - tolerance. **t~ieren** *vt* tolerate

toll *adj* crazy, mad; (🄸: *prima*) fantastic; (*schlimm*) awful ● *adv* (*sehr*) very; (*schlimm*) badly. **t~kühn** *adj* foolhardy. **T~wut** *f* rabies. **t~wütig** *adj* rabid

Tölpel *m* -s,- fool

Tomate *f* -,-n tomato. **T~nmark** *nt* tomato purée

Tombola *f* -,-s raffle

Ton[1] *m* -[e]s clay

Ton[2] *m* -[e]s,¨e tone; (*Klang*) sound; (*Note*) note; (*Betonung*) stress; (*Farb-*) shade; **der gute Ton** (*fig*) good form. **T~abnehmer** *m* -s,- pick-up. **t~angebend** *adj* (*fig*) leading. **T~art** *f* tone [of voice]; (*Mus*) key. **T~band** *nt* (*pl* **-bänder**) tape. **T~bandgerät** *nt* tape recorder

tönen *vi* (*haben*) sound ● *vt* tint

Tonleiter *f* scale

Tonne *f* -,-n barrel, cask: (*Müll-*)

bin; (*Maß*) tonne, metric ton

Topf *m* **-[e]s,⸚e** pot; (*Koch-*) pan

Topfen *m* **-s** (Aust) ≈ curd cheese

Töpferei *f* **-,-en** pottery

Topf|lappen *m* oven-cloth. **T∼pflanze** *f* potted plant

Tor *nt* **-[e]s,-e** gate; (*Einfahrt*) gateway; (*Sport*) goal

Torf *m* **-s** peat

torkeln *vi* (*sein/habe*) stagger

Tornister *m* **-s,-** knapsack; (*Sch*) satchel

Torpedo *m* **-s,-s** torpedo

Torpfosten *m* goal-post

Torte *f* **-,-n** gateau; (*Obst-*) flan

Tortur *f* **-,-en** torture

Torwart *m* **-s,-e** goalkeeper

tot *adj* dead; **tot geboren** stillborn; **sich tot stellen** pretend to be dead

total *adj* total. **T∼schaden** *m* ≈ write-off

Tote|(r) *m/f* dead man/woman; (*Todesopfer*) fatality; **die T∼n** the dead *pl*

töten *vt* kill

Toten|gräber *m* **-s,-** grave-digger. **T∼kopf** *m* skull. **T∼schein** *m* death certificate

totfahren† *vt sep* run over and kill

Toto *nt & m* **-s** football pools *pl*. **T∼schein** *m* pools coupon

tot|schießen† *vt sep* shoot dead. **T∼schlag** *m* (*Jur*) manslaughter. **t∼schlagen**† *vt sep* kill

Tötung *f* **-,-en** killing; **fahrlässige T∼** (*Jur*) manslaughter

Toup|et /tu'pe:/ *nt* **-s,-s** toupee. **t∼ieren** *vt* back-comb

Tour /tu:ɐ̯/ *f* **-,-en** tour; (*Ausflug*) trip; (*Auto-*) drive; (*Rad-*) ride; (*Strecke*) distance; (*Techn*) revolution; (🅸: *Weise*) way

Touris|mus /tu'rɪsmʊs/ *m* **-** tourism. **T∼t** *m* **-en,-en** tourist

Tournee /tʊr'ne:/ *f* **-,-n** tour

Trab *m* **-[e]s** trot

Trabant *m* **-en,-en** satellite

traben *vi* (*haben/sein*) trot

Tracht *f* **-,-en** [national] costume

Tradition /-'tsi̯o:n/ *f* **-,-en** tradition. **t∼ell** *adj* traditional

Trag|bahre *f* stretcher. **t∼bar** *adj* portable; (*Kleidung*) wearable

tragen† *vt* carry; (*an-/ aufhaben*) wear; (*fig*) bear ●*vi* (*haben*) carry; **gut t∼** (*Baum:*) produce a good crop

Träger *m* **-s,-** porter; (*Inhaber*) bearer; (*eines Ordens*) holder; (*Bau-*) beam; (*Stahl-*) girder; (*Achsel-*) [shoulder] strap. **T∼kleid** *nt* pinafore dress

Trag|etasche *f* carrier bag. **T∼flächenboot**, **T∼flügelboot** *nt* hydrofoil

Trägheit *f* **-** sluggishness; (*Faulheit*) laziness; (*Phys*) inertia

Trag|ik *f* **-** tragedy. **t∼isch** *adj* tragic

Tragödie /-i̯ə/ *f* **-,-n** tragedy

Train|er /'trɛ:nɐ/ *m* **-s,-** trainer; (*Tennis-*) coach. **t∼ieren** *vt/i* (*haben*) train

Training /'trɛ:nɪŋ/ *nt* **-s** training. **T∼sanzug** *m* tracksuit. **T∼sschuhe** *mpl* trainers

Traktor *m* **-s,-en** tractor

trampeln *vi* (*haben*) stamp one's feet ●*vi* (*sein*) trample (**auf** + *acc* on) ●*vt* trample

trampen /'trɛmpən/ *vi* (*sein*) 🅸 hitch-hike

Tranchiermesser /trã'ʃi:ɐ̯-/ *nt* carving knife

Träne *f* **-,-n** tear. **t∼n** *vi* (*haben*) water. **T∼ngas** *nt* tear-gas

Tränke *f* **-,-n** watering place; (*Trog*) drinking trough. **t∼n** *vt* water

t

(*Pferd*); (*nässen*) soak (mit with)

Trans|formator *m* **-s,-en** transformer. **T~fusion** *f* **-,-en** [blood] transfusion

Transit /tran'zi:t/ *m* **-s** transit

Transparent *nt* **-[e]s,-e** banner; (*Bild*) transparency

transpirieren *vi* (*haben*) perspire

Transport *m* **-[e]s,-e** transport; (*Güter-*) consignment. **t~ieren** *vt* transport

Trapez *nt* **-es,-e** trapeze

Tratte *f* **-,-n** (*Comm*) draft

Traube *f* **-,-n** bunch of grapes; (*Beere*) grape; (*fig*) cluster. **T~nzucker** *m* glucose

trauen *vi* (*haben*) (+ *dat*) trust ● *vt* marry; **sich t~** dare (**etw zu tun** [to] do sth); venture (**in** + *acc*/**aus** into/out of)

Trauer *f* **-** mourning; (*Schmerz*) grief (**um** for); **T~ tragen** be [dressed] in mourning. **T~fall** *m* bereavement. **T~feier** *f* funeral service. **t~n** *vi* (*haben*) grieve; **t~n um** mourn [for]. **T~spiel** *nt* tragedy. **T~weide** *f* weeping willow

Traum *m* **-[e]s, Träume** dream

Trauma *nt* **-s,-men** trauma

träumen *vt/i* (*haben*) dream

traumhaft *adj* dreamlike; (*schön*) fabulous

traurig *adj* sad; (*erbärmlich*) sorry. **T~keit** *f* **-** sadness

Trau|ring *m* wedding-ring. **T~schein** *m* marriage certificate. **T~ung** *f* **-,-en** wedding [ceremony]

Treff *nt* **-s,-s** (*Karten*) spades *pl*

treff|en† *vt* hit; (*Blitz:*) strike; (*fig: verletzen*) hurt; (*zusammenkommen mit*) meet; take (*Maßnahme*); **sich t~en** meet (**mit jdm** s.o.); **sich gut t~en** be convenient; **es gut/schlecht t~en** be lucky/unlucky ● *vi* (*haben*) hit the target; **t~en auf** (+ *acc*) meet; (*fig*) meet with. **T~en** *nt* **-s,-** meeting. **T~er** *m* **-s,-** hit; (*Los*) winner. **T~punkt** *m* meeting-place

treiben† *vt* drive; (*sich befassen mit*) do; carry on (*Gewerbe*); indulge in (*Luxus*); get up to (*Unfug*); **Handel t~** trade ● *vi* (*sein*) drift; (*schwimmen*) float ● *vi* (*haben*) (*Bot*) sprout. **T~** *nt* **-s** activity

Treib|haus *nt* hothouse. **T~hauseffekt** *m* greenhouse effect. **T~holz** *nt* driftwood. **T~riemen** *m* transmission belt. **T~sand** *m* quicksand. **T~stoff** *m* fuel

trenn|bar *adj* separable. **t~en** *vt* separate/(*abmachen*) detach (**von** from); divide, split (*Wort*); **sich t~en** separate; (*auseinander gehen*) part; **sich t~en von** leave; (*fortgeben*) part with. **T~ung** *f* **-,-en** separation; (*Silben-*) division. **T~ungsstrich** *m* hyphen. **T~wand** *f* partition

trepp|ab *adv* downstairs. **t~auf** *adv* upstairs

Treppe *f* **-,-n** stairs *pl*; (*Außen-*) steps *pl*. **T~ngeländer** *nt* banisters *pl*

Tresor *m* **-s,-e** safe

Tresse *f* **-,-n** braid

Treteimer *m* pedal bin

treten† *vi* (*sein/haben*) step; (*versehentlich*) tread; (*ausschlagen*) kick (**nach** at); **in Verbindung t~** get in touch ● *vt* tread; (*mit Füßen*) kick

treu *adj* faithful; (*fest*) loyal. **T~e** *f* **-** faithfulness; loyalty; (*eheliche*) fidelity. **T~ekarte** *f* loyalty card. **T~händer** *m* **-s,-** trustee. **t~los** *adj* disloyal; (*untreu*) unfaithful

Tribüne *f* **-,-n** platform; (*Zuschauer-*) stand

Trichter *m* **-s,-** funnel; (*Bomben-*) crater

Trick *m* **-s,-s** trick. **T~film** *m* cartoon. **t~reich** *adj* clever

Trieb *m* **-[e]s,-e** drive, urge; (*Instinkt*) instinct; (*Bot*) shoot. **T~verbrecher** *m* sex offender. **T~werk** *nt* (*Aviat*) engine; (*Uhr-*) mechanism

triefen† *vi* (*haben*) drip; (*nass sein*) be dripping (**von/vor** + *dat* with)

Trigonometrie *f* - trigonometry

Trikot[1] /tri'ko:/ *m* **-s** (*Textiles*) jersey

Trikot[2] *nt* **-s,-s** (*Sport*) jersey; (*Fußball-*) shirt

Trimester *nt* **-s,-** term

Trimm-dich *nt* **-s** keep-fit

trimmen *vt* trim; tune (*Motor*); **sich t~** keep fit

trink|en† *vt/i* (*haben*) drink. **T~er(in)** *m* **-s,-** (*f* **-,-nen**) alcoholic. **T~geld** *nt* tip. **T~spruch** *m* toast

trist *adj* dreary

Tritt *m* **-[e]s,-e** step; (*Fuß-*) kick. **T~brett** *nt* step

Triumph *m* **-s,-e** triumph. **t~ieren** *vi* (*haben*) rejoice

trocken *adj* dry. **T~haube** *f* drier. **T~heit** *f* **-,-en** dryness; (*Dürre*) drought. **t~legen** *vt sep* change (*Baby*); drain (*Sumpf*). **T~milch** *f* powdered milk

trockn|en *vt/i* (*sein*) dry. **T~er** *m* **-s,-** drier

Trödel *m* **-s** [F] junk. **t~n** *vi* (*haben*) dawdle

Trödler *m* **-s,-** [F] slowcoach; (*Händler*) junk-dealer

Trog *m* **-[e]s,⸚e** trough

Trommel *f* **-,-n** drum. **T~fell** *nt* ear-drum. **t~n** *vi* (*haben*) drum

Trommler *m* **-s,-** drummer

Trompete *f* **-,-n** trumpet. **T~r** *m* **-s,-** trumpeter

Tropen *pl* tropics

Tropf *m* **-[e]s,-e** (*Med*) drip

tröpfeln *vt/i* (*sein/haben*) drip

tropfen *vt/i* (*sein/haben*) drip. **T~** *m* **-s,-** drop; (*fallend*) drip. **t~weise** *adv* drop by drop

Trophäe /tro'fɛ:ə/ *f* **-,-n** trophy

tropisch *adj* tropical

Trost *m* **-[e]s** consolation, comfort

tröst|en *vt* console, comfort; **sich t~en** console oneself. **t~lich** *adj* comforting

trost|los *adj* desolate; (*elend*) wretched; (*reizlos*) dreary. **T~preis** *m* consolation prize

Trott *m* **-s** amble; (*fig*) routine

Trottel *m* **-s,-** [F] idiot

Trottoir /trɔ'to̯a:ɐ̯/ *nt* **-s,-s** pavement

trotz *prep* (+ *gen*) despite, in spite of. **T~** *m* **-es** defiance. **t~dem** *adv* nevertheless. **t~ig** *adj* defiant; stubborn

trübe *adj* dull; (*Licht*) dim; (*Flüssigkeit*) cloudy; (*fig*) gloomy

Trubel *m* **-s** bustle

trüben *vt* dull; make cloudy (*Flüssigkeit*); (*fig*) spoil; strain (*Verhältnis*) **sich t~** (*Flüssigkeit:*) become cloudy; (*Himmel:*) cloud over; (*Augen:*) dim

Trüb|sal *f* - misery. **T~sinn** *m* melancholy. **t~sinnig** *adj* melancholy

trügen† *vt* deceive ● *vi* (*haben*) be deceptive

Trugschluss *m* fallacy

Truhe *f* **-,-n** chest

Trümmer *pl* rubble *sg*; (*T~teile*) wreckage *sg*, (*fig*) ruins

Trumpf *m* **-[e]s,⸚e** trump [card]. **t~en** *vi* (*haben*) play trumps

Trunk *m* **-[e]s** drink. **T~enheit** *f* -

t

drunkenness; **T~enheit am Steuer** drink-driving

Trupp *m* **-s,-s** group; (*Mil*) squad. **T~e** *f* **-,-n** (*Mil*) unit; (*Theat*) troupe; **T~en** troops

Truthahn *m* turkey

Tschech|e *m* **-n,-n, T~in** *f* **-,-nen** Czech. **t~isch** *adj* Czech. **T~oslowakei (die)** - Czechoslovakia

tschüs, tschüss *int* bye, cheerio

Tuba *f* **-,-ben** (*Mus*) tuba

Tube *f* **-,-n** tube

Tuberkulose *f* - tuberculosis

Tuch *nt* **-[e]s,⸚er** cloth; (*Hals-, Kopf-*) scarf; (*Schulter-*) shawl

tüchtig *adj* competent; (*reichlich, beträchtlich*) good; (*groß*) big ●*adv* competently; (*ausreichend*) well

Tück|e *f* **-,-n** malice. **t~isch** *adj* malicious; (*gefährlich*) treacherous

Tugend *f* **-,en** virtue. **t~haft** *adj* virtuous

Tülle *f* **-,-n** spout

Tulpe *f* **-,-n** tulip

Tümmler *m* **-s,-** porpoise

Tumor *m* **-s,-en** tumour

Tümpel *m* **-[e]s,-** pond

Tumult *m* **-[e]s,-e** commotion; (*Aufruhr*) riot

tun† *vt* do; take (*Schritt, Blick*); work (*Wunder*); (*bringen*) put (**in** + *acc* into); **sich tun** happen; **jdm etwas tun** hurt s.o.; **das tut nichts** it doesn't matter ●*vi* (*haben*) act (**als ob** as if); **er tut nur so** he's just pretending; **jdm/etw gut tun** do s.o./sth good; **zu tun haben** have things/work to do; **[es] zu tun haben mit** have to deal with. **Tun** *nt* **-s** actions *pl*

Tünche *f* **-,-n** whitewash; (*fig*) veneer. **t~n** *vt* whitewash

Tunesien /-i̯ən/ *nt* **-s** Tunisia

Tunfisch *m* **Thunfisch**

Tunnel *m* **-s,-** tunnel

tupf|en *vt* dab ●*vi* (*haben*) **t~en an/auf** (+ *acc*) touch. **T~en** *m* **-s,-** spot. **T~er** *m* **-s,-** spot; (*Med*) swab

Tür *f* **-,-en** door

Turban *m* **-s,-e** turban

Turbine *f* **-,-n** turbine

Türk|e *m* **-n,-n** Turk. **T~ei (die)** - Turkey. **T~in** *f* **-,-nen** Turk

türkis *inv adj* turquoise

türkisch *adj* Turkish

Turm *m* **-[e]s,⸚e** tower; (*Schach*) rook, castle

Türm|chen *nt* **-s,-** turret. **t~en** *vt* pile [up]; **sich t~en** pile up

Turmspitze *f* spire

turn|en *vi* (*haben*) do gymnastics. **T~en** *nt* **-s** gymnastics *sg*; (*Sch*) physical education, [I] gym. **T~er(in)** *m* **-s,-** (*f* **-,-nen**) gymnast. **T~halle** *f* gymnasium

Turnier *nt* **-s,-e** tournament; (*Reit-*) show

Turnschuhe *mpl* gym shoes; trainers

Türschwelle *f* doorstep, threshold

Tusche *f* **-,-n** [drawing] ink

tuscheln *vt/i* (*haben*) whisper

Tüte *f* **-,-n** bag; (*Comm*) packet; (*Eis-*) cornet; **in die T~ blasen** [I] be breathalysed

TÜV *m* - ≈ MOT [test]

Typ *m* **-s,-en** type; ([I]: *Kerl*) bloke. **T~e** *f* **-,-n** type

Typhus *m* - typhoid

typisch *adj* typical (**für** of)

Typus *m* **-, Typen** type

Tyrann *m* **-en,-en** tyrant. **T~ei** *f* - tyranny. **t~isch** *adj* tyrannical. **t~isieren** *vt* tyrannize

Uu

U-Bahn *f* underground
übel *adj* bad; (*hässlich*) nasty; **mir ist ü~** I feel sick; **jdm etw ü~ nehmen** hold sth against s.o. **Ü~keit** *f* - nausea
üben *vt/i* (*haben*) practise
über *prep* (+ *dat/acc*) over; (*höher als*) above; (*betreffend*) about; (*Buch, Vortrag*) on; (*Scheck, Rechnung*) for; (*quer ü~*) across; **ü~ Köln fahren** go via Cologne; **ü~ Ostern** over Easter; **die Woche ü~** during the week; **Fehler ü~ Fehler** mistake after mistake ● *adv* **ü~ und ü~** all over; **jdm ü~ sein** be better/(*stärker*) stronger than s.o. ● *adj* ⓘ **ü~ sein** be left over; **etw ü~ sein** be fed up with sth
überall *adv* everywhere
überanstrengen *vt insep* overtax; strain (*Augen*)
überarbeiten *vt insep* revise; **sich ü~en** overwork
überbieten† *vt insep* outbid; (*übertreffen*) surpass
Überblick *m* overall view; (*Abriss*) summary
überblicken *vt insep* overlook; (*abschätzen*) assess
überbringen† *vt insep* deliver
überbrücken *vt insep* (*fig*) bridge
überbuchen *vt insep* overbook
überdies *adv* moreover
überdimensional *adj* oversized
Überdosis *f* overdose
überdrüssig *adj* **ü~ sein/werden** be/grow tired (*gen* of)
übereignen *vt insep* transfer
übereilt *adj* over-hasty
übereinander *adv* one on top of/above the other; (*sprechen*) about each other
überein|kommen† *vi sep* (*sein*) agree. **Ü~kunft** *f* - agreement. **ü~stimmen** *vi sep* (*haben*) agree; (*Zahlen:*) tally; (*Ansichten:*) coincide; (*Farben:*) match. **Ü~stimmung** *f* agreement
überfahren† *vt insep* run over
Überfahrt *f* crossing
Überfall *m* attack; (*Bank-*) raid
überfallen† *vt insep* attack; raid (*Bank*); (*bestürmen*) bombard (**mit** with)
Überfluss *m* abundance; (*Wohlstand*) affluence
überflüssig *adj* superfluous
überfordern *vt insep* overtax
überführ|en *vt insep* transfer; (*Jur*) convict (*gen* of). **Ü~ung** *f* transfer; (*Straße*) flyover; (*Fußgänger-*) foot-bridge
überfüllt *adj* overcrowded
Übergabe *f* handing over; transfer
Übergang *m* crossing; (*Wechsel*) transition
übergeben† *vt insep* hand over; (*übereignen*) transfer; **sich ü~** be sick
übergehen† *vt insep* (*fig*) pass over; (*nicht beachten*) ignore; (*auslassen*) leave out
Übergewicht *nt* excess weight; (*fig*) predominance; **Ü~ haben** be overweight
über|greifen† *vi sep* (*haben*) spread (**auf** + *acc* to). **Ü~griff** *m* infringement
über|groß *adj* outsize; (*übertrieben*) exaggerated. **Ü~größe** *f* outsize
überhand *adv* **ü~ nehmen**

increase alarmingly
überhäufen *vt insep* inundate (**mit** with)
überhaupt *adv* (*im Allgemeinen*) altogether; (*eigentlich*) anyway; (*überdies*) besides; **ü~ nicht/nichts** not/nothing at all
überheblich *adj* arrogant. **Ü~keit** *f* - arrogance
überhol|en *vt insep* overtake; (*reparieren*) overhaul. **ü~t** *adj* outdated. **Ü~ung** *f* -,-en overhaul. **Ü~verbot** *nt* '**Ü~verbot**' 'no overtaking'
überhören *vt insep* fail to hear; (*nicht beachten*) ignore
überirdisch *adj* supernatural
überkochen *vi sep* (*sein*) boil over
überlassen† *vt insep* **jdm etw ü~** leave sth to s.o.; (*geben*) let s.o. have sth; **sich** (*dat*) **selbst ü~ sein** be left to one's own devices
Überlauf *m* overflow
überlaufen† *vi sep* (*sein*) overflow; (*Mil, Pol*) defect
Überläufer *m* defector
überleben *vt/i insep* (*haben*) survive. **Ü~de(r)** *m/f* survivor
überlegen[1] *vt sep* put over
überlegen[2] *v insep* ●*vt* [**sich** *dat*] **ü~** think over, consider; **es sich** (*dat*) **anders ü~** change one's mind ●*vi* (*haben*) think, reflect
U
überlegen[3] *adj* superior. **Ü~heit** *f* - superiority
Überlegung *f* -,-en reflection
überliefer|n *vt insep* hand down. **Ü~ung** *f* tradition
überlisten *vt insep* outwit
Übermacht *f* superiority
übermäßig *adj* excessive
Übermensch *m* superman. **ü~lich** *adj* superhuman
übermitteln *vt insep* convey; (*senden*) transmit
übermorgen *adv* the day after tomorrow
übermüdet *adj* overtired
Über|mut *m* high spirits *pl*. **ü~mütig** *adj* high-spirited
übernächst|e(r,s) *adj* next but one; **ü~es Jahr** the year after next
übernacht|en *vi insep* (*haben*) stay overnight. **Ü~ung** *f* -,-en overnight stay; **Ü~ung und Frühstück** bed and breakfast
Übernahme *f* - taking over; (*Comm*) take-over
übernatürlich *adj* supernatural
übernehmen† *vt insep* take over; (*annehmen*) take on; **sich ü~** overdo things; (*finanziell*) overreach oneself
überqueren *vt insep* cross
überrasch|en *vt insep* surprise. **ü~end** *adj* surprising; (*unerwartet*) unexpected. **Ü~ung** *f* -,-en surprise
überreden *vt insep* persuade
Überreste *mpl* remains
Überschall- *prefix* supersonic
überschätzen *vt insep* overestimate
Überschlag *m* rough estimate; (*Sport*) somersault
überschlagen[1]† *vt sep* cross (*Beine*)
überschlagen[2]† *vt insep* estimate roughly; (*auslassen*) skip; **sich ü~** somersault; (*Ereignisse:*) happen fast ●*adj* tepid
überschneiden† **(sich)** *vr insep* intersect, cross; (*zusammenfallen*) overlap
überschreiten† *vt insep* cross; (*fig*) exceed
Überschrift *f* heading; (*Zeitungs-*)

headline
Über|schuss *m* surplus. **ü~schüssig** *adj* surplus
überschwemm|en *vt insep* flood; (*fig*) inundate. **Ü~ung** *f* -,-en flood
Übersee in/nach Ü~ overseas; **aus/von Ü~** from overseas. **Ü~dampfer** *m* ocean liner. **ü~isch** *adj* overseas
übersehen† *vt insep* look out over; (*abschätzen*) assess; (*nicht sehen*) overlook, miss; (*ignorieren*) ignore
übersenden† *vt insep* send
übersetzen[1] *vi sep* (*haben/sein*) cross [over]
übersetz|en[2] *vt insep* translate. **Ü~er(in)** *m* **-s,-** (*f* **-,-nen**) translator. **Ü~ung** *f* **-,-en** translation
Übersicht *f* overall view; (*Abriss*) summary; (*Tabelle*) table. **ü~lich** *adj* clear
Übersiedlung *f* move
überspielen *vt insep* (*fig*) cover up; **auf Band ü~** tape
überstehen† *vt insep* come through; get over (*Krankheit*); (*überleben*) survive
übersteigen† *vt insep* climb [over]; (*fig*) exceed
überstimmen *vt insep* outvote
Überstunden *fpl* overtime *sg*; **Ü~ machen** work overtime
überstürz|en *vt insep* rush; **sich ü~en** (*Ereignisse:*) happen fast. **ü~t** *adj* hasty
übertrag|bar *adj* transferable; (*Med*) infectious. **ü~en**† *vt insep* transfer; (*übergeben*) assign (*dat* to); (*Techn, Med*) transmit; (*Radio, TV*) broadcast; (*übersetzen*) translate; (*anwenden*) apply (**auf** + *acc* to) ● *adj* transferred, figurative. **Ü~ung** *f* **-,-en** transfer; transmission; broadcast; translation, application
übertreffen† *vt insep* surpass; (*übersteigen*) exceed; **sich selbst ü~** excel oneself
übertreib|en† *vt insep* exaggerate; (*zu weit treiben*) overdo. **Ü~ung** *f* **-,-en** exaggeration
übertreten[1]† *vi sep* (*sein*) step over the line; (*Pol*) go over/(*Relig*) convert (**zu** to)
übertret|en[2]† *vt insep* infringe; break (*Gesetz*). **Ü~ung** *f* **-,-en** infringement; breach
übertrieben *adj* exaggerated
übervölkert *adj* overpopulated
überwachen *vt insep* supervise; (*kontrollieren*) monitor; (*bespitzeln*) keep under surveillance
überwältigen *vt insep* overpower; (*fig*) overwhelm
überweis|en† *vt insep* transfer; refer (*Patienten*). **Ü~ung** *f* transfer; (*ärztliche*) referral
überwiegen† *v insep* ● *vi* (*haben*) predominate. ● *vt* outweigh
überwind|en† *vt insep* overcome; **sich ü~en** force oneself. **Ü~ung** *f* effort
Über|zahl *f* majority. **ü~zählig** *adj* spare
überzeug|en *vt insep* convince; **sich [selbst] ü~en** satisfy oneself. **ü~end** *adj* convincing. **Ü~ung** *f* **-,-en** conviction
überziehen[1]† *vt sep* put on
überziehen[2]† *vt insep* cover; overdraw (*Konto*)
Überzug *m* cover; (*Schicht*) coating
üblich *adj* usual; (*gebräuchlich*) customary
U-Boot *nt* submarine
übrig *adj* remaining; (*andere*) other;

alles Ü~e [all] the rest; **im Ü~en** besides; (*ansonsten*) apart from that; **ü~ sein** *od* **bleiben** be left [over]; **etw ü~ lassen** leave sth [over]; **uns blieb nichts anderes ü~** we had no choice

Übung *f* **-,-en** exercise; (*Üben*) practice; **außer** *od* **aus der Ü~** out of practice

Ufer *nt* **-s,-** shore; (*Fluss-*) bank

Uhr *f* **-,-en** clock; (*Armband-*) watch; (*Zähler*) meter; **um ein U~** at one o'clock; **wie viel U~ ist es?** what's the time? **U~macher** *m* **-s,-** watch and clockmaker. **U~werk** *nt* clock/ watch mechanism. **U~zeiger** *m* [clock-/watch-]hand. **U~zeit** *f* time

Uhu *m* **-s,-s** eagle owl

UKW *abbr* (*Ultrakurzwelle*) VHF

ulkig *adj* funny; (*seltsam*) odd

Ulme *f* **-,-n** elm

Ultimatum *nt* **-s,-ten** ultimatum

Ultra|kurzwelle *f* very high frequency. **U~leichtflugzeug** *nt* microlight [aircraft]

Ultraschall *m* ultrasound

ultraviolett *adj* ultraviolet

um *prep* (+ *acc*) [a]round; (*Uhrzeit*) at; (*bitten*) for; (*streiten*) over; (*sich sorgen*) about; (*betrügen*) out of; (*bei Angabe einer Differenz*) by; **um [... herum]** around, [round] about; **Tag um Tag** day after day; **um seinetwillen** for his sake ● *adv* (*ungefähr*) around, about; **um sein** ⊡ be over; (*Zeit*) be up ● *conj* **um zu** to; (*Absicht*) [in order] to; **zu müde, um zu ...** too tired to ...

umarm|en *vt insep* embrace, hug. **U~ung** *f* **-,-en** embrace, hug

Umbau *m* rebuilding; conversion (**zu** into). **u~en** *vt sep* rebuild; convert (**zu** into)

Umbildung *f* reorganization; (*Pol*) reshuffle

umbinden† *vt sep* put on

umblättern *v sep* ● *vt* turn [over] ● *vi* (*haben*) turn the page

umbringen† *vt sep* kill; **sich u~** kill oneself

umbuchen *v sep* ● *vt* change; (*Comm*) transfer ● *vi* (*haben*) change one's booking

umdrehen *v sep* ● *vt* turn round/(*wenden*) over; turn (*Schlüssel*); (*umkrempeln*) turn inside out; **sich u~** turn round; (*im Liegen*) turn over ● *vi* (*haben/sein*) turn back

Umdrehung *f* turn; (*Motor-*) revolution

umeinander *adv* around each other; **sich u~ sorgen** worry about each other

umfahren[1]† *vt sep* run over

umfahren[2]† *vt insep* go round; bypass (*Ort*)

umfallen† *vi sep* (*sein*) fall over; (*Person:*) fall down

Umfang *m* girth; (*Geometry*) circumference; (*Größe*) size

umfangreich *adj* extensive; (*dick*) big

umfassen *vt insep* consist of, comprise; (*umgeben*) surround. **u~d** *adj* comprehensive

Umfrage *f* survey, poll

umfüllen *vt sep* transfer

umfunktionieren *vt sep* convert

Umgang *m* [social] contact; (*Umgehen*) dealing (**mit** with)

Umgangssprache *f* colloquial language

umgeb|en† *vt/i insep* (*haben*) surround ● *adj* **u~en von** surrounded by. **U~ung** *f* **-,-en** surroundings *pl*

umgehen† *vt insep* avoid; (*nicht beachten*) evade; (*Straße:*) bypass

umgehend *adj* immediate

Umgehungsstraße *f* bypass
umgekehrt *adj* inverse; (*Reihenfolge*) reverse; **es war u~** it was the other way round
umgraben† *vt sep* dig [over]
Umhang *m* cloak
umhauen† *vt sep* knock down; (*fällen*) chop down
umhören (sich) *vr sep* ask around
Umkehr *f* - turning back. **u~en** *v sep* ●*vi* (*sein*) turn back ●*vt* turn round; turn inside out (*Tasche*); (*fig*) reverse
umkippen *v sep* ●*vt* tip over; (*versehentlich*) knock over ●*vi* (*sein*) fall over; (*Boot:*) capsize
Umkleide|kabine *f* changing-cubicle. **u~n (sich)** *vr sep* change. **U~raum** *m* changing-room
umknicken *v sep* ●*vt* bend; (*falten*) fold ●*vi* (*sein*) bend; (*mit dem Fuß*) go over on one's ankle
umkommen† *vi sep* (*sein*) perish
Umkreis *m* surroundings *pl*; **im U~ von** within a radius of
umkreisen *vt insep* circle; (*Astronomy*) revolve around; (*Satellit:*) orbit
umkrempeln *vt sep* turn up; (*von innen nach außen*) turn inside out; (*ändern*) change radically
Umlauf *m* circulation; (*Astronomy*) revolution. **U~bahn** *f* orbit
Umlaut *m* umlaut
umlegen *vt sep* lay *or* put down; flatten (*Getreide*); turn down (*Kragen*); put on (*Schal*); throw (*Hebel*); (*verlegen*) transfer; (🅃: *töten*) kill
umleit|en *vt sep* divert. **U~ung** *f* diversion
umliegend *adj* surrounding
umpflanzen *vt sep* transplant
umranden *vt insep* edge
umräumen *vt sep* rearrange
umrechn|en *vt sep* convert. **U~ung** *f* conversion
umreißen† *vt insep* outline
Umriss *m* outline
umrühren *vt/i sep* (*haben*) stir
ums *pron* = **um das**
Umsatz *m* (*Comm*) turnover
umschalten *vt/i sep* (*haben*) switch over; **auf Rot u~** (*Ampel:*) change to red
Umschau *f* **U~ halten nach** look out for
Umschlag *m* cover; (*Schutz-*) jacket; (*Brief-*) envelope; (*Med*) compress; (*Hosen-*) turn-up. **u~en**† *v sep* ●*vt* turn up; turn over (*Seite*); (*fällen*) chop down ●*vi* (*sein*) topple over; (*Wetter:*) change; (*Wind:*) veer
umschließen† *vt insep* enclose
umschreib|en *vt insep* define; (*anders ausdrücken*) paraphrase
umschulen *vt sep* retrain; (*Sch*) transfer to another school
Umschwung *m* (*fig*) change; (*Pol*) U-turn
umsehen† **(sich)** *vr sep* look round; (*zurück*) look back; **sich u~ nach** look for
umsein* *vi sep* (*sein*) **um sein**, *s.* **um**
umseitig *adj & adv* overleaf
umsetzen *vt sep* move; (*umpflanzen*) transplant; (*Comm*) sell
umsied|eln *v sep* ●*vt* resettle ●*vi* (*sein*) move. **U~lung** *f* resettlement
umso *conj* **~ besser/mehr** all the better/more; **je mehr, ~ besser** the more the better
umsonst *adv* in vain; (*grundlos*) without reason; (*gratis*) free
Umstand *m* circumstance; (*Tatsache*) fact; (*Aufwand*) fuss; (*Mühe*) trouble; **unter U~en** possibly; **jdm U~e machen** put s.o. to trouble; **in**

andern U~en pregnant
umständlich *adj* laborious; (*kompliziert*) involved
Umstands|kleid *nt* maternity dress. **U~wort** *nt* (*pl* **-wörter**) adverb
Umstehende *pl* bystanders
umsteigen† *vi sep* (*sein*) change
umstellen[1] *vt insep* surround
umstell|en[2] *vt sep* rearrange; transpose (*Wörter*); (*anders einstellen*) reset; (*Techn*) convert; (*ändern*) change; **sich u~en** adjust. **U~ung** *f* rearrangement; transposition; resetting; conversion; change; adjustment
umstritten *adj* controversial; (*ungeklärt*) disputed
umstülpen *vt sep* turn upside down; (*von innen nach außen*) turn inside out
Um|sturz *m* coup. **u~stürzen** *v sep* ● *vt* overturn; (*Pol*) overthrow ● *vi* (*sein*) fall over
umtaufen *vt sep* rename
Umtausch *m* exchange. **u~en** *vt sep* change; exchange (**gegen** for)
umwechseln *vt sep* change
Umweg *m* detour; **auf U~en** (*fig*) in a roundabout way
Umwelt *f* environment. **u~freundlich** *adj* environmentally friendly. **U~schutz** *m* protection of the environment
umwerfen† *vt sep* knock over; (*fig*) upset (*Plan*)
umziehen† *v sep* ● *vi* (*sein*) move ● *vt* change; **sich u~** change
umzingeln *vt insep* surround
Umzug *m* move; (*Prozession*) procession
unabänderlich *adj* irrevocable; (*Tatsache*) unalterable
unabhängig *adj* independent; **u~ davon, ob** irrespective of whether. **U~keit** *f* - independence
unablässig *adj* incessant
unabsehbar *adj* incalculable
unabsichtlich *adj* unintentional
unachtsam *adj* careless
unangebracht *adj* inappropriate
unangenehm *adj* unpleasant; (*peinlich*) embarrassing
Unannehmlichkeiten *fpl* trouble *sg*
unansehnlich *adj* shabby
unanständig *adj* indecent
unappetitlich *adj* unappetizing
Unart *f* -,-en bad habit. **u~ig** *adj* naughty
unauffällig *adj* inconspicuous; unobtrusive
unaufgefordert *adv* without being asked
unauf|haltsam *adj* inexorable. **u~hörlich** *adj* incessant
unaufmerksam *adj* inattentive
unaufrichtig *adj* insincere
unausbleiblich *adj* inevitable
unausstehlich *adj* insufferable
unbarmherzig *adj* merciless
unbeabsichtigt *adj* unintentional
unbedenklich *adj* harmless ● *adv* without hesitation
unbedeutend *adj* insignificant; (*geringfügig*) slight
unbedingt *adj* absolute; **nicht u~** not necessarily
unbefriedig|end *adj* unsatisfactory. **u~t** *adj* dissatisfied
unbefugt *adj* unauthorized ● *adv* without authorization
unbegreiflich *adj* incomprehensible
unbegrenzt *adj* unlimited ● *adv* indefinitely

u

unbegründet *adj* unfounded
Unbehagen *nt* unease; (*körperlich*) discomfort
unbekannt *adj* unknown; (*nicht vertraut*) unfamiliar. **U~e(r)** *m/f* stranger
unbekümmert *adj* unconcerned; (*unbeschwert*) carefree
unbeliebt *adj* unpopular. **U~heit** *f* unpopularity
unbemannt *adj* unmanned
unbemerkt *adj & adv* unnoticed
unbenutzt *adj* unused
unbequem *adj* uncomfortable; (*lästig*) awkward
unberechenbar *adj* unpredictable
unberechtigt *adj* unjustified; (*unbefugt*) unauthorized
unberührt *adj* untouched; (*fig*) virgin; (*Landschaft*) unspoilt
unbescheiden *adj* presumptuous
unbeschrankt *adj* unguarded
unbeschränkt *adj* unlimited ● *adv* without limit
unbeschwert *adj* carefree
unbesiegt *adj* undefeated
unbespielt *adj* blank
unbeständig *adj* inconsistent; (*Wetter*) unsettled
unbestechlich *adj* incorruptible
unbestimmt *adj* indefinite: (*Alter*) indeterminate; (*ungewiss*) uncertain; (*unklar*) vague
unbestritten *adj* undisputed ● *adv* indisputably
unbeteiligt *adj* indifferent; **u~ an** (+ *dat*) not involved in
unbetont *adj* unstressed
unbewacht *adj* unguarded
unbewaffnet *adj* unarmed
unbeweglich *adj & adv* motionless, still
unbewohnt *adj* uninhabited
unbewusst *adj* unconscious
unbezahlbar *adj* priceless
unbrauchbar *adj* useless
und *conj* and; **und so weiter** and so on; **nach und nach** bit by bit
Undank *m* ingratitude. **u~bar** *adj* ungrateful; (*nicht lohnend*) thankless. **U~barkeit** *f* ingratitude
undeutlich *adj* indistinct; vague
undicht *adj* leaking; **u~e Stelle** leak
Unding *nt* absurdity
undiplomatisch *adj* undiplomatic
unduldsam *adj* intolerant
undurch|dringlich *adj* impenetrable; (*Miene*) inscrutable. **u~führbar** *adj* impracticable
undurch|lässig *adj* impermeable. **u~sichtig** *adj* opaque; (*fig*) doubtful
uneben *adj* uneven. **U~heit** *f* **-,-en** unevenness; (*Buckel*) bump
unecht *adj* false; **u~er Schmuck** imitation jewellery
unehelich *adj* illegitimate
uneinig *adj* (*fig*) divided; [**sich** (*dat*)] **u~ sein** disagree
uneins *adj* **~ sein** be at odds
unempfindlich *adj* insensitive (**gegen** to); (*widerstandsfähig*) tough; (*Med*) immune
unendlich *adj* infinite; (*endlos*) endless. **U~keit** *f* **-** infinity
unentbehrlich *adj* indispensable
unentgeltlich *adj* free, (*Arbeit*) unpaid ● *adv* free of charge
unentschieden *adj* undecided; (*Sport*) drawn; **u~ spielen** draw. **U~** *nt* **-s,-** draw
unentschlossen *adj* indecisive; (*unentschieden*) undecided
unentwegt *adj* persistent; (*unauf-*

hörlich) incessant
unerfahren *adj* inexperienced. **U~heit** *f* - inexperience
unerfreulich *adj* unpleasant
unerhört *adj* enormous; (*empörend*) outrageous
unerklärlich *adj* inexplicable
unerlässlich *adj* essential
unerlaubt *adj* unauthorized ●*adv* without permission
unerschwinglich *adj* prohibitive
unersetzlich *adj* irreplaceable; (*Verlust*) irreparable
unerträglich *adj* unbearable
unerwartet *adj* unexpected
unerwünscht *adj* unwanted; (*Besuch*) unwelcome
unfähig *adj* incompetent; **u~, etw zu tun** incapable of doing sth; (*nicht in der Lage*) unable to do sth. **U~keit** *f* incompetence; inability (**zu** to)
unfair *adj* unfair
Unfall *m* accident. **U~flucht** *f* failure to stop after an accident. **U~station** *f* casualty department
unfassbar *adj* incomprehensible
Unfehlbarkeit *f* - infallibility
unfolgsam *adj* disobedient
unförmig *adj* shapeless
unfreiwillig *adj* involuntary; (*unbeabsichtigt*) unintentional
unfreundlich *adj* unfriendly; (*unangenehm*) unpleasant. **U~keit** *f* unfriendliness; unpleasantness
Unfriede[n] *m* discord
unfruchtbar *adj* infertile; (*fig*) unproductive. **U~keit** *f* infertility
Unfug *m* **-s** mischief; (*Unsinn*) nonsense
Ungar|(in) *m* **-n,-n** (*f* **-,-nen**) Hungarian. **u~isch** *adj* Hungarian. **U~n** *nt* **-s** Hungary
ungeachtet *prep* (+ *gen*) in spite of; **dessen u~** notwithstanding [this]. **ungebraucht** *adj* unused. **ungedeckt** *adj* uncovered; (*Sport*) unmarked; (*Tisch*) unlaid
Ungeduld *f* impatience. **u~ig** *adj* impatient
ungeeignet *adj* unsuitable
ungefähr *adj* approximate, rough
ungefährlich *adj* harmless
ungeheuer *adj* enormous. **U~** *nt* **-s,-** monster
ungehorsam *adj* disobedient. **U~** *m* disobedience
ungeklärt *adj* unsolved; (*Frage*) unsettled; (*Ursache*) unknown
ungelegen *adj* inconvenient
ungelernt *adj* unskilled
ungemütlich *adj* uncomfortable; (*unangenehm*) unpleasant
ungenau *adj* inaccurate; vague. **U~igkeit** *f* **-,-en** inaccuracy
ungeniert /ˈʊnʒeniːɐ̯t/ *adj* uninhibited ●*adv* openly
ungenießbar *adj* inedible; (*Getränk*) undrinkable. **ungenügend** *adj* inadequate; (*Sch*) unsatisfactory. **ungepflegt** *adj* neglected; (*Person*) unkempt. **ungerade** *adj* (*Zahl*) odd
ungerecht *adj* unjust. **U~igkeit** *f* **-,-en** injustice
ungern *adv* reluctantly
ungesalzen *adj* unsalted
Ungeschick|lichkeit *f* clumsiness. **u~t** *adj* clumsy
ungeschminkt *adj* without make-up; (*Wahrheit*) unvarnished. **ungesetzlich** *adj* illegal. **ungestört** *adj* undisturbed. **ungesund** *adj* unhealthy. **ungesüßt** *adj* unsweetened. **ungetrübt** *adj* perfect
Ungetüm *nt* **-s,-e** monster
ungewiss *adj* uncertain; **im Ungewissen sein/lassen** be/leave in

the dark. **U~heit** *f* uncertainty

ungewöhnlich *adj* unusual. **ungewohnt** *adj* unaccustomed; (*nicht vertraut*) unfamiliar

Ungeziefer *nt* **-s** vermin

ungezogen *adj* naughty

ungezwungen *adj* informal; (*natürlich*) natural

ungläubig *adj* incredulous

unglaublich *adj* incredible, unbelievable

ungleich *adj* unequal; (*verschieden*) different. **U~heit** *f* **-** inequality. **u~mäßig** *adj* uneven

Unglück *nt* **-s,-e** misfortune; (*Pech*) bad luck; (*Missgeschick*) mishap; (*Unfall*) accident. **u~lich** *adj* unhappy; (*ungünstig*) unfortunate. **u~licherweise** *adv* unfortunately

ungültig *adj* invalid; (*Jur*) void

ungünstig *adj* unfavourable; (*unpassend*) inconvenient

Unheil *nt* **-s** disaster; **U~ anrichten** cause havoc

unheilbar *adj* incurable

unheimlich *adj* eerie; (*gruselig*) creepy; (!: *groß*) terrific ● *adv* eerily; (!: *sehr*) terribly

unhöflich *adj* rude. **U~keit** *f* rudeness

unhygienisch *adj* unhygienic

Uni *f* **-,-s** ! university

uni /y'ni:/ *inv adj* plain

Uniform *f* **-,-en** uniform

uninteressant *adj* uninteresting

Union *f* **-,-en** union

universell *adj* universal

Universität *f* **-,-en** university

Universum *nt* **-s** universe

unkenntlich *adj* unrecognizable

unklar *adj* unclear; (*ungewiss*) uncertain; (*vage*) vague; **im U~en (u~en) sein** be in the dark

unkompliziert *adj* uncomplicated

Unkosten *pl* expenses

Unkraut *nt* weed; (*coll*) weeds *pl*; **U~ jäten** weed. **U~vertilgungsmittel** *nt* weed-killer

unlängst *adv* recently

unlauter *adj* dishonest; (*unfair*) unfair

unleserlich *adj* illegible

unleugbar *adj* undeniable

unlogisch *adj* illogical

Unmenge *f* enormous amount/(*Anzahl*) number

Unmensch *m* ! brute. **u~lich** *adj* inhuman

unmerklich *adj* imperceptible

unmittelbar *adj* immediate; (*direkt*) direct

unmöbliert *adj* unfurnished

unmodern *adj* old-fashioned

unmöglich *adj* impossible. **U~keit** *f* **-** impossibility

Unmoral *f* immorality. **u~isch** *adj* immoral

unmündig *adj* under-age

Unmut *m* displeasure

unnatürlich *adj* unnatural

unnormal *adj* abnormal

unnötig *adj* unnecessary

unord|entlich *adj* untidy; (*nachlässig*) sloppy. **U~nung** *f* disorder; (*Durcheinander*) muddle

unorthodox *adj* unorthodox ● *adv* in an unorthodox manner

unparteiisch *adj* impartial

unpassend *adj* inappropriate; (*Moment*) inopportune

unpersönlich *adj* impersonal

unpraktisch *adj* impractical

unpünktlich *adj* unpunctual ● *adv* late

unrealistisch *adj* unrealistic

unrecht *adj* wrong ● *n* **jdm u~**

tun do s.o. an injustice. **U~** *nt* wrong; **zu U~** wrongly; **U~ haben** be wrong; **jdm U~ geben** disagree with s.o. **u~mäßig** *adj* unlawful

unregelmäßig *adj* irregular

unreif *adj* unripe; (*fig*) immature

unrein *adj* impure; (*Luft*) polluted; (*Haut*) bad; **ins U~e schreiben** make a rough draft of

unrentabel *adj* unprofitable

Unruh|e *f* **-,-n** restlessness; (*Erregung*) agitation; (*Besorgnis*) anxiety; **U~en** (*Pol*) unrest *sg*. **u~ig** *adj* restless; (*laut*) noisy; (*besorgt*) anxious

uns *pron* (*acc/dat of* **wir**) us; (*reflexive*) ourselves; (*einander*) each other

unsauber *adj* dirty; (*nachlässig*) sloppy

unschädlich *adj* harmless

unscharf *adj* blurred

unschätzbar *adj* inestimable

unscheinbar *adj* inconspicuous

unschlagbar *adj* unbeatable

unschlüssig *adj* undecided

Unschuld *f* - innocence; (*Jungfräulichkeit*) virginity. **u~ig** *adj* innocent

unselbstständig, **unselbständig** *adj* dependent ●*adv* **u~ denken** not think for oneself

unser *poss pron* our. **u~e(r,s)** *poss pron* ours. **u~erseits** *adv* for our part. **u~twegen** *adv* for our sake; (*wegen uns*) because of us, on our account

unsicher *adj* unsafe; (*ungewiss*) uncertain; (*nicht zuverlässig*) unreliable; (*Schritte, Hand*) unsteady; (*Person*) insecure ●*adv* unsteadily. **U~heit** *f* uncertainty; unreliability; insecurity

unsichtbar *adj* invisible

Unsinn *m* nonsense. **u~ig** *adj* nonsensical, absurd

Unsitt|e *f* bad habit. **u~lich** *adj* indecent

unsportlich *adj* not sporty; (*unfair*) unsporting

uns|re(r,s) *poss pron* = **unsere(r,s)**. **u~rige** *poss pron* **der/die/das u~rige** ours

unsterblich *adj* immortal. **U~keit** *f* immortality

Unsumme *f* vast sum

unsympathisch *adj* unpleasant; **er ist mir u~** I don't like him

untätig *adj* idle

untauglich *adj* unsuitable; (*Mil*) unfit

unten *adv* at the bottom; (*auf der Unterseite*) underneath; (*eine Treppe tiefer*) downstairs; (*im Text*) below; **hier/da u~** down here/there; **nach u~** down[wards]; (*die Treppe hinunter*) downstairs; **siehe u~** see below

unter *prep* (+ *dat/acc*) under; (*niedriger als*) below; (*inmitten, zwischen*) among; **u~ anderem** among other things; **u~ der Woche** during the week; **u~ sich** by themselves

Unter|arm *m* forearm. **U~bewusstsein** *nt* subconscious

unterbieten† *vt insep* undercut; beat (*Rekord*)

unterbinden† *vt insep* stop

unterbrech|en† *vt insep* interrupt; break (*Reise*). **U~ung** *f* **-,-en** interruption, break

unterbringen† *vt sep* put; (*beherbergen*) put up

unterdessen *adv* in the meantime

Unterdrückung *f* - suppression; oppression

untere(r,s) *adj* lower

untereinander *adv* one below the other; (*miteinander*) among ourselves/yourselves/themselves

unterernähr|t *adj* undernourished. **U~ung** *f* malnutrition

Unterführung *f* underpass; (*Fußgänger-*) subway

Untergang *m* (*der Sonne*) setting; (*Naut*) sinking; (*Zugrundegehen*) disappearance; (*der Welt*) end

Untergebene(r) *m/f* subordinate

untergehen† *vi sep* (*sein*) (*Astronomy*) set; (*versinken*) go under; (*Schiff:*) go down, sink; (*zugrunde gehen*) disappear; (*Welt:*) come to an end

Untergeschoss *nt* basement

Untergrund *m* foundation; (*Hintergrund*) background. **U~bahn** *f* underground [railway]

unterhaken *vt sep* **jdn u~** take s.o.'s arm; **untergehakt** arm in arm

unterhalb *adv & prep* (+ *gen*) below

Unterhalt *m* maintenance

unterhalt|en† *vt insep* maintain; (*ernähren*) support; (*betreiben*) run; (*erheitern*) entertain; **sich u~en** talk; (*sich vergnügen*) enjoy oneself. **U~ung** *f* -,-en maintenance; (*Gespräch*) conversation; (*Zeitvertreib*) entertainment

Unter|haus *nt* (*Pol*) lower house; (*in UK*) House of Commons. **U~hemd** *nt* vest. **U~hose** *f* underpants *pl*. **u~irdisch** *adj & adv* underground

Unterkiefer *m* lower jaw

unterkommen† *vi sep* (*sein*) find accommodation; (*eine Stellung finden*) get a job

Unterkunft *f* -,-künfte accommodation

Unterlage *f* pad; **U~n** papers

Unterlass *m* **ohne U~** incessantly

Unterlassung *f* -,-en omission

unterlegen *adj* inferior; (*Sport*) losing; **zahlenmäßig u~** outnumbered (*dat* by). **U~e(r)** *m/f* loser

Unterleib *m* abdomen

unterliegen† *vi insep* (*sein*) lose (*dat* to); (*unterworfen sein*) be subject (*dat* to)

Unterlippe *f* lower lip

Untermiete *f* **zur U~ wohnen** be a lodger. **U~r(in)** *m*(*f*) lodger

unternehm|en† *vt insep* undertake; take (*Schritte*); **etw/nichts u~en** do sth/nothing. **U~en** *nt* **-s,-** undertaking, enterprise (*Betrieb*) concern. **U~er** *m* **-s,-** employer; (*Bau-*) contractor; (*Industrieller*) industrialist. **u~ungslustig** *adj* enterprising

Unteroffizier *m* non-commissioned officer

unterordnen *vt sep* subordinate

Unterredung *f* -,-en talk

Unterricht *m* **-[e]s** teaching; (*Privat-*) tuition; (*U~sstunden*) lessons *pl*

unterrichten *vt/i insep* (*haben*) teach; (*informieren*) inform; **sich u~** inform oneself

Unterrock *m* slip

untersagen *vt insep* forbid

Untersatz *m* mat; (*mit Füßen*) stand; (*Gläser-*) coaster

unterscheid|en† *vt/i insep* (*haben*) distinguish; (*auseinander halten*) tell apart; **sich u~en** differ. **U~ung** *f* -,-en distinction

Unterschied *m* **-[e]s,-e** difference; (*Unterscheidung*) distinction; **im U~ zu ihm** unlike him. **u~lich** *adj* different; (*wechselnd*) varying

unterschlag|en† *vt insep* embezzle; (*verheimlichen*) suppress. **U~ung** *f* -,-en embezzlement;

suppression
Unterschlupf *m* -[e]s shelter; (*Versteck*) hiding-place
unterschreiben† *vt/i insep* (*haben*) sign
Unter|schrift *f* signature; (*Bild-*) caption. **U~seeboot** *nt* submarine
Unterstand *m* shelter
unterste(r,s) *adj* lowest, bottom
unterstehen† *v insep* ● *vi* (*haben*) be answerable (*dat* to); (*unterliegen*) be subject (*dat* to)
unterstellen[1] *vt sep* put underneath; (*abstellen*) store; **sich u~** shelter
unterstellen[2] *vt insep* place under the control (*dat* of); (*annehmen*) assume; (*fälschlich zuschreiben*) impute (*dat* to)
unterstreichen† *vt insep* underline
unterstütz|en *vt insep* support; (*helfen*) aid. **U~ung** *f* -,-en support; (*finanziell*) aid; (*regelmäßiger Betrag*) allowance; (*Arbeitslosen-*) benefit
untersuch|en *vt insep* examine; (*Jur*) investigate; (*prüfen*) test; (*überprüfen*) check; (*durchsuchen*) search. **U~ung** *f* -,-en examination; investigation; test; check; search. **U~ungshaft** *f* detention on remand
Untertan *m* -s & -en,-en subject
Untertasse *f* saucer
Unterteil *nt* bottom (part)
Untertitel *m* subtitle
untervermieten *vt/i insep* (*haben*) sublet
Unterwäsche *f* underwear
unterwegs *adv* on the way; (*außer Haus*) out; (*verreist*) away
Unterwelt *f* underworld
unterzeichnen *vt insep* sign
unterziehen† *vt insep* **etw einer Untersuchung/Überprüfung u~** examine/ check sth; **sich einer Operation/Prüfung u~** have an operation/take a test
Untier *nt* monster
untragbar *adj* intolerable
untrennbar *adj* inseparable
untreu *adj* disloyal; (*in der Ehe*) unfaithful. **U~e** *f* disloyalty; infidelity
untröstlich *adj* inconsolable
unübersehbar *adj* obvious; (*groß*) immense
ununterbrochen *adj* incessant
unveränderlich *adj* invariable; (*gleichbleibend*) unchanging
unverändert *adj* unchanged
unverantwortlich *adj* irresponsible
unverbesserlich *adj* incorrigible
unverbindlich *adj* non-committal; (*Comm*) not binding ● *adv* without obligation
unverdaulich *adj* indigestible
unver|gesslich *adj* unforgettable. **u~gleichlich** *adj* incomparable. **u~heiratet** *adj* unmarried. **u~käuflich** *adj* not for sale; (*Muster*) free
unverkennbar *adj* unmistakable
unverletzt *adj* unhurt
unvermeidlich *adj* inevitable
unver|mindert *adj & adv* undiminished. **u~mutet** *adj* unexpected
Unver|nunft *f* folly. **u~nünftig** *adj* foolish
unverschämt *adj* insolent; (*[F]: ungeheuer*) outrageous. **U~heit** *f* -,-en insolence
unver|sehens *adv* suddenly. **u~sehrt** *adj* unhurt; (*unbeschädigt*) intact
unverständlich *adj* incomprehensible; (*undeutlich*) indistinct

unverträglich *adj* incompatible; (*Person*) quarrelsome; (*unbekömmlich*) indigestible

unver|wundbar *adj* invulnerable. **u~wüstlich** *adj* indestructible; (*Person, Humor*) irrepressible; (*Gesundheit*) robust. **u~zeihlich** *adj* unforgivable

unverzüglich *adj* immediate

unvollendet *adj* unfinished

unvollkommen *adj* imperfect; (*unvollständig*) incomplete

unvollständig *adj* incomplete

unvor|bereitet *adj* unprepared. **u~hergesehen** *adj* unforeseen

unvorsichtig *adj* careless

unvorstellbar *adj* unimaginable

unvorteilhaft *adj* unfavourable; (*nicht hübsch*) unattractive

unwahr *adj* untrue. **U~heit** *f* **-,-en** untruth. **u~scheinlich** *adj* unlikely; (*unglaublich*) improbable; ([!]: *groß*) incredible

unweit *adv & prep* (+ *gen*) not far

unwesentlich *adj* unimportant

Unwetter *nt* **-s,-** storm

unwichtig *adj* unimportant

unwider|legbar *adj* irrefutable. **u~stehlich** *adj* irresistible

Unwill|e *m* displeasure. **u~ig** *adj* angry; (*widerwillig*) reluctant

unwirklich *adj* unreal

unwirksam *adj* ineffective

unwirtschaftlich *adj* uneconomic

unwissen|d *adj* ignorant. **U~heit** *f* **-** ignorance

unwohl *adj* unwell; (*unbehaglich*) uneasy

unwürdig *adj* unworthy (*gen* of)

Unzahl *f* vast number. **unzählig** *adj* innumerable, countless

unzerbrechlich *adj* unbreakable

unzerstörbar *adj* indestructible

unzertrennlich *adj* inseparable

Unzucht *f* sexual offence; **gewerbsmäßige U~** prostitution

unzüchtig *adj* indecent; (*Schriften*) obscene

unzufrieden *adj* dissatisfied; (*innerlich*) discontented. **U~heit** *f* dissatisfaction

unzulässig *adj* inadmissible

unzurechnungsfähig *adj* insane. **U~keit** *f* insanity

unzusammenhängend *adj* incoherent

unzutreffend *adj* inapplicable; (*falsch*) incorrect

unzuverlässig *adj* unreliable

unzweifelhaft *adj* undoubted

üppig *adj* luxuriant; (*überreichlich*) lavish

uralt *adj* ancient

Uran *nt* **-s** uranium

Uraufführung *f* first performance

Urenkel *m* great-grandson; (*pl*) great-grandchildren

Urgroß|mutter *f* great-grandmother. **U~vater** *m* great-grandfather

Urheber *m* **-s,-** originator; (*Verfasser*) author. **U~recht** *nt* copyright

Urin *m* **-s,-e** urine

Urkunde *f* **-,-n** certificate; (*Dokument*) document

Urlaub *m* **-s** holiday; (*Mil, Admin*) leave; **auf U~** on holiday/leave; **U~ haben** be on holiday/leave. **U~er(in)** *m* **-s,-** (*f* **-,-nen**) holidaymaker. **U~sort** *m* holiday resort

Urne *f* **-,-n** urn; (*Wahl-*) ballot-box

Ursache *f* cause; (*Grund*) reason; **keine U~!** don't mention it!

Ursprung *m* origin

ursprünglich *adj* original; (*anfänglich*) initial; (*natürlich*) natural

Urteil *nt* **-s,-e** judgement; (*Meinung*) opinion; (*U~sspruch*) verdict; (*Strafe*) sentence. **u~en** *vi* (*haben*) judge

Urwald *m* primeval forest; (*tropischer*) jungle

Urzeit *f* primeval times *pl*

USA *pl* USA *sg*

usw. *abbr* (**und so weiter**) etc.

utopisch *adj* Utopian

Vv

Vakuum /ˈva:kuʊm/ *nt* **-s** vacuum. **v~verpackt** *adj* vacuum-packed

Vanille /vaˈnɪljə/ *f* **-** vanilla

variieren *vt/i* (*haben*) vary

Vase /ˈva:zə/ *f* **-,-n** vase

Vater *m* **-s,⸚** father. **V~land** *nt* fatherland

väterlich *adj* paternal; (*fürsorglich*) fatherly. **v~erseits** *adv* on one's/the father's side

Vater|schaft *f* **-** fatherhood; (*Jur*) paternity. **V~unser** *nt* **-s,-** Lord's Prayer

v. Chr. *abbr* (**vor Christus**) BC

Vegetar|ier(in) /vegeˈta:riɐ, -iərɪn/ *m*(*f*) **-s,-** (*f* **-,-nen**) vegetarian. **v~isch** *adj* vegetarian

Veilchen *nt* **-s,-n** violet

Vene /ˈve:nə/ *f* **-,-n** vein

Venedig /veˈne:dɪç/ *nt* **-s** Venice

Ventil /vɛnˈti:l/ *nt* **-s,-e** valve. **V~ator** *m* **-s,-en** fan

verabred|en *vt* arrange; **sich [mit jdm] v~en** arrange to meet [s.o.]. **V~ung** *f* **-,-en** arrangement; (*Treffen*) appointment

verabschieden *vt* say goodbye to; (*aus dem Dienst*) retire; pass (*Gesetz*); **sich v~** say goodbye

verachten *vt* despise

Verachtung *f* **-** contempt

verallgemeinern *vt/i* (*haben*) generalize

veränder|lich *adj* changeable; (*Math*) variable. **v~n** *vt* change; **sich v~n** change; (*beruflich*) change one's job. **V~ung** *f* change

verängstigt *adj* frightened, scared

verankern *vt* anchor

veranlag|t *adj* **künstlerisch/musikalisch v~t sein** have an artistic/a musical bent; **praktisch v~t** practically minded. **V~ung** *f* **-,-en** disposition; (*Neigung*) tendency; (*künstlerisch*) bent

veranlassen *vt* (*reg*) arrange for; (*einleiten*) institute; **jdn v~** prompt s.o. (**zu** to)

veranschlagen *vt* (*reg*) estimate

veranstalt|en *vt* organize; hold, give (*Party*); make (*Lärm*). **V~er** *m* **-s,-** organizer. **V~ung** *f* **-,-en** event

verantwort|lich *adj* responsible; **v~lich machen** hold responsible. **V~ung** *f* **-** responsibility. **v~ungsbewusst** *adj* responsible. **v~ungslos** *adj* irresponsible. **v~ungsvoll** *adj* responsible

verarbeiten *vt* use; (*Techn*) process; (*verdauen & fig*) digest

verärgern *vt* annoy

verausgaben (sich) *vr* spend all one's money (*or*) strength

veräußern *vt* sell

Verb /vɛrp/ *nt* **-s,-en** verb

Verband *m* **-[e]s,⸚e** association; (*Mil*) unit; (*Med*) bandage; (*Wund-*) dressing. **V~szeug** *nt* first-aid kit

verbann|en *vt* exile; (*fig*) banish. **V~ung** *f* **-** exile

verbergen† *vt* hide; **sich v~** hide

verbesser|n *vt* improve; (*berichtigen*) correct. **V~ung** *f* **-,-en** improvement; correction

verbeug|en (sich) *vr* bow. **V~ung** *f* bow

verbeulen *vt* dent

verbiegen† *vt* bend

verbieten† *vt* forbid; (*Admin*) prohibit, ban

verbillig|en *vt* reduce [in price]. **v~t** *adj* reduced

verbinden† *vt* connect (**mit** to); (*zusammenfügen*) join; (*verknüpfen*) combine; (*in Verbindung bringen*) associate; (*Med*) bandage; dress (*Wunde*); **jdm verbunden sein** (*fig*) be obliged to s.o.

verbindlich *adj* friendly; (*bindend*) binding

Verbindung *f* connection; (*Verknüpfung*) combination; (*Kontakt*) contact; (*Vereinigung*) association; **chemiche V~** chemical compound; **in V~ stehen/sich in V~ setzen** be/get in touch

verbissen *adj* grim

verbitter|n *vt* make bitter. **v~t** *adj* bitter. **V~ung** *f* **-** bitterness

verblassen *vi* (*sein*) fade

Verbleib *m* **-s** whereabouts *pl*

verbleit *adj* (*Benzin*) leaded

verblüff|en *vt* amaze, astound. **V~ung** *f* **-** amazement

verblühen *vi* (*sein*) wither, fade

verbluten *vi* (*sein*) bleed to death

verborgen *vt* lend

Verbot *nt* **-[e]s,-e** ban. **v~en** *adj* forbidden; (*Admin*) prohibited

Verbrauch *m* **-[e]s** consumption. **v~en** *vt* use; consume (*Lebensmittel*); (*erschöpfen*) use up. **V~er** *m* **-s,-** consumer

Verbrechen† *nt* **-s,-** crime

Verbrecher *m* **-s,-** criminal

verbreit|en *vt* spread. **v~et** *adj* widespread. **V~ung** *f* **-** spread; (*Verbreiten*) spreading

verbrenn|en† *vt/i* (*sein*) burn; cremate (*Leiche*). **V~ung** *f* **-,-en** burning; cremation; (*Wunde*) burn

verbringen† *vt* spend

verbrühen *vt* scald

verbuchen *vt* enter

verbünd|en (sich) *vr* form an alliance. **V~ete(r)** *m/f* ally

verbürgen *vt* guarantee; **sich v~ für** vouch for

Verdacht *m* **-[e]s** suspicion; **in** *or* **im V~ haben** suspect

verdächtig *adj* suspicious. **v~en** *vt* suspect (*gen* of). **V~te(r)** *m/f* suspect

verdamm|en *vt* condemn; (*Relig*) damn. **v~t** *adj & adv* ⊠ damned; **v~t!** damn!

verdampfen *vt/i* (*sein*) evaporate

verdanken *vt* owe (*dat* to)

verdau|en *vt* digest. **v~lich** *adj* digestible. **V~ung** *f* **-** digestion

Verdeck *nt* **-[e]s,-e** hood; (*Oberdeck*) top deck

verderb|en† *vi* (*sein*) spoil; (*Lebensmittel:*) go bad ● *vt* spoil; **ich habe mir den Magen verdorben** I have an upset stomach. **V~en** *nt* **-s** ruin. **v~lich** *adj* perishable; (*schädlich*) pernicious

verdien|en *vt/i* (*haben*) earn; (*fig*) deserve. **V~er** *m* **-s,-** wage-earner

Verdienst[1] *m* **-[e]s** earnings *pl*

Verdienst[2] *nt* **-[e]s,-e** merit

verdient *adj* well-deserved

verdoppeln *vt* double

verdorben *adj* spoilt, ruined; (*Magen*) upset; (*moralisch*) corrupt; (*verkommen*) depraved

verdreh|en *vt* twist; roll (*Augen*);

(*fig*) distort. **v~t** *adj* [I] crazy

verdreifachen *vt* treble, triple

verdrücken *vt* crumple; ([I]: *essen*) polish off; **sich v~** [I] slip away

Verdruss *m* **-es** annoyance

verdünnen *vt* dilute; **sich v~** taper off

verdunst|en *vi* (*sein*) evaporate. **V~ung** *f* - evaporation

verdursten *vi* (*sein*) die of thirst

veredeln *vt* refine; (*Horticulture*) graft

verehr|en *vt* revere; (*Relig*) worship; (*bewundern*) admire; (*schenken*) give. **V~er(in)** *m* **-s,-** (*f* **-,-nen**) admirer. **V~ung** *f* - veneration; worship; admiration

vereidigen *vt* swear in

Verein *m* **-s,-e** society; (*Sport-*) club

vereinbar *adj* compatible. **v~en** *vt* arrange. **V~ung** *f* **-,-en** agreement

vereinfachen *vt* simplify

vereinheitlichen *vt* standardize

vereinig|en *vt* unite; merge (*Firmen*); **wieder v~en** reunite; reunify (*Land*); **sich v~en** unite; **V~te Staaten [von Amerika]** United States *sg* [of America]. **V~ung** *f* **-,-en** union; (*Organisation*) organization

vereinzelt *adj* isolated ●*adv* occasionally

vereist *adj* frozen; (*Straße*) icy

vereitert *adj* septic

verenden *vi* (*sein*) die

verengen *vt* restrict; **sich v~** narrow; (*Pupille:*) contract

vererb|en *vt* leave (*dat* to); (*Biology* & *fig*) pass on (*dat* to). **V~ung** *f* - heredity

verfahren† *vi* (*sein*) proceed; **v~ mit** deal with ●*vr* **sich v~** lose one's way ●*adj* muddled. **V~** *nt* **-s,-** procedure; (*Techn*) process; (*Jur*) proceedings *pl*

Verfall *m* decay; (*eines Gebäudes*) dilapidation; (*körperlich* & *fig*) decline; (*Ablauf*) expiry. **v~en**† *vi* (*sein*) decay; (*Person, Sitten:*) decline; (*ablaufen*) expire; **v~en in** (+ *acc*) lapse into; **v~en auf** (+ *acc*) hit on (*Idee*)

verfärben (sich) *vr* change colour; (*Stoff:*) discolour

verfass|en *vt* write; (*Jur*) draw up; (*entwerfen*) draft. **V~er** *m* **-s,-** author. **V~ung** *f* (*Pol*) constitution; (*Zustand*) state

verfaulen *vi* (*sein*) rot, decay

verfechten† *vt* advocate

verfehlen *vt* miss

verfeinde|n (sich) *vr* become enemies; **v~t sein** be enemies

verfeinern *vt* refine; (*verbessern*) improve

verfilmen *vt* film

verfluch|en *vt* curse. **v~t** *adj* & *adv* [I] damned; **v~t!** damn!

verfolg|en *vt* pursue; (*folgen*) follow; (*bedrängen*) pester; (*Pol*) persecute; **strafrechtlich v~en** prosecute. **V~er** *m* **-s,-** pursuer. **V~ung** *f* - pursuit; persecution

verfrüht *adj* premature

verfügbar *adj* available

verfüg|en *vt* order; (*Jur*) decree ●*vi* (*haben*) **v~en über** (+ *acc*) have at one's disposal. **V~ung** *f* **-,-en** order; (*Jur*) decree; **jdm zur V~ung stehen** be at s.o.'s disposal

verführ|en *vt* seduce; tempt. **V~ung** *f* seduction; temptation

vergangen *adj* past; (*letzte*) last. **V~heit** *f* - past; (*Gram*) past tense

vergänglich *adj* transitory

vergas|en *vt* gas. **V~er** *m* **-s,-**

carburettor

vergeb|en† *vt* award (**an** + *dat* to); (*weggeben*) give away; (*verzeihen*) forgive. **v~lich** *adj* futile, vain ● *adv* in vain. **V~ung** *f* - forgiveness

vergehen† *vi* (*sein*) pass; **sich v~** violate (**gegen etw** sth). **V~** *nt* -s,- offence

vergelt|en† *vt* repay. **V~ung** *f* - retaliation; (*Rache*) revenge

vergessen† *vt* forget; (*liegen lassen*) leave behind

vergesslich *adj* forgetful. **V~keit** *f* - forgetfulness

vergeuden *vt* waste, squander

vergewaltig|en *vt* rape. **V~ung** *f* -,-en rape

vergießen† *vt* spill; shed (*Tränen, Blut*)

vergift|en *vt* poison. **V~ung** *f* -,-en poisoning

Vergissmeinnicht *nt* -[e]s,-[e] forget-me-not

vergittert *adj* barred

verglasen *vt* glaze

Vergleich *m* -[e]s,-e comparison; (*Jur*) settlement. **v~bar** *adj* comparable. **v~en**† *vt* compare (**mit** with/to)

vergnüg|en (sich) *vr* enjoy oneself. **V~en** *nt* -s,- pleasure; (*Spaß*) fun; **viel V~en!** have a good time! **v~t** *adj* cheerful; (*zufrieden*) happy. **V~ungen** *fpl* entertainments

vergolden *vt* gild; (*plattieren*) gold-plate

vergraben† *vt* bury

vergriffen *adj* out of print

vergrößer|n *vt* enlarge; (*Linse:*) magnify; (*vermehren*) increase; (*erweitern*) extend; expand (*Geschäft*); **sich v~n** grow bigger; (*Firma:*) expand; (*zunehmen*) increase. **V~ung** *f* -,-en magnification; increase; expansion; (*Phot*) enlargement. **V~ungsglas** *nt* magnifying glass

vergüt|en *vt* pay for; **jdm etw v~en** reimburse s.o. for sth. **V~ung** *f* -,-en remuneration; (*Erstattung*) reimbursement

verhaft|en *vt* arrest. **V~ung** *f* -,-en arrest

verhalten† **(sich)** *vr* behave; (*handeln*) act; (*beschaffen sein*) be. **V~** *nt* -s behaviour, conduct

Verhältnis *nt* -ses,-se relationship; (*Liebes-*) affair; (*Math*) ratio; **V~se** circumstances; conditions. **v~mäßig** *adv* comparatively, relatively

verhand|eln *vt* discuss; (*Jur*) try ● *vi* (*haben*) negotiate. **V~lung** *f* (*Jur*) trial; **V~lungen** negotiations

Verhängnis *nt* -ses fate, doom

verhärten *vt/i* (*sein*) harden

verhasst *adj* hated

verhätscheln *vt* spoil

verhauen† *vt* [F] beat; make a mess of (*Prüfung*)

verheilen *vi* (*sein*) heal

verheimlichen *vt* keep secret

verheirat|en (sich) *vr* get married (**mit** to); **sich wieder v~en** remarry. **v~et** *adj* married

verhelfen† *vi* (*haben*) **jdm zu etw v~** help s.o. get sth

verherrlichen *vt* glorify

verhexen *vt* bewitch

verhindern *vt* prevent; **v~t sein** be unable to come

Verhör *nt* -s,-e interrogation; **ins V~ nehmen** interrogate. **v~en** *vt* interrogate; **sich v~en** mishear

verhungern *vi* (*sein*) starve

verhüt|en *vt* prevent. **V~ung** *f* - prevention. **V~ungsmittel** *nt* contraceptive

verirren (sich) *vr* get lost

verjagen *vt* chase away
verjüngen *vt* rejuvenate
verkalkt *adj* [!] senile
verkalkulieren (sich) *vr* miscalculate
Verkauf *m* sale; **zum V~** for sale. **v~en** *vt* sell; **zu v~en** for sale
Verkäufer(in) *m(f)* seller; (*im Geschäft*) shop assistant
Verkehr *m* **-s** traffic; (*Kontakt*) contact; (*Geschlechts-*) intercourse; **aus dem V~ ziehen** take out of circulation. **v~en** *vi* (*haben*) operate; (*Bus, Zug:*) run; (*Umgang haben*) associate, mix (**mit** with); (*Gast sein*) visit (**bei jdm** s.o.)
Verkehrs|ampel *f* traffic lights *pl*. **V~unfall** *m* road accident. **V~verein** *m* tourist office. **V~zeichen** *nt* traffic sign
verkehrt *adj* wrong; **v~ herum** *adv* the wrong way round; (*links*) inside out
verklagen *vt* sue (**auf** + *acc* for)
verkleid|en *vt* disguise; (*Techn*) line; **sich v~en** disguise oneself; (*für Kostümfest*) dress up. **V~ung** *f* **-,-en** disguise; (*Kostüm*) fancy dress; (*Techn*) lining
verkleiner|n *vt* reduce [in size]. **V~ung** *f* **-** reduction
verknittern *vt/i* (*sein*) crumple
verknüpfen *vt* knot together
verkommen† *vi* (*sein*) be neglected; (*sittlich*) go to the bad; (*verfallen*) decay; (*Haus:*) fall into disrepair; (*Gegend:*) become run-down; (*Lebensmittel:*) go bad ●*adj* neglected; (*sittlich*) depraved; (*Haus*) dilapidated; (*Gegend*) run-down
verkörpern *vt* embody, personify
verkraften *vt* cope with
verkrampft *adj* (*fig*) tense
verkriechen† **(sich)** *vr* hide
verkrümmt *adj* crooked, bent
verkrüppelt *adj* crippled; (*Glied*) deformed
verkühl|en (sich) *vr* catch a chill. **V~ung** *f* **-,-en** chill
verkümmern *vi* (*sein*) waste/(*Pflanze:*) wither away
verkünden *vt* announce; pronounce (*Urteil*)
verkürzen *vt* shorten; (*verringern*) reduce; (*abbrechen*) cut short; while away (*Zeit*)
Verlag *m* **-[e]s,-e** publishing firm
verlangen *vt* ask for; (*fordern*) demand; (*berechnen*) charge. **V~** *nt* **-s** desire; (*Bitte*) request
verlänger|n *vt* extend; lengthen (*Kleid*); (*zeitlich*) prolong; renew (*Pass, Vertrag*); (*Culin*) thin down. **V~ung** *f* **-,-en** extension; renewal. **V~ungsschnur** *f* extension cable
verlassen† *vt* leave; (*im Stich lassen*) desert; **sich v~ auf** (+ *acc*) rely or depend on ●*adj* deserted. **V~heit** *f* **-** desolation
verlässlich *adj* reliable
Verlauf *m* course; **im V~** (+ *gen*) in the course of. **v~en**† *vi* (*sein*) run; (*ablaufen*) go; **gut v~en** go [off] well ●*vr* **sich v~en** lose one's way
verlegen *vt* move; (*verschieben*) postpone; (*vor-*) bring forward; (*verlieren*) mislay; (*versperren*) block; (*legen*) lay (*Teppich, Rohre*); (*veröffentlichen*) publish; **sich v~ auf** (+ *acc*) take up (*Beruf*); resort to (*Bitten*) ●*adj* embarrassed. **V~heit** *f* **-** embarrassment
Verleger *m* **-s,-** publisher
verleihen† *vt* lend; (*gegen Gebühr*) hire out; (*überreichen*) award, confer; (*fig*) give
verlernen *vt* forget
verletz|en *vt* injure; (*kränken*)

hurt; (*verstoßen gegen*) infringe; violate (*Grenze*). **v∼end** *adj* hurtful, wounding. **V∼te(r)** *m/f* injured person; (*bei Unfall*) casualty. **V∼ung** *f* **-,-en** (*Verstoß*) infringement; violation

verleugnen *vt* deny; disown (*Freund*)

verleumd|en *vt* slander; (*schriftlich*) libel. **v∼erisch** *adj* slanderous; libellous. **V∼ung** *f* **-,-en** slander; (*schriftlich*) libel

verlieben (sich) *vr* fall in love (**in** + *acc* with); **verliebt sein** be in love (**in** + *acc* with)

verlier|en† *vt* lose; shed (*Laub*) ●*vi* (*haben*) lose (**an etw** *dat* sth). **V∼er** *m* **-s,-** loser

verlob|en (sich) *vr* get engaged (**mit** to); **v∼t sein** be engaged. **V∼te** *f* fiancée. **V∼te(r)** *m* fiancé. **V∼ung** *f* **-,-en** engagement

verlock|en *vt* tempt. **V∼ung** *f* **-,-en** temptation

verloren *adj* lost; **v∼ gehen** get lost

verlos|en *vt* raffle. **V∼ung** *f* **-,-en** raffle; (*Ziehung*) draw

Verlust *m* **-[e]s,-e** loss

vermachen *vt* leave, bequeath

Vermächtnis *nt* **-ses,-se** legacy

vermähl|en (sich) *vr* marry. **V∼ung** *f* **-,-en** marriage

vermehren *vt* increase; propagate (*Pflanzen*); **sich v∼** increase; (*sich fortpflanzen*) breed

vermeiden† *vt* avoid

Vermerk *m* **-[e]s,-e** note. **v∼en** note [down]

vermessen† *vt* measure; survey (*Gelände*) ●*adj* presumptuous

vermiet|en *vt* let, rent [out]; hire out (*Boot, Auto*); **zu v∼en** to let; (*Boot:*) for hire. **V∼er** *m* landlord. **V∼erin** *f* landlady

vermindern *vt* reduce

vermischen *vt* mix

vermissen *vt* miss

vermisst *adj* missing

vermitteln *vi* (*haben*) mediate ●*vt* arrange; (*beschaffen*) find; place (*Arbeitskräfte*)

Vermittl|er *m* **-s,-** agent; (*Schlichter*) mediator. **V∼ung** *f* **-,-en** arrangement; (*Agentur*) agency; (*Teleph*) exchange; (*Schlichtung*) mediation

Vermögen *nt* **-s,-** fortune. **v∼d** *adj* wealthy

vermut|en *vt* suspect; (*glauben*) presume. **v∼lich** *adj* probable ●*adv* presumably. **V∼ung** *f* **-,-en** supposition; (*Verdacht*) suspicion

vernachlässigen *vt* neglect

vernehm|en† *vt* hear; (*verhören*) question; (*Jur*) examine. **V∼ung** *f* **-,-en** questioning

verneigen (sich) *vr* bow

verneln|en *vt* answer in the negative; (*ablehnen*) reject. **v∼end** *adj* negative. **V∼ung** *f* **-,-en** negative answer

vernicht|en *vt* destroy; (*ausrotten*) exterminate. **V∼ung** *f* **-** destruction; extermination

Vernunft *f* **-** reason

vernünftig *adj* reasonable, sensible

veröffentlich|en *vt* publish. **V∼ung** *f* **-,-en** publication

verordn|en *vt* prescribe (*dat* for). **V∼ung** *f* **-,-en** prescription; (*Verfügung*) decree

verpachten *vt* lease [out]

verpack|en *vt* pack; (*einwickeln*) wrap. **V∼ung** *f* packaging; wrapping

verpassen *vt* miss; (🄵: *geben*) give

verpfänden *vt* pawn
verpflanzen *vt* transplant
verpfleg|en *vt* feed: **sich selbst v~en** cater for oneself. **V~ung** *f* - board; (*Essen*) food; **Unterkunft und V~ung** board and lodging
verpflicht|en *vt* oblige; (*einstellen*) engage; (*Sport*) sign; **sich v~en** undertake/(*versprechen*) promise (**zu** to); (*vertraglich*) sign a contract. **V~ung** *f* -,-**en** obligation, commitment
verprügeln *vt* beat up, thrash
Verputz *m* -**es** plaster. **v~en** *vt* plaster
Verrat *m* -[**e**]**s** betrayal, treachery. **v~en**† *vt* betray; give away (*Geheimnis*)
Verräter *m* -**s**,- traitor
verrech|nen *vt* settle; clear (*Scheck*); **sich v~nen** make a mistake; (*fig*) miscalculate. **V~nungsscheck** *m* crossed cheque
verreisen *vi* (*sein*) go away; **verreist sein** be away
verrenken *vt* dislocate
verrichten *vt* perform, do
verriegeln *vt* bolt
verringer|n *vt* reduce; **sich v~n** decrease. **V~ung** *f* - reduction; decrease
verrost|en *vi* (*sein*) rust. **v~et** *adj* rusty
verrückt *adj* crazy, mad. **V~e(r)** *m*/*f* lunatic, **V~heit** *f* -,-**en** madness; (*Torheit*) folly
verrühren *vt* mix
verrunzelt *adj* wrinkled
verrutschen *vt* (*sein*) slip
Vers /fɛrs/ *m* -**es**,-**e** verse
versag|en *vi* (*haben*) fail ● *vt* **sich etw v~en** deny oneself sth. **V~en** *nt* -**s**,- failure. **V~er** *m* -**s**,- failure
versalzen† *vt* put too much salt in/on; (*fig*) spoil
versamm|eln *vt* assemble. **V~lung** *f* assembly, meeting
Versand *m* -[**e**]**s** dispatch. **V~haus** *nt* mail-order firm
versäumen *vt* miss; lose (*Zeit*); (*unterlassen*) neglect; **[es] v~en, etw zu tun** fail to do sth
verschärfen *vt* intensify; tighten (*Kontrolle*); increase (*Tempo*); aggravate (*Lage*); **sich v~** intensify; increase; (*Lage:*) worsen
verschätzen (sich) *vr* **sich v~ in** (+ *dat*) misjudge
verschenken *vt* give away
verscheuchen *vt* shoo/(*jagen*) chase away
verschicken *vt* send; (*Comm*) dispatch
verschieb|en† *vt* move; (*aufschieben*) put off, postpone; **sich v~en** move, shift; (*verrutschen*) slip; (*zeitlich*) be postponed. **V~ung** *f* shift; postponement
verschieden *adj* different; **v~e** *pl* different; (*mehrere*) various; **V~es** some things; (*dieses und jenes*) various things; **das ist v~** it varies ● *adv* differently; **v~ groß** of different sizes. **v~artig** *adj* diverse
verschimmel|n *vi* (*sein*) go mouldy. **v~t** *adj* mouldy
verschlafen† *vi* (*haben*) oversleep ● *vt* sleep through (*Tag*); **sich v~** oversleep ● *adj* sleepy
verschlagen† *vt* lose (*Seite*); **jdm die Sprache/den Atem v~** leave s.o. speechless/take s.o.'s breath away ● *adj* sly
verschlechter|n *vt* make worse; **sich v~n** get worse, deteriorate. **V~ung** *f* -,-**en** deterioration
Verschleiß *m* -**es** wear and tear
verschleppen *vt* carry off; (*entführen*) abduct; spread (*Seuche*);

neglect (*Krankheit*); (*hinausziehen*) delay

verschleudern *vt* sell at a loss

verschließen† *vt* close; (*abschließen*) lock; (*einschließen*) lock up

verschlimmer|n *vt* make worse; aggravate (*Lage*); **sich v~n** get worse, deteriorate. **V~ung** *f* -,-en deterioration

verschlossen *adj* reserved. **V~heit** *f* - reserve

verschlucken *vt* swallow; **sich v~** choke (**an** + *dat* on)

Verschluss *m* **-es,⸚e** fastener, clasp; (*Koffer-*) catch; (*Flaschen-*) top; (*luftdicht*) seal; (*Phot*) shutter

verschlüsselt *adj* coded

verschmelzen† *vt/i* (*sein*) fuse

verschmerzen *vt* get over

verschmutz|en *vt* soil; pollute (*Luft*) ● *vi* (*sein*) get dirty. **V~ung** *f* - pollution

verschneit *adj* snow-covered

verschnörkelt *adj* ornate

verschnüren *vt* tie up

verschollen *adj* missing

verschonen *vt* spare

verschossen *adj* faded

verschränken *vt* cross

verschreiben† *vt* prescribe; **sich v~** make a slip of the pen

verschulden *vt* be to blame for. **V~** *nt* -s fault

verschuldet *adj* **v~ sein** be in debt

verschütten *vt* spill; (*begraben*) bury

verschweigen† *vt* conceal, hide

verschwend|en *vt* waste. **V~ung** *f* - extravagance; (*Vergeudung*) waste

verschwiegen *adj* discreet

verschwinden† *vi* (*sein*) disappear; **[mal] v~** Ⓘ spend a penny

verschwommen *adj* blurred

verschwör|en† **(sich)** *vr* conspire. **V~ung** *f* -,-en conspiracy

versehen† *vt* perform; hold (*Posten*); keep (*Haushalt*); **v~ mit** provide with; **sich v~** make a mistake. **V~** *nt* **-s,-** oversight; (*Fehler*) slip; **aus V~** by mistake. **v~tlich** *adv* by mistake

Versehrte(r) *m* disabled person

versengen *vt* singe; (*stärker*) scorch

versenken *vt* sink

versessen *adj* keen (**auf** + *acc* on)

versetz|en *vt* move; transfer (*Person*); (*Sch*) move up; (*verpfänden*) pawn; (*verkaufen*) sell; (*vermischen*) blend; **jdn v~en** (Ⓘ: *warten lassen*) stand s.o. up; **jdm in Angst/Erstaunen v~en** frighten/astonish s.o.; **sich in jds Lage v~en** put oneself in s.o.'s place. **V~ung** *f* -,-en move; transfer; (*Sch*) move to a higher class

verseuchen *vt* contaminate

versicher|n *vt* insure; (*bekräftigen*) affirm; **jdm v~n** assure s.o. (**dass** that). **V~ung** *f* -,-en insurance; assurance

versiegeln *vt* seal

versiert /vɛrˈʒiːɐ̯t/ *adj* experienced

versilbert *adj* silver-plated

Versmaß /ˈfɛrs-/ *nt* metre

versöhn|en *vt* reconcile; **sich v~en** become reconciled. **V~ung** *f* -,-en reconciliation

versorg|en *vt* provide, supply (**mit** with); provide for (*Familie*); (*betreuen*) look after. **V~ung** *f* - provision, supply; (*Betreuung*) care

verspät|en (sich) *vr* be late. **v~et** *adj* late; (*Zug*) delayed; (*Dank*) belated. **V~ung** *f* - lateness; **V~ung haben** be late

versperren *vt* block; bar (*Weg*)

verspiel|en *vt* gamble away. **v~t** *adj* playful
verspotten *vt* mock, ridicule
versprech|en† *vt* promise; **sich v~en** make a slip of the tongue; **sich** (*dat*) **viel v~en von** have high hopes of; **ein viel v~ender Anfang** a promising start. **V~en** *nt* **-s,-** promise. **V~ungen** *fpl* promises
verstaatlich|en *vt* nationalize. **V~ung** *f* **-** nationalization
Verstand *m* **-[e]s** mind; (*Vernunft*) reason; **den V~ verlieren** go out of one's mind
verständig *adj* sensible; (*klug*) intelligent. **v~en** *vt* notify, inform; **sich v~en** communicate; (*sich verständlich machen*) make oneself understood. **V~ung** *f* **-** notification; communication; (*Einigung*) agreement
verständlich *adj* comprehensible; (*deutlich*) clear; (*begreiflich*) understandable; **sich v~ machen** make oneself understood. **v~erweise** *adv* understandably
Verständnis *nt* **-ses** understanding
verstärk|en *vt* strengthen, reinforce; (*steigern*) intensify, increase; amplify (*Ton*). **V~er** *m* **-s,-** amplifier. **V~ung** *f* reinforcement; increase; amplification; (*Truppen*) reinforcements *pl*
verstaubt *adj* dusty
verstauchen *vt* sprain
Versteck *nt* **-[e]s,-e** hiding-place; **V~ spielen** play hide-and-seek. **v~en** *vt* hide; **sich v~en** hide
verstehen† *vt* understand; (*können*) know; **falsch v~** misunderstand; **sich v~** understand one another; (*auskommen*) get on
versteiger|n *vt* auction. **V~ung** *f* auction
versteinert *adj* fossilized
verstell|en *vt* adjust; (*versperren*) block; (*verändern*) disguise; **sich v~en** pretend. **V~ung** *f* **-** pretence
versteuern *vt* pay tax on
verstimm|t *adj* disgruntled; (*Magen*) upset; (*Mus*) out of tune. **V~ung** *f* **-** ill humour; (*Magen-*) upset
verstockt *adj* stubborn
verstopf|en *vt* plug; (*versperren*) block; **v~t** blocked; (*Person*) constipated. **V~ung** *f* **-,-en** blockage; (*Med*) constipation
verstorben *adj* late, deceased. **V~e(r)** *m/f* deceased
verstört *adj* bewildered
Verstoß *m* infringement. **v~en**† *vt* disown ● *vi* (*haben*) **v~en gegen** contravene, infringe
verstreuen *vt* scatter
verstümmeln *vt* mutilate; garble (*Text*)
Versuch *m* **-[e]s,-e** attempt; (*Experiment*) experiment. **v~en** *vt* (*haben*) try; **v~t sein** be tempted (**zu** to). **V~ung** *f* **-,-en** temptation
vertagen *vt* adjourn; (*aufschieben*) postpone; **sich v~** adjourn
vertauschen *vt* exchange; (*verwechseln*) mix up
verteidig|en *vt* defend. **V~er** *m* **-s,-** defender; (*Jur*) defence counsel. **V~ung** *f* **-,-en** defence
verteil|en *vt* distribute; (*zuteilen*) allocate; (*ausgeben*) hand out; (*verstreichen*) spread. **V~ung** *f* **-** distribution; allocation
vertief|en *vt* deepen; **v~t sein in** (+ *acc*) be engrossed in. **V~ung** *f* **-,-en** hollow, depression
vertikal /vɛrti'ka:l/ *adj* vertical
vertilgen *vt* exterminate; kill [off] (*Unkraut*)

vertippen (sich) *vr* make a typing mistake
vertonen *vt* set to music
Vertrag *m* **-[e]s,⸚e** contract; (*Pol*) treaty
vertragen† *vt* tolerate, stand; take (*Kritik, Spaß*); **sich v~** get on
vertraglich *adj* contractual
verträglich *adj* good-natured; (*bekömmlich*) digestible
vertrauen *vi* (*haben*) trust (**jdm/etw** s.o./sth; **auf** + *acc* in). **V~** *nt* **-s** trust, confidence (**zu** in); **im V~** in confidence. **v~swürdig** *adj* trustworthy
vertraulich *adj* confidential; (*intim*) familiar
vertraut *adj* intimate; (*bekannt*) familiar. **V~heit** *f* **-** intimacy; familiarity
vertreib|en† *vt* drive away; drive out (*Feind*); (*Comm*) sell; **sich** (*dat*) **die Zeit v~en** pass the time. **V~ung** *f* **-,-en** expulsion
vertret|en† *vt* represent; (*einspringen für*) stand in *or* deputize for; (*verfechten*) support; hold (*Meinung*); **sich** (*dat*) **den Fuß v~en** twist one's ankle. **V~er** *m* **-s,-** representative; deputy; (*Arzt-*) locum; (*Verfechter*) supporter. **V~ung** *f* **-,-en** representation; (*Person*) deputy; (*eines Arztes*) locum; (*Handels-*) agency
Vertrieb *m* **-[e]s** (*Comm*) sale
vertrocknen *vi* (*sein*) dry up
verüben *vt* commit
verunglücken *vi* (*sein*) be involved in an accident; (**!**: *missglücken*) go wrong; **tödlich v~** be killed in an accident
verunreinigen *vt* pollute; (*verseuchen*) contaminate
verursachen *vt* cause
verurteil|en *vt* condemn; (*Jur*) convict (**wegen** of); sentence (**zum Tode** to death). **V~ung** *f* **-** condemnation; (*Jur*) conviction
vervielfachen *vt* multiply
vervielfältigen *vt* duplicate
vervollständigen *vt* complete
verwählen (sich) *vr* misdial
verwahren *vt* keep; (*verstauen*) put away
verwahrlost *adj* neglected; (*Haus*) dilapidated
Verwahrung *f* **-** keeping; **in V~ nehmen** take into safe keeping
verwaist *adj* orphaned
verwalt|en *vt* administer; (*leiten*) manage; govern (*Land*). **V~er** *m* **-s,-** administrator; manager. **V~ung** *f* **-,-en** administration; management; government
verwand|eln *vt* transform, change (**in** + *acc* into) **sich v~eln** change, turn (**in** + *acc* into). **V~lung** *f* transformation
verwandt *adj* related (**mit** to). **V~e(r)** *m/f* relative. **V~schaft** *f* **-** relationship; (*Menschen*) relatives *pl*
verwarn|en *vt* warn, caution. **V~ung** *f* warning, caution
verwechs|eln *vt* mix up, confuse; (*halten für*) mistake (**mit** for). **V~lung** *f* **-,-en** mix-up
verweiger|n *vt/i* (*haben*) refuse (**jdm etw** s.o. sth). **V~ung** *f* refusal
Verweis *m* **-es,-e** reference (**auf** + *acc* to); (*Tadel*) reprimand; **v~en**† *vt* refer (**auf/an** + *acc* to); (*tadeln*) reprimand; **von der Schule v~en** expel
verwelken *vi* (*sein*) wilt
verwend|en† *vt* use; spend (*Zeit, Mühe*). **V~ung** *f* use
verwerten *vt* utilize, use
verwesen *vi* (*sein*) decompose

verwick|eln *vt* involve (**in** + *acc* in); **sich v~eln** get tangled up. **v~elt** *adj* complicated

verwildert *adj* wild; (*Garten*) overgrown; (*Aussehen*) unkempt

verwinden† *vt* (*fig*) get over

verwirklichen *vt* realize

verwirr|en *vt* tangle up; (*fig*) confuse; **sich v~en** get tangled; (*fig*) become confused. **v~t** *adj* confused. **V~ung** *f* - confusion

verwischen *vt* smudge

verwittert *adj* weathered

verwitwet *adj* widowed

verwöhn|en *vt* spoil. **v~t** *adj* spoilt

verworren *adj* confused

verwund|bar *adj* vulnerable. **v~en** *vt* wound

verwunder|lich *adj* surprising. **v~n** *vt* surprise; **sich v~n** be surprised. **V~ung** *f* - surprise

Verwund|ete(r) *m* wounded soldier; **die V~eten** the wounded *pl*. **V~ung** *f* **-,-en** wound

verwüst|en *vt* devastate, ravage. **V~ung** *f* **-,-en** devastation

verzählen (sich) *vr* miscount

verzaubern *vt* bewitch; (*fig*) enchant; **v~ in** (+ *acc*) turn into

Verzehr *m* **-s** consumption. **v~en** *vt* eat

verzeih|en† *vt* forgive; **v~en Sie!** excuse me! **V~ung** *f* - forgiveness; **um V~ung bitten** apologize; **V~ung!** sorry! (*bei Frage*) excuse me!

Verzicht *m* **-[e]s** renunciation (**auf** + *acc* of). **v~en** *vi* (*haben*) do without; **v~en auf** (+ *acc*) give up; renounce (*Recht, Erbe*)

verziehen† *vt* pull out of shape; (*verwöhnen*) spoil; **sich v~** lose shape; (*Holz:*) warp; (*Gesicht:*) twist; (*verschwinden*) disappear; (*Nebel:*) disperse; (*Gewitter:*) pass ● *vi* (*sein*) move [away]

verzier|en *vt* decorate. **V~ung** *f* **-,-en** decoration

verzinsen *vt* pay interest on

verzöger|n *vt* delay; (*verlangsamen*) slow down. **V~ung** *f* **-,-en** delay

verzollen *vt* pay duty on; **haben Sie etwas zu v~?** have you anything to declare?

verzweif|eln *vi* (*sein*) despair. **v~elt** *adj* desperate. **V~lung** *f* - despair; (*Ratlosigkeit*) desperation

verzweigen (sich) *vr* branch [out]

Veto /ˈveːto/ *nt* **-s,-s** veto

Vetter *m* **-s,-n** cousin

vgl. *abbr* (**vergleiche**) cf.

Viadukt /vi̯aˈdʊkt/ *nt* **-[e]s,-e** viaduct

Video /ˈviːdeo/ *nt* **-s,-s** video. **V~handy** *nt* vision phone. **V~kassette** *f* video cassette. **V~recorder** *m* **-s,-** video recorder

Vieh *nt* **-[e]s** livestock; (*Rinder*) cattle *pl*; ([T]: *Tier*) creature

viel *pron* a great deal/[T] a lot of; (*pl*) many, [T] a lot of; (*substantivisch*) **v~[es]** much, [T] a lot; **nicht/so/wie/zu v~** not/so/how/too much/ (*pl*) many; **v~e** *pl* many; **das v~e Geld** all that money ● *adv* much, [T] a lot; **v~ mehr/weniger** much more/less; **v~zu groß/klein** much *or* far too big/small; **so v~ wie möglich** as much as possible; **so/zu v~ arbeiten** work so/too much

viel|deutig *adj* ambiguous. **v~fach** *adj* multiple ● *adv* many times; ([T]: *oft*) frequently. **V~falt** *f* - diversity, [great] variety

vielleicht *adv* perhaps, maybe;

(Ⓘ: *wirklich*) really

vielmals *adv* very much

vielmehr *adv* rather; (*im Gegenteil*) on the contrary

vielseitig *adj* varied; (*Person*) versatile. **V∼keit** *f* - versatility

vielversprechend* *adj* **viel versprechend**, *s.* **versprechen**

vier *inv adj*, **V∼** *f* **-,-en** four; (*Sch*) ≈ fair. **V∼eck** *nt* **-[e]s,-e** oblong, rectangle; (*Quadrat*) square. **v∼eckig** *adj* oblong, rectangular; square. **V∼linge** *mpl* quadruplets

viertel /'fɪrtəl/ *inv adj* quarter; **um v∼ neun** at [a] quarter past eight; **um drei v∼ neun** at [a] quarter to nine. **V∼** *nt* **-s,-** quarter; (*Wein*) quarter litre; **V∼ vor/nach sechs** [a] quarter to/past six. **V∼finale** *nt* quarter-final. **V∼jahr** *nt* three months *pl*; (*Comm*) quarter. **v∼jährlich** *adj & adv* quarterly. **V∼stunde** *f* quarter of an hour

vier|zehn /'fɪr-/ *inv adj* fourteen. **v∼zehnte(r,s)** *adj* fourteenth. **v∼zig** *inv adj* forty. **v∼zigste(r,s)** *adj* fortieth

Villa /'vɪla/ *f* **-,-len** villa

violett /vi̯o'lɛt/ *adj* violet

Vio|line /vi̯o'li:nə/ *f* **-,-n** violin. **V∼linschlüssel** *m* treble clef

Virus /'vi:rʊs/ *nt* **-,-ren** virus

Visier /vi'zi:ɐ̯/ *nt* **-s,-e** visor

Visite /vi'zi:tə/ *f* **-,-n** round; **V∼ machen** do one's round

Visum /'vi:zʊm/ *nt* **-s,-sa** visa

Vitamin /vita'mi:n/ *nt* **-s,-e** vitamin

Vitrine /vi'tri:nə/ *f* **-,-n** display cabinet/(*im Museum*) case

Vizepräsident /'fi:tsə-/ *m* vice president

Vogel *m* **-s,⸚** bird; **einen V∼ haben** Ⓘ have a screw loose. **V∼scheuche** *f* **-,-n** scarecrow

Vokabeln /vo'ka:bəln/ *fpl* vocabulary *sg*

Vokal /vo'ka:l/ *m* **-s,-e** vowel

Volant /vo'lã:/ *m* **-s,-s** flounce

Volk *nt* **-[e]s,⸚er** people *sg*; (*Bevölkerung*) people *pl*

Völker|kunde *f* ethnology. **V∼mord** *m* genocide. **V∼recht** *nt* international law

Volks|abstimmung *f* plebiscite. **V∼fest** *nt* public festival. **V∼hochschule** *f* adult education classes *pl*/(*Gebäude*) centre. **V∼lied** *nt* folk-song. **V∼tanz** *m* folk-dance. **v∼tümlich** *adj* popular. **V∼wirt** *m* economist. **V∼wirtschaft** *f* economics *sg*. **V∼zählung** *f* [national] census

voll *adj* full (**von** *od* **mit** of); (*Haar*) thick; (*Erfolg, Ernst*) complete; (*Wahrheit*) whole; **v∼ machen** fill up; **v∼ tanken** fill up with petrol ● *adv* (*ganz*) completely; (*arbeiten*) full-time; (*auszahlen*) in full; **v∼ und ganz** completely

Vollblut *nt* thoroughbred

vollende|n *vt insep* complete. **v∼t** *adj* perfect

Vollendung *f* completion; (*Vollkommenheit*) perfection

voller *inv adj* full of

Volleyball /'vɔli-/ *m* volleyball

vollführen *vt insep* perform

vollfüllen *vt sep* fill up

Vollgas *nt* **V∼ geben** put one's foot down; **mit V∼** flat out

völlig *adj* complete

volljährig *adj* **v∼ sein** (*Jur*) be of age. **V∼keit** *f* - (*Jur*) majority

Vollkaskoversicherung *f* fully comprehensive insurance

vollkommen *adj* perfect; (*völlig*) complete

Voll|kornbrot *nt* wholemeal

bread. **V~macht** *f* **-,-en** authority; (*Jur*) power of attorney. **V~mond** *m* full moon. **V~pension** *f* full board

vollständig *adj* complete

vollstrecken *vt insep* execute; carry out (*Urteil*)

volltanken* *vi sep* (*haben*) **voll tanken**, *s.* **voll**

Volltreffer *m* direct hit

vollzählig *adj* complete

vollziehen† *vt insep* carry out; perform (*Handlung*); consummate (*Ehe*); **sich v~** take place

Volt /vɔlt/ *nt* **-[s],-** volt

Volumen /vo'lu:mən/ *nt* **-s,-** volume

vom *prep* = **von dem**

von

● *preposition* (+ *dative*)

! Note that **von dem** can become **vom**

····➤ (*räumlich*) from; (*nach Richtungen*) of. **von hier an** from here on[ward]. **von Wien aus** [starting] from Vienna. **nördlich/südlich von Mannheim** [to the] north/south of Mannheim. **rechts/links von mir** to the right/left of me; on my right/left

····➤ (*zeitlich*) from. **von jetzt an** from now on. **von heute/morgen an** [as] from today/tomorrow; starting today/tomorrow

····➤ (*zur Angabe des Urhebers, der Ursache; nach Passiv*) by. **der Roman ist von Fontane** the novel is by Fontane. **sie hat ein Kind von ihm.** she has a child by him. **er ist vom Blitz erschlagen worden** he was killed by lightning

····➤ (*anstelle eines Genitivs; Hingehören, Beschaffenheit, Menge etc.*) of. **ein Stück von dem Kuchen** a piece of the cake. **einer von euch** one of you. **eine Fahrt von drei Stunden** a drive of three hours; a three-hour drive. **das Brot von gestern** yesterday's bread. **ein Tal von erstaunlicher Schönheit** a valley of extraordinary beauty

····➤ (*beftreffend*) about. **handeln/wissen/erzählen** *od* **reden von** ... be/know/talk about .... **eine Geschichte von zwei Elefanten** a story about *or* of two elephants

voneinander *adv* from each other; (*abhängig*) on each other

vonseiten *prep* (+ *gen*) on the part of

vonstatten *adv* **v~ gehen** take place

vor *prep* (+ *dat/acc*) in front of; (*zeitlich, Reihenfolge*) before; (+ *dat*) (*bei Uhrzeit*) to; (*warnen, sich fürchten*) of; (*schützen, davonlaufen*) from; (*Respekt haben*) for; **vor Angst zittern** tremble with fear; **vor drei Tagen** three days ago; **vor allen Dingen** above all ● *adv* forward; **vor und zurück** backwards and forwards

Vorabend *m* eve

voran *adv* at the front; (*voraus*) ahead; (*vorwärts*) forward. **v~gehen**† *vi sep* (*sein*) lead the way; (*Fortschritte machen*) make progress. **v~kommen**† *vi sep* (*sein*) make progress; (*fig*) get on

Vor|anschlag *m* estimate. **V~anzeige** *f* advance notice. **V~arbeiter** *m* foreman

voraus *adv* ahead (*dat* of); (*vorn*) at the front; (*vorwärts*) forward ● **im Voraus** in advance. **v~bezahlen** *vt sep* pay in advance. **v~gehen**† *vi sep* (*sein*) go on ahead; **jdm/etw v~gehen** precede s.o./sth. **V~sage** *f* **-,-n** prediction. **v~sagen** *vt sep* predict

voraussetz|en *vt sep* take for granted; (*erfordern*) require; **vorausgesetzt, dass** provided that. **V~ung** *f* **-,-en** assumption; (*Erfordernis*) prerequisite

voraussichtlich *adj* anticipated, expected ● *adv* probably

Vorbehalt *m* **-[e]s,-e** reservation

vorbei *adv* past (**an jdm/etw** s.o./sth); (*zu Ende*) over. **v~fahren**† *vi sep* (*sein*) drive/go past. **v~gehen**† *vi sep* (*sein*) go past; (*verfehlen*) miss; (*vergehen*) pass; (🅸: *besuchen*) drop in (**bei** on)

vorbereit|en *vt sep* prepare; prepare for (*Reise*); **sich v~en** prepare [oneself] (**auf** + *acc* for). **V~ung** *f* **-,-en** preparation

vorbestellen *vt sep* order/(*im Theater, Hotel*) book in advance

vorbestraft *adj* **v~ sein** have a [criminal] record

Vorbeugung *f* **-** prevention

Vorbild *nt* model. **v~lich** *adj* exemplary, model ● *adv* in an exemplary manner

vorbringen† *vt sep* put forward; offer (*Entschuldigung*)

vordatieren *vt sep* post-date

Vorder|bein *nt* foreleg. **v~e(r,s)** *adj* front. **V~grund** *m* foreground. **V~rad** *nt* front wheel. **V~seite** *f* front; (*einer Münze*) obverse. **v~ste(r,s)** *adj* front, first. **V~teil** *nt* front

vor|drängeln (sich) *vr sep* 🅸 jump the queue. **v~drängen (sich)** *vr sep* push forward. **v~dringen**† *vi sep* (*sein*) advance

voreilig *adj* rash

voreingenommen *adj* biased, prejudiced. **V~heit** *f* **-** bias

vorenthalten† *vt sep* withhold

vorerst *adv* for the time being

Vorfahr *m* **-en,-en** ancestor

Vorfahrt *f* right of way; **'V~ beachten'** 'give way'. **V~sstraße** *f* ≈ major road

Vorfall *m* incident. **v~en**† *vi sep* (*sein*) happen

vorfinden† *vt sep* find

Vorfreude *f* [happy] anticipation

vorführ|en *vt sep* present, show; (*demonstrieren*) demonstrate; (*aufführen*) perform. **V~ung** *f* presentation; demonstration; performance

Vor|gabe *f* (*Sport*) handicap. **V~gang** *m* occurrence; (*Techn*) process. **V~gänger(in)** *m* **-s,-** (*f* **-,-nen**) predecessor

vorgehen† *vi sep* (*sein*) go forward; (*voraus-*) go on ahead; (*Uhr:*) be fast; (*wichtig sein*) take precedence; (*verfahren*) act, proceed; (*geschehen*) happen, go on. **V~** *nt* **-s** action

vor|geschichtlich *adj* prehistoric. **V~geschmack** *m* foretaste. **V~gesetzte(r)** *m/f* superior. **v~gestern** *adv* the day before yesterday; **v~gestern Abend** the evening before last

vorhaben† *vt sep* propose, intend (**zu** to); **etw v~** have sth planned. **V~** *nt* **-s,-** plan

Vorhand *f* (*Sport*) forehand

vorhanden *adj* existing; **v~ sein** exist; be available

Vorhang *m* curtain

Vorhängeschloss *nt* padlock

vorher *adv* before[hand]

vorhergehend *adj* previous
vorherrschend *adj* predominant
Vorher|sage *f* **-,-n** prediction: (*Wetter-*) forecast. **v~sagen** *vt sep* predict; forecast (*Wetter*). **v~sehen**† *vt sep* foresee
vorhin *adv* just now
vorige(r,s) *adj* last, previous
Vor|kehrungen *fpl* precautions. **V~kenntnisse** *fpl* previous knowledge *sg*
vorkommen† *vi sep* (*sein*) happen; (*vorhanden sein*) occur; (*nach vorn kommen*) come forward; (*hervorkommen*) come out; (*zu sehen sein*) show; **jdm bekannt v~** seem familiar to s.o.
Vorkriegszeit *f* pre-war period
vorlad|en† *vt sep* (*Jur*) summons. **V~ung** *f* summons
Vorlage *f* model; (*Muster*) pattern; (*Gesetzes-*) bill
vorlassen† *vt sep* admit; **jdn v~** [T] let s.o. pass; (*den Vortritt lassen*) let s.o. go first
Vor|lauf *m* (*Sport*) heat. **V~läufer** *m* forerunner. **v~läufig** *adj* provisional; (*zunächst*) for the time being. **v~laut** *adj* forward. **V~leben** *nt* past
vorleg|en *vt sep* put on (*Kette*); (*unterbreiten*) present; (*vorzeigen*) show. **V~er** *m* **-s,-** mat; (*Bett-*) rug
vorles|en† *vt sep* read [out]; **jdm v~en** read to s.o. **V~ung** *f* lecture
vorletzt|e(r,s) *adj* last ... but one; **v~es Jahr** the year before last
Vorliebe *f* preference
vorliegen† *vt sep* (*haben*) be present/(*verfügbar*) available; (*bestehen*) exist, be
vorlügen† *vt sep* lie (*dat* to)
vormachen *vt sep* put up; put on (*Kette*); push (*Riegel*); (*zeigen*) demonstrate; **jdm etwas v~** ([T]: *täuschen*) kid s.o.
Vormacht *f* supremacy
vormals *adv* formerly
vormerken *vt sep* make a note of; (*reservieren*) reserve
Vormittag *m* morning; **gestern/heute V~** yesterday/this morning. **v~s** *adv* in the morning
Vormund *m* **-[e]s,-munde** & **-münder** guardian
vorn *adv* at the front; **nach v~** to the front; **von v~** from the front/(*vom Anfang*) beginning; **von v~ anfangen** start afresh
Vorname *m* first name
vorne *adv* = **vorn**
vornehm *adj* distinguished; smart
vornehmen† *vt sep* carry out; **sich** (*dat*) **v~, etw zu tun** plan to do sth
vornherein *adv* **von v~herein** from the start
Vor|ort *m* suburb. **V~rang** *m* priority, precedence (**vor** + *dat* over). **V~rat** *m* **-[e]s,-e** supply, stock (**an** + *dat* of). **v~rätig** *adj* available; **v~rätig haben** have in stock. **V~ratskammer** *f* larder. **V~recht** *nt* privilege. **V~richtung** *f* device
Vorrunde *f* qualifying round
vorsagen *vt/i sep* (*haben*) recite; **jdm v~** tell s.o. the answer
Vor|satz *m* resolution. **v~sätzlich** *adj* deliberate; (*Jur*) premeditated
Vorschau *f* preview; (*Film-*) trailer
Vorschein *m* **zum V~kommen** appear
Vorschlag *m* suggestion, proposal. **v~en**† *vt sep* suggest, propose
vorschnell *adj* rash
vorschreiben† *vt sep* lay down; dictate (*dat* to); **vorgeschriebene Dosis** prescribed dose

V

Vorschrift *f* regulation; (*Anweisung*) instruction; **jdm V~en machen** tell s.o. what to do. **v~smäßig** *adj* correct

Vorschule *f* nursery school

Vorschuss *m* advance

vorseh|en† *v sep* ● *vt* intend (**für**/**als** for/as); (*planen*) plan; **sich v~en** be careful (**vor** + *dat* of) ● *vi* (*haben*) peep out. **V~ung** *f* - providence

Vorsicht *f* - care; (*bei Gefahr*) caution; **V~!** careful! (*auf Schild*) 'caution'. **v~ig** *adj* careful; cautious. **V~smaßnahme** *f* precaution

Vorsilbe *f* prefix

Vorsitz *m* chairmanship; **den V~ führen** be in the chair. **V~ende(r)** *m*/*f* chairman

Vorsorge *f* **V~ treffen** take precautions; make provisions (**für** for). **v~n** *vi sep* (*haben*) provide (**für** for)

Vorspeise *f* starter

Vorspiel *nt* prelude. **v~en** *v sep* ● *vt* perform/ (*Mus*) play (*dat* for) ● *vi* (*haben*) audition

vorsprechen† *v sep* ● *vt* recite; (*zum Nachsagen*) say (*dat* to) ● *vi* (*haben*) (*Theat*) audition; **bei jdm v~** call on s.o.

Vor|sprung *m* projection; (*Fels-*) ledge; (*Vorteil*) lead (**vor** + *dat* over). **V~stadt** *f* suburb. **V~stand** *m* board [of directors]; (*Vereins-*) committee; (*Partei-*) executive

vorsteh|en† *vi sep* (*haben*) project, protrude; **einer Abteilung v~en** be in charge of a department. **V~er** *m* **-s,-** head

vorstell|en *vt sep* put forward (*Bein, Uhr*); (*darstellen*) represent; (*bekanntmachen*) introduce; **sich v~en** introduce oneself; (*als Bewerber*) go for an interview; **sich** (*dat*) **etw v~en** imagine sth. **V~ung** *f* introduction; (*bei Bewerbung*) interview; (*Aufführung*) performance; (*Idee*) idea; (*Phantasie*) imagination. **V~ungsgespräch** *nt* interview

Vorstoß *m* advance

Vorstrafe *f* previous conviction

Vortag *m* day before

vortäuschen *vt sep* feign, fake

Vorteil *m* advantage. **v~haft** *adj* advantageous; flattering

Vortrag *m* **-[e]s,⸚e** talk; (*wissenschaftlich*) lecture. **v~en**† *vt sep* perform; (*aufsagen*) recite; (*singen*) sing; (*darlegen*) present (*dat* to)

vortrefflich *adj* excellent

Vortritt *m* precedence; **jdm den V~ lassen** let s.o. go first

vorüber *adv* **v~ sein** be over; **an etw** (*dat*) **v~** past sth. **v~gehend** *adj* temporary

Vor|urteil *nt* prejudice. **V~verkauf** *m* advance booking

vorverlegen *vt sep* bring forward

Vor|wahl[nummer] *f* dialling code. **V~wand** *m* **-[e]s,⸚e** pretext; (*Ausrede*) excuse

vorwärts *adv* forward[s]; **v~ kommen** make progress; (*fig*) get on *or* ahead

vorwegnehmen† *vt sep* anticipate

vorweisen† *vt sep* show

vorwiegend *adv* predominantly

Vorwort *nt* (*pl* **-worte**) preface

Vorwurf *m* reproach; **jdm Vorwürfe machen** reproach s.o. **v~svoll** *adj* reproachful

Vorzeichen *nt* sign; (*fig*) omen

vorzeigen *vt sep* show

vorzeitig *adj* premature

vorziehen† *vt sep* pull forward; draw (*Vorhang*); (*lieber mögen*) prefer; favour

Vor|zimmer *nt* anteroom; (*Büro*)

outer office. **V~zug** *m* preference; (*gute Eigenschaft*) merit, virtue; (*Vorteil*) advantage

vorzüglich *adj* excellent

vulgär /vʊlˈgɛːɐ̯/ *adj* vulgar ● *adv* in a vulgar way

Vulkan /vʊlˈkaːn/ *m* **-s,-e** volcano

Ww

Waage *f* **-,-n** scales *pl*; (*Astrology*) Libra. **w~recht** *adj* horizontal

Wabe *f* **-,-n** honeycomb

wach *adj* awake; (*aufgeweckt*) alert; **w~ werden** wake up

Wach|e *f* **-,-n** guard; (*Posten*) sentry; (*Dienst*) guard duty; (*Naut*) watch; (*Polizei-*) station; **W~e halten** keep watch. **W~hund** *m* guard-dog

Wacholder *m* **-s** juniper

Wachposten *m* sentry

Wachs *nt* **-es** wax

wach|sam *adj* vigilant. **W~keit** *f* **-** vigilance

wachsen†[1] *vi* (*sein*) grow

wachs|en[2] *vt* (*reg*) wax. **W~figur** *f* waxwork

Wachstum *nt* **-s** growth

Wächter *m* **-s,-** guard; (*Park-*) keeper; (*Parkplatz-*) attendant

Wacht|meister *m* [police] constable. **W~posten** *m* sentry

wackel|ig *adj* wobbly; (*Stuhl*) rickety; (*Person*) shaky. **W~kontakt** *m* loose connection. **w~n** *vi* (*haben*) wobble; (*zittern*) shake

Wade *f* **-,-n** (*Anat*) calf

Waffe *f* **-,-n** weapon; **W~n** arms

Waffel *f* **-,-n** waffle; (*Eis-*) wafer

Waffen|ruhe *f* cease-fire. **W~schein** *m* firearms licence. **W~stillstand** *m* armistice

Wagemut *m* daring

wagen *vt* risk; **es w~, etw zu tun** dare [to] do sth; **sich w~** (*gehen*) venture

Wagen *m* **-s,-** cart; (*Eisenbahn-*) carriage, coach; (*Güter-*) wagon; (*Kinder-*) pram; (*Auto*) car. **W~heber** *m* **-s,-** jack

Waggon /vaˈgõː/ *m* **-s,-s** wagon

Wahl *f* **-,-en** choice; (*Pol, Admin*) election; (*geheime*) ballot; **zweite W~** (*Comm*) seconds *pl*

wähl|en *vt/i* (*haben*) choose; (*Pol, Admin*) elect; (*stimmen*) vote; (*Teleph*) dial. **W~er(in)** *m* **-s,-** (*f* **-,-nen**) voter. **w~erisch** *adj* choosy, fussy

Wahl|fach *nt* optional subject. **w~frei** *adj* optional. **W~kampf** *m* election campaign. **W~kreis** *m* constituency. **W~lokal** *nt* polling-station. **w~los** *adj* indiscriminate

Wahl|spruch *m* motto. **W~urne** *f* ballot-box

Wahn *m* **-[e]s** delusion; (*Manie*) mania

Wahnsinn *m* madness. **w~ig** *adj* mad, insane; (*[F]: unsinnig*) crazy; (*[F]: groß*) terrible; **w~ig werden** go mad ● *adv* [F] terribly. **W~ige(r)** *m/f* maniac

wahr *adj* true; (*echt*) real; **du kommst doch, nicht w~?** you are coming, aren't you?

während *prep* (+ *gen*) during ● *conj* while; (*wohingegen*) whereas

Wahrheit *f* **-,-en** truth. **w~sgemäß** *adj* truthful

wahrnehm|en† *vt sep* notice; (*nutzen*) take advantage of; exploit (*Vorteil*); look after (*Interessen*).

W~ung *f* **-,-en** perception

Wahrsagerin *f* **-,-nen** fortune teller

wahrscheinlich *adj* probable. **W~keit** *f* **-** probability

Währung *f* **-,-en** currency

Wahrzeichen *nt* symbol

Waise *f* **-,-n** orphan. **W~nhaus** *nt* orphanage. **W~nkind** *nt* orphan

Wal *m* **-[e]s,-e** whale

Wald *m* **-[e]s,⸚er** wood; (*groß*) forest. **w~ig** *adj* wooded

> **Waldorfschule** An increasingly popular type of private school originally inspired by the Austrian educationist Rudolf Steiner (1861-1925) in the 1920s. The main aim of Waldorf schools is to develop pupils' creative and cognitive abilities through music, art and crafts.

Waliser *m* **-s,-** Welshman

Waliserin *f* **-,-nen** Welshwoman

w~isch *adj* Welsh

Wall *m* **-[e]s,⸚e** mound

Wallfahr|er(in) *m(f)* pilgrim. **W~t** *f* pilgrimage

Walnuss *f* walnut

Walze *f* **-,-n** roller. **w~n** *vt* roll

Walzer *m* **-s,-** waltz

Wand *f* **-,⸚e** wall; (*Trenn-*) partition; (*Seite*) side; (*Fels-*) face

Wandel *m* **-s** change

Wander|er *m* **-s,-**, **W~in** *f* **-,-nen** hiker, rambler. **w~n** *vi* (*sein*) hike, ramble; (*ziehen*) travel; (*gemächlich gehen*) wander; (*ziellos*) roam. **W~schaft** *f* **-** travels *pl*. **W~ung** *f* **-,-en** hike, ramble. **W~weg** *m* footpath

Wandlung *f* **-,-en** change, transformation

Wand|malerei *f* mural. **W~tafel** *f* blackboard. **W~teppich** *m* tapestry

Wange *f* **-,-n** cheek

wann *adv* when

Wanne *f* **-,-n** tub

Wanze *f* **-,-n** bug

Wappen *nt* **-s,-** coat of arms. **W~kunde** *f* heraldry

> **Bundeswappen** The federal coat of arms features a heraldic eagle, which was originally the emblem of Roman emperors. It was incorporated into the coat of arms of the German Empire when it was founded in 1871. In 1950 it was revived as the official coat of arms of the Federal Republic of Germany.

war, wäre *s.* **sein**[1]

Ware *f* **-,-n** article; (*Comm*) commodity; (*coll*) merchandise; **W~n** goods. **W~nhaus** *nt* department store. **W~nprobe** *f* sample. **W~nzeichen** *nt* trademark

warm *adj* warm; (*Mahlzeit*) hot; **w~ machen** heat ●*adv* warmly; **w~ essen** have a hot meal

Wärm|e *f* **-** warmth; (*Phys*) heat; **10 Grad W~e** 10 degrees above zero. **w~en** *vt* warm; heat (*Essen, Wasser*). **W~flasche** *f* hot-water bottle

Warn|blinkanlage *f* hazard [warning] lights *pl*. **w~en** *vt/i* (*haben*) warn (**vor** + *dat* of). **W~ung** *f* **-,-en** warning

Warteliste *f* waiting list

warten *vi* (*haben*) wait (**auf** + *acc* for) ●*vt* service

Wärter(in) *m* **-s,-** (*f* **-,-nen**) keeper; (*Museums-*) attendant; (*Gefängnis-*) warder; (*Kranken-*) orderly

Warte|raum, W~saal *m* waiting-room. **W~zimmer** *nt* (*Med*) waiting-room

Wartung *f* - (*Techn*) service

warum *adv* why

Warze *f* -,-n wart

was *pron* what ● *rel pron* that; **alles, was ich brauche** all [that] I need ● *indefinite pronoun* (🅔: *etwas*) something; (*fragend, verneint*) anything; **so was Ärgerliches!** what a nuisance! ● *adv* 🅔 (*warum*) why; (*wie*) how

wasch|bar *adj* washable. **W~becken** *nt* wash-basin

Wäsche *f* - washing; (*Unter-*) underwear

waschecht *adj* colour-fast

Wäscheklammer *f* clothes-peg

waschen† *vt* wash; **sich w~** have a wash; **W~ und Legen** shampoo and set ● *vi* (*haben*) do the washing

Wäscherei *f* -,-en laundry

Wäsche|schleuder *f* spin-drier. **W~trockner** *m* tumble-drier

Wasch|küche *f* laundry-room. **W~lappen** *m* face-flannel. **W~maschine** *f* washing machine. **W~mittel** *nt* detergent. **W~pulver** *nt* washing-powder. **W~salon** *m* launderette. **W~zettel** *m* blurb

Wasser *nt* -s water. **W~ball** *m* beach-ball; (*Spiel*) water polo. **w~dicht** *adj* watertight; (*Kleidung*) waterproof. **W~fall** *m* waterfall. **W~farbe** *f* water-colour. **W~hahn** *m* tap. **W~kraft** *f* water-power. **W~kraftwerk** *nt* hydroelectric power-station. **W~leitung** *f* water-main; **aus der W~leitung** from the tap. **W~mann** *m* (*Astrology*) Aquarius

wässern *vt* soak; (*begießen*) water ● *vi* (*haben*) water

Wasser|ski *nt* -s water-skiing. **W~stoff** *m* hydrogen. **W~straße** *f* waterway. **W~waage** *f* spirit-level

wässrig *adj* watery

watscheln *vi* (*sein*) waddle

Watt *nt* -s,- (*Phys*) watt

Watt|e *f* - cotton wool. **w~iert** *adj* padded; (*gesteppt*) quilted

WC /ve'tse:/ *nt* -s,-s WC

Web|cam *f* -,-s web camera. **W~design** *nt* web design

web|en *vt/i* (*haben*) weave. **W~er** *m* -s,- weaver

Web|seite /'vep-/ *f* web page. **W~site** *f* -, -s website

Wechsel *m* -s,- change; (*Tausch*) exchange; (*Comm*) bill of exchange. **W~geld** *nt* change. **w~haft** *adj* changeable. **W~jahre** *npl* menopause *sg*. **W~kurs** *m* exchange rate. **w~n** *vt* change; (*tauschen*) exchange ● *vi* (*haben*) change; vary. **w~nd** *adj* changing; varying. **W~strom** *m* alternating current. **W~stube** *f* bureau de change

weck|en *vt* wake [up]; (*fig*) awaken ● *vi* (*haben*) (*Wecker:*) go off. **W~er** *m* -s,- alarm [clock]

wedeln *vi* (*haben*) wave; **mit dem Schwanz w~** wag its tail

weder *conj* **w~ ... noch** neither ... nor

Weg *m* -[e]s,-e way; (*Fuß-*) path; (*Fahr-*) track; (*Gang*) errand; **sich auf den Weg machen** set off

weg *adv* away, off; (*verschwunden*) gone; **weg sein** be away; (*gegangen/verschwunden*) have gone; **Hände weg!** hands off!

wegen *prep* (+ *gen*) because of; (*um ... willen*) for the sake of; (*bezüglich*) about

weg|fahren† *vi sep* (*sein*) go away; (*abfahren*) leave. **W~fahrsperre** *f* immobilizer. **w~fallen**† *vi sep* (*sein*) be dropped/(*ausgelassen*) omitted; (*entfallen*) no longer apply.

W

w∼geben† *vt sep* give away. **w∼gehen**† *vi sep* (*sein*) leave, go away; (*ausgehen*) go out. **w∼kommen**† *vi sep* (*sein*) get away; (*verloren gehen*) disappear; **schlecht w∼kommen** [T] get a raw deal. **w∼lassen**† *vt sep* let go; (*auslassen*) omit. **w∼laufen**† *vi sep* (*sein*) run away. **w∼räumen** *vt sep* put away; (*entfernen*) clear away. **w∼schicken** *vt sep* send away; (*abschicken*) send off. **w∼tun**† *vt sep* put away; (*wegwerfen*) throw away

Wegweiser *m* **-s,-** signpost

weg|werfen† *vt sep* throw away. **w∼ziehen**† *v sep* ● *vt* pull away ● *vi* (*sein*) move away

weh *adj* sore; **weh tun** hurt; (*Kopf, Rücken:*) ache; **jdm weh tun** hurt s.o.

wehe *int* alas; **w∼ [dir/euch]!** (*drohend*) don't you dare!

wehen *vi* (*haben*) blow; (*flattern*) flutter ● *vt* blow

Wehen *fpl* contractions

Wehr[1] *nt* **-[e]s,-e** weir

Wehr[2] *f* **sich zur W∼ setzen** resist. **W∼dienst** *m* military service. **W∼dienstverweigerer** *m* **-s,-** conscientious objector

wehren (sich) *vr* resist; (*gegen Anschuldigung*) protest; (*sich sträuben*) refuse

wehr|los *adj* defenceless. **W∼macht** *f* armed forces *pl*. **W∼pflicht** *f* conscription

Weib *nt* **-[e]s,-er** woman; (*Ehe-*) wife. **W∼chen** *nt* **-s,-** (*Zool*) female. **w∼lich** *adj* feminine; (*Biology*) female

weich *adj* soft; (*gar*) done

Weiche *f* **-,-n** (*Rail*) points *pl*

Weich|heit *f* **-** softness. **w∼lich** *adj* soft; (*Charakter*) weak. **W∼spüler** *m* **-s,-** (*Textiles*) conditioner.

W∼tier *nt* mollusc

Weide[1] *f* **-,-n** (*Bot*) willow

Weide[2] *f* **-,-n** pasture. **w∼n** *vt/i* (*haben*) graze

weiger|n (sich) *vr* refuse. **W∼ung** *f* **-,-en** refusal

Weihe *f* **-,-n** consecration; (*Priester-*) ordination. **w∼n** *vt* consecrate; (*zum Priester*) ordain

Weiher *m* **-s,-** pond

Weihnacht|en *nt* **-s** & *pl* Christmas. **w∼lich** *adj* Christmassy. **W∼sbaum** *m* Christmas tree. **W∼slied** *nt* Christmas carol. **W∼smann** *m* (*pl* **-männer**) Father Christmas. **W∼stag** *m* **erster/zweiter W∼stag** Christmas Day/Boxing Day

> *i* **Weihnachtsmarkt** During the weeks of Advent, Christmas markets are held in most German towns. Visitors can buy Christmas decorations, handmade toys and crib figures, traditional Christmas biscuits, and mulled wine to sustain them while they shop.

Weih|rauch *m* incense. **W∼wasser** *nt* holy water

weil *conj* because; (*da*) since

Weile *f* **-** while

Wein *m* **-[e]s,-e** wine; (*Bot*) vines *pl*; (*Trauben*) grapes *pl*. **W∼bau** *m* winegrowing. **W∼berg** *m* vineyard. **W∼brand** *m* **-[e]s** brandy

weinen *vt/i* (*haben*) cry, weep

Wein|glas *nt* wine glass. **W∼karte** *f* wine list. **W∼lese** *f* grape harvest. **W∼liste** *f* wine list. **W∼probe** *f* wine tasting. **W∼rebe** *f*, **W∼stock** *m* vine. **W∼stube** *f* wine bar. **W∼traube** *f* bunch of grapes; (*W∼beere*) grape

weise *adj* wise

Weise *f* **-,-n** way; (*Melodie*) tune

Weisheit *f* **-,-en** wisdom. **W~szahn** *m* wisdom tooth

weiß *adj*, **W~** *nt* **-,-** white

weissag|en *vt/i insep* (*haben*) prophesy. **W~ung** *f* **-,-en** prophecy

Weiß|brot *nt* white bread. **W~e(r)** *m/f* white man/woman. **w~en** *vt* whitewash. **W~wein** *m* white wine

Weisung *f* **-,-en** instruction; (*Befehl*) order

weit *adj* wide; (*ausgedehnt*) extensive; (*lang*) long ● *adv* widely; (*offen, öffnen*) wide; (*lang*) far; **von w~em** from a distance; **bei w~em** by far; **w~ und breit** far and wide; **ist es noch w~?** is it much further? **so w~ wie möglich** as far as possible; **ich bin so w~** I'm ready; **w~ verbreitet** widespread; **w~ reichende Folgen** far-reaching consequences

Weite *f* **-,-n** expanse; (*Entfernung*) distance; (*Größe*) width. **w~n** *vt* widen; stretch (*Schuhe*)

weiter *adj* further ● *adv* further; (*außerdem*) in addition; (*anschließend*) then; **etw w~ tun** go on doing sth; **w~ nichts/niemand** nothing/no one else; **und so w~** and so on

weiter|e(r,s) *adj* further; **ohne w~es** just like that; (*leicht*) easily

weiter|erzählen *vt sep* go on with; (*w~sagen*) repeat. **w~fahren**† *vi sep* (*sein*) go on. **w~geben**† *vt sep* pass on. **w~hin** *adv* (*immer noch*) still; (*in Zukunft*) in future; (*außerdem*) furthermore; **etw w~hin tun** go on doing sth. **w~machen** *vi sep* (*haben*) carry on

W

weit|gehend *adj* extensive ● *adv* to a large extent. **w~sichtig** *adj* long-sighted; (*fig*) far-sighted. **W~sprung** *m* long jump. **w~verbreitet** *adj* = **w~ verbreitet**, *s.* **weit**

Weizen *m* **-s** wheat

welch *inv pron* what; **w~ ein(e)** what a. **w~e(r,s)** *pron* which; **um w~e Zeit?** at what time? ● *rel pron* which; (*Person*) who ● *indefinite pronoun* some; (*fragend*) any; **was für w~e?** what sort of?

Wellblech *nt* corrugated iron

Well|e *f* **-,-n** wave; (*Techn*) shaft. **W~enlänge** *f* wavelength. **W~enlinie** *f* wavy line. **W~enreiten** *nt* surfing. **W~ensittich** *m* **-s,-e** budgerigar. **w~ig** *adj* wavy.

Wellness *f* **-** mental and physical wellbeing

Welt *f* **-,-en** world; **auf der W~** in the world; **auf die** *od* **zur W~ kommen** be born. **W~all** *nt* universe. **w~berühmt** *adj* world-famous. **w~fremd** *adj* unworldly. **W~kugel** *f* globe. **w~lich** *adj* worldly; (*nicht geistlich*) secular

Weltmeister|(in) *m(f)* world champion. **W~schaft** *f* world championship

Weltraum *m* space. **W~fahrer** *m* astronaut

Weltrekord *m* world record

wem *pron* (*dat of* **wer**) to whom

wen *pron* (*acc of* **wer**) whom

Wende *f* **-,-n** change. **W~kreis** *m* (*Geog*) tropic

Wendeltreppe *f* spiral staircase

wenden[1] *vt* (*reg*) turn ● *vi* (*haben*) turn [round]

wenden[2]† (& *reg*) *vt* turn; **sich w~** turn; **sich an jdn w~** turn/(*schriftlich*) write to s.o.

Wend|epunkt *m* (*fig*) turning-point. **W~ung** *f* **-,-en** turn; (*Biegung*) bend; (*Veränderung*) change

wenig *pron* little; (*pl*) few; **so/zu w~** so/too little/(*pl*) few; **w~e** *pl* few ● *adv* little; (*kaum*) not much; **so w~ wie möglich** as little as possible. **w~er** *pron* less; (*pl*) fewer; **immer w~er** less and less ● *adv & conj* less. **w~ste(r,s)** least; **am w~sten** least [of all]. **w~stens** *adv* at least

wenn *conj* if; (*sobald*) when; **immer w~** whenever; **w~ nicht** *od* **außer w~** unless; **w~ auch** even though

wer *pron* who; (🅸: *jemand*) someone; (*fragend*) anyone

Werbe|agentur *f* advertising agency. **w~n†** *vt* recruit; attract (*Kunden, Besucher*) ● *vi* (*haben*) **w~n für** advertise; canvass for (*Partei*). **W~spot** *m* **-s,-s** commercial

Werbung *f* **-** advertising

werden†

● *intransitive verb (sein)*

····➤ (+ *adjective*) become; get; (*allmählich*) grow. **müde/alt/länger werden** become *or* get/grow tired/old/longer. **taub/blind/wahnsinnig werden** go deaf/blind/mad. **blass werden** become *or* turn pale. **krank werden** become *or* fall ill. **es wird warm/dunkel** it is getting warm/dark. **mir wurde schlecht/schwindlig** I began to feel sick/dizzy

····➤ (+ *noun*) become. **Arzt/Lehrer/Mutter werden** become a doctor/teacher/mother. **er will Lehrer werden** he wants to be a teacher. **was ist aus ihm geworden?** what has become of him?

····➤ **werden zu** become; turn into. **das Erlebnis wurde zu einem Albtraum** the experience became *or* turned into a nightmare. **zu Eis werden** turn into ice

● *auxiliary verb*

····➤ (*Zukunft*) will; shall. **er wird bald hier sein** he will *or* he'll soon be here. **wir werden sehen** we shall see. **es wird bald regnen** it's going to rain soon

····➤ (*Konjunktiv*) **würde(n)** would. **ich würde es kaufen, wenn ...** I would buy it if .... **würden Sie so nett sein?** would you be so kind?

····➤ (*beim Passiv; pp* **worden**) be. **geliebt/geboren werden** be loved/born. **du wirst gerufen** you are being called. **er wurde gebeten** he was asked. **es wurde gemunkelt** it was rumoured. **mir wurde gesagt, dass ...** I was told that .... **das Haus ist soeben/1995 renoviert worden** the house has just been renovated/was renovated in 1995

werfen† *vt* throw; cast (*Blick, Schatten*); **sich w~** (*Holz:*) warp

Werft *f* **-,-en** shipyard

Werk *nt* **-[e]s,-e** work; (*Fabrik*) works *sg*, factory; (*Trieb-*) mechanism. **W~en** *nt* **-s** (*Sch*) handicraft. **W~statt** *f* **-,¨en** workshop; (*Auto-*) garage. **W~tag** *m* weekday. **w~tags** *adv* on weekdays. **w~tätig** *adj* working

Werkzeug *nt* tool; (*coll*) tools *pl*. **W~leiste** *f* toolbar

Wermut *m* **-s** vermouth

wert *adj* **viel w~** worth a lot; **nichts w~ sein** be worthless; **jds w~ sein** be worthy of s.o. **W~** *m* **-[e]s,-e** value; (*Nenn-*) denomination; **im W~ von** worth. **w~en**

vt rate

Wert|gegenstand *m* object of value. **w~los** *adj* worthless. **W~minderung** *f* depreciation. **W~papier** *nt* (*Comm*) security. **W~sachen** *fpl* valuables. **w~voll** *adj* valuable

Wesen *nt* **-s,-** nature; (*Lebe-*) being; (*Mensch*) creature

wesentlich *adj* essential; (*grundlegend*) fundamental ● *adv* considerably, much

weshalb *adv* why

Wespe *f* **-,-n** wasp

wessen *pron* (*gen of* **wer**) whose

westdeutsch *adj* West German

Weste *f* **-,-n** waistcoat

Westen *m* **-s** west

Western *m* **-[s],-** western

Westfalen *nt* **-s** Westphalia

Westindien *nt* West Indies *pl*

west|lich *adj* western; (*Richtung*) westerly ● *adv* & *prep* (+ *gen*) **w~lich [von] der Stadt** [to the] west of the town. **w~wärts** *adv* westwards

weswegen *adv* why

Wettbewerb *m* **-s,-e** competition

Wette *f* **-,-n** bet; **um die W~ laufen** race (**mit jdm** s.o.)

wetten *vt/i* (*haben*) bet (**auf** + *acc* on); **mit jdm w~** have a bet with s.o.

Wetter *nt* **-s,-** weather; (*Un-*) storm. **W~bericht** *m* weather report. **W~vorhersage** *f* weather forecast. **W~warte** *f* **-,-n** meteorological station

Wett|kampf *m* contest. **W~kämpfer(in)** *m*(*f*) competitor. **W~lauf** *m* race. **W~rennen** *nt* race. **W~streit** *m* contest

Whisky *m* **-s** whisky

wichtig *adj* important; **w~ nehmen** take seriously. **W~keit** *f* **-** importance

Wicke *f* **-,-n** sweet pea

Wickel *m* **-s,-** compress

wickeln *vt* wind; (*ein-*) wrap; (*bandagieren*) bandage; **ein Kind frisch w~** change a baby

Widder *m* **-s,-** ram; (*Astrology*) Aries

wider *prep* (+ *acc*) against; (*entgegen*) contrary to; **w~ Willen** against one's will

widerlegen *vt insep* refute

wider|lich *adj* repulsive. **W~rede** *f* contradiction; **keine W~rede!** don't argue!

widerrufen† *vt/i insep* (*haben*) retract; revoke (*Befehl*)

Widersacher *m* **-s,-** adversary

widersetzen (sich) *vr insep* resist (**jdm/etw** s.o./sth)

widerspiegeln *vt sep* reflect

widersprechen† *vi insep* (*haben*) contradict (**jdm/etw** s.o./something)

Wider|spruch *m* contradiction; (*Protest*) protest. **w~sprüchlich** *adj* contradictory. **w~spruchslos** *adv* without protest

Widerstand *m* resistance; **W~ leisten** resist. **w~sfähig** *adj* resistant; (*Bot*) hardy

widerstehen† *vi insep* (*haben*) resist (**jdm/etw** s.o./sth); (*anwidern*) be repugnant (**jdm** to *s.o.*)

Widerstreben *nt* **-s** reluctance

widerwärtig *adj* disagreeable

Widerwill|e *m* aversion, repugnance. **w~ig** *adj* reluctant

widm|en *vt* dedicate (*dat* to); (*verwenden*) devote (*dat* to); **sich w~en** (+ *dat*) devote oneself to. **W~ung** *f* **-,-en** dedication

wie *adv* how; **wie viel** how much/(*pl*) many; **um wie viel Uhr?** at what time? **wie viele?** how many? **wie ist Ihr Name?** what is your name? **wie ist das Wetter?** what is the weather like? ● *conj* as; (*gleich wie*) like; (*sowie*) as well as; (*als*) when, as; **so gut wie** as good as; **nichts wie** nothing but

wieder *adv* again; **jdn/etw w∼ erkennen** recognize s.o./something; **etw w∼ verwenden/verwerten** reuse/recycle sth; **etw w∼ gutmachen** make up for (*Schaden*); redress (*Unrecht*); (*bezahlen*) pay for sth

Wiederaufbau *m* reconstruction

wieder|bekommen† *vt sep* get back. **W∼belebung** *f* - resuscitation. **w∼bringen**† *vt sep* bring back. **w∼erkennen**† *vt sep* * **w∼ erkennen**, *s.* **wieder**. **w∼geben**† *vt sep* give back, return; (*darstellen*) portray; (*ausdrücken, übersetzen*) render; (*zitieren*) quote. **W∼geburt** *f* reincarnation

Wiedergutmachung *f* - reparation; (*Entschädigung*) compensation

wiederherstellen *vt sep* reestablish; restore (*Gebäude*); restore to health (*Kranke*)

wiederhol|en *vt insep* repeat; (*Sch*) revise; **sich w∼en** recur; (*Person:*) repeat oneself. **w∼t** *adj* repeated. **W∼ung** *f* -,-en repetition; (*Sch*) revision

Wieder|hören *nt* **auf W∼hören!** goodbye! **W∼käuer** *m* -s,- ruminant. **W∼kehr** *f* - return; (*W∼holung*) recurrence. **w∼kommen**† *vi sep* (*sein*) come back

wiedersehen* *vt sep* **wieder sehen**, *s.* **sehen**. **W∼** *nt* -s,- reunion; **auf W∼!** goodbye!

wiedervereinig|en* *vt sep* **wieder vereinigen**, *s.* **vereinigen**. **W∼ung** *f* reunification

> **i** **Wiedervereinigung** The reunification of Germany officially took place on 3 October 1990, when the former German Democratic Republic (East Germany) was incorporated into the Federal Republic. It followed the collapse of Communism in 1989 and the fall of *die Mauer* (the Berlin Wall).

wieder|verwenden† *vt sep** **w∼ verwenden**, *s.* **wieder**. **w∼verwerten*** *vt sep* **w∼ verwerten**, *s.* **wieder**

Wiege *f* -,-n cradle

wiegen[1]† *vt/i* (*haben*) weigh

wiegen[2] *vt* (*reg*) rock. **W∼lied** *nt* lullaby

wiehern *vi* (*haben*) neigh

Wien *nt* -s Vienna. **W∼er** *adj* Viennese ● *m* -s,- Viennese ● *f* -,- ≈ frankfurter. **w∼erisch** *adj* Viennese

Wiese *f* -,-n meadow

Wiesel *nt* -s,- weasel

wieso *adv* why

wieviel* *pron* **wie viel**, *s.* **wie**. **w∼te(r,s)** *adj* which; **der W∼te ist heute?** what is the date today?

wieweit *adv* how far

wild *adj* wild; (*Stamm*) savage; **w∼er Streik** wildcat strike; **w∼ wachsen** grow wild. **W∼** *nt* -[e]s game; (*Rot-*) deer; (*Culin*) venison. **W∼e(r)** *m/f* savage

Wilder|er *m* -s,- poacher. **w∼n** *vt/i* (*haben*) poach

Wild|heger, W∼hüter *m* -s,- gamekeeper. **W∼leder** *nt* suede. **W∼nis** *f* - wilderness. **W∼schwein** *nt* wild boar. **W∼westfilm** *m* western

Wille *m* -ns will

Willenskraft *f* will-power
willig *adj* willing
willkommen *adj* welcome; **w~ heißen** welcome. **W~** *nt* **-s** welcome
wimmeln *vi* (*haben*) swarm
wimmern *vi* (*haben*) whimper
Wimpel *m* **-s,-** pennant
Wimper *f* **-,-n** [eye]lash; **W~n-tusche** *f* mascara
Wind *m* **-[e]s,-e** wind
Winde *f* **-,-n** (*Techn*) winch
Windel *f* **-,-n** nappy
winden† *vt* wind; make (*Kranz*); **in die Höhe w~** winch up; **sich w~** wind (**um** round); (*sich krümmen*) writhe
Wind|hund *m* greyhound. **w~ig** *adj* windy. **W~mühle** *f* windmill. **W~park** *m* wind farm. **W~pocken** *fpl* chickenpox *sg*. **W~schutzscheibe** *f* windscreen. **W~stille** *f* calm. **W~stoß** *m* gust of wind. **W~surfen** *nt* windsurfing
Windung *f* **-,-en** bend; (*Spirale*) spiral
Winkel *m* **-s,-** angle; (*Ecke*) corner. **W~messer** *m* **-s,-** protractor
winken *vi* (*haben*) wave
Winter *m* **-s,-** winter. **w~lich** *adj* wintry; (*Winter-*) winter **W~schlaf** *m* hibernation; **W~sport** *m* winter sports *pl*
Winzer *m* **-s,-** winegrower
winzig *adj* tiny, minute
Wipfel *m* **-s,-** [tree-]top
Wippe *f* **-,-n** see-saw
wir *pron* **we; wir sind es** it's us
Wirbel *m* **-s,-** eddy; (*Drehung*) whirl; (*Trommel-*) roll; (*Anat*) vertebra; (*Haar-*) crown; (*Aufsehen*) fuss. **w~n** *vt/i* (*sein/haben*) whirl. **W~säule** *f* spine. **W~sturm** *m* cyclone. **W~tier** *nt* vertebrate. **W~wind** *m* whirlwind
wird *s.* **werden**
wirken *vi* (*haben*) have an effect (**auf** + *acc* on); (*zur Geltung kommen*) be effective; (*tätig sein*) work; (*scheinen*) seem ●*vt* (*Textiles*) knit
wirklich *adj* real. **W~keit** *f* **-,-en** reality
wirksam *adj* effective
Wirkung *f* **-,-en** effect. **w~slos** *adj* ineffective. **w~svoll** *adj* effective
wirr *adj* tangled; (*Haar*) tousled; (*verwirrt, verworren*) confused
Wirt *m* **-[e]s,-e** landlord. **W~in** *f* **-,-nen** landlady
Wirtschaft *f* **-,-en** economy; (*Gast-*) restaurant; (*Kneipe*) pub. **w~en** *vi* (*haben*) manage one's finances. **w~lich** *adj* economic; (*sparsam*) economical. **W~sflüchtling** *m* economic refugee. **W~sgeld** *nt* housekeeping [money]. **W~sprüfer** *m* auditor
Wirtshaus *nt* inn; (*Kneipe*) pub
wischen *vt/i* (*haben*) wipe; wash (*Fußboden*)
wissen† *vt/i* (*haben*) know; **weißt du noch?** do you remember? **nichts w~ wollen von** not want anything to do with. **W~** *nt* **-s** knowledge; **meines W~s** to my knowledge
Wissenschaft *f* **-,-en** science. **W~ler** *m* **-s,-** academic; (*Natur-*) scientist. **w~lich** *adj* academic; scientific
wissenswert *adj* worth knowing
witter|n *vt* scent; (*ahnen*) sense. **W~ung** *f* **-** scent; (*Wetter*) weather
Witwe *f* **-,-n** widow. **W~r** *m* **-s,-** widower
Witz *m* **-es,-e** joke; (*Geist*) wit. **W~bold** *m* **-[e]s,-e** joker. **w~ig** *adj* funny; witty

wo *adv* where; (*als*) when; (*irgendwo*) somewhere; **wo immer** wherever ●*conj* seeing that; (*obwohl*) although; (*wenn*) if

woanders *adv* somewhere else

wobei *adv* how; (*relativ*) during the course of which

Woche *f* **-,-n** week. **W~nende** *nt* weekend. **W~nkarte** *f* weekly ticket. **w~nlang** *adv* for weeks. **W~ntag** *m* day of the week; (*Werktag*) weekday. **w~tags** *adv* on weekdays

wöchentlich *adj & adv* weekly

Wodka *m* **-s** vodka

wofür *adv* what ... for; (*relativ*) for which

Woge *f* **-,-n** wave

woher *adv* where from; **woher weißt du das?** how do you know that? **wohin** *adv* where [to]; **wohin gehst du?** where are you going?

wohl *adv* well; (*vermutlich*) probably; (*etwa*) about; (*zwar*) perhaps; **w~ kaum** hardly; **sich w~ fühlen** feel well/(*behaglich*) comfortable; **jdm w~ tun** do s.o. good. **W~** *nt* **-[e]s** welfare, well-being; **zum W~** (+ *gen*) for the good of; **zum W~!** cheers!

Wohl|befinden *nt* well-being. **W~behagen** *nt* feeling of well-being. **W~ergehen** *nt* **-s** welfare. **w~erzogen** *adj* well brought-up

Wohlfahrt *f* - welfare. **W~sstaat** *m* Welfare State

wohl|habend *adj* prosperous, well-to-do. **w~ig** *adj* comfortable. **w~schmeckend** *adj* tasty

Wohlstand *m* prosperity. **W~sgesellschaft** *f* affluent society

Wohltat *f* [act of] kindness; (*Annehmlichkeit*) treat; (*Genuss*) bliss

Wohltät|er *m* benefactor. **w~ig** *adj* charitable

wohl|tuend *adj* agreeable. **w~tun*** *vi sep* (*haben*) **w~ tun**, *s.* **wohl**

Wohlwollen *nt* **-s** goodwill; (*Gunst*) favour. **w~d** *adj* benevolent

Wohn|block *m* block of flats. **w~en** *vi* (*haben*) live; (*vorübergehend*) stay. **W~gegend** *f* residential area. **w~haft** *adj* resident. **W~haus** *nt* house. **W~heim** *nt* hostel; (*Alten-*) home. **w~lich** *adj* comfortable. **W~mobil** *nt* **-s,-e** camper. **W~ort** *m* place of residence. **W~sitz** *m* place of residence

Wohnung *f* **-,-en** flat; (*Unterkunft*) accommodation. **W~snot** *f* housing shortage

Wohn|wagen *m* caravan. **W~zimmer** *nt* living-room

wölb|en *vt* curve; arch (*Rücken*). **W~ung** *f* **-,-en** curve; (*Architecture*) vault

Wolf *m* **-[e]s,⸚e** wolf; (*Fleisch-*) mincer; (*Reiß-*) shredder

Wolk|e *f* **-,-n** cloud. **W~enbruch** *m* cloudburst. **W~enkratzer** *m* skyscraper. **w~enlos** *adj* cloudless. **w~ig** *adj* cloudy

Woll|decke *f* blanket. **W~e** *f* **-,-n** wool

wollen†[1]

●*auxiliary verb*

····➤(*den Wunsch haben*) want to. **ich will nach Hause gehen** I want to go home. **ich wollte Sie fragen, ob ...** I wanted to ask you if ...

····➤(*im Begriff sein*) be about to. **wir wollten gerade gehen** we were just about to go

····➤(*sich in der gewünschten Weise verhalten*) **will nicht** refuses to.

der Motor will nicht anspringen the engine won't start

● *intransitive verb*

····➤ want to. **ob du willst oder nicht** whether you want to or not. **ganz wie du willst** just as you like

····➤ ([!]: *irgendwohin zu gehen wünschen*) **ich will nach Hause** I want to go home. **zu wem wollen Sie?** who[m] do you want to see?

····➤ ([!]: *funktionieren*) **will nicht** won't go. **meine Beine wollen nicht mehr** my legs are giving up [!]

● *transitive verb*

····➤ want; (*beabsichtigen*) intend. **er will nicht, dass du ihm hilfst** he does not want you to help him. **das habe ich nicht gewollt** I never intended *or* meant that to happen

Wollsachen *fpl* woollens

womit *adv* what ... with; (*relativ*) with which. **wonach** *adv* what ... after/(*suchen*) for/(*riechen*) of; (*relativ*) after/for/of which

woran *adv* what ... on/(*denken, sterben*) of; (*relativ*) on/of which; **woran hast du ihn erkannt?** how did you recognize him? **worauf** *adv* what on .../(*warten*) for; (*relativ*) on/for which; (*woraufhin*) whereupon. **woraus** *adv* what ... from; (*relativ*) from which

Wort *nt* **-[e]s,⸚er & -e** word; **jdm ins W~ fallen** interrupt s.o.

Wörterbuch *nt* dictionary

Wort|führer *m* spokesman. **w~getreu** *adj & adv* word-for-word. **w~karg** *adj* taciturn. **W~laut** *m* wording

wörtlich *adj* literal; (*wortgetreu*) word-for-word

wort|los *adj* silent ● *adv* without a word. **W~schatz** *m* vocabulary. **W~spiel** *nt* pun, play on words

worüber *adv* what ... over/(*lachen, sprechen*) about; (*relativ*) over/about which. **worum** *adv* what ... round/(*bitten, kämpfen*) for; (*relativ*) round/for which; **worum geht es?** what is it about? **wovon** *adv* what ... from/(*sprechen*) about; (*relativ*) from/about which. **wovor** *adv* what ... in front of; (*sich fürchten*) what of; (*relativ*) in front of which; of which. **wozu** *adv* what ... to/(*brauchen, benutzen*) for; (*relativ*) to/for which; **wozu?** what for?

Wrack *nt* **-s,-s** wreck

wringen† *vt* wring

Wucher|preis *m* extortionate price. **W~ung** *f* **-,-en** growth

Wuchs *m* **-es** growth; (*Gestalt*) stature

Wucht *f* **-** force

wühlen *vi* (*haben*) rummage; (*in der Erde*) burrow ● *vt* dig

Wulst *m* **-[e]s,⸚e** bulge; (*Fett-*) roll

wund *adj* sore; **w~ reiben** chafe; **sich w~ liegen** get bedsores. **W~brand** *m* gangrene

Wunde *f* **-,-n** wound

Wunder *nt* **-s,-** wonder, marvel; (*übernatürliches*) miracle; **kein W~!** no wonder! **w~bar** *adj* miraculous; (*herrlich*) wonderful. **W~kind** *nt* infant prodigy. **w~n** *vt* surprise; **sich w~n** be surprised (**über** + *acc* at). **w~schön** *adj* beautiful

Wundstarrkrampf *m* tetanus

Wunsch *m* **-[e]s,⸚e** wish; (*Verlangen*) desire; (*Bitte*) request

wünschen *vt* want; **sich** (*dat*) **etw w~** want sth; (*bitten um*) ask for sth; **jdm Glück/gute Nacht w~** wish s.o. luck/good night; **Sie w~?** can I help you? **w~swert** *adj* desirable

Wunschkonzert *nt* musical request programme

wurde, **würde** *s.* **werden**

Würde *f* **-,-n** dignity; (*Ehrenrang*) honour. **w∼los** *adj* undignified. **W∼nträger** *m* dignitary. **w∼voll** *adj* dignified ●*adv* with dignity

würdig *adj* dignified; (*wert*) worthy

Wurf *m* **-[e]s,⸚e** throw; (*Junge*) litter

Würfel *m* **-s,-** cube; (*Spiel-*) dice; (*Zucker-*) lump. **w∼n** *vi* (*haben*) throw the dice; **w∼n um** play dice for ●*vt* throw; (*in Würfel schneiden*) dice. **W∼zucker** *m* cube sugar

würgen *vt* choke ●*vi* (*haben*) retch; choke (**an** + *dat* on)

Wurm *m* **-[e]s,⸚er** worm; (*Made*) maggot. **w∼en** *vi* (*haben*) **jdn w∼en** [I] rankle [with s.o.]

Wurst *f* **-,⸚e** sausage; **das ist mir W∼** [I] I couldn't care less

Würze *f* **-,-n** spice; (*Aroma*) aroma

Wurzel *f* **-,-n** root; **W∼n schlagen** take root. **w∼n** *vi* (*haben*) root

würz|en *vt* season. **w∼ig** *adj* tasty; (*aromatisch*) aromatic; (*pikant*) spicy

wüst *adj* chaotic; (*wirr*) tangled; (*öde*) desolate; (*wild*) wild; (*schlimm*) terrible

Wüste *f* **-,-n** desert

Wut *f* **-** rage, fury. **W∼anfall** *m* fit of rage

wüten *vi* (*haben*) rage. **w∼d** *adj* furious; **w∼d machen** infuriate

x /ɪks/ *inv adj* (*Math*) x; [I] umpteen. **X-Beine** *ntpl* knock-knees. **x-beinig**, **X-beinig** *adj* knock-kneed. **x-beliebig** *adj* [I] any. **x-mal** *adv* [I] umpteen times

Yoga /ˈjo:ga/ *m & nt* **-[s]** yoga

Zz

Zack|e *f* **-,-n** point; (*Berg-*) peak; (*Gabel-*) prong. **z∼ig** *adj* jagged; (*gezackt*) serrated

zaghaft *adj* timid; (*zögernd*) tentative

zäh *adj* tough; (*hartnäckig*) tenacious. **z∼flüssig** *adj* viscous; (*Verkehr*) slow-moving. **Z∼igkeit** *f* **-** toughness; tenacity

Zahl *f* **-,-en** number; (*Ziffer, Betrag*) figure

zahlen *vt/i* (*haben*) pay; (*bezahlen*) pay for; **bitte z∼!** the bill please!

zählen *vi* (*haben*) count; **z∼ zu** (*fig*) be one/(*pl*) some of ●*vt* count; **z∼ zu** add to; (*fig*) count among

zahlenmäßig *adj* numerical

Zähler *m* **-s,-** meter
Zahl|grenze *f* fare-stage. **Z~karte** *f* paying-in slip. **z~los** *adj* countless. **z~reich** *adj* numerous; (*Anzahl, Gruppe*) large ● *adv* in large numbers. **Z~ung** *f* **-,-en** payment; **in Z~ung nehmen** take in part-exchange
Zählung *f* **-,-en** count
Zahlwort *nt* (*pl* **-wörter**) numeral
zahm *adj* tame
zähmen *vt* tame; (*fig*) restrain
Zahn *m* **-[e]s,¨e** tooth; (*am Zahnrad*) cog. **Z~arzt** *m*, **Z~ärztin** *f* dentist. **Z~belag** *m* plaque. **Z~bürste** *f* toothbrush. **Z~fleisch** *nt* gums *pl*. **z~los** *adj* toothless. **Z~pasta** *f* **-,-en** toothpaste. **Z~rad** *nt* cog-wheel. **Z~schmelz** *m* enamel. **Z~schmerzen** *mpl* toothache *sg*. **Z~spange** *f* brace. **Z~stein** *m* tartar. **Z~stocher** *m* **-s,-** toothpick
Zange *f* **-,-n** pliers *pl*; (*Kneif-*) pincers *pl*; (*Kohlen-, Zucker-*) tongs *pl*; (*Geburts-*) forceps *pl*
Zank *m* **-[e]s** squabble. **z~en** *vr* **sich z~en** squabble
Zäpfchen *nt* **-s,-** (*Anat*) uvula; (*Med*) suppository
zapfen *vt* tap, draw. **Z~streich** *m* (*Mil*) tattoo
Zapf|hahn *m* tap. **Z~säule** *f* petrol-pump
zappeln *vi* (*haben*) wriggle; (*Kind:*) fidget
zart *adj* delicate; (*weich, zärtlich*) tender; (*sanft*) gentle. **Z~gefühl** *nt* tact
zärtlich *adj* tender; (*liebevoll*) loving. **Z~keit** *f* **-,-en** tenderness; (*Liebkosung*) caress
Zauber *m* **-s** magic; (*Bann*) spell. **Z~er** *m* **-s,-** magician. **z~haft** *adj* enchanting. **Z~künstler** *m* conjuror. **z~n** *vi* (*haben*) do magic; (*Zaubertricks ausführen*) do conjuring tricks ● *vt* produce as if by magic. **Z~stab** *m* magic wand. **Z~trick** *m* conjuring trick
Zaum *m* **-[e]s,Zäume** bridle
Zaun *m* **-[e]s,Zäune** fence
z.B. *abbr* (**zum Beispiel**) e.g.
Zebra *nt* **-s,-s** zebra. **Z~streifen** *m* zebra crossing
Zeche *f* **-,-n** bill; (*Bergwerk*) pit
zechen *vi* (*haben*) [!] drink
Zeder *f* **-,-n** cedar
Zeh *m* **-[e]s,-en** toe. **Z~e** *f* **-,-n** toe; (*Knoblauch-*) clove
zehn *inv adj*, **Z~** *f* **-,-en** ten. **z~te(r,s)** *adj* tenth. **Z~tel** *nt* **-s,-** tenth
Zeichen *nt* **-s,-** sign; (*Signal*) signal. **Z~setzung** *f* **-** punctuation. **Z~trickfilm** *m* cartoon
zeichn|en *vt/i* (*haben*) draw; (*kenn-*) mark; (*unter-*) sign. **Z~ung** *f* **-,-en** drawing
Zeige|finger *m* index finger. **z~n** *vt* show; **sich z~n** appear; (*sich herausstellen*) become clear ● *vi* (*haben*) point (**auf** + *acc* to). **Z~r** *m* **-s,-** pointer; (*Uhr-*) hand
Zeile *f* **-,-n** line; (*Reihe*) row
Zeit *f* **-,-en** time; **sich** (*dat*) **Z~ lassen** take one's time; **es hat Z~** theres's no hurry; **mit der Z~** in time; **in nächster Z~** in the near future; **zur Z~** (*rechtzeitig*) in time; *(*derzeit*) s. **zurzeit**; **eine Z~ lang** for a time or while
Zeit|alter *nt* age, era. **z~gemäß** *adj* modern, up-to-date. **Z~genosse** *m*, **Z~genossin** *f* contemporary. **z~genössisch** *adj* contemporary. **z~ig** *adj* & *adv* early
zeitlich *adj* (*Dauer*) in time; (*Folge*) chronological. ● *adv* **z~ begrenzt** for a limited time

zeit|los *adj* timeless. **Z~lupe** *f* slow motion. **Z~punkt** *m* time. **z~raubend** *adj* time-consuming. **Z~raum** *m* period. **Z~schrift** *f* magazine, periodical

Zeitung *f* -,-en newspaper. **Z~spapier** *nt* newspaper

Zeit|verschwendung *f* waste of time. **Z~vertreib** *m* pastime. **z~weise** *adv* at times. **Z~wort** *nt* (*pl* **-wörter**) verb. **Z~zünder** *m* time fuse

Zelle *f* -,-n cell; (*Telefon-*) box

Zelt *nt* -[e]s,-e tent; (*Fest-*) marquee. **z~en** *vi* (*haben*) camp. **Z~en** *nt* -s camping. **Z~plane** *f* tarpaulin. **Z~platz** *m* campsite

Zement *m* -[e]s cement

zen|sieren *vt* (*Sch*) mark; censor (*Presse, Film*). **Z~sur** *f* -,-en (*Sch*) mark; (*Presse-*) censorship

Zentimeter *m* & *nt* centimetre. **Z~maß** *nt* tape-measure

Zentner *m* -s,- [metric] hundredweight (*50 kg*)

zentral *adj* central. **Z~e** *f* -,-n central office; (*Partei-*) headquarters *pl*; (*Teleph*) exchange. **Z~heizung** *f* central heating

Zentrum *nt* -s,-tren centre

zerbrech|en† *vt/i* (*sein*) break. **z~lich** *adj* fragile

zerdrücken *vt* crush

Zeremonie *f* -,-n ceremony

Zerfall *m* disintegration; (*Verfall*) decay. **z~en**† *vi* (*sein*) disintegrate; (*verfallen*) decay

zergehen† *vi* (*sein*) melt; (*sich auflösen*) dissolve

zerkleinern *vt* chop/(*schneiden*) cut up; (*mahlen*) grind

zerknüllen *vt* crumple [up]

zerkratzen *vt* scratch

zerlassen† *vt* melt

zerlegen *vt* take to pieces, dismantle; (*zerschneiden*) cut up; (*tranchieren*) carve

zerlumpt *adj* ragged

zermalmen *vt* crush

zermürben *vt* (*fig*) wear down

zerplatzen *vi* (*sein*) burst

zerquetschen *vt* squash; crush

Zerrbild *nt* caricature

zerreißen† *vt* tear; (*in Stücke*) tear up; break (*Faden, Seil*) ● *vi* (*sein*) tear; break

zerren *vt* drag; pull (*Muskel*) ● *vi* (*haben*) pull (**an** + *dat* at)

zerrissen *adj* torn

zerrütten *vt* ruin, wreck; shatter (*Nerven*)

zerschlagen† *vt* smash; smash up (*Möbel*); **sich z~** (*fig*) fall through; (*Hoffnung:*) be dashed

zerschmettern *vt/i* (*sein*) smash

zerschneiden† *vt* cut; (*in Stücke*) cut up

zersplittern *vi* (*sein*) splinter; (*Glas:*) shatter ● *vt* shatter

zerspringen† *vi* (*sein*) shatter; (*bersten*) burst

Zerstäuber *m* -s,- atomizer

zerstör|en *vt* destroy; (*zunichte machen*) wreck. **Z~er** *m* -s,- destroyer. **Z~ung** *f* destruction

zerstreu|en *vt* scatter; disperse (*Menge*); dispel (*Zweifel*); **sich z~en** disperse; (*sich unterhalten*) amuse oneself. **z~t** *adj* absent-minded

Zertifikat *nt* -[e]s,-e certificate

zertrümmern *vt* smash [up]; wreck (*Gebäude, Stadt*)

Zettel *m* -s,- piece of paper; (*Notiz*) note; (*Bekanntmachung*) notice

Zeug *nt* -s ◻ stuff; (*Sachen*) things *pl*; (*Ausrüstung*) gear; **dummes Z~** nonsense

Zeuge *m* -n,-n witness. **z~n** *vi*

(*haben*) testify; **z~n von** (*fig*) show ● *vt* father. **Z~naussage** *f* testimony. **Z~nstand** *m* witness box

Zeugin *f* -,-nen witness

Zeugnis *nt* **-ses,-se** certificate; (*Sch*) report; (*Referenz*) reference; (*fig: Beweis*) evidence

Zickzack *m* **-[e]s,-e** zigzag

Ziege *f* -,-n goat

Ziegel *m* **-s,-** brick; (*Dach-*) tile. **Z~stein** *m* brick

ziehen† *vt* pull; (*sanfter; zücken; zeichnen*) draw; (*heraus-*) pull out; extract (*Zahn*); raise (*Hut*); put on (*Bremse*); move (*Schachfigur*); (*dehnen*) stretch; make (*Grimasse, Scheitel*); (*züchten*) breed; grow (*Rosen*); **nach sich z~** (*fig*) entail ● *vr* **sich z~** (*sich erstrecken*) run; (*sich verziehen*) warp ● *vi* (*haben*) pull (**an** + *dat* on/at); (*Tee, Ofen:*) draw; (*Culin*) simmer; **es zieht** there is a draught; **solche Filme z~ nicht mehr** films like that are no longer popular ● *vi* (*sein*) (*um-*) move (**nach** to); (*Menge:*) march; (*Vögel:*) migrate; (*Wolken, Nebel:*) drift

Ziehharmonika *f* accordion

Ziehung *f* -,-en draw

Ziel *nt* **-[e]s,-e** destination; (*Sport*) finish; (*Z~scheibe & Mil*) target; (*Zweck*) aim, goal. **z~bewusst** *adj* purposeful. **z~en** *vi* (*haben*) aim (**auf** + *acc* at). **z~los** *adj* aimless. **Z~scheibe** *f* target

ziemlich *adj* ⓘ fair ● *adv* rather, fairly

Zier|de *f* -,-n ornament. **z~en** *vt* adorn

zierlich *adj* dainty

Ziffer *f* -,-n figure, digit; (*Zahlzeichen*) numeral. **Z~blatt** *nt* dial

Zigarette *f* -,-n cigarette

Zigarre *f* -,-n cigar

Zigeuner(in) *m* **-s,-** (*f* **-,-nen**) gypsy

Zimmer *nt* **-s,-** room. **Z~mädchen** *nt* chambermaid. **Z~mann** *m* (*pl* **-leute**) carpenter. **Z~nachweis** *m* accommodation bureau. **Z~pflanze** *f* house plant

Zimt *m* **-[e]s** cinnamon

Zink *nt* **-s** zinc

Zinn *m* **-s** tin; (*Gefäße*) pewter

Zins|en *mpl* interest *sg*; **Z~en tragen** earn interest. **Z~eszins** *m* **-es,-en** compound interest. **Z~fuß, Z~satz** *m* interest rate

Zipfel *m* **-s,-** corner; (*Spitze*) point

zirka *adv* about

Zirkel *m* **-s,-** [pair of] compasses *pl*; (*Gruppe*) circle

Zirkul|ation /-ˈtsi̯oːn/ *f* **-** circulation. **z~ieren** *vi* (*sein*) circulate

Zirkus *m* **-,-se** circus

zirpen *vi* (*haben*) chirp

zischen *vi* (*haben*) hiss; (*Fett:*) sizzle ● *vt* hiss

Zit|at *nt* **-[e]s,-e** quotation. **z~ieren** *vt/i* (*haben*) quote

Zitr|onat *nt* **-[e]s** candied lemon-peel. **Z~one** *f* -,-n lemon

zittern *vi* (*haben*) tremble; (*vor Kälte*) shiver; (*beben*) shake

zittrig *adj* shaky

Zitze *f* -,-n teat

zivil *adj* civilian; (*Ehe, Recht*) civil. **Z~** *nt* **-s** civilian clothes *pl*. **Z~dienst** *m* community service

Zivili|sation /-ˈtsi̯oːn/ *f* **-,-en** civilization. **z~sieren** *vt* civilize. **z~siert** *adj* civilized ● *adv* in a civilized manner

Zivilist *m* **-en,-en** civilian

zögern *vi* (*haben*) hesitate. **Z~** *nt* **-s** hesitation. **z~d** *adj* hesitant

Zoll[1] *m* **-[e]s,-** inch

Zoll[2] *m* **-[e]s,⸚e** [customs] duty; (*Behörde*) customs *pl*. **Z~abferti-**

gung *f* customs clearance. **Z～beamte(r)** *m* customs officer. **z～frei** *adj & adv* duty-free. **Z～kontrolle** *f* customs check

Zone *f* **-,-n** zone

Zoo *m* **-s,-s** zoo

zoologisch *adj* zoological

Zopf *m* **-[e]s,¨-e** plait

Zorn *m* **-[e]s** anger. **z～ig** *adj* angry

zu

● *preposition (+ dative)*

! Note that **zu dem** can become **zum** and **zu der, zur**

····➤ (*Richtung*) to; (*bei Beruf*) into. **wir gehen zur Schule** we are going to school. **ich muss zum Arzt** I must go to the doctor's. **zu ... hin** towards. **er geht zum Theater/Militär** he is going into the theatre/army

····➤ (*zusammen mit*) with. **zu dem Käse gab es Wein** there was wine with the cheese. **zu etw passen** go with sth

····➤ (*räumlich; zeitlich*) at. **zu Hause** at home. **zu ihren Füßen** at her feet. **zu Ostern** at Easter. **zur Zeit** (+ *gen*) at the time of

····➤ (*preislich*) at; for. **zum halben Preis** at half price. **das Stück zu zwei Euro** at *or* for two euros each. **eine Marke zu 60 Cent** a 60-cent stamp

····➤ (*Zweck, Anlass*) for. **zu diesem Zweck** for this purpose. **zum Spaß** for fun. **zum Lesen** for reading. **zum Geburtstag bekam ich** ... for my birthday I got ... . **zum ersten Mal** for the first time

····➤ (*Art und Weise*) **zu meinem Erstaunen/Entsetzen** to my surprise/horror. **zu Fuß/Pferde** on foot/horseback. **zu Dutzenden** by the dozen. **wir waren zu dritt/viert** there were three/four of us

····➤ (*Zahlenverhältnis*) to. **es steht 5 zu 3** the score is 5–3

····➤ (*Ziel, Ergebnis*) into. **zu etw werden** turn into sth

····➤ (*gegenüber*) to; towards. **freundlich/hässlich zu jdm sein** be friendly/nasty to s.o.

····➤ (*über*) on; about. **sich zu etw äußern** to comment on sth

● *adverb*

····➤ (*allzu*) too. **zu groß/viel/weit** too big/much/far

····➤ (*Richtung*) towards. **nach dem Fluss zu** towards the river

····➤ (*geschlossen*) closed; (*an Schalter, Hahn*) off. **Augen zu!** close your eyes! **Tür zu!** shut the door!

● *conjunction*

····➤ to. **etwas zu essen** something to eat. **nicht zu glauben** unbelievable. **zu erörternde Probleme** problems to be discussed

zuallererst *adv* first of all. **z～letzt** *adv* last of all

Zubehör *nt* **-s** accessories *pl*

zubereiten *vt sep* prepare. **Z～ung** *f* **-** preparation; (*in Rezept*) method

zubinden† *vt sep* tie [up]

zubringen† *vt sep* spend. **Z～er** *m* **-s,-** access road; (*Bus*) shuttle

Zucchini /tsu'ki:ni/ *pl* courgettes

Zucht *f* **-,-en** breeding; (*Pflanzen-*) cultivation; (*Art, Rasse*) breed; (*von Pflanzen*) strain; (*Z～farm*) farm; (*Pferde-*) stud

züchtlen *vt* breed; cultivate, grow (*Rosen*). **Z~er** *m* **-s,-** breeder; grower

Zuchthaus *nt* prison

Züchtung *f* **-,-en** breeding; (*Pflanzen-*) cultivation; (*Art, Rasse*) breed; (*von Pflanzen*) strain

zucken *vi* (*haben*) twitch; (*sich z~d bewegen*) jerk; (*Blitz:*) flash; (*Flamme:*) flicker ● *vt* **die Achseln z~** shrug one's shoulders

Zucker *m* **-s** sugar. **Z~dose** *f* sugar basin. **Z~guss** *m* icing. **z~krank** *adj* diabetic. **Z~krankheit** *f* diabetes. **z~n** *vt* sugar. **Z~rohr** *nt* sugar cane. **Z~rübe** *f* sugar beet. **Z~watte** *f* candyfloss

zudecken *vt sep* cover up; (*im Bett*) tuck up; cover (*Topf*)

zudem *adv* moreover

zudrehen *vt sep* turn off

zueinander *adv* to one another; **z~ passen** go together; **z~ halten** (*fig*) stick together

zuerkennen† *vt sep* award (*dat* to)

zuerst *adv* first; (*anfangs*) at first

zufahr|en† *vi sep* (*sein*) **z~en auf** (+ *acc*) drive towards. **Z~t** *f* access; (*Einfahrt*) drive

Zufall *m* chance; (*Zusammentreffen*) coincidence; **durch Z~** by chance/coincidence. **z~en**† *vi sep* (*sein*) close, shut; **jdm z~en** (*Aufgabe:*) fall/(*Erbe:*) go to s.o.

zufällig *adj* chance, accidental ● *adv* by chance

Zuflucht *f* refuge; (*Schutz*) shelter

zufolge *prep* (+ *dat*) according to

zufrieden *adj* contented; (*befriedigt*) satisfied; **sich z~ geben** be satisfied; **jdn z~ lassen** leave s.o. in peace; **jdn z~ stellen** satisfy s.o.; **z~ stellend** satisfactory. **Z~heit** *f* - contentment; satisfaction

zufrieren† *vi sep* (*sein*) freeze over

zufügen *vt sep* inflict (*dat* on); do (*Unrecht*) (*dat* to)

Zufuhr *f* - supply

Zug *m* **-[e]s,⸚e** train; (*Kolonne*) column; (*Um-*) procession; (*Mil*) platoon; (*Vogelschar*) flock; (*Ziehen, Zugkraft*) pull; (*Wandern, Ziehen*) migration; (*Schluck, Luft-*) draught; (*Atem-*) breath; (*beim Rauchen*) puff; (*Schach-*) move; (*beim Schwimmen, Rudern*) stroke; (*Gesichts-*) feature; (*Wesens-*) trait

Zugabe *f* (*Geschenk*) [free] gift; (*Mus*) encore

Zugang *m* access

zugänglich *adj* accessible; (*Mensch:*) approachable

Zugbrücke *f* drawbridge

zugeben† *vt sep* add; (*gestehen*) admit; (*erlauben*) allow

zugehen† *vi sep* (*sein*) close; **jdm z~** be sent to s.o.; **z~ auf** (+ *acc*) go towards; **dem Ende z~** draw to a close; (*Vorräte:*) run low; **auf der Party ging es lebhaft zu** the party was pretty lively

Zugehörigkeit *f* - membership

Zügel *m* **-s,-** rein

zugelassen *adj* registered

zügel|los *adj* unrestrained. **z~n** *vt* rein in; (*fig*) curb

Zuge|ständnis *nt* concession. **z~stehen**† *vt sep* grant

zügig *adj* quick

Zugkraft *f* pull; (*fig*) attraction

zugleich *adv* at the same time

Zugluft *f* draught

zugreifen† *vi sep* (*haben*) grab it/them; (*bei Tisch*) help oneself; (*bei Angebot*) jump at it; (*helfen*) lend a hand

zugrunde *adv* **z~ richten** destroy; **z~ gehen** be destroyed; (*sterben*) die; **z~ liegen** form the basis (*dat* of)

zugunsten *prep* (+ *gen*) in favour of; (*Sammlung*) in aid of

zugute *adv* **jdm/etw z~ kommen** benefit s.o./something

Zugvogel *m* migratory bird

zuhalten† *v sep* ●*vt* keep closed; (*bedecken*) cover; **sich** (*dat*) **die Nase z~** hold one's nose

Zuhälter *m* **-s,-** pimp

zuhause *adv* = **zu Hause**, *s.* **Haus**. **Z~** *nt* **-s,-** home

zuhör|en *vi sep* (*haben*) listen (*dat* to). **Z~er(in)** *m*(*f*) listener

zujubeln *vi sep* (*haben*) **jdm z~** cheer s.o.

zukleben *vt sep* seal

zuknöpfen *vt sep* button up

zukommen† *vi sep* (*sein*) **z~ auf** (+ *acc*) come towards; (*sich nähern*) approach; **z~ lassen** send (**jdm** s.o.); devote (*Pflege*) (*dat* to); **jdm z~** be s.o.'s right

Zukunft *f* - future. **zukünftig** *adj* future ●*adv* in future

zulächeln *vi sep* (*haben*) smile (*dat* at)

zulangen *vi sep* (*haben*) help oneself

zulassen† *vt sep* allow, permit; (*teilnehmen lassen*) admit; (*Admin*) license, register; (*geschlossen lassen*) leave closed; leave unopened (*Brief*)

zulässig *adj* permissible

Zulassung *f* **-,-en** admission; registration; (*Lizenz*) licence

zuleide *adv* **jdm etwas z~ tun** hurt s.o.

zuletzt *adv* last; (*schließlich*) in the end

zuliebe *adv* **jdm/etw z~** for the sake of someone/something

zum *prep* = **zu dem; zum Spaß** for fun; **etw zum Lesen** sth to read

zumachen *v sep* ●*vt* close, shut; do up (*Jacke*); seal (*Umschlag*); turn off (*Hahn*); (*stilllegen*) close down ●*vi* (*haben*) close, shut; (*stillgelegt werden*) close down

zumal *adv* especially ●*conj* especially since

zumindest *adv* at least

zumutbar *adj* reasonable

zumute *adv* **mir ist nicht danach z~** I don't feel like it

zumut|en *vt sep* **jdm etw z~en** ask *or* expect sth of s.o.; **sich** (*dat*) **zu viel z~en** overdo things. **Z~ung** *f* - imposition

zunächst *adv* first [of all]; (*anfangs*) at first; (*vorläufig*) for the moment ●*prep* (+ *dat*) nearest to

Zunahme *f* **-,-n** increase

Zuname *m* surname

zünd|en *vt/i* (*haben*) ignite. **Z~er** *m* **-s,-** detonator, fuse. **Z~holz** *nt* match. **Z~kerze** *f* sparking-plug. **Z~schlüssel** *m* ignition key. **Z~schnur** *f* fuse. **Z~ung** *f* **-,-en** ignition

zunehmen† *vi sep* (*haben*) increase (**an** + *dat* in); (*Mond:*) wax; (*an Gewicht*) put on weight. **z~d** *adj* increasing

Zuneigung *f* - affection

Zunft *f* **-,¨e** guild

Zunge *f* **-,-n** tongue. **Z~nbrecher** *m* tongue-twister

zunutze *adj* **sich** (*dat*) **etw z~ machen** make use of sth; (*ausnutzen*) take advantage of sth

zuoberst *adv* right at the top

zuordnen *vt sep* assign (*dat* to)

zupfen *vt/i* (*haben*) pluck (**an** + *dat* at); pull out (*Unkraut*)

zur *prep* = **zu der; zur Schule** to

school; **zur Zeit** at present

zurate *adv* **z~ ziehen** consult

> **Zürcher Festspiele** The Zurich festival in Switzerland is an annual celebration of classical music, opera, dance and art, with special performances held throughout the city. The festival concludes with a brilliant Midsummer Night's Ball in central Zurich.

zurechnungsfähig *adj* of sound mind

zurecht|finden† **(sich)** *vr sep* find one's way. **z~kommen**† *vi sep* (*sein*) cope (**mit** with); (*rechtzeitig kommen*) be in time. **z~legen** *vt sep* put out ready; **sich** (*dat*) **eine Ausrede z~legen** have an excuse all ready. **z~machen** *vt sep* get ready. **Z~weisung** *f* reprimand

zureden *vi sep* (*haben*) **jdm z~** try to persuade s.o.

zurichten *vt sep* prepare; (*beschädigen*) damage; (*verletzen*) injure

zuriegeln *vt sep* bolt

zurück *adv* back; **Berlin, hin und z~** return to Berlin. **z~bekommen**† *vt sep* get back. **z~bleiben**† *vi sep* (*sein*) stay behind; (*nicht mithalten*) lag behind. **z~bringen**† *vt sep* bring back; (*wieder hinbringen*) take back. **z~erstatten** *vt sep* refund. **z~fahren**† *v sep* ● *vt* drive back ● *vi* (*sein*) return, go back; (*im Auto*) drive back; (*z~weichen*) recoil. **z~finden**† *vi sep* (*haben*) find one's way back. **z~führen** *v sep* ● *vt* take back; (*fig*) attribute (**auf** + *acc* to) ● *vi* (*haben*) lead back. **z~geben**† *vt sep* give back, return. **z~geblieben** *adj* retarded. **z~gehen**† *vi sep* (*sein*) go back, return; (*abnehmen*) go down; **z~gehen auf** (+ *acc*) (*fig*) go back to

zurückgezogen *adj* secluded. **Z~heit** *f* - seclusion

zurückhalt|en† *vt sep* hold back; (*abhalten*) stop; **sich z~en** restrain oneself. **z~end** *adj* reserved. **Z~ung** *f* - reserve

zurück|kehren *vi sep* (*sein*) return. **z~kommen**† *vi sep* (*sein*) come back, return; (*ankommen*) get back. **z~lassen**† *vt sep* leave behind; (*z~kehren lassen*) allow back. **z~legen** *vt sep* put back; (*reservieren*) keep; (*sparen*) put by; cover (*Strecke*). **z~liegen**† *vi sep* (*haben*) be in the past; (*Sport*) be behind; **das liegt lange zurück** that was long ago. **z~melden (sich)** *vr sep* report back. **z~schicken** *vt sep* send back. **z~schlagen**† *v sep* ● *vi* (*haben*) hit back ● *vt* hit back; (*umschlagen*) turn back. **z~schrecken**† *vi sep* (*sein*) shrink back, recoil; (*fig*) shrink (**vor** + *dat* from). **z~stellen** *vt sep* put back; (*reservieren*) keep; (*fig*) put aside; (*aufschieben*) postpone. **z~stoßen**† *v sep* ● *vt* push back ● *vi* (*sein*) reverse, back. **z~treten**† *vi sep* (*sein*) step back; (*vom Amt*) resign; (*verzichten*) withdraw. **z~weisen**† *vt sep* turn away; (*fig*) reject. **z~zahlen** *vt sep* pay back. **z~ziehen**† *vt sep* draw back; (*fig*) withdraw; **sich z~ziehen** withdraw; (*vom Beruf*) retire

Zuruf *m* shout. **z~en**† *vt sep* shout (*dat* to)

zurzeit *adv* at present

Zusage *f* -,-n acceptance; (*Versprechen*) promise. **z~n** *v sep* ● *vt* promise ● *vi* (*haben*) accept

zusammen *adv* together; (*insgesamt*) altogether; **z~ sein** be together. **Z~arbeit** *f* co-operation. **z~arbeiten** *vi sep* (*haben*) co-operate. **z~bauen** *vt sep* assemble.

z~bleiben† *vi sep* (*sein*) stay together. **z~brechen**† *vi sep* (*sein*) collapse. **Z~bruch** *m* collapse; (*Nerven- & fig*) breakdown. **z~fallen**† *vi sep* (*sein*) collapse; (*zeitlich*) coincide. **z~fassen** *vt sep* summarize, sum up. **Z~fassung** *f* summary. **z~fügen** *vt sep* fit together. **z~gehören** *vi sep* (*haben*) belong together; (*z~passen*) go together. **z~gesetzt** *adj* (*Gram*) compound. **z~halten**† *v sep* ●*vt* hold together; (*beisammenhalten*) keep together ●*vi* (*haben*) (*fig*) stick together. **Z~hang** *m* connection; (*Kontext*) context. **z~hanglos** *adj* incoherent. **z~klappen** *v sep* ●*vt* fold up ●*vi* (*sein*) collapse. **z~kommen**† *vi sep* (*sein*) meet; (*sich sammeln*) accumulate. **Z~kunft** *f* **-,⸚e** meeting. **z~laufen**† *vi sep* (*sein*) gather; (*Flüssigkeit:*) collect; (*Linien:*) converge. **z~leben** *vi sep* (*haben*) live together. **z~legen** *v sep* ●*vt* put together; (*z~falten*) fold up; (*vereinigen*) amalgamate; pool (*Geld*) ●*vi* (*haben*) club together. **z~nehmen**† *vt sep* gather up; summon up (*Mut*); collect (*Gedanken*); **sich z~nehmen** pull oneself together. **z~passen** *vi sep* (*haben*) go together, match. **Z~prall** *m* collision. **z~rechnen** *vt sep* add up. **z~schlagen**† *vt sep* smash up; (*prügeln*) beat up. **z~schließen**† **(sich)** *vr sep* join together; (*Firmen:*) merge. **Z~schluss** *m* union; (*Comm*) merger

Zusammensein *nt* **-s** get-together

zusammensetz|en *vt sep* put together; (*Techn*) assemble; **sich z~en** sit [down] together; (*bestehen*) be made up (**aus** from). **Z~ung** *f* **-,-en** composition; (*Techn*) assembly; (*Wort*) compound

zusammen|stellen *vt sep* put together; (*gestalten*) compile. **Z~stoß** *m* collision; (*fig*) clash. **z~treffen**† *vi sep* (*sein*) meet; (*zeitlich*) coincide. **z~zählen** *vt sep* add up. **z~ziehen**† *v sep* ●*vt* draw together; (*addieren*) add up; (*konzentrieren*) mass; **sich z~ziehen** contract; (*Gewitter:*) gather ●*vi* (*sein*) move in together; move in (**mit** with)

Zusatz *m* addition; (*Jur*) rider; (*Lebensmittel-*) additive. **zusätzlich** *adj* additional ●*adv* in addition

zuschau|en *vi sep* (*haben*) watch. **Z~er(in)** *m* **-s,-** (*f* **-,-nen**) spectator; (*TV*) viewer

Zuschlag *m* surcharge; (*Zug*) supplement. **z~pflichtig** *adj* (*Zug*) for which a supplement is payable

zuschließen† *v sep* ●*vt* lock ●*vi* (*haben*) lock up

zuschneiden† *vt sep* cut out; cut to size (*Holz*)

zuschreiben† *vt sep* attribute (*dat* to); **jdm die Schuld z~** blame s.o.

Zuschrift *f* letter; (*auf Annonce*) reply

zuschulden *adv* **sich** (*dat*) **etwas z~ kommen lassen** do wrong

Zuschuss *m* contribution; (*staatlich*) subsidy

zusehends *adv* visibly

zusein* *vi sep* (*sein*) **zu sein**, *s.* **zu**

zusenden† *vt sep* send (*dat* to)

zusetzen *v sep* ●*vt* add; (*einbüßen*) lose

zusicher|n *vt sep* promise. **Z~ung** *f* promise.

zuspielen *vt sep* (*Sport*) pass

zuspitzen (sich) *vr sep* (*fig*) become critical

Zustand *m* condition, state

zustande *adv* **z~ bringen/kom-**

men bring/come about
zuständig *adj* competent; (*verantwortlich*) responsible
zustehen† *vi sep* (*haben*) **jdm z~** be s.o.'s right; (*Urlaub:*) be due to s.o.
zusteigen† *vi sep* (*sein*) get on; **noch jemand zugestiegen?** ≈ tickets please; (*im Bus*) ≈ any more fares please?
zustell|en *vt sep* block; (*bringen*) deliver. **Z~ung** *f* delivery
zusteuern *v sep* ● *vi* (*sein*) head (**auf** + *acc* for) ● *vt* contribute
zustimm|en *vi sep* (*haben*) agree; (*billigen*) approve (*dat* of). **Z~ung** *f* consent; approval
zustoßen† *vi sep* (*sein*) happen (*dat* to)
Zustrom *m* influx
Zutat *f* (*Culin*) ingredient
zuteil|en *vt sep* allocate; assign (*Aufgabe*). **Z~ung** *f* allocation
zutiefst *adv* deeply
zutragen† *vt sep* carry/(*fig*) report (*dat* to); **sich z~** happen
zutrau|en *vt sep* **jdm etw z~** believe s.o. capable of sth. **Z~en** *nt* -s confidence
zutreffen† *vi sep* (*haben*) be correct; **z~ auf** (+ *acc*) apply to
Zutritt *m* admittance
zuunterst *adv* right at the bottom
zuverlässig *adj* reliable. **Z~keit** *f* - reliability
Zuversicht *f* - confidence. **z~lich** *adj* confident
zuviel* *pron & adv* **zu viel**, *s.* **viel**
zuvor *adv* before; (*erst*) first
zuvorkommen† *vi sep* (*sein*) (+ *dat*) anticipate. **z~d** *adj* obliging
Zuwachs *m* **-es** increase
Zuwanderung *f* immigration
zuwege *adv* **z~ bringen** achieve
zuweilen *adv* now and then
zuweisen† *vt sep* assign
Zuwendung *f* donation; (*Fürsorge*) care
zuwenig* *pron & adv* **zu wenig**, *s.* **wenig**
zuwerfen† *vt sep* slam (*Tür*); **jdm etw z~** throw s.o. sth
zuwider *adv* **jdm z~ sein** be repugnant to s.o. ● *prep* (+ *dat*) contrary to
zuzahlen *vt sep* pay extra
zuziehen† *v sep* ● *vt* pull tight; draw (*Vorhänge*); (*hinzu-*) call in; **sich** (*dat*) **etw z~** contract (*Krankheit*); sustain (*Verletzung*); incur (*Zorn*) ● *vi* (*sein*) move into the area
zuzüglich *prep* (+ *gen*) plus
Zwang *m* **-[e]s,⸚e** compulsion; (*Gewalt*) force; (*Verpflichtung*) obligation
zwängen *vt* squeeze
zwanglos *adj* informal. **Z~igkeit** *f* - informality
Zwangsjacke *f* straitjacket
zwanzig *inv adj* twenty. **z~ste(r,s)** *adj* twentieth
zwar *adv* admittedly
Zweck *m* **-[e]s,-e** purpose; (*Sinn*) point. **z~los** *adj* pointless. **z~mäßig** *adj* suitable; (*praktisch*) functional
zwei *inv adj*, **Z~** *f* **-,-en** two; (*Sch*) ≈ B. **Z~bettzimmer** *nt* twin-bedded room
zweideutig *adj* ambiguous
zwei|erlei *inv adj* two kinds of ● *pron* two things. **z~fach** *adj* double
Zweifel *m* **-s,-** doubt. **z~haft** *adj* doubtful; (*fragwürdig*) dubious. **z~los** *adv* undoubtedly. **z~n** *vi* (*haben*) doubt (**an etw** *dat* sth)

Zweig *m* **-[e]s,-e** branch. **Z~stelle** *f* branch [office]

Zwei|kampf *m* duel. **z~mal** *adv* twice. **z~reihig** *adj* (Anzug) double-breasted. **z~sprachig** *adj* bilingual

zweit *adv* **zu z~** in twos; **wir waren zu z~** there were two of us. **z~beste(r,s)** *adj* second-best. **z~e(r,s)** *adj* second

zweitens *adv* secondly

Zwerchfell *nt* diaphragm

Zwerg *m* **-[e]s,-e** dwarf

Zwickel *m* **-s,-** gusset

zwicken *vt/i* (*haben*) pinch

Zwieback *m* **-[e]s,¨e** rusk

Zwiebel *f* **-,-n** onion; (*Blumen-*)bulb

Zwielicht *nt* half-light; (*Dämmerlicht*) twilight. **z~ig** *adj* shady

Zwiespalt *m* conflict

Zwilling *m* **-s,-e** twin; **Z~e** (*Astrology*) Gemini

zwingen† *vt* force; **sich z~** force oneself. **z~d** *adj* compelling

Zwinger *m* **-s,-** run; (*Zucht-*) kennels *pl*

zwinkern *vi* (*haben*) blink; (*als Zeichen*) wink

Zwirn *m* **-[e]s** button thread

zwischen *prep* (+ *dat/acc*) between; (*unter*) among[st]. **Z~bemerkung** *f* interjection. **z~durch** *adv* in between; (*in der Z~zeit*) in the meantime. **Z~fall** *m* incident. **Z~landung** *f* stopover. **Z~raum** *m* gap, space. **Z~wand** *f* partition. **Z~zeit** *f* **in der Z~zeit** in the meantime

Zwist *m* **-[e]s,-e** discord; (*Streit*) feud

zwitschern *vi* (*haben*) chirp

zwo *inv adj* two

zwölf *inv adj* twelve. **z~te(r,s)** *adj* twelfth

Zylind|er *m* **-s,-** cylinder; (*Hut*) top hat. **z~risch** *adj* cylindrical

Zyn|iker *m* **-s,-** cynic. **z~isch** *adj* cynical. **Z~ismus** *m* **-** cynicism

Zypern *nt* **-s** Cyprus

Zypresse *f* **-,-n** cypress

Zyste /ˈtsʏstə/ *f* **-,-n** cyst

Phrasefinder/Sprachführer

Key phrases Nützliche Redewendungen

yes, please	ja bitte
no, thank you	nein danke
sorry!	Entschuldigung!
you're welcome	nichts zu danken
I don't understand	ich verstehe das nicht

Meeting people Wir lernen uns kennen

hello/goodbye	hallo!/auf Wiedersehen!
how are you?	wie geht es Ihnen?/wie geht's?
fine, thank you	danke, gut
see you later!	bis nachher!

Asking questions	Fragen
do you speak English/German?	sprechen Sie/sprichst du Englisch/ Deutsch?
what's your name?	wie heißen Sie?/wie heißt du?
where are you from?	woher kommen Sie?/ woher kommst du?
how much is it?	wie viel kostet das?
how far is it?	wie weit ist es?

About you	Alles über mich
my name is...	ich heiße...
I'm English	ich bin Engländer/Engländerin
I don't speak German/English very well	ich kann nicht gut Deutsch/Englisch sprechen
I'm here on holiday	ich bin im Urlaub hier
I live near Manchester/Hamburg	ich wohne in der Nähe von Manchester/Hamburg

Emergencies	Im Notfall
can you help me, please?	können Sie mir bitte helfen?
I'm lost	ich habe mich verlaufen
call an ambulance	rufen Sie einen Krankenwagen
get the police/a doctor	holen Sie die Polizei/einen Arzt
watch out!	Vorsicht!, Achtung!

Going Places/Unterwegs

By rail and underground / Mit Bahn und U-Bahn

By rail and underground	Mit Bahn und U-Bahn
where can I buy a ticket?	wo kann ich eine Fahrkarte kaufen?
what time is the next train to Berlin/New York?	wann geht der nächste Zug nach Berlin/New York?
do I have to change?	muss ich umsteigen?
can I take my bike on the train?	kann ich mein Rad im Zug mitnehmen?
which platform for the train to Cologne/Bath?	von welchem Bahnsteig fährt der Zug nach Köln/Bath ab?
a single/return, (*Amer* round trip) to Baltimore/Frankfurt, please	einmal einfach/eine Rückfahrkarte nach Baltimore/Frankfurt, bitte
I'd like a cheap day return/ an all-day ticket	ich möchte eine Tagesrückfahrkarte/ Tageskarte
I'd like to reserve a seat	ich möchte einen Platz reservieren
is there a student/senior citizen discount?	gibt es eine Ermäßigung für Studenten/Senioren?
is this the train for...?	ist dies der Zug nach...?
what time does the train arrive in Cologne/Washington?	wann kommt der Zug in Köln/ Washington an?
have I missed the train?	habe ich den Zug verpasst?
which line do I need to take for the castle?	mit welcher Linie komme ich zum Schloss?

YOU WILL HEAR:	SIE HÖREN:
der Zug fährt auf Gleis 2 ein	the train is arriving at platform 2
um 10 Uhr fährt ein Zug nach Berlin/York	there's a train to Berlin/York at 10 o'clock
der Zug hat Verspätung/ ist pünktlich	the train is delayed/on time
die nächste Haltestelle ist ...	the next stop is...
Ihre Fahrkarte ist ungültig	your ticket isn't valid

MORE USEFUL WORDS:	NÜTZLICHE WÖRTER:
underground station, (*Amer*) subway station	U-Bahnhof, U-Bahn-Station
timetable	Fahrplan
connection	Anschluss
express train	Schnellzug
local train	Nahverkehrszug
seat reservation	Platzreservierung
high-speed train	ICE, Intercity-Express

DID YOU KNOW...?	WUSSTEN SIE SCHON...?
At weekends and during busy times, it is advisable to get a seat reservation when you buy your train ticket. There is a small charge for this service.	Wenn Sie in Großbritannien Zugfahrkahrten einige Wochen im Voraus kaufen, können Sie viel Geld sparen.

At the airport — Am Flughafen

when's the next flight to Paris/Rome?	wann geht der nächste Flug nach Paris/Rom?
what time do I have to check in?	um wie viel Uhr muss ich einchecken?
where do I check in?	wo checkt man ein?
I'd like to confirm/cancel my flight	ich möchte meinen Flug bestätigen/stornieren
I'd like a window seat/an aisle seat	ich möchte einen Fensterplatz/Platz am Gang
can I change my booking?	kann ich umbuchen?
can I carry this in my hand, (*Amer*) carry-on luggage?	kann ich das im Handgepäck mitnehmen?
my luggage hasn't arrived	mein Gepäck ist nicht angekommen

YOU WILL HEAR:	SIE HÖREN:
Flug BA7057 ist zum Einsteigen bereit/ist verspätet/wurde gestrichen	flight BA7057 is now boarding/ delayed/cancelled
gehen Sie bitte zum Flugsteig 29	please go to gate 29
darf ich Ihre Bordkarte sehen?	could I see your boarding card?

MORE USEFUL WORDS:	NÜTZLICHE WÖRTER:
arrivals	Ankunft
departures	Abflug
baggage claim	Gepäckausgabe

Asking how to get there — Nach dem Weg fragen

how do I get to the airport/ city centre, (*Amer* center)?	wie komme ich zum Flughafen/ Stadtzentrum?
how long will it take me to walk there?	wie lange braucht man zu Fuß?
how far is it from here?	wie weit ist das von hier?
which bus do I take for the cathedral?	mit welchem Bus komme ich zum Dom?
where does this bus go?	wohin fährt dieser Bus?
where do I get the bus for...?	wo fährt der Bus nach...ab?
does this bus/train go to...?	fährt dieser Bus/Zug nach...?
which bus goes to...?	welcher Bus fährt nach...?
where do I get off?	wo muss ich aussteigen?
how much is the fare to the town centre (*Amer* center)?	was kostet es ins Stadtzentrum?
what time is the last bus?	wann fährt der letzte Bus?
where's the nearest underground station (*Amer* subway station)?	wo ist die nächste U-Bahn-Station?
is this the turning for...?	ist das die Abzweigung nach...?
can you call me a taxi?	können Sie mir ein Taxi bestellen?

YOU WILL HEAR:	SIE HÖREN:
nehmen Sie die erste Straße rechts	take the first turning (*Amer* turn) on the right
gehen Sie an der Ampel/ gleich nach der Kirche links	turn left at the traffic lights/ just past the church

Disabled travellers — Reisende mit Behinderungen

I'm disabled	ich habe eine Behinderung
is there wheelchair access?	gibt es einen stufenfreien Zugang?
are guide dogs permitted?	sind Blindenhunde zugelassen?

On the road — Auf der Straße

where's the nearest petrol station, (*Amer*) gas station?	wo ist die nächste Tankstelle?
what's the best way to get there?	wie komme ich am besten dorthin?
I've got a puncture, (*Amer*) flat tire	ich habe eine Reifenpanne
I'd like to hire, (*Amer*) rent a bike/car	ich möchte ein Rad/Auto mieten
where can I park around here?	wo kann man hier parken?
there's been an accident	es ist ein Unfall passiert
my car's broken down	mein Auto hat eine Panne
the car won't start	der Wagen springt nicht an
where's the nearest garage?	wo ist die nächste Autowerkstatt?
pump number six, please	Zapfsäule Nummer sechs, bitte
fill it up, please	bitte volltanken
can I wash my car here?	kann ich hier mein Auto waschen?
can I park here?	kann ich hier parken?
there's a problem with the brakes/lights	mit den Bremsen/der Beleuchtung stimmt etwas nicht
the clutch/gearstick isn't working	die Kupplung/Gangschaltung ist kaputt

take the third exit off the roundabout, (*Amer* traffic circle)	nehmen Sie im Kreisverkehr die dritte Ausfahrt
turn right at the next junction	biegen Sie an der nächsten Kreuzung rechts ab
slow down	fahren Sie langsamer
I can't drink, I'm driving	ich kann leider nichts trinken, ich muss noch fahren
can I buy a road map here?	kann ich hier eine Straßenkarte kaufen?

YOU WILL HEAR:	SIE HÖREN:
darf ich Ihren Führerschein sehen?	can I see your driving licence?
Sie müssen einen Unfallbericht ausfüllen	you need to fill out an accident report
dies ist eine Einbahnstraße	this road is one-way
das Tempolimit ist 50 Stundenkilometer	the speed limit is 50 kilometres per hour
Sie können hier nicht parken	you can't park here

MORE USEFUL WORDS:	NÜTZLICHE WÖRTER:
diesel	Diesel
unleaded	bleifreies Benzin
motorway, (*Amer* expressway)	Autobahn
toll/toll road	Maut/Mautstraße
satnav, (*Amer* GPS)	Satellitennavigationssystem
speed camera	Radarfalle
roundabout	Kreisverkehr
crossroads	Kreuzung
bus lane	Busspur
dual carriageway, (*Amer* divided highway)	vierspurige Schnellstraße
traffic lights	Ampel
driver	Fahrer/-in

DID YOU KNOW...?	WUSSTEN SIE SCHON...?
Heavy goods vehicles over 7.5 tons are not allowed to travel on German motorways on Sundays and Bank Holidays. Exceptions apply to HGVs transporting perishable goods.	Radarfallen (Starenkästen) sind in Großbritannien meist gelb angestrichen und daher von Weitem gut zu erkennen. Oft weist ein Schild mit einem Kamera-Symbol auf Radarkontrollen hin.

COMMON ROAD SIGNS

Achtung Kinder	Careful - children
Anlieger frei	Residents only
Ausfahrt	Exit
Einbahnstraße	One-way street
Fahrradstraße	Priority for cyclists
H	Bus/tram stop
P	Car park, parking
Spielstraße	Home zone
Stop	Stop
Umleitung	Diversion

STRASSENSCHILDER

Get in lane	Einordnen
Give way	Vorfahrt gewähren
Level crossing	Bahnübergang
No overtaking (*Amer* Do not pass)	Überholverbot
No stopping/parking	Halteverbot/Parkverbot
P	Parkplatz
Reduce speed now	Jetzt das Tempo verlangsamen
Slow	Langsam
Stop	Stopp!, Halt!

Keeping in touch/In Verbindung bleiben

On the phone	Am Telefon
where can I buy a phone card?	wo kann man Telefonkarten kaufen?
may I use your phone?	darf ich Ihr Telefon benutzen?
do you have a mobile, (*Amer* cell phone?)	haben Sie ein Handy?
what is your phone number?	was ist Ihre Telefonnummer?
what is the area code for Leipzig/ Sheffield?	was ist die Vorwahl von Leipzig/ Sheffield?
I'd like to make a phone call	ich möchte gern telefonieren
I'd like to reverse the charges (*Amer* call collect)	ich möchte ein R-Gespräch anmelden
the line's engaged/busy	es ist besetzt
there's no answer	es meldet sich niemand
hello, this is Natalie	hallo, hier spricht Natalie
can I speak to Simon, please?	kann ich bitte Simon sprechen?
who's calling?	wer ist am Apparat?
sorry, I must have the wrong number	Entschuldigung, ich habe mich verwählt
just a moment, please	einen Augenblick bitte
please hold the line	bleiben Sie bitte am Apparat
it's a business/personal call	es ist ein geschäftliches/privates Gespräch
I'll put you through	ich verbinde Sie
he cannot come to the phone at the moment	er kann jetzt nicht an den Apparat kommen
please tell him/her I called	richten Sie ihm/ihr bitte aus, dass ich angerufen habe
can I leave a message for Eva?	kann ich eine Nachricht für Eva hinterlassen?
I'll try again later	ich versuche es später noch einmal
please tell her that Danielle called	sagen Sie ihr bitte, dass Danielle angerufen hat

can he/she call me back?	kann er/sie mich zurückrufen?
my home number is...	meine Privatnummer ist...
my business number is...	meine Nummer im Büro ist...
my fax number is...	meine Faxnummer ist...
can I send a fax from here?	kann ich von hier faxen?
we were cut off	wir sind unterbrochen worden
I'll call you later	ich rufe Sie später an
I need to top up my mobile phone (*Amer* cell phone)	ich muss mein Handy-Guthaben aufladen
the battery's run out	die Batterie ist leer
I'm running low on credit	mein Handy-Guthaben ist fast aufgebraucht
send me a text	schicken Sie mir eine SMS
there's no signal here	hier ist kein Empfang
you're breaking up	ich kann Sie nicht mehr hören
could you speak a little louder?	könnten Sie etwas lauter sprechen?

YOU WILL HEAR:	SIE HÖREN:
hallo	hello
rufen Sie mich auf meinem Handy an	call me on my mobile (*Amer* cell phone)
der Teilnehmer ist nicht erreichbar	the person you are calling is unavailable
bitte drücken Sie die Rautetaste	please press the hash key
möchten Sie eine Nachricht hinterlassen?	Would you like to leave a message?
Bitte hinterlassen Sie eine Nachricht nach dem Ton	please leave a message after the tone

MORE USEFUL WORDS:	NÜTZLICHE WÖRTER:
text message	SMS
top-up card	Aufladekarte
phone box, (*Amer* phone booth)	Telefonzelle
dial	wählen

Writing Schreiben

can you give me your address?	können Sie mir Ihre/kannst du mir deine Adresse geben?
where is the nearest post office?	wo ist die nächste Post?
two one-euro stamps	zwei Briefmarken zu einem Euro
I'd like a stamp for a letter to Germany/Italy	ich hätte gern eine Briefmarke für einen Brief nach Deutschland/Italien
can I have stamps for two postcards to England/the USA, please?	kann ich bitte Briefmarken für zwei Postkarten nach England/in die USA haben?
I'd like to send a parcel	ich möchte ein Paket abschicken
is there a postbox (*Amer* mailbox) near here?	gibt es hier in der Nähe einen Briefkasten?
dear Isabel/Fred	Liebe Isabel/Lieber Fred
dear Sir or Madam	Sehr geehrte Damen und Herren
yours sincerely	Mit freundlichen Grüßen
yours faithfully	Mit freundlichen Grüßen
best wishes	Viele Grüße

YOU WILL HEAR:	SIE HÖREN:
möchten Sie es per Luftpost schicken?	would you like to send it by air mail?
ist es wertvoll?	is it valuable?

MORE USEFUL WORDS:	NÜTZLICHE WÖRTER:
postcode (*Amer* ZIP code)	Postleitzahl
airmail	Luftpost
fragile	zerbrechlich
urgent	dringend
registered post (*Amer* mail)	Einschreiben

On line — Online

are you on the Internet?	hast du Zugang zum Internet?
what's your e-mail address?	was ist deine E-Mail-Adresse?
I'll e-mail it to you	ich schicke es Ihnen per E-Mail
I've looked for it on the Internet	ich habe es im Internet gesucht
he found the information surfing the net	er hat die Informationen beim Surfen im Internet gefunden
my e-mail address is jane dot smith at new99 dot com	meine E-Mail-Adresse ist jane Punkt smith at-Zeichen new99 Punkt com
can I check my e-mail here?	kann ich hier meine E-Mails ansehen?
I have broadband/dial-up	ich habe Breitband/eine Einwahlverbindung
do you have wireless internet access here?	gibt es hier einen drahtlosen Internetzugang?
I spend a lot of time surfing the Net	ich surfe viel im Internet
I'll send you the file as an attachment	ich schicke Ihnen die Datei als Anhang

YOU MAY SEE:	SIE SEHEN:
Suche	search
auf das Symbol doppelklicken	double-click on the icon
Anwendung öffnen	open (up) the application
Datei herunterladen	download file

MORE USEFUL WORDS:	NÜTZLICHE WÖRTER:
subject (of an email)	Betreff
password	Passwort
social networking site	soziales Netzwerk
search engine	Suchmaschine
mouse	Maus
keyboard	Tastatur

Meeting up | Verabredungen

what shall we do this evening?	was machen wir heute Abend?
do you want to go out tonight?	möchten Sie/möchtest du heute Abend ausgehen?
where shall we meet?	wo treffen wir uns?
see you outside the cinema at 6 o'clock	ich treffe Sie/dich um sechs Uhr vor dem Kino
do you fancy joining in?	hast du/haben Sie Lust mitzumachen?
I can't today, I'm busy	ich kann heute nicht, ich habe keine Zeit
shall we go for something to eat?	sollen wir etwas essen gehen?
let's meet for a coffee in town	treffen wir uns in der Stadt zum Kaffeetrinken
would you like to see a show/film (*Amer* movie)?	möchten Sie/möchtest du eine Show/einen Film ansehen?
I'm sorry, I've got something planned	es tut mir leid, ich habe schon etwas vor
what about next week instead?	wie wäre es stattdessen nächste Woche?

YOU WILL HEAR:	SIE HÖREN:
freut mich, Sie kennenzulernen	nice to meet you
kann ich Sie zu einem Gläschen einladen?	can I buy you a drink?

MORE USEFUL WORDS:	NÜTZLICHE WÖRTER:
bar	Bar
bar *(serving counter in a bar/pub)*	Theke
meal	Essen
snack	Imbiss
date	Verabredung
cigarette	Zigarette

Food and Drink/Essen und trinken

Booking a table / Vorbestellungen

can you recommend a good restaurant?	können Sie uns/mir ein gutes Restaurant empfehlen?
I'd like to reserve a table for four	ich möchte einen Tisch für vier Personen bestellen
I booked a table for two	ich habe einen Tisch für zwei Personen bestellt

Ordering / Wir möchten bestellen

could we see the menu/ wine list, please?	können wir bitte die Speisekarte Weinkarte haben?
do you have a vegetarian/children's menu?	haben Sie vegetarische Gerichte/ Kinderportionen?
could we have some more bread?	noch etwas Brot, bitte
what would you recommend?	was würden Sie mir/uns empfehlen?
I'd like a white/black coffee	ich möchte einen Kaffee mit Milch/ einen Kaffee ohne Milch
... an espresso	... einen Espresso
... a decaffeinated coffee	... einen entkoffeinierten Kaffee
the bill, (*Amer*) check, please	Rechnung, bitte

YOU WILL HEAR:	SIE HÖREN:
hätten Sie gern einen Aperitif?	would you like an aperitif?
haben Sie schon bestellt?	are you ready to order?
möchten Sie eine Vorspeise?	would you like a starter?
was nehmen Sie als Hauptgericht?	what will you have for the main course?
möchten Sie eine Nachspeise?	would you like a dessert?
haben Sie noch einen Wunsch?	anything else?
guten Appetit!	enjoy your meal!
die Bedienung ist (nicht) inbegriffen	service is (not) included

The menu Die Speisekarte

starters	Vorspeisen
canapés	Häppchen
hors d'oeuvres	Horsd'oeuvres, Vorspeisen
omelette	Omelett
soup	Suppe
fish	**Fisch**
bass	Barsch
cod	Kabeljau
eel	Aal
haddock	Schellfisch
hake	Seehecht
herring	Hering
monk fish	Anglerfisch
mullet	Meeräsche
mussels	Muscheln
oysters	Austern
plaice	Scholle
prawns	Garnelen
red mullet	Meerbarbe
salmon	Lachs
sardines	Sardinen
shrimps	Krabben
sole	Seezunge
squid	Calamares
trout	Forelle
tuna	Thunfisch
turbot	Steinbutt

Vorspeisen	starters
Häppchen	canapés
Horsd'oeuvres, Vorspeisen	hors d'oeuvres
Omelett	omelette
Suppe	soup
Fisch	**fish**
Aal	eel
Austern	oysters
Barsch	bass
Calamares	squid
Forelle	trout
Garnelen	prawns
Hering	herring
Kabeljau	cod
Krabben	shrimps
Lachs	salmon
Meeräsche	mullet
Muscheln	mussels
Sardinen	sardines
Schellfisch	haddock
Scholle	plaice
Seehecht	hake
Seezunge	sole
Steinbutt	turbot

meat	Fleisch
chicken	Hühnchen
duck	Ente
goose	Gans
guinea fowl	Perlhuhn
hare	Hase
kidneys	Nieren
lamb	Lammfleisch
liver	Leber
pork	Schweinefleisch
rabbit	Kaninchen
veal	Kalbfleisch
wild boar	Wildschwein

Fleisch	meat
Ente	duck
Gans	goose
Hase	hare
Hühnchen	chicken
Kalbfleisch	veal
Kaninchen	rabbit
Lammfleisch	lamb
Leber	liver
Nieren	kidneys
Sauerbraten	braised beef
Schweinefleisch	pork
Wiener Schnitzel	breaded escalope
Wildschwein	wild boar

vegetables	Gemüse
artichokes	Artischocken
asparagus	Spargel
beans	Bohnen
cabbage	Kohl
carrots	Möhren, Karotten
cauliflower	Blumenkohl
celery	Sellerie
endive	Endivie
mushrooms	Pilze
onions	Zwiebeln
peas	Erbsen
peppers	Paprikaschoten
potatoes	Kartoffeln
red cabbage	Rotkohl, Blaukraut (*Aust.*)

Gemüse	vegetables
Artischocken	artichokes
Blaukraut (*Aust.*)	red cabbage
Blumenkohl	cauliflower
Bohnen	beans
Endivie	endive
Erbsen	peas
Kartoffeln	potatoes
Kohl	cabbage
Möhren, Karotten	carrots
Paprikaschoten	peppers
Pilze	mushrooms
Rotkohl	red cabbage
Sellerie	celeriac; celery
Spargel	asparagus
Zwiebeln	onions

the way it's cooked	wie es zubereitet wird
boiled	gekocht
fried	gebraten, in der Pfanne gebraten
grilled	gegrillt
medium	halb durchgebraten
puréed	püriert
rare	englisch gebraten, schwach gebraten
roast	gebraten, geröstet
stewed	geschmort
well done	durch

wie es zubereitet wird	the way it's cooked
englisch gebraten	rare
gebraten, geröstet	roast
gebraten, in der Pfanne gebraten	fried
gegrillt	grilled
geschmort	stewed
durch	well done
halb durchgebraten	medium
püriert	puréed
schwach gebraten	rare

desserts	Nachspeisen
cheese	Käse
cheeseboard	Käseplatte
chocolate gateau	Schokoladentorte
fruit	Obst
fruit tart	Obsttorte
ice cream	Eis
pie	Obstkuchen

Nachspeisen	desserts
Kaiserschmarren (*Aust.*)	pancake strips sprinkled with sugar and raisins
Kompott	stewed fruit
Kuchen	cake
Nockerln (*Aust.*)	sweet dumplings
rote Grütze	red-berry compote

side dishes/ condiments	Beilagen/ Gewürze
bread	Brot
butter	Butter
herbs	Gewürzkräuter
mayonnaise	Majonäse
mustard	Senf

Beilagen/ Gewürze	side dishes/ condiments
Brot	bread
Brötchen	rolls
Butter	butter
Essig	vinegar
Gewürze	seasoning

olive oil	Olivenöl
pepper	Pfeffer
rolls	Brötchen, Semmeln (*Aust.*)
salt	Salz
sauce	Soße
seasoning	Gewürze
vinegar	Essig

drinks	**Getränke**
beer	Bier
bottle	Flasche
carbonated	mit Kohlensäure
draught beer	Bier vom Fass
half-bottle	eine halbe Flasche
liqueur	Likör
red wine	Rotwein
rosé	Rosé
soft drink	alkoholfreies Getränk
spritzer	Schorle
still	ohne Kohlensäure
table wine	Tafelwein
white wine	Weißwein
wine	Wein

Gewürzkräuter	herbs
Majonäse	mayonnaise
Olivenöl	olive oil
Pfeffer	pepper
Salz	salt
Semmeln (*Aust.*)	rolls
Senf	mustard
Soße	sauce

Getränke	**drinks**
alkoholfreies Getränk	soft drink
Bier	beer
Bier vom Fass	draught beer
Flasche	bottle
Likör	liqueur
mit Kohlensäure	carbonated
ohne Kohlensäure	still
Rosé	rosé
Rotwein	red wine
Schoppenwein	wine by the glass
Schorle	spritzer
Tafelwein	table wine
Wein	wine
Weißwein	white wine

Places to stay/Unterkunft

Camping | Camping

we're looking for a campsite	wir suchen einen Campingplatz
can we pitch our tent here?	können wir hier zelten?
can we park our caravan here?	können wir unseren Wohnwagen hier parken?
do you have space for a caravan/tent?	haben Sie Platz für einen Wohnwagen/ein Zelt?
are there shopping facilities?	gibt es Einkaufsmöglichkeiten?
how much is it per night?	was kostet es pro Nacht?

At the hotel | Im Hotel

I'd like a double/single room with bath	ich möchte ein Doppelzimmer/ Einzelzimmer mit Bad
we have a reservation in the name of Milnes	wir haben auf den Namen Milnes reservieren lassen
I reserved two rooms	ich habe zwei Zimmer reservieren lassen
for three nights, from Friday to Sunday	für drei Nächte, von Freitag bis Sonntag
how much does the room cost?	was kostet das Zimmer?
I'd like to see the room first, please	ich möchte das Zimmer erst sehen, bitte
what time is breakfast?	wann gibt es Frühstück?
can I leave this in the safe?	kann ich das im Safe lassen?
bed and breakfast	Zimmer mit Frühstück
we'd like to stay another night	wir möchten noch eine Nacht bleiben
please call me at 7:30	bitte wecken Sie mich um 7:30
are there any messages for me?	hat jemand eine Nachricht für mich hinterlassen?

Hostels | Jugendherbergen und Heime

could you tell me where the youth hostel is?	können Sie mir sagen, wo die Jugendherberge ist?
what time does the hostel close?	um wie viel Uhr macht das Heim zu?
I spent the night in a youth hostel	ich habe in einer Jugendherberge übernachtet
the hostel we're staying in is great value	unsere Herberge ist sehr preiswert
I'm staying in a youth hostel	ich wohne in einer Jugendherberge
I know a really good youth hostel in Dublin	ich kenne eine sehr gute Jugendherberge in Dublin
I'd like to go backpacking in Australia	ich würde gern in Australien mit dem Rucksack herum reisen

Rooms to rent | Zimmer zu vermieten

I'm looking for a room with a reasonable rent	ich suche ein preiswertes Zimmer
I'd like to rent an apartment for three weeks	ich möchte eine Wohnung für drei Wochen mieten
where do I find out about rooms to let?	wo kann man sich nach Fremdenzimmern erkundigen?
what's the weekly rent for the apartment?	was kostet die Wohnung pro Woche?
I'm staying with friends at the moment	ich wohne zur Zeit bei Freunden
I rent an apartment on the outskirts of town	ich habe eine Wohnung am Stadtrand gemietet
the room's fine—I'll take it	das Zimmer ist gut—ich nehme es

Shopping and money/Einkaufen und Geld

At the bank / In der Bank

At the bank	In der Bank
I'd like to change some money	ich möchte gern Geld wechseln
I want to change 100 euros into pounds	ich möchte 100 Euro[s] in Pfund wechseln
do you take Eurocheques?	nehmen Sie Euroschecks?
what's the exchange rate today?	wie steht der Wechselkurs heute?
I prefer traveller's cheques (*Amer* traveler's checks) to cash	mir sind Reiseschecks lieber als Bargeld
I'd like to transfer some money from my account	ich möchte Geld von meinem Konto überweisen
I'll get some money from the cash machine/ATM	ich hole mir Geld vom Automaten
a £50 cheque (*Amer* check)	ein Scheck über 50 Pfund
can I cash this cheque (*Amer* check) here?	kann ich diesen Scheck hier einlösen?
can I get some cash with my credit card?	kann ich auf meine Kreditkarte Bargeld bekommen?

Finding the right shop / Das richtige Geschäft finden

Finding the right shop	Das richtige Geschäft finden
where's the main shopping district?	wo ist das Haupteinkaufsviertel?
is the shopping centre (*Amer* mall) far from here?	ist das Einkaufszentrum weit von hier?
where's a good place to buy shoes/sunglasses?	wo kauft man am besten Schuhe/ eine Sonnenbrille?
where can I buy batteries/ postcards?	wo kann ich Batterien/Postkarten kaufen?
where's the nearest pharmacy (*Amer* drugstore)?	wo ist die nächste Apotheke?
what time do the shops open/close?	um wie viel Uhr machen die Läden auf/zu?
where did you get those?	wo hast du die her?
I'm looking for a present for my mother	ich suche ein Geschenk für meine Mutter

Are you being served? Werden Sie schon bedient?

how much does that cost?	was kostet das?
can I try it on?	kann ich es anprobieren?
can you keep it for me?	können Sie es mir zurücklegen?
could you gift-wrap it for me, please?	können Sie es bitte als Geschenk einpacken?
please wrap it up well	verpacken Sie es bitte gut
can I pay by credit card/cheque (*Amer* check)?	kann ich mit Kreditkarte/Scheck zahlen?
do you have this in another colour?	haben Sie das in einer anderen Farbe?
I'm just looking	ich sehe mich nur um
a receipt, please	eine Quittung bitte
I need a bigger size	ich brauche die nächste Größe
I take a size...	ich habe Größe...
it doesn't suit me	das steht mir nicht

Changing things Umtauschen

can I have a refund?	kann ich mein Geld zurückbekommen?
can you mend it for me?	können Sie es mir reparieren?
can I speak to the manager?	kann ich den Geschäftsführer/ die Geschäftsführerin sprechen?
it doesn't work	es funktioniert nicht
I'd like to change the dress	ich möchte das Kleid umtauschen
I bought this here yesterday	ich habe das gestern hier gekauft

Currency Convertor Währungsumrechner

€/$	£/$	£/$	€/$
0.25		0.25	
0.50		0.50	
0.75		0.75	
1		1	
1.5		1.5	
2		2	
3		3	
5		5	
10		10	
20		20	
30		30	
40		40	
50		50	
100		100	
200		200	
1000		1000	

Sport and leisure/Freizeit und Sport

Keeping fit — Wir halten uns fit

Keeping fit	Wir halten uns fit
where can we play badminton/squash?	wo kann man Badminton/Squash spielen?
is there a local sports centre (*Amer* center)?	gibt es hier ein Sportzentrum?
we want to hire (*Amer* rent) skis/snowboards	wir möchten Skier/Snowboards mieten
what's the charge per day?	was kostet das pro Tag?
is there a reduction for children/a student discount?	gibt es eine Ermäßigung für Kinder/Studenten?
where can we go swimming/play football?	wo kann man schwimmen gehen/Fußball spielen?
are there any yoga/pilates classes here?	gibt es hier Yogakurse/Pilateskurse?
I want to do aerobics	ich möchte Aerobic machen
is there a hotel gym?	hat das Hotel ein Fitnesscenter?
do you have to be a member?	muss man Mitglied sein?
I would like to go fishing/riding	ich würde gern angeln gehen/reiten
I love playing baseball/tennis	ich spiele gern Baseball/Tennis
I play golf on Mondays	ich spiele jeden Montag Golf
would you like to play tennis/badminton?	möchten Sie Tennis/Badminton spielen?

Watching sport / Zuschauen

is there a match (*Amer* game) on Saturday?	gibt es am Samstag ein Spiel?
who's playing?	wer spielt?
which teams are playing?	welche Mannschaften spielen?
where can I get tickets?	wo kann man Karten bekommen?
can you get me a ticket?	kannst du mir eine Karte besorgen?
I'd like to see a rugby match	ich würde gern ein Rugbyspiel sehen
let's watch the match on TV	sehen wir uns das Spiel im Fernsehen an
my favourite (*Amer* favorite) team is Bayern	ich bin ein Bayern-Fan
who's winning?	wer gewinnt?
the reds are winning 3-1	die Roten liegen 3 zu 1 in Führung

SPORTS

basketball	Basketball
cricket	Kricket
cycling	Radfahren
football/American football	American Football
football/soccer	Fußball
golf	Golf
hiking	Wandern
horse-riding	Reiten
ice-skating	Eislaufen
roller-blading	Inlineskaten
running	Laufen
skiing	Skifahren
snowboarding	Snowboarden
surfing	Surfen
swimming	Schwimmen

SPORTARTEN

Basketball	**basketball**
Bergsteigen	**climbing**
Eislaufen	**ice-skating**
Fußball	**football/soccer**
Handball	**handball**
Inlineskaten	**roller-blading**
Laufen	**running**
Leichtathlethik	**athletics**
Radfahren	**cycling**
Reiten	**horse-riding**
Schwimmen	**swimming**
Skifahren	**skiing**
Snowboarden	**snowboarding**
Surfen	**surfing**
Wandern	**hiking**

Going to the cinema/theatre/club — Wir gehen ins Kino/Theater/in einen Club

what's on at the cinema/ (*Amer*) at the movies?	was läuft im Kino?
what's on at the theatre?	was wird im Theater gespielt?
how long is the performance?	wie lange dauert die Vorstellung?
when does the box office open/close?	wann macht die Kasse auf/zu?
what time does the performance start?	um wie viel Uhr fängt die Aufführung an?
what time does the film (*Amer* movie) finish?	wann ist der Film zu Ende?
are there any tickets left?	gibt es noch Karten?
how much are the tickets?	was kosten die Karten?
where can I get a programme (*Amer* program)?	wo kann man ein Programm kaufen?
I want to book tickets for tonight	ich möchte für heute Abend Karten bestellen
I'd rather have seats in the stalls (*Amer* orchestra)/circle	ich hätte lieber Plätze im Parkett/auf dem Balkon
we'd like to go to a club	wir wollen in einen Club gehen
I go clubbing every weekend	ich gehe am Wochenende immer in Clubs

Hobbies — Hobbys

do you have any hobbies?	hast du irgendwelche Hobbys?
what do you do at (*Amer* on) weekends?	was machst du/machen Sie immer am Wochenende?
I like reading/listening to music/going out	ich lese gerne/höre gerne Musik/gehe gerne aus
do you like watching TV/shopping/travelling?	sehen Sie gerne fern?/gehen Sie gerne einkaufen?/verreisen Sie gerne?
I collect comics	ich sammle Comichefte/Comics

Good timing/Der richtige Zeitpunkt

Telling the time / Uhrzeit

could you tell me the time?	können Sie mir sagen, wie spät es ist?
what time is it?	wie viel Uhr ist es?
it's 2 o'clock	es ist zwei Uhr
at about 8 o'clock	gegen acht Uhr
at 9 o'clock tomorrow	morgen um neun Uhr
from 10 o'clock onwards	ab zehn Uhr
the meeting starts at 8 p.m.	die Besprechung fängt um zwanzig Uhr an/um acht Uhr abends
at 5 o'clock in the morning/ afternoon	um fünf Uhr morgens/um fünf Uhr nachmittags (um siebzehn Uhr)
at exactly 1 o'clock	um Punkt eins
it's five past.../quarter past...	es ist fünf nach.../Viertel nach...
it's half past one	es ist halb zwei
it's twenty-five to one	es ist fünf nach halb eins
it's quarter to/five to one	es ist Viertel vor/fünf vor eins
a quarter of an hour	eine Viertelstunde
three quarters of an hour	eine Dreiviertelstunde

Days and dates / Wochentage und Datum

Sunday, Monday, Tuesday, Wednesday, Thursday, Friday, Saturday	Sonntag, Montag, Dienstag, Mittwoch, Donnerstag, Freitag, Samstag/Sonnabend
January, February, March, April, May, June, July, August, September, October, November, December	Januar, Februar, März, April, Mai, Juni, Juli, August, September, Oktober, November, Dezember
what's the date?	der Wievielte ist heute?

it's the second of June	heute ist der zweite Juni
we meet up every Monday	wir treffen uns jeden Montag
she comes on Tuesdays	sie kommt immer dienstags
we're going away in August	wir verreisen im August
I forgot it was the first of April today	ich habe ganz vergessen, dass heute der erste April ist
on November 8th	am achten November
about the 8th of June	um den 8. Juni

Public holidays and special days — Feste und Feiertage

Bank holiday	gesetzlicher Feiertag
New Year's Day (Jan 1)	Neujahr
Epiphany (Jan 6)	Heilige Drei Könige
St Valentine's Day (Feb 14)	Valentinstag
Shrove Tuesday	Fastnachtsdienstag/ Faschingsdienstag
Ash Wednesday	Aschermittwoch
Mothering Sunday/Mother's Day	Muttertag
Palm Sunday	Palmsonntag
Maundy Thursday	Gründonnerstag
Good Friday	Karfreitag
Easter Day	Ostersonntag
Easter Monday	Ostermontag
May Day (May 1)	der Erste Mai, Maifeiertag
Father's Day	Vatertag
Day of German Unity (Oct 3)	Tag der Deutschen Einheit
First Sunday in Advent	erster Advent
St Nicholas' Day (Dec 6)	Nikolaus
Christmas Eve	Heiligabend
Christmas Day (Dec 25)	erster Weihnachtstag
Boxing Day (Dec 26)	zweiter Weihnachtstag
New Year's Eve (Dec 31)	Silvester

Health and Beauty/ Gesundheit und Schönheit

At the doctor's / Beim Arzt

At the doctor's	Beim Arzt
can I see a doctor?	kann ich einen Arzt sehen?
I don't feel well	ich fühle mich schlecht
it hurts here	es tut hier weh
I have a migraine/headache	ich habe Migräne/Kopfschmerzen
the pain is getting worse	die Schmerzen werden immer schlimmer
I have a sore ankle/wrist/knee	mein Knöchel/Handgelenk/Knie tut weh
are there any side effects?	gibt es Nebenwirkungen?

YOU WILL HEAR:	SIE HÖREN:
Sie müssen sich einen Termin geben lassen	you need to make an appointment
bitte setzen Sie sich	please take a seat
haben Sie eine Europäische Versicherungskarte?	do you have a European Health Insurance Card?
haben Sie Krankenversicherung?	do you have health insurance?
ich muss Ihren Blutdruck messen	I need to take your blood pressure

MORE USEFUL WORDS:	NÜTZLICHE WÖRTER:
nurse	Krankenschwester
antibiotics	Antibiotika
medicine	Medikament
infection	Infektion
treatment	Behandlung
(bed)rest	(Bett)ruhe

At the pharmacy | In der Apotheke

can I have some painkillers?	kann ich ein Schmerzmittel haben?
I have asthma/hay fever/eczema	ich habe Asthma/Heuschnupfen/ ein Ekzem
I've been stung by a wasp/bee	mich hat eine Wespe/Biene gestochen
I've got a cold/cough/the flu	ich bin erkältet/ich habe Husten/ Grippe
I need something for diarrhoea/ stomachache	ich brauche etwas gegen Durchfall/ Magenschmerzen
I'm pregnant	ich bin schwanger

YOU WILL HEAR:	SIE HÖREN:
haben Sie diese Tabletten schon einmal eingenommen?	have you taken these tablets before?
tragen Sie diese Salbe dreimal täglich auf	apply this ointment three times a day
zu den Mahlzeiten/auf nüchternen Magen einnehmen	take at mealtimes/on an empty stomach
sind Sie gegen irgendetwas allergisch?	are you allergic to anything?
nehmen Sie andere Medikamente ein?	are you taking any other medication?

MORE USEFUL WORDS:	NÜTZLICHE WÖRTER:
plasters (*Amer* Band-Aid™)	Pflaster
insect repellent	Insektenschutzmittel
contraception	Verhütungsmittel
sun cream	Sonnencreme
aftersun	After-Sun-Produkt
dosage	Dosierung

At the hairdresser's/salon — Beim Friseur

I'd like a cut and blow dry	bitte schneiden und föhnen
just a trim please	bitte nur nachschneiden
a short back and sides	ein kurzer Haarschnitt
I'd like my hair washed first please	bitte waschen Sie mir zuerst die Haare
can I have a manicure/pedicure/ facial?	kann ich eine Maniküre/Pediküre/ Gesichtsbehandlung haben?
how much is a head/back massage?	was kostet eine Kopfmassage/ Rückenmassage?
can I see a price list?	kann ich eine Preisliste sehen?
do you offer reflexology/ aromatherapy treatments?	bieten Sie Reflexzonenmassage/ Aromatherapie an?

YOU WILL HEAR:	SIE HÖREN:
möchten Sie die Haare geföhnt haben?	would you like your hair blow-dried?
wo tragen Sie den Scheitel?	where is your parting (*Amer* part)?
möchten Sie die Haare stufig geschnitten haben?	would you like your hair layered?

MORE USEFUL WORDS:	NÜTZLICHE WÖRTER:
dry/greasy/fine/flyaway/frizzy	trocken/fettig/fein/fliegend/kraus
highlights	helle Strähnchen
extensions	Haarverlängerung
sunbed	Sonnenbank
leg/arm/bikini wax	Wachsbehandlung der Beine/Arme/Bikinizone

At the dentist's Beim Zahnarzt

I have toothache	ich habe Zahnschmerzen
I'd like an emergency appointment	ich hätte gern einen Notfalltermin
I have cracked a tooth	ich habe mir einen Zahn angebrochen
my gums are bleeding	mein Zahnfleisch blutet

YOU WILL HEAR:	SIE HÖREN:
machen Sie den Mund auf	open your mouth
Sie brauchen eine Füllung	you need a filling
wir müssen eine Röntgenaufnahme machen	we need to take an X-ray
bitte den Mund ausspülen	please rinse

MORE USEFUL WORDS:	NÜTZLICHE WÖRTER:
anaesthetic	Betäubung
root canal treatment	Wurzelkanalbehandlung
injection	Spritze
floss	Zahnseide

Weights & measures/Maße u. Gewichte

Length/Längenmaße

inches/Zoll	0.39	3.9	7.8	11.7	15.6	19.7	39
cm/Zentimeter	1	10	20	30	40	50	100

Distance/Entfernungen

miles/Meilen	0.62	6.2	12.4	18.6	24.9	31	62
km/Kilometer	1	10	20	30	40	50	100

Weight/Gewichte

pounds/Pfund	2.2	22	44	66	88	110	220
kg/Kilogramm	1	10	20	30	40	50	100

Capacity/Hohlmaße

gallons/Gallonen	0.22	2.2	4.4	6.6	8.8	11	22
litres/Liter	1	10	20	30	40	50	100

Temperature/Temperatur

°C	0	5	10	15	20	25	30	37	38	40
°F	32	41	50	59	68	77	86	98.4	100	104

Clothing and shoe sizes/Kleider- und Schuhgrößen

Women's clothing sizes/Damengrößen

UK	8	10	12	14	16	18
US	6	8	10	12	14	16
Continent	36	38	40	42	44	46

Men's clothing sizes/Herrengrößen

UK/US	36	38	40	42	44	46
Continent	46	48	50	52	54	56

Men's and women's shoes/Schuhgrößen

UK women	4	5	6	7	7.5	8			
UK men			6	7	8	9	10	11	
US	6.5	7.5	8.5	9.5	10.5	11.5	12.5	13.5	14.5
Continent	37	38	39	40	41	42	43	44	45

Aa

a /ə/, *betont* /eɪ/

vor einem Vokal **an**

● *indefinite article*

····▸ ein (*m*), eine (*f*), ein (*nt*). **a problem** ein Problem. **an apple** ein Apfel. **a cat** eine Katze. **have you got a pencil?** hast du einen Bleistift? **I gave it to a beggar** ich gab es einem Bettler

! There are some cases where **a** is not translated, such as when talking about people's professions or nationalities: **she is a lawyer** sie ist Rechtsanwältin. **he's an Italian** er ist Italiener

····▸ (*with 'not'*) kein (*m*), keine (*f*), kein (*nt*), keine (*pl*). **that's not a problem/not a good idea** das ist kein Problem/keine gute Idee. **there was not a chance that ...** es bestand keine Möglichkeit, dass .... **she did not say a word** sie sagte kein Wort. **I didn't tell a soul** ich habe es keinem Menschen gesagt

····▸ (*per; each*) pro. **£300 a week** 300 Pfund pro Woche. **30 miles an hour** 30 Meilen pro Stunde. (*in prices*) **it costs 90p a pound** es kostet 90 Pence das Pfund.

aback /ə'bæk/ *adv* **be taken ~** verblüfft sein

abandon /ə'bændən/ *vt* verlassen; (*give up*) aufgeben

abate /ə'beɪt/ *vi* nachlassen

abattoir /'æbətwɑ:(r)/ *n* Schlachthof *m*

abb|ey /'æbɪ/ *n* Abtei *f*. **~ot** *n* Abt *m*

abbreviat|e /ə'bri:vɪeɪt/ *vt* abkürzen. **~ion** *n* Abkürzung *f*

abdicat|e /'æbdɪkeɪt/ *vi* abdanken. **~ion** *n* Abdankung *f*

abdom|en /'æbdəmən/ *n* Unterleib *m*. **~inal** *adj* Unterleibs-

abduct /əb'dʌkt/ *vt* entführen. **~ion** *n* Entführung *f*

aberration /æbə'reɪʃn/ *n* Abweichung *f*; (*mental*) Verwirrung *f*

abeyance /ə'beɪəns/ *n* **in ~** [zeitweilig] außer Kraft

abhor /əb'hɔ:(r)/ *vt* (*pt/pp* **abhorred**) verabscheuen. **~rent** *adj* abscheulich

abide /ə'baɪd/ *vt* (*pt/pp* **abided**) (*tolerate*) aushalten; ausstehen (*person*)

ability /ə'bɪlətɪ/ *n* Fähigkeit *f*; (*talent*) Begabung *f*

abject /'æbdʒekt/ *adj* erbärmlich; (*humble*) demütig

ablaze /ə'bleɪz/ *adj* in Flammen

able /'eɪbl/ *adj* (**-r,-st**) fähig; **be ~ to do sth** etw tun können. **~-'bodied** *adj* körperlich gesund

ably /'eɪblɪ/ *adv* gekonnt

abnormal /æb'nɔ:ml/ *adj* anormal; (*Med*) abnorm. **~ity** *n* Abnormität *f*. **~ly** *adv* ungewöhnlich

aboard /ə'bɔ:d/ *adv & prep* an Bord (+ *gen*)

abol|ish /ə'bɒlɪʃ/ *vt* abschaffen.

a

~ition *n* Abschaffung *f*
abominable /ə'bɒmɪnəbl/ *adj*, **-bly** *adv* abscheulich
aborigines /æbə'rɪdʒəni:z/ *npl* Ureinwohner *pl*
abort /ə'bɔ:t/ *vt* abtreiben. **~ion** *n* Abtreibung *f*. **~ive** *adj* (*attempt*) vergeblich
about /ə'baʊt/ *adv* umher, herum; (*approximately*) ungefähr; **be ~** (*in circulation*) umgehen; (*in existence*) vorhanden sein; **be ~ to do sth** im Begriff sein, etw zu tun; **there was no one ~** es war kein Mensch da; **run/play ~** herumlaufen/-spielen ● *prep* um (+ *acc*) [... herum]; (*concerning*) über (+ *acc*); **what is it ~?** worum geht es? (*book:*) wovon handelt es? **I know nothing ~ it** ich weiß nichts davon; **talk/know ~** reden/wissen von
about: ~-'face *n*, **-'turn** *n* Kehrtwendung *f*
above /ə'bʌv/ *adv* oben ● *prep* über (+ *dat/acc*); **~ all** vor allem
above: ~-'board *adj* legal. **~-mentioned** *adj* oben erwähnt
abrasive /ə'breɪsɪv/ *adj* Scheuer-; (*remark*) verletzend ● *n* Scheuermittel *nt*; (*Techn*) Schleifmittel *nt*
abreast /ə'brest/ *adv* nebeneinander; **keep ~ of** Schritt halten mit
abridge /ə'brɪdʒ/ *vt* kürzen
abroad /ə'brɔ:d/ *adv* im Ausland; **go ~** ins Ausland fahren
abrupt /ə'brʌpt/ *adj* abrupt; (*sudden*) plötzlich; (*curt*) schroff
abscess /'æbsɪs/ *n* Abszess *m*
absence /'æbsəns/ *n* Abwesenheit *f*
absent /'æbsənt/ *adj* abwesend; **be ~** fehlen
absentee /æbsən'ti:/ *n* Abwesende(r) *m/f*
absent-minded /æbsənt'maɪndɪd/ *adj* geistesabwesend; (*forgetful*) zerstreut
absolute /'æbsəlu:t/ *adj* absolut
absorb /əb'sɔ:b/ *vt* absorbieren, aufsaugen; **~ed in** vertieft in (+ *acc*). **~ent** *adj* saugfähig
absorption /əb'sɔ:pʃn/ *n* Absorption *f*
abstain /əb'steɪn/ *vi* sich enthalten (**from** *gen*)
abstemious /əb'sti:mɪəs/ *adj* enthaltsam
abstention /əb'stenʃn/ *n* (*Pol*) [Stimm]enthaltung *f*
abstract /'æbstrækt/ *adj* abstrakt ● *n* (*summary*) Abriss *m*
absurd /əb'sɜ:d/ *adj* absurd. **~ity** *n* Absurdität *f*
abundan|ce /ə'bʌndəns/ *n* Fülle *f* (**of** an + *dat*). **~t** *adj* reichlich
abuse[1] /ə'bju:z/ *vt* missbrauchen; (*insult*) beschimpfen
abus|e[2] /ə'bju:s/ *n* Missbrauch *m*; (*insults*) Beschimpfungen *pl*. **~ive** ausfallend
abysmal /ə'bɪʒml/ *adj* ! katastrophal
abyss /ə'bɪs/ *n* Abgrund *m*
academic /ækə'demɪk/ *adj*, **-ally** *adv* akademisch
academy /ə'kædəmɪ/ *n* Akademie *f*
accelerat|e /ək'seləreɪt/ *vt/i* beschleunigen. **~ion** *n* Beschleunigung *f*. **~or** *n* (*Auto*) Gaspedal *nt*
accent /'æksənt/ *n* Akzent *m*
accept /ək'sept/ *vt* annehmen; (*fig*) akzeptieren ● *vi* zusagen. **~able** *adj* annehmbar. **~ance** *n* Annahme *f*; (*of invitation*) Zusage *f*
access /'ækses/ *n* Zugang *m*. **~ible** *adj* zugänglich
accessor|y /ək'sesərɪ/ *n* (*Jur*) Mitschuldige(r) *m/f*; **~ies** *pl* (*fashion*)

Accessoires *pl*; (*Techn*) Zubehör *nt*

accident /'æksɪdənt/ *n* Unfall *m*; (*chance*) Zufall *m*; **by ~** zufällig; (*unintentionally*) versehentlich. **~al** *adj* zufällig; (*unintentional*) versehentlich

acclaim /ə'kleɪm/ *vt* feiern (**as** als)

acclimatize /ə'klaɪmətaɪz/ *vt* **become ~d** sich akklimatisieren

accommodat|e /ə'kɒmədeɪt/ *vt* unterbringen. **~ing** *adj* entgegenkommend. **~ion** *n* (*rooms*) Unterkunft *f*

accompan|iment /ə'kʌmpənɪmənt/ *n* Begleitung *f*. **~ist** *n* (*Mus*) Begleiter(in) *m*(*f*)

accompany /ə'kʌmpənɪ/ *vt* (*pt*/*pp* **-ied**) begleiten

accomplice /ə'kʌmplɪʃ/ *n* Komplize/-zin *m*/*f*

accomplish /ə'kʌmplɪʃ/ *vt* erfüllen (*task*); (*achieve*) erreichen. **~ed** *adj* fähig. **~ment** *n* Fertigkeit *f*; (*achievement*) Leistung *f*

accord /ə'kɔ:d/ *n* **of one's own ~** aus eigenem Antrieb. **~ance** *n* **in ~ance with** entsprechend (+ *dat*)

according /ə'kɔ:dɪŋ/ *adv* **~ to** nach (+ *dat*). **~ly** *adv* entsprechend

accordion /ə'kɔ:dɪən/ *n* Akkordeon *nt*

account /ə'kaʊnt/ *n* Konto *nt*; (*bill*) Rechnung *f*; (*description*) Darstellung *f*; (*report*) Bericht *m*; **~s** *pl* (*Comm*) Bücher *pl*; **on ~ of** wegen (+ *gen*); **on no ~** auf keinen Fall; **take into ~** in Betracht ziehen, berücksichtigen ● *vi* **~ for** Rechenschaft ablegen für; (*explain*) erklären

accountant /ə'kaʊntənt/ *n* Buchhalter(in) *m*(*f*); (*chartered*) Wirtschaftsprüfer *m*

accumulat|e /ə'kju:mjʊleɪt/ *vt* ansammeln, anhäufen ● *vi* sich ansammeln, sich anhäufen. **~ion** *n* Ansammlung *f*, Anhäufung *f*

accura|cy /'ækʊrəsɪ/ *n* Genauigkeit *f*. **~te** *adj* genau

accusation /ækju:'zeɪʃn/ *n* Anklage *f*

accusative /ə'kju:zətɪv/ *adj* & *n* **~ [case]** (*Gram*) Akkusativ *m*

accuse /ə'kju:z/ *vt* (*Jur*) anklagen (**of** *gen*); **~ s.o. of doing sth** jdn beschuldigen, etw getan zu haben

accustom /ə'kʌstəm/ *vt* gewöhnen (**to** an + *dat*); **grow** *or* **get ~ed to** sich gewöhnen an (+ *acc*). **~ed** *adj* gewohnt

ace /eɪs/ *n* (*Cards, Sport*) Ass *nt*

ache /eɪk/ *n* Schmerzen *pl* ● *vi* weh tun, schmerzen

achieve /ə'tʃi:v/ *vt* leisten; (*gain*) erzielen; (*reach*) erreichen. **~ment** *n* (*feat*) Leistung *f*

acid /'æsɪd/ *adj* sauer; (*fig*) beißend ● *n* Säure *f*. **~ity** *n* Säure *f*. **~'rain** *n* saurer Regen *m*

acknowledge /ək'nɒlɪdʒ/ *vt* anerkennen; (*admit*) zugeben; erwidern (*greeting*); **~ receipt of** den Empfang bestätigen (+ *gen*). **~ment** *n* Anerkennung *f*; (*of letter*) Empfangsbestätigung *f*

acne /'æknɪ/ *n* Akne *f*

acorn /'eɪkɔ:n/ *n* Eichel *f*

acoustic /ə'ku:stɪk/ *adj*, **-ally** *adv* akustisch. **~s** *npl* Akustik *f*

acquaint /ə'kweɪnt/ *vt* **be ~ed with** kennen; vertraut sein mit (*fact*). **~ance** *n* (*person*) Bekannte(r) *m*/*f*; **make s.o.'s ~ance** jdn kennen lernen

acquire /ə'kwaɪə(r)/ *vt* erwerben

acquisit|ion /ækwɪ'zɪʃn/ *n* Erwerb *m*; (*thing*) Erwerbung *f*. **~ive** *adj* habgierig

acquit /ə'kwɪt/ *vt* (*pt*/*pp* **acquitted**) freisprechen

acre /'eɪkə(r)/ *n* ≈ Morgen *m*

a

acrimon|ious /ˈækrɪˈməʊnɪəs/ *adj* bitter

acrobat /ˈækrəbæt/ *n* Akrobat(in) *m(f)*. **~ic** *adj* akrobatisch

across /əˈkrɒs/ *adv* hinüber/herüber; (*wide*) breit; (*not lengthwise*) quer; (*in crossword*) waagerecht; **come ~ sth** auf etw (*acc*) stoßen; **go ~** hinübergehen; **bring ~** herüberbringen ● *prep* über (+ *acc*); (*on the other side of*) auf der anderen Seite (+ *gen*)

act /ækt/ *n* Tat *f*; (*action*) Handlung *f*; (*law*) Gesetz *nt*; (*Theat*) Akt *m*; (*item*) Nummer *f* ● *vi* handeln; (*behave*) sich verhalten; (*Theat*) spielen; (*pretend*) sich verstellen; **~ as** fungieren als ● *vt* spielen (*role*). **~ing** *adj* (*deputy*) stellvertretend ● *n* (*Theat*) Schauspielerei *f*

action /ˈækʃn/ *n* Handlung *f*; (*deed*) Tat *f*; (*Mil*) Einsatz *m*; (*Jur*) Klage *f*; (*effect*) Wirkung *f*; (*Techn*) Mechanismus *m*; **out of ~** (*machine:*) außer Betrieb; **take ~** handeln; **killed in ~** gefallen

activate /ˈæktɪveɪt/ *vt* betätigen

activ|e /ˈæktɪv/ *adj* aktiv; **on ~e service** im Einsatz. **~ity** *n* Aktivität *f*

act|or /ˈæktə(r)/ *n* Schauspieler *m*. **~ress** *n* Schauspielerin *f*

actual /ˈæktʃʊəl/ *adj* eigentlich; (*real*) tatsächlich

acupuncture /ˈækjʊ-/ *n* Akupunktur *f*

acute /əˈkjuːt/ *adj* scharf; (*angle*) spitz; (*illness*) akut. **~ly** *adv* sehr

ad /æd/ *n* [I] = **advertisement**

AD *abbr* (**Anno Domini**) n.Chr.

adamant /ˈædəmənt/ *adj* **be ~ that** darauf bestehen, dass

adapt /əˈdæpt/ *vt* anpassen; bearbeiten (*play*) ● *vi* sich anpassen. **~able** *adj* anpassungsfähig

adaptation /ædæpˈteɪʃn/ *n* (*Theat*) Bearbeitung *f*

add /æd/ *vt* hinzufügen; (*Math*) addieren ● *vi* zusammenzählen, addieren; **~ to** hinzufügen zu; (*fig: increase*) steigern; (*compound*) verschlimmern. **~ up** *vt* zusammenzählen (*figures*) ● *vi* zusammenzählen, addieren

adder /ˈædə(r)/ *n* Kreuzotter *f*

addict /ˈædɪkt/ *n* Süchtige(r) *m/f*

addict|ed /əˈdɪktɪd/ *adj* süchtig; **~ed to drugs** drogensüchtig. **~ion** *n* Sucht *f*

addition /əˈdɪʃn/ *n* Hinzufügung *f*; (*Math*) Addition *f*; (*thing added*) Ergänzung *f*; **in ~** zusätzlich. **~al** *adj* zusätzlich

additive /ˈædɪtɪv/ *n* Zusatz *m*

address /əˈdres/ *n* Adresse *f*, Anschrift *f*; (*speech*) Ansprache *f* ● *vt* adressieren (**to** an + *acc*); (*speak to*) anreden (*person*); sprechen vor (+ *dat*) (*meeting*). **~ee** *n* Empfänger *m*

adequate /ˈædɪkwət/ *adj* ausreichend

adhere /ədˈhɪə(r)/ *vi* kleben/(*fig*) festhalten (**to** an + *dat*)

adhesive /ədˈhiːsɪv/ *adj* klebend ● *n* Klebstoff *m*

adjacent /əˈdʒeɪsnt/ *adj* angrenzend

adjective /ˈædʒɪktɪv/ *n* Adjektiv *nt*

adjoin /əˈdʒɔɪn/ *vt* angrenzen an (+ *acc*). **~ing** *adj* angrenzend

adjourn /əˈdʒɜːn/ *vt* vertagen (**until** auf + *acc*) ● *vi* sich vertagen. **~ment** *n* Vertagung *f*

adjudicate /əˈdʒuːdɪkeɪt/ *vi* (*in competition*) Preisrichter sein

adjust /əˈdʒʌst/ *vt* einstellen; (*alter*) verstellen ● *vi* sich anpassen (**to** *dat*). **~able** *adj* verstellbar. **~ment** *n* Einstellung *f*; Anpassung *f*

ad lib /ædˈlɪb/ *adv* aus dem Stegreif ● *vi* (*pt/pp* **ad libbed**) 🄸 improvisieren

administer /əd'mɪnɪstə(r)/ *vt* verwalten; verabreichen (*medicine*)

administration /ədmɪnɪ'streɪʃn/ *n* Verwaltung *f*; (*Pol*) Regierung *f*

admirable /'ædmərəbl/ *adj* bewundernswert

admiral /'ædmərəl/ *n* Admiral *m*

admiration /ædmə'reɪʃn/ *n* Bewunderung *f*

admire /əd'maɪə(r)/ *vt* bewundern. **~r** *n* Verehrer(in) *m*(*f*)

admission /əd'mɪʃn/ *n* Eingeständnis *nt*; (*entry*) Eintritt *m*

admit /əd'mɪt/ *vt* (*pt/pp* **admitted**) (*let in*) hereinlassen; (*acknowledge*) zugeben; **~ to sth** etw zugeben. **~tance** *n* Eintritt *m*. **~tedly** *adv* zugegebenermaßen

admonish /əd'mɒnɪʃ/ *vt* ermahnen

adolescen|ce /ædə'lesns/ *n* Jugend *f*, Pubertät *f*. **~t** *adj* Jugend-; (*boy, girl*) halbwüchsig ● *n* Jugendliche(r) *m/f*

adopt /ə'dɒpt/ *vt* adoptieren; ergreifen (*measure*); (*Pol*) annehmen (*candidate*). **~ion** *n* Adoption *f*

ador|able /ə'dɔːrəbl/ *adj* bezaubernd. **~ation** *n* Anbetung *f*

adore /ə'dɔː(r)/ *vt* (*worship*) anbeten; (🄸*: like*) lieben

adorn /ə'dɔːn/ *vt* schmücken. **~ment** *n* Schmuck *m*

Adriatic /eɪdrɪ'ætɪk/ *adj & n* **~ [Sea]** Adria *f*

adrift /ə'drɪft/ *adj* **be ~** treiben

adroit /ə'drɔɪt/ *adj* gewandt, geschickt

adulation /ædjʊ'leɪʃn/ *n* Schwärmerei *f*

adult /'ædʌlt/ *n* Erwachsene(r) *m/f*

adulterate /ə'dʌltəreɪt/ *vt* verfälschen; panschen (*wine*)

adultery /ə'dʌltərɪ/ *n* Ehebruch *m*

advance /əd'vɑːns/ *n* Fortschritt *m*; (*Mil*) Vorrücken *nt*; (*payment*) Vorschuss *m*; **in ~** im Voraus ● *vi* vorankommen; (*Mil*) vorrücken; (*make progress*) Fortschritte machen ● *vt* fördern (*cause*); vorbringen (*idea*); vorschießen (*money*). **~d** *adj* fortgeschritten; (*progressive*) fortschrittlich. **~ment** *n* Förderung *f*; (*promotion*) Beförderung *f*

advantage /əd'vɑːntɪdʒ/ *n* Vorteil *m*; **take ~ of** ausnutzen. **~ous** *adj* vorteilhaft

adventur|e /əd'ventʃə(r)/ *n* Abenteuer *nt*. **~er** *n* Abenteurer *m*. **~ous** *adj* abenteuerlich; (*person*) abenteuerlustig

adverb /'ædvɜːb/ *n* Adverb *nt*

adverse /'ædvɜːs/ *adj* ungünstig

advert /'ædvɜːt/ *n* 🄸 = **advertisement**

advertise /'ædvətaɪz/ *vt* Reklame machen für; (*by small ad*) inserieren ● *vi* Reklame machen; inserieren

advertisement /əd'vɜːtɪsmənt/ *n* Anzeige *f*; (*publicity*) Reklame *f*; (*small ad*) Inserat *nt*

advertis|er /'ædvətaɪzə(r)/ *n* Inserent *m*. **~ing** *n* Werbung *f*

advice /əd'vaɪs/ *n* Rat *m*

advisable /əd'vaɪzəbl/ *adj* ratsam

advis|e /əd'vaɪz/ *vt* raten (**s.o.** jdm); (*counsel*) beraten; (*inform*) benachrichtigen; **~e s.o. against sth** jdm von etw abraten ● *vi* raten. **~er** *n* Berater(in) *m*(*f*). **~ory** *adj* beratend

advocate[1] /'ædvəkət/ *n* (*supporter*) Befürworter *m*

advocate[2] /'ædvəkeɪt/ *vt* befürworten

aerial /'eərɪəl/ *adj* Luft- ● *n*

Antenne *f*

aerobics /eəˈrəʊbɪks/ *n* Aerobic *nt*

aero|drome /ˈeərədrəʊm/ *n* Flugplatz *m*. **~plane** *n* Flugzeug *nt*

aerosol /ˈeərəsɒl/ *n* Spraydose *f*

aesthetic /iːsˈθetɪk/ *adj* ästhetisch

affair /əˈfeə(r)/ *n* Angelegenheit *f*, Sache *f*; (*scandal*) Affäre *f*; **[love-]~** [Liebes]verhältnis *nt*

affect /əˈfekt/ *vt* sich auswirken auf (+ *acc*); (*concern*) betreffen; (*move*) rühren; (*pretend*) vortäuschen. **~ation** *n* Affektiertheit *f*. **~ed** *adj* affektiert

affection /əˈfekʃn/ *n* Liebe *f*. **~ate** *adj* liebevoll

affirm /əˈfɜːm/ *vt* behaupten

affirmative /əˈfɜːmətɪv/ *adj* bejahend ● *n* Bejahung *f*

afflict /əˈflɪkt/ *vt* **be ~ed with** behaftet sein mit. **~ion** *n* Leiden *nt*

affluen|ce /ˈæfluəns/ *n* Reichtum *m*. **~t** *adj* wohlhabend. **~t society** *n* Wohlstandsgesellschaft *f*

afford /əˈfɔːd/ *vt* **be able to ~ sth** sich (*dat*) etw leisten können. **~able** *adj* erschwinglich

affront /əˈfrʌnt/ *n* Beleidigung *f* ● *vt* beleidigen

afloat /əˈfləʊt/ *adj* **be ~** (*ship:*) flott sein; **keep ~** (*person:*) sich über Wasser halten

afraid /əˈfreɪd/ *adj* **be ~** Angst haben (**of** vor + *dat*); **I'm ~ not** leider nicht; **I'm ~ so** [ja] leider

Africa /ˈæfrɪkə/ *n* Afrika *nt*. **~n** *adj* afrikanisch ● *n* Afrikaner(in) *m*(*f*)

after /ˈɑːftə(r)/ *adv* danach ● *prep* nach (+ *dat*); **~ that** danach; **~ all** schließlich; **the day ~ tomorrow** übermorgen; **be ~** aus sein auf (+ *acc*) ● *conj* nachdem

after: ~-effect *n* Nachwirkung *f*. **~math** /-mɑːθ/ *n* Auswirkungen *pl*. **~ˈnoon** *n* Nachmittag *m*; **good ~noon!** guten Tag! **~-sales service** *n* Kundendienst *m*. **~shave** *n* Rasierwasser *nt*. **~thought** *n* nachträglicher Einfall *m*. **~wards** *adv* nachher

again /əˈgen/ *adv* wieder; (*once more*) noch einmal; **~ and ~** immer wieder

against /əˈgenst/ *prep* gegen (+ *acc*)

age /eɪdʒ/ *n* Alter *nt*; (*era*) Zeitalter *nt*; **~s** [I] ewig; **under ~** minderjährig; **of ~** volljährig; **two years of ~** zwei Jahre alt ● *v* (*pres p* **ageing**) ● *vt* älter machen ● *vi* altern; (*mature*) reifen

aged[1] /eɪdʒd/ *adj* **~ two** zwei Jahre alt

aged[2] /ˈeɪdʒɪd/ *adj* betagt ● *n* **the ~** *pl* die Alten

ageless /ˈeɪdʒlɪʃ/ *adj* ewig jung

agency /ˈeɪdʒənsɪ/ *n* Agentur *f*; (*office*) Büro *nt*

agenda /əˈdʒendə/ *n* Tagesordnung *f*

agent /ˈeɪdʒənt/ *n* Agent(in) *m*(*f*); (*Comm*) Vertreter(in) *m*(*f*); (*substance*) Mittel *nt*

aggravat|e /ˈægrəveɪt/ *vt* verschlimmern; ([I]: *annoy*) ärgern. **~ion** *n* [I] Ärger *m*

aggregate /ˈægrɪgət/ *adj* gesamt ● *n* Gesamtzahl *f*; (*sum*) Gesamtsumme *f*

aggress|ion /əˈgreʃn/ *n* Aggression *f*. **~ive** *adj* aggressiv. **~or** *n* Angreifer(in) *m*(*f*)

aggro /ˈægrəʊ/ *n* [I] Ärger *m*

aghast /əˈgɑːst/ *adj* entsetzt

agil|e /ˈædʒaɪl/ *adj* flink, behände; (*mind*) wendig. **~ity** *n* Flinkheit *f*, Behändigkeit *f*

agitat|e /ˈædʒɪteɪt/ *vt* bewegen; (*shake*) schütteln ● *vi* (*fig*) **~ for** agitieren für. **~ed** *adj* erregt. **~ion**

n Erregung *f*; (*Pol*) Agitation *f*

ago /ə'gəʊ/ *adv* vor (+ *dat*); **a long time ~** vor langer Zeit; **how long ~ is it?** wie lange ist es her?

agony /'ægənɪ/ *n* Qual *f*; **be in ~** furchtbare Schmerzen haben

agree /ə'gri:/ *vt* vereinbaren; (*admit*) zugeben; **~ to do sth** sich bereit erklären, etw zu tun ● *vi* (*people, figures:*) übereinstimmen; (*reach agreement*) sich einigen; (*get on*) gut miteinander auskommen; (*consent*) einwilligen (**to** in + *acc*); **~ with s.o.** jdm zustimmen; (*food:*) jdm bekommen; **~ with sth** (*approve of*) mit etw einverstanden sein

agreeable /ə'gri:əbl/ *adj* angenehm

agreed /ə'gri:d/ *adj* vereinbart

agreement /ə'gri:mənt/ *n* Übereinstimmung *f*; (*consent*) Einwilligung *f*; (*contract*) Abkommen *nt*; **reach ~** sich einigen

agricultur|al /ægrɪ'kʌltʃərəl/ *adj* landwirtschaftlich. **~e** *n* Landwirtschaft *f*

aground /ə'graʊnd/ *adj* gestrandet; **run ~** (*ship:*) stranden

ahead /ə'hed/ *adv* **straight ~** geradeaus; **be ~ of s.o./sth** vor jdm/etw sein; (*fig*) voraus sein; **go on ~** vorgehen; **get ~** vorankommen; **go ~!** [!] bitte! **look/plan ~** vorausblicken/-planen

aid /eɪd/ *n* Hilfe *f*; (*financial*) Unterstützung *f*; **in ~ of** zugunsten (+ *gen*) ● *vt* helfen (+ *dat*)

Aids /eɪdz/ *n* Aids *nt*

aim /eɪm/ *n* Ziel *nt*; **take ~** zielen ● *vt* richten (**at** auf + *acc*); ● *vi* zielen (**at** auf + *acc*); **~ to do sth** beabsichtigen, etw zu tun. **~less** *adj* ziellos

air /eə(r)/ *n* Luft *f*; (*expression*) Miene *f*; (*appearance*) Anschein *m*; **be on the ~** (*programme:*) gesendet werden; (*person:*) auf Sendung sein; **by ~** auf dem Luftweg; (*airmail*) mit Luftpost ● *vt* lüften; vorbringen (*views*)

air: ~ bag *n* (*Auto*) Airbag *m*. **~-conditioned** *adj* klimatisiert. **~-conditioning** *n* Klimaanlage *f*. **~craft** *n* Flugzeug *nt*. **~field** *n* Flugplatz *m*. **~ force** *n* Luftwaffe *f*. **~ freshener** *n* Raumspray *nt*. **~gun** *n* Luftgewehr *nt*. **~ hostess** *n* Stewardess *f*. **~ letter** *n* Aerogramm *nt*. **~line** *n* Fluggesellschaft *f*. **~mail** *n* Luftpost *f*. **~man** *n* Flieger *m*. **~plane** *n* (*Amer*) Flugzeug *nt*. **~port** *n* Flughafen *m*. **~-raid** *n* Luftangriff *m*. **~-raid shelter** *n* Luftschutzbunker *m*. **~ship** *n* Luftschiff *nt*. **~ ticket** *n* Flugschein *m*. **~tight** *adj* luftdicht. **~-traffic controller** *n* Fluglotse *m*

airy /'eərɪ/ *adj* luftig; (*manner*) nonchalant

aisle /aɪl/ *n* Gang *m*

ajar /ə'dʒɑ:(r)/ *adj* angelehnt

alarm /əlɑ:m/ *n* Alarm *m*; (*device*) Alarmanlage *f*; (*clock*) Wecker *m*; (*fear*) Unruhe *f* ● *vt* erschrecken

alas /ə'læs/ *int* ach!

album /'ælbəm/ *n* Album *nt*

alcohol /'ælkəhɒl/ *n* Alkohol *m*. **~ic** *adj* alkoholisch ● *n* Alkoholiker(in) *m(f)*. **~ism** *n* Alkoholismus *m*

alert /ə'lɜ:t/ *adj* aufmerksam ● *n* Alarm *m*

algebra /'ældʒɪbrə/ *n* Algebra *f*

Algeria /æl'dʒɪərɪə/ *n* Algerien *nt*

alias /'eɪlɪəs/ *n* Deckname *m* ● *adv* alias

alibi /'ælɪbaɪ/ *n* Alibi *nt*

alien /'eɪlɪən/ *adj* fremd ● *n* Ausländer(in) *m(f)*

alienate /'eɪlɪəneɪt/ *vt* entfremden

a

alight¹ /əˈlaɪt/ *vi* aussteigen (**from** aus)

alight² *adj* **be ~** brennen; **set ~** anzünden

align /əˈlaɪn/ *vt* ausrichten. **~ment** *n* Ausrichtung *f*

alike /əˈlaɪk/ *adj & adv* ähnlich; (*same*) gleich; **look ~** sich (*dat*) ähnlich sehen

alive /əˈlaɪv/ *adj* lebendig; **be ~** leben; **be ~ with** wimmeln von

all /ɔːl/

● *adjective*

····➤ (*plural*) alle. **all [the] children** alle Kinder. **all our children** alle unsere Kinder. **all the books** alle Bücher. **all the others** alle anderen

····➤ (*singular = whole*) ganz. **all the wine** der ganze Wein. **all the town** die ganze Stadt. **all my money** mein ganzes Geld; all mein Geld. **all day** den ganzen Tag. **all Germany** ganz Deutschland

● *pronoun*

····➤ (*plural = all persons/things*) alle. **all are welcome** alle sind willkommen. **they all came** sie sind alle gekommen. **are we all here?** sind wir alle da? **the best pupils of all** die besten Schüler (von allen). **the most beautiful of all** der/die/das schönste von allen

····➤ (*singular = everything*) alles. **that is all** das ist alles. **all that I possess** alles, was ich besitze

····➤ **all of** ganz; (*with plural*) alle. **all of the money** das ganze Geld. **all of the paintings** alle Gemälde. **all of you/them** Sie/sie alle

····➤ (*in phrases*) **all in all** alles in allem. **in all** insgesamt. **most of all** am meisten. **once and for all** ein für alle Mal. **not at all** gar nicht

● *adverb*

····➤ (*completely*) ganz. **she was all alone** sie war ganz allein. **I was all dirty** ich war ganz schmutzig

····➤ (*in scores*) **four all** vier zu vier

····➤ **all right** (*things*) in Ordnung. **is everything all right?** ist alles in Ordnung? **is that all right for you?** passt das Ihnen? **I'm all right** mir geht es gut. **did you get home all right?** sind Sie gut nach Hause gekommen? **is it all right to go in?** kann ich reingehen? **yes, all right** ja, gut. **work out all right** gut gehen; klappen ⓘ

····➤ (*in phrases*) **all but** (*almost*) fast. **all at once** auf einmal. **all the better** umso besser. **all the same** (*nevertheless*) trotzdem

allege /əˈledʒ/ *vt* behaupten. **~d** *adj* angeblich

allegiance /əˈliːdʒəns/ *n* Treue *f*

allerg|ic /əˈlɜːdʒɪk/ *adj* allergisch (**to** gegen). **~y** *n* Allergie *f*

alleviate /əˈliːvɪeɪt/ *vt* lindern

alley /ˈælɪ/ *n* Gasse *f*; (*for bowling*) Bahn *f*

alliance /əˈlaɪəns/ *n* Verbindung *f*; (*Pol*) Bündnis *nt*

allied /ˈælaɪd/ *adj* alliiert

alligator /ˈælɪgeɪtə(r)/ *n* Alligator *m*

allocat|e /ˈæləkeɪt/ *vt* zuteilen; (*share out*) verteilen. **~ion** *n* Zuteilung *f*

allot /əˈlɒt/ *vt* (*pt/pp* **allotted**) zuteilen (**s.o.** jdm)

allow /əˈlaʊ/ *vt* erlauben; (*give*)

geben; (*grant*) gewähren; (*reckon*) rechnen; (*agree, admit*) zugeben; **~ for** berücksichtigen; **~ s.o. to do sth** jdm erlauben, etw zu tun; **be ~ed to do sth** etw tun dürfen

allowance /ə'laʊəns/ *n* [finanzielle] Unterstützung *f*; **make ~s for** berücksichtigen

alloy /'ælɔɪ/ *n* Legierung *f*

allude /ə'lu:d/ *vi* anspielen (**to** auf + *acc*)

allusion /ə'lu:ʒn/ *n* Anspielung *f*

ally[1] /'ælaɪ/ *n* Verbündete(r) *m/f*; **the Allies** *pl* die Alliierten

ally[2] /ə'laɪ/ *vt* (*pt/pp* **-ied**) verbinden; **~ oneself with** sich verbünden mit

almighty /ɔ:l'maɪtɪ/ *adj* allmächtig; (⊡: *big*) Riesen- ●*n* **the A~** der Allmächtige

almond /'ɑ:mənd/ *n* (*Bot*) Mandel *f*

almost /'ɔ:lməʊst/ *adv* fast, beinahe

alone /ə'ləʊn/ *adj & adv* allein; **leave me ~** lass mich in Ruhe; **leave that ~!** lass die Finger davon! **let ~** ganz zu schweigen von

along /ə'lɒŋ/ *prep* entlang (+ *acc*); **~ the river** den Fluss entlang ●*adv* **~ with** zusammen mit; **all ~** die ganze Zeit; **come ~** komm doch; **I'll bring it ~** ich bringe es mit

along'side *adv* daneben ●*prep* neben (+ *dat*)

aloud /ə'laʊd/ *adv* laut

alphabet /'ælfəbet/ *n* Alphabet *nt*. **~ical** *adj* alphabetisch

alpine /'ælpaɪn/ *adj* alpin; **A~** Alpen-

Alps /ælps/ *npl* Alpen *pl*

already /ɔ:l'redɪ/ *adv* schon

Alsace /æl'sæs/ *n* Elsass *nt*

Alsatian /æl'seɪʃn/ *n* (*dog*) [deutscher] Schäferhund *m*

also /'ɔ:lsəʊ/ *adv* auch

altar /'ɔ:ltə(r)/ *n* Altar *m*

alter /'ɔ:ltə(r)/ *vt* ändern ●*vi* sich verändern. **~ation** *n* Änderung *f*

alternate[1] /'ɔ:ltəneɪt/ *vi* [sich] abwechseln ●*vt* abwechseln

alternate[2] /ɔ:l'tɜ:nət/ *adj* abwechselnd; **on ~ days** jeden zweiten Tag

alternative /ɔ:l'tɜ:nətɪv/ *adj* andere(r,s); **~ medicine** Alternativmedizin *f* ●*n* Alternative *f*. **~ly** *adv* oder aber

although /ɔ:l'ðəʊ/ *conj* obgleich, obwohl

altitude /'æltɪtju:d/ *n* Höhe *f*

altogether /ɔ:ltə'geðə(r)/ *adv* insgesamt; (*on the whole*) alles in allem

aluminium /æljʊ'mɪnɪəm/ *n*, (*Amer*) **aluminum** *n* Aluminium *nt*

always /'ɔ:lweɪz/ *adv* immer

am /æm/ *see* **be**

a.m. *abbr* (**ante meridiem**) vormittags

amass /ə'mæs/ *vt* anhäufen

amateur /'æmətə(r)/ *n* Amateur *m* ●*attrib* Amateur-; (*Theat*) Laien-. **~ish** *adj* laienhaft

amaze /ə'meɪz/ *vt* erstaunen. **~d** *adj* erstaunt. **~ment** *n* Erstaunen *nt*

amazing /ə'meɪzɪŋ/ *adj* erstaunlich

ambassador /æm'bæsədə(r)/ *n* Botschafter *m*

amber /'æmbə(r)/ *n* Bernstein *m* ●*adj* (*colour*) gelb

ambigu|ity /æmbɪ'gju:ətɪ/ *n* Zweideutigkeit *f*. **~ous** *adj* **-ly** *adv* zweideutig

ambiti|on /æm'bɪʃn/ *n* Ehrgeiz *m*; (*aim*) Ambition *f*. **~ous** *adj* ehrgeizig

a

amble /'æmbl/ *vi* schlendern

ambulance /'æmbjʊləns/ *n* Krankenwagen *m*. ~ **man** *n* Sanitäter *m*

ambush /'æmbʊʃ/ *n* Hinterhalt *m* ● *vt* aus dem Hinterhalt überfallen

amen /ɑː'men/ *int* amen

amend /ə'mend/ *vt* ändern. **~ment** *n* Änderung *f*

amenities /ə'miːnətɪz/ *npl* Einrichtungen *pl*

America /ə'merɪkə/ *n* Amerika *nt*. **~n** *adj* amerikanisch ● *n* Amerikaner(in) *m*(*f*). **~nism** *n* Amerikanismus *m*

American dream Der Glaube, dass Amerika das Land unbegrenzter Möglichkeiten ist, in dem jeder sein Leben erfolgreich gestalten kann. Für Minderheiten und Einwanderer bedeutet der Traum weitgehende Toleranz und Anspruch auf eigene freie Lebensgestaltung. Der *American dream* verkörpert eine optimistische allgemeine Grundhaltung mit auf Erfolg gerichtetem Denken und Handeln.

amiable /'eɪmɪəbl/ *adj* nett

amicable /'æmɪkəbl/ *adj*, **-bly** *adv* freundschaftlich; (*agreement*) gütlich

amid[st] /ə'mɪd[st]/ *prep* inmitten (+ *gen*)

ammonia /ə'məʊnɪə/ *n* Ammoniak *nt*

ammunition /æmjʊ'nɪʃn/ *n* Munition *f*

amnesty /'æmnəstɪ/ *n* Amnestie *f*

among[st] /ə'mʌŋ[st]/ *prep* unter (+ *dat*/*acc*); ~ **yourselves** untereinander

amoral /eɪ'mɒrəl/ *adj* amoralisch

amorous /'æmərəs/ *adj* zärtlich

amount /ə'maʊnt/ *n* Menge *f*; (*sum of money*) Betrag *m*; (*total*) Gesamtsumme *f* ● *vi* ~ **to** sich belaufen auf (+ *acc*); (*fig*) hinauslaufen auf (+ *acc*)

amphibi|an /æm'fɪbɪən/ *n* Amphibie *f*. **~ous** *adj* amphibisch

amphitheatre /'æmfɪ-/ *n* Amphitheater *nt*

ample /'æmpl/ *adj* (**-r,-st**) reichlich; (*large*) füllig

amplif|ier /'æmplɪfaɪə(r)/ *n* Verstärker *m*. **~y** *vt* (*pt*/*pp* **-ied**) weiter ausführen; verstärken (*sound*)

amputat|e /'æmpjʊteɪt/ *vt* amputieren. **~ion** *n* Amputation *f*

amuse /ə'mjuːz/ *vt* amüsieren, belustigen; (*entertain*) unterhalten. **~ment** *n* Belustigung *f*; Unterhaltung *f*

amusing /ə'mjuːzɪŋ/ *adj* amüsant

an /ən/, *betont* /æn/ *see* **a**

anaem|ia /ə'niːmɪə/ *n* Blutarmut *f*, Anämie *f*. **~ic** *adj* blutarm

anaesthetic /ænəs'θetɪk/ *n* Narkosemittel *nt*, Betäubungsmittel *nt*; **under [an]** ~ in Narkose

anaesthetist /ə'niːsθətɪst/ *n* Narkosearzt *m*

analogy /ə'nælədʒɪ/ *n* Analogie *f*

analyse /'ænəlaɪz/ *vt* analysieren

analysis /ə'næləsɪs/ *n* Analyse *f*

analyst /'ænəlɪst/ *n* Chemiker(in) *m*(*f*); (*psychologist*) Analytiker *m*

analytical /ænə'lɪtɪkl/ *adj* analytisch

anarch|ist /'ænəkɪst/ *n* Anarchist *m*. **~y** *n* Anarchie *f*

anatom|ical /ænə'tɒmɪkl/ *adj* anatomisch. **~y** *n* Anatomie *f*

ancest|or /'ænsestə(r)/ *n* Vorfahr *m*. **~ry** *n* Abstammung *f*

anchor /'æŋkə(r)/ *n* Anker *m* ● *vi* ankern ● *vt* verankern

ancient /'eɪnʃənt/ *adj* alt

and /ənd/, *betont* /ænd/ *conj* und; ~ **so on** und so weiter; **six hundred** ~ **two** sechshundertzwei; **more** ~ **more** immer mehr; **nice** ~ **warm** schön warm

anecdote /ˈænɪkdəʊt/ *n* Anekdote *f*

angel /ˈeɪndʒl/ *n* Engel *m*. ~**ic** *adj* engelhaft

anger /ˈæŋgə(r)/ *n* Zorn *m* ● *vt* zornig machen

angle /ˈæŋgl/ *n* Winkel *m*; (*fig*) Standpunkt *m*; **at an** ~ schräg

angler /ˈæŋglə(r)/ *n* Angler *m*

Anglican /ˈæŋglɪkən/ *adj* anglikanisch ● *n* Anglikaner(in) *m*(*f*)

Anglo-Saxon /æŋgləʊˈsæksn/ *adj* angelsächsich ● *n* (*Lang*) Angelsächsisch *nt*

angry /ˈæŋgrɪ/ *adj*, **-ily** *adv* zornig; **be** ~ **with** böse sein auf (+ *acc*)

anguish /ˈæŋgwɪʃ/ *n* Qual *f*

angular /ˈæŋgjʊlə(r)/ *adj* eckig; (*features*) kantig

animal /ˈænɪml/ *n* Tier *nt* ● *adj* tierisch

animat|e /ˈænɪmeɪt/ *vt* beleben. ~**ed** *adj* lebhaft

animosity /ænɪˈmɒsətɪ/ *n* Feindseligkeit *f*

ankle /ˈæŋkl/ *n* [Fuß]knöchel *m*

annex[e] /ˈæneks/ *n* Nebengebäude *nt*; (*extension*) Anbau *m*

annihilate /əˈnaɪəleɪt/ *vt* vernichten

anniversary /ænɪˈvɜːsərɪ/ *n* Jahrestag *m*

annotate /ˈænəteɪt/ *vt* kommentieren

announce /əˈnaʊns/ *vt* bekannt geben; (*over loudspeaker*) durchsagen; (*at reception*) ankündigen; (*Radio, TV*) ansagen; (*in newspaper*) anzeigen. ~**ment** *n* Bekanntgabe *f*, Bekanntmachung *f*; Durchsage *f*; Ansage *f*; Anzeige *f*. ~**r** *n* Ansager(in) *m*(*f*)

annoy /əˈnɔɪ/ *vt* ärgern; (*pester*) belästigen; **get** ~**ed** sich ärgern. ~**ance** *n* Ärger *m*. ~**ing** *adj* ärgerlich

annual /ˈænjʊəl/ *adj* jährlich ● *n* (*book*) Jahresalbum *nt*

anonymous /əˈnɒnɪməs/ *adj* anonym

anorak /ˈænəræk/ *n* Anorak *m*

anorexi|a /ænəˈreksɪə/ *n* Magersucht *f*; **be** ~**c** an Magersucht leiden

another /əˈnʌðə(r)/ *adj & pron* ein anderer/eine andere/ein anderes; (*additional*) noch ein(e); ~ **[one]** noch einer/eine/eins; ~ **time** ein andermal; **one** ~ einander

answer /ˈɑːnsə(r)/ *n* Antwort *f*; (*solution*) Lösung *f* ● *vt* antworten (**s.o.** jdm); beantworten (*question, letter*); ~ **the door/telephone** an die Tür/ans Telefon gehen ● *vi* antworten; (*Teleph*) sich melden; ~ **back** eine freche Antwort geben. ~**ing machine** *n* (*Teleph*) Anrufbeantworter *m*

ant /ænt/ *n* Ameise *f*

antagonis|m /ænˈtægənɪzm/ *n* Antagonismus *m*. ~**tic** *adj* feindselig

Antarctic /æntˈɑːktɪk/ *n* Antarktis *f*

antelope /ˈæntɪləʊp/ *n* Antilope *f*

antenatal /æntɪˈneɪtl/ *adj* ~ **care** Schwangerschaftsfürsorge *f*

antenna /ænˈtenə/ *n* Fühler *m*; (*Amer: aerial*) Antenne *f*

anthem /ˈænθəm/ *n* Hymne *f*

anthology /ænˈθɒlədʒɪ/ *n* Anthologie *f*

anthrax /ˈænθræks/ *n* Milzbrand *m*, Anthrax *m*

a

anthropology /ænθrəˈpɒlədʒɪ/ *n* Anthropologie *f*

antibiotic /æntɪbaɪˈɒtɪk/ *n* Antibiotikum *nt*

anticipat|e /ænˈtɪsɪpeɪt/ *vt* vorhersehen; (*forestall*) zuvorkommen (+ *dat*); (*expect*) erwarten. **~ion** *n* Erwartung *f*

antiˈclimax *n* Enttäuschung *f*

antiˈclockwise *adj & adv* gegen den Uhrzeigersinn

antics /ˈæntɪks/ *npl* Mätzchen *pl*

antidote /ˈæntɪdəʊt/ *n* Gegengift *nt*

ˈantifreeze *n* Frostschutzmittel *nt*

antipathy /ænˈtɪpəθɪ/ *n* Abneigung *f*, Antipathie *f*

antiquated /ˈæntɪkweɪtɪd/ *adj* veraltet

antique /ænˈtiːk/ *adj* antik ● *n* Antiquität *f*. **~ dealer** *n* Antiquitätenhändler *m*

antiquity /ænˈtɪkwətɪ/ *n* Altertum *nt*

antiˈseptic *adj* antiseptisch ● *n* Antiseptikum *nt*

antiˈsocial *adj* asozial; 🄵 ungesellig

antlers /ˈæntləz/ *npl* Geweih *nt*

anus /ˈeɪnəs/ *n* After *m*

anvil /ˈænvɪl/ *n* Amboss *m*

anxiety /æŋˈzaɪətɪ/ *n* Sorge *f*

anxious /ˈæŋkʃəs/ *adj* ängstlich; (*worried*) besorgt; **be ~ to do sth** etw gerne machen wollen

any /ˈenɪ/ *adj* irgendein(e); *pl* irgendwelche; (*every*) jede(r,s); *pl* alle; (*after negative*) kein(e); *pl* keine; **~ colour/number you like** eine beliebige Farbe/Zahl; **have you ~ wine/apples?** haben Sie Wein/Äpfel? ● *pron* [irgend]einer/eine/eins; *pl* [irgend]welche; (*some*) welche(r,s); *pl* welche; (*all*) alle *pl*; (*negative*) keiner/keine/keins; *pl* keine; **I don't want ~ of it** ich will nichts davon; **there aren't ~** es gibt keine ● *adv* noch; **~ quicker/slower** noch schneller/langsamer; **is it ~ better?** geht es etwas besser? **would you like ~ more?** möchten Sie noch [etwas]? **I can't eat ~ more** ich kann nichts mehr essen

ˈanybody *pron* [irgend]jemand; (*after negative*) niemand; **~ can do that** das kann jeder

ˈanyhow *adv* jedenfalls; (*nevertheless*) trotzdem; (*badly*) irgendwie

ˈanyone *pron* = **anybody**

ˈanything *pron* [irgend]etwas; (*after negative*) nichts; (*everything*) alles

ˈanyway *adv* jedenfalls; (*in any case*) sowieso

ˈanywhere *adv* irgendwo; (*after negative*) nirgendwo; (*be, live*) überall; (*go*) überallhin

apart /əˈpɑːt/ *adv* auseinander; **live ~** getrennt leben; **~ from** abgesehen von

apartment /əˈpɑːtmənt/ *n* Zimmer *nt*; (*flat*) Wohnung *f*

ape /eɪp/ *n* [Menschen]affe *m* ● *vt* nachäffen

aperitif /əˈperətiːf/ *n* Aperitif *m*

apologetic /əpɒləˈdʒetɪk/ *adj*, **-ally** *adv* entschuldigend; **be ~** sich entschuldigen

apologize /əˈpɒlədʒaɪz/ *vi* sich entschuldigen (**to** bei)

apology /əˈpɒlədʒɪ/ *n* Entschuldigung *f*

apostle /əˈpɒsl/ *n* Apostel *m*

apostrophe /əˈpɒstrəfɪ/ *n* Apostroph *m*

appal /əˈpɔːl/ *vt* (*pt/pp* **appalled**) entsetzen. **~ling** *adj* entsetzlich

apparatus /æpəˈreɪtəs/ *n* Apparatur *f*; (*Sport*) Geräte *pl*; (*single piece*)

Gerät *nt*

apparent /ə'pærənt/ *adj* offenbar; (*seeming*) scheinbar. **~ly** *adv* offenbar, anscheinend

appeal /ə'pi:l/ *n* Appell *m*, Aufruf *m*; (*request*) Bitte *f*; (*attraction*) Reiz *m*; (*Jur*) Berufung *f* ● *vi* appellieren (**to** an + *acc*); (*ask*) bitten (**for** um); (*be attractive*) zusagen (**to** *dat*); (*Jur*) Berufung einlegen. **~ing** *adj* ansprechend

appear /ə'pɪə(r)/ *vi* erscheinen; (*seem*) scheinen; (*Theat*) auftreten. **~ance** *n* Erscheinen *nt*; (*look*) Aussehen *nt*; **to all ~ances** allem Anschein nach

appendicitis /əpendɪ'saɪtɪs/ *n* Blinddarmentzündung *f*

appendix /ə'pendɪks/ *n* (*pl* **-ices** /-ɪsi:z/) (*of book*) Anhang *m* ● (*pl* **-es**) (*Anat*) Blinddarm *m*

appetite /'æpɪtaɪt/ *n* Appetit *m*

appetizing /'æpɪtaɪzɪŋ/ *adj* appetitlich

applau|d /ə'plɔ:d/ *vt/i* Beifall klatschen (+ *dat*). **~se** *n* Beifall *m*

apple /'æpl/ *n* Apfel *m*

appliance /ə'plaɪəns/ *n* Gerät *nt*

applicable /'æplɪkəbl/ *adj* anwendbar (**to** auf + *acc*); (*on form*) **not ~** nicht zutreffend

applicant /'æplɪkənt/ *n* Bewerbe-r(in) *m(f)*

application /æplɪ'keɪʃn/ *n* Anwendung *f*; (*request*) Antrag *m*; (*for job*) Bewerbung *f*; (*diligence*) Fleiß *m*

applied /ə'plaɪd/ *adj* angewandt

apply /ə'plaɪ/ *vt* (*pt/pp* **-ied**) auftragen (*paint*); anwenden (*force, rule*) ● *vi* zutreffen (**to** auf + *acc*); **~ for** beantragen; sich bewerben um (*job*)

appoint /ə'pɔɪnt/ *vt* ernennen; (*fix*) festlegen. **~ment** *n* Ernennung *f*; (*meeting*) Verabredung *f*; (*at doctor's, hairdresser's*) Termin *m*; (*job*) Posten *m*; **make an ~ment** sich anmelden

appreciable /ə'pri:ʃəbl/ *adj* merklich; (*considerable*) beträchtlich

appreciat|e /ə'pri:ʃɪeɪt/ *vt* zu schätzen wissen; (*be grateful for*) dankbar sein für; (*enjoy*) schätzen; (*understand*) verstehen ● *vi* (*increase in value*) im Wert steigen. **~ion** *n* (*gratitude*) Dankbarkeit *f*. **~ive** *adj* dankbar

apprehens|ion /æprɪ'henʃn/ *n* Festnahme *f*; (*fear*) Angst *f*. **~ive** *adj* ängstlich

apprentice /ə'prentɪs/ *n* Lehrling *m*. **~ship** *n* Lehre *f*

approach /ə'prəʊtʃ/ *n* Näherkommen *nt*; (*of time*) Nahen *nt*; (*access*) Zugang *m*; (*road*) Zufahrt *f* ● *vi* sich nähern; (*time:*) nahen ● *vt* sich nähern (+ *dat*); (*with request*) herantreten an (+ *acc*); (*set about*) sich heranmachen an (+ *acc*). **~able** *adj* zugänglich

appropriate /ə'prəʊprɪət/ *adj* angebracht, angemessen

approval /ə'pru:vl/ *n* Billigung *f*; **on ~** zur Ansicht

approv|e /ə'pru:v/ *vt* billigen ● *vi* **~e of sth/s.o.** mit etw/jdm einverstanden sein. **~ing** *adj* anerkennend

approximate /ə'prɒksɪmət/ *adj*, **-ly** *adv* ungefähr

approximation /əprɒksɪ'meɪʃn/ *n* Schätzung *f*

apricot /'eɪprɪkɒt/ *n* Aprikose *f*

April /'eɪprəl/ *n* April *m*; **make an ~ fool of** in den April schicken

apron /'eɪprən/ *n* Schürze *f*

apt /æpt/ *adj* passend; **be ~ to do sth** dazu neigen, etw zu tun

aqualung /'ækwəlʌŋ/ *n* Tauchgerät *nt*

a

aquarium /ə'kweərɪəm/ *n* Aquarium *nt*
aquatic /ə'kwætɪk/ *adj* Wasser-
Arab /'ærəb/ *adj* arabisch ● *n* Araber(in) *m(f)*. **~ian** *adj* arabisch
Arabic /'ærəbɪk/ *adj* arabisch
arbitrary /'ɑ:bɪtrərɪ/ *adj*, **-ily** *adv* willkürlich
arbitrat|e /'ɑ:bɪtreɪt/ *vi* schlichten. **~ion** *n* Schlichtung *f*
arc /ɑ:k/ *n* Bogen *m*
arcade /ɑ:'keɪd/ *n* Laubengang *m*; (*shops*) Einkaufspassage *f*
arch /ɑ:tʃ/ *n* Bogen *m*; (*of foot*) Gewölbe *nt* ● *vt* **~ its back** (*cat:*) einen Buckel machen
archaeological /ɑ:kɪə'lɒdʒɪkl/ *adj* archäologisch
archaeolog|ist /ɑ:kɪ'ɒlədʒɪst/ *n* Archäologe *m*/-login *f*. **~y** *n* Archäologie *f*
archaic /ɑ:'keɪɪk/ *adj* veraltet
arch'bishop /ɑ:tʃ-/ *n* Erzbischof *m*
archer /'ɑ:tʃə(r)/ *n* Bogenschütze *m*. **~y** *n* Bogenschießen *nt*
architect /'ɑ:kɪtekt/ *n* Architekt(in) *m(f)*. **~ural** *adj* architektonisch
architecture /'ɑ:kɪtektʃə(r)/ *n* Architektur *f*
archives /'ɑ:kaɪvz/ *npl* Archiv *nt*
archway /'ɑ:tʃweɪ/ *n* Torbogen *m*
Arctic /'ɑ:ktɪk/ *adj* arktisch ● *n* **the ~** die Arktis
ardent /'ɑ:dənt/ *adj* leidenschaftlich
ardour /'ɑ:də(r)/ *n* Leidenschaft *f*
arduous /'ɑ:djʊəs/ *adj* mühsam
are /ɑ:(r)/ *see* **be**
area /'eərɪə/ *n* (*surface*) Fläche *f*; (*Geometry*) Flächeninhalt *m*; (*region*) Gegend *f*; (*fig*) Gebiet *nt*
arena /ə'ri:nə/ *n* Arena *f*
Argentina /ɑ:dʒən'ti:nə/ *n* Argentinien *nt*
Argentin|e /'ɑ:dʒəntaɪn/, **~ian** /-'tɪnɪən/ *adj* argentinisch
argue /'ɑ:gju:/ *vi* streiten (**about** über + *acc*); (*two people:*) sich streiten; (*debate*) diskutieren; **don't ~!** keine Widerrede! ● *vt* (*debate*) diskutieren; (*reason*) **~ that** argumentieren, dass
argument /'ɑ:gjʊmənt/ *n* Streit *m*, Auseinandersetzung *f*; (*reasoning*) Argument *nt*; **have an ~** sich streiten. **~ative** *adj* streitlustig
aria /'ɑ:rɪə/ *n* Arie *f*
arise /ə'raɪz/ *vi* (*pt* **arose**, *pp* **arisen**) sich ergeben (**from** aus)
aristocracy /ærɪ'stɒkrəsɪ/ *n* Aristokratie *f*
aristocrat /'ærɪstəkræt/ *n* Aristokrat(in) *m(f)*. **~ic** *adj* aristokratisch
arithmetic /ə'rɪθmətɪk/ *n* Rechnen *nt*
arm /ɑ:m/ *n* Arm *m*; (*of chair*) Armlehne *f*; **~s** *pl* (*weapons*) Waffen *pl*; (*Heraldry*) Wappen *nt* ● *vt* bewaffnen
armament /'ɑ:məmənt/ *n* Bewaffnung *f*; **~s** *pl* Waffen *pl*
'armchair *n* Sessel *m*
armed /ɑ:md/ *adj* bewaffnet; **~ forces** Streitkräfte *pl*
armour /'ɑ:mə(r)/ *n* Rüstung *f*. **~ed** *adj* Panzer-
'armpit *n* Achselhöhle *f*
army /'ɑ:mɪ/ *n* Heer *nt*; (*specific*) Armee *f*; **join the ~** zum Militär gehen
aroma /ə'rəʊmə/ *n* Aroma *nt*, Duft *m*. **~tic** *adj* aromatisch
arose /ə'rəʊz/ *see* **arise**
around /ə'raʊnd/ *adv* **[all] ~** rings herum; **he's not ~** er ist nicht da; **travel ~** herumreisen ● *prep* um (+ *acc*) ... herum; (*approximately*,

nearly) gegen

arouse /ə'raʊz/ *vt* aufwecken; (*excite*) erregen

arrange /ə'reɪndʒ/ *vt* arrangieren; anordnen (*furniture, books*); (*settle*) abmachen. **~ment** *n* Anordnung *f*; (*agreement*) Vereinbarung *f*; (*of flowers*) Gesteck *nt*; **make ~ments** Vorkehrungen treffen

arrest /ə'rest/ *n* Verhaftung *f*; **under ~** verhaftet ● *vt* verhaften

arrival /ə'raɪvl/ *n* Ankunft *f*; **new ~s** *pl* Neuankömmlinge *pl*

arrive /ə'raɪv/ *vi* ankommen; **~ at** (*fig*) gelangen zu

arrogan|ce /'ærəgəns/ *n* Arroganz *f*. **~t** *adj* arrogant

arrow /'ærəʊ/ *n* Pfeil *m*

arse /ɑ:s/ *n* (*vulgar*) Arsch *m*

arson /'ɑ:sn/ *n* Brandstiftung *f*. **~ist** *n* Brandstifter *m*

art /ɑ:t/ *n* Kunst *f*; **work of ~** Kunstwerk *nt*; **~s and crafts** *pl* Kunstgewerbe *nt*; **A~s** *pl* (*Univ*) Geisteswissenschaften *pl*

artery /'ɑ:tərɪ/ *n* Schlagader *f*, Arterie *f*

'art gallery *n* Kunstgalerie *f*

arthritis /ɑ:'θraɪtɪs/ *n* Arthritis *f*

artichoke /'ɑ:tɪtʃəʊk/ *n* Artischocke *f*

article /'ɑ:tɪkl/ *n* Artikel *m*; (*object*) Gegenstand *m*; **~ of clothing** Kleidungsstück *nt*

artificial /ɑ:tɪ'fɪʃl/ *adj* künstlich

artillery /ɑ:'tɪlərɪ/ *n* Artillerie *f*

artist /'ɑ:tɪst/ *n* Künstler(in) *m*(*f*)

artiste /ɑ:'ti:st/ *n* (*Theat*) Artist(in) *m*(*f*)

artistic /ɑ:'tɪstɪk/ *adj*, **-ally** *adv* künstlerisch

as /æz/ *conj* (*because*) da; (*when*) als; (*while*) während ● *prep* als; **as a child/foreigner** als Kind/Ausländer ● *adv* **as well** auch; **as soon as** sobald; **as much as** so viel wie; **as quick as you** so schnell wie du; **as you know** wie Sie wissen; **as far as I'm concerned** was mich betrifft

asbestos /æz'bestɒs/ *n* Asbest *m*

ascend /ə'send/ *vi* [auf]steigen ● *vt* besteigen (*throne*)

ascent /ə'sent/ *n* Aufstieg *m*

ascertain /æsə'teɪn/ *vt* ermitteln

ash¹ /æʃ/ *n* (*tree*) Esche *f*

ash² *n* Asche *f*

ashamed /ə'ʃeɪmd/ *adj* beschämt; **be ~** sich schämen (**of** über + *acc*)

ashore /ə'ʃɔ:(r)/ *adv* an Land

'ashtray *n* Aschenbecher *m*

Asia /'eɪʃə/ *n* Asien *nt*. **~n** *adj* asiatisch ● *n* Asiat(in) *m*(*f*). **~tic** *adj* asiatisch

aside /ə'saɪd/ *adv* beiseite

ask /ɑ:sk/ *vt/i* **fragen**; stellen (*question*); (*invite*) einladen; **~ for** bitten um; verlangen (*s.o.*); **~ after** sich erkundigen nach; **~ s.o. in** jdn hereinbitten; **~ s.o. to do sth** jdn bitten, etw zu tun

asleep /ə'sli:p/ *adj* **be ~** schlafen; **fall ~** einschlafen

asparagus /ə'spærəgəs/ *n* Spargel *m*

aspect /'æspekt/ *n* Aspekt *m*

asphalt /'æsfælt/ *n* Asphalt *m*

aspire /ə'spaɪə(r)/ *vi* **~ to** streben nach

ass /æs/ *n* Esel *m*

assail /ə'seɪl/ *vt* bestürmen. **~ant** *n* Angreifer(in) *m*(*f*)

assassin /ə'sæsɪn/ *n* Mörder(in) *m*(*f*). **~ate** *vt* ermorden. **~ation** *n* [politischer] Mord *m*

assault /ə'sɔ:lt/ *n* (*Mil*) Angriff *m*; (*Jur*) Körperverletzung *f* ● *vt* [tätlich] angreifen

assemble /ə'sembl/ *vi* sich versammeln ● *vt* versammeln; (*Techn*) montieren

assembly /əˈsemblɪ/ *n* Versammlung *f*; (*Sch*) Andacht *f*; (*Techn*) Montage *f*. **~ line** *n* Fließband *nt*

assent /əˈsent/ *n* Zustimmung *f*

assert /əˈsɜːt/ *vt* behaupten; **~ oneself** sich durchsetzen. **~ion** *n* Behauptung *f*

assess /əˈses/ *vt* bewerten; (*fig & for tax purposes*) einschätzen: schätzen (*value*). **~ment** *n* Einschätzung *f*; (*of tax*) Steuerbescheid *m*

asset /ˈæset/ *n* Vorteil *m*; **~s** *pl* (*money*) Vermögen *nt*; (*Comm*) Aktiva *pl*

assign /əˈsaɪn/ *vt* zuweisen (**to** *dat*). **~ment** *n* (*task*) Aufgabe *f*

assist /əˈsɪst/ *vt/i* helfen (+ *dat*). **~ance** *n* Hilfe *f*. **~ant** *adj* Hilfs- ● *n* Assistent(in) *m(f)*; (*in shop*) Verkäufer(in) *m(f)*

associat|e¹ /əˈsəʊʃɪeɪt/ *vt* verbinden; (*Psychology*) assoziieren ● *vi* **~ with** verkehren mit. **~ion** *n* Verband *m*

associate² /əˈsəʊʃɪət/ *adj* assoziiert ● *n* Kollege *m*/-gin *f*

assort|ed /əˈsɔːtɪd/ *adj* gemischt. **~ment** *n* Mischung *f*

assum|e /əˈsjuːm/ *vt* annehmen; übernehmen (*office*); **~ing that** angenommen, dass

assumption /əˈsʌmpʃn/ *n* Annahme *f*; **on the ~** in der Annahme (**that** dass)

assurance /əˈʃʊərəns/ *n* Versicherung *f*; (*confidence*) Selbstsicherheit *f*

assure /əˈʃʊə(r)/ *vt* versichern (**s.o.** jdm); **I ~ you [of that]** das versichere ich Ihnen. **~d** *adj* sicher

asterisk /ˈæstərɪsk/ *n* Sternchen *nt*

asthma /ˈæsmə/ *n* Asthma *nt*

astonish /əˈstɒnɪʃ/ *vt* erstaunen. **~ing** *adj* erstaunlich. **~ment** *n* Erstaunen *nt*

astray /əˈstreɪ/ *adv* **go ~** verloren gehen; (*person:*) sich verlaufen

astride /əˈstraɪd/ *adv* rittlings ● *prep* rittlings auf (+ *dat*/*acc*)

astrolog|er /əˈstrɒlədʒə(r)/ *n* Astrologe *m*/-gin *f*. **~y** *n* Astrologie *f*

astronaut /ˈæstrənɔːt/ *n* Astronaut(in) *m(f)*

astronom|er /əˈstrɒnəmə(r)/ *n* Astronom *m*. **~ical** *adj* astronomisch. **~y** *n* Astronomie *f*

astute /əˈstjuːt/ *adj* scharfsinnig

asylum /əˈsaɪləm/ *n* Asyl *nt*; **[lunatic] ~** Irrenanstalt *f*. **~-seeker** *n* Asylbewerber(in) *m(f)*

at /æt/, *unbetont* /ət/

● *preposition*

····➤ (*expressing place*) an (+ *dat*). **at the station** am Bahnhof. **at the end** am Ende. **at the corner** an der Ecke. **at the same place** an der gleichen Stelle

····➤ (*at s.o.'s house or shop*) bei (+ *dat*). **at Lisa's** bei Lisa. **at my uncle's** bei meinem Onkel. **at the baker's**/**butcher's** beim Bäcker/Fleischer

····➤ (*inside a building*) in (+ *dat*). **at the theatre**/**supermarket** im Theater/Supermarkt. **we spent the night at a hotel** wir übernachteten in einem Hotel. **he is still at the office** er ist noch im Büro

····➤ (*expressing time*) (*with clock time*) um; (*with main festivals*) zu. **at six o'clock** um sechs Uhr. **at midnight** um Mitternacht. **at midday** um zwölf Uhr mittags. **at Christmas**/**Easter** zu

Weihnachten/Ostern

····➤ (*expressing age*) mit. **at [the age of] forty** mit vierzig; im Alter von vierzig

····➤ (*expressing price*) zu. **at £2.50 [each]** zu *od* für [je] 2,50 Pfund

····➤ (*expressing speed*) mit. **at 30 m.p.h.** mit dreißig Meilen pro Stunde

····➤ (*in phrases*) **good/bad at languages** gut/schlecht in Sprachen. **two at a time** zwei auf einmal. **at that** (*at that point*) dabei; (*at that provocation*) daraufhin; (*moreover*) noch dazu

ate /et/ *see* **eat**

atheist /'eɪθɪɪst/ *n* Atheist(in) *m*(*f*)

athlet|e /'æθli:t/ *n* Athlet(in) *m*(*f*). **~ic** *adj* sportlich. **~ics** *n* Leichtathletik *f*

Atlantic /ət'læntɪk/ *adj* & *n* **the ~ [Ocean]** der Atlantik

atlas /'ætləs/ *n* Atlas *m*

atmosphere /'ætməsfɪə(r)/ *n* Atmosphäre *f*

atom /'ætəm/ *n* Atom *nt*. **~ bomb** *n* Atombombe *f*

atomic /ə'tɒmɪk/ *adj* Atom-

atrocious /ə'trəʊʃəs/ *adj* abscheulich

atrocity /ə'trɒsətɪ/ *n* Gräueltat *f*

attach /ə'tætʃ/ *vt* befestigen (**to** an + *dat*); beimessen (*importance*) (**to** *dat*); **be ~ed to** (*fig*) hängen an (+ *dat*). **~ment** *n* (*to email*) Anhang *m*

attack /ə'tæk/ *n* Angriff *m*; (*Med*) Anfall *m* ● *vt/i* angreifen. **~er** *n* Angreifer *m*

attain /ə'teɪn/ *vt* erreichen. **~able** *adj* erreichbar

attempt /ə'tempt/ *n* Versuch *m* ● *vt* versuchen

attend /ə'tend/ *vt* anwesend sein bei; (*go regularly to*) besuchen; (*take part in*) teilnehmen an (+ *dat*); (*accompany*) begleiten; (*doctor:*) behandeln ● *vi* anwesend sein; (*pay attention*) aufpassen; **~ to** sich kümmern um; (*in shop*) bedienen. **~ance** *n* Anwesenheit *f*; (*number*) Besucherzahl *f*. **~ant** *n* Wärter(in) *m*(*f*); (*in car park*) Wächter *m*

attention /ə'tenʃn/ *n* Aufmerksamkeit *f*; **~!** (*Mil*) stillgestanden! **pay ~** aufpassen; **pay ~ to** beachten, achten auf (+ *acc*)

attentive /ə'tentɪv/ *adj* aufmerksam

attic /'ætɪk/ *n* Dachboden *m*

attitude /'ætɪtju:d/ *n* Haltung *f*

attorney /ə'tɜ:nɪ/ *n* (*Amer: lawyer*) Rechtsanwalt *m*; **power of ~** Vollmacht *f*

attract /ə'trækt/ *vt* anziehen; erregen (*attention*); **~ s.o.'s attention** jds Aufmerksamkeit auf sich (*acc*) lenken. **~ion** *n* Anziehungskraft *f*; (*charm*) Reiz *m*; (*thing*) Attraktion *f*. **~ive** *adj*, -ly *adv* attraktiv

attribute /ə'trɪbju:t/ *vt* zuschreiben (**to** *dat*)

aubergine /'əʊbəʒi:n/ *n* Aubergine *f*

auburn /'ɔ:bən/ *adj* kastanienbraun

auction /'ɔ:kʃn/ *n* Auktion *f* Versteigerung *f* ● *vt* versteigern. **~eer** *n* Auktionator *m*

audaci|ous /ɔ:'deɪʃəs/ *adj* verwegen. **~ty** *n* Verwegenheit *f*; (*impudence*) Dreistigkeit *f*

audible /'ɔ:dəbl/ *adj*, **-bly** *adv* hörbar

audience /'ɔ:dɪəns/ *n* Publikum *nt*; (*Theat, TV*) Zuschauer *pl*; (*Radio*) Zuhörer *pl*; (*meeting*) Audienz *f*

audit /'ɔ:dɪt/ *n* Bücherrevision *f* ● *vt* (*Comm*) prüfen

audition /ɔ:'dɪʃn/ *n* (*Theat*) Vorsprechen *nt*; (*Mus*) Vorspielen *nt* (*for singer*) Vorsingen *nt* ● *vi* vorsprechen; vorspielen; vorsingen

auditor /'ɔːdɪtə(r)/ *n* Buchprüfer *m*

auditorium /ɔːdɪ'tɔːrɪəm/ *n* Zuschauerraum *m*

August /'ɔːgəst/ *n* August *m*

aunt /ɑːnt/ *n* Tante *f*

au pair /əʊ'peə(r)/ *n* ~ **[girl]** Au-pair-Mädchen *nt*

aura /'ɔːrə/ *n* Fluidum *nt*

auspicious /ɔː'spɪʃəs/ *adj* günstig; (*occasion*) freudig

auster|e /ɒ'stɪə(r)/ *adj* streng; (*simple*) nüchtern. **~ity** *n* Strenge *f*; (*hardship*) Entbehrung *f*

Australia /ɒ'streɪlɪə/ *n* Australien *nt*. **~n** *adj* australisch ● *n* Australier(in) *m*(*f*)

Austria /'ɒstrɪə/ *n* Österreich *nt* **~n** *adj* österreichisch ● *n* Österreicher(in) *m*(*f*)

authentic /ɔː'θentɪk/ *adj* echt, authentisch. **~ate** *vt* beglaubigen. **~ity** *n* Echtheit *f*

author /'ɔːθə(r)/ *n* Schriftsteller *m*, Autor *m*; (*of document*) Verfasser *m*

authoritarian /ɔːθɒrɪ'teərɪən/ *adj* autoritär

authoritative /ɔː'θɒrɪtətɪv/ *adj* maßgebend

authority /ɔː'θɒrətɪ/ *n* Autorität *f*; (*public*) Behörde *f*; **in** ~ verantwortlich

authorization /ɔːθəraɪ'zeɪʃn/ *n* Ermächtigung *f*

authorize /'ɔːθəraɪz/ *vt* ermächtigen (*s.o.*); genehmigen (*sth*)

autobi'ography /ɔːtə-/ *n* Autobiographie *f*

autograph /'ɔːtə-/ *n* Autogramm *nt*

automatic /ɔːtə'mætɪk/ *adj*, **-ally** *adv* automatisch

automation /ɔːtə'meɪʃn/ *n* Automation *f*

automobile /'ɔːtəməbiːl/ *n* Auto *nt*

autonom|ous /ɔː'tɒnəməs/ *adj* autonom. **~y** *n* Autonomie *f*

autumn /'ɔːtəm/ *n* Herbst *m*. **~al** *adj* herbstlich

auxiliary /ɔːg'zɪlɪərɪ/ *adj* Hilfs- ● *n* Helfer(in) *m*(*f*), Hilfskraft *f*

avail /ə'veɪl/ *n* **to no** ~ vergeblich

available /ə'veɪləbl/ *adj* verfügbar; (*obtainable*) erhältlich

avalanche /'ævəlɑːnʃ/ *n* Lawine *f*

avenge /ə'vendʒ/ *vt* rächen

avenue /'ævənjuː/ *n* Allee *f*

average /'ævərɪdʒ/ *adj* Durchschnitts-, durchschnittlich ● *n* Durchschnitt *m*; **on** ~ im Durchschnitt, durchschnittlich ● *vt* durchschnittlich schaffen

averse /ə'vɜːs/ *adj* **not be ~e to sth** etw (*dat*) nicht abgeneigt sein

avert /ə'vɜːt/ *vt* abwenden

aviary /'eɪvɪərɪ/ *n* Vogelhaus *nt*

aviation /eɪvɪ'eɪʃn/ *n* Luftfahrt *f*

avocado /ævə'kɑːdəʊ/ *n* Avocado *f*

avoid /ə'vɔɪd/ *vt* vermeiden; ~ **s.o.** jdm aus dem Weg gehen. **~able** *adj* vermeidbar. **~ance** *n* Vermeidung *f*

await /ə'weɪt/ *vt* warten auf (+ *acc*)

awake /ə'weɪk/ *adj* wach; **wide** ~ hellwach ● *vi* (*pt* **awoke**, *pp* **awoken**) erwachen

awaken /ə'weɪkn/ *vt* wecken ● *vi* erwachen. **~ing** *n* Erwachen *nt*

award /ə'wɔːd/ *n* Auszeichnung *f*; (*prize*) Preis *m* ● *vt* zuerkennen (**to s.o.** *dat*); verleihen (*prize*)

aware /ə'weə(r)/ *adj* **become** ~ gewahr werden (**of** *gen*); **be** ~ **that** wissen, dass. **~ness** *n* Bewusstsein *nt*

away /ə'weɪ/ *adv* weg, fort; (*absent*) abwesend; **four kilometres ~** vier Kilometer entfernt; **play ~** (*Sport*) auswärts spielen. **~ game** *n* Auswärtsspiel *nt*

awful /'ɔ:fl/ *adj* furchtbar

awkward /'ɔ:kwəd/ *adj* schwierig; (*clumsy*) ungeschickt; (*embarrassing*) peinlich; (*inconvenient*) ungünstig. **~ly** *adv* ungeschickt; (*embarrassedly*) verlegen

awning /'ɔ:nɪŋ/ *n* Markise *f*

awoke(n) /ə'wəʊk(n)/ *see* **awake**

axe /æks/ *n* Axt *f* ● *vt* (*pres p* **axing**) streichen

axle /'æksl/ *n* (*Techn*) Achse *f*

Bb

B /bi:/ *n* (*Mus*) H *nt*

baboon /bə'bu:n/ *n* Pavian *m*

baby /'beɪbɪ/ *n* Baby *nt*; (*Amer*, [I]) Schätzchen *nt*

baby: ~ish *adj* kindisch. **~-sit** *vi* babysitten. **~-sitter** *n* Babysitter *m*

bachelor /'bætʃələ(r)/ *n* Junggeselle *m*

back /bæk/ *n* Rücken *m*; (*reverse*) Rückseite *f*; (*of chair*) Rückenlehne *f*; (*Sport*) Verteidiger *m*; **at**/(*Auto*) **in the ~** hinten; **on the ~** auf der Rückseite; **~ to front** verkehrt ● *adj* Hinter- ● *adv* zurück; **~ here**/**there** hier/da hinten; **~ at home** zu Hause; **go**/**pay ~** zurückgehen/-zahlen ● *vt* (*support*) unterstützen; (*with money*) finanzieren; (*Auto*) zurücksetzen; (*Betting*) [Geld] setzen auf (+ *acc*); (*cover the back of*) mit einer Verstärkung versehen ● *vi* (*Auto*) zurücksetzen. **~ down** *vi* klein beigeben. **~ in** *vi* rückwärts hineinfahren. **~ out** *vi* rückwärts hinaus-/herausfahren; (*fig*) aussteigen (**of** aus). **~ up** *vt* unterstützen; (*confirm*) bestätigen ● *vi* (*Auto*) zurücksetzen

back: ~ache *n* Rückenschmerzen *pl*. **~biting** *n* gehässiges Gerede *nt*. **~bone** *n* Rückgrat *nt*. **~date** *vt* rückdatieren; **~dated to** rückwirkend von. **~ 'door** *n* Hintertür *f*

backer /'bækə(r)/ *n* Geldgeber *m*

back: ~'fire *vi* (*Auto*) fehlzünden; (*fig*) fehlschlagen. **~ground** *n* Hintergrund *m*; **family ~ground** Familienverhältnisse *pl*. **~hand** *n* (*Sport*) Rückhand *f*. **~'handed** *adj* (*complIment*) zweifelhaft

backing /'bækɪŋ/ *n* (*support*) Unterstützung *f*; (*material*) Verstärkung *f*

back: ~lash *n* (*fig*) Gegenschlag *m*. **~log** *n* Rückstand *m* (**of** an + *dat*). **~pack** *n* Rucksack *m*. **~ 'seat** *n* Rücksitz *m*. **~side** *n* [I] Hintern *m*. **~stroke** *n* Rückenschwimmen *nt*. **~-up** *n* Unterstützung *f*; (*Amer: traffic jam*) Stau *m*

backward /'bækwəd/ *adj* zurückgeblieben; (*country*) rückständig ● *adv* rückwärts. **~s** rückwärts; **~s and forwards** hin und her

back'yard *n* Hinterhof *m*; **not in my ~yard** [I] nicht vor meiner Haustür

bacon /'beɪkn/ *n* [Schinken]speck *m*

bacteria /bæk'tɪərɪə/ *npl* Bakterien *pl*

bad /bæd/ *adj* (**worse, worst**) schlecht; (*serious*) schwer, schlimm; (*naughty*) unartig; **~ language** gemeine Ausdrucksweise *f*; **feel ~** sich schlecht fühlen; (*feel guilty*) ein schlechtes Gewissen haben

b

badge /bædʒ/ *n* Abzeichen *nt*

badger /'bædʒə(r)/ *n* Dachs *m* ● *vt* plagen

badly /'bædlɪ/ *adv* schlecht; (*seriously*) schwer; ~ **off** schlecht gestellt; ~ **behaved** unerzogen; **want** ~ sich (*dat*) sehnsüchtig wünschen; **need** ~ dringend brauchen

bad-'mannered *adj* mit schlechten Manieren

badminton /'bædmɪntən/ *n* Federball *m*

bad-'tempered *adj* schlecht gelaunt

baffle /'bæfl/ *vt* verblüffen

bag /bæg/ *n* Tasche *f*; (*of paper*) Tüte *f*; (*pouch*) Beutel *m*; **~s of** [!] jede Menge ● *vt* ([!]: *reserve*) in Beschlag nehmen

baggage /'bægɪdʒ/ *n* [Reise]gepäck *nt*

baggy /'bægɪ/ *adj* (*clothes*) ausgebeult

'bagpipes *npl* Dudelsack *m*

bail /beɪl/ *n* Kaution *f*; **on** ~ gegen Kaution ● *vt* ~ **s.o. out** jdn gegen Kaution freibekommen; (*fig*) jdm aus der Patsche helfen

bait /beɪt/ *n* Köder *m* ● *vt* mit einem Köder versehen; (*fig: torment*) reizen

bake /beɪk/ *vt/i* backen

baker /'beɪkə(r)/ *n* Bäcker *m*; **~'s [shop]** Bäckerei *f*. **~y** *n* Bäckerei *f*

baking /'beɪkɪŋ/ *n* Backen *nt*. **~-powder** *n* Backpulver *nt*

balance /'bæləns/ *n* (*equilibrium*) Gleichgewicht *nt*, Balance *f*; (*scales*) Waage *f*; (*Comm*) Saldo *m*; (*outstanding sum*) Restbetrag *m*; **[bank]** ~ Kontostand *m*; **in the** ~ (*fig*) in der Schwebe ● *vt* balancieren; (*equalize*) ausgleichen; (*Comm*) abschließen (*books*) ● *vi* balancieren; (*fig & Comm*) sich ausgleichen. **~d** *adj* ausgewogen

balcony /'bælkənɪ/ *n* Balkon *m*

bald /bɔːld/ *adj* (**-er, -est**) kahl; (*person*) kahlköpfig

bald|ly *adv* unverblümt. **~ness** *n* Kahlköpfigkeit *f*

ball[1] /bɔːl/ *n* Ball *m*; (*Billiards, Croquet*) Kugel *f*; (*of yarn*) Knäuel *m* & *nt*; **on the** ~ [!] auf Draht

ball[2] *n* (*dance*) Ball *m*

ball-'bearing *n* Kugellager *nt*

ballerina /bælə'riːnə/ *n* Ballerina *f*

ballet /'bæleɪ/ *m* Ballett *nt*. ~ **dancer** *n* Balletttänzer(in) *m*(*f*)

balloon /bə'luːn/ *n* Luftballon *m*; (*Aviat*) Ballon *m*

ballot /'bælət/ *n* [geheime] Wahl *f*; (*on issue*) [geheime] Abstimmung *f*. **~-box** *n* Wahlurne *f*. **~-paper** *n* Stimmzettel *m*

ball: ~point ['pen] *n* Kugelschreiber *m*. **~room** *n* Ballsaal *m*

balm /bɑːm/ *n* Balsam *m*

balmy /'bɑːmɪ/ *adj* sanft

Baltic /'bɔːltɪk/ *adj* & *n* **the ~ [Sea]** die Ostsee

bamboo /bæm'buː/ *n* Bambus *m*

ban /bæn/ *n* Verbot *nt* ● *vt* (*pt/pp* **banned**) verbieten

banal /bə'nɑːl/ *adj* banal. **~ity** *n* Banalität *f*

banana /bə'nɑːnə/ *n* Banane *f*

band /bænd/ *n* Band *nt*; (*stripe*) Streifen *m*; (*group*) Schar *f*; (*Mus*) Kapelle *f*

bandage /'bændɪdʒ/ *n* Verband *m*; (*for support*) Bandage *f* ● *vt* verbinden; bandagieren (*limb*)

b. & b. *abbr* **bed and breakfast**

bandit /'bændɪt/ *n* Bandit *m*

band: ~stand *n* Musikpavillon *m*. **~wagon** *n* **jump on the ~wagon**

(*fig*) sich einer erfolgreichen Sache anschließen

bang /bæŋ/ *n* (*noise*) Knall *m*; (*blow*) Schlag *m* ● *adv* **go ~** knallen ● *int* bums! peng! ● *vt* knallen; (*shut noisily*) zuknallen; (*strike*) schlagen auf (+ *acc*); **~ one's head** sich (*dat*) den Kopf stoßen (**on** an + *acc*) ● *vi* schlagen; (*door*:) zuknallen

banger /'bæŋə(r)/ *n* (*firework*) Knallfrosch *m*; (🅧: *sausage*) Wurst *f*; **old ~** (🅧: *car*) Klapperkiste *f*

bangle /'bæŋgl/ *n* Armreifen *m*

banish /'bænɪʃ/ *vt* verbannen

banisters /'bænɪstəz/ *npl* [Treppen]geländer *nt*

banjo /'bændʒəʊ/ *n* Banjo *nt*

bank¹ /bæŋk/ *n* (*of river*) Ufer *nt*; (*slope*) Hang *m* ● *vi* (*Aviat*) in die Kurve gehen

bank² *n* Bank *f* ● **~ on** *vt* sich verlassen auf (+ *acc*)

'bank account *n* Bankkonto *nt*

banker /'bæŋkə(r)/ *n* Bankier *m*

bank: ~ 'holiday *n* gesetzlicher Feiertag *m*. **~ing** *n* Bankwesen *nt*. **~note** *n* Banknote *f*

bankrupt /'bæŋkrʌpt/ *adj* bankrott; **go ~** Bankrott machen ● *n* Bankrotteur *m* ● *vt* Bankrott machen. **~cy** *n* Bankrott *m*

banner /'bænə(r)/ *n* Banner *nt*; (*carried by demonstrators*) Transparent *nt*, Spruchband *nt*

banquet /'bæŋkwɪt/ *n* Bankett *nt*

baptism /'bæptɪzm/ *n* Taufe *f*

baptize /bæp'taɪz/ *vt* taufen

bar /bɑ:(r)/ *n* Stange *f*; (*of cage*) [Gitter]stab *m*; (*of gold*) Barren *m*; (*of chocolate*) Tafel *f*; (*of soap*) Stück *nt*; (*long*) Riegel *m*; (*café*) Bar *f*; (*counter*) Theke *f*; (*Mus*) Takt *m*; (*fig: obstacle*) Hindernis *nt*; **parallel ~s** (*Sport*) Barren *m*; **behind ~s** 🅧 hinter Gittern ● *vt* (*pt/pp* **barred**) versperren (*way, door*); ausschließen (*person*)

barbar|ic /bɑ:'bærɪk/ *adj* barbarisch. **~ity** *n* Barbarei *f*. **~ous** *adj* barbarisch

barbecue /'bɑ:bɪkju:/ *n* Grill *m*; (*party*) Grillfest *nt* ● *vt* [im Freien] grillen

barbed /'bɑ:bd/ *adj* **~ wire** Stacheldraht *m*

barber /'bɑ:bə(r)/ *n* [Herren]friseur *m*

'bar code *n* Strichkode *m*

bare /beə(r)/ *adj* (**-r, -st**) nackt, bloß; (*tree*) kahl; (*empty*) leer; (*mere*) bloß

bare: ~back *adv* ohne Sattel. **~faced** *adj* schamlos. **~foot** *adv* barfuß. **~'headed** *adj* mit unbedecktem Kopf

barely /'beəlɪ/ *adv* kaum

bargain /'bɑ:gɪn/ *n* (*agreement*) Geschäft *nt*; (*good buy*) Gelegenheitskauf *m*; **into the ~** noch dazu; **make a ~** sich einigen ● *vi* handeln; (*haggle*) feilschen; **~ for** (*expect*) rechnen mit

barge /bɑ:dʒ/ *n* Lastkahn *m*; (*towed*) Schleppkahn *m* ● *vi* **~ in** 🅧 hereinplatzen

baritone /'bærɪtəʊn/ *n* Bariton *m*

bark¹ /bɑ:k/ *n* (*of tree*) Rinde *f*

bark² *n* Bellen *nt* ● *vi* bellen

barley /'bɑ:lɪ/ *n* Gerste *f*

bar: ~maid *n* Schankmädchen *nt*. **~man** Barmann *m*

barmy /'bɑ:mɪ/ *adj* 🅧 verrückt

barn /bɑ:n/ *n* Scheune *f*

barometer /bə'rɒmɪtə(r)/ *n* Barometer *nt*

baron /'bærn/ *n* Baron *m*. **~ess** *n* Baronin *f*

barracks /ˈbærəks/ *npl* Kaserne *f*

barrage /ˈbærɑːʒ/ *n* (*in river*) Wehr *nt*; (*Mil*) Sperrfeuer *nt*; (*fig*) Hagel *m*

barrel /ˈbærl/ *n* Fass *nt*; (*of gun*) Lauf *m*; (*of cannon*) Rohr *nt*. **~-organ** *n* Drehorgel *f*

barren /ˈbærn/ *adj* unfruchtbar; (*landscape*) öde

barricade /bærɪˈkeɪd/ *n* Barrikade *f* ● *vt* verbarrikadieren

barrier /ˈbærɪə(r)/ *n* Barriere *f*; (*across road*) Schranke *f*; (*Rail*) Sperre *f*; (*fig*) Hindernis *nt*

barrow /ˈbærəʊ/ *n* Karre *f*, Karren *m*

base /beɪs/ *n* Fuß *m*; (*fig*) Basis *f*; (*Mil*) Stützpunkt *m* ● *vt* stützen (**on** auf + *acc*); **be ~d on** basieren auf (+ *dat*)

base: ~ball *n* Baseball *m*. **~less** *adj* unbegründet. **~ment** *n* Kellergeschoss *nt*

bash /bæʃ/ *n* Schlag *m*; **have a ~!** [!] probier es mal! ● *vt* hauen

basic /ˈbeɪsɪk/ *adj* Grund-; (*fundamental*) grundlegend; (*essential*) wesentlich; (*unadorned*) einfach; **the ~s** das Wesentliche. **~ally** *adv* grundsätzlich

basin /ˈbeɪsn/ *n* Becken *nt*; (*for washing*) Waschbecken *nt*; (*for food*) Schüssel *f*

basis /ˈbeɪsɪs/ *n* (*pl* **-ses** /-siːz/) Basis *f*

bask /bɑːsk/ *vi* sich sonnen

basket /ˈbɑːskɪt/ *n* Korb *m*. **~ball** *n* Basketball *m*

Basle /bɑːl/ *n* Basel *nt*

bass /beɪs/ *adj* Bass-; **~ voice** Bassstimme *f* ● *n* Bass *m*; (*person*) Bassist *m*

bassoon /bəˈsuːn/ *n* Fagott *nt*

bastard /ˈbɑːstəd/ *n* [✖] Schuft *m*

bat¹ /bæt/ *n* Schläger *m*; **off one's own ~** [!] auf eigene Faust ● *vt* (*pt/pp* **batted**) schlagen; **not ~ an eyelid** (*fig*) nicht mit der Wimper zucken

bat² *n* (*Zool*) Fledermaus *f*

batch /bætʃ/ *n* (*of people*) Gruppe *f*; (*of papers*) Stoß *m*; (*of goods*) Sendung *f*; (*of bread*) Schub *m*

bath /bɑːθ/ *n* (*pl* **~s** /bɑːðz/) Bad *nt*; (*tub*) Badewanne *f*; **~s** *pl* Badeanstalt *f*; **have a ~** baden

bathe /beɪð/ *n* Bad *nt* ● *vt/i* baden. **~r** *n* Badende(r) *m/f*

bathing /ˈbeɪðɪŋ/ *n* Baden *nt*. **~-cap** *n* Bademütze *f*. **~-costume** *n* Badeanzug *m*

bath: ~-mat *n* Badematte *f*. **~room** *n* Badezimmer *nt*. **~-towel** *n* Badetuch *nt*

battalion /bəˈtælɪən/ *n* Bataillon *nt*

batter /ˈbætə(r)/ *n* (*Culin*) flüssiger Teig *m* ● *vt* schlagen. **~ed** *adj* (*car*) verbeult; (*wife*) misshandelt

battery /ˈbætərɪ/ *n* Batterie *f*

battle /ˈbætl/ *n* Schlacht *f*; (*fig*) Kampf *m* ● *vi* (*fig*) kämpfen (**for** um)

battle: ~field *n* Schlachtfeld *nt*. **~ship** *n* Schlachtschiff *nt*

batty /ˈbætɪ/ *adj* [!] verrückt

Bavaria /bəˈveərɪə/ *n* Bayern *nt*. **~n** *adj* bayrisch ● *n* Bayer(in) *m(f)*

bawl /bɔːl/ *vt/i* brüllen

bay¹ /beɪ/ *n* (*Geog*) Bucht *f*; (*in room*) Erker *m*

bay² *n* (*Bot*) [echter] Lorbeer *m*. **~-leaf** *n* Lorbeerblatt *nt*

bayonet /ˈbeɪənet/ *n* Bajonett *nt*

bay ˈwindow *n* Erkerfenster *nt*

bazaar /bəˈzɑː(r)/ *n* Basar *m*

BC *abbr* (**before Christ**) v.Chr.

be /biː/

(*pres* **am, are, is,** *pl* **are**; *pt* **was,** *pl* **were**; *pp* **been**)

● *intransitive verb*

····➤ (*expressing identity, nature, state, age etc.*) sein. **he is a teacher** er ist Lehrer. **she is French** sie ist Französin. **he is very nice** er ist sehr nett. **I am tall** ich bin groß. **you are thirty** du bist dreißig. **it was very cold** es war sehr kalt

····➤ (*expressing general position*) sein; (*lie*) liegen; (*stand*) stehen. **where is the bank?** wo ist die Bank? **the book is on the table** das Buch liegt auf dem Tisch. **the vase is on the shelf** die Vase steht auf dem Brett

····➤ (*feel*) **I am cold/hot** mir ist kalt/heiß. **I am ill** ich bin krank. **I am well** mir geht es gut. **how are you?** wie geht es Ihnen?

····➤ (*date*) **it is the 5th today** heute haben wir den Fünften

····➤ (*go, come, stay*) sein. **I have been to Vienna** ich bin in Wien gewesen. **have you ever been to London?** bist du schon einmal in London gewesen? **has the postman been?** war der Briefträger schon da? **I've been here for an hour** ich bin seit einer Stunde hier

····➤ (*origin*) **where are you from?** woher stammen *od* kommen Sie? **she is from Australia** sie stammt *od* ist aus Australien

····➤ (*cost*) kosten. **how much are the eggs?** was kosten die Eier?

····➤ (*in calculations*) **two threes are six** zweimal drei ist *od* sind sechs

····➤ (*exist*) **there is/are** es gibt (+ *acc*). **there's no fish left** es gibt keinen Fisch mehr

● *auxiliary verb*

····➤ (*forming continuous tenses: not translated*) **I'm working** ich arbeite. **I'm leaving tomorrow** ich reise morgen [ab]. **they were singing** sie sangen. **they will be coming on Tuesday** sie kommen am Dienstag

····➤ (*forming passive*) werden. **the child was found** das Kind wurde gefunden. **German is spoken here** hier wird Deutsch gesprochen; hier spricht man Deutsch

····➤ (*expressing arrangement, obligation, destiny*) sollen. **I am to go/inform you** ich soll gehen/Sie unterrichten. **they were to fly today** sie sollten heute fliegen. **you are to do that immediately** das sollst du sofort machen. **you are not to ...** (*prohibition*) du darfst nicht .... **they were never to meet again** (*destiny*) sie sollten sich nie wieder treffen

····➤ (*in short answers*) **Are you disappointed? — Yes I am** Bist du enttäuscht? — Ja. (*negating previous statement*) **Aren't you coming? — Yes I am!** Kommst du nicht? — Doch!

····➤ (*in tag questions*) **isn't it? wasn't she? aren't they?** *etc.* nicht wahr. **it's a beautiful house, isn't it?** das Haus ist sehr schön, nicht wahr?

beach /biːtʃ/ *n* Strand *m*

bead /biːd/ *n* Perle *f*

beak /biːk/ *n* Schnabel *m*

b

beam /biːm/ *n* Balken *m*; (*of light*) Strahl *m* ● *vi* strahlen. **~ing** *adj* [freude]strahlend

bean /biːn/ *n* Bohne *f*

bear[1] /beə(r)/ *n* Bär *m*

bear[2] *vt/i* (*pt* **bore**, *pp* **borne**) tragen; (*endure*) ertragen; gebären (*child*); **~ right** sich rechts halten. **~able** *adj* erträglich

beard /bɪəd/ *n* Bart *m*. **~ed** *adj* bärtig

bearer /ˈbeərə(r)/ *n* Träger *m*; (*of news, cheque*) Überbringer *m*; (*of passport*) Inhaber(in) *m*(*f*)

bearing /ˈbeərɪŋ/ *n* Haltung *f*; (*Techn*) Lager *nt*; **get one's ~s** sich orientieren

beast /biːst/ *n* Tier *nt*; (!: *person*) Biest *nt*

beastly /ˈbiːstlɪ/ *adj* ! scheußlich; (*person*) gemein

beat /biːt/ *n* Schlag *m*; (*of policeman*) Runde *f*; (*rhythm*) Takt *m* ● *vt/i* (*pt* **beat**, *pp* **beaten**) schlagen; (*thrash*) verprügeln; klopfen (*carpet*); (*hammer*) hämmern (**on** an + *acc*); **~ it!** ! hau ab! **it ~s me** ! das begreife ich nicht. **~ up** *vt* zusammenschlagen

beat|en /ˈbiːtn/ *adj* **off the ~en track** abseits. **~ing** *n* Prügel *pl*

beauti|ful /ˈbjuːtɪfl/ *adj* schön. **~fy** *vt* (*pt/pp* **-ied**) verschönern

beauty /ˈbjuːtɪ/ *n* Schönheit *f*. **~ parlour** *n* Kosmetiksalon *m*. **~ spot** *n* Schönheitsfleck *m*; (*place*) landschaftlich besonders reizvolles Fleckchen *nt*.

beaver /ˈbiːvə(r)/ *n* Biber *m*

became /bɪˈkeɪm/ *see* **become**

because /bɪˈkɒz/ *conj* weil ● *adv* **~ of** wegen (+ *gen*)

becom|e /bɪˈkʌm/ *vt/i* (*pt* **became**, *pp* **become**) werden. **~ing** *adj* (*clothes*) kleidsam

bed /bed/ *n* Bett *nt*; (*layer*) Schicht *f*; (*of flowers*) Beet *nt*; **in ~** im Bett; **go to ~** ins *od* zu Bett gehen; **~ and breakfast** Zimmer mit Frühstück. **~clothes** *npl*, **~ding** *n* Bettzeug *nt*. **~room** *n* Schlafzimmer *nt*

i

bed and breakfast Überall in Großbritannien sieht man Schilder mit der Aufschrift *Bed & Breakfast* oder *B & B*. Sie weisen auf Privathäuser hin, die preisgünstige Unterkunft anbieten, wobei im Zimmerpreis das Frühstück mit eingeschlossen ist. Zum traditionellen Frühstück gehört vor allem, Cornflakes, *bacon and eggs* (Spiegelei mit Speck), Toast und Orangenmarmelade und Tee.

ˈbedside *n* **at his ~** an seinem Bett. **~ ˈlamp** *n* Nachttischlampe *f*. **~ ˈtable** *n* Nachttisch *m*

bed: ~ˈsitter *n*, **~-ˈsitting-room** *n* Wohnschlafzimmer *nt*. **~spread** *n* Tagesdecke *f*. **~time** *n* **at ~time** vor dem Schlafengehen

bee /biː/ *n* Biene *f*

beech /biːtʃ/ *n* Buche *f*

beef /biːf/ *n* Rindfleisch *nt*. **~burger** *n* Hamburger *m*

bee: ~hive *n* Bienenstock *m*. **~-line** *n* **make a ~-line for** ! zusteuern auf (+ *acc*)

been /biːn/ *see* **be**

beer /bɪə(r)/ *n* Bier *nt*

beet /biːt/ *n* (*Amer: beetroot*) rote Bete *f*; **[sugar] ~** Zuckerrübe *f*

beetle /ˈbiːtl/ *n* Käfer *m*

ˈbeetroot *n* rote Bete *f*

before /bɪˈfɔː(r)/ *prep* vor (+ *dat*/*acc*); **the day ~ yesterday** vorgestern; **~ long** bald ● *adv* vorher; (*already*) schon; **never ~** noch nie; **~ that** davor ● *conj* (*time*) ehe, bevor. **~hand** *adv* vorher, im Voraus

beg /beg/ *v* (*pt/pp* **begged**) ● *vi* betteln ● *vt* (*entreat*) anflehen; (*ask*) bitten (**for** um)

began /bɪ'gæn/ *see* **begin**

beggar /'begə(r)/ *n* Bettler(in) *m(f)*; [!] Kerl *m*

begin /bɪ'gɪn/ *vt/i* (*pt* **began**, *pp* **begun**, *pres p* **beginning**) anfangen, beginnen; **to ~ with** anfangs. **~ner** *n* Anfänger(in) *m(f)*. **~ning** *n* Anfang *m*, Beginn *m*

begun /bɪ'gʌn/ *see* **begin**

behalf /bɪ'hɑːf/ *n* **on ~ of** im Namen von; **on my ~** meinetwegen

behave /bɪ'heɪv/ *vi* sich verhalten; **~ oneself** sich benehmen

behaviour /bɪ'heɪvjə(r)/ *n* Verhalten *nt*; **good/bad ~** gutes/schlechtes Benehmen *nt*

behind /bɪ'haɪnd/ *prep* hinter (+ *dat/acc*); **be ~ sth** hinter etw (*dat*) stecken ● *adv* hinten; (*late*) im Rückstand; **a long way ~** weit zurück ● *n* [!] Hintern *m*. **~hand** *adv* im Rückstand

beige /beɪʒ/ *adj* beige

being /'biːɪŋ/ *n* Dasein *nt*; **living ~** Lebewesen *nt*; **come into ~** entstehen

belated /bɪ'leɪtɪd/ *adj* verspätet

belfry /'belfrɪ/ *n* Glockenstube *f*; (*tower*) Glockenturm *m*

Belgian /'beldʒən/ *adj* belgisch ● *n* Belgier(in) *m(f)*

Belgium /'beldʒəm/ *n* Belgien *nt*

belief /bɪ'liːf/ *n* Glaube *m*

believable /bɪ'liːvəbl/ *adj* glaubhaft

believe /bɪ'liːv/ *vt/i* glauben (**s.o.** jdm; **in** an + *acc*). **~r** *n* (*Relig*) Gläubige(r) *m/f*

belittle /bɪ'lɪtl/ *vt* herabsetzen

bell /bel/ *n* Glocke *f*; (*on door*) Klingel *f*

bellow /'beləʊ/ *vt/i* brüllen

belly /'belɪ/ *n* Bauch *m*

belong /bɪ'lɒŋ/ *vi* gehören (**to** *dat*); (*be member*) angehören (**to** *dat*). **~ings** *npl* Sachen *pl*

beloved /bɪ'lʌvɪd/ *adj* geliebt ● *n* Geliebte(r) *m/f*

below /bɪ'ləʊ/ *prep* unter (+ *dat/acc*) ● *adv* unten; (*Naut*) unter Deck

belt /belt/ *n* Gürtel *m*; (*area*) Zone *f*; (*Techn*) [Treib]riemen *m* ● *vi* ([!]: *rush*) rasen ● *vt* ([!]: *hit*) hauen

bench /bentʃ/ *n* Bank *f*; (*work-*) Werkbank *f*

bend /bend/ *n* Biegung *f*; (*in road*) Kurve *f*; **round the ~** [!] verrückt ● *v* (*pt/pp* **bent**) ● *vt* biegen; beugen (*arm, leg*) ● *vi* sich bücken; (*thing:*) sich biegen; (*road:*) eine Biegung machen. **~ down** *vi* sich bücken. **~ over** *vi* sich vornüberbeugen

beneath /bɪ'niːθ/ *prep* unter (+ *dat/acc*); **~ him** (*fig*) unter seiner Würde ● *adv* darunter

benefactor /'benɪfæktə(r)/ *n* Wohltäter(in) *m(f)*

beneficial /benɪ'fɪʃl/ *adj* nützlich

benefit /'benɪfɪt/ *n* Vorteil *m*; (*allowance*) Unterstützung *f*; (*insurance*) Leistung *f*; **sickness ~** Krankengeld *nt* ● *v* (*pt/pp* **-fited**, *pres p* **-fiting**) ● *vt* nützen (+ *dat*) ● *vi* profitieren (**from** von)

benevolen|ce /bɪ'nevələns/ *n* Wohlwollen *nt*. **~t** *adj* wohlwollend

bent /bent/ *see* **bend** ● *adj* (*person*) gebeugt; (*distorted*) verbogen; ([!]: *dishonest*) korrupt; **be ~ on doing sth** darauf erpicht sein, etw zu tun ● *n* Hang *m*, Neigung *f* (**for** zu); **artistic ~** künstlerische Ader *f*

b

bequeath /bɪ'kwi:ð/ *vt* vermachen (to *dat*)
bereave|d /bɪ'ri:vd/ *n* **the ~d** *pl* die Hinterbliebenen
beret /'bereɪ/ *n* Baskenmütze *f*
Berne /bɜ:n/ *n* Bern *nt*
berry /'berɪ/ *n* Beere *f*
berth /bɜ:θ/ *n* (*on ship*) [Schlaf]koje *f*; (*ship's anchorage*) Liegeplatz *m*; **give a wide ~ to** [I] einen großen Bogen machen um
beside /bɪ'saɪd/ *prep* neben (+ *dat/acc*); **~ oneself** außer sich (*dat*)
besides /bɪ'saɪdz/ *prep* außer (+ *dat*) ● *adv* außerdem
besiege /bɪ'si:dʒ/ *vt* belagern
best /best/ *adj & n* beste(r,s); **the ~** der/die/das Beste; **at ~** bestenfalls; **all the ~!** alles Gute! **do one's ~** sein Bestes tun; **the ~ part of a year** fast ein Jahr; **to the ~ of my knowledge** so viel ich weiß; **make the ~ of it** das Beste daraus machen ● *adv* am besten; **as ~ I could** so gut ich konnte. **~'man** *n* ≈ Trauzeuge *m*. **~'seller** *n* Bestseller *m*
bet /bet/ *n* Wette *f* ● *v* (*pt/pp* **bet** *or* **betted**) ● *vt* **~ s.o. £5** mit jdm um £5 wetten ● *vi* wetten; **~ on** [Geld] setzen auf (+ *acc*)
betray /bɪ'treɪ/ *vt* verraten. **~al** *n* Verrat *m*
better /'betə(r)/ *adj* besser; **get ~** sich bessern; (*after illness*) sich erholen ● *adv* besser; **~ off** besser dran; **~ not** lieber nicht; **all the ~** umso besser; **the sooner the ~** je eher, desto besser; **think ~ of sth** sich eines Besseren besinnen; **you'd ~ stay** du bleibst am besten hier ● *vt* verbessern; (*do better than*) übertreffen; **~ oneself** sich verbessern
between /bɪ'twi:n/ *prep* zwischen (+ *dat/acc*); **~ you and me** unter uns; **~ us** (*together*) zusammen ● *adv* **[in] ~** dazwischen
beware /bɪ'weə(r)/ *vi* sich in Acht nehmen (**of** vor + *dat*); **~ of the dog!** Vorsicht, bissiger Hund!
bewilder /bɪ'wɪldə(r)/ *vt* verwirren. **~ment** *n* Verwirrung *f*
bewitch /bɪ'wɪtʃ/ *vt* verzaubern; (*fig*) bezaubern
beyond /bɪ'jɒnd/ *prep* über (+ *acc*) ... hinaus; (*further*) weiter als; **~ reach** außer Reichweite; **~ doubt** ohne jeden Zweifel; **it's ~ me** [I] das geht über meinen Horizont ● *adv* darüber hinaus
bias /'baɪəs/ *n* Voreingenommenheit *f*; (*preference*) Vorliebe *f*; (*Jur*) Befangenheit *f* ● *vt* (*pt/pp* **biased**) (*influence*) beeinflussen. **~ed** *adj* voreingenommen; (*Jur*) befangen
bib /bɪb/ *n* Lätzchen *nt*
Bible /'baɪbl/ *n* Bibel *f*
biblical /'bɪblɪkl/ *adj* biblisch
bibliography /bɪblɪ'ɒgrəfɪ/ *n* Bibliographie *f*
bicycle /'baɪsɪkl/ *n* Fahrrad *nt* ● *vi* mit dem Rad fahren
bid /bɪd/ *n* Gebot *nt*; (*attempt*) Versuch *m* ● *vt/i* (*pt/pp* **bid**, *pres p* **bidding**) bieten (**for** auf + *acc*); (*Cards*) reizen
bidder /'bɪdə(r)/ *n* Bieter(in) *m*(*f*)
bide /baɪd/ *vt* **~ one's time** den richtigen Moment abwarten
big /bɪg/ *adj* (**bigger, biggest**) groß ● *adv* **talk ~** [I] angeben
bigam|ist /'bɪgəmɪst/ *n* Bigamist *m*. **~y** *n* Bigamie *f*
big-'headed *adj* [I] eingebildet
bigot /'bɪgət/ *n* Eiferer *m*. **~ed** *adj* engstirnig
'bigwig *n* [I] hohes Tier *nt*
bike /baɪk/ *n* [I] [Fahr]rad *nt*
bikini /bɪ'ki:nɪ/ *n* Bikini *m*

bile /baɪl/ *n* Galle *f*
bilingual /baɪˈlɪŋgwəl/ *adj* zweisprachig
bilious /ˈbɪljəs/ *adj* (*Med*) ~ **attack** verdorbener Magen *m*
bill[1] /bɪl/ *n* Rechnung *f*; (*poster*) Plakat *nt*; (*Pol*) Gesetzentwurf *m*; (*Amer: note*) Banknote *f*; ~ **of exchange** Wechsel *m* ●*vt* eine Rechnung schicken (+ *dat*)
bill[2] *n* (*beak*) Schnabel *m*
ˈbillfold *n* (*Amer*) Brieftasche *f*
billiards /ˈbɪljədz/ *n* Billard *nt*
billion /ˈbɪljən/ *n* (*thousand million*) Milliarde *f*; (*million million*) Billion *f*
bin /bɪn/ *n* Mülleimer *m*
bind /baɪnd/ *vt* (*pt/pp* **bound**) binden (**to** an + *acc*); (*bandage*) verbinden; (*Jur*) verpflichten; (*cover the edge of*) einfassen. ~**ing** *adj* verbindlich ●*n* Einband *m*; (*braid*) Borte *f*; (*on ski*) Bindung *f*
binge /bɪndʒ/ *n* ▣ **go on the ~** eine Sauftour machen
binoculars /bɪˈnɒkjʊləz/ *npl* **[pair of]** ~ Fernglas *nt*
bio|ˈchemistry /baɪəʊ-/ *n* Biochemie *f*. ~**degradable** *adj* biologisch abbaubar
biofuel /ˈbaɪəʊfju:əl/ *n* Biokraftstoff *m*
biograph|er /baɪˈɒgrəfə(r)/ *n* Biograph(in) *m*(*f*). ~**y** *n* Biographie *f*
biological /baɪəˈlɒdʒɪkl/ *adj* biologisch
biolog|ist /baɪˈɒlədʒɪst/ *n* Biologe *m*. ~**y** *n* Biologie *f*
bioˈterrorism /baɪəʊ-/ *n* Bioterrorismus *m*
birch /bɜ:tʃ/ *n* Birke *f*; (*whip*) Rute *f*
bird /bɜ:d/ *n* Vogel *m*; (▣: *girl*) Mädchen *nt*; **kill two ~s with one stone** zwei Fliegen mit einer Klappe schlagen
Biro ® /ˈbaɪrəʊ/ *n* Kugelschreiber *m*
birth /bɜ:θ/ *n* Geburt *f*
birth: ~ **certificate** *n* Geburtsurkunde *f*. ~**-control** *n* Geburtenregelung *f*. ~**day** *n* Geburtstag *m*. ~**-rate** *n* Geburtenziffer *f*
biscuit /ˈbɪskɪt/ *n* Keks *m*
bishop /ˈbɪʃəp/ *n* Bischof *m*
bit[1] /bɪt/ *n* Stückchen *nt*; (*for horse*) Gebiss *nt*; (*Techn*) Bohreinsatz *m*; **a ~** ein bisschen; ~ **by** ~ nach und nach; **a ~ of bread** ein bisschen Brot; **do one's ~** sein Teil tun
bit[2] *see* **bite**
bitch /bɪtʃ/ *n* Hündin *f*; ▣ Luder *nt*. ~**y** *adj* gehässig
bit|e /baɪt/ *n* Biss *m*; **[insect] ~** Stich *m*; (*mouthful*) Bissen *m* ●*vt/i* (*pt* **bit**, *pp* **bitten**) beißen; (*insect:*) stechen; kauen (*one's nails*). ~**ing** *adj* beißend
bitten /ˈbɪtn/ *see* **bite**
bitter /ˈbɪtə(r)/ *adj* bitter; ~**ly cold** bitterkalt ●*n* bitteres Bier *nt*. ~**ness** *n* Bitterkeit *f*
bitty /ˈbɪtɪ/ *adj* zusammengestoppelt
bizarre /bɪˈzɑ:(r)/ *adj* bizarr
black /blæk/ *adj* (**-er, -est**) schwarz; **be ~and blue** grün und blau sein ●*n* Schwarz *nt*; (*person*) Schwarze(r) *m/f* ●*vt* schwärzen; boykottieren (*goods*)
black: ~**berry** *n* Brombeere *f*. ~**bird** *n* Amsel *f*. ~**board** *n* (*Sch*) [Wand]tafel *f*. ~**ˈcurrant** *n* schwarze Johannisbeere *f*
blacken *vt/i* schwärzen
black: ~ **ˈeye** *n* blaues Auge *nt*. **B ~ ˈForest** *n* Schwarzwald *m*. ~ **ˈice** *n* Glatteis *nt*. ~**list** *vt* auf die schwarze Liste setzen. ~**mail** *n* Erpressung *f* ●*vt* erpressen. ~**mailer** *n* Erpresser(in) *m*(*f*). ~ **ˈmarket** *n* schwarzer Markt *m*. ~**-out** *n* **have**

a ~-out (*Med*) das Bewusstsein verlieren. ~ '**pudding** *n* Blutwurst *f*

b

bladder /'blædə(r)/ *n* (*Anat*) Blase *f*

blade /bleɪd/ *n* Klinge *f*; (*of grass*) Halm *m*

blame /bleɪm/ *n* Schuld *f* ● *vt* die Schuld geben (+ *dat*); **no one is to** ~ keiner ist schuld daran. ~**less** *adj* schuldlos

bland /blænd/ *adj* (**-er, -est**) mild

blank /blæŋk/ *adj* leer; (*look*) ausdruckslos ● *n* Lücke *f*; (*cartridge*) Platzpatrone *f*. ~ '**cheque** *n* Blankoscheck *m*

blanket /'blæŋkɪt/ *n* Decke *f*; **wet** ~ 🄸 Spielverderber(in) *m*(*f*)

blare /bleə(r)/ *vt*/*i* schmettern

blasé /'blɑːzeɪ/ *adj* blasiert

blast /blɑːst/ *n* (*gust*) Luftstoß *m*; (*sound*) Schmettern *nt*; (*of horn*) Tuten *nt* ● *vt* sprengen ● *int* ☒ verdammt. ~**ed** *adj* ☒ verdammt

blatant /'bleɪtənt/ *adj* offensichtlich

blaze /bleɪz/ *n* Feuer *nt* ● *vi* brennen

blazer /'bleɪzə(r)/ *n* Blazer *m*

bleach /bliːtʃ/ *n* Bleichmittel *nt* ● *vt*/*i* bleichen

bleak /bliːk/ *adj* (**-er, -est**) öde; (*fig*) trostlos

bleary-eyed /'blɪərɪ-/ *adj* mit trüben/(*on waking up*) verschlafenen Augen

bleat /bliːt/ *vi* blöken

bleed /bliːd/ *v* (*pt*/*pp* **bled**) ● *vi* bluten ● *vt* entlüften (*radiator*)

bleep /bliːp/ *n* Piepton *m* ● *vi* piepsen ● *vt* mit dem Piepser rufen. ~**er** *n* Piepser *m*

blemish /'blemɪʃ/ *n* Makel *m*

blend /blend/ *n* Mischung *f* ● *vt* mischen ● *vi* sich vermischen

bless /bles/ *vt* segnen. ~**ed** *adj* heilig; ☒ verflixt. ~**ing** *n* Segen *m*

blew /bluː/ *see* **blow**[2]

blight /blaɪt/ *n* (*Bot*) Brand *m*

blind /blaɪnd/ *adj* blind; (*corner*) unübersichtlich; ~ **man**/**woman** Blinde(r) *m*/*f* ● *n* [**roller**] ~ Rouleau *nt* ● *vt* blenden

blind: ~ '**alley** *n* Sackgasse *f*. ~**fold** *adj* & *adv* mit verbundenen Augen ● *n* Augenbinde *f* ● *vt* die Augen verbinden (+ *dat*). ~**ly** *adv* blindlings. ~**ness** *n* Blindheit *f*

blink /blɪŋk/ *vi* blinzeln; (*light:*) blinken

bliss /blɪs/ *n* Glückseligkeit *f*. ~**ful** *adj* glücklich

blister /'blɪstə(r)/ *n* (*Med*) Blase *f*

blitz /blɪts/ *n* 🄸 Großaktion *f*

blizzard /'blɪzəd/ *n* Schneesturm *m*

bloated /'bləʊtɪd/ *adj* aufgedunsen

blob /blɒb/ *n* Klecks *m*

block /blɒk/ *n* Block *m*; (*of wood*) Klotz *m*; (*of flats*) [Wohn]block *m* ● *vt* blockieren. ~ **up** *vt* zustopfen

blockade /blɒ'keɪd/ *n* Blockade *f* ● *vt* blockieren

blockage /'blɒkɪdʒ/ *n* Verstopfung *f*

block: ~**head** *n* 🄸 Dummkopf *m*. ~ '**letters** *npl* Blockschrift *f*

blog /blɒg/ *n* Online-Tagebuch *nt*, Blog *f*/*m*

bloke /bləʊk/ *n* 🄸 Kerl *m*

blonde /blɒnd/ *adj* blond ● *n* Blondine *f*

blood /blʌd/ *n* Blut *nt*

blood: ~**-curdling** *adj* markerschütternd. ~ **donor** *n* Blutspender *m*. ~ **group** *n* Blutgruppe *f*. ~**hound** *n* Bluthund *m*. ~**-poisoning** *n* Blutvergiftung *f*. ~ **pressure** *n* Blutdruck *m*. ~**shed** *n* Blutvergießen *nt*. ~**shot** *adj* blutunterlaufen. ~ **sports** *npl* Jagdsport *m*. ~**-stained** *adj* blutbefleckt. ~ **test** *n* Blutprobe *f*. ~**thirsty** *adj* blutdürstig. ~**-vessel** *n* Blutgefäß *nt*

bloody /'blʌdɪ/ *adj* blutig; ☒ verdammt. ~**-'minded** *adj* ☒ stur

bloom /blu:m/ *n* Blüte *f* ● *vi* blühen

blossom /'blɒsəm/ *n* Blüte *f* ● *vi* blühen

blot /blɒt/ *n* [Tinten]klecks *m*; (*fig*) Fleck *m* ● ~ **out** *vt* (*fig*) auslöschen

blotch /blɒtʃ/ *n* Fleck *m*. ~**y** *adj* fleckig

'blotting-paper *n* Löschpapier *nt*

blouse /blaʊz/ *n* Bluse *f*

blow¹ /bləʊ/ *n* Schlag *m*

blow² *v* (*pt* **blew**, *pp* **blown**) ● *vt* blasen; (*fam; squander*) verpulvern; ~ **one's nose** sich (*dat*) die Nase putzen ● *vi* blasen; (*fuse:*) durchbrennen. ~ **away** *vt* wegblasen ● *vi* wegfliegen. ~ **down** *vt* umwehen ● *vi* umfallen. ~ **out** *vt* (*extinguish*) ausblasen. ~ **over** *vi* umfallen; (*fig: die down*) vorübergehen. ~ **up** *vt* (*inflate*) aufblasen; (*enlarge*) vergrößern; (*shatter by explosion*) sprengen ● *vi* explodieren

'blowlamp *n* Lötlampe *f*

blown /bləʊn/ *see* **blow²**

'blowtorch *n* (*Amer*) Lötlampe *f*

blowy /'bləʊɪ/ *adj* windig

blue /blu:/ *adj* (**-r**, **-st**) blau; **feel** ~ deprimiert sein ● *n* Blau *nt*; **have the** ~**s** deprimiert sein; **out of the** ~ aus heiterem Himmel

blue: ~**bell** *n* Sternhyazinthe *f*. ~**berry** *n* Heidelbeere *f*. ~**bottle** *n* Schmeißfliege *f*. ~ **film** *n* Pornofilm *m*. ~**print** *n* (*fig*) Entwurf *m*

bluff /blʌf/ *n* Bluff *m* ● *vi* bluffen

blunder /'blʌndə(r)/ *n* Schnitzer *m* ● *vi* einen Schnitzer machen

blunt /blʌnt/ *adj* stumpf; (*person*) geradeheraus. ~**ly** *adv* unverblümt, geradeheraus

blur /blɜ:(r)/ *n* **it's all a** ~ alles ist verschwommen ● *vt* (*pt/pp* **blurred**) verschwommen machen; ~**red** verschwommen

blush /blʌʃ/ *n* Erröten *nt* ● *vi* erröten

bluster /'blʌstə(r)/ *n* Großtuerei *f*. ~**y** *adj* windig

boar /bɔ:(r)/ *n* Eber *m*

board /bɔ:d/ *n* Brett *nt*; (*for notices*) schwarzes Brett *nt*; (*committee*) Ausschuss *m*; (*of directors*) Vorstand *m*; **on** ~ an Bord; **full** ~ Vollpension *f*; ~ **and lodging** Unterkunft und Verpflegung *pl* ● *vt* einsteigen in (+ *acc*); (*Naut, Aviat*) besteigen ● *vi* an Bord gehen. ~ **up** *vt* mit Brettern verschlagen

boarder /'bɔ:də(r)/ *n* Pensionsgast *m*; (*Sch*) Internatsschüler(in) *m(f)*

board: ~**-game** *n* Brettspiel *nt*. ~**ing-house** *n* Pension *f*. ~**ing-school** *n* Internat *nt*

boast /bəʊst/ *vt* sich rühmen (+ *gen*) ● *vi* prahlen (**about** mit). ~**ful** *adj* prahlerisch

boat /bəʊt/ *n* Boot *nt*; (*ship*) Schiff *nt*

> *i*
>
> **Boat Race** Seit 1829 findet jährlich (meist am Samstag vor Ostern) ein Ruderrennen auf der Themse in London statt. Das Achterrennen wird von den Rudermannschaften der Universitäten Oxford und Cambridge ausgetragen. Im Gegensatz zu anderen sportlichen Universitätswettbewerben wird dieses Ruderrennen landesweit im Fernsehen übertragen.

b

bob /bɒb/ *vi* (*pt/pp* **bobbed**) ~ **up and down** sich auf und ab bewegen

'**bob-sleigh** *n* Bob *m*

bodily /'bɒdɪlɪ/ *adj* körperlich ● *adv* (*forcibly*) mit Gewalt

body /'bɒdɪ/ *n* Körper *m*; (*corpse*) Leiche *f*; (*corporation*) Körperschaft *f*. ~**guard** *n* Leibwächter *m*. ~ **part** *n* Leichenteil *nt*. ~**work** *n* (*Auto*) Karosserie *f*

bog /bɒg/ *n* Sumpf *m*

bogus /'bəʊgəs/ *adj* falsch

boil[1] /bɔɪl/ *n* Furunkel *m*

boil[2] *n* **bring/come to the** ~ zum Kochen bringen/kommen ● *vt/i* kochen; ~**ed potatoes** Salzkartoffeln *pl*. ~ **down** *vi* (*fig*) hinauslaufen (**to** auf + *acc*). ~ **over** *vi* überkochen

boiler /'bɔɪlə(r)/ *n* Heizkessel *m*

'**boiling point** *n* Siedepunkt *m*

boisterous /'bɔɪstərəs/ *adj* übermütig

bold /bəʊld/ *adj* (**-er, -est**) kühn; (*Printing*) fett. ~**ness** *n* Kühnheit *f*

bolster /'bəʊlstə(r)/ *n* Nackenrolle *f* ● *vt* ~ **up** Mut machen (+ *dat*)

bolt /bəʊlt/ *n* Riegel *m*; (*Techn*) Bolzen *m* ● *vt* schrauben (**to** an + *acc*); verriegeln (*door*); hinunterschlingen (*food*) ● *vi* abhauen; (*horse:*) durchgehen

bomb /bɒm/ *n* Bombe *f* ● *vt* bombardieren

bombard /bɒm'bɑ:d/ *vt* beschießen; (*fig*) bombardieren

bombastic /bɒm'bæstɪk/ *adj* bombastisch

bomber /'bɒmə(r)/ *n* (*Aviat*) Bomber *m*; (*person*) Bombenleger(in) *m*(*f*)

bond /bɒnd/ *n* (*fig*) Band *nt*; (*Comm*) Obligation *f*

bone /bəʊn/ *n* Knochen *m*; (*of fish*) Gräte *f* ● *vt* von den Knochen lösen (*meat*); entgräten (*fish*). ~-'**dry** *adj* knochentrocken

bonfire /'bɒn-/ *n* Gartenfeuer *nt*; (*celebratory*) Freudenfeuer *nt*

bonus /'bəʊnəs/ *n* Prämie *f*; (*gratuity*) Gratifikation *f*; (*fig*) Plus *nt*

bony /'bəʊnɪ/ *adj* knochig; (*fish*) grätig

boo /bu:/ *int* buh! ● *vt* ausbuhen ● *vi* buhen

boob /bu:b/ *n* ([!]: *mistake*) Schnitzer *m*

book /bʊk/ *n* Buch *nt*; (*of tickets*) Heft *nt*; **keep the** ~**s** (*Comm*) die Bücher führen ● *vt/i* buchen; (*reserve*) [vor]bestellen; (*for offence*) aufschreiben

book: ~**case** *n* Bücherregal *nt*. ~-**ends** *npl* Buchstützen *pl*. ~**ing-office** *n* Fahrkartenschalter *m*. ~**keeping** *n* Buchführung *f*. ~**let** *n* Broschüre *f*. ~**maker** *n* Buchmacher *m*. ~**mark** *n* Lesezeichen *nt*. ~**seller** *n* Buchhändler(in) *m*(*f*). ~**shop** *n* Buchhandlung *f*. ~**stall** *n* Bücherstand *m*

boom /bu:m/ *n* (*Comm*) Hochkonjunktur *f*; (*upturn*) Aufschwung *m* ● *vi* dröhnen; (*fig*) blühen

boon /bu:n/ *n* Segen *m*

boost /bu:st/ *n* Auftrieb *m* ● *vt* Auftrieb geben (+ *dat*)

boot /bu:t/ *n* Stiefel *m*; (*Auto*) Kofferraum *m*

booth /bu:ð/ *n* Bude *f*; (*cubicle*) Kabine *f*

booty /'bu:tɪ/ *n* Beute *f*

booze /bu:z/ *n* [!] Alkohol *m* ● *vi* [!] saufen

border /'bɔ:də(r)/ *n* Rand *m*; (*frontier*) Grenze *f*; (*in garden*) Rabatte *f* ● *vi* ~ **on** grenzen an (+ *acc*). ~**line case** *n* Grenzfall *m*

bore[1] /bɔ:(r)/ *see* **bear**[2]

bor|e[2] *n* (*of gun*) Kaliber *nt*; (*person*) langweiliger Mensch *m*; (*thing*) langweilige Sache *f* ● *vt* langweilen; **be ~ed** sich langweilen. **~edom** *n* Langeweile *f*. **~ing** *adj* langweilig

born /bɔ:n/ *pp* **be ~** geboren werden ● *adj* geboren

borne /bɔ:n/ *see* **bear**[2]

borrow /ˈbɒrəʊ/ *vt* [sich (*dat*)] borgen *od* leihen (**from** von)

bosom /ˈbʊzm/ *n* Busen *m*

boss /bɒs/ *n* 🄸 Chef *m* ● *vt* herumkommandieren. **~y** *adj* herrschsüchtig

botanical /bəˈtænɪkl/ *adj* botanisch

botan|ist /ˈbɒtənɪst/ *n* Botaniker(in) *m*(*f*). **~y** *n* Botanik *f*

both /bəʊθ/ *adj & pron* beide; **~[of] the children** beide Kinder; **~ of them** beide [von ihnen] ● *adv* **~ men and women** sowohl Männer als auch Frauen

bother /ˈbɒðə(r)/ *n* Mühe *f*; (*minor trouble*) Ärger *m* ● *int* 🄸 verflixt! ● *vt* belästigen; (*disturb*) stören ● *vi* sich kümmern (**about** um)

bottle /ˈbɒtl/ *n* Flasche *f* ● *vt* auf Flaschen abfüllen; (*preserve*) einmachen

bottle: ~-neck *n* (*fig*) Engpass *m*. **~-opener** *n* Flaschenöffner *m*

bottom /ˈbɒtəm/ *adj* unterste(r,s) ● *n* (*of container*) Boden *m*; (*of river*) Grund *m*; (*of page, hill*) Fuß *m*; (*buttocks*) Hintern *m*; **at the ~** unten; **get to the ~ of sth** (*fig*) hinter etw (*acc*) kommen

bought /bɔ:t/ *see* **buy**

bounce /baʊns/ *vi* [auf]springen; (*cheque:*) 🄸 nicht gedeckt sein ● *vt* aufspringen lassen (*ball*)

bouncer /ˈbaʊnsə(r)/ *n* 🄸 Rausschmeißer *m*

bound[1] /baʊnd/ *n* Sprung *m* ● *vi* springen

bound[2] *see* **bind** ● *adj* **~ for** (*ship*) mit Kurs auf (+ *acc*); **be ~ to do sth** etw bestimmt machen; (*obliged*) verpflichtet sein, etw zu machen

boundary /ˈbaʊndərɪ/ *n* Grenze *f*

bounds /baʊndz/ *npl* (*fig*) Grenzen *pl*; **out of ~** verboten

bouquet /bʊˈkeɪ/ *n* [Blumen-]strauß *m*; (*of wine*) Bukett *nt*

bourgeois /ˈbʊəʒwɑ:/ *adj* (*pej*) spießbürgerlich

bout /baʊt/ *n* (*Med*) Anfall *m*; (*Sport*) Kampf *m*

bow[1] /bəʊ/ *n* (*weapon & Mus*) Bogen *m*; (*knot*) Schleife *f*

bow[2] /baʊ/ *n* Verbeugung *f* ● *vi* sich verbeugen ● *vt* neigen (*head*)

bow[3] /baʊ/ *n* (*Naut*) Bug *m*

bowel /ˈbaʊəl/ *n* Darm *m*. **~s** *pl* Eingeweide *pl*

bowl[1] /bəʊl/ *n* Schüssel *f*; (*shallow*) Schale *f*

bowl[2] *n* (*ball*) Kugel *f* ● *vt/i* werfen. **~ over** *vt* umwerfen

bowler /ˈbəʊlə(r)/ *n* (*Sport*) Werfer *m*

bowling /ˈbəʊlɪŋ/ *n* Kegeln *nt*. **~-alley** *n* Kegelbahn *f*

bowls /bəʊlz/ *n* Bowlsspiel *nt*

bow-ˈtie /bəʊ-/ *n* Fliege *f*

box[1] /bɒks/ *n* Schachtel *f*; (*wooden*) Kiste *f*; (*cardboard*) Karton *m*; (*Theat*) Loge *f*

box[2] *vt/i* (*Sport*) boxen

box|er /ˈbɒksə(r)/ *n* Boxer *m*. **~ing** *n* Boxen *nt*. **B~ing Day** *n* zweiter Weihnachtstag *m*

box: ~-office *n* (*Theat*) Kasse *f*. **~-room** *n* Abstellraum *m*

boy /bɔɪ/ *n* Junge *m*. **~ band** *n* Jungenband *f*

b

boycott /ˈbɔɪkɒt/ *n* Boykott *m* ● *vt* boykottieren

boy: ~friend *n* Freund *m*. **~ish** *adj* jungenhaft

bra /brɑː/ *n* BH *m*

brace /breɪs/ *n* Strebe *f*, Stütze *f*; (*dental*) Zahnspange *f*; **~s** *npl* Hosenträger *mpl*

bracelet /ˈbreɪslɪt/ *n* Armband *nt*

bracing /ˈbreɪsɪŋ/ *adj* stärkend

bracket /ˈbrækɪt/ *n* Konsole *f*; (*group*) Gruppe *f*; (*Printing*) **round/square ~s** runde/eckige Klammern ● *vt* einklammern

brag /bræg/ *vi* (*pt/pp* **bragged**) prahlen (**about** mit)

braille /breɪl/ *n* Blindenschrift *f*

brain /breɪn/ *n* Gehirn *nt*; **~s** (*fig*) Intelligenz *f*

brain: ~less *adj* dumm. **~wash** *vt* einer Gehirnwäsche unterziehen. **~wave** *n* Geistesblitz *m*

brainy /ˈbreɪnɪ/ *adj* klug

brake /breɪk/ *n* Bremse *f* ● *vt/i* bremsen. **~-light** *n* Bremslicht *nt*

bramble /ˈbræmbl/ *n* Brombeerstrauch *m*

branch /brɑːntʃ/ *n* Ast *m*; (*fig*) Zweig *m*; (*Comm*) Zweigstelle *f*; (*shop*) Filiale *f* ● *vi* sich gabeln

brand /brænd/ *n* Marke *f* ● *vt* (*fig*) brandmarken als

brandish /ˈbrændɪʃ/ *vt* schwingen

brand-ˈnew *adj* nagelneu

brandy /ˈbrændɪ/ *n* Weinbrand *m*

brash /bræʃ/ *adj* nassforsch

brass /brɑːs/ *n* Messing *nt*; (*Mus*) Blech *nt*; **top ~** [!] hohe Tiere *pl*. **~ band** *n* Blaskapelle *f*

brassy /ˈbrɑːsɪ/ *adj* [!] ordinär

brat /bræt/ *n* (*pej*) Balg *nt*

bravado /brəˈvɑːdəʊ/ *n* Forschheit *f*

brave /breɪv/ *adj* (**-r, -st**) tapfer ● *vt* die Stirn bieten (+ *dat*). **~ry** *n* Tapferkeit *f*

bravo /brɑːˈvəʊ/ *int* bravo!

brawl /brɔːl/ *n* Schlägerei *f*

brawn /brɔːn/ *n* (*Culin*) Sülze *f*

brawny /ˈbrɔːnɪ/ *adj* muskulös

bray /breɪ/ *vi* iahen

brazen /ˈbreɪzn/ *adj* unverschämt

Brazil /brəˈzɪl/ *n* Brasilien *nt*. **~ian** *adj* brasilianisch. **~ nut** *n* Paranuss *f*

breach /briːtʃ/ *n* Bruch *m*; (*Mil & fig*) Bresche *f*; **~ of contract** Vertragsbruch *m*

bread /bred/ *n* Brot *nt*; **slice of ~ and butter** Butterbrot *nt*. **~crumbs** *npl* Brotkrümel *pl*; (*Culin*) Paniermehl *nt*

breadth /bredθ/ *n* Breite *f*

break /breɪk/ *n* Bruch *m*; (*interval*) Pause *f*; (*interruption*) Unterbrechung *f*; ([!]: *chance*) Chance *f* ● *v* (*pt* **broke**, *pp* **broken**) ● *vt* brechen; (*smash*) zerbrechen; (*damage*) kaputtmachen [!]; (*interrupt*) unterbrechen; **~ one's arm** sich (*dat*) den Arm brechen ● *vi* brechen; (*day:*) anbrechen; (*storm:*) losbrechen; (*thing:*) kaputtgehen [!]; (*rope, thread:*) reißen; (*news:*) bekannt werden; **his voice is ~ing** er ist im Stimmbruch. **~ away** *vi* sich losreißen/(*fig*) sich absetzen (**from** von). **~ down** *vi* zusammenbrechen; (*Techn*) eine Panne haben; (*negotiations:*) scheitern ● *vt* aufbrechen (*door*); aufgliedern (*figures*). **~ in** *vi* einbrechen. **~ off** *vt/i* abbrechen; lösen (*engagement*). **~ out** *vi* ausbrechen. **~ up** *vt* zerbrechen ● *vi* (*crowd:*) sich zerstreuen; (*marriage, couple:*) auseinander gehen; (*Sch*) Ferien bekommen

break|able /ˈbreɪkəbl/ *adj* zerbrechlich. **~age** *n* Bruch *m*. **~down** *n* (*Techn*) Panne *f*; (*Med*)

Zusammenbruch *m*; (*of figures*) Aufgliederung *f*. **~er** *n* (*wave*) Brecher *m*

breakfast /'brekfəst/ *n* Frühstück *nt*

break: ~through *n* Durchbruch *m*. **~water** *n* Buhne *f*

breast /brest/ *n* Brust *f*. **~bone** *n* Brustbein *nt*. **~-feed** *vt* stillen. **~-stroke** *n* Brustschwimmen *nt*

breath /breθ/ *n* Atem *m*; **out of ~** außer Atem; **under one's ~** vor sich (*acc*) hin

breathe /bri:ð/ *vt/i* atmen. **~ in** *vt/i* einatmen. **~ out** *vt/i* ausatmen

breathing *n* Atmen *nt*

breath: /'breθ/: **~less** *adj* atemlos. **~-taking** *adj* atemberaubend

bred /bred/ *see* **breed**

breed /bri:d/ *n* Rasse *f* ● *v* (*pt/pp* **bred**) ● *vt* züchten; (*give rise to*) erzeugen ● *vi* sich vermehren. **~er** *n* Züchter *m*. **~ing** *n* Zucht *f*; (*fig*) [gute] Lebensart *f*

breez|e /bri:z/ *n* Lüftchen *nt*; (*Naut*) Brise *f*. **~y** *adj* windig

brevity /'brevətɪ/ *n* Kürze *f*

brew /bru:/ *n* Gebräu *nt* ● *vt* brauen; kochen (*tea*). **~er** *n* Brauer *m*. **~ery** *n* Brauerei *f*

bribe /braɪb/ *n* (*money*) Bestechungsgeld *nt* ● *vt* bestechen. **~ry** *n* Bestechung *f*

brick /brɪk/ *n* Ziegelstein *m*, Backstein *m*

'bricklayer *n* Maurer *m*

bridal /'braɪdl/ *adj* Braut-

bride /braɪd/ *n* Braut *f*. **~groom** *n* Bräutigam *m*. **~smaid** *n* Brautjungfer *f*

bridge[1] /brɪdʒ/ *n* Brücke *f*; (*of nose*) Nasenrücken *m*; (*of spectacles*) Steg *m*

bridge[2] *n* (*Cards*) Bridge *nt*

bridle /'braɪdl/ *n* Zaum *m*

brief[1] /bri:f/ *adj* (**-er, -est**) kurz; **be ~** (*person:*) sich kurz fassen

brief[2] *n* Instruktionen *pl*; (*Jur: case*) Mandat *nt*. **~case** *n* Aktentasche *f*

brief|ing /'bri:fɪŋ/ *n* Informationsgespräch *nt*. **~ly** *adv* kurz. **~ness** *n* Kürze *f*

briefs /bri:fs/ *npl* Slip *m*

brigade /brɪ'geɪd/ *n* Brigade *f*

bright /braɪt/ *adj* (**-er, -est**) hell; (*day*) heiter; **~ red** hellrot

bright|en /'braɪtn/ *v* **~en [up]** ● *vt* aufheitern ● *vi* sich aufheitern. **~ness** *n* Helligkeit *f*

brilliance /'brɪljəns/ *n* Glanz *m*; (*of person*) Genialität *f*

brilliant /'brɪljənt/ *adj* glänzend; (*person*) genial

brim /brɪm/ *n* Rand *m*; (*of hat*) Krempe *f*

bring /brɪŋ/ *vt* (*pt/pp* **brought**) bringen; **~ them with you** bring sie mit; **I can't b~ myself to do it** ich bringe es nicht fertig. **~ about** *vt* verursachen. **~ along** *vt* mitbringen. **~ back** *vt* zurückbringen. **~ down** *vt* herunterbringen; senken (*price*). **~ off** *vt* vollbringen. **~ on** *vt* (*cause*) verursachen. **~ out** *vt* herausbringen. **~ round** *vt* vorbeibringen; (*persuade*) überreden; wieder zum Bewusstsein bringen (*unconscious person*). **~ up** *vt* heraufbringen; (*vomit*) erbrechen; aufziehen (*children*); erwähnen (*question*)

brink /brɪŋk/ *n* Rand *m*

brisk /brɪsk/ *adj* (**-er, -est,**) **-ly** *adv* lebhaft; (*quick*) schnell

bristle /'brɪsl/ *n* Borste *f*

Brit|ain /'brɪtn/ *n* Großbritannien *nt*. **~ish** *adj* britisch; **the ~ish** die Briten *pl*. **~on** *n* Brite *m*/Britin *f*

Brittany /'brɪtənɪ/ *n* die Bretagne

b

brittle /ˈbrɪtl/ *adj* brüchig, spröde

broad /brɔːd/ *adj* (-**er**, -**est**) breit; (*hint*) deutlich; **in ~ daylight** am helllichten Tag. **~ beans** *npl* dicke Bohnen *pl*

broadband /ˈbrɔːdbænd/ *n* Breitband *nt*

ˈ**broadcast** *n* Sendung *f* ● *vt/i* (*pt/pp* -**cast**) senden. **~er** *n* Rundfunk- und Fernsehpersönlichkeit *f*. **~ing** *n* Funk und Fernsehen *pl*

broaden /ˈbrɔːdn/ *vt* verbreitern; (*fig*) erweitern ● *vi* sich verbreitern

broadly /ˈbrɔːdlɪ/ *adv* breit; **~ speaking** allgemein gesagt

broadˈminded *adj* tolerant

broccoli /ˈbrɒkəlɪ/ *n inv* Brokkoli *pl*

brochure /ˈbrəʊʃə(r)/ *n* Broschüre *f*

broke /brəʊk/ *see* **break** ● *adj* 🄸 pleite

broken /ˈbrəʊkn/ *see* **break** ● *adj* zerbrochen, 🄸 kaputt. **~-hearted** *adj* untröstlich

broker /ˈbrəʊkə(r)/ *n* Makler *m*

brolly /ˈbrɒlɪ/ *n* 🄸 Schirm *m*

bronchitis /brɒŋˈkaɪtɪs/ *n* Bronchitis *f*

bronze /brɒnz/ *n* Bronze *f*

brooch /brəʊtʃ/ *n* Brosche *f*

brood /bruːd/ *vi* (*fig*) grübeln

broom /bruːm/ *n* Besen *m*; (*Bot*) Ginster *m*

broth /brɒθ/ *n* Brühe *f*

brothel /ˈbrɒθl/ *n* Bordell *nt*

brother /ˈbrʌðə(r)/ *n* Bruder *m*

brother: ~-in-law *n* (*pl* **-s-in-law**) Schwager *m*. **~ly** *adj* brüderlich

brought /brɔːt/ *see* **bring**

brow /braʊ/ *n* Augenbraue *f*; (*forehead*) Stirn *f*; (*of hill*) [Berg]kuppe *f*

brown /braʊn/ *adj* (-**er**, -**est**) braun; **~ ˈpaper** Packpapier *nt* ● *n* Braun *nt* ● *vt* bräunen ● *vi* braun werden

browse /braʊz/ *vi* (*read*) schmökern; (*in shop*) sich umsehen. **~r** *n* (*Computing*) Browser *m*

bruise /bruːz/ *n* blauer Fleck *m* ● *vt* beschädigen (*fruit*); **~ one's arm** sich (*dat*) den Arm quetschen

brunette /bruːˈnet/ *n* Brünette *f*

brush /brʌʃ/ *n* Bürste *f*; (*with handle*) Handfeger *m*; (*for paint, pastry*) Pinsel *m*; (*bushes*) Unterholz *nt*; (*fig: conflict*) Zusammenstoß *m* ● *vt* bürsten; putzen (*teeth*); **~ against** streifen [gegen]; **~ aside** (*fig*) abtun. **~ off** *vt* abbürsten. **~ up** *vt/i* (*fig*) **~ up [on]** auffrischen

brusque /brʊsk/ *adj* brüsk

Brussels /ˈbrʌslz/ *n* Brüssel *nt*. **~ sprouts** *npl* Rosenkohl *m*

brutal /ˈbruːtl/ *adj* brutal. **~ity** *n* Brutalität *f*

brute /bruːt/ *n* Unmensch *m*. **~ force** *n* rohe Gewalt *f*

BSE *abbr* (**bovine spongiform encephalopathy**) BSE *f*

bubble /ˈbʌbl/ *n* [Luft]blase *f* ● *vi* sprudeln

buck¹ /bʌk/ *n* (*deer & Gym*) Bock *m*; (*rabbit*) Rammler *m* ● *vi* (*horse:*) bocken

buck² *n* (*Amer* 🄸) Dollar *m*

buck³ *n* **pass the ~** die Verantwortung abschieben

bucket /ˈbʌkɪt/ *n* Eimer *m*

buckle /ˈbʌkl/ *n* Schnalle *f* ● *vt* zuschnallen ● *vi* sich verbiegen

bud /bʌd/ *n* Knospe *f*

buddy /ˈbʌdɪ/ *n* 🄸 Freund *m*

budge /bʌdʒ/ *vt* bewegen ● *vi* sich [von der Stelle] rühren

budget /ˈbʌdʒɪt/ *n* Budget *nt*; (*Pol*) Haushaltsplan *m*; (*money available*)

Etat *m* ● *vi* (*pt/pp* **budgeted**) ~ **for sth** **etw** einkalkulieren

buff /bʌf/ *adj* (*colour*) sandfarben ● *n* Sandfarbe *f*; ▣ Fan *m* ● *vt* polieren

buffalo /ˈbʌfələʊ/ *n* (*inv or pl* **-es**) Büffel *m*

buffer /ˈbʌfə(r)/ *n* (*Rail*) Puffer *m*

buffet¹ /ˈbʊfeɪ/ *n* Büfett *nt*; (*on station*) Imbissstube *f*

buffet² /ˈbʌfɪt/ *vt* (*pt/pp* **buffeted**) hin und her werfen

bug /bʌg/ *n* Wanze *f*; (▣: *virus*) Bazillus *m*; (▣: *device*) Abhörgerät *nt*, ▣ Wanze *f* ● *vt* (*pt/pp* **bugged**) ▣ verwanzen (*room*); abhören (*telephone*); (*Amer: annoy*) ärgern

bugle /ˈbju:gl/ *n* Signalhorn

build /bɪld/ *n* (*of person*) Körperbau *m* ● *vt/i* (*pt/pp* **built**) bauen. ~ **on** *vt* anbauen (**to** an + *acc*). ~ **up** *vt* aufbauen ● *vi* zunehmen

builder /ˈbɪldə(r)/ *n* Bauunternehmer *m*

building /ˈbɪldɪŋ/ *n* Gebäude *nt*. ~ **site** *n* Baustelle *f*. ~ **society** *n* Bausparkasse *f*

built /bɪlt/ *see* **build.** ~**-in** *adj* eingebaut. ~**-in** ˈ**cupboard** *n* Einbauschrank *m*. ~**-up area** *n* bebautes Gebiet *nt*; (*Auto*) geschlossene Ortschaft *f*

bulb /bʌlb/ *n* [Blumen]zwiebel *f*; (*Electr*) [Glüh]birne *f*

bulbous /ˈbʌlbəs/ *adj* bauchig

Bulgaria /bʌlˈgeərɪə/ *n* Bulgarien *nt*

bulg|e /bʌldʒ/ *n* Ausbauchung *f* ● *vi* sich ausbauchen. ~**ing** *adj* prall; (*eyes*) hervorquellend

bulk /bʌlk/ *n* Masse *f*; (*greater part*) Hauptteil *m*. ~**y** *adj* sperrig; (*large*) massig

bull /bʊl/ *n* Bulle *m*, Stier *m*

ˈ**bulldog** *n* Bulldogge *f*

bulldozer /ˈbʊldəʊzə(r)/ *n* Planierraupe *f*

bullet /ˈbʊlɪt/ *n* Kugel *f*

bulletin /ˈbʊlɪtɪn/ *n* Bulletin *nt*

ˈ**bullet-proof** *adj* kugelsicher

ˈ**bullfight** *n* Stierkampf *m*. ~**er** *n* Stierkämpfer *m*

ˈ**bullfinch** *n* Dompfaff *m*

bullock /ˈbʊlək/ *n* Ochse *m*

bull: ~**ring** *n* Stierkampfarena *f*. ~**'s-eye** *n* **score a** ~**'s-eye** ins Schwarze treffen

bully /ˈbʊlɪ/ *n* Tyrann *m* ● *vt* tyrannisieren

bum /bʌm/ *n* ▣ Hintern *m*

bumble-bee /ˈbʌmbl-/ *n* Hummel *f*

bump /bʌmp/ *n* Bums *m*; (*swelling*) Beule *f*; (*in road*) holperige Stelle *f* ● *vt* stoßen; ~ **into** stoßen gegen; (*meet*) zufällig treffen. ~ **off** *vt* ▣ um die Ecke bringen

bumper /ˈbʌmpə(r)/ *adj* Rekord- ● *n* (*Auto*) Stoßstange *f*

bumpy /ˈbʌmpɪ/ *adj* holperig

bun /bʌn/ *n* Milchbrötchen *nt*; (*hair*) [Haar]knoten *m*

bunch /bʌntʃ/ *n* (*of flowers*) Strauß *m*; (*of radishes, keys*) Bund *m*; (*of people*) Gruppe *f*; ~ **of grapes** [ganze] Weintraube *f*

bundle /ˈbʌndl/ *n* Bündel *nt* ● *vt* ~ **[up]** bündeln

bungalow /ˈbʌŋgələʊ/ *n* Bungalow *m*

bungle /ˈbʌŋgl/ *vt* verpfuschen

bunk /bʌŋk/ *n* [Schlaf]koje *f*. ~**-beds** *npl* Etagenbett *nt*

bunker /ˈbʌŋkə(r)/ *n* Bunker *m*

bunny /ˈbʌnɪ/ *n* ▣ Kaninchen *nt*

buoy /bɔɪ/ *n* Boje *f*

buoyan|cy /ˈbɔɪənsɪ/ *n* Auftrieb *m*. ~**t** *adj* **be** ~**t** schwimmen

burden /ˈbɜ:dn/ *n* Last *f*

bureau /ˈbjʊərəʊ/ *n* (*pl* **-x** *or* **~s**) (*desk*) Sekretär *m*; (*office*) Büro *nt*

b **bureaucracy** /bjʊəˈrɒkrəsɪ/ *n* Bürokratie *f*

bureaucratic /bjʊərəkrætɪk/ *adj* bürokratisch

burger /ˈbɜːgə(r)/ *n* Hamburger *m*

burglar /ˈbɜːglə(r)/ *n* Einbrecher *m*. **~ alarm** *n* Alarmanlage *f*

burglary *n* Einbruch *m*

burgle /ˈbɜːgl/ *vt* einbrechen in (+ *acc*); **they have been ~d** bei ihnen ist eingebrochen worden

burial /ˈberɪəl/ *n* Begräbnis *nt*

burly /ˈbɜːlɪ/ *adj* stämmig

Burm|a /ˈbɜːmə/ *n* Birma *nt*. **~ese** *adj* birmanisch

burn /bɜːn/ *n* Verbrennung *f*; (*on skin*) Brandwunde *f*; (*on material*) Brandstelle *f* ● *v* (*pt/pp* **burnt** *or* **burned**) ● *vt* verbrennen ● *vi* brennen; (*food:*) anbrennen. **~ down** *vt/i* niederbrennen

burner /ˈbɜːnə(r)/ *n* Brenner *m*

burnt /bɜːnt/ *see* **burn**

burp /bɜːp/ *vi* [!] aufstoßen

burrow /ˈbʌrəʊ/ *n* Bau *m* ● *vi* wühlen

burst /bɜːst/ *n* Bruch *m*; (*surge*) Ausbruch *m* ● *v* (*pt/pp* **burst**) ● *vt* platzen machen ● *vi* platzen; (*bud:*) aufgehen; **~ into tears** in Tränen ausbrechen

bury /ˈberɪ/ *vt* (*pt/pp* **-ied**) begraben; (*hide*) vergraben

bus /bʌs/ *n* [Auto]bus *m*

bush /bʊʃ/ *n* Strauch *m*; (*land*) Busch *m*. **~y** *adj* buschig

busily /ˈbɪzɪlɪ/ *adv* eifrig

business /ˈbɪznɪs/ *n* Angelegenheit *f*; (*Comm*) Geschäft *nt*; **on ~** geschäftlich; **he has no ~** er hat kein Recht (**to** zu); **mind one's own ~** sich um seine eigenen Angelegenheiten kümmern; **that's none of your ~** das geht Sie nichts an. **~-like** *adj* geschäftsmäßig. **~man** *n* Geschäftsmann *m*

ˈbus-stop *n* Bushaltestelle *f*

bust¹ /bʌst/ *n* Büste *f*

bust² *adj* [!] kaputt; **go ~** Pleite gehen ● *v* (*pt/pp* **busted** *or* **bust**) [!] ● *vt* kaputtmachen ● *vi* kaputtgehen

busy /ˈbɪzɪ/ *adj* beschäftigt; (*day*) voll; (*street*) belebt; (*with traffic*) stark befahren; (*Amer Teleph*) besetzt; **be ~** zu tun haben ● *vt* **~ oneself** sich beschäftigen (**with** mit)

but /bʌt/, *unbetont* /bət/ *conj* aber; (*after negative*) sondern ● *prep* außer (+ *dat*); **~ for** (*without*) ohne (+ *acc*); **the last ~ one** der/die/das vorletzte; **the next ~ one** der/die/das übernächste ● *adv* nur

butcher /ˈbʊtʃə(r)/ *n* Fleischer *m*, Metzger *m*; **~'s [shop]** Fleischerei *f*, Metzgerei *f* ● *vt* [ab]schlachten

butler /ˈbʌtlə(r)/ *n* Butler *m*

butt /bʌt/ *n* (*of gun*) [Gewehr]kolben *m*; (*fig: target*) Zielscheibe *f*; (*of cigarette*) Stummel *m*; (*for water*) Regentonne *f* ● *vi* **~ in** unterbrechen

butter /ˈbʌtə(r)/ *n* Butter *f* ● *vt* mit Butter bestreichen. **~ up** *vt* [!] schmeicheln (+ *dat*)

butter: ~cup *adj* Butterblume *f*, Hahnenfuß *m*. **~fly** *n* Schmetterling *m*

buttocks /ˈbʌtəks/ *npl* Gesäß *nt*

button /ˈbʌtn/ *n* Knopf *m* ● *vt* **~ [up]** zuknöpfen. **~hole** *n* Knopfloch *nt*

buy /baɪ/ *n* Kauf *m* ● *vt* (*pt/pp* **bought**) kaufen. **~er** *n* Käufer(in) *m*(*f*)

buzz /bʌz/ *n* Summen *nt* ● *vi*

summen

buzzer /ˈbʌzə(r)/ *n* Summer *m*

by /baɪ/ *prep* (*close to*) bei (+ *dat*); (*next to*) neben (+ *dat*/*acc*); (*past*) an (+ *dat*) ... vorbei; (*to the extent of*) um (+ *acc*); (*at the latest*) bis; (*by means of*) durch; **by Mozart/ Dickens** von Mozart/Dickens; ~ **oneself** allein; ~ **the sea** am Meer; ~ **car/bus** mit dem Auto/Bus; ~ **sea** mit dem Schiff; ~ **day/night** bei Tag/Nacht; ~ **the hour** pro Stunde; ~ **the metre** meterweise; **six metres** ~ **four** sechs mal vier Meter; **win** ~ **a length** mit einer Länge Vorsprung gewinnen; **miss the train** ~ **a minute** den Zug um eine Minute verpassen ● *adv* ~ **and large** im Großen und Ganzen; **put** ~ beiseite legen; **go/pass** ~ vorbeigehen

bye /baɪ/ *int* 🅃 tschüs

by: ~**-election** *n* Nachwahl *f*. ~**pass** *n* Umgehungsstraße *f*; (*Med*) Bypass *m* ● *vt* umfahren. ~**-product** *n* Nebenprodukt *m*. ~**stander** *n* Zuschauer(in) *m*(*f*)

Cc

cab /kæb/ *n* Taxi *nt*; (*of lorry, train*) Führerhaus *nt*

cabaret /ˈkæbəreɪ/ *n* Kabarett *nt*

cabbage /ˈkæbɪdʒ/ *n* Kohl *m*

cabin /ˈkæbɪn/ *n* Kabine *f*; (*hut*) Hütte *f*

cabinet /ˈkæbɪnɪt/ *n* Schrank *m*; **[display]** ~ Vitrine *f*; **C**~ (*Pol*) Kabinett *nt*

cable /ˈkeɪbl/ *n* Kabel *nt*; (*rope*) Tau *nt*. ~ **'railway** *n* Seilbahn *f*. ~ **'television** *n* Kabelfernsehen *nt*

cackle /ˈkækl/ *vi* gackern

cactus /ˈkæktəs/ *n* (*pl* **-ti** *or* **-tuses**) Kaktus *m*

cadet /kəˈdet/ *n* Kadett *m*

cadge /kædʒ/ *vt*/*i* 🅃 schnorren

Caesarean /sɪˈzeərɪən/ *adj* & *n* ~ **[section]** Kaiserschnitt *m*

café /ˈkæfeɪ/ *n* Café *nt*

cafeteria /kæfəˈtɪərɪə/ *n* Selbstbedienungsrestaurant *nt*

cage /keɪdʒ/ *n* Käfig *m*

cagey /ˈkeɪdʒɪ/ *adj* 🅃 **be** ~ mit der Sprache nicht herauswollen

cake /keɪk/ *n* Kuchen *m*; (*of soap*) Stück *nt*. ~**d** *adj* verkrustet **(with** mit)

calamity /kəˈlæmətɪ/ *n* Katastrophe *f*

calculat|e /ˈkælkjʊleɪt/ *vt* berechnen; (*estimate*) kalkulieren. ~**ing** *adj* (*fig*) berechnend. ~**ion** *n* Rechnung *f*, Kalkulation *f*. ~**or** *n* Rechner *m*

calendar /ˈkælɪndə(r)/ *n* Kalender *m*

calf¹ /kɑːf/ *n* (*pl* **calves**) Kalb *nt*

calf² *n* (*pl* **calves**) (*Anat*) Wade *f*

calibre /ˈkælɪbə(r)/ *n* Kaliber *nt*

call /kɔːl/ *n* Ruf *m*; (*Teleph*) Anruf *m*; (*visit*) Besuch *m* ● *vt* rufen; (*Teleph*) anrufen; (*wake*) wecken; ausrufen (*strike*) (*name*) nennen; **be** ~**ed** heißen ● *vi* rufen; ~ **[in** *or* **round]** vorbeikommen. ~ **back** *vt* zurückrufen ● *vi* noch einmal vorbeikommen. ~ **for** *vt* rufen nach; (*demand*) verlangen; (*fetch*) abholen. ~ **off** *vt* zurückrufen (*dog*); (*cancel*) absagen. ~ **on** *vt* bitten (**for** um); (*appeal to*) appellieren an (+ *acc*); (*visit*) besuchen. ~ **out** *vt* rufen; aufrufen (*names*) ● *vi* rufen. ~ **up** *vt* (*Mil*) einberufen; (*Teleph*) anrufen

call: ~**-box** *n* Telefonzelle *f*. ~

C

centre *n* Callcenter *nt*. **~er** *n* Besucher *m*; (*Teleph*) Anrufer *m*. **~ing** *n* Berufung *f*. **~-up** *n* (*Mil*) Einberufung *f*

calm /kɑːm/ *adj* (**-er, -est**) ruhig ● *n* Ruhe *f* ● *vt* **~ [down]** beruhigen ● *vi* **~ down** sich beruhigen. **~ness** *n* Ruhe *f*; (*of sea*) Stille *f*

calorie /ˈkælərɪ/ *n* Kalorie *f*

calves /kɑːvz/ *npl see* **calf**[1] & [2]

camcorder /ˈkæmkɔːdə(r)/ *n* Camcorder *m*

came /keɪm/ *see* **come**

camel /ˈkæml/ *n* Kamel *nt*

camera /ˈkæmərə/ *n* Kamera *f*

camouflage /ˈkæməflɑːʒ/ *n* Tarnung *f* ● *vt* tarnen

camp /kæmp/ *n* Lager *nt* ● *vi* campen; (*Mil*) kampieren

campaign /kæmˈpeɪn/ *n* Feldzug *m*; (*Comm, Pol*) Kampagne *f* ● *vi* (*Pol*) im Wahlkampf arbeiten

camp: ~-bed *n* Feldbett *nt*. **~er** *n* Camper *m*; (*Auto*) Wohnmobil *nt*. **~ing** *n* Camping *nt*. **~site** *n* Campingplatz *m*

can[1] /kæn/ *n* (*for petrol*) Kanister *m*; (*tin*) Dose *f*, Büchse *f*; **a ~ of beer** eine Dose Bier

can[2] /kæn/, *unbetont* /kən/

pres **can**, *pt* **could**

● *modal verb*

····➤ (*be able to*) können. **I can't** *or* **cannot go** ich kann nicht gehen. **she couldn't** *or* **could not go** (*was unable to*) sie konnte nicht gehen; (*would not be able to*) sie könnte nicht gehen. **he could go if he had time** er könnte gehen, wenn er Zeit hätte. **if I could go** wenn ich gehen könnte. **that cannot be true** das kann nicht stimmen

····➤ (*know how to*) können. **can you swim?** können Sie schwimmen? **she can drive** sie kann Auto fahren

····➤ (*be allowed to*) dürfen. **you can't smoke here** hier dürfen Sie nicht rauchen. **can I go?** kann ich gehen?

····➤ (*in requests*) können. **can I have a glass of water, please?** kann ich ein Glas Wasser haben, bitte? **could you ring me tomorrow?** könnten Sie mich morgen anrufen?

····➤ **could** (*expressing possibility*) könnte. **that could be so** das könnte *od* kann sein. **I could have killed him** ich hätte ihn umbringen können

Canad|a /ˈkænədə/ *n* Kanada *nt*. **~ian** *adj* kanadisch ● *n* Kanadier(in) *m*(*f*)

canal /kəˈnæl/ *n* Kanal *m*

canary /kəˈneərɪ/ *n* Kanarienvogel *m*

cancel /ˈkænsl/ *vt/i* (*pt/pp* **cancelled**) absagen; abbestellen (*newspaper*); (*Computing*) abbrechen; **be ~led** ausfallen. **~lation** *n* Absage *f*

cancer /ˈkænsə(r)/ *n* (*also Astrology*) **C~** Krebs *m*. **~ous** *adj* krebsig

candid /ˈkændɪd/ *adj* offen

candidate /ˈkændɪdət/ *n* Kandidat(in) *m*(*f*)

candle /ˈkændl/ *n* Kerze *f*. **~stick** *n* Kerzenständer *m*, Leuchter *m*

candy /ˈkændɪ/ *n* (*Amer*) Süßigkeiten *pl*; **[piece of] ~** Bonbon *m*

cane /keɪn/ *n* Rohr *nt*; (*stick*) Stock *m* ● *vt* mit dem Stock züchtigen

canine /ˈkeɪnaɪn/ *adj* Hunde-. **~ tooth** *n* Eckzahn *m*

cannabis /ˈkænəbɪs/ *n* Haschisch *nt*

canned /kænd/ *adj* Dosen-, Büchsen-

cannibal /ˈkænɪbl/ *n* Kannibale *m*. **~ism** *n* Kannibalismus *m*

cannon /ˈkænən/ *n inv* Kanone *f*

cannot /ˈkænɒt/ *see* **can**[2]

canoe /kəˈnuː/ *n* Paddelboot *nt*; (*Sport*) Kanu *nt*

ˈcan-opener *n* Dosenöffner *m*

can't /kɑːnt/ = **cannot.** *See* **can**[2]

canteen /kænˈtiːn/ *n* Kantine *f*; **~ of cutlery** Besteckkasten *m*

canter /ˈkæntə(r)/ *n* Kanter *m* ● *vi* kantern

canvas /ˈkænvəs/ *n* Segeltuch *nt*; (*Art*) Leinwand *f*; (*painting*) Gemälde *nt*

canvass /ˈkænvəs/ *vi* um Stimmen werben

canyon /ˈkænjən/ *n* Cañon *m*

cap /kæp/ *n* Kappe *f*, Mütze *f*; (*nurse's*) Haube *f*; (*top, lid*) Verschluss *m*

capability /keɪpəˈbɪlətɪ/ *n* Fähigkeit *f*

capable /ˈkeɪpəbl/ *adj*, **-bly** *adv* fähig; **be ~ of doing sth** fähig sein, etw zu tun

capacity /kəˈpæsətɪ/ *n* Fassungsvermögen *nt*; (*ability*) Fähigkeit *f*; **in my ~ as** in meiner Eigenschaft als

cape[1] /keɪp/ *n* (*cloak*) Cape *nt*

cape[2] *n* (*Geog*) Kap *nt*

capital /ˈkæpɪtl/ *adj* (*letter*) groß ● *n* (*town*) Hauptstadt *f*; (*money*) Kapital *nt*; (*letter*) Großbuchstabe *m*

capital|ism /ˈkæpɪtəlɪzm/ *n* Kapitalismus *m*. **~ist** *adj* kapitalistisch ● *n* Kapitalist *m*. **~ ˈletter** *n* Großbuchstabe *m*. **~ ˈpunishment** *n* Todesstrafe *f*

Capitol Der Sitz des amerikanischen ▸**CONGRESS** auf dem Capitol Hill in Washington D.C.

capsize /kæpˈsaɪz/ *vi* kentern ● *vt* zum Kentern bringen

captain /ˈkæptɪn/ *n* Kapitän *m*; (*Mil*) Hauptmann *m* ● *vt* anführen (*team*)

caption /ˈkæpʃn/ *n* Überschrift *f*; (*of illustration*) Bildtext *m*

captivate /ˈkæptɪveɪt/ *vt* bezaubern

captiv|e /ˈkæptɪv/ *adj* **hold/take ~e** gefangen halten/nehmen ● *n* Gefangene(r) *m/f*. **~ity** *n* Gefangenschaft *f*

capture /ˈkæptʃə(r)/ *n* Gefangennahme *f* ● *vt* gefangen nehmen; [ein]fangen (*animal*); (*Mil*) einnehmen (*town*)

car /kɑː(r)/ *n* Auto *nt*, Wagen *m*; **by ~** mit dem Auto *od* Wagen

caramel /ˈkærəmel/ *n* Karamell *m*

carat /ˈkærət/ *n* Karat *nt*

caravan /ˈkærəvæn/ *n* Wohnwagen *m*; (*procession*) Karawane *f*

carbon /ˈkɑːbən/ *n* Kohlenstoff *m*; (*copy*) Durchschlag *m*

carbon: ~ copy *n* Durchschlag *m*. **~ footprint** *n* CO_2-Fußabdruck *m*. **~ paper** *n* Kohlepapier *nt*

carburettor /kɑːbjʊˈretə(r)/ *n* Vergaser *m*

carcass /ˈkɑːkəs/ *n* Kadaver *m*

card /kɑːd/ *n* Karte *f*

ˈcardboard *n* Pappe *f*, Karton *m*. **~ ˈbox** *n* Pappschachtel *f*; (*large*) [Papp]karton *m*

ˈcard-game *n* Kartenspiel *nt*

cardigan /ˈkɑːdɪgən/ *n* Strickjacke *f*

cardinal /ˈkɑːdɪnl/ *adj* Kardinal-

c

C

● *n* (*Relig*) Kardinal *m*

card 'index *n* Kartei *f*

care /keə(r)/ *n* Sorgfalt *f*; (*caution*) Vorsicht *f*; (*protection*) Obhut *f*; (*looking after*) Pflege *f*; (*worry*) Sorge *f*; ~ **of** (*on letter abbr* **c/o**) bei; **take** ~ vorsichtig sein; **take into** ~ in Pflege nehmen; **take** ~ **of** sich kümmern um ● *vi* ~ **for** (*like*) mögen; (*look after*) betreuen; **I don't** ~ das ist mir gleich

career /kə'rɪə(r)/ *n* Laufbahn *f*; (*profession*) Beruf *m* ● *vi* rasen

care: ~**free** *adj* sorglos. ~**ful** *adj* sorgfältig; (*cautious*) vorsichtig. ~**less** *adj* nachlässig. ~**lessness** *n* Nachlässigkeit *f*. ~**r** *n* Pflegende(r) *m/f*

'caretaker *n* Hausmeister *m*

'car ferry *n* Autofähre *f*

cargo /'kɑːgəʊ/ *n* (*pl* **-es**) Ladung *f*

Caribbean /kærɪ'biːən/ *n* **the** ~ die Karibik

caricature /'kærɪkətjʊə(r)/ *n* Karikatur *f* ● *vt* karikieren

caring /'keərɪŋ/ *adj* (*parent*) liebevoll; (*profession, attitude*) sozial

carnation /kɑː'neɪʃn/ *n* Nelke *f*

carnival /'kɑːnɪvl/ *n* Karneval *m*

carol /'kærl/ *n* **[Christmas]** ~ Weihnachtslied *nt*

carp[1] /kɑːp/ *n inv* Karpfen *m*

carp[2] *vi* nörgeln

'car park *n* Parkplatz *m*; (*multistorey*) Parkhaus *nt*; (*underground*) Tiefgarage *f*

carpent|er /'kɑːpɪntə(r)/ *n* Zimmermann *m*; (*joiner*) Tischler *m*. ~**ry** *n* Tischlerei *f*

carpet /'kɑːpɪt/ *n* Teppich *m*

carriage /'kærɪdʒ/ *n* Kutsche *f*; (*Rail*) Wagen *m*; (*of goods*) Beförderung *f*; (*cost*) Frachtkosten *pl*; (*bearing*) Haltung *f*

carrier /'kærɪə(r)/ *n* Träger(in) *m*(*f*); (*Comm*) Spediteur *m*; ~ **[-bag]** Tragetasche *f*

carrot /'kærət/ *n* Möhre *f*, Karotte *f*

carry /'kærɪ/ *vt/i* (*pt/pp* **-ied**) tragen; **be carried away** [!] hingerissen sein. ~ **off** *vt* wegtragen; gewinnen (*prize*). ~ **on** *vi* weitermachen; ~ **on with** [!] eine Affäre haben mit ● *vt* führen; (*continue*) fortführen. ~ **out** *vt* hinaus-/heraustragen; (*perform*) ausführen

cart /kɑːt/ *n* Karren *m*; **put the** ~ **before the horse** das Pferd beim Schwanz aufzäumen ● *vt* karren; ([!]: *carry*) schleppen

carton /'kɑːtn/ *n* [Papp]karton *m*; (*for drink*) Tüte *f*; (*of cream, yoghurt*) Becher *m*

cartoon /kɑː'tuːn/ *n* Karikatur *f*; (*joke*) Witzzeichnung *f*; (*strip*) Comic Strips *pl*; (*film*) Zeichentrickfilm *m*. ~**ist** *n* Karikaturist *m*

cartridge /'kɑːtrɪdʒ/ *n* Patrone *f*; (*for film*) Kassette *f*

carve /kɑːv/ *vt* schnitzen; (*in stone*) hauen; (*Culin*) aufschneiden

carving /'kɑːvɪŋ/ *n* Schnitzerei *f*. ~**-knife** *n* Tranchiermesser *nt*

'car wash *n* Autowäsche *f*; (*place*) Autowaschanlage *f*

case[1] /keɪs/ *n* Fall *m*; **in any** ~ auf jeden Fall; **just in** ~ für alle Fälle; **in** ~ **he comes** falls er kommt

case[2] *n* Kasten *m*; (*crate*) Kiste *f*; (*for spectacles*) Etui *nt*; (*suitcase*) Koffer *m*; (*for display*) Vitrine *f*

cash /kæʃ/ *n* Bargeld *nt*; **pay [in]** ~ [in] bar bezahlen; ~ **on delivery** per Nachnahme ● *vt* einlösen (*cheque*). ~ **desk** *n* Kasse *f*

cashier /kæ'ʃɪə(r)/ *n* Kassierer(in) *m*(*f*)

cash: ~**point [machine]** *n* Geldautomat *m*. ~ **register** *n* Registrierkasse *f*

cassette /kə'set/ *n* Kassette *f*. ~ **recorder** *n* Kassettenrecorder *m*

cast /kɑ:st/ *n* (*mould*) Form *f*; (*model*) Abguss *m*; (*Theat*) Besetzung *f*; **[plaster]** ~ (*Med*) Gipsverband *m* ● *vt* (*pt/pp* **cast**) (*throw*) werfen; (*shed*) abwerfen; abgeben (*vote*); gießen (*metal*); (*Theat*) besetzen (*role*). ~ **off** *vi* (*Naut*) ablegen

castle /'kɑ:sl/ *n* Schloss *nt*; (*fortified*) Burg *f*; (*Chess*) Turm *m*

'cast-offs *npl* abgelegte Kleidung *f*

castor /'kɑ:stə(r)/ *n* (*wheel*) [Lauf]rolle *f*

'castor sugar *n* Streuzucker *m*

casual /'kæʒʊəl/ *adj* (*chance*) zufällig; (*offhand*) lässig; (*informal*) zwanglos; (*not permanent*) Gelegenheits-; ~ **wear** Freizeitbekleidung *f*

casualty /'kæʒʊəltɪ/ *n* [Todes]opfer *nt*; (*injured person*) Verletzte(r) *m/f*; ~ **[department]** Unfallstation *f*

cat /kæt/ *n* Katze *f*

catalogue /'kætəlɒg/ *n* Katalog *m* ● *vt* katalogisieren

catapult /'kætəpʌlt/ *n* Katapult *nt* ● *vt* katapultieren

cataract /'kætərækt/ *n* (*Med*) grauer Star *m*

catarrh /kə'tɑ:(r)/ *n* Katarrh *m*

catastroph|e /kə'tæstrəfɪ/ *n* Katastrophe *f*. ~**ic** *adj* katastrophal

catch /kætʃ/ *n* (*of fish*) Fang *m*; (*fastener*) Verschluss *m*; (*on door*) Klinke *f*; (🄸: *snag*) Haken *m* 🄸 ● *v* (*pt/pp* **caught**) ● *vt* fangen; (*be in time for*) erreichen; (*travel by*) fahren mit; bekommen (*illness*); ~ **a cold** sich erkälten; ~ **sight of** erblicken; ~ **s.o. stealing** jdn beim Stehlen erwischen; ~ **one's finger in the door** sich (*dat*) den Finger in der Tür [ein]klemmen ● *vi* (*burn*) anbrennen; (*get stuck*) klemmen. ~ **on** *vi* 🄸 (*understand*) kapieren; (*become popular*) sich durchsetzen. ~ **up** *vt* einholen ● *vi* aufholen; ~ **up with** einholen (*s.o.*); nachholen (*work*)

catching /'kætʃɪŋ/ *adj* ansteckend

catch: ~**-phrase** *n*, ~**word** *n* Schlagwort *nt*

catchy /'kætʃɪ/ *adj* einprägsam

categor|ical /kætɪ'gɒrɪkl/ *adj* kategorisch. ~**y** *n* Kategorie *f*

cater /'keɪtə(r)/ *vi* ~ **for** beköstigen; (*firm:*) das Essen liefern für (*party*); (*fig*) eingestellt sein auf (+ *acc*). ~**ing** *n* (*trade*) Gaststättengewerbe *nt*

caterpillar /'kætəpɪlə(r)/ *n* Raupe *f*

cathedral /kə'θi:drl/ *n* Dom *m*, Kathedrale *f*

Catholic /'kæθəlɪk/ *adj* katholisch ● *n* Katholik(in) *m*(*f*). **C** ~**ism** *n* Katholizismus *m*

cattle /'kætl/ *npl* Vieh *nt*

catty /'kætɪ/ *adj* boshaft

caught /kɔ:t/ *see* **catch**

cauliflower /'kɒlɪ-/ *n* Blumenkohl *m*

cause /kɔ:z/ *n* Ursache *f*; (*reason*) Grund *m*; **good** ~ gute Sache *f* ● *vt* verursachen; ~ **s.o. to do sth** jdn veranlassen, etw zu tun

caution /'kɔ:ʃn/ *n* Vorsicht *f*; (*warning*) Verwarnung *f* ● *vt* (*Jur*) verwarnen

cautious /'kɔ:ʃəs/ *adj* vorsichtig

cavalry /'kævəlrɪ/ *n* Kavallerie *f*

cave /keɪv/ *n* Höhle *f* ● *vi* ~ **in** einstürzen

cavern /'kævən/ *n* Höhle *f*

caviare /'kævɪɑ:(r)/ *n* Kaviar *m*

c

cavity /ˈkævətɪ/ *n* Hohlraum *m*; (*in tooth*) Loch *nt*

CCTV *abbr* (**closed-circuit television**) CCTV *nt*; (*surveillance*) Videoüberwachung *f*

CD *abbr* (**compact disc**) CD *f*; **~-ROM** CD-ROM *f*

cease /siːs/ *vt/i* aufhören. **~-fire** *n* Waffenruhe *f*. **~less** *adj* unaufhörlich

cedar /ˈsiːdə(r)/ *n* Zeder *f*

ceiling /ˈsiːlɪŋ/ *n* [Zimmer]decke *f*; (*fig*) oberste Grenze *f*

celebrat|e /ˈselɪbreɪt/ *vt/i* feiern. **~ed** *adj* berühmt (**for** wegen). **~ion** *n* Feier *f*

celebrity /sɪˈlebrətɪ/ *n* Berühmtheit *f*

celery /ˈselərɪ/ *n* [Stangen]sellerie *m* & *f*

cell /sel/ *n* Zelle *f*

cellar /ˈselə(r)/ *n* Keller *m*

cellist /ˈtʃelɪst/ *n* Cellist(in) *m*(*f*)

cello /ˈtʃeləʊ/ *n* Cello *nt*

cellphone /ˈselfəʊn/ *n* Handy *nt*

Celsius /ˈselsɪəs/ *adj* Celsius

Celt /kelt/ *n* Kelte *m*/ Keltin *f*. **~ic** *adj* keltisch

cement /sɪˈment/ *n* Zement *m*; (*adhesive*) Kitt *m*

cemetery /ˈsemətrɪ/ *n* Friedhof *m*

censor /ˈsensə(r)/ *n* Zensor *m* ● *vt* zensieren. **~ship** *n* Zensur *f*

census /ˈsensəs/ *n* Volkszählung *f*

cent /sent/ *n* Cent *m*

centenary /senˈtiːnərɪ/ *n*, (*Amer*) **centennial** *n* Hundertjahrfeier *f*

center /ˈsentə(r)/ *n* (*Amer*) = centre

centi|grade /ˈsentɪ-/ *adj* Celsius. **~metre** *n* Zentimeter *m* & *nt*

central /ˈsentrəl/ *adj* zentral. **~ ˈheating** *n* Zentralheizung *f*. **~ize** *vt* zentralisieren

centre /ˈsentə(r)/ *n* Zentrum *nt*; (*middle*) Mitte *f* ● *v* (*pt/pp* **centred**) ● *vt* zentrieren. **~-ˈforward** *n* Mittelstürmer *m*

century /ˈsentʃərɪ/ *n* Jahrhundert *nt*

ceramic /sɪˈræmɪk/ *adj* Keramik-

cereal /ˈsɪərɪəl/ *n* Getreide *nt*; (*breakfast food*) Frühstücksflocken *pl*

ceremon|ial /serɪˈməʊnɪəl/ *adj* zeremoniell, feierlich ● *n* Zeremoniell *nt*. **~ious** *adj* formell

ceremony /ˈserɪmənɪ/ *n* Zeremonie *f*, Feier *f*

certain /ˈsɜːtn/ *adj* sicher; (*not named*) gewiss; **for ~** mit Bestimmtheit; **make ~** (*check*) sich vergewissern (**that** dass); (*ensure*) dafür sorgen (**that** dass); **he is ~ to win** er wird ganz bestimmt siegen. **~ly** *adv* bestimmt, sicher; **~ly not!** auf keinen Fall! **~ty** *n* Sicherheit *f*, Gewissheit *f*; **it's a ~ty** es ist sicher

certificate /səˈtɪfɪkət/ *n* Bescheinigung *f*; (*Jur*) Urkunde *f*; (*Sch*) Zeugnis *nt*

certify /ˈsɜːtɪfaɪ/ *vt* (*pt/pp* **-ied**) bescheinigen; (*declare insane*) für geisteskrank erklären

cf. *abbr* (*compare*) vgl.

chafe /tʃeɪf/ *vt* wund reiben

chaffinch /ˈtʃæfɪntʃ/ *n* Buchfink *m*

chain /tʃeɪn/ *n* Kette *f* ● *vt* ketten (**to** an + *acc*). **~ up** *vt* anketten

chain: ~ reˈaction *n* Kettenreaktion *f*. **~-smoker** *n* Kettenraucher *m*. **~ store** *n* Kettenladen *m*

chair /tʃeə(r)/ *n* Stuhl *m*; (*Univ*) Lehrstuhl *m*; (*Adm*) Vorsitzende(r) *m/f*. **~-lift** *n* Sessellift *m*. **~man** *n* Vorsitzende(r) *m/f*

chalet /ˈʃæleɪ/ *n* Chalet *nt*

chalk /tʃɔːk/ *n* Kreide *f*

challeng|e /ˈtʃælɪndʒ/ *n* Herausforderung *f*; (*Mil*) Anruf *m* ● *vt* herausfordern; (*Mil*) anrufen; (*fig*) anfechten (*statement*). **~er** *n* Herausforderer *m*. **~ing** *adj* herausfordernd; (*demanding*) anspruchsvoll

chamber /ˈtʃeɪmbə(r)/ *n* Kammer *f*; **C~ of Commerce** Handelskammer *f*. **~ music** *n* Kammermusik *f*

chamois /ˈʃæmɪ/ *n* **~[-leather]** Ledertuch *nt*

champagne /ʃæmˈpeɪn/ *n* Champagner *m*

champion /ˈtʃæmpɪən/ *n* (*Sport*) Meister(in) *m*(*f*); (*of cause*) Verfechter *m* ● *vt* sich einsetzen für. **~ship** *n* (*Sport*) Meisterschaft *f*

chance /tʃɑːns/ *n* Zufall *m*; (*prospect*) Chancen *pl*; (*likelihood*) Aussicht *f*; (*opportunity*) Gelegenheit *f*; **by ~** zufällig; **take a ~** ein Risiko eingehen; **give s.o. a ~** jdm eine Chance geben ● *attrib* zufällig ● *vt* **~ it** es riskieren

chancellor /ˈtʃɑːnsələ(r)/ *n* Kanzler *m*; (*Univ*) Rektor *m*

chancy /ˈtʃɑːnsɪ/ *adj* riskant

change /tʃeɪndʒ/ *n* Veränderung *f*; (*alteration*) Änderung *f*; (*money*) Wechselgeld *nt*; **for a ~** zur Abwechslung ● *vt* wechseln; (*alter*) ändern; (*exchange*) umtauschen (**for** gegen); (*transform*) verwandeln; trocken legen (*baby*); **~ one's clothes** sich umziehen; **~ trains** umsteigen ● *vi* sich verändern; (**~** *clothes*) sich umziehen; (**~** *trains*) umsteigen; **all ~!** alles aussteigen!

changeable /ˈtʃeɪndʒəbl/ *adj* wechselhaft

ˈchanging-room *n* Umkleideraum *m*

channel /ˈtʃænl/ *n* Rinne *f*; (*Radio, TV*) Kanal *m*; (*fig*) Weg *m*; **the [English] C~** der Ärmelkanal; **the C~ Islands** die Kanalinseln

chant /tʃɑːnt/ *vt* singen; (*demonstrators:*) skandieren

chao|s /ˈkeɪɒs/ *n* Chaos *nt*. **~tic** *adj* chaotisch

chap /tʃæp/ *n* 🄸 Kerl *m*

chapel /ˈtʃæpl/ *n* Kapelle *f*

chaplain /ˈtʃæplɪn/ *n* Geistliche(r) *m*

chapped /tʃæpt/ *adj* (*skin*) aufgesprungen

chapter /ˈtʃæptə(r)/ *n* Kapitel *nt*

character /ˈkærɪktə(r)/ *n* Charakter *m*; (*in novel, play*) Gestalt *f*; (*Printing*) Schriftzeichen *nt*; **out of ~** uncharakteristisch; **quite a ~** 🄸 ein Original

characteristic /kærɪktəˈrɪstɪk/ *adj*, **-ally** *adv* charakteristisch (**of** für) ● *n* Merkmal *nt*

characterize /ˈkærɪktəraɪz/ *vt* charakterisieren

charge /tʃɑːdʒ/ *n* (*price*) Gebühr *f*; (*Electr*) Ladung *f*; (*attack*) Angriff *m*; (*Jur*) Anklage *f*; **free of ~** kostenlos; **be in ~** verantwortlich sein (**of** für); **take ~** die Aufsicht übernehmen (**of** über + *acc*) ● *vt* berechnen (*fee*); (*Electr*) laden; (*attack*) angreifen; (*Jur*) anklagen (**with** *gen*); **~ s.o. for sth** jdm etw berechnen

charitable /ˈtʃærɪtəbl/ *adj* wohltätig; (*kind*) wohlwollend

charity /ˈtʃærətɪ/ *n* Nächstenliebe *f*; (*organization*) wohltätige Einrichtung *f*; **for ~** für Wohltätigkeitszwecke

charm /tʃɑːm/ *n* Reiz *m*; (*of person*) Charme *f*; (*object*) Amulett *nt* ● *vt* bezaubern. **~ing** *adj* reizend; (*person, smile*) charmant

chart /tʃɑːt/ *n* Karte *f*; (*table*) Tabelle *f*

charter /ˈtʃɑːtə(r)/ *n* **~ [flight]** Charterflug *m* ● *vt* chartern; **~ed accountant** Wirtschaftsprüfer,

Wirtschaftsprüferin *m(f)*

chase /tʃeɪs/ *n* Verfolgungsjagd *f* ● *vt* jagen, verfolgen. **~ away** *or* **off** *vt* wegjagen

chassis /ˈʃæsɪ/ *n* (*pl* **chassis**) Chassis *nt*

chaste /tʃeɪst/ *adj* keusch

chat /tʃæt/ *n* Plauderei *f*; **have a ~ with** plaudern mit ● *vi* (*pt/pp* **chatted**) plaudern. **~ show** *n* Talkshow *f*

chatter /ˈtʃætə(r)/ *n* Geschwätz *nt* ● *vi* schwatzen; (*child:*) plappern; (*teeth:*) klappern. **~box** *n* ⓘ Plappermaul *nt*

chatty /ˈtʃætɪ/ *adj* geschwätzig

chauffeur /ˈʃəʊfə(r)/ *n* Chauffeur *m*

cheap /tʃi:p/ *adj & adv* (**-er, -est**) billig. **~en** *vt* entwürdigen

cheat /tʃi:t/ *n* Betrüger(in) *m(f)*; (*at games*) Mogler *m* ● *vt* betrügen ● *vi* (*at games*) mogeln ⓘ

check¹ /tʃek/ *adj* (*squared*) kariert ● *n* Karo *nt*

check² *n* Überprüfung *f*; (*inspection*) Kontrolle *f*; (*Chess*) Schach *nt*; (*Amer: bill*) Rechnung *f*; (*Amer: cheque*) Scheck *m*; (*Amer: tick*) Haken *m*; **keep a ~ on** kontrollieren ● *vt* [über]prüfen; (*inspect*) kontrollieren; (*restrain*) hemmen; (*stop*) aufhalten ● *vi* **[go and] ~** nachsehen. **~ in** *vi* sich anmelden; (*Aviat*) einchecken ● *vt* abfertigen; einchecken. **~ out** *vi* sich abmelden. **~ up** *vi* prüfen, kontrollieren; **~ up on** überprüfen

checked /tʃekt/ *adj* kariert

check: ~-out *n* Kasse *f*. **~room** *n* (*Amer*) Garderobe *f*. **~-up** *n* (*Med*) [Kontroll]untersuchung *f*

cheek /tʃi:k/ *n* Backe *f*; (*impudence*) Frechheit *f*. **~y** *adj*, **-ily** *adv* frech

cheer /tʃɪə(r)/ *n* Beifallsruf *m*; **three ~s** ein dreifaches Hoch (**for** auf + *acc*); **~s!** prost! (*goodbye*) tschüs! ● *vt* zujubeln (+ *dat*) ● *vi* jubeln. **~ up** *vt* aufmuntern; aufheitern ● *vi* munterer werden. **~ful** *adj* fröhlich. **~fulness** *n* Fröhlichkeit *f*

cheerio /tʃɪərɪˈəʊ/ *int* ⓘ tschüs!

cheese /tʃi:z/ *n* Käse *m*. **~cake** *n* Käsekuchen *m*

chef /ʃef/ *n* Koch *m*

chemical /ˈkemɪkl/ *adj* chemisch ● *n* Chemikalie *f*

chemist /ˈkemɪst/ *n* (*pharmacist*) Apotheker(in) *m(f)*; (*scientist*) Chemiker(in) *m(f)*; **~'s [shop]** Drogerie *f*; (*dispensing*) Apotheke *f*. **~ry** *n* Chemie *f*

cheque /tʃek/ *n* Scheck *m*. **~-book** *n* Scheckbuch *nt*. **~ card** *n* Scheckkarte *f*

cherish /ˈtʃerɪʃ/ *vt* lieben; (*fig*) hegen

cherry /ˈtʃerɪ/ *n* Kirsche *f* ● *attrib* Kirsch-

chess /tʃes/ *n* Schach *nt*

chess: ~board *n* Schachbrett *nt*. **~-man** *n* Schachfigur *f*

chest /tʃest/ *n* Brust *f*; (*box*) Truhe *f*

chestnut /ˈtʃesnʌt/ *n* Esskastanie *f*, Marone *f*; (*horse-*) [Ross]kastanie *f*

chest of ˈdrawers *n* Kommode *f*

chew /tʃu:/ *vt* kauen. **~ing-gum** *n* Kaugummi *m*

chick /tʃɪk/ *n* Küken *nt*

chicken /ˈtʃɪkɪn/ *n* Huhn *nt* ● *attrib* Hühner- ● *adj* ⓘ feige

chief /tʃi:f/ *adj* Haupt- ● *n* Chef *m*; (*of tribe*) Häuptling *m*. **~ly** *adv* hauptsächlich

child /tʃaɪld/ *n* (*pl* **~ren**) Kind *nt*

child: ~birth *n* Geburt *f*. **~hood**

n Kindheit *f*. **~ish** *adj* kindisch. **~less** *adj* kinderlos. **~like** *adj* kindlich. **~-minder** *n* Tagesmutter *f*

children /ˈtʃɪldrən/ *npl see* **child**

Chile /ˈtʃɪlɪ/ *n* Chile *nt*

chill /tʃɪl/ *n* Kälte *f*; (*illness*) Erkältung *f* ● *vt* kühlen

chilly /ˈtʃɪlɪ/ *adj* kühl; **I felt ~** mich fröstelte [es]

chime /tʃaɪm/ *vi* läuten; (*clock:*) schlagen

chimney /ˈtʃɪmnɪ/ *n* Schornstein *m*. **~-pot** *n* Schornsteinaufsatz *m*. **~-sweep** *n* Schornsteinfeger *m*

chin /tʃɪn/ *n* Kinn *nt*

china /ˈtʃaɪnə/ *n* Porzellan *nt*

Chin|a *n* China *nt*. **~ese** *adj* chinesisch ● *n* (*Lang*) Chinesisch *nt*; **the ~ese** *pl* die Chinesen

chink[1] /tʃɪŋk/ *n* (*slit*) Ritze *f*

chink[2] *n* Geklirr *nt* ● *vi* klirren; (*coins:*) klimpern

chip /tʃɪp/ *n* (*fragment*) Span *m*; (*in china, paintwork*) angeschlagene Stelle *f*; (*Computing, Gambling*) Chip *m*; **~s** *pl* (*Culin*) Pommes frites *pl*; (*Amer: crisps*) Chips *pl* ● *vt* (*pt/pp* **chipped**) (*damage*) anschlagen. **~ped** *adj* angeschlagen

chirp /tʃɜːp/ *vi* zwitschern; (*cricket:*) zirpen. **~y** *adj* [!] munter

chit /tʃɪt/ *n* Zettel *m*

chocolate /ˈtʃɒkələt/ *n* Schokolade *f*; (*sweet*) Praline *f*

choice /tʃɔɪs/ *n* Wahl *f*; (*variety*) Auswahl *f* ● *adj* auserlesen

choir /ˈkwaɪə(r)/ *n* Chor *m*. **~boy** *n* Chorknabe *m*

choke /tʃəʊk/ *n* (*Auto*) Choke *m* ● *vt* würgen; (*to death*) erwürgen ● *vi* sich verschlucken; **~ on** [fast] ersticken an (+ *dat*)

choose /tʃuːz/ *vt/i* (*pt* **chose**, *pp* **chosen**) wählen; (*select*) sich (*dat*) aussuchen; **~ to do/go** [freiwillig] tun/gehen; **as you ~** wie Sie wollen

choos[e]y /ˈtʃuːzɪ/ *adj* [!] wählerisch

chop /tʃɒp/ *n* (*blow*) Hieb *m*; (*Culin*) Kotelett *nt* ● *vt* (*pt/pp* **chopped**) hacken. **~ down** *vt* abhacken; fällen (*tree*). **~ off** *vt* abhacken

chop|per /ˈtʃɒpə(r)/ *n* Beil *nt*; [!] Hubschrauber *m*. **~py** *adj* kabbelig

ˈchopsticks *npl* Essstäbchen *pl*

choral /ˈkɔːrəl/ *adj* Chor-

chord /kɔːd/ *n* (*Mus*) Akkord *m*

chore /tʃɔː(r)/ *n* lästige Pflicht *f*; **[household] ~s** Hausarbeit *f*

chorus /ˈkɔːrəs/ *n* Chor *m*; (*of song*) Refrain *m*

chose, **chosen** *see* **choose**

Christ /kraɪst/ *n* Christus *m*

christen /ˈkrɪsn/ *vt* taufen

Christian /ˈkrɪstʃən/ *adj* christlich ● *n* Christ(in) *m*(*f*). **~ity** *n* Christentum *nt*. **~ name** *n* Vorname *m*

Christmas /ˈkrɪsməs/ *n* Weihnachten *nt*. **~ card** *n* Weihnachtskarte *f*. **~ ˈDay** *n* erster Weihnachtstag *m*. **~ ˈEve** *n* Heiligabend *m*. **~ tree** *n* Weihnachtsbaum *m*

chrome /krəʊm/ *n*, **chromium** *n* Chrom *nt*

chronic /ˈkrɒnɪk/ *adj* chronisch

chronicle /ˈkrɒnɪkl/ *n* Chronik *f*

chrysanthemum /krɪˈsænθəməm/ *n* Chrysantheme *f*

chubby /ˈtʃʌbɪ/ *adj* mollig

chuck /tʃʌk/ *vt* [!] schmeißen. **~ out** *vt* [!] rausschmeißen

chuckle /ˈtʃʌkl/ *vi* in sich (*acc*) hineinlachen

chum /tʃʌm/ *n* Freund(in) *m*(*f*)

chunk /tʃʌŋk/ *n* Stück *nt*

church /tʃɜːtʃ/ *n* Kirche *f*. **~yard** *n* Friedhof *m*

churn /tʃɜ:n/ *vt* ~ **out** am laufenden Band produzieren

cider /'saɪdə(r)/ *n* ≈ Apfelwein *m*

cigar /sɪ'gɑ:(r)/ *n* Zigarre *f*

cigarette /sɪgə'ret/ *n* Zigarette *f*

cine-camera /'sɪnɪ-/ *n* Filmkamera *f*

cinema /'sɪnɪmə/ *n* Kino *nt*

cinnamon /'sɪnəmən/ *n* Zimt *m*

circle /'sɜ:kl/ *n* Kreis *m*; (*Theat*) Rang *m* ● *vt* umkreisen ● *vi* kreisen

circuit /'sɜ:kɪt/ *n* Runde *f*; (*racetrack*) Rennbahn *f*; (*Electr*) Stromkreis *m*. **~ous** *adj* ~ **route** Umweg *m*

circular /'sɜ:kjʊlə(r)/ *adj* kreisförmig ● *n* Rundschreiben *nt*. ~ **'saw** *n* Kreissäge *f*. ~ **'tour** *n* Rundfahrt *f*

circulat|e /'sɜ:kjʊleɪt/ *vt* in Umlauf setzen ● *vi* zirkulieren. **~ion** *n* Kreislauf *m*; (*of newspaper*) Auflage *f*

circumference /ʃə'kʌmfərəns/ *n* Umfang *m*

circumstance /'sɜ:kəmstəns/ *n* Umstand *m*; **~s** *pl* Umstände *pl*; (*financial*) Verhältnisse *pl*

circus /'sɜ:kəs/ *n* Zirkus *m*

cistern /'sɪstən/ *n* (*tank*) Wasserbehälter *m*; (*of WC*) Spülkasten *m*

cite /saɪt/ *vt* zitieren

citizen /'sɪtɪzn/ *n* Bürger(in) *m*(*f*). **~ship** *n* Staatsangehörigkeit *f*

citrus /'sɪtrəs/ *n* ~ **[fruit]** Zitrusfrucht *f*

city /'sɪtɪ/ *n* [Groß]stadt *f*

> *i*
>
> **City** *The City of London* ist das Gebiet innerhalb der alten Stadtgrenzen von London. Heute ist es das Geschäfts- und Finanzzentrum Londons und viele Banken und andere Geldinstitute haben dort ihre Hauptstellen. Wenn Leute über die *City* sprechen, beziehen sie sich oft auf diese Institutionen und nicht auf den Ort.

civic /'sɪvɪk/ *adj* Bürger-

civil /'ʃɪvl/ *adj* bürgerlich; (*aviation, defence*) zivil; (*polite*) höflich. ~ **engi'neering** *n* Hoch- und Tiefbau *m*

civilian /sɪ'vɪljən/ *adj* Zivil-; **in** ~ **clothes** in Zivil ● *n* Zivilist *m*

civiliz|ation /sɪvəlaɪ'zeɪʃn/ *n* Zivilisation *f*. **~e** *vt* zivilisieren

civil: **~'partnership** *n* Lebenspartnerschaft *f*. **~'servant** *n* Beamte(r) *m*/Beamtin *f*. **C~ 'Service** *n* Staatsdienst *m*

claim /kleɪm/ *n* Anspruch *m*; (*application*) Antrag *m*; (*demand*) Forderung *f*; (*assertion*) Behauptung *f* ● *vt* beanspruchen; (*apply for*) beantragen; (*demand*) fordern; (*assert*) behaupten; (*collect*) abholen

clam /klæm/ *n* Klaffmuschel *f*

clamber /'klæmbə(r)/ *vi* klettern

clammy /'klæmɪ/ *adj* feucht

clamour /'klæmə(r)/ *n* Geschrei *nt* ● *vi* ~ **for** schreien nach

clamp /klæmp/ *n* Klammer *f*; **[wheel]** ~ Parkkralle *f* ● *vt* [ein]spannen ● *vi* [!] ~ **down on** vorgehen gegen

clan /klæn/ *n* Clan *m*

clang /klæŋ/ *n* Schmettern *nt*. **~er** *n* [!] Schnitzer *m*

clank /klæŋk/ *vi* klirren

clap /klæp/ *n* **give s.o. a** ~ jdm Beifall klatschen; ~ **of thunder** Donnerschlag *m* ● *vt/i* (*pt/pp* **clapped**) Beifall klatschen (+ *dat*); ~ **one's hands** [in die Hände] klatschen

clari|fication /klærɪfɪ'keɪʃn/ *n* Klärung *f*. **~fy** *vt/i* (*pt/pp* **-ied**) klären

clarinet /klærɪ'net/ *n* Klarinette *f*

clarity /'klærətɪ/ *n* Klarheit *f*

clash /klæʃ/ *n* Geklirr *nt*; (*fig*) Konflikt *m* ● *vi* klirren; (*colours:*) sich beißen; (*events:*) ungünstig zusammenfallen

clasp /klɑ:sp/ *n* Verschluss *m* ● *vt* ergreifen; (*hold*) halten

class /klɑ:s/ *n* Klasse *f*; **travel first/second ~** erster/zweiter Klasse reisen ● *vt* einordnen

classic /ˈklæsɪk/ *adj* klassisch ● *n* Klassiker *m*. **~al** *adj* klassisch

classi|fication /klæsɪfɪˈkeɪʃn/ *n* Klassifikation *f*. **~fy** *vt* (*pt/pp* **-ied**) klassifizieren

ˈclassroom *n* Klassenzimmer *nt*

classy /ˈklɑ:sɪ/ *adj* [F] schick

clatter /ˈklætə(r)/ *n* Geklapper *nt* ● *vi* klappern

clause /klɔ:z/ *n* Klausel *f*; (*Gram*) Satzteil *m*

claw /klɔ:/ *n* Kralle *f*; (*of bird of prey & Techn*) Klaue *f*; (*of crab, lobster*) Schere *f* ● *vt* kratzen

clay /kleɪ/ *n* Lehm *m*; (*pottery*) Ton *m*

clean /kli:n/ *adj* (**-er, -est**) sauber ● *adv* glatt ● *vt* sauber machen; putzen (*shoes, windows*); **~ one's teeth** sich (*dat*) die Zähne putzen; **have sth ~ed** etw reinigen lassen. **~ up** *vt* sauber machen

cleaner /ˈkli:nə(r)/ *n* Putzfrau *f*; (*substance*) Reinigungsmittel *nt*; **[dry] ~'s** chemische Reinigung *f*

cleanliness /ˈklenlɪnɪs/ *n* Sauberkeit *f*

cleanse /klenz/ *vt* reinigen

clear /klɪə(r)/ *adj* (**-er, -est**) klar; (*obvious*) eindeutig; (*distinct*) deutlich; (*conscience*) rein; (*without obstacles*) frei; **make sth ~** etw klarmachen (**to** *dat*) ● *adv* **stand ~** zurücktreten; **keep ~ of** aus dem Wege gehen (+ *dat*) ● *vt* räumen; abräumen (*table*); (*acquit*) freisprechen; (*authorize*) genehmigen; (*jump over*) überspringen; **~ one's throat** sich räuspern ● *vi* (*fog:*) sich auflösen. **~ away** *vt* wegräumen. **~ off** *vi* [F] abhauen. **~ out** *vt* ausräumen ● *vi* [F] abhauen. **~ up** *vt* (*tidy*) aufräumen; (*solve*) aufklären ● *vi* (*weather*): sich aufklären

clearance /ˈklɪərəns/ *n* Räumung *f*; (*authorization*) Genehmigung *f*; (*customs*) [Zoll]abfertigung *f*; (*Techn*) Spielraum *m*. **~ sale** *n* Räumungsverkauf *m*

clench /klentʃ/ *vt* **~ one's fist** die Faust ballen; **~ one's teeth** die Zähne zusammenbeißen

clergy /ˈklɜ:dʒɪ/ *npl* Geistlichkeit *f*. **~man** *n* Geistliche(r) *m*

clerk /klɑ:k/, *Amer*: /klɜ:k/ *n* Büroangestellte(r) *m/f*; (*Amer: shop assistant*) Verkäufer(in) *m*(*f*)

clever /ˈklevə(r)/ *adj* (**-er, -est**), **-ly** *adv* klug; (*skilful*) geschickt

cliché /ˈkli:ʃeɪ/ *n* Klischee *nt*

click /klɪk/ *vi* klicken

client /ˈklaɪənt/ *n* Kunde *m*/ Kundin *f*; (*Jur*) Klient(in) *m*(*f*)

cliff /klɪf/ *n* Kliff *nt*

climat|e /ˈklaɪmət/ *n* Klima *nt*. **~e change** *n* Klimawandel *m*

climax /ˈklaɪmæks/ *n* Höhepunkt *m*

climb /klaɪm/ *n* Aufstieg *m* ● *vt* besteigen (*mountain*); steigen auf (+ *acc*) (*ladder, tree*) ● *vi* klettern; (*rise*) steigen; (*road:*) ansteigen. **~ down** *vi* hinunter-/herunterklettern; (*from ladder, tree*) heruntersteigen; [F] nachgeben

climber /ˈklaɪmə(r)/ *n* Bergsteiger *m*; (*plant*) Kletterpflanze *f*

cling /klɪŋ/ *vi* (*pt/pp* **clung**) sich klammern (**to** an + *acc*); (*stick*) haften (**to** an + *dat*). **~ film** *n* Sichtfolie *f* mit Hafteffekt

clinic /ˈklɪnɪk/ *n* Klinik *f*. **~al** *adj*

c

klinisch

clink /klɪŋk/ *vi* klirren

clip¹ /klɪp/ *n* Klammer *f*; (*jewellery*) Klipp *m* ● *vt* (*pt/pp* **clipped**) anklammern (**to** an + *acc*)

clip² *n* (*extract*) Ausschnitt *m* ● *vt* schneiden; knipsen (*ticket*). **~ping** *n* (*extract*) Ausschnitt *m*

cloak /kləʊk/ *n* Umhang *m*. **~room** *n* Garderobe *f*; (*toilet*) Toilette *f*

clobber /ˈklɒbə(r)/ *n* [!] Zeug *nt* ● *vt* ([!]: *hit, defeat*) schlagen

clock /klɒk/ *n* Uhr *f*; ([!]: *speedometer*) Tacho *m* ● *vi* **~ in/out** stechen

clock: ~wise *adj* & *adv* im Uhrzeigersinn. **~work** *n* Uhrwerk *nt*; (*of toy*) Aufziehmechanismus *m*; **like ~work** [!] wie am Schnürchen

clod /klɒd/ *n* Klumpen *m*

clog /klɒg/ *vt/i* (*pt/pp* **clogged**) **~ [up]** verstopfen

cloister /ˈklɔɪstə(r)/ *n* Kreuzgang *m*

clone /kləʊn/ *n* Klon *m* ● *vt* klonen

close¹ /kləʊs/ *adj* (**-r, -st**) nah[e] (**to** *dat*); (*friend*) eng; (*weather*) schwül; **have a ~ shave** [!] mit knapper Not davonkommen ● *adv* nahe ● *n* (*street*) Sackgasse *f*

close² /kləʊz/ *n* Ende *nt*; **draw to a ~** sich dem Ende nähern ● *vt* zumachen, schließen; (*bring to an end*) beenden; sperren (*road*) ● *vi* sich schließen; (*shop:*) schließen, zumachen; (*end*) enden. **~ down** *vt* schließen; stilllegen (*factory*) ● *vi* schließen; (*factory:*) stillgelegt werden

closely /ˈkləʊslɪ/ *adv* eng, nah[e]; (*with attention*) genau

closet /ˈklɒzɪt/ *n* (*Amer*) Schrank *m*

close-up /ˈkləʊs-/ *n* Nahaufnahme *f*

closure /ˈkləʊʒə(r)/ *n* Schließung *f*; (*of factory*) Stilllegung *f*; (*of road*) Sperrung *f*

clot /klɒt/ *n* [Blut]gerinnsel *nt*; ([!]: *idiot*) Trottel *m*

cloth /klɒθ/ *n* Tuch *nt*

clothe /kləʊð/ *vt* kleiden

clothes /kləʊðz/ *npl* Kleider *pl*. **~-line** *n* Wäscheleine *f*

clothing /ˈkləʊðɪŋ/ *n* Kleidung *f*

cloud /klaʊd/ *n* Wolke *f* ● *vi* **~ over** sich bewölken

cloudy /ˈklaʊdɪ/ *adj* wolkig, bewölkt; (*liquid*) trübe

clout /klaʊt/ *n* [!] Schlag *m*; (*influence*) Einfluss *m*

clove /kləʊv/ *n* [Gewürz]nelke *f*; **~ of garlic** Knoblauchzehe *f*

clover /ˈkləʊvə(r)/ *n* Klee *m*. **~ leaf** *n* Kleeblatt *nt*

clown /klaʊn/ *n* Clown *m* ● *vi* **~ [about]** herumalbern

club /klʌb/ *n* Klub *m*; (*weapon*) Keule *f*; (*Sport*) Schläger *m*; **~s** *pl* (*Cards*) Kreuz *nt*, Treff *nt*

clue /kluː/ *n* Anhaltspunkt *m*; (*in crossword*) Frage *f*; **I haven't a ~** [!] ich habe keine Ahnung

clump /klʌmp/ *n* Gruppe *f*

clumsiness /ˈklʌmzɪnɪs/ *n* Ungeschicklichkeit *f*

clumsy /ˈklʌmzɪ/ *adj*, **-ily** *adv* ungeschickt; (*unwieldy*) unförmig

clung /klʌŋ/ *see* **cling**

clutch /klʌtʃ/ *n* Griff *m*; (*Auto*) Kupplung *f*; **be in s.o.'s ~es** [!] in jds Klauen sein ● *vt* festhalten; (*grab*) ergreifen ● *vi* **~ at** greifen nach

clutter /ˈklʌtə(r)/ *n* Kram *m* ● *vt* **~ [up]** vollstopfen

c/o *abbr* (**care of**) bei

coach /kəʊtʃ/ *n* [Reise]bus *m*; (*Rail*) Wagen *m*; (*horse-drawn*) Kutsche *f*;

(*Sport*) Trainer *m* ● *vt* Nachhilfestunden geben (+ *dat*); (*Sport*) trainieren

coal /kəʊl/ *n* Kohle *f*

coalition /kəʊə'lɪʃn/ *n* Koalition *f*

'coal-mine *n* Kohlenbergwerk *nt*

coarse /kɔːs/ *adj* (**-r, -st**) grob

coast /kəʊst/ *n* Küste *f* ● *vi* (*freewheel*) im Freilauf fahren; (*Auto*) im Leerlauf fahren. **~er** *n* (*mat*) Untersatz *m*

coast: ~guard *n* Küstenwache *f*. **~line** *n* Küste *f*

coat /kəʊt/ *n* Mantel *m*; (*of animal*) Fell *nt*; (*of paint*) Anstrich *m*; **~ of arms** Wappen *nt* ● *vt* überziehen; (*with paint*) streichen. **~-hanger** *n* Kleiderbügel *m*. **~-hook** *n* Kleiderhaken *m*

coating /'kəʊtɪŋ/ *n* Überzug *m*, Schicht *f*; (*of paint*) Anstrich *m*

coax /kəʊks/ *vt* gut zureden (+ *dat*)

cobble[1] /'kɒbl/ *n* Kopfstein *m*; **~s** *pl* Kopfsteinpflaster *nt*

cobble[2] *vt* flicken. **~r** *n* Schuster *m*

cobweb /'kɒb-/ *n* Spinnengewebe *nt*

cock /kɒk/ *n* Hahn *m*; (*any male bird*) Männchen *nt* ● *vt* (*animal*:) **~ its ears** die Ohren spitzen; **~ the gun** den Hahn spannen

cockerel /'kɒkərəl/ *n* [junger] Hahn *m*

cockney /'kɒknɪ/ *n* (*dialect*) Cockney *nt*; (*person*) Cockney *m*

cock: ~pit *n* (*Aviat*) Cockpit *nt*. **~roach** /-rəʊtʃ/ *n* Küchenschabe *f*. **~tail** *n* Cocktail *m*. **~-up** *n* ☒ **make a ~-up** Mist bauen (**of** bei)

cocky /'kɒkɪ/ *adj* ☐ eingebildet

cocoa /'kəʊkəʊ/ *n* Kakao *m*

coconut /'kəʊkənʌt/ *n* Kokosnuß *f*

cod /kɒd/ *n inv* Kabeljau *m*

COD *abbr* (**cash on delivery**) per Nachnahme

coddle /'kɒdl/ *vt* verhätscheln

code /kəʊd/ *n* Kode *m*; (*Computing*) Code *m*; (*set of rules*) Kodex *m*. **~d** *adj* verschlüsselt

coerc|e /kəʊ'ɜːs/ *vt* zwingen. **~ion** *n* Zwang *m*

coffee /'kɒfɪ/ *n* Kaffee *m*

coffee: ~-grinder *n* Kaffeemühle *f*. **~-pot** *n* Kaffeekanne *f*. **~-table** *n* Couchtisch *m*

coffin /'kɒfɪn/ *n* Sarg *m*

cogent /'kəʊdʒənt/ *adj* überzeugend

coherent /kəʊ'hɪərənt/ *adj* zusammenhängend; (*comprehensible*) verständlich

coil /kɔɪl/ *n* Rolle *f*; (*Electr*) Spule *f*; (*one ring*) Windung *f* ● *vt* **~[up]** zusammenrollen

coin /kɔɪn/ *n* Münze *f* ● *vt* prägen

coincide /kəʊɪn'saɪd/ *vi* zusammenfallen; (*agree*) übereinstimmen

coinciden|ce /kəʊ'ɪnsɪdəns/ *n* Zufall *m*. **~tal** *adj* zufällig

coke /kəʊk/ *n* Koks *m*

Coke (R) *n* (*drink*) Cola *f*

cold /kəʊld/ *adj* (**-er, -est**) kalt; **I am** *or* **feel ~** mir ist kalt ● *n* Kälte *f*; (*Med*) Erkältung *f*

cold: ~-'blooded *adj* kaltblütig. **~-'hearted** *adj* kaltherzig. **~ly** *adv* (*fig*) kalt, kühl. **~ness** *n* Kälte *f*

collaborat|e /kə'læbəreɪt/ *vi* zusammenarbeiten (**with** mit); **~e on sth** mitarbeiten bei etw. **~ion** *n* Zusammenarbeit *f*, Mitarbeit *f*; (*with enemy*) Kollaboration *f*. **~or** *n* Mitarbeiter(in) *m*(*f*); Kollaborateur *m*

collaps|e /kə'læps/ *n* Zusammenbruch *m*; Einsturz *m* ● *vi* zusammenbrechen; (*roof, building*) einstürzen. **~ible** *adj* zusammenklappbar

collar /'kɒlə(r)/ *n* Kragen *m*; (*for*

animal) Halsband *nt*. **~-bone** *n* Schlüsselbein *nt*

colleague /ˈkɒliːg/ *n* Kollege *m*/Kollegin *f*

collect /kəˈlekt/ *vt* sammeln; (*fetch*) abholen; einsammeln (*tickets*); einziehen (*taxes*) ● *vi* sich [an]sammeln ● *adv* **call ~** (*Amer*) ein R-Gespräch führen

collection /kəˈlekʃn/ *n* Sammlung *f*; (*in church*) Kollekte *f*; (*of post*) Leerung *f*; (*designer's*) Kollektion *f*

collector /kəˈlektə(r)/ *n* Sammler(in) *m*(*f*)

college /ˈkɒlɪdʒ/ *n* College *nt*

collide /kəˈlaɪd/ *vi* zusammenstoßen

colliery /ˈkɒlɪərɪ/ *n* Kohlengrube *f*

collision /kəˈlɪʒn/ *n* Zusammenstoß *m*

colloquial /kəˈləʊkwɪəl/ *adj* umgangssprachlich

Cologne /kəˈləʊn/ *n* Köln *nt*

colon /ˈkəʊlən/ *n* Doppelpunkt

colonel /ˈkɜːnl/ *n* Oberst *m*

colonial /kəˈləʊnɪəl/ *adj* Kolonial-

colony /ˈkɒlənɪ/ *n* Kolonie *f*

colossal /kəˈlɒsl/ *adj* riesig

colour /ˈkʌlə(r)/ *n* Farbe *f*; (*complexion*) Gesichtsfarbe *f*; (*race*) Hautfarbe *f*; **off ~** [T] nicht ganz auf der Höhe ● *vt* färben; **~ [in]** ausmalen

colour: ~-blind *adj* farbenblind. **~ed** *adj* farbig ● *n* (*person*) Farbige(r) *m*/*f*. **~-fast** *adj* farbecht. **~ film** *n* Farbfilm *m*. **~ful** *adj* farbenfroh. **~less** *adj* farblos. **~ photo-[graph]** *n* Farbaufnahme *f*. **~ television** *n* Farbfernsehen *nt*

column /ˈkɒləm/ *n* Säule *f*; (*of soldiers, figures*) Kolonne *f*; (*Printing*) Spalte *f*; (*newspaper*) Kolumne *f*

comb /kəʊm/ *n* Kamm *m* ● *vt* kämmen; (*search*) absuchen; **~ one's hair** sich (*dat*) [die Haare] kämmen

combat /ˈkɒmbæt/ *n* Kampf *m*

combination /kɒmbɪˈneɪʃn/ *n* Kombination *f*

combine[1] /kəmˈbaɪn/ *vt* verbinden ● *vi* sich verbinden; (*people:*) sich zusammenschließen

combine[2] /ˈkɒmbaɪn/ *n* (*Comm*) Konzern *m*

combustion /kəmˈbʌstʃn/ *n* Verbrennung *f*

come /kʌm/ *vi* (*pt* **came**, *pp* **come**) kommen; (*reach*) reichen (**to** an + *acc*); **that ~s to £10** das macht £10; **~ into money** zu Geld kommen; **~ true** wahr werden; **~ in two sizes** in zwei Größen erhältlich sein; **the years to ~** die kommenden Jahre; **how ~?** [T] wie das? **~ about** *vi* geschehen. **~ across** *vi* herüberkommen; [T] klar werden ● *vt* stoßen auf (+ *acc*). **~ apart** *vi* sich auseinander nehmen lassen; (*accidentally*) auseinander gehen. **~ away** *vi* weggehen; (*thing:*) abgehen. **~ back** *vi* zurückkommen. **~ by** *vi* vorbeikommen ● *vt* (*obtain*) bekommen. **~ in** *vi* hereinkommen. **~ off** *vi* abgehen; (*take place*) stattfinden; (*succeed*) klappen [T]. **~ out** *vi* herauskommen; (*book:*) erscheinen; (*stain:*) herausgehen. **~ round** *vi* vorbeikommen; (*after fainting*) [wieder] zu sich kommen; (*change one's mind*) sich umstimmen lassen. **~ to** *vi* [wieder] zu sich kommen. **~ up** *vi* heraufkommen; (*plant:*) aufgehen; (*reach*) reichen (**to** bis); **~ up with** sich (*dat*) einfallen lassen

ˈcome-back *n* Comeback *nt*

comedian /kəˈmiːdɪən/ *n* Komiker *m*

ˈcome-down *n* Rückschritt *m*

comedy /ˈkɒmədɪ/ *n* Komödie *f*

comet /ˈkɒmɪt/ *n* Komet *m*

comfort /ˈkʌmfət/ *n* Bequemlichkeit *f*; (*consolation*) Trost *m* ● *vt* trösten

comfortable /ˈkʌmfətəbl/ *adj*, **-bly** *adv* bequem

ˈcomfort station *n* (*Amer*) öffentliche Toilette *f*

comfy /ˈkʌmfɪ/ *adj* ⓘ bequem

comic /ˈkɒmɪk/ *adj* komisch ● *n* Komiker *m*; (*periodical*) Comic-Heft *nt*

coming /ˈkʌmɪŋ/ *adj* kommend ● *n* Kommen *nt*

comma /ˈkɒmə/ *n* Komma *nt*

command /kəˈmɑːnd/ *n* Befehl *m*; (*Mil*) Kommando *nt*; (*mastery*) Beherrschung *f* ● *vt* befehlen (+ *dat*); kommandieren (*army*)

command|er /kəˈmɑːndə(r)/ *n* Befehlshaber *m*. **~ing officer** *n* Befehlshaber *m*

commemorat|e /kəˈmeməreɪt/ *vt* gedenken (+ *gen*). **~ion** *n* Gedenken *nt*

commence /kəˈmens/ *vt/i* anfangen, beginnen

commend /kəˈmend/ *vt* loben; (*recommend*) empfehlen (**to** *dat*)

comment /ˈkɒment/ *n* Bemerkung *f*; **no ~!** kein Kommentar! ● *vi* sich äußern (**on** zu); **~ on** (*an event*) kommentieren

commentary /ˈkɒməntrɪ/ *n* Kommentar *m*; **[running] ~** (*Radio, TV*) Reportage *f*

commentator /ˈkɒmənteɪtə(r)/ *n* Kommentator *m*; (*Sport*) Reporter *m*

commerce /ˈkɒmɜːs/ *n* Handel *m*

commercial /kəˈmɜːʃl/ *adj* kommerziell ● *n* (*Radio, TV*) Werbespot *m*

commission /kəˈmɪʃn/ *n* (*order for work*) Auftrag *m*; (*body of people*) Kommission *f*; (*payment*) Provision *f*; (*Mil*) [Offiziers]patent *nt*; **out of ~** außer Betrieb ● *vt* beauftragen (*s.o.*); in Auftrag geben (*thing*); (*Mil*) zum Offizier ernennen

commit /kəˈmɪt/ *vt* (*pt/pp* **committed**) begehen; (*entrust*) anvertrauen (**to** *dat*); (*consign*) einweisen (**to** in + *acc*); **~ oneself** sich festlegen; (*involve oneself*) sich engagieren. **~ment** *n* Verpflichtung *f*; (*involvement*) Engagement *nt*. **~ted** *adj* engagiert

committee /kəˈmɪtɪ/ *n* Ausschuss *m*, Komitee *nt*

common /ˈkɒmən/ *adj* (**-er, -est**) gemeinsam; (*frequent*) häufig; (*ordinary*) gewöhnlich; (*vulgar*) ordinär ● *n* Gemeindeland *nt*; **have in ~** gemeinsam haben; **House of C~s** Unterhaus *nt*

common: **~ly** *adv* allgemein. **C~ ˈMarket** *n* Gemeinsamer Markt *m*. **~place** *adj* häufig. **~-room** *n* Aufenthaltsraum *m*. **~ ˈsense** *n* gesunder Menschenverstand *m*

Commonwealth Seit 1931 ist das Commonwealth die Gemeinschaft der 53 unabhängigen Staaten des ehemaligen britischen Weltreichs. Die Mitgliedsländer, die jetzt bildungs- und kulturpolitisch miteinander verbunden sind, nehmen alle zwei Jahre an den Commonwealth-Konferenzen teil. Alle vier Jahre finden die Commonwealth-Spiele statt. In den USA ist *Commonwealth* die offizielle Bezeichnung der vier US-Staaten: Kentucky, Massachusetts, Pennsylvania und Virginia.

commotion /kəˈməʊʃn/ *n* Tumult *m*

C

communal /'kɒmjʊnl/ *adj* gemeinschaftlich

communicate /kə'mju:nɪkeɪt/ *vt* mitteilen (**to** *dat*); übertragen (disease) ● *vi* sich verständigen

communication /kəmju:nɪ'keɪʃn/ *n* Verständigung *f*; (*contact*) Verbindung *f*; (*message*) Mitteilung *f*; **~s** *pl* (*technology*) Nachrichtenwesen *nt*

communicative /kə'mju:nɪkətɪv/ *adj* mitteilsam

Communion /kə'mju:nɪən/ *n* [**Holy**] **~** das [heilige] Abendmahl; (*Roman Catholic*) die [heilige] Kommunion

communis|m /'kɒmjʊnɪzm/ *n* Kommunismus *m*. **~t** *adj* kommunistisch ● *n* Kommunist(in) *m(f)*

community /kə'mju:nətɪ/ *n* Gemeinschaft *f*; **local ~** Gemeinde *f*

commute /kə'mju:t/ *vi* pendeln. **~r** *n* Pendler(in) *m(f)*

compact /kəm'pækt/ *adj* kompakt

companion /kəm'pænjən/ *n* Begleiter(in) *m(f)*. **~ship** *n* Gesellschaft *f*

company /'kʌmpənɪ/ *n* Gesellschaft *f*; (*firm*) Firma *f*; (*Mil*) Kompanie *f*; (*[I]*: *guests*) Besuch *m*. **~ car** *n* Firmenwagen *m*

comparable /'kɒmpərəbl/ *adj* vergleichbar

comparative /kəm'pærətɪv/ *adj* vergleichend; (*relative*) relativ ● *n* (*Gram*) Komparativ *m*. **~ly** *adv* verhältnismäßig

compare /kəm'peə(r)/ *vt* vergleichen (**with**/**to** mit) ● *vi* sich vergleichen lassen

comparison /kəm'pærɪsn/ *n* Vergleich *m*

compartment /kəm'pɑ:tmənt/ *n* Fach *nt*; (*Rail*) Abteil *nt*

compass /'kʌmpəs/ *n* Kompass *m*

compassion /kəm'pæʃn/ *n* Mitleid *nt*. **~ate** *adj* mitfühlend

compatible /kəm'pætəbl/ *adj* vereinbar; (*drugs*) verträglich; (*Techn*) kompatibel; **be ~** (*people*:) [gut] zueinander passen

compatriot /kəm'pætrɪət/ *n* Landsmann *m* /-männin *f*

compel /kəm'pel/ *vt* (*pt*/*pp* **compelled**) zwingen

compensat|e /'kɒmpənseɪt/ *vt* entschädigen. **~ion** *n* Entschädigung *f*; (*fig*) Ausgleich *m*

compete /kəm'pi:t/ *vi* konkurrieren; (*take part*) teilnehmen (**in** an + *dat*)

competen|ce /'kɒmpɪtəns/ *n* Fähigkeit *f*. **~t** *adj* fähig

competition /kɒmpə'tɪʃn/ *n* Konkurrenz *f*; (*contest*) Wettbewerb *m*; (*in newspaper*) Preisausschreiben *nt*

competitive /kəm'petətɪv/ *adj* (*Comm*) konkurrenzfähig

competitor /kəm'petɪtə(r)/ *n* Teilnehmer *m*; (*Comm*) Konkurrent *m*

compile /kəm'paɪl/ *vt* zusammenstellen

complacen|cy /kəm'pleɪsənsɪ/ *n* Selbstzufriedenheit *f*. **~t** *adj* selbstzufrieden

complain /kəm'pleɪn/ *vi* klagen (**about**/**of** über + *acc*); (*formally*) sich beschweren. **~t** *n* Klage *f*; (*formal*) Beschwerde *f*; (*Med*) Leiden *nt*

complement[1] /'kɒmplɪmənt/ *n* Ergänzung *f*; **full ~** volle Anzahl *f*

complement[2] /'kɒmplɪment/ *vt* ergänzen

complete /kəm'pli:t/ *adj* vollständig; (*finished*) fertig; (*utter*) völlig ● *vt* vervollständigen; (*finish*) abschließen; (*fill in*) ausfüllen. **~ly** *adv* völlig

completion /kəm'pli:ʃn/ *n* Vervollständigung *f*; (*end*) Abschluss *m*

complex /ˈkɒmpleks/ *adj* komplex ● *n* Komplex *m*

complexion /kəmˈplekʃn/ *n* Teint *m*; (*colour*) Gesichtsfarbe *f*

complexity /kəmˈpleksətɪ/ *n* Komplexität *f*

complicat|e /ˈkɒmplɪkeɪt/ *vt* komplizieren. **~ed** *adj* kompliziert. **~ion** *n* Komplikation *f*

compliment /ˈkɒmplɪmənt/ *n* Kompliment *nt*; **~s** *pl* Grüße *pl* ● *vt* ein Kompliment machen (+ *dat*). **~ary** *adj* schmeichelhaft; (*given free*) Frei-

comply /kəmˈplaɪ/ *vi* (*pt*/*pp* **-ied**) **~ with** nachkommen (+ *dat*)

compose /kəmˈpəʊz/ *vt* verfassen; (*Mus*) komponieren; **be ~d of** sich zusammensetzen aus. **~r** *n* Komponist *m*

composition /kɒmpəˈzɪʃn/ *n* Komposition *f*; (*essay*) Aufsatz *m*

compost /ˈkɒmpɒst/ *n* Kompost *m*

composure /kəmˈpəʊʒə(r)/ *n* Fassung *f*

compound /ˈkɒmpaʊnd/ *adj* zusammengesetzt; (*fracture*) kompliziert ● *n* (*Chemistry*) Verbindung *f*; (*Gram*) Kompositum *nt*

comprehen|d /kɒmprɪˈhend/ *vt* begreifen, verstehen. **~sible** *adj*, **-bly** *adv* verständlich. **~sion** *n* Verständnis *nt*

comprehensive /kɒmprɪˈhensɪv/ *adj & n* umfassend; **~ [school]** Gesamtschule *f*. **~ insurance** *n* (*Auto*) Vollkaskoversicherung *f*

compress /kəmˈpres/ *vt* zusammenpressen; **~ed air** Druckluft *f*

comprise /kəmˈpraɪz/ *vt* umfassen, bestehen aus

compromise /ˈkɒmprəmaɪz/ *n* Kompromiss *m* ● *vt* kompromittieren (*person*) ● *vi* einen Kompromiss schließen

compuls|ion /kəmˈpʌlʃn/ *n* Zwang *m*. **~ive** *adj* zwanghaft. **~ory** *adj* obligatorisch

comput|e /kəmˈpjuːt/ *vb* berechnen. **~er** Computer *m*. **~er game** *n* Computerspiel. **~erize** *vt* computerisieren (*data*); auf Computer umstellen (*firm*). **~-ˈliterate** *adj* mit Computern vertraut. **~ing** *n* Computertechnik *f*

comrade /ˈkɒmreɪd/ *n* Kamerad *m*; (*Pol*) Genosse *m*/Genossin *f*

con¹ /kɒn/ *see* **pro**

con² *n* [!] Schwindel *m* ● *vt* (*pt*/*pp* **conned**) [!] beschwindeln

concave /ˈkɒŋkeɪv/ *adj* konkav

conceal /kənˈsiːl/ *vt* verstecken; (*keep secret*) verheimlichen

concede /kənˈsiːd/ *vt* zugeben; (*give up*) aufgeben

conceit /kənˈsiːt/ *n* Einbildung *f*. **~ed** *adj* eingebildet

conceivable /kənˈsiːvəbl/ *adj* denkbar

conceive /kənˈsiːv/ *vt* (*child*) empfangen; (*fig*) sich (*dat*) ausdenken ● *vi* schwanger werden

concentrat|e /ˈkɒnsəntreɪt/ *vt* konzentrieren ● *vi* sich konzentrieren. **~ion** *n* Konzentration *f*

concern /kənˈsɜːn/ *n* Angelegenheit *f*; (*worry*) Sorge *f*; (*Comm*) Unternehmen *nt* ● *vt* (*be about, affect*) betreffen; (*worry*) kümmern; **be ~ed about** besorgt sein um; **~ oneself with** sich beschäftigen mit; **as far as I am ~ed** was mich angeht *od* betrifft. **~ing** *prep* bezüglich (+ *gen*)

concert /ˈkɒnsət/ *n* Konzert *nt*

concerto /kənˈtʃeətəʊ/ *n* Konzert *nt*

concession /kənˈseʃn/ *n* Zuge-

C

ständnis *nt*; (*Comm*) Konzession *f*; (*reduction*) Ermäßigung *f*

concise /kən'saɪs/ *adj* kurz

conclude /kən'klu:d/ *vt/i* schließen

conclusion /kən'klu:ʒn/ *n* Schluss *m*; **in ~** abschließend, zum Schluss

conclusive /kən'klu:sɪv/ *adj* schlüssig

concoct /kən'kɒkt/ *vt* zusammenstellen; (*fig*) fabrizieren. **~ion** *n* Zusammenstellung *f*; (*drink*) Gebräu *nt*

concrete /'kɒnkri:t/ *adj* konkret ● *n* Beton *m* ● *vt* betonieren

concurrently /kən'kʌrəntlɪ/ *adv* gleichzeitig

concussion /kən'kʌʃn/ *n* Gehirnerschütterung *f*

condemn /kən'dem/ *vt* verurteilen; (*declare unfit*) für untauglich erklären. **~ation** *n* Verurteilung *f*

condensation /kɒnden'seɪʃn/ *n* Kondensation *f*

condense /kən'dens/ *vt* zusammenfassen

condescend /kɒndɪ'send/ *vi* sich herablassen (**to** zu). **~ing** *adj* herablassend

condition /kən'dɪʃn/ *n* Bedingung *f*; (*state*) Zustand *m*; **~s** *pl* Verhältnisse *pl*; **on ~ that** unter der Bedingung, dass ● *vt* (*mentally*) konditionieren. **~al** *adj* bedingt ● *n* (*Gram*) Konditional *m*. **~er** *n* Pflegespülung *f*; (*for fabrics*) Weichspüler *m*

condolences /kən'dəʊlənsɪz/ *npl* Beileid *nt*

condom /'kɒndəm/ *n* Kondom *nt*

condominium /kɒndə'mɪnɪəm/ *n* (*Amer*) ≈ Eigentumswohnung *f*

conduct¹ /'kɒndʌkt/ *n* Verhalten *nt*; (*Sch*) Betragen *nt*

conduct² /kən'dʌkt/ *vt* führen; (*Phys*) leiten; (*Mus*) dirigieren. **~or** *n* Dirigent *m*; (*of bus*) Schaffner *m*; (*Phys*) Leiter *m*

cone /kəʊn/ Kegel *m*; (*Bot*) Zapfen *m*; (*for ice-cream*) [Eis]tüte *f*; (*Auto*) Leitkegel *m*

confectioner /kən'fekʃənə(r)/ *n* Konditor *m*. **~y** *n* Süßwaren *pl*

conference /'kɒnfərəns/ *n* Konferenz *f*

confess /kən'fes/ *vt/i* gestehen; (*Relig*) beichten. **~ion** *n* Geständnis *nt*; (*Relig*) Beichte *f*

confetti /kən'fetɪ/ *n* Konfetti *nt*

confide /kən'faɪd/ *vt* anvertrauen ● *vi* **~ in s.o.** sich jdm anvertrauen

confidence /'kɒnfɪdəns/ *n* (*trust*) Vertrauen *nt*; (*self-assurance*) Selbstvertrauen *nt*; (*secret*) Geheimnis *nt*; **in ~** im Vertrauen. **~ trick** *n* Schwindel *m*

confident /'kɒnfɪdənt/ *adj* zuversichtlich; (*self-assured*) selbstsicher

confidential /kɒnfɪ'denʃl/ *adj* vertraulich

configuration /kənfɪgə'reɪʃn/ *n* Anordnung *f*, Konfiguration *f*

confine /kən'faɪn/ *vt* beschränken (**to** auf + *acc*). **~d** *adj* (*narrow*) eng

confirm /kən'fɜ:m/ *vt* bestätigen; (*Relig*) konfirmieren; (*Roman Catholic*) firmen. **~ation** *n* Bestätigung *f*; Konfirmation *f*; Firmung *f*

confiscat|e /'kɒnfɪskeɪt/ *vt* beschlagnahmen. **~ion** *n* Beschlagnahme *f*

conflict¹ /'kɒnflɪkt/ *n* Konflikt *m*

conflict² /kən'flɪkt/ *vi* im Widerspruch stehen (**with** zu). **~ing** *adj* widersprüchlich

conform /kən'fɔ:m/ *vi* (*person:*) sich anpassen; (*thing:*) entsprechen (**to** *dat*). **~ist** *n* Konformist *m*

confounded /kən'faʊndɪd/ *adj* ! verflixt

confront /kən'frʌnt/ *vt* konfrontieren. **~ation** *n* Konfrontation *f*

confus|e /kən'fju:z/ *vt* verwirren; (*mistake for*) verwechseln (**with** mit). **~ing** *adj* verwirrend. **~ion** *n* Verwirrung *f*; (*muddle*) Durcheinander *nt*

congenial /kən'dʒi:nɪəl/ *adj* angenehm

congest|ed /kən'dʒestɪd/ *adj* verstopft; (*with people*) überfüllt. **~ion** *n* Verstopfung *f*; Überfüllung *f*

congratulat|e /kən'grætjʊleɪt/ *vt* gratulieren (+ *dat*) (**on** zu). **~ions** *npl* Glückwünsche *pl*; **~ions!** [ich] gratuliere!

congregation /kɒŋgrɪ'geɪʃn/ *n* (*Relig*) Gemeinde *f*

congress /'kɒŋgres/ *n* Kongress *m*. **~man** *n* Kongressabgeordnete(r) *m*

> **Congress** Die nationale gesetzgebende Versammlung in den Vereinigten Staaten. Der Kongress tritt im ▸**CAPITOL** zusammen und besteht aus zwei Kammern, dem Senat und dem Repräsentantenhaus. Der Kongress erlässt Gesetze, die von beiden Kammern angenommen und anschließend vom Präsidenten verabschiedet werden.

conical /'kɒnɪkl/ *adj* kegelförmig

conifer /'kɒnɪfə(r)/ *n* Nadelbaum *m*

conjecture /kən'dʒektʃə(r)/ *n* Mutmaßung *f*

conjunction /kən'dʒʌŋkʃn/ *n* Konjunktion *f*; **in ~ with** zusammen mit

conjur|e /'kʌndʒə(r)/ *vi* zaubern ● *vt* **~e up** heraufbeschwören. **~or** *n* Zauberkünstler *m*

conk /kɒŋk/ *vi* **~ out** [!] (*machine:*) kaputtgehen

conker /'kɒŋkə(r)/ *n* [!] Kastanie *f*

'con-man *n* [!] Schwindler *m*

connect /kə'nekt/ *vt* verbinden (**to** mit); (*Electr*) anschließen (**to** an + *acc*) ● *vi* verbunden sein; (*train:*) Anschluss haben (**with** an + *acc*); **be ~ed with** zu tun haben mit; (*be related to*) verwandt sein mit

connection /kə'nekʃn/ *n* Verbindung *f*; (*Rail, Electr*) Anschluss *m*; **in ~ with** in Zusammenhang mit. **~s** *npl* Beziehungen *pl*

connoisseur /kɒnə'sɜ:(r)/ *n* Kenner *m*

conquer /'kɒŋkə(r)/ *vt* erobern; (*fig*) besiegen. **~or** *n* Eroberer *m*

conquest /'kɒŋkwest/ *n* Eroberung *f*

conscience /'kɒnʃəns/ *n* Gewissen *nt*

conscientious /kɒnʃɪ'enʃəs/ *adj* gewissenhaft

conscious /'kɒnʃəs/ *adj* bewusst; **[fully] ~** bei [vollem] Bewusstsein; **be/become ~ of sth** sich (*dat*) etw (*gen*) bewusst sein/werden. **~ness** *n* Bewusstsein *nt*

conscript /'kɒnskrɪpt/ *n* Einberufene(r) *m*

consecrat|e /'kɒnsɪkreɪt/ *vt* weihen; einweihen (*church*). **~ion** *n* Weihe *f*; Einweihung *f*

consecutive /kən'sekjʊtɪv/ *adj* aufeinanderfolgend. **-ly** *adv* fortlaufend

consent /kən'sent/ *n* Einwilligung *f*, Zustimmung *f* ● *vi* einwilligen (**to** in + *acc*), zustimmen (**to** *dat*)

consequen|ce /'kɒnsɪkwəns/ *n* Folge *f*. **~t** *adj* daraus folgend. **~tly** *adv* folglich

conservation /kɒnsə'veɪʃn/ *n* Erhaltung *f*, Bewahrung *f*. **~ist** *n* Umweltschützer *m*

conservative /kən'sɜ:vətɪv/ *adj* konservativ; (*estimate*) vorsichtig.

C~ (*Pol*) *adj* konservativ ● *n* Konservative(r) *m/f*

conservatory /kən'sɜːvətrɪ/ *n* Wintergarten *m*

conserve /kən'sɜːv/ *vt* erhalten, bewahren; sparen (*energy*)

consider /kən'sɪdə(r)/ *vt* erwägen; (*think over*) sich (*dat*) überlegen; (*take into account*) berücksichtigen; (*regard as*) betrachten als; ~ **doing sth** erwägen, etw zu tun. **~able** *adj*, **-ably** *adv* erheblich

consider|ate /kən'sɪdərət/ *adj* rücksichtsvoll. **~ation** *n* Erwägung *f*; (*thoughtfulness*) Rücksicht *f*; (*payment*) Entgelt *nt*; **take into ~ation** berücksichtigen. **~ing** *prep* wenn man bedenkt (**that** dass)

consist /kən'sɪst/ *vi* ~ **of** bestehen aus

consisten|cy /kən'sɪstənsɪ/ *n* Konsequenz *f*; (*density*) Konsistenz *f*. **~t** *adj* konsequent; (*unchanging*) gleichbleibend. **~tly** *adv* konsequent; (*constantly*) ständig

consolation /kɒnsə'leɪʃn/ *n* Trost *m*. ~ **prize** *n* Trostpreis *m*

console /kən'səʊl/ *vt* trösten

consonant /'kɒnsənənt/ *n* Konsonant *m*

conspicuous /kən'spɪkjʊəs/ *adj* auffällig

conspiracy /kən'spɪrəsɪ/ *n* Verschwörung *f*

constable /'kʌnstəbl/ *n* Polizist *m*

constant /'kɒnstənt/ *adj* beständig; (*continuous*) ständig

constipat|ed /'kɒnstɪpeɪtɪd/ *adj* verstopft. **~ion** *n* Verstopfung *f*

constituency /kən'stɪtjʊənsɪ/ *n* Wahlkreis *m*

constitut|e /'kɒnstɪtjuːt/ *vt* bilden. **~ion** *n* (*Pol*) Verfassung *f*; (*of person*) Konstitution *f*

constraint /kən'streɪnt/ *n* Zwang *m*; (*restriction*) Beschränkung *f*; (*strained manner*) Gezwungenheit *f*

construct /kən'strʌkt/ *vt* bauen. **~ion** *n* Bau *m*; (*Gram*) Konstruktion *f*; (*interpretation*) Deutung *f*; **under ~ion** im Bau

consul /'kɒnsl/ *n* Konsul *m*. **~ate** *n* Konsulat *nt*

consult /kən'sʌlt/ *vt* [um Rat] fragen; konsultieren (*doctor*); nachschlagen in (+ *dat*) (*book*). **~ant** *n* Berater *m*; (*Med*) Chefarzt *m*. **~ation** *n* Beratung *f*; (*Med*) Konsultation *f*

consume /kɒn'sjuːm/ *vt* verzehren; (*use*) verbrauchen. **~r** *n* Verbraucher *m*

consumption /kən'sʌmpʃn/ *n* Konsum *m*; (*use*) Verbrauch *m*

contact /'kɒntækt/ *n* Kontakt *m*; (*person*) Kontaktperson *f* ● *vt* sich in Verbindung setzen mit. ~ **'lenses** *npl* Kontaktlinsen *pl*

contagious /kən'teɪdʒəs/ *adj* direkt übertragbar

contain /kən'teɪn/ *vt* enthalten; (*control*) beherrschen. **~er** *n* Behälter *m*; (*Comm*) Container *m*

contaminat|e /kən'tæmɪneɪt/ *vt* verseuchen. **~ion** *n* Verseuchung *f*

contemplat|e /'kɒntəmpleɪt/ *vt* betrachten; (*meditate*) nachdenken über (+ *acc*). **~ion** *n* Betrachtung *f*; Nachdenken *nt*

contemporary /kən'tempərərɪ/ *adj* zeitgenössisch ● *n* Zeitgenosse *m*/ -genossin *f*

contempt /kən'tempt/ *n* Verachtung *f*; **beneath** ~ verabscheuungswürdig. **~ible** *adj* verachtenswert. **~uous** *adj* verächtlich

content[1] /'kɒntent/ *n* (*also* **contents**) *pl* Inhalt *m*

content[2] /kən'tent/ *adj* zufrieden ● *n* **to one's heart's** ~ nach Herzenslust • *vt* ~ **oneself** sich begnügen (**with** mit). ~**ed** *adj* zufrieden

contentment /kən'tentmənt/ *n* Zufriedenheit *f*

contest /'kɒntest/ *n* Kampf *m*; (*competition*) Wettbewerb *m*. ~**ant** *n* Teilnehmer *m*

context /'kɒntekst/ *n* Zusammenhang *m*

continent /'kɒntɪnənt/ *n* Kontinent *m*

continental /kɒntɪ'nentl/ *adj* Kontinental-. ~ **breakfast** *n* kleines Frühstück *nt*. ~ **quilt** *n* Daunendecke *f*

continual /kən'tɪnjʊəl/ *adj* dauernd

continuation /kəntɪnjʊ'eɪʃn/ *n* Fortsetzung *f*

continue /kən'tɪnju:/ *vt* fortsetzen; ~ **doing** *or* **to do sth** fortfahren, etw zu tun; **to be** ~**d** Fortsetzung folgt • *vi* weitergehen; (*doing sth*) weitermachen; (*speaking*) fortfahren; (*weather:*) anhalten

continuity /kɒntɪ'nju:ətɪ/ *n* Kontinuität *f*

continuous /kən'tɪnjʊəs/ *adj* anhaltend, ununterbrochen

contort /kən'tɔ:t/ *vt* verzerren. ~**ion** *n* Verzerrung *f*

contour /'kɒntʊə(r)/ *n* Kontur *f*; (*line*) Höhenlinie *f*

contracep|tion /kɒntrə'sepʃn/ *n* Empfängnisverhütung *f*. ~**tive** *n* Empfängnisverhütungsmittel *nt*

contract[1] /'kɒntrækt/ *n* Vertrag *m*

contract[2] /kən'trækt/ *vi* sich zusammenziehen. ~**or** *n* Unternehmer *m*

contradict /kɒntrə'dɪkt/ *vt* widersprechen (+ *dat*). ~**ion** *n* Widerspruch *m*. ~**ory** *adj* widersprüchlich

contralto /kən'træltəʊ/ *n* Alt *m*; (*singer*) Altistin *f*

contraption /kən'træpʃn/ *n* [!] Apparat *m*

contrary /'kɒntrərɪ/ *adj & adv* entgegengesetzt; ~ **to** entgegen (+ *dat*) • *n* Gegenteil *nt*; **on the** ~ im Gegenteil

contrast[1] /'kɒntrɑ:st/ *n* Kontrast *m*

contrast[2] /kən'trɑ:st/ *vt* gegenüberstellen (**with** *dat*) • *vi* einen Kontrast bilden (**with** zu). ~**ing** *adj* gegensätzlich; (*colour*) Kontrast-

contribut|e /kən'trɪbju:t/ *vt/i* beitragen; beisteuern (*money*); (*donate*) spenden. ~**ion** *n* Beitrag *m*; (*donation*) Spende *f*. ~**or** *n* Beitragende(r) *m*/*f*

contrivance /kən'traɪvəns/ *n* Vorrichtung *f*

control /kən'trəʊl/ *n* Kontrolle *f*; (*mastery*) Beherrschung *f*; (*Techn*) Regler *m*; ~**s** *pl* (*of car, plane*) Steuerung *f*; **get out of** ~ außer Kontrolle geraten • *vt* (*pt/pp* **controlled**) kontrollieren; (*restrain*) unter Kontrolle halten; ~ **oneself** sich beherrschen

controvers|ial /kɒntrə'vɜ:ʃl/ *adj* umstritten. ~**y** *n* Kontroverse *f*

convalesce /kɒnvə'les/ *vi* sich erholen. ~**nce** *n* Erholung *f*

convalescent /kɒnvə'lesnt/ *adj* ~ **home** *n* Erholungsheim *nt*

convenience /kən'vi:nɪəns/ *n* Bequemlichkeit *f*; **[public]** ~ öffentliche Toilette *f*; **with all modern** ~**s** mit allem Komfort

convenient /kən'vi:nɪənt/ *adj* günstig; **be** ~ **for s.o.** jdm gelegen sein *od* jdm passen; **if it is** ~ **[for you]** wenn es Ihnen passt

convent /'kɒnvənt/ *n* [Nonnen]kloster *nt*

convention /kən'venʃn/ *n* (*cus-*

tom) Brauch *m*, Sitte *f*. **~al** *adj* konventionell

converge /kən'vɜːdʒ/ *vi* zusammenlaufen

conversation /kɒnvə'seɪʃn/ *n* Gespräch *nt*; (*Sch*) Konversation *f*

conversion /kən'vɜːʃn/ *n* Umbau *m*; (*Relig*) Bekehrung *f*; (*calculation*) Umrechnung *f*

convert¹ /'kɒnvɜːt/ *n* Bekehrte(r) *m/f*, Konvertit *m*

convert² /kən'vɜːt/ *vt* bekehren (*person*); (*change*) umwandeln (**into** in + *acc*); umbauen (*building*); (*calculate*) umrechnen; (*Techn*) umstellen. **~ible** a verwandelbar ● *n* (*Auto*) Kabrio[lett] *nt*

convex /'kɒnveks/ *adj* konvex

convey /kən'veɪ/ *vt* befördern; vermitteln (*idea, message*). **~or belt** *n* Förderband *nt*

convict¹ /'kɒnvɪkt/ *n* Sträfling *m*

convict² /kən'vɪkt/ *vt* verurteilen (of wegen). **~ion** *n* Verurteilung *f*; (*belief*) Überzeugung *f*; **previous ~ion** Vorstrafe *f*

convinc|e /kən'vɪns/ *vt* überzeugen. **~ing** *adj* überzeugend

convoy /'kɒnvɔɪ/ *n* Konvoi *m*

convulse /kən'vʌls/ *vt* **be ~ed** sich krümmen (**with** vor + *dat*)

coo /kuː/ *vi* gurren

cook /kʊk/ *n* Koch *m*/ Köchin *f* ● *vt/i* kochen; **is it ~ed?** ist es gar? **~ the books** 🄸 die Bilanz frisieren. **~book** *n* Kochbuch *nt*

cooker /'kʊkə(r)/ *n* [Koch]herd *m*; (*apple*) Kochapfel *m*. **~y** *n* Kochen *nt*. **~y book** *n* Kochbuch *nt*

cookie /'kʊkɪ/ *n* (*Amer*) Keks *m*

cool /kuːl/ *adj* (**-er, -est**) kühl ● *n* Kühle *f* ● *vt* kühlen ● *vi* abkühlen. **~-box** *n* Kühlbox *f*. **~ness** *n* Kühle *f*

coop /kuːp/ *vt* **~ up** einsperren

co-operat|e /kəʊ'ɒpəreɪt/ *vi* zusammenarbeiten. **~ion** *n* Kooperation *f*

co-operative /kəʊ'ɒpərətɪv/ *adj* hilfsbereit ● *n* Genossenschaft *f*

cop /kɒp/ *n* 🄸 Polizist *m*

cope /kəʊp/ *vi* 🄸 zurechtkommen; **~ with** fertig werden mit

copious /'kəʊpɪəs/ *adj* reichlich

copper¹ /'kɒpə(r)/ *n* Kupfer *nt* ● *adj* kupfern

copper² *n* 🄸 Polizist *m*

copper 'beech *n* Blutbuche *f*

coppice /'kɒpɪs/ *n*, **copse** *n* Gehölz *nt*

copy /'kɒpɪ/ *n* Kopie *f*; (*book*) Exemplar *nt* ● *vt* (*pt/pp* **-ied**) kopieren; (*imitate*) nachahmen; (*Sch*) abschreiben

copy: ~right *n* Copyright *nt*. **~-writer** *n* Texter *m*

coral /'kɒrl/ *n* Koralle *f*

cord /kɔːd/ *n* Schnur *f*; (*fabric*) Cordsamt *m*; **~s** *pl* Cordhose *f*

cordial /'kɔːdɪəl/ *adj* herzlich ● *n* Fruchtsirup *m*

cordon /'kɔːdn/ *n* Kordon *m* ● *vt* **~ off** absperren

corduroy /'kɔːdərɔɪ/ *n* Cordsamt *m*

core /kɔː(r)/ *n* Kern *m*; (*of apple, pear*) Kerngehäuse *nt*

cork /kɔːk/ *n* Kork *m*; (*for bottle*) Korken *m*. **~screw** *n* Korkenzieher *m*

corn¹ /kɔːn/ *n* Korn *nt*; (*Amer: maize*) Mais *m*

corn² *n* (*Med*) Hühnerauge *nt*

corned beef /kɔːnd'biːf/ *n* Cornedbeef *nt*

corner /'kɔːnə(r)/ *n* Ecke *f*; (*bend*) Kurve *f*; (*football*) Eckball *m* ● *vt* (*fig*) in die Enge treiben; (*Comm*) monopolisieren (*market*). **~-stone**

n Eckstein *m*

cornet /ˈkɔːnɪt/ *n* (*Mus*) Kornett *nt*; (*for ice-cream*) [Eis]tüte *f*

corn: ~flour *n*, (*Amer*) **~starch** *n* Stärkemehl *nt*

corny /ˈkɔːnɪ/ *adj* Ⓘ abgedroschen

coronation /kɒrəˈneɪʃn/ *n* Krönung *f*

coroner /ˈkɒrənə(r)/ *n* Beamte(r) *m*, der verdächtige Todesfälle untersucht

corporal /ˈkɔːpərəl/ *n* (*Mil*) Stabsunteroffizier *m*

corps /kɔː(r)/ *n* (*pl* **corps** /kɔːz/) Korps *nt*

corpse /kɔːps/ *n* Leiche *f*

correct /kəˈrekt/ *adj* richtig; (*proper*) korrekt ● *vt* verbessern; (*text, school work*) korrigieren. **~ion** *n* Verbesserung *f*; (*Typ*) Korrektur *f*

correspond /kɒrɪˈspɒnd/ *vi* entsprechen (**to** *dat*); (*two things:*) sich entsprechen; (*write*) korrespondieren. **~ence** *n* Briefwechsel *m*; (*Comm*) Korrespondenz *f*. **~ent** *n* Korrespondent(in) *m*(*f*). **~ing** *adj* entsprechend

corridor /ˈkɒrɪdɔː(r)/ *n* Gang *m*; (*Pol, Aviat*) Korridor *m*

corro|de /kəˈrəʊd/ *vt* zerfressen ● *vi* rosten. **~sion** *n* Korrosion *f*

corrugated /ˈkɒrəgeɪtɪd/ *adj* gewellt. **~ iron** *n* Wellblech *nt*

corrupt /kəˈrʌpt/ *adj* korrupt ● *vt* korrumpieren; (*spoil*) verderben. **~ion** *n* Korruption *f*

corset /ˈkɔːsɪt/ *n* Korsett *nt*

Corsica /ˈkɔːsɪkə/ *n* Korsika *nt*

cosh /kɒʃ/ *n* Totschläger *m*

cosmetic /kɒzˈmetɪk/ *adj* kosmetisch ● *n* **~s** *pl* Kosmetika *pl*

cosset /ˈkɒsɪt/ *vt* verhätscheln

cost /kɒst/ *n* Kosten *pl*; **~s** *pl* (*Jur*) Kosten; **at all ~s** um jeden Preis ● *vt* (*pt/pp* **cost**) kosten; **it ~ me £20** es hat mich £20 gekostet ● *vt* (*pt/pp* **costed**) **~ [out]** die Kosten kalkulieren für

costly /ˈkɒstlɪ/ *adj* teuer

cost: ~ of ˈliving *n* Lebenshaltungskosten *pl*. **~ price** *n* Selbstkostenpreis *m*

costume /ˈkɒstjuːm/ *n* Kostüm *nt*; (*national*) Tracht *f*. **~ jewellery** *n* Modeschmuck *m*

cosy /ˈkəʊzɪ/ *adj* gemütlich ● *n* (*tea-, egg-*) Wärmer *m*

cot /kɒt/ *n* Kinderbett *nt*; (*Amer: camp bed*) Feldbett *nt*

cottage /ˈkɒtɪdʒ/ *n* Häuschen *nt*. **~ ˈcheese** *n* Hüttenkäse *m*

cotton /ˈkɒtn/ *n* Baumwolle *f*; (*thread*) Nähgarn *nt* ● *adj* baumwollen ● *vi* **~ on** Ⓘ kapieren

cotton ˈwool *n* Watte *f*

couch /kaʊtʃ/ *n* Liege *f*

couchette /kuːˈʃet/ *n* (*Rail*) Liegeplatz *m*

cough /kɒf/ *n* Husten *m* ● *vi* husten. **~ up** *vt/i* husten; (Ⓘ*: pay*) blechen

ˈcough mixture *n* Hustensaft *m*

could /kʊd/, *unbetont* /kəd/ *see* can[2]

council /ˈkaʊnsl/ *n* Rat *m*; (*Admin*) Stadtverwaltung *f*; (*rural*) Gemeindeverwaltung *f*. **~ house** *n* ≈ Sozialwohnung *f*

councillor /ˈkaʊnsələ(r)/ *n* Ratsmitglied *nt*

ˈcouncil tax *n* Gemeindesteuer *f*

count[1] /kaʊnt/ *n* Graf *m*

count[2] *n* Zählung *f*; **keep ~** zählen ● *vt/i* zählen. **~ on** *vt* rechnen auf (+ *acc*)

counter[1] /ˈkaʊntə(r)/ *n* (*in shop*) Ladentisch *m*; (*in bank*) Schalter *m*; (*in café*) Theke *f*; (*Games*)

C

Spielmarke *f*

counter² *adj* Gegen- ●*vt/i* kontern

counter'act *vt* entgegenwirken (+ *dat*)

'counterfeit /-fɪt/ *adj* gefälscht

'counterfoil *n* Kontrollabschnitt *m*

'counterpart *n* Gegenstück *nt*

counter-pro'ductive *adj* **be ~** das Gegenteil bewirken

'countersign *vt* gegenzeichnen

countess /'kaʊntɪs/ *n* Gräfin *f*

countless /'kaʊntlɪs/ *adj* unzählig

country /'kʌntrɪ/ *n* Land *nt*; (*native land*) Heimat *f*; (*countryside*) Landschaft *f*; **in the ~** auf dem Lande. **~man** *n* **[fellow] ~man** Landsmann *m*. **~side** *n* Landschaft *f*

county /'kaʊntɪ/ *n* Grafschaft *f*

coup /ku:/ *n* (*Pol*) Staatsstreich *m*

couple /'kʌpl/ *n* Paar *nt*; **a ~ of** (*two*) zwei ●*vt* verbinden

coupon /'ku:pɒn/ *n* Kupon *m*; (*voucher*) Gutschein *m*; (*entry form*) Schein *m*

courage /'kʌrɪdʒ/ *n* Mut *m*. **~ous** *adj* mutig

courgettes /kʊə'ʒets/ *npl* Zucchini *pl*

courier /'kʊrɪə(r)/ *n* Bote *m*; (*diplomatic*) Kurier *m*; (*for tourists*) Reiseleiter(in) *m*(*f*)

course /kɔ:s/ *n* (*Naut, Sch*) Kurs *m*; (*Culin*) Gang *m*; (*for golf*) Platz *m*; **~ of treatment** (*Med*) Kur *f*; **of ~** natürlich, selbstverständlich; **in the ~ of** im Lauf[e] (+ *gen*)

court /kɔ:t/ *n* Hof *m*; (*Sport*) Platz *m*; (*Jur*) Gericht *nt*

courteous /'kɜ:tɪəs/ *adj* höflich

courtesy /'kɜ:təsɪ/ *n* Höflichkeit *f*

court: ~ 'martial *n* (*pl* **~s martial**) Militärgericht *nt*. **~yard** *n* Hof *m*

cousin /'kʌzn/ *n* Vetter *m*, Cousin *m*; (*female*) Kusine *f*

cove /kəʊv/ *n* kleine Bucht *f*

cover /'kʌvə(r)/ *n* Decke *f*; (*of cushion*) Bezug *m*; (*of umbrella*) Hülle *f*; (*of typewriter*) Haube *f*; (*of book, lid*) Deckel *m*; (*of magazine*) Umschlag *m*; (*protection*) Deckung *f*, Schutz *m*; **take ~** Deckung nehmen; **under separate ~** mit getrennter Post ●*vt* bedecken; beziehen (*cushion*); decken (*costs, needs*); zurücklegen (*distance*); berichten über (+ *acc*) *event*; (*insure*) versichern. **~ up** *vt* zudecken; (*fig*) vertuschen

coverage /'kʌvərɪdʒ/ *n* (*Journalism*) Berichterstattung *f* (**of** über + *acc*)

cover: ~ing *n* Decke *f*; (*for floor*) Belag *m*. **~-up** *n* Vertuschung *f*

cow /kaʊ/ *n* Kuh *f*

coward /'kaʊəd/ *n* Feigling *m*. **~ice** *n* Feigheit *f*. **~ly** *adj* feige

'cowboy *n* Cowboy *m*; [I] unsolider Handwerker *m*

cower /'kaʊə(r)/ *vi* sich [ängstlich] ducken

'cowshed *n* Kuhstall *m*

cox /kɒks/ *n*, **coxswain** *n* Steuermann *m*

coy /kɔɪ/ *adj* (**-er, -est**) gespielt schüchtern

crab /kræb/ *n* Krabbe *f*

crack /kræk/ *n* Riss *m*; (*in china, glass*) Sprung *m*; (*noise*) Knall *m*; ([I]: *joke*) Witz *m*; ([I]: *attempt*) Versuch *m* ●*adj* [I] erstklassig ●*vt* knacken (*nut, code*); einen Sprung machen in (+ *acc*) (*china, glass*); [I] reißen (*joke*); [I] lösen (*problem*) ●*vi* (*china, glass:*) springen; (*whip:*) knallen. **~ down** *vi* [I] durchgreifen

cracked /krækt/ *adj* gesprungen; (*rib*) angebrochen; ([!]: *crazy*) verrückt

cracker /ˈkrækə(r)/ *n* (*biscuit*) Kräcker *m*; (*firework*) Knallkörper *m*; **[Christmas] ~** Knallbonbon *m*. **~s** *adj* **be ~s** [!] einen Knacks haben

crackle /ˈkrækl/ *vi* knistern

cradle /ˈkreɪdl/ *n* Wiege *f*

craft *n* Handwerk *nt*; (*technique*) Fertigkeit *f*. **~sman** *n* Handwerker *m*

crafty /ˈkrɑːftɪ/ *adj* , **-ily** *adv* gerissen

crag /kræg/ *n* Felszacken *m*

cram /kræm/ *v* (*pt/pp* **crammed**) ● *vt* hineinstopfen (**into** in + *acc*); vollstopfen (**with** mit) ● *vi* (*for exams*) pauken

cramp /kræmp/ *n* Krampf *m*. **~ed** *adj* eng

cranberry /ˈkrænbərɪ/ *n* (*Culin*) Preiselbeere *f*

crane /kreɪn/ *n* Kran *m*; (*bird*) Kranich *m*

crank /kræŋk/ *n* [!] Exzentriker *m*

ˈ**crankshaft** *n* Kurbelwelle *f*

crash /kræʃ/ *n* (*noise*) Krach *m*; (*Auto*) Zusammenstoß *m*; (*Aviat*) Absturz *m* ● *vi* krachen (**into** gegen); (*cars:*) zusammenstoßen; (*plane:*) abstürzen ● *vt* einen Unfall haben mit (*car*)

crash: ~-helmet *n* Sturzhelm *m*. **~-landing** *n* Bruchlandung *f*

crate /kreɪt/ *n* Kiste *f*

crater /ˈkreɪtə(r)/ *n* Krater *m*

crawl /krɔːl/ *n* (*Swimming*) Kraul *nt*; **do the ~** kraulen; **at a ~** im Kriechtempo ● *vi* kriechen; (*baby:*) krabbeln; **~ with** wimmeln von

crayon /ˈkreɪən/ *n* Wachsstift *m*; (*pencil*) Buntstift *m*

craze /kreɪz/ *n* Mode *f*

crazy /ˈkreɪzɪ/ *adj* verrückt; **be ~ about** verrückt sein nach

creak /kriːk/ *vi* knarren

cream /kriːm/ *n* Sahne *f*; (*Cosmetic, Med, Culin*) Creme *f* ● *adj* (*colour*) cremefarben ● *vt* (*Culin*) cremig rühren. **~y** *adj* sahnig; (*smooth*) cremig

crease /kriːs/ *n* Falte *f*; (*unwanted*) Knitterfalte *f* ● *vt* falten; (*accidentally*) zerknittern ● *vi* knittern

creat|e /kriːˈeɪt/ *vt* schaffen. **~ion** *n* Schöpfung *f*. **~ive** *adj* schöpferisch. **~or** *n* Schöpfer *m*

creature /ˈkriːtʃə(r)/ *n* Geschöpf *nt*

crèche /kreʃ/ *n* Kinderkrippe *f*

credibility /kredəˈbɪlətɪ/ *n* Glaubwürdigkeit *f*

credible /ˈkredəbl/ *adj* glaubwürdig

credit /ˈkredɪt/ *n* Kredit *m*; (*honour*) Ehre *f* ● *vt* glauben; **~ s.o. with sth** (*Comm*) jdm etw gutschreiben; (*fig*) jdm etw zuschreiben. **~able** *adj* lobenswert

credit: ~ card *n* Kreditkarte *f*. **~or** *n* Gläubiger *m*

creep /kriːp/ *vi* (*pt/pp* **crept**) schleichen ● *n* [!] fieser Kerl *m*; **it gives me the ~s** es ist mir unheimlich. **~er** *n* Kletterpflanze *f*. **~y** *adj* gruselig

cremat|e /krɪˈmeɪt/ *vt* einäschern. **~ion** *n* Einäscherung *f*

crêpe /kreɪp/ *n* Krepp *m*. **~ paper** *n* Krepppapier *nt*

crept /krept/ *see* **creep**

crescent /ˈkresənt/ *n* Halbmond *m*

cress /kres/ *n* Kresse *f*

crest /krest/ *n* Kamm *m*; (*coat of arms*) Wappen *nt*

crew /kruː/ *n* Besatzung *f*; (*gang*) Bande *f*. **~ cut** *n* Bürstenschnitt *m*

C

crib¹ /krɪb/ *n* Krippe *f*
crib² *vt/i* (*pt/pp* **cribbed**) [!] abschreiben
cricket /ˈkrɪkɪt/ *n* Kricket *nt*. **~er** *n* Kricketspieler *m*
crime /kraɪm/ *n* Verbrechen *nt*; (*rate*) Kriminalität *f*
criminal /ˈkrɪmɪnl/ *adj* kriminell, verbrecherisch; (*law, court*) Straf- ● *n* Verbrecher *m*
crimson /ˈkrɪmzn/ *adj* purpurrot
crinkle /ˈkrɪŋkl/ *vt/i* knittern
cripple /ˈkrɪpl/ *n* Krüppel *m* ● *vt* zum Krüppel machen; (*fig*) lahmlegen. **~d** *adj* verkrüppelt
crisis /ˈkraɪsɪs/ *n* (*pl* **-ses** /-siːz/) Krise *f*
crisp /krɪsp/ *adj* (**-er, -est**) knusprig. **~bread** *n* Knäckebrot *nt*. **~s** *npl* Chips *pl*
criss-cross /ˈkrɪs-/ *adj* schräg gekreuzt
criterion /kraɪˈtɪərɪən/ *n* (*pl* **-ria** /-rɪə/) Kriterium *nt*
critic /ˈkrɪtɪk/ *n* Kritiker *m*. **~al** *adj* kritisch. **~ally** *adv* kritisch; **~ally ill** schwer krank
criticism /ˈkrɪtɪsɪzm/ *n* Kritik *f*
criticize /ˈkrɪtɪsaɪz/ *vt* kritisieren
croak /krəʊk/ *vi* krächzen; (*frog:*) quaken
crockery /ˈkrɒkərɪ/ *n* Geschirr *nt*
crocodile /ˈkrɒkədaɪl/ *n* Krokodil *nt*
crocus /ˈkrəʊkəs/ *n* (*pl* **-es**) Krokus *m*
crony /ˈkrəʊnɪ/ *n* Kumpel *m*
crook /krʊk/ *n* (*stick*) Stab *m*; ([!]: *criminal*) Schwindler *m*, Gauner *m*
crooked /ˈkrʊkɪd/ *adj* schief; (*bent*) krumm; ([!]: *dishonest*) unehrlich
crop /krɒp/ *n* Feldfrucht *f*; (*harvest*) Ernte *f* ● *v* (*pt/pp* **cropped**) ● *vt* stutzen ● *vi* **~ up** [!] zur Sprache kommen; (*occur*) dazwischenkommen
croquet /ˈkrəʊkeɪ/ *n* Krocket *nt*
cross /krɒs/ *adj* (*annoyed*) böse (**with** auf + *acc*); **talk at ~ purposes** aneinander vorbeireden ● *n* Kreuz *nt*; (*Bot, Zool*) Kreuzung *f* ● *vt* kreuzen (*cheque, animals*); überqueren (*road*); **~ oneself** sich bekreuzigen; **~ one's arms** die Arme verschränken; **~ one's legs** die Beine übereinander schlagen; **keep one's fingers ~ed for s.o.** jdm die Daumen drücken; **it ~ed my mind** es fiel mir ein ● *vi* (*go across*) hinübergehen/-fahren; (*lines:*) sich kreuzen. **~ out** *vt* durchstreichen
cross: ~-ˈcountry *n* (*Sport*) Crosslauf *m*. **~-ˈeyed** *adj* schielend; **be ~-eyed** schielen. **~fire** *n* Kreuzfeuer *nt*. **~ing** *n* Übergang *m*; (*sea journey*) Überfahrt *f*. **~roads** *n* [Straßen]kreuzung *f*. **~-ˈsection** *n* Querschnitt *m*. **~wise** *adv* quer. **~word** *n* **~word [puzzle]** Kreuzworträtsel *nt*
crotchety /ˈkrɒtʃɪtɪ/ *adj* griesgrämig
crouch /kraʊtʃ/ *vi* kauern
crow /krəʊ/ *n* Krähe *f*; **as the ~ flies** Luftlinie
crowd /kraʊd/ *n* [Menschen]menge *f* ● *vi* sich drängen. **~ed** *adj* [gedrängt] voll
crown /kraʊn/ *n* Krone *f* ● *vt* krönen; überkronen (*tooth*)
crucial /ˈkruːʃl/ *adj* höchst wichtig; (*decisive*) entscheidend (**to** für)
crude /ˈkruːd/ *adj* (**-r, -st**) primitiv; (*raw*) roh
cruel /ˈkruːəl/ *adj* (**crueller, cruellest**) grausam (**to** gegen). **~ty** *n* Grausamkeit *f*
cruis|e /kruːz/ *n* Kreuzfahrt *f* ● *vi*

kreuzen; (*car:*) fahren. **~er** *n* (*Mil*) Kreuzer *m*; (*motor boat*) Kajütboot *nt*

crumb /krʌm/ *n* Krümel *m*

crumb|le /ˈkrʌmbl/ *vt/i* krümeln; (*collapse*) einstürzen

crumple /ˈkrʌmpl/ *vt* zerknittern ● *vi* knittern

crunch /krʌntʃ/ *n* 🅃 **when it comes to the ~** wenn es [wirklich] drauf ankommt ● *vt* mampfen ● *vi* knirschen

crusade /kru:ˈseɪd/ *n* Kreuzzug *m*; (*fig*) Kampagne *f*. **~r** *n* Kreuzfahrer *m*; (*fig*) Kämpfer *m*

crush /krʌʃ/ *n* (*crowd*) Gedränge *nt* ● *vt* zerquetschen; zerknittern (*clothes*); (*fig: subdue*) niederschlagen

crust /krʌst/ *n* Kruste *f*

crutch /krʌtʃ/ *n* Krücke *f*

cry /kraɪ/ *n* Ruf *m*; (*shout*) Schrei *m*; **a far ~ from** (*fig*) weit entfernt von ● *vi* (*pt/pp* **cried**) (*weep*) weinen; (*baby:*) schreien; (*call*) rufen

crypt /krɪpt/ *n* Krypta *f*. **~ic** *adj* rätselhaft

crystal /ˈkrɪstl/ *n* Kristall *m*; (*glass*) Kristall *nt*

cub /kʌb/ *n* (*Zool*) Junge(s) *nt*

Cuba /ˈkju:bə/ *n* Kuba *nt*

cubby-hole /ˈkʌbɪ-/ *n* Fach *nt*

cub|e /kju:b/ *n* Würfel *m*. **~ic** *adj* Kubik-

cubicle /ˈkju:bɪkl/ *n* Kabine *f*

cuckoo /ˈkʊku:/ *n* Kuckuck *m*. **~ clock** *n* Kuckucksuhr *f*

cucumber /ˈkju:kʌmbə(r)/ *n* Gurke *f*

cuddl|e /ˈkʌdl/ *vt* herzen ● *vi* **~e up to** sich kuscheln an (+ *acc*). **~y** *adj* kuschelig

cue[1] /kju:/ *n* Stichwort *nt*

cue[2] *n* (*Billiards*) Queue *nt*

cuff /kʌf/ *n* Manschette *f*; (*Amer: turn-up*) [Hosen]aufschlag *m*; (*blow*) Klaps *m*; **off the ~** 🅃 aus dem Stegreif. **~-link** *n* Manschettenknopf *m*

cul-de-sac /ˈkʌldəsæk/ *n* Sackgasse *f*

culinary /ˈkʌlɪnərɪ/ *adj* kulinarisch

culprit /ˈkʌlprɪt/ *n* Täter *m*

cult /kʌlt/ *n* Kult *m*

cultivate /ˈkʌltɪveɪt/ *vt* anbauen (*crop*); bebauen (*land*)

cultural /ˈkʌltʃərəl/ *adj* kulturell

culture /ˈkʌltʃə(r)/ *n* Kultur *f*. **~d** *adj* kultiviert

cumbersome /ˈkʌmbəsəm/ *adj* hinderlich; (*unwieldy*) unhandlich

cunning /ˈkʌnɪŋ/ *adj* listig ● *n* List *f*

cup /kʌp/ *n* Tasse *f*; (*prize*) Pokal *m*

cupboard /ˈkʌbəd/ *n* Schrank *m*

Cup ˈFinal *n* Pokalendspiel *nt*

curable /ˈkjʊərəbl/ *adj* heilbar

curate /ˈkjʊərət/ *n* Vikar *m*; (*Roman Catholic*) Kaplan *m*

curb /kɜ:b/ *vt* zügeln

curdle /ˈkɜ:dl/ *vi* gerinnen

cure /kjʊə(r)/ *n* [Heil]mittel *nt* ● *vt* heilen; (*salt*) pökeln; (*smoke*) räuchern; gerben (*skin*)

curiosity /kjʊərɪˈɒsətɪ/ *n* Neugier *f*; (*object*) Kuriosität *f*

curious /ˈkjʊərɪəs/ *adj* neugierig; (*strange*) merkwürdig, seltsam

curl /kɜ:l/ *n* Locke *f* ● *vt* locken ● *vi* sich locken

curly /ˈkɜ:lɪ/ *adj* lockig

currant /ˈkʌrənt/ *n* (*dried*) Korinthe *f*

currency /ˈkʌrənsɪ/ *n* Geläufigkeit *f*; (*money*) Währung *f*; **foreign ~** Devisen *pl*

current /ˈkʌrənt/ *adj* augenblicklich, gegenwärtig; (*in general use*) geläufig, gebräuchlich ● *n* Strömung *f*; (*Electr*) Strom *m*. ~ **affairs** *or* **events** *npl* Aktuelle(s) *nt*. ~**ly** *adv* zurzeit

curriculum /kəˈrɪkjʊləm/ *n* Lehrplan *m*. ~ **vitae** *n* Lebenslauf *m*

curry /ˈkʌrɪ/ *n* Curry *nt* & *m*; (*meal*) Currygericht *nt*

curse /kɜːs/ *n* Fluch *m* ● *vt* verfluchen ● *vi* fluchen

cursor /ˈkɜːsə(r)/ *n* Cursor *m*

cursory /ˈkɜːsərɪ/ *adj* flüchtig

curt /kɜːt/ *adj* barsch

curtain /ˈkɜːtn/ *n* Vorhang *m*

curtsy /ˈkɜːtsɪ/ *n* Knicks *m* ● *vi* (*pt*/*pp* **-ied**) knicksen

curve /kɜːv/ *n* Kurve *f* ● *vi* einen Bogen machen; ~ **to the right/left** nach rechts/links biegen. ~**d** *adj* gebogen

cushion /ˈkʊʃn/ *n* Kissen *nt* ● *vt* dämpfen; (*protect*) beschützen

cushy /ˈkʊʃɪ/ *adj* 🅃 bequem

custard /ˈkʌstəd/ *n* Vanillesoße *f*

custom /ˈkʌstəm/ *n* Brauch *m*; (*habit*) Gewohnheit *f*; (*Comm*) Kundschaft *f*. ~**ary** *adj* üblich; (*habitual*) gewohnt. ~**er** *n* Kunde *m*/Kundin *f*

customs /ˈkʌstəmz/ *npl* Zoll *m*. ~ **officer** *n* Zollbeamte(r) *m*

cut /kʌt/ *n* Schnitt *m*; (*Med*) Schnittwunde *f*; (*reduction*) Kürzung *f*; (*in price*) Senkung *f*; ~ **[of meat]** [Fleisch]stück *nt* ● *vt/i* (*pt*/*pp* **cut**, *pres p* **cutting**) schneiden; (*mow*) mähen; abheben (*cards*); (*reduce*) kürzen; senken (*price*); ~ **one's finger** sich in den Finger schneiden; ~ **s.o.'s hair** jdm die Haare schneiden; ~ **short** abkürzen. ~ **back** *vt* zurückschneiden; (*fig*) einschränken, kürzen. ~ **down** *vt* fällen; (*fig*) einschränken. ~ **off** *vt* abschneiden; (*disconnect*) abstellen; **be** ~ **off** (*Teleph*) unterbrochen werden. ~ **out** *vt* ausschneiden; (*delete*) streichen; **be** ~ **out for** 🅃 geeignet sein zu. ~ **up** *vt* zerschneiden; (*slice*) aufschneiden

ˈcut-back *n* Kürzung *f*

cute /kjuːt/ *adj* (**-r, -st**) 🅃 niedlich

cut ˈglass *n* Kristall *nt*

cutlery /ˈkʌtlərɪ/ *n* Besteck *nt*

cutlet /ˈkʌtlɪt/ *n* Kotelett *nt*

ˈcut-price *adj* verbilligt

cutting /ˈkʌtɪŋ/ *adj* (*remark*) bissig ● *n* (*from newspaper*) Ausschnitt *m*; (*of plant*) Ableger *m*

CV *abbr* **curriculum vitae**

cyberspace /ˈsaɪbəspeɪs/ *n* Cyberspace *m*

cycl|e /ˈsaɪkl/ *n* Zyklus *m*; (*bicycle*) [Fahr]rad *nt* ● *vi* mit dem Rad fahren. ~**ing** *n* Radfahren *nt*. ~**ist** *n* Radfahrer(in) *m*(*f*)

cylind|er /ˈsɪlɪndə(r)/ *n* Zylinder *m*. ~**rical** *adj* zylindrisch

cynic /ˈsɪnɪk/ *n* Zyniker *m*. ~**al** *adj* zynisch. ~**ism** *n* Zynismus *m*

Cyprus /ˈsaɪprəs/ *n* Zypern *nt*

Czech /tʃek/ *adj* tschechisch; ~ **Republic** Tschechische Republik *f* ● *n* Tscheche *m*/ Tschechin *f*

Dd

dab /dæb/ *n* Tupfer *m*; (*of butter*) Klecks *m*

dabble /ˈdæbl/ *vi* ~ **in sth** (*fig*) sich nebenbei mit etw befassen

dachshund /ˈdækshʊnd/ *n* Dackel *m*

dad[dy] /ˈdæd[i]/ *n* 🅃 Vati *m*

daddy-ˈlong-legs *n* [Kohl]schnake *f*; (*Amer: spider*) Weberknecht *m*

daffodil /ˈdæfədɪl/ *n* Osterglocke *f*, gelbe Narzisse *f*

daft /dɑːft/ *adj* (**-er, -est**) dumm

dagger /ˈdægə(r)/ *n* Dolch *m*

dahlia /ˈdeɪlɪə/ *n* Dahlie *f*

> *i* **Dáil Éireann** Das Repräsentantenhaus, der *Dáil Éireann* (ausgesprochen da:l'ern) ist das Unterhaus und gesetzgebende Organ des irischen Parlaments in der Republik Irland. Es setzt sich aus 166 Abgeordneten zusammen, die für fünf Jahre durch allgemeine Wahlen (Verhältniswahlsystem) bestimmt werden. Die Verfassung sorgt dafür, dass ein Abgeordneter je 20- bis 30 000 Einwohner vertritt.

daily /ˈdeɪlɪ/ *adj & adv* täglich

dainty /ˈdeɪntɪ/ *adj* zierlich

dairy /ˈdeərɪ/ *n* Molkerei *f*; (*shop*) Milchgeschäft *nt*. ~ **products** *pl* Milchprodukte *pl*

daisy /ˈdeɪzɪ/ *n* Gänseblümchen *nt*

dam /dæm/ *n* [Stau]damm *m* ● *vt* (*pt/pp* **dammed**) eindämmen

damag|e /ˈdæmɪdʒ/ *n* Schaden *m* (**to** an + *dat*); **~es** *pl* (*Jur*) Schadenersatz *m* ● *vt* beschädigen; (*fig*) beeinträchtigen

damn /dæm/ *adj, int & adv* [T] verdammt ● *n* **I don't care** *or* **give a ~** [T] ich schere mich einen Dreck darum ● *vt* verdammen. **~ation** *n* Verdammnis *f*

damp /dæmp/ *adj* (**-er, -est**) feucht ● *n* Feuchtigkeit *f*

damp|en *vt* anfeuchten; (*fig*) dämpfen. **~ness** *n* Feuchtigkeit *f*

dance /dɑːns/ *n* Tanz *m*; (*function*) Tanzveranstaltung *f* ● *vt/i* tanzen. ~ **music** *n* Tanzmusik *f*

dancer /ˈdɑːnsə(r)/ *n* Tänzer(in) *m*(*f*)

dandelion /ˈdændɪlaɪən/ *n* Löwenzahn *m*

dandruff /ˈdændrʌf/ *n* Schuppen *pl*

Dane /deɪn/ *n* Däne *m*/Dänin *f*

danger /ˈdeɪndʒə(r)/ *n* Gefahr *f*; **in/out of ~** in/außer Gefahr. **~ous** *adj* gefährlich; **~ously ill** schwer erkrankt

dangle /ˈdæŋgl/ *vi* baumeln ● *vt* baumeln lassen

Danish /ˈdeɪnɪʃ/ *adj* dänisch. ~ ˈ**pastry** *n* Hefeteilchen *nt*

Danube /ˈdænjuːb/ *n* Donau *f*

dare /deə(r)/ *vt/i* (*challenge*) herausfordern (**to** zu); ~ **[to] do sth** [es] wagen, etw zu tun. **~devil** *n* Draufgänger *m*

daring /ˈdeərɪŋ/ *adj* verwegen ● *n* Verwegenheit *f*

dark /dɑːk/ *adj* (**-er, -est**) dunkel; ~ **blue/brown** dunkelblau/ -braun; ~ **horse** (*fig*) stilles Wasser *nt* ● *n* Dunkelheit *f*; **after ~** nach Einbruch der Dunkelheit; **in the ~** im Dunkeln

dark|en /ˈdɑːkn/ *vt* verdunkeln ● *vi* dunkler werden. **~ness** *n* Dunkelheit *f*

ˈ**dark-room** *n* Dunkelkammer *f*

darling /ˈdɑːlɪŋ/ *adj* allerliebst ● *n* Liebling *m*

darn /dɑːn/ *vt* stopfen

dart /dɑːt/ *n* Pfeil *m*; **~s** *sg* (*game*) [Wurf]pfeil *m* ● *vi* flitzen

dash /dæʃ/ *n* (*Printing*) Gedankenstrich *m*; **a ~ of milk** ein Schuss Milch ● *vi* rennen ● *vt* schleudern. ~ **off** *vi* losstürzen ● *vt* (*write quickly*) hinwerfen

ˈ**dashboard** *n* Armaturenbrett *nt*

data /ˈdeɪtə/ *npl & sg* Daten *pl*. ~ **processing** *n* Datenverarbeitung *f*

d

date¹ /deɪt/ *n* (*fruit*) Dattel *f*

date² *n* Datum *nt*; [!] Verabredung *f*; **to ~** bis heute; **out of ~** überholt; (*expired*) ungültig; **be up to ~** auf dem Laufenden sein ● *vt/i* datieren; (*Amer, fam: go out with*) ausgehen mit

dated /ˈdeɪtɪd/ *adj* altmodisch

dative /ˈdeɪtɪv/ *adj* & *n* (*Gram*) **~** [case] Dativ *m*

daub /dɔːb/ *vt* beschmieren (**with** mit); schmieren (*paint*)

daughter /ˈdɔːtə(r)/ *n* Tochter *f*. **~-in-law** *n* (*pl* **~s-in-law**) Schwiegertochter *f*

dawdle /ˈdɔːdl/ *vi* trödeln

dawn /dɔːn/ *n* Morgendämmerung *f*; **at ~** bei Tagesanbruch ● *vi* anbrechen; **it ~ed on me** (*fig*) es ging mir auf

day /deɪ/ *n* Tag *m*; **~ by ~** Tag für Tag; **~ after ~** Tag um Tag; **these ~s** heutzutage; **in those ~s** zu der Zeit

day: ~-dream *n* Tagtraum *m* ● *vi* [mit offenen Augen] träumen. **~light** *n* Tageslicht *nt*. **~time** *n* **in the ~time** am Tage

daze /deɪz/ *n* **in a ~** wie benommen. **~d** *adj* benommen

dazzle /ˈdæzl/ *vt* blenden

dead /ded/ *adj* tot; (*flower*) verwelkt; (*numb*) taub; **~ body** Leiche *f*; **~ centre** genau in der Mitte ● *adv* **~ tired** todmüde; **~ slow** sehr langsam ● *n* **the ~** *pl* die Toten; **in the ~ of night** mitten in der Nacht

deaden /ˈdedn/ *vt* dämpfen (*sound*); betäuben (*pain*)

dead: ~ 'end *n* Sackgasse *f*. **~ 'heat** *n* totes Rennen *nt*. **~line** *n* [letzter] Termin *m*

deadly /ˈdedlɪ/ *adj* tödlich; ([!]: *dreary*) sterbenslangweilig

deaf /def/ *adj* (**-er, -est**) taub; **~ and dumb** taubstumm

deaf|en /ˈdefn/ *vt* betäuben; (*permanently*) taub machen. **~ening** *adj* ohrenbetäubend. **~ness** *n* Taubheit *f*

deal /diːl/ *n* (*transaction*) Geschäft *nt*; **whose ~?** (*Cards*) wer gibt? **a good** *or* **great ~** eine Menge; **get a raw ~** [!] schlecht wegkommen ● *v* (*pt/pp* **dealt** /delt/) ● *vt* (*Cards*) geben; **~ out** austeilen ● *vi* **~ in** handeln mit; **~ with** zu tun haben mit; (*handle*) sich befassen mit; (*cope with*) fertig werden mit; (*be about*) handeln von; **that's been dealt with** das ist schon erledigt

deal|er /ˈdiːlə(r)/ *n* Händler *m*

dean /diːn/ *n* Dekan *m*

dear /dɪə(r)/ *adj* (**-er, -est**) lieb; (*expensive*) teuer; (*in letter*) liebe(r,s)/ (*formal*) sehr geehrte(r,s) ● *n* Liebe(r) *m/f* ● *int* **oh ~!** oje! **~ly** *adv* (*love*) sehr; (*pay*) teuer

death /deθ/ *n* Tod *m*; **three ~s** drei Todesfälle. **~ certificate** *n* Sterbeurkunde *f*

deathly *adj* **~ silence** Totenstille *f* ● *adv* **~ pale** totenblass

death: ~ penalty *n* Todesstrafe *f*. **~-trap** *n* Todesfalle *f*

debatable /dɪˈbeɪtəbl/ *adj* strittig

debate /dɪˈbeɪt/ *n* Debatte *f* ● *vt/i* debattieren

debauchery /dɪˈbɔːtʃərɪ/ *n* Ausschweifung *f*

debit /ˈdebɪt/ *n* **~ [side]** Soll *nt* ● *vt* (*pt/pp* **debited**) belasten; abbuchen (*sum*)

debris /ˈdebriː/ *n* Trümmer *pl*

debt /det/ *n* Schuld *f*; **in ~** verschuldet. **~or** *n* Schuldner *m*

début /ˈdeɪbuː/ *n* Debüt *nt*

decade /ˈdekeɪd/ *n* Jahrzehnt *nt*

decaden|ce /ˈdekədəns/ *n* Dekadenz *f.* **~t** *adj* dekadent

decaffeinated /dɪ'kæfɪneɪtɪd/ *adj* koffeinfrei

decay /dɪ'keɪ/ *n* Verfall *m*; (*rot*) Verwesung *f*; (*of tooth*) Zahnfäule *f* ● *vi* verfallen; (*rot*) verwesen; (*tooth:*) schlecht werden

deceased /dɪ'si:sd/ *adj* verstorben ● *n* **the ~d** der/die Verstorbene

deceit /dɪ'si:t/ *n* Täuschung *f*. **~ful** *adj* unaufrichtig

deceive /dɪ'si:v/ *vt* täuschen; (*be unfaithful to*) betrügen

December /dɪ'sembə(r)/ *n* Dezember *m*

decency /'di:sənsɪ/ *n* Anstand *m*

decent /'di:sənt/ *adj* anständig

decept|ion /dɪ'sepʃn/ *n* Täuschung *f*; (*fraud*) Betrug *m*. **~ive** *adj* täuschend

decide /dɪ'saɪd/ *vt* entscheiden ● *vi* sich entscheiden (**on** für)

decided /dɪ'saɪdɪd/ *adj* entschieden

decimal /'desɪml/ *adj* Dezimal- ● *n* Dezimalzahl *f*. **~ 'point** *n* Komma *nt*

decipher /dɪ'saɪfə(r)/ *vt* entziffern

decision /dɪ'sɪʒn/ *n* Entscheidung *f*; (*firmness*) Entschlossenheit *f*

decisive /dɪ'saɪsɪv/ *adj* ausschlaggebend; (*firm*) entschlossen

deck[1] /dek/ *vt* schmücken

deck[2] *n* (*Naut*) Deck *nt*; **on ~** an Deck; **~ of cards** (*Amer*) [Karten]-spiel *nt*. **~-chair** *n* Liegestuhl *m*

declaration /deklə'reɪʃn/ *n* Erklärung *f*

declare /dɪ'kleə(r)/ *vt* erklären; angeben (*goods*); **anything to ~?** etwas zu verzollen?

decline /dɪ'klaɪn/ *n* Rückgang *m*; (*in health*) Verfall *m* ● *vt* ablehnen; (*Gram*) deklinieren ● *vi* ablehnen; (*fall*) sinken; (*decrease*) nachlassen

decommission /di:kə'mɪʃn/ *vt* stilllegen; außer Dienst stellen (*Schiff*)

décor /'deɪkɔ:(r)/ *n* Ausstattung *f*

decorat|e /'dekəreɪt/ *vt* (*adorn*) schmücken; verzieren (*cake*); (*paint*) streichen; (*wallpaper*) tapezieren; (*award medal to*) einen Orden verleihen (+ *dat*). **~ion** *n* Verzierung *f*; (*medal*) Orden *m*; **~ions** *pl* Schmuck *m*. **~ive** *adj* dekorativ. **~or** *n* **painter and ~or** Maler und Tapezierer *m*

d

decoy /'di:kɔɪ/ *n* Lockvogel *m*

decrease[1] /'di:kri:s/ *n* Verringerung *f*; (*in number*) Rückgang *m*

decrease[2] /dɪ'kri:s/ *vt* verringern; herabsetzen (*price*) ● *vi* sich verringern; (*price:*) sinken

decrepit /dɪ'krepɪt/ *adj* altersschwach

dedicat|e /'dedɪkeɪt/ *vt* widmen; (*Relig*) weihen. **~ed** *adj* hingebungsvoll; (*person*) aufopfernd. **~ion** *n* Hingabe *f*; (*in book*) Widmung *f*

deduce /dɪ'dju:s/ *vt* folgern (**from** aus)

deduct /dɪ'dʌkt/ *vt* abziehen

deduction /dɪ'dʌkʃn/ *n* Abzug *m*; (*conclusion*) Folgerung *f*

deed /di:d/ *n* Tat *f*; (*Jur*) Urkunde *f*

deep /di:p/ *adj* (**-er, -est**) tief; **go off the ~ end** [!] auf die Palme gehen ● *adv* tief

deepen /'di:pn/ *vt* vertiefen

deep-'freeze *n* Gefriertruhe *f*; (*upright*) Gefrierschrank *m*

deer /dɪə(r)/ *n inv* Hirsch *m*; (*roe*) Reh *nt*

deface /dɪ'feɪs/ *vt* beschädigen

default /dɪ'fɔ:lt/ *n* **win by ~** (*Sport*) kampflos gewinnen

d

defeat /dɪ'fi:t/ *n* Niederlage *f*; (*defeating*) Besiegung *f*; (*rejection*) Ablehnung *f* ●*vt* besiegen; ablehnen; (*frustrate*) vereiteln

defect /'di:fekt/ *n* Fehler *m*; (*Techn*) Defekt *m*. **~ive** *adj* fehlerhaft; (*Techn*) defekt

defence /dɪ'fens/ *n* Verteidigung *f*. **~less** *adj* wehrlos

defend /dɪ'fend/ *vt* verteidigen; (*justify*) rechtfertigen. **~ant** *n* (*Jur*) Beklagte(r) *m/f*; (*in criminal court*) Angeklagte(r) *m/f*

defensive /dɪ'fensɪv/ *adj* defensiv

defer /dɪ'fɜ:(r)/ *vt* (*pt/pp* **deferred**) (*postpone*) aufschieben

deferen|ce /'defərəns/ *n* Ehrerbietung *f*. **~tial** *adj* ehrerbietig

defian|ce /dɪ'faɪəns/ *n* Trotz *m*; **in ~ce of** zum Trotz (+ *dat*). **~t** *adj* aufsässig

deficien|cy /dɪ'fɪʃənsɪ/ *n* Mangel *m*. **~t** *adj* mangelhaft

deficit /'defɪsɪt/ *n* Defizit *nt*

define /dɪ'faɪn/ *vt* bestimmen; definieren (*word*)

definite /'defɪnɪt/ *adj* bestimmt; (*certain*) sicher

definition /defɪ'nɪʃn/ *n* Definition *f*; (*Phot, TV*) Schärfe *f*

definitive /dɪ'fɪnətɪv/ *adj* endgültig; (*authoritative*) maßgeblich

deflat|e /dɪ'fleɪt/ *vt* die Luft auslassen aus. **~ion** *n* (*Comm*) Deflation *f*

deflect /dɪ'flekt/ *vt* ablenken

deform|ed /dɪ'fɔ:md/ *adj* missgebildet. **~ity** *n* Missbildung *f*

defraud /dɪ'frɔ:d/ *vt* betrügen (**of** um)

defray /dɪ'freɪ/ *vt* bestreiten

defrost /di:'frɒst/ *vt* entfrosten; abtauen (*fridge*); auftauen (*food*)

deft /deft/ *adj* (**-er, -est**) geschickt. **~ness** *n* Geschicklichkeit *f*

defuse /di:'fju:z/ *vt* entschärfen

defy /dɪ'faɪ/ *vt* (*pt/pp* **-ied**) trotzen (+ *dat*); widerstehen (+ *dat*) (*attempt*)

degrading /dɪ'greɪdɪŋ/ *adj* entwürdigend

degree /dɪ'gri:/ *n* Grad *m*; (*Univ*) akademischer Grad *m*; **20 ~s** 20 Grad

de-ice /di:'aɪs/ *vt* enteisen

deity /'di:ɪtɪ/ *n* Gottheit *f*

dejected /dɪ'dʒektɪd/ *adj* niedergeschlagen

delay /dɪ'leɪ/ *n* Verzögerung *f*; (*of train, aircraft*) Verspätung *f*; **without ~** unverzüglich ●*vt* aufhalten; (*postpone*) aufschieben ●*vi* zögern

delegate¹ /'delɪgət/ *n* Delegierte(r) *m/f*

delegat|e² /'delɪgeɪt/ *vt* delegieren. **~ion** *n* Delegation *f*

delet|e /dɪ'li:t/ *vt* streichen. **~ion** *n* Streichung *f*

deliberate /dɪ'lɪbərət/ *adj* absichtlich; (*slow*) bedächtig

delicacy /'delɪkəsɪ/ *n* Feinheit *f*; Zartheit *f*; (*food*) Delikatesse *f*

delicate /'delɪkət/ *adj* fein; (*fabric, health*) zart; (*situation*) heikel; (*mechanism*) empfindlich

delicatessen /delɪkə'tesn/ *n* Delikatessengeschäft *nt*

delicious /dɪ'lɪʃəs/ *adj* köstlich

delight /dɪ'laɪt/ *n* Freude *f* ●*vt* entzücken ●*vi* **~ in** sich erfreuen an (+ *dat*). **~ed** *adj* hocherfreut; **be ~ed** sich sehr freuen. **~ful** *adj* reizend

delinquent /dɪ'lɪŋkwənt/ *adj* straffällig ●*n* Straffällige(r) *m/f*

deli|rious /dɪ'lɪrɪəs/ *adj* **be ~rious** im Delirium sein. **~rium** *n* Delirium *nt*

deliver /dɪ'lɪvə(r)/ *vt* liefern; zustellen (*post, newspaper*); halten (*speech*); überbringen (*message*); versetzen (*blow*); (*set free*) befreien; **~ a baby** ein Kind zur Welt bringen. **~y** *n* Lieferung *f*; (*of post*) Zustellung *f*; (*Med*) Entbindung *f*. **cash on ~y** per Nachnahme

delta /'deltə/ *n* Delta *nt*

deluge /'delju:dʒ/ *n* Flut *f*; (*heavy rain*) schwerer Guss *m*

delusion /dɪ'lu:ʒn/ *n* Täuschung *f*

de luxe /də'lʌks/ *adj* Luxus-

demand /dɪ'mɑ:nd/ *n* Forderung *f*; (*Comm*) Nachfrage *f*; **in ~** gefragt; **on ~** auf Verlangen ● *vt* verlangen, fordern (**of/from** von). **~ing** *adj* anspruchsvoll

demented /dɪ'mentɪd/ *adj* verrückt

demister /di:'mɪstə(r)/ *n* (*Auto*) Defroster *m*

demo /'deməʊ/ *n* (*pl* **~s**) [I] Demonstration *f*

democracy /dɪ'mɒkrəsɪ/ *n* Demokratie *f*

democrat /'deməkræt/ *n* Demokrat *m*. **~ic** *adj*, **-ally** *adv* demokratisch

demo|lish /dɪ'mɒlɪʃ/ *vt* abbrechen; (*destroy*) zerstören. **~lition** *n* Abbruch *m*

demon /'di:mən/ *n* Dämon *m*

demonstrat|e /'demənstreɪt/ *vt* beweisen; vorführen (*appliance*) ● *vi* (*Pol*) demonstrieren. **~ion** *n* Vorführung *f*; (*Pol*) Demonstration *f*

demonstrator /'demənstreɪtə(r)/ *n* Vorführer *m*; (*Pol*) Demonstrant *m*

demoralize /dɪ'mɒrəlaɪz/ *vt* demoralisieren

demote /dɪ'məʊt/ *vt* degradieren

demure /dɪ'mjʊə(r)/ *adj* sittsam

den /den/ *n* Höhle *f*; (*room*) Bude *f*

denial /dɪ'naɪəl/ *n* Leugnen *nt*; **official ~** Dementi *nt*

denim /'denɪm/ *n* Jeansstoff *m*; **~s** *pl* Jeans *pl*

Denmark /'denmɑ:k/ *n* Dänemark *nt*

denounce /dɪ'naʊns/ *vt* denunzieren; (*condemn*) verurteilen

dens|e /dens/ *adj* (**-r, -st**) dicht; ([I]: *stupid*) blöd[e]. **~ity** *n* Dichte *f*

dent /dent/ *n* Delle *f*, Beule *f* ● *vt* einbeulen; **~ed** verbeult

dental /'dentl/ *adj* Zahn-; (*treatment*) zahnärztlich. **~ floss** *n* Zahnseide *f*. **~ surgeon** *n* Zahnarzt *m*

dentist /'dentɪst/ *n* Zahnarzt *m*/-ärztin *f*. **~ry** *n* Zahnmedizin *f*

denture /'dentʃə(r)/ *n* Zahnprothese *f*; **~s** *pl* künstliches Gebiss *nt*

deny /dɪ'naɪ/ *vt* (*pt/pp* **-ied**) leugnen; (*officially*) dementieren; **~ s.o. sth** jdm etw verweigern

deodorant /di:'əʊdərənt/ *n* Deodorant *nt*

depart /dɪ'pɑ:t/ *vi* abfahren; (*Aviat*) abfliegen; (*go away*) weggehen/-fahren; (*deviate*) abweichen (**from** von)

department /dɪ'pɑ:tmənt/ *n* Abteilung *f*; (*Pol*) Ministerium *nt*. **~ store** *n* Kaufhaus *nt*

departure /dɪ'pɑ:tʃə(r)/ *n* Abfahrt *f*; (*Aviat*) Abflug *m*; (*from rule*) Abweichung *f*

depend /dɪ'pend/ *vi* abhängen (**on** von); (*rely*) sich verlassen (**on** auf + *acc*); **it all ~s** das kommt darauf an. **~able** *adj* zuverlässig. **~ant** *n* Abhängige(r) *m/f*. **~ence** *n* Abhängigkeit *f*. **~ent** *adj* abhängig (**on** von)

depict /dɪ'pɪkt/ *vt* darstellen

deplor|able /dɪ'plɔ:rəbl/ *adj* bedauerlich. **~e** *vt* bedauern

deploy /dɪ'plɔɪ/ *vt* (*Mil*) einsetzen

d

depopulate /di:ˈpɒpjʊleɪt/ *vt* entvölkern

deport /dɪˈpɔ:t/ *vt* deportieren, ausweisen. **~ation** *n* Ausweisung *f*

depose /dɪˈpəʊz/ *vt* absetzen

deposit /dɪˈpɒzɪt/ *n* Anzahlung *f*; (*against damage*) Kaution *f*; (*on bottle*) Pfand *nt*; (*sediment*) Bodensatz *m*; (*Geology*) Ablagerung *f* ● *vt* (*pt/pp* **deposited**) legen; (*for safety*) deponieren; (*Geology*) ablagern. **~ account** *n* Sparkonto *nt*

depot /ˈdepəʊ/ *n* Depot *nt*; (*Amer: railway station*) Bahnhof *m*

deprav|e /dɪˈpreɪv/ *vt* verderben. **~ed** *adj* verkommen

depreciat|e /dɪˈpri:ʃɪeɪt/ *vi* an Wert verlieren. **~ion** *n* Wertminderung *f*; (*Comm*) Abschreibung *f*

depress /dɪˈpres/ *vt* deprimieren; (*press down*) herunterdrücken. **~ed** *adj* deprimiert. **~ing** *adj* deprimierend. **~ion** *n* Vertiefung *f*; (*Med*) Depression *f*; (*weather*) Tiefdruckgebiet *nt*

deprivation /deprɪˈveɪʃn/ *n* Entbehrung *f*

deprive /dɪˈpraɪv/ *vt* **~ s.o. of sth** jdm etw entziehen. **~d** *adj* benachteiligt

depth /depθ/ *n* Tiefe *f*; **in ~** gründlich; **in the ~s of winter** im tiefsten Winter

deputize /ˈdepjʊtaɪz/ *vi* **~ for** vertreten

deputy /ˈdepjʊtɪ/ *n* Stellvertreter *m* ● *attrib* stellvertretend

derail /dɪˈreɪl/ *vt* **be ~ed** entgleisen. **~ment** *n* Entgleisung *f*

derelict /ˈderəlɪkt/ *adj* verfallen; (*abandoned*) verlassen

derisory /dɪˈraɪsərɪ/ *adj* höhnisch; (*offer*) lächerlich

derivation /derɪˈveɪʃn/ *n* Ableitung *f*

derivative /dɪˈrɪvətɪv/ *adj* abgeleitet ● *n* Ableitung *f*

derive /dɪˈraɪv/ *vt/i* (*obtain*) gewinnen (**from** aus); **be ~d from** (*word:*) hergeleitet sein aus

derogatory /dɪˈrɒgətrɪ/ *adj* abfällig

derv /dɜ:v/ *n* Diesel[kraftstoff] *m*

descend /dɪˈsend/ *vt/i* hinunter-/heruntergehen; (*vehicle, lift:*) hinunter-/herunterfahren; **be ~ed from** abstammen von. **~ant** *n* Nachkomme *m*

descent /dɪˈsent/ *n* Abstieg *m*; (*lineage*) Abstammung *f*

describe /dɪˈskraɪb/ *vt* beschreiben

descrip|tion /dɪˈskrɪpʃn/ *n* Beschreibung *f*; (*sort*) Art *f*. **~tive** *adj* beschreibend; (*vivid*) anschaulich

desecrate /ˈdesɪkreɪt/ *vt* entweihen

desert[1] /ˈdezət/ *n* Wüste *f*. **~ island** verlassene Insel *f*

desert[2] /dɪˈzɜ:t/ *vt* verlassen ● *vt* desertieren. **~ed** *adj* verlassen. **~er** *n* (*Mil*) Deserteur *m*. **~ion** *n* Fahnenflucht *f*

deserv|e /dɪˈzɜ:v/ *vt* verdienen. **~edly** *adv* verdientermaßen. **~ing** *adj* verdienstvoll

design /dɪˈzaɪn/ *n* Entwurf *m*; (*pattern*) Muster *nt*; (*construction*) Konstruktion *f*; (*aim*) Absicht *f* ● *vt* entwerfen; (*construct*) konstruieren; **be ~ed for** bestimmt sein für

designer /dɪˈzaɪnə(r)/ *n* Designer *m*; (*Techn*) Konstrukteur *m*; (*Theat*) Bühnenbildner *m*

desirable /dɪˈzaɪrəbl/ *adj* wünschenswert; (*sexually*) begehrenswert

desire /dɪˈzaɪə(r)/ *n* Wunsch *m*; (*longing*) Verlangen *nt* (**for** nach); (*sexual*) Begierde *f* ● *vt* [sich (*dat*)] wünschen; (*sexually*) begehren

desk /desk/ *n* Schreibtisch *m*; (*Sch*) Pult *nt*

desolat|e /ˈdesələt/ *adj* trostlos. **~ion** *n* Trostlosigkeit *f*

despair /dɪˈspeə(r)/ *n* Verzweiflung *f*; **in ~** verzweifelt ● *vi* verzweifeln

desperat|e /ˈdespərət/ *adj* verzweifelt; (*urgent*) dringend; **be ~e for** dringend brauchen. **~ion** *n* Verzweiflung *f*

despicable /dɪˈspɪkəbl/ *adj* verachtenswert

despise /dɪˈspaɪz/ *vt* verachten

despite /dɪˈspaɪt/ *prep* trotz (+ *gen*)

despondent /dɪˈspɒndənt/ *adj* niedergeschlagen

dessert /dɪˈzɜ:t/ *n* Dessert *nt*, Nachtisch *m*. **~ spoon** *n* Dessertlöffel *m*

destination /destɪˈneɪʃn/ *n* [Reise]ziel *nt*; (*of goods*) Bestimmungsort *m*

destiny /ˈdestɪnɪ/ *n* Schicksal *nt*

destitute /ˈdestɪtju:t/ *adj* völlig mittellos

destroy /dɪˈstrɔɪ/ *vt* zerstören; (*totally*) vernichten. **~er** *n* (*Naut*) Zerstörer *m*

destruc|tion /dɪˈstrʌkʃn/ *n* Zerstörung *f*; Vernichtung *f*. **-tive** *adj* zerstörerisch; (*fig*) destruktiv

detach /dɪˈtætʃ/ *vt* abnehmen; (*tear off*) abtrennen. **~able** *adj* abnehmbar. **~ed** *adj* **~ed house** Einzelhaus *nt*

detail /ˈdi:teɪl/ *n* Einzelheit *f*, Detail *nt*; **in ~** ausführlich ● *vt* einzeln aufführen. **~ed** *adj* ausführlich

detain /dɪˈteɪn/ *vt* aufhalten; (*police:*) in Haft behalten; (*take into custody*) in Haft nehmen

detect /dɪˈtekt/ *vt* entdecken; (*perceive*) wahrnehmen. **~ion** *n* Entdeckung *f*

detective /dɪˈtektɪv/ *n* Detektiv *m*. **~ story** *n* Detektivroman *m*

detention /dɪˈtenʃn/ *n* Haft *f*; (*Sch*) Nachsitzen *nt*

deter /dɪˈtɜ:(r)/ *vt* (*pt/pp* **deterred**) abschrecken; (*prevent*) abhalten

detergent /dɪˈtɜ:dʒənt/ *n* Waschmittel *nt*

deteriorat|e /dɪˈtɪərɪəreɪt/ *vi* sich verschlechtern. **~ion** *n* Verschlechterung *f*

determination /dɪtɜ:mɪˈneɪʃn/ *n* Entschlossenheit *f*

determine /dɪˈtɜ:mɪn/ *vt* bestimmen. **~d** *adj* entschlossen

deterrent /dɪˈterənt/ *n* Abschreckungsmittel *nt*

detest /dɪˈtest/ *vt* verabscheuen. **~able** *adj* abscheulich

detonate /ˈdetəneɪt/ *vt* zünden

detour /ˈdi:tʊə(r)/ *n* Umweg *m*

detract /dɪˈtrækt/ *vi* **~ from** beeinträchtigen

detriment /ˈdetrɪmənt/ *n* **to the ~ (of)** zum Schaden (+ *gen*). **~al** *adj* schädlich (**to** *dat*)

deuce /dju:s/ *n* (*Tennis*) Einstand *m*

devaluation /di:væljʊˈeɪʃn/ *n* Abwertung *f*

deˈvalue *vt* abwerten (*currency*)

devastat|e /ˈdevəsteɪt/ *vt* verwüsten. **~ing** *adj* verheerend. **~ion** *n* Verwüstung *f*

develop /dɪˈveləp/ *vt* entwickeln; bekommen (*illness*); erschließen (*area*) ● *vi* sich entwickeln (**into** zu). **~er** *n* **[property] ~er** Bodenspekulant *m*

development /dɪˈveləpmənt/ *n* Entwicklung *f*

deviat|e /ˈdi:vɪeɪt/ *vi* abweichen. **~ion** *n* Abweichung *f*

device /dɪˈvaɪs/ *n* Gerät *nt*; (*fig*)

Mittel *nt*

devil /'devl/ *n* Teufel *m*. **~ish** *adj* teuflisch

devious /'di:vɪəs/ *adj* verschlagen

devise /dɪ'vaɪz/ *vt* sich (*dat*) ausdenken

devot|e /dɪ'vəʊt/ *vt* widmen (**to** *dat*). **~ed** *adj* ergeben; (*care*) liebevoll; **be ~ed to s.o.** sehr an jdm hängen

devotion /dɪ'vəʊʃn/ *n* Hingabe *f*

devour /dɪ'vaʊə(r)/ *vt* verschlingen

devout /dɪ'vaʊt/ *adj* fromm

dew /dju:/ *n* Tau *m*

dexterity /dek'sterətɪ/ *n* Geschicklichkeit *f*

diabet|es /daɪə'bi:ti:z/ *n* Zuckerkrankheit *f*. **~ic** *n* Diabetiker(in) *m*(*f*)

diabolical /daɪə'bɒlɪkl/ *adj* teuflisch

diagnose /daɪəg'nəʊz/ *vt* diagnostizieren

diagnosis /daɪəg'nəʊsɪs/ *n* (*pl* **-oses** /-si:z/) Diagnose *f*

diagonal /daɪ'ægənl/ *adj* diagonal ● *n* Diagonale *f*

diagram /'daɪəgræm/ *n* Diagramm *nt*

dial /'daɪəl/ *n* (*of clock*) Zifferblatt *nt*; (*Techn*) Skala *f*; (*Teleph*) Wählscheibe *f* ● *vt/i* (*pt/pp* **dialled**) (*Teleph*) wählen; **~ direct** durchwählen

dialect /'daɪəlekt/ *n* Dialekt *m*

dialling: ~ code *n* Vorwahlnummer *f*. **~ tone** *n* Amtszeichen *nt*

dialogue /'daɪəlɒg/ *n* Dialog *m*

diameter /daɪ'æmɪtə(r)/ *n* Durchmesser *m*

diamond /'daɪəmənd/ *n* Diamant *m*; (*cut*) Brillant *m*; (*shape*) Raute *f*; **~s** *pl* (*Cards*) Karo *nt*

diaper /'daɪəpə(r)/ *n* (*Amer*) Windel *f*

diarrhoea /daɪə'ri:ə/ *n* Durchfall *m*

diary /'daɪərɪ/ *n* Tagebuch *nt*; (*for appointments*) [Termin]kalender *m*

dice /daɪs/ *n inv* Würfel *m*

dictat|e /dɪk'teɪt/ *vt/i* diktieren. **~ion** *n* Diktat *nt*

dictator /dɪk'teɪtə(r)/ *n* Diktator *m*. **~ial** *adj* diktatorisch. **~ship** *n* Diktatur *f*

dictionary /'dɪkʃənrɪ/ *n* Wörterbuch *nt*

did /dɪd/ *see* **do**

didn't /'dɪdnt/ = **did not**

die[1] /daɪ/ *n* (*Techn*) Prägestempel *m*; (*metal mould*) Gussform *f*

die[2] *vi* (*pres p* **dying**) sterben (**of** an + *dat*); (*plant, animal:*) eingehen; (*flower:*) verwelken; **be dying to do sth** [!] darauf brennen, etw zu tun; **be dying for sth** [!] sich nach etw sehnen. **~ down** *vi* nachlassen; (*fire:*) herunterbrennen. **~ out** *vi* aussterben

diesel /'di:zl/ *n* Diesel *m*. **~ engine** *n* Dieselmotor *m*

diet /'daɪət/ *n* Kost *f*; (*restricted*) Diät *f*; (*for slimming*) Schlankheitskur *f*; **be on a ~** Diät leben; eine Schlankheitskur machen ● *vi* Diät leben; eine Schlankheitskur machen

differ /'dɪfə(r)/ *vi* sich unterscheiden; (*disagree*) verschiedener Meinung sein

differen|ce /'dɪfrəns/ *n* Unterschied *m*; (*disagreement*) Meinungsverschiedenheit *f*. **~t** *adj* andere(r,s); (*various*) verschiedene; **be ~t** anders sein (**from** als)

differential /dɪfə'renʃl/ *adj* Differenzial- ● *n* Unterschied *m*; (*Techn*) Differenzial *nt*

differentiate /dɪfə'renʃɪeɪt/ *vt/i* unterscheiden (**between**

zwischen + *dat*)

differently /'dɪfrəntlɪ/ *adv* anders

difficult /'dɪfɪkəlt/ *adj* schwierig, schwer. **~y** *n* Schwierigkeit *f*

diffiden|ce /'dɪfɪdəns/ *n* Zaghaftigkeit *f*. **~t** *adj* zaghaft

dig /dɪg/ *n* (*poke*) Stoß *m*; (*remark*) spitze Bemerkung *f*; (*archaeological*) Ausgrabung *f* ● *vt*/*i* (*pt*/*pp* **dug**, *pres p* **digging**) graben; umgraben (*garden*). **~ out** *vt* ausgraben. **~ up** *vt* ausgraben; umgraben (*garden*); aufreißen (*street*)

digest /dɪ'dʒest/ *vt* verdauen. **~ible** *adj* verdaulich. **~ion** *n* Verdauung *f*

digit /'dɪdʒɪt/ *n* Ziffer *f*; (*finger*) Finger *m*; (*toe*) Zehe *f*. **~ize** *vt* digitalisieren

digital /'dɪdʒɪtl/ *adj* Digital-; **~ camera** Digitalkamera *f*; **~ television** Digitalfernsehen *nt*

dignified /'dɪgnɪfaɪd/ *adj* würdevoll

dignity /'dɪgnɪtɪ/ *n* Würde *f*

dilapidated /dɪ'læpɪdeɪtɪd/ *adj* baufällig

dilatory /'dɪlətərɪ/ *adj* langsam

dilemma /dɪ'lemə/ *n* Dilemma *nt*

dilettante /dɪlɪ'tæntɪ/ *n* Dilettant(in) *m*(*f*)

diligen|ce /'dɪlɪdʒəns/ *n* Fleiß *m*. **~t** *adj* fleißig

dilute /daɪ'lu:t/ *vt* verdünnen

dim /dɪm/ *adj* (**dimmer, dimmest**). **-ly** *adv* (*weak*) schwach; (*dark*) trüb[e]; (*indistinct*) undeutlich; (🄸: *stupid*) dumm, 🄸 doof ● *v* (*pt*/*pp* **dimmed**) ● *vt* dämpfen

dime /daɪm/ *n* (*Amer*) Zehncentstück *nt*

dimension /daɪ'menʃn/ *n* Dimension *f*; **~s** *pl* Maße *pl*

diminutive /dɪ'mɪnjʊtɪv/ *adj* winzig ● *n* Verkleinerungsform *f*

dimple /'dɪmpl/ *n* Grübchen *nt*

din /dɪn/ *n* Krach *m*, Getöse *nt*

dine /daɪn/ *vi* speisen. **~r** *n* Speisende(r) *m*/*f*; (*Amer: restaurant*) Eslokal *nt*

d

dinghy /'dɪŋgɪ/ *n* Dinghi *nt*; (*inflatable*) Schlauchboot *nt*

dingy /'dɪndʒɪ/ *adj* trübe

dining /'daɪnɪŋ/: **~-car** *n* Speisewagen *m*. **~-room** *n* Esszimmer *nt*. **~-table** *n* Esstisch *m*

dinner /'dɪnə(r)/ *n* Abendessen *nt*; (*at midday*) Mittagessen *nt*; (*formal*) Essen *nt*. **~-jacket** *n* Smoking *m*

dinosaur /'daɪnəsɔ:(r)/ *n* Dinosaurier *m*

diocese /'daɪəsɪs/ *n* Diözese *f*

dip /dɪp/ *n* (*in ground*) Senke *f*; (*Culin*) Dip *m* ● *v* (*pt*/*pp* **dipped**) *vt* [ein]tauchen; **~ one's headlights** (*Auto*) [die Scheinwerfer] abblenden ● *vi* sich senken

diploma /dɪ'pləʊmə/ *n* Diplom *nt*

diplomacy /dɪ'pləʊməsɪ/ *n* Diplomatie *f*

diplomat /'dɪpləmæt/ *n* Diplomat *m*. **~ic** *adj*, **-ally** *adv* diplomatisch

'dip-stick *n* (*Auto*) Ölmessstab *m*

dire /'daɪə(r)/ *adj* (**-r, -st**) bitter; (*consequences*) furchtbar

direct /dɪ'rekt/ *adj & adv* direkt ● *vt* (*aim*) richten (**at** auf / (*fig*) an + *acc*); (*control*) leiten; (*order*) anweisen; **~ a film**/**play** bei einem Film/Theaterstück Regie führen

direction /dɪ'rekʃn/ *n* Richtung *f*; (*control*) Leitung *f*; (*of play, film*) Regie *f*; **~s** *pl* Anweisungen *pl*; **~s for use** Gebrauchsanweisung *f*

directly /dɪ'rektlɪ/ *adv* direkt; (*at once*) sofort

director /dɪ'rektə(r)/ *n* (*Comm*) Direktor *m*; (*of play, film*) Regisseur *m*, Regisseurin *f*

directory /dɪ'rektərɪ/ *n* Verzeichnis *nt*; (*Teleph*) Telefonbuch *nt*

dirt /dɜ:t/ *n* Schmutz *m*; (*soil*) Erde *f*; ~ **cheap** 🅸 spottbillig

d

dirty /'dɜ:tɪ/ *adj* schmutzig

dis|a'bility /dɪs-/ *n* Behinderung *f*. **~abled** *adj* [körper]behindert

disad'vantage *n* Nachteil *m*; **at a ~** im Nachteil. **~d** *adj* benachteiligt

disa'gree *vi* nicht übereinstimmen (**with** mit); **I ~** ich bin anderer Meinung; **oysters ~ with me** Austern bekommen mir nicht

disa'greeable *adj* unangenehm

disa'greement *n* Meinungsverschiedenheit *f*

disap'pear *vi* verschwinden. **~ance** *n* Verschwinden *nt*

disap'point *vt* enttäuschen. **~ment** *n* Enttäuschung *f*

disap'proval *n* Missbilligung *f*

disap'prove *vi* dagegen sein; **~ of** missbilligen

dis'arm *vt* entwaffnen ● *vi* (*Mil*) abrüsten. **~ament** *n* Abrüstung *f*. **~ing** *adj* entwaffnend

disast|er /dɪ'zɑ:stə(r)/ *n* Katastrophe *f*; (*accident*) Unglück *nt*. **~rous** *adj* katastrophal

disbe'lief *n* Ungläubigkeit *f*; **in ~** ungläubig

disc /dɪsk/ *n* Scheibe *f*; (*record*) [Schall]platte *f*; (*CD*) CD *f*

discard /dɪ'skɑ:d/ *vt* ablegen; (*throw away*) wegwerfen

discerning /dɪ'sɜ:nɪŋ/ *adj* anspruchsvoll

'discharge¹ *n* Ausstoßen *nt*; (*Naut, Electr*) Entladung *f*; (*dismissal*) Entlassung *f*; (*Jur*) Freispruch *m*; (*Med*) Ausfluss *m*

dis'charge² *vt* ausstoßen; (*Naut, Electr*) entladen; (*dismiss*) entlassen; (*Jur*) freisprechen (*accused*)

disciplinary /'dɪsɪplɪnərɪ/ *adj* disziplinarisch

discipline /'dɪsɪplɪn/ *n* Disziplin *f* ● *vt* Disziplin beibringen (+ *dat*); (*punish*) bestrafen

'disc jockey *n* Diskjockey *m*

dis'claim *vt* abstreiten. **~er** *n* Verzichterklärung *f*

dis'clos|e *vt* enthüllen. **~ure** *n* Enthüllung *f*

disco /'dɪskəʊ/ *n* 🅸 Disko *f*

dis'colour *vt* verfärben ● *vi* sich verfärben

dis'comfort *n* Beschwerden *pl*; (*fig*) Unbehagen *nt*

discon'nect *vt* trennen; (*Electr*) ausschalten; (*cut supply*) abstellen

discon'tent *n* Unzufriedenheit *f*. **~ed** *adj* unzufrieden

discon'tinue *vt* einstellen; (*Comm*) nicht mehr herstellen

'discord *n* Zwietracht *f*; (*Mus & fig*) Missklang *m*

discothèque /'dɪskətek/ *n* Diskothek *f*

'discount *n* Rabatt *m*

dis'courage *vt* entmutigen; (*dissuade*) abraten (+ *dat*)

dis'courteous *adj* unhöflich

discover /dɪ'skʌvə(r)/ *vt* entdecken. **~y** *n* Entdeckung *f*

discreet /dɪ'skri:t/ *adj* diskret

discretion /dɪ'skreʃn/ *n* Diskretion *f*; (*judgement*) Ermessen *nt*

discriminat|e /dɪ'skrɪmɪneɪt/ *vi* unterscheiden (**between** zwischen + *dat*); **~e against** diskriminieren. **~ing** *adj* anspruchsvoll. **~ion** *n* Diskriminierung *f*

discus /'dɪskəs/ *n* Diskus *m*

discuss /dɪ'skʌs/ *vt* besprechen; (*examine critically*) diskutieren.

~**ion** *n* Besprechung *f*; Diskussion *f*
disdain /dɪs'deɪn/ *n* Verachtung *f*
disease /dɪ'zi:z/ *n* Krankheit *f*
disem'bark *vi* an Land gehen
disen'chant *vt* ernüchtern
disen'gage *vt* losmachen
disen'tangle *vt* entwirren
dis'figure *vt* entstellen
dis'grace *n* Schande *f*; **in** ~ in Ungnade ● *vt* Schande machen (+ *dat*). ~**ful** *adj* schändlich
disgruntled /dɪs'grʌntld/ *adj* verstimmt
disguise /dɪs'gaɪz/ *n* Verkleidung *f*; **in** ~ verkleidet ● *vt* verkleiden; verstellen (*voice*)
disgust /dɪs'gʌst/ *n* Ekel *m*; **in** ~ empört ● *vt* anekeln; (*appal*) empören. ~**ing** *adj* eklig; (*appalling*) abscheulich
dish /dɪʃ/ *n* Schüssel *f*; (*shallow*) Schale *f*; (*small*) Schälchen *nt*; (*food*) Gericht *nt*. ~ **out** *vt* austeilen. ~ **up** *vt* auftragen
'dishcloth *n* Spültuch *nt*
dis'hearten *vt* entmutigen
dis'honest *adj* **-ly** *adv* unehrlich. ~**y** *n* Unehrlichkeit *f*
dis'honour *n* Schande *f*. ~**able** *adj*, **-bly** *adv* unehrenhaft
'dishwasher *n* Geschirrspülmaschine *f*
disil'lusion *vt* ernüchtern. ~**ment** *n* Ernüchterung *f*
disin'fect *vt* desinfizieren. ~**ant** *n* Desinfektionsmittel *nt*
disin'herit *vt* enterben
dis'integrate *vi* zerfallen
dis'jointed *adj* unzusammenhängend
disk /dɪsk/ *n* = **disc**
dis'like *n* Abneigung *f* ● *vt* nicht mögen
dislocate /'dɪsləkeɪt/ *vt* ausrenken
dis'lodge *vt* entfernen
dis'loyal *adj* illoyal. ~**ty** *n* Illoyalität *f*
dismal /'dɪzməl/ *adj* trüb[e]; (*person*) trübselig
dismantle /dɪs'mæntl/ *vt* auseinander nehmen; (*take down*) abbauen
dis'may *n* Bestürzung *f*. ~**ed** *adj* bestürzt
dis'miss *vt* entlassen; (*reject*) zurückweisen. ~**al** *n* Entlassung *f*; Zurückweisung *f*
diso'bedien|ce *n* Ungehorsam *m*. ~**t** *adj* ungehorsam
diso'bey *vt/i* nicht gehorchen (+ *dat*); nicht befolgen (*rule*)
dis'order *n* Unordnung *f*; (*Med*) Störung *f*. ~**ly** *adj* unordentlich
dis'organized *adj* unorganisiert
dis'own *vt* verleugnen
disparaging /dɪ'spærɪdʒɪŋ/ *adj* abschätzig
dispassionate /dɪ'spæʃənət/ *adj* gelassen; (*impartial*) unparteiisch
dispatch /dɪ'spætʃ/ *n* (*Comm*) Versand *m*; (*Mil*) Nachricht *f*; (*report*) Bericht *m* ● *vt* [ab]senden; (*kill*) töten
dispel /dɪ'spel/ *vt* (*pt/pp* **dispelled**) vertreiben
dispensary /dɪ'spensərɪ/ *n* Apotheke *f*
dispense /dɪ'spens/ *vt* austeilen; ~ **with** verzichten auf (+ *acc*). ~**r** *n* (*device*) Automat *m*
disperse /dɪ'spɜ:s/ *vt* zerstreuen ● *vi* sich zerstreuen
dispirited /dɪ'spɪrɪtɪd/ *adj* entmutigt
display /dɪ'spleɪ/ *n* Ausstellung *f*; (*Comm*) Auslage *f*; (*performance*) Vorführung *f* ● *vt* zeigen; ausstellen (*goods*)

dis'please *vt* missfallen (+ *dat*)
dis'pleasure *n* Missfallen *nt*
disposable /dɪ'spəʊzəbl/ *adj* Wegwerf-; (*income*) verfügbar
disposal /dɪ'spəʊzl/ *n* Beseitigung *f*; **be at s.o.'s ~** jdm zur Verfügung stehen
dispose /dɪ'spəʊz/ *vi* **~ of** beseitigen; (*deal with*) erledigen
disposition /dɪspə'zɪʃn/ *n* Veranlagung *f*; (*nature*) Wesensart *f*
disproportionate /dɪsprə'pɔ:ʃənət/ *adj* unverhältnismäßig
dis'prove *vt* widerlegen
dispute /dɪ'spju:t/ *n* Disput *m*; (*quarrel*) Streit *m* • *vt* bestreiten
disqualifi'cation *n* Disqualifikation *f*
dis'qualify *vt* disqualifizieren; **~ s.o. from driving** jdm den Führerschein entziehen
disre'gard *vt* nicht beachten
disre'pair *n* **fall into ~** verfallen
dis'reputable *adj* verrufen
disre'pute *n* Verruf *m*
disre'spect *n* Respektlosigkeit *f*. **~ful** *adj* respektlos
disrupt /dɪs'rʌpt/ *vt* stören. **~ion** *n* Störung *f*
dissatis'faction *n* Unzufriedenheit *f*
dis'satisfied *adj* unzufrieden
dissect /dɪ'sekt/ *vt* zergliedern; (*Med*) sezieren. **~ion** *n* Zergliederung *f*; (*Med*) Sektion *f*
dissent /dɪ'sent/ *n* Nichtübereinstimmung *f* • *vi* nicht übereinstimmen
dissident /'dɪsɪdənt/ *n* Dissident *m*
dis'similar *adj* unähnlich (**to** *dat*)
dissociate /dɪ'səʊʃɪeɪt/ *vt* **~ oneself** sich distanzieren (**from** von)
dissolute /'dɪsəlu:t/ *adj* zügellos; (*life*) ausschweifend
dissolve /dɪ'zɒlv/ *vt* auflösen • *vi* sich auflösen
dissuade /dɪ'sweɪd/ *vt* abbringen (**from** von)
distance /'dɪstəns/ *n* Entfernung *f*; **long/short ~** lange/kurze Strecke *f*; **in the/from a ~** in/aus der Ferne
distant /'dɪstənt/ *adj* fern; (*aloof*) kühl; (*relative*) entfernt
dis'tasteful *adj* unangenehm
distil /dɪ'stɪl/ *vt* (*pt/pp* **distilled**) brennen; (*Chemistry*) destillieren. **~lery** *n* Brennerei *f*
distinct /dɪ'stɪŋkt/ *adj* deutlich; (*different*) verschieden. **~ion** *n* Unterschied *m*; (*Sch*) Auszeichnung *f*. **~ive** *adj* kennzeichnend; (*unmistakable*) unverwechselbar. **~ly** *adv* deutlich
distinguish /dɪ'stɪŋgwɪʃ/ *vt/i* unterscheiden; (*make out*) erkennen; **~ oneself** sich auszeichnen. **~ed** *adj* angesehen; (*appearance*) distinguiert
distort /dɪ'stɔ:t/ *vt* verzerren; (*fig*) verdrehen. **~ion** *n* Verzerrung *f*; (*fig*) Verdrehung *f*
distract /dɪ'strækt/ *vt* ablenken. **~ion** *n* Ablenkung *f*; (*despair*) Verzweiflung *f*
distraught /dɪ'strɔ:t/ *adj* [völlig] aufgelöst
distress /dɪ'stres/ *n* Kummer *m*; (*pain*) Schmerz *m*; (*poverty, danger*) Not *f* • *vt* Kummer/Schmerz bereiten (+ *dat*); (*sadden*) bekümmern; (*shock*) erschüttern. **~ing** *adj* schmerzlich; (*shocking*) erschütternd
distribut|e /dɪ'strɪbju:t/ *vt* verteilen; (*Comm*) vertreiben. **~ion** *n* Verteilung *f*; Vertrieb *m*. **~or** *n* Verteiler *m*
district /'dɪstrɪkt/ *n* Gegend *f*; (*Admin*) Bezirk *m*

dis'trust *n* Misstrauen *nt* ● *vt* misstrauen (+ *dat*). **~ful** *adj* misstrauisch
disturb /dɪ'stɜ:b/ *vt* stören; (*perturb*) beunruhigen; (*touch*) anrühren. **~ance** *n* Unruhe *f*; (*interruption*) Störung *f*. **~ed** *adj* beunruhigt; **[mentally] ~ed** geistig gestört. **~ing** *adj* beunruhigend
dis'used *adj* stillgelegt; (*empty*) leer
ditch /dɪtʃ/ *n* Graben *m* ● *vt* (!: *abandon*) fallen lassen (*plan*)
dither /'dɪðə(r)/ *vi* zaudern
ditto /'dɪtəʊ/ *n* dito; ! ebenfalls
dive /daɪv/ *n* [Kopf]sprung *m*; (*Aviat*) Sturzflug *m*; (!: *place*) Spelunke *f* ● *vi* einen Kopfsprung machen; (*when in water*) tauchen; (*Aviat*) einen Sturzflug machen; (!: *rush*) stürzen
diver /'daɪvə(r)/ *n* Taucher *m*; (*Sport*) [Kunst]springer *m*
diverse /daɪ'vɜ:s/ *adj* verschieden
diversify /daɪ'vɜ:sɪfaɪ/ *vt/i* (*pt/pp* **-ied**) variieren; (*Comm*) diversifizieren
diversion /daɪ'vɜ:ʃn/ *n* Umleitung *f*; (*distraction*) Ablenkung *f*
diversity /daɪ'vɜ:sətɪ/ *n* Vielfalt *f*
divert /daɪ'vɜ:t/ *vt* umleiten; ablenken (*attention*); (*entertain*) unterhalten
divide /dɪ'vaɪd/ *vt* teilen; (*separate*) trennen; (*Math*) dividieren (**by** durch) ● *vi* sich teilen
dividend /'dɪvɪdend/ *n* Dividende *f*
divine /dɪ'vaɪn/ *adj* göttlich
diving /'daɪvɪŋ/ *n* (*Sport*) Kunstspringen *nt*. **~-board** *n* Sprungbrett *nt*
divinity /dɪ'vɪnətɪ/ *n* Göttlichkeit *f*; (*subject*) Theologie *f*
division /dɪ'vɪʒn/ *n* Teilung *f*; (*separation*) Trennung *f*; (*Math, Mil*) Division *f*; (*Parl*) Hammelsprung *m*; (*line*) Trennlinie *f*; (*group*) Abteilung *f*
divorce /dɪ'vɔ:s/ *n* Scheidung *f* ● *vt* sich scheiden lassen von. **~d** *adj* geschieden; **get ~d** sich scheiden lassen
DIY *abbr* **do-it-yourself**
dizziness /'dɪzɪnɪs/ *n* Schwindel *m*
dizzy /'dɪzɪ/ *adj* schwindlig; **I feel ~** mir ist schwindlig

d

do /du:/, *unbetont* /də/

3 sg pres tense **does**; *pt* **did**; *pp* **done**

● *transitive verb*
····➤ (*perform*) machen (*homework, housework, exam, handstand etc*); tun (*duty, favour, something, nothing*); vorführen (*trick, dance*); durchführen (*test*). **what are you doing?** was tust *od* machst du? **what can I do for you?** was kann ich für Sie tun? **do something!** tu doch etwas! **have you nothing better to do?** hast du nichts Besseres zu tun? **do the washing-up /cleaning** abwaschen/ sauber machen
····➤ (*as job*) **what does your father do?** was macht dein Vater?; was ist dein Vater von Beruf?
····➤ (*clean*) putzen; (*arrange*) [zurecht]machen (*hair*)
····➤ (*cook*) kochen; (*roast, fry*) braten. **well done** (*meat*) durch[gebraten]. **the potatoes aren't done yet** die Kartoffeln sind noch nicht richtig durch
····➤ (*solve*) lösen (*problem, riddle*); machen (*puzzle*)

d

····➤ ([I]: *swindle*) reinlegen. **do s.o. out of sth** jdn um etw bringen

● *intransitive verb*

····➤ (*with as or adverb*) es tun; es machen. **do as they do** mach es wie sie. **he can do as he likes** er kann tun *od* machen, was er will. **you did well** du hast es gut gemacht

····➤ (*get on*) vorankommen; (*in exams*) abschneiden. **do well/badly at school** gut/schlecht in der Schule sein. **how are you doing?** wie geht's dir? **how do you do?** (*formal*) guten Tag!

····➤ **will do** (*serve purpose*) es tun; (*suffice*) [aus]reichen; (*be suitable*) gehen. **that won't do** das geht nicht. **that will do!** jetzt aber genug!

● *auxiliary verb*

····➤ (*in questions*) **do you know him?** kennst du ihn? **what does he want?** was will er?

····➤ (*in negation*) **I don't** *or* **do not wish to take part** ich will nicht teilnehmen. **don't be so noisy!** seid [doch] nicht so laut!

····➤ (*as verb substitute*) **you mustn't act as he does** du darfst nicht so wie er handeln. **come in, do!** komm doch herein!

····➤ (*in tag questions*) **don't you, doesn't he** *etc.* nicht wahr. **you went to Paris, didn't you?** du warst in Paris, nicht wahr?

····➤ (*in short questions*) **Does he live in London? — Yes, he does** Wohnt er in London? — Ja, stimmt

····➤ (*for special emphasis*) **I do love Greece** Griechenland gefällt mir wirklich gut

····➤ (*for inversion*) **little did he know that ...** er hatte keine Ahnung, dass ...

● *noun*

pl **do's** *or* **dos** /du:z/

····➤ ([I]: *celebration*) Feier *f*

● *phrasal verbs*

● **do away with** *vt* abschaffen. ● **do for** *vt* [I]: **do for s.o.** jdn fertig machen [I]; **be done for** erledigt sein. ● **do in** *vt* (*sl: kill*) kaltmachen [x]. ● **do up** *vt* (*fasten*) zumachen; binden (*shoe-lace, bow-tie*); (*wrap*) einpacken; (*renovate*) renovieren. ● **do with** *vt*: **I could do with** ... ich brauche .... ● **do without** *vt*: **do without sth** auf etw (*acc*) verzichten; *vi* darauf verzichten

docile /ˈdəʊsaɪl/ *adj* fügsam

dock[1] /dɒk/ *n* (*Jur*) Anklagebank *f*

dock[2] *n* Dock *nt* ● *vi* anlegen. **~er** *n* Hafenarbeiter *m*. **~yard** *n* Werft *f*

doctor /ˈdɒktə(r)/ *n* Arzt *m*/ Ärztin *f*; (*Univ*) Doktor *m* ● *vt* kastrieren; (*spay*) sterilisieren

doctrine /ˈdɒktrɪn/ *n* Lehre *f*

document /ˈdɒkjʊmənt/ *n* Dokument *nt*. **~ary** *adj* Dokumentar- ● *n* Dokumentarbericht *m*; (*film*) Dokumentarfilm *m*

dodge /dɒdʒ/ *n* [I] Trick *m*, Kniff *m* ● *vt/i* ausweichen (+ *dat*)

dodgy /ˈdɒdʒɪ/ *adj* [I] (*awkward*) knifflig; (*dubious*) zweifelhaft

doe /dəʊ/ *n* Ricke *f*; (*rabbit*) [Kaninchen]weibchen *nt*

does /dʌz/ *see* **do**

doesn't /ˈdʌznt/ = **does not**

dog /dɒg/ *n* Hund *m*

dog: ~-biscuit *n* Hundekuchen *m*.

~**-collar** *n* Hundehalsband *nt*; (*Relig*, 🅸) Kragen *m* eines Geistlichen. ~**-eared** *adj* **be ~-eared** Eselsohren haben

dogged /'dɒgɪd/ *adj* beharrlich

dogma /'dɒgmə/ *n* Dogma *nt*. ~**tic** *adj* dogmatisch

do-it-yourself /du:ɪtjə'self/ *n* Heimwerken *nt*. ~ **shop** *n* Heimwerkerladen *m*

doldrums /'dɒldrəmz/ *npl* **be in the ~** niedergeschlagen sein; (*business:*) daniederliegen

dole /dəʊl/ *n* 🅸 Stempelgeld *nt*; **be on the ~** arbeitslos sein ● *vt* ~ **out** austeilen

doll /dɒl/ *n* Puppe *f* ● *vt* 🅸 ~ **oneself up** sich herausputzen

dollar /'dɒlə(r)/ *n* Dollar *m*

dolphin /'dɒlfɪn/ *n* Delphin *m*

domain /də'meɪn/ *n* Gebiet *nt*

dome /dəʊm/ *n* Kuppel *m*

domestic /də'mestɪk/ *adj* häuslich; (*Pol*) Innen-; (*Comm*) Binnen-. ~ **animal** *n* Haustier *nt*. ~ **flight** *n* Inlandflug *m*

domestic flight *n* Inlandflug *m*

dominant /'dɒmɪnənt/ *adj* vorherrschend

dominat|e /'dɒmɪneɪt/ *vt* beherrschen ● *vi* dominieren. ~**ion** *n* Vorherrschaft *f*

domineering /dɒmɪ'nɪə(r)iŋ/ *adj* herrschsüchtig

domino /'dɒmɪnəʊ/ *n* (*pl* **-es**) Dominostein *m*; ~**es** *sg* (*game*) Domino *nt*

donat|e /dəʊ'neɪt/ *vt* spenden. ~**ion** *n* Spende *f*

done /dʌn/ *see* **do**

donkey /'dɒŋkɪ/ *n* Esel *m*; ~**'s years** 🅸 eine Ewigkeit. ~**-work** *n* Routinearbeit *f*

donor /'dəʊnə(r)/ *n* Spender *m*, Spenderin *f*

don't /dəʊnt/ = **do not**

doom /du:m/ *n* Schicksal *nt*; (*ruin*) Verhängnis *nt*

door /dɔ:(r)/ *n* Tür *f*; **out of ~s** im Freien

door: ~**man** *n* Portier *m*. ~**mat** *n* [Fuß]abtreter *m*. ~**step** *n* Türschwelle *f*; **on the ~step** vor der Tür. ~**way** *n* Türöffnung *f*

dope /dəʊp/ *n* 🅸 Drogen *pl*; (🅸*: information*) Informationen *pl*; (🅸*: idiot*) Trottel *m* ● *vt* betäuben; (*Sport*) dopen

dormant /'dɔ:mənt/ *adj* ruhend

dormitory /'dɔ:mɪtərɪ/ *n* Schlafsaal *m*

dormouse /'dɔ:-/ *n* Haselmaus *f*

dosage /'dəʊsɪdʒ/ *n* Dosierung *f*

dose /dəʊs/ *n* Dosis *f*

dot /dɒt/ *n* Punkt *m*; **on the ~** pünktlich

dote /dəʊt/ *vi* ~ **on** vernarrt sein in (+ *acc*)

dotted /'dɒtɪd/ *adj* ~ **line** punktierte Linie *f*; **be ~ with** bestreut sein mit

dotty /'dɒtɪ/ *adj* 🅸 verdreht

double /'dʌbl/ *adj & adv* doppelt; (*bed, chin*) Doppel-; (*flower*) gefüllt ● *n* das Doppelte; (*person*) Doppelgänger *m*; ~**s** *pl* (*Tennis*) Doppel *nt*; ● *vt* verdoppeln; (*fold*) falten ● *vi* sich verdoppeln. ~ **up** *vi* sich krümmen (**with** vor + *dat*)

double: ~**-'bass** *n* Kontrabass *m*. ~**-breasted** *adj* zweireihig. ~**-click** *vt/i* doppelklicken (**on** auf + *acc*). ~**-'cross** *vt* ein Doppelspiel treiben mit. ~**-'decker** *n* Doppeldecker *m*. ~ **'glazing** *n* Doppelverglasung *f*. ~ **'room** *n* Doppelzimmer *nt*

doubly /'dʌblɪ/ *adv* doppelt

doubt /daʊt/ *n* Zweifel *m* ● *vt* bezweifeln. ~**ful** *adj* zweifelhaft; (*dis-*

believing) skeptisch. **~less** *adv* zweifellos

dough /dəʊ/ *n* [fester] Teig *m*; (☐: *money*) Pinke *f*. **~nut** *n* Berliner [Pfannkuchen] *m*

dove /dʌv/ *n* Taube *f*

dowdy /ˈdaʊdɪ/ *adj* unschick

down[1] /daʊn/ *n* (*feathers*) Daunen *pl*

down[2] *adv* unten; (*with movement*) nach unten; **go ~** hinuntergehen; **come ~** herunterkommen; **~ there** da unten; **£50 ~** £50 Anzahlung; **~!** (*to dog*) Platz! **~ with ...!** nieder mit ...! ● *prep* **~ the road/stairs** die Straße/Treppe hinunter; **~ the river** den Fluss abwärts ● *vt* ☐ (*drink*) runterkippen; **~ tools** die Arbeit niederlegen

down: ~cast *adj* niedergeschlagen. **~fall** *n* Sturz *m*; (*ruin*) Ruin *m*. **~-ˈhearted** *adj* entmutigt. **~ˈhill** *adv* bergab. **~load** *vt* herunterladen. **~ payment** *n* Anzahlung *f*. **~pour** *n* Platzregen *m*. **~right** *adj* & *adv* ausgesprochen. **~size** *vt* verschlanken ● *vi* abspecken. **~ˈstairs** *adv* unten; (*go*) nach unten ● *adj* im Erdgeschoss. **~ˈstream** *adv* stromabwärts. **~-to-ˈearth** *adj* sachlich. **~town** *adv* (*Amer*) im Stadtzentrum. **~ward** *adj* nach unten; (*slope*) abfallend ● *adv* **~[s]** abwärts, nach unten

> *i*
>
> **Downing Street** Der Name einer Straße im Zentrum von London. Das Haus mit der Nummer 10 in der *Downing Street* ist der offizielle Sitz des Premierministers und das mit der Nummer 11 der des Finanzministers. Unter Journalisten bezieht sich der Ausdruck *Downing Street* oder *Number 10* auf den Amtssitz des Premierministers.

doze /dəʊz/ *n* Nickerchen *nt* ● *vi* dösen. **~ off** *vi* einnicken

dozen /ˈdʌzn/ *n* Dutzend *nt*

Dr *abbr* **doctor**

draft[1] /drɑːft/ *n* Entwurf *m*; (*Comm*) Tratte *f*; (*Amer Mil*) Einberufung *f* ● *vt* entwerfen; (*Amer Mil*) einberufen

draft[2] *n* (*Amer*) = **draught**

drag /dræg/ *n* **in ~** ☐ (*man*) als Frau gekleidet ● *vt* (*pt/pp* **dragged**) schleppen; absuchen (*river*). **~ on** *vi* sich in die Länge ziehen

dragon /ˈdrægən/ *n* Drache *m*. **~-fly** *n* Libelle *f*

drain /dreɪn/ *n* Abfluss *m*; (*underground*) Kanal *m*; **the ~s** die Kanalisation ● *vt* entwässern (*land*); ablassen (*liquid*); das Wasser ablassen aus (*tank*); abgießen (*vegetables*); austrinken (*glass*) ● *vi* **~ [away]** ablaufen

drain|age /ˈdreɪnɪdʒ/ *n* Kanalisation *f*; (*of land*) Dränage *f*. **~ing board** *n* Abtropfbrett *nt*. **~-pipe** *n* Abflussrohr *nt*

drake /dreɪk/ *n* Enterich *m*

drama /ˈdrɑːmə/ *n* Drama *nt*

dramatic /drəˈmætɪk/ *adj*, **-ally** *adv* dramatisch

dramat|ist /ˈdræmətɪst/ *n* Dramatiker *m*. **~ize** *vt* für die Bühne bearbeiten; (*fig*) dramatisieren

drank /dræŋk/ *see* **drink**

drape /dreɪp/ *n* (*Amer*) Vorhang *m* ● *vt* drapieren

drastic /ˈdræstɪk/ *adj*, **-ally** *adv* drastisch

draught /drɑːft/ *n* [Luft]zug *m*; **~s** *sg* (*game*) Damespiel *nt*; **there is a ~** es zieht

draught beer *n* Bier *nt* vom Fass

draughty /ˈdrɑːftɪ/ *adj* zugig

draw /drɔː/ *n* Attraktion *f*; (*Sport*)

Unentschieden *nt*; (*in lottery*) Ziehung *f* ●*v* (*pt* **drew**, *pp* **drawn**) ●*vt* ziehen; (*attract*) anziehen; zeichnen (*picture*); abheben (*money*); ~ **the curtains** die Vorhänge zuziehen/ (*back*) aufziehen ●*vi* (*Sport*) unentschieden spielen. ~ **back** *vt* zurückziehen ●*vi* (*recoil*) zurückweichen. ~ **in** *vt* einziehen ●*vi* einfahren. ~ **out** *vt* herausziehen; abheben (*money*) ●*vi* ausfahren. ~ **up** *vt* aufsetzen (*document*); herrücken (*chair*) ●*vi* [an]halten

draw: ~**back** *n* Nachteil *m*. ~**bridge** *n* Zugbrücke *f*

drawer /drɔ:(r)/ *n* Schublade *f*

drawing /'drɔ:ɪŋ/ *n* Zeichnung *f*

drawing: ~**-board** *n* Reißbrett *nt*. ~**-pin** *n* Reißzwecke *f*. ~**-room** *n* Wohnzimmer *nt*

drawl /drɔ:l/ *n* schleppende Aussprache *f*

drawn /drɔ:n/ *see* **draw**

dread /dred/ *n* Furcht *f* (**of** vor + *dat*) ●*vt* fürchten. ~**ful** *adj*, **-fully** *adv* fürchterlich

dream /dri:m/ *n* Traum *m* ●*vt/i* (*pt/pp* **dreamt** *or* **dreamed**) träumen (**about**/**of** von)

dreary /'drɪərɪ/ *adj* trüb[e]; (*boring*) langweilig

dregs /dregz/ *npl* Bodensatz *m*

drench /drentʃ/ *vt* durchnässen

dress /dres/ *n* Kleid *nt*; (*clothing*) Kleidung *f* ●*vt* anziehen; (*Med*) verbinden; ~ **oneself, get** ~**ed** sich anziehen ●*vi* sich anziehen. ~ **up** *vi* sich schön anziehen; (*in disguise*) sich verkleiden (**as** als)

dress: ~ **circle** *n* (*Theat*) erster Rang *m*. ~**er** *n* (*furniture*) Anrichte *f*; (*Amer: dressing-table*) Frisiertisch *m*

dressing *n* (*Culin*) Soße *f*; (*Med*) Verband *m*

dressing: ~**-gown** *n* Morgenmantel *m*. ~**-room** *n* Ankleidezimmer *nt*; (*Theat*) [Künstler]garderobe *f*. ~**-table** *n* Frisiertisch *m*

dress: ~**maker** *n* Schneiderin *f*. ~ **rehearsal** *n* Generalprobe *f*

drew /dru:/ *see* **draw**

dried /draɪd/ *adj* getrocknet; ~ **fruit** Dörrobst *nt*

drier /'draɪə(r)/ *n* Trockner *m*

drift /drɪft/ *n* Abtrift *f*; (*of snow*) Schneewehe *f*; (*meaning*) Sinn *m* ●*vi* treiben; (*off course*) abtreiben; (*snow:*) Wehen bilden; (*fig*) (*person:*) sich treiben lassen

drill /drɪl/ *n* Bohrer *m*; (*Mil*) Drill *m* ●*vt/i* bohren (**for** nach); (*Mil*) drillen

drily /'draɪlɪ/ *adv* trocken

drink /drɪŋk/ *n* Getränk *nt*; (*alcoholic*) Drink *m*; (*alcohol*) Alkohol *m* ●*vt/i* (*pt* **drank**, *pp* **drunk**) trinken. ~ **up** *vt/i* austrinken

drink|able /'drɪŋkəbl/ *adj* trinkbar. ~**er** *n* Trinker *m*

'drinking-water *n* Trinkwasser *nt*

drip /drɪp/ *n* Tropfen *nt*; (*drop*) Tropfen *m*; (*Med*) Tropf *m*; (🅸: *person*) Niete *f* ●*vi* (*pt/pp* **dripped**) tropfen

drive /draɪv/ *n* [Auto]fahrt *f*; (*entrance*) Einfahrt *f*; (*energy*) Elan *m*; (*Psychology*) Trieb *m*; (*Pol*) Aktion *f*; (*Sport*) Treibschlag *m*; (*Techn*) Antrieb *m* ●*v* (*pt* **drove**, *pp* **driven**) ●*vt* treiben; fahren (*car*); (*Sport: hit*) schlagen; (*Techn*) antreiben; ~ **s.o. mad** 🅸 jdn verrückt machen; **what are you driving at?** 🅸 worauf willst du hinaus? ●*vi* fahren. ~ **away** *vt* vertreiben ●*vi* abfahren. ~ **off** *vt* vertreiben ●*vi* abfahren. ~ **on** *vi* weiterfahren. ~ **up** *vi* vorfahren

d

drivel /'drɪvl/ *n* 🄵 Quatsch *m*
driven /'drɪvn/ *see* **drive**
driver /'draɪvə(r)/ *n* Fahrer(in) *m(f)*; (*of train*) Lokführer *m*
driving: ~ **lesson** *n* Fahrstunde *f*. ~ **licence** *n* Führerschein *m*. ~ **school** *n* Fahrschule *f*. ~ **test** Fahrprüfung *f*
drizzle /'drɪzl/ *n* Nieselregen *m* ● *vi* nieseln
drone /drəʊn/ *n* (*sound*) Brummen *nt*
droop /dru:p/ *vi* herabhängen
drop /drɒp/ *n* Tropfen *m*; (*fall*) Fall *m*; (*in price, temperature*) Rückgang *m* ● *v* (*pt/pp* **dropped**) ● *vt* fallen lassen; abwerfen (*bomb*); (*omit*) auslassen; (*give up*) aufgeben ● *vi* fallen; (*fall lower*) sinken; (*wind:*) nachlassen. ~ **in** *vi* vorbeikommen. ~ **off** *vt* absetzen (*person*) ● *vi* abfallen; (*fall asleep*) einschlafen. ~ **out** *vi* herausfallen; (*give up*) aufgeben
drought /draʊt/ *n* Dürre *f*
drove /drəʊv/ *see* **drive**
drown /draʊn/ *vi* ertrinken ● *vt* ertränken; übertönen (*noise*); **be** ~**ed** ertrinken
drowsy /'draʊzɪ/ *adj* schläfrig
drudgery /'drʌdʒərɪ/ *n* Plackerei *f*
drug /drʌg/ *n* Droge *f* ● *vt* (*pt/pp* **drugged**) betäuben
drug: ~ **addict** *n* Drogenabhängige(r) *m/f*. ~**store** *n* (*Amer*) Drogerie *f*; (*dispensing*) Apotheke *f*
drum /drʌm/ *n* Trommel *f*; (*for oil*) Tonne *f* ● *v* (*pt/pp* **drummed**) ● *vi* trommeln ● *vt* ~**sth into s.o.** 🄵 jdm etw einbläuen. ~**mer** *n* Trommler *m*; (*in pop-group*) Schlagzeuger *m*. ~**stick** *n* Trommelschlegel *m*; (*Culin*) Keule *f*
drunk /drʌŋk/ *see* **drink** ● *adj* betrunken; **get** ~ sich betrinken ● *n* Betrunkene(r) *m*
drunk|ard /'drʌŋkəd/ *n* Trinker *m*. ~**en** *adj* betrunken
dry /draɪ/ *adj* (**drier, driest**) trocken ● *vt/i* trocknen. ~ **up** *vt/i* austrocknen
dry: ~-'**clean** *vt* chemisch reinigen. ~-'**cleaner's** *n* (*shop*) chemische Reinigung *f*. ~**ness** *n* Trockenheit *f*
dual /'dju:əl/ *adj* doppelt
dual 'carriageway *n* ≈ Schnellstraße *f*
dubious /'dju:bɪəs/ *adj* zweifelhaft
duchess /'dʌtʃɪs/ *n* Herzogin *f*
duck /dʌk/ *n* Ente *f* ● *vt* (*in water*) untertauchen ● *vi* sich ducken
duct /dʌkt/ *n* Rohr *nt*; (*Anat*) Gang *m*
dud /dʌd/ *adj* 🄵 nutzlos; (*coin*) falsch; (*cheque*) ungedeckt; (*forged*) gefälscht
due /dju:/ *adj* angemessen; **be** ~ fällig sein; (*baby:*) erwartet werden; (*train:*) planmäßig ankommen; ~ **to** (*owing to*) wegen (+ *gen*); **be** ~ **to** zurückzuführen sein auf (+ *acc*) ● *adv* ~ **west** genau westlich
duel /'dju:əl/ *n* Duell *nt*
duet /dju:'et/ *n* Duo *nt*; (*vocal*) Duett *nt*
dug /dʌg/ *see* **dig**
duke /dju:k/ *n* Herzog *m*
dull /dʌl/ *adj* (**-er, -est**) (*overcast, not bright*) trüb[e]; (*not shiny*) matt; (*sound*) dumpf; (*boring*) langweilig; (*stupid*) schwerfällig
duly /'dju:lɪ/ *adv* ordnungsgemäß
dumb /dʌm/ *adj* (**-er, -est**) stumm. ~ **down** *vt/i* verflachen
dummy /'dʌmɪ/ *n* (*tailor's*) [Schneider]puppe *f*; (*for baby*) Schnuller *m*; (*Comm*) Attrappe *f*
dump /dʌmp/ *n* Abfallhaufen *m*; (*for refuse*) Müllhalde *f*, Deponie *f*; (🄵: *town*) Kaff *nt*; **be down in the**

~s ⓘ deprimiert sein ● *vt* abladen
dumpling /'dʌmplɪŋ/ *n* Kloß *m*
dunce /dʌns/ *n* Dummkopf *m*
dune /dju:n/ *n* Düne *f*
dung /dʌŋ/ *n* Mist *m*
dungarees /dʌŋgə'ri:z/ *npl* Latzhose *f*
dungeon /'dʌndʒən/ *n* Verlies *nt*
dunk /dʌŋk/ *vt* eintunken
duo /'dju:əʊ/ *n* Paar *nt*; (*Mus*) Duo *nt*
dupe /dju:p/ *n* Betrogene(r) *m/f* ● *vt* betrügen
duplicate¹ /'dju:plɪkət/ *n* Doppel *nt*; **in** ~ in doppelter Ausfertigung *f*
duplicat|e² /'dju:plɪkeɪt/ *vt* kopieren; (*do twice*) zweimal machen
durable /'djʊərəbl/ *adj* haltbar
duration /djʊə'reɪʃn/ *n* Dauer *f*
during /'djʊərɪŋ/ *prep* während (+ *gen*)
dusk /dʌsk/ *n* [Abend]dämmerung *f*
dust /dʌst/ *n* Staub *m* ● *vt* abstauben; (*sprinkle*) bestäuben (**with** mit) ● *vi* Staub wischen
dust: ~**bin** *n* Mülltonne *f*. ~**-cart** *n* Müllwagen *m*. ~**er** *n* Staubtuch *nt*. ~**-jacket** *n* Schutzumschlag *m*. ~**man** *n* Müllmann *m*. ~**pan** *n* Kehrschaufel *f*
dusty /'dʌstɪ/ *adj* staubig
Dutch /dʌtʃ/ *adj* holländisch ● *n* (*Lang*) Holländisch *nt*; **the** ~ *pl* die Holländer. ~**man** *n* Holländer *m*
dutiful /'dju:tɪfl/ *adj* pflichtbewusst
duty /'dju:tɪ/ *n* Pflicht *f*; (*task*) Aufgabe *f*; (*tax*) Zoll *m*; **be on** ~ Dienst haben. ~**-free** *adj* zollfrei
duvet /'du:veɪ/ *n* Steppdecke *f*
DVD *abbr* (**digital versatile disc**) DVD *f*
dwarf /dwɔ:f/ *n* (*pl* **-s** *or* **dwarves**) Zwerg *m*
dwell /dwel/ *vi* (*pt/pp* **dwelt**); ~ **on** (*fig*) verweilen bei. ~**ing** *n* Wohnung *f*
dwindle /'dwɪndl/ *vi* abnehmen, schwinden
dye /daɪ/ *n* Farbstoff *m* ● *vt* (*pres p* **dyeing**) färben
dying /'daɪɪŋ/ *see* **die²**
dynamic /daɪ'næmɪk/ *adj* dynamisch
dynamite /'daɪnəmaɪt/ *n* Dynamit *nt*
dyslex|ia /dɪs'leksɪə/ *n* Legasthenie *f*. ~**ic** *adj* legasthenisch; **be** ~**ic** Legastheniker sein

Ee

each /i:tʃ/ *adj & pron* jede(r,s); (*per*) je; ~ **other** einander; **£1** ~ £1 pro Person; (*for thing*) pro Stück
eager /'i:gə(r)/ *adj* eifrig; **be** ~ **to do sth** etw gerne machen wollen. ~**ness** *n* Eifer *m*
eagle /'i:gl/ *n* Adler *m*
ear *n* Ohr *nt*. ~**ache** *n* Ohrenschmerzen *pl*. ~**-drum** *n* Trommelfell *nt*
earl /ɜ:l/ *n* Graf *m*
early /'ɜ:lɪ/ *adj & adv* (**-ier, -iest**) früh; (*reply*) baldig; **be** ~ früh dran sein
earn /ɜ:n/ *vt* verdienen
earnest /'ɜ:nɪst/ *adj* ernsthaft ● *n* **in** ~ im Ernst
earnings /'ɜ:nɪŋz/ *npl* Verdienst *m*
ear: ~**phones** *npl* Kopfhörer *pl*. ~**-ring** *n* Ohrring *m*; (*clip-on*) Ohrklips *m*. ~**shot** *n* **within/out of** ~**shot** in/außer Hörweite

earth /ɜ:θ/ *n* Erde *f*; (*of fox*) Bau *m* ● *vt* (*Electr*) erden

earthenware /'ɜ:θn-/ *n* Tonwaren *pl*

earthly /'ɜ:θlɪ/ *adj* irdisch; **be no ~ use** [!] völlig nutzlos sein

'earthquake *n* Erdbeben *nt*

e

earthy /'ɜ:θɪ/ *adj* erdig; (*coarse*) derb

ease /i:z/ *n* Leichtigkeit *f* ● *vt* erleichtern; lindern (*pain*) ● *vi* (*pain:*) nachlassen; (*situation:*) sich entspannen

easily /'i:zɪlɪ/ *adv* leicht, mit Leichtigkeit

east /i:st/ *n* Osten *m*; **to the ~ of** östlich von ● *adj* Ost-, ost- ● *adv* nach Osten

Easter /'i:stə(r)/ *n* Ostern *nt* ● *attrib* Oster-. **~ egg** *n* Osterei *nt*

east|erly /'i:stəlɪ/ *adj* östlich. **~ern** *adj* östlich. **~ward[s]** *adv* nach Osten

easy /'i:zɪ/ *adj* leicht; **take it ~** [!] sich schonen; **go ~ with** [!] sparsam umgehen mit

easy: ~ chair *n* Sessel *m*. **~'going** *adj* gelassen

eat /i:t/ *vt/i* (*pt* **ate**, *pp* **eaten**) essen; (*animal:*) fressen. **~ up** *vt* aufessen

eatable /'i:təbl/ *adj* genießbar

eau-de-Cologne /əʊdəkə'ləʊn/ *n* Kölnisch Wasser *nt*

eaves /i:vz/ *npl* Dachüberhang *m*. **~drop** *vi* (*pt/pp* **~ dropped**) [heimlich] lauschen

ebb /eb/ *n* (*tide*) Ebbe *f* ● *vi* zurückgehen; (*fig*) verebben

ebony /'ebənɪ/ *n* Ebenholz *nt*

EC *abbr* (**European Community**) EG *f*

eccentric /ɪk'sentrɪk/ *adj* exzentrisch ● *n* Exzentriker *m*

ecclesiastical /ɪkli:zɪ'æstɪkl/ *adj* kirchlich

echo /'ekəʊ/ *n* (*pl* **-es**) Echo *nt*, Widerhall *m* ● *v* (*pt/pp* **echoed**, *pres p* **echoing**) ● *vi* widerhallen (**with** von)

eclipse /ɪ'klɪps/ *n* (*Astronomy*) Finsternis *f*

ecolog|ical /i:kə'lɒdʒɪkl/ *adj* ökologisch. **~y** *n* Ökologie *f*

e-commerce /i:'kɒmɜ:s/ *n* E-Commerce *m*

economic /i:kə'nɒmɪk/ *adj* wirtschaftlich. **~al** *adj* sparsam. **~ally** *adv* wirtschaftlich; (*thriftily*) sparsam. **~ refugee** *n* Wirtschaftsflüchtling *m*. **~s** *n* Volkswirtschaft *f*

economist /ɪ'kɒnəmɪst/ *n* Volkswirt *m*; (*Univ*) Wirtschaftswissenschaftler *m*

economize /ɪ'kɒnəmaɪz/ *vi* sparen (**on** an + *dat*)

economy /ɪ'kɒnəmɪ/ *n* Wirtschaft *f*; (*thrift*) Sparsamkeit *f*

ecstasy /'ekstəsɪ/ *n* Ekstase *f*

ecstatic /ɪk'stætɪk/ *adj*, **-ally** *adv* ekstatisch

eczema /'eksɪmə/ *n* Ekzem *nt*

eddy /'edɪ/ *n* Wirbel *m*

edge /edʒ/ *n* Rand *m*; (*of table, lawn*) Kante *f*; (*of knife*) Schneide *f*; **on ~** [!] nervös ● *vt* einfassen. **~ forward** *vi* sich nach vorn schieben

edgy /'edʒɪ/ *adj* [!] nervös

edible /'edɪbl/ *adj* essbar

edifice /'edɪfɪs/ *n* [großes] Gebäude *nt*

Edinburgh Festival *i*

Großbritanniens berühmtestes Kunst- und Theaterfestival findet seit 1947 jedes Jahr im August in der schottischen Hauptstadt statt. Die Festspiele ziehen Besucher aus aller Welt an. Ergänzt wird das Programm durch das gleichzeitig stattfindende *Edinburgh Festival Fringe*, das ein Forum für unbekannte Künstler, experimentelle Kunst und alternative Veranstaltungen ist.

edit /ˈedɪt/ *vt* (*pt/pp* **edited**) redigieren; herausgeben (*anthology, dictionary*); schneiden (*film, tape*)

edition /ɪˈdɪʃn/ *n* Ausgabe *f*; (*impression*) Auflage *f*

editor /ˈedɪtə(r)/ *n* Redakteur *m*; (*of anthology, dictionary*) Herausgeber *m*; (*of newspaper*) Chefredakteur *m*; (*of film*) Cutter(in) *m*(*f*)

editorial /edɪˈtɔːrɪəl/ *adj* redaktionell, Redaktions- ● *n* (*in newspaper*) Leitartikel *m*

educate /ˈedjʊkeɪt/ *vt* erziehen. **~d** *adj* gebildet

education /edjʊˈkeɪʃn/ *n* Erziehung *f*; (*culture*) Bildung *f*. **~al** *adj* pädagogisch; (*visit*) kulturell

eel /iːl/ *n* Aal *m*

eerie /ˈɪərɪ/ *adj* unheimlich

effect /ɪˈfekt/ *n* Wirkung *f*, Effekt *m*; **take ~** in Kraft treten

effective /ɪˈfektɪv/ *adj* wirksam, effektiv; (*striking*) wirkungsvoll, effektvoll; (*actual*) tatsächlich. **~ness** *n* Wirksamkeit *f*

effeminate /ɪˈfemɪnət/ *adj* unmännlich

effervescent /efəˈvesnt/ *adj* sprudelnd

efficiency /ɪˈfɪʃənsɪ/ *n* Tüchtigkeit *f*; (*of machine, organization*) Leistungsfähigkeit *f*

efficient /ɪˈfɪʃənt/ *adj* tüchtig; (*machine, organization*) leistungsfähig; (*method*) rationell. **~ly** *adv* gut; (*function*) rationell

effort /ˈefət/ *n* Anstrengung *f*; **make an ~** sich (*dat*) Mühe geben. **~less** *adj* mühelos

e.g. *abbr* (**exempli gratia**) z.B.

egalitarian /ɪgælɪˈteərɪən/ *adj* egalitär

egg *n* Ei *nt*. **~-cup** *n* Eierbecher *m*. **~shell** *n* Eierschale *f*

ego /ˈiːgəʊ/ *n* Ich *nt*. **~ism** *n* Egoismus *m*. **~ist** *n* Egoist *m*. **~tism** *n* Ichbezogenheit *f*. **~tist** *n* ichbezogener Mensch *m*

Egypt /ˈiːdʒɪpt/ *n* Ägypten *nt*. **~ian** *adj* ägyptisch ● *n* Ägypter(in) *m*(*f*)

eiderdown /ˈaɪdə-/ *n* (*quilt*) Daunendecke *f*

eigh|t /eɪt/ *adj* acht ● *n* Acht *f*; (*boat*) Achter *m*. **~ˈteen** *adj* achtzehn. **~ˈteenth** *adj* achtzehnte(r,s)

eighth /eɪtθ/ *adj* achte(r,s) ● *n* Achtel *nt*

eightieth /ˈeɪtɪɪθ/ *adj* achtzigste(r,s)

eighty /ˈeɪtɪ/ *adj* achtzig

either /ˈaɪðə(r)/ *adj & pron* **~ [of them]** einer von [den] beiden; (*both*) beide; **on ~ side** auf beiden Seiten ● *adv* **I don't ~** ich auch nicht ● *conj* **~ ... or** entweder ... oder

eject /ɪˈdʒekt/ *vt* hinauswerfen

elaborate /ɪˈlæbərət/ *adj* kunstvoll; (*fig*) kompliziert

elapse /ɪˈlæps/ *vi* vergehen

elastic /ɪˈlæstɪk/ *adj* elastisch. **~ ˈband** *n* Gummiband *nt*

elasticity /ɪlæsˈtɪsətɪ/ *n* Elastizität *f*

elated /ɪˈleɪtɪd/ *adj* überglücklich

elbow /ˈelbəʊ/ *n* Ellbogen *m*

elder¹ /ˈeldə(r)/ *n* Holunder *m*

eld|er² *adj* ältere(r,s) ● *n* **the ~er** der/die Ältere. **~erly** *adj* alt. **~est** *adj* älteste(r,s) ● *n* **the ~est**

der/die Älteste

elect /ɪ'lekt/ *vt* wählen. **~ion** *n* Wahl *f*

elector /ɪ'lektə(r)/ *n* Wähler(in) *m(f)*. **~ate** *n* Wählerschaft *f*

electric /ɪ'lektrɪk/ *adj*, **-ally** *adv* elektrisch

e

electrical /ɪ'lektrɪkl/ *adj* elektrisch; **~ engineering** Elektrotechnik *f*

electric: ~ 'blanket *n* Heizdecke *f*. **~ 'fire** *n* elektrischer Heizofen *m*

electrician /ɪlek'trɪʃn/ *n* Elektriker *m*

electricity /ɪlek'trɪsətɪ/ *n* Elektrizität *f*; (*supply*) Strom *m*

electrify /ɪ'lektrɪfaɪ/ *vt* (*pt/pp* **-ied**) elektrifizieren. **~ing** *adj* (*fig*) elektrisierend

electrocute /ɪ'lektrəkju:t/ *vt* durch einen elektrischen Schlag töten

electrode /ɪ'lektrəʊd/ *n* Elektrode *f*

electronic /ɪlek'trɒnɪk/ *adj* elektronisch. **~s** *n* Elektronik *f*

elegance /'elɪgəns/ *n* Eleganz *f*

elegant /'elɪgənt/ *adj* elegant

elegy /'elɪdʒɪ/ *n* Elegie *f*

element /'elɪmənt/ *n* Element *nt*. **~ary** *adj* elementar

elephant /'elɪfənt/ *n* Elefant *m*

elevat|e /'elɪveɪt/ *vt* heben; (*fig*) erheben. **~ion** *n* Erhebung *f*

elevator /'elɪveɪtə(r)/ *n* (*Amer*) Aufzug *m*, Fahrstuhl *m*

eleven /ɪ'levn/ *adj* elf ● *n* Elf *f*. **~th** *adj* elfte(r,s); **at the ~th hour** [!] in letzter Minute

eligible /'elɪdʒəbl/ *adj* berechtigt

eliminate /ɪ'lɪmɪneɪt/ *vt* ausschalten

élite /eɪ'li:t/ *n* Elite *f*

elm /elm/ *n* Ulme *f*

elocution /elə'kju:ʃn/ *n* Sprecherziehung *f*

elope /ɪ'əʊp/ *vi* durchbrennen [!]

eloquen|ce /'eləkwəns/ *n* Beredsamkeit *f*. **~t** *adj*, **~ly** *adv* beredt

else /els/ *adv* sonst; **nothing ~** sonst nichts; **or ~** oder; (*otherwise*) sonst; **someone/somewhere ~** jemand/irgendwo anders; **anyone ~** jeder andere; (*as question*) sonst noch jemand? **anything ~** alles andere; (*as question*) sonst noch etwas? **~where** *adv* woanders

elucidate /ɪ'lu:sɪdeɪt/ *vt* erläutern

elusive /ɪ'lu:sɪv/ *adj* **be ~** schwer zu fassen sein

emaciated /ɪ'meɪsɪeɪtɪd/ *adj* abgezehrt

e-mail /'i:meɪl/ *n* E-Mail *f* ● *vt* per E-Mail übermitteln (*Ergebnisse, Datei usw.*); **~ s.o.** jdm eine E-Mail schicken. **~ address** *n* E-Mail-Adresse *f*. **~ message** *n* E-Mail *f*

emancipat|ed /ɪ'mænsɪpeɪtɪd/ *adj* emanzipiert. **~ion** *n* Emanzipation *f*; (*of slaves*) Freilassung *f*

embankment /ɪm'bæŋkmənt/ *n* Böschung *f*; (*of railway*) Bahndamm *m*

embark /ɪm'bɑ:k/ *vi* sich einschiffen. **~ation** *n* Einschiffung *f*

embarrass /ɪm'bærəs/ *vt* in Verlegenheit bringen. **~ed** *adj* verlegen. **~ing** *adj* peinlich. **~ment** *n* Verlegenheit *f*

embassy /'embəsɪ/ *n* Botschaft *f*

embellish /ɪm'belɪʃ/ *vt* verzieren; (*fig*) ausschmücken

embezzle /ɪm'bezl/ *vt* unterschlagen. **~ment** *n* Unterschlagung *f*

emblem /'embləm/ *n* Emblem *nt*

embodiment /ɪm'bɒdɪmənt/ *n* Verkörperung *f*

embody /ɪm'bɒdɪ/ *vt* (*pt/pp* **-ied**) verkörpern; (*include*) enthalten

embrace /ɪm'breɪs/ *n* Umarmung *f* ● *vt* umarmen; (*fig*) umfassen ● *vi* sich umarmen
embroider /ɪm'brɔɪdə(r)/ *vt* besticken; sticken (*design*) ● *vi* sticken. **~y** *n* Stickerei *f*
embryo /'embrɪəʊ/ *n* Embryo *m*
emerald /'emərəld/ *n* Smaragd *m*
emer|ge /ɪ'mɜ:dʒ/ *vi* auftauchen (**from** aus); (*become known*) sich herausstellen; (*come into being*) entstehen. **~gence** *n* Auftauchen *nt*; Entstehung *f*
emergency /ɪ'mɜ:dʒənsɪ/ *n* Notfall *m*. **~ exit** *n* Notausgang *m*
emigrant /'emɪgrənt/ *n* Auswanderer *m*
emigrat|e /'emɪgreɪt/ *vi* auswandern. **~ion** *n* Auswanderung *f*
eminent /'emɪnənt/ *adj* eminent
emission /ɪ'mɪʃn/ *n* Ausstrahlung *f*; (*of pollutant*) Emission *f*
emit /ɪ'mɪt/ *vt* (*pt/pp* **emitted**) ausstrahlen (*light, heat*); ausstoßen (*smoke, fumes, cry*)
emotion /ɪ'məʊʃn/ *n* Gefühl *nt*. **~al** *adj* emotional; **become ~al** sich erregen
empathy /'empəθɪ/ *n* Einfühlungsvermögen *nt*
emperor /'empərə(r)/ *n* Kaiser *m*
emphasis /'emfəsɪs/ *n* Betonung *f*
emphasize /'emfəsaɪz/ *vt* betonen
emphatic /ɪm'fætɪk/ *adj*, **-ally** *adv* nachdrücklich
empire /'empaɪə(r)/ *n* Reich *nt*
employ /ɪm'plɔɪ/ *vt* beschäftigen; (*appoint*) einstellen; (*fig*) anwenden. **~ee** *n* Beschäftigte(r) *m/f*; (*in contrast to employer*) Arbeitnehmer *m*. **~er** *n* Arbeitgeber *m*. **~ment** *n* Beschäftigung *f*; (*work*) Arbeit *f*. **~ment agency** *n* Stellenvermittlung *f*
empress /'emprɪs/ *n* Kaiserin *f*
emptiness /'emptɪnɪs/ *n* Leere *f*
empty /'emptɪ/ *adj* leer ● *vt* leeren; ausleeren (*container*) ● *vi* sich leeren
emulsion /ɪ'mʌlʃn/ *n* Emulsion *f*
enable /ɪ'neɪbl/ *vt* **~ s.o. to** es jdm möglich machen, zu
enact /ɪ'nækt/ *vt* (*Theat*) aufführen
enamel /ɪ'næml/ *n* Email *nt*; (*on teeth*) Zahnschmelz *m*; (*paint*) Lack *m*
enchant /ɪn'tʃɑ:nt/ *vt* bezaubern. **~ing** *adj* bezaubernd. **~ment** *n* Zauber *m*
encircle /ɪn'sɜ:kl/ *vt* einkreisen
enclos|e /ɪn'kləʊz/ *vt* einschließen; (*in letter*) beilegen (**with** *dat*). **~ure** *n* (*at zoo*) Gehege *nt*; (*in letter*) Anlage *f*
encore /'ɒŋkɔ:(r)/ *n* Zugabe *f* ● *int* bravo!
encounter /ɪn'kaʊntə(r)/ *n* Begegnung *f* ● *vt* begegnen (+ *dat*); (*fig*) stoßen auf (+ *acc*)
encourag|e /ɪn'kʌrɪdʒ/ *vt* ermutigen; (*promote*) fördern. **~ement** *n* Ermutigung *f*. **~ing** *adj* ermutigend
encroach /ɪn'krəʊtʃ/ *vi* **~ on** eindringen in (+ *acc*) (*land*)
encyclopaed|ia /ɪnsaɪklə'pi:dɪə/ *n* Enzyklopädie *f*, Lexikon *nt*. **~ic** *adj* enzyklopädisch
end /end/ *n* Ende *nt*; (*purpose*) Zweck *m*; **in the ~** schließlich; **at the ~ of May** Ende Mai; **on ~** hochkant; **for days on ~** tagelang; **make ~s meet** ⊡ [gerade] auskommen; **no ~ of** ⊡ unheimlich viel(e) ● *vt* beenden ● *vi* enden; **~ up in** (⊡: *arrive at*) landen in (+ *dat*)
endanger /ɪn'deɪndʒə(r)/ *vt* gefährden
endeavour /ɪn'devə(r)/ *n* Bemühung *f* ● *vi* sich bemühen (**to** zu)

e

ending /'endɪŋ/ *n* Schluss *m*, Ende *nt*; (*Gram*) Endung *f*

endless /'endlɪs/ *adj* endlos

endorse /en'dɔ:s/ *vt* (*Comm*) indossieren; (*confirm*) bestätigen. **~ment** *n* (*Comm*) Indossament *nt*; (*fig*) Bestätigung *f*; (*on driving licence*) Strafvermerk *m*

endow /ɪn'daʊ/ *vt* stiften; **be ~ed with** (*fig*) haben

endurance /ɪn'djʊərəns/ *n* Durchhaltevermögen *nt*

endure /ɪn'djʊə(r)/ *vt* ertragen

enemy /'enəmɪ/ *n* Feind *m* ● *attrib* feindlich

energetic /enə'dʒetɪk/ *adj* tatkräftig; **be ~** voller Energie sein

energy /'enədʒɪ/ *n* Energie *f*. **~-efficient** *adj* energieeffizient

enforce /ɪn'fɔ:s/ *vt* durchsetzen. **~d** *adj* unfreiwillig

engage /ɪn'geɪdʒ/ *vt* einstellen (*staff*); (*Theat*) engagieren; (*Auto*) einlegen (*gear*) ● *vi* sich beteiligen (**in** an + *dat*); (*Techn*) ineinandergreifen. **~d** *adj* besetzt; (*person*) beschäftigt; (*to be married*) verlobt; **get ~d** sich verloben (**to** mit). **~ment** *n* Verlobung *f*; (*appointment*) Verabredung *f*; (*Mil*) Gefecht *nt*

engaging /ɪn'geɪdʒɪŋ/ *adj* einnehmend

engine /'endʒɪn/ *n* Motor *m*; (*Naut*) Maschine *f*; (*Rail*) Lokomotive *f*; (*of jet plane*) Triebwerk *nt*. **~-driver** *n* Lokomotivführer *m*

engineer /endʒɪ'nɪə(r)/ *n* Ingenieur *m*; (*service, installation*) Techniker *m*; (*Naut*) Maschinist *m*; (*Amer*) Lokomotivführer *m*. **~ing** *n* **[mechanical] ~ing** Maschinenbau *m*

England /'ɪŋglənd/ *n* England *nt*

English /'ɪŋglɪʃ/ *adj* englisch; **the ~ Channel** der Ärmelkanal ● *n* (*Lang*) Englisch *nt*; **in ~** auf Englisch; **into ~** ins Englische; **the ~** *pl* die Engländer. **~man** *n* Engländer *m*. **~woman** *n* Engländerin *f*

engrav|e /ɪn'greɪv/ *vt* eingravieren. **~ing** *n* Stich *m*

enhance /ɪn'hɑ:ns/ *vt* verschönern; (*fig*) steigern

enigma /ɪ'nɪgmə/ *n* Rätsel *nt*. **~tic** *adj* rätselhaft

enjoy /ɪn'dʒɔɪ/ *vt* genießen; **~ oneself** sich amüsieren; **~ cooking** gern kochen; **I ~ed it** es hat mir gut gefallen/ (*food:*) geschmeckt. **~able** *adj* angenehm, nett. **~ment** *n* Vergnügen *nt*

enlarge /ɪn'lɑ:dʒ/ *vt* vergrößern. **~ment** *n* Vergrößerung *f*

enlist /ɪn'lɪst/ *vt* (*Mil*) einziehen; **~ s.o.'s help** jdn zur Hilfe heranziehen ● *vi* (*Mil*) sich melden

enliven /ɪn'laɪvn/ *vt* beleben

enmity /'enmətɪ/ *n* Feindschaft *f*

enormity /ɪ'nɔ:mətɪ/ *n* Ungeheuerlichkeit *f*

enormous /ɪ'nɔ:məs/ *adj* riesig

enough /ɪ'nʌf/ *a, adv* & *n* genug; **be ~** reichen; **funnily ~** komischerweise

enquir|e /ɪn'kwaɪə(r)/ *vi* sich erkundigen (**about** nach). **~y** *n* Erkundigung *f*; (*investigation*) Untersuchung *f*

enrage /ɪn'reɪdʒ/ *vt* wütend machen

enrich /ɪn'rɪtʃ/ *vt* bereichern

enrol /ɪn'rəʊl/ *v* (*pt/pp* **-rolled**) ● *vt* einschreiben ● *vi* sich einschreiben

ensemble /ɒn'sɒmbl/ *n* (*clothing* & *Mus*) Ensemble *nt*

enslave /ɪn'sleɪv/ *vt* versklaven

ensue /ɪn'sju:/ *vi* folgen; (*result*) sich ergeben (**from** aus)

ensure /ɪn'ʃʊə(r)/ *vt* sicherstellen; ~ **that** dafür sorgen, dass

entail /ɪn'teɪl/ *vt* erforderlich machen; **what does it ~?** was ist damit verbunden?

entangle /ɪn'tæŋgl/ *vt* **get ~d** sich verfangen (**in** in + *dat*)

enter /'entə(r)/ *vt* eintreten/ (*vehicle:*) einfahren in (+ *acc*); einreisen in (+ *acc*) (*country*); (*register*) eintragen; sich anmelden zu (*competition*) ● *vi* eintreten; (*vehicle:*) einfahren; (*Theat*) auftreten; (*register as competitor*) sich anmelden; (*take part*) sich beteiligen (**in** an + *dat*)

enterpris|e /'entəpraɪz/ *n* Unternehmen *nt*; (*quality*) Unternehmungsgeist *m*. **~ing** *adj* unternehmend

entertain /entə'teɪn/ *vt* unterhalten; (*invite*) einladen; (*to meal*) bewirten (*guest*) ● *vi* unterhalten; (*have guests*) Gäste haben. **~er** *n* Unterhalter *m*. **~ment** *n* Unterhaltung *f*

enthral /ɪn'θrɔːl/ *vt* (*pt/pp* **enthralled**) **be ~led** gefesselt sein (**by** von)

enthuse /ɪn'θjuːz/ *vi* ~ **over** schwärmen von

enthusias|m /ɪn'θjuːzɪæzm/ *n* Begeisterung *f*. **~t** *n* Enthusiast *m*. **~tic** *adj*, **-ally** *adv* begeistert

entice /ɪn'taɪs/ *vt* locken. **~ment** *n* Anreiz *m*

entire /ɪn'taɪə(r)/ *adj* ganz. **~ly** *adv* ganz, völlig. **~ty** *n* **in its ~ty** in seiner Gesamtheit

entitle /ɪn'taɪtl/ *vt* berechtigen; **~d** ... mit dem Titel ...; **be ~d to sth** das Recht auf etw (*acc*) haben. **~ment** *n* Berechtigung *f*; (*claim*) Anspruch *m* (**to** auf + *acc*)

entrance /'entrəns/ *n* Eintritt *m*; (*Theat*) Auftritt *m*; (*way in*) Eingang *m*; (*for vehicle*) Einfahrt *f*. ~ **fee** *n* Eintrittsgebühr *f*

entrant /'entrənt/ *n* Teilnehmer(in) *m*(*f*)

entreat /ɪn'triːt/ *vt* anflehen (**for** um)

entrust /ɪn'trʌst/ *vt* ~ **s.o. with sth,** ~ **sth to s.o.** jdm etw anvertrauen

entry /'entrɪ/ *n* Eintritt *m*; (*into country*) Einreise *f*; (*on list*) Eintrag *m*; **no** ~ Zutritt/ (*Auto*) Einfahrt verboten

envelop /ɪn'veləp/ *vt* (*pt/pp* **enveloped**) einhüllen

envelope /'envələʊp/ *n* [Brief]umschlag *m*

enviable /'envɪəbl/ *adj* beneidenswert

envious /'envɪəs/ *adj* neidisch (**of** auf + *acc*)

environment /ɪn'vaɪərənmənt/ *n* Umwelt *f*

environmental /ɪnvaɪərən'mentl/ *adj* Umwelt-. **~ist** *n* Umweltschützer *m*. **~ly** *adv* **~ly friendly** umweltfreundlich

envisage /ɪn'vɪzɪdʒ/ *vt* sich (*dat*) vorstellen

envoy /'envɔɪ/ *n* Gesandte(r) *m*

envy /'envɪ/ *n* Neid *m* ● *vt* (*pt/pp* **-ied**) ~ **s.o. sth** jdn um etw beneiden

epic /'epɪk/ *adj* episch ● *n* Epos *nt*

epidemic /epɪ'demɪk/ *n* Epidemie *f*

epilep|sy /'epɪlepsɪ/ *n* Epilepsie *f*. **~tic** *adj* epileptisch ● *n* Epileptiker(in) *m*(*f*)

epilogue /'epɪlɒg/ *n* Epilog *m*

episode /'epɪsəʊd/ *n* Episode *f*; (*instalment*) Folge *f*

epitome /ɪ'pɪtəmɪ/ *n* Inbegriff *m*

epoch /'iːpɒk/ *n* Epoche *f*. **~-mak-**

e

ing *adj* epochemachend

equal /'i:kwl/ *adj* gleich (**to** *dat*); **be ~ to a task** einer Aufgabe gewachsen sein ● *n* Gleichgestellte(r) *m/f* ● *vt* (*pt/pp* **equalled**) gleichen (+ *dat*); (*fig*) gleichkommen (+ *dat*). **~ity** *n* Gleichheit *f*

equalize /'i:kwəlaɪz/ *vt/i* ausgleichen

equally /'i:kwəlɪ/ *adv* gleich; (*divide*) gleichmäßig; (*just as*) genauso

equat|e /ɪ'kweɪt/ *vt* gleichsetzen (**with** mit). **~ion** *n* (*Math*) Gleichung *f*

equator /ɪ'kweɪtə(r)/ *n* Äquator *m*

equestrian /ɪ'kwestrɪən/ *adj* Reit-

equilibrium /i:kwɪ'lɪbrɪəm/ *n* Gleichgewicht *nt*

equinox /'i:kwɪnɒks/ *n* Tagundnachtgleiche *f*

equip /ɪ'kwɪp/ *vt* (*pt/pp* **equipped**) ausrüsten; (*furnish*) ausstatten. **~ment** *n* Ausrüstung *f*, Ausstattung *f*

equity /'ekwətɪ/ *n* Gerechtigkeit *f*

equivalent /ɪ'kwɪvələnt/ *adj* gleichwertig; (*corresponding*) entsprechend ● *n* Äquivalent *nt*; (*value*) Gegenwert *m*; (*counterpart*) Gegenstück *nt*

era /'ɪərə/ *n* Ära *f*, Zeitalter *nt*

eradicate /ɪ'rædɪkeɪt/ *vt* ausrotten

erase /ɪ'reɪz/ *vt* ausradieren; (*from tape*) löschen

erect /ɪ'rekt/ *adj* aufrecht ● *vt* errichten. **~ion** *n* Errichtung *f*; (*building*) Bau *m*; (*Physiology*) Erektion *f*

ero|de /ɪ'rəʊd/ *vt* (*water:*) auswaschen; (*acid:*) angreifen. **~sion** *n* Erosion *f*

erotic /ɪ'rɒtɪk/ *adj* erotisch

errand /'erənd/ *n* Botengang *m*

erratic /ɪ'rætɪk/ *adj* unregelmäßig; (*person*) unberechenbar

erroneous /ɪ'rəʊnɪəs/ *adj* falsch; (*belief, assumption*) irrig

error /'erə(r)/ *n* Irrtum *m*; (*mistake*) Fehler *m*; **in ~** irrtümlicherweise

erupt /ɪ'rʌpt/ *vi* ausbrechen. **~ion** *n* Ausbruch *m*

escalat|e /'eskəleɪt/ *vt/i* eskalieren. **~or** *n* Rolltreppe *f*

escape /ɪ'skeɪp/ *n* Flucht *f*; (*from prison*) Ausbruch *m*; **have a narrow ~** gerade noch davonkommen ● *vi* flüchten; (*prisoner:*) ausbrechen; entkommen (**from** aus; **from s.o.** jdm); (*gas:*) entweichen ● *vt* **the name ~s me** der Name entfällt mir

escapism /ɪ'skeɪpɪzm/ *n* Eskapismus *m*

escort¹ /'eskɔ:t/ *n* (*of person*) Begleiter *m*; (*Mil*) Eskorte *f*

escort² /ɪ'skɔ:t/ *vt* begleiten; (*Mil*) eskortieren

Eskimo /'eskɪməʊ/ *n* Eskimo *m*

esoteric /esə'terɪk/ *adj* esoterisch

especially /ɪ'speʃəlɪ/ *adv* besonders

espionage /'espɪənɑ:ʒ/ *n* Spionage *f*

essay /'eseɪ/ *n* Aufsatz *m*

essence /'esns/ *n* Wesen *nt*; (*Chemistry, Culin*) Essenz *f*

essential /ɪ'senʃl/ *adj* wesentlich; (*indispensable*) unentbehrlich ● *n* **the ~s** das Wesentliche; (*items*) das Nötigste. **~ly** *adv* im Wesentlichen

establish /ɪ'stæblɪʃ/ *vt* gründen; (*form*) bilden; (*prove*) beweisen

estate /ɪ'steɪt/ *n* Gut *nt*; (*possessions*) Besitz *m*; (*after death*) Nachlass *m*; (*housing*) [Wohn]siedlung *f*. **~ agent** *n* Immobilienmakler *m*. **~ car** *n* Kombi[wagen] *m*

esteem /ɪ'sti:m/ *n* Achtung *f* ● *vt* hochschätzen

estimate[1] /ˈestɪmət/ *n* Schätzung *f*; (*Comm*) [Kosten]voranschlag *m*; **at a rough ~** grob geschätzt

estimat|e[2] /ˈestɪmeɪt/ *vt* schätzen. **~ion** *n* Einschätzung *f*

estuary /ˈestjʊərɪ/ *n* Mündung *f*

etc. /etˈsetərə/ *abbr* (**et cetera**) und so weiter, usw.

eternal /ɪˈtɜːnl/ *adj* ewig

eternity /ɪˈθɜːnətɪ/ *n* Ewigkeit *f*

ethical /ˈeθɪkl/ *adj* ethisch; (*morally correct*) moralisch einwandfrei. **~s** *n* Ethik *f*

Ethiopia /iːθɪˈəʊpɪə/ *n* Äthiopien *nt*

ethnic /ˈeθnɪk/ *adj* ethnisch. **~ cleansing** *n* ethnische Säuberung

etiquette /ˈetɪket/ *n* Etikette *f*

EU *abbr* (**European Union**) EU *f*

eulogy /ˈjuːlədʒɪ/ *n* Lobrede *f*

euphemis|m /ˈjuːfəmɪzm/ *n* Euphemismus *m*. **~tic** *adj*, **-ally** *adv* verhüllend

euro /ˈjʊərəʊ/ *n* Euro *m*. **E~cheque** *n* Euroscheck *m*. **E~land** *n* Euroland *nt*

Europe /ˈjʊərəp/ *n* Europa *nt*

European /jʊərəˈpiːən/ *adj* europäisch; **~ Union** Europäische Union *f* ● *n* Europäer(in) *m*(*f*)

eurosceptic /ˈjʊərəʊskeptɪk/ *n* Euroskeptiker(in) *m*(*f*)

evacuat|e /ɪˈvækjʊeɪt/ *vt* evakuieren; räumen (*building, area*). **~ion** *n* Evakuierung *f*, Räumung *f*

evade /ɪˈveɪd/ *vt* sich entziehen (+ *dat*); hinterziehen (*taxes*)

evaluat|e /ɪvæljʊˈeɪt/ *vt* einschätzen **~ion** *n* Beurteilung *f*, Einschätzung *f*

evange|lical /iːvænˈdʒelɪkl/ *adj* evangelisch. **~list** *n* Evangelist *m*

evaporat|e /ɪˈvæpəreɪt/ *vi* verdunsten. **~ion** *n* Verdampfung *f*

evasion /ɪˈveɪʒn/ *n* Ausweichen *nt*; **tax ~** Steuerhinterziehung *f*

evasive /ɪˈveɪsɪv/ *adj* ausweichend; **be ~** ausweichen

even /ˈiːvn/ *adj* (*level*) eben; (*same, equal*) gleich; (*regular*) gleichmäßig; (*number*) gerade; **get ~ with** 🅸 es jdm heimzahlen ● *adv* sogar, selbst; **~ so** trotzdem; **not ~** nicht einmal ● *vt* **~ the score** ausgleichen

evening /ˈiːvnɪŋ/ *n* Abend *m*; **this ~** heute Abend; **in the ~** abends, am Abend. **~ class** *n* Abendkurs *m*

evenly /ˈiːvnlɪ/ *adv* gleichmäßig

event /ɪˈvent/ *n* Ereignis *nt*; (*function*) Veranstaltung *f*; (*Sport*) Wettbewerb *m*. **~ful** *adj* ereignisreich

eventual /ɪˈventjʊəl/ *adj* **his ~ success** der Erfolg, der ihm schließlich zuteil wurde. **~ly** *adv* schließlich

ever /ˈevə(r)/ *adv* je[mals]; **not ~** nie; **for ~** für immer; **hardly ~** fast nie; **~ since** seitdem

ˈevergreen *n* immergrüner Strauch *m*/ (*tree*) Baum *m*

everˈlasting *adj* ewig

every /ˈevrɪ/ *adj* jede(r,s); **~ one** jede(r,s) Einzelne; **~ other day** jeden zweiten Tag

every: ~body *pron* jeder[mann]; alle *pl*. **~day** *adj* alltäglich. **~ one** *pron* jeder[mann]; alle *pl*. **~thing** *pron* alles. **~where** *adv* überall

evict /ɪˈvɪkt/ *vt* [aus der Wohnung] hinausweisen. **~ion** *n* Ausweisung *f*

eviden|ce /ˈevɪdəns/ *n* Beweise *pl*; (*Jur*) Beweismaterial *nt*; (*testimony*) Aussage *f*; **give ~ce** aussagen. **~t** *adj* offensichtlich

evil /ˈiːvl/ *adj* böse ● *n* Böse *nt*

evoke /ɪˈvəʊk/ *vt* heraufbeschwören

evolution /iːvəˈluːʃn/ *n* Evolution *f*

e

evolve /ɪ'vɒlv/ *vt* entwickeln ● *vi* sich entwickeln

ewe /ju:/ *n* Schaf *nt*

exact /ɪg'zækt/ *adj* genau; **not ~ly** nicht gerade. **~ness** *n* Genauigkeit *f*

exaggerat|e /ɪg'zædʒəreɪt/ *vt/i* übertreiben. **~ion** *n* Übertreibung *f*

exam /ɪg'zæm/ *n* [I] Prüfung *f*

examination /ɪgzæmɪ'neɪʃn/ *n* Untersuchung *f*; (*Sch*) Prüfung *f*

examine /ɪg'zæmɪn/ *vt* untersuchen; (*Sch*) prüfen

example /ɪg'zɑ:mpl/ *n* Beispiel *nt* (**of** für); **for ~** zum Beispiel; **make an ~ of** ein Exempel statuieren an (+ *dat*)

exasperat|e /ɪg'zæspəreɪt/ *vt* zur Verzweiflung treiben. **~ion** *n* Verzweiflung *f*

excavat|e /'ekskəveɪt/ *vt* ausschachten; ausgraben (*site*). **~ion** *n* Ausgrabung *f*

exceed /ɪk'si:d/ *vt* übersteigen. **~ingly** *adv* äußerst

excel /ɪk'sel/ *v* (*pt/pp* **excelled**) *vi* sich auszeichnen ● *vt* **~ oneself** sich selbst übertreffen

excellen|ce /'eksələns/ *n* Vorzüglichkeit *f*. **~t** *adj* ausgezeichnet, vorzüglich

except /ɪk'sept/ *prep* außer (+ *dat*); **~ for** abgesehen von ● *vt* ausnehmen

exception /ɪk'sepʃn/ *n* Ausnahme *f*. **~al** *adj* außergewöhnlich

excerpt /'eksɜ:pt/ *n* Auszug *m*

excess /ɪk'ses/ *n* Übermaß *nt* (**of** an + *dat*); (*surplus*) Überschuss *m*; **~es** *pl* Exzesse *pl*

excessive /ɪk'sesɪv/ *adj* übermäßig

exchange /ɪks'tʃeɪndʒ/ *n* Austausch *m*; (*Teleph*) Fernsprechamt *nt*; (*Comm*) [Geld]wechsel *m*; **in ~** dafür ● *vt* austauschen (**for** gegen); tauschen (*places*). **~ rate** *n* Wechselkurs *m*

excitable /ɪk'saɪtəbl/ *adj* [leicht] erregbar

excit|e /ɪk'saɪt/ *vt* aufregen; (*cause*) erregen. **~ed** *adj* aufgeregt; **get ~ed** sich aufregen. **~ement** *n* Aufregung *f*; Erregung *f*. **~ing** *adj* aufregend; (*story*) spannend

exclaim /ɪk'skleɪm/ *vt/i* ausrufen

exclamation /eksklə'meɪʃn/ *n* Ausruf *m*. **~ mark** *n*, (*Amer*) **~ point** *n* Ausrufezeichen *nt*

exclu|de /ɪk'sklu:d/ *vt* ausschließen. **~ding** *prep* ausschließlich (+ *gen*). **~sion** *n* Ausschluss *m*

exclusive /ɪk'sklu:sɪv/ *adj* ausschließlich; (*select*) exklusiv

excrement /'ekskrɪmənt/ *n* Kot *m*

excrete /ɪk'skri:t/ *vt* ausscheiden

excruciating /ɪk'skru:ʃɪeɪtɪŋ/ *adj* grässlich

excursion /ɪk'skɜ:ʃn/ *n* Ausflug *m*

excusable /ɪk'skju:zəbl/ *adj* entschuldbar

excuse[1] /ɪk'skju:s/ *n* Entschuldigung *f*; (*pretext*) Ausrede *f*

excuse[2] /ɪk'skju:z/ *vt* entschuldigen; **~ me!** Entschuldigung!

ex-di'rectory *adj* **be ~** nicht im Telefonbuch stehen

execute /'eksɪkju:t/ *vt* ausführen; (*put to death*) hinrichten

execution /eksɪ'kju:ʃn/ *n* Ausführung *f*; Hinrichtung *f*

executive /ɪg'zekjʊtɪv/ *adj* leitend ● *n* leitende(r) Angestellte(r) *m/f*; (*Pol*) Exekutive *f*

exemplary /ɪg'zemplərɪ/ *adj* beispielhaft

exemplify /ɪg'zemplɪfaɪ/ *vt* (*pt/pp* **-ied**) veranschaulichen

exempt /ɪg'zempt/ *adj* befreit ● *vt* befreien (**from** von). **~ion** *n* Befreiung *f*

exercise /'eksəsaɪz/ *n* Übung *f*; **physical ~** körperliche Bewegung *f* ● *vt* (*use*) ausüben; bewegen (*horse*) ● *vi* sich bewegen. **~ book** *n* [Schul]heft *nt*

exert /ɪg'zɜːt/ *vt* ausüben; **~ oneself** sich anstrengen. **~ion** *n* Anstrengung *f*

exhale /eks'heɪl/ *vt/i* ausatmen

exhaust /ɪg'zɔːst/ *n* (*Auto*) Auspuff *m*; (*fumes*) Abgase *pl* ● *vt* erschöpfen. **~ed** *adj* erschöpft. **~ing** *adj* anstrengend. **~ion** *n* Erschöpfung *f*. **~ive** *adj* (*fig*) erschöpfend

exhibit /ɪg'zɪbɪt/ *n* Ausstellungsstück *nt*; (*Jur*) Beweisstück *nt* ● *vt* ausstellen

exhibition /eksɪ'bɪʃn/ *n* Ausstellung *f*; (*Univ*) Stipendium *nt*. **~ist** *n* Exhibitionist(in) *m(f)*

exhibitor /ɪg'zɪbɪtə(r)/ *n* Aussteller *m*

exhilarat|ing /ɪg'zɪləreɪtɪŋ/ *adj* berauschend. **~ion** *n* Hochgefühl *nt*

exhume /ɪg'zjuːm/ *vt* exhumieren

exile /'eksaɪl/ *n* Exil *nt*; (*person*) im Exil Lebende(r) *m/f* ● *vt* ins Exil schicken

exist /ɪg'zɪst/ *vi* bestehen, existieren. **~ence** *n* Existenz *f*; **be in ~ence** existieren

exit /'eksɪt/ *n* Ausgang *m*; (*Auto*) Ausfahrt *f*; (*Theat*) Abgang *m*

exorbitant /ɪg'zɔːbɪtənt/ *adj* übermäßig hoch

exotic /ɪg'zɒtɪk/ *adj* exotisch

expand /ɪk'spænd/ *vt* ausdehnen; (*explain better*) weiter ausführen ● *vi* sich ausdehnen; (*Comm*) expandieren

expans|e /ɪk'spæns/ *n* Weite *f*. **~ion** *n* Ausdehnung *f*; (*Techn, Pol, Comm*) Expansion *f*

expect /ɪk'spekt/ *vt* erwarten; (*suppose*) annehmen; **I ~ so** wahrscheinlich

expectan|cy /ɪk'spektənsɪ/ *n* Erwartung *f*. **~t** *adj* erwartungsvoll; **~t mother** werdende Mutter *f*

expectation /ekspek'teɪʃn/ *n* Erwartung *f*

expedient /ɪk'spiːdɪənt/ *adj* zweckdienlich

expedite /'ekspɪdaɪt/ *vt* beschleunigen

expedition /ekspɪ'dɪʃn/ *n* Expedition *f*

expel /ɪk'spel/ *vt* (*pt/pp* **expelled**) ausweisen (**from** aus); (*from school*) von der Schule verweisen

expenditure /ɪk'spendɪtʃə(r)/ *n* Ausgaben *pl*

expense /ɪk'spens/ *n* Kosten *pl*; **business ~s** *pl* Spesen *pl*; **at my ~** auf meine Kosten

expensive /ɪk'spensɪv/ *adj* teuer

experience /ɪk'spɪərɪəns/ *n* Erfahrung *f*; (*event*) Erlebnis *nt* ● *vt* erleben. **~d** *adj* erfahren

experiment /ɪk'sperɪmənt/ *n* Versuch *m*, Experiment *nt* ● /-ment/ *vi* experimentieren. **~al** *adj* experimentell

expert /'ekspɜːt/ *adj* fachmännisch ● *n* Fachmann *m*, Experte *m*

expertise /ekspɜː'tiːz/ *n* Sachkenntnis *f*

expire /ɪk'spaɪə(r)/ *vi* ablaufen

expiry /ɪk'spaɪərɪ/ *n* Ablauf *m*

explain /ɪk'spleɪn/ *vt* erklären

explana|tion /eksplə'neɪʃn/ *n* Erklärung *f*. **~tory** *adj* erklärend

explicit /ɪk'splɪsɪt/ *adj* deutlich

explode /ɪk'spləʊd/ *vi* explodieren ● *vt* zur Explosion bringen

e

exploit[1] /ˈeksplɔɪt/ *n* [Helden]tat *f*

exploit[2] /ɪkˈsplɔɪt/ *vt* ausbeuten. **~ation** *n* Ausbeutung *f*

exploration /ekspləˈreɪʃn/ *n* Erforschung *f*

explore /ɪkˈsplɔː(r)/ *vt* erforschen. **~r** *n* Forschungsreisende(r) *m*

e

explos|ion /ɪkˈspləʊʒn/ *n* Explosion *f*. **~ive** *adj* explosiv ● *n* Sprengstoff *m*

export[1] /ˈekspɔːt/ *n* Export *m*, Ausfuhr *f*

export[2] /ɪkˈspɔːt/ *vt* exportieren, ausführen. **~er** *n* Exporteur *m*

expos|e /ɪkˈspəʊz/ *vt* freilegen; (*to danger*) aussetzen (**to** *dat*); (*reveal*) aufdecken; (*Phot*) belichten. **~ure** *n* Aussetzung *f*; (*Med*) Unterkühlung *f*; (*Phot*) Belichtung *f*; **24 ~ures** 24 Aufnahmen

express /ɪkˈspres/ *adv* (*send*) per Eilpost ● *n* (*train*) Schnellzug *m* ● *vt* ausdrücken; **~ oneself** sich ausdrücken. **~ion** *n* Ausdruck *m*. **~ive** *adj* ausdrucksvoll. **~ly** *adv* ausdrücklich

expulsion /ɪkˈspʌlʃn/ *n* Ausweisung *f*; (*Sch*) Verweisung *f* von der Schule

exquisite /ekˈskwɪzɪt/ *adj* erlesen

extend /ɪkˈstend/ *vt* verlängern; (*stretch out*) ausstrecken; (*enlarge*) vergrößern ● *vi* sich ausdehnen; (*table:*) sich ausziehen lassen

extension /ɪkˈstenʃn/ *n* Verlängerung *f*; (*to house*) Anbau *m*; (*Teleph*) Nebenanschluss *m*

extensive /ɪkˈstensɪv/ *adj* weit; (*fig*) umfassend. **~ly** *adv* viel

extent /ɪkˈstent/ *n* Ausdehnung *f*; (*scope*) Ausmaß *nt*, Umfang *m*; **to a certain ~** in gewissem Maße

exterior /ɪkˈstɪərɪə(r)/ *adj* äußere(r,s) ● *n* **the ~** das Äußere

exterminat|e /ɪkˈstɜːmɪneɪt/ *vt* ausrotten. **~ion** *n* Ausrottung *f*

external /ɪkˈstɜːnl/ *adj* äußere(r,s); **for ~ use only** (*Med*) nur äußerlich. **~ly** *adv* äußerlich

extinct /ɪkˈstɪŋkt/ *adj* ausgestorben; (*volcano*) erloschen. **~ion** *n* Aussterben *nt*

extinguish /ɪkˈstɪŋgwɪʃ/ *vt* löschen. **~er** *n* Feuerlöscher *m*

extort /ɪkˈstɔːt/ *vt* erpressen. **~ion** *n* Erpressung *f*

extortionate /ɪkˈstɔːʃənət/ *adj* übermäßig hoch

extra /ˈekstrə/ *adj* zusätzlich ● *adv* extra; (*especially*) besonders ● *n* (*Theat*) Statist(in) *m*(*f*); **~s** *pl* Nebenkosten *pl*; (*Auto*) Extras *pl*

extract[1] /ˈekstrækt/ *n* Auszug *m*

extract[2] /ɪkˈstrækt/ *vt* herausziehen; ziehen (*tooth*)

extraordinary /ɪkˈstrɔːdɪnərɪ/ *adj*, **-ily** *adv* außerordentlich; (*strange*) seltsam

extravagan|ce /ɪkˈstrævəgəns/ *n* Verschwendung *f*; **an ~ce** ein Luxus *m*. **~t** *adj* verschwenderisch

extrem|e /ɪkˈstriːm/ *adj* äußerste(r,s); (*fig*) extrem ● *n* Extrem *nt*; **in the ~e** im höchsten Grade. **~ely** *adv* äußerst. **~ist** *n* Extremist *m*

extricate /ˈekstrɪkeɪt/ *vt* befreien

extrovert /ˈekstrəvɜːt/ *n* extravertierter Mensch *m*

exuberant /ɪgˈzjuːbərənt/ *adj* überglücklich

exude /ɪgˈzjuːd/ *vt* absondern; (*fig*) ausstrahlen

exult /ɪgˈzʌlt/ *vi* frohlocken

eye /aɪ/ *n* Auge *nt*; (*of needle*) Öhr *nt*; (*for hook*) Öse *f*; **keep an ~ on** aufpassen auf (+ *acc*) ● *vt* (*pt/pp* **eyed**, *pres p* **ey[e]ing**) ansehen

eye: ~brow *n* Augenbraue *f*. **~lash** *n* Wimper *f*. **~lid** *n* Augenlid *nt.* **~-shadow** *n* Lidschatten *m.* **~sight** *n* Sehkraft *f.* **~sore** *n* ① Schandfleck *m.* **~witness** *n* Augenzeuge *m*

Ff

fable /'feɪbl/ *n* Fabel *f*
fabric /'fæbrɪk/ *n* Stoff *m*
fabrication /fæbrɪ'keɪʃn/ *n* Erfindung *f*
fabulous /'fæbjʊləs/ *adj* ① phantastisch
façade /fə'sɑ:d/ *n* Fassade *f*
face /feɪs/ *n* Gesicht *nt*; (*surface*) Fläche *f*; (*of clock*) Zifferblatt *nt*; **pull ~s** Gesichter schneiden; **in the ~ of** angesichts (+ *gen*); **on the ~ of it** allem Anschein nach ● *vt/i* gegenüberstehen (+ *dat*); **~ north** (*house:*) nach Norden liegen; **~ the fact that** sich damit abfinden, dass
face: ~-flannel *n* Waschlappen *m.* **~less** *adj* anonym. **~-lift** *n* Gesichtsstraffung *f*
facet /'fæsɪt/ *n* Facette *f*; (*fig*) Aspekt *m*
facetious /fə'si:ʃəs/ *adj* spöttisch
facial /'feɪʃl/ *adj* Gesichts-
facile /'fæsaɪl/ *adj* oberflächlich
facilitate /fə'sɪlɪteɪt/ *vt* erleichtern
facility /fə'sɪlətɪ/ *n* Leichtigkeit *f*; (*skill*) Gewandtheit *f*; **~ies** *pl* Einrichtungen *pl*
facsimile /fæk'sɪməlɪ/ *n* Faksimile *nt*
fact /fækt/ *n* Tatsache *f*; **in ~** tatsächlich; (*actually*) eigentlich
faction /'fækʃn/ *n* Gruppe *f*
factor /'fæktə(r)/ *n* Faktor *m*
factory /'fæktərɪ/ *n* Fabrik *f*
factual /'fæktʃʊəl/ *adj* sachlich
faculty /'fækəltɪ/ *n* Fähigkeit *f*; (*Univ*) Fakultät *f*
fad /fæd/ *n* Fimmel *m*
fade /feɪd/ *vi* verblassen; (*material:*) verbleichen; (*sound:*) abklingen; (*flower:*) verwelken.
fag /fæg/ *n* (*chore*) Plage *f*; (①: *cigarette*) Zigarette *f*
fail /feɪl/ *n* **without ~** unbedingt ● *vi* (*attempt:*) scheitern; (*grow weak*) nachlassen; (*break down*) versagen; (*in exam*) durchfallen; **~ to do sth** etw nicht tun ● *vt* nicht bestehen (*exam*); durchfallen lassen (*candidate*); (*disappoint*) enttäuschen
failing /'feɪlɪŋ/ *n* Fehler *m*
failure /'feɪljə(r)/ *n* Misserfolg *m*; (*breakdown*) Versagen *nt*; (*person*) Versager *m*
faint /feɪnt/ *adj* (**-er, -est**) schwach; **I feel ~** mir ist schwach ● *n* Ohnmacht *f* ● *vi* ohnmächtig werden. **~ness** *n* Schwäche *f*
fair[1] /feə(r)/ *n* Jahrmarkt *m*; (*Comm*) Messe *f*
fair[2] *adj* (**-er, -est**) (*hair*) blond; (*skin*) hell; (*weather*) heiter; (*just*) gerecht, fair; (*quite good*) ziemlich gut; (*Sch*) genügend; **a ~ amount** ziemlich viel ● *adv* **play ~** fair sein. **~ly** *adv* gerecht; (*rather*) ziemlich. **~ness** *n* Blondheit *f*; Helle *f*; Gerechtigkeit *f*; (*Sport*) Fairness *f*
fairy /'feərɪ/ *n* Elfe *f*; **good/wicked ~** gute/böse Fee *f*. **~ story, ~-tale** *n* Märchen *nt*
faith /feɪθ/ *n* Glaube *m*; (*trust*) Vertrauen *nt* (**in** zu)
faithful /'feɪθfl/ *adj* treu; (*exact*) genau; **Yours ~ly** Hochachtungsvoll. **~ness** *n* Treue *f*; Genauigkeit *f*
fake /feɪk/ *adj* falsch ● *n* Fälschung *f*; (*person*) Schwindler *m* ● *vt* fäl-

schen; (*pretend*) vortäuschen

falcon /'fɔːlkən/ *n* Falke *m*

fall /fɔːl/ *n* Fall *m*; (*heavy*) Sturz *m*; (*in prices*) Fallen *nt*; (*Amer: autumn*) Herbst *m*; **have a ~** fallen ● *vi* (*pt* **fell**, *pp* **fallen**) fallen; (*heavily*) stürzen; (*night:*) anbrechen; **~ in love** sich verlieben; **~ back on** zurückgreifen auf (+ *acc*); **~ for s.o.** [T] sich in jdn verlieben; **~ for sth** [T] auf etw (*acc*) hereinfallen. **~ about** *vi* (*with laughter*) sich [vor Lachen] kringeln. **~ down** *vi* umfallen; (*thing:*) herunterfallen; (*building:*) einstürzen. **~ in** *vi* hineinfallen; (*collapse*) einfallen; (*Mil*) antreten; **~ in with** sich anschließen (+ *dat*). **~ off** *vi* herunterfallen; (*diminish*) abnehmen. **~ out** *vi* herausfallen; (*hair:*) ausfallen; (*quarrel*) sich überwerfen. **~ over** *vi* hinfallen. **~ through** *vi* durchfallen; (*plan:*) ins Wasser fallen

fallacy /'fæləsɪ/ *n* Irrtum *m*

fallible /'fæləbl/ *adj* fehlbar

'fall-out *n* [radioaktiver] Niederschlag *m*

false /fɔːls/ *adj* falsch; (*artificial*) künstlich. **~hood** *n* Unwahrheit *f*. **~ly** *adv* falsch

false 'teeth *npl* [künstliches] Gebiss *nt*

falsify /'fɔːlsɪfaɪ/ *vt* (*pt/pp* **-ied**) fälschen

falter /'fɔːltə(r)/ *vi* zögern

fame /feɪm/ *n* Ruhm *m*.

familiar /fə'mɪljə(r)/ *adj* vertraut; (*known*) bekannt; **too ~** familiär. **~ity** *n* Vertrautheit *f*. **~ize** *vt* vertraut machen (**with** mit)

family /'fæməlɪ/ *n* Familie *f*

family: ~ 'doctor *n* Hausarzt *m*. **~ 'life** *n* Familienleben *nt*. **~ 'planning** *n* Familienplanung *f*. **~ 'tree** *n* Stammbaum *m*

famine /'fæmɪn/ *n* Hungersnot *f*

famished /'fæmɪʃt/ *adj* sehr hungrig

famous /'feɪməs/ *adj* berühmt

fan¹ /fæn/ *n* Fächer *m*; (*Techn*) Ventilator *m*

fan² *n* (*admirer*) Fan *m*

fanatic /fə'nætɪk/ *n* Fanatiker *m*. **~al** *adj* fanatisch. **~ism** *n* Fanatismus *m*

fanciful /'fænsɪfl/ *adj* phantastisch; (*imaginative*) phantasiereich

fancy /'fænsɪ/ *n* Phantasie *f*; **I have taken a real ~ to him** er hat es mir angetan ● *adj* ausgefallen ● *vt* (*believe*) meinen; (*imagine*) sich (*dat*) einbilden; ([T]: *want*) Lust haben auf (+ *acc*); **~ that!** stell dir vor! (*really*) tatsächlich! **~ 'dress** *n* Kostüm *nt*

fanfare /'fænfeə(r)/ *n* Fanfare *f*

fang /fæŋ/ *n* Fangzahn *m*

'fan heater *n* Heizlüfter *m*

fantas|ize /'fæntəsaɪz/ *vi* phantasieren. **~tic** *adj* phantastisch. **~y** *n* Phantasie *f*

far /fɑː(r)/ *adv* weit; (*much*) viel; **by ~** bei weitem; **~ away** weit weg; **as ~ as I know** soviel ich weiß; **as ~ as the church** bis zur Kirche ● *adj* **at the ~ end** am anderen Ende; **the F~ East** der Ferne Osten

farc|e /fɑːs/ *n* Farce *f*. **~ical** *adj* lächerlich

fare /feə(r)/ *n* Fahrpreis *m*; (*money*) Fahrgeld *nt*; (*food*) Kost *f*; **air ~** Flugpreis *m*

farewell /feə'wel/ *int* (*literary*) lebe wohl! ● *n* Lebewohl *nt*

far-'fetched *adj* weit hergeholt

farm /fɑːm/ *n* Bauernhof *m* ● *vi* Landwirtschaft betreiben ● *vt* bewirtschaften (*land*). **~er** *n* Landwirt *m*

farm: ~house *n* Bauernhaus *nt*. **~ing** *n* Landwirtschaft *f*.

~yard *n* Hof *m*

far: ~-'reaching *adj* weit reichend. **~-'sighted** *adj* (*fig*) umsichtig; (*Amer: long-sighted*) weitsichtig

farther /'fɑ:ðə(r)/ *adv* weiter; **~ off** weiter entfernt

fascinat|e /'fæsɪneɪt/ *vt* faszinieren. **~ing** *adj* faszinierend. **~ion** *n* Faszination *f*

fascis|m /'fæʃɪzm/ *n* Faschismus *m*. **~t** *n* Faschist *m* ● *adj* faschistisch

fashion /'fæʃn/ *n* Mode *f*; (*manner*) Art *f*. **~able** *adj*, **-bly** *adv* modisch

fast /fɑ:st/ *adj* & *adv* (**-er, -est**) schnell; (*firm*) fest; (*colour*) waschecht; **be ~** (*clock:*) vorgehen; **be ~ asleep** fest schlafen

fasten /'fɑ:sn/ *vt* zumachen; (*fix*) befestigen (**to** an + *dat*). **~er** *n*, **~ing** *n* Verschluss *m*

fastidious /fə'stɪdɪəs/ *adj* wählerisch; (*particular*) penibel

fat /fæt/ *adj* (**fatter, fattest**) dick; (*meat*) fett ● *n* Fett *nt*

fatal /'feɪtl/ *adj* tödlich; (*error*) verhängnisvoll. **~ity** *n* Todesopfer *nt*. **~ly** *adv* tödlich

fate /feɪt/ *n* Schicksal *nt*. **~ful** *adj* verhängnisvoll

'fat-head *n* [!] Dummkopf *m*

father /'fɒ:ðə(r)/ *n* Vater *m*; **F ~ Christmas** der Weihnachtsmann ● *vt* zeugen

father: ~hood *n* Vaterschaft *f*. **~-in-law** *n* (*pl* **~s-in-law**) Schwiegervater *m*. **~ly** *adj* väterlich

fathom /'fæðəm/ *n* (*Naut*) Faden *m* ● *vt* verstehen

fatigue /fə'ti:g/ *n* Ermüdung *f*

fatten /'fætn/ *vt* mästen (*animal*)

fatty /'fætɪ/ *adj* fett; (*foods*) fetthaltig

fatuous /'fætjʊəs/ *adj* albern

fault /fɔ:lt/ *n* Fehler *m*; (*Techn*) Defekt *m*; (*Geology*) Verwerfung *f*; **at ~** im Unrecht; **find ~ with** etwas auszusetzen haben an (+ *dat*); **it's your ~** du bist schuld. **~less** *adj* fehlerfrei

faulty /'fɔ:ltɪ/ *adj* fehlerhaft

favour /'feɪvə(r)/ *n* Gunst *f*; **I am in ~** ich bin dafür; **do s.o. a ~** jdm einen Gefallen tun ● *vt* begünstigen; (*prefer*) bevorzugen. **~able** *adj*, **-bly** *adv* günstig; (*reply*) positiv

favourit|e /'feɪvərɪt/ *adj* Lieblings- ● *n* Liebling *m*; (*Sport*) Favorit(in) *m*(*f*). **~ism** *n* Bevorzugung *f*

fawn /fɔ:n/ *adj* rehbraun ● *n* Hirschkalb *nt*

fax /fæks/ *n* Fax *nt* ● *vt* faxen (**s.o.** jdm). **~ machine** *n* Faxgerät *nt*

fear /fɪə(r)/ *n* Furcht *f*, Angst *f* (**of** vor + *dat*) ● *vt/i* fürchten

fear|ful /'fɪəfl/ *adj* besorgt; (*awful*) furchtbar. **~less** *adj* furchtlos

feas|ibility /fi:zə'bɪlətɪ/ *n* Durchführbarkeit *f*. **~ible** *adj* durchführbar; (*possible*) möglich

feast /fi:st/ *n* Festmahl *nt*; (*Relig*) Fest *nt* ● *vi* **~ [on]** schmausen

feat /fi:t/ *n* Leistung *f*

feather /'feðə(r)/ *n* Feder *f*

feature /'fi:tʃə(r)/ *n* Gesichtszug *m*; (*quality*) Merkmal *nt*; (*article*) Feature *nt* ● *vt* darstellen

February /'februərɪ/ *n* Februar *m*

fed /fed/ *see* **feed** ● *adj* **be ~ up** [!] die Nase voll haben (**with** von)

federal /'fedərəl/ *adj* Bundes-

federation /fedə'reɪʃn/ *n* Föderation *f*

fee /fi:/ *n* Gebühr *f*; (*professional*) Honorar *nt*

feeble /'fi:bl/ *adj* (**-r, -st**), **-bly** *adv* schwach

f

feed /fi:d/ *n* Futter *nt*; (*for baby*) Essen *nt* ● *v* (*pt/pp* **fed**) ● *vt* füttern; (*support*) ernähren; (*into machine*) eingeben; speisen (*computer*) ● *vi* sich ernähren (**on** von)

'feedback *n* Feedback *nt*

feel /fi:l/ *v* (*pt/pp* **felt**) ● *vt* fühlen; (*experience*) empfinden; (*think*) meinen ● *vi* sich fühlen; ~ **soft/hard** sich weich/hart anfühlen; **I** ~ **hot/ill** mir ist heiß/schlecht; **~ing** *n* Gefühl *nt*; **no hard ~ings** nichts für ungut

feet /fi:t/ *see* **foot**

feline /'fi:laɪn/ *adj* Katzen-; (*catlike*) katzenartig

fell[1] /fel/ *vt* fällen

fell[2] *see* **fall**

fellow /'feləʊ/ *n* (🅸: *man*) Kerl *m*

fellow: **~-'countryman** *n* Landsmann *m*. **~ men** *pl* Mitmenschen *pl*

felt[1] /felt/ *see* **feel**

felt[2] *n* Filz *m*. **~[-tipped] 'pen** *n* Filzstift *m*

female /'fi:meɪl/ *adj* weiblich ● *nt* Weibchen *nt*; (*pej: woman*) Weib *nt*

femin|ine /'femmɪn/ *adj* weiblich ● *n* (*Gram*) Femininum *nt*. **~inity** *n* Weiblichkeit *f*. **~ist** *adj* feministisch ● *n* Feminist(in) *m*(*f*)

fenc|e /fens/ *n* Zaun *m*; (🅸: *person*) Hehler *m* ● *vi* (*Sport*) fechten ● *vt* **~e in** einzäunen. **~er** *n* Fechter *m*. **~ing** *n* Zaun *m*; (*Sport*) Fechten *nt*

fender /'fendə(r)/ *n* Kaminvorsetzer *m*; (*Naut*) Fender *m*; (*Amer: wing*) Kotflügel *m*

ferment /fə'ment/ *vi* gären ● *vt* gären lassen

fern /fɜ:n/ *n* Farn *m*

feroc|ious /fə'rəʊʃəs/ *adj* wild. **~ity** *n* Wildheit *f*

ferry /'ferɪ/ *n* Fähre *f*

fertil|e /'fɜ:taɪl/ *adj* fruchtbar. **~ity** *n* Fruchtbarkeit *f*

fertilize /'fɜ:təlaɪz/ *vt* befruchten; düngen (*land*). **~r** *n* Dünger *m*

fervent /'fɜ:vənt/ *adj* leidenschaftlich

fervour /'fɜ:və(r)/ *n* Leidenschaft *f*

festival /'festɪvl/ *n* Fest *nt*; (*Mus, Theat*) Festspiele *pl*

festiv|e /'festɪv/ *adj* festlich. **~ities** *npl* Feierlichkeiten *pl*

festoon /fe'stu:n/ *vt* behängen (**with** mit)

fetch /fetʃ/ *vt* holen; (*collect*) abholen; (*be sold for*) einbringen

fetching /'fetʃɪŋ/ *adj* anziehend

fête /feɪt/ *n* Fest *nt* ● *vt* feiern

feud /fju:d/ *n* Fehde *f*

feudal /'fju:dl/ *adj* Feudal-

fever /'fi:və(r)/ *n* Fieber *nt*. **~ish** *adj* fiebrig; (*fig*) fieberhaft

few /fju:/ *adj* (**-er, -est**) wenige; **every ~ days** alle paar Tage ● *n* **a ~** ein paar; **quite a ~** ziemlich viele

fiancé /fɪ'ɒnseɪ/ *n* Verlobte(r) *m*. **fiancée** *n* Verlobte *f*

fiasco /fɪ'æskəʊ/ *n* Fiasko *nt*

fib /fɪb/ *n* kleine Lüge

fibre /'faɪbə(r)/ *n* Faser *f*

fiction /'fɪkʃn/ *n* Erfindung *f*; **[works of] ~** Erzählungsliteratur *f*. **~al** *adj* erfunden

fictitious /fɪk'tɪʃəs/ *adj* [frei] erfunden

fiddle /'fɪdl/ *n* 🅸 Geige *f*; (*cheating*) Schwindel *m* ● *vi* herumspielen (**with** mit) ● *vt* 🅸 frisieren (*accounts*)

fiddly /'fɪdlɪ/ *adj* knifflig

fidelity /fɪ'delətɪ/ *n* Treue *f*

fidget /'fɪdʒɪt/ *vi* zappeln. **~y** *adj* zappelig

field /fi:ld/ *n* Feld *nt*; (*meadow*)

Wiese *f*; (*subject*) Gebiet *nt*

field: ~ **events** *npl* Sprung- und Wurfdisziplinen *pl*. **F**~ '**Marshal** *n* Feldmarschall *m*

fiendish /'fi:ndɪʃ/ *adj* teuflisch

fierce /fɪəs/ *adj* (**-r, -st**) wild; (*fig*) heftig. ~**ness** *n* Wildheit *f*; (*fig*) Heftigkeit *f*

fiery /'faɪərɪ/ *adj* feurig

fifteen /fɪf'ti:n/ *adj* fünfzehn ● *n* Fünfzehn *f*. ~**th** *adj* fünfzehnte(r,s)

fifth /fɪfθ/ *adj* fünfte(r,s)

fiftieth /'fɪftɪɪθ/ *adj* fünfzigste(r,s)

fifty /'fɪftɪ/ *adj* fünfzig

fig /fɪg/ *n* Feige *f*

fight /faɪt/ *n* Kampf *m*; (*brawl*) Schlägerei *f*; (*between children, dogs*) Rauferei *f* ● *v* (*pt*/*pp* **fought**) ● *vt* kämpfen gegen; (*fig*) bekämpfen ● *vi* kämpfen; (*brawl*) sich schlagen; (*children, dogs:*) sich raufen. ~**er** *n* Kämpfer *m*; (*Aviat*) Jagdflugzeug *nt*. ~**ing** *n* Kampf *m*

figurative /'fɪgjərətɪv/ *adj* bildlich, übertragen

figure /'fɪgə(r)/ *n* (*digit*) Ziffer *f*; (*number*) Zahl *f*; (*sum*) Summe *f*; (*carving, sculpture, woman's*) Figur *f*; (*form*) Gestalt *f*; (*illustration*) Abbildung *f*; **good at** ~**s** gut im Rechnen ● *vi* (*appear*) erscheinen ● *vt* (*Amer: think*) glauben

filch /fɪltʃ/ *vt* 🅸 klauen

file[1] /faɪl/ *n* Akte *f*; (*for documents*) [Akten]ordner *m* ● *vt* ablegen (*documents*); (*Jur*) einreichen

file[2] *n* (*line*) Reihe *f*; **in single** ~ im Gänsemarsch

file[3] *n* (*Techn*) Feile *f* ● *vt* feilen

fill /fɪl/ *n* **eat one's** ~ sich satt essen ● *vt* füllen; plombieren (*tooth*) ● *vi* sich füllen. ~ **in** *vt* auffüllen; ausfüllen (*form*). ~ **out** *vt* ausfüllen (*form*). ~ **up** *vi* sich füllen ● *vt* vollfüllen; (*Auto*) volltanken; ausfüllen (*questionnaire*)

fillet /'fɪlɪt/ *n* Filet *nt* ● *vt* (*pt*/*pp* **filleted**) entgräten

filling /'fɪlɪŋ/ *n* Füllung *f*; (*of tooth*) Plombe *f*. ~ **station** *n* Tankstelle *f*

filly /'fɪlɪ/ *n* junge Stute *f*

film /fɪlm/ *n* Film *m* ● *vt*/*i* filmen; verfilmen (*book*). ~ **star** *n* Filmstar *m*

filter /'fɪltə(r)/ *n* Filter *m* ● *vt* filtern

filth /fɪlθ/ *n* Dreck *m*. ~**y** *adj* dreckig

fin /fɪn/ *n* Flosse *f*

final /'faɪnl/ *adj* letzte(r,s); (*conclusive*) endgültig ● *n* (*Sport*) Endspiel *nt*; ~**s** *pl* (*Univ*) Abschlussprüfung *f*

finale /fɪ'nɑ:lɪ/ *n* Finale *nt*

final|ist /'faɪnəlɪst/ *n* Finalist(in) *m*(*f*)

final|ize /'faɪnəlaɪz/ *vt* endgültig festlegen. ~**ly** *adv* schließlich

finance /faɪ'næns/ *n* Finanz *f* ● *vt* finanzieren

financial /faɪ'nænʃl/ *adj* finanziell

find /faɪnd/ *n* Fund *m* ● *vt* (*pt*/*pp* **found**) finden; (*establish*) feststellen; **go and** ~ holen; **try to** ~ suchen. ~ **out** *vt* herausfinden; (*learn*) erfahren ● *vi* (*enquire*) sich erkundigen

fine[1] /faɪn/ *n* Geldstrafe *f* ● *vt* zu einer Geldstrafe verurteilen

fine[2] *adj* (**-r, -st,**) **-ly** *adv* fein; (*weather*) schön; **he's** ~ es geht ihm gut ● *adv* gut; **cut it** ~ 🅸 sich (*dat*) wenig Zeit lassen

finesse /fɪ'nes/ *n* Gewandtheit *f*

finger /'fɪŋgə(r)/ *n* Finger *m* ● *vt* anfassen

finger: ~**-nail** *n* Fingernagel *m*. ~**print** *n* Fingerabdruck *m*. ~**tip** *n* Fingerspitze *f*

finicky /'fɪnɪkɪ/ *adj* knifflig; (*choosy*) wählerisch

finish /'fɪnɪʃ/ *n* Schluss *m*; (*Sport*)

f

Finish *nt*; (*line*) Ziel *nt*; (*of product*) Ausführung *f* ● *vt* beenden; (*use up*) aufbrauchen; ~ **one's drink** austrinken; ~ **reading** zu Ende lesen ● *vi* fertig werden; (*performance:*) zu Ende sein; (*runner:*) durchs Ziel gehen

Finland /'fɪnlənd/ *n* Finnland *nt*

Finn /fɪn/ *n* Finne *m*/ Finnin *f*. ~**ish** *adj* finnisch

f

fir /fɜː(r)/ *n* Tanne *f*

fire /'faɪə(r)/ *n* Feuer *nt*; (*forest, house*) Brand *m*; **be on** ~ brennen; **catch** ~ Feuer fangen; **set** ~ **to** anzünden; (*arsonist:*) in Brand stecken; **under** ~ unter Beschuss ● *vt* brennen (*pottery*); abfeuern (*shot*); schießen mit (*gun*); (Ⓘ: *dismiss*) feuern ● *vi* schießen (**at** auf + *acc*); (*engine:*) anspringen

fire: ~ **alarm** *n* Feuermelder *m*. ~ **brigade** *n* Feuerwehr *f*. ~**-engine** *n* Löschfahrzeug *nt*. ~ **extinguisher** *n* Feuerlöscher *m*. ~**man** *n* Feuerwehrmann *m*. ~**place** *n* Kamin *m*. ~**side** *n* **by** *or* **at the** ~**side** am Kamin. ~ **station** *n* Feuerwache *f*. ~**wood** *n* Brennholz *nt*. ~**work** *n* Feuerwerkskörper *m*; ~**works** *pl* (*display*) Feuerwerk *nt*

firm[1] /fɜːm/ *n* Firma *f*

firm[2] *adj* (**-er, -est**) fest; (*resolute*) entschlossen; (*strict*) streng

first /fɜːst/ *adj* & *n* erste(r,s); **at** ~ zuerst; **at** ~ **sight** auf den ersten Blick; **from the** ~ von Anfang an ● *adv* zuerst; (*firstly*) erstens

first: ~ **'aid** *n* erste Hilfe. ~**-'aid kit** *n* Verbandkasten *m*. ~**-class** *adj* erstklassig; (*Rail*) erster Klasse ● /-'-/ *adv* (*travel*) erster Klasse. ~ **'floor** *n* erster Stock; (*Amer: ground floor*) Erdgeschoss *nt*. ~**ly** *adv* erstens. ~**name** *n* Vorname *m*. ~**-rate** *adj* erstklassig

fish /fɪʃ/ *n* Fisch *m* ● *vt*/*i* fischen; (*with rod*) angeln

fish: ~**bone** *n* Gräte *f*. ~**erman** *n* Fischer *m*. ~ **'finger** *n* Fischstäbchen *nt*

fishing /'fɪʃɪŋ/ *n* Fischerei *f*. ~ **boat** *n* Fischerboot *nt*. ~**-rod** *n* Angel[rute] *f*

fish: ~**monger** /-mʌŋgə(r)/ *n* Fischhändler *m*. ~**y** *adj* Fisch-; (Ⓘ: *suspicious*) verdächtig

fission /'fɪʃn/ *n* (*Phys*) Spaltung *f*

fist /fɪst/ *n* Faust *f*

fit[1] /fɪt/ *n* (*attack*) Anfall *m*

fit[2] *adj* (**fitter, fittest**) (*suitable*) geeignet; (*healthy*) gesund; (*Sport*) fit; ~ **to eat** essbar

fit[3] *n* (*of clothes*) Sitz *m*; **be a good** ~ gut passen ● *v* (*pt*/*pp* **fitted**) ● *vi* (*be the right size*) passen ● *vt* anbringen (**to** an + *dat*); (*install*) einbauen; ~ **with** versehen mit. ~ **in** *vi* hineinpassen; (*adapt*) sich einfügen (**with** in + *acc*) ● *vt* (*accommodate*) unterbringen

fit|ness *n* Eignung *f*; **[physical]** ~**ness** Gesundheit *f*; (*Sport*) Fitness *f*. ~ **ted** *adj* eingebaut; (*garment*) tailliert

fitted: ~ **'carpet** *n* Teppichboden *m*. ~ **'kitchen** *n* Einbauküche *f*. ~ **'sheet** *n* Spannlaken *nt*

fitting /'fɪtɪŋ/ *adj* passend ● *n* (*of clothes*) Anprobe *f*; (*of shoes*) Weite *f*; (*Techn*) Zubehörteil *nt*; ~**s** *pl* Zubehör *nt*

five /faɪv/ *adj* fünf ● *n* Fünf *f*. ~**r** *n* Fünfpfundschein *m*

fix /fɪks/ *n* (*sl: drugs*) Fix *m*; **be in a** ~ Ⓘ in der Klemme sitzen ● *vt* befestigen (**to** an + *dat*); (*arrange*) festlegen; (*repair*) reparieren; (*Phot*) fixieren; ~ **a meal** Essen machen

fixed /fɪkst/ *adj* fest

fixture /'fɪkstʃə(r)/ *n* (*Sport*) Veranstaltung *f*; ~**s and fittings** zu einer Wohnung gehörende Einrichtungen *pl*

fizz /fɪz/ *vi* sprudeln

fizzle /'fɪzl/ *vi* ~ **out** verpuffen

fizzy /'fɪzɪ/ *adj* sprudelnd. ~ **drink** *n* Brause[limonade] *f*

flabbergasted /'flæbəgɑ:stɪd/ *adj* **be** ~ platt sein [!]

flabby /'flæbɪ/ *adj* schlaff

flag /flæg/ *n* Fahne *f*; (*Naut*) Flagge *f*

'**flag-pole** *n* Fahnenstange *f*

flagrant /'fleɪgrənt/ *adj* flagrant

'**flagstone** *n* [Pflaster]platte *f*

flair /fleə(r)/ *n* Begabung *f*

flake /fleɪk/ *n* Flocke *f* ● *vi* ~**[off]** abblättern

flamboyant /flæm'bɔɪənt/ *adj* extravagant

flame /fleɪm/ *n* Flamme *f*

flan /flæn/ *n* **[fruit]** ~ Obsttorte *f*

flank /flæŋk/ *n* Flanke *f*

flannel /'flænl/ *n* Flanell *m*; (*for washing*) Waschlappen *m*

flap /flæp/ *n* Klappe *f*; **in a** ~ [!] aufgeregt ● *v* (*pt/pp* **flapped**) *vi* flattern; [!] sich aufregen ● *vt* ~ **its wings** mit den Flügeln schlagen

flare /fleə(r)/ *n* Leuchtsignal *nt*. ● *vi* ~ **up** auflodern; ([!]: *get angry*) aufbrausen

flash /flæʃ/ *n* Blitz *m*; **in a** ~ [!] im Nu ● *vi* blitzen; (*repeatedly*) blinken; ~ **past** vorbeirasen

flash: ~**back** *n* Rückblende *f*. ~**er** *n* (*Auto*) Blinker *m*. ~**light** *n* (*Phot*) Blitzlicht *nt*; (*Amer: torch*) Taschenlampe *f*. ~**y** a auffällig

flask /fla:sk/ *n* Flasche *f*

flat /flæt/ *adj* (**flatter, flattest**) flach; (*surface*) eben; (*refusal*) glatt; (*beer*) schal; (*battery*) verbraucht/ (*Auto*) leer; (*tyre*) platt; (*Mus*) **A** ~ As *nt*; **B** ~ B *nt* ● *n* Wohnung *f*; ([!]: *puncture*) Reifenpanne *f*

flat: ~**ly** *adv* (*refuse*) glatt. ~ **rate** *n* Einheitspreis *m*

flatten /'flætn/ *vt* platt drücken

flatter /'flætə(r)/ *vt* schmeicheln (+ *dat*). ~**y** *n* Schmeichelei *f*

flat 'tyre *n* Reifenpanne *f*

flaunt /flɔ:nt/ *vt* prunken mit

flautist /'flɔ:tɪst/ *n* Flötist(in) *m*(*f*)

flavour /'fleɪvə(r)/ *n* Geschmack *m* ● *vt* abschmecken. ~**ing** *n* Aroma *nt*

flaw /flɔ:/ *n* Fehler *m*. ~**less** *adj* tadellos; (*complexion*) makellos

flea /fli:/ *n* Floh *m*

fleck /flek/ *n* Tupfen *m*

fled /fled/ *see* **flee**

flee /fli:/ *v* (*pt/pp* **fled**) ● *vi* fliehen (**from** vor + *dat*) ● *vt* flüchten aus

fleec|e /fli:s/ *n* Vlies *nt* ● *vt* [!] schröpfen

fleet /fli:t/ *n* Flotte *f*; (*of cars*) Wagenpark *m*

fleeting /'fli:tɪŋ/ *adj* flüchtig

Flemish /'flemɪʃ/ *adj* flämisch

flesh /fleʃ/ *n* Fleisch *nt*

flew /flu:/ *see* **fly**[2]

flex[1] /fleks/ *vt* anspannen (*muscle*)

flex[2] *n* (*Electr*) Schnur *f*

flexib|ility /fleksə'bɪlətɪ/ *n* Biegsamkeit *f*; (*fig*) Flexibilität *f*. ~**le** *adj* biegsam; (*fig*) flexibel

flick /flɪk/ *vt* schnippen

flicker /'flɪkə(r)/ *vi* flackern

flier /'flaɪə(r)/ *n* = **flyer**

flight[1] /flaɪt/ *n* (*fleeing*) Flucht *f*

flight[2] *n* (*flying*) Flug *m*; ~ **of stairs** Treppe *f*

'**flight recorder** *n* Flugschreiber *m*

flimsy /'flɪmzɪ/ *adj* dünn; (*excuse*) fadenscheinig

flinch /flɪntʃ/ *vi* zurückzucken

fling /flɪŋ/ *vt* (*pt/pp* **flung**) schleudern

flint /flɪnt/ *n* Feuerstein *m*

flip /flɪp/ *vt/i* schnippen; ~ **through** durchblättern

flippant /ˈflɪpənt/ *adj* leichtfertig

flirt /flɜːt/ *n* kokette Frau *f* ● *vi* flirten

flirtat|ion /flɜːˈteɪʃn/ *n* Flirt *m*. **~ious** *adj* kokett

flit /flɪt/ *vi* (*pt/pp* **flitted**) flattern

float /fləʊt/ *n* Schwimmer *m*; (*in procession*) Festwagen *m*; (*money*) Wechselgeld *nt* ● *vi* (*thing:*) schwimmen; (*person:*) sich treiben lassen; (*in air*) schweben

flock /flɒk/ *n* Herde *f*; (*of birds*) Schwarm *m* ● *vi* strömen

flog /flɒg/ *vt* (*pt/pp* **flogged**) auspeitschen; ([!]: *sell*) verkloppen

flood /flʌd/ *n* Überschwemmung *f*; (*fig*) Flut *f* ● *vt* überschwemmen

ˈfloodlight *n* Flutlicht *nt* ● *vt* (*pt/pp* **floodlit**) anstrahlen

floor /flɔː(r)/ *n* Fußboden *m*; (*storey*) Stock *m*

floor: ~ **board** *n* Dielenbrett *nt*. **~-polish** *n* Bohnerwachs *nt*. ~ **show** *n* Kabarettvorstellung *f*

flop /flɒp/ *n* [!] (*failure*) Reinfall *m*; (*Theat*) Durchfall *m* ● *vi* (*pt/pp* **flopped**) [!] (*fail*) durchfallen

floppy /ˈflɒpɪ/ *adj* schlapp. ~ **ˈdisc** *n* Diskette *f*

floral /ˈflɔːrl/ *adj* Blumen-

florid /ˈflɒrɪd/ *adj* (*complexion*) gerötet; (*style*) blumig

florist /ˈflɒrɪst/ *n* Blumenhändler(in) *m*(*f*)

flounder /ˈflaʊndə(r)/ *vi* zappeln

flour /ˈflaʊə(r)/ *n* Mehl *nt*

flourish /ˈflʌrɪʃ/ *n* große Geste *f*; (*scroll*) Schnörkel *m* ● *vi* gedeihen; (*fig*) blühen ● *vt* schwenken

flout /flaʊt/ *vt* missachten

flow /fləʊ/ *n* Fluss *m*; (*of traffic, blood*) Strom *m* ● *vi* fließen

flower /ˈflaʊə(r)/ *n* Blume *f* ● *vi* blühen

flower: **~-bed** *n* Blumenbeet *nt*. **~pot** *n* Blumentopf *m*. **~y** *adj* blumig

flown /fləʊn/ *see* **fly**[2]

flu /fluː/ *n* [!] Grippe *f*

fluctuat|e /ˈflʌktjʊeɪt/ *vi* schwanken. **~ion** *n* Schwankung *f*

fluent /ˈfluːənt/ *adj* fließend

fluff /flʌf/ *n* Fusseln *pl*; (*down*) Flaum *m*. **~y** *adj* flauschig

fluid /ˈfluːɪd/ *adj* flüssig, (*fig*) veränderlich ● *n* Flüssigkeit *f*

fluke /fluːk/ *n* [glücklicher] Zufall *m*

flung /flʌŋ/ *see* **fling**

fluorescent /flʊəˈresnt/ *adj* fluoreszierend

fluoride /ˈflʊəraɪd/ *n* Fluor *nt*

flush /flʌʃ/ *n* (*blush*) Erröten *nt* ● *vi* rot werden ● *vt* spülen ● *adj* in einer Ebene (**with** mit); ([!]: *affluent*) gut bei Kasse

flustered /ˈflʌstəd/ *adj* nervös

flute /fluːt/ *n* Flöte *f*

flutter /ˈflʌtə(r)/ *n* Flattern *nt* ● *vi* flattern

fly[1] /flaɪ/ *n* (*pl* **flies**) Fliege *f*

fly[2] *v* (*pt* **flew**, *pp* **flown**) ● *vi* fliegen; (*flag:*) wehen; (*rush*) sausen ● *vt* fliegen; führen (*flag*)

fly[3] *n* & **flies** *pl* (*on trousers*) Hosenschlitz *m*

flyer /ˈflaɪə(r)/ *n* Flieger(in) *m*(*f*); (*leaflet*) Flugblatt *nt*

foal /fəʊl/ *n* Fohlen *nt*

foam /fəʊm/ *n* Schaum *m*; (*synthetic*) Schaumstoff *m* ● *vi* schäumen

fob /fɒb/ *vt* (*pt/pp* **fobbed**) ~ **sth off** etw andrehen (**on s.o.** jdm); ~

s.o. **off** jdn abspeisen (**with** mit)

focal /'fəʊkl/ *n* Brenn-

focus /'fəʊkəs/ *n* Brennpunkt *m*; **in ~** scharf eingestellt ● *v* (*pt/pp* **focused** *or* **focussed**) ● *vt* einstellen (**on auf** + *acc*) ● *vi* (*fig*) sich konzentrieren (**on** auf + *acc*)

fog /fɒg/ *n* Nebel *m*

foggy /'fɒgɪ/ *adj* (**foggier, foggiest**) neblig

'fog-horn *n* Nebelhorn *nt*

foible /'fɔɪbl/ *n* Eigenart *f*

foil[1] /fɔɪl/ *n* Folie *f*; (*Culin*) Alufolie *f*

foil[2] *vt* (*thwart*) vereiteln

foil[3] *n* (*Fencing*) Florett *nt*

fold *n* Falte *f*; (*in paper*) Kniff *m* ● *vt* falten; **~ one's arms** die Arme verschränken ● *vi* sich falten lassen; (*fail*) eingehen. **~ up** *vt* zusammenfalten; zusammenklappen (*chair*) ● *vi* sich zusammenfalten/-klappen lassen; 🅃 (*business:*) eingehen

fold|er /'fəʊldə(r)/ *n* Mappe *f*. **~ing** *adj* Klapp-

foliage /'fəʊlɪɪdʒ/ *n* Blätter *pl*; (*of tree*) Laub *nt*

folk /fəʊk/ *npl* Leute *pl*

folk: ~-dance *n* Volkstanz *m*. **~-song** *n* Volkslied *nt*

follow /'fɒləʊ/ *vt/i* folgen (+ *dat*); (*pursue*) verfolgen; (*in vehicle*) nachfahren (+ *dat*). **~ up** *vt* nachgehen (+ *dat*)

follow|er /'fɒləʊə(r)/ *n* Anhänger(in) *m*(*f*). **~ing** *adj* folgend ● *n* Folgende(s) *nt*; (*supporters*) Anhängerschaft *f* ● *prep* im Anschluss an (+ *acc*)

folly /'fɒlɪ/ *n* Torheit *f*

fond /fɒnd/ *adj* (**-er, -est**) liebevoll; **be ~ of** gern haben; gern essen (*food*)

fondle /'fɒndl/ *vt* liebkosen

fondness /'fɒndnɪs/ *n* Liebe *f* (**for** zu)

food /fu:d/ *n* Essen *nt*; (*for animals*) Futter *nt*; (*groceries*) Lebensmittel *pl*. **~ poisoning** *n* Lebensmittelvergiftung *f*

food poisoning *n* Lebensmittelvergiftung *f*

fool[1] /fu:l/ *n* (*Culin*) Fruchtcreme *f*

fool[2] *n* Narr *m*; **make a ~ of oneself** sich lächerlich machen ● *vt* hereinlegen ● *vi* **~ around** herumalbern

'fool|hardy *adj* tollkühn. **~ish** *adj* dumm. **~ishness** *n* Dummheit *f*. **~proof** *adj* narrensicher

foot /fʊt/ *n* (*pl* **feet**) Fuß *m*; (*measure*) Fuß *m* (*30,48 cm*); (*of bed*) Fußende *nt*; **on ~** zu Fuß; **on one's feet** auf den Beinen; **put one's ~ in it** 🅃 ins Fettnäpfchen treten

foot: ~-and-'mouth [disease] *n* Maul- und Klauenseuche *f*. **~ball** *n* Fußball *m*. **~baller** *n* Fußballspieler *m*. **~ball pools** *npl* Fußballtoto *nt*. **~-bridge** *n* Fußgängerbrücke *f*. **~hills** *npl* Vorgebirge *nt*. **~hold** *n* Halt *m*. **~ing** *n* Halt *m*. **~lights** *npl* Rampenlicht *nt*. **~note** *n* Fußnote *f*. **~path** *n* Fußweg *m*. **~print** *n* Fußabdruck *m*. **~step** *n* Schritt *m*; **follow in s.o.'s ~steps** (*fig*) in jds Fußstapfen treten. **~wear** *n* Schuhwerk *nt*

for /fɔ:(r)/, *unstressed* /fə(r)/

● *preposition*

····➤ (*on behalf of; in place of; in favour of*) für (+ *acc*). **I did it for you** ich habe es für dich gemacht. **I work for him/for a bank** ich arbeite für ihn/für eine Bank. **be for doing sth** dafür sein, etw zu tun. **cheque/bill for £5** Scheck/Rechnung über 5 Pfund. **for nothing** umsonst.

what have you got for a cold? was haben Sie gegen Erkältungen?

····➤ (*expressing reason*) wegen (+ *gen*); (*with emotion*) aus. **famous for these wines** berühmt wegen dieser Weine *od* für diese Weine. **he was sentenced to death for murder** er wurde wegen Mordes zum Tode verurteilt. **were it not for you/your help** ohne dich/ deine Hilfe. **for fear/love of** aus Angst vor (+ *dat*)/aus Liebe zu (+ *dat*)

····➤ (*expressing purpose*) (*with action, meal*) zu (+ *dat*); (*with object*) für (+ *acc*). **it's for washing the car** es ist zum Autowaschen. **we met for a discussion** wir trafen uns zu einer Besprechung. **for pleasure** zum Vergnügen. **meat for lunch** Fleisch zum Mittagessen. **what is that for?** wofür *od* wozu ist das? **a dish for nuts** eine Schale für Nüsse

····➤ (*expressing direction*) nach (+ *dat*); (*less precise*) in Richtung. **the train for Oxford** der Zug nach Oxford. **they were heading** *or* **making for London** sie fuhren in Richtung London

····➤ (*expressing time*) (*completed process*) ... lang; (*continuing process*) seit (+ *dat*). **I lived here for two years** ich habe zwei Jahre [lang] hier gewohnt. **I have been living here for two years** ich wohne hier seit zwei Jahren. **we are staying for a week** wir werden eine Woche bleiben

····➤ (*expressing difficulty, impossibility, embarrassment etc.*) + *dat*. **it's impossible/inconvenient for her** es ist ihr unmöglich/ungelegen. **it was embarrassing for our teacher** unserem Lehrer war es peinlich

● *conjunction*

····➤ denn. **he's not coming for he has no money** er kommt nicht mit, denn er hat kein Geld

forbade /fəˈbæd/ *see* **forbid**

forbid /fəˈbɪd/ *vt* (*pt* **forbade**, *pp* **forbidden**) verbieten (**s.o.** jdm). **~ding** *adj* bedrohlich; (*stern*) streng

force /fɔːs/ *n* Kraft *f*; (*of blow*) Wucht *f*; (*violence*) Gewalt *f*; **in ~** gültig; (*in large numbers*) in großer Zahl; **come into ~** in Kraft treten; **the ~s** *pl* die Streitkräfte *pl* ● *vt* zwingen; (*break open*) aufbrechen

forced /fɔːst/ *adj* gezwungen; **~ landing** Notlandung *f*

force: ~-ˈfeed *vt* (*pt/pp* **-fed**) zwangsernähren. **~ful** *adj* energisch

forceps /ˈfɔːseps/ *n inv* Zange *f*

forcible /ˈfɔːsəbl/ *adj* gewaltsam

ford /fɔːd/ *n* Furt *f* ● *vt* durchwaten; (*in vehicle*) durchfahren

fore /fɔː(r)/ *adj* vordere(r,s)

fore: ~arm *n* Unterarm *m*. **~cast** *n* Voraussage *f*; (*for weather*) Vorhersage *f* ● *vt* (*pt/pp* **~cast**) voraussagen, vorhersagen. **~finger** *n* Zeigefinger *m*. **~gone** *adj* **be a ~gone conclusion** von vornherein feststehen. **~ground** *n* Vordergrund *m*. **~head** /ˈfɒrɪd/ *n* Stirn *f*. **~hand** *n* Vorhand *f*

foreign /ˈfɒrən/ *adj* ausländisch; (*country*) fremd; **he is ~** er ist Ausländer. **~ currency** *n* Devisen *pl*. **~er** *n* Ausländer(in) *m*(*f*). **~ language** *n* Fremdsprache *f*

Foreign: ~ Office *n* ≈ Außenministerium *nt*. **~ ˈSecretary** *n* ≈ Außenminister *m*

fore: ~leg *n* Vorderbein *nt*. **~man**

n Vorarbeiter *m*. **~most** *a* führend ● *adv* **first and ~most** zuallererst. **~name** *n* Vorname *m*. **~runner** *n* Vorläufer *m*

fore'see *vt* (*pt* **-saw**, *pp* **-seen**) voraussehen, vorhersehen. **~able** *adj* **in the ~able future** in absehbarer Zeit

'foresight *n* Weitblick *m*

forest /'fɒrɪst/ *n* Wald *m*. **~er** *n* Förster *m*

forestry /'fɒrɪstrɪ/ *n* Forstwirtschaft *f*

'foretaste *n* Vorgeschmack *m*

forever /fə'revə(r)/ *adv* für immer

fore'warn *vt* vorher warnen

foreword /'fɔ:wɜ:d/ *n* Vorwort *nt*

forfeit /'fɔ:fɪt/ *n* (*in game*) Pfand *nt* ● *vt* verwirken

forgave /fə'geɪv/ *see* **forgive**

forge /fɔ:dʒ/ *n* Schmiede *f* ● *vt* schmieden; (*counterfeit*) fälschen. **~r** *n* Fälscher *m*. **~ry** *n* Fälschung *f*

forget /fə'get/ *vt/i* (*pt* **-got**, *pp* **-gotten**) vergessen; verlernen (*language, skill*). **~ful** *adj* vergesslich. **~fulness** *n* Vergesslichkeit *f*. **~-me-not** *n* Vergissmeinnicht *nt*

forgive /fə'gɪv/ *vt* (*pt* **-gave**, *pp* **-given**) **~ s.o. for sth** jdm etw vergeben *od* verzeihen

forgot(ten) /fə'gɒt(n)/ *see* **forget**

fork /fɔ:k/ *n* Gabel *f*; (*in road*) Gabelung *f* ● *vi* (*road:*) sich gabeln; **~ right** rechts abzweigen

fork-lift 'truck *n* Gabelstapler *m*

forlorn /fə'lɔ:n/ *adj* verlassen; (*hope*) schwach

form /fɔ:m/ *n* Form *f*; (*document*) Formular *nt*; (*bench*) Bank *f*; (*Sch*) Klasse *f* ● *vt* formen (**into** zu); (*create*) bilden ● *vi* sich bilden; (*idea:*) Gestalt annehmen

formal /'fɔ:ml/ *adj* formell, förmlich. **~ity** *n* Förmlichkeit *f*; (*requirement*) Formalität *f*

format /'fɔ:mæt/ *n* Format *nt* ● *vt* formatieren

formation /fɔ:'meɪʃn/ *n* Formation *f*

former /'fɔmə(r)/ *adj* ehemalig; **the ~** der/die/das Erstere. **~ly** *adv* früher

formidable /'fɔmɪdəbl/ *adj* gewaltig

formula /'fɔ:mjʊlə/ *n* (*pl* **-ae** *or* **-s**) Formel *f*

formulate /'fɔ:mjʊleɪt/ *vt* formulieren

forsake /fə'seɪk/ *vt* (*pt* **-sook** /-sʊk/, *pp* **-saken**) verlassen

fort /fɔ:t/ *n* (*Mil*) Fort *nt*

forth /fɔ:θ/ *adv* **back and ~** hin und her; **and so ~** und so weiter

forth: ~'coming *adj* bevorstehend; (🄸: *communicative*) mitteilsam. **~right** *adj* direkt

fortieth /'fɔ:tɪɪθ/ *adj* vierzigste(r,s)

fortification /fɔ:tɪfɪ'keɪʃn/ *n* Befestigung *f*

fortify /'fɔ:tɪfaɪ/ *vt* (*pt/pp* **-ied**) befestigen; (*fig*) stärken

fortnight /'fɔ:t-/ *n* vierzehn Tage *pl*. **~ly** *adj* vierzehntäglich ● *adv* alle vierzehn Tage

fortress /'fɔ:trɪs/ *n* Festung *f*

fortunate /'fɔ:tʃʊnət/ *adj* glücklich; **be ~** Glück haben. **~ly** *adv* glüklicherweise

fortune /'fɔ:tʃu:n/ *n* Glück *nt*; (*money*) Vermögen *nt*. **~-teller** *n* Wahrsagerin *f*

forty /'fɔ:tɪ/ *adj* vierzig

forward /'fɔ:wəd/ *adv* vorwärts; (*to the front*) nach vorn ● *adj* Vorwärts-; (*presumptuous*) anmaßend ● *n* (*Sport*) Stürmer *m* ● *vt* nachsenden (*letter*). **~s** *adv* vorwärts

fossil /'fɒsl/ *n* Fossil *nt*
foster /'fɒstə(r)/ *vt* fördern; in Pflege nehmen (*child*). **~-child** *n* Pflegekind *nt*. **~-mother** *n* Pflegemutter *f*
fought /fɔ:t/ *see* **fight**
foul /faʊl/ *adj* (**-er, -est**) widerlich; (*language*) unflätig; **~ play** (*Jur*) Mord *m* ● *n* (*Sport*) Foul *nt* ● *vt* verschmutzen; (*obstruct*) blockieren; (*Sport*) foulen
found[1] /faʊnd/ *see* **find**
found[2] *vt* gründen
foundation /faʊn'deɪʃn/ *n* (*basis*) Gundlage *f*; (*charitable*) Stiftung *f*; **~s** *pl* Fundament *nt*
founder /'faʊndə(r)/ *n* Gründer(in) *m*(*f*)
foundry /'faʊndrɪ/ *n* Gießerei *f*
fountain /'faʊntɪn/ *n* Brunnen *m*
four /fɔ:(r)/ *adj* vier ● *n* Vier *f*
four: ~'teen *adj* vierzehn ● *n* Vierzehn *f*. **~'teenth** *adj* vierzehnte(r,s)
fourth /fɔ:θ/ *adj* vierte(r,s)
fowl /faʊl/ *n* Geflügel *nt*
fox /fɒks/ *n* Fuchs *m* ● *vt* (*puzzle*) verblüffen
foyer /'fɔɪeɪ/ *n* Foyer *nt*; (*in hotel*) Empfangshalle *f*
fraction /'frækʃn/ *n* Bruchteil *m*; (*Math*) Bruch *m*
fracture /'fræktʃə(r)/ *n* Bruch *m* ● *vt/i* brechen
fragile /'frædʒaɪl/ *adj* zerbrechlich
fragment /'frægmənt/ *n* Bruchstück *nt*, Fragment *nt*
fragran|ce /'freɪgrəns/ *n* Duft *m*. **~t** *adj* duftend
frail /freɪl/ *adj* (**-er, -est**) gebrechlich
frame /freɪm/ *n* Rahmen *m*; (*of spectacles*) Gestell *nt*; (*Anat*) Körperbau *m* ● *vt* einrahmen; (*fig*) formulieren; ⊠ ein Verbrechen anhängen (+ *dat*). **~work** *n* Gerüst *nt*; (*fig*) Gerippe *nt*
franc /fræŋk/ *n* (*French, Belgian*) Franc *m*; (*Swiss*) Franken *m*
France /frɑ:ns/ *n* Frankreich *nt*
franchise /'fræntʃaɪz/ *n* (*Pol*) Wahlrecht *nt*; (*Comm*) Franchise *nt*
frank /fræŋk/ *adj* offen
frankfurter /'fræŋkfɜ:tə(r)/ *n* Frankfurter *f*
frantic /'fræntɪk/ *adj*, **-ally** *adv* verzweifelt; außer sich (*dat*) (**with** vor)
fraternal /frə'tɜ:nl/ *adj* brüderlich
fraud /frɔ:d/ *n* Betrug *m*; (*person*) Betrüger(in) *m*(*f*)
fray /freɪ/ *vi* ausfransen
freak /fri:k/ *n* Missbildung *f*; (*person*) Missgeburt *f* ● *adj* anormal
freckle /'frekl/ *n* Sommersprosse *f*
free /fri:/ *adj* (**freer, freest**) frei; (*ticket, copy, time*) Frei-; (*lavish*) freigebig; **~ [of charge]** kostenlos; **set ~** freilassen; (*rescue*) befreien ● *vt* (*pt/pp* **freed**) freilassen; (*rescue*) befreien; (*disentangle*) freibekommen
free: ~dom *n* Freiheit *f*. **~hold** *n* [freier] Grundbesitz *m*. **~lance** *adj* & *adv* freiberuflich. **~ly** *adv* frei; (*voluntarily*) freiwillig; (*generously*) großzügig. **F~mason** *n* Freimaurer *m*. **~-range** *adj* **~-range eggs** Landeier *pl*. **~ 'sample** *n* Gratisprobe *f*. **~style** *n* Freistil *m*. **~way** *n* (*Amer*) Autobahn *f*
freez|e /fri:z/ *vt* (*pt* **froze**, *pp* **frozen**) einfrieren; stoppen (*wages*) ● *vi* **it's ~ing** es friert.
freez|er /'fri:zə(r)/ *n* Gefriertruhe *f*; (*upright*) Gefrierschrank *m*. **freezing** *adj* eiskalt ● *n* **five degrees below ~ing** fünf Grad unter Null

freight /freɪt/ *n* Fracht *f*. **~er** *n* Frachter *m*. **~ train** *n* Güterzug *m*

French /frentʃ/ *adj* französisch ● *n* (*Lang*) Französisch *nt*; **the ~** *pl* die Franzosen

French: ~ 'beans *npl* grüne Bohnen *pl*. **~ 'bread** *n* Stangenbrot *nt*. **~' fries** *npl* Pommes frites *pl*. **~man** *n* Franzose *m*. **~ 'window** *n* Terrassentür *f*. **~woman** *n* Französin *f*

frenzy /'frenzɪ/ *n* Raserei *f*

frequency /'fri:kwənsɪ/ *n* Häufigkeit *f*; (*Phys*) Frequenz *f*

frequent[1] /'fri:kwənt/ *adj* häufig

frequent[2] /frɪ'kwent/ *vt* regelmäßig besuchen

fresh /freʃ/ *adj* (**-er, -est**) frisch; (*new*) neu; (*cheeky*) frech

freshness /'freʃnɪs/ *n* Frische *f*

'freshwater *adj* Süßwasser-

fret /fret/ *vi* (*pt/pp* **fretted**) sich grämen. **~ful** *adj* weinerlich

'fretsaw *n* Laubsäge *f*

friction /'frɪkʃn/ *n* Reibung *f*; (*fig*) Reibereien *pl*

Friday /'fraɪdeɪ/ *n* Freitag *m*

fridge /frɪdʒ/ *n* Kühlschrank *m*

fried /fraɪd/ *see* **fry**[2] ● *adj* gebraten; **~ egg** Spiegelei *nt*

friend /frend/ *n* Freund(in) *m*(*f*). **~liness** *n* Freundlichkeit *f*. **~ly** *adj* freundlich; **~ly with** befreundet mit. **~ship** *n* Freundschaft *f*

fright /fraɪt/ *n* Schreck *m*

frighten /'fraɪtn/ *vt* Angst machen (+ *dat*); (*startle*) erschrecken; **be ~ed** Angst haben (**of** vor + *dat*). **~ing** *adj* Angst erregend

frightful /'fraɪtfl/ *adj* schrecklich

frigid /'frɪdʒɪd/ *adj* frostig; (*sexually*) frigide. **~ity** *n* Frostigkeit *f*; Frigidität *f*

frill /frɪl/ *n* Rüsche *f*; (*paper*) Manschette *f*. **~y** *adj* rüschenbesetzt

fringe /frɪndʒ/ *n* Fransen *pl*; (*of hair*) Pony *m*; (*fig: edge*) Rand *m*

frisk /frɪsk/ *vi* herumspringen ● *vt* (*search*) durchsuchen

frisky /'frɪskɪ/ *adj* lebhaft

fritter /'frɪtə(r)/ *vt* **~ [away]** verplempern [!]

frivol|ity /frɪ'vɒlətɪ/ *n* Frivolität *f*. **~ous** *adj* frivol, leichtfertig

fro /frəʊ/ *see* **to**

frock /frɒk/ *n* Kleid *nt*

frog /frɒk/ *n* Frosch *m*. **~man** *n* Froschmann *m*

frolic /'frɒlɪk/ *vi* (*pt/pp* **frolicked**) herumtollen

from /frɒm/ *prep* von (+ *dat*); (*out of*) aus (+ *dat*); (*according to*) nach (+ *dat*); **~ Monday** ab Montag; **~ that day** seit dem Tag

front /frʌnt/ *n* Vorderseite *f*; (*fig*) Fassade *f*; (*of garment*) Vorderteil *nt*; (*sea~*) Strandpromenade *f*; (*Mil, Pol, Meteorol*) Front *f*; **in ~ of** vor; **in** or **at the ~** vorne; **to the ~** nach vorne ● *adj* vordere(r,s); (*page, row*) erste(r,s); (*tooth, wheel*) Vorder-

front: ~ 'door *n* Haustür *f*. **~ 'garden** *n* Vorgarten *m*

frontier /'frʌntɪə(r)/ *n* Grenze *f*

frost /frɒst/ *n* Frost *m*; (*hoar-~*) Raureif *m*; **ten degrees of ~** zehn Grad Kälte. **~bite** *n* Erfrierung *f*. **~bitten** *adj* erfroren

frost|ed /'frɒstɪd/ *adj* **~ed glass** Mattglas *nt*. **~ing** *n* (*Amer Culin*) Zuckerguss *m*. **~y** *adj*, **-ily** *adv* frostig

froth /frɒθ/ *n* Schaum *m* ● *vi* schäumen. **~y** *adj* schaumig

frown /fraʊn/ *n* Stirnrunzeln *nt* ● *vi* die Stirn runzeln

froze /frəʊz/ *see* **freeze**

frozen /'frəʊzn/ *see* **freeze** ● *adj*

gefroren; (*Culin*) tiefgekühlt; **I'm ~** [!] mir ist eiskalt. **~ food** *n* Tiefkühlkost *f*
frugal /'fru:gl/ *adj* sparsam; (*meal*) frugal
fruit /fru:t/ *n* Frucht *f*; (*collectively*) Obst *nt*. **~ cake** *n* englischer [Tee-]kuchen *m*
fruitful *adj* fruchtbar
fruit: ~ juice *n* Obstsaft *m*. **~less** *adj* fruchtlos. **~ 'salad** *n* Obstsalat *m*
fruity /'fru:tɪ/ *adj* fruchtig
frustrat|e /frʌ'streɪt/ *vt* vereiteln; (*Psychology*) frustrieren. **~ion** *n* Frustration *f*
fry /fraɪ/ *vt*/*i* (*pt*/*pp* **fried**) [in der Pfanne] braten. **~ing-pan** *n* Bratpfanne *f*
fuel /'fju:əl/ *n* Brennstoff *m*; (*for car*) Kraftstoff *m*; (*for aircraft*) Treibstoff *m*
fugitive /'fju:dʒətɪv/ *n* Flüchtling *m*
fulfil /fʊl'fɪl/ *vt* (*pt*/*pp* **-filled**) erfüllen. **~ment** *n* Erfüllung *f*
full /fʊl/ *adj* & *adv* (**-er, -est**) voll; (*detailed*) ausführlich; (*skirt*) weit; **~ of** voll von (+ *dat*), voller (+ *gen*); **at ~ speed** in voller Fahrt ● *n* **in ~** vollständig
full: ~ 'moon *n* Vollmond *m*. **~-scale** *adj* (*model*) in Originalgröße; (*rescue, alert*) großangelegt. **~ 'stop** *n* Punkt *m*. **~-time** *adj* ganztägig ● *adv* ganztags
fully /'fʊlɪ/ *adv* völlig; (*in detail*) ausführlich
fumble /'fʌmbl/ *vi* herumfummeln (**with** an + *dat*)
fume /fju:m/ *vi* vor Wut schäumen
fumes /fju:mz/ *npl* Dämpfe *pl*; (*from car*) Abgase *pl*
fun /fʌn/ *n* Spaß *m*; **for ~** aus *od* zum Spaß; **make ~ of** sich lustig machen über (+ *acc*); **have ~!** viel Spaß!
function /'fʌŋkʃn/ *n* Funktion *f*; (*event*) Veranstaltung *f* ● *vi* funktionieren; (*serve*) dienen (**as** als). **~al** *adj* zweckmäßig
fund /fʌnd/ *n* Fonds *m*; (*fig*) Vorrat *m*; **~s** *pl* Geldmittel *pl* ● *vt* finanzieren
fundamental /fʌndə'mentl/ *adj* grundlegend; (*essential*) wesentlich
funeral /'fju:nərl/ *n* Beerdigung *f*; (*cremation*) Feuerbestattung *f*
funeral: ~ march *n* Trauermarsch *m*. **~ service** *n* Trauergottesdienst *m*
'funfair *n* Jahrmarkt *m*
fungus /'fʌŋgəs/ *n* (*pl* **-gi** /-gaɪ/) Pilz *m*
funnel /'fʌnl/ *n* Trichter *m*; (*on ship, train*) Schornstein *m*
funnily /'fʌnɪlɪ/ *adv* komisch; **~ enough** komischerweise
funny /'fʌnɪ/ *adj* komisch
fur /fɜ:(r)/ *n* Fell *nt*; (*for clothing*) Pelz *m*; (*in kettle*) Kesselstein *m*. **~ 'coat** *n* Pelzmantel *m*
furious /'fjʊərɪəs/ *adj* wütend (**with** auf + *acc*)
furnace /'fɜ:nɪs/ *n* (*Techn*) Ofen *m*
furnish /'fɜ:nɪʃ/ *vt* einrichten; (*supply*) liefern. **~ed** *adj* **~ed room** möbliertes Zimmer *nt*. **~ings** *npl* Einrichtungsgegenstände *pl*
furniture /'fɜ:nɪtʃə(r)/ *n* Möbel *pl*
further /'fɜ:ðə(r)/ *adj* weitere(r,s); **at the ~ end** am anderen Ende; **until ~ notice** bis auf weiteres ● *adv* weiter; **~ off** weiter entfernt ● *vt* fördern
furthermore /fɜ:ðə'mɔ:(r)/ *adv* außerdem
furthest /'fɜ:ðɪst/ *adj* am weitesten entfernt ● *adv* am weitesten

fury /ˈfjʊərɪ/ *n* Wut *f*
fuse¹ /fjuːz/ *n* (*of bomb*) Zünder *m*; (*cord*) Zündschnur *f*
fuse² *n* (*Electr*) Sicherung *f* ● *vt/i* verschmelzen; **the lights have ~d** die Sicherung [für das Licht] ist durchgebrannt. **~-box** *n* Sicherungskasten *m*
fuselage /ˈfjuːzəlɑːʒ/ *n* (*Aviat*) Rumpf *m*
fuss /fʌs/ *n* Getue *nt*; **make a ~ of** verwöhnen; (*caress*) liebkosen ● *vi* Umstände machen
fussy /ˈfʌsɪ/ *adj* wählerisch; (*particular*) penibel
futil|e /ˈfjuːtaɪl/ *adj* zwecklos. **~ity** *n* Zwecklosigkeit *f*
future /ˈfjuːtʃə(r)/ *adj* zukünftig ● *n* Zukunft *f*; (*Gram*) [erstes] Futur *nt*
futuristic /fjuːtʃəˈrɪstɪk/ *adj* futuristisch
fuzzy /ˈfʌzɪ/ *adj* (*hair*) kraus; (*blurred*) verschwommen

Gg

gabble /ˈgæbl/ *vi* schnell reden
gable /ˈgeɪbl/ *n* Giebel *m*
gadget /ˈgædʒɪt/ *n* [kleines] Gerät *nt*
Gaelic /ˈgeɪlɪk/ *n* Gälisch *nt*
gag /gæg/ *n* Knebel *m*; (*joke*) Witz *m*; (*Theat*) Gag *m* ● *vt* (*pt/pp* **gagged**) knebeln
gaiety /ˈgeɪətɪ/ *n* Fröhlichkeit *f*
gaily /ˈgeɪlɪ/ *adv* fröhlich
gain /geɪn/ *n* Gewinn *m*; (*increase*) Zunahme *f* ● *vt* gewinnen; (*obtain*) erlangen; **~ weight** zunehmen ● *vi* (*clock:*) vorgehen
gait /geɪt/ *n* Gang *m*
gala /ˈgɑːlə/ *n* Fest *nt* ● *attrib* Gala-
galaxy /ˈgæləksɪ/ *n* Galaxie *f*; **the G~** die Milchstraße
gale /geɪl/ *n* Sturm *m*
gallant /ˈgælənt/ *adj* tapfer; (*chivalrous*) galant. **~ry** *n* Tapferkeit *f*
ˈgall-bladder *n* Gallenblase *f*
gallery /ˈgælərɪ/ *n* Galerie *f*
galley /ˈgælɪ/ *n* (*ship's kitchen*) Kombüse *f*; **~ [proof]** [Druck-]fahne *f*
gallon /ˈgælən/ *n* Gallone *f* (*= 4,5 l; Amer = 3,785 l*)
gallop /ˈgæləp/ *n* Galopp *m* ● *vi* galoppieren
gallows /ˈgæləʊz/ *n* Galgen *m*
galore /gəˈlɔ(r)/ *adv* in Hülle und Fülle
gamble /ˈgæmbl/ *n* (*risk*) Risiko *nt* ● *vi* [um Geld] spielen; **~ on** (*rely*) sich verlassen auf (+ *acc*). **~r** *n* Spieler(in) *m*(*f*)
game /geɪm/ *n* Spiel *nt*; (*animals, birds*) Wild *nt*; **~s** (*Sch*) Sport *m* ● *adj* (*brave*) tapfer; (*willing*) bereit (**for** zu). **~keeper** *n* Wildhüter *m*
gammon /ˈgæmən/ *n* [geräucherter] Schinken *m*
gang /gæŋ/ *n* Bande *f*; (*of workmen*) Kolonne *f*
gangling /ˈgæŋglɪŋ/ *adj* schlaksig
gangmaster /ˈgæŋmɑːstə(r)/ *n* Aufseher(in) *m*(*f*) von (meist illegalen) Gelegenheitsarbeitern
gangrene /ˈgæŋgriːn/ *n* Wundbrand *m*
gangster /ˈgæŋstə(r)/ *n* Gangster *m*
gangway /ˈgæŋweɪ/ *n* Gang *m*; (*Naut, Aviat*) Gangway *f*
gaol /dʒeɪl/ *n* Gefängnis *nt* ● *vt* ins Gefängnis sperren. **~er** *n*

Gefängniswärter *m*

gap /gæp/ *n* Lücke *f*; (*interval*) Pause *f*; (*difference*) Unterschied *m*

gap|e /geɪp/ *vi* gaffen; **~e at** anstarren. **~ing** *adj* klaffend

> **gap year** Britische Schulabsolventen legen vor Universitätsbeginn oft eine einjährige Pause ein. In diesem *gap year* jobben sie, um Arbeitserfahrung zu erwerben oder Geld für ihr Studium zu verdienen. Viele reisen um die Welt, lernen die Kultur anderer Länder kennen, sammeln Auslandserfahrungen, belegen Sprachkurse oder arbeiten ehrenamtlich in Entwickungsländern.

garage /ˈgærɑːʒ/ *n* Garage *f*; (*for repairs*) Werkstatt *f*; (*for petrol*) Tankstelle *f*

garbage /ˈgɑːbɪdʒ/ *n* Müll *m*. **~ can** *n* (*Amer*) Mülleimer *m*

garbled /ˈgɑːbld/ *adj* verworren

garden /ˈgɑːdn/ *n* Garten *m*; **[public] ~s** *pl* [öffentliche] Anlagen *pl* ● *vi* im Garten arbeiten. **~er** *n* Gärtner(in) *m*(*f*). **~ing** *n* Gartenarbeit *f*

gargle /ˈgɑːgl/ *n* (*liquid*) Gurgelwasser *nt* ● *vi* gurgeln

garish /ˈgeərɪʃ/ *adj* grell

garland /ˈgɑːlənd/ *n* Girlande *f*

garlic /ˈgɑːlɪk/ *n* Knoblauch *m*

garment /ˈgɑːmənt/ *n* Kleidungsstück *nt*

garnet /ˈgɑːnɪt/ *n* Granat *m*

garnish /ˈgɑːnɪʃ/ *n* Garnierung *f* ● *vt* garnieren

garrison /ˈgærɪsn/ *n* Garnison *f*

garrulous /ˈgærʊləs/ *adj* geschwätzig

garter /ˈgɑːtə(r)/ *n* Strumpfband *nt*; (*Amer: suspender*) Strumpfhalter *m*

gas /gæs/ *n* Gas *nt*; (*Amer, fam: petrol*) Benzin *nt* ● *v* (*pt/pp* **gassed**) ● *vt* vergasen ● *vi* [T] schwatzen. **~ cooker** *n* Gasherd *m*. **~ ˈfire** *n* Gasofen *m*

gash /gæʃ/ *n* Schnitt *m*; (*wound*) klaffende Wunde *f*

gasket /ˈgæskɪt/ *n* (*Techn*) Dichtung *f*

gas: ~ mask *n* Gasmaske *f*. **~-meter** *n* Gaszähler *m*

gasoline /ˈgæsəliːn/ *n* (*Amer*) Benzin *nt*

gasp /gɑːsp/ *vi* keuchen; (*in surprise*) hörbar die Luft einziehen

ˈgas station *n* (*Amer*) Tankstelle *f*

gastric /ˈgæstrɪk/ *adj* Magen-

gastronomy /gæˈstrɒnəmɪ/ *n* Gastronomie *f*

gate /geɪt/ *n* Tor *nt*; (*to field*) Gatter *nt*; (*barrier*) Schranke *f*; (*at airport*) Flugsteig *m*

gate: ~crasher *n* ungeladener Gast *m*. **~way** *n* Tor *nt*

gather /ˈgæðə(r)/ *vt* sammeln; (*pick*) pflücken; (*conclude*) folgern (**from** aus) ● *vi* sich versammeln; (*storm:*) sich zusammenziehen. **~ing** *n* **family ~ing** Familientreffen *nt*

gaudy /ˈgɔːdɪ/ *adj* knallig

gauge /geɪdʒ/ *n* Stärke *f*; (*Rail*) Spurweite *f*; (*device*) Messinstrument *nt*

gaunt /gɔːnt/ *adj* hager

gauze /gɔːz/ *n* Gaze *f*

gave /geɪv/ *see* **give**

gawky /ˈgɔːkɪ/ *adj* schlaksig

gay /geɪ/ *adj* (**-er, -est**) fröhlich; (*homosexual*) homosexuell

gaze /geɪz/ *n* [langer] Blick *m* ● *vi* sehen; **~ at** ansehen

GB *abbr* **Great Britain**

gear /gɪə(r)/ *n* Ausrüstung *f*; (*Techn*) Getriebe *nt*; (*Auto*) Gang *m*; **change ~** schalten

gear: ~box *n* (*Auto*) Getriebe *nt*. **~-lever** *n*, (*Amer*) **~-shift** *n* Schalthebel *m*

geese /gi:s/ *see* **goose**

gel /dʒel/ *n* Gel *nt*

gelatine /ˈdʒelətɪn/ *n* Gelatine *f*

gem /dʒem/ *n* Juwel *nt*

gender /ˈdʒendə(r)/ *n* (*Gram*) Geschlecht *nt*

gene /dʒi:n/ *n* Gen *nt*

genealogy /dʒi:nɪˈælədʒɪ/ *n* Genealogie *f*

general /ˈdʒenrəl/ *adj* allgemein ● *n* General *m*; **in ~** im Allgemeinen. **~ eˈlection** *n* allgemeine Wahlen *pl*

generaliz|ation /dʒenrəlaɪˈzeɪʃn/ *n* Verallgemeinerung *f*. **~e** *vi* verallgemeinern

generally /ˈdʒenrəlɪ/ *adv* im Allgemeinen

general pracˈtitioner *n* praktischer Arzt *m*

generate /ˈdʒenəreɪt/ *vt* erzeugen

generation /dʒenəˈreɪʃn/ *n* Generation *f*

generator /ˈdʒenəreɪtə(r)/ *n* Generator *m*

generosity /dʒenəˈrɒsɪtɪ/ *n* Großzügigkeit *f*

generous /ˈdʒenərəs/ *adj* großzügig

genetic /dʒəˈnetɪk/ *adj*, **-ally** *adv* genetisch. **~ally modified** gentechnisch verändert; genmanipuliert. **~ engineering** *n* Gentechnologie *f*

Geneva /dʒɪˈni:və/ *n* Genf *nt*

genial /ˈdʒi:nɪəl/ *adj* freundlich

genitals /ˈdʒenɪtlz/ *pl* [äußere] Geschlechtsteile *pl*

genitive /ˈdʒenɪtɪv/ *adj & n* ~ [case] Genitiv *m*

genius /ˈdʒi:nɪəs/ *n* (*pl* **-uses**) Genie *nt*; (*quality*) Genialität *f*

genome /ˈdʒi:nəʊm/ *n* Genom *nt*

genre /ˈʒɑ̃rə/ *n* Gattung *f*, Genre *nt*

gent /dʒent/ *n* 🄸 Herr *m*; **the ~s** *sg* die Herrentoilette *f*

genteel /dʒenˈti:l/ *adj* vornehm

gentle /ˈdʒentl/ *adj* (**-r**, **-st**) sanft

gentleman /ˈdʒentlmən/ *n* Herr *m*; (*well-mannered*) Gentleman *m*

gent|leness /ˈdʒentlnɪs/ *n* Sanftheit *f*. **~ly** *adv* sanft

genuine /ˈdʒenjʊɪn/ *adj* echt; (*sincere*) aufrichtig. **~ly** *adv* (*honestly*) ehrlich

geograph|ical /dʒɪəˈgræfɪkl/ *adj* geographisch. **~y** *n* Geographie *f*, Erdkunde *f*

geological /dʒɪəˈlɒdʒɪkl/ *adj* geologisch

geolog|ist /dʒɪˈɒlədʒɪst/ *n* Geologe *m*/-gin *f*. **~y** *n* Geologie *f*

geometr|ic(al) /dʒɪəˈmetrɪk(l)/ *adj* geometrisch. **~y** *n* Geometrie *f*

geranium /dʒəˈreɪnɪəm/ *n* Geranie *f*

geriatric /dʒerɪˈætrɪk/ *adj* geriatrisch ● *n* geriatrischer Patient *m*

germ /dʒɜ:m/ *n* Keim *m*; **~s** *pl* 🄸 Bazillen *pl*

German /ˈdʒɜ:mən/ *adj* deutsch ● *n* (*person*) Deutsche(r) *m/f*; (*Lang*) Deutsch *nt*; **in ~** auf Deutsch; **into ~** ins Deutsche

Germanic /dʒəˈmænɪk/ *adj* germanisch

Germany /ˈdʒɜ:mənɪ/ *n* Deutschland *nt*

germinate /ˈdʒɜ:mɪneɪt/ *vi* keimen

gesticulate /dʒeˈstɪkjʊleɪt/ *vi* gestikulieren

gesture /ˈdʒestʃə(r)/ *n* Geste *f*

get /get/ *v*

pt **got**, *pp* **got** (*Amer also* **gotten**), *pres p* **getting**

● *transitive verb*

····> (*obtain, receive*) bekommen, [!] kriegen; (*procure*) besorgen; (*buy*) kaufen; (*fetch*) holen. **get a job/taxi for s.o.** jdm einen Job verschaffen/ein Taxi besorgen. **I must get some bread** ich muss Brot holen. **get permission** die Erlaubnis erhalten. **I couldn't get her on the phone** ich konnte sie nicht telefonisch erreichen

····> (*prepare*) machen (*meal*). **he got the breakfast** er machte das Frühstück

····> (*cause*) **get s.o. to do sth** jdn dazu bringen, etw zu tun. **get one's hair cut** sich (*dat*) die Haare schneiden lassen. **get one's hands dirty** sich (*dat*) die Hände schmutzig machen

····> **get the bus/train**. (*travel by*) den Bus/Zug nehmen; (*be in time for, catch*) den Bus/Zug erreichen

····> **have got** ([!]: *have*) haben. **I've got a cold** ich habe eine Erkältung

····> **have got to do sth** etw tun müssen. **I've got to hurry** ich muss mich beeilen

····> ([!]: *understand*) kapieren [!]. **I don't get it** ich kapiere nicht

● *intransitive verb*

····> (*become*) werden. **get older** älter werden. **the weather got worse** das Wetter wurde schlechter. **get to** kommen zu /nach (*town*); (*reach*) erreichen. **get dressed** sich anziehen. **get married** heiraten.

● *phrasal verbs*

● **get about** *vi* (*move*) sich bewegen; (*travel*) herumkommen; (*spread*) sich verbreiten. ● **get at** *vt* (*have access*) herankommen an (+ *acc*); ([!]: *criticize*) anmachen [!]. (*mean*) **what are you getting at?** worauf willst du hinaus? ● **get away** *vi* (*leave*) wegkommen; (*escape*) entkommen. ● **get back** *vi* zurückkommen; *vt* (*recover*) zurückbekommen; **get one's own back** sich revanchieren. ● **get by** *vi* vorbeikommen; (*manage*) sein Auskommen haben. ● **get down** *vi* heruntersteigen; *vt* (*depress*) deprimieren; **get down to** sich [heran]machen an (+ *acc*). ● **get in** *vi* (*into bus*) einsteigen; *vt* (*fetch*) hereinholen. ● **get off** *vi* (*dismount*) absteigen; (*from bus*) aussteigen; (*leave*) wegkommen; (*Jur*) freigesprochen werden; *vt* (*remove*) abbekommen. ● **get on** *vi* (*mount*) aufsteigen; (*to bus*) einsteigen; (*be on good terms*) gut auskommen (**with** mit + *dat*); (*make progress*) Fortschritte machen; **how are you getting on?** wie geht's? ● **get out** *vi* herauskommen; (*of car*) aussteigen; **get out of** (*avoid doing*) sich drücken um; *vt* (*take out*) herausholen; herausbekommen (*cork, stain*). ● **get over** *vi* hinübersteigen; *vt* (*fig*) hinwegkommen über (+ *acc*). ● **get round** *vi* herumkommen; **I never get round to it** ich komme nie dazu; *vt* herumkriegen; (*avoid*) umgehen. ● **get through** *vi* durchkommen.
● **get up** *vi* aufstehen

get: ~**away** *n* Flucht *f*. ~**-up** *n* Aufmachung *f*

ghastly /ˈgɑːstlɪ/ *adj* grässlich; (*pale*) blass

gherkin /ˈgɜːkɪn/ *n* Essiggurke *f*

ghost /gəʊst/ *n* Geist *m*, Gespenst *nt*. ~**ly** *adj* geisterhaft

ghoulish /ˈguːlɪʃ/ *adj* makaber

giant /ˈdʒaɪənt/ *n* Riese *m* ● *adj* riesig

gibberish /ˈdʒɪbərɪʃ/ *n* Kauderwelsch *nt*

giblets /ˈdʒɪblɪts/ *npl* Geflügelklein *nt*

giddiness /ˈgɪdɪnɪs/ *n* Schwindel *m*

giddy /ˈgɪdɪ/ *adj* schwindlig

gift /gɪft/ *n* Geschenk *nt*; (*to charity*) Gabe *f*; (*talent*) Begabung *f*. ~**ed** *adj* begabt

gigantic /dʒaɪˈgæntɪk/ *adj* riesig, riesengroß

giggle /ˈgɪgl/ *n* Kichern *nt* ● *vi* kichern

gild /gɪld/ *vt* vergolden

gilt /gɪlt/ *adj* vergoldet ● *n* Vergoldung *f*. ~**-edged** *adj* (*Comm*) mündelsicher

gimmick /ˈgɪmɪk/ *n* Trick *m*

gin /dʒɪn/ *n* Gin *m*

ginger /ˈdʒɪndʒə(r)/ *adj* rotblond; (*cat*) rot ● *n* Ingwer *m*. ~**bread** *n* Pfefferkuchen *m*

gingerly /ˈdʒɪndʒəlɪ/ *adv* vorsichtig

gipsy /ˈdʒɪpsɪ/ *n* = **gypsy**

giraffe /dʒɪˈrɑːf/ *n* Giraffe *f*

girder /ˈgɜːdə(r)/ *n* (*Techn*) Träger *m*

girl /gɜːl/ *n* Mädchen *nt*; (*young woman*) junge Frau *f*. ~ **band** *n* Mädchenband *f*. ~**friend** *n* Freundin *f*. ~**ish** *adj* mädchenhaft

gist /dʒɪst/ *n* **the** ~ das Wesentliche

give /gɪv/ *n* Elastizität *f* ● *v* (*pt* **gave**, *pp* **given**) ● *vt* geben/(*as present*) schenken (**to** *dat*); (*donate*) spenden; (*lecture*) halten; (*one's name*) angeben ● *vi* geben; (*yield*) nachgeben. ~ **away** *vt* verschenken; (*betray*) verraten; (*distribute*) verteilen. ~ **back** *vt* zurückgeben. ~ **in** *vt* einreichen ● *vi* (*yield*) nachgeben. ~ **off** *vt* abgeben. ~ **up** *vt*/*i* aufgeben; ~ **oneself up** sich stellen. ~ **way** *vi* nachgeben; (*Auto*) die Vorfahrt beachten

glacier /ˈglæsɪə(r)/ *n* Gletscher *m*

glad /glæd/ *adj* froh (**of** über + *acc*)

gladly /ˈglædlɪ/ *adv* gern[e]

glamorous /ˈglæmərəs/ *adj* glanzvoll; (*film star*) glamourös

glamour /ˈglæmə(r)/ *n* [betörender] Glanz *m*

glance /glɑːns/ *n* [flüchtiger] Blick *m* ● *vi* ~ **at** einen Blick werfen auf (+ *acc*). ~ **up** *vi* aufblicken

gland /glænd/ *n* Drüse *f*

glare /gleə(r)/ *n* grelles Licht *nt*; (*look*) ärgerlicher Blick *m* ● *vi* ~ **at** böse ansehen

glaring /ˈgleərɪŋ/ *adj* grell; (*mistake*) krass

glass /glɑːs/ *n* Glas *nt*; (*mirror*) Spiegel *m*; ~**es** *pl* (*spectacles*) Brille *f*. ~**y** *adj* glasig

glaze /gleɪz/ *n* Glasur *f*

gleam /gliːm/ *n* Schein *m* ● *vi* glänzen

glib /glɪb/ *adj* (*pej*) gewandt

glid|e /glaɪd/ *vi* gleiten; (*through the air*) schweben. ~**er** *n* Segelflugzeug *nt*. ~**ing** *n* Segelfliegen *nt*

glimmer /ˈglɪmə(r)/ *n* Glimmen *nt* ● *vi* glimmen

glimpse /glɪmps/ *vt* flüchtig sehen

glint /glɪnt/ *n* Blitzen *nt* ● *vi* blitzen

g

glisten /ˈglɪsn/ *vi* glitzern

glitter /ˈglɪtə(r)/ *vi* glitzern

global /ˈgləʊbl/ *adj* global

globaliz|e /ˈgləʊbəlaɪz/ *vt* globalisieren. **~ation** *n* Globalisierung *f*

globe /gləʊb/ *n* Kugel *f*; (*map*) Globus *m*

gloom /glu:m/ *n* Düsterkeit *f*; (*fig*) Pessimismus *m*

gloomy /ˈglu:mɪ/ *adj* , **-ily** *adv* düster; (*fig*) pessimistisch

glorif|y /ˈglɔ:rɪfaɪ/ *vt* (*pt/pp* **-ied**) verherrlichen

glorious /ˈglɔ:rɪəs/ *adj* herrlich; (*deed, hero*) glorreich

glory /ˈglɔ:rɪ/ *n* Ruhm *m*; (*splendour*) Pracht *f* ● *vi* ~ **in** genießen

gloss /glɒs/ *n* Glanz *m* ● *adj* Glanz- ● *vi* ~ **over** beschönigen

glossary /ˈglɒsərɪ/ *n* Glossar *nt*

glossy /ˈglɒsɪ/ *adj* glänzend

glove /glʌv/ *n* Handschuh *m*

glow /gləʊ/ *n* Glut *f*; (*of candle*) Schein *m* ● *vi* glühen; (*candle:*) scheinen. **~ing** *adj* glühend; (*account*) begeistert

glucose /ˈglu:kəʊs/ *n* Traubenzucker *m*, Glukose *f*

glue /glu:/ *n* Klebstoff *m* ● *vt* (*pres p* **gluing**) kleben (**to** an + *acc*)

glum /glʌm/ *adj* (**glummer, glummest**) niedergeschlagen

glut /glʌt/ *n* Überfluss *m* (**of** an + *dat*)

glutton /ˈglʌtən/ *n* Vielfraß *m*

GM *abbr* (**genetically modified**); ~ **crops/food** gentechnisch veränderte Feldfrüchte/Nahrungsmittel

gnash /næʃ/ *vt* ~ **one's teeth** mit den Zähnen knirschen

gnat /næt/ *n* Mücke *f*

gnaw /nɔ:/ *vt/i* nagen (**at** an + *dat*)

go /gəʊ/

3 sg pres tense **goes**; *pt* **went**; *pp* **gone**

● *intransitive verb*

····➤ gehen; (*in vehicle*) fahren. **go by air** fliegen. **where are you going?** wo gehst du hin? **I'm going to France** ich fahre nach Frankreich. **go to the doctor's/dentist's** zum Arzt/Zahnarzt gehen. **go to the theatre/cinema** ins Theater/Kino gehen. **I must go to Paris/to the doctor's** ich muss nach Paris/zum Arzt. **go shopping** einkaufen gehen. **go swimming** schwimmen gehen. **go to see s.o.** jdn besuchen [gehen]

····➤ (*leave*) weggehen; (*on journey*) abfahren. **I must go now** ich muss jetzt gehen. **we're going on Friday** wir fahren am Freitag

····➤ (*work, function*) (*engine, clock*) gehen

····➤ (*become*) werden. **go deaf** taub werden. **go mad** verrückt werden. **he went red** er wurde rot

····➤ (*pass*) (*time*) vergehen

····➤ (*disappear*) weggehen; (*coat, hat, stain*) verschwinden. **my headache/my coat/the stain has gone** mein Kopfweh/mein Mantel/der Fleck ist weg

····➤ (*turn out, progress*) gehen; verlaufen. **everything's going very well** alles geht *od* verläuft sehr gut. **how did the party go?** wie war die Party? **go smoothly/according to plan** reibungslos/planmäßig verlaufen

····➤ (*match*) zusammenpassen. **the two colours don't go [together]** die beiden Farben passen nicht zusammen

····➤ (*cease to function*) kaputtgehen; (*fuse*) durchbrennen. **his memory is going** sein Gedächtnis lässt nach

● *auxiliary verb*

····➤ **be going to** werden + *inf.* **it's going to rain** es wird regnen. **I'm not going to** ich werde es nicht tun

● *noun*

pl **goes**

····➤ (*turn*) **it's your go** du bist jetzt an der Reihe *od* dran

····➤ (*attempt*) Versuch. **have a go at doing sth** versuchen, etw zu tun. **have another go!** versuch's noch mal!

····➤ (*energy, drive*) Energie

····➤ (*in phrases*) **on the go** auf Trab. **make a go of sth** das Beste aus etw machen

● *phrasal verbs*

● **go across** *vi* hinübergehen/-fahren; *vt* überqueren. ● **go after** *vt* (*pursue*) jagen. ● **go away** *vi* weggehen/-fahren; (*on holiday or business*) verreisen. ● **go back** *vi* zurückgehen/-fahren. ● **go back on** *vt* nicht [ein]halten (*promise*). ● **go by** *vi* vorbeigehen/-fahren; (*time*) vergehen. ● **go down** *vi* hinuntergehen/-fahren; (*sun, ship*) untergehen; (*prices*) fallen; (*temperature, swelling*) zurückgehen. ● **go for** *vt* holen; ([!]: *attack*) losgehen auf (+ *acc*). ● **go in** *vi* hineingehen/-fahren; ● **go in for** teilnehmen an (+ *dat*) (*competition*); (*take up*) sich verlegen auf (+ *acc*). ● **go off** *vi* weggehen/-fahren; (*alarm clock*) klingeln; (*alarm, gun, bomb*) losgehen; (*light*) ausgehen; (*go bad*) schlecht werden; *vt*: **go off sth** von etw abkommen. ● **go off well** gut verlaufen. ● **go on** *vi* weitergehen/-fahren; (*light*) angehen; (*continue*) weitermachen; (*talking*) fortfahren; (*happen*) vorgehen. ● **go on at** [!] herumnörgeln an (+ *dat*). ● **go out** *vi* (*from home*) ausgehen; (*leave*) hinausgehen/-fahren; (*fire, light*) ausgehen; **go out to work/for a meal** arbeiten/essen gehen; **go out with s.o.** ([!]: *date s.o.*) mit jdm gehen [!]. ● **go over** *vi* hinübergehen/-fahren; *vt* (*rehearse*) durchgehen. ● **go round** *vi* herumgehen/-fahren; (*visit*) vorbeigehen; (*turn*) sich drehen; (*be enough*) reichen. ● **go through** *vi* durchgehen/-fahren; *vt* (*suffer*) durchmachen; (*rehearse*) durchgehen; (*bags*) durchsuchen. ● **go through with** *vt* zu Ende machen. ● **go under** *vi* untergehen/-fahren; (*fail*) scheitern. ● **go up** *vi* hinaufgehen/-fahren; (*lift*) hochfahren; (*prices*) steigen. ● **go without** *vt*: **go without sth** auf etw (*acc*) verzichten; *vi* darauf verzichten

ˈgo-ahead *adj* fortschrittlich; (*enterprising*) unternehmend ● *n* (*fig*) grünes Licht *nt*

goal /gəʊl/ *n* Ziel *nt*; (*sport*) Tor *nt*. **~keeper** *n* Torwart *m*. **~-post** *n* Torpfosten *m*

goat /gəʊt/ *n* Ziege *f*

gobble /ˈgɒbl/ *vt* hinunterschlingen

God, god /gɒd/ *n* Gott *m*

god: **~child** *n* Patenkind *nt.* **~-daughter** *n* Patentochter *f.* **~dess** *n* Göttin *f.* **~father** *n* Pate *m.* **~mother** *n* Patin *f.* **~parents** *npl* Paten *pl.* **~send** *n* Segen *m.* **~son** *n* Patensohn *m*

goggles /'gɒglz/ *npl* Schutzbrille *f*

going /'gəʊɪŋ/ *adj* (*price, rate*) gängig; (*concern*) gut gehend ● *n* **it is hard ~** es ist schwierig

g

gold /gəʊld/ *n* Gold *nt* ● *adj* golden

golden /'gəʊldn/ *adj* golden. **~ 'wedding** *n* goldene Hochzeit *f*

gold: **~fish** *n inv* Goldfisch *m.* **~-mine** *n* Goldgrube *f.* **~-plated** *adj* vergoldet. **~smith** *n* Goldschmied *m*

golf /gɒlf/ *n* Golf *nt*

golf: **~-club** *n* Golfklub *m*; (*implement*) Golfschläger *m.* **~-course** *n* Golfplatz *m.* **~er** *m* Golfspieler(in) *m*(*f*)

gone /gɒn/ *see* **go**

good /gʊd/ *adj* (**better, best**) gut; (*well-behaved*) brav, artig; **~ at** gut in (+ *dat*); **a ~ deal** ziemlich viel; **~ morning/evening** guten Morgen/Abend ● *n* **for ~** für immer; **do ~** Gutes tun; **do s.o. ~** jdm gut tun; **it's no ~** es ist nutzlos; (*hopeless*) da ist nichts zu machen

goodbye /gʊd'baɪ/ *int* auf Wiedersehen; (*Teleph, Radio*) auf Wiederhören

good: **G~ 'Friday** *n* Karfreitag *m.* **~-'looking** *adj* gut aussehend. **~-'natured** *adj* gutmütig

goodness /'gʊdnɪs/ *n* Güte *f*; **thank ~!** Gott sei Dank!

goods /gʊdz/ *npl* Waren *pl.* **~ train** *n* Güterzug *m*

good'will *n* Wohlwollen *nt*; (*Comm*) Goodwill *m*

gooey /'gu:ɪ/ *adj* [!] klebrig

google /'gu:gl/ ® *vt, vi* googeln

goose /gu:s/ *n* (*pl* **geese**) Gans *f*

gooseberry /'gʊzbərɪ/ *n* Stachelbeere *f*

goose: /gu:s/ **~-flesh** *n*, **~-pimples** *npl* Gänsehaut *f*

gorge /gɔ:dʒ/ *n* (*Geog*) Schlucht *f* ● *vt* **~ oneself** sich vollessen

gorgeous /'gɔ:dʒəs/ *adj* prachtvoll; [!] herrlich

gorilla /gə'rɪlə/ *n* Gorilla *m*

gormless /'gɔ:mlɪs/ *adj* [!] doof

gorse /gɔ:s/ *n inv* Stechginster *m*

gory /'gɔ:rɪ/ *adj* blutig; (*story*) blutrünstig

gosh /gɒʃ/ *int* [!] Mensch!

gospel /'gɒspl/ *n* Evangelium *nt*

gossip /'gɒsɪp/ *n* Klatsch *m*; (*person*) Klatschbase *f* ● *vi* klatschen

got /gɒt/ *see* **get; have ~** haben; **have ~ to** müssen; **have ~ to do sth** etw tun müssen

Gothic /'gɒθɪk/ *adj* gotisch

gotten /'gɒtn/ *see* **get**

goulash /'gu:læʃ/ *n* Gulasch *nt*

gourmet /'gʊəmeɪ/ *n* Feinschmecker *m*

govern /'gʌvn/ *vt/i* regieren; (*determine*) bestimmen

government /'gʌvnmənt/ *n* Regierung *f*

governor /'gʌvənə(r)/ *n* Gouverneur *m*; (*on board*) Vorstandsmitglied *nt*; (*of prison*) Direktor *m*; ([!]: *boss*) Chef *m*

gown /gaʊn/ *n* [elegantes] Kleid *nt*; (*Univ, Jur*) Talar *m*

GP *abbr* **general practitioner**

GPS *abbr* (**Global Positioning System**) GPS *nt*

grab /græb/ *vt* (*pt/pp* **grabbed**) ergreifen; **~ [hold of]** packen

grace /greɪs/ *n* Anmut *f*; (*before meal*) Tischgebet *nt*; **three days' ~** drei Tage Frist. **~ful** *adj* anmutig

gracious /'greɪʃəs/ *adj* gnädig; (*elegant*) vornehm

grade /greɪd/ *n* Stufe *f*; (*Comm*) Güteklasse *f*; (*Sch*) Note *f*; (*Amer, Sch: class*) Klasse *f*; (*Amer*) = **gradient** ● *vt* einstufen; (*Comm*) sortieren. **~ crossing** *n* (*Amer*) Bahnübergang *m*

gradient /'greɪdɪənt/ *n* Steigung *f*; (*downward*) Gefälle *nt*

gradual /'grædʒʊəl/ *adj* allmählich

graduate /'grædʒʊət/ *n* Akademiker(in) *m*(*f*)

graffiti /grə'fi:ti/ *npl* Graffiti *pl*

graft /grɑ:ft/ *n* (*Bot*) Pfropfreis *nt*; (*Med*) Transplantat *nt*; ([!]: *hard work*) Plackerei *f*

grain /greɪn/ *n* (*sand, salt, rice*) Korn *nt*; (*cereals*) Getreide *nt*; (*in wood*) Maserung *f*

gram /græm/ *n* Gramm *nt*

grammar /'græmə(r)/ *n* Grammatik *f*. **~ school** *n* ≈ Gymnasium *nt*

grammatical /grə'mætɪkl/ *adj* grammatisch

grand /grænd/ *adj* (**-er, -est**) großartig

grandad /'grændæd/ *n* [!] Opa *m*

'grandchild *n* Enkelkind *nt*

'granddaughter *n* Enkelin *f*

grandeur /'grændʒə(r)/ *n* Pracht *f*

'grandfather *n* Großvater *m*. **~ clock** *n* Standuhr *f*

grandiose /'grændɪəʊs/ *adj* grandios

grand: ~mother *n* Großmutter *f*. **~parents** *npl* Großeltern *pl*. **~ pi'ano** *n* Flügel *m*. **~son** *n* Enkel *m*. **~stand** *n* Tribüne *f*

granite /'grænɪt/ *n* Granit *m*

granny /'grænɪ/ *n* [!] Oma *f*

grant /grɑ:nt/ *n* Subvention *f*; (*Univ*) Studienbeihilfe *f* ● *vt* gewähren; (*admit*) zugeben; **take sth for ~ed** etw als selbstverständlich hinnehmen

grape /greɪp/ *n* [Wein]traube *f*; **bunch of ~s** [ganze] Weintraube *f*

grapefruit /'greɪp-/ *n invar* Grapefruit *f*

graph /grɑ:f/ grafische Darstellung *f*

graphic /'græfɪk/ *adj*, **-ally** *adv* grafisch; (*vivid*) anschaulich

'graph paper *n* Millimeterpapier *nt*

grapple /'græpl/ *vi* ringen

grasp /grɑ:sp/ *n* Griff *m* ● *vt* ergreifen; (*understand*) begreifen. **~ing** *adj* habgierig

grass /grɑ:s/ *n* Gras *nt*; (*lawn*) Rasen *m*. **~hopper** *n* Heuschrecke *f*

grassy /'grɑ:sɪ/ *adj* grasig

grate¹ /greɪt/ *n* Feuerrost *m*; (*hearth*) Kamin *m*

grate² *vt* (*Culin*) reiben

grateful /'greɪtfl/ *adj* dankbar (**to** *dat*)

grater /'greɪtə(r)/ *n* (*Culin*) Reibe *f*

gratify /'grætɪfaɪ/ *vt* (*pt/pp* **-ied**) befriedigen. **~ing** *adj* erfreulich

gratis /'grɑ:tɪs/ *adv* gratis

gratitude /'grætɪtju:d/ *n* Dankbarkeit *f*

gratuitous /grə'tju:ɪtəs/ *adj* (*uncalled for*) überflüssig

grave¹ /greɪv/ *adj* (**-r, -st**) ernst; **~ly ill** schwer krank

grave² *n* Grab *nt*. **~-digger** *n* Totengräber *m*

gravel /'grævl/ *n* Kies *m*

grave: ~stone *n* Grabstein *m*. **~yard** *n* Friedhof *m*

gravity /'grævətɪ/ *n* Ernst *m*; (*force*) Schwerkraft *f*

gravy /'greɪvɪ/ *n* [Braten]soße *f*

gray /greɪ/ *adj* (*Amer*) = **grey**

graze¹ /greɪz/ *vi* (*animal:*) weiden
graze² *n* Schürfwunde *f* ● *vt* (*car*) streifen; (*knee*) aufschürfen
grease /gri:s/ *n* Fett *nt*; (*lubricant*) Schmierfett *nt* ● *vt* einfetten; (*lubricate*) schmieren
greasy /ˈgri:sɪ/ *adj* fettig
great /greɪt/ *adj* (**-er, -est**) groß; ([!]: *marvellous*) großartig
great: **~-ˈaunt** *n* Großtante *f*. **G~ˈBritain** *n* Großbritannien *nt*. **~-ˈgrandchildren** *npl* Urenkel *pl*. **~-ˈgrandfather** *n* Urgroßvater *m*. **~-ˈgrandmother** *n* Urgroßmutter *f*
great|ly /ˈgreɪtlɪ/ *adv* sehr. **~ness** *n* Größe *f*
great-ˈuncle *n* Großonkel *m*
Greece /gri:s/ *n* Griechenland *nt*
greed /gri:d/ *n* [Hab]gier *f*
greedy /ˈgri:dɪ/ *adj* , **-ily** *adv* gierig
Greek /gri:k/ *adj* griechisch ● *n* Grieche *m*/Griechin *f*; (*Lang*) Griechisch *nt*
green /gri:n/ *adj* (**-er, -est**) grün; (*fig*) unerfahren ● *n* Grün *nt*; (*grass*) Wiese *f*; **~s** *pl* Kohl *m*; **the G~s** *pl* (*Pol*) die Grünen *pl*

> **green card** Ein offizielles Dokument, das nichtamerikanische Bürger zur Erwerbstätigkeit in den USA berechtigt. Die *green card* braucht jeder, der beabsichtigt, eine feste Stelle in den USA anzutreten. In Europa ist die grüne Karte ein vom Versicherungsverband ausgestellter grüner Ausweis, mit dem ein Kraftfahrer beim Grenzübertritt nachweist, dass er haftpflichtversichert ist.

greenery /ˈgri:nərɪ/ *n* Grün *nt*
green: **~fly** *n* Blattlaus *f*. **~grocer** *n* Obst- und Gemüsehändler *m*. **~house** *n* Gewächshaus *nt*
Greenland /ˈgri:nlənd/ *n* Grönland *nt*
greet /gri:t/ *vt* grüßen; (*welcome*) begrüßen. **~ing** *n* Gruß *m*; (*welcome*) Begrüßung *f*
grew /gru:/ *see* **grow**
grey /greɪ/ *adj* (**-er, -est**) grau ● *n* Grau *nt* ● *vi* grau werden. **~hound** *n* Windhund *m*
grid /grɪd/ *n* Gitter *nt*
grief /gri:f/ *n* Trauer *f*
grievance /ˈgri:vəns/ *n* Beschwerde *f*
grieve /gri:v/ *vi* trauern (**for** um)
grill /grɪl/ *n* Gitter *nt*; (*Culin*) Grill *m*; **mixed ~** Gemischtes *nt* vom Grill ● *vt/i* grillen; (*interrogate*) [streng] verhören
grille /grɪl/ *n* Gitter *nt*
grim /grɪm/ *adj* (**grimmer, grimmest**) ernst; (*determination*) verbissen
grimace /grɪˈmeɪs/ *n* Grimasse *f* ● *vi* Grimassen schneiden
grime /graɪm/ *n* Schmutz *m*
grimy /ˈgraɪmɪ/ *adj* schmutzig
grin /grɪn/ *n* Grinsen *nt* ● *vi* (*pt/pp* **grinned**) grinsen
grind /graɪnd/ *n* ([!]: *hard work*) Plackerei *f* ● *vt* (*pt/pp* **ground**) mahlen; (*smooth, sharpen*) schleifen; (*Amer: mince*) durchdrehen
grip /grɪp/ *n* Griff *m*; (*bag*) Reisetasche *f* ● *vt* (*pt/pp* **gripped**) ergreifen; (*hold*) festhalten
gripping /ˈgrɪpɪŋ/ *adj* fesselnd
grisly /ˈgrɪzlɪ/ *adj* grausig
gristle /ˈgrɪsl/ *n* Knorpel *m*
grit /grɪt/ *n* [grober] Sand *m*; (*for roads*) Streugut *nt*; (*courage*) Mut *m* ● *vt* (*pt/pp* **gritted**) streuen (*road*)
groan /grəʊn/ *n* Stöhnen *nt* ● *vi* stöhnen
grocer /ˈgrəʊsə(r)/ *n* Lebensmittel-

händler *m*; **~'s [shop]** Lebensmittelgeschäft *nt*. **~ies** *npl* Lebensmittel *pl*

groin /grɔɪn/ *n* (*Anat*) Leiste *f*

groom /gru:m/ *n* Bräutigam *m*; (*for horse*) Pferdepfleger(in) *m*(*f*) ● *vt* striegeln (*horse*)

groove /gru:v/ *n* Rille *f*

grope /grəʊp/ *vi* tasten (**for** nach)

gross /grəʊs/ *adj* (**-er, -est**) fett; (*coarse*) derb; (*glaring*) grob; (*Comm*) brutto; (*salary, weight*) Brutto-. **~ly** *adv* (*very*) sehr

grotesque /grəʊ'tesk/ *adj* grotesk

ground[1] /graʊnd/ *see* **grind**

ground[2] *n* Boden *m*; (*terrain*) Gelände *nt*; (*reason*) Grund *m*; (*Amer, Electr*) Erde *f*; **~s** *pl* (*park*) Anlagen *pl*; (*of coffee*) Satz *m*

ground: ~ floor *n* Erdgeschoss *nt*. **~ing** *n* Grundlage *f*. **~less** *adj* grundlos. **~sheet** *n* Bodenplane *f*. **~work** *n* Vorarbeiten *pl*

group /gru:p/ *n* Gruppe *f* ● *vt* gruppieren ● *vi* sich gruppieren

grouse *vi* [T] meckern

grovel /'grɒvl/ *vi* (*pt/pp* **grovelled**) kriechen

grow /grəʊ/ *v* (*pt* **grew**, *pp* **grown**) ● *vi* wachsen; (*become*) werden; (*increase*) zunehmen ● *vt* anbauen. **~ up** *vi* aufwachsen; (*town:*) entstehen

growl /graʊl/ *n* Knurren *nt* ● *vi* knurren

grown /grəʊn/ *see* **grow**. **~-up** *adj* erwachsen ● *n* Erwachsene(r) *m/f*

growth /grəʊθ/ *n* Wachstum *nt*; (*increase*) Zunahme *f*; (*Med*) Gewächs *nt*

grub /grʌb/ *n* (*larva*) Made *f*; ([T]: *food*) Essen *nt*

grubby /'grʌbɪ/ *adj* schmuddelig

grudg|e /grʌdʒ/ *n* Groll *m* ● *vt* **~e s.o. sth** jdm etw missgönnen. **~ing** *adj* widerwillig

gruelling /'gru:əlɪŋ/ *adj* strapaziös

gruesome /'gru:səm/ *adj* grausig

gruff /grʌf/ *adj* barsch

grumble /'grʌmbl/ *vi* schimpfen (**at** mit)

grumpy /'grʌmpɪ/ *adj* griesgrämig

grunt /grʌnt/ *n* Grunzen *nt* ● *vi* grunzen

g

guarantee /gærən'ti:/ *n* Garantie *f*; (*document*) Garantieschein *m* ● *vt* garantieren; garantieren für (*quality, success*)

guard /gɑ:d/ *n* Wache *f*; (*security*) Wächter *m*; (*on train*) ≈ Zugführer *m*; (*Techn*) Schutz *m*; **be on ~** Wache stehen; **on one's ~** auf der Hut ● *vt* bewachen; (*protect*) schützen ● *vi* **~ against** sich hüten vor (+ *dat*). **~-dog** *n* Wachhund *m*

guarded /'gɑ:dɪd/ *adj* vorsichtig

guardian /'gɑ:dɪən/ *n* Vormund *m*

guess /ges/ *n* Vermutung *f* ● *vt* erraten ● *vi* raten; (*Amer: believe*) glauben. **~work** *n* Vermutung *f*

guest /gest/ *n* Gast *m*. **~-house** *n* Pension *f*

guidance /'gaɪdəns/ *n* Führung *f*, Leitung *f*; (*advice*) Beratung *f*

guide /gaɪd/ *n* Führer(in) *m*(*f*); (*book*) Führer *m*; **[Girl] G~** Pfadfinderin *f* ● *vt* führen, leiten. **~book** *n* Führer *m*

guided /'gaɪdɪd/ *adj* **~ tour** Führung *f*

guide: ~-dog *n* Blindenhund *m*. **~lines** *npl* Richtlinien *pl*

guilt /gɪlt/ *n* Schuld *f*. **~ily** *adv* schuldbewusst

guilty /'gɪltɪ/ *adj adj* schuldig (**of** *gen*); (*look*) schuldbewusst; (*conscience*) schlecht

guinea-pig /'gɪnɪ-/ *n* Meerschweinchen *nt*; (*person*) Versuchskaninchen *nt*

guitar /gɪ'tɑ:(r)/ *n* Gitarre *f*. **~ist** *n* Gitarrist(in) *m*(*f*)

gulf /gʌlf/ *n* (*Geog*) Golf *m*; (*fig*) Kluft *f*

gull /gʌl/ *n* Möwe *f*

gullible /'gʌlɪbl/ *adj* leichtgläubig

gully /'gʌlɪ/ *n* Schlucht *f*; (*drain*) Rinne *f*

g

h

gulp /gʌlp/ *n* Schluck *m* ● *vi* schlucken ● *vt* **~ down** hinunterschlucken

gum¹ /gʌm/ *n* (*also pl* **-s**) (*Anat*) Zahnfleisch *nt*

gum² *n* Gummi[harz] *nt*; (*glue*) Klebstoff *m*; (*chewing gum*) Kaugummi *m*

gummed /gʌmd/ ● *adj* (*label*) gummiert

gun /gʌn/ *n* Schusswaffe *f*; (*pistol*) Pistole *f*; (*rifle*) Gewehr *nt*; (*cannon*) Geschütz *nt*

gun: ~fire *n* Geschützfeuer *nt*. **~man** bewaffneter Bandit *m*

gunner /'gʌnə(r)/ *n* Artillerist *m*

gunpowder *n* Schießpulver *nt*

gurgle /'gɜ:gl/ *vi* gluckern; (*of baby*) glucksen

gush /gʌʃ/ *vi* strömen; (*enthuse*) schwärmen (**over** von)

gust /gʌst/ *n* (*of wind*) Windstoß *m*; (*Naut*) Bö *f*

gusto /'gʌstəʊ/ *n* **with ~** mit Schwung

gusty /'gʌstɪ/ *adj* böig

gut /gʌt/ *n* Darm *m*; **~s** *pl* Eingeweide *pl*; (🅘: *courage*) Schneid *m* ● *vt* (*pt/pp* **gutted**) (*Culin*) ausnehmen; **~ted by fire** ausgebrannt

gutter /'gʌtə(r)/ *n* Rinnstein *m*; (*fig*) Gosse *f*; (*on roof*) Dachrinne *f*

guy /gaɪ/ *n* 🅘 Kerl *m*

guzzle /'gʌzl/ *vt/i* schlingen; (*drink*) schlürfen

gym /dʒɪm/ *n* 🅘 Turnhalle *f*; (*gymnastics*) Turnen *nt*

gymnasium /dʒɪm'neɪzɪəm/ *n* Turnhalle *f*

gymnast /'dʒɪmnæst/ *n* Turner(in) *m*(*f*). **~ics** *n* Turnen *nt*

gym shoes *pl* Turnschuhe *pl*

gynaecolog|ist /gaɪnɪ'kɒlədʒɪst/ *n* Frauenarzt *m* /-ärztin *f*. **~y** *n* Gynäkologie *f*

gypsy /'dʒɪpsɪ/ *n* Zigeuner(in) *m*(*f*)

habit /'hæbɪt/ *n* Gewohnheit *f*; (*Relig: costume*) Ordenstracht *f*; **be in the ~** die Angewohnheit haben (**of zu**)

habitat /'hæbɪtæt/ *n* Habitat *nt*

habitation /hæbɪ'teɪʃn/ *n* **unfit for human ~** für Wohnzwecke ungeeignet

habitual /hə'bɪtjʊəl/ *adj* gewohnt; (*inveterate*) gewohnheitsmäßig. **~ly** *adv* gewohnheitsmäßig; (*constantly*) ständig

hack¹ /hæk/ *n* (*writer*) Schreiberling *m*; (*hired horse*) Mietpferd *nt*

hack² *vt* hacken; **~ to pieces** zerhacken

hackneyed /'hæknɪd/ *adj* abgedroschen

'hacksaw *n* Metallsäge *f*

had /hæd/ *see* **have**

haddock /'hædək/ *n inv* Schellfisch *m*

haggard /'hægəd/ *adj* abgehärmt

haggle /'hægl/ *vi* feilschen

(over um)

hail¹ /heɪl/ *vt* begrüßen; herbeirufen (*taxi*) ● *vi* ~ **from** kommen aus

hail² *n* Hagel *m* ● *vi* hageln. ~**stone** *n* Hagelkorn *nt*

hair /heə(r)/ *n* Haar *nt*; **wash one's** ~ sich (*dat*) die Haare waschen

hair: ~**brush** *n* Haarbürste *f*. ~**cut** *n* Haarschnitt *m*; **have a** ~**cut** sich (*dat*) die Haare schneiden lassen. ~**-do** *n* [!] Frisur *f*. ~**dresser** *n* Friseur *m*/Friseuse *f*. ~**-drier** *n* Haartrockner *m*; (*hand-held*) Föhn *m*. ~**pin** *n* Haarnadel *f*. ~**pin 'bend** *n* Haarnadelkurve *f*. ~**-raising** *adj* haarsträubend. ~**-style** *n* Frisur *f*

hairy /'heərɪ/ *adj* behaart; (*excessively*) haarig; ([!] *frightening*) brenzlig

hake /heɪk/ *n inv* Seehecht *m*

half /hɑ:f/ *n* (*pl* **halves**) Hälfte *f*; **cut in** ~ halbieren; **one and a** ~ eineinhalb, anderthalb; ~ **a dozen** ein halbes Dutzend; ~ **an hour** eine halbe Stunde ● *adj & adv* halb; ~ **past two** halb drei; **[at]** ~ **price** zum halben Preis

half: ~**-'hearted** *adj* lustlos. ~**-'term** *n* schulfreie Tage nach dem halben Trimester. ~**-'timbered** *adj* Fachwerk-. ~**-'time** *n* (*Sport*) Halbzeit *f*. ~**-'way** *adj* **the** ~**-way mark/stage** die Hälfte ● *adv* auf halbem Weg

halibut /'hælɪbət/ *n inv* Heilbutt *m*

hall /hɔ:l/ *n* Halle *f*; (*room*) Saal *m*; (*Sch*) Aula *f*; (*entrance*) Flur *m*; (*mansion*) Gutshaus *nt*; ~ **of residence** (*Univ*) Studentenheim *nt*

'hallmark *n* [Feingehalts]stempel *m*; (*fig*) Kennzeichen *nt* (**of** für)

hallo /hə'ləʊ/ *int* [guten] Tag! [!] hallo!

hallucination /həlu:sɪ'neɪʃn/ *n* Halluzination *f*

halo /'heɪləʊ/ *n* (*pl* **-es**) Heiligenschein *m*; (*Astronomy*) Hof *m*

halt /hɔ:lt/ *n* Halt *m*; **come to a** ~ stehen bleiben; (*traffic*:) zum Stillstand kommen ● *vi* Halt machen; ~**!** halt! ~**ing** *adj*, *adv* **-ly** zögernd

halve /hɑ:v/ *vt* halbieren; (*reduce*) um die Hälfte reduzieren

ham /hæm/ *n* Schinken *m*

hamburger /'hæmbɜ:gə(r)/ *n* Hamburger *m*

hammer /'hæmə(r)/ *n* Hammer *m* ● *vt/i* hämmern (**at** an + *acc*)

hammock /'hæmək/ *n* Hängematte *f*

hamper *vt* behindern

hamster /'hæmstə(r)/ *n* Hamster *m*

hand /hænd/ *n* Hand *f*; (*of clock*) Zeiger *m*; (*writing*) Handscrift *f*; (*worker*) Arbeiter(in) *m*(*f*); (*Cards*) Blatt *nt*; **on the one/other** ~ einer-/andererseits; **out of** ~ außer Kontrolle; (*summarily*) kurzerhand; **in** ~ unter Kontrolle; (*available*) verfügbar; **give s.o. a** ~ jdm behilflich sein ● *vt* reichen (**to** *dat*). ~ **in** *vt* abgeben. ~ **out** *vt* austeilen. ~ **over** *vt* überreichen

hand: ~**bag** *n* Handtasche *f*. ~**book** *n* Handbuch *nt*. ~**brake** *n* Handbremse *f*. ~**cuffs** *npl* Handschellen *pl*. ~**ful** *n* Handvoll *f*; **be [quite] a** ~**ful** [!] nicht leicht zu haben sein

handicap /'hændɪkæp/ *n* Behinderung *f*; (*Sport & fig*) Handikap *nt*. ~**ped** *adj* **mentally/physically** ~**ped** geistig/körperlich behindert

handkerchief /'hæŋkətʃɪf/ *n* (*pl* ~**s** & **-chieves**) Taschentuch *nt*

handle /'hændl/ *n* Griff *m*; (*of door*) Klinke *f*; (*of cup*) Henkel *m*; (*of broom*) Stiel *m* ● *vt* handhaben; (*treat*) umgehen mit; (*touch*) anfas-

h

sen. ~**bars** *npl* Lenkstange *f*

hand: ~**made** *adj* handgemacht. ~**shake** *n* Händerdruck *m*

handsome /'hænsəm/ *adj* gut aussehend; (*generous*) großzügig; (*large*) beträchtlich

hand: ~**writing** *n* Handschrift *f*. ~-'**written** *adj* handgeschrieben

handy /'hændɪ/ *adj* handlich; (*person*) geschickt; **have**/**keep** ~ griffbereit haben/halten

h

hang /hæŋ/ *vt*/*i* (*pt*/*pp* **hung**) hängen; ~ **wallpaper** tapezieren ● *vt* (*pt*/*pp* **hanged**) hängen (*criminal*) ● *n* **get the** ~ **of it** 🅸 den Dreh herauskriegen. ~ **about** *vi* sich herumdrücken. ~ **on** *vi* sich festhalten (**to** an + *dat*); (🅸: *wait*) warten. ~ **out** *vi* heraushängen; (🅸: *live*) wohnen ● *vt* draußen aufhängen (*washing*). ~ **up** *vt*/*i* aufhängen

hangar /'hæŋə(r)/ *n* Flugzeughalle *f*

hanger /'hæŋə(r)/ *n* [Kleider]bügel *m*

hang: ~-**glider** *n* Drachenflieger *m*. ~-**gliding** *n* Drachenfliegen *nt*. ~**man** *n* Henker *m*. ~**over** *n* 🅸 Kater *m* 🅸. ~-**up** *n* 🅸 Komplex *m*

hanker /'hæŋkə(r)/ *vi* ~ **after sth** sich (*dat*) etw wünschen

hanky /'hæŋkɪ/ *n* 🅸 Taschentuch *nt*

haphazard /hæp'hæzəd/ *adj* planlos

happen /'hæpn/ *vi* geschehen, passieren; **I** ~**ed to be there** ich war zufällig da; **what has** ~**ed to him?** was ist mit ihm los? (*become of*) was ist aus ihm geworden? ~**ing** *n* Ereignis *nt*

happi|ly /'hæpɪlɪ/ *adv* glücklich; (*fortunately*) glücklicherweise. ~**ness** *n* Glück *nt*

happy /'hæpɪ/ *adj* glücklich. ~-**go**-'**lucky** *adj* sorglos

harass /'hærəs/ *vt* schikanieren. ~**ed** *adj* abgehetzt. ~**ment** *n* Schikane *f*; (*sexual*) Belästigung *f*

harbour /'hɑːbə(r)/ *n* Hafen *m*

hard /hɑːd/ *adj* (**-er, -est**) hart; (*difficult*) schwer; ~ **of hearing** schwerhörig ● *adv* hart; (*work*) schwer; (*pull*) kräftig; (*rain, snow*) stark; **be** ~ **up** 🅸 knapp bei Kasse sein

hard: ~**back** *n* gebundene Ausgabe *f*. ~**board** *n* Hartfaserplatte *f*. ~-**boiled** *adj* hart gekocht ~**disk** *n* Festplatte *f*

harden /'hɑːdn/ *vi* hart werden

hard-'hearted *adj* hartherzig

hard|ly /'hɑːdlɪ/ *adv* kaum; ~**ly ever** kaum [jemals]. ~**ness** *n* Härte *f*. ~**ship** *n* Not *f*

hard: ~ '**shoulder** *n* (*Auto*) Randstreifen *m*. ~**ware** *n* Haushaltswaren *pl*; (*Computing*) Hardware *f*. ~-'**wearing** *adj* strapazierfähig. ~-'**working** *adj* fleißig

hardy /'hɑːdɪ/ *adj* abgehärtet; (*plant*) winterhart

hare /heə(r)/ *n* Hase *m*

harm /hɑːm/ *n* Schaden *m*; **it won't do any** ~ es kann nichts schaden ● *vt* ~ **s.o.** jdm etwas antun. ~**ful** *adj* schädlich. ~**less** *adj* harmlos

harmonious /hɑː'məʊnɪəs/ *adj* harmonisch

harmon|ize /'hɑːmənaɪz/ *vi* (*fig*) harmonieren. ~**y** *n* Harmonie *f*

harness /'hɑːnɪs/ *n* Geschirr *nt*; (*of parachute*) Gurtwerk *nt* ● *vt* anschirren (*horse*); (*use*) nutzbar machen

harp /hɑːp/ *n* Harfe *f*. ~**ist** *n* Harfenist(in) *m*(*f*)

harpsichord /'hɑːpsɪkɔːd/ *n* Cembalo *nt*

harrowing /'hærəʊɪŋ/ *adj*

grauenhaft

harsh /hɑːʃ/ *adj* (**-er, -est**) hart; (*voice*) rau; (*light*) grell. **~ness** *n* Härte *f*; Rauheit *f*

harvest /ˈhɑːvɪst/ *n* Ernte *f* ● *vt* ernten

has /hæz/ *see* **have**

hassle /ˈhæsl/ *n* [T] Ärger *m* ● *vt* schikanieren

haste /heɪst/ *n* Eile *f*

hasten /ˈheɪsn/ *vi* sich beeilen (**to** zu); (*go quickly*) eilen ● *vt* beschleunigen

hasty /ˈheɪstɪ/ *adj* , **-ily** *adv* hastig; (*decision*) voreilig

hat /hæt/ *n* Hut *m*; (*knitted*) Mütze *f*

hatch[1] /hætʃ/ *n* (*for food*) Durchreiche *f*; (*Naut*) Luke *f*

hatch[2] *vi* **~[out]** ausschlüpfen ● *vt* ausbrüten

ˈ**hatchback** *n* (*Auto*) Modell *nt* mit Hecktür

hate /heɪt/ *n* Hass *m* ● *vt* hassen. **~ful** *adj* abscheulich

hatred /ˈheɪtrɪd/ *n* Hass *m*

haughty /ˈhɔːtɪ/ *adj* , **-ily** *adv* hochmütig

haul /hɔːl/ *n* (*loot*) Beute *f* ● *vt/i* ziehen (**on** an + *dat*)

haunt /hɔːnt/ *n* Lieblingsaufenthalt *m* ● *vt* umgehen in (+ *dat*); **this house is ~ed** in diesem Haus spukt es

have /hæv/, *unbetont* /həv/, /əv/

3 sg pres tense **has**; *pt and pp* **had**

● *transitive verb*

····➤ (*possess*) haben. **he has [got] a car** er hat ein Auto. **she has [got] a brother** sie hat einen Bruder. **we have [got] five minutes** wir haben fünf Minuten

····➤ (*eat*) essen; (*drink*) trinken; (*smoke*) rauchen. **have a cup of tea** eine Tasse Tee trinken. **have a pizza** eine Pizza essen. **have a cigarette** eine Zigarette rauchen. **have breakfast/dinner/lunch** frühstücken/zu Abend essen/zu Mittag essen

····➤ (*take esp. in shop, restaurant*) nehmen. **I'll have the soup/the red dress** ich nehme die Suppe/das rote Kleid. **have a cigarette!** nehmen Sie eine Zigarette!

····➤ (*get, receive*) bekommen. **I had a letter from her** ich bekam einen Brief von ihr. **have a baby** ein Baby bekommen

····➤ (*suffer*) haben (*illness, pain, disappointment*); erleiden (*shock*)

····➤ (*organize*) **have a party** eine Party veranstalten. **they had a meeting** sie hielten eine Versammlung ab

····➤ (*take part in*) **have a game of football** Fußball spielen. **have a swim** schwimmen

····➤ (*as guest*) **have s.o. to stay** jdn zu Besuch haben

····➤ **have had it** [T] (*thing*) ausgedient haben; (*person*) geliefert sein. **you've had it now** jetzt ist es aus

····➤ **have sth done** etw machen lassen. **we had the house painted** wir haben das Haus malen lassen. **have a dress made** sich (*dat*) ein Kleid machen lassen. **have a tooth out** sich (*dat*) einen Zahn ziehen lassen. **have one's hair cut** sich (*dat*) die Haare schneiden lassen

····➤ **have to do sth** etw tun

müssen. **I have to go now** ich muss jetzt gehen

● *auxiliary verb*

····➤ (*forming perfect and past perfect tenses*) haben; (*with verbs of motion and some others*) sein. **I have seen him** ich habe ihn gesehen. **he has never been there** er ist nie da gewesen. **I had gone** ich war gegangen. **if I had known ...** wenn ich gewusst hätte ...

h

····➤ (*in tag questions*) nicht wahr. **you've met her, haven't you?** du kennst sie, nicht wahr?

····➤ (*in short answers*) **Have you seen the film? — Yes, I have** Hast du den Film gesehen? — Ja [, stimmt]

● **have on** *vt* (*be wearing*) anhaben; (*dupe*) anführen

havoc /'hævək/ *n* Verwüstung *f*

hawk /hɔ:k/ *n* Falke *m*

hawthorn /'hɔ:-/ *n* Hagedorn *m*

hay /heɪ/ *n* Heu *nt*. ~ **fever** *n* Heuschnupfen *m*. **~stack** *n* Heuschober *m*

hazard /'hæzəd/ *n* Gefahr *f*; (*risk*) Risiko *nt* ● *vt* riskieren. **~ous** *adj* gefährlich; (*risky*) riskant

haze /'heɪz/ *n* Dunst *m*

hazel /'heɪzl/ *n* Haselbusch *m*. **~-nut** *n* Haselnuss *f*

hazy /'heɪzɪ/ *adj* dunstig; (*fig*) unklar

he /hi:/ *pron* er

head /hed/ *n* Kopf *m*; (*chief*) Oberhaupt *nt*; (*of firm*) Chef(in) *m*(*f*); (*of school*) Schulleiter(in) *m*(*f*); (*on beer*) Schaumkrone *f*; (*of bed*) Kopfende *nt*; ~ **first** kopfüber ● *vt* anführen; (*Sport*) köpfen (*ball*) ● *vi* ~ **for** zusteuern auf (+ *acc*). **~ache** *n* Kopfschmerzen *pl*

head|er /'hedə(r)/ *n* Kopfball *m*; (*dive*) Kopfsprung *m*. **~ing** *n* Überschrift *f*

head: ~lamp, **~light** *n* (*Auto*) Scheinwerfer *m*. **~line** *n* Schlagzeile *f*. **~long** *adv* kopfüber. **~'master** *n* Schulleiter *m*. **~'mistress** *n* Schulleiterin *f*. **~-on** *adj* & *adv* frontal. **~phones** *npl* Kopfhörer *m*. **~quarters** *npl* Hauptquartier *nt*; (*Pol*) Zentrale *f*. **~-rest** *n* Kopfstütze *f*. **~room** *n* lichte Höhe *f*. **~scarf** *n* Kopftuch *nt*. **~strong** *adj* eigenwillig. **~way** *n* **make ~way** Fortschritte machen. **~word** *n* Stichwort *nt*

heady /'hedɪ/ *adj* berauschend

heal /hi:l/ *vt*/*i* heilen

health /helθ/ *n* Gesundheit *f*

health: ~ **farm** *n* Schönheitsfarm *f*. ~ **foods** *npl* Reformkost *f*. **~-food shop** *n* Reformhaus *nt*. ~ **insurance** *n* Krankenversicherung *f*

healthy /'helθɪ/ *adj*, **-ily** *adv* gesund

heap /hi:p/ *n* Haufen *m*; **~s** 🅃 jede Menge ● *vt* ~ **[up]** häufen

hear /hɪə(r)/ *vt*/*i* (*pt*/*pp* **heard**) hören; **~,~!** hört, hört! **he would not ~ of it** er ließ es nicht zu

hearing /'hɪərɪŋ/ *n* Gehör *nt*; (*Jur*) Verhandlung *f*. **~-aid** *n* Hörgerät *nt*

hearse /hɜ:s/ *n* Leichenwagen *m*

heart /hɑ:t/ *n* Herz *nt*; (*courage*) Mut *m*; **~s** *pl* (*Cards*) Herz *nt*; **by ~** auswendig

heart: ~ache *n* Kummer *m*. **~attack** *n* Herzanfall *m*. **~beat** *n* Herzschlag *m*. **~-breaking** *adj* herzzerreißend. **~-broken** *adj* untröstlich. **~burn** *n* Sodbrennen *nt*. **~en** *vt* ermutigen. **~felt** *adj* herzlich[st]

hearth /hɑ:θ/ *n* Herd *m*; (*fireplace*) Kamin *m*

heart|ily /'hɑ:tɪlɪ/ *adv* herzlich;

(*eat*) viel. **~less** *adj* herzlos. **~y** *adj* herzlich; (*meal*) groß; (*person*) burschikos

heat /hi:t/ *n* Hitze *f*; (*Sport*) Vorlauf *m* ● *vt* heiß machen; heizen (*room*). **~ed** *adj* geheizt; (*swimming pool*) beheizt; (*discussion*) hitzig. **~er** *n* Heizgerät *nt*; (*Auto*) Heizanlage *f*

heath /hi:θ/ *n* Heide *f*

heathen /'hi:ðn/ *adj* heidnisch ● *n* Heide *m*/Heidin *f*

heather /'heðə(r)/ *n* Heidekraut *nt*

heating /'hi:tɪŋ/ *n* Heizung *f*

heat wave *n* Hitzewelle *f*

heave /hi:v/ *vt/i* ziehen; (*lift*) heben; ([I]: *throw*) schmeißen

heaven /'hevn/ *n* Himmel *m*. **~ly** *adj* himmlisch

heavy /'hevɪ/ *adj* , **-ily** *adv* schwer; (*traffic, rain*) stark. **~weight** *n* Schwergewicht *nt*

heckle /'hekl/ *vt* [durch Zwischenrufe] unterbrechen. **~r** *n* Zwischenrufer *m*

hectic /'hektɪk/ *adj* hektisch

hedge /hedʒ/ *n* Hecke *f*. **~hog** *n* Igel *m*

heed /hi:d/ *vt* beachten

heel[1] /hi:l/ *n* Ferse *f*; (*of shoe*) Absatz *m*; **down at ~** heruntergekommen

heel[2] *vi* **~ over** (*Naut*) sich auf die Seite legen

hefty /'heftɪ/ *adj* kräftig; (*heavy*) schwer

height /haɪt/ *n* Höhe *f*; (*of person*) Größe *f*. **~en** *vt* (*fig*) steigern

heir /eə(r)/ *n* Erbe *m*. **~ess** *n* Erbin *f*. **~loom** *n* Erbstück *nt*

held /held/ *see* **hold**[2]

helicopter /'helɪkɒptə(r)/ *n* Hubschrauber *m*

hell /hel/ *n* Hölle *f*; **go to ~!** [x] geh zum Teufel! ● *int* verdammt!

hello /hə'ləʊ/ *int* [guten] Tag! [I] hallo!

helm /helm/ *n* [Steuer]ruder *nt*

helmet /'helmɪt/ *n* Helm *m*

help /help/ *n* Hilfe *f*; (*employees*) Hilfskräfte *pl*; **that's no ~** das nützt nichts ● *vt/i* helfen (**s.o.** jdm); **~ oneself to sth** sich (*dat*) etw nehmen; **~ yourself** (*at table*) greif zu; **I could not ~ laughing** ich musste lachen; **it cannot be ~ed** es lässt sich nicht ändern; **I can't ~ it** ich kann nichts dafür

help|er /'helpə(r)/ *n* Helfer(in) *m*(*f*). **~ful** *adj*, -ly *adv* hilfsbereit; (*advice*) nützlich. **~ing** *n* Portion *f*. **~less** *adj* hilflos

hem /hem/ *n* Saum *m* ● *vt* (*pt*/*pp* **hemmed**) säumen; **~ in** umzingeln

hemisphere /'hemɪ-/ *n* Hemisphäre *f*

'hem-line *n* Rocklänge *f*

hen /hen/ *n* Henne *f*; (*any female bird*) Weibchen *nt*

hence /hens/ *adv* daher; **five years ~** in fünf Jahren. **~'forth** *adv* von nun an

'henpecked *adj* **~ husband** Pantoffelheld *m*

her /hɜ:(r)/ *adj* ihr ● *pron* (*acc*) sie; (*dat*) ihr

herald /'herəld/ *vt* verkünden. **~ry** *n* Wappenkunde *f*

herb /hɜ:b/ *n* Kraut *nt*

herbaceous /hɜ:'beɪʃəs/ *adj* **~ border** Staudenrabatte *f*

herd /hɜ:d/ *n* Herde *f*. **~ together** *vt* zusammentreiben

here /hɪə(r)/ *adv* hier; (*to this place*) hierher; **in ~** hier drinnen; **come/bring ~** herkommen/herbringen

hereditary /hə'redɪtərɪ/ *adj* erblich

here|sy /'herəsɪ/ *n* Ketzerei *f*. **~tic** *n* Ketzer(in) *m*(*f*)

here'with *adv* (*Comm*) beiliegend
heritage /'herɪtɪdʒ/ *n* Erbe *nt*. **~ tourism** *n* Kulturtourismus *m*
hero /'hɪərəʊ/ *n* (*pl* **-es**) Held *m*
heroic /hɪ'rəʊɪk/ *adj*, **-ally** *adv* heldenhaft
heroin /'herəʊɪn/ *n* Heroin *nt*
hero|ine /'herəʊɪn/ *n* Heldin *f*. **~ism** *n* Heldentum *nt*
heron /'hern/ *n* Reiher *m*
herring /'herɪŋ/ *n* Hering *m*
hers /hɜːz/ *poss pron* ihre(r), ihrs; **a friend of ~** ein Freund von ihr; **that is ~** das gehört ihr
her'self *pron* selbst; (*reflexive*) sich; **by ~** allein
hesitant /'hezɪtənt/ *adj* zögernd
hesitat|e /'hezɪteɪt/ *vi* zögern. **~ion** *n* Zögern *nt*; **without ~ion** ohne zu zögern
hexagonal /hek'sægənl/ *adj* sechseckig
heyday /'heɪ-/ *n* Glanzzeit *f*
hi /haɪ/ *int* he! (*hallo*) Tag!
hiatus /haɪ'eɪtəs/ *n* (*pl* **-tuses**) Lücke *f*
hibernat|e /'haɪbəneɪt/ *vi* Winterschlaf halten. **~ion** *n* Winterschlaf *m*
hiccup /'hɪkʌp/ *n* Hick *m*; (🄸: *hitch*) Panne *f*; **have the ~s** den Schluckauf haben ● *vi* hick machen
hid /hɪd/, **hidden** *see* **hide**²
hide *v* (*pt* **hid**, *pp* **hidden**) ● *vt* verstecken; (*keep secret*) verheimlichen ● *vi* sich verstecken
hideous /'hɪdɪəs/ *adj* hässlich; (*horrible*) grässlich
'hide-out *n* Versteck *nt*
hiding¹ /'haɪdɪŋ/ *n* 🄸 **give s.o. a ~** jdn verdreschen
hiding² *n* **go into ~** untertauchen
hierarchy /'haɪərɑːkɪ/ *n* Hierarchie *f*
high /haɪ/ *adj* (**-er, -est**) hoch; *attrib* hohe(r,s); (*meat*) angegangen; (*wind*) stark; (*on drugs*) high; **it's ~ time** es ist höchste Zeit ● *adv* hoch; **~ and low** überall ● *n* Hoch *nt*; (*temperature*) Höchsttemperatur *f*
high: ~brow *adj* intellektuell. **~chair** *n* Kinderhochstuhl *m*. **~'-handed** *adj* selbstherrlich. **~-'heeled** *adj* hochhackig. **~ jump** *n* Hochsprung *m*
'highlight *n* (*fig*) Höhepunkt *m*; **~s** *pl* (*in hair*) helle Strähnen *pl* ● *vt* (*emphasize*) hervorheben
highly /'haɪlɪ/ *adv* hoch; **speak ~ of** loben; **think ~ of** sehr schätzen. **~-'strung** *adj* nervös
Highness /'haɪnɪs/ *n* Hoheit *f*

> *i*
> **high school** Eine weiterführende Schule in den USA, normalerweise für Schüler von vierzehn bis achtzehn Jahren. Schüler erwerben einen Highschoolabschluss durch Nachweis von *credits* (Punkten) in bestimmten Pflicht- und Wahlkursen. Der Abschluss ist Voraussetzung zum Besuch einer Hochschule. Auch in Großbritannien werden einige weiterführende Schulen als *high schools* bezeichnet.

high: ~ season *n* Hochsaison *f*. **~ street** *n* Hauptstraße *f*. **~ 'tide** *n* Hochwasser *nt*. **~way** *n* **public ~way** öffentliche Straße *f*
hijack /'haɪdʒæk/ *vt* entführen. **~er** *n* Entführer *m*
hike /haɪk/ *n* Wanderung *f* ● *vi* wandern. **~r** *n* Wanderer *m*
hilarious /hɪ'leərɪəs/ *adj* sehr komisch
hill /hɪl/ *n* Berg *m*; (*mound*) Hügel *m*; (*slope*) Hang *m*
hill: ~side *n* Hang *m*. **~y** *adj*

hügelig

him /hɪm/ *pron* (*acc*) ihn; (*dat*) ihm. **~'self** *pron* selbst; (*reflexive*) sich; by **~self** allein

hind /haɪnd/ *adj* Hinter-

hind|er /'hɪndə(r)/ *vt* hindern. **~rance** *n* Hindernis *nt*

hindsight /'haɪnd-/ *n* **with ~** rückblickend

Hindu /'hɪndu:/ *n* Hindu *m* ● *adj* Hindu-. **~ism** *n* Hinduismus *m*

hinge /hɪndʒ/ *n* Scharnier *nt*; (*on door*) Angel *f*

hint /hɪnt/ *n* Wink *m*, Andeutung *f*; (*advice*) Hinweis *m*; (*trace*) Spur *f* ● *vi* **~ at** anspielen auf (+ *acc*)

hip /hɪp/ *n* Hüfte *f*

hip 'pocket *n* Gesäßtasche *f*

hippopotamus /hɪpə'pɒtəməs/ *n* (*pl* **-muses** *or* **-mi** /-maɪ/) Nilpferd *nt*

hire /'haɪə(r)/ *vt* mieten (*car*); leihen (*suit*); einstellen (*person*); **~[out]** vermieten; verleihen

his /hɪz/ *adj* sein ● *poss pron* seine(r), seins; **a friend of ~** ein Freund von ihm; **that is ~** das gehört ihm

hiss /hɪs/ *n* Zischen *nt* ● *vt/i* zischen

historian /hɪ'stɔ:rɪən/ *n* Historiker(in) *m*(*f*)

historic /hɪ'stɒrɪk/ *adj* historisch. **~al** *adj* geschichtlich, historisch

history /'hɪstərɪ/ *n* Geschichte *f*

hit /hɪt/ *n* (*blow*) Schlag *m*; ([!]: *success*) Erfolg *m*; **direct ~** Volltreffer *m* ● *vt/i* (*pt/pp* **hit**, *pres p* **hitting**) schlagen; (*knock against, collide with, affect*) treffen; **~ the target** das Ziel treffen; **~ on** (*fig*) kommen auf (+ *acc*); **~ it off** gut auskommen (**with** mit); **~ one's head on sth** sich (*dat*) den Kopf an etw (*dat*) stoßen

hitch /hɪtʃ/ *n* Problem *nt*; **technical ~** Panne *f* ● *vt* festmachen (**to** an + *dat*); **~ up** hochziehen. **~-hike** *vi* [!] trampen. **~-hiker** *n* Anhalter(in) *m*(*f*)

hive /haɪv/ *n* Bienenstock *m*

hoard /hɔ:d/ *n* Hort *m* ● *vt* horten, hamstern

hoarding /'hɔ:dɪŋ/ *n* Bauzaun *m*; (*with advertisements*) Reklamewand *f*

hoar-frost /'hɔ:-/ *n* Raureif *m*

hoarse /hɔ:s/ *adj* (**-r**, **-st**) heiser. **~ness** *n* Heiserkeit *f*

hoax /həʊks/ *n* übler Scherz *m*; (*false alarm*) blinder Alarm *m*

hobble /'hɒbl/ *vi* humpeln

hobby /'hɒbɪ/ *n* Hobby *nt*. **~-horse** *n* (*fig*) Lieblingsthema *nt*

hockey /'hɒkɪ/ *n* Hockey *nt*

hoe /həʊ/ *n* Hacke *f* ● *vt* (*pres p* **hoeing**) hacken

hog /hɒg/ *vt* (*pt/pp* **hogged**) [!] mit Beschlag belegen

hoist /hɔɪst/ *n* Lastenaufzug *m* ● *vt* hochziehen; hissen (*flag*)

hold¹ /həʊld/ *n* (*Naut*) Laderaum *m*

hold² *n* Halt *m*; (*Sport*) Griff *m*; (*fig: influence*) Einfluss *m*; **get ~ of** fassen; ([!]: *contact*) erreichen ● *v* (*pt/pp* **held**) ● *vt* halten; (*container:*) fassen; (*believe*) meinen; (*possess*) haben; anhalten (*breath*) ● *vi* (*rope:*) halten; (*weather:*) sich halten. **~ back** *vt* zurückhalten ● *vi* zögern. **~ on** *vi* (*wait*) warten; (*on telephone*) am Apparat bleiben; **~ on to** (*keep*) behalten; (*cling to*) sich festhalten an (+ *dat*). **~ out** *vt* hinhalten ● *vi* (*resist*) aushalten. **~ up** *vt* hochhalten; (*delay*) aufhalten; (*rob*) überfallen

'hold|all *n* Reisetasche *f*. **~er** *n* Inhaber(in) *m*(*f*); (*container*) Halter *m*. **~-up** *n* Verzögerung *f*; (*attack*) Überfall *m*

hole /həʊl/ *n* Loch *nt*

holiday /ˈhɒlədeɪ/ *n* Urlaub *m*; (*Sch*) Ferien *pl*; (*public*) Feiertag *m*; (*day off*) freier Tag *m*; **go on ~** in Urlaub fahren

holiness /ˈhəʊlɪnɪs/ *n* Heiligkeit *f*

Holland /ˈhɒlənd/ *n* Holland *nt*

hollow /ˈhɒləʊ/ *adj* hohl; (*promise*) leer ● *n* Vertiefung *f*; (*in ground*) Mulde *f*. **~ out** *vt* aushöhlen

holly /ˈhɒlɪ/ *n* Stechpalme *f*

holster /ˈhəʊlstə(r)/ *n* Pistolentasche *f*

h

holy /ˈhəʊlɪ/ *adj* (**-ier, -est**) heilig. **H~ Ghost** *or* **Spirit** *n* Heiliger Geist *m*

homage /ˈhɒmɪdʒ/ *n* Huldigung *f*; **pay ~ to** huldigen (+ *dat*)

home /həʊm/ *n* Zuhause *nt* (*house*) Haus *nt*; (*institution*) Heim *nt*; (*native land*) Heimat *f* ● *adv* **at ~** zu Hause; **come**/**go ~** nach Hause kommen/gehen

home: ~ adˈdress *n* Heimatanschrift *f*. **~ game** *n* Heimspiel *nt*. **~ help** *n* Haushaltshilfe *f*. **~land** *n* Heimatland *nt*. **~land security** innere Sicherheit *f*. **~less** *adj* obdachlos

homely /ˈhəʊmlɪ/ *adj adj* gemütlich; (*Amer: ugly*) unscheinbar

home: ~-ˈmade *adj* selbst gemacht. **H~ Office** *n* Innenministerium *nt*. **~ page** *n* Homepage *f*. **H~ ˈSecretary** Innenminister *m*. **~sick** *adj* **be ~sick** Heimweh haben (**for** nach). **~sickness** *n* Heimweh *nt*. **~ ˈtown** *n* Heimatstadt *f*. **~work** *n* (*Sch*) Hausaufgaben *pl*

homoˈsexual *adj* homosexuell ● *n* Homosexuelle(r) *m/f*

honest /ˈɒnɪst/ *adj* ehrlich. **~y** *n* Ehrlichkeit *f*

honey /ˈhʌnɪ/ *n* Honig *m* ([!]: *darling*) Schatz *m*

honey: ~comb *n* Honigwabe *f*. **~moon** *n* Flitterwochen *pl*; (*journey*) Hochzeitsreise *f*

honorary /ˈɒnərərɪ/ *adj* ehrenamtlich; (*member, doctorate*) Ehren-

honour /ˈɒnə(r)/ *n* Ehre *f* ● *vt* ehren; honorieren (*cheque*). **~able** *adj*, **-bly** *adv* ehrenhaft

hood /hʊd/ *n* Kapuze *f*; (*of car, pram*) [Klapp]verdeck *nt*; (*over cooker*) Abzugshaube *f*; (*Auto, Amer*) Kühlerhaube *f*

hoof /hu:f/ *n* (*pl* **~s** *or* **hooves**) Huf *m*

hook /hʊk/ *n* Haken *m* ● *vt* festhaken (**to** an + *acc*)

hook|ed /hʊkt/ *adj* **~ed nose** Hakennase *f*; **~ed on** [!] abhängig von; (*keen on*) besessen von. **~er** *n* (*Amer*, [✖]) Nutte *f*

hookey /ˈhʊkɪ/ *n* **play ~** (*Amer*, [!]) schwänzen

hooligan /ˈhu:lɪgən/ *n* Rowdy *m*. **~ism** *n* Rowdytum *nt*

hooray /hʊˈreɪ/ *int & n* = **hurrah**

hoot /hu:t/ *n* Ruf *m*; **~s of laughter** schallendes Gelächter *nt* ● *vi* (*owl:*) rufen; (*car:*) hupen; (*jeer*) johlen. **~er** *n* (*of factory*) Sirene *f*; (*Auto*) Hupe *f*

hoover /ˈhu:və(r)/ *n* **H~** ® Staubsauger *m* ● *vt/i* [staub]saugen

hop¹ /hɒp/ *n*, & **~s** *pl* Hopfen *m*

hop² *vi* (*pt/pp* **hopped**) hüpfen; **~ it!** [!] hau ab!

hope /həʊp/ *n* Hoffnung *f*; (*prospect*) Aussicht *f* (**of** auf + *acc*) ● *vt/i* hoffen (**for** auf + acc); **I ~ so** hoffentlich

hope|ful /ˈhəʊpfl/ *adj* hoffnungsvoll; **be ~ful that** hoffen, dass. **~fully** *adv* hoffnungsvoll; (*it is hoped*) hoffentlich. **~less** *adj* hoffnungslos; (*useless*) nutzlos; (*incompetent*) untauglich

horde /hɔ:d/ *n* Horde *f*
horizon /həˈraɪzn/ *n* Horizont *m*
horizontal /hɒrɪˈzɒntl/ *adj* horizontal. ~ ˈ**bar** *n* Reck *nt*
horn /hɔ:n/ *n* Horn *nt*; (*Auto*) Hupe *f*
hornet /ˈhɔ:nɪt/ *n* Hornisse *f*
horoscope /ˈhɒrəskəʊp/ *n* Horoskop *nt*
horrible /ˈhɒrɪbl/ *adj*, **-bly** *adv* schrecklich
horrid /ˈhɒrɪd/ *adj* grässlich
horrific /həˈrɪfɪk/ *adj* entsetzlich
horrify /ˈhɒrɪfaɪ/ *vt* (*pt/pp* **-ied**) entsetzen
horror /ˈhɒrə(r)/ *n* Entsetzen *nt*
hors-d'œuvre /ɔ:ˈdɜ:vr/ *n* Vorspeise *f*
horse /hɔ:s/ *n* Pferd *nt*
horse: ~**back** *n* **on** ~**back** zu Pferde. ~**man** *n* Reiter *m*. ~**power** *n* Pferdestärke *f*. ~**-racing** *n* Pferderennen *nt*. ~**radish** *n* Meerrettich *m*. ~**shoe** *n* Hufeisen *nt*
ˈ**horticulture** *n* Gartenbau *m*
hose /həʊz/ *n* (*pipe*) Schlauch *m* ● *vt* ~ **down** abspritzen
hosiery /ˈhəʊzɪərɪ/ *n* Strumpfwaren *pl*
hospitable /hɒˈspɪtəbl/ *adj*, **-bly** *adv* gastfreundlich
hospital /ˈhɒspɪtl/ *n* Krankenhaus *nt*
hospitality /hɒspɪˈtælətɪ/ *n* Gastfreundschaft *f*
host /həʊst/ *n* Gastgeber *m*
hostage /ˈhɒstɪdʒ/ *n* Geisel *f*
hostel /ˈhɒstl/ *n* [Wohn]heim *nt*
hostess /ˈhəʊstɪs/ *n* Gastgeberin *f*
hostile /ˈhɒstaɪl/ *adj* feindlich; (*unfriendly*) feindselig
hostilit|y /hɒˈstɪlətɪ/ *n* Feindschaft *f*; ~**ies** *pl* Feindseligkeiten *pl*
hot /hɒt/ *adj* (**hotter, hottest**) heiß; (*meal*) warm; (*spicy*) scharf; **I am** *or* **feel** ~ mir ist heiß
hotel /həʊˈtel/ *n* Hotel *nt*
hot: ~**head** *n* Hitzkopf *m*. ~**house** *n* Treibhaus *nt*. ~**ly** *adv* (*fig*) heiß, heftig. ~**plate** *n* Tellerwärmer *m*; (*of cooker*) Kochplatte *f*. ~ **tap** *n* Warmwasserhahn *m*. ~**-tempered** *adj* jähzornig. ~**-ˈwaterbottle** *n* Wärmflasche *f*
hound /haʊnd/ *n* Jagdhund *m* ● *vt* (*fig*) verfolgen
hour /ˈaʊə(r)/ *n* Stunde *f*. ~**ly** *adj* & *adv* stündlich
house[1] /haʊs/ *n* Haus *nt*; **at my** ~ bei mir
house[2] /haʊz/ *vt* unterbringen
house: /haʊs/ ~**breaking** *n* Einbruch *m*. ~**hold** *n* Haushalt *m*. ~**holder** *n* Hausinhaber(in) *m*(*f*). ~**keeper** *n* Haushälterin *f*. ~**keeping** *n* Hauswirtschaft *f*; (*money*) Haushaltsgeld *nt*. ~**-plant** *n* Zimmerpflanze *f*. ~**-trained** *adj* stubenrein. ~**-warming** *n* **have a** ~**-warming party** Einstand feiern. ~**wife** *n* Hausfrau *f*. ~**work** *n* Hausarbeit *f*
housing /ˈhaʊzɪŋ/ *n* Wohnungen *pl*; (*Techn*) Gehäuse *nt*
hovel /ˈhɒvl/ *n* elende Hütte *f*
hover /ˈhɒvə(r)/ *vi* schweben. ~**craft** *n* Luftkissenfahrzeug *nt*
how /haʊ/ *adv* wie; ~ **do you do?** guten Tag!; **and** ~**!** und ob!
how'ever *adv* (*in question*) wie; (*nevertheless*) jedoch, aber; ~ **small** wie klein es auch sein mag
howl /haʊl/ *n* Heulen *nt* ● *vi* heulen; (*baby:*) brüllen
hub /hʌb/ *n* Nabe *f*
huddle /ˈhʌdl/ *vi* ~ **together** sich zusammendrängen
huff /hʌf/ *n* **in a** ~ beleidigt
hug /hʌg/ *n* Umarmung *f* ● *vt* (*pt/*

pp **hugged**) umarmen
huge /hju:dʒ/ *adj* riesig
hull /hʌl/ *n* (*Naut*) Rumpf *m*
hullo /hə'ləʊ/ *int* = **hallo**
hum /hʌm/ *n* Summen *nt*; Brummen *nt* ● *vt/i* (*pt/pp* **hummed**) summen; (*motor:*) brummen
human /'hju:mən/ *adj* menschlich ● *n* Mensch *m*. ~ **'being** *n* Mensch *m*
humane /hju:'meɪn/ *adj* human
humanitarian /hju:mænɪ'teərɪən/ *adj* humanitär
humanity /hju:'mænətɪ/ *n* Menschheit *f*
humble /'hʌmbl/ *adj* (**-r**, **-st**), **-bly** *adv* demütig ● *vt* demütigen
'humdrum *adj* eintönig
humid /'hju:mɪd/ *adj* feucht. ~**ity** *n* Feuchtigkeit *f*
humiliat|e /hju:'mɪlɪeɪt/ *vt* demütigen. ~**ion** *n* Demütigung *f*
humility /hju:'mɪlətɪ/ *n* Demut *f*
humorous /'hju:mərəs/ *adj* humorvoll; (*story*) humoristisch
humour /'hju:mə(r)/ *n* Humor *m*; (*mood*) Laune *f*; **have a sense of ~** Humor haben
hump /hʌmp/ *n* Buckel *m*; (*of camel*) Höcker *m* ● *vt* schleppen
hunch /hʌntʃ/ *n* (*idea*) Ahnung *f*
'hunch|back *n* Bucklige(r) *m/f*
hundred /'hʌndrəd/ *adj* **one/a ~** [ein]hundert ● *n* Hundert *nt*; (*written figure*) Hundert *f*. ~**th** *adj* hundertste(r,s) ● *n* Hundertstel *nt*. ~**weight** *n* ≈ Zentner *m*
hung /hʌŋ/ *see* **hang**
Hungarian /hʌŋ'geərɪən/ *adj* ungarisch ● *n* Ungar(in) *m(f)*
Hungary /'hʌŋgərɪ/ *n* Ungarn *nt*
hunger /'hʌŋgə(r)/ *n* Hunger *m*. ~**-strike** *n* Hungerstreik *m*
hungry /'hʌŋgrɪ/ *adj* , **-ily** *adv* hungrig; **be ~** Hunger haben
hunt /hʌnt/ *n* Jagd *f*; (*for criminal*) Fahndung *f* ● *vt/i* jagen; fahnden nach (*criminal*); ~ **for** suchen. ~**er** *n* Jäger *m*; (*horse*) Jagdpferd *nt*. ~**ing** *n* Jagd *f*
hurdle /'hɜ:dl/ *n* (*Sport & fig*) Hürde *f*
hurl /hɜ:l/ *vt* schleudern
hurrah /hʊ'rɑ:/, **hurray** /hʊ'reɪ/ *int* hurra! ● *n* Hurra *nt*
hurricane /'hʌrɪkən/ *n* Orkan *m*
hurried /'hʌrɪd/ *adj* eilig; (*superficial*) flüchtig
hurry /'hʌrɪ/ *n* Eile *f*; **be in a ~** es eilig haben ● *vi* (*pt/pp* **-ied**) sich beeilen; (*go quickly*) eilen. ~ **up** *vi* sich beeilen ● *vt* antreiben
hurt /hɜ:t/ *n* Schmerz *m* ● *vt/i* (*pt/pp* **hurt**) weh tun (+ *dat*); (*injure*) verletzen; (*offend*) kränken
hurtle /'hɜ:tl/ *vi* ~ **along** rasen
husband /'hʌzbənd/ *n* [Ehe]mann *m*
hush /hʌʃ/ *n* Stille *f* ● *vt* ~ **up** vertuschen. ~**ed** *adj* gedämpft
husky /'hʌskɪ/ *adj* heiser; (*burly*) stämmig
hustle /'hʌsl/ *vt* drängen ● *n* Gedränge *nt*
hut /hʌt/ *n* Hütte *f*
hutch /hʌtʃ/ *n* [Kaninchen]stall *m*
hybrid /'haɪbrɪd/ *adj* hybrid ● *n* Hybride *f*
hydraulic /haɪ'drɔ:lɪk/ *adj*, **-ally** *adv* hydraulisch
hydroe'lectric /haɪdrəʊ-/ *adj* hydroelektrisch
hydrogen /'haɪdrədʒən/ *n* Wasserstoff *m*
hygien|e /'haɪdʒi:n/ *n* Hygiene *f*. ~**ic** *adj*, **-ally** *adv* hygienisch
hymn /hɪm/ *n* Kirchenlied *nt*. ~**-book** *n* Gesangbuch *nt*

hyphen /'haɪfn/ *n* Bindestrich *m*. **~ate** *vt* mit Bindestrich schreiben

hypno|sis /hɪp'nəʊsɪs/ *n* Hypnose *f*. **~tic** *adj* hypnotisch

hypno|tism /'hɪpnətɪzm/ *n* Hypnotik *f*. **~tist** *n* Hypnotiseur *m*. **~tize** *vt* hypnotisieren

hypochondriac /haɪpə'kɒndrɪæk/ *n* Hypochonder *m*

hypocrisy /hɪ'pɒkrəsɪ/ *n* Heuchelei *f*

hypocrit|e /'hɪpəkrɪt/ *n* Heuchler(in) *m*(*f*)

hypodermic /haɪpə'dɜ:mɪk/ *adj* & *n* ~ [**syringe**] Injektionsspritze *f*

hypothe|sis /haɪ'pɒθəsɪs/ *n* Hypothese *f*. **~tical** *adj* hypothetisch

hyster|ia /hɪ'stɪərɪə/ *n* Hysterie *f*. **~ical** *adj* hysterisch. **~ics** *npl* hysterischer Anfall *m*

Ii

I /aɪ/ *pron* ich

ice /aɪs/ *n* Eis *nt* ● *vt* mit Zuckerguss überziehen (*cake*)

ice: ~berg /-bɜ:g/ *n* Eisberg *m*. **~box** *n* (*Amer*) Kühlschrank *m*. **~-'cream** *n* [Speise]eis *nt*. **~-cube** *n* Eiswürfel *m*

Iceland /'aɪslənd/ *n* Island *nt*

ice: ~'lolly *n* Eis *nt* am Stiel. **~ rink** *n* Eisbahn *f*

icicle /'aɪsɪkl/ *n* Eiszapfen *m*

icing /'aɪsɪŋ/ *n* Zuckerguss *m*. **~ sugar** *n* Puderzucker *m*

icon /'aɪkɒn/ *n* Ikone *f*

icy /'aɪsɪ/ *adj* , **-ily** *adv* eisig; (*road*) vereist

idea /aɪ'dɪə/ *n* Idee *f*; (*conception*) Vorstellung *f*; **I have no ~!** ich habe keine Ahnung!

ideal /aɪ'dɪəl/ *adj* ideal ● *n* Ideal *nt*. **~ism** *n* Idealismus *m*. **~ist** *n* Idealist(in) *m*(*f*). **~istic** *adj* idealistisch. **~ize** *vt* idealisieren. **~ly** *adv* ideal; (*in ideal circumstances*) idealerweise

identical /aɪ'dentɪkl/ *adj* identisch; (*twins*) eineiig

identi|fication /aɪdentɪfɪ'keɪʃn/ *n* Identifizierung *f*; (*proof of identity*) Ausweispapiere *pl*. **~fy** *vt* (*pt*/*pp* **-ied**) identifizieren

identity /aɪ'dentətɪ/ *n* Identität *f*. **~ card** *n* [Personal]ausweis *m*. **~ theft** Identitätsdiebstahl *m*

idiom /'ɪdɪəm/ *n* [feste] Redewendung *f*. **~atic** *adj*, **-ally** *adv* idiomatisch

idiosyncrasy /ɪdɪə'sɪŋkrəsɪ/ *n* Eigenart *f*

idiot /'ɪdɪət/ *n* Idiot *m*. **~ic** *adj* idiotisch

idle /'aɪdl/ *adj* (**-r, -st**) untätig; (*lazy*) faul; (*empty*) leer; (*machine*) nicht in Betrieb ● *vi* faulenzen; (*engine:*) leer laufen. **~ness** *n* Untätigkeit *f*; Faulheit *f*

idol /'aɪdl/ *n* Idol *nt*. **~ize** *vt* vergöttern

idyllic /ɪ'dɪlɪk/ *adj* idyllisch

i.e. *abbr* (**id est**) d.h.

if /ɪf/ *conj* wenn; (*whether*) ob; **as if** als ob

ignition /ɪg'nɪʃn/ *n* (*Auto*) Zündung *f*. **~ key** *n* Zündschlüssel *m*

ignoramus /ɪgnə'reɪməs/ *n* Ignorant *m*

ignoran|ce /'ɪgnərəns/ *n* Unwissenheit *f*. **~t** *adj* unwissend

ignore /ɪg'nɔ:(r)/ *vt* ignorieren

ill /ɪl/ *adj* krank; (*bad*) schlecht; **feel ~ at ease** sich unbehaglich fühlen ● *adv* schlecht

illegal /ɪ'li:gl/ *adj* illegal

illegible /ɪ'ledʒəbl/ *adj*, **-bly** *adv* unleserlich

illegitimate /ɪlɪ'dʒɪtɪmət/ *adj* unehelich; (*claim*) unberechtigt

illicit /ɪ'lɪsɪt/ *adj* illegal

illiterate /ɪ'lɪtərət/ *adj* **be ~te** nicht lesen und schreiben können

illness /'ɪlnɪs/ *n* Krankheit *f*

illogical /ɪ'lɒdʒɪkl/ *adj* unlogisch

ill-treat /ɪl'tri:t/ *vt* misshandeln. **~ment** *n* Misshandlung *f*

illuminat|e /ɪ'lu:mɪneɪt/ *vt* beleuchten. **~ion** *n* Beleuchtung *f*

illusion /ɪ'lu:ʒn/ *n* Illusion *f*; **be under the ~ that** sich (*dat*) einbilden, dass

illustrat|e /'ɪləstreɪt/ *vt* illustrieren. **~ion** *n* Illustration *f*

illustrious /ɪ'lʌstrɪəs/ *adj* berühmt

image /'ɪmɪdʒ/ *n* Bild *nt*; (*statue*) Standbild *nt*; (*exact likeness*) Ebenbild *nt*; **[public] ~** Image *nt*

imagin|able /ɪ'mædʒɪnəbl/ *adj* vorstellbar. **~ary** *adj* eingebildet

imaginat|ion /ɪmædʒɪ'neɪʃn/ *n* Phantasie *f*; (*fancy*) Einbildung *f*. **~ive** *adj* phantasievoll; (*full of ideas*) einfallsreich

imagine /ɪ'mædʒɪn/ *vt* sich (*dat*) vorstellen; (*wrongly*) sich (*dat*) einbilden

im'balance *n* Unausgeglichenheit *f*

imbecile /'ɪmbəsi:l/ *n* Schwachsinnige(r) *m/f*; (*pej*) Idiot *m*

imitat|e /'ɪmɪteɪt/ *vt* nachahmen, imitieren. **~ion** *n* Nachahmung *f*, Imitation *f*

immaculate /ɪ'mækjʊlət/ *adj* tadellos; (*Relig*) unbefleckt

imma'ture *adj* unreif

immediate /ɪ'mi:dɪət/ *adj* sofortig; (*nearest*) nächste(r,s). **~ly** *adv* sofort; **~ly next to** unmittelbar neben ● *conj* sobald

immemorial /ɪmə'mɔ:rɪəl/ *adj* **from time ~** seit Urzeiten

immense /ɪ'mens/ *adj* riesig; ! enorm

immerse /ɪ'mɜ:s/ *vt* untertauchen

immigrant /'ɪmɪgrənt/ *n* Einwanderer *m*

immigration /ɪmɪ'greɪʃn/ *n* Einwanderung *f*

imminent /'ɪmɪnənt/ *adj* **be ~** unmittelbar bevorstehen

immobil|e /ɪ'məʊbaɪl/ *adj* unbeweglich. **~ize** *vt* (*fig*) lähmen; (*Med*) ruhig stellen. **~izer** *n* (*Auto*) Wegfahrsperre *f*

immodest /ɪ'mɒdɪst/ *adj* unbescheiden

immoral /ɪ'mɒrəl/ *adj* unmoralisch. **~ity** *n* Unmoral *f*

immortal /ɪ'mɔ:tl/ *adj* unsterblich. **~ity** *n* Unsterblichkeit *f*. **~ize** *vt* verewigen

immune /ɪ'mju:n/ *adj* immun (**to/from** gegen)

immunity /ɪ'mju:nətɪ/ *n* Immunität *f*

imp /ɪmp/ *n* Kobold *m*

impact /'ɪmpækt/ *n* Aufprall *m*; (*collision*) Zusammenprall *m*; (*of bomb*) Einschlag *m*; (*fig*) Auswirkung *f*

impair /ɪm'peə(r)/ *vt* beeinträchtigen

impart /ɪm'pɑ:t/ *vt* übermitteln (**to** *dat*); vermitteln (*knowledge*)

im'parti|al *adj* unparteiisch. **~'ality** *n* Unparteilichkeit *f*

im'passable *adj* unpassierbar

impassioned /ɪm'pæʃnd/ *adj* leidenschaftlich

im'passive *adj* unbeweglich

im'patien|ce *n* Ungeduld *f*. **~t**

adj ungeduldig
impeccable /ɪm'pekəbl/ *adj*, **-bly** *adv* tadellos
impede /ɪm'pi:d/ *vt* behindern
impediment /ɪm'pedɪmənt/ *n* Hindernis *nt*; (*in speech*) Sprachfehler *m*
impel /ɪm'pel/ *vt* (*pt/pp* **impelled**) treiben
impending /ɪm'pendɪŋ/ *adj* bevorstehend
impenetrable /ɪm'penɪtrəbl/ *adj* undurchdringlich
imperative /ɪm'perətɪv/ *adj* **be ~** dringend notwendig sein ● *n* (*Gram*) Imperativ *m*
imper'ceptible *adj* nicht wahrnehmbar
im'perfect *adj* unvollkommen; (*faulty*) fehlerhaft ● *n* (*Gram*) Imperfekt *nt*. **~ion** *n* Unvollkommenheit *f*; (*fault*) Fehler *m*
imperial /ɪm'pɪərɪəl/ *adj* kaiserlich. **~ism** *n* Imperialismus *m*
im'personal *adj* unpersönlich
impersonat|e /ɪm'pɜ:səneɪt/ *vt* sich ausgeben als; (*Theat*) nachahmen, imitieren. **~or** *n* Imitator *m*
impertinen|ce /ɪm'pɜ:tɪnəns/ *n* Frechheit *f*. **~t** *adj* frech
imperturbable /ɪmpə'tɜ:bəbl/ *adj* unerschütterlich
impetuous /ɪm'petjʊəs/ *adj* ungestüm
impetus /'ɪmpɪtəs/ *n* Schwung *m*
implacable /ɪm'plækəbl/ *adj* unerbittlich
im'plant *vt* einpflanzen
implement[1] /'ɪmplɪmənt/ *n* Gerät *nt*
implement[2] /'ɪmplɪment/ *vt* ausführen. **~ation** *n* Ausführung *f*, Durchführung *f*
implication /ɪmplɪ'keɪʃn/ *n* Verwicklung *f*; **~s** *pl* Auswirkungen *pl*; **by ~** implizit
implicit /ɪm'plɪsɪt/ *adj* unausgesprochen; (*absolute*) unbedingt
implore /ɪm'plɔ:(r)/ *vt* anflehen
imply /ɪm'plaɪ/ *vt* (*pt/pp* **-ied**) andeuten; **what are you ~ing?** was wollen Sie damit sagen?
impo'lite *adj* unhöflich
import[1] /'ɪmpɔ:t/ *n* Import *m*, Einfuhr *f*
import[2] /ɪm'pɔ:t/ *vt* importieren, einführen
importan|ce /ɪm'pɔ:tns/ *n* Wichtigkeit *f*. **~t** *adj* wichtig
importer /ɪm'pɔ:tə(r)/ *n* Importeur *m*
impos|e /ɪm'pəʊz/ *vt* auferlegen (**on** *dat*) ● *vi* sich aufdrängen (**on** *dat*). **~ing** *adj* eindrucksvoll
impossi'bility *n* Unmöglichkeit *f*
im'possible *adj*, **-bly** *adv* unmöglich
impostor /ɪm'pɒstə(r)/ *n* Betrüger(in) *m*(*f*)
impoten|ce /'ɪmpətəns/ *n* Machtlosigkeit *f*; (*Med*) Impotenz *f*. **~t** *adj* machtlos; (*Med*) impotent
impoverished /ɪm'pɒvərɪʃt/ *adj* verarmt
im'practicable *adj* undurchführbar
im'practical *adj* unpraktisch
impre'cise *adj* ungenau
im'press *vt* beeindrucken; **~ sth [up]on s.o.** jdm etw einprägen
impression /ɪm'preʃn/ *n* Eindruck *m*; (*imitation*) Nachahmung *f*; (*edition*) Auflage *f*. **~ism** *n* Impressionismus *m*
impressive /ɪm'presɪv/ *adj* eindrucksvoll
im'prison *vt* gefangen halten; (*put in prison*) ins Gefängnis sperren

im'probable *adj* unwahrscheinlich

impromptu /ɪm'prɒmptju:/ *adj* improvisiert ● *adv* aus dem Stegreif

im'proper *adj* inkorrekt; (*indecent*) unanständig

impro'priety *n* Unkorrektheit *f*

improve /ɪm'pru:v/ *vt* verbessern; verschönern (*appearance*) ● *vi* sich bessern; ~ **[up]on** übertreffen. **~ment** *n* Verbesserung *f*; (*in health*) Besserung *f*

improvise /'ɪmprəvaɪz/ *vt/i* improvisieren

im'prudent *adj* unklug

impuden|ce /'ɪmpjʊdəns/ *n* Frechheit *f*. **~t** *adj* frech

impuls|e /'ɪmpʌls/ *n* Impuls *m*; **on [an] ~e** impulsiv. **~ive** *adj* impulsiv

im'pur|e *adj* unrein. **~ity** *n* Unreinheit *f*

in /ɪn/ *prep* in (+ *dat*/(*into*) + *acc*); **sit in the garden** im Garten sitzen; **go in the garden** in den Garten gehen; **in May** im Mai; **in 1992** [im Jahre] 1992; **in this heat** bei dieser Hitze; **in the evening** am Abend; **in the sky** am Himmel; **in the world** auf der Welt; **in the street** auf der Straße; **deaf in one ear** auf einem Ohr taub; **in the army** beim Militär; **in English/German** auf Englisch/Deutsch; **in ink/pencil** mit Tinte/Bleistift; **in a soft/loud voice** mit leiser/lauter Stimme; **in doing this, he ...** indem er das tut/tat, ... er ● *adv* (*at home*) zu Hause; (*indoors*) drinnen; **he's not in yet** er ist noch nicht da; **all in** alles inbegriffen; (🄸: *exhausted*) kaputt; **day in, day out** tagaus, tagein; **have it in for s.o.** 🄸 es auf jdn abgesehen haben; **send/go in** hineinschicken/-gehen; **come/bring in** hereinkommen/-bringen ● *adj* (🄸: *in fashion*) in ● *n* **the ins and outs** alle Einzelheiten *pl*

ina'bility *n* Unfähigkeit *f*

inac'cessible *adj* unzugänglich

in'accura|cy *n* Ungenauigkeit *f*. **~te** *adj* ungenau

in'ac|tive *adj* untätig. **~'tivity** *n* Untätigkeit *f*

in'adequate *adj* unzulänglich

inad'missable *adj* unzulässig

inadvertently /ɪnəd'vɜ:təntlɪ/ *adv* versehentlich

inad'visable *adj* nicht ratsam

inane /ɪ'neɪn/ *adj* albern

in'animate *adj* unbelebt

in'applicable *adj* nicht zutreffend

inap'propriate *adj* unangebracht

inar'ticulate *adj* undeutlich; **be ~** sich nicht gut ausdrücken können

inat'tentive *adj* unaufmerksam

in'audible *adj*, **-bly** *adv* unhörbar

inaugural /ɪ'nɔ:gjʊrl/ *adj* Antritts-

inau'spicious *adj* ungünstig

inborn /'ɪnbɔ:n/ *adj* angeboren

inbred /ɪn'bred/ *adj* angeboren

incalculable /ɪn'kælkjʊləbl/ *adj* nicht berechenbar; (*fig*) unabsehbar

in'capable *adj* unfähig; **be ~ of doing sth** nicht fähig sein, etw zu tun

incapacitate /ɪnkə'pæsɪteɪt/ *vt* unfähig machen

incarnation /ɪnkɑ:'neɪʃn/ *n* Inkarnation *f*

incendiary /ɪn'sendɪərɪ/ *adj* & *n* **~ [bomb]** Brandbombe *f*

incense¹ /'ɪnsens/ *n* Weihrauch *m*

incense² /ɪn'sens/ *vt* wütend machen

incentive /ɪn'sentɪv/ *n* Anreiz *m*

incessant /ɪn'sesnt/ *adj* unaufhörlich

incest /'ɪnsest/ *n* Inzest *m*,

Blutschande *f*

inch /ɪntʃ/ *n* Zoll *m* ● *vi* ~ **forward** sich ganz langsam vorwärts schieben

incident /ˈɪnsɪdənt/ *n* Zwischenfall *m*

incidental /ɪnsɪˈdentl/ *adj* nebensächlich; (*remark*) beiläufig; (*expenses*) Neben-. **~ly** *adv* übrigens

incinerat|e /ɪnˈsɪnəreɪt/ *vt* verbrennen

incision /ɪnˈsɪʒn/ *n* Einschnitt *m*

incisive /ɪnˈsaɪsɪv/ *adj* scharfsinnig

incite /ɪnˈsaɪt/ *vt* aufhetzen. **~ment** *n* Aufhetzung *f*

inˈclement *adj* rau

inclination /ɪnklɪˈneɪʃn/ *n* Neigung *f*

incline /ɪnˈklaɪn/ *vt* neigen; **be ~d to do sth** dazu neigen, etw zu tun ● *vi* sich neigen

inclu|de /ɪnˈkluːd/ *vt* einschließen; (*contain*) enthalten; (*incorporate*) aufnehmen (**in** in + *acc*). **~ding** *prep* einschließlich (+ *gen*). **~sion** *n* Aufnahme *f*

inclusive /ɪnˈkluːsɪv/ *adj* Inklusiv-; ~ of einschließlich (+ *gen*)

incognito /ɪnkɒgˈniːtəʊ/ *adv* inkognito

incoˈherent *adj* zusammenhanglos; (*incomprehensible*) unverständlich

income /ˈɪnkəm/ *n* Einkommen *nt*. ~ **tax** *n* Einkommensteuer *f*

ˈincoming *adj* ankommend; (*mail, call*) eingehend

inˈcomparable *adj* unvergleichlich

incomˈpatible *adj* unvereinbar; **be** ~ (*people:*) nicht zueinander passen

inˈcompeten|ce *n* Unfähigkeit *f*. **~t** *adj* unfähig

incomˈplete *adj* unvollständig

incompreˈhensible *adj* unverständlich

inconˈceivable *adj* undenkbar

inconˈclusive *adj* nicht schlüssig

incongruous /ɪnˈkɒŋgrʊəs/ *adj* unpassend

inconˈsiderate *adj* rücksichtslos

inconˈsistent *adj* widersprüchlich; (*illogical*) inkonsequent; **be** ~ nicht übereinstimmen

inconsolable /ɪnkənˈsəʊləbl/ *adj* untröstlich

inconˈspicuous *adj* unauffällig

incontinen|ce /ɪnˈkɒntɪnəns/ *n* Inkontinenz *f*. **~t** *adj* inkontinent

inconˈvenien|ce *n* Unannehmlichkeit *f*; (*drawback*) Nachteil *m*. **~t** *adj* ungünstig; **be ~t for s.o.** jdm nicht passen

incorporate /ɪnˈkɔːpəreɪt/ *vt* aufnehmen; (*contain*) enthalten

incorˈrect *adj* inkorrekt

incorrigible /ɪnˈkɒrɪdʒəbl/ *adj* unverbesserlich

incorruptible /ɪnkəˈrʌptəbl/ *adj* unbestechlich

increase[1] /ˈɪnkriːs/ *n* Zunahme *f*; (*rise*) Erhöhung *f*; **be on the** ~ zunehmen

increas|e[2] /ɪnˈkriːs/ *vt* vergrößern; (*raise*) erhöhen ● *vi* zunehmen; (*rise*) sich erhöhen. **~ing** *adj* zunehmend

inˈcredi|ble *adj*, **-bly** *adv* unglaublich

incredulous /ɪnˈkredjʊləs/ *adj* ungläubig

incriminate /ɪnˈkrɪmɪneɪt/ *vt* (*Jur*) belasten

incur /ɪnˈkɜː(r)/ *vt* (*pt/pp* **incurred**) sich (*dat*) zuziehen; machen (*debts*)

inˈcura|ble *adj*, **-bly** *adv* unheilbar

indebted /ɪnˈdetɪd/ *adj* verpflichtet (**to** *dat*)

in'decent *adj* unanständig

inde'cision *n* Unentschlossenheit *f*

inde'cisive *adj* ergebnislos; (*person*) unentschlossen

indeed /ɪn'di:d/ *adv* in der Tat, tatsächlich; **very much ~** sehr

indefatigable /ɪndɪ'fætɪgəbl/ *adj* unermüdlich

in'definite *adj* unbestimmt. **~ly** *adv* unbegrenzt; (*postpone*) auf unbestimmte Zeit

indent /ɪn'dent/ *vt* (*Printing*) einrücken. **~ation** *n* Einrückung *f*; (*notch*) Kerbe *f*

inde'penden|ce *n* Unabhängigkeit *f*; (*self-reliance*) Selbstständigkeit *f*. **~t** *adj* unabhängig; selbstständig

indescriba|ble /ɪndɪ'skraɪbəbl/ *adj*, **-bly** *adv* unbeschreiblich

indestructible /ɪndɪ'strʌktəbl/ *adj* unzerstörbar

indeterminate /ɪndɪ'tɜ:mɪnət/ *adj* unbestimmt

index /'ɪndeks/ *n* Register *nt*

index: ~ card *n* Karteikarte *f*. **~ finger** *n* Zeigefinger *m*. **~-linked** *adj* (*pension*) dynamisch

India /'ɪndɪə/ *n* Indien *nt*. **~n** *adj* indisch; (*American*) indianisch ● *n* Inder(in) *m*(*f*); (*American*) Indianer(in) *m*(*f*)

Indian 'summer *n* Nachsommer *m*

indicat|e /'ɪndɪkeɪt/ *vt* zeigen; (*point at*) zeigen auf (+ *acc*); (*hint*) andeuten; (*register*) anzeigen ● *vi* (*Auto*) blinken. **~ion** *n* Anzeichen *nt*

indicative /ɪn'dɪkətɪv/ *n* (*Gram*) Indikativ *m*

indicator /'ɪndɪkeɪtə(r)/ *n* (*Auto*) Blinker *m*

in'differen|ce *n* Gleichgültigkeit *f*. **~t** *adj* gleichgültig; (*not good*) mittelmäßig

indi'gest|ible *adj* unverdaulich; (*difficult to digest*) schwer verdaulich. **~ion** *n* Magenverstimmung *f*

indigna|nt /ɪn'dɪgnənt/ *adj* entrüstet, empört. **~tion** *n* Entrüstung *f*, Empörung *f*

in'dignity *n* Demütigung *f*

indi'rect *adj* indirekt

indi'screet *adj* indiskret

indis'cretion *n* Indiskretion *f*

indi'spensable *adj* unentbehrlich

indisposed /ɪndɪ'spəʊzd/ *adj* indisponiert

indisputable /ɪndɪ'spju:təbl/ *adj*, **-bly** *adv* unbestreitbar

indi'stinct *adj* undeutlich

indistinguishable /ɪndɪ'stɪŋgwɪʃəbl/ *adj* **be ~** nicht zu unterscheiden sein

individual /ɪndɪ'vɪdjʊəl/ *adj* individuell; (*single*) einzeln ● *n* Individuum *nt*. **~ity** *n* Individualität *f*

indi'visible *adj* unteilbar

indoctrinate /ɪn'dɒktrɪneɪt/ *vt* indoktrinieren

indolen|ce /'ɪndələns/ *n* Faulheit *f*. **~t** *adj* faul

indomitable /ɪn'dɒmɪtəbl/ *adj* unbeugsam

indoor /'ɪndɔ:(r)/ *adj* Innen-; (*clothes*) Haus-; (*plant*) Zimmer-; (*Sport*) Hallen-. **~s** *adv* im Haus, drinnen; **go ~s** ins Haus gehen

indulge /ɪn'dʌldʒ/ *vt* frönen (+ *dat*); verwöhnen (*child*) ● *vi* **~ in** frönen (+ *dat*). **~nce** *n* Nachgiebigkeit *f*; (*leniency*) Nachsicht *f*. **~nt** *adj* [zu] nachgiebig; nachsichtig

industrial /ɪn'dʌstrɪəl/ *adj* Industrie-. **~ist** *n* Industrielle(r) *m*

industr|ious /ɪn'dʌstrɪəs/ *adj* fleißig. **~y** *n* Industrie *f*; (*zeal*) Fleiß *m*

inebriated /ɪ'ni:brɪeɪtɪd/ *adj*

betrunken

in'edible *adj* nicht essbar

inef'fective *adj* unwirksam; (*person*) untauglich

inef'ficient *adj* unfähig; (*organization*) nicht leistungsfähig; (*method*) nicht rationell

in'eligible *adj* nicht berechtigt

inept /ɪ'nept/ *adj* ungeschickt

ine'quality *n* Ungleichheit *f*

inertia /ɪ'nɜːʃə/ *n* Trägheit *f*

inescapable /ɪnɪ'skeɪpəbl/ *adj* unvermeidlich

inestimable /ɪn'estɪməbl/ *adj* unschätzbar

inevitab|le /ɪn'evɪtəbl/ *adj* unvermeidlich. **~ly** *adv* zwangsläufig

ine'xact *adj* ungenau

inex'cusable *adj* unverzeihlich

inexhaustible /ɪnɪg'zɔːstəbl/ *adj* unerschöpflich

inex'pensive *adj* preiswert

inex'perience *n* Unerfahrenheit *f*. **~d** *adj* unerfahren

inexplicable /ɪnɪk'splɪkəbl/ *adj* unerklärlich

in'fallible *adj* unfehlbar

infamous /'ɪnfəməs/ *adj* niederträchtig; (*notorious*) berüchtigt

infan|cy /'ɪnfənsɪ/ *n* frühe Kindheit *f*; (*fig*) Anfangsstadium *nt*. **~t** *n* Kleinkind *nt*. **~tile** *adj* kindisch

infantry /'ɪnfəntrɪ/ *n* Infanterie *f*

infatuated /ɪn'fætʃʊeɪtɪd/ *adj* vernarrt (**with** in + *acc*)

infect /ɪn'fekt/ *vt* anstecken, infizieren; **become ~ed** (*wound:*) sich infizieren. **~ion** *n* Infektion *f*. **~ious** *adj* ansteckend

inferior /ɪn'fɪərɪə(r)/ *adj* minderwertig; (*in rank*) untergeordnet ● *n* Untergebene(r) *m*/*f*

inferiority /ɪnfɪərɪ'ɒrətɪ/ *n* Minderwertigkeit *f*. **~ complex** *n* Minderwertigkeitskomplex *m*

infern|al /ɪn'fɜːnl/ *adj* höllisch. **~o** *n* flammendes Inferno *nt*

in'fertile *adj* unfruchtbar

infest /ɪn'fest/ *vt* **be ~ed with** befallen sein von; (*place*) verseucht sein mit

infi'delity *n* Untreue *f*

infighting /'ɪnfaɪtɪŋ/ *n* (*fig*) interne Machtkämpfe *pl*

infinite /'ɪnfɪnət/ *adj* unendlich

infinitive /ɪn'fɪnətɪv/ *n* (*Gram*) Infinitiv *m*

infinity /ɪn'fɪnətɪ/ *n* Unendlichkeit *f*

inflame /ɪn'fleɪm/ *vt* entzünden. **~d** *adj* entzündet

in'flammable *adj* feuergefährlich

inflammation /ɪnflə'meɪʃn/ *n* Entzündung *f*

inflammatory /ɪn'flæmətrɪ/ *adj* aufrührerisch

inflat|e /ɪn'fleɪt/ *vt* aufblasen; (*with pump*) aufpumpen. **~ion** *n* Inflation *f*. **~ionary** *adj* inflationär

in'flexible *adj* starr; (*person*) unbeugsam

inflict /ɪn'flɪkt/ *vt* zufügen (**on** *dat*); versetzen (*blow*) (**on** *dat*)

influen|ce /'ɪnflʊəns/ *n* Einfluss *m* ● *vt* beeinflussen. **~tial** *adj* einflussreich

influenza /ɪnflʊ'enzə/ *n* Grippe *f*

inform /ɪn'fɔːm/ *vt* benachrichtigen; (*officially*) informieren; **~ s.o. of sth** jdm etw mitteilen; **keep s.o. ~ed** jdn auf dem Laufenden halten ● *vi* **~ against** denunzieren

in'for|mal *adj* zwanglos; (*unofficial*) inoffiziell. **~'mality** *n* Zwanglosigkeit *f*

informant /ɪn'fɔːmənt/ *n* Gewährsmann *m*

informat|ion /ɪnfə'meɪʃn/ *n* Auskunft *f*; **a piece of ~ion** eine Auskunft. **~ive** *adj* aufschlussreich; (*instructive*) lehrreich

informer /ɪn'fɔ:mə(r)/ *n* Spitzel *m*; (*Pol*) Denunziant *m*

infra-'red /ɪnfrə-/ *adj* infrarot

in'frequent *adj* selten

infringe /ɪn'frɪndʒ/ *vt/i* **~ [on]** verstoßen gegen. **~ment** *n* Verstoß *m*

infuriat|e /ɪn'fjʊərɪeɪt/ *vt* wütend machen. **~ing** *adj* ärgerlich

ingenious /ɪn'dʒi:nɪəs/ *adj* erfinderisch; (*thing*) raffiniert

ingenuity /ɪndʒɪ'nju:ətɪ/ *n* Geschicklichkeit *f*

ingrained /ɪn'greɪnd/ *adj* eingefleischt; **be ~** (*dirt:*) tief sitzen

ingratiate /ɪn'greɪʃɪeɪt/ *vt* **~ oneself** sich einschmeicheln (**with** bei)

in'gratitude *n* Undankbarkeit *f*

ingredient /ɪn'gri:dɪənt/ *n* (*Culin*) Zutat *f*

ingrowing /'ɪngrəʊɪŋ/ *adj* (*nail*) eingewachsen

inhabit /ɪn'hæbɪt/ *vt* bewohnen. **~ant** *n* Einwohner(in) *m*(*f*)

inhale /ɪn'heɪl/ *vt/i* einatmen; (*Med & when smoking*) inhalieren

inherent /ɪn'hɪərənt/ *adj* natürlich

inherit /ɪn'herɪt/ *vt* erben. **~ance** *n* Erbschaft *f*, Erbe *nt*

inhibit|ed /ɪn'hɪbɪtɪd/ *adj* gehemmt. **~ion** *n* Hemmung *f*

inho'spitable *adj* ungastlich

in'human *adj* unmenschlich

inimitable /ɪ'nɪmɪtəbl/ *adj* unnachahmlich

initial /ɪ'nɪʃl/ *adj* anfänglich, Anfangs- ● *n* Anfangsbuchstabe *m*; **my ~s** meine Initialen. **~ly** *adv* anfangs, am Anfang

initiat|e /ɪ'nɪʃɪeɪt/ *vt* einführen. **~ion** *n* Einführung *f*

initiative /ɪ'nɪʃətɪv/ *n* Initiative *f*

inject /ɪn'dʒekt/ *vt* einspritzen, injizieren. **~ion** *n* Spritze *f*, Injektion *f*

injur|e /'ɪndʒə(r)/ *vt* verletzen. **~y** *n* Verletzung *f*

in'justice *n* Ungerechtigkeit *f*; **do s.o. an ~** jdm unrecht tun

ink /ɪŋk/ *n* Tinte *f*

inlaid /ɪn'leɪd/ *adj* eingelegt

inland /'ɪnlənd/ *adj* Binnen- ● *adv* landeinwärts. **I~ Revenue** (*UK*) ≈ Finanzamt *nt*

in-laws /'ɪnlɔ:z/ *npl* [!] Schwiegereltern *pl*

inlay /'ɪnleɪ/ *n* Einlegearbeit *f*

inlet /'ɪnlet/ *n* schmale Bucht *f*; (*Techn*) Zuleitung *f*

inmate /'ɪnmeɪt/ *n* Insasse *m*

inn /ɪn/ *n* Gasthaus *nt*

innate /ɪ'neɪt/ *adj* angeboren

inner /'ɪnə(r)/ *adj* innere(r,s). **~most** *adj* innerste(r,s)

innocen|ce /'ɪnəsəns/ *n* Unschuld *f*. **~t** *adj* unschuldig. **~tly** *adv* in aller Unschuld

innocuous /ɪ'nɒkjʊəs/ *adj* harmlos

innovat|ion /ɪnə'veɪʃn/ *n* Neuerung *f*. **~ive** *adj* innovativ. **~or** *n* Neuerer *m*

innumerable /ɪ'nju:mərəbl/ *adj* unzählig

inoculat|e /ɪ'nɒkjʊleɪt/ *vt* impfen. **~ion** *n* Impfung *f*

inof'fensive *adj* harmlos

in'operable *adj* nicht operierbar

in'opportune *adj* unpassend

inor'ganic *adj* anorganisch

'in-patient *n* [stationär behandelter] Krankenhauspatient *m*

input /'ɪnpʊt/ *n* Input *m* & *nt*

inquest /'ɪnkwest/ *n* gerichtliche Untersuchung *f* der Todesursache

inquir|e /ɪn'kwaɪə(r)/ *vi* sich erkundigen (**about** nach); **~e into** untersuchen ● *vt* sich erkundigen nach. **~y** *n* Erkundigung *f*; (*investigation*) Untersuchung *f*

inquisitive /ɪn'kwɪzətɪv/ *adj* neugierig

in'sane *adj* geisteskrank; (*fig*) wahnsinnig

in'sanitary *adj* unhygienisch

in'sanity *n* Geisteskrankheit *f*

insatiable /ɪn'seɪʃəbl/ *adj* unersättlich

inscription /ɪn'skrɪpʃn/ *n* Inschrift *f*

inscrutable /ɪn'skru:təbl/ *adj* unergründlich; (*expression*) undurchdringlich

insect /'ɪnsekt/ *n* Insekt *nt*. **~icide** *n* Insektenvertilgungsmittel *nt*

inse'cur|e *adj* nicht sicher; (*fig*) unsicher. **~ity** *n* Unsicherheit *f*

in'sensitive *adj* gefühllos; **~ to** unempfindlich gegen

in'separable *adj* untrennbar; (*people*) unzertrennlich

insert¹ /'ɪnsɜ:t/ *n* Einsatz *m*

insert² /ɪn'sɜ:t/ *vt* einfügen, einsetzen; einstecken (*key*); einwerfen (*coin*). **~ion** *n* (*insert*) Einsatz *m*; (*in text*) Einfügung *f*

inside /ɪn'saɪd/ *n* Innenseite *f*; (*of house*) Innere(s) *nt* ● *attrib* Innen- ● *adv* innen; (*indoors*) drinnen; **go ~** hineingehen; **come ~** hereinkommen; **~ out** links [herum]; **know sth ~ out** etw in- und auswendig kennen ● *prep* **~ [of]** in (+ *dat*/ (*into*) + *acc*)

insight /'ɪnsaɪt/ *n* Einblick *m* (**into** in + *acc*); (*understanding*) Einsicht *f*

insig'nificant *adj* unbedeutend

insin'cere *adj* unaufrichtig

insinuat|e /ɪn'sɪnjʊeɪt/ *vt* andeuten. **~ion** *n* Andeutung *f*

insipid /ɪn'sɪpɪd/ *adj* fade

insist /ɪn'sɪst/ *vi* darauf bestehen; **~ on** bestehen auf (+ *dat*) ● *vt* **~ that** darauf bestehen, dass. **~ence** *n* Bestehen *nt*. **~ent** *adj* beharrlich; **be ~ent** darauf bestehen

'insole *n* Einlegesohle *f*

insolen|ce /'ɪnsələns/ *n* Unverschämtheit *f*. **~t** *adj* unverschämt

in'soluble *adj* unlöslich; (*fig*) unlösbar

in'solvent *adj* zahlungsunfähig

insomnia /ɪn'sɒmnɪə/ *n* Schlaflosigkeit *f*

inspect /ɪn'spekt/ *vt* inspizieren; (*test*) prüfen; kontrollieren (*ticket*). **~ion** *n* Inspektion *f*. **~or** *n* Inspektor *m*; (*of tickets*) Kontrolleur *m*

inspiration /ɪnspə'reɪʃn/ *n* Inspiration *f*

inspire /ɪn'spaɪə(r)/ *vt* inspirieren

insta'bility *n* Unbeständigkeit *f*; (*of person*) Labilität *f*

install /ɪn'stɔ:l/ *vt* installieren. **~ation** *n* Installation *f*

instalment /ɪn'stɔ:lmənt/ *n* (*Comm*) Rate *f*; (*of serial*) Fortsetzung *f*; (*Radio, TV*) Folge *f*

instance /'ɪnstəns/ *n* Fall *m*; (*example*) Beispiel *nt*; **in the first ~** zunächst; **for ~** zum Beispiel

instant /'ɪnstənt/ *adj* sofortig; (*Culin*) Instant- ● *n* Augenblick *m*, Moment *m*. **~aneous** *adj* unverzüglich, unmittelbar

instant 'coffee *n* Pulverkaffee *m*

instantly /'ɪnstəntlɪ/ *adv* sofort

instead /ɪn'sted/ *adv* statt dessen; **~ of** statt (+ *gen*), anstelle von; **~ of me** an meiner Stelle; **~ of going** anstatt zu gehen

'instep *n* Spann *m*, Rist *m*

instigat|e /'ɪnstɪgeɪt/ *vt* anstiften; einleiten (*proceedings*). **~ion** *n* Anstiftung *f*; **at his ~ion** auf seine

Veranlassung

instil /ɪnˈstɪl/ *vt* (*pt/pp* **instilled**) einprägen (**into s.o.** jdm)

instinct /ˈɪnstɪŋkt/ *n* Instinkt *m*. **~ive** *adj* instinktiv

institut|e /ˈɪnstɪtjuːt/ *n* Institut *nt*. **~ion** *n* Institution *f*; (*home*) Anstalt *f*

instruct /ɪnˈstrʌkt/ *vt* unterrichten; (*order*) anweisen. **~ion** *n* Unterricht *m*; Anweisung *f*; **~ions** *pl* **for use** Gebrauchsanweisung *f*. **~ive** *adj* lehrreich. **~or** *n* Lehrer(in) *m*(*f*); (*Mil*) Ausbilder *m*

i

instrument /ˈɪnstrʊmənt/ *n* Instrument *nt*. **~al** *adj* Instrumental-

insuˈbordi|nate *adj* ungehorsam. **~nation** *n* Ungehorsam *m*; (*Mil*) Insubordination *f*

insufˈficient *adj* nicht genügend

insulat|e /ˈɪnsjʊleɪt/ *vt* isolieren. **~ing tape** *n* Isolierband *nt*. **~ion** *n* Isolierung *f*

insult¹ /ˈɪnsʌlt/ *n* Beleidigung *f*

insult² /ɪnˈsʌlt/ *vt* beleidigen

insur|ance /ɪnˈʃʊərəns/ *n* Versicherung *f*. **~e** *vt* versichern

intact /ɪnˈtækt/ *adj* unbeschädigt; (*complete*) vollständig

ˈintake *n* Aufnahme *f*

inˈtangible *adj* nicht greifbar

integral /ˈɪntɪgrl/ *adj* wesentlich

integrat|e /ˈɪntɪgreɪt/ *vt* integrieren ● *vi* sich integrieren. **~ion** *n* Integration *f*

integrity /ɪnˈtegrətɪ/ *n* Integrität *f*

intellect /ˈɪntəlekt/ *n* Intellekt *m*. **~ual** *adj* intellektuell

intelligen|ce /ɪnˈtelɪdʒəns/ *n* Intelligenz *f*; (*Mil*) Nachrichtendienst *m*; (*information*) Meldungen *pl*. **~t** *adj* intelligent

intelligible /ɪnˈtelɪdʒəbl/ *adj* verständlich

intend /ɪnˈtend/ *vt* beabsichtigen; **be ~ed for** bestimmt sein für

intense /ɪnˈtens/ *adj* intensiv; (*pain*) stark. **~ly** *adv* äußerst; (*study*) intensiv

intensify /ɪnˈtensɪfaɪ/ *v* (*pt/pp* **-ied**) ● *vt* intensivieren ● *vi* zunehmen

intensity /ɪnˈtensətɪ/ *n* Intensität *f*

intensive /ɪnˈtensɪv/ *adj* intensiv; **be in ~ care** auf der Intensivstation sein

intent /ɪnˈtent/ *adj* aufmerksam; **~ on** (*absorbed in*) vertieft in (+ *acc*) ● *n* Absicht *f*

intention /ɪnˈtenʃn/ *n* Absicht *f*. **~al** *adj* absichtlich

interˈacti|on *n* Wechselwirkung *f*. **~ve** *adj* interactiv

intercede /ɪntəˈsiːd/ *vi* Fürsprache einlegen (**on behalf of** für)

intercept /ɪntəˈsept/ *vt* abfangen

ˈinterchange *n* Austausch *m*; (*Auto*) Autobahnkreuz *nt*

intercom /ˈɪntəkɒm/ *n* [Gegen]-sprechanlage *f*

ˈintercourse *n* (*sexual*) Geschlechtsverkehr *m*

interest /ˈɪntrəst/ *n* Interesse *nt*; (*Comm*) Zinsen *pl* ● *vt* interessieren; **be ~ed** sich interessieren (**in** für). **~ing** *adj* interessant. **~ rate** *n* Zinssatz *m*

interface /ˈɪntəfeɪs/ *n* Schnittstelle *f*

interfere /ɪntəˈfɪə(r)/ *vi* sich einmischen. **~nce** *n* Einmischung *f*; (*Radio, TV*) Störung *f*

interim /ˈɪntərɪm/ *adj* Zwischen-; (*temporary*) vorläufig

interior /ɪnˈtɪərɪə(r)/ *adj* innere(r,s), Innen- ● *n* Innere(s) *nt*

interject /ɪntəˈdʒekt/ *vt* einwerfen. **~ion** *n* Interjektion *f*; (*remark*) Einwurf *m*

interlude /ˈɪntəluːd/ *n* Pause *f*;

(*performance*) Zwischenspiel *nt*

inter'marry *vi* untereinander heiraten; (*different groups:*) Mischehen schließen

intermediary /ɪntəˈmiːdɪərɪ/ *n* Vermittler(in) *m(f)*

intermediate /ɪntəˈmiːdɪət/ *adj* Zwischen-

interminable /ɪnˈtɜːmɪnəbl/ *adj* endlos [lang]

intermittent /ɪntəˈmɪtənt/ *adj* in Abständen auftretend

internal /ɪnˈtɜːnl/ *adj* innere(r,s); (*matter, dispute*) intern. **I~ Revenue** (*USA*) ≈ Finanzamt *nt*. **~ly** *adv* innerlich; (*deal with*) intern

inter'national *adj* international ● *n* Länderspiel *nt*; (*player*) Nationalspieler(in) *m(f)*

'Internet *n* Internet *nt*; **on the ~** im Internet

internment /ɪnˈtɜːnmənt/ *n* Internierung *f*

'interplay *n* Wechselspiel *nt*

interpolate /ɪnˈtɜːpəleɪt/ *vt* einwerfen

interpret /ɪnˈtɜːprɪt/ *vt* interpretieren; auslegen (*text*); deuten (*dream*); (*translate*) dolmetschen ● *vi* dolmetschen. **~ation** *n* Interpretation *f*. **~er** *n* Dolmetscher(in) *m(f)*

interrogat|e /ɪnˈterəgeɪt/ *vt* verhören. **~ion** *n* Verhör *nt*

interrogative /ɪntəˈrɒgətɪv/ *adj* & *n* **~ [pronoun]** Interrogativpronomen *nt*

interrupt /ɪntəˈrʌpt/ *vt/i* unterbrechen; **don't ~!** red nicht dazwischen! **~ion** *n* Unterbrechung *f*

intersect /ɪntəˈsekt/ *vi* sich kreuzen; (*of lines*) sich schneiden. **~ion** *n* Kreuzung *f*

interspersed /ɪntəˈspɜːst/ *adj* **~ with** durchsetzt mit

inter'twine *vi* sich ineinanderschlingen

interval /ˈɪntəvl/ *n* Abstand *m*; (*Theat*) Pause *f*; (*Mus*) Intervall *nt*; **at hourly ~s** alle Stunde; **bright ~s** *pl* Aufheiterungen *pl*

interven|e /ɪntəˈviːn/ *vi* eingreifen; (*occur*) dazwischenkommen. **~tion** *n* Eingreifen *nt*; (*Mil, Pol*) Intervention *f*

interview /ˈɪntəvjuː/ *n* (*in media*) Interview *nt*; (*for job*) Vorstellungsgespräch *nt* ● *vt* interviewen; ein Vorstellungsgespräch führen mit. **~er** *n* Interviewer(in) *m(f)*

intimacy /ˈɪntɪməsɪ/ *n* Vertrautheit *f*; (*sexual*) Intimität *f*

intimate /ˈɪntɪmət/ *adj* vertraut; (*friend*) eng; (*sexually*) intim

intimidat|e /ɪnˈtɪmɪdeɪt/ *vt* einschüchtern. **~ion** *n* Einschüchterung *f*

into /ˈɪntə/, *vor einem Vokal* /ˈɪntʊ/ *prep* in (+ *acc*); **be ~** 🅃 sich auskennen mit; **7 ~ 21** 21 [geteilt] durch 7

in'tolerable *adj* unerträglich

in'toleran|ce *n* Intoleranz *f*. **~t** *adj* intolerant

intonation /ɪntəˈneɪʃn/ *n* Tonfall *m*

intoxicat|ed /ɪnˈtɒksɪkeɪtɪd/ *adj* betrunken; (*fig*) berauscht. **~ion** *n* Rausch *m*

intransigent /ɪnˈtrænsɪdʒənt/ *adj* unnachgiebig

in'transitive *adj* intransitiv

intrepid /ɪnˈtrepɪd/ *adj* kühn, unerschrocken

intricate /ˈɪntrɪkət/ *adj* kompliziert

intrigu|e /ɪnˈtriːg/ *n* Intrige *f* ● *vt* faszinieren. **~ing** *adj* faszinierend

intrinsic /ɪnˈtrɪnsɪk/ *adj* **~ value** Eigenwert *m*

introduce /ɪntrəˈdjuːs/ *vt* vorstellen; (*bring in, insert*) einführen

introduct|ion /ɪntrəˈdʌkʃn/ *n* Einführung *f*; (*to person*) Vorstellung *f*; (*to book*) Einleitung *f*. **~ory** *adj* einleitend

introvert /ˈɪntrəvɜːt/ *n* introvertierter Mensch *m*

intru|de /ɪnˈtruːd/ *vi* stören. **~der** *n* Eindringling *m*. **~sion** *n* Störung *f*

intuit|ion /ɪntjuːˈɪʃn/ *n* Intuition *f*. **~ive** *adj* intuitiv

inundate /ˈɪnəndeɪt/ *vt* überschwemmen

i

invade /ɪnˈveɪd/ *vt* einfallen in (+ *acc*). **~r** *n* Angreifer *m*

invalid[1] /ˈɪnvəlɪd/ *n* Kranke(r) *m*/*f*

invalid[2] /ɪnˈvælɪd/ *adj* ungültig

inˈvaluable *adj* unschätzbar; (*person*) unersetzlich

inˈvariab|le *adj* unveränderlich. **~ly** *adv* immer

invasion /ɪnˈveɪʒn/ *n* Invasion *f*

invent /ɪnˈvent/ *vt* erfinden. **~ion** *n* Erfindung *f*. **~ive** *adj* erfinderisch. **~or** *n* Erfinder *m*

inventory /ˈɪnvəntrɪ/ *n* Bestandsliste *f*

invert /ɪnˈvɜːt/ *vt* umkehren. **~ed commas** *npl* Anführungszeichen *pl*

invest /ɪnˈvest/ *vt* investieren, anlegen; **~ in** (![]: *buy*) sich (*dat*) zulegen

investigat|e /ɪnˈvestɪgeɪt/ *vt* untersuchen. **~ion** *n* Untersuchung *f*

invest|ment /ɪnˈvestmənt/ *n* Anlage *f*; **be a good ~ment** (*fig*) sich bezahlt machen. **~or** *n* Kapitalanleger *m*

invidious /ɪnˈvɪdɪəs/ *adj* unerfreulich; (*unfair*) ungerecht

invincible /ɪnˈvɪnsəbl/ *adj* unbesiegbar

inviolable /ɪnˈvaɪələbl/ *adj* unantastbar

inˈvisible *adj* unsichtbar

invitation /ɪnvɪˈteɪʃn/ *n* Einladung *f*

invit|e /ɪnˈvaɪt/ *vt* einladen. **~ing** *adj* einladend

invoice /ˈɪnvɔɪs/ *n* Rechnung *f* ● *vt* **~ s.o.** jdm eine Rechnung schicken

inˈvoluntary *adj*, **-ily** *adv* unwillkürlich

involve /ɪnˈvɒlv/ *vt* beteiligen; (*affect*) betreffen; (*implicate*) verwickeln; (*entail*) mit sich bringen; (*mean*) bedeuten; **be ~d in** beteiligt sein an (+ *dat*); (*implicated*) verwickelt sein in (+ *acc*); **get ~d with s.o.** sich mit jdm einlassen. **~d** *adj* kompliziert. **~ment** *n* Verbindung *f*

inˈvulnerable *adj* unverwundbar; (*position*) unangreifbar

inward /ˈɪnwəd/ *adj* innere(r,s). **~s** *adv* nach innen

iodine /ˈaɪədiːn/ *n* Jod *nt*

IOU *abbr* Schuldschein *m*

Iran /ɪˈrɑːn/ *n* der Iran

Iraq /ɪˈrɑːk/ *n* der Irak

irascible /ɪˈræsəbl/ *adj* aufbrausend

irate /aɪˈreɪt/ *adj* wütend

Ireland /ˈaɪələnd/ *n* Irland *nt*

iris /ˈaɪərɪs/ *n* (*Anat*) Regenbogenhaut *f*, Iris *f*; (*Bot*) Schwertlilie *f*

Irish /ˈaɪərɪʃ/ *adj* irisch ● *n* **the ~** *pl* die Iren. **~man** *n* Ire *m*. **~woman** *n* Irin *f*

iron /ˈaɪən/ *adj* Eisen-; (*fig*) eisern ● *n* Eisen *nt*; (*appliance*) Bügeleisen *nt* ● *vt/i* bügeln

ironic[al] /aɪˈrɒnɪk[l]/ *adj* ironisch

ironing /ˈaɪənɪŋ/ *n* Bügeln *nt*; (*articles*) Bügelwäsche *f*. **~-board** *n* Bügelbrett *nt*

ironmonger /ˈ-mʌŋgə(r)/ *n* **~'s [shop]** Haushaltswarengeschäft *nt*

irony /ˈaɪərənɪ/ *n* Ironie *f*
irrational /ɪˈræʃənl/ *adj* irrational
irreconcilable /ɪˈrekənsaɪləbl/ *adj* unversöhnlich
irrefutable /ɪrɪˈfju:təbl/ *adj* unwiderlegbar
irregular /ɪˈregjʊlə(r)/ *adj* unregelmäßig; (*against rules*) regelwidrig. **~ity** *n* Unregelmäßigkeit *f*; Regelwidrigkeit *f*
irrelevant /ɪˈreləvənt/ *adj* irrelevant
irreparable /ɪˈrepərəbl/ *adj* nicht wieder gutzumachen
irreplaceable /ɪrɪˈpleɪsəbl/ *adj* unersetzlich
irrepressible /ɪrɪˈpresəbl/ *adj* unverwüstlich; **be ~** (*person:*) nicht unterzukriegen sein
irresistible /ɪrɪˈzɪstəbl/ *adj* unwiderstehlich
irresolute /ɪˈrezəlu:t/ *adj* unentschlossen
irrespective /ɪrɪˈspektɪv/ *adj* **~ of** ungeachtet (+ *gen*)
irresponsible /ɪrɪˈspɒnsəbl/ *adj*, **-bly** *adv* unverantwortlich; (*person*) verantwortungslos
irreverent /ɪˈrevərənt/ *adj* respektlos
irrevocable /ɪˈrevəkəbl/ *adj*, **-bly** *adv* unwiderruflich
irrigat|e /ˈɪrɪgeɪt/ *vt* bewässern. **~ion** *n* Bewässerung *f*
irritable /ˈɪrɪtəbl/ *adj* reizbar
irritant /ˈɪrɪtənt/ *n* Reizstoff *m*
irritat|e /ˈɪrɪteɪt/ *vt* irritieren; (*Med*) reizen. **~ion** *n* Ärger *m*; (*Med*) Reizung *f*
is /ɪz/ *see* **be**
Islam /ˈɪzlɑ:m/ *n* der Islam. **~ic** *adj* islamisch
island /ˈaɪlənd/ *n* Insel *f*. **~er** *n* Inselbewohner(in) *m(f)*
isolat|e /ˈaɪsəleɪt/ *vt* isolieren. **~ed** *adj* (*remote*) abgelegen; (*single*) einzeln. **~ion** *n* Isoliertheit *f*; (*Med*) Isolierung *f*
Israel /ˈɪzreɪl/ *n* Israel *nt*. **~i** *adj* israelisch ● *n* Israeli *m/f*
issue /ˈɪʃu:/ *n* Frage *f*; (*outcome*) Ergebnis *nt*; (*of magazine, stamps*) Ausgabe *f*; (*offspring*) Nachkommen *pl* ● *vt* ausgeben; ausstellen (*passport*); erteilen (*order*); herausgeben (*book*); **be ~d with sth** etw erhalten

it /ɪt/

● *pronoun*

····➤ (*as subject*) er (*m*), sie (*f*), es (*nt*); (*in impersonal sentence*) es. **where is the spoon? It's on the table** wo ist der Löffel? Er liegt auf dem Tisch. **it was very kind of you** es war sehr nett von Ihnen. **it's five o'clock** es ist fünf Uhr

····➤ (*as direct object*) ihn (*m*), sie (*f*), es (*nt*). **that's my pencil — give it to me** das ist mein Bleistift — gib ihn mir.

····➤ (*as dative object*) ihm (*m*), ihr (*f*), ihm (*nt*). **he found a track and followed it** er fand eine Spur und folgte ihr.

····➤ (*after prepositions*)

! Combinations such as *with it*, *from it*, *to it* are translated by the prepositions with the prefix **da-** (**damit, davon, dazu**). Prepositions beginning with a vowel insert an 'r' (**daran, darauf, darüber**). **I can't do anything with it** ich kann nichts damit anfangen. **don't lean on it!** lehn dich nicht daran!

····➤ (*the person in question*) es.

it's me ich bin's. **is it you, Dad?** bist du es, Vater? **who is it?** wer ist da?

Italian /ɪ'tæljən/ *adj* italienisch ● *n* Italiener(in) *m(f)*; (*Lang*) Italienisch *nt*

italics /ɪ'tælɪks/ *npl* Kursivschrift *f*; **in ~s** kursiv

Italy /'ɪtəlɪ/ *n* Italien *nt*

itch /ɪtʃ/ *n* Juckreiz *m*; **I have an ~** es juckt mich ● *vi* jucken; **I'm ~ing** [!] es juckt mich (**to** zu). **~y** *adj* **be ~y** jucken

item /'aɪtəm/ *n* Gegenstand *m*; (*Comm*) Artikel *m*; (*on agenda*) Punkt *m*; (*on invoice*) Posten *m*; (*act*) Nummer *f*

itinerary /aɪ'tɪnərərɪ/ *n* [Reise]-route *f*

its /ɪts/ *poss pron* sein; (*f*) ihr

it's = **it is, it has**

itself /ɪt'self/ *pron* selbst; (*reflexive*) sich; **by ~** von selbst; (*alone*) allein

ivory /'aɪvərɪ/ *n* Elfenbein *nt* ● *attrib* Elfenbein-

ivy /'aɪvɪ/ *n* Efeu *m*

i

Ivy League Amerikanische Universitäten sind in Grupppen von Institutionen aufgeteilt, die untereinander sportliche Veranstaltungen durchführen. Die exklusivste Gruppe ist die *Ivy League* im Nordosten der USA. (Efeuliga, nach den mit Efeu bewachsenen, alten Universitätsgebäuden.) Harvard und Yale haben den besten akademischen Ruf der acht Eliteuniversitäten. Viele amerikanische Politiker haben an einer *Ivy-League* Universität studiert.

Jj

jab /dʒæb/ *n* Stoß *m*; ([!]: *injection*) Spritze *f* ● *vt* (*pt/pp* **jabbed**) stoßen

jabber /'dʒæbə(r)/ *vi* plappern

jack /dʒæk/ *n* (*Auto*) Wagenheber *m*; (*Cards*) Bube *m* ● *vt* **~ up** (*Auto*) aufbocken

jacket /'dʒækɪt/ *n* Jacke *f*; (*of book*) Schutzumschlag *m*

'jackpot *n* **hit the ~** das große Los ziehen

jade /dʒeɪd/ *n* Jade *m*

jagged /'dʒægɪd/ *adj* zackig

jail /dʒeɪl/ = **gaol**

jam¹ /dʒæm/ *n* Marmelade *f*

jam² *n* Gedränge *nt*; (*Auto*) Stau *m*; (*fam. difficulty*) Klemme *f* ● *v* (*pt/pp* **jammed**) ● *vt* klemmen (**in** in + *acc*); stören (*broadcast*) ● *vi* klemmen

Jamaica /dʒə'meɪkə/ *n* Jamaika *nt*

jangle /'dʒæŋgl/ *vi* klimpern ● *vt* klimpern mit

January /'dʒænjʊərɪ/ *n* Januar *m*

Japan /dʒə'pæn/ *n* Japan *nt*. **~ese** *adj* japanisch ● *n* Japaner(in) *m(f)*; (*Lang*) Japanisch *nt*

jar /dʒɑ:(r)/ *n* Glas *nt*; (*earthenware*) Topf *m*

jargon /'dʒɑ:gən/ *n* Jargon *m*

jaunt /dʒɔ:nt/ *n* Ausflug *m*

jaunt|y /'dʒɔ:ntɪ/ *adj* **-ily** *adv* keck

javelin /'dʒævlɪn/ *n* Speer *m*

jaw /dʒɔ:/ *n* Kiefer *m*

jazz /dʒæz/ *n* Jazz *m*. **~y** *adj* knallig

jealous /'dʒeləs/ *adj* eifersüchtig (**of** auf + *acc*). **~y** *n* Eifersucht *f*

jeans /dʒi:nz/ *npl* Jeans *pl*

jeer /dʒɪə(r)/ *vi* johlen; **~ at**

verhöhnen

jelly /ˈdʒelɪ/ *n* Gelee *nt*; (*dessert*) Götterspeise *f*. **~fish** *n* Qualle *f*

jeopar|dize /ˈdʒepədaɪz/ *vt* gefährden. **~dy** *n* **in ~dy** gefährdet

jerk /dʒɜːk/ *n* Ruck *m* ● *vt* stoßen; (*pull*) reißen ● *vi* rucken; (*limb, muscle:*) zucken. **~ily** *adv* ruckweise. **~y** *adj* ruckartig

jersey /ˈdʒɜːzɪ/ *n* Pullover *m*; (*Sport*) Trikot *nt*; (*fabric*) Jersey *m*

jest /dʒest/ *n* **in ~** im Spaß

jet *n* (*of water*) [Wasser]strahl *m*; (*nozzle*) Düse *f*; (*plane*) Düsenflugzeug *nt*

jet: ~-ˈblack *adj* pechschwarz. **~-proˈpelled** *adj* mit Düsenantrieb

jetty /ˈdʒetɪ/ *n* Landesteg *m*; (*breakwater*) Buhne *f*

Jew /dʒuː/ *n* Jude *m* /Jüdin *f*

jewel /ˈdʒuːəl/ *n* Edelstein *m*; (*fig*) Juwel *nt*. **~ler** *n* Juwelier *m*; **~ler's [shop]** Juweliergeschäft *nt*. **~lery** *n* Schmuck *m*

Jew|ess /ˈdʒuːɪs/ *n* Jüdin *f*. **~ish** *adj* jüdisch

jib /dʒɪb/ *vi* (*pt/pp* **jibbed**) (*fig*) sich sträuben (**at** gegen)

jigsaw /ˈdʒɪgsɔː/ *n* **~ [puzzle]** Puzzlespiel *nt*

jilt /dʒɪlt/ *vt* sitzen lassen

jingle /ˈdʒɪŋgl/ *n* (*rhyme*) Verschen *nt* ● *vi* klimpern

jinx /dʒɪŋks/ *n* 🅸 **it's got a ~ on it** es ist verhext

jittery /ˈdʒɪtərɪ/ *adj* 🅸 nervös

job /dʒɒb/ *n* Aufgabe *f*; (*post*) Stelle *f*, 🅸 Job *m*; **be a ~** 🅸 nicht leicht sein; **it's a good ~ that** es ist [nur] gut, dass. **~less** *adj* arbeitslos

jockey /ˈdʒɒkɪ/ *n* Jockei *m*

jocular /ˈdʒɒkjʊlə(r)/ *adj* spaßhaft

jog /ˈdʒɒg/ *n* Stoß *m* ● *v* (*pt/pp* **jogged**) ● *vt* anstoßen; **~ s.o.'s memory** jds Gedächtnis nachhelfen ● *vi* (*Sport*) joggen. **~ging** *n* Jogging *nt*

john /dʒɒn/ *n* (*Amer*, 🅸) Klo *nt*

join /dʒɔɪn/ *n* Nahtstelle *f* ● *vt* verbinden (**to** mit); sich anschließen (+ *dat*) (*person*); (*become member of*) beitreten (+ *dat*); eintreten in (+ *acc*) (*firm*) ● *vi* (*roads:*) sich treffen. **~ in** *vi* mitmachen. **~ up** *vi* (*Mil*) Soldat werden ● *vt* zusammenfügen

joint /dʒɔɪnt/ *adj* gemeinsam ● *n* Gelenk *nt*; (*in wood, brickwork*) Fuge *f*; (*Culin*) Braten *m*; (🅸*: bar*) Lokal *nt*

jok|e /dʒəʊk/ *n* Scherz *m*; (*funny story*) Witz *m*; (*trick*) Streich *m* ● *vi* scherzen. **~er** *n* Witzbold *m*; (*Cards*) Joker *m*. **~ing** *n* **~ing apart** Spaß beiseite. **~ingly** *adv* im Spaß

jolly /ˈdʒɒlɪ/ *adj* lustig ● *adv* 🅸 sehr

jolt /dʒəʊlt/ *n* Ruck *m* ● *vt* einen Ruck versetzen (+ *dat*) ● *vi* holpern

Jordan /ˈdʒɔːdn/ *n* Jordanien *nt*

jostle /ˈdʒɒsl/ *vt* anrempeln

jot /dʒɒt/ *vt* (*pt/pp* **jotted**) **~ [down]** sich (*dat*) notieren

journal /ˈdʒɜːnl/ *n* Zeitschrift *f*; (*diary*) Tagebuch *nt*. **~ese** *n* Zeitungsjargon *m*. **~ism** *n* Journalismus *m*. **~ist** *n* Journalist(in) *m*(*f*)

journey /ˈdʒɜːnɪ/ *n* Reise *f*

jovial /ˈdʒəʊvɪəl/ *adj* lustig

joy /dʒɔɪ/ *n* Freude *f*. **~ful** *adj* freudig, froh. **~ride** *n* 🅸 Spritztour *f* [im gestohlenen Auto]

jubil|ant /ˈdʒuːbɪlənt/ *adj* überglücklich. **~ation** *n* Jubel *m*

jubilee /ˈdʒuːbɪliː/ *n* Jubiläum *nt*

judder /ˈdʒʌdə(r)/ *vi* rucken

judge /dʒʌdʒ/ *n* Richter *m*; (*of competition*) Preisrichter *m* ● *vt* beurteilen; (*estimate*) [ein]schätzen ● *vi* urteilen (**by** nach). **~ment** *n* Beurteilung *f*; (*Jur*) Urteil *nt*; (*fig*)

J

Urteilsvermögen *nt*

judic|ial /dʒu:ˈdɪʃl/ *adj* gerichtlich. **~ious** *adj* klug

jug /dʒʌg/ *n* Kanne *f*; (*small*) Kännchen *nt*; (*for water, wine*) Krug *m*

juggle /ˈdʒʌgl/ *vi* jonglieren. **~r** *n* Jongleur *m*

juice /dʒu:s/ *n* Saft *m*

juicy /ˈdʒu:sɪ/ *adj* saftig; ▣ (*story*) pikant

juke-box /ˈdʒu:k-/ *n* Musikbox *f*

July /dʒʊˈlaɪ/ *n* Juli *m*

jumble /ˈdʒʌmbl/ *n* Durcheinander *nt* ● *vt* ~ **[up]** durcheinander bringen. ~ **sale** *n* [Wohltätigkeits]-basar *m*

jump /dʒʌmp/ *n* Sprung *m*; (*in prices*) Anstieg *m*; (*in horse racing*) Hindernis *nt* ● *vi* springen; (*start*) zusammenzucken; **make s.o.** ~ jdn erschrecken; ~ **at** (*fig*) sofort zugreifen bei (*offer*); ~ **to conclusions** voreilige Schlüsse ziehen ● *vt* überspringen. ~ **up** *vi* aufspringen

jumper /ˈdʒʌmpə(r)/ *n* Pullover *m*, Pulli *m*

jumpy /ˈdʒʌmpɪ/ *adj* nervös

junction /ˈdʒʌŋkʃn/ *n* Kreuzung *f*; (*Rail*) Knotenpunkt *m*

June /dʒu:n/ *n* Juni *m*

jungle /ˈdʒʌŋgl/ *n* Dschungel *m*

junior /ˈdʒu:nɪə(r)/ *adj* jünger; (*in rank*) untergeordnet; (*Sport*) Junioren- ● *n* Junior *m*

junk /dʒʌŋk/ *n* Gerümpel *nt*, Trödel *m*

junkie /ˈdʒʌŋkɪ/ *n* ▣ Fixer *m*

ˈjunk-shop *n* Trödelladen *m*

jurisdiction /dʒʊərɪsˈdɪkʃn/ *n* Gerichtsbarkeit *f*

jury /ˈdʒʊərɪ/ *n* **the** ~ die Geschworenen *pl*; (*for competition*) die Jury

just /dʒʌst/ *adj* gerecht ● *adv* gerade; (*only*) nur; (*simply*) einfach; (*exactly*) genau; ~ **as tall** ebenso groß; **I'm** ~ **going** ich gehe schon

justice /ˈdʒʌstɪs/ *n* Gerechtigkeit *f*; **do** ~ **to** gerecht werden (+ *dat*)

justifiab|le /ˈdʒʌstɪfaɪəbl/ *adj* berechtigt. **~ly** *adv* berechtigterweise

justi|fication /dʒʌstɪfɪˈkeɪʃn/ *n* Rechtfertigung *f*. **~fy** *vt* (*pt*/*pp* **-ied**) rechtfertigen

justly /ˈdʒʌstlɪ/ *adv* zu Recht

jut /dʒʌt/ *vi* (*pt*/*pp* **jutted**) ~ **out** vorstehen

juvenile /ˈdʒu:vənaɪl/ *adj* jugendlich; (*childish*) kindisch ● *n* Jugendliche(r) *m*/*f*. ~ **delinquency** *n* Jugendkriminalität *f*

Kk

kangaroo /kæŋgəˈru:/ *n* Känguru *nt*

kebab /kɪˈbæb/ *n* Spießchen *nt*

keel /ki:l/ *n* Kiel *m* ● *vi* ~ **over** umkippen; (*Naut*) kentern

keen /ki:n/ *adj* (**-er, -est**) (*sharp*) scharf; (*intense*) groß; (*eager*) eifrig, begeistert; ~ **on** ▣ erpicht auf (+ *acc*); ~ **on s.o.** von jdm sehr angetan; **be** ~ **to do sth** etw gerne machen wollen. **~ly** *adv* tief. **~ness** *n* Eifer *m*, Begeisterung *f*

keep /ki:p/ *n* (*maintenance*) Unterhalt *m*; (*of castle*) Bergfried *m*; **for ~s** für immer ● *v* (*pt*/*pp* **kept**) ● *vt* behalten; (*store*) aufbewahren; (*not throw away*) aufheben; (*support*) unterhalten; (*detain*) aufhalten; freihalten (*seat*); halten (*promise, animals*); führen, haben (*shop*); einhalten (*law, rules*); ~ **s.o. waiting** jdn warten lassen; ~ **sth to oneself** etw nicht weitersagen ● *vi (remain)* bleiben; (*food:*) sich halten; ~ **left/ right** sich links/rechts halten; ~ **on doing sth** etw weitermachen; (*repeatedly*) etw dauernd machen; ~ **in with** sich gut stellen mit. ~ **up** *vi* Schritt halten ● *vt (continue)* weitermachen

keep|er /ˈkiːpə(r)/ *n* Wärter(in) *m(f)*. ~**ing** *n* **be in** ~**ing with** passen zu

kennel /ˈkenl/ *n* Hundehütte *f*; ~**s** *pl (boarding)* Hundepension *f*; *(breeding)* Zwinger *m*

Kenya /ˈkenjə/ *n* Kenia *nt*

kept /kept/ *see* **keep**

kerb /kɜːb/ *n* Bordstein *m*

kernel /ˈkɜːnl/ *n* Kern *m*

ketchup /ˈketʃʌp/ *n* Ketschup *m*

kettle /ˈketl/ *n* [Wasser]kessel *m*; **put the** ~ **on** Wasser aufsetzen

key /kiː/ *n* Schlüssel *m*; *(Mus)* Tonart *f*; *(of piano, typewriter)* Taste *f* ● *vt* ~ **in** eintasten

key: ~**board** *n* Tastatur *f*; *(Mus)* Klaviatur *f*. ~**hole** *n* Schlüsselloch *nt*. ~**-ring** *n* Schlüsselring *m*

khaki /ˈkɑːkɪ/ *adj* khakifarben ● *n* Khaki *nt*

kick /kɪk/ *n* [Fuß]tritt *m*; **for** ~**s** [I] zum Spaß ● *vt* treten; ~ **the bucket** [I] abkratzen ● *vi (animal)* ausschlagen

kid /kɪd/ *n* ([I]: *child*) Kind *nt* ● *vt* (*pt/pp* **kidded**) [I] ~ **s.o.** jdm etwas vormachen

kidnap /ˈkɪdnæp/ *vt* (*pt/pp* **-napped**) entführen. ~**per** *n* Entführer *m*. ~**ping** *n* Entführung *f*

kidney /ˈkɪdnɪ/ *n* Niere *f*

kill /kɪl/ *vt* töten; [I] totschlagen *(time)*: ~ **two birds with one stone** zwei Fliegen mit einer Klappe schlagen. ~**er** *n* Mörder(in) *m(f)*. ~**ing** *n* Tötung *f*; *(murder)* Mord *m*

ˈ**killjoy** *n* Spielverderber *m*

kilo /ˈkiːləʊ/ *n* Kilo *nt*

kilo: /ˈkɪlə/: ~**gram** *n* Kilogramm *nt*. ~**metre** *n* Kilometer *m*. ~**watt** *n* Kilowatt *nt*

kilt /kɪlt/ *n* Schottenrock *m*

kind[1] /kaɪnd/ *n* Art *f*; *(brand, type)* Sorte *f*; **what** ~ **of car?** was für ein Auto? ~ **of** [I] irgendwie

kind[2] *adj* (**-er, -est**) nett; ~ **to animals** gut zu Tieren

kind|ly /ˈkaɪndlɪ/ *adj* nett ● *adv* netterweise; *(if you please)* gefälligst. ~**ness** *n* Güte *f*; *(favour)* Gefallen *m*

king /kɪŋ/ *n* König *m*; *(Draughts)* Dame *f*. ~**dom** *n* Königreich *nt*; *(fig & Relig)* Reich *nt*

king: ~**fisher** *n* Eisvogel *m*. ~**-sized** *adj* extragroß

kink /kɪŋk/ *n* Knick *m*. ~**y** *adj* [I] pervers

kiosk /ˈkiːɒsk/ *n* Kiosk *m*

kip /kɪp/ *n* **have a** ~ [I] pennen ● *vi* (*pt/pp* **kipped**) [I] pennen

kipper /ˈkɪpə(r)/ *n* Räucherhering *m*

kiss /kɪs/ *n* Kuss *m* ● *vt/i* küssen

kit /kɪt/ *n* Ausrüstung *f*; *(tools)* Werkzeug *nt*; *(construction* ~*)* Bausatz *m* ● *vt* (*pt/pp* **kitted**) ~**out** ausrüsten

kitchen /ˈkɪtʃɪn/ *n* Küche *f* ● *attrib* Küchen-. ~**ette** *n* Kochnische *f*

kitchen: ~ˈ**garden** *n* Gemüsegarten *m*. ~ˈ**sink** *n* Spülbecken *nt*

kite /kaɪt/ *n* Drachen *m*

kitten /ˈkɪtn/ *n* Kätzchen *nt*

kitty /ˈkɪtɪ/ *n (money)* [gemeinsame] Kasse *f*

knack /næk/ *n* Trick *m*, Dreh *m*

knead /niːd/ *vt* kneten

knee /niː/ *n* Knie *nt*. ~**cap** *n*

Kniescheibe *f*

kneel /ni:l/ *vi* (*pt/pp* **knelt**) knien; ~ **[down]** sich [nieder]knien

knelt /nelt/ *see* **kneel**

knew /nju:/ *see* **know**

knickers /ˈnɪkəz/ *npl* Schlüpfer *m*

knife /naɪf/ *n* (*pl* **knives**) Messer *nt* ●*vt* einen Messerstich versetzen (+ *dat*)

knight /naɪt/ *n* Ritter *m*; (*Chess*) Springer *m* ●*vt* adeln

knit /nɪt/ *vt/i* (*pt/pp* **knitted**) stricken; ~ **one's brow** die Stirn runzeln. **~ting** *n* Stricken *nt*; (*work*) Strickzeug *nt*. **~ting-needle** *n* Stricknadel *f*. **~wear** *n* Strickwaren *pl*

knives /naɪvz/ *npl see* **knife**

knob /nɒb/ *n* Knopf *m*; (*on door*) Knauf *m*; (*small lump*) Beule *f*. **~bly** *adj* knorrig; (*bony*) knochig

knock /nɒk/ *n* Klopfen *nt*; (*blow*) Schlag *m*; **there was a** ~ es klopfte ●*vt* anstoßen; (Ⓘ: *criticize*) heruntermachen; ~ **a hole in sth** ein Loch in etw (*acc*) schlagen; ~ **one's head** sich (*dat*) den Kopf stoßen (**on** an + *dat*) ●*vi* klopfen. ~ **about** *vt* schlagen ●*vi* Ⓘ herumkommen. ~ **down** *vt* herunterwerfen; (*with fist*) niederschlagen; (*in car*) anfahren; (*demolish*) abreißen; (Ⓘ: *reduce*) herabsetzen. ~ **off** *vt* herunterwerfen; (Ⓘ: *steal*) klauen; (Ⓘ: *complete quickly*) hinhauen ●*vi* (Ⓘ: *cease work*) Feierabend machen. ~ **out** *vt* ausschlagen; (*make unconscious*) bewusstlos schlagen; (*Boxing*) k.o. schlagen. ~ **over** *vt* umwerfen; (*in car*) anfahren

knock: ~-down *adj* **~-down prices** Schleuderpreise *pl*. **~er** *n* Türklopfer *m*. **~-out** *n* (*Boxing*) K.o. *m*

knot /nɒt/ *n* Knoten *m* ●*vt* (*pt/pp* **knotted**) knoten

know /nəʊ/ *vt/i* (*pt* **knew**, *pp* **known**) wissen; kennen (*person*); können (*language*); **get to** ~ kennen lernen ●*n* **in the** ~ Ⓘ im Bild

know: ~-all *n* Ⓘ Alleswisser *m*. **~-how** *n* Ⓘ [Sach]kenntnis *f*. **~ing** *adj* wissend. **~ingly** *adv* wissend; (*intentionally*) wissentlich

knowledge /ˈnɒlɪdʒ/ *n* Kenntnis *f* (**of** von/*gen*); (*general*) Wissen *nt*; (*specialized*) Kenntnisse *pl*. **~able** *adj* **be ~able** viel wissen

knuckle /ˈnʌkl/ *n* [Finger]knöchel *m*; (*Culin*) Hachse *f*

kosher /ˈkəʊʃə(r)/ *adj* koscher

kudos /ˈkju:dɒs/ *n* Ⓘ Prestige *nt*

L

lab /læb/ *n* Ⓘ Labor *nt*

label /ˈleɪbl/ *n* Etikett *nt* ●*vt* (*pt/pp* **labelled**) etikettieren

laboratory /ləˈbɒrətrɪ/ *n* Labor *nt*

laborious /ləˈbɔ:rɪəs/ *adj* mühsam

labour /ˈleɪbə(r)/ *n* Arbeit *f*; (*workers*) Arbeitskräfte *pl*; (*Med*) Wehen *pl*; **L~** (*Pol*) die Labourpartei ●*attrib* Labour- ●*vi* arbeiten ●*vt* (*fig*) sich lange auslassen über (+ *acc*). **~er** *n* Arbeiter *m*

ˈ**labour-saving** *adj* arbeitssparend

lace /leɪs/ *n* Spitze *f*; (*of shoe*) Schnürsenkel *m* ●*vt* schnüren

lack /læk/ *n* Mangel *m* (**of** an + *dat*) ●*vt* **I** ~ **the time** mir fehlt die Zeit ●*vi* **be ~ing** fehlen

laconic /ləˈkɒnɪk/ *adj*, **-ally** *adv* lakonisch

lacquer /ˈlækə(r)/ *n* Lack *m*; (*for hair*) [Haar]spray *m*

lad /læd/ *n* Junge *m*

ladder /ˈlædə(r)/ *n* Leiter *f*; (*in fabric*) Laufmasche *f*

ladle /ˈleɪdl/ *n* [Schöpf]kelle *f* ● *vt* schöpfen

lady /ˈleɪdɪ/ *n* Dame *f*; (*title*) Lady *f*

lady: ~bird *n*, (*Amer*) **~bug** *n* Marienkäfer *m*. **~like** *adj* damenhaft

lag[1] /læg/ *vi* (*pt/pp* **lagged**) **~ behind** zurückbleiben; (*fig*) nachhinken

lag[2] *vt* (*pt/pp* **lagged**) umwickeln (*pipes*)

lager /ˈlɑːgə(r)/ *n* Lagerbier *nt*

laid /leɪd/ *see* **lay**[3]

lain /leɪn/ *see* **lie**[2]

lake /leɪk/ *n* See *m*

lamb /læm/ *n* Lamm *nt*

lame /leɪm/ *adj* (**-r, -st**) lahm

lament /ləˈment/ *n* Klage *f*; (*song*) Klagelied *nt* ● *vt* beklagen ● *vi* klagen

laminated /ˈlæmɪneɪtɪd/ *adj* laminiert

lamp /læmp/ *n* Lampe *f*; (*in street*) Laterne *f*. **~post** *n* Laternenpfahl *m*. **~shade** *n* Lampenschirm *m*

lance /lɑːns/ *vt* (*Med*) aufschneiden

land /lænd/ *n* Land *nt*; **plot of ~** Grundstück *nt* ● *vt/i* landen; **~ s.o. with sth** [!] jdm etw aufhalsen

landing /ˈlændɪŋ/ *n* Landung *f*; (*top of stairs*) Treppenflur *m*. **~-stage** *n* Landesteg *m*

land: ~lady *n* Wirtin *f*. **~lord** *n* Wirt *m*; (*of land*) Grundbesitzer *m*; (*of building*) Hausbesitzer *m*. **~mark** *n* Erkennungszeichen *nt*; (*fig*) Meilenstein *m*. **~owner** *n* Grundbesitzer *m*. **~scape** /-skeɪp/ *n* Landschaft *f*. **~slide** *n* Erdrutsch *m*

lane /leɪn/ *n* kleine Landstraße *f*; (*Auto*) Spur *f*; (*Sport*) Bahn *f*; **'get in ~'** (*Auto*) 'bitte einordnen'

language /ˈlæŋgwɪdʒ/ *n* Sprache *f*; (*speech, style*) Ausdrucksweise *f*

languid /ˈlæŋgwɪd/ *adj* träge

languish /ˈlæŋgwɪʃ/ *vi* schmachten

lanky /ˈlæŋkɪ/ *adj* schlaksig

lantern /ˈlæntən/ *n* Laterne *f*

lap[1] /læp/ *n* Schoß *m*

lap[2] *n* (*Sport*) Runde *f*; (*of journey*) Etappe *f* ● *vi* (*pt/pp* **lapped**) plätschern (**against** gegen)

lap[3] *vt* (*pt/pp* **lapped**) **~ up** aufschlecken

lapel /ləˈpel/ *n* Revers *nt*

lapse /læps/ *n* Fehler *m*; (*moral*) Fehltritt *m*; (*of time*) Zeitspanne *f* ● *vi* (*expire*) erlöschen; **~ into** verfallen in (+ *acc*)

laptop /ˈlæptɒp/ *n* Laptop *m*

lard /lɑːd/ *n* [Schweine]schmalz *nt*

larder /ˈlɑːdə(r)/ *n* Speisekammer *f*

large /lɑːdʒ/ *adj* (**-r, -st**) & *adv* groß; **by and ~** im Großen und Ganzen; **at ~** auf freiem Fuß. **~ly** *adv* großenteils

lark[1] /lɑːk/ *n* (*bird*) Lerche *f*

lark[2] *n* (*joke*) Jux *m* ● *vi* **~ about** herumalbern

laryngitis /lærɪnˈdʒaɪtɪs/ *n* Kehlkopfentzündung *f*

larynx /ˈlærɪŋks/ *n* Kehlkopf *m*

laser /ˈleɪzə(r)/ *n* Laser *m*

lash /læʃ/ *n* Peitschenhieb *m*; (*eyelash*) Wimper *f* ● *vt* peitschen; (*tie*) festbinden (**to** an + *acc*). **~ out** *vi* um sich schlagen; (*spend*) viel Geld ausgeben (**on** für)

lass /læs/ *n* Mädchen *nt*

lasso /ləˈsuː/ *n* Lasso *nt*

last /lɑːst/ *adj* & *n* letzte(r,s); **~ night** heute *od* gestern Nacht;

l

(*evening*) gestern Abend; **at ~** endlich; **for the ~ time** zum letzten Mal; **the ~ but one** der/die/das vorletzte ● *adv* zuletzt; (*last time*) das letzte Mal; **he/she went ~** er-/sie ging als Letzter/Letzte ● *vi* dauern; (*weather:*) sich halten; (*relationship:*) halten. **~ing** *adj* dauerhaft. **~ly** *adv* schließlich, zum Schluss

latch /lætʃ/ *n* [einfache] Klinke *f*

late /leɪt/ *adj & adv* (**-r, -st**) spät; (*delayed*) verspätet; (*deceased*) verstorben; **the ~st news** die neuesten Nachrichten; **stay up ~** bis spät aufbleiben; **arrive ~** zu spät ankommen; **I am ~** ich komme zu spät *od* habe mich verspätet; **the train is ~** der Zug hat Verspätung. **~comer** *n* Zuspätkommende(r) *m/f*. **~ly** *adv* in letzter Zeit. **~ness** *n* Zuspätkommen *nt*; (*delay*) Verspätung *f*

later /ˈleɪtə(r)/ *adj & adv* später; **~ on** nachher

lateral /ˈlætərəl/ *adj* seitlich

lather /ˈlɑːðə(r)/ *n* [Seifen]-schaum *m*

Latin /ˈlætɪn/ *adj* lateinisch ● *n* Latein *nt*. **~ Aˈmerica** *n* Lateinamerika *nt*

latitude /ˈlætɪtjuːd/ *n* (*Geog*) Breite *f*; (*fig*) Freiheit *f*

latter /ˈlætə(r)/ *adj & n* **the ~** der/die/das Letztere

Latvia /ˈlætvɪə/ *n* Lettland *nt*

laudable /ˈlɔːdəbl/ *adj* lobenswert

laugh /lɑːf/ *n* Lachen *nt*; **with a ~** lachend ● *vi* lachen (**at/about** über + *acc*); **~ at s.o.** (*mock*) jdn auslachen. **~able** *adj* lachhaft, lächerlich

laughter /ˈlɑːftə(r)/ *n* Gelächter *nt*

launch¹ /lɔːntʃ/ *n* (*boat*) Barkasse *f*

launch² *n* Stapellauf *m*; (*of rocket*) Abschuss *m*; (*of product*) Lancierung *f* ● *vt* vom Stapel lassen (*ship*); zu Wasser lassen (*lifeboat*); abschießen (*rocket*); starten (*attack*); (*Comm*) lancieren (*product*)

laund(e)rette /lɔːndret/ *n* Münzwäscherei *f*

laundry /ˈlɔːndrɪ/ *n* Wäscherei *f*; (*clothes*) Wäsche *f*

laurel /ˈlɒrl/ *n* Lorbeer *m*

lava /ˈlɑːvə/ *n* Lava *f*

lavatory /ˈlævətrɪ/ *n* Toilette *f*

lavender /ˈlævəndə(r)/ *n* Lavendel *m*

lavish /ˈlævɪʃ/ *adj* großzügig; (*wasteful*) verschwenderisch ● *vt* **~ sth on s.o.** jdn mit etw überschütten

law /lɔː/ *n* Gesetz *nt*; (*system*) Recht *nt*; **study ~** Jura studieren; **~ and order** Recht und Ordnung

law: ~-abiding *adj* gesetzestreu. **~court** *n* Gerichtshof *m*. **~ful** *adj* rechtmäßig. **~less** *adj* gesetzlos

lawn /lɔːn/ *n* Rasen *m*. **~-mower** *n* Rasenmäher *m*

lawyer /ˈlɔːjə(r)/ *n* Rechtsanwalt *m* /-anwältin *f*

lax /læks/ *adj* lax, locker

laxative /ˈlæksətɪv/ *n* Abführmittel *nt*

laxity /ˈlæksətɪ/ *n* Laxheit *f*

lay¹ /leɪ/ *see* **lie²**

lay² *vt* (*pt/pp* **laid**) legen; decken (*table*); **~ a trap** eine Falle stellen. **~ down** *vt* hinlegen; festlegen (*rules, conditions*). **~ off** *vt* entlassen (*workers*) ● *vi* (I: *stop*) aufhören. **~ out** *vt* hinlegen; aufbahren (*corpse*); anlegen (*garden*); (*Typography*) gestalten

lay-by *n* Parkbucht *f*

layer /ˈleɪə(r)/ *n* Schicht *f*

lay: ~man *n* Laie *m*. **~out** *n* Anordnung *f*; (*design*) Gestaltung *f*; (*Typography*) Layout *nt*

laze /leɪz/ *vi* ~**[about]** faulenzen
laziness /ˈleɪzɪnɪs/ *n* Faulheit *f*
lazy /ˈleɪzɪ/ *adj* faul. ~**-bones** *n* Faulenzer *m*
lead[1] /led/ *n* Blei *nt*; (*of pencil*) [Bleistift]mine *f*
lead[2] /liːd/ *n* Führung *f*; (*leash*) Leine *f*; (*flex*) Schnur *f*; (*clue*) Hinweis *m*, Spur *f*; (*Theat*) Hauptrolle *f*; (*distance ahead*) Vorsprung *m*; **be in the** ~ in Führung liegen ● *vt/i* (*pt/pp* **led**) führen; leiten (*team*); (*induce*) bringen; (*at cards*) ausspielen; ~ **the way** vorangehen; ~ **up to sth** (*fig*) etw (*dat*) vorangehen
leader /ˈliːdə(r)/ *n* Führer *m*; (*of expedition, group*) Leiter(in) *m*(*f*); (*of orchestra*) Konzertmeister *m*; (*in newspaper*) Leitartikel *m*. ~**ship** *n* Führung *f*; Leitung *f*
leading /ˈliːdɪŋ/ *adj* führend; ~ **lady** Hauptdarstellerin *f*
leaf /liːf/ *n* (*pl* **leaves**) Blatt *nt* ● *vi* ~ **through sth** etw durchblättern. ~**let** *n* Merkblatt *nt*; (*advertising*) Reklameblatt *nt*; (*political*) Flugblatt *nt*
league /liːg/ *n* Liga *f*
leak /liːk/ *n* (*hole*) undichte Stelle *f*; (*Naut*) Leck *nt*; (*of gas*) Gasausfluss *m* ● *vi* undicht sein; (*ship:*) leck sein, lecken; (*liquid:*) auslaufen; (*gas:*) ausströmen ● *vt* auslaufen lassen; ~ **sth to s.o.** (*fig*) jdm etw zuspielen. ~**y** *adj* undicht; (*Naut*) leck
lean[1] /liːn/ *adj* (**-er, -est**) mager
lean[2] *v* (*pt/pp* **leaned** *or* **leant** /lent/) ● *vt* lehnen (**against**/**on** an + *acc*) ● *vi* (*person*) sich lehnen (**against**/**on** an + *acc*); (*not be straight*) sich neigen; **be** ~**ing against** lehnen an (+ *dat*). ~ **back** *vi* sich zurücklehnen. ~ **forward** *vi* sich vorbeugen. ~ **out** *vi* sich hinauslehnen. ~ **over** *vi* sich vorbeugen
leaning /ˈliːnɪŋ/ *adj* schief ● *n* Neigung *f*
leap /liːp/ *n* Sprung *m* ● *vi* (*pt/pp* **leapt** *or* **leaped**) springen; **he leapt at it** [!] er griff sofort zu. ~ **year** *n* Schaltjahr *nt*
learn /lɜːn/ *vt/i* (*pt/pp* **learnt** *or* **learned**) lernen; (*hear*) erfahren; ~ **to swim** schwimmen lernen
learn|ed /ˈlɜːnɪd/ *adj* gelehrt. ~**er** *n* Anfänger *m*; ~**er [driver]** Fahrschüler(in) *m*(*f*). ~**ing** *n* Gelehrsamkeit *f*; ~**ing curve** Lernkurve *f*
lease /liːs/ *n* Pacht *f*; (*contract*) Mietvertrag *m* ● *vt* pachten
leash /liːʃ/ *n* Leine *f*
least /liːst/ *adj* geringste(r,s) ● *n* **the** ~ das wenigste; **at** ~ wenigstens, mindestens; **not in the** ~ nicht im Geringsten ● *adv* am wenigsten
leather /ˈleðə(r)/ *n* Leder *nt*
leave /liːv/ *n* Erlaubnis *f*; (*holiday*) Urlaub *m*; **on** ~ auf Urlaub; **take one's** ~ sich verabschieden ● *v* (*pt/pp* **left**) ● *vt* lassen; (*go out of, abandon*) verlassen; (*forget*) liegen lassen; (*bequeath*) vermachen (**to** *dat*); ~ **it to me!** überlassen Sie es mir! **there is nothing left** es ist nichts mehr übrig ● *vi* [weg]gehen/-fahren; (*train, bus:*) abfahren. ~ **behind** *vt* zurücklassen; (*forget*) liegen lassen. ~ **out** *vt* liegen lassen; (*leave outside*) draußen lassen; (*omit*) auslassen
leaves /liːvz/ *see* **leaf**
Lebanon /ˈlebənən/ *n* Libanon *m*
lecherous /ˈletʃərəs/ *adj* lüstern
lecture /ˈlektʃə(r)/ *n* Vortrag *m*; (*Univ*) Vorlesung *f*; (*reproof*) Strafpredigt *f* ● *vi* einen Vortrag/eine Vorlesung halten (**on** über + *acc*) ● *vt* ~ **s.o.** jdm eine Strafpredigt halten. ~**r** *n* Vortragende(r) *m*/*f*;

l

(*Univ*) Dozent(in) *m*(*f*)

led /led/ *see* **lead**[2]

ledge /ledʒ/ *n* Leiste *f*; (*shelf, of window*) Sims *m*; (*in rock*) Vorsprung *m*

ledger /ˈledʒə(r)/ *n* Hauptbuch *nt*

leech /liːtʃ/ *n* Blutegel *m*

leek /liːk/ *n* Stange *f* Porree; **~s** *pl* Porree *m*

left[1] /left/ *see* **leave**

left[2] *adj* linke(r,s) ● *adv* links; (*go*) nach links ● *n* linke Seite *f*; **on the ~** links; **from/to the ~** von/nach links; **the ~** (*Pol*) die Linke

left: ~-ˈhanded *adj* linkshändig. **~-ˈluggage [office]** *n* Gepäckaufbewahrung *f*. **~overs** *npl* Reste *pl*. **~-ˈwing** *adj* (*Pol*) linke(r,s)

leg /leg/ *n* Bein *nt*; (*Culin*) Keule *f*; (*of journey*) Etappe *f*

legacy /ˈlegəsɪ/ *n* Vermächtnis *nt*, Erbschaft *f*

legal /ˈliːgl/ *adj* gesetzlich; (*matters*) rechtlich; (*department, position*) Rechts-; **be ~** [gesetzlich] erlaubt sein

legality /lɪˈgælətɪ/ *n* Legalität *f*

legend /ˈledʒənd/ *n* Legende *f*. **~ary** *adj* legendär

legi|ble /ˈledʒəbl/ *adj*, **-bly** *adv* leserlich

legion /ˈliːdʒn/ *n* Legion *f*

legislat|e /ˈledʒɪsleɪt/ *vi* Gesetze erlassen. **~ion** *n* Gesetzgebung *f*; (*laws*) Gesetze *pl*

legislative /ˈledʒɪslətɪv/ *adj* gesetzgebend

legitimate /lɪˈdʒɪtɪmət/ *adj* rechtmäßig; (*justifiable*) berechtigt

leisure /ˈleʒə(r)/ *n* Freizeit *f*; **at your ~** wenn Sie Zeit haben. **~ly** *adj* gemächlich

lemon /ˈlemən/ *n* Zitrone *f*. **~ade** *n* Zitronenlimonade *f*

lend /lend/ *vt* (*pt/pp* **lent**) leihen (**s.o. sth** jdm etw)

length /leŋθ/ *n* Länge *f*; (*piece*) Stück *nt*; (*of wallpaper*) Bahn *f*; (*of time*) Dauer *f*

length|en /ˈleŋθən/ *vt* länger machen ● *vi* länger werden. **~ways** *adv* der Länge nach

lengthy /ˈleŋθɪ/ *adj* langwierig

lenient /ˈliːnɪənt/ *adj* nachsichtig

lens /lenz/ *n* Linse *f*; (*Phot*) Objektiv *nt*; (*of spectacles*) Glas *nt*

lent /lent/ *see* **lend**

Lent *n* Fastenzeit *f*

lentil /ˈlentl/ *n* (*Bot*) Linse *f*

leopard /ˈlepəd/ *n* Leopard *m*

leotard /ˈliːətɑːd/ *n* Trikot *nt*

lesbian /ˈlezbɪən/ *adj* lesbisch ● *n* Lesbierin *f*

less /les/ *a, adv, n & prep* weniger; **~ and ~** immer weniger

lessen /ˈlesn/ *vt* verringern ● *vi* nachlassen; (*value:*) abnehmen

lesser /ˈlesə(r)/ *adj* geringere(r,s)

lesson /ˈlesn/ *n* Stunde *f*; (*in textbook*) Lektion *f*; (*Relig*) Lesung *f*; **teach s.o. a ~** (*fig*) jdm eine Lehre erteilen

lest /lest/ *conj* (*literary*) damit ... nicht

let /let/ *vt* (*pt/pp* **let**, *pres p* **letting**) lassen; (*rent*) vermieten; **~ alone** (*not to mention*) geschweige denn; **~ us go** gehen wir; **~ me know** sagen Sie mir Bescheid; **~ oneself in for sth** [!] sich (*dat*) etw einbrocken. **~ down** *vt* hinunter-/herunterlassen; (*lengthen*) länger machen; **~ s.o. down** [!] jdn im Stich lassen; (*disappoint*) jdn enttäuschen. **~ in** *vt* hereinlassen. **~ off** *vt* abfeuern (*gun*); hochgehen lassen (*firework, bomb*); (*emit*) ausstoßen; (*excuse from*) befreien von; (*not punish*) frei ausgehen lassen. **~ out** *vt* hinaus-/

herauslassen; (*make larger*) auslassen. ~ **through** *vt* durchlassen. ~ **up** *vi* [T] nachlassen

'let-down *n* Enttäuschung *f*, [T] Reinfall *m*

lethal /'li:θl/ *adj* tödlich

letharg|ic /lɪ'θɑ:dʒɪk/ *adj* lethargisch. **~y** *n* Lethargie *f*

letter /'letə(r)/ *n* Brief *m*; (*of alphabet*) Buchstabe *m*. **~-box** *n* Briefkasten *m*. **~-head** *n* Briefkopf *m*. **~ing** *n* Beschriftung *f*

lettuce /'letɪs/ *n* [Kopf]salat *m*

'let-up *n* [T] Nachlassen *nt*

level /'levl/ *adj* eben; (*horizontal*) waagerecht; (*in height*) auf gleicher Höhe; (*spoonful*) gestrichen; **one's ~ best** sein Möglichstes ● *n* Höhe *f*; (*fig*) Ebene *f*, Niveau *nt*; (*stage*) Stufe *f*; **on the ~** [T] ehrlich ● *vt* (*pt/pp* **levelled**) einebnen

level 'crossing *n* Bahnübergang *m*

lever /'li:və(r)/ *n* Hebel *m* ● *vt* ~ **up** mit einem Hebel anheben. **~age** *n* Hebelkraft *f*

lewd /lju:d/ *adj* (**-er, -est**) anstößig

liabilit|y /laɪə'bɪlətɪ/ *n* Haftung *f*; **~ies** *pl* Verbindlichkeiten *pl*

liable /'laɪəbl/ *adj* haftbar; **be ~ to do sth** etw leicht tun können

liaise /lɪ'eɪz/ *vi* [T] Verbindungsperson sein

liaison /lɪ'eɪzɒn/ *n* Verbindung *f*; (*affair*) Verhältnis *nt*

liar /'laɪə(r)/ *n* Lügner(in) *m*(*f*)

libel /'laɪbl/ *n* Verleumdung *f* ● *vt* (*pt/pp* **libelled**) verleumden. **~lous** *adj* verleumderisch

liberal /'lɪbərl/ *adj* tolerant; (*generous*) großzügig. **L~** *adj* (*Pol*) liberal ● *n* Liberale(r) *m*/*f*

liberat|e /'lɪbəreɪt/ *vt* befreien. **~ed** *adj* (*woman*) emanzipiert. **~ion** *n* Befreiung *f*. **~or** *n* Befreier *m*

liberty /'lɪbətɪ/ *n* Freiheit *f*; **take liberties** sich (*dat*) Freiheiten erlauben

librarian /laɪ'breərɪən/ *n* Bibliothekar(in) *m*(*f*)

library /'laɪbrərɪ/ *n* Bibliothek *f*

Libya /'lɪbɪə/ *n* Libyen *nt*

lice /laɪs/ *see* **louse**

licence /'laɪsns/ *n* Genehmigung *f*; (*Comm*) Lizenz *f*; (*for TV*) ≈ Fernsehgebühr *f*; (*for driving*) Führerschein *m*; (*for alcohol*) Schankkonzession *f*

license /'laɪsns/ *vt* eine Genehmigung/(*Comm*) Lizenz erteilen (+ *dat*); **be ~d** (*car:*) zugelassen sein; (*restaurant:*) Schankkonzession haben. **~-plate** *n* (*Amer*) Nummernschild *nt*

lick /lɪk/ *n* Lecken *nt*; **a ~ of paint** ein bisschen Farbe ● *vt* lecken; ([T]: *defeat*) schlagen

lid /lɪd/ *n* Deckel *m*; (*of eye*) Lid *nt*

lie¹ /laɪ/ *n* Lüge *f*; **tell a ~** lügen ● *vi* (*pt/pp* **lied**, *pres p* **lying**) lügen; **~ to** belügen

lie² *vi* (*pt* **lay**, *pp* **lain**, *pres p* **lying**) liegen; **here ~s ...** hier ruht ... ~ **down** *vi* sich hinlegen

'lie-in *n* **have a ~** [sich] ausschlafen

lieu /lju:/ *n* **in ~ of** statt (+ *gen*)

lieutenant /lef'tenənt/ *n* Oberleutnant *m*

life /laɪf/ *n* (*pl* **lives**) Leben *nt*; **lose one's ~** ums Leben kommen

life: ~-boat *n* Rettungsboot *nt*. **~ coach** *n* Lebensberater(in) *m*(*f*). **~-guard** *n* Lebensretter *m*. **~-jacket** *n* Schwimmweste *f*. **~less** *adj* leblos. **~like** *adj* naturgetreu. **~long** *adj* lebenslang. **~ preserver** *n* (*Amer*) Rettungsring *m*. **~-size(d)** *adj* ... in Lebensgröße.

~**time** *n* Leben *nt*; **in s.o.'s ~time** zu jds Lebzeiten; **the chance of a ~time** eine einmalige Gelegenheit

lift /lɪft/ *n* Aufzug *m*, Lift *m*; **give s.o. a ~** jdn mitnehmen; **get a ~** mitgenommen werden ● *vt* heben; aufheben (*restrictions*) ● *vi* (*fog:*) sich lichten. **~ up** *vt* hochheben

light[1] /laɪt/ *adj* (**-er, -est**) (*not dark*) hell; **~ blue** hellblau ● *n* Licht *nt*; (*lamp*) Lampe *f*; **have you [got] a ~?** haben Sie Feuer? ● *vt* (*pt/pp* **lit** *or* **lighted**) anzünden (*fire, cigarette*); (*illuminate*) beleuchten. **~ up** *vi* (*face:*) sich erhellen

light[2] *adj* (**-er, -est**) (*not heavy*) leicht; **~ sentence** milde Strafe *f* ● *adv* **travel ~** mit wenig Gepäck reisen

'light-bulb *n* Glühbirne *f*

lighten[1] /'laɪtn/ *vt* heller machen

lighten[2] *vt* leichter machen (*load*)

lighter /'laɪtə(r)/ *n* Feuerzeug *nt*

light: ~-'hearted *adj* unbekümmert. **~house** *n* Leuchtturm *m*. **~ing** *n* Beleuchtung *f*. **~ly** *adv* leicht; **get off ~ly** glimpflich davonkommen

lightning /'laɪtnɪŋ/ *n* Blitz *m*

'lightweight *adj* leicht ● *n* (*Boxing*) Leichtgewicht *nt*

like[1] /laɪk/ *adj* ähnlich; (*same*) gleich ● *prep* wie; (*similar to*) ähnlich (+ *dat*); **~ this** so; **what's he ~?** wie ist er denn? ● *conj* (🅸: *as*) wie; (*Amer: as if*) als ob

like[2] *vt* mögen; **I should/would ~** ich möchte; **I ~ the car** das Auto gefällt mir; **~ dancing/singing** gern tanzen/singen ● *n* **~s and dislikes** *pl* Vorlieben und Abneigungen *pl*

like|able /'laɪkəbl/ *adj* sympathisch. **~lihood** *n* Wahrscheinlichkeit *f*. **~ly** *adj* & *adv* wahrscheinlich; **not ~ly!** 🅸 auf gar keinen Fall!

'like-minded *adj* gleich gesinnt

liken /'laɪkən/ *vt* vergleichen (**to** mit)

like|ness /'laɪknɪs/ *n* Ähnlichkeit *f*. **~wise** *adv* ebenso

liking /'laɪkɪŋ/ *n* Vorliebe *f*; **is it to your ~?** gefällt es Ihnen?

lilac /'laɪlək/ *n* Flieder *m*

lily /'lɪlɪ/ *n*. Lilie *f*

limb /lɪm/ *n* Glied *nt*

lime /laɪm/ *n* (*fruit*) Limone *f*; (*tree*) Linde *f*. **~light** *n* **be in the ~light** im Rampenlicht stehen

limit /'lɪmɪt/ *n* Grenze *f*; (*limitation*) Beschränkung *f*; **that's the ~!** 🅸 das ist doch die Höhe! ● *vt* beschränken (**to** auf + *acc*). **~ation** *n* Beschränkung *f*; **~ed** *adj* beschränkt. **~ed company** Gesellschaft *f* mit beschränkter Haftung

limousine /'lɪməzi:n/ *n* Limousine *f*

limp[1] /lɪmp/ *n* Hinken *nt* ● *vi* hinken

limp[2] *adj* (**-er -est**) schlaff

limpid /'lɪmpɪd/ *adj* klar

line[1] /laɪn/ *n* Linie *f*; (*length of rope, cord*) Leine *f*; (*Teleph*) Leitung *f*; (*of writing*) Zeile *f*; (*row*) Reihe *f*; (*wrinkle*) Falte *f*; (*of business*) *f*; (*Amer: queue*) Schlange *f*; **in ~ with** gemäß (+ *dat*) ● *vt* säumen (*street*)

line[2] *vt* füttern (*garment*); (*Techn*) auskleiden

lined[1] /laɪnd/ *adj* (*wrinkled*) faltig; (*paper*) liniert

lined[2] *adj* (*garment*) gefüttert

'line dancing *n* Linedance-Tanzen *nt*

linen /'lɪnɪn/ *n* Leinen *nt*; (*articles*) Wäsche *f*

liner /'laɪnə(r)/ *n* Passagierschiff *nt*

'linesman *n* (**-men**) (*Sport*)

Linienrichter *m*

linger /ˈlɪŋgə(r)/ *vi* [zurück]bleiben

lingerie /ˈlæ̃ʒərɪ/ *n* Damenunterwäsche *f*

linguist /ˈlɪŋgwɪst/ *n* Sprachkundige(r) *m/f*

linguistic /lɪŋˈgwɪstɪk/ *adj*, **-ally** *adv* sprachlich

lining /ˈlaɪnɪŋ/ *n* (*of garment*) Futter *nt*; (*Techn*) Auskleidung *f*

link /lɪŋk/ *n* (*of chain*) Glied *nt* (*fig*) Verbindung *f* ● *vt* verbinden; ~ arms sich unterhaken

links /lɪŋks/ *n or npl* Golfplatz *m*

lint /lɪnt/ *n* Verbandstoff *m*

lion /ˈlaɪən/ *n* Löwe *m*; **~'s share** (*fig*) Löwenanteil *m*. **~ess** *n* Löwin *f*

lip /lɪp/ *n* Lippe *f*; (*edge*) Rand *m*; (*of jug*) Schnabel *m*

lip: ~-reading *n* Lippenlesen *nt*. **~-service** *n* **pay ~-service** ein Lippenbekenntnis ablegen (**to** zu). **~stick** *n* Lippenstift *m*

liqueur /lɪˈkjʊə(r)/ *n* Likör *m*

liquid /ˈlɪkwɪd/ *n* Flüssigkeit *f* ● *adj* flüssig

liquidation /lɪkwɪˈdeɪʃn/ *n* Liquidation *f*

liquidize /ˈlɪkwɪdaɪz/ *vt* [im Mixer] pürieren. **~r** *n* Mixer *m*

liquor /ˈlɪkə(r)/ *n* Alkohol *m*. **~ store** *n* (*Amer*) Spirituosengeschäft *nt*

lisp /lɪsp/ *n* Lispeln *nt* ● *vt/i* lispeln

list¹ /lɪst/ *n* Liste *f* ● *vt* aufführen

list² *vi* (*ship:*) Schlagseite haben

listen /ˈlɪsn/ *vi* zuhören (**to** *dat*); **~ to the radio** Radio hören. **~er** *n* Zuhörer(in) *m*(*f*); (*Radio*) Hörer(in) *m*(*f*)

listless /ˈlɪstlɪs/ *adj* lustlos

lit /lɪt/ *see* **light¹**

literacy /ˈlɪtərəsɪ/ *n* Lese- und Schreibfertigkeit *f*

literal /ˈlɪtərl/ *adj* wörtlich. **~ly** *adv* buchstäblich

literary /ˈlɪtərərɪ/ *adj* literarisch

literate /ˈlɪtərət/ *adj* **be ~** lesen und schreiben können

literature /ˈlɪtrətʃə(r)/ *n* Literatur *f*; 🅘 Informationsmaterial *nt*

lithe /laɪð/ *adj* geschmeidig

Lithuania /lɪθjʊˈeɪnɪə/ *n* Litauen *nt*

litre /ˈliːtə(r)/ *n* Liter *m & nt*

litter /ˈlɪtə(r)/ *n* Abfall *m*; (*Zool*) Wurf *m*. **~-bin** *n* Abfalleimer *m*

little /ˈlɪtl/ *adj* klein; (*not much*) wenig ● *adv & n* wenig; **a ~** ein bisschen/wenig; **~ by ~** nach und nach

live¹ /laɪv/ *adj* lebendig; (*ammunition*) scharf; **~ broadcast** Live-Sendung *f*; **be ~** (*Electr*) unter Strom stehen

live² /lɪv/ *vi* leben; (*reside*) wohnen. **~ on** *vt* leben von; (*eat*) sich ernähren von ● *vi* weiterleben

liveli|hood /ˈlaɪvlɪhʊd/ *n* Lebensunterhalt *m*. **~ness** *n* Lebendigkeit *f*

lively /ˈlaɪvlɪ/ *adj* lebhaft, lebendig

liver /ˈlɪvə(r)/ *n* Leber *f*

lives /laɪvz/ *see* life

livid /ˈlɪvɪd/ *adj* 🅘 wütend

living /ˈlɪvɪŋ/ *adj* lebend ● *n* **earn one's ~** seinen Lebensunterhalt verdienen. **~-room** *n* Wohnzimmer *nt*

lizard /ˈlɪzəd/ *n* Eidechse *f*

load /ləʊd/ *n* Last *f*; (*quantity*) Ladung *f*; (*Electr*) Belastung *f*; **~s of** 🅘 jede Menge ● *vt* laden (*goods, gun*); beladen (*vehicle*); **~ a camera** einen Film in eine Kamera einlegen. **~ed** *adj* beladen; (🅘: *rich*) steinreich

loaf /ləʊf/ *n* (*pl* **loaves**) Brot *nt*

loan /ləʊn/ *n* Leihgabe *f*; (*money*) Darlehen *nt*; **on ~** geliehen ● *vt* leihen (*to dat*)

loath /ləʊθ/ *adj* **be ~ to do sth** etw ungern tun

loath|e /ləʊð/ *vt* verabscheuen. **~ing** *n* Abscheu *m*

loaves /ləʊvz/ *see* **loaf**[1]

lobby /ˈlɒbɪ/ *n* Foyer *nt*; (*anteroom*) Vorraum *m*; (*Pol*) Lobby *f*

lobster /ˈlɒbstə(r)/ *n* Hummer *m*

local /ˈləʊkl/ *adj* hiesig; (*time, traffic*) Orts-; **~ anaesthetic** örtliche Betäubung; **I'm not ~** ich bin nicht von hier ● *n* Hiesige(r) *m/f*; (🄸: *public house*) Stammkneipe *f*. **~ call** *n* (*Teleph*) Ortsgespräch *nt*

locality /ləʊˈkælətɪ/ *n* Gegend *f*

localization /ləʊkəlaɪˈzeɪʃn/ *n* Lokalisierung *f*

locally /ˈləʊkəlɪ/ *adv* am Ort

locat|e /ləʊˈkeɪt/ *vt* ausfindig machen; **be ~ed** sich befinden. **~ion** *n* Lage *f*; **filmed on ~ion** als Außenaufnahme gedreht

lock[1] /lɒk/ *n* (*hair*) Strähne *f*

lock[2] *n* (*on door*) Schloss *nt*; (*on canal*) Schleuse *f* ● *vt* abschließen ● *vi* sich abschließen lassen. **~ in** *vt* einschließen. **~ out** *vt* ausschließen. **~ up** *vt* abschließen; einsperren (*person*)

locker /ˈlɒkə(r)/ *n* Schließfach *nt*; (*Mil*) Spind *m*

lock: ~-out *n* Aussperrung *f*. **~smith** *n* Schlosser *m*

locomotive /ləʊkəˈməʊtɪv/ *n* Lokomotive *f*

locum /ˈləʊkəm/ *n* Vertreter(in) *m(f)*

locust /ˈləʊkəst/ *n* Heuschrecke *f*

lodge /lɒdʒ/ *n* (*porter's*) Pförtnerhaus *nt* ● *vt* (*submit*) einreichen; (*deposit*) deponieren ● *vi* zur Untermiete wohnen (**with** bei); (*become fixed*) stecken bleiben. **~r** *n* Untermieter(in) *m(f)*

lodging /ˈlɒdʒɪŋ/ *n* Unterkunft *f*; **~s** *npl* möbliertes Zimmer *nt*

loft /lɒft/ *n* Dachboden *m*

lofty /ˈlɒftɪ/ *adj* hoch

log /lɒg/ *n* Baumstamm *m*; (*for fire*) [Holz]scheit *nt*; **sleep like a ~** 🄸 wie ein Murmeltier schlafen ● *vi* **~ off** sich abmelden; **~ on** sich anmelden

loggerheads /ˈlɒgə-/ *npl* **be at ~** 🄸 sich in den Haaren liegen

logic /ˈlɒdʒɪk/ *n* Logik *f*. **~al** *adj* logisch

logo /ˈləʊgəʊ/ *n* Symbol *nt*, Logo *nt*

loiter /ˈlɔɪtə(r)/ *vi* herumlungern

loll /lɒl/ *vi* sich lümmeln

loll|ipop /ˈlɒlɪpɒp/ *n* Lutscher *m*. **~y** *n* Lutscher *m*; (🄸: *money*) Moneten *pl*

London /ˈlʌndən/ *n* London *nt* ● *attrib* Londoner. **~er** *n* Londoner(in) *m(f)*

lone /ləʊn/ *adj* einzeln. **~liness** *n* Einsamkeit *f*

lonely /ˈləʊnlɪ/ *adj* einsam

lone|r /ˈləʊnə(r)/ *n* Einzelgänger *m*. **~some** *adj* einsam

long[1] /lɒŋ/ *adj* **(-er** /ˈlɒŋgə(r)/, **-est** /ˈlɒŋgɪst/) lang; (*journey*) weit; **a ~ time** lange; **a ~ way** weit; **in the ~ run** auf lange Sicht; (*in the end*) letzten Endes ● *adv* lange; **all day ~** den ganzen Tag; **not ~ ago** vor kurzem; **before ~** bald; **no ~er** nicht mehr; **as** *or* **so ~as** solange; **so ~!** 🄸 tschüs!

long[2] *vi* **~ for** sich sehnen nach

long-ˈdistance *adj* Fern-; (*Sport*) Langstrecken-

longing /ˈlɒŋɪŋ/ *adj* sehnsüchtig ● *n* Sehnsucht *f*

longitude /ˈlɒŋgɪtju:d/ *n*

(*Geog*) Länge *f*

long: ~ **jump** *n* Weitsprung *m*. **~-lived** /-lɪvd/ *adj* langlebig. **~-range** *adj* (*Mil, Aviat*) Langstrecken-; (*forecast*) langfristig. **~-sighted** *adj* weitsichtig. **~-sleeved** *adj* langärmelig. **~-suffering** *adj* langmütig. **~-term** *adj* langfristig. ~ **wave** *n* Langwelle. **~-winded** /-ˈwɪndɪd/ *adj* langatmig

loo /luː/ *n* 🄵 Klo *nt*

look /lʊk/ *n* Blick *m*; (*appearance*) Aussehen *nt*; **[good] ~s** *pl* [gutes] Aussehen *nt*; **have a ~ at** sich (*dat*) ansehen; **go and have a ~** sieh mal nach ● *vi* sehen; (*search*) nachsehen; (*seem*) aussehen; **don't ~** sieh nicht hin; **~ here!** hören Sie mal! **~ at** ansehen; **~ for** suchen; **~ forward to** sich freuen auf (+ *acc*); **~ in on** vorbeischauen bei; **~ into** (*examine*) nachgehen (+ *dat*); **~ like** aussehen wie; **~ on to** (*room:*) gehen auf (+ *acc*). **~ after** *vt* betreuen. **~ down** *vi* hinuntersehen; **~ down on s.o.** (*fig*) auf jdn herabsehen. **~ out** *vi* hinaus-/heraussehen; (*take care*) aufpassen; **~ out for** Ausschau halten nach; **~ out!** Vorsicht! **~ round** *vi* sich umsehen. **~ up** *vi* aufblicken; **~ up to s.o.** (*fig*) zu jdm aufsehen ● *vt* nachschlagen (*word*)

ˈlook-out *n* Wache *f*; (*prospect*) Aussicht *f*; **be on the ~ for** Ausschau halten nach

loom¹ /luːm/ *n* Webstuhl *m*

loom² *vi* auftauchen

loony /ˈluːnɪ/ *adj* 🄵 verrückt

loop /luːp/ *n* Schlinge *f*; (*in road*) Schleife *f*. **~hole** *n* Hintertürchen *nt*; (*in the law*) Lücke *f*

loose /luːs/ *adj* (**-r, -st**) lose; (*not tight enough*) locker; (*inexact*) frei; **be at a ~ end** nichts zu tun haben. **~ ˈchange** *n* Kleingeld *nt*

loosen /ˈluːsn/ *vt* lockern

loot /luːt/ *n* Beute *f* ● *vt/i* plündern. **~er** *n* Plünderer *m*

lop /lɒp/ *vt* (*pt/pp* **lopped**) stutzen

lopˈsided *adj* schief

lord /lɔːd/ *n* Herr *m*; (*title*) Lord *m*; **House of L~s** ≈ Oberhaus *nt*; **the L~'s Prayer** das Vaterunser

lorry /ˈlɒrɪ/ *n* Last[kraft]wagen *m*

lose /luːz/ *v* (*pt/pp* **lost**) ● *vt* verlieren; (*miss*) verpassen ● *vi* verlieren; (*clock:*) nachgehen; **get lost** verloren gehen; (*person*) sich verlaufen. **~r** *n* Verlierer *m*

loss /lɒs/ *n* Verlust *m*; **be at a ~** nicht mehr weiter wissen

lost /lɒst/ *see* **lose**. **~ ˈproperty office** *n* Fundbüro *nt*

lot¹ /lɒt/ Los *nt*; (*at auction*) Posten *m*; **draw ~s** losen (**for** um)

lot² *n* **the ~** alle; (*everything*) alles; **a ~ [of]** viel; (*many*) viele; **~s of** 🄵 eine Menge; **it has changed a ~** es hat sich sehr verändert

lotion /ˈləʊʃn/ *n* Lotion *f*

lottery /ˈlɒtərɪ/ *n* Lotterie *f*. **~ ticket** *n* Los *nt*

loud /laʊd/ *adj* (**-er, -est**) laut; (*colours*) grell ● *adv* **[out] ~** laut. **~ˈspeaker** *n* Lautsprecher *m*

lounge /laʊndʒ/ *n* Wohnzimmer *nt*; (*in hotel*) Aufenthaltsraum *m*. ● *vi* sich lümmeln

louse /laʊs/ *n* (*pl* **lice**) Laus *f*

lousy /ˈlaʊzɪ/ *adj* 🄵 lausig

lout /laʊt/ *n* Flegel *m*, Lümmel *m*

lovable /ˈlʌvəbl/ *adj* liebenswert

love /lʌv/ *n* Liebe *f*; (*Tennis*) null; **in ~** verliebt ● *vt* lieben; **~ doing sth** etw sehr gerne machen. **~-affair** *n* Liebesverhältnis *nt*. **~ letter** *n* Liebesbrief *m*

lovely /ˈlʌvlɪ/ *adj* schön

lover /ˈlʌvə(r)/ *n* Liebhaber *m*

love: ~ **song** *n* Liebeslied *nt*. ~ **story** *n* Liebesgeschichte *f*

loving /ˈlʌvɪŋ/ *adj* liebevoll

low /ləʊ/ *adj* (**-er, -est**) niedrig; (*cloud, note*) tief; (*voice*) leise; (*depressed*) niedergeschlagen ● *adv* niedrig; (*fly, sing*) tief; (*speak*) leise ● *n* (*weather*) Tief *nt*; (*fig*) Tiefstand *m*

low: ~**brow** *adj* geistig anspruchslos. ~**-cut** *adj* (*dress*) tief ausgeschnitten

lower /ˈləʊə(r)/ *adj* & *adv see* **low** ● *vt* niedriger machen; (*let down*) herunterlassen; (*reduce*) senken

low: ~**-ˈfat** *adj* fettarm. ~**lands** /-ləndz/ *npl* Tiefland *nt*. ~ **ˈtide** *n* Ebbe *f*

loyal /ˈlɔɪəl/ *adj* treu. ~**ty** *n* Treue *f*. ~**ty card** *n* Treuekarte *f*

lozenge /ˈlɒzɪndʒ/ *n* Pastille *f*

Ltd *abbr* (**Limited**) GmbH

lubricant /ˈluːbrɪkənt/ *n* Schmiermittel *nt*

lubricat|e /ˈluːbrɪkeɪt/ *vt* schmieren. ~**ion** *n* Schmierung *f*

lucid /ˈluːsɪd/ *adj* klar. ~**ity** *n* Klarheit *f*

luck /lʌk/ *n* Glück *nt*; **bad** ~ Pech *nt*; **good** ~! viel Glück! ~**ily** *adv* glücklicherweise, zum Glück

lucky /ˈlʌkɪ/ *adj* glücklich; (*day, number*) Glücks-; **be** ~ Glück haben; (*thing:*) Glück bringen

lucrative /ˈluːkrətɪv/ *adj* einträglich

ludicrous /ˈluːdɪkrəs/ *adj* lächerlich

lug /lʌɡ/ *vt* (*pt/pp* **lugged**) 🄵 schleppen

luggage /ˈlʌɡɪdʒ/ *n* Gepäck *nt*

luggage: ~**-rack** *n* Gepäckablage *f*. ~**-van** *n* Gepäckwagen *m*

lukewarm /ˈluːk-/ *adj* lauwarm

lull /lʌl/ *n* Pause *f* ● *vt* ~ **to sleep** einschläfern

lullaby /ˈlʌləbaɪ/ *n* Wiegenlied *nt*

lumber /ˈlʌmbə(r)/ *n* Gerümpel *nt*; (*Amer: timber*) Bauholz *nt* ● *vt* ~ **s.o. with sth** jdm etw aufhalsen. ~**jack** *n* (*Amer*) Holzfäller *m*

luminous /ˈluːmɪnəs/ *adj* leuchtend

lump /lʌmp/ *n* Klumpen *m*; (*of sugar*) Stück *nt*; (*swelling*) Beule *f*; (*in breast*) Knoten *m*; (*tumour*) Geschwulst *f*; **a** ~ **in one's throat** 🄵 ein Kloß im Hals

lump: ~ **sugar** *n* Würfelzucker *m*. ~ **ˈsum** *n* Pauschalsumme *f*

lumpy /ˈlʌmpɪ/ *adj* klumpig

lunacy /ˈluːnəsɪ/ *n* Wahnsinn *m*

lunar /ˈluːnə(r)/ *adj* Mond-

lunatic /ˈluːnətɪk/ *n* Wahnsinnige(r) *m*/*f*

lunch /lʌntʃ/ *n* Mittagessen *nt* ● *vi* zu Mittag essen

luncheon /ˈlʌntʃn/ *n* Mittagessen *nt*. ~ **voucher** *n* Essensbon *m*

lunch: ~**-hour** *n* Mittagspause *f*. ~**-time** *n* Mittagszeit *f*

lung /lʌŋ/ *n* Lungenflügel *m*; ~**s** *pl* Lunge *f*

lunge /lʌndʒ/ *vi* sich stürzen (**at** auf + *acc*)

lurch[1] /lɜːtʃ/ *n* **leave in the** ~ 🄵 im Stich lassen

lurch[2] *vi* (*person:*) torkeln

lure /ljʊə(r)/ *vt* locken

lurid /ˈlʊərɪd/ *adj* grell; (*sensational*) reißerisch

lurk /lɜːk/ *vi* lauern

luscious /ˈlʌʃəs/ *adj* lecker, köstlich

lush /lʌʃ/ *adj* üppig

lust /lʌst/ *n* Begierde *f*. ~**ful** *adj* lüstern

lustre /ˈlʌstə(r)/ *n* Glanz *m*

lusty /ˈlʌstɪ/ *adj* kräftig
luxuriant /lʌgˈʒʊərɪənt/ *adj* üppig
luxurious /lʌgˈʒʊərɪəs/ *adj* luxuriös
luxury /ˈlʌkʃərɪ/ *n* Luxus *m* ● *attrib* Luxus-
lying /ˈlaɪɪŋ/ *see* **lie**[1], **lie**[2]
lynch /lɪntʃ/ *vt* lynchen
lyric /ˈlɪrɪk/ *adj* lyrisch. **~al** *adj* lyrisch; (*enthusiastic*) schwärmerisch. **~ poetry** *n* Lyrik *f*. **~s** *npl* [Lied]text *m*

Mm

mac /mæk/ *n* 🄵 Regenmantel *m*
macabre /məˈkɑːbr/ *adj* makaber
macaroni /mækəˈrəʊnɪ/ *n* Makkaroni *pl*
machinations /mækɪˈneɪʃnz/ *pl* Machenschaften *pl*
machine /məˈʃiːn/ *n* Maschine *f* ● *vt* (*sew*) mit der Maschine nähen; (*Techn*) maschinell bearbeiten. **~-gun** *n* Maschinengewehr *nt*
machinery /məˈʃiːnərɪ/ *n* Maschinerie *f*
mackerel /ˈmækrl/ *n inv* Makrele *f*
mackintosh /ˈmækɪntoʃ/ *n* Regenmantel *m*
mad /mæd/ *adj* (**madder, maddest**) verrückt; (*dog*) tollwütig; (🄵: *angry*) böse (**at** auf + *acc*)
madam /ˈmædəm/ *n* gnädige Frau *f*
mad 'cow disease *n* 🄵 Rinderwahnsinn *m*
madden /ˈmædn/ *vt* (*make angry*) wütend machen
made /meɪd/ *see* **make**; **~ to measure** maßgeschneidert
mad|ly /ˈmædlɪ/ *adv* 🄵 wahnsinnig. **~man** *n* Irre(r) *m*. **~ness** *n* Wahnsinn *m*
madonna /məˈdɒnə/ *n* Madonna *f*
magazine /mægəˈziːn/ *n* Zeitschrift *f*; (*Mil, Phot*) Magazin *nt*
maggot /ˈmægət/ *n* Made *f*
magic /ˈmædʒɪk/ *n* Zauber *m*; (*tricks*) Zauberkunst *f* ● *adj* magisch; (*word, wand*) Zauber-. **~al** *adj* zauberhaft
magician /məˈdʒɪʃn/ *n* Zauberer *m*; (*entertainer*) Zauberkünstler *m*
magistrate /ˈmædʒɪstreɪt/ *n* ≈ Friedensrichter *m*
magnet /ˈmægnɪt/ *n* Magnet *m*. **~ic** *adj* magnetisch. **~ism** *n* Magnetismus *m*
magnification /mægnɪfɪˈkeɪʃn/ *n* Vergrößerung *f*
magnificen|ce /mægˈnɪfɪsəns/ *n* Großartigkeit *f*. **~t** *adj* großartig
magnify /ˈmægnɪfaɪ/ *vt* (*pt/pp* **-ied**) vergrößern; (*exaggerate*) übertreiben. **~ing glass** *n* Vergrößerungsglas *nt*
magnitude /ˈmægnɪtjuːd/ *n* Größe *f*; (*importance*) Bedeutung *f*
magpie /ˈmægpaɪ/ *n* Elster *f*
mahogany /məˈhɒgənɪ/ *n* Mahagoni *nt*
maid /meɪd/ *n* Dienstmädchen *nt*; **old ~** (*pej*) alte Jungfer *f*
maiden /ˈmeɪdn/ *adj* (*speech, voyage*) Jungfern-. **~ name** *n* Mädchenname *m*
mail /meɪl/ *n* Post *f* ● *vt* mit der Post schicken
mail: ~-bag *n* Postsack *m*. **~box** *n* (*Amer*) Briefkasten *m*. **~ing list** *n* Postversandliste *f*. **~man** *n* (*Amer*) Briefträger *m*. **~-order firm** *n* Versandhaus *nt*

maim /meɪm/ *vt* verstümmeln
main /meɪn/ *adj* Haupt- ● *n* (*water, gas, electricity*) Hauptleitung *f*
main: ~land /-lənd/ *n* Festland *nt*. **~ly** *adv* hauptsächlich. **~stay** *n* (*fig*) Stütze *f*. **~ street** *n* Hauptstraße *f*
maintain /meɪn'teɪn/ *vt* aufrechterhalten; (*keep in repair*) instand halten; (*support*) unterhalten; (*claim*) behaupten
maintenance /'meɪntənəns/ *n* Aufrechterhaltung *f*; (*care*) Instandhaltung *f*; (*allowance*) Unterhalt *m*
maize /meɪz/ *n* Mais *m*
majestic /mə'dʒestɪk/ *adj*, **-ally** *adv* majestätisch
majesty /'mædʒəstɪ/ *n* Majestät *f*
major /'meɪdʒə(r)/ *adj* größer ● *n* (*Mil*) Major *m*; (*Mus*) Dur *nt* ● *vi* **~ in** als Hauptfach studieren
majority /mə'dʒɒrətɪ/ *n* Mehrheit *f*; **in the ~** in der Mehrzahl
major road *n* Hauptverkehrsstraße *f*
make /meɪk/ *n* (*brand*) Marke *f* ● *v* (*pt/pp* **made**) ● *vt* machen; (*force*) zwingen; (*earn*) verdienen; halten (*speech*); treffen (*decision*); erreichen (*destination*) ● *vi* **~ do** *vi* zurechtkommen (**with** mit). **~ for** *vi* zusteuern auf (+ *acc*). **~ off** *vi* sich davonmachen (**with** mit). **~ out** *vt* (*distinguish*) ausmachen; (*write out*) ausstellen; (*assert*) behaupten. **~ up** *vt* (*constitute*) bilden; (*invent*) erfinden; (*apply cosmetics to*) schminken; **~ up one's mind** sich entschließen ● *vi* sich versöhnen; **~ up for sth** etw wieder gutmachen; **~ up for lost time** verlorene Zeit aufholen
'make-believe *n* Phantasie *f*
maker /'meɪkə(r)/ *n* Hersteller *m*
make: ~ shift *adj* behelfsmäßig ● *n* Notbehelf *m*. **~-up** *n* Make-up *nt*
maladjusted /mælə'dʒʌstɪd/ *adj* verhaltensgestört
male /meɪl/ *adj* männlich ● *n* Mann *m*; (*animal*) Männchen *nt*. **~ nurse** *n* Krankenpfleger *m*. **~ voice 'choir** *n* Männerchor *m*
malice /'mælɪs/ *n* Bosheit *f*
malicious /mə'lɪʃəs/ *adj* böswillig
malign /mə'laɪŋ/ *vt* verleumden
malignant /mə'lɪgnənt/ *adj* bösartig
mallet /'mælɪt/ *n* Holzhammer *m*
malnu'trition /mæl-/ *n* Unterernährung *f*
mal'practice *n* Berufsvergehen *nt*
malt /mɔːlt/ *n* Malz *nt*
mal'treat /mæl-/ *vt* misshandeln. **~ment** *n* Misshandlung *f*
mammal /'mæml/ *n* Säugetier *nt*
mammoth /'mæməθ/ *adj* riesig
man /mæn/ *n* (*pl* **men**) Mann *m*; (*mankind*) der Mensch; (*chess*) Figur *f*; (*draughts*) Stein *m* ● *vt* (*pt/pp* **manned**) bemannen (*ship*); bedienen (*pump*); besetzen (*counter*)
manage /'mænɪdʒ/ *vt* leiten; verwalten (*estate*); (*cope with*) fertig werden mit; **~ to do sth** es schaffen, etw zu tun ● *vi* zurechtkommen; **~ on** auskommen mit. **~able** *adj* (*tool*) handlich; (*person*) fügsam. **~ment** *n* Leitung *f*; **the ~ment** die Geschäftsleitung *f*
manager /'mænɪdʒə(r)/ *n* Geschäftsführer *m*; (*of bank*) Direktor *m*; (*of estate*) Verwalter *m*; (*Sport*) [Chef]trainer *m*. **~ess** *n* Geschäftsführerin *f*. **~ial** *adj* **~ial staff** Führungskräfte *pl*
managing /'mænɪdʒɪŋ/ *adj* **~ director** Generaldirektor *m*
mandat|e /'mændeɪt/ *n* Mandat *nt*. **~ory** *adj* obligatorisch

mane /meɪn/ *n* Mähne *f*

manful /ˈmænfl/ *adj* mannhaft

man: **~ˈhandle** *vt* grob behandeln (*person*). **~hole** *n* Kanalschacht *m*. **~hood** *n* Mannesalter *nt*; (*quality*) Männlichkeit *f*. **~-hour** *n* Arbeitsstunde *f*. **~-hunt** *n* Fahndung *f*

man|ia /ˈmeɪnɪə/ *n* Manie *f*. **~iac** *n* Wahnsinnige(r) *m*/*f*

manicure /ˈmænɪkjʊə(r)/ *n* Maniküre *f* ● *vt* maniküren

manifest /ˈmænɪfest/ *adj* offensichtlich

manifesto /mænɪˈfestəʊ/ *n* Manifest *nt*

manifold /ˈmænɪfəʊld/ *adj* mannigfaltig

manipulat|e /məˈnɪpjʊleɪt/ *vt* handhaben; (*pej*) manipulieren. **~ion** *n* Manipulation *f*

manˈkind *n* die Menschheit

manly /ˈmænlɪ/ *adj* männlich

ˈman-made *adj* künstlich. **~ fibre** *n* Kunstfaser *f*

manner /ˈmænə(r)/ *n* Weise *f*; (*kind, behaviour*) Art *f*; **[good/bad] ~s** [gute/schlechte] Manieren *pl*. **~ism** *n* Angewohnheit *f*

manœuvrable /məˈnu:vrəbl/ *adj* manövrierfähig

manœuvre /məˈnu:və(r)/ *n* Manöver *nt* ● *vt/i* manövrieren

manor /ˈmænə(r)/ *n* Gutshof *m*; (*house*) Gutshaus *nt*

ˈmanpower *n* Arbeitskräfte *pl*

mansion /ˈmænʃn/ *n* Villa *f*

ˈmanslaughter *n* Totschlag *m*

mantelpiece /ˈmæntl-/ *n* Kaminsims *m* & *nt*

manual /ˈmænjʊəl/ *adj* Hand- ● *n* Handbuch *nt*

manufacture /mænjʊˈfæktʃə(r)/ *vt* herstellen ● *n* Herstellung *f*. **~r** *n* Hersteller *m*

manure /məˈnjʊə(r)/ *n* Mist *m*

manuscript /ˈmænjʊskrɪpt/ *n* Manuskript *nt*

many /ˈmenɪ/ *adj* viele ● *n* **a good/great ~** sehr viele

map /mæp/ *n* Landkarte *f*; (*of town*) Stadtplan *m*

maple /ˈmeɪpl/ *n* Ahorn *m*

mar /mɑ:(r)/ *vt* (*pt/pp* **marred**) verderben

marathon /ˈmærəθən/ *n* Marathon *m*

marble /ˈmɑ:bl/ *n* Marmor *m*; (*for game*) Murmel *f*

March /mɑ:tʃ/ *n* März *m*

march *n* Marsch *m* ● *vi* marschieren ● *vt* marschieren lassen; **~ s.o. off** jdn abführen

mare /ˈmeə(r)/ *n* Stute *f*

margarine /mɑ:dʒəˈri:n/ *n* Margarine *f*

margin /ˈmɑ:dʒɪn/ *n* Rand *m*; (*leeway*) Spielraum *m*; (*Comm*) Spanne *f*. **~al** *adj* geringfügig

marigold /ˈmærɪgəʊld/ *n* Ringelblume *f*

marina /məˈri:nə/ *n* Jachthafen *m*

marine /məˈri:n/ *adj* Meeres- ● *n* Marine *f*; (*sailor*) Marineinfanterist *m*

marital /ˈmærɪtl/ *adj* ehelich. **~ status** *n* Familienstand *m*

maritime /ˈmærɪtaɪm/ *adj* See-

mark[1] /mɑ:k/ *n* (*former German currency*) Mark *f*

mark[2] *n* Fleck *m*; (*sign*) Zeichen *nt*; (*trace*) Spur *f*; (*target*) Ziel *nt*; (*Sch*) Note *f* ● *vt* markieren; (*spoil*) beschädigen; (*characterize*) kennzeichnen; (*Sch*) korrigieren; (*Sport*) decken; **~ time** (*Mil*) auf der Stelle treten; (*fig*) abwarten. **~ out** *vt* markieren

marked /mɑ:kt/ *adj*, **~ly** *adv* deutlich; (*pronounced*) ausgeprägt

m

market /ˈmɑːkɪt/ *n* Markt *m* ● *vt* vertreiben; (*launch*) auf den Markt bringen. **~ing** *n* Marketing *nt*. **~ reˈsearch** *n* Marktforschung *f*

marking /ˈmɑːkɪŋ/ *n* Markierung *f*; (*on animal*) Zeichnung *f*

marksman /ˈmɑːksmən/ *n* Scharfschütze *m*

marmalade /ˈmɑːməleɪd/ *n* Orangenmarmelade *f*

maroon /məˈruːn/ *adj* dunkelrot

marooned /məˈruːnd/ *adj* (*fig*) von der Außenwelt abgeschnitten

marquee /mɑːˈkiː/ *n* Festzelt *nt*

marquetry /ˈmɑːkɪtrɪ/ *n* Einlegearbeit *f*

marriage /ˈmærɪdʒ/ *n* Ehe *f*; (*wedding*) Hochzeit *f*. **~able** *adj* heiratsfähig

married /ˈmærɪd/ *see* **marry** ● *adj* verheiratet. **~ life** *n* Eheleben *nt*

m

marrow /ˈmærəʊ/ *n* (*Anat*) Mark *nt*; (*vegetable*) Kürbis *m*

marr|y /ˈmærɪ/ *vt/i* (*pt/pp* **married**) heiraten; (*unite*) trauen; **get ~ied** heiraten

marsh /mɑːʃ/ *n* Sumpf *m*

marshal /ˈmɑːʃl/ *n* Marschall *m*; (*steward*) Ordner *m*

marshy /ˈmɑːʃɪ/ *adj* sumpfig

martial /ˈmɑːʃl/ *adj* kriegerisch. **~ ˈlaw** *n* Kriegsrecht *nt*

martyr /ˈmɑːtə(r)/ *n* Märtyrer(in) *m(f)*. **~dom** *n* Martyrium *nt*

marvel /ˈmɑːvl/ *n* Wunder *nt* ● *vi* (*pt/pp* **marvelled**) staunen (**at** über + *acc*). **~lous** a, **-ly** adv wunderbar

Marxis|m /ˈmɑːksɪzm/ *n* Marxismus *m*. **~t** *adj* marxistisch ● *n* Marxist(in) *m(f)*

marzipan /ˈmɑːzɪpæn/ *n* Marzipan *nt*

mascot /ˈmæskət/ *n* Maskottchen *nt*

masculin|e /ˈmæskjʊlɪn/ *adj* männlich ● *n* (*Gram*) Maskulinum *nt*. **~ity** *n* Männlichkeit *f*

mash /mæʃ/ *n* ⊡, **~ed potatoes** *npl* Kartoffelpüree *nt*

mask /mɑːsk/ *n* Maske *f* ● *vt* maskieren

masochis|m /ˈmæsəkɪzm/ *n* Masochismus *m*. **~t** *n* Masochist *m*

mason /ˈmeɪsn/ *n* Steinmetz *m*. **~ry** *n* Mauerwerk *nt*

mass[1] /mæs/ *n* (*Relig*) Messe *f*

mass[2] *n* Masse *f* ● *vi* sich sammeln; (*Mil*) sich massieren

massacre /ˈmæsəkə(r)/ *n* Massaker *nt* ● *vt* niedermetzeln

massage /ˈmæsɑːʒ/ *n* Massage *f* ● *vt* massieren

masseu|r /mæˈsɜː(r)/ *n* Masseur *m*. **~se** *n* Masseuse *f*

massive /ˈmæsɪv/ *adj* massiv; (*huge*) riesig

mass: ~ ˈmedia *npl* Massenmedien *pl*. **~-proˈduce** *vt* in Massenproduktion herstellen. **~proˈduction** *n* Massenproduktion *f*

mast /mɑːst/ *n* Mast *m*

master /ˈmɑːstə(r)/ *n* Herr *m*; (*teacher*) Lehrer *m*; (*craftsman, artist*) Meister *m*; (*of ship*) Kapitän *m* ● *vt* meistern; beherrschen (*language*)

master: ~ly *adj* meisterhaft. **~-mind** *n* führender Kopf *m* ● *vt* der führende Kopf sein von. **~piece** *n* Meisterwerk *nt*. **~y** *n* (*of subject*) Beherrschung *f*

mat /mæt/ *n* Matte *f*; (*on table*) Untersatz *m*

match[1] /mætʃ/ *n* Wettkampf *m*; (*in ball games*) Spiel *nt*; (*Tennis*) Match *nt*; (*marriage*) Heirat *f*; **be a good ~** (*colours:*) gut zusammenpassen; **be no ~ for s.o.** jdm nicht gewachsen sein ● *vt* (*equal*) gleichkommen (+ *dat*); (*be like*) passen zu; (*find sth similar*) etwas Passendes finden zu ● *vi* zusammenpassen

match[2] *n* Streichholz *nt*. **~box** *n* Streichholzschachtel *f*

mate[1] /meɪt/ *n* Kumpel *m*; (*assistant*) Gehilfe *m*; (*Naut*) Maat *m*; (*Zool*) Männchen *nt*; (*female*) Weibchen *nt* ● *vi* sich paaren

mate[2] *n* (*Chess*) Matt *nt*

material /məˈtɪərɪəl/ *n* Material *nt*; (*fabric*) Stoff *m*; **raw ~s** Rohstoffe *pl* ● *adj* materiell

material|ism /məˈtɪərɪəlɪzm/ *n* Materialismus *m*. **~istic** *adj* materialistisch. **~ize** *vi* sich verwirklichen

maternal /məˈtɜːnl/ *adj* mütterlich

maternity /məˈtɜːnətɪ/ *n* Mutterschaft *f*. **~ clothes** *npl* Umstandskleidung *f*. **~ ward** *n* Entbindungsstation *f*

mathematic|al /mæθəˈmætɪkl/ *adj* mathematisch. **~ian** *n* Mathematiker(in) *m*(*f*)

mathematics /mæθəˈmætɪks/ *n* Mathematik *f*

maths /mæθs/ *n* [!] Mathe *f*

matinée /ˈmætɪneɪ/ *n* (*Theat*) Nachmittagsvorstellung *f*

matrimony /ˈmætrɪmənɪ/ *n* Ehe *f*

matron /ˈmeɪtrən/ *n* (*of hospital*) Oberin *f*; (*of school*) Hausmutter *f*

matt /mæt/ *adj* matt

matted /ˈmætɪd/ *adj* verfilzt

matter /ˈmætə(r)/ *n* (*affair*) Sache *f*; (*Phys: substance*) Materie *f*; **money ~s** Geldangelegenheiten *pl*; **what is the ~?** was ist los? ● *vi* wichtig sein; **~ to s.o.** jdm etwas ausmachen; **it doesn't ~** es macht nichts. **~-of-fact** *adj* sachlich

mattress /ˈmætrɪs/ *n* Matratze *f*

matur|e /məˈtjʊə(r)/ *adj* reif; (*Comm*) fällig ● *vi* reifen; (*person:*) reifer werden; (*Comm*) fällig werden ● *vt* reifen lassen. **~ity** *n* Reife *f*; (*Comm*) Fälligkeit *f*

mauve /məʊv/ *adj* lila

maximum /ˈmæksɪməm/ *adj* maximal ● *n* (*pl* **-ima**) Maximum *nt*. **~ speed** *n* Höchstgeschwindigkeit *f*

may /meɪ/

pres **may**, *pt* **might**

● *modal verb*

····➤ (*expressing possibility*) können. **she may come** es kann sein, dass sie kommt; es ist möglich, dass sie kommt. **she might come** (*more distant possibility*) sie könnte kommen. **it may/might rain** es könnte regnen. **I may be wrong** vielleicht irre ich mich. **he may have missed his train** vielleicht hat er seinen Zug verpasst

····➤ (*expressing permission*) dürfen. **may I come in?** darf ich reinkommen? **you may smoke** Sie dürfen rauchen

····➤ (*expressing wish*) **may the best man win!** auf dass der Beste gewinnt!

····➤ (*expressing concession*) **he may be slow but he's accurate** mag *od* kann sein, dass er langsam ist, aber dafür ist er auch genau

····➤ **may/might as well** ebenso gut können. **we may/might as well go** wir könnten eigentlich ebensogut [auch] gehen. **we might as well give up** da können wir gleich aufgeben

May *n* Mai *m*

maybe /ˈmeɪbiː/ *adv* vielleicht

ˈMay Day *n* der Erste Mai

mayonnaise /meɪəˈneɪz/ *n*

m

Mayonnaise *f*
mayor /ˈmeə(r)/ *n* Bürgermeister *m*. **~ess** *n* Bürgermeisterin *f*; (*wife of mayor*) Frau Bürgermeister *f*
maze /meɪz/ *n* Irrgarten *m*; (*fig*) Labyrinth *nt*
me /miː/ *pron* (*acc*) mich; (*dat*) mir; **it's ~** [!] ich bin es
meadow /ˈmedəʊ/ *n* Wiese *f*
meagre /ˈmiːgə(r)/ *adj* dürftig
meal /miːl/ *n* Mahlzeit *f*; (*food*) Essen *nt*; (*grain*) Schrot *m*
mean[1] /miːn/ *adj* (**-er, -est**) (*miserly*) geizig; (*unkind*) gemein; (*poor*) schäbig
mean[2] *adj* mittlere(r,s) ● *n* (*average*) Durchschnitt *m*
mean[3] *vt* (*pt/pp* **meant**) heißen; (*signify*) bedeuten; (*intend*) beabsichtigen; **I ~ it** das ist mein Ernst; **~ well** es gut meinen; **be meant for** (*present:*) bestimmt sein für; (*remark:*) gerichtet sein an (+ *acc*)
meaning /ˈmiːnɪŋ/ *n* Bedeutung *f*. **~ful** *adj* bedeutungsvoll. **~less** *adj* bedeutungslos
means /miːnz/ *n* Möglichkeit *f*, Mittel *nt*; **~ of transport** Verkehrsmittel *nt*; **by ~ of** durch; **by all ~!** aber natürlich! **by no ~** keineswegs ● *npl* (*resources*) [Geld]mittel *pl*
meant /ment/ *see* **mean**[3]
ˈmeantime *n* **in the ~** in der Zwischenzeit ● *adv* inzwischen
ˈmeanwhile *adv* inzwischen
measles /ˈmiːzlz/ *n* Masern *pl*
measure /ˈmeʒə(r)/ *n* Maß *nt*; (*action*) Maßnahme *f* ● *vt/i* messen; **~ up to** (*fig*) herankommen an (+ *acc*). **~d** *adj* gemessen. **~ment** *n* Maß *nt*
meat /miːt/ *n* Fleisch *nt*
mechan|ic /mɪˈkænɪk/ *n* Mechaniker *m*. **~ical** *adj* mechanisch. **~ical engineering** Maschinenbau *m*

m

mechan|ism /ˈmekənɪzm/ *n* Mechanismus *m*. **~ize** *vt* mechanisieren
medal /ˈmedl/ *n* Orden *m*; (*Sport*) Medaille *f*
medallist /ˈmedəlɪst/ *n* Medaillengewinner(in) *m*(*f*)
meddle /ˈmedl/ *vi* sich einmischen (**in** in + *acc*); (*tinker*) herumhantieren (**with** an + *acc*)
media /ˈmiːdɪə/ *see* **medium** ● *n pl* **the ~** die Medien *pl*
mediat|e /ˈmiːdɪeɪt/ *vi* vermitteln. **~or** *n* Vermittler(in) *m*(*f*)
medical /ˈmedɪkl/ *adj* medizinisch; (*treatment*) ärztlich ● *n* ärztliche Untersuchung *f*. **~ insurance** *n* Krankenversicherung *f*. **~ student** *n* Medizinstudent *m*
medicat|ed /ˈmedɪkeɪtɪd/ *adj* medizinisch. **~ion** *n* (*drugs*) Medikamente *pl*
medicinal /mɪˈdɪsɪnl/ *adj* medizinisch; (*plant*) heilkräftig
medicine /ˈmedsən/ *n* Medizin *f*; (*preparation*) Medikament *nt*
medieval /medɪˈiːvl/ *adj* mittelalterlich
mediocr|e /miːdɪˈəʊkə(r)/ *adj* mittelmäßig. **~ity** *n* Mittelmäßigkeit *f*
meditat|e /ˈmedɪteɪt/ *vi* nachdenken (**on** über + *acc*). **~ion** *n* Meditation *f*
Mediterranean /medɪtəˈreɪnɪən/ *n* Mittelmeer *nt* ● *adj* Mittelmeer-
medium /ˈmiːdɪəm/ *adj* mittlere(r,s); (*steak*) medium; **of ~ size** von mittlerer Größe ● *n* (*pl* **media**) Medium *nt*: (*means*) Mittel *nt*
medium: ~-sized *adj* mittelgroß. **~ wave** *n* Mittelwelle *f*
medley /ˈmedlɪ/ *n* Gemisch *nt*; (*Mus*) Potpourri *nt*
meek /miːk/ *adj* (**-er, -est**) sanftmütig; (*unprotesting*, compliant)

widerspruchslos

meet /mi:t/ *v* (*pt/pp* **met**) ● *vt* treffen; (*by chance*) begegnen (+ *dat*); (*at station*) abholen; (*make the acquaintance of*) kennen lernen; stoßen auf (+ *acc*) (*problem*); bezahlen (*bill*); erfüllen (*requirements*) ● *vi* sich treffen; (*for the first time*) sich kennen lernen

meeting /'mi:tɪŋ/ *n* Treffen *nt*; (*by chance*) Begegnung *f*; (*discussion*) Besprechung *f*; (*of committee*) Sitzung *f*; (*large*) Versammlung *f*

megalomania /megələ'meɪnɪə/ *n* Größenwahnsinn *m*

megaphone /'megəfəʊn/ *n* Megaphon *nt*

melancholy /'melənkəlɪ/ *adj* melancholisch ● *n* Melancholie *f*

mellow /'meləʊ/ *adj*(**-er, -est**) (*fruit*) ausgereift; (*sound, person*) sanft ● *vi* reifer werden

melodious /mɪ'ləʊdɪəs/ *adj* melodiös

melodramatic /melədrə'mætɪk/ *adj*, **-ally** *adv* melodramatisch

melody /'melədɪ/ *n* Melodie *f*

melon /'melən/ *n* Melone *f*

melt /melt/ *vt/i* schmelzen

member /'membə(r)/ *n* Mitglied *nt*; (*of family*) Angehörige(r) *m/f*; **M~ of Parliament** Abgeordnete(r) *m/f*. **~ship** *n* Mitgliedschaft *f*; (*members*) Mitgliederzahl *f*

memento /mɪ'mentəʊ/ *n* Andenken *nt*

memo /'meməʊ/ *n* Mitteilung *f*

memoirs /'memwɑ:z/ *n pl* Memoiren *pl*

memorable /'memərəbl/ *adj* denkwürdig

memorial /mɪ'mɔ:rɪəl/ *n* Denkmal *nt*. **~ service** *n* Gedenkfeier *f*

memorize /'meməraɪz/ *vt* sich (*dat*) einprägen

memory /'memərɪ/ *n* Gedächtnis *nt*; (*thing remembered*) Erinnerung *f*; (*of computer*) Speicher *m*; **from ~** auswendig; **in ~ of** zur Erinnerung an (+ *acc*). **~ stick** *n* Memorystick *m*

men /men/ *see* **man**

menac|e /'menɪs/ *n* Drohung *f*; (*nuisance*) Plage *f* ● *vt* bedrohen. **~ing** *adj*, **~ly** *adv* drohend

mend /mend/ *vt* reparieren; (*patch*) flicken; ausbessern (*clothes*)

'menfolk *n pl* Männer *pl*

menial /'mi:nɪəl/ *adj* niedrig

menopause /'menə-/ *n* Wechseljahre *pl*

mental /'mentl/ *adj* geistig; (🅘: *mad*) verrückt. **~ a'rithmetic** *n* Kopfrechnen *nt*. **~ 'illness** *n* Geisteskrankheit *f*

mentality /men'tælətɪ/ *n* Mentalität *f*

mention /'menʃn/ *n* Erwähnung *f* ● *vt* erwähnen; **don't ~ it** keine Ursache; bitte

menu /'menju:/ *n* Speisekarte *f*

merchandise /'mɜ:tʃəndaɪz/ *n* Ware *f*

merchant /'mɜ:tʃənt/ *n* Kaufmann *m*; (*dealer*) Händler *m*. **~ 'navy** *n* Handelsmarine *f*

merci|ful /'mɜ:sɪfl/ *adj* barmherzig. **~fully** *adv* 🅘 glücklicherweise. **~less** *adj* erbarmungslos

mercury /'mɜ:kjʊrɪ/ *n* Quecksilber *nt*

mercy /'mɜ:sɪ/ *n* Barmherzigkeit *f*, Gnade *f*; **be at s.o.'s ~** jdm ausgeliefert sein

mere /mɪə(r)/ *adj* bloß

merest /'mɪərɪst/ *adj* kleinste(r,s)

merge /mɜ:dʒ/ *vi* zusammenlaufen; (*Comm*) fusionieren

merger /'mɜ:dʒə(r)/ *n* Fusion *f*

meringue /mə'ræŋ/ *n* Baiser *nt*

merit /ˈmerɪt/ *n* Verdienst *nt*; (*advantage*) Vorzug *m*; (*worth*) Wert *m* ● *vt* verdienen

merry /ˈmerɪ/ *adj* fröhlich

merry-go-round *n* Karussell *nt*

mesh /meʃ/ *n* Masche *f*

mesmerized /ˈmezməraɪzd/ *adj* (*fig*) [wie] gebannt

mess /mes/ *n* Durcheinander *nt*; (*trouble*) Schwierigkeiten *pl*; (*something spilt*) Bescherung *f* [I]; (*Mil*) Messe *f*; **make a ~ of** (*botch*) verpfuschen ● *vt* **~ up** in Unordnung bringen; (*botch*) verpfuschen ● *vi* **~ about** herumalbern; (*tinker*) herumspielen (**with** mit)

message /ˈmesɪdʒ/ *n* Nachricht *f*; **give s.o. a ~** jdm etwas ausrichten

messenger /ˈmesɪndʒə(r)/ *n* Bote *m*

m

Messrs /ˈmesəz/ *n pl see* **Mr**; (*on letter*) **~ Smith** Firma Smith

messy /ˈmesɪ/ *adj* schmutzig; (*untidy*) unordentlich

met /met/ *see* **meet**

metal /ˈmetl/ *n* Metall *nt* ● *adj* Metall-. **~lic** *adj* metallisch

metaphor /ˈmetəfə(r)/ *n* Metapher *f*. **~ical** *adj* metaphorisch

meteor /ˈmiːtɪə(r)/ *n* Meteor *m*. **~ic** *adj* kometenhaft

meteorological /miːtɪərəˈlɒdʒɪkl/ *adj* Wetter-

meteorolog|ist /miːtɪəˈrɒlədʒɪst/ *n* Meteorologe *m*/ -gin *f*. **~y** *n* Meteorologie *f*

meter¹ /ˈmiːtə(r)/ *n* Zähler *m*

meter² *n* (*Amer*) = **metre**

method /ˈmeθəd/ *n* Methode *f*; (*Culin*) Zubereitung *f*

methodical /mɪˈθɒdɪkl/ *adj* systematisch, methodisch

methylated /ˈmeθɪleɪtɪd/ *adj* **~ spirit[s]** Brennspiritus *m*

meticulous /mɪˈtɪkjʊləs/ *adj* sehr genau

metre /ˈmiːtə(r)/ *n* Meter *m* & *n*; (*rhythm*) Versmaß *nt*

metric /ˈmetrɪk/ *adj* metrisch

metropolis /mɪˈtrɒpəlɪs/ *n* Metropole *f*

metropolitan /metrəˈpɒlɪtən/ *adj* hauptstädtisch; (*international*) weltstädtisch

mew /mjuː/ *n* Miau *nt* ● *vi* miauen

Mexican /ˈmeksɪkən/ *adj* mexikanisch ● *n* Mexikaner(in) *m*(*f*). **ˈMexico** *n* Mexiko *nt*

miaow /mɪˈaʊ/ *n* Miau *nt* ● *vi* miauen

mice /maɪs/ *see* **mouse**

micro: ~film *n* Mikrofilm *m*. **~light [aircraft]** *n* Ultraleichtflugzeug *nt*. **~phone** *n* Mikrofon *nt*. **~scope** /-skəʊp/ *n* Mikroskop *nt*. **~scopic** /-ˈskɒpɪk/ *adj* mikroskopisch. **~wave [oven]** *n* Mikrowellenherd *m*

mid /mɪd/ *adj* **~ May** Mitte Mai; **in ~ air** in der Luft

midday /mɪdˈdeɪ/ *n* Mittag *m*

middle /ˈmɪdl/ *adj* mittlere(r,s); **the M~ Ages** das Mittelalter; **the ~ class[es]** der Mittelstand; **the M~ East** der Nahe Osten ● *n* Mitte *f*; **in the ~ of the night** mitten in der Nacht

middle: ~-aged *adj* mittleren Alters. **~-class** *adj* bürgerlich

midge /mɪdʒ/ *n* [kleine] Mücke *f*

midget /ˈmɪdʒɪt/ *n* Liliputaner(in) *m*(*f*)

Midlands /ˈmɪdləndz/ *npl* **the ~** Mittelengland *n*

ˈmidnight *n* Mitternacht *f*

midriff /ˈmɪdrɪf/ *n* [I] Taille *f*

midst /mɪdst/ *n* **in the ~ of** mitten in (+ *dat*); **in our ~** unter uns

mid: ~summer *n* Hochsommer *m*. **~way** *adv* auf halbem Wege. **~wife** *n* Hebamme *f*. **~'winter** *n* Mitte *f* des Winters

might¹ /maɪt/ *modal verb* **I ~** vielleicht; **it ~ be true** es könnte wahr sein; **he asked if he ~ go** er fragte, ob er gehen dürfte; **you ~ have drowned** du hättest ertrinken können

might² *n* Macht *f*

mighty /ˈmaɪtɪ/ *adj* mächtig

migraine /ˈmiːgreɪn/ *n* Migräne *f*

migrat|e /maɪˈgreɪt/ *vi* abwandern; (*birds:*) ziehen. **~ion** *n* Wanderung *f*; (*of birds*) Zug *m*

mike /maɪk/ *n* 🄵 Mikrofon *nt*

mild /maɪld/ *adj* (**-er, -est**) mild

mild|ly /ˈmaɪldlɪ/ *adv* leicht; **to put it ~ly** gelinde gesagt. **~ness** *n* Milde *f*

mile /maɪl/ *n* Meile *f* (= *1,6 km*); **~s too big** 🄵 viel zu groß

mile|age /-ɪdʒ/ *n* Meilenzahl *f*; (*of car*) Meilenstand *m*

militant /ˈmɪlɪtənt/ *adj* militant

military /ˈmɪlɪtrɪ/ *adj* militärisch. **~ service** *n* Wehrdienst *m*

milk /mɪlk/ *n* Milch *f* ● *vt* melken

milk: ~man *n* Milchmann *m*. **~shake** *n* Milchmixgetränk *nt*. **~tooth** *n* Milchzahn *m*

milky /ˈmɪlkɪ/ *adj* milchig. **M~ Way** *n* (*Astronomy*) Milchstraße *f*

mill /mɪl/ *n* Mühle *f*; (*factory*) Fabrik *f*

millennium /mɪˈlenɪəm/ *n* Jahrtausend *nt*

milli|gram /ˈmɪlɪ-/ *n* Milligramm *nt*. **~metre** *n* Millimeter *m* & *nt*

million /ˈmɪljən/ *n* Million *f*; **a ~ pounds** eine Million Pfund. **~aire** *n* Millionär(in) *m*(*f*)

mime /maɪm/ *n* Pantomime *f* ● *vt* pantomimisch darstellen

mimic /ˈmɪmɪk/ *n* Imitator *m* ● *vt* (*pt/pp* **mimicked**) nachahmen

mince /mɪns/ *n* Hackfleisch *nt* ● *vt* (*Culin*) durchdrehen; **not ~ words** kein Blatt vor den Mund nehmen

mince: ~meat *n* Masse *f* aus Korinthen, Zitronat *usw*; **make ~meat of** (*fig*) vernichtend schlagen. **~'pie** *n* mit 'mincemeat' gefülltes Pastetchen *nt*

mincer /ˈmɪnsə(r)/ *n* Fleischwolf *m*

mind /maɪnd/ *n* Geist *m*; (*sanity*) Verstand *m*; **give s.o. a piece of one's ~** jdm gehörig die Meinung sagen; **make up one's ~** sich entschließen; **be out of one's ~** nicht bei Verstand sein; **have sth in ~** etw im Sinn haben; **bear sth in ~** an etw (*acc*) denken; **have a good ~ to** große Lust haben, zu; **I have changed my ~** ich habe es mir anders überlegt ● *vt* aufpassen auf (+ *acc*); **I don't ~ the noise** der Lärm stört mich nicht; **~ the step!** Achtung Stufe! ● *vi* (*care*) sich kümmern (**about** um); **I don't ~** mir macht es nichts aus; **never ~!** macht nichts! **do you ~ if?** haben Sie etwas dagegen, wenn? **~ out** *vi* aufpassen

'mindless *adj* geistlos

mine¹ /maɪn/ *poss pron* meine(r), meins; **a friend of ~** ein Freund von mir; **that is ~** das gehört mir

mine² *n* Bergwerk *nt*; (*explosive*) Mine *f* ● *vt* abbauen; (*Mil*) verminen

miner /ˈmaɪnə(r)/ *n* Bergarbeiter *m*

mineral /ˈmɪnərl/ *n* Mineral *nt*. **~ water** *n* Mineralwasser *nt*

minesweeper /ˈmaɪn-/ *n* Minenräumboot *nt*

mingle /ˈmɪŋgl/ *vi* **~ with** sich mischen unter (+ *acc*)

miniature /ˈmɪnɪtʃə(r)/ *adj* Klein-

● *n* Miniatur *f*

mini|bus /ˈmɪnɪ-/ *n* Kleinbus *m*. **~cab** *n* Kleintaxi *nt*

minim|al /ˈmɪnɪməl/ *adj* minimal. **~um** *n* (*pl* **-ima**) Minimum *nt* ● *adj* Mindest-

mining /ˈmaɪnɪŋ/ *n* Bergbau *m*

miniskirt /ˈmɪnɪ-/ *n* Minirock *m*

minist|er /ˈmɪnɪstə(r)/ *n* Minister *m*; (*Relig*) Pastor *m*. **~erial** *adj* ministeriell

ministry /ˈmɪnɪstrɪ/ *n* (*Pol*) Ministerium *nt*

mink /mɪŋk/ *n* Nerz *m*

minor /ˈmaɪnə(r)/ *adj* kleiner; (*less important*) unbedeutend ● *n* Minderjährige(r) *m/f*; (*Mus*) Moll *nt*

minority /maɪˈnɒrətɪ/ *n* Minderheit *f*

minor road *n* Nebenstraße *f*

m

mint[1] /mɪnt/ *n* Münzstätte *f* ● *adj* (*stamp*) postfrisch; **in ~ condition** wie neu ● *vt* prägen

mint[2] *n* (*herb*) Minze *f*; (*sweet*) Pfefferminzbonbon *m* & *nt*

minus /ˈmaɪnəs/ *prep* minus, weniger; ([!]: *without*) ohne

minute[1] /ˈmɪnɪt/ *n* Minute *f*; **in a ~** (*shortly*) gleich; **~s** *pl* (*of meeting*) Protokoll *nt*

minute[2] /maɪˈnju:t/ *adj* winzig

mirac|le /ˈmɪrəkl/ *n* Wunder *nt*. **~ulous** *adj* wunderbar

mirror /ˈmɪrə(r)/ *n* Spiegel *m* ● *vt* widerspiegeln

mirth /mɜ:θ/ *n* Heiterkeit *f*

misadˈventure /mɪs-/ *n* Missgeschick *nt*

misappreˈhension *n* Missverständnis *nt*; **be under a ~** sich irren

misbeˈhav|e *vi* sich schlecht benehmen. **~iour** *n* schlechtes Benehmen *nt*

misˈcalcu|late *vt* falsch berechnen ● *vi* sich verrechnen. **~ˈlation** *n* Fehlkalkulation *f*

ˈmiscarriage *n* Fehlgeburt *f*

miscellaneous /mɪsəˈleɪnɪəs/ *adj* vermischt

mischief /ˈmɪstʃɪf/ *n* Unfug *m*

mischievous /ˈmɪstʃɪvəs/ *adj* schelmisch; (*malicious*) boshaft

misconˈception *n* falsche Vorstellung *f*

misˈconduct *n* unkorrektes Verhalten *nt*; (*adultery*) Ehebruch *m*

miser /ˈmaɪzə(r)/ *n* Geizhals *m*

miserable /ˈmɪzrəbl/ *adj*, **-bly** *adv* unglücklich; (*wretched*) elend

miserly /ˈmaɪzəlɪ/ *adv* geizig

misery /ˈmɪzərɪ/ *n* Elend *nt*; ([!]: *person*) Miesepeter *m*

misˈfire *vi* fehlzünden; (*go wrong*) fehlschlagen

ˈmisfit *n* Außenseiter(in) *m*(*f*)

misˈfortune *n* Unglück *nt*

misˈgivings *npl* Bedenken *pl*

misˈguided *adj* töricht

mishap /ˈmɪshæp/ *n* Missgeschick *nt*

misinˈform *vt* falsch unterrichten

misinˈterpret *vt* missdeuten

misˈjudge *vt* falsch beurteilen

misˈlay *vt* (*pt/pp* **-laid**) verlegen

misˈlead *vt* (*pt/pp* **-led**) irreführen. **~ing** *adj* irreführend

misˈmanage *vt* schlecht verwalten. **~ment** *n* Misswirtschaft *f*

misnomer /mɪsˈnəʊmə(r)/ *n* Fehlbezeichnung *f*

ˈmisprint *n* Druckfehler *m*

misˈquote *vt* falsch zitieren

misrepreˈsent *vt* falsch darstellen

miss /mɪs/ *n* Fehltreffer *m* ● *vt* verpassen; (*fail to hit or find*) verfehlen; (*fail to attend*) versäumen; (*fail to notice*) übersehen; (*feel the loss of*) vermissen ●*vi* (*fail to hit*) nicht treffen. ~ **out** *vt* auslassen

Miss *n* (*pl* **-es**) Fräulein *nt*

missile /'mɪsaɪl/ *n* [Wurf]geschoss *nt*; (*Mil*) Rakete *f*

missing /'mɪsɪŋ/ *adj* fehlend; (*lost*) verschwunden; (*Mil*) vermisst; **be** ~ fehlen

mission /'mɪʃn/ *n* Auftrag *m*; (*Mil*) Einsatz *m*; (*Relig*) Mission *f*

missionary /'mɪʃənrɪ/ *n* Missionar(in) *m*(*f*)

mis'spell *vt* (*pt/pp* **-spelt** or **-spelled**) falsch schreiben

mist /mɪst/ *n* Dunst *m*; (*fog*) Nebel *m*; (*on window*) Beschlag *m* ●*vi* ~ **up** beschlagen

mistake /mɪ'steɪk/ *n* Fehler *m*; **by** ~ aus Versehen ●*vt* (*pt* **mistook**, *pp* **mistaken**); ~ **for** verwechseln mit

mistaken /mɪ'steɪkən/ *adj* falsch; **be** ~ sich irren. ~**ly** *adv* irrtümlicherweise

mistletoe /'mɪsltəʊ/ *n* Mistel *f*

mistress /'mɪstrɪs/ *n* Herrin *f*; (*teacher*) Lehrerin *f*; (*lover*) Geliebte *f*

mis'trust *n* Misstrauen *nt* ●*vt* misstrauen (+ *dat*)

misty /'mɪstɪ/ *adj* dunstig; (*foggy*) neblig; (*fig*) unklar

misunder'stand *vt* (*pt/pp* **-stood**) missverstehen. ~**ing** *n* Missverständnis *nt*

misuse[1] /mɪs'ju:z/ *vt* missbrauchen

misuse[2] /mɪs'ju:s/ *n* Missbrauch *m*

mitigating /'mɪtɪgeɪtɪŋ/ *adj* mildernd

mix /mɪks/ *n* Mischung *f* ●*vt* mischen ●*vi* sich mischen; ~ **with** (*associate with*) verkehren mit. ~ **up** *vt* mischen; (*muddle*) durcheinander bringen; (*mistake for*) verwechseln (**with** mit)

mixed /mɪkst/ *adj* gemischt; **be** ~ **up** durcheinander sein

mixer /'mɪksə(r)/ *n* Mischmaschine *f*; (*Culin*) Küchenmaschine *f*

mixture /'mɪkstʃə(r)/ *n* Mischung *f*; (*medicine*) Mixtur *f*; (*Culin*) Teig *m*

'mix-up *n* Durcheinander *nt*; (*confusion*) Verwirrung *f*; (*mistake*) Verwechslung *f*

moan /məʊn/ *n* Stöhnen *nt* ●*vi* stöhnen; (*complain*) jammern

mob /mɒb/ *n* Horde *f*; (*rabble*) Pöbel *m*; (🄸: *gang*) Bande *f* ●*vt* (*pt/pp* **mobbed**) herfallen über (+ *acc*); belagern (*celebrity*)

mobile /'məʊbaɪl/ *adj* beweglich ●*n* Mobile *nt*; (*telephone*) Handy *nt*. ~ **'home** *n* Wohnwagen *m*. ~ **'phone** *n* Handy *nt*

mobility /mə'bɪlətɪ/ *n* Beweglichkeit *f*

mock /mɒk/ *adj* Schein- ●*vt* verspotten. ~**ery** *n* Spott *m*

'mock-up *n* Modell *nt*

mode /məʊd/ *n* [Art und] Weise *f*; (*fashion*) Mode *f*

model /'mɒdl/ *n* Modell *nt*; (*example*) Vorbild *nt*; **[fashion]** ~ Mannequin *nt* ●*adj* Modell-; (*exemplary*) Muster- ●*v* (*pt/pp* **modelled**) ●*vt* formen, modellieren; vorführen (*clothes*) ●*vi* Mannequin sein; (*for artist*) Modell stehen

moderate[1] /'mɒdəreɪt/ *vt* mäßigen

moderate[2] /'mɒdərət/ *adj* mäßig; (*opinion*) gemäßigt. ~**ly** *adv* mäßig; (*fairly*) einigermaßen

moderation /mɒdə'reɪʃn/ *n* Mäßigung *f*; **in** ~ mit Maß[en]

modern /'mɒdn/ *adj* modern. ~**ize** *vt* modernisieren. ~ **'languages** *npl* neuere Sprachen *pl*

modest /ˈmɒdɪst/ *adj* bescheiden; (*decorous*) schamhaft. **~y** *n* Bescheidenheit *f*

modif|ication /mɒdɪfɪˈkeɪʃn/ *n* Abänderung *f*. **~y** *vt* (*pt/pp* **-fied**) abändern

module /ˈmɒdju:l/ *n* Element *nt*; (*of course*) Kurseinheit *f*

moist /mɔɪst/ *adj* (**-er, -est**) feucht

moisten /ˈmɔɪsn/ *vt* befeuchten

moistur|e /ˈmɔɪstʃə(r)/ *n* Feuchtigkeit *f*. **~izer** *n* Feuchtigkeitscreme *f*

molar /ˈməʊlə(r)/ *n* Backenzahn *m*

mole[1] /məʊl/ *n* Leberfleck *m*

mole[2] *n* (*Zool*) Maulwurf *m*

molecule /ˈmɒlɪkju:l/ *n* Molekül *nt*

molest /məˈlest/ *vt* belästigen

mollify /ˈmɒlɪfaɪ/ *vt* (*pt/pp* **-ied**) besänftigen

m

mollycoddle /ˈmɒlɪkɒdl/ *vt* verzärteln

molten /ˈməʊltən/ *adj* geschmolzen

mom /mɒm/ *n* (*Amer fam*) Mutti *f*

moment /ˈməʊmənt/ *n* Moment *m*, Augenblick *m*; **at the ~** im Augenblick, augenblicklich. **~ary** *adj* vorübergehend

momentous /məˈmentəs/ *adj* bedeutsam

momentum /məˈmentəm/ *n* Schwung *m*

monarch /ˈmɒnək/ *n* Monarch(in) *m(f)*. **~y** *n* Monarchie *f*

monastery /ˈmɒnəstrɪ/ *n* Kloster *nt*

Monday /ˈmʌndeɪ/ *n* Montag *m*

money /ˈmʌnɪ/ *n* Geld *nt*

money: ~-box *n* Sparbüchse *f*. **~-lender** *n* Geldverleiher *m*. **~ order** *n* Zahlungsanweisung *f*

mongrel /ˈmʌŋgrəl/ *n* Promenadenmischung *f*

monitor /ˈmɒnɪtə(r)/ *n* (*Techn*) Monitor *m* ● *vt* überwachen (*progress*); abhören (*broadcast*)

monk /mʌŋk/ *n* Mönch *m*

monkey /ˈmʌŋkɪ/ *n* Affe *m*

mono /ˈmɒnəʊ/ *n* Mono *nt*

monogram /ˈmɒnəgræm/ *n* Monogramm *nt*

monologue /ˈmɒnəlɒg/ *n* Monolog *m*

monopol|ize /məˈnɒpəlaɪz/ *vt* monopolisieren. **~y** *n* Monopol *nt*

monosyllable /ˈmɒnəsɪləbl/ *n* einsilbiges Wort *nt*

monotone /ˈmɒnətəʊn/ *n* **in a ~** mit monotoner Stimme

monoton|ous /məˈnɒtənəs/ *adj* eintönig, monoton; (*tedious*) langweilig. **~y** *n* Eintönigkeit *f*, Monotonie *f*

monster /ˈmɒnstə(r)/ *n* Ungeheuer *nt*; (*cruel person*) Unmensch *m*

monstrosity /mɒnˈstrɒsətɪ/ *n* Monstrosität *f*

monstrous /ˈmɒnstrəs/ *adj* ungeheuer; (*outrageous*) ungeheuerlich

month /mʌnθ/ *n* Monat *m*. **~ly** *adj & adv* monatlich ● *n* (*periodical*) Monatszeitschrift *f*

monument /ˈmɒnjʊmənt/ *n* Denkmal *nt*. **~al** *adj* (*fig*) monumental

moo /mu:/ *n* Muh *nt* ● *vi* (*pt/pp* **mooed**) muhen

mood /mu:d/ *n* Laune *f*; **be in a good/bad ~** gute/schlechte Laune haben

moody /ˈmu:dɪ/ *adj* launisch

moon /mu:n/ *n* Mond *m*; **over the ~** ! überglücklich

moon: ~light *n* Mondschein *m*. **~lighting** *n* ! ≈ Schwarzarbeit *f*.

~lit *adj* mondhell

moor[1] /mʊə(r)/ *n* Moor *nt*

moor[2] *vt* (*Naut*) festmachen ● *vi* anlegen

mop /mɒp/ *n* Mopp *m*; **~ of hair** Wuschelkopf *m* ● *vt* (*pt/pp* **mopped**) wischen. **~ up** *vt* aufwischen

moped /ˈməʊped/ *n* Moped *nt*

moral /ˈmɒrl/ *adj* moralisch, sittlich; (*virtuous*) tugendhaft ● *n* Moral *f*; **~s** *pl* Moral *f*

morale /məˈrɑːl/ *n* Moral *f*

morality /məˈrælətɪ/ *n* Sittlichkeit *f*

morbid /ˈmɔːbɪd/ *adj* krankhaft; (*gloomy*) trübe

more /mɔː(r)/ *a, adv* & *n* mehr; (*in addition*) noch; **a few ~** noch ein paar; **any ~** noch etwas; **once ~** noch einmal; **~ or less** mehr oder weniger; **some ~ tea?** noch etwas Tee? **~ interesting** interessanter; **~ [and ~] quickly** [immer] schneller

moreover /mɔːˈrəʊvə(r)/ *adv* außerdem

morgue /mɔːg/ *n* Leichenschauhaus *nt*

morning /ˈmɔːnɪŋ/ *n* Morgen *m*; **in the ~** morgens, am Morgen; (*tomorrow*) morgen früh

Morocco /məˈrɒkəʊ/ *n* Marokko *nt*

moron /ˈmɔːrɒn/ *n* [!] Idiot *m*

morose /məˈrəʊs/ *adj* mürrisch

morsel /ˈmɔːsl/ *n* Happen *m*

mortal /ˈmɔːtl/ *adj* sterblich; (*fatal*) tödlich ● *n* Sterbliche(r) *m/f*. **~ity** *n* Sterblichkeit *f*. **~ly** *adv* tödlich

mortar /ˈmɔːtə(r)/ *n* Mörtel *m*

mortgage /ˈmɔːgɪdʒ/ *n* Hypothek *f* ● *vt* hypothekarisch belasten

mortuary /ˈmɔːtjʊərɪ/ *n* Leichenhalle *f*; (*public*) Leichenschauhaus *nt*; (*Amer*: *undertaker's*) Bestattungsinstitut *nt*

mosaic /məʊˈzeɪɪk/ *n* Mosaik *nt*

Moscow /ˈmɒskəʊ/ *n* Moskau *nt*

mosque /mɒsk/ *n* Moschee *f*

mosquito /mɒsˈkiːtəʊ/ *n* (*pl* **-es**) [Stech]mücke *f*, Schnake *f*; (*tropical*) Moskito *m*

moss /mɒs/ *n* Moos *nt*. **~y** *adj* moosig

most /məʊst/ *adj* der/die/das meiste; (*majority*) die meisten; **for the ~ part** zum größten Teil ● *adv* am meisten; (*very*) höchst; **the ~ interesting day** der interessanteste Tag; **~ unlikely** höchst unwahrscheinlich ● *n* das meiste; **~ of them** die meisten [von ihnen]; **at [the] ~** höchstens; **~ of the time** die meiste Zeit. **~ly** *adv* meist

MOT *n* ≈ TÜV *m*

motel /məʊˈtel/ *n* Motel *nt*

moth /mɒθ/ *n* Nachtfalter *m*; [clothes-] **~** Motte *f*

ˈmothball *n* Mottenkugel *f*

mother /ˈmʌðə(r)/ *n* Mutter *f*

mother: ~hood *n* Mutterschaft *f*. **~-in-law** *n* (*pl* **~s-in-law**) Schwiegermutter *f*. **~land** *n* Mutterland *nt*. **~ly** *adj* mütterlich. **~-of-pearl** *n* Perlmutter *f*. **~-to-be** *n* werdende Mutter *f*

mothproof /ˈmɒθ-/ *adj* mottenfest

motif /məʊˈtiːf/ *n* Motiv *nt*

motion /ˈməʊʃn/ *n* Bewegung *f*; (*proposal*) Antrag *m*. **~less** *adj* bewegungslos

motivat|e /ˈməʊtɪveɪt/ *vt* motivieren. **~ion** *n* Motivation *f*

motive /ˈməʊtɪv/ *n* Motiv *nt*

motor /ˈməʊtə(r)/ *n* Motor *m*; (*car*) Auto *nt* ● *adj* Motor-; (*Anat*) motorisch ● *vi* [mit dem Auto] fahren

motor: ~ **bike** *n* [!] Motorrad *nt*. ~ **boat** *n* Motorboot *nt*. ~ **car** *n* Auto *nt*, Wagen *m*. ~ **cycle** *n* Motorrad *nt*. ~**-cyclist** *n* Motorradfahrer *m*. ~**ing** *n* Autofahren *nt*. ~**ist** *n* Autofahrer(in) *m*(*f*). ~ **vehicle** *n* Kraftfahrzeug *nt*. ~**way** *n* Autobahn *f*

mottled /'mɒtld/ *adj* gesprenkelt

motto /'mɒtəʊ/ *n* (*pl* **-es**) Motto *nt*

mould[1] /məʊld/ *n* (*fungus*) Schimmel *m*

mould[2] *n* Form *f* ● *vt* formen (**into** zu). ~**ing** *n* (*decorative*) Fries *m*

mouldy /'məʊldɪ/ *adj* schimmelig; ([!]: *worthless*) schäbig

mound /maʊnd/ *n* Hügel *m*; (*of stones*) Haufen *m*

mount *n* (*animal*) Reittier *nt*; (*of jewel*) Fassung *f*; (*of photo, picture*) Passepartout *nt* ● *vt* (*get on*) steigen auf (+ *acc*); (*on pedestal*) montieren auf (+ *acc*); besteigen (*horse*); fassen (*jewel*); aufziehen (*photo, picture*) ● *vi* aufsteigen; (*tension:*) steigen. ~ **up** *vi* sich häufen; (*add up*) sich anhäufen

m

mountain /'maʊntɪn/ *n* Berg *m*

mountaineer /maʊntɪ'nɪə(r)/ *n* Bergsteiger(in) *m*(*f*). ~**ing** *n* Bergsteigen *nt*

mountainous /'maʊntɪnəs/ *adj* bergig, gebirgig

mourn /mɔːn/ *vt* betrauern ● *vi* trauern (**for** um). ~**er** *n* Trauernde(r) *m*/*f*. ~**ful** *adj* trauervoll. ~**ing** *n* Trauer *f*

mouse /maʊs/ *n* (*pl* **mice**) Maus *f*. ~**trap** *n* Mausefalle *f*

moustache /mə'stɑːʃ/ *n* Schnurrbart *m*

mouth[1] /maʊð/ *vt* ~ **sth** etw lautlos mit den Lippen sagen

mouth[2] /maʊθ/ *n* Mund *m*; (*of animal*) Maul *nt*; (*of river*) Mündung *f*

mouth: ~**ful** *n* Mundvoll *m*; (*bite*) Bissen *m*. ~**-organ** *n* Mundharmonika *f*. ~**wash** *n* Mundwasser *nt*

movable /'muːvəbl/ *adj* beweglich

move /muːv/ *n* Bewegung *f*; (*fig*) Schritt *m*; (*moving house*) Umzug *m*; (*in board game*) Zug *m*; **on the** ~ unterwegs; **get a** ~ **on** [!] sich beeilen ● *vt* bewegen; (*emotionally*) rühren; (*move along*) rücken; (*in board game*) ziehen; (*take away*) wegnehmen; wegfahren (*car*); (*rearrange*) umstellen; (*transfer*) versetzen (*person*); verlegen (*office*); (*propose*) beantragen; ~ **house** umziehen ● *vi* sich bewegen; (*move house*) umziehen; **don't** ~**!** stillhalten! (*stop*) stillstehen! ~ **along** *vt*/*i* weiterrücken. ~ **away** *vt*/*i* wegrücken; (*move house*) wegziehen. ~ **in** *vi* einziehen. ~ **off** *vi* (*vehicle:*) losfahren. ~ **out** *vi* ausziehen. ~ **over** *vt*/*i* [zur Seite] rücken. ~ **up** *vi* aufrücken

movement /'muːvmənt/ *n* Bewegung *f*; (*Mus*) Satz *m*; (*of clock*) Uhrwerk *nt*

movie /'muːvɪ/ *n* (*Amer*) Film *m*; **go to the** ~**s** ins Kino gehen

moving /'muːvɪŋ/ *adj* beweglich; (*touching*) rührend

mow /məʊ/ *vt* (*pt* **mowed**, *pp* **mown** *or* **mowed**) mähen

mower /'məʊə(r)/ *n* Rasenmäher *m*

MP *abbr* **Member of Parliament**

Mr /'mɪstə(r)/ *n* (*pl* **Messrs**) Herr *m*

Mrs /'mɪsɪz/ *n* Frau *f*

Ms /mɪz/ *n* Frau *f*

much /mʌtʃ/ *a, adv* & *n* viel; **as** ~ **as** so viel wie; ~ **loved** sehr geliebt

muck /mʌk/ *n* Mist *m*; ([!]: *filth*) Dreck *m*. ~ **about** *vi* herumalbern; (*tinker*) herumspielen (**with** mit). ~

out *vt* ausmisten. ~ **up** *vt* [!] vermasseln; (*make dirty*) schmutzig machen

mucky /ˈmʌkɪ/ *adj* dreckig

mud /mʌd/ *n* Schlamm *m*

muddle /ˈmʌdl/ *n* Durcheinander *nt*; (*confusion*) Verwirrung *f* ● *vt* ~ [**up**] durcheinander bringen

muddy /ˈmʌdɪ/ *adj* schlammig; (*shoes*) schmutzig

ˈ**mudguard** *n* Kotflügel *m*; (*on bicycle*) Schutzblech *nt*

muffle /ˈmʌfl/ *vt* dämpfen

muffler /ˈmʌflə(r)/ *n* Schal *m*; (*Amer, Auto*) Auspufftopf *m*

mug[1] /mʌg/ *n* Becher *m*; (*for beer*) Bierkrug *m*; ([!]: *face*) Visage *f*; ([!]: *simpleton*) Trottel *m*

mug[2] *vt* (*pt/pp* **mugged**) überfallen. ~**ger** *n* Straßenräuber *m*. ~**ging** *n* Straßenraub *m*

muggy /ˈmʌgɪ/ *adj* schwül

mule /mju:l/ *n* Maultier *nt*

mulled /mʌld/ *adj* ~ **wine** Glühwein *m*

multi /ˈmʌltɪ/: ~**coloured** *adj* vielfarbig, bunt. ~**lingual** *adj* mehrsprachig. ~ˈ**national** *adj* multinational

multiple /ˈmʌltɪpl/ *adj* vielfach; (*with pl*) mehrere ● *n* Vielfache(s) *nt*

multiplication /mʌltɪplɪˈkeɪʃn/ *n* Multiplikation *f*

multiply /ˈmʌltɪplaɪ/ *v* (*pt/pp* **-ied**) ● *vt* multiplizieren (**by** mit) ● *vi* sich vermehren

multistorey *adj* ~ **car park** Parkhaus *nt*

mum/mʌm/ *n* [!] Mutti *f*

mumble /ˈmʌmbl/ *vt/i* murmeln

mummy[1] /ˈmʌmɪ/ *n* [!] Mutti *f*

mummy[2] *n* (*Archaeology*) Mumie *f*

mumps /mʌmps/ *n* Mumps *m*

munch /mʌntʃ/ *vt/i* mampfen

municipal /mju:ˈnɪsɪpl/ *adj* städtisch

munitions /mju:ˈnɪʃnz/ *npl* Kriegsmaterial *nt*

mural /ˈmjʊərəl/ *n* Wandgemälde *nt*

murder /ˈmɜ:də(r)/ *n* Mord *m* ● *vt* ermorden. ~**er** *n* Mörder *m*. ~**ess** *n* Mörderin *f*. ~**ous** *adj* mörderisch

murky /ˈmɜ:kɪ/ *adj* düster

murmur /ˈmɜ:mə(r)/ *n* Murmeln *nt* ● *vt/i* murmeln

muscle /ˈmʌsl/ *n* Muskel *m*

muscular /ˈmʌskjʊlə(r)/ *adj* Muskel-; (*strong*) muskulös

museum /mju:ˈzɪəm/ *n* Museum *nt*

mushroom /ˈmʌʃrʊm/ *n* [essbarer] Pilz *m*, *esp* Champignon *m* ● *vi* (*fig*) wie Pilze aus dem Boden schießen

mushy /ˈmʌʃɪ/ *adj* breiig

music /ˈmju:zɪk/ *n* Musik *f*; (*written*) Noten *pl*; **set to** ~ vertonen

musical /ˈmju:zɪkl/ *adj* musikalisch ● *n* Musical *nt*. ~ **box** *n* Spieldose *f*. ~ **instrument** *n* Musikinstrument *nt*

musician /mju:ˈzɪʃn/ *n* Musiker(in) *m*(*f*)

ˈ**music-stand** *n* Notenständer *m*

Muslim /ˈmʊzlɪm/ *adj* mohammedanisch ● *n* Mohammedaner(in) *m*(*f*)

must /mʌst/ *modal verb* (*nur Präsens*) müssen; (*with negative*) dürfen ● *n* **a** ~ [!] ein Muss *nt*

mustard /ˈmʌstəd/ *n* Senf *m*

musty /ˈmʌstɪ/ *adj* muffig

mute /mju:t/ *adj* stumm

mutilat|e /ˈmju:tɪleɪt/ *vt* verstümmeln. ~**ion** *n* Verstümmelung *f*

mutin|ous /ˈmju:tɪnəs/ *adj* meuterisch. ~**y** *n* Meuterei *f* ● *vi* (*pt/pp*

-ied) meutern

mutter /ˈmʌtə(r)/ *n* Murmeln *nt* ● *vt/i* murmeln

mutton /ˈmʌtn/ *n* Hammelfleisch *nt*

mutual /ˈmjuːtjʊəl/ *adj* gegenseitig; (🄸: *common*) gemeinsam. **~ly** *adv* gegenseitig

muzzle /ˈmʌzl/ *n* (*of animal*) Schnauze *f*; (*of firearm*) Mündung *f*; (*for dog*) Maulkorb *m*

my /maɪ/ *adj* mein

myself /maɪˈself/ *pron* selbst; (*reflexive*) mich; **by ~** allein; **I thought to ~** ich habe mir gedacht

mysterious /mɪˈstɪərɪəs/ *adj* geheimnisvoll; (*puzzling*) mysteriös, rätselhaft

mystery /ˈmɪstərɪ/ *n* Geheimnis *nt*; (*puzzle*) Rätsel *nt*; **~ [story]** Krimi *m*

mysti|c[al] /ˈmɪstɪk[l]/ *adj* mystisch. **~cism** *n* Mystik *f*

mystified /ˈmɪstɪfaɪd/ *adj* **be ~** vor einem Rätsel stehen

mystique /mɪˈstiːk/ *n* geheimnisvoller Zauber *m*

myth /mɪθ/ *n* Mythos *m*; (🄸: *untruth*) Märchen *nt*. **~ical** *adj* mythisch; (*fig*) erfunden

mythology /mɪˈθɒlədʒɪ/ *n* Mythologie *f*

Nn

nab /næb/ *vt* (*pt/pp* **nabbed**) 🄸 erwischen

nag¹ /næg/ *n* (*horse*) Gaul *m*

nag² *vt/i* (*pp/pp* **nagged**) herumnörgeln (**s.o.** an jdm)

nail /neɪl/ *n* (*Anat, Techn*) Nagel *m*; **on the ~** 🄸 sofort ● *vt* nageln (**to** an + *acc*)

nail: ~-brush *n* Nagelbürste *f*. **~-file** *n* Nagelfeile *f*. **~ scissors** *npl* Nagelschere *f*. **~ varnish** *n* Nagellack *m*

naïve /naɪˈiːv/ *adj* naiv. **~ty** *n* Naivität *f*

naked /ˈneɪkɪd/ *adj* nackt; (*flame*) offen; **with the ~ eye** mit bloßem Auge. **~ness** *n* Nacktheit *f*

name /neɪm/ *n* Name *m*; (*reputation*) Ruf *m*; **by ~** dem Namen nach; **by the ~ of** namens; **call s.o. ~s** 🄸 jdn beschimpfen ● *vt* nennen; (*give a name to*) einen Namen geben (+ *dat*); (*announce publicly*) den Namen bekannt geben von. **~less** *adj* namenlos. **~ly** *adv* nämlich

name: ~-plate *n* Namensschild *nt*. **~sake** *n* Namensvetter *m*/Namensschwester *f*

nanny /ˈnænɪ/ *n* Kindermädchen *nt*

nap /næp/ *n* Nickerchen *nt*

napkin /ˈnæpkɪn/ *n* Serviette *f*

nappy /ˈnæpɪ/ *n* Windel *f*

narcotic /nɑːˈkɒtɪk/ *n* (*drug*) Rauschgift *nt*

narrat|e /nəˈreɪt/ *vt* erzählen. **~ion** *n* Erzählung *f*

narrative /ˈnærətɪv/ *n* Erzählung *f*

narrator /nəˈreɪtə(r)/ *n* Erzähler(in) *m*(*f*)

narrow /ˈnærəʊ/ *adj* (**-er, -est**) schmal; (*restricted*) eng; (*margin, majority*) knapp; **have a ~ escape** mit knapper Not davonkommen ● *vi* sich verengen. **~-ˈminded** *adj* engstirnig

nasal /ˈneɪzl/ *adj* nasal; (*Med & Anat*) Nasen-

nasty /ˈnɑːstɪ/ *adj* übel; (*unpleasant*) unangenehm; (*unkind*) boshaft;

(*serious*) schlimm

nation /'neɪʃn/ *n* Nation *f*; (*people*) Volk *nt*

national /'næʃənl/ *adj* national; (*newspaper*) überregional; (*campaign*) landesweit ● *n* Staatsbürger(in) *m*(*f*)

national: ~ **'anthem** *n* Nationalhymne *f*. **N~ 'Health Service** *n* staatlicher Gesundheitsdienst *m*. **N~ In'surance** *n* Sozialversicherung *f*

nationalism /'næʃənəlɪzm/ *n* Nationalismus *m*

nationality /næʃə'nælətɪ/ *n* Staatsangehörigkeit *f*

national|ization /næʃənəlaɪ'zeɪʃn/ *n* Verstaatlichung *f*. **~ize** *vt* verstaatlichen

> i
> **National Trust** Eine Stiftung zur Erhaltung und Pflege von Stätten von historischem Interesse oder besonderen Naturschönheiten. Der *National Trust* finanziert sich aus Stiftungsgeldern und privaten Spenden und ist der größte Privateigentümer von Land in Großbritannien. Er hat riesige Landflächen, Dörfer und Häuser gekauft oder erhalten, von denen viele öffentlich zugänglich sind.

native /'neɪtɪv/ *adj* einheimisch; (*innate*) angeboren ● *n* Eingeborene(r) *m*/*f*; (*local inhabitant*) Einheimische(r) *m*/*f*; **a ~ of Vienna** ein gebürtiger Wiener

native: ~ **'land** *n* Heimatland *nt*. ~ **'language** *n* Muttersprache *f*

natter /'nætə(r)/ *vi* [!] schwatzen

natural /'nætʃrəl/ *adj* natürlich; **~[-coloured]** naturfarben

natural: ~ **'gas** *n* Erdgas *nt*. ~ **'history** *n* Naturkunde *f*

naturalist /'nætʃrəlɪst/ *n* Naturforscher *m*

natural|ization /nætʃrəlaɪ'zeɪʃn/ *n* Einbürgerung *f*. **~ize** *vt* einbürgern

nature /'neɪtʃə(r)/ *n* Natur *f*; (*kind*) Art *f*; **by ~** von Natur aus. ~ **reserve** *n* Naturschutzgebiet *nt*

naughty /'nɔːtɪ/ *adj* , **-ily** *adv* unartig; (*slightly indecent*) gewagt

nausea /'nɔːzɪə/ *n* Übelkeit *f*

nautical /'nɔːtɪkl/ *adj* nautisch. ~ **mile** *n* Seemeile *f*

naval /'neɪvl/ *adj* Marine-

nave /neɪv/ *n* Kirchenschiff *nt*

navel /'neɪvl/ *n* Nabel *m*

navigable /'nævɪgəbl/ *adj* schiffbar

navigat|e /'nævɪgeɪt/ *vi* navigieren ● *vt* befahren (*river*). **~ion** *n* Navigation *f*

navy /'neɪvɪ/ *n* [Kriegs]marine *f* ● *adj* ~ **[blue]** marineblau

near /nɪə(r)/ *adj* (**-er, -est**) nah[e]; **the ~est bank** die nächste Bank ● *adv* nahe; **draw ~** sich nähern ● *prep* nahe an (+ *dat*/*acc*); in der Nähe von

near: ~by *adj* nahe gelegen, nahe liegend. **~ly** *adv* fast, beinahe; **not ~ly** bei weitem nicht. **~ness** *n* Nähe *f*. ~ **side** *n* Beifahrerseite *f*. **~-sighted** *adj* (*Amer*) kurzsichtig

neat /niːt/ *adj* (**-er, -est**) adrett; (*tidy*) ordentlich; (*clever*) geschickt; (*undiluted*) pur. **~ness** *n* Ordentlichkeit *f*

necessarily /'nesəserəlɪ/ *adv* notwendigerweise; **not ~** nicht unbedingt

necessary /'nesəsərɪ/ *adj* nötig, notwendig

necessit|ate /nɪ'sesɪteɪt/ *vt* notwendig machen. **~y** *n* Notwendigkeit *f*; **work from ~y** arbeiten, weil man es nötig hat

neck /nek/ *n* Hals *m*; **~ and ~** Kopf an Kopf

necklace /'neklɪs/ *n* Halskette *f*

necklinen Halsausschnitt *m*

née /neɪ/ *adj* **~ X** geborene X

need /ni:d/ *n* Bedürfnis *nt*; (*misfortune*) Not *f*; **be in ~ of** brauchen; **in case of ~** notfalls; **if ~ be** wenn nötig; **there is a ~ for** es besteht ein Bedarf an (+ *dat*); **there is no ~ for that** das ist nicht nötig ● *vt* brauchen; **you ~ not go** du brauchst nicht zu gehen; **~ I come?** muss ich kommen? **I ~ to know** ich muss es wissen

needle /'ni:dl/ *n* Nadel *f*

needless /'ni:dlɪs/ *adj* unnötig; **~ to say** selbstverständlich, natürlich

'needlework *n* Nadelarbeit *f*

needy /'ni:dɪ/ *adj* bedürftig

negation /nɪ'geɪʃn/ *n* Verneinung *f*

n

negative /'negətɪv/ *adj* negativ ● *n* Verneinung *f*; (*photo*) Negativ *nt*

neglect /nɪ'glekt/ *n* Vernachlässigung *f* ● *vt* vernachlässigen; (*omit*) versäumen (**to** zu). **~ed** *adj* verwahrlost. **~ful** *adj* nachlässig

negligen|ce /'neglɪdʒəns/ *n* Nachlässigkeit *f*. **~t** *adj* nachlässig

negligible /'neglɪdʒəbl/ *adj* unbedeutend

negotiat|e /nɪ'gəʊʃɪeɪt/ *vt* aushandeln; (*Auto*) nehmen (*bend*) ● *vi* verhandeln. **~ion** *n* Verhandlung *f*. **~or** *n* Unterhändler(in) *m*(*f*)

Negro /'ni:grəʊ/ *adj* Neger- ● *n* (*pl* **-es**) Neger *m*

neigh /neɪ/ *vi* wiehern

neighbour /'neɪbə(r)/ *n* Nachbar(in) *m*(*f*). **~hood** *n* Nachbarschaft *f*. **~ing** *adj* Nachbar-. **~ly** *adj* [gut]nachbarlich

neither /'naɪðə(r)/ *adj & pron* keine(r, s) [von beiden] ● *adv* **~... nor** weder ... noch ● *conj* auch nicht

neon /'ni:ɒn/ *n* Neon *nt*

nephew /'nevju:/ *n* Neffe *m*

nepotism /'nepətɪzm/ *n* Vetternwirtschaft *f*

nerve /nɜ:v/ *n* Nerv *m*; ([!]: *courage*) Mut *m*; ([!]: *impudence*) Frechheit *f*. **~-racking** *adj* nervenaufreibend

nervous /'nɜ:vəs/ *adj* (*afraid*) ängstlich; (*highly strung*) nervös; (*Anat, Med*) Nerven-. **~ 'breakdown** *n* Nervenzusammenbruch *m*. **~ness** Ängstlichkeit *f*

nervy /'nɜ:vɪ/ *adj* nervös; (*Amer: impudent*) frech

nest /nest/ *n* Nest *nt* ● *vi* nisten

nestle /'nesl/ *vi* sich schmiegen (**against** an + *acc*)

net¹ /net/ *n* Netz *nt*; (*curtain*) Store *m*

net² *adj* netto; (*salary, weight*) Netto-

'netball *n* ≈ Korbball *m*

Netherlands /'neðələndz/ *npl* **the ~** die Niederlande *pl*

nettle /'netl/ *n* Nessel *f*

'network *n* Netz *nt*

neurolog|ist /njʊə'rɒlədʒɪst/ *n* Neurologe *m*/ -gin *f*. **~y** *n* Neurologie *f*

neur|osis /njʊə'rəʊsɪs/ *n* (*pl* **-oses** /-si:z/) Neurose *f*. **~otic** *adj* neurotisch

neuter /'nju:tə(r)/ *adj* (*Gram*) sächlich ● *n* (*Gram*) Neutrum *nt* ● *vt* kastrieren; (*spay*) sterilisieren

neutral /'nju:trl/ *adj* neutral ● *n* **in ~** (*Auto*) im Leerlauf. **~ity** *n* Neutralität *f*

never /'nevə(r)/ *adv* nie, niemals; ([!]: *not*) nicht; **~ mind** macht nichts; **well I ~!** ja so was! **~-ending** *adj* endlos

nevertheless /nevəðə'les/ *adv* dennoch, trotzdem

new /nju:/ *adj* (**-er, -est**) neu

new: ~comer *n* Neuankömmling *m*. **~fangled** /-'fæŋgld/ *adj* (*pej*) neumodisch. **~-laid** *adj* frisch gelegt

'newly *adv* frisch. **~-weds** *npl* Jungverheiratete *pl*

new: ~ 'moon *n* Neumond *m*. **~ness** *n* Neuheit *f*

news /nju:z/ *n* Nachricht *f*; (*Radio, TV*) Nachrichten *pl*; **piece of ~** Neuigkeit *f*

news: ~agent *n* Zeitungshändler *m*. **~ bulletin** *n* Nachrichtensendung *f*. **~letter** *n* Mitteilungsblatt *nt*. **~paper** *n* Zeitung *f*; (*material*) Zeitungspapier *nt*. **~reader** *n* Nachrichtensprecher(in) *m*(*f*)

New: ~ Year's 'Day *n* Neujahr *nt*. **~ Year's 'Eve** *n* Silvester *nt*. **~ Zealand** /'zi:lənd/ *n* Neuseeland *nt*

next /nekst/ *adj* & *n* nächste(r, s); **who's ~?** wer kommt als Nächster dran? **the ~ best** das nächstbeste; **~ door** nebenan; **my ~ of kin** mein nächster Verwandter; **~ to nothing** fast gar nichts; **the week after ~** übernächste Woche ● *adv* als Nächstes; **~ to** neben

nib /nɪb/ *n* Feder *f*

nibble /'nɪbl/ *vt/i* knabbern (**at** an + *dat*)

nice /naɪs/ *adj* (**-r, -st**) nett; (*day, weather*) schön; (*food*) gut; (*distinction*) fein. **~ly** *adv* nett; (*well*) gut

niche /ni:ʃ/ *n* Nische *f*; (*fig*) Platz *m*

nick /nɪk/ *n* Kerbe *f*; (🅘: *prison*) Knast *m*; (🅘: *police station*) Revier *nt*; **in good ~** 🅘 in gutem Zustand ● *vt* einkerben; (*steal*) klauen; (🅘: *arrest*) schnappen

nickel /'nɪkl/ *n* Nickel *nt*; (*Amer*) Fünfcentstück *nt*

'nickname *n* Spitzname *m*

nicotine /'nɪkəti:n/ *n* Nikotin *nt*

niece /ni:s/ *n* Nichte *f*

Nigeria /naɪ'dʒɪərɪə/ *n* Nigeria *nt*. **~n** *adj* nigerianisch ● *n* Nigeriane-r(in) *m*(*f*)

night /naɪt/ *n* Nacht *f*; (*evening*) Abend *m*; **at ~** nachts

night: ~-club *n* Nachtklub *m*. **~-dress** *n* Nachthemd *nt*. **~fall** *n* **at ~fall** bei Einbruch der Dunkelheit. **~-gown** *n*, 🅘 **~ie** /'naɪtɪ/ *n* Nachthemd *nt*

nightingale /'naɪtɪŋgeɪl/ *n* Nachtigall *f*

night: ~-life *n* Nachtleben *nt*. **~ly** *adj* nächtlich ● *adv* jede Nacht. **~mare** *n* Albtraum *m*. **~-time** *n* **at ~-time** bei Nacht

nil /nɪl/ *n* null

nimble /'nɪmbl/ *adj* (**-r, -st**), **-bly** *adv* flink

nine /naɪn/ *adj* neun ● *n* Neun *f*. **~'teen** *adj* neunzehn. **~'teenth** *adj* neunzehnte(r, s)

ninetieth /'naɪntɪɪθ/ *adj* neunzigste(r, s)

ninety /'naɪntɪ/ *adj* neunzig

ninth /naɪnθ/ *adj* neunte(r, s)

nip /nɪp/ *vt* kneifen; (*bite*) beißen; **~ in the bud** (*fig*) im Keim ersticken ● *vi* (🅘: *run*) laufen

nipple /'nɪpl/ *n* Brustwarze *f*; (*Amer: on bottle*) Sauger *m*

nitwit /'nɪtwɪt/ *n* 🅘 Dummkopf *m*

no /nəʊ/ *adv* nein ● *n* (*pl* **noes**) Nein *nt* ● *adj* kein(e); (*pl*) keine; **in no time** [sehr] schnell; **no parking/smoking** Parken/Rauchen verboten; **no one = nobody**

nobility /nəʊ'bɪlətɪ/ *n* Adel *m*

n

noble /ˈnəʊbl/ *adj* (**-r, -st**) edel; (*aristocratic*) adlig. **~man** *n* Adlige(r) *m*

nobody /ˈnəʊbədɪ/ *pron* niemand, keiner ● *n* **a ~** ein Niemand *m*

nocturnal /nɒkˈtɜːnl/ *adj* nächtlich; (*animal, bird*) Nacht-

nod /nɒd/ *n* Nicken *nt* ● *v* (*pt/pp* **nodded**) ● *vi* nicken ● *vt* **~ one's head** mit dem Kopf nicken

noise /nɔɪz/ *n* Geräusch *nt*; (*loud*) Lärm *m*. **~less** *adj* geräuschlos

noisy /ˈnɔɪzɪ/ *adj* , **-ily** *adv* laut; (*eater*) geräuschvoll

nomad /ˈnəʊmæd/ *n* Nomade *m*. **~ic** *adj* nomadisch; (*life, tribe*) Nomaden-

nominal /ˈnɒmɪnl/ *adj* nominell

nominat|e /ˈnɒmɪneɪt/ *vt* nominieren, aufstellen; (*appoint*) ernennen. **~ion** *n* Nominierung *f*; Ernennung *f*

n

nominative /ˈnɒmɪnətɪv/ *adj* & *n* (*Gram*) **~[case]** Nominativ *m*

nonchalant /ˈnɒnʃələnt/ *adj* nonchalant; (*gesture*) lässig

nondescript /ˈnɒndɪskrɪpt/ *adj* unbestimmbar; (*person*) unscheinbar

none /nʌn/ *pron* keine(r)/keins; **~ of it/this** nichts davon ● *adv* **~ too** nicht gerade; **~ too soon** [um] keine Minute zu früh; **~ the less** dennoch

nonentity /nɒˈnentətɪ/ *n* Null *f*

non-exˈistent *adj* nicht vorhanden

non-ˈfiction *n* Sachliteratur *f*

nonplussed /nɒnˈplʌst/ *adj* verblüfft

nonsens|e /ˈnɒnsəns/ *n* Unsinn *m*. **~ical** *adj* unsinnig

non-ˈsmoker *n* Nichtraucher *m*

non-ˈstop *adv* ununterbrochen; (*fly*) nonstop

non-ˈswimmer *n* Nichtschwimmer *m*

non-ˈviolent *adj* gewaltlos

noodles /ˈnuːdlz/ *npl* Bandnudeln *pl*

noon /nuːn/ *n* Mittag *m*; **at ~** um 12 Uhr mittags

noose /nuːs/ *n* Schlinge *f*

nor /nɔː(r)/ *adv* noch ● *conj* auch nicht

Nordic /ˈnɔːdɪk/ *adj* nordisch

norm /nɔːm/ *n* Norm *f*

normal /ˈnɔːml/ *adj* normal. **~ity** *n* Normalität *f*. **~ly** *adv* normal; (*usually*) normalerweise

north /nɔːθ/ *n* Norden *m*; **to the ~ of** nördlich von ● *adj* Nord-, nord- ● *adv* nach Norden

north: N~ America *n* Nordamerika *nt*. **~-east** *adj* Nordost- ● *n* Nordosten *m*

norther|ly /ˈnɔːðəlɪ/ *adj* nördlich. **~n** *adj* nördlich. **N~n Ireland** *n* Nordirland *nt*

north: N~ ˈPole *n* Nordpol *m*. **N~ ˈSea** *n* Nordsee *f*. **~ward[s]** /-wəd[z]/ *adv* nach Norden. **~-west** *adj* Nordwest- ● *n* Nordwesten *m*

Nor|way /ˈnɔːweɪ/ *n* Norwegen *nt*. **~wegian** *adj* norwegisch ● *n* Norweger(in) *m*(*f*)

nose /nəʊz/ *n* Nase

ˈnosebleed *n* Nasenbluten *nt*

nostalg|ia /nɒˈstældʒɪə/ *n* Nostalgie *f*. **~ic** *adj* nostalgisch

nostril /ˈnɒstrəl/ *n* Nasenloch *nt*

nosy /ˈnəʊzɪ/ *adj* [!] neugierig

not /nɒt/

● *adverb*

····> nicht. **I don't know** ich weiß nicht. **isn't she pretty?** ist sie nicht hübsch?

····➤ **not a** kein. **he is not a doctor** er ist kein Arzt. **she didn't wear a hat** sie trug keinen Hut. **there was not a person to be seen** es gab keinen Menschen zu sehen. **not a thing** gar nichts. **not a bit** kein bisschen

····➤ (*in elliptical phrases*) **I hope not** ich hoffe nicht. **of course not** natürlich nicht. **not at all** überhaupt nicht; (*in polite reply to thanks*) keine Ursache; gern geschehen. **certainly not!** auf keinen Fall! **not I** ich nicht

····➤ **not ... but ...** nicht ... sondern .... **it was not a small town but a big one** es war keine kleine Stadt, sondern eine große

notab|le /ˈnəʊtəbl/ *adj* bedeutend; (*remarkable*) bemerkenswert. **~ly** *adv* insbesondere

notation /nəʊˈteɪʃn/ *n* Notation *f*; (*Mus*) Notenschrift *f*

notch /nɒtʃ/ *n* Kerbe *f*

note /nəʊt/ *n* (*written comment*) Notiz *f*, Anmerkung *f*; (*short letter*) Briefchen *nt*, Zettel *m*; (*bank* ~) Banknote *f*, Schein *m*; (*Mus*) Note *f*; (*sound*) Ton *m*; (*on piano*) Taste *f*; **half/whole ~** (*Amer*) halbe/ganze Note *f*; **of ~** von Bedeutung; **make a ~ of** notieren ● *vt* beachten; (*notice*) bemerken (**that** dass)

ˈnotebook *n* Notizbuch *nt*

noted /ˈnəʊtɪd/ *adj* bekannt (**for** für)

note: ~paper *n* Briefpapier *nt*. **~worthy** *adj* beachtenswert

nothing /ˈnʌθɪŋ/ *n, pron & adv* nichts; **for ~** umsonst; **~ but** nichts als; **~ much** nicht viel; **~ interesting** nichts Interessantes

notice /ˈnəʊtɪs/ *n* (*on board*) Anschlag *m*, Bekanntmachung *f*; (*announcement*) Anzeige *f*; (*review*) Kritik *f*; (*termination of lease, employment*) Kündigung *f*; **give [in one's] ~** kündigen; **give s.o. ~** jdm kündigen; **take no ~!** ignoriere es! ● *vt* bemerken. **~able** /-əbl/, *adj*, **-bly** *adv* merklich. **~-board** *n* Anschlagbrett *nt*

noti|fication /nəʊtɪfɪˈkeɪʃn/ *n* Benachrichtigung *f*. **~fy** *vt* (*pt/pp* **-ied**) benachrichtigen

notion /ˈnəʊʃn/ *n* Idee *f*

notorious /nəʊˈtɔːrɪəs/ *adj* berüchtigt

notwithˈstanding *prep* trotz (+ *gen*) ● *adv* trotzdem, dennoch

nought /nɔːt/ *n* Null *f*

noun /naʊn/ *n* Substantiv *nt*

nourish /ˈnʌrɪʃ/ *vt* nähren. **~ing** *adj* nahrhaft. **~ment** *n* Nahrung *f*

novel /ˈnɒvl/ *adj* neu[artig] ● *n* Roman *m*. **~ist** *n* Romanschriftsteller(in) *m*(*f*). **~ty** *n* Neuheit *f*

November /nəʊˈvembə(r)/ *n* November *m*

novice /ˈnɒvɪs/ *n* Neuling *m*; (*Relig*) Novize *m*/Novizin *f*

now /naʊ/ *adv & conj* jetzt; **~ [that]** jetzt, wo; **just ~** gerade, eben; **right ~** sofort; **~ and again** hin und wieder; **now, now!** na, na!

ˈnowadays *adv* heutzutage

nowhere /ˈnəʊ-/ *adv* nirgendwo, nirgends

nozzle /ˈnɒzl/ *n* Düse *f*

nuance /ˈnjuːɑ̃s/ *n* Nuance *f*

nuclear /ˈnjuːklɪə(r)/ *adj* Kern-. **~ deˈterrent** *n* nukleares Abschreckungsmittel *nt*

nucleus /ˈnjuːklɪəs/ *n* (*pl* **-lei** /-lɪaɪ/) Kern *m*

nude /njuːd/ *adj* nackt ● *n* (*Art*) Akt *m*; **in the ~** nackt

nudge /nʌdʒ/ *vt* stupsen

nud|ist /ˈnjuːdɪst/ *n* Nudist *m*. **~ity** *n* Nacktheit *f*

nuisance /ˈnjuːsns/ *n* Ärgernis *nt*; (*pest*) Plage *f*; **be a ~** ärgerlich sein

null /nʌl/ *adj* **~ and void** null und nichtig

numb /nʌm/ *adj* gefühllos, taub ● *vt* betäuben

number /ˈnʌmbə(r)/ *n* Nummer *f*; (*amount*) Anzahl *f*; (*Math*) Zahl *f* ● *vt* nummerieren; (*include*) zählen (**among** zu). **~-plate** *n* Nummernschild *nt*

numeral /ˈnjuːmərl/ *n* Ziffer *f*

numerical /njuːˈmerɪkl/ *adj* numerisch; **in ~ order** zahlenmäßig geordnet

numerous /ˈnjuːmərəs/ *adj* zahlreich

nun /nʌn/ *n* Nonne *f*

nurse /nɜːs/ *n* [Kranken]schwester *f*; (*male*) Krankenpfleger *m*; **children's ~** Kindermädchen *nt* ● *vt* pflegen

nursery /ˈnɜːsərɪ/ *n* Kinderzimmer *nt*; (*for plants*) Gärtnerei *f*; **[day] ~** Kindertagesstätte *f*. **~ rhyme** *n* Kinderreim *m*. **~ school** *n* Kindergarten *m*

nursing /ˈnɜːsɪŋ/ *n* Krankenpflege *f*. **~ home** *n* Pflegeheim *nt*

nut /nʌt/ *n* Nuss *f*; (*Techn*) [Schrauben]mutter *f*; ([!]: *head*) Birne *f* [!]; **be ~s** [!] spinnen [!]. **~crackers** *npl* Nussknacker *m*. **~meg** *n* Muskat *m*

nutrient /ˈnjuːtrɪənt/ *n* Nährstoff *m*

nutrit|ion /njuːˈtrɪʃn/ *n* Ernährung *f*. **~ious** *adj* nahrhaft

ˈnutshell *n* Nussschale *f*; **in a ~** (*fig*) kurz gesagt

nylon /ˈnaɪlɒn/ *n* Nylon *nt*

O /əʊ/ *n* (*Teleph*) null

oak /əʊk/ *n* Eiche *f*

OAP *abbr* (**old-age pensioner**) Rentner(in) *m*(*f*)

oar /ɔː(r)/ *n* Ruder *nt*. **~sman** *n* Ruderer *m*

oasis /əʊˈeɪsɪs/ *n* (*pl* **oases** /-siːz/) Oase *f*

oath /əʊθ/ *n* Eid *m*; (*swear-word*) Fluch *m*

oatmeal /ˈəʊt-/ *n* Hafermehl *nt*

oats /əʊts/ *npl* Hafer *m*; (*Culin*) **[rolled] ~** Haferflocken *pl*

obedien|ce /əˈbiːdɪəns/ *n* Gehorsam *m*. **~t** *adj* gehorsam

obey /əˈbeɪ/ *vt/i* gehorchen (+ *dat*); befolgen (*instructions, rules*)

obituary /əˈbɪtjʊərɪ/ *n* Nachruf *m*; (*notice*) Todesanzeige *f*

object[1] /ˈɒbdʒɪkt/ *n* Gegenstand *m*; (*aim*) Zweck *m*; (*intention*) Absicht *f*; (*Gram*) Objekt *nt*; **money is no ~** Geld spielt keine Rolle

object[2] /əbˈdʒekt/ *vi* Einspruch erheben (**to** gegen); (*be against*) etwas dagegen haben

objection /əbˈdʒekʃn/ *n* Einwand *m*; **have no ~** nichts dagegen haben. **~able** *adj* anstößig; (*person*) unangenehm

objectiv|e /əbˈdʒektɪv/ *adj* objektiv ● *n* Ziel *nt*. **~ity** *n* Objektivität *f*

objector /əbˈdʒektə(r)/ *n* Gegner *m*

obligation /ɒblɪˈgeɪʃn/ *n* Pflicht *f*; **without ~** unverbindlich

obligatory /əˈblɪgətrɪ/ *adj* obligatorisch; **be ~** Vorschrift sein

oblig|e /əˈblaɪdʒ/ *vt* verpflichten;

(*compel*) zwingen; (*do a small service*) einen Gefallen tun (+ *dat*). **~ing** *adj* entgegenkommend

oblique /ə'bli:k/ *adj* schräg; (*angle*) schief; (*fig*) indirekt

obliterate /ə'blɪtəreɪt/ *vt* auslöschen

oblivion /ə'blɪvɪən/ *n* Vergessenheit *f*

oblivious /ə'blɪvɪəs/ *adj* **be ~** sich (*dat*) nicht bewusst sein (of *gen*)

oblong /'ɒblɒŋ/ *adj* rechteckig ● *n* Rechteck *nt*

obnoxious /əb'nɒkʃəs/ *adj* widerlich

oboe /'əʊbəʊ/ *n* Oboe *f*

obscen|e /əb'si:n/ *adj* obszön. **~ity** *n* Obszönität *f*

obscur|e /əb'skjʊə(r)/ *adj* dunkel; (*unknown*) unbekannt ● *vt* verdecken; (*confuse*) verwischen. **~ity** *n* Dunkelheit *f*; Unbekanntheit *f*

observa|nce /əb'zɜ:vns/ *n* (*of custom*) Einhaltung *f*. **~nt** *adj* aufmerksam. **~tion** *n* Beobachtung *f*; (*remark*) Bemerkung *f*

observatory /əb'zɜ:vətrɪ/ *n* Sternwarte *f*

observe /əb'zɜ:v/ *vt* beobachten; (*say, notice*) bemerken; (*keep, celebrate*) feiern; (*obey*) einhalten. **~r** *n* Beobachter *m*

obsess /əb'ses/ *vt* **be ~ed by** besessen sein von. **~ion** *n* Besessenheit *f*; (*persistent idea*) fixe Idee *f*. **~ive** *adj* zwanghaft

obsolete /'ɒbsəli:t/ *adj* veraltet

obstacle /'ɒbstəkl/ *n* Hindernis *nt*

obstina|cy /'ɒbstɪnəsɪ/ *n* Starrsinn *m*. **~te** *adj* starrsinnig; (*refusal*) hartnäckig

obstruct /əb'strʌkt/ *vt* blockieren; (*hinder*) behindern. **~ion** *n* Blockierung *f*; Behinderung *f*; (*obstacle*) Hindernis *nt*. **~ive** *adj* **be ~ive** Schwierigkeiten bereiten

obtain /əb'teɪn/ *vt* erhalten. **~able** *adj* erhältlich

obtrusive /əb'tru:sɪv/ *adj* aufdringlich; (*thing*) auffällig

obtuse /əb'tju:s/ *adj* begriffsstutzig

obvious /'ɒbvɪəs/ *adj* offensichtlich, offenbar

occasion /ə'keɪʒn/ *n* Gelegenheit *f*; (*time*) Mal *nt*; (*event*) Ereignis *nt*; (*cause*) Anlass *m*, Grund *m*; **on the ~ of** anlässlich (+ *gen*)

occasional /ə'keɪʒənl/ *adj* gelegentlich. **~ly** *adv* gelegentlich, hin und wieder

occult /ɒ'kʌlt/ *adj* okkult

occupant /'ɒkjʊpənt/ *n* Bewohner(in) *m*(*f*); (*of vehicle*) Insasse *m*

occupation /ɒkjʊ'peɪʃn/ *n* Beschäftigung *f*; (*job*) Beruf *m*; (*Mil*) Besetzung *f*; (*period*) Besatzung *f*. **~al** *adj* Berufs-. **~al therapy** *n* Beschäftigungstherapie *f*

occupier /'ɒkjʊpaɪə(r)/ *n* Bewohner(in) *m*(*f*)

occupy /'ɒkjʊpaɪ/ *vt* (*pt/pp* **occupied**) besetzen (*seat*, (*Mil*) *country*); einnehmen (*space*); in Anspruch nehmen (*time*); (*live in*) bewohnen; (*fig*) bekleiden (*office*); (*keep busy*) beschäftigen

occur /ə'kɜ:(r)/ *vi* (*pt/pp* **occurred**) geschehen; (*exist*) vorkommen, auftreten; **it ~red to me that** es fiel mir ein, dass. **~rence** *n* Auftreten *nt*; (*event*) Ereignis *nt*

ocean /'əʊʃn/ *n* Ozean *m*

o'clock /ə'klɒk/ *adv* **[at] 7 ~** [um] 7 Uhr

octagonal /ɒk'tægənl/ *adj* achteckig

October /ɒk'təʊbə(r)/ *n* Oktober *m*

octopus /'ɒktəpəs/ *n* (*pl* **-puses**)

O

Tintenfisch *m*

odd /ɒd/ *adj* (**-er, -est**) seltsam, merkwürdig; (*number*) ungerade; (*not of set*) einzeln; **forty ~** über vierzig; **~ jobs** Gelegenheitsarbeiten *pl*; **the ~ one out** die Ausnahme; **at ~ moments** zwischendurch

odd|ity /ˈɒdɪtɪ/ *n* Kuriosität *f*. **~ly** *adv* merkwürdig; **~ly enough** merkwürdigerweise **~ment** *n* (*of fabric*) Rest *m*

odds /ɒdz/ *npl* (*chances*) Chancen *pl*; **at ~** uneinig; **~ and ends** Kleinkram *m*

ode /əʊd/ *n* Ode *f*

odious /ˈəʊdɪəs/ *adj* widerlich

odour /ˈəʊdə(r)/ *n* Geruch *m*. **~less** *adj* geruchlos

of /ɒv/, *unbetont* /əv/

● *preposition*

····➤ (*indicating belonging, origin*) von (+ *dat*); genitive. **the mother of twins** die Mutter von Zwillingen. **the mother of the twins** die Mutter der Zwillinge *or* von den Zwillingen. **the Queen of England** die Königin von England. **a friend of mine** ein Freund von mir. **a friend of the teacher's** ein Freund des Lehrers. **the brother of her father** der Bruder ihres Vaters. **the works of Shakespeare** Shakespeares Werke. **it was nice of him** es war nett von ihm

····➤ (*made of*) aus (+ *dat*). **a dress of cotton** ein Kleid aus Baumwolle

····➤ (*following number*) **five of us** fünf von uns. **the two of us** wir zwei. **there were four of us waiting** wir waren vier, die warteten

····➤ (*followed by number, description*) von (+ *dat*). **a girl of ten** ein Mädchen von zehn Jahren. **a distance of 50 miles** eine Entfernung von 50 Meilen. **a man of character** ein Mann von Charakter. **a woman of exceptional beauty** eine Frau von außerordentlicher Schönheit. **a person of strong views** ein Mensch mit festen Ansichten

! **of** is not translated after measures and in some other cases: **a pound of apples** ein Pfund Äpfel; **a cup of tea** eine Tasse Tee; **a glass of wine** ein Glas Wein; **the city of Chicago** die Stadt Chicago; **the fourth of January** der vierte Januar

off /ɒf/ *prep* von (+ *dat*); **~ the coast** vor der Küste; **get ~ the ladder/bus** von der Leiter/aus dem Bus steigen ● *adv* weg; (*button, lid, handle*) ab; (*light*) aus; (*brake*) los; (*machine*) abgeschaltet; (*tap*) zu; (*on appliance*) **'off'** 'aus'; **2 kilometres ~** 2 Kilometer entfernt; **a long way ~** weit weg; (*time*) noch lange hin; **~ and on** hin und wieder; **with his hat/coat ~** ohne Hut/Mantel; **20% ~** 20% Nachlass; **be ~** (*leave*) [weg]gehen; (*Sport*) starten; (*food:*) schlecht sein; **be well ~** gut dran sein; (*financially*) wohlhabend sein; **have a day ~** einen freien Tag haben

offal /ˈɒfl/ *n* (*Culin*) Innereien *pl*

i **off-Broadway** *Off-Broadway* ist eine Bezeichnung für das nichtkommerzielle amerikanische Theater. Diese experimentale Gegenrichtung mit kleineren Truppen und Bühnen gewann nach 1952 an Bedeutung. Viele junge Intendanten sind nicht an kommerziellen Aufführungen interessiert, und ihre Inszenierungen finden in alten Lagerhäusern abseits des *Broadway*, der großen New Yorker Theaterstraße, statt.

offence /ə'fens/ *n* (*illegal act*) Vergehen *nt*; **give/take ~** Anstoß erregen/nehmen (**at** an + *dat*)

offend /ə'fend/ *vt* beleidigen. **~er** *n* (*Jur*) Straftäter *m*

offensive /ə'fensɪv/ *adj* anstößig; (*Mil, Sport*) offensiv ● *n* Offensive *f*

offer /'ɒfə(r)/ *n* Angebot *nt*; **on (special) ~** im Sonderangebot ● *vt* anbieten (**to** *dat*); leisten (*resistance*); **~ to do sth** sich anbieten, etw zu tun. **~ing** *n* Gabe *f*

off'hand *adj* brüsk; (*casual*) lässig

office /'ɒfɪs/ *n* Büro *nt*; (*post*) Amt *nt*

officer /'ɒfɪsə(r)/ *n* Offizier *m*; (*official*) Beamte(r) *m*/ Beamtin *f*; (*police*) Polizeibeamte(r) *m*/-beamtin *f*

official /ə'fɪʃl/ *adj* offiziell, amtlich ● *n* Beamte(r) *m*/ Beamtin *f*; (*Sport*) Funktionär *m*. **~ly** *adv* offiziell

officious /ə'fɪʃəs/ *adj* übereifrig

'off-licence *n* Wein- und Spirituosenhandlung *f*

off-licence Ein britischer Wein- und Spirituosenladen, der eine Konzession für den Verkauf alkoholisher Getränke hat. *Off-licence*-Läden haben längere Öffnungszeiten als andere Geschäfte und bleiben geöffnet, wenn Bars und Wirtshäuser geschlossen sind. Sie verkaufen auch alkoholfreie Getränke, Süßigkeiten und Tabakwaren und verleihen Gläser für Partys.

off-'load *vt* ausladen

'off-putting *adj* ⊡ abstoßend

off'set *vt* (*pt/pp* **-set**, *pres p* **-setting**) ausgleichen

'offshoot *n* Schössling *m*; (*fig*) Zweig *m*

'offshore *adj* (*oil field*) im Meer; (*breeze*) vom Land kommend ● *adv* im/ins Ausland

off'side *adj* (*Sport*) abseits

off'stage *adv* hinter den Kulissen

off-'white *adj* fast weiß

often /'ɒfn/ *adv* oft; **every so ~** von Zeit zu Zeit

oh /əʊ/ *int* oh! ach! **oh dear**! o weh!

oil /ɔɪl/ *n* Öl *nt*; (*petroleum*) Erdöl *nt* ● *vt* ölen

oil: ~field *n* Ölfeld *nt*. **~-painting** *n* Ölgemälde *nt*. **~ refinery** *n* [Erd]ölraffinerie *f*. **~-tanker** *n* Öltanker *m*. **~ well** *n* Ölquelle *f*

oily /'ɔɪlɪ/ *adj* ölig

ointment /'ɔɪntmənt/ *n* Salbe *f*

OK /əʊ'keɪ/ *adj & int* ⊡ in Ordnung; okay ● *adv* (*well*) gut ● *vt* (*auch* **okay**) (*pt/pp* **okayed**) genehmigen

old /əʊld/ *adj* (**-er, -est**) alt; (*former*) ehemalig

old: ~ 'age *n* Alter *nt*. **~-age 'pensioner** *n* Rentner(in) *m*(*f*). **~ boy** *n* ehemaliger Schüler. **~-'fashioned** *adj* altmodisch. **~ girl** ehemalige Schülerin *f*

olive /'ɒlɪv/ *n* Olive *f*; (*colour*) Oliv *nt* ● *adj* olivgrün. **~ 'oil** *n* Olivenöl *nt*

Olympic /ə'lɪmpɪk/ *adj* olympisch ● *n* **the ~s** die Olympischen Spiele *pl*

omelette /'ɒmlɪt/ *n* Omelett *nt*

ominous /'ɒmɪnəs/ *adj* bedrohlich

omission /ə'mɪʃn/ *n* Auslassung *f*; (*failure to do*) Unterlassung *f*

omit /ə'mɪt/ *vt* (*pt/pp* **omitted**)

auslassen; ~ **to do sth** es unterlassen, etw zu tun

omnipotent /ɒm'nɪpətənt/ *adj* allmächtig

on /ɒn/ *prep* auf (+ *dat*/(*on to*) + *acc*); (*on vertical surface*) an (+ *dat*/(*on to*) + *acc*); (*about*) über (+ *acc*); **on Monday** [am] Montag; **on Mondays** montags; **on the first of May** am ersten Mai; **on arriving** als ich ankam; **on one's finger** am Finger; **on the right**/**left** rechts/links; **on the Rhine** am Rhein; **on the radio**/**television** im Radio/Fernsehen; **on the bus**/**train** im Bus/Zug; **go on the bus**/**train** mit dem Bus/Zug fahren; **on me** (*with me*) bei mir; **it's on me** ☐ das spendiere ich ● *adv* (*further on*) weiter; (*switched on*) an; (*brake*) angezogen; (*machine*) angeschaltet; (*on appliance*) **'on'** 'ein'; **with**/**without his hat**/**coat on** mit/ohne Hut/Mantel; **be on** (*film:*) laufen; (*event:*) stattfinden; **be on at** ☐ bedrängen **(zu** to**)**; **it's not on** ☐ das geht nicht; **on and on** immer weiter; **on and off** hin und wieder; **and so on** und so weiter

o

once /wʌns/ *adv* einmal; (*formerly*) früher; **at** ~ sofort; (*at the same time*) gleichzeitig; ~ **and for all** ein für alle Mal ● *conj* wenn; (*with past tense*) als

'oncoming *adj* ~ **traffic** Gegenverkehr *m*

one /wʌn/ *adj* ein(e); (*only*) einzig; **not** ~ kein(e); ~ **day**/**evening** eines Tages/Abends ● *n* Eins *f* ● *pron* eine(r)/eins; (*impersonal*) man; **which** ~ welche(r,s); ~ **another** einander; ~ **by** ~ einzeln; ~ **never knows** man kann nie wissen

one: ~**-parent 'family** *n* Einelternfamilie *f*. ~**'self** *pron* selbst; (*reflexive*) sich; **by** ~**self** allein. ~**-sided** *adj* einseitig. ~**-way** *adj* (*street*) Einbahn-; (*ticket*) einfach

onion /'ʌnjən/ *n* Zwiebel *f*

on-'line *adv* online

'onlooker *n* Zuschauer(in) *m*(*f*)

only /'əʊnlɪ/ *adj* einzige(r,s); **an** ~ **child** ein Einzelkind *nt* ● *adv & conj* nur; ~ **just** gerade erst; (*barely*) gerade noch

'onset *n* Beginn *m*; (*of winter*) Einsetzen *nt*

'on-shore *adj* (*oil field*) an Land; (*breeze*) vom Meer kommend

onward[s] /'ɒnwəd[z]/ *adv* vorwärts; **from then** ~ von der Zeit an

ooze /uːz/ *vi* sickern

opaque /əʊ'peɪk/ *adj* undurchsichtig

open /'əʊpən/ *adj* offen; **be** ~ (*shop:*) geöffnet sein; **in the** ~ **air** im Freien ● *n* **in the** ~ im Freien ● *vt* öffnen, aufmachen; (*start, set up*) eröffnen ● *vi* sich öffnen; (*flower:*) aufgehen; (*shop:*) öffnen, aufmachen; (*be started*) eröffnet werden. ~ **up** *vt* öffnen, aufmachen

'open day *n* Tag *m* der offenen Tür

opener /'əʊpənə(r)/ *n* Öffner *m*

opening /'əʊpənɪŋ/ *n* Öffnung *f*; (*beginning*) Eröffnung *f*; (*job*) Einstiegsmöglichkeit *f*. ~ **hours** *npl* Öffnungszeiten *pl*

open: ~**-'minded** *adj* aufgeschlossen. ~ **'sandwich** *n* belegtes Brot *nt*

Open University - OU
Eine britische Fernuniversität, die 1969 gegründet wurde und vor allem Berufstätigen im Fernstudium Kurse auf verschiedenem Niveau bietet. Studenten jeder Altersgruppe, selbst

solche ohne die erforderlichen Schulabschlüsse, können das Studium mit dem *Bachelor's degree* und dem *Master's degree* abschließen. Teilnehmer studieren von zu Hause und können auch an Direktunterricht teilnehmen.

opera /ˈɒpərə/ *n* Oper *f*. ~ **glasses** *pl* Opernglas *n* ~**-house** *n* Opernhaus *nt*. ~**-singer** *n* Opernsänger(in) *m(f)*

operate /ˈɒpəreɪt/ *vt* bedienen (*machine, lift*); betätigen (*lever, brake*); (*fig: run*) betreiben ● *vi* (*Techn*) funktionieren; (*be in action*) in Betrieb sein; (*Mil & fig*) operieren; ~ **[on]** (*Med*) operieren

operatic /ɒpəˈrætɪk/ *adj* Opern-

operation /ɒpəˈreɪʃn/ *n* (*see* **operate**) Bedienung *f*; Betätigung *f*; Operation *f*; **in** ~ (*Techn*) in Betrieb; **come into** ~ (*fig*) in Kraft treten; **have an** ~ (*Med*) operiert werden. ~**al** *adj* einsatzbereit; **be** ~**al** in Betrieb sein; (*law:*) in Kraft sein

operative /ˈɒpərətɪv/ *adj* wirksam

operator /ˈɒpərəreɪtə(r)/ *n* (*user*) Bedienungsperson *f*; (*Teleph*) Vermittlung *f*

operetta /ɒpəˈretə/ *n* Operette *f*

opinion /əˈpɪnjən/ *n* Meinung *f*; **in my** ~ meiner Meinung nach. ~**ated** *adj* rechthaberisch

opponent /əˈpəʊnənt/ *n* Gegner(in) *m(f)*

opportun|e /ˈɒpətjuːn/ *adj* günstig. ~**ist** *n* Opportunist *m*

opportunity /ɒpəˈtjuːnətɪ/ *n* Gelegenheit *f*

oppos|e /əˈpəʊz/ *vt* Widerstand leisten (+ *dat*); (*argue against*) sprechen gegen; **be** ~**ed to sth** gegen etw sein; **as** ~**ed to** im Gegensatz zu. ~**ing** *adj* gegnerisch

opposite /ˈɒpəzɪt/ *adj* entgegengesetzt; (*house, side*) gegenüberliegend; ~ **number** (*fig*) Gegenstück *nt*; **the** ~ **sex** das andere Geschlecht ● *n* Gegenteil *nt* ● *adv* gegenüber ● *prep* gegenüber (+ *dat*)

opposition /ɒpəˈzɪʃn/ *n* Widerstand *m*; (*Pol*) Opposition *f*

oppress /əˈpres/ *vt* unterdrücken. ~**ion** *n* Unterdrücken *f*. ~**ive** *adj* tyrannisch; (*heat*) drückend

opt /ɒpt/ *vi* ~ **for** sich entscheiden für

optical /ˈɒptɪkl/ *adj* optisch

optician /ɒpˈtɪʃn/ *n* Optiker *m*

optimis|m /ˈɒptɪmɪzm/ *n* Optimismus *m*. ~**t** *n* Optimist *m*. ~**tic** *adj*, **-ally** *adv* optimistisch

optimum /ˈɒptɪməm/ *adj* optimal

option /ˈɒpʃn/ *n* Wahl *f*; (*Comm*) Option *f*. ~**al** *adj* auf Wunsch erhältlich; (*subject*) wahlfrei

opu|lence /ˈɒpjʊləns/ *n* Prunk *m*. ~**lent** *adj* prunkvoll

or /ɔː(r)/ *conj* oder; (*after negative*) noch; **or [else]** sonst; **in a year or two** in ein bis zwei Jahren

oral /ˈɔːrl/ *adj* mündlich; (*Med*) oral ● *n* Mündliche(s) *nt*

orange /ˈɒrɪndʒ/ *n* Apfelsine *f*, Orange *f*; (*colour*) Orange *nt* ● *adj* orangefarben

oratorio /ɒrəˈtɔːrɪəʊ/ *n* Oratorium *nt*

oratory /ˈɒrətərɪ/ *n* Redekunst *f*

orbit /ˈɔːbɪt/ *n* Umlaufbahn *f* ● *vt* umkreisen

orchard /ˈɔːtʃəd/ *n* Obstgarten *m*

orches|tra /ˈɔːkɪstrə/ *n* Orchester *nt*. ~**tral** *adj* Orchester-. ~**trate** *vt* orchestrieren

ordeal /ɔːˈdiːl/ *n* (*fig*) Qual *f*

order /ˈɔːdə(r)/ *n* Ordnung *f*; (*se-*

quence) Reihenfolge *f*; (*condition*) Zustand *m*; (*command*) Befehl *m*; (*in restaurant*) Bestellung *f*; (*Comm*) Auftrag *m*; (*Relig, medal*) Orden *m*; **out of ~** (*machine*) außer Betrieb; **in ~ that** damit; **in ~ to help** um zu helfen ● *vt* (*put in ~*) ordnen; (*command*) befehlen (+ *dat*); (*Comm, in restaurant*) bestellen; (*prescribe*) verordnen

orderly /'ɔːdəlɪ/ *adj* ordentlich; (*not unruly*) friedlich ● *n* (*Mil, Med*) Sanitäter *m*

ordinary /'ɔːdɪnərɪ/ *adj* gewöhnlich, normal

ore /ɔː(r)/ *n* Erz *nt*

organ /'ɔːgən/ *n* (*Biology*) Organ *nt*; (*Mus*) Orgel *f*

organic /ɔː'gænɪk/ *adj*, **-ally** *adv* organisch; (*without chemicals*) biodynamisch; (*crop*) biologisch angebaut; (*food*) Bio-. **~ farming** *n* biologischer Anbau *m*

organism /'ɔːgənɪzm/ *n* Organismus *m*

organist /'ɔːgənɪst/ *n* Organist *m*

organization /ɔːgənaɪ'zeɪʃn/ *n* Organisation *f*

organize /'ɔːgənaɪz/ *vt* organisieren; veranstalten (*event*). **~r** *n* Organisator *m*; Veranstalter *m*

orgy /'ɔːdʒɪ/ *n* Orgie *f*

Orient /'ɔːrɪənt/ *n* Orient *m*. **o~al** *adj* orientalisch ● *n* Orientale *m*/Orientalin *f*

orientation /'ɔːrɪən'teɪʃn/ *n* Orientierung *f*

origin /'ɒrɪdʒɪn/ *n* Ursprung *m*; (*of person, goods*) Herkunft *f*

original /ə'rɪdʒənl/ *adj* ursprünglich; (*not copied*) original; (*new*) originell ● *n* Original *nt*. **~ity** *n* Originalität *f*. **~ly** *adv* ursprünglich

originate /ə'rɪdʒɪneɪt/ *vi* entstehen

ornament /'ɔːnəmənt/ *n* Ziergegenstand *m*; (*decoration*) Verzierung *f*. **~al** *adj* dekorativ

ornate /ɔː'neɪt/ *adj* reich verziert

ornithology /ɔːnɪ'θɒlədʒɪ/ *n* Vogelkunde *f*

orphan /'ɔːfn/ *n* Waisenkind *nt*, Waise *f*. **~age** *n* Waisenhaus *nt*

orthodox /'ɔːθədɒks/ *adj* orthodox

ostensible /ɒ'stensəbl/ *adj*, **-bly** *adv* angeblich

ostentat|ion /ɒsten'teɪʃn/ *n* Protzerei *f* [!]. **~ious** *adj* protzig [!]

osteopath /'ɒstɪəpæθ/ *n* Osteopath *m*

ostrich /'ɒstrɪtʃ/ *n* Strauß *m*

other /'ʌðə(r)/ *adj, pron & n* andere(r,s); **the ~ [one]** der/die/das andere; **the ~ two** die zwei anderen; **no ~s** sonst keine; **any ~ questions?** sonst noch Fragen? **every ~ day** jeden zweiten Tag; **the ~ day** neulich; **the ~ evening** neulich abends; **someone/something or ~** irgendjemand/-etwas ● *adv* anders; **~ than him** außer ihm; **somehow/somewhere or ~** irgendwie/irgendwo

'otherwise *adv* sonst; (*differently*) anders

ought /ɔːt/ *modal verb* **I/we ~ to stay** ich sollte/wir sollten eigentlich bleiben; **he ~ not to have done it** er hätte es nicht machen sollen

ounce /aʊns/ *n* Unze *f* (*28,35 g*)

our /'aʊə(r)/ *adj* unser

ours /'aʊəz/ *poss pron* unsere(r,s); **a friend of ~** ein Freund von uns; **that is ~** das gehört uns

ourselves /aʊə'selvz/ *pron* selbst; (*reflexive*) uns; **by ~** allein

out /aʊt/ *adv* (*not at home*) weg; (*outside*) draußen; (*not alight*) aus; (*unconscious*) bewusstlos; **be ~**

(*sun:*) scheinen; (*flower*) blühen; (*workers*) streiken; (*calculation:*) nicht stimmen; (*Sport*) aus sein; (*fig: not feasible*) nicht infrage kommen; **~ and about** unterwegs; **have it ~ with s.o.** [!] jdn zur Rede stellen; **get ~!** [!] raus! **~ with it!** [!] heraus damit! ● *prep* **~ of** aus (+ *dat*); **go ~ (of) the door** zur Tür hinausgehen; **be ~ of bed/the room** nicht im Bett/im Zimmer sein; **~ of breath/danger** außer Atem/Gefahr; **~ of work** arbeitslos; **nine ~ of ten** neun von zehn; **be ~ of sugar** keinen Zucker mehr haben

'outboard *adj* **~ motor** Außenbordmotor *m*

'outbreak *n* Ausbruch *m*

'outbuilding *n* Nebengebäude *nt*

'outburst *n* Ausbruch *m*

'outcast *n* Ausgestoßene(r) *m/f*

'outcome *n* Ergebnis *nt*

'outcry *n* Aufschrei *m* [der Entrüstung]

out'dated *adj* überholt

out'do *vt* (*pt* **-did**, *pp* **-done**) übertreffen, übertrumpfen

'outdoor *adj* (*life, sports*) im Freien; **~ swimming pool** Freibad *nt*

out'doors *adv* draußen; **go ~** nach draußen gehen

'outer *adj* äußere(r,s)

'outfit *n* Ausstattung *f*; (*clothes*) Ensemble *nt*; ([!]: *organization*) Laden *m*

'outgoing *adj* ausscheidend; (*mail*) ausgehend; (*sociable*) kontaktfreudig. **~s** *npl* Ausgaben *pl*

out'grow *vi* (*pt* **-grew**, *pp* **-grown**) herauswachsen aus

outing /'aʊtɪŋ/ *n* Ausflug *m*

'outlaw *n* Geächtete(r) *m/f* ● *vt* ächten

'outlay *n* Auslagen *pl*

'outlet *n* Abzug *m*; (*for water*) Abfluss *m*; (*fig*) Ventil *nt*; (*Comm*) Absatzmöglichkeit *f*

'outline *n* Umriss *m*; (*summary*) kurze Darstellung *f* ● *vt* umreißen

out'live *vt* überleben

'outlook *n* Aussicht *f*; (*future prospect*) Aussichten *pl*; (*attitude*) Einstellung *f*

out'moded *adj* überholt

out'number *vt* zahlenmäßig überlegen sein (+ *dat*)

'out-patient *n* ambulanter Patient *m*

'outpost *n* Vorposten *m*

'output *n* Leistung *f*; Produktion *f*

'outrage *n* Gräueltat *f*; (*fig*) Skandal *m*; (*indignation*) Empörung *f*. **~ous** *adj* empörend

'outright[1] *adj* völlig, total; (*refusal*) glatt

out'right[2] *adv* ganz; (*at once*) sofort; (*frankly*) offen

'outset *n* Anfang *m*

'outside[1] *adj* äußere(r,s); **~ wall** Außenwand *f* ● *n* Außenseite *f*; **from the ~** von außen; **at the ~** höchstens

out'side[2] *adv* außen; (*out of doors*) draußen; **go ~** nach draußen gehen ● *prep* außerhalb (+ *gen*); (*in front of*) vor (+ *dat/acc*)

out'sider *n* Außenseiter *m*

'outsize *adj* übergroß

'outskirts *npl* Rand *m*

out'spoken *adj* offen; **be ~** kein Blatt vor den Mund nehmen

out'standing *adj* hervorragend; (*conspicuous*) bemerkenswert; (*Comm*) ausstehend

'outstretched *adj* ausgestreckt

out'vote *vt* überstimmen

'outward /-wəd/ *adj* äußerlich; ~ **journey** Hinreise *f* ● *adv* nach außen. **~ly** *adv* nach außen hin, äußerlich. **~s** *adv* nach außen

out'wit *vt* (*pt/pp* **-witted**) überlisten

oval /'əʊvl/ *adj* oval ● *n* Oval *nt*

> **Oval Office** Das *Oval Office* ist das Büro des amerikanishen Präsidenten. Es befindet sich im westlichen Flügel des Weißen Hauses und sein Name bezieht sich auf die ovale Form des Raumes. George Washington (1. Präsident der USA) bestand auf ein ovales Büro, damit er bei Besprechungen allen Anwesenden in die Augen sehen konnte.

ovation /əʊ'veɪʃn/ *n* Ovation *f*

oven /'ʌvn/ *n* Backofen *m*

o

over /'əʊvə(r)/ *prep* über (+ *acc/dat*); ~ **dinner** beim Essen; ~ **the phone** am Telefon; ~ **the page** auf der nächsten Seite ● *adv* (*remaining*) übrig; (*ended*) zu Ende; ~ **again** noch einmal; ~ **and** ~ immer wieder; ~ **here/there** hier/da drüben; **all** ~ (*everywhere*) überall; **it's all** ~ es ist vorbei; **I ache all** ~ mir tut alles weh

overall[1] /'əʊvərɔːl/ *n* Kittel *m*; **~s** *pl* Overall *m*

overall[2] /əʊvər'ɔːl/ *adj* gesamt; (*general*) allgemein ● *adv* insgesamt

over'balance *vi* das Gleichgewicht verlieren

over'bearing *adj* herrisch

'overboard *adv* (*Naut*) über Bord

'overcast *adj* bedeckt

over'charge *vt* ~ **s.o.** jdm zu viel berechnen ● *vi* zu viel verlangen

'overcoat *n* Mantel *m*

over'come *vt* (*pt* **-came**, *pp* **-come**) überwinden; **be ~ by** überwältigt werden von

over'crowded *adj* überfüllt

over'do *vt* (*pt* **-did**, *pp* **-done**) übertreiben; (*cook too long*) zu lange kochen; ~ **it** (🄸: *do too much*) sich übernehmen

'overdose *n* Überdosis *f*

'overdraft *n* [Konto]überziehung *f*; **have an** ~ sein Konto überzogen haben

over'due *adj* überfällig

over'estimate *vt* überschätzen

'overflow[1] *n* Überschuss *m*; (*outlet*) Überlauf *m*; ~ **car park** zusätzlicher Parkplatz *m*

over'flow[2] *vi* überlaufen

over'grown *adj* (*garden*) überwachsen

'overhang[1] *n* Überhang *m*

over'hang[2] *vt/i* (*pt/pp* **-hung**) überhängen (über + *acc*)

'overhaul[1] *n* Überholung *f*

over'haul[2] *vt* (*Techn*) überholen

over'head[1] *adv* oben

'overhead[2] *adj* Ober-; (*ceiling*) Decken-. **~s** *npl* allgemeine Unkosten *pl*

over'hear *vt* (*pt/pp* **-heard**) mit anhören (*conversation*)

over'heat *vi* zu heiß werden

over'joyed *adj* überglücklich

'overland *adj & adv* /--'-/ auf dem Landweg; ~ **route** Landroute *f*

over'lap *vi* (*pt/pp* **-lapped**) sich überschneiden

over'leaf *adv* umseitig

over'load *vt* überladen

over'look *vt* überblicken; (*fail to see, ignore*) übersehen

over'night¹ *adv* über Nacht; stay ~ übernachten

'overnight² *adj* Nacht-; ~ **stay** Übernachtung *f*

'overpass *n* Überführung *f*

over'pay *vt* (*pt/pp* **-paid**) überbezahlen

over'populated *adj* übervölkert

over'power *vt* überwältigen. **~ing** *adj* überwältigend

over'priced *adj* zu teuer

over'rated *adj* überbewertet

overre'act *vi* überreagieren. **~ion** *n* Überreaktion *f*

over'riding *adj* Haupt-

over'rule *vt* ablehnen; **we were ~d** wir wurden überstimmt

over'run *vt* (*pt* **-ran**, *pp* **-run**, *pres p* **-running**) überrennen; überschreiten (*time*); **be ~ with** überlaufen sein von

over'seas¹ *adv* in Übersee; **go ~** nach Übersee gehen

'overseas² *adj* Übersee-

over'see *vt* (*pt* **-saw**, *pp* **-seen**) beaufsichtigen

over'shadow *vt* überschatten

over'shoot *vt* (*pt/pp* **-shot**) hinausschießen über (+ *acc*)

'oversight *n* Versehen *nt*

over'sleep *vi* (*pt/pp* **-slept**) [sich] verschlafen

over'step *vt* (*pt/pp* **-stepped**) überschreiten

overt /əʊ'vɜːt/ *adj* offen

over'take *vt/i* (*pt* **-took**, *pp* **-taken**) überholen

over'throw *vt* (*pt* **-threw**, *pp* **-thrown**) (*Pol*) stürzen

'overtime *n* Überstunden *pl* ● *adv* **work ~** Überstunden machen

over'tired *adj* übermüdet

overture /'əʊvətjʊə(r)/ *n* (*Mus*) Ouvertüre *f*; **~s** *pl* (*fig*) Annäherungsversuche *pl*

over'turn *vt* umstoßen ● *vi* umkippen

over'weight *adj* übergewichtig; **be ~** Übergewicht haben

overwhelm /-'welm/ *vt* überwältigen. **~ing** *adj* überwältigend

over'work *n* Überarbeitung *f* ● *vt* überfordern ● *vi* sich überarbeiten

over'wrought *adj* überreizt

ow|e /əʊ/ *vt* schulden/ (*fig*) verdanken (**[to] s.o.** jdm); **~e s.o. sth** jdm etw schuldig sein. **'~ing to** *prep* wegen (+ *gen*)

owl /aʊl/ *n* Eule *f*

own¹ /əʊn/ *adj & pron* eigen; **it's my ~** es gehört mir; **a car of my ~** mein eigenes Auto; **on one's ~** allein; **get one's ~ back** [!] sich revanchieren

own² *vt* besitzen; **I don't ~ it** es gehört mir nicht. **~ up** *vi* es zugeben

owner /'əʊnə(r)/ *n* Eigentümer(in) *m*(*f*), Besitzer(in) *m*(*f*); (*of shop*) Inhaber(in) *m*(*f*). **~ship** *n* Besitz *m*

i

Oxbridge Eine Wortbildung aus den Namen Oxford und Cambridge. Diese umgangssprachliche Zusammensetzung wird als Sammelbegriff für die zwei Eliteuniversitäten in England verwendet, um sie von anderen Hochschulen zu unterscheiden. Oxford und Cambridge sind die ältesten britischen Universitäten mit dem besten akademischen Ruf. *Oxbridge*-Absolventen werden häufig von Arbeitgebern bevorzugt.

oxygen /'ɒksɪdʒən/ *n* Sauerstoff *m*

oyster /'ɔɪstə(r)/ *n* Auster *f*

O

Pp

pace /peɪs/ *n* Schritt *m*; (*speed*) Tempo *nt*; **keep ~ with** Schritt halten mit ● *vi* **~ up and down** auf und ab gehen. **~-maker** *n* (*Sport & Med*) Schrittmacher *m*

Pacific /pəˈsɪfɪk/ *adj & n* **the ~** [Ocean] der Pazifik

pacifist /ˈpæsɪfɪst/ *n* Pazifist *m*

pacify /ˈpæsɪfaɪ/ *vt* (*pt/pp* **-ied**) beruhigen

pack /pæk/ *n* Packung *f*; (*Mil*) Tornister *m*; (*of cards*) [Karten]spiel *nt*; (*gang*) Bande *f*; (*of hounds*) Meute *f*; (*of wolves*) Rudel *nt*; **a ~ of lies** ein Haufen Lügen ● *vt/i* packen; einpacken (*article*); **be ~ed** (*crowded*) [gedrängt] voll sein. **~ up** *vt* einpacken ● *vi* 🄸 (*machine:*) kaputtgehen

package /ˈpækɪdʒ/ *n* Paket *nt*. **~ holiday** *n* Pauschalreise *f*

packet /ˈpækɪt/ *n* Päckchen *nt*

P

packing /ˈpækɪŋ/ *n* Verpackung *f*

pact /pækt/ *n* Pakt *m*

pad /pæd/ *n* Polster *nt*; (*for writing*) [Schreib]block *m* ● *vt* (*pt/pp* **padded**) polstern

padding /ˈpædɪŋ/ *n* Polsterung *f*; (*in written work*) Füllwerk *nt*

paddle[1] /ˈpædl/ *n* Paddel *nt* ● *vt* (*row*) paddeln

paddle[2] *vi* waten

paddock /ˈpædək/ *n* Koppel *f*

padlock /ˈpædlɒk/ *n* Vorhängeschloss *nt* ● *vt* mit einem Vorhängeschloss verschließen

paediatrician /piːdɪəˈtrɪʃn/ *n* Kinderarzt *m* /-ärztin *f*

pagan /ˈpeɪgən/ *adj* heidnisch ● *n* Heide *m*/Heidin *f*

page[1] /peɪdʒ/ *n* Seite *f*

page[2] *n* (*boy*) Page *m* ● *vt* ausrufen (*person*)

paid /ˈpeɪd/ *see* **pay** ● *adj* bezahlt; **put ~ to** 🄸 zunichte machen

pail /peɪl/ *n* Eimer *m*

pain /peɪn/ *n* Schmerz *m*; **be in ~** Schmerzen haben; **take ~s** sich (*dat*) Mühe geben; **~ in the neck** 🄸 Nervensäge *f*

pain: ~ful *adj* schmerzhaft; (*fig*) schmerzlich. **~-killer** *n* schmerzstillendes Mittel *nt*. **~less** *adj* schmerzlos

painstaking /ˈpeɪnzteɪkɪŋ/ *adj* sorgfältig

paint /peɪnt/ *n* Farbe *f* ● *vt/i* streichen; (*artist:*) malen. **~brush** *n* Pinsel *m*. **~er** *n* Maler *m*; (*decorator*) Anstreicher *m*. **~ing** *n* Malerei *f*; (*picture*) Gemälde *nt*

pair /peə(r)/ *n* Paar *nt*; **~ of trousers** Hose *f* ● *vi* **~ off** Paare bilden

pajamas /pəˈdʒɑːməz/ *n pl* (*Amer*) Schlafanzug *m*

Pakistan /pɑːkɪˈstɑːn/ *n* Pakistan *nt*. **~i** *adj* pakistanisch ● *n* Pakistaner(in) *m*(*f*)

pal /pæl/ *n* Freund(in) *m*(*f*)

palace /ˈpælɪs/ *n* Palast *m*

palatable /ˈpælətəbl/ *adj* schmackhaft

palate /ˈpælət/ *n* Gaumen *m*

palatial /pəˈleɪʃl/ *adj* palastartig

pale *adj* (**-r**, **-st**) blass ● *vi* blass werden. **~ness** *n* Blässe *f*

Palestin|e /ˈpælɪstaɪn/ *n* Palästina *nt*. **~ian** *adj* palästinensisch ● *n* Palästinenser(in) *m*(*f*)

palette /ˈpælɪt/ *n* Palette *f*

palm /pɑːm/ *n* Handfläche *f*; (*tree, symbol*) Palme *f* ● *vt* **~ sth off on s.o.** jdm etw andrehen. **P~ˈSunday** *n* Palmsonntag *m*

palpable /ˈpælpəbl/ *adj* tastbar; (*perceptible*) spürbar

palpitations /ˈpælpɪˈteɪʃnz/ *npl* Herzklopfen *nt*

paltry /ˈpɔːltrɪ/ *adj* armselig

pamper /ˈpæmpə(r)/ *vt* verwöhnen

pamphlet /ˈpæmflɪt/ *n* Broschüre *f*

pan /pæn/ *n* Pfanne *f*; (*saucepan*) Topf *m*; (*of scales*) Schale *f*

panacea /pænəˈsiːə/ *n* Allheilmittel *nt*

ˈ**pancake** *n* Pfannkuchen *m*

panda /ˈpændə/ *n* Panda *m*

pandemonium /pændɪˈməʊnɪəm/ *n* Höllenlärm *m*

pane /peɪn/ *n* [Glas]scheibe *f*

panel /ˈpænl/ *n* Tafel *f*, Platte *f*; ~ **of experts** Expertenrunde *f*; ~ **of judges** Jury *f*. ~**ling** *n* Täfelung *f*

pang /pæŋ/ *n* ~**s of hunger** Hungergefühl *nt*; ~**s of conscience** Gewissensbisse *pl*

panic /ˈpænɪk/ *n* Panik *f* ● *vi* (*pt/pp* **panicked**) in Panik geraten. ~**-stricken** *adj* von Panik ergriffen

panoram|a /pænəˈrɑːmə/ *n* Panorama *nt*. ~**ic** *adj* Panorama-

pansy /ˈpænzɪ/ *n* Stiefmütterchen *nt*

pant /pænt/ *vi* keuchen; (*dog:*) hecheln

panther /ˈpænθə(r)/ *n* Panther *m*

panties /ˈpæntɪz/ *npl* [Damen]slip *m*

pantomime /ˈpæntəmaɪm/ *n* [zu Weihnachten aufgeführte] Märchenvorstellung *f*

pantry /ˈpæntrɪ/ *n* Speisekammer *f*

pants /pænts/ *npl* Unterhose *f*; (*woman's*) Schlüpfer *m*; (*trousers*) Hose *f*

ˈ**pantyhose** *n* (*Amer*) Strumpfhose *f*

paper /ˈpeɪpə(r)/ *n* Papier *nt*; (*newspaper*) Zeitung *f*; (*exam*~) Testbogen *m*; (*exam*) Klausur *f*; (*treatise*) Referat *nt*; ~**s** *pl* (*documents*) Unterlagen *pl*; (*for identification*) [Ausweis]papiere *pl* ● *vt* tapezieren

paper: ~**back** *n* Taschenbuch *nt*. ~**-clip** *n* Büroklammer *f*. ~**weight** *n* Briefbeschwerer *m*. ~**work** *n* Schreibarbeit *f*

par /pɑː(r)/ *n* (*Golf*) Par *nt*; **on a** ~ gleichwertig (**with** *dat*)

parable /ˈpærəbl/ *n* Gleichnis *nt*

parachut|e /ˈpærəʃuːt/ *n* Fallschirm *m* ● *vi* [mit dem Fallschirm] abspringen. ~**ist** *n* Fallschirmspringer *m*

parade /pəˈreɪd/ *n* Parade *f*; (*procession*) Festzug *m* ● *vt* (*show off*) zur Schau stellen

paradise /ˈpærədaɪs/ *n* Paradies *nt*

paradox /ˈpærədɒks/ *n* Paradox *nt*. ~**ical** paradox

paraffin /ˈpærəfɪn/ *n* Paraffin *nt*

paragraph /ˈpærəgrɑːf/ *n* Absatz *m*

parallel /ˈpærəlel/ *adj* & *adv* parallel ● *n* (*Geog*) Breitenkreis *m*; (*fig*) Parallele *f*

Paralympics /pærəˈlɪmpɪks/ *npl* **the** ~ die Paralympics *pl*

paralyse /ˈpærəlaɪz/ *vt* lähmen; (*fig*) lahmlegen

paralysis /pəˈræləsɪs/ *n* (*pl* **-ses** /-siːz/) Lähmung *f*

paramedic /pærəˈmedɪk/ *n* Rettungssanitäter(in) *m*(*f*)

parameter /pəˈræmɪtə(r)/ *n* Parameter *m*, Rahmen *m*

paranoid /ˈpærənɔɪd/ *adj* [krankhaft] misstrauisch

parapet /ˈpærəpɪt/ *n* Brüstung *f*

P

paraphernalia /pærəfə'neɪlɪə/ *n* Kram *m*
parasite /'pærəsaɪt/ *n* Parasit *m*, Schmarotzer *m*
paratrooper /'pærətru:pə(r)/ *n* Fallschirmjäger *m*
parcel /'pɑ:sl/ *n* Paket *nt*
parch /pɑ:tʃ/ *vt* austrocknen; **be ~ed** (*person*:) einen furchtbaren Durst haben
parchment /'pɑ:tʃmənt/ *n* Pergament *nt*
pardon /'pɑ:dn/ *n* Verzeihung *f*; (*Jur*) Begnadigung *f*; **~?** ! bitte? **I beg your ~** wie bitte? (*sorry*) Verzeihung! ● *vt* verzeihen; (*Jur*) begnadigen
parent /'peərənt/ *n* Elternteil *m*; **~s** *pl* Eltern *pl*. **~al** *adj* elterlich
parenthesis /pə'renθəsɪs/ *n* (*pl* **-ses** /-si:z/) Klammer *f*
parish /'pærɪʃ/ *n* Gemeinde *f*. **~ioner** *n* Gemeindemitglied *nt*
park /pɑ:k/ *n* Park *m* ● *vt/i* parken. **~-and-ride** *n* Park-and-ride-Platz *m*
parking /'pɑ:kɪŋ/ *n* Parken *nt*; **'no ~'** 'Parken verboten'. **~-lot** *n* (*Amer*) Parkplatz *m*. **~-meter** *n* Parkuhr *f*. **~ space** *n* Parkplatz *m*
parliament /'pɑ:ləmənt/ *n* Parlament *nt*. **~ary** *adj* parlamentarisch

Parliament Das britische Parlament ist die oberste gesetzgebende Gewalt in Großbritannien und besteht aus dem Souverän (dem König oder der Königin), dem *House of Lords* (Oberhaus) und dem *House of Commons* (Unterhaus). Die Partei mit der Mehrheit im Unterhaus bildet die Regierung. ▷**DÁIL ÉIREANN**, ▷**SCOTTISH PARLIAMENT**, ▷**WELSH ASSEMBLY**.

parochial /pə'rəʊkɪəl/ *adj* Gemeinde-; (*fig*) beschränkt
parody /'pærədɪ/ *n* Parodie *f* ● *vt* (*pt/pp* **-ied**) parodieren
parole /pə'rəʊl/ *n* **on ~** auf Bewährung
parquet /'pɑ:keɪ/ *n* **~ floor** Parkett *nt*
parrot /'pærət/ *n* Papagei *m*
parsley /'pɑ:slɪ/ *n* Petersilie *f*
parsnip /'pɑ:snɪp/ *n* Pastinake *f*
parson /'pɑ:sn/ *n* Pfarrer *m*
part /pɑ:t/ *n* Teil *m*; (*Techn*) Teil *nt*; (*area*) Gegend *f*; (*Theat*) Rolle *f*; (*Mus*) Part *m*; **spare ~** Ersatzteil *nt*; **for my ~** meinerseits; **on the ~ of** vonseiten (+ *gen*); **take s.o.'s ~** für jdn Partei ergreifen; **take ~ in** teilnehmen an (+ *dat*) ● *adv* teils ● *vt* trennen; scheiteln (*hair*) ● *vi* (*people*:) sich trennen; **~ with** sich trennen von
partial /'pɑ:ʃl/ *adj* Teil-; **be ~ to** mögen. **-ly** *adv* teilweise
particip|ant /pɑ:'tɪsɪpənt/ *n* Teilnehmer(in) *m*(*f*). **~ate** *vi* teilnehmen (**in** an + *dat*). **~ation** *n* Teilnahme *f*
particle /'pɑ:tɪkl/ *n* Körnchen *nt*; (*Phys*) Partikel *nt*; (*Gram*) Partikel *f*
particular /pə'tɪkjʊlə(r)/ *adj* besondere(r,s); (*precise*) genau; (*fastidious*) penibel; **in ~** besonders. **~ly** *adv* besonders. **~s** *npl* nähere Angaben *pl*
parting /'pɑ:tɪŋ/ *n* Abschied *m*; (*in hair*) Scheitel *m*
partition /pɑ:'tɪʃn/ *n* Trennwand *f*; (*Pol*) Teilung *f* ● *vt* teilen
partly /'pɑ:tlɪ/ *adv* teilweise
partner /'pɑ:tnə(r)/ *n* Partner(in) *m*(*f*); (*Comm*) Teilhaber *m*. **~ship** *n* Partnerschaft *f*; (*Comm*) Teilhaberschaft *f*
partridge /'pɑ:trɪdʒ/ *n* Rebhuhn *nt*

part-'time *adj & adv* Teilzeit-; **be** *or* **work** ~ Teilzeitarbeit machen

party /'pɑːtɪ/ *n* Party *f*, Fest *nt*; (*group*) Gruppe *f*; (*Pol, Jur*) Partei *f*

pass /pɑːs/ *n* Ausweis *m*; (*Geog, Sport*) Pass *m*; (*Sch*) ≈ ausreichend; **get a** ~ bestehen ● *vt* vorbeigehen/-fahren an (+ *dat*); (*overtake*) überholen; (*hand*) reichen; (*Sport*) abgeben, abspielen; (*approve*) annehmen; (*exceed*) übersteigen; bestehen (*exam*); machen (*remark*); fällen (*judgement*); (*Jur*) verhängen (*sentence*); ~ **the time** sich (*dat*) die Zeit vertreiben; ~ **one's hand over sth** mit der Hand über etw (*acc*) fahren ● *vi* vorbeigehen/-fahren; (*get by*) vorbeikommen; (*overtake*) überholen; (*time:*) vergehen; (*in exam*) bestehen; ~ **away** *vi* sterben. ~ **down** *vt* herunterreichen; (*fig*) weitergeben. ~ **out** *vi* ohnmächtig werden. ~ **round** *vt* herumreichen. ~ **up** *vt* heraufreichen; (!: *miss*) vorübergehen lassen

passable /'pɑːsəbl/ *adj* (*road*) befahrbar; (*satisfactory*) passabel

passage /'pæsɪdʒ/ *n* Durchgang *m*; (*corridor*) Gang *m*; (*voyage*) Überfahrt *f*; (*in book*) Passage *f*

passenger /'pæsɪndʒə(r)/ *n* Fahrgast *m*; (*Naut, Aviat*) Passagier *m*; (*in car*) Mitfahrer *m*. ~ **seat** *n* Beifahrersitz *m*

passer-by /pɑːsə'baɪ/ *n* (*pl* **-s-by**) Passant(in) *m*(*f*)

passion /'pæʃn/ *n* Leidenschaft *f*. ~**ate** *adj* leidenschaftlich

passive /'pæsɪv/ *adj* passiv ● *n* Passiv *nt*

pass: ~**port** *n* [Reise]pass *m*. ~**word** *n* Kennwort *nt*; (*Mil*) Losung *f*

past /pɑːst/ *adj* vergangene(r,s); (*former*) ehemalig; **that's all** ~ das ist jetzt vorbei ● *n* Vergangenheit *f* ● *prep* an (+ *dat*) ... vorbei; (*after*) nach; **at ten** ~ **two** um zehn nach zwei ● *adv* vorbei; **go** ~ vorbeigehen

pasta /'pæstə/ *n* Nudeln *pl*

paste /peɪst/ *n* Brei *m*; (*adhesive*) Kleister *m*; (*jewellery*) Strass *m* ● *vt* kleistern

pastel /'pæstl/ *n* Pastellfarbe *f*; (*drawing*) Pastell *nt* ● *attrib* Pastell-

pastime /'pɑːstaɪm/ *n* Zeitvertreib *m*

pastr|y /'peɪstrɪ/ *n* Teig *m*; **cakes and** ~**ies** Kuchen und Gebäck

pasture /'pɑːstʃə(r)/ *n* Weide *f*

pasty[1] /'pæstɪ/ *n* Pastete *f*

pat /pæt/ *n* Klaps *m*; (*of butter*) Stückchen *nt* ● *vt* (*pt/pp* **patted**) tätscheln; ~ **s.o. on the back** jdm auf die Schulter klopfen

patch /pætʃ/ *n* Flicken *m*; (*spot*) Fleck *m*; **not a** ~ **on** ! gar nicht zu vergleichen mit ● *vt* flicken. ~ **up** *vt* [zusammen]flicken; beilegen (*quarrel*)

patchy /'pætʃɪ/ *adj* ungleichmäßig

patent /'peɪtnt/ *n* Patent *nt* ● *vt* patentieren. ~ **leather** *n* Lackleder *nt*

paternal /pə'tɜːnl/ *adj* väterlich

path /pɑːθ/ *n* (*pl* ~**s** /pɑːðz/) [Fuß]weg *m*, Pfad *m*; (*orbit, track*) Bahn *f*; (*fig*) Weg *m*

pathetic /pə'θetɪk/ *adj* mitleiderregend; (*attempt*) erbärmlich

patience /'peɪʃns/ *n* Geduld *f*; (*game*) Patience *f*

patient /'peɪʃnt/ *adj* geduldig ● *n* Patient(in) *m*(*f*)

patio /'pætɪəʊ/ *n* Terrasse *f*

patriot /'pætrɪət/ *n* Patriot(in) *m*(*f*). ~**ic** *adj* patriotisch. ~**ism** *n* Patriotismus *m*

patrol /pəˈtrəʊl/ *n* Patrouille *f* ● *vt/i* patrouillieren [in (+ *dat*)]; (*police*:) auf Streife gehen/fahren [in (+ *dat*)]. ~ **car** *n* Streifenwagen *m*

patron /ˈpeɪtrən/ *n* Gönner *m*; (*of charity*) Schirmherr *m*; (*of the arts*) Mäzen *m*; (*customer*) Kunde *m*/Kundin *f*; (*Theat*) Besucher *m*. ~**age** *n* Schirmherrschaft *f*

patroniz|e /ˈpætrənaɪz/ *vt* (*fig*) herablassend behandeln. ~**ing** *adj* gönnerhaft

patter *n* (*speech*) Gerede *nt*

pattern /ˈpætn/ *n* Muster *nt*

paunch /pɔːntʃ/ *n* [Schmer]bauch *m*

pause /pɔːz/ *n* Pause *f* ● *vi* innehalten

pave /peɪv/ *vt* pflastern; ~ **the way** den Weg bereiten (**for** *dat*). ~**ment** *n* Bürgersteig *m*

paw /pɔː/ *n* Pfote *f*; (*of large animal*) Pranke *f*, Tatze *f*

pawn[1] /pɔːn/ *n* (*Chess*) Bauer *m*; (*fig*) Schachfigur *f*

pawn[2] *vt* verpfänden. ~ **broker** *n* Pfandleiher *m*

P

pay /peɪ/ *n* Lohn *m*; (*salary*) Gehalt *nt*; **be in the** ~ **of** bezahlt werden von ● *v* (*pt/pp* **paid**) ● *vt* bezahlen; zahlen (*money*); ~ **s.o. a visit** jdm einen Besuch abstatten; ~ **s.o. a compliment** jdm ein Kompliment machen ● *vi* zahlen; (*be profitable*) sich bezahlt machen; (*fig*) sich lohnen; ~ **for sth** etw bezahlen. ~ **back** *vt* zurückzahlen. ~ **in** *vt* einzahlen. ~ **off** *vt* abzahlen (*debt*) ● *vi* (*fig*) sich auszahlen

payable /ˈpeɪəbl/ *adj* zahlbar; **make** ~ **to** ausstellen auf (+ *acc*)

payment /ˈpeɪmənt/ *n* Bezahlung *f*; (*amount*) Zahlung *f*

pea /piː/ *n* Erbse *f*

peace /piːs/ *n* Frieden *m*; **for my** ~ **of mind** zu meiner eigenen Beruhigung

peace|ful *adj* friedlich. ~**maker** *n* Friedensstifter *m*

peach /piːtʃ/ *n* Pfirsich *m*

peacock /ˈpiːkɒk/ *n* Pfau *m*

peak /piːk/ *n* Gipfel *m*; (*fig*) Höhepunkt *m*. ~**ed** ˈ**cap** *n* Schirmmütze *f*. ~ **hours** *npl* Hauptbelastungszeit *f*; (*for traffic*) Hauptverkehrszeit *f*

peal /piːl/ *n* (*of bells*) Glockengeläut *nt*; ~**s of laughter** schallendes Gelächter *nt*

ˈ**peanut** *n* Erdnuss *f*

pear /peə(r)/ *n* Birne *f*

pearl /pɜːl/ *n* Perle *f*

peasant /ˈpeznt/ *n* Bauer *m*

peat /piːt/ *n* Torf *m*

pebble /ˈpebl/ *n* Kieselstein *m*

peck /pek/ *n* Schnabelhieb *m*; (*kiss*) flüchtiger Kuss *m* ● *vt/i* picken/(*nip*) hacken (**at** nach)

peculiar /pɪˈkjuːlɪə(r)/ *adj* eigenartig, seltsam; ~ **to** eigentümlich (+ *dat*). ~**ity** *n* Eigenart *f*

pedal /ˈpedl/ *n* Pedal *nt* ● *vt* fahren (*bicycle*) ● *vi* treten

pedantic /pɪˈdæntɪk/ *adj*, **-ally** *adv* pedantisch

pedestal /ˈpedɪstl/ *n* Sockel *m*

pedestrian /pɪˈdestrɪən/ *n* Fußgänger(in) *m*(*f*) ● *adj* (*fig*) prosaisch. ~ ˈ**crossing** *n* Fußgängerüberweg *m*. ~ ˈ**precinct** *n* Fußgängerzone *f*

pedigree /ˈpedɪgriː/ *n* Stammbaum *m* ● *attrib* (*animal*) Rasse-

pedlar /ˈpedlə(r)/ *n* Hausierer *m*

peek /piːk/ *vi* [!] gucken

peel /piːl/ *n* Schale *f* ● *vt* schälen; ● *vi* (*skin*:) sich schälen; (*paint*:) abblättern. ~ **ings** *npl* Schalen *pl*

peep /piːp/ *n* kurzer Blick *m* ● *vi* gucken. ~**-hole** *n* Guckloch *nt*

peer[1] /pɪə(r)/ *vi* ~ **at** forschend ansehen

peer[2] *n* Peer *m*; **his** ~**s** *pl* seinesgleichen

peg /peg/ *n* (*hook*) Haken *m*; (*for tent*) Pflock *m*, Hering *m*; (*for clothes*) [Wäsche]klammer *f*; **off the** ~ [!] von der Stange

pejorative /pɪˈdʒɒrətɪv/ *adj* abwertend

pelican /ˈpelɪkən/ *n* Pelikan *m*

pellet /ˈpelɪt/ *n* Kügelchen *nt*

pelt[1] /pelt/ *n* (*skin*) Pelz *m*, Fell *nt*

pelt[2] *vt* bewerfen ● *vi* ~ **[down]** (*rain:*) [hernieder]prasseln

pelvis /ˈpelvɪs/ *n* (*Anat*) Becken *nt*

pen[1] /pen/ *n* (*for animals*) Hürde *f*

pen[2] *n* Federhalter *m*; (*ballpoint*) Kugelschreiber *m*

penal /ˈpi:nl/ *adj* Straf-. ~**ize** *vt* bestrafen; (*fig*) benachteiligen

penalty /ˈpenltɪ/ *n* Strafe *f*; (*fine*) Geldstrafe *f*; (*Sport*) Strafstoß *m*; (*Football*) Elfmeter *m*

penance /ˈpenəns/ *n* Buße *f*

pence /pens/ *see* **penny**

pencil /ˈpensɪl/ *n* Bleistift *m* ● *vt* (*pt/pp* **pencilled**) mit Bleistift schreiben. ~**-sharpener** *n* Bleistiftspitzer *m*

pendulum /ˈpendjʊləm/ *n* Pendel *nt*

penetrat|e /ˈpenɪtreɪt/ *vt* durchdringen; ~**e into** eindringen in (+ *acc*). ~**ing** *adj* durchdringend. ~**ion** *n* Durchdringen *nt*

ˈ**penfriend** *n* Brieffreund(in) *m*(*f*)

penguin /ˈpeŋgwɪn/ *n* Pinguin *m*

penicillin /penɪˈsɪlɪn/ *n* Penizillin *nt*

peninsula /pəˈnɪnsʊlə/ *n* Halbinsel *f*

penis /ˈpi:nɪs/ *n* Penis *m*

penitentiary /penɪˈtenʃərɪ/ *n* (*Amer*) Gefängnis *nt*

pen: ~**knife** *n* Taschenmesser *nt*. ~**-name** *n* Pseudonym *nt*

penniless /ˈpenɪlɪs/ *adj* mittellos

penny /ˈpenɪ/ *n* (*pl* **pence**; *single coins* **pennies**) Penny *m*; (*Amer*) Centstück *nt*; **the** ~**'s dropped** [!] der Groschen ist gefallen

pension /ˈpenʃn/ *n* Rente *f*; (*of civil servant*) Pension *f*. ~**er** *n* Rentner(in) *m*(*f*); Pensionär(in) *m*(*f*)

pensive /ˈpensɪv/ *adj* nachdenklich

pent-up /ˈpentʌp/ *adj* angestaut

penultimate /peˈnʌltɪmət/ *adj* vorletzte(r,s)

people /ˈpi:pl/ *npl* Leute *pl*, Menschen *pl*; (*citizens*) Bevölkerung *f*; **the** ~ das Volk; **English** ~ die Engländer; ~ **say** man sagt; **for four** ~ für vier Personen ● *vt* bevölkern

pepper /ˈpepə(r)/ *n* Pfeffer *m*; (*vegetable*) Paprika *m*

pepper: ~**mint** *n* Pfefferminz *nt*; (*Bot*) Pfefferminze *f*. ~**pot** *n* Pfefferstreuer *m*

per /pɜ:(r)/ *prep* pro; ~ **cent** Prozent *nt*

percentage /pəˈsentɪdʒ/ *n* Prozentsatz *m*; (*part*) Teil *m*

perceptible /pəˈseptəbl/ *adj* wahrnehmbar

percept|ion /pəˈsepʃn/ *n* Wahrnehmung *f*. ~**ive** *adj* feinsinnig

perch[1] /pɜ:tʃ/ *n* Stange *f* ● *vi* (*bird:*) sich niederlassen

perch[2] *n inv* (*fish*) Barsch *m*

percussion /pəˈkʌʃn/ *n* Schlagzeug *nt*. ~ **instrument** *n* Schlaginstrument *nt*

perennial /pəˈrenɪəl/ *adj* (*problem*) immer wiederkehrend ● *n* (*Bot*) mehrjährige Pflanze *f*

perfect[1] /ˈpɜ:fɪkt/ *adj* perfekt, vollkommen; ([!]: *utter*) völlig ● *n*

(*Gram*) Perfekt *nt*
perfect² /pəˈfekt/ *vt* vervollkommnen. **~ion** *n* Vollkommenheit *f*; **to ~ion** perfekt
perfectly /ˈpɜːfɪktlɪ/ *adv* perfekt; (*completely*) vollkommen, völlig
perforated /ˈpɜːfəreɪtɪd/ *adj* perforiert
perform /pəˈfɔːm/ *vt* ausführen; erfüllen (*duty*); (*Theat*) aufführen (*play*); spielen (*role*) ● *vi* (*Theat*) auftreten; (*Techn*) laufen. **~ance** *n* Aufführung *f*; (*at theatre, cinema*) Vorstellung *f*; (*Techn*) Leistung *f*. **~er** *n* Künstler(in) *m*(*f*)
perfume /ˈpɜːfjuːm/ *n* Parfüm *nt*; (*smell*) Duft *m*
perhaps /pəˈhæps/ *adv* vielleicht
perilous /ˈperələs/ *adj* gefährlich
perimeter /pəˈrɪmɪtə(r)/ *n* [äußere] Grenze *f*; (*Geometry*) Umfang *m*
period /ˈpɪərɪəd/ *n* Periode *f*; (*Sch*) Stunde *f*; (*full stop*) Punkt *m* ● *attrib* (*costume*) zeitgenössisch; (*furniture*) antik. **~ic** *adj*, **-ally** *adv* periodisch. **~ical** *n* Zeitschrift *f*
peripher|al /pəˈrɪfərl/ *adj* nebensächlich. **~y** *n* Peripherie *f*
perish /ˈperɪʃ/ *vi* (*rubber:*) verrotten; (*food:*) verderben; (*to die*) ums Leben kommen. **~able** *adj* leicht verderblich. **~ing** *adj* (🄸: *cold*) eiskalt
perjur|e /ˈpɜːdʒə(r)/ *vt* **~e oneself** einen Meineid leisten. **~y** *n* Meineid *m*
perk¹ /pɜːk/ *n* 🄸 [Sonder]vergünstigung *f*
perk² *vi* **~ up** munter werden
perm /pɜːm/ *n* Dauerwelle *f* ● *vt* **~ s.o.'s hair** jdm eine Dauerwelle machen
permanent /ˈpɜːmənənt/ *adj* ständig; (*job, address*) fest. **~ly** *adv* ständig; (*work, live*) dauernd, permanent; (*employed*) fest
permissible /pəˈmɪsəbl/ *adj* erlaubt
permission /pəˈmɪʃn/ *n* Erlaubnis *f*
permit¹ /pəˈmɪt/ *vt* (*pt/pp* **-mitted**) erlauben (**s.o.** jdm)
permit² /ˈpɜːmɪt/ *n* Genehmigung *f*
perpendicular /pɜːpənˈdɪkjʊlə(r)/ *adj* senkrecht ● *n* Senkrechte *f*
perpetual /pəˈpetjʊəl/ *adj* ständig, dauernd
perpetuate /pəˈpetjʊeɪt/ *vt* bewahren; verewigen (*error*)
perplex /pəˈpleks/ *vt* verblüffen. **~ed** *adj* verblüfft
persecut|e /ˈpɜːsɪkjuːt/ *vt* verfolgen. **~ion** *n* Verfolgung *f*
perseverance /pɜːsɪˈvɪərəns/ *n* Ausdauer *f*
persevere /pɜːsɪˈvɪə(r)/ *vi* beharrlich weitermachen
Persia /ˈpɜːʃə/ *n* Persien *nt*
Persian /ˈpɜːʃn/ *adj* persisch; (*cat, carpet*) Perser-
persist /pəˈsɪst/ *vi* beharrlich weitermachen; (*continue*) anhalten; (*view:*) weiter bestehen; **~ in doing sth** dabei bleiben, etw zu tun. **~ence** *n* Beharrlichkeit *f*. **~ent** *adj* beharrlich; (*continuous*) anhaltend
person /ˈpɜːsn/ *n* Person *f*; **in ~** persönlich
personal /ˈpɜːsənl/ *adj* persönlich. **~ ˈhygiene** *n* Körperpflege *f*
personality /pɜːsəˈnælətɪ/ *n* Persönlichkeit *f*
personify /pəˈsɒnɪfaɪ/ *vt* (*pt/pp* **-ied**) personifizieren, verkörpern
personnel /pɜːsəˈnel/ *n* Personal *nt*

perspective /pəˈspektɪv/ *n* Perspektive *f*

persp|iration /pɜːspɪˈreɪʃn/ *n* Schweiß *m*. **~ire** *vi* schwitzen

persua|de /pəˈsweɪd/ *vt* überreden; (*convince*) überzeugen. **~sion** *n* Überredung *f*; (*powers of* **~***sion*) Überredungskunst *f*

persuasive /pəˈsweɪsɪv/ *adj* beredsam; (*convincing*) überzeugend

pertinent /ˈpɜːtɪnənt/ *adj* relevant (**to** für)

perturb /pəˈtɜːb/ *vt* beunruhigen

peruse /pəˈruːz/ *vt* lesen

pervers|e /pəˈvɜːs/ *adj* eigensinnig. **~ion** *n* Perversion *f*

pervert[1] /pəˈvɜːt/ *vt* verdrehen; verführen (*person*)

pervert[2] /ˈpɜːvɜːt/ *n* Perverse(r) *m*

pessimis|m /ˈpesɪmɪzm/ *n* Pessimismus *m*. **~t** *n* Pessimist *m*. **~tic** *adj*, **-ally** *adv* pessimistisch

pest /pest/ *n* Schädling *m*; ([!]: *person*) Nervensäge *f*

pester /ˈpestə(r)/ *vt* belästigen

pesticide /ˈpestɪsaɪd/ *n* Schädlingsbekämpfungsmittel *nt*

pet /pet/ *n* Haustier *nt*; (*favourite*) Liebling *m* ● *vt* (*pt/pp* **petted**) liebkosen

petal /ˈpetl/ *n* Blütenblatt *nt*

peter /ˈpiːtə(r)/ *vi* **~ out** allmählich aufhören

petition /pəˈtɪʃn/ *n* Bittschrift *f*

pet 'name *n* Kosename *m*

petrified /ˈpetrɪfaɪd/ *adj* vor Angst wie versteinert

petrol /ˈpetrl/ *n* Benzin *nt*

petroleum /pɪˈtrəʊlɪəm/ *n* Petroleum *nt*

petrol: ~-pump *n* Zapfsäule *f*. **~ station** *n* Tankstelle *f*. **~ tank** *n* Benzintank *m*

petticoat /ˈpetɪkəʊt/ *n* Unterrock *m*

petty /ˈpetɪ/ *adj* kleinlich. **~ 'cash** *n* Portokasse *f*

petulant /ˈpetjʊlənt/ *adj* gekränkt

pew /pjuː/ *n* [Kirchen]bank *f*

pharmaceutical /fɑːməˈsjuːtɪkl/ *adj* pharmazeutisch

pharmac|ist /ˈfɑːməsɪst/ *n* Apotheker(in) *m*(*f*). **~y** *n* Pharmazie *f*; (*shop*) Apotheke *f*

phase /feɪz/ *n* Phase *f* ● *vt* **~ in/out** allmählich einführen/abbauen

Ph.D. (*abbr* **Doctor of Philosophy**) Dr. phil.

pheasant /ˈfeznt/ *n* Fasan *m*

phenomen|al /fɪˈnɒmɪnl/ *adj* phänomenal. **~on** *n* (*pl* **-na**) Phänomen *nt*

philharmonic /fɪlɑːˈmɒnɪk/ *n* (*orchestra*) Philharmoniker *pl*

Philippines /ˈfɪlɪpiːnz/ *npl* Philippinen *pl*

philistine /ˈfɪlɪstaɪn/ *n* Banause *m*

philosoph|er /fɪˈlɒsəfə(r)/ *n* Philosoph *m*. **~ical** *adj* philosophisch. **~y** *n* Philosophie *f*

phlegmatic /flegˈmætɪk/ *adj* phlegmatisch

phobia /ˈfəʊbɪə/ *n* Phobie *f*

phone /fəʊn/ *n* Telefon *nt*; **be on the ~** Telefon haben; (*be phoning*) telefonieren ● *vt* anrufen ● *vi* telefonieren. **~ back** *vt/i* zurückrufen. **~ book** *n* Telefonbuch *nt*. **~ box** *n* Telefonzelle *f*. **~ card** *n* Telefonkarte *f*. **~-in** *n* (*Radio*) Hörersendung *f*. **~ number** *n* Telefonnummer *f*

phonetic /fəˈnetɪk/ *adj* phonetisch. **~s** *n* Phonetik *f*

phoney /ˈfəʊnɪ/ *adj* falsch; (*forged*) gefälscht

photo /ˈfəʊtəʊ/ *n* Foto *nt*, Aufnahme *f*. **~copier** *n* Fotokopiergerät *nt*. **~copy** *n* Fotokopie *f* ● *vt* fotokopieren

photogenic /fəʊtəʊˈdʒenɪk/ *adj* fotogen

photograph /ˈfəʊtəgrɑːf/ *n* Fotografie *f*, Aufnahme *f* ● *vt* fotografieren

photograph|er /fəˈtɒgrəfə(r)/ *n* Fotograf(in) *m*(*f*). **~ic** *adj*, **-ally** *adv* fotografisch. **~y** *n* Fotografie *f*

phrase /freɪz/ *n* Redensart *f* ● *vt* formulieren. **~-book** *n* Sprachführer *m*

physical /ˈfɪzɪkl/ *adj* körperlich

physician /fɪˈzɪʃn/ *n* Arzt *m*/ Ärztin *f*

physic|ist /ˈfɪzɪsɪst/ *n* Physiker(in) *m*(*f*). **~s** *n* Physik *f*

physioˈtherap|ist /fɪzɪəʊ-/ *n* Physiotherapeut(in) *m*(*f*). **~y** *n* Physiotherapie *f*

physique /fɪˈziːk/ *n* Körperbau *m*

pianist /ˈpɪənɪst/ *n* Klavierspieler(in) *m*(*f*); (*professional*) Pianist(in) *m*(*f*)

P

piano /pɪˈænəʊ/ *n* Klavier *nt*

pick[1] /pɪk/ *n* Spitzhacke *f*

pick[2] *n* Auslese *f*; **take one's ~** sich (*dat*) aussuchen ● *vt/i* (*pluck*) pflücken; (*select*) wählen, sich (*dat*) aussuchen; **~ and choose** wählerisch sein; **~ a quarrel** einen Streit anfangen; **~ holes in** [!] kritisieren; **~ at one's food** im Essen herumstochern. **~ on** *vt* wählen; ([!]: *find fault with*) herumhacken auf (+ *dat*). **~ up** *vt* in die Hand nehmen; (*off the ground*) aufheben; hochnehmen (*baby*); (*learn*) lernen; (*acquire*) erwerben; (*buy*) kaufen; (*Teleph*) abnehmen (*receiver*); auffangen (*signal*); (*collect*) abholen; aufnehmen (*passengers*); (*police:*) aufgreifen (*criminal*); sich holen (*illness*); [!] aufgabeln (*girl*); **~ oneself up** aufstehen ● *vi* (*improve*) sich bessern

ˈpickaxe *n* Spitzhacke *f*

picket /ˈpɪkɪt/ *n* Streikposten *m*

pickle /ˈpɪkl/ *n* (*Amer: gherkin*) Essiggurke *f*; **~s** *pl* [Mixed] Pickles *pl* ● *vt* einlegen

pick: ~pocket *n* Taschendieb *m*. **~-up** *n* (*truck*) Lieferwagen *m*

picnic /ˈpɪknɪk/ *n* Picknick *nt* ● *vi* (*pt/pp* **-nicked**) picknicken

picture /ˈpɪktʃə(r)/ *n* Bild *nt*; (*film*) Film *m*; **as pretty as a ~** bildhübsch; **put s.o. in the ~** (*fig*) jdn ins Bild setzen ● *vt* (*imagine*) sich (*dat*) vorstellen

picturesque /pɪktʃəˈresk/ *adj* malerisch

pie /paɪ/ *n* Pastete *f*; (*fruit*) Kuchen *m*

piece /piːs/ *n* Stück *nt*; (*of set*) Teil *nt*; (*in game*) Stein *m*; (*writing*) Artikel *m*; **a ~ of bread/paper** ein Stück Brot/Papier; **a ~ of news/advice** eine Nachricht/ein Rat; **take to ~s** auseinander nehmen ● *vt* **~ together** zusammensetzen; (*fig*) zusammenstückeln. **~meal** *adv* stückweise

pier /pɪə(r)/ *n* Pier *m*; (*pillar*) Pfeiler *m*

pierc|e /pɪəs/ *vt* durchstechen. **~ing** *adj* durchdringend

pig /pɪg/ *n* Schwein *nt*

pigeon /ˈpɪdʒɪn/ *n* Taube *f*. **~-hole** *n* Fach *nt*

piggy|back /ˈpɪgɪbæk/ *n* **give s.o. a ~back** jdn huckepack tragen. **~ bank** *n* Sparschwein *nt*

pigˈheaded *adj* [!] starrköpfig

pigment /ˈpɪgmənt/ *n* Pigment *nt*

pig: ~skin *n* Schweinsleder *nt*. **~sty** *n* Schweinestall *m*. **~tail** *n* [!] Zopf *m*

pilchard /ˈpɪltʃəd/ *n* Sardine *f*

pile¹ /paɪl/ *n* (*of fabric*) Flor *m*
pile² *n* Haufen *m* ● *vt* ~ **sth on to sth** etw auf etw (*acc*) häufen. ~ **up** *vt* häufen ● *vi* sich häufen
piles /paɪlz/ *npl* Hämorrhoiden *pl*
'pile-up *n* Massenkarambolage *f*
pilgrim /'pɪlgrɪm/ *n* Pilger(in) *m*(*f*). ~**age** *n* Pilgerfahrt *f*, Wallfahrt *f*
pill /pɪl/ *n* Pille *f*
pillar /'pɪlə(r)/ *n* Säule *f*. ~**-box** *n* Briefkasten *m*
pillow /'pɪləʊ/ *n* Kopfkissen *nt*. ~**case** *n* Kopfkissenbezug *m*
pilot /'paɪlət/ *n* Pilot *m*; (*Naut*) Lotse *m* ● *vt* fliegen (*plane*); lotsen (*ship*). ~**-light** *n* Zündflamme *f*
pimple /'pɪmpl/ *n* Pickel *m*
pin /pɪn/ *n* Stecknadel *f*; (*Techn*) Bolzen *m*, Stift *m*; (*Med*) Nagel *m*; **I have ~s and needles in my leg** 🄸 mein Bein ist eingeschlafen ● *vt* (*pt/pp* **pinned**) anstecken (**to/on** an + *acc*); (*sewing*) stecken; (*hold down*) festhalten
PIN /pɪn/ *n* PIN *f*, Geheimnummer *f*
pinafore /'pɪnəfɔ:(r)/ *n* Schürze *f*. ~ **dress** *n* Kleiderrock *m*
pincers /'pɪnsəz/ *npl* Kneifzange *f*; (*Zool*) Scheren *pl*
pinch /pɪntʃ/ *n* Kniff *m*; (*of salt*) Prise *f*; **at a** ~ 🄸 zur Not ● *vt* kneifen, zwicken; (*fam; steal*) klauen; ~ **one's finger** sich (*dat*) den Finger klemmen ● *vi* (*shoe*:) drücken
pine¹ /paɪn/ *n* (*tree*) Kiefer *f*
pine² *vi* ~ **for** sich sehnen nach
pineapple /'paɪn-/ *n* Ananas *f*
pink /pɪŋk/ *adj* rosa
pinnacle /'pɪnəkl/ *n* Gipfel *m*; (*on roof*) Turmspitze *f*
pin: ~**point** *vt* genau festlegen. ~**stripe** *n* Nadelstreifen *m*
pint /paɪnt/ *n* Pint *nt* (0,57 *l*, *Amer:* 0,47 *l*)
pioneer /paɪə'nɪə(r)/ *n* Pionier *m* ● *vt* bahnbrechende Arbeit leisten für
pious /'paɪəs/ *adj* fromm
pip¹ /pɪp/ *n* (*seed*) Kern *m*
pip² *n* (*sound*) Tonsignal *nt*
pipe /paɪp/ *n* Pfeife *f*; (*for water, gas*) Rohr *nt* ● *vt* in Rohren leiten; (*Culin*) spritzen
pipe: ~**-dream** *n* Luftschloss *nt*. ~**line** *n* Pipeline *f*; **in the ~line** 🄸 in Vorbereitung
piping /'paɪpɪŋ/ *adj* ~ **hot** kochend heiß
pirate /'paɪərət/ *n* Pirat *m*
piss /pɪs/ *vi* ⊠ pissen
pistol /'pɪstl/ *n* Pistole *f*
piston /'pɪstən/ *n* (*Techn*) Kolben *m*
pit /pɪt/ *n* Grube *f*; (*for orchestra*) Orchestergraben *m*; (*for audience*) Parkett *nt*; (*motor racing*) Box *f*
pitch¹ /pɪtʃ/ *n* (*steepness*) Schräge *f*; (*of voice*) Stimmlage *f*; (*of sound*) [Ton]höhe *f*; (*Sport*) Feld *nt*; (*of street-trader*) Standplatz *m*; (*fig: degree*) Grad *m* ● *vt* werfen; aufschlagen (*tent*) ● *vi* fallen
pitch² *n* (*tar*) Pech *nt*. ~**-'black** *adj* pechschwarz. ~**-'dark** *adj* stockdunkel
piteous /'pɪtɪəs/ *adj* erbärmlich
'pitfall *n* (*fig*) Falle *f*
pith /pɪθ/ *n* (*Bot*) Mark *nt*; (*of orange*) weiße Haut *f*
pithy /'pɪθɪ/ *adj* (*fig*) prägnant
piti|ful /'pɪtɪfl/ *adj* bedauernswert. ~**less** *adj* mitleidslos
'pit stop *n* Boxenstopp *m*
pittance /'pɪtns/ *n* Hungerlohn *m*
pity /'pɪtɪ/ *n* Mitleid *nt*, Erbarmen *nt*; **[what a] ~!** [wie] schade! **take ~ on** sich erbarmen über (+ *acc*) ● *vt* bemitleiden

P

pivot /ˈpɪvət/ *n* Drehzapfen *m* ● *vi* sich drehen (**on** um)

pizza /ˈpiːtsə/ *n* Pizza *f*

placard /ˈplækɑːd/ *n* Plakat *nt*

placate /pləˈkeɪt/ *vt* beschwichtigen

place /pleɪs/ *n* Platz *m*; (*spot*) Stelle *f*; (*town, village*) Ort *m*; (🅘: *house*) Haus *nt*; **out of ~** fehl am Platze; **take ~** stattfinden ● *vt* setzen; (*upright*) stellen; (*flat*) legen; (*remember*) unterbringen 🅘; **~ an order** eine Bestellung aufgeben; **be ~d** (*in race*) sich platzieren. **~-mat** *n* Set *nt*

placid /ˈplæsɪd/ *adj* gelassen

plague /pleɪg/ *n* Pest *f* ● *vt* plagen

plaice /pleɪs/ *n inv* Scholle *f*

plain /pleɪn/ *adj* (**-er, -est**) klar; (*simple*) einfach; (*not pretty*) nicht hübsch; (*not patterned*) einfarbig; (*chocolate*) zartbitter; **in ~ clothes** in Zivil ● *adv* (*simply*) einfach ● *n* Ebene *f*. **~ly** *adv* klar, deutlich; (*simply*) einfach; (*obviously*) offensichtlich

P

plaintiff /ˈpleɪntɪf/ *n* Kläger(in) *m*(*f*)

plait /plæt/ *n* Zopf *m* ● *vt* flechten

plan /plæn/ *n* Plan *m* ● *vt* (*pt/pp* **planned**) planen; (*intend*) vorhaben

plane¹ /pleɪn/ *n* (*tree*) Platane *f*

plane² *n* Flugzeug *nt*; (*Geometry & fig*) Ebene *f*

plane³ *n* (*Techn*) Hobel *m* ● *vt* hobeln

planet /ˈplænɪt/ *n* Planet *m*

plank /plæŋk/ *n* Brett *nt*; (*thick*) Planke *f*

planning /ˈplænɪŋ/ *n* Planung *f*

plant /plɑːnt/ *n* Pflanze *f*; (*Techn*) Anlage *f*; (*factory*) Werk *nt* ● *vt* pflanzen; (*place in position*) setzen; **~ oneself** sich hinstellen. **~ation** *n* Plantage *f*

plaque /plɑːk/ *n* [Gedenk]tafel *f*; (*on teeth*) Zahnbelag *m*

plaster /ˈplɑːstə(r)/ *n* Verputz *m*; (*sticking ~*) Pflaster *nt*; **~ [of Paris]** Gips *m* ● *vt* verputzen (*wall*); (*cover*) bedecken mit

plastic /ˈplæstɪk/ *n* Kunststoff *m*, Plastik *nt* ● *adj* Kunststoff-, Plastik-; (*malleable*) formbar, plastisch

plastic ˈsurgery *n* plastische Chirurgie *f*

plate /pleɪt/ *n* Teller *m*; (*flat sheet*) Platte *f*; (*with name, number*) Schild *nt*; (*gold and silverware*) vergoldete/versilberte Ware *f*; (*in book*) Tafel *f* ● *vt* (*with gold*) vergolden; (*with silver*) versilbern

platform /ˈplætfɔːm/ *n* Plattform *f*; (*stage*) Podium *nt*; (*Rail*) Bahnsteig *m*; **~ 5** Gleis 5

platinum /ˈplætɪnəm/ *n* Platin *nt*

platitude /ˈplætɪtjuːd/ *n* Plattitüde *f*

plausible /ˈplɔːzəbl/ *adj* plausibel

play /pleɪ/ *n* Spiel *nt*; [Theater]stück *nt*; (*Radio*) Hörspiel *nt*; (*TV*) Fernsehspiel *nt*; **~ on words** Wortspiel *nt* ● *vt/i* spielen; ausspielen (*card*); **~ safe** sichergehen. **~ down** *vt* herunterspielen. **~ up** *vi* 🅘 Mätzchen machen

play: ~er *n* Spieler(in) *m*(*f*). **~ful** *adj* verspielt. **~ground** *n* Spielplatz *m*; (*Sch*) Schulhof *m*. **~group** *n* Kindergarten *m*

playing: ~-card *n* Spielkarte *f*. **~-field** *n* Sportplatz *m*

play: ~mate *n* Spielkamerad *m*. **~thing** *n* Spielzeug *nt*. **~wright** /-raɪt/ *n* Dramatiker *m*

plc *abbr* (**public limited company**) ≈ GmbH

plea /pliː/ *n* Bitte *f*; **make a ~ for** bitten um

plead /pliːd/ *vi* flehen (**for** um); **~**

guilty sich schuldig bekennen; ~ **with s.o.** jdn anflehen

pleasant /ˈplezənt/ *adj* angenehm; (*person*) nett. **~ly** *adv* angenehm; (*say, smile*) freundlich

pleas|e /pliːz/ *adv* bitte ● *vt* gefallen (+ *dat*); **~e s.o.** jdm eine Freude machen; **~e oneself** tun, was man will. **~ed** *adj* erfreut; **be ~ed with/about sth** sich über etw (*acc*) freuen. **~ing** *adj* erfreulich

pleasure /ˈpleʒə(r)/ *n* Vergnügen *nt*; (*joy*) Freude *f*; **with ~** gern[e]

pleat /pliːt/ *n* Falte *f* ● *vt* fälteln

pledge /pledʒ/ *n* Versprechen *nt* ● *vt* verpfänden; versprechen

plentiful /ˈplentɪfl/ *adj* reichlich

plenty /ˈplentɪ/ *n* eine Menge; (*enough*) reichlich; ~ **of money/people** viel Geld/viele Leute

pliable /ˈplaɪəbl/ *adj* biegsam

pliers /ˈplaɪəz/ *npl* [Flach]zange *f*

plight /plaɪt/ *n* [Not]lage *f*

plinth /plɪnθ/ *n* Sockel *m*

plod /plɒd/ *vi* (*pt/pp* **plodded**) trotten; (*work*) sich abmühen

plonk /plɒŋk/ *n* [!] billiger Wein *m*

plot /plɒt/ *n* Komplott *nt*; (*of novel*) Handlung *f*; ~ **of land** Stück *nt* Land ● *vt* einzeichnen ● *vi* ein Komplott schmieden

plough /plaʊ/ *n* Pflug *m* ● *vt/i* pflügen

ploy /plɔɪ/ *n* [!] Trick *m*

pluck /plʌk/ *n* Mut *m* ● *vt* zupfen; rupfen (*bird*); pflücken (*flower*); ~ **up courage** Mut fassen

plucky /ˈplʌkɪ/ *adj* tapfer, mutig

plug /plʌg/ *n* Stöpsel *m*; (*wood*) Zapfen *m*; (*cotton wool*) Bausch *m*; (*Electr*) Stecker *m*; (*Auto*) Zündkerze *f*; ([!]: *advertisement*) Schleichwerbung *f* ● *vt* zustopfen; ([!]: *advertise*) Schleichwerbung machen für. ~ **in** *vt* (*Electr*) einstecken

plum /plʌm/ *n* Pflaume *f*

plumage /ˈpluːmɪdʒ/ *n* Gefieder *nt*

plumb|er /ˈplʌmə(r)/ *n* Klempner *m*. **~ing** *n* Wasserleitungen *pl*

plume /pluːm/ *n* Feder *f*

plump /plʌmp/ *adj* (**-er, -est**) mollig, rundlich ● *vt* ~ **for** wählen

plunge /plʌndʒ/ *n* Sprung *m*; **take the ~** [!] den Schritt wagen ● *vt/i* tauchen

plural /ˈplʊərl/ *adj* pluralisch ● *n* Mehrzahl *f*, Plural *m*

plus /plʌs/ *prep* plus (+ *dat*) ● *adj* Plus- ● *n* Pluszeichen *nt*; (*advantage*) Plus *nt*

plush[y] /ˈplʌʃ[ɪ]/ *adj* luxuriös

ply /plaɪ/ *vt* (*pt/pp* **plied**) ausüben (*trade*); ~ **s.o. with drink** jdm ein Glas nach dem anderen eingießen. **~wood** *n* Sperrholz *nt*

p.m. *adv* (*abbr* **post meridiem**) nachmittags

pneumatic /njuːˈmætɪk/ *adj* pneumatisch. ~ **ˈdrill** *n* Presslufthammer *m*

pneumonia /njuːˈməʊnɪə/ *n* Lungenentzündung *f*

poach /pəʊtʃ/ *vt* (*Culin*) pochieren; (*steal*) wildern. **~er** *n* Wilddieb *m*

pocket /ˈpɒkɪt/ *n* Tasche *f*; **be out of ~** [an einem Geschäft] verlieren ● *vt* einstecken. **~-book** *n* Notizbuch *nt*; (*wallet*) Brieftasche *f*. **~-money** *n* Taschengeld *nt*

pod /pɒd/ *n* Hülse *f*

poem /ˈpəʊɪm/ *n* Gedicht *nt*

poet /ˈpəʊɪt/ *n* Dichter(in) *m*(*f*). **~ic** *adj* dichterisch

poetry /ˈpəʊɪtrɪ/ *n* Dichtung *f*

poignant /ˈpɔɪnjənt/ *adj* ergreifend

point /pɔɪnt/ *n* Punkt *m*; (*sharp end*) Spitze *f*; (*meaning*) Sinn *m*;

P

(*purpose*) Zweck *m*; (*Electr*) Steckdose *f*; **~s** *pl* (*Rail*) Weiche *f*; **~ of view** Standpunkt *m*; **good/bad ~s** gute/schlechte Seiten; **what is the ~?** wozu? **the ~ is** es geht darum; **up to a ~** bis zu einem gewissen Grade; **be on the ~ of doing sth** im Begriff sein, etw zu tun ● *vt* richten (**at** auf + *acc*); ausfugen (*brickwork*) ● *vi* deuten (**at/to** auf + *acc*); (*with finger*) mit dem Finger zeigen. **~ out** *vt* zeigen auf (+ *acc*); **~ sth out to s.o.** jdn auf etw (*acc*) hinweisen

point-'blank *adj* aus nächster Entfernung; (*fig*) rundweg

point|ed /'pɔɪntɪd/ *adj* spitz; (*question*) gezielt. **~less** *adj* zwecklos, sinnlos

poise /pɔɪz/ *n* Haltung *f*

poison /'pɔɪzn/ *n* Gift *nt* ● *vt* vergiften. **~ous** *adj* giftig

poke /pəʊk/ *n* Stoß *m* ● *vt* stoßen; schüren (*fire*); (*put*) stecken

poker[1] /'pəʊkə(r)/ *n* Schüreisen *nt*

poker[2] *n* (*Cards*) Poker *nt*

P **poky** /'pəʊkɪ/ *adj* eng

Poland /'pəʊlənd/ *n* Polen *nt*

polar /'pəʊlə(r)/ *adj* Polar-. **~'bear** *n* Eisbär *m*

Pole /pəʊl/ *n* Pole *m*/Polin *f*

pole[1] *n* Stange *f*

pole[2] *n* (*Geog, Electr*) Pol *m*

'pole-vault *n* Stabhochsprung *m*

police /pə'li:s/ *npl* Polizei *f*

police: ~man *n* Polizist *m*. **~ station** *n* Polizeiwache *f*. **~woman** *n* Polizistin *f*

policy[1] /'pɒlɪsɪ/ *n* Politik *f*

policy[2] *n* (*insurance*) Police *f*

Polish /'pəʊlɪʃ/ *adj* polnisch

polish /'pɒlɪʃ/ *n* (*shine*) Glanz *m*; (*for shoes*) [Schuh]creme *f*; (*for floor*) Bohnerwachs *m*; (*for furniture*) Politur *f*; (*for silver*) Putzmittel *nt*; (*for nails*) Lack *m*; (*fig*) Schliff *m* ● *vt* polieren; bohnern (*floor*). **~ off** *vt* [T] verputzen (*food*); erledigen (*task*)

polite /pə'laɪt/ *adj* höflich. **~ness** *n* Höflichkeit *f*

politic|al /pə'lɪtɪkl/ *adj* politisch. **~ian** *n* Politiker(in) *m*(*f*)

politics /'pɒlətɪks/ *n* Politik *f*

poll /pəʊl/ *n* Abstimmung *f*; (*election*) Wahl *f*; **[opinion] ~** [Meinungs]umfrage *f*

pollen /'pɒlən/ *n* Blütenstaub *m*, Pollen *m*

polling /'pəʊlɪŋ/: **~-booth** *n* Wahlkabine *f*. **~-station** *n* Wahllokal *nt*

pollut|e /pə'lu:t/ *vt* verschmutzen. **~ion** *n* Verschmutzung *f*

polo /'pəʊləʊ/ *n* Polo *nt*. **~-neck** *n* Rollkragen *m*

polystyrene /pɒlɪ'staɪri:n/ *n* Polystyrol *nt*; (*for packing*) Styropor® *nt*

polythene /'pɒlɪθi:n/ *n* Polyäthylen *nt*. **~ bag** *n* Plastiktüte *f*

pomp /pɒmp/ *n* Pomp *m*

pompous /'pɒmpəs/ *adj* großspurig

pond /pɒnd/ *n* Teich *m*

ponder /'pɒndə(r)/ *vi* nachdenken

ponderous /'pɒndərəs/ *adj* schwerfällig

pony /'pəʊnɪ/ *n* Pony *nt*. **~-tail** *n* Pferdeschwanz *m*

poodle /'pu:dl/ *n* Pudel *m*

pool /pu:l/ *n* [Schwimm]becken *nt*; (*pond*) Teich *m*; (*of blood*) Lache *f*; (*common fund*) [gemeinsame] Kasse *f*; **~s** *pl* [Fußball]toto *nt* ● *vt* zusammenlegen

poor /pʊə(r)/ *adj* (**-er, -est**) arm; (*not good*) schlecht; **in ~ health**

nicht gesund. **~ly** *adj* **be ~ly** krank sein ● *adv* ärmlich; (*badly*) schlecht

pop[1] /pɒp/ *n* Knall *m* ● *v* (*pt/pp* **popped**) ● *vt* (🄸: *put*) stecken (**in** in + *acc*) ● *vi* knallen; (*burst*) platzen. **~ in** *vi* 🄸 reinschauen. **~ out** *vi* 🄸 kurz rausgehen

pop[2] *n* 🄸 Popmusik *f*, Pop *m* ● *attrib* Pop-

'popcorn *n* Puffmais *m*

pope /pəʊp/ *n* Papst *m*

poplar /'pɒplə(r)/ *n* Pappel *f*

poppy /'pɒpɪ/ *n* Mohn *m*

popular /'pɒpjʊlə(r)/ *adj* beliebt, populär; (*belief*) volkstümlich. **~ity** *n* Beliebtheit *f*, Popularität *f*

populat|e /'pɒpjʊleɪt/ *vt* bevölkern. **~ion** *n* Bevölkerung *f*

pop-up /'pɒpʌp/ *n* Pop-up-Werbefenster *nt*

porcelain /'pɔ:səlɪn/ *n* Porzellan *nt*

porch /pɔ:tʃ/ *n* Vorbau *m*; (*Amer*) Veranda *f*

porcupine /'pɔ:kjʊpaɪn/ *n* Stachelschwein *nt*

pore /pɔ:(r)/ *n* Pore *f*

pork /pɔ:k/ *n* Schweinefleisch *nt*

porn /pɔ:n/ *n* 🄸 Porno *m*

pornograph|ic /pɔ:nə'græfɪk/ *adj* pornographisch. **~y** *n* Pornographie *f*

porridge /'pɒrɪdʒ/ *n* Haferbrei *m*

port[1] /pɔ:t/ *n* Hafen *m*; (*town*) Hafenstadt *f*

port[2] *n* (*Naut*) Backbord *nt*

port[3] *n* (*wine*) Portwein *m*

portable /'pɔ:təbl/ *adj* tragbar

porter /'pɔ:tə(r)/ *n* Portier *m*; (*for luggage*) Gepäckträger *m*

'porthole *n* Bullauge *nt*

portion /'pɔ:ʃn/ *n* Portion *f*; (*part, share*) Teil *nt*

portrait /'pɔ:trɪt/ *n* Porträt *nt*

portray /pɔ:'treɪ/ *vt* darstellen. **~al** *n* Darstellung *f*

Portug|al /'pɔ:tjʊgl/ *n* Portugal *nt*. **~uese** *adj* portugiesisch ● *n* Portugiese *m*/-giesin *f*

pose /pəʊz/ *n* Pose *f* ● *vt* aufwerfen (*problem*); stellen (*question*) ● *vi* posieren; (*for painter*) Modell stehen

posh /pɒʃ/ *adj* 🄸 feudal

position /pə'zɪʃn/ *n* Platz *m*; (*posture*) Haltung *f*; (*job*) Stelle *f*; (*situation*) Lage *f*, Situation *f*; (*status*) Stellung *f* ● *vt* platzieren; **~ oneself** sich stellen

positive /'pɒzətɪv/ *adj* positiv; (*definite*) eindeutig; (*real*) ausgesprochen ● *n* Positiv *nt*

possess /pə'zes/ *vt* besitzen. **~ion** *n* Besitz *m*; **~ions** *pl* Sachen *pl*

possess|ive /pə'zesɪv/ *adj* Possessiv-; **be ~ive about s.o.** zu sehr an jdm hängen

possibility /pɒsə'bɪlətɪ/ *n* Möglichkeit *f*

possib|le /'pɒsəbl/ *adj* möglich. **~ly** *adv* möglicherweise; **not ~ly** unmöglich

post[1] /pəʊst/ *n* (*pole*) Pfosten *m*

post[2] *n* (*place of duty*) Posten *m*; (*job*) Stelle *f*

post[3] *n* (*mail*) Post *f*; **by ~** mit der Post ● *vt* aufgeben (*letter*); (*send by* ~) mit der Post schicken; **keep s.o. ~ed** jdn auf dem Laufenden halten

postage /'pəʊstɪdʒ/ *n* Porto *nt*

postal /'pəʊstl/ *adj* Post-. **~ order** *n* ≈ Geldanweisung *f*

post: ~-box *n* Briefkasten *m*. **~card** *n* Postkarte *f*; (*picture*) Ansichtskarte *f*. **~code** *n* Postleitzahl *f*. **~-'date** *vt* vordatieren

poster /'pəʊstə(r)/ *n* Plakat *nt*

posterity /pɒ'sterətɪ/ *n* Nachwelt *f*

posthumous /'pɒstjʊməs/ *adj*

postum

post: **~man** *n* Briefträger *m*. **~mark** *n* Poststempel *m*

post-mortem /-'mɔːtəm/ *n* Obduktion *f*

'post office *n* Post *f*

postpone /pəʊst'pəʊn/ *vt* aufschieben; **~ until** verschieben auf (+ *acc*). **~ment** *n* Verschiebung *f*

postscript /'pəʊstskrɪpt/ *n* Nachschrift *f*

posture /'pɒstʃə(r)/ *n* Haltung *f*

pot /pɒt/ *n* Topf *m*; (*for tea, coffee*) Kanne *f*; **~s of money** [!] eine Menge Geld

potato /pə'teɪtəʊ/ *n* (*pl* **-es**) Kartoffel *f*

potent /'pəʊtənt/ *adj* stark

potential /pə'tenʃl/ *adj* potenziell ● *n* Potenzial *nt*

pot: **~-hole** *n* Höhle *f*; (*in road*) Schlagloch *nt*. **~-shot** *n* **take a ~-shot at** schießen auf (+ *acc*)

potter /'pɒtə(r)/ *n* Töpfer(in) *m(f)*. **~y** *n* Töpferei *f*; (*articles*) Töpferwaren *pl*

potty /'pɒtɪ/ *adj* [!] verrückt ● *n* Töpfchen *nt*

pouch /paʊtʃ/ *n* Beutel *m*

poultry /'pəʊltrɪ/ *n* Geflügel *nt*

pounce /paʊns/ *vi* zuschlagen; **~ on** sich stürzen auf (+ *acc*)

pound[1] /paʊnd/ *n* (*money & 0,454 kg*) Pfund *nt*

pound[2] *vi* (*heart:*) hämmern; (*run heavily*) stampfen

pour /pɔː(r)/ *vt* gießen; einschenken (*drink*) ● *vi* strömen; (*with rain*) gießen. **~ out** *vi* ausströmen ● *vt* ausschütten; einschenken (*drink*)

pout /paʊt/ *vi* einen Schmollmund machen

poverty /'pɒvətɪ/ *n* Armut *f*

powder /'paʊdə(r)/ *n* Pulver *nt*; (*cosmetic*) Puder *m* ● *vt* pudern

power /'paʊə(r)/ *n* Macht *f*; (*strength*) Kraft *f*; (*Electr*) Strom *m*; (*nuclear*) Energie *f*; (*Math*) Potenz *f*. **~ cut** *n* Stromsperre *f*. **~ed** *adj* betrieben (**by** mit); **~ed by electricity** mit Elektroantrieb. **~ful** *adj* mächtig; (*strong*) stark. **~less** *adj* machtlos. **~-station** *n* Kraftwerk *nt*

practicable /'præktɪkəbl/ *adj* durchführbar, praktikabel

practical /'præktɪkl/ *adj* praktisch. **~ 'joke** *n* Streich *m*

practice /'præktɪs/ *n* Praxis *f*; (*custom*) Brauch *m*; (*habit*) Gewohnheit *f*; (*exercise*) Übung *f*; (*Sport*) Training *nt*; **in ~** (*in reality*) in der Praxis; **out of ~** außer Übung; **put into ~** ausführen

practise /'præktɪs/ *vt* üben; (*carry out*) praktizieren; ausüben (*profession*) ● *vi* üben; (*doctor:*) praktizieren. **~d** *adj* geübt

praise /preɪz/ *n* Lob *nt* ● *vt* loben. **~worthy** *adj* lobenswert

pram /præm/ *n* Kinderwagen *m*

prank /præŋk/ *n* Streich *m*

prawn /prɔːn/ *n* Garnele *f*, Krabbe *f*

pray /preɪ/ *vi* beten. **~er** *n* Gebet *nt*

preach /priːtʃ/ *vt/i* predigen. **~er** *n* Prediger *m*

pre-ar'range /priː-/ *vt* im Voraus arrangieren

precarious /prɪ'keərɪəs/ *adj* unsicher

precaution /prɪ'kɔːʃn/ *n* Vorsichtsmaßnahme *f*

precede /prɪ'siːd/ *vt* vorangehen (+ *dat*)

preceden|ce /'presɪdəns/ *n* Vorrang *m*. **~t** *n* Präzedenzfall *m*

preceding /prɪ'siːdɪŋ/ *adj* vorhergehend

precinct /ˈpriːsɪŋkt/ *n* Bereich *m*; (*traffic-free*) Fußgängerzone *f*; (*Amer: district*) Bezirk *m*

precious /ˈpreʃəs/ *adj* kostbar; (*style*) preziös ● *adv* Ⓕ ~ **little** recht wenig

precipice /ˈpresɪpɪs/ *n* Steilabfall *m*

precipitation /prɪsɪpɪˈteɪʃn/ *n* (*rain*) Niederschlag *m*

precis|e /prɪˈsaɪs/ *adj* genau. **~ion** *n* Genauigkeit *f*

precocious /prɪˈkəʊʃəs/ *adj* frühreif

pre|con'ceived /priː-/ *adj* vorgefasst. **~con'ception** *n* vorgefasste Meinung *f*

predator /ˈpredətə(r)/ *n* Raubtier *nt*

predecessor /ˈpriːdɪsesə(r)/ *n* Vorgänger(in) *m*(*f*)

predicat|e /ˈpredɪkət/ *n* (*Gram*) Prädikat *nt*. **~ive** *adj* prädikativ

predict /prɪˈdɪkt/ *vt* voraussagen. **~able** *adj* voraussehbar; (*person*) berechenbar. **~ion** *n* Voraussage *f*

pre'domin|ant /prɪ-/ *adj* vorherrschend. **~antly** *adv* hauptsächlich, überwiegend. **~ate** *vi* vorherrschen

preen /priːn/ *vt* putzen

pre|fab /ˈpriːfæb/ *n* Ⓕ [einfaches] Fertighaus *nt*. **~'fabricated** *adj* vorgefertigt

preface /ˈprefɪs/ *n* Vorwort *nt*

prefect /ˈpriːfekt/ *n* Präfekt *m*

prefer /prɪˈfɜː(r)/ *vt* (*pt/pp* **preferred**) vorziehen; **I ~ to walk** ich gehe lieber zu Fuß; **I ~ wine** ich trinke lieber Wein

prefera|ble /ˈprefərəbl/ *adj* **be ~ble** vorzuziehen sein (**to** *dat*). **~bly** *adv* vorzugsweise

preferen|ce /ˈprefərəns/ *n* Vorzug *m*. **~tial** *adj* bevorzugt

pregnan|cy /ˈpregnənsɪ/ *n* Schwangerschaft *f*. **~t** *adj* schwanger; (*animal*) trächtig

prehi'storic /priː-/ *adj* prähistorisch

prejudice /ˈpredʒʊdɪs/ *n* Vorurteil *nt*; (*bias*) Voreingenommenheit *f* ● *vt* einnehmen (**against** gegen). **~d** *adj* voreingenommen

preliminary /prɪˈlɪmɪnərɪ/ *adj* Vor-

prelude /ˈpreljuːd/ *n* Vorspiel *nt*

premature /ˈpremətjʊə(r)/ *adj* vorzeitig; (*birth*) Früh-. **~ly** *adv* zu früh

pre'meditated /priː-/ *adj* vorsätzlich

premier /ˈpremɪə(r)/ *adj* führend ● *n* (*Pol*) Premier[minister] *m*

première /ˈpremɪeə(r)/ *n* Premiere *f*

premise /ˈpremɪs/ *n* Prämisse *f*, Voraussetzung *f*

premises /ˈpremɪsɪz/ *npl* Räumlichkeiten *pl*; **on the ~** im Haus

premium /ˈpriːmɪəm/ *n* Prämie *f*; **be at a ~** hoch im Kurs stehen

premonition /preməˈnɪʃn/ *n* Vorahnung *f*

preoccupied /prɪˈɒkjʊpaɪd/ *adj* [in Gedanken] beschäftigt

preparation /prepəˈreɪʃn/ *n* Vorbereitung *f*; (*substance*) Präparat *nt*

preparatory /prɪˈpærətrɪ/ *adj* Vor-

prepare /prɪˈpeə(r)/ *vt* vorbereiten; anrichten (*meal*) ● *vi* sich vorbereiten (**for** auf + *acc*); **~d to** bereit zu

preposition /prepəˈzɪʃn/ *n* Präposition *f*

preposterous /prɪˈpɒstərəs/ *adj* absurd

prerequisite /priːˈrekwɪzɪt/ *n*

P

Voraussetzung *f*

Presbyterian /prezbɪ'tɪərɪən/ *adj* presbyterianisch ● *n* Presbyterianer(in) *m(f)*

prescribe /prɪ'skraɪb/ *vt* vorschreiben; (*Med*) verschreiben

prescription /prɪ'skrɪpʃn/ *n* (*Med*) Rezept *nt*

presence /'prezns/ *n* Anwesenheit *f*, Gegenwart *f*; ~ **of mind** Geistesgegenwart *f*

present[1] /'preznt/ *adj* gegenwärtig; **be** ~ anwesend sein; (*occur*) vorkommen ● *n* Gegenwart *f*; (*Gram*) Präsens *nt*; **at** ~ zurzeit; **for the** ~ vorläufig

present[2] *n* (*gift*) Geschenk *nt*

present[3] /prɪ'zent/ *vt* überreichen; (*show*) zeigen; vorlegen (*cheque*); (*introduce*) vorstellen; ~ **s.o. with** sth jdm etw überreichen. ~**able** *adj* **be** ~**able** sich zeigen lassen können

presentation /prezn'teɪʃn/ *n* Überreichung *f*

presently /'prezntlɪ/ *adv* nachher; (*Amer: now*) zurzeit

preservation /prezə'veɪʃn/ *n* Erhaltung *f*

preservative /prɪ'zɜ:vətɪv/ *n* Konservierungsmittel *nt*

preserve /prɪ'zɜ:v/ *vt* erhalten; (*Culin*) konservieren; (*bottle*) einmachen ● *n* (*Hunting & fig*) Revier *nt*; (*jam*) Konfitüre *f*

preside /prɪ'zaɪd/ *vi* den Vorsitz haben (**over** bei)

presidency /'prezɪdənsɪ/ *n* Präsidentschaft *f*

president /'prezɪdənt/ *n* Präsident *m*; (*Amer: chairman*) Vorsitzende(r) *m/f*. ~**ial** *adj* Präsidenten-; (*election*) Präsidentschafts-

press /pres/ *n* Presse *f* ● *vt/i* drücken; drücken auf (+ *acc*) (*button*); pressen (*flower*); (*iron*) bügeln; (*urge*) bedrängen; ~ **for** drängen auf (+ *acc*); **be** ~**ed for time** in Zeitdruck sein. ~ **on** *vi* weitergehen/-fahren; (*fig*) weitermachen

press: ~ **cutting** *n* Zeitungsausschnitt *m*. ~**ing** *adj* dringend

pressure /'preʃə(r)/ *n* Druck *m*. ~**-cooker** *n* Schnellkochtopf *m*

pressurize /'preʃəraɪz/ *vt* Druck ausüben auf (+ *acc*). ~**d** *adj* Druck-

prestig|e /pre'sti:ʒ/ *n* Prestige *nt*. ~**ious** *adj* Prestige-

presumably /prɪ'zju:məblɪ/ *adv* vermutlich

presume /prɪ'zju:m/ *vt* vermuten

presumpt|ion /prɪ'zʌmpʃn/ *n* Vermutung *f*; (*boldness*) Anmaßung *f*. ~**uous** *adj* anmaßend

pretence /prɪ'tens/ *n* Verstellung *f*; (*pretext*) Vorwand *m*

pretend /prɪ'tend/ *vt* (*claim*) vorgeben; ~ **that** so tun, als ob; ~ **to be** sich ausgeben als

pretentious /prɪ'tenʃəs/ *adj* protzig

pretext /'pri:tekst/ *n* Vorwand *m*

prett|y /'prɪtɪ/ *adj* , ~**ily** *adv* hübsch ● *adv* (☐: *fairly*) ziemlich

prevail /prɪ'veɪl/ *vi* siegen; (*custom*:) vorherrschen; ~ **on s.o. to do sth** jdn dazu bringen, etw zu tun

prevalen|ce /'prevələns/ *n* Häufigkeit *f*. ~**t** *adj* vorherrschend

prevent /prɪ'vent/ *vt* verhindern, verhüten; ~ **s.o. [from] doing sth** jdn daran hindern, etw zu tun. ~**ion** *n* Verhinderung *f*, Verhütung *f*. ~**ive** *adj* vorbeugend

preview /'pri:vju:/ *n* Voraufführung *f*

previous /'pri:vɪəs/ *adj* vorhergehend; ~ to vor (+ *dat*). **~ly** *adv* vorher, früher

prey /preɪ/ *n* Beute *f*; **bird of ~** Raubvogel *m*

price /praɪs/ *n* Preis *m* ● *vt* (*Comm*) auszeichnen. **~less** *adj* unschätzbar; (*fig*) unbezahlbar

prick /prɪk/ *n* Stich *m* ● *vt/i* stechen

prickl|e /ˈprɪkl/ *n* Stachel *m*; (*thorn*) Dorn *m*. **~y** *adj* stachelig; (*sensation*) stechend

pride /praɪd/ *n* Stolz *m*; (*arrogance*) Hochmut *m* ● *vt* **~ oneself on** stolz sein auf (+ *acc*)

priest /pri:st/ *n* Priester *m*

prim /prɪm/ *adj* (**primmer, primmest**) prüde

primarily /ˈpraɪmərɪlɪ/ *adv* hauptsächlich, in erster Linie

primary /ˈpraɪmərɪ/ *adj* Haupt-. **~ school** *n* Grundschule *f*

prime¹ /praɪm/ *adj* Haupt-; (*first-rate*) erstklassig

prime² *vt* scharf machen (*bomb*); grundieren (*surface*)

Prime Minister /praɪ ˈmɪnɪstə(r)/ *n* Premierminister(in) *m*(*f*)

primitive /ˈprɪmɪtɪv/ *adj* primitiv

primrose /ˈprɪmrəʊz/ *n* gelbe Schlüsselblume *f*

prince /prɪns/ *n* Prinz *m*

princess /prɪnˈses/ *n* Prinzessin *f*

principal /ˈprɪnsəpl/ *adj* Haupt- ● *n* (*Sch*) Rektor(in) *m*(*f*)

principally /ˈprɪnsəplɪ/ *adv* hauptsächlich

principle /ˈprɪnsəpl/ *n* Prinzip *nt*, Grundsatz *m*; **in/on ~** im/aus Prinzip

print /prɪnt/ *n* Druck *m*; (*Phot*) Abzug *m*; **in ~** gedruckt; (*available*) erhältlich; **out of ~** vergriffen ● *vt* drucken; (*write in capitals*) in Druckschrift schreiben; (*Computing*) ausdrucken; (*Phot*) abziehen. **~ed matter** *n* Drucksache *f*

print|er /ˈprɪntə(r)/ *n* Drucker *m*. **~ing** *n* Druck *m*

ˈprintout *n* (*Computing*) Ausdruck *m*

prior /ˈpraɪə(r)/ *adj* frühere(r,s); **~ to** vor (+ *dat*)

priority /praɪˈɒrətɪ/ *n* Priorität *f*, Vorrang *m*

prise /praɪz/ *vt* **~ open/up** aufstemmen/hochstemmen

prison /ˈprɪzn/ *n* Gefängnis *nt*. **~er** *n* Gefangene(r) *m*/*f*

privacy /ˈprɪvəsɪ/ *n* Privatsphäre *f*; **have no ~** nie für sich sein

private /ˈpraɪvət/ *adj* privat; (*confidential*) vertraulich; (*car, secretary, school*) Privat- ● *n* (*Mil*) [einfacher] Soldat *m*; **in ~** privat; (*confidentially*) vertraulich

privation /praɪˈveɪʃn/ *n* Entbehrung *f*

privilege /ˈprɪvəlɪdʒ/ *n* Privileg *nt*. **~d** *adj* privilegiert

prize /praɪz/ *n* Preis *m* ● *vt* schätzen

pro /prəʊ/ *n* 🅸 Profi *m*; **the ~s and cons** das Für und Wider

probability /prɒbəˈbɪlətɪ/ *n* Wahrscheinlichkeit *f*

proba|ble /ˈprɒbəbl/ *adj*, **-bly** *adv* wahrscheinlich

probation /prəˈbeɪʃn/ *n* (*Jur*) Bewährung *f*

probe /prəʊb/ *n* Sonde *f*; (*fig: investigation*) Untersuchung *f*

problem /ˈprɒbləm/ *n* Problem *nt*; (*Math*) Textaufgabe *f*. **~atic** *adj* problematisch

procedure /prəˈsi:dʒə(r)/ *n*

Verfahren *nt*

proceed /prə'si:d/ *vi* gehen; (*in vehicle*) fahren; (*continue*) weitergehen/-fahren; (*speaking*) fortfahren; (*act*) verfahren

proceedings /prə'si:dɪŋz/ *npl* Verfahren *nt*; (*Jur*) Prozess *m*

proceeds /'prəʊsi:dz/ *npl* Erlös *m*

process /'prəʊses/ *n* Prozess *m*; (*procedure*) Verfahren *nt*; **in the ~** dabei ● *vt* verarbeiten; (*Admin*) bearbeiten; (*Phot*) entwickeln

procession /prə'seʃn/ *n* Umzug *m*, Prozession *f*

processor /'prəʊsesə(r)/ *n* Prozessor *m*

proclaim /prə'kleɪm/ *vt* ausrufen

proclamation /prɒklə'meɪʃn/ *n* Proklamation *f*

procure /prə'kjʊə(r)/ *vt* beschaffen

prod /prɒd/ *n* Stoß *m* ● *vt* stoßen

prodigy /'prɒdɪdʒɪ/ *n* **[infant] ~** Wunderkind *nt*

produce[1] /'prɒdju:s/ *n* landwirtschaftliche Erzeugnisse *pl*

produce[2] /prə'dju:s/ *vt* erzeugen, produzieren; (*manufacture*) herstellen; (*bring out*) hervorholen; (*cause*) hervorrufen; inszenieren. (*play*); (*Radio, TV*) redigieren. **~r** *n* Erzeuger *m*, Produzent *m*; Hersteller *m*; (*Theat*) Regisseur *m*; (*Radio, TV*) Redakteur(in) *m*(*f*)

product /'prɒdʌkt/ *n* Erzeugnis *nt*, Produkt *nt*. **~ion** *n* Produktion *f*; (*Theat*) Inszenierung *f*

productiv|e /prə'dʌktɪv/ *adj* produktiv; (*land, talks*) fruchtbar. **~ity** *n* Produktivität *f*

profession /prə'feʃn/ *n* Beruf *m*. **~al** *adj* beruflich; (*not amateur*) Berufs-; (*expert*) fachmännisch; (*Sport*) professionell ● *n* Fachmann *m*; (*Sport*) Profi *m*

professor /prə'fesə(r)/ *n* Professor *m*

proficien|cy /prə'fɪʃnsɪ/ *n* Können *nt*. **~t** *adj* **be ~t in** beherrschen

profile /'prəʊfaɪl/ *n* Profil *nt*; (*character study*) Porträt *nt*

profit /'prɒfɪt/ *n* Gewinn *m*, Profit *m* ● *vi* **~ from** profitieren von. **~able** *adj*, **-bly** *adv* gewinnbringend; (*fig*) nutzbringend

profound /prə'faʊnd/ *adj* tief

program /'prəʊgræm/ *n* Programm *nt*; ● *vt* (*pt/pp* **programmed**) programmieren

programme /'prəʊgræm/ *n* Programm *nt*; (*Radio, TV*) Sendung *f*. **~r** *n* (*Computing*) Programmierer(in) *m*(*f*)

progress[1] /'prəʊgres/ *n* Vorankommen *nt*; (*fig*) Fortschritt *m*; **in ~** im Gange; **make ~** (*fig*) Fortschritte machen

progress[2] /prə'gres/ *vi* vorankommen; (*fig*) fortschreiten. **~ion** *n* Folge *f*; (*development*) Entwicklung *f*

progressive /prə'gresɪv/ *adj* fortschrittlich. **~ly** *adv* zunehmend

prohibit /prə'hɪbɪt/ *vt* verbieten (**s.o.** jdm). **~ive** *adj* unerschwinglich

project[1] /'prɒdʒekt/ *n* Projekt *nt*; (*Sch*) Arbeit *f*

project[2] /prə'dʒekt/ *vt* projizieren (*film*); (*plan*) planen ● *vi* (*jut out*) vorstehen

projector /prə'dʒektə(r)/ *n* Projektor *m*

prolific /prə'lɪfɪk/ *adj* fruchtbar; (*fig*) produktiv

prologue /'prəʊlɒg/ *n* Prolog *m*

prolong /prə'lɒŋ/ *vt* verlängern

promenade /prɒmə'nɑ:d/ *n* Promenade *f* ● *vi* spazieren gehen

prominent /ˈprɒmɪnənt/ *adj* vorstehend; (*important*) prominent; (*conspicuous*) auffällig

promiscuous /prəˈmɪskjʊəs/ *adj* **be ~ous** häufig den Partner wechseln

promis|e /ˈprɒmɪs/ *n* Versprechen *nt* ● *vt/i* versprechen (**s.o.** jdm). **~ing** *adj* viel versprechend

promot|e /prəˈməʊt/ *vt* befördern; (*advance*) fördern; (*publicize*) Reklame machen für; **be ~ed** (*Sport*) aufsteigen. **~ion** *n* Beförderung *f*; (*Sport*) Aufstieg *m*; (*Comm*) Reklame *f*

prompt /prɒmpt/ *adj* prompt, unverzüglich; (*punctual*) pünktlich ● *adv* pünktlich ● *vt/i* veranlassen (**to** zu); (*Theat*) soufflieren (+ *dat*). **~er** *n* Souffleur *m*/Souffleuse *f*. **~ly** *adv* prompt

i

Proms Die Proms, offiziell *BBC Henry Wood Promenade Concerts*, finden jeden Sommer in der Londoner Royal Albert Hall statt. Bei den Promenadekonzerten steht ein Teil des Publikums vor dem Orchester. In den USA bezeichnet *Prom* einen Ball, den eine ▷HIGH SCHOOL veranstaltet, um das Ende des Schuljahrs zu feiern.

prone /prəʊn/ *adj* **be** *or* **lie ~** auf dem Bauch liegen; **be ~ to** neigen zu

pronoun /ˈprəʊnaʊn/ *n* Fürwort *nt*, Pronomen *nt*

pronounce /prəˈnaʊns/ *vt* aussprechen; (*declare*) erklären. **~d** *adj* ausgeprägt; (*noticeable*) deutlich. **~ment** *n* Erklärung *f*

pronunciation /prənʌnsɪˈeɪʃn/ *n* Aussprache *f*

proof /pruːf/ *n* Beweis *m*; (*Typography*) Korrekturbogen *m*. **~-reader** *n* Korrektor *m*

prop¹ /prɒp/ *n* Stütze *f* ● *vt* (*pt/pp* **propped**) **~ against** lehnen an (+ *acc*). **~ up** *vt* stützen

prop² *n* (*Theat*, [!]) Requisit *nt*

propaganda /prɒpəˈgændə/ *n* Propaganda *f*

propel /prəˈpel/ *vt* (*pt/pp* **propelled**) [an]treiben. **~ler** *n* Propeller *m*

proper /ˈprɒpə(r)/ *adj* richtig; (*decent*) anständig

property /ˈprɒpətɪ/ *n* Eigentum *nt*; (*quality*) Eigenschaft *f*; (*Theat*) Requisit *nt*; (*land*) [Grund]besitz *m*; (*house*) Haus *nt*

prophecy /ˈprɒfəsɪ/ *n* Prophezeiung *f*

prophesy /ˈprɒfɪsaɪ/ *vt* (*pt/pp* **-ied**) prophezeien

prophet /ˈprɒfɪt/ *n* Prophet *m*. **~ic** *adj* prophetisch

proportion /prəˈpɔːʃn/ *n* Verhältnis *nt*; (*share*) Teil *m*; **~s** *pl* Proportionen; (*dimensions*) Maße. **~al** *adj* proportional

proposal /prəˈpəʊzl/ *n* Vorschlag *m*; (*of marriage*) [Heirats]antrag *m*

propose /prəˈpəʊz/ *vt* vorschlagen; (*intend*) vorhaben; einbringen (*motion*) ● *vi* einen Heiratsantrag machen

proposition /prɒpəˈzɪʃn/ *n* Vorschlag *m*

proprietor /prəˈpraɪətə(r)/ *n* Inhaber(in) *m*(*f*)

propriety /prəˈpraɪətɪ/ *n* Korrektheit *f*; (*decorum*) Anstand *m*

prose /prəʊz/ *n* Prosa *f*

prosecut|e /ˈprɒsɪkjuːt/ *vt* strafrechtlich verfolgen. **~ion** *n* strafrechtliche Verfolgung *f*; **the ~ion**

die Anklage. **~or** *n* **[Public] P~or** Staatsanwalt *m*

prospect /'prɒspekt/ *n* Aussicht *f*

prospect|ive /prə'spektɪv/ *adj* (*future*) zukünftig. **~or** *n* Prospektor *m*

prospectus /prə'spektəs/ *n* Prospekt *m*

prosper /'prɒspə(r)/ *vi* gedeihen, florieren; (*person*) Erfolg haben. **~ity** *n* Wohlstand *m*

prosperous /'prɒspərəs/ *adj* wohlhabend

prostitut|e /'prɒstɪtju:t/ *n* Prostituierte *f*. **~ion** *n* Prostitution *f*

prostrate /'prɒstreɪt/ *adj* ausgestreckt

protagonist /prəʊ'tægənɪst/ *n* Kämpfer *m*; (*fig*) Protagonist *m*

protect /prə'tekt/ *vt* schützen (**from** vor + *dat*); beschützen (*person*). **~ion** *n* Schutz *m*. **~ive** *adj* Schutz-; (*fig*) beschützend. **~or** *n* Beschützer *m*

protein /'prəʊti:n/ *n* Eiweiß *nt*

P **protest¹** /'prəʊtest/ *n* Protest *m*

protest² /prə'test/ *vi* protestieren

Protestant /'prɒtɪstənt/ *adj* protestantisch ● *n* Protestant(in) *m*(*f*)

protester /prə'testə(r)/ *n* Protestierende(r) *m*/*f*

prototype /'prəʊtə-/ *n* Prototyp *m*

protrude /prə'tru:d/ *vi* [her]vorstehen

proud /praʊd/ *adj* stolz (**of** auf + *acc*)

prove /pru:v/ *vt* beweisen ● *vi* **~to be** sich erweisen als

proverb /'prɒvɜ:b/ *n* Sprichwort *nt*

provide /prə'vaɪd/ *vt* zur Verfügung stellen; spenden (*shade*); **~ s.o. with sth** jdn mit etw versorgen *od* versehen ● *vi* **~ for** sorgen für

provided /prə'vaɪdɪd/ *conj* **~ [that]** vorausgesetzt [dass]

providen|ce /'prɒvɪdəns/ *n* Vorsehung *f*. **~tial** *adj* **be ~tial** ein Glück sein

provinc|e /'prɒvɪns/ *n* Provinz *f*; (*fig*) Bereich *m*. **~ial** *adj* provinziell

provision /prə'vɪʒn/ *n* Versorgung *f* (**of** mit); **~s** *pl* Lebensmittel *pl*. **~al** *adj* vorläufig

provocat|ion /prɒvə'keɪʃn/ *n* Provokation *f*. **~ive** *adj* provozierend; (*sexually*) aufreizend

provoke /prə'vəʊk/ *vt* provozieren; (*cause*) hervorrufen

prow /praʊ/ *n* Bug *m*

prowl /praʊl/ *vi* herumschleichen

proximity /prɒk'sɪmətɪ/ *n* Nähe *f*

pruden|ce /'pru:dns/ *n* Umsicht *f*. **~t** *adj* umsichtig; (*wise*) klug

prudish /'pru:dɪʃ/ *adj* prüde

prune¹ /pru:n/ *n* Backpflaume *f*

prune² *vt* beschneiden

pry /praɪ/ *vi* (*pt*/*pp* **pried**) neugierig sein

psalm /sɑ:m/ *n* Psalm *m*

psychiatric /saɪkɪ'ætrɪk/ *adj* psychiatrisch

psychiatr|ist /saɪ'kaɪətrɪst/ *n* Psychiater(*in*) *m*(*f*). **~y** *n* Psychiatrie *f*

psychic /'saɪkɪk/ *adj* übersinnlich

psycho|a'nalysis /saɪkəʊ-/ *n* Psychoanalyse *f*. **~'analyst** Psychoanalytiker(in) *m*(*f*)

psychological /saɪkə'lɒdʒɪkl/ *adj* psychologisch; (*illness*) psychisch

psycholog|ist /saɪ'kɒlədʒɪst/ *n* Psychologe *m*/ -login *f*. **~y** *n* Psychologie *f*

P.T.O. *abbr* (**please turn over**) b.w.

pub /pʌb/ *n* [!] Kneipe *f*

pub Ein *pub*, kurz für *public house*, ist ein englisches Wirtshaus. *Pubs* sind bei allen Schichten der britschen Gesellschaft beliebt und Gäste haben oft eine Stammkneipe, wo sie Bier trinken und Darts oder Pool spielen. Öffnungszeiten sind meist von 11-23 Uhr und in vielen *pubs* kann man auch essen.

puberty /ˈpjuːbətɪ/ *n* Pubertät *f*

public /ˈpʌblɪk/ *adj* öffentlich; **make ~** publik machen ● *n* **the ~** die Öffentlichkeit

publican /ˈpʌblɪkən/ *n* [Gast]wirt *m*

publication /pʌblɪˈkeɪʃn/ *n* Veröffentlichung *f*

public: ~ ˈholiday *n* gesetzlicher Feiertag *m*. **~ ˈhouse** *n* [Gast]wirtschaft *f*

publicity /pʌbˈlɪsətɪ/ *n* Publicity *f*; (*advertising*) Reklame *f*

publicize /ˈpʌblɪsaɪz/ *vt* Reklame machen für

public: ~ ˈschool *n* Privatschule *f*; (*Amer*) staatliche Schule *f*. **~-ˈspirited** *adj* **be ~-spirited** Gemeinsinn haben

public school Eine Privatschule in England und Wales für Schüler im Alter von dreizehn bis achtzehn Jahren. Die meisten *public schools* sind Internate, normalerweise entweder für Jungen oder Mädchen. Die Eltern zahlen Schulgeld für die Ausbildung ihrer Kinder. In Schottland und den USA ist eine *public school* eine staatliche Schule.

publish /ˈpʌblɪʃ/ *vt* veröffentlichen. **~er** *n* Verleger(in) *m(f)*; (*firm*) Verlag *m*. **~ing** *n* Verlagswesen *nt*

pudding /ˈpʊdɪŋ/ *n* Pudding *m*; (*course*) Nachtisch *m*

puddle /ˈpʌdl/ *n* Pfütze *f*

puff /pʌf/ *n* (*of wind*) Hauch *m*; (*of smoke*) Wölkchen *nt* ● *vt* blasen, pusten; **~ out** ausstoßen. ● *vi* keuchen; **~ at** paffen an (+ *dat*) (*pipe*). **~ed** *adj* (*out of breath*) aus der Puste. **~ pastry** *n* Blätterteig *m*

pull /pʊl/ *n* Zug *m*; (*jerk*) Ruck *m*; ([!]: *influence*) Einfluss *m* ● *vt* ziehen; ziehen an (+ *dat*) (*rope*); **~ a muscle** sich (*dat*) einen Muskel zerren; **~ oneself together** sich zusammennehmen; **~ one's weight** tüchtig mitarbeiten; **~ s.o.'s leg** [!] jdn auf den Arm nehmen. **~ down** *vt* herunterziehen; (*demolish*) abreißen. **~ in** *vt* hereinziehen ● *vi* (*Auto*) einscheren. **~ off** *vt* abziehen; [!] schaffen. **~ out** *vt* herausziehen ● *vi* (*Auto*) ausscheren. **~ through** *vt* durchziehen ● *vi* (*recover*) durchkommen. **~ up** *vt* heraufziehen; ausziehen (*plant*) ● *vi* (*Auto*) anhalten

pullover /ˈpʊləʊvə(r)/ *n* Pullover *m*

pulp /pʌlp/ *n* Brei *m*; (*of fruit*) [Frucht]fleisch *nt*

pulpit /ˈpʊlpɪt/ *n* Kanzel *f*

pulse /pʌls/ *n* Puls *m*

pulses /ˈpʌlsɪz/ *npl* Hülsenfrüchte *pl*

pummel /ˈpʌml/ *vt* (*pt/pp* **pummelled**) mit den Fäusten bearbeiten

pump /pʌmp/ *n* Pumpe *f* ● *vt* pumpen; [!] aushorchen. **~ up** *vt* (*inflate*) aufpumpen

pumpkin /ˈpʌmpkɪn/ *n* Kürbis *m*

pun /pʌn/ *n* Wortspiel *nt*

punch[1] /pʌntʃ/ *n* Faustschlag *m*; (*device*) Locher *m* ● *vt* boxen; lochen (*ticket*); stanzen (*hole*)

punch² *n* (*drink*) Bowle *f*

punctual /'pʌŋktjʊəl/ *adj* pünktlich. **~ity** *n* Pünktlichkeit *f*

punctuat|e /'pʌŋktjʊeɪt/ *vt* mit Satzzeichen versehen. **~ion** *n* Interpunktion *f*

puncture /'pʌŋktʃə(r)/ *n* Loch *nt*; (*tyre*) Reifenpanne *f* ● *vt* durchstechen

punish /'pʌnɪʃ/ *vt* bestrafen. **~able** *adj* strafbar. **~ment** *n* Strafe *f*

punt /pʌnt/ *n* (*boat*) Stechkahn *m*

puny /'pju:nɪ/ *adj* mickerig

pup /pʌp/ *n* = **puppy**

pupil /'pju:pl/ *n* Schüler(in) *m*(*f*); (*of eye*) Pupille *f*

puppet /'pʌpɪt/ *n* Puppe *f*; (*fig*) Marionette *f*

puppy /'pʌpɪ/ *n* junger Hund *m*

purchase /'pɜ:tʃəs/ *n* Kauf *m*; (*leverage*) Hebelkraft *f* ● *vt* kaufen. **~r** *n* Käufer *m*

pure /pjʊə(r)/ *adj* (**-r**, **-st**,) **-ly** *adv* rein

P

purge /pɜ:dʒ/ *n* (*Pol*) Säuberungsaktion *f* ● *vt* reinigen

puri|fication /pjʊərɪfɪ'keɪʃn/ *n* Reinigung *f*. **~fy** *vt* (*pt*/*pp* **-ied**) reinigen

puritanical /pjʊərɪ'tænɪkl/ *adj* puritanisch

purity /'pjʊərɪtɪ/ *n* Reinheit *f*

purple /'pɜ:pl/ *adj* [dunkel]lila

purpose /'pɜ:pəs/ *n* Zweck *m*; (*intention*) Absicht *f*; (*determination*) Entschlossenheit *f*; **on ~** absichtlich. **~ful** *adj* entschlossen. **~ly** *adv* absichtlich

purr /pɜ:(r)/ *vi* schnurren

purse /pɜ:s/ *n* Portemonnaie *nt*; (*Amer: handbag*) Handtasche *f*

pursue /pə'sju:/ *vt* verfolgen; (*fig*) nachgehen (+ *dat*). **~r** *n* Verfolger(in) *m*(*f*)

pursuit /pə'sju:t/ *n* Verfolgung *f*; Jagd *f*; (*pastime*) Beschäftigung *f*

pus /pʌs/ *n* Eiter *m*

push /pʊʃ/ *n* Stoß *m*; **get the ~** [!] hinausfliegen ● *vt*/*i* schieben; (*press*) drücken; (*roughly*) stoßen. **~ off** *vt* hinunterstoßen ● *vi* ([!]: *leave*) abhauen. **~ on** *vi* (*continue*) weitergehen/-fahren; (*with activity*) weitermachen. **~ up** *vt* hochschieben; hochtreiben (*price*)

push: ~-button *n* Druckknopf *m*. **~-chair** *n* [Kinder]sportwagen *m*

pushy /'pʊʃɪ/ *adj* [!] aufdringlich

puss /pʊs/ *n*, **pussy** *n* Mieze *f*

put /pʊt/ *vt* (*pt*/*pp* **put**, *pres p* **putting**) tun; (*place*) setzen; (*upright*) stellen; (*flat*) legen; (*express*) ausdrücken; (*say*) sagen; (*estimate*) schätzen (**at** auf + *acc*); **~ aside** *or* **by** beiseite legen ● *vi* **~ to sea** auslaufen ● *adj* **stay ~** dableiben. **~ away** *vt* wegräumen. **~ back** *vt* wieder hinsetzen/-stellen/-legen; zurückstellen (*clock*). **~ down** *vt* hinsetzen/-stellen/-legen; (*suppress*) niederschlagen; (*kill*) töten; (*write*) niederschreiben; (*attribute*) zuschreiben (**to** *dat*). **~ forward** *vt* vorbringen; vorstellen (*clock*). **~ in** *vt* hineinsetzen/-stellen/-legen; (*insert*) einstecken; (*submit*) einreichen ● *vi* **~ in for** beantragen. **~ off** *vt* ausmachen (*light*); (*postpone*) verschieben; **~ s.o. off** jdn abbestellen; (*disconcert*) jdn aus der Fassung bringen. **~ on** *vt* anziehen (*clothes, brake*); sich (*dat*) aufsetzen (*hat*); (*Culin*) aufsetzen; anmachen (*light*); aufführen (*play*); annehmen (*accent*); **~ on weight** zunehmen. **~ out** *vt* hinaussetzen/-stellen/-legen; ausmachen (*fire, light*); ausstrecken (*hand*); (*disconcert*) aus der Fassung bringen; **~ s.o./oneself out** jdm/

sich Umstände machen. ~ **through** *vt* durchstecken; (*Teleph*) verbinden (**to** mit). ~ **up** *vt* errichten (*building*); aufschlagen (*tent*); aufspannen (*umbrella*); anschlagen (*notice*); erhöhen (*price*); unterbringen (*guest*) ● *vi* (*at hotel*) absteigen in (+ *dat*); ~ **up with sth** sich (*dat*) etw bieten lassen

putrid /ˈpju:trɪd/ faulig

putt /pʌt/ *n* Putt *m*

putty /ˈpʌtɪ/ *n* Kitt *m*

puzzl|e /ˈpʌzl/ *n* Rätsel *nt*; (*jigsaw*) Puzzlespiel *nt* ● *vt* **it** ~**es me** es ist mir rätselhaft. ~**ing** *adj* rätselhaft

pyjamas /pəˈdʒɑ:məz/ *npl* Schlafanzug *m*

pylon /ˈpaɪlən/ *n* Mast *m*

pyramid /ˈpɪrəmɪd/ *n* Pyramide *f*

python /ˈpaɪθn/ *n* Pythonschlange *f*

Qq

quack /kwæk/ *n* Quaken *nt*; (*doctor*) Quacksalber *m* ● *vi* quaken

quadrangle /ˈkwɒdræŋgl/ *n* Viereck *nt*; (*court*) Hof *m*

quadruped /ˈkwɒdrʊped/ *n* Vierfüßer *m*

quadruple /ˈkwɒdrʊpl/ *adj* vierfach ● *vt* vervierfachen ● *vi* sich vervierfachen

quaint /kweɪnt/ *adj* (**-er, -est**) malerisch; (*odd*) putzig

quake /kweɪk/ *n* 🅸 Erdbeben *nt* ● *vi* beben; (*with fear*) zittern

qualif|ication /kwɒlɪfɪˈkeɪʃn/ *n* Qualifikation *f*; (*reservation*) Einschränkung *f*. ~**ied** *adj* qualifiziert; (*trained*) ausgebildet; (*limited*) bedingt

qualify /ˈkwɒlɪfaɪ/ *v* (*pt/pp* **-ied**) ● *vt* qualifizieren; (*entitle*) berechtigen; (*limit*) einschränken ● *vi* sich qualifizieren

quality /ˈkwɒlətɪ/ *n* Qualität *f*; (*characteristic*) Eigenschaft *f*

qualm /kwɑ:m/ *n* Bedenken *pl*

quantity /ˈkwɒntətɪ/ *n* Quantität *f*, Menge *f*; **in** ~ in großen Mengen

quarantine /ˈkwɒrəntɪ:n/ *n* Quarantäne *f*

quarrel /ˈkwɒrl/ *n* Streit *m* ● *vi* (*pt/pp* **quarrelled**) sich streiten. ~**some** *adj* streitsüchtig

quarry[1] /ˈkwɒrɪ/ *n* (*prey*) Beute *f*

quarry[2] *n* Steinbruch *m*

quart /kwɔ:t/ *n* Quart *nt*

quarter /ˈkwɔ:tə(r)/ *n* Viertel *nt*; (*of year*) Vierteljahr *nt*; (*Amer*) 25-Cent-Stück *nt*; ~**s** *pl* Quartier *nt*; **at [a]** ~ **to six** um Viertel vor sechs ● *vt* vierteln; (*Mil*) einquartieren (**on** bei). ~-ˈ**final** *n* Viertelfinale *nt*

quarterly /ˈkwɔ:təlɪ/ *adj & adv* vierteljährlich

quartet /kwɔ:ˈtet/ *n* Quartett *nt*

quartz /kwɔ:ts/ *n* Quarz *m*

quay /ki:/ *n* Kai *m*

queasy /ˈkwi:zɪ/ *adj* **I feel** ~ mir ist übel

queen /kwi:n/ *n* Königin *f*; (*Cards, Chess*) Dame *f*

queer /kwɪə(r)/ *adj* (**-er, -est**) eigenartig; (*dubious*) zweifelhaft; (*ill*) unwohl

quell /kwel/ *vt* unterdrücken

quench /kwentʃ/ *vt* löschen

query /ˈkwɪərɪ/ *n* Frage *f*; (*question mark*) Fragezeichen *nt* ● *vt* (*pt/pp* **-ied**) infrage stellen; reklamieren (*bill*)

quest /kwest/ *n* Suche *f* (**for** nach)

question /'kwestʃn/ *n* Frage *f*; (*for discussion*) Thema *nt*; **out of the ~** ausgeschlossen; **the person in ~** die fragliche Person ● *vt* infrage stellen; **~ s.o.** jdn ausfragen; (*police*:) jdn verhören. **~able** *adj* zweifelhaft. **~ mark** *n* Fragezeichen *nt*

questionnaire /kwestʃə'neə(r)/ *n* Fragebogen *m*

queue /kju:/ *n* Schlange *f* ● *vi* **~ [up]** Schlange stehen, sich anstellen (**for** nach)

quibble /'kwɪbl/ *vi* Haarspalterei treiben

quick /kwɪk/ *adj* (**-er, -est**) schnell; **be ~!** mach schnell! ● *adv* schnell. **~en** *vt* beschleunigen ● *vi* sich beschleunigen

quick: ~sand *n* Treibsand *m*. **~-tempered** *adj* aufbrausend

quid /kwɪd/ *n inv* [!] Pfund *nt*

quiet /'kwaɪət/ *adj* (**-er, -est**) still; (*calm*) ruhig; (*soft*) leise; **keep ~ about** [!] nichts sagen von ● *n* Stille *f*; Ruhe *f*

quiet|en /'kwaɪətn/ *vt* beruhigen ● *vi* **~en down** ruhig werden. **~ness** *n* Stille *f*; Ruhe *f*

quilt /kwɪlt/ *n* Steppdecke *f*. **~ed** *adj* Stepp-

quintet /kwɪn'tet/ *n* Quintett *nt*

quirk /kwɜ:k/ *n* Eigenart *f*

quit /kwɪt/ *v* (*pt/pp* **quitted** or **quit**) ● *vt* verlassen; (*give up*) aufgeben; **~ doing sth** aufhören, etw zu tun ● *vi* gehen

quite /kwaɪt/ *adv* ganz; (*really*) wirklich; **~ [so]!** genau! **~ a few** ziemlich viele

quits /kwɪts/ *adj* quitt

quiver /'kwɪvə(r)/ *vi* zittern

quiz /kwɪz/ *n* Quiz *nt* ● *vt* (*pt/pp* **quizzed**) ausfragen. **~zical** *adj* fragend

quota /'kwəʊtə/ *n* Anteil *m*; (*Comm*) Kontingent *nt*

quotation /kwəʊ'teɪʃn/ *n* Zitat *nt*; (*price*) Kostenvoranschlag *m*; (*of shares*) Notierung *f*. **~ marks** *npl* Anführungszeichen *pl*

quote /kwəʊt/ *n* [!] = **quotation; in ~s** in Anführungszeichen ● *vt/i* zitieren

Rr

rabbi /'ræbaɪ/ *n* Rabbiner *m*; (*title*) Rabbi *m*

rabbit /'ræbɪt/ *n* Kaninchen *nt*

rabid /'ræbɪd/ *adj* fanatisch; (*animal*) tollwütig

rabies /'reɪbi:z/ *n* Tollwut *f*

race[1] /reɪs/ *n* Rasse *f*

race[2] *n* Rennen *nt*; (*fig*) Wettlauf *m* ● *vi* [am Rennen] teilnehmen; (*athlete, horse*:) laufen; ([!]: *rush*) rasen ● *vt* um die Wette laufen mit; an einem Rennen teilnehmen lassen (*horse*)

race: ~course *n* Rennbahn *f*. **~horse** *n* Rennpferd *nt*. **~track** *n* Rennbahn *f*

racial /'reɪʃl/ *adj* rassisch; (*discrimination*) Rassen-

racing /'reɪsɪŋ/ *n* Rennsport *m*; (*horse-*) Pferderennen *nt*. **~ car** *n* Rennwagen *m*. **~ driver** *n* Rennfahrer *m*

racis|m /'reɪsɪzm/ *n* Rassismus *m*. **~t** *adj* rassistisch ● *n* Rassist *m*

rack[1] /ræk/ *n* Ständer *m*; (*for plates*) Gestell *nt* ● *vt* **~ one's brains** sich (*dat*) den Kopf zerbrechen

rack² *n* **go to ~ and ruin** verfallen; (*fig*) herunterkommen

racket /'rækɪt/ *n* (*Sport*) Schläger *m*; (*din*) Krach *m*; (*swindle*) Schwindelgeschäft *nt*

racy /'reɪsɪ/ *adj* schwungvoll; (*risqué*) gewagt

radar /'reɪdɑ:(r)/ *n* Radar *m*

radian|ce /'reɪdɪəns/ *n* Strahlen *nt*. **~t** *adj* strahlend

radiat|e /'reɪdɪeɪt/ *vt* ausstrahlen ● *vi* (*heat:*) ausgestrahlt werden; (*roads:*) strahlenförmig ausgehen. **~ion** *n* Strahlung *f*

radiator /'reɪdɪeɪtə(r)/ *n* Heizkörper *m*; (*Auto*) Kühler *m*

radical /'rædɪkl/ *adj* radikal ● *n* Radikale(r) *m/f*

radio /'reɪdɪəʊ/ *n* Radio *nt*; **by ~** über Funk ● *vt* funken (*message*)

radio|'active *adj* radioaktiv. **~ac'tivity** *n* Radioaktivität *f*

radish /'rædɪʃ/ *n* Radieschen *nt*

radius /'reɪdɪəs/ *n* (*pl* **-dii** /-dɪaɪ/) Radius *m*, Halbmesser *m*

raffle /'ræfl/ *n* Tombola *f*

raft /rɑ:ft/ *n* Floß *nt*

rafter /'rɑ:ftə(r)/ *n* Dachsparren *m*

rag /ræg/ *n* Lumpen *m*; (*pej: newspaper*) Käseblatt *nt*

rage /reɪdʒ/ *n* Wut *f*; **all the ~** [!] der letzte Schrei ● *vi* rasen

ragged /'rægɪd/ *adj* zerlumpt; (*edge*) ausgefranst

raid /reɪd/ *n* Überfall *m*; (*Mil*) Angriff *m*; (*police*) Razzia *f* ● *vt* überfallen; (*Mil*) angreifen; (*police*) eine Razzia durchführen in (+ *dat*); (*break in*) eindringen in (+ *acc*). **~er** *n* Eindringling *m*; (*of bank*) Bankräuber *m*

rail /reɪl/ *n* Schiene *f*; (*pole*) Stange *f*; (*hand~*) Handlauf *m*; (*Naut*) Reling *f*; **by ~** mit der Bahn

railings /'reɪlɪŋz/ *npl* Geländer *nt*

'railroad *n* (*Amer*) = **railway**

'railway *n* [Eisen]bahn *f*. **~ station** *n* Bahnhof *m*

rain /reɪn/ *n* Regen *m* ● *vi* regnen

rain: ~bow *n* Regenbogen *m*. **~coat** *n* Regenmantel *m*. **~fall** *n* Niederschlag *m*

rainy /'reɪnɪ/ *adj* regnerisch

raise /reɪz/ *n* (*Amer*) Lohnerhöhung *f* ● *vt* erheben; (*upright*) aufrichten; (*make higher*) erhöhen; (*lift*) [hoch]heben; aufziehen (*child, animal*); aufwerfen (*question*); aufbringen (*money*)

raisin /'reɪzn/ *n* Rosine *f*

rake /reɪk/ *n* Harke *f*, Rechen *m* ● *vt* harken, rechen

rally /'rælɪ/ *n* Versammlung *f*; (*Auto*) Rallye *f*; (*Tennis*) Ballwechsel *m* ● *vt* sammeln

ram /ræm/ *n* Schafbock *m* ● *vt* (*pt/pp* **rammed**) rammen

rambl|e /'ræmbl/ *n* Wanderung *f* ● *vi* wandern; (*in speech*) irrereden. **~er** *n* Wanderer *m*; (*rose*) Kletterrose *f*. **~ing** *adj* weitschweifig; (*club*) Wander-

ramp /ræmp/ *n* Rampe *f*; (*Aviat*) Gangway *f*

rampage¹ /'ræmpeɪdʒ/ *n* **be/go on the ~** randalieren

rampage² /ræm'peɪdʒ/ *vi* randalieren

ramshackle /'ræmʃækl/ *adj* baufällig

ran /ræn/ *see* **run**

ranch /rɑ:ntʃ/ *n* Ranch *f*

random /'rændəm/ *adj* willkürlich; **a ~ sample** eine Stichprobe ● *n* **at ~** aufs Geratewohl; (*choose*) willkürlich

rang /ræŋ/ *see* **ring²**

range /reɪndʒ/ *n* Serie *f*, Reihe *f*;

r

(*Comm*) Auswahl *f*, Angebot *nt* (**of** an + *dat*); (*of mountains*) Kette *f*; (*Mus*) Umfang *m*; (*distance*) Reichweite *f*; (*for shooting*) Schießplatz *m*; (*stove*) Kohlenherd *m* ● *vi* reichen; ~ **from ... to** gehen von ... bis. ~**r** *n* Aufseher *m*

rank /ræŋk/ *n* (*row*) Reihe *f*; (*Mil*) Rang *m*; (*social position*) Stand *m*; **the ~ and file** die breite Masse ● *vt/i* einstufen; ~ **among** zählen zu

ransack /'rænsæk/ *vt* durchwühlen; (*pillage*) plündern

ransom /'rænsəm/ *n* Lösegeld *nt*; **hold s.o. to ~** Lösegeld für jdn fordern

rape /reɪp/ *n* Vergewaltigung *f* ● *vt* vergewaltigen

rapid /'ræpɪd/ *adj* schnell. ~**ity** *n* Schnelligkeit *f*

rapist /'reɪpɪst/ *n* Vergewaltiger *m*

raptur|e /'ræptʃə(r)/ *n* Entzücken *nt*. ~**ous** *adj* begeistert

rare[1] /reə(r)/ *adj* (**-r**, **-st**) selten

rare[2] *adj* (*Culin*) englisch gebraten

rarefied /'reərɪfaɪd/ *adj* dünn

rarity /'reərətɪ/ *n* Seltenheit *f*

rascal /'rɑ:skl/ *n* Schlingel *m*

rash[1] /ræʃ/ *n* (*Med*) Ausschlag *m*

rash[2] *adj* (**-er**, **-est**) voreilig

rasher /'ræʃə(r)/ *n* Speckscheibe *f*

raspberry /'rɑ:zbərɪ/ *n* Himbeere *f*

rat /ræt/ *n* Ratte *f*; ([!]: *person*) Schuft *m*; **smell a ~** [!] Lunte riechen

rate /reɪt/ *n* Rate *f*; (*speed*) Tempo *nt*; (*of payment*) Satz *m*; (*of exchange*) Kurs *m*; ~**s** *pl* (*taxes*) ≈ Grundsteuer *f*; **at any ~** auf jeden Fall; **at this ~** auf diese Weise ● *vt* einschätzen; ~ **among** zählen zu ● *vi* ~ **as** gelten als

rather /'rɑ:ðə(r)/ *adv* lieber; (*fairly*) ziemlich; ~**!** und ob!

rating /'reɪtɪŋ/ *n* Einschätzung *f*; (*class*) Klasse *f*; (*sailor*) [einfacher] Matrose *m*; ~**s** *pl* (*Radio, TV*) ≈ Einschaltquote *f*

ratio /'reɪʃɪəʊ/ *n* Verhältnis *nt*

ration /'ræʃn/ *n* Ration *f* ● *vt* rationieren

rational /'ræʃənl/ *adj* rational. ~**ize** *vt/i* rationalisieren

rattle /'rætl/ *n* Rasseln *nt*; (*of windows*) Klappern *nt*; (*toy*) Klapper *f* ● *vi* rasseln; klappern ● *vt* rasseln mit

raucous /'rɔ:kəs/ *adj* rau

rave /reɪv/ *vi* toben; ~ **about** schwärmen von

raven /'reɪvn/ *n* Rabe *m*

ravenous /'rævənəs/ *adj* heißhungrig

ravine /rə'vi:n/ *n* Schlucht *f*

raving /'reɪvɪŋ/ *adj* ~ **mad** [!] total verrückt

ravishing /'rævɪʃɪŋ/ *adj* hinreißend

raw /rɔ:/ *adj* (**-er**, **-est**) roh; (*not processed*) Roh-; (*skin*) wund; (*weather*) nasskalt; (*inexperienced*) unerfahren; **get a ~ deal** [!] schlecht wegkommen. ~ **ma'terials** *npl* Rohstoffe *pl*

ray /reɪ/ *n* Strahl *m*

razor /'reɪzə(r)/ *n* Rasierapparat *m*. ~ **blade** *n* Rasierklinge *f*

re /ri:/ *prep* betreffs (+ *gen*)

reach /ri:tʃ/ *n* Reichweite *f*; (*of river*) Strecke *f*; **within/out of ~** in/außer Reichweite ● *vt* erreichen; (*arrive at*) ankommen in (+ *dat*); (~ *as far as*) reichen bis zu; kommen zu (*decision, conclusion*); (*pass*) reichen ● *vi* reichen (**to** bis zu); ~ **for** greifen nach

re'act /ri:'ækt/ *vi* reagieren

(**to** auf + *acc*)

re'action /rɪ-/ *n* Reaktion *f*. **~ary** *adj* reaktionär

reactor /rɪ'æktə(r)/ *n* Reaktor *m*

read /ri:d/ *vt/i* (*pt/pp* **read** /red/) lesen; (*aloud*) vorlesen (**to** *dat*); (*Univ*) studieren; ablesen (*meter*). **~ out** *vt* vorlesen

readable /'ri:dəbl/ *adj* lesbar

reader /'ri:də(r)/ *n* Leser(in) *m*(*f*); (*book*) Lesebuch *nt*

readily /'redɪlɪ/ *adv* bereitwillig; (*easily*) leicht

reading /'ri:dɪŋ/ *n* Lesen *nt*; (*Pol, Relig*) Lesung *f*

rea'djust /ri:-/ *vt* neu einstellen ● *vi* sich umstellen (**to** auf + *acc*)

ready /'redɪ/ *adj* fertig; (*willing*) bereit; (*quick*) schnell; **get ~** sich fertig machen; (*prepare to*) sich bereitmachen

ready: ~-'made *adj* fertig. **~-to--'wear** *adj* Konfektions-

real /rɪəl/ *adj* wirklich; (*genuine*) echt; (*actual*) eigentlich ● *adv* (*Amer*, [!]) echt. **~ estate** *n* Immobilien *pl*

realis|m /'rɪəlɪzm/ *n* Realismus *m*. **~t** *n* Realist *m*. **~tic** *adj*, **-ally** *adv* realistisch

reality /rɪ'ælətɪ/ *n* Wirklichkeit *f*

realization /rɪəlaɪ'zeɪʃn/ *n* Erkenntnis *f*

realize /'rɪəlaɪz/ *vt* einsehen; (*become aware*) gewahr werden; verwirklichen (*hopes, plans*); einbringen (*price*)

really /'rɪəlɪ/ *adv* wirklich; (*actually*) eigentlich

realm /relm/ *n* Reich *nt*

realtor /'ri:əltə(r)/ *n* (*Amer*) Immobilienmakler *m*

reap /ri:p/ *vt* ernten

reap'pear /ri:-/ *vi* wiederkommen

rear¹ /rɪə(r)/ *adj* Hinter-; (*Auto*) Heck- ● *n* **the ~** der hintere Teil; **from the ~** von hinten

rear² *vt* aufziehen ● *vi* **~ [up]** (*horse:*) sich aufbäumen

rear'range /ri:-/ *vt* umstellen

reason /'ri:zn/ *n* Grund *m*; (*good sense*) Vernunft *f*; (*ability to think*) Verstand *m*; **within ~** in vernünftigen Grenzen ● *vi* argumentieren; **~ with** vernünftig reden mit. **~able** *adj* vernünftig; (*not expensive*) preiswert. **~ably** *adv* (*fairly*) ziemlich

reas'sur|ance /ri:-/ *n* Beruhigung *f*; Versicherung *f*. **~e** *vt* beruhigen; **~e s.o. of sth** jdm etw (*gen*) versichern

rebel¹ /'rebl/ *n* Rebell *m*

rebel² /rɪ'bel/ *vi* (*pt/pp* **rebelled**) rebellieren. **~lion** *n* Rebellion *f*. **~lious** *adj* rebellisch

re'bound¹ /rɪ-/ *vi* abprallen

'rebound² /ri:-/ *n* Rückprall *m*

re'build /ri:-/ *vt* (*pt/pp* **-built**) wieder aufbauen

rebuke /rɪ'bju:k/ *n* Tadel *m* ● *vt* tadeln

re'call /rɪ-/ *n* Erinnerung *f* ● *vt* zurückrufen; abberufen (*diplomat*); (*remember*) sich erinnern an (+ *acc*)

recant /rɪ'kænt/ *vi* widerrufen

recap /'ri:kæp/ *vt/i* [!] = **recapitulate**

recapitulate /ri:kə'pɪtjʊleɪt/ *vt/i* zusammenfassen; rekapitulieren

re'capture /ri:-/ *vt* wieder gefangen nehmen (*person*); wieder einfangen (*animal*)

reced|e /rɪ'si:d/ *vi* zurückgehen. **~ing** *adj* (*forehead, chin*) fliehend

receipt /rɪ'si:t/ *n* Quittung *f*; (*receiving*) Empfang *m*; **~s** *pl* (*Comm*) Einnahmen *pl*

receive /rɪ'si:v/ *vt* erhalten, bekommen; empfangen (*guests*). **~r** *n*

(*Teleph*) Hörer *m*; (*of stolen goods*) Hehler *m*

recent /ˈriːsənt/ *adj* kürzlich erfolgte(r,s). **~ly** *adv* vor kurzem

receptacle /rɪˈseptəkl/ *n* Behälter *m*

reception /rɪˈsepʃn/ *n* Empfang *m*; **~ [desk]** (*in hotel*) Rezeption *f*. **~ist** *n* Empfangsdame *f*

receptive /rɪˈseptɪv/ *adj* aufnahmefähig; **~ to** empfänglich für

recess /rɪˈses/ *n* Nische *f*; (*holiday*) Ferien *pl*

recession /rɪˈseʃn/ *n* Rezession *f*

re'charge /riː-/ *vt* [wieder] aufladen

recipe /ˈresəpɪ/ *n* Rezept *nt*

recipient /rɪˈsɪpɪənt/ *n* Empfänger *m*

recital /rɪˈsaɪtl/ *n* (*of poetry, songs*) Vortrag *m*; (*on piano*) Konzert *nt*

recite /rɪˈsaɪt/ *vt* aufsagen; (*before audience*) vortragen

reckless /ˈreklɪs/ *adj* leichtsinnig; (*careless*) rücksichtslos. **~ness** *n* Leichtsinn *m*; Rücksichtslosigkeit *f*

reckon /ˈrekən/ *vt* rechnen; (*consider*) glauben ● *vi* **~ on/with** rechnen mit

r

re'claim /rɪ-/ *vt* zurückfordern; zurückgewinnen (*land*)

reclin|e /rɪˈklaɪn/ *vi* liegen. **~ing seat** *n* Liegesitz *m*

recluse /rɪˈkluːs/ *n* Einsiedler(in) *m*(*f*)

recognition /rekəgˈnɪʃn/ *n* Erkennen *nt*; (*acknowledgement*) Anerkennung *f*; **in ~** als Anerkennung (**of** *gen*)

recognize /ˈrekəgnaɪz/ *vt* erkennen; (*know again*) wieder erkennen; (*acknowledge*) anerkennen

re'coil /rɪ-/ *vi* zurückschnellen; (*in fear*) zurückschrecken

recollect /rekəˈlekt/ *vt* sich erinnern an (+ *acc*). **~ion** *n* Erinnerung *f*

recommend /rekəˈmend/ *vt* empfehlen. **~ation** *n* Empfehlung *f*

recon|cile /ˈrekənsaɪl/ *vt* versöhnen; **~cile oneself to** sich abfinden mit. **~ciliation** *n* Versöhnung *f*

reconnaissance /rɪˈkɒnɪsns/ *n* (*Mil*) Aufklärung *f*

reconnoitre /rekəˈnɔɪtə(r)/ *vi* (*pres p* **-tring**) auf Erkundung ausgehen

recon'sider /riː-/ *vt* sich (*dat*) noch einmal überlegen

recon'struct /riː-/ *vt* wieder aufbauen; rekonstruieren (*crime*)

record[1] /rɪˈkɔːd/ *vt* aufzeichnen; (*register*) registrieren; (*on tape*) aufnehmen

record[2] /ˈrekɔːd/ *n* Aufzeichnung *f*; (*Jur*) Protokoll *nt*; (*Mus*) [Schall]platte *f*; (*Sport*) Rekord *m*; **~s** *pl* Unterlagen *pl*; **off the ~** inoffiziell; **have a [criminal] ~** vorbestraft sein

recorder /rɪˈkɔːdə(r)/ *n* (*Mus*) Blockflöte *f*

recording /rɪˈkɔːdɪŋ/ *n* Aufnahme *f*

re-'count[1] /riː-/ *vt* nachzählen

're-count[2] /riː-/ *n* (*Pol*) Nachzählung *f*

recover /rɪˈkʌvə(r)/ *vt* zurückbekommen ● *vi* sich erholen. **~y** *n* Wiedererlangung *f*; (*of health*) Erholung *f*

recreation /rekrɪˈeɪʃn/ *n* Erholung *f*; (*hobby*) Hobby *nt*. **~al** *adj* Freizeit-; **be ~al** erholsam sein

recruit /rɪˈkruːt/ *n* (*Mil*) Rekrut *m*; **new ~** (*member*) neues Mitglied *nt*; (*worker*) neuer Mitarbeiter *m* ● *vt* rekrutieren; anwerben (*staff*). **~ment** *n* Rekrutierung *f*;

Anwerbung *f*

rectang|le /'rektæŋgl/ *n* Rechteck *nt*. **~ular** *adj* rechteckig

rectify /'rektɪfaɪ/ *vt* (*pt/pp* **-ied**) berichtigen

rector /'rektə(r)/ *n* Pfarrer *m*; (*Univ*) Rektor *m*. **~y** *n* Pfarrhaus *nt*

recur /rɪ'kɜ:(r)/ *vi* (*pt/pp* **recurred**) sich wiederholen; (*illness:*) wiederkehren

recurren|ce /rɪ'kʌrəns/ *n* Wiederkehr *f*. **~t** *adj* wiederkehrend

recycle /ri:'saɪkl/ *vt* wieder verwerten

red /red/ *adj* (**redder, reddest**) rot ● *n* Rot *nt*

redd|en /'redn/ *vt* röten ● *vi* rot werden. **~ish** *adj* rötlich

re'decorate /ri:-/ *vt* renovieren; (*paint*) neu streichen; (*wallpaper*) neu tapezieren

redeem /rɪ'di:m/ *vt* einlösen; (*Relig*) erlösen

redemption /rɪ'dempʃn/ *n* Erlösung *f*

red: **~-haired** *adj* rothaarig. **~-'handed** *adj* **catch s.o. ~-handed** jdn auf frischer Tat ertappen. **~ 'herring** *n* falsche Spur *f*. **~-hot** *adj* glühend heiß. **~ 'light** *n* (*Auto*) rote Ampel *f*. **~ness** *n* Röte *f*

re'do /ri:-/ *vt* (*pt* **-did**, *pp* **-done**) noch einmal machen

re'double /ri:-/ *vt* verdoppeln

red 'tape *n* ▣ Bürokratie *f*

reduc|e /rɪ'dju:s/ *vt* verringern, vermindern; (*in size*) verkleinern; ermäßigen (*costs*); herabsetzen (*price, goods*); (*Culin*) einkochen lassen. **~tion** *n* Verringerung *f*; (*in price*) Ermäßigung *f*; (*in size*) Verkleinerung *f*

redundan|cy /rɪ'dʌndənsɪ/ *n* Beschäftigungslosigkeit *f*. **~t** *adj* überflüssig; **make ~t** entlassen; **be made ~t** beschäftigungslos werden

reed /ri:d/ *n* [Schilf]rohr *nt*; **~s** *pl* Schilf *nt*

reef /ri:f/ *n* Riff *nt*

reek /ri:k/ *vi* riechen (**of** nach)

reel /ri:l/ *n* Rolle *f*, Spule *f* ● *vi* (*stagger*) taumeln ● *vt* **~ off** (*fig*) herunterrasseln

refectory /rɪ'fektərɪ/ *n* Refektorium *nt*; (*Univ*) Mensa *f*

refer /rɪ'fɜ:(r)/ *v* (*pt/pp* **referred**) ● *vt* verweisen (**to** an + *acc*); übergeben, weiterleiten (*matter*) (**to** an + *acc*) ● *vi* **~ to** sich beziehen auf (+ *acc*); (*mention*) erwähnen; (*concern*) betreffen; (*consult*) sich wenden an (+ *acc*); nachschlagen in (+ *dat*) (*book*); **are you ~ring to me?** meinen Sie mich?

referee /refə'ri:/ *n* Schiedsrichter *m*; (*Boxing*) Ringrichter *m*; (*for job*) Referenz *f* ● *vt/i* (*pt/pp* **refereed**) Schiedsrichter/Ringrichter sein (bei)

reference /'refərəns/ *n* Erwähnung *f*; (*in book*) Verweis *m*; (*for job*) Referenz *f*; **with ~ to** in Bezug auf (+ *acc*); **make [a] ~ to** erwähnen. **~ book** *n* Nachschlagewerk *nt*

referendum /refə'rendəm/ *n* Volksabstimmung *f*

re'fill[1] /ri:-/ *vt* nachfüllen

'refill[2] /ri:-/ *n* (*for pen*) Ersatzmine *f*

refine /rɪ'faɪn/ *vt* raffinieren. **~d** *adj* fein, vornehm. **~ment** *n* Vornehmheit *f*; (*Techn*) Verfeinerung *f*. **~ry** *n* Raffinerie *f*

reflect /rɪ'flekt/ *vt* reflektieren; (*mirror:*) [wider]spiegeln; **be ~ed in** sich spiegeln in (+ *dat*) ● *vi* nachdenken (**on** über + *acc*). **~ion** *n* Reflexion *f*; (*image*) Spiegelbild *nt*; **on ~ion** nach nochmaliger Überlegung. **~or** *n* Rückstrahler *m*

reflex /ˈriːfleks/ *n* Reflex *m*
reflexive /rɪˈfleksɪv/ *adj* reflexiv
reform /rɪˈfɔːm/ *n* Reform *f* ● *vt* reformieren ● *vi* sich bessern
refrain[1] /rɪˈfreɪn/ *n* Refrain *m*
refrain[2] *vi* ~ **from doing sth** etw nicht tun
refresh /rɪˈfreʃ/ *vt* erfrischen. ~**ing** *adj* erfrischend. ~**ments** *npl* Erfrischungen *pl*
refrigerat|e /rɪˈfrɪdʒəreɪt/ *vt* kühlen. ~**or** *n* Kühlschrank *m*
re'fuel /riː-/ *vt/i* (*pt/pp* **-fuelled**) auftanken
refuge /ˈrefjuːdʒ/ *n* Zuflucht *f*; take ~ Zuflucht nehmen
refugee /refjʊˈdʒiː/ *n* Flüchtling *m*
'refund[1] /riː-/ **get a** ~ sein Geld zurückbekommen
re'fund[2] /rɪ-/ *vt* zurückerstatten
refusal /rɪˈfjuːzl/ *n* (*see* **refuse**[1]) Ablehnung *f*; Weigerung *f*
refuse[1] /rɪˈfjuːz/ *vt* ablehnen; (*not grant*) verweigern; ~ **to do sth** sich weigern, etw zu tun ● *vi* ablehnen; sich weigern
refuse[2] /ˈrefjuːs/ *n* Müll *m*
refute /rɪˈfjuːt/ *vt* widerlegen
re'gain /rɪ-/ *vt* wiedergewinnen
regal /ˈriːgl/ *adj* königlich
regard /rɪˈgɑːd/ *n* (*heed*) Rücksicht *f*; (*respect*) Achtung *f*; ~**s** *pl* Grüße *pl*; **with** ~ **to** in Bezug auf (+ *acc*) ● *vt* ansehen, betrachten (**as** als). ~**ing** *prep* bezüglich (+ *gen*). ~**less** *adv* ohne Rücksicht (**of** auf + *acc*)
regatta /rɪˈgætə/ *n* Regatta *f*
regime /reɪˈʒiːm/ *n* Regime *nt*
regiment /ˈredʒɪmənt/ *n* Regiment *nt*. ~**al** *adj* Regiments-
region /ˈriːdʒən/ *n* Region *f*; **in the** ~ **of** (*fig*) ungefähr. ~**al** *adj* regional
register /ˈredʒɪstə(r)/ *n* Register *nt*; (*Sch*) Anwesenheitsliste *f* ● *vt* registrieren; (*report*) anmelden; einschreiben (*letter*); aufgeben (*luggage*) ● *vi* (*report*) sich anmelden
registrar /redʒɪˈstrɑː(r)/ *n* Standesbeamte(r) *m*
registration /redʒɪˈstreɪʃn/ *n* Registrierung *f*; Anmeldung *f*. ~ **number** *n* Autonummer *f*
registry office /ˈredʒɪstrɪ-/ *n* Standesamt *nt*
regret /rɪˈgret/ *n* Bedauern *nt* ● *vt* (*pt/pp* **regretted**) bedauern. ~**fully** *adv* mit Bedauern
regrettab|le /rɪˈgretəbl/ *adj* bedauerlich. ~**ly** *adv* bedauerlicherweise
regular /ˈregjʊlə(r)/ *adj* regelmäßig; (*usual*) üblich ● *n* (*in pub*) Stammgast *m*; (*in shop*) Stammkunde *m*. ~**ity** *n* Regelmäßigkeit *f*
regulat|e /ˈregjʊleɪt/ *vt* regulieren. ~**ion** *n* (*rule*) Vorschrift *f*
rehears|al /rɪˈhɜːsl/ *n* (*Theat*) Probe *f*. ~**e** *vt* proben
reign /reɪn/ *n* Herrschaft *f* ● *vi* herrschen, regieren
rein /reɪn/ *n* Zügel *m*
reindeer /ˈreɪndɪə(r)/ *n inv* Rentier *nt*
reinforce /riːɪnˈfɔːs/ *vt* verstärken. ~**ment** *n* Verstärkung *f*; **send** ~**ments** Verstärkung schicken
reiterate /riːˈɪtəreɪt/ *vt* wiederholen
reject /rɪˈdʒekt/ *vt* ablehnen. ~**ion** *n* Ablehnung *f*
rejects /ˈriːdʒekts/ *npl* (*Comm*) Ausschussware *f*
rejoic|e /rɪˈdʒɔɪs/ *vi* (*literary*) sich freuen. ~**ing** *n* Freude *f*
re'join /rɪ-/ *vt* sich wieder anschließen (+ *dat*); wieder beitreten (+ *dat*) (*club, party*)
rejuvenate /rɪˈdʒuːvəneɪt/ *vt*

verjüngen

relapse /rɪˈlæps/ *n* Rückfall *m* ● *vi* einen Rückfall erleiden

relate /rɪˈleɪt/ *vt* (*tell*) erzählen; (*connect*) verbinden

relation /rɪˈleɪʃn/ *n* Beziehung *f*; (*person*) Verwandte(r) *m/f*. **~ship** *n* Beziehung *f*; (*link*) Verbindung *f*; (*blood tie*) Verwandtschaft *f*; (*affair*) Verhältnis *nt*

relative /ˈrelətɪv/ *n* Verwandte(r) *m/f* ● *adj* relativ; (*Gram*) Relativ-. **~ly** *adv* relativ, verhältnismäßig

relax /rɪˈlæks/ *vt* lockern, entspannen ● *vi* sich lockern, sich entspannen. **~ation** *n* Entspannung *f*. **~ing** *adj* entspannend

relay[1] /riːˈleɪ/ *vt* (*pt/pp* **-layed**) weitergeben; (*Radio, TV*) übertragen

relay[2] /ˈriːleɪ/ *n*. **~ [race]** *n* Staffel *f*

release /rɪˈliːs/ *n* Freilassung *f*, Entlassung *f*; (*Techn*) Auslöser *m* ● *vt* freilassen; (*let go of*) loslassen; (*Techn*) auslösen; veröffentlichen (*information*)

relent /rɪˈlent/ *vi* nachgeben. **~less** *adj* erbarmungslos; (*unceasing*) unaufhörlich

relevan|ce /ˈreləvəns/ *n* Relevanz *f*. **~t** *adj* relevant (**to** für)

reliab|ility /rɪlaɪəˈbɪlətɪ/ *n* Zuverlässigkeit *f*. **~le** *adj* zuverlässig

relian|ce /rɪˈlaɪəns/ *n* Abhängigkeit *f* (**on** von). **~t** *adj* angewiesen (**on** auf + *acc*)

relic /ˈrelɪk/ *n* Überbleibsel *nt*; (*Relig*) Reliquie *f*

relief /rɪˈliːf/ *n* Erleichterung *f*; (*assistance*) Hilfe *f*; (*replacement*) Ablösung *f*; (*Art*) Relief *nt*

relieve /rɪˈliːv/ *vt* erleichtern; (*take over from*) ablösen; **~ of** entlasten von

religion /rɪˈlɪdʒən/ *n* Religion *f*

religious /rɪˈlɪdʒəs/ *adj* religiös

relinquish /rɪˈlɪŋkwɪʃ/ *vt* loslassen; (*give up*) aufgeben

relish /ˈrelɪʃ/ *n* Genuss *m*; (*Culin*) Würze *f* ● *vt* genießen

reluctan|ce /rɪˈlʌktəns/ *n* Widerstreben *nt*. **~t** *adj* widerstrebend; **be ~t** zögern (**to** zu). **~tly** *adv* ungern, widerstrebend

rely /rɪˈlaɪ/ *vi* (*pt/pp* **-ied**) **~ on** sich verlassen auf (+ *acc*); (*be dependent on*) angewiesen sein auf (+ *acc*)

remain /rɪˈmeɪn/ *vi* bleiben; (*be left*) übrig bleiben. **~der** *n* Rest *m*. **~ing** *adj* restlich. **~s** *npl* Reste *pl*; **[mortal] ~s** [sterbliche] Überreste *pl*

remand /rɪˈmɑːnd/ *n* **on ~** in Untersuchungshaft ● *vt* **~ in custody** in Untersuchungshaft schicken

remark /rɪˈmɑːk/ *n* Bemerkung *f* ● *vt* bemerken. **~able** *adj*, **-bly** *adv* bemerkenswert

re|marry /riː-/ *vi* wieder heiraten

remedy /ˈremədɪ/ *n* [Heil]mittel *nt* (**for** gegen); (*fig*) Abhilfe *f* ● *vt* (*pt/pp* **-ied**) abhelfen (+ *dat*); beheben (*fault*)

rememb|er /rɪˈmembə(r)/ *vt* sich erinnern an (+ *acc*); **~er to do sth** daran denken, etw zu tun ● *vi* sich erinnern

remind /rɪˈmaɪnd/ *vt* erinnern (**of** an + *acc*). **~er** *n* Andenken *nt*; (*letter, warning*) Mahnung *f*

reminisce /remɪˈnɪs/ *vi* sich seinen Erinnerungen hingeben. **~nces** *npl* Erinnerungen *pl*. **~nt** *adj* **be ~nt of** erinnern an (+ *acc*)

remnant /ˈremnənt/ *n* Rest *m*

remorse /rɪˈmɔːs/ *n* Reue *f*. **~ful** *adj* reumütig. **~less** *adj* unerbittlich

remote /rɪˈməʊt/ *adj* fern; (*isolated*) abgelegen; (*slight*) gering. **~**

con'trol *n* Fernsteuerung *f*; (*for TV*) Fernbedienung *f*
remotely /rɪ'məʊtlɪ/ *adv* entfernt; **not ~** nicht im Entferntesten
re'movable /rɪ-/ *adj* abnehmbar
removal /rɪ'mu:vl/ *n* Entfernung *f*; (*from house*) Umzug *m*. **~ van** *n* Möbelwagen *m*
remove /rɪ'mu:v/ *vt* entfernen; (*take off*) abnehmen; (*take out*) herausnehmen
render /'rendə(r)/ *vt* machen; erweisen (*service*); (*translate*) wiedergeben; (*Mus*) vortragen
renegade /'renɪgeɪd/ *n* Abtrünnige(r) *m*/*f*
renew /rɪ'nju:/ *vt* erneuern; verlängern (*contract*). **~al** *n* Erneuerung *f*; Verlängerung *f*
renounce /rɪ'naʊns/ *vt* verzichten auf (+ *acc*)
renovat|e /'renəveɪt/ *vt* renovieren. **~ion** *n* Renovierung *f*
renown /rɪ'naʊn/ *n* Ruf *m*. **~ed** *adj* berühmt
rent /rent/ *n* Miete *f* ● *vt* mieten; (*hire*) leihen; **~ [out]** vermieten; verleihen. **~al** *n* Mietgebühr *f*; Leihgebühr *f*
renunciation /rɪnʌnsɪ'eɪʃn/ *n* Verzicht *m*
re'open /ri:-/ *vt*/*i* wieder aufmachen
re'organize /ri:-/ *vt* reorganisieren
rep /rep/ *n* ☐ Vertreter *m*
repair /rɪ'peə(r)/ *n* Reparatur *f*; **in good/bad ~** in gutem/schlechtem Zustand ● *vt* reparieren
repatriat|e /ri:'pætrɪeɪt/ *vt* repatriieren
re'pay /ri:-/ *vt* (*pt*/*pp* **-paid**) zurückzahlen; **~ s.o. for sth** jdm etw zurückzahlen. **~ment** *n* Rückzahlung *f*
repeal /rɪ'pi:l/ *n* Aufhebung *f* ● *vt* aufheben
repeat /rɪ'pi:t/ *n* Wiederholung *f* ● *vt*/*i* wiederholen; **~ after me** sprechen Sie mir nach. **~ed** *adj* wiederholt
repel /rɪ'pel/ *vt* (*pt*/*pp* **repelled**) abwehren; (*fig*) abstoßen. **~lent** *adj* abstoßend
repent /rɪ'pent/ *vi* Reue zeigen. **~ance** *n* Reue *f*. **~ant** *adj* reuig
repercussions /ri:pə'kʌʃnz/ *npl* Auswirkungen *pl*
repertoire /'repətwɑ:(r)/, **repertory** *n* Repertoire *nt*
repetit|ion /repɪ'tɪʃn/ *n* Wiederholung *f*. **~ive** *adj* eintönig
re'place /rɪ-/ *vt* zurücktun; (*take the place of*) ersetzen; (*exchange*) austauschen. **~ment** *n* Ersatz *m*
'replay /ri:-/ *n* (*Sport*) Wiederholungsspiel *nt*; **[action] ~** Wiederholung *f*
replenish /rɪ'plenɪʃ/ *vt* auffüllen (*stocks*); (*refill*) nachfüllen
replica /'replɪkə/ *n* Nachbildung *f*
reply /rɪ'plaɪ/ *n* Antwort *f* (**to** auf + *acc*) ● *vt*/*i* (*pt*/*pp* **replied**) antworten
report /rɪ'pɔ:t/ *n* Bericht *m*; (*Sch*) Zeugnis *nt*; (*rumour*) Gerücht *nt*; (*of gun*) Knall *m* ● *vt* berichten; (*notify*) melden; **~ s.o. to the police** jdn anzeigen ● *vi* berichten (**on** über + *acc*); (*present oneself*) sich melden (**to** bei). **~er** *n* Reporter(in) *m*(*f*)
reprehensible /reprɪ'hensəbl/ *adj* tadelnswert
represent /reprɪ'zent/ *vt* darstellen; (*act for*) vertreten, repräsentieren. **~ation** *n* Darstellung *f*
representative /reprɪ'zentətɪv/ *adj* repräsentativ (**of** für) ● *n* Bevollmächtigte(r) *m*/(*f*); (*Comm*) Vertreter(in) *m*(*f*); (*Amer, Politics*)

Abgeordnete(r) *m/f*

repress /rɪ'pres/ *vt* unterdrücken. **~ion** *n* Unterdrückung *f*. **~ive** *adj* repressiv

reprieve /rɪ'pri:v/ *n* Begnadigung *f*; (*fig*) Gnadenfrist *f* ● *vt* begnadigen

reprimand /'reprɪmɑ:nd/ *n* Tadel *m* ● *vt* tadeln

'reprint¹ /ri:-/ *n* Nachdruck *m*

re'print² /ri:-/ *vt* neu auflegen

reprisal /rɪ'praɪzl/ *n* Vergeltungsmaßnahme *f*

reproach /rɪ'prəʊtʃ/ *n* Vorwurf *m* ● *vt* Vorwürfe *pl* machen (+ *dat*). **~ful** *adj* vorwurfsvoll

repro'duc|e /ri:-/ *vt* wiedergeben, reproduzieren ● *vi* sich fortpflanzen. **~tion** *n* Reproduktion *f*; (*Biology*) Fortpflanzung *f*

reptile /'reptaɪl/ *n* Reptil *nt*

republic /rɪ'pʌblɪk/ *n* Republik *f*. **~an** *adj* republikanisch ● *n* Republikaner(in) *m*(*f*)

repugnan|ce /rɪ'pʌgnəns/ *n* Widerwille *m*. **~t** *adj* widerlich

repuls|ion /rɪ'pʌlʃn/ *n* Widerwille *m*. **~ive** *adj* abstoßend, widerlich

reputable /'repjʊtəbl/ *adj* (*firm*) von gutem Ruf; (*respectable*) anständig

reputation /repjʊ'teɪʃn/ *n* Ruf *m*

request /rɪ'kwest/ *n* Bitte *f* ● *vt* bitten

require /rɪ'kwaɪə(r)/ *vt* (*need*) brauchen; (*demand*) erfordern; **be ~d to do sth** etw tun müssen. **~ment** *n* Bedürfnis *nt*; (*condition*) Erfordernis *nt*

re'sale /ri:-/ *n* Weiterverkauf *m*

rescue /'reskju:/ *n* Rettung *f* ● *vt* retten. **~r** *n* Retter *m*

research /rɪ'sɜ:tʃ/ *n* Forschung *f* ● *vt* erforschen; (*in media*) recherchieren. **~er** *n* Forscher *m*; (*for media*) Rechercheur *m*

resem|blance /rɪ'zembləns/ *n* Ähnlichkeit *f*. **~ble** *vt* ähneln (+ *dat*)

resent /rɪ'zent/ *vt* übel nehmen; einen Groll hegen gegen (*person*). **~ful** *adj* verbittert. **~ment** *n* Groll *m*

reservation /rezə'veɪʃn/ *n* Reservierung *f*; (*doubt*) Vorbehalt *m*; (*enclosure*) Reservat *nt*

reserve /rɪ'zɜ:v/ *n* Reserve *f*; (*for animals*) Reservat *nt*; (*Sport*) Reservespieler(in) *m*(*f*) ● *vt* reservieren; (*client:*) reservieren lassen; (*keep*) aufheben; sich (*dat*) vorbehalten (*right*). **~d** *adj* reserviert

reservoir /'rezəvwɑ:(r)/ *n* Reservoir *nt*

re'shuffle /ri:-/ *n* (*Pol*) Umbildung *f* ● *vt* (*Pol*) umbilden

residence /'rezɪdəns/ *n* Wohnsitz *m*; (*official*) Residenz *f*; (*stay*) Aufenthalt *m*

resident /'rezɪdənt/ *adj* ansässig (**in** in + *dat*); (*housekeeper, nurse*) im Haus wohnend ● *n* Bewohner(in) *m*(*f*); (*of street*) Anwohner *m*. **~ial** *adj* Wohn-

residue /'rezɪdju:/ *n* Rest *m*; (*Chemistry*) Rückstand *m*

resign /rɪ'zaɪn/ *vt* **~ oneself to** sich abfinden mit ● *vi* kündigen; (*from public office*) zurücktreten. **~ation** *n* Resignation *f*; (*from job*) Kündigung *f*; Rücktritt *m*. **~ed** *adj* resigniert

resilient /rɪ'zɪlɪənt/ *adj* federnd; (*fig*) widerstandsfähig

resin /'rezɪn/ *n* Harz *nt*

resist /rɪ'zɪst/ *vt/i* sich widersetzen (+ *dat*), (*fig*) widerstehen (+ *dat*). **~ance** *n* Widerstand *m*. **~ant** *adj* widerstandsfähig

r

resolut|e /ˈrezəluːt/ *adj* entschlossen. **~ion** *n* Entschlossenheit *f*; (*intention*) Vorsatz *m*; (*Pol*) Resolution *f*

resolve /rɪˈzɒlv/ *n* Entschlossenheit *f*; (*decision*) Beschluss *m* ● *vt* beschließen; (*solve*) lösen

resort /rɪˈzɔːt/ *n* (*place*) Urlaubsort *m*; **as a last ~** wenn alles andere fehlschlägt ● *vi* **~ to** (*fig*) greifen zu

resound /rɪˈzaʊnd/ *vi* widerhallen

resource /rɪˈsɔːs/ *n* **~s** *pl* Ressourcen *pl*. **~ful** *adj* findig

respect /rɪˈspekt/ *n* Respekt *m*, Achtung *f* (**for** vor + *dat*); (*aspect*) Hinsicht *f*; **with ~ to** in Bezug auf (+ *acc*) ● *vt* respektieren, achten

respect|able /rɪˈspektəbl/ *adj*, **-bly** *adv* ehrbar; (*decent*) anständig; (*considerable*) ansehnlich. **~ful** *adj* respektvoll

respective /rɪˈspektɪv/ *adj* jeweilig. **~ly** *adv* beziehungsweise

respiration /respəˈreɪʃn/ *n* Atmung *f*

respite /ˈrespaɪt/ *n* [Ruhe]pause *f*; (*delay*) Aufschub *m*

respond /rɪˈspɒnd/ *vi* antworten; (*react*) reagieren (**to** auf + *acc*)

r

response /rɪˈspɒns/ *n* Antwort *f*; Reaktion *f*

responsibility /rɪspɒnsɪˈbɪlətɪ/ *n* Verantwortung *f*; (*duty*) Verpflichtung *f*

responsib|le /rɪˈspɒnsəbl/ *adj* verantwortlich; (*trustworthy*) verantwortungsvoll. **~ly** *adv* verantwortungsbewusst

rest¹ /rest/ *n* Ruhe *f*; (*holiday*) Erholung *f*; (*interval & Mus*) Pause *f*; **have a ~** eine Pause machen; (*rest*) sich ausruhen ● *vt* ausruhen; (*lean*) lehnen (**on** an/auf + *acc*) ● *vi* ruhen; (*have a rest*) sich ausruhen

rest² *n* **the ~** der Rest; (*people*) die Übrigen *pl* ● *vi* **it ~s with you** es ist an Ihnen (**to** zu)

restaurant /ˈrest(ə)rɒnt/ *n* Restaurant *nt*, Gaststätte *f*

restful /ˈrestfl/ *adj* erholsam

restive /ˈrestɪv/ *adj* unruhig

restless /ˈrestlɪs/ *adj* unruhig

restoration /restəˈreɪʃn/ *n* (*of building*) Restaurierung *f*

restore /rɪˈstɔː(r)/ *vt* wiederherstellen; restaurieren (*building*)

restrain /rɪˈstreɪn/ *vt* zurückhalten; **~ oneself** sich beherrschen. **~ed** *adj* zurückhaltend. **~t** *n* Zurückhaltung *f*

restrict /rɪˈstrɪkt/ *vt* einschränken; **~ to** beschränken auf (+ *acc*). **~ion** *n* Einschränkung *f*; Beschränkung *f*. **~ive** *adj* einschränkend

ˈrest room *n* (*Amer*) Toilette *f*

result /rɪˈzʌlt/ *n* Ergebnis *nt*, Resultat *nt*; (*consequence*) Folge *f*; **as a ~** als Folge (**of** *gen*) ● *vi* sich ergeben (**from** aus); **~ in** enden in (+ *dat*); (*lead to*) führen zu

resume /rɪˈzjuːm/ *vt* wieder aufnehmen ● *vi* wieder beginnen

résumé /ˈrezʊmeɪ/ *n* Zusammenfassung *f*

resumption /rɪˈzʌmpʃn/ *n* Wiederaufnahme *f*

resurrect /rezəˈrekt/ *vt* (*fig*) wieder beleben. **~ion** *n* **the R ~ion** (*Relig*) die Auferstehung

resuscitat|e /rɪˈsʌsɪteɪt/ *vt* wieder beleben. **~ion** *n* Wiederbelebung *f*

retail /ˈriːteɪl/ *n* Einzelhandel *m* ● *adj* Einzelhandels- ● *adv* im Einzelhandel ● *vt* im Einzelhandel verkaufen ● *vi* **~ at** im Einzelhandel kosten. **~er** *n* Einzelhändler *m*

retain /rɪˈteɪn/ *vt* behalten

retaliat|e /rɪˈtælɪeɪt/ *vi* zurückschlagen. **~ion** *n* Vergeltung *f*; **in**

∼ion als Vergeltung

retarded /rɪ'tɑːdɪd/ *adj* zurückgeblieben

reticen|ce /'retɪsns/ *n* Zurückhaltung *f*. **∼t** *adj* zurückhaltend

retina /'retɪnə/ *n* Netzhaut *f*

retinue /'retɪnjuː/ *n* Gefolge *nt*

retire /rɪ'taɪə(r)/ *vi* in den Ruhestand treten; (*withdraw*) sich zurückziehen. **∼d** *adj* im Ruhestand. **∼ment** *n* Ruhestand *m*

retiring /rɪ'taɪərɪŋ/ *adj* zurückhaltend

retort /rɪ'tɔːt/ *n* scharfe Erwiderung *f*; (*Chemistry*) Retorte *f* ● *vt* scharf erwidern

re'trace /rɪ-/ *vt* **∼ one's steps** denselben Weg zurückgehen

re'train /riː-/ *vt* umschulen ● *vi* umgeschult werden

retreat /rɪ'triːt/ *n* Rückzug *m*; (*place*) Zufluchtsort *m* ● *vi* sich zurückziehen

re'trial /riː-/ *n* Wiederaufnahmeverfahren *nt*

retrieve /rɪ'triːv/ *vt* zurückholen; (*from wreckage*) bergen; (*Computing*) wieder auffinden

retrograde /'retrəgreɪd/ *adj* rückschrittlich

retrospect /'retrəspekt/ *n* **in ∼** rückblickend. **∼ive** *adj* rückwirkend; (*looking back*) rückblickend

return /rɪ'tɜːn/ *n* Rückkehr *f*; (*giving back*) Rückgabe *f*; (*Comm*) Ertrag *m*; (*ticket*) Rückfahrkarte *f*; (*Aviat*) Rückflugschein *m*; **by ∼ [of post]** postwendend; **in ∼** dafür; **in ∼ for** für; **many happy ∼s!** herzlichen Glückwunsch zum Geburtstag! ● *vt* zurückgehen/-fahren; (*come back*) zurückkommen ● *vt* zurückgeben; (*put back*) zurückstellen/-legen; (*send back*) zurückschicken

return ticket *n* Rückfahrkarte *f*; (*Aviat*) Rückflugschein *m*

reunion /riː'juːnɪən/ *n* Wiedervereinigung *f*; (*social gathering*) Treffen *nt*

reunite /riːjuː'naɪt/ *vt* wieder vereinigen

re'use *vt* wieder verwenden

rev /rev/ *n* (*Auto*, [!]) Umdrehung *f* ● *vt/i* **∼ [up]** den Motor auf Touren bringen

reveal /rɪ'viːl/ *vt* zum Vorschein bringen; (*fig*) enthüllen. **∼ing** *adj* (*fig*) aufschlussreich

revel /'revl/ *vi* (*pt/pp* **revelled**) **∼ in sth** etw genießen

revelation /revə'leɪʃn/ *n* Offenbarung *f*, Enthüllung *f*

revenge /rɪ'vendʒ/ *n* Rache *f*; (*fig & Sport*) Revanche *f* ● *vt* rächen

revenue /'revənjuː/ *n* [Staats]einnahmen *pl*

revere /rɪ'vɪə(r)/ *vt* verehren. **∼nce** *n* Ehrfurcht *f*

Reverend /'revərənd/ *adj* **the ∼ X** Pfarrer X; (*Catholic*) Hochwürden X

reverent /'revərənt/ *adj* ehrfürchtig

reversal /rɪ'vɜːsl/ *n* Umkehrung *f*

reverse /rɪ'vɜːs/ *adj* umgekehrt ● *n* Gegenteil *nt*; (*back*) Rückseite *f*; (*Auto*) Rückwärtsgang *m* ● *vt* umkehren; (*Auto*) zurücksetzen ● *vi* zurücksetzen

revert /rɪ'vɜːt/ *vi* **∼ to** zurückfallen an (+ *acc*)

review /rɪ'vjuː/ *n* Rückblick *m* (**of** auf + *acc*); (*re-examination*) Überprüfung *f*; (*Mil*) Truppenschau *f*; (*of book, play*) Kritik *f*, Rezension *f* ● *vt* zurückblicken auf (+ *acc*); überprüfen (*situation*); rezensieren (*book, play*). **∼er** *n* Kritiker *m*, Rezensent *m*

revis|e /rɪ'vaɪz/ *vt* revidieren; (*for*

exam) wiederholen. **~ion** *n* Revision *f*; Wiederholung *f*

revival /rɪ'vaɪvl/ *n* Wiederbelebung *f*

revive /rɪ'vaɪv/ *vt* wieder beleben; (*fig*) wieder aufleben lassen ● *vi* wieder aufleben

revolt /rɪ'vəʊlt/ *n* Aufstand *m* ● *vi* rebellieren ● *vt* anwidern. **~ing** *adj* widerlich, eklig

revolution /revə'lu:ʃn/ *n* Revolution *f*; (*Auto*) Umdrehung *f*. **~ary** *adj* revolutionär. **~ize** *vt* revolutionieren

revolve /rɪ'vɒlv/ *vi* sich drehen; **~ around** kreisen um

revolv|er /rɪ'vɒlvə(r)/ *n* Revolver *m*. **~ing** *adj* Dreh-

revue /rɪ'vju:/ *n* Revue *f*; (*satirical*) Kabarett *nt*

revulsion /rɪ'vʌlʃn/ *n* Abscheu *m*

reward /rɪ'wɔ:d/ *n* Belohnung *f* ● *vt* belohnen. **~ing** *adj* lohnend

re'write /ri:-/ *vt* (*pt* **rewrote**, *pp* **rewritten**) noch einmal [neu] schreiben; (*alter*) umschreiben

rhetoric /'retərɪk/ *n* Rhetorik *f*. **~al** *adj* rhetorisch

rheumatism /'ru:mətɪzm/ *n* Rheumatismus *m*, Rheuma *nt*

r

Rhine /raɪn/ *n* Rhein *m*

rhinoceros /raɪ'nɒsərəs/ *n* Nashorn *nt*, Rhinozeros *nt*

rhubarb /'ru:bɑ:b/ *n* Rhabarber *m*

rhyme /raɪm/ *n* Reim *m* ● *vt* reimen ● *vi* sich reimen

rhythm /'rɪðm/ *n* Rhythmus *m*. **~ic[al]** *adj*, **-ally** *adv* rhythmisch

rib /rɪb/ *n* Rippe *f*

ribbon /'rɪbən/ *n* Band *nt*; (*for typewriter*) Farbband *nt*

rice /raɪs/ *n* Reis *m*

rich /rɪtʃ/ *adj* (**-er, -est**) reich; (*food*) gehaltvoll; (*heavy*) schwer ● *n* **the ~** *pl* die Reichen; **~es** *pl* Reichtum *m*

ricochet /'rɪkəʃeɪ/ *vi* abprallen

rid /rɪd/ *vt* (*pt/pp* **rid**, *pres p* **ridding**) befreien (**of** von); **get ~ of** loswerden

riddance /'rɪdns/ *n* **good ~!** auf Nimmerwiedersehen!

ridden /'rɪdn/ *see* **ride**

riddle /'rɪdl/ *n* Rätsel *nt*

riddled /'rɪdld/ *adj* **~ with** durchlöchert mit

ride /raɪd/ *n* Ritt *m*; (*in vehicle*) Fahrt *f*; **take s.o. for a ~** [!] jdn reinlegen ● *v* (*pt* **rode**, *pp* **ridden**) ● *vt* reiten (*horse*); fahren mit (*bicycle*) ● *vi* reiten; (*in vehicle*) fahren. **~r** *n* Reiter(in) *m*(*f*); (*on bicycle*) Fahrer(in) *m*(*f*)

ridge /rɪdʒ/ *n* Erhebung *f*; (*on roof*) First *m*; (*of mountain*) Grat *m*, Kamm *m*

ridicule /'rɪdɪkju:l/ *n* Spott *m* ● *vt* verspotten, spotten über (+ *acc*)

ridiculous /rɪ'dɪkjʊləs/ *adj* lächerlich

riding /'raɪdɪŋ/ *n* Reiten *nt* ● *attrib* Reit-

riff-raff /'rɪfræf/ *n* Gesindel *nt*

rifle /'raɪfl/ *n* Gewehr *nt* ● *vt* plündern; **~ through** durchwühlen

rift /rɪft/ *n* Spalt *m*; (*fig*) Riss *m*

rig /rɪg/ *n* Ölbohrturm *m*; (*at sea*) Bohrinsel *f* ● *vt* (*pt/pp* **rigged**) **~ out** ausrüsten; **~ up** aufbauen

right /raɪt/ *adj* richtig; (*not left*) rechte(r,s); **be ~** (*person:*) Recht haben; (*clock:*) richtig gehen; **put ~** wieder in Ordnung bringen; (*fig*) richtig stellen; **that's ~!** das stimmt! ● *adv* richtig; (*directly*) direkt; (*completely*) ganz; (*not left*) rechts; (*go*) nach rechts; **~ away** sofort ● *n* Recht *nt*; (*not left*) rechte Seite *f*; **on the ~** rechts; **from/to**

the ~ von/nach rechts; **be in the ~** Recht haben; **by ~s** eigentlich; the R~ (*Pol*) die Rechte. **~ angle** *n* rechter Winkel *m*

rightful /'raɪtfl/ *adj* rechtmäßig

right-'handed *adj* rechtshändig

rightly /'raɪtlɪ/ *adv* mit Recht

right-'wing *adj* (*Pol*) rechte(r,s)

rigid /'rɪdʒɪd/ *adj* starr; (*strict*) streng. **~ity** *n* Starrheit *f*; Strenge *f*

rigorous /'rɪgərəs/ *adj* streng

rigour /'rɪgə(r)/ *n* Strenge *f*

rim /rɪm/ *n* Rand *m*; (*of wheel*) Felge *f*

rind /raɪnd/ *n* (*on fruit*) Schale *f*; (*on cheese*) Rinde *f*; (*on bacon*) Schwarte *f*

ring¹ /rɪŋ/ *n* Ring *m*; (*for circus*) Manege *f*; **stand in a ~** im Kreis stehen ● *vt* umringen

ring² *n* Klingeln *nt*; **give s.o. a ~** (*Teleph*) jdn anrufen ● *v* (*pt* **rang**, *pp* **rung**) ● *vt* läuten; **~ [up]** (*Teleph*) anrufen ● *vi* (*bells:*) läuten; (*telephone:*) klingeln. **~ back** *vt/i* (*Teleph*) zurückrufen

ring: ~leader *n* Rädelsführer *m*. **~ road** *n* Umgehungsstraße *f*

rink /rɪŋk/ *n* Eisbahn *f*

rinse /rɪns/ *n* Spülung *f*; (*hair colour*) Tönung *f* ● *vt* spülen

riot /'raɪət/ *n* Aufruhr *m*; **~s** *pl* Unruhen *pl*; **run ~** randalieren ● *vi* randalieren. **~er** *n* Randalierer *m*. **~ous** *adj* aufrührerisch; (*boisterous*) wild

rip /rɪp/ *n* Riss *m* ● *vt/i* (*pt/pp* **ripped**) zerreißen; **~ open** aufreißen. **~ off** *vt* 🅸 neppen

ripe /raɪp/ *adj* (**-r, -st**) reif

ripen /'raɪpn/ *vi* reifen ● *vt* reifen lassen

ripeness /'raɪpnɪs/ *n* Reife *f*

'rip-off *n* 🅸 Nepp *m*

ripple /'rɪpl/ *n* kleine Welle *f*

rise /raɪz/ *n* Anstieg *m*; (*fig*) Aufstieg *m*; (*increase*) Zunahme *f*; (*in wages*) Lohnerhöhung *f*; (*in salary*) Gehaltserhöhung *f*; **give ~ to** Anlass geben zu ● *vi* (*pt* **rose**, *pp* **risen**) steigen; (*ground:*) ansteigen; (*sun, dough:*) aufgehen; (*river:*) entspringen; (*get up*) aufstehen; (*fig*) aufsteigen (**to** zu). **~r** *n* **early ~r** Frühaufsteher *m*

rising /'raɪzɪn/ *adj* steigend; (*sun*) aufgehend ● *n* (*revolt*) Aufstand *m*

risk /rɪsk/ *n* Risiko *nt*; **at one's own ~** auf eigene Gefahr ● *vt* riskieren

risky /'rɪskɪ/ *adj* riskant

rite /raɪt/ *n* Ritus *m*

ritual /'rɪtjʊəl/ *adj* rituell ● *n* Ritual *nt*

rival /'raɪvl/ *adj* rivalisierend ● *n* Rivale *m*/Rivalin *f*. **~ry** *n* Rivalität *f*; (*Comm*) Konkurrenzkampf *m*

river /'rɪvə(r)/ *n* Fluss *m*

rivet /'rɪvɪt/ *n* Niete *f* ● *vt* [ver]nieten; **~ed by** (*fig*) gefesselt von

road /rəʊd/ *n* Straße *f*; (*fig*) Weg *m*

road: ~-map *n* Straßenkarte *f*. **~ safety** *n* Verkehrssicherheit *f*. **~side** *n* Straßenrand *m*. **~way** *n* Fahrbahn *f*. **~-works** *npl* Straßenarbeiten *pl*. **~worthy** *adj* verkehrssicher

roam /rəʊm/ *vi* wandern

roar /rɔː(r)/ *n* Gebrüll *nt*; **~s of laughter** schallendes Gelächter *nt* ● *vi* brüllen; (*with laughter*) schallend lachen. **~ing** *adj* (*fire*) prasselnd; **do a ~ing trade** 🅸 ein Bombengeschäft machen

roast /rəʊst/ *adj* gebraten, Brat-; **~ beef/pork** Rinder-/Schweinebraten *m* ● *n* Braten *m* ● *vt/i* braten; rösten (*coffee, chestnuts*)

rob /rɒb/ *vt* (*pt/pp* **robbed**) berau-

r

ben (**of** *gen*); ausrauben (*bank*). **~ber** *n* Räuber *m*. **~bery** *n* Raub *m*

robe /rəʊb/ *n* Robe *f*; (*Amer: bath-robe*) Bademantel *m*

robin /'rɒbɪn/ *n* Rotkehlchen *nt*

robot /'rəʊbɒt/ *n* Roboter *m*

robust /rəʊ'bʌst/ *adj* robust

rock[1] /rɒk/ *n* Fels *m*; **on the ~s** (*ship*) aufgelaufen; (*marriage*) kaputt; (*drink*) mit Eis

rock[2] *vt/i* schaukeln

rock[3] *n* (*Mus*) Rock *m*

rockery /'rɒkərɪ/ *n* Steingarten *m*

rocket /'rɒkɪt/ *n* Rakete *f*

rocking: ~-chair *n* Schaukelstuhl *m*. **~-horse** *n* Schaukelpferd *nt*

rocky /'rɒkɪ/ *adj* felsig; (*unsteady*) wackelig

rod /rɒd/ *n* Stab *m*; (*stick*) Rute *f*; (*for fishing*) Angel[rute] *f*

rode /rəʊd/ *see* **ride**

rodent /'rəʊdnt/ *n* Nagetier *nt*

rogue /rəʊg/ *n* Gauner *m*

role /rəʊl/ *n* Rolle *f*

roll /rəʊl/ *n* Rolle *f*; (*bread*) Brötchen *nt*; (*list*) Liste *f*; (*of drum*) Wirbel *m* ●*vi* rollen; **be ~ing in money** 🅸 Geld wie Heu haben ●*vt* rollen; walzen (*lawn*); ausrollen (*pastry*). **~ over** *vi* sich auf die andere Seite rollen. **~ up** *vt* aufrollen; hochkrempeln (*sleeves*) ●*vi* 🅸 auftauchen

roller /'rəʊlə(r)/ *n* Rolle *f*; (*lawn, road*) Walze *f*; (*hair*) Lockenwickler *m*. **~ blind** *n* Rollo *nt*. **R~blades®** *npl* Rollerblades® *mpl*. **~-coaster** *n* Berg-und-Talbahn *f*. **~-skate** *n* Rollschuh *m*

'rolling-pin *n* Teigrolle *f*

Roman /'rəʊmən/ *adj* römisch ●*n* Römer(in) *m(f)*

romance /rə'mæns/ *n* Romantik *f*; (*love-affair*) Romanze *f*; (*book*) Liebesgeschichte *f*

Romania /rəʊ'meɪnɪə/ *n* Rumänien *nt*. **~n** *adj* rumänisch ●*n* Rumäne *m*/-nin *f*

romantic /rəʊ'mæntɪk/ *adj*, **-ally** *adv* romantisch. **~ism** *n* Romantik *f*

Rome /rəʊm/ *n* Rom *nt*

romp /rɒmp/ *vi* [herum]tollen

roof /ru:f/ *n* Dach *nt*; (*of mouth*) Gaumen *m* ●*vt* **~ [over]** überdachen. **~-top** *n* Dach *nt*

rook /rʊk/ *n* Saatkrähe *f*; (*Chess*) Turm *m*

room /ru:m/ *n* Zimmer *nt*; (*for functions*) Saal *m*; (*space*) Platz *m*. **~y** *adj* geräumig

roost /ru:st/ *n* Hühnerstange *f*

root[1] /ru:t/ *n* Wurzel *f*; **take ~** anwachsen ●*vi* Wurzeln schlagen. **~ out** *vt* (*fig*) ausrotten

root[2] *vi* **~ about** wühlen; **~ for s.o.** 🅸 für jdn sein

rope /rəʊp/ *n* Seil *nt*; **know the ~s** 🅸 sich auskennen. **~ in** *vt* 🅸 einspannen

rose[1] /rəʊz/ *n* Rose *f*; (*of watering-can*) Brause *f*

rose[2] *see* **rise**

rostrum /'rɒstrəm/ *n* Podium *nt*

rosy /'rəʊzɪ/ *adj* rosig

rot /rɒt/ *n* Fäulnis *f*; (🅸: *nonsense*) Quatsch *m* ●*vi* (*pt/pp* **rotted**) [ver-]faulen

rota /'rəʊtə/ *n* Dienstplan *m*

rotary /'rəʊtərɪ/ *adj* Dreh-; (*Techn*) Rotations-

rotat|e /rəʊ'teɪt/ *vt* drehen ●*vi* sich drehen; (*Techn*) rotieren. **~ion** *n* Drehung *f*; **in ~ion** im Wechsel

rote /rəʊt/ *n* **by ~** auswendig

rotten /'rɒtn/ *adj* faul; 🅸 mies; (*person*) fies

rough /rʌf/ *adj* (**-er, -est**) rau; (*uneven*) uneben; (*coarse, not gentle*) grob; (*brutal*) roh; (*turbulent*) stürmisch; (*approximate*) ungefähr ● *adv* **sleep ~** im Freien übernachten ● *vt* **~ it** primitiv leben. **~ out** *vt* im Groben entwerfen

roughage /ˈrʌfɪdʒ/ *n* Ballaststoffe *pl*

rough ˈdraft *n* grober Entwurf *m*

rough|ly /ˈrʌflɪ/ *adv* (*see* **rough**) rau; grob; roh; ungefähr. **~ness** *n* Rauheit *f*

ˈrough paper *n* Konzeptpapier *nt*

round /raʊnd/ *adj* (**-er, -est**) rund ● *n* Runde *f*; (*slice*) Scheibe *f*; **do one's ~s** seine Runde machen ● *prep* um (+ *acc*); **~ the clock** rund um die Uhr ● *adv* **all ~** ringsherum; **ask s.o. ~** jdn einladen ● *vt* biegen um (*corner*). **~ off** *vt* abrunden. **~ up** *vt* aufrunden; zusammentreiben (*animals*); festnehmen (*criminals*)

roundabout /ˈraʊndəbaʊt/ *adj* **~ route** Umweg *m* ● *n* Karussell *nt*; (*for traffic*) Kreisverkehr *m*

round ˈtrip *n* Rundreise *f*

rous|e /raʊz/ *vt* wecken; (*fig*) erregen. **~ing** *adj* mitreißend

route /ru:t/ *n* Route *f*; (*of bus*) Linie *f*

routine /ru:ˈti:n/ *adj* routinemäßig ● *n* Routine *f*; (*Theat*) Nummer *f*

row[1] /rəʊ/ *n* (*line*) Reihe *f*

row[2] *vt/i* rudern

row[3] /raʊ/ *n* 🄸 Krach *m* ● *vi* 🄸 sich streiten

rowdy /ˈraʊdɪ/ *adj* laut

rowing boat /ˈrəʊɪŋ-/ *n* Ruderboot *nt*

royal /rɔɪəl/ *adj* königlich

royalt|y /ˈrɔɪəltɪ/ *n* Königtum *nt*; (*persons*) Mitglieder *pl* der königlichen Familie; **-ies** *pl* (*payments*) Tantiemen *pl*

RSI *abbr* (**repetitive strain injury**) chronisches Überlastungssyndrom *nt*

rub /rʌb/ *vt* (*pt/pp* **rubbed**) reiben; (*polish*) polieren; **don't ~ it in** 🄸 reib es mir nicht unter die Nase. **~ off** *vt* abreiben ● *vi* abgehen. **~ out** *vt* ausradieren

rubber /ˈrʌbə(r)/ *n* Gummi *m*; (*eraser*) Radiergummi *m*. **~ band** *n* Gummiband *nt*

rubbish /ˈrʌbɪʃ/ *n* Abfall *m*, Müll *m*; (🄸: *nonsense*) Quatsch *m*; (🄸: *junk*) Plunder *m*. **~ bin** *n* Abfalleimer *m*. **~ dump** *n* Abfallhaufen *m*; (*official*) Müllhalde *f*

rubble /ˈrʌbl/ *n* Trümmer *pl*

ruby /ˈru:bɪ/ *n* Rubin *m*

rudder /ˈrʌdə(r)/ *n* [Steuer]ruder *nt*

rude /ru:d/ *adj* (**-r, -st**) unhöflich; (*improper*) unanständig. **~ness** *n* Unhöflichkeit *f*

rudimentary /ru:dɪˈmentərɪ/ *adj* elementar; (*Biology*) rudimentär

ruffian /ˈrʌfɪən/ *n* Rüpel *m*

ruffle /ˈrʌfl/ *vt* zerzausen

rug /rʌg/ *n* Vorleger *m*, [kleiner] Teppich *m*; (*blanket*) Decke *f*

rugged /ˈrʌgɪd/ *adj* (*coastline*) zerklüftet

ruin /ˈru:ɪn/ *n* Ruine *f*; (*fig*) Ruin *m* ● *vt* ruinieren

rule /ru:l/ *n* Regel *f*; (*control*) Herrschaft *f*; (*government*) Regierung *f*; (*for measuring*) Lineal *nt*; **as a ~** in der Regel ● *vt* regieren, herrschen über (+ *acc*); (*fig*) beherrschen; (*decide*) entscheiden; ziehen (*line*) ● *vi* regieren, herrschen. **~ out** *vt* ausschließen

ruled /ru:ld/ *adj* (*paper*) liniert

ruler /ˈruːlə(r)/ *n* Herrscher(in) *m(f)*; (*measure*) Lineal *nt*

ruling /ˈruːlɪŋ/ *adj* herrschend; (*factor*) entscheidend; (*Pol*) regierend ● *n* Entscheidung *f*

rum /rʌm/ *n* Rum *m*

rumble /ˈrʌmbl/ *n* Grollen *nt* ● *vi* grollen; (*stomach:*) knurren

rummage /ˈrʌmɪdʒ/ *vi* wühlen; **~ through** durchwühlen

rumour /ˈruːmə(r)/ *n* Gerücht *nt* ● *vt* **it is ~ed that** es geht das Gerücht, dass

rump /rʌmp/ *n* Hinterteil *nt*. **~ steak** *n* Rumpsteak *nt*

run /rʌn/ *n* Lauf *m*; (*journey*) Fahrt *f*; (*series*) Serie *f*, Reihe *f*; (*Theat*) Laufzeit *f*; (*Skiing*) Abfahrt *f*; (*enclosure*) Auslauf *m*; (*Amer: ladder*) Laufmasche *f*; **~ of bad luck** Pechsträhne *f*; **be on the ~** flüchtig sein; **in the long ~** auf lange Sicht ● *v* (*pt* **ran**, *pp* **run**, *pres p* **running**) ● *vi* laufen; (*flow*) fließen; (*eyes:*) tränen; (*bus:*) verkehren; (*butter, ink:*) zerfließen; (*colours:*) [ab]färben; (*in election*) kandidieren ● *vt* laufen lassen; einlaufen lassen (*bath*); (*manage*) führen, leiten; (*drive*) fahren; eingehen (*risk*); (*Journalism*) bringen (*story*); **~ one's hand over sth** mit der Hand über etw (*acc*) fahren. **~ away** *vi* weglaufen. **~ down** *vi* hinunter-/herunterlaufen; (*clockwork:*) ablaufen; (*stocks:*) sich verringern ● *vt* (*run over*) überfahren; (*reduce*) verringern; (🅸: *criticize*) heruntermachen. **~ in** *vi* hinein-/hereinlaufen. **~ off** *vi* weglaufen ● *vt* abziehen (*copies*). **~ out** *vi* hinaus-/herauslaufen; (*supplies, money:*) ausgehen; **I've ~ out of sugar** ich habe keinen Zucker mehr. **~ over** *vt* überfahren. **~ up** *vi* hinauf-/herauflaufen; (*towards*) hinlaufen ● *vt* machen (*debts*); auflaufen lassen (*bill*); (*sew*) schnell nähen

ˈrunaway *n* Ausreißer *m*

run-ˈdown *adj* (*area*) verkommen

rung[1] /rʌŋ/ *n* (*of ladder*) Sprosse *f*

rung[2] *see* **ring**[2]

runner /ˈrʌnə(r)/ *n* Läufer *m*; (*Bot*) Ausläufer *m*; (*on sledge*) Kufe *f*. **~ bean** *n* Stangenbohne *f*. **~-up** *n* Zweite(r) *m/f*

running /ˈrʌnɪŋ/ *adj* laufend; (*water*) fließend; **four times ~** viermal nacheinander ● *n* Laufen *nt*; (*management*) Führung *f*, Leitung *f*; **be/not be in the ~** eine/keine Chance haben

runny /ˈrʌnɪ/ *adj* flüssig

run: ~-up *n* (*Sport*) Anlauf *m*; (*to election*) Zeit *f* vor der Wahl. **~way** *n* Start- und Landebahn *f*

rupture /ˈrʌptʃə(r)/ *n* Bruch *m* ● *vt/i* brechen

rural /ˈrʊərəl/ *adj* ländlich

ruse /ruːz/ *n* List *f*

rush[1] /rʌʃ/ *n* (*Bot*) Binse *f*

rush[2] *n* Hetze *f*; **in a ~** in Eile ● *vi* sich hetzen; (*run*) rasen; (*water:*) rauschen ● *vt* hetzen, drängen. **~-hour** *n* Hauptverkehrszeit *f*, Stoßzeit *f*

Russia /ˈrʌʃə/ *n* Russland *nt*. **~n** *adj* russisch ● *n* Russe *m*/Russin *f*; (*Lang*) Russisch *nt*

rust /rʌst/ *n* Rost *m* ● *vi* rosten

rustle /ˈrʌsl/ *vi* rascheln ● *vt* rascheln mit; (*Amer*) stehlen (*cattle*). **~ up** *vt* 🅸 improvisieren

ˈrustproof *adj* rostfrei

rusty /ˈrʌstɪ/ *adj* rostig

rut /rʌt/ *n* Furche *f*

ruthless /ˈruːθlɪs/ *adj* rücksichtslos. **~ness** *n* Rücksichtslosigkeit *f*

rye /raɪ/ *n* Roggen *m*

Ss

sabbath /'sæbəθ/ *n* Sabbat *m*
sabot|age /'sæbətɑ:ʒ/ *n* Sabotage *f* ● *vt* sabotieren
sachet /'sæʃeɪ/ *n* Beutel *m*; (*scented*) Kissen *nt*
sack *n* Sack *m*; **get the ~** ⓕ rausgeschmissen werden ● *vt* ⓕ rausschmeißen
sacred /'seɪkrɪd/ *adj* heilig
sacrifice /'sækrɪfaɪs/ *n* Opfer *nt* ● *vt* opfern
sacrilege /'sækrɪlɪdʒ/ *n* Sakrileg *nt*
sad /sæd/ *adj* (**sadder, saddest**) traurig: (*loss, death*) schmerzlich. **~den** *vt* traurig machen
saddle /'sædl/ *n* Sattel *m* ● *vt* satteln; **~ s.o. with sth** ⓕ jdm etw aufhalsen
sadist /'seɪdɪst/ *n* Sadist *m*. **~ic** *adj*, **-ally** *adv* sadistisch
sad|ly /'sædlɪ/ *adv* traurig; (*unfortunately*) leider. **~ness** *n* Traurigkeit *f*
safe /seɪf/ *adj* (**-r, -st**) sicher; (*journey*) gut; (*not dangerous*) ungefährlich; **~ and sound** gesund und wohlbehalten ● *n* Safe *m*. **~guard** *n* Schutz *m* ● *vt* schützen. **~ly** *adv* sicher; (*arrive*) gut
safety /'seɪftɪ/ *n* Sicherheit *f*. **~-belt** *n* Sicherheitsgurt *m*. **~-pin** *n* Sicherheitsnadel *f*. **~-valve** *n* [Sicherheits]ventil *nt*
sag /sæg/ *vi* (*pt/pp* **sagged**) durchhängen
saga /'sɑ:gə/ *n* Saga *f*; (*fig*) Geschichte *f*
said /sed/ *see* **say**
sail /seɪl/ *n* Segel *nt*; (*trip*) Segelfahrt *f* ● *vi* segeln; (*on liner*) fahren; (*leave*) abfahren (**for** nach) ● *vt* segeln mit
sailing /'seɪlɪŋ/ *n* Segelsport *m*. **~-boat** *n* Segelboot *nt*. **~-ship** *n* Segelschiff *nt*
sailor /'seɪlə(r)/ *n* Seemann *m*; (*in navy*) Matrose *m*
saint /seɪnt/ *n* Heilige(r) *m/f*. **~ly** *adj* heilig
sake /seɪk/ *n* **for the ~ of ...** um ... (*gen*) willen; **for my/your ~** um meinet-/deinetwillen
salad /'sæləd/ *n* Salat *m*. **~-dressing** *n* Salatsoße *f*
salary /'sælərɪ/ *n* Gehalt *nt*
sale /seɪl/ *n* Verkauf *m*; (*event*) Basar *m*; (*at reduced prices*) Schlussverkauf *m*; **for ~** zu verkaufen
sales|man *n* Verkäufer *m*. **~woman** *n* Verkäuferin *f*
saliva /sə'laɪvə/ *n* Speichel *m*
salmon /'sæmən/ *n* Lachs *m*
saloon /sə'lu:n/ *n* Salon *m*; (*Auto*) Limousine *f*; (*Amer: bar*) Wirtschaft *f*
salt /sɔ:lt/ *n* Salz *nt* ● *adj* salzig; (*water, meat*) Salz- ● *vt* salzen; (*cure*) pökeln; streuen (*road*). **~-cellar** *n* Salzfass *nt*. **~ 'water** *n* Salzwasser *nt*. **~y** *adj* salzig
salute /sə'lu:t/ *n* (*Mil*) Gruß *m* ● *vt/i* (*Mil*) grüßen
salvage /'sælvɪdʒ/ *n* (*Naut*) Bergung *f* ● *vt* bergen
salvation /sæl'veɪʃn/ *n* Rettung *f*; (*Relig*) Heil *nt*
same /seɪm/ *adj & pron* **the ~** der/die/das gleiche; (*pl*) die gleichen; (*identical*) der-/die-/dasselbe; (*pl*) dieselben ● *adv* **the ~** gleich; **all the ~** trotzdem
sample /'sɑ:mpl/ *n* Probe *f*; (*Comm*) Muster *nt* ● *vt* probieren; kosten (*food*)
sanatorium /sænə'tɔ:rɪəm/ *n*

Sanatorium *nt*

sanction /ˈsæŋkʃn/ *n* Sanktion *f* ● *vt* sanktionieren

sanctuary /ˈsæŋktjʊərɪ/ *n* (*Relig*) Heiligtum *nt*; (*refuge*) Zuflucht *f*; (*for wildlife*) Tierschutzgebiet *nt*

sand /sænd/ *n* Sand *m* ● *vt* **~ [down]** [ab]schmirgeln

sandal /ˈsændl/ *n* Sandale *f*

sand: ~bank *n* Sandbank *f*. **~paper** *n* Sandpapier *nt*. **~-pit** *n* Sandkasten *m*

sandwich /ˈsænwɪdʒ/ *n*; Sandwich *m* ● *vt* **~ed between** eingeklemmt zwischen

sandy /ˈsændɪ/ *adj* sandig; (*beach, soil*) Sand-; (*hair*) rotblond

sane /seɪn/ *adj* (**-r, -st**) geistig normal; (*sensible*) vernünftig

sang /sæŋ/ *see* **sing**

sanitary /ˈsænɪtərɪ/ *adj* hygienisch; (*system*) sanitär. **~ napkin** *n* (*Amer*), **~ towel** *n* [Damen]binde *f*

sanitation /sænɪˈteɪʃn/ *n* Kanalisation und Abfallbeseitigung *pl*

sanity /ˈsænətɪ/ *n* [gesunder] Verstand *m*

sank /sæŋk/ *see* **sink**

sap /sæp/ *n* (*Bot*) Saft *m* ● *vt* (*pt/pp* **sapped**) schwächen

sarcas|m /ˈsɑːkæzm/ *n* Sarkasmus *m*. **~tic** *adj*, **-ally** *adv* sarkastisch

sardine /sɑːˈdiːn/ *n* Sardine *f*

sash /sæʃ/ *n* Schärpe *f*

sat /sæt/ *see* **sit**

satchel /ˈsætʃl/ *n* Ranzen *m*

satellite /ˈsætəlaɪt/ *n* Satellit *m*. **~television** *n* Satellitenfernsehen *nt*

satin /ˈsætɪn/ *n* Satin *m*

satire /ˈsætaɪə(r)/ *n* Satire *f*

satirical /səˈtɪrɪkl/ *adj* satirisch

satirist /ˈsætərɪst/ *n* Satiriker(in) *m(f)*

satisfaction /sætɪsˈfækʃn/ *n* Befriedigung *f*; to **my ~** zu meiner Zufriedenheit

satisfactory /sætɪsˈfæktərɪ/ *adj*, **-ily** *adv* zufrieden stellend

satisf|y /ˈsætɪsfaɪ/ *vt* (*pp/pp* **-fied**) befriedigen; zufrieden stellen (*customer*); (*convince*) überzeugen; **be ~ied** zufrieden sein. **~ying** *adj* befriedigend; (*meal*) sättigend

satphone /ˈsætfəʊn/ *n* Satellitentelefon *nt*

saturate /ˈsætʃəreɪt/ *vt* durchtränken; (*Chemistry & fig*) sättigen

Saturday /ˈsætədeɪ/ *n* Samstag *m*

sauce /sɔːs/ *n* Soße *f*; (*cheek*) Frechheit *f*. **~pan** *n* Kochtopf *m*

saucer /ˈsɔːsə(r)/ *n* Untertasse *f*

saucy /ˈsɔːʃɪ/ *adj* frech

Saudi Arabia /saʊdɪəˈreɪbɪə/ *n* Saudi-Arabien *n*

sauna /ˈsɔːnə/ *n* Sauna *f*

saunter /ˈsɔːntə(r)/ *vi* schlendern

sausage /ˈsɒsɪdʒ/ *n* Wurst *f*

savage /ˈsævɪdʒ/ *adj* wild; (*fierce*) scharf; (*brutal*) brutal ● *n* Wilde(r) *m/f*. **~ry** *n* Brutalität *f*

save /seɪv/ *n* (*Sport*) Abwehr *f* ● *vt* retten (**from** vor + *dat*); (*keep*) aufheben; (*not waste*) sparen; (*collect*) sammeln; (*avoid*) ersparen; (*Sport*) verhindern (*goal*) ● *vi* **~ [up]** sparen

saver /ˈseɪvə(r)/ *n* Sparer *m*

saving /ˈseɪvɪŋ/ *n* (*see* **save**) Rettung *f*; Sparen *nt*; Ersparnis *f*; **~s** *pl* (*money*) Ersparnisse *pl*

savour /ˈseɪvə(r)/ *n* Geschmack *m* ● *vt* auskosten. **~y** *adj* würzig

saw[1] /sɔː/ *see* **see**[1]

saw[2] *n* Säge *f* ● *vt/i* (*pt* **sawed**, *pp* **sawn** *or* **sawed**) sägen

saxophone /ˈsæksəfəʊn/ *n* Saxophon *nt*

say /seɪ/ *n* Mitspracherecht *nt*; **have one's ~** seine Meinung sagen ● *vt/i* (*pt/pp* **said**) sagen; sprechen (*prayer*); **that is to ~** das heißt; **that goes without ~ing** das versteht sich von selbst. **~ing** *n* Redensart *f*

scab /skæb/ *n* Schorf *m*; (*pej*) Streikbrecher *m*

scaffolding /ˈskæfəldɪŋ/ *n* Gerüst *nt*

scald /skɔːld/ *vt* verbrühen

scale¹ /skeɪl/ *n* (*of fish*) Schuppe *f*

scale² *n* Skala *f*; (*Mus*) Tonleiter *f*; (*ratio*) Maßstab *m* ● *vt* (*climb*) erklettern. **~ down** *vt* verkleinern

scales /skeɪlz/ *npl* (*for weighing*) Waage *f*

scalp /skælp/ *n* Kopfhaut *f*

scamper /ˈskæmpə(r)/ *vi* huschen

scan /skæn/ *n* (*Med*) Szintigramm *nt* ● *v* (*pt/pp* **scanned**) ● *vt* absuchen; (*quickly*) flüchtig ansehen; (*Med*) szintigraphisch untersuchen

scandal /ˈskændl/ *n* Skandal *m*; (*gossip*) Skandalgeschichten *pl*. **~ize** *vt* schockieren. **~ous** *adj* skandalös

Scandinavia /skændɪˈneɪvɪə/ *n* Skandinavien *nt*. **~n** *adj* skandinavisch ● *n* Skandinavier(in) *m(f)*

scanner /ˈskænə(r)/ *n* Scanner *m*

scanty /ˈskæntɪ/ *adj*, **-ily** *adv* spärlich; (*clothing*) knapp

scapegoat /ˈskeɪp-/ *n* Sündenbock *m*

scar /skɑː(r)/ *n* Narbe *f*

scarc|e /skeəs/ *adj* (**-r, -st**) knapp; **make oneself ~e** 🅸 sich aus dem Staub machen. **~ely** *adv* kaum. **~ity** *n* Knappheit *f*

scare /skeə(r)/ *n* Schreck *m*; (*panic*) [allgemeine] Panik *f* ● *vt* Angst machen (+ *dat*); **be ~d** Angst haben (**of** vor + *dat*)

scarf /skɑːf/ *n* (*pl* **scarves**) Schal *m*; (*square*) Tuch *nt*

scarlet /ˈskɑːlət/ *adj* scharlachrot

scary /ˈskeərɪ/ *adj* unheimlich

scathing /ˈskeɪðɪŋ/ *adj* bissig

scatter /ˈskætə(r)/ *vt* verstreuen; (*disperse*) zerstreuen ● *vi* sich zerstreuen. **~ed** *adj* verstreut; (*showers*) vereinzelt

scatty /ˈskætɪ/ *adj* 🅸 verrückt

scene /siːn/ *n* Szene *f*; (*sight*) Anblick *m*; (*place of event*) Schauplatz *m*; **behind the ~s** hinter den Kulissen

scenery /ˈsiːnərɪ/ *n* Landschaft *f*; (*Theat*) Szenerie *f*

scenic /ˈsiːnɪk/ *adj* landschaftlich schön

scent /sent/ *n* Duft *m*; (*trail*) Fährte *f*; (*perfume*) Parfüm *nt*. **~ed** *adj* parfümiert

sceptic|al /ˈskeptɪkl/ *adj* skeptisch. **~ism** *n* Skepsis *f*

schedule /ˈʃedjuːl/ *n* Programm *nt*; (*of work*) Zeitplan *m*; (*timetable*) Fahrplan *m*; **behind ~** im Rückstand; **according to ~** planmäßig ● *vt* planen

scheme /skiːm/ *n* Programm *nt*; (*plan*) Plan *m*; (*plot*) Komplott *nt* ● *vi* Ränke schmieden

schizophrenic /skɪtsəˈfrenɪk/ *adj* schizophren

scholar /ˈskɒlə(r)/ *n* Gelehrte(r) *m/f*. **~ly** *adj* gelehrt. **~ship** *n* Gelehrtheit *f*; (*grant*) Stipendium *nt*

school /skuːl/ *n* Schule *f*; (*Univ*) Fakultät *f* ● *vt* schulen

school: ~boy *n* Schüler *m*. **~girl** *n* Schülerin *f*. **~ing** *n* Schulbildung *f*. **~master** *n* Lehrer *m*. **~mistress** *n* Lehrerin *f*. **~-teacher** *n* Lehrer(in) *m(f)*

scien|ce /ˈsaɪəns/ *n* Wissenschaft *f*. **~tific** *adj* wissenschaftlich. **~tist** *n*

S

Wissenschaftler(in) *m(f)*

scissors /ˈsɪzəz/ *npl* Schere *f*; **a pair of ~** eine Schere

scoff¹ /skɒf/ *vi* **~ at** spotten über (+ *acc*)

scoff² *vt* ⓘ verschlingen

scold /skəʊld/ *vt* ausschimpfen

scoop /sku:p/ *n* Schaufel *f*; (*Culin*) Portionierer *m*; (*story*) Exklusivmeldung *f* ● *vt* **~ out** aushöhlen; (*remove*) auslöffeln

scooter /sku:tə(r)/ *n* Roller *m*

scope /skəʊp/ *n* Bereich *m*; (*opportunity*) Möglichkeiten *pl*

scorch /skɔ:tʃ/ *vt* versengen. **~ing** *adj* glühend heiß

score /skɔ:(r)/ *n* [Spiel]stand *m*; (*individual*) Punktzahl *f*; (*Mus*) Partitur *f*; (*Cinema*) Filmmusik *f*; **on that ~** was das betrifft ● *vt* erzielen; schießen (*goal*); (*cut*) einritzen ● *vi* Punkte erzielen; (*Sport*) ein Tor schießen; (*keep score*) Punkte zählen. **~r** *n* Punktezähler *m*; (*of goals*) Torschütze *m*

scorn /skɔ:n/ *n* Verachtung *f* ● *vt* verachten. **~ful** *adj* verächtlich

Scot /skɒt/ *n* Schotte *m*/Schottin *f*

Scotch /skɒtʃ/ *adj* schottisch ● *n* (*whisky*) Scotch *m*

Scot|land /ˈskɒtlənd/ *n* Schottland *nt*. **~s, ~tish** *adj* schottisch

S

> **Scottish Parliament** Das schottische Parlament, dessen Mitglieder im *Holyrood Building* in der Hauptstadt Edinburgh zusammentreten. Es wurde 1999 (nach einer Volksabstimmung) eröffnet und verleiht Schottland eine größere Autonomie gegenüber dem britischen Parlament in London. Von den 129 schottischen Abgeordneten werden 73 direkt gewählt und 56 nach dem Verhältniswahlrecht bestimmt.

scoundrel /ˈskaʊndrl/ *n* Schurke *m*

scour /ˈskaʊə(r)/ *vt* (*search*) absuchen; (*clean*) scheuern

scout /skaʊt/ *n* (*Mil*) Kundschafter *m*; **[Boy] S~** Pfadfinder *m*

scowl /skaʊl/ *n* böser Gesichtsausdruck *m* ● *vi* ein böses Gesicht machen

scram /skræm/ *vi* ⓘ abhauen

scramble /ˈskræmbl/ *n* Gerangel *nt* ● *vi* klettern; **~ for** sich drängen nach. **~d ˈegg[s]** *n[pl]* Rührei *nt*

scrap¹ /skræp/ *n* (ⓘ: *fight*) Rauferei *f* ● *vi* sich raufen

scrap² *n* Stückchen *nt*; (*metal*) Schrott *m*; **~s** *pl* Reste; **not a ~** kein bisschen ● *vt* (*pt/pp* **scrapped**) aufgeben

ˈscrapbook *n* Sammelalbum *nt*

scrape /skreɪp/ *vt* schaben; (*clean*) abkratzen; (*damage*) [ver]schrammen. **~ through** *vi* gerade noch durchkommen. **~ together** *vt* zusammenkriegen

scrappy /ˈskræpɪ/ *adj* lückenhaft

ˈscrapyard *n* Schrottplatz *m*

scratch /skrætʃ/ *n* Kratzer *m*; **start from ~** von vorne anfangen; **not be up to ~** zu wünschen übrig lassen ● *vt/i* kratzen; (*damage*) zerkratzen

scrawl /skrɔ:l/ *n* Gekrakel *nt* ● *vt/i* krakeln

scream /skri:m/ *n* Schrei *m* ● *vt/i* schreien

screech /skri:tʃ/ *n* Kreischen *nt* ● *vt/i* kreischen

screen /skri:n/ *n* Schirm *m*; (*Cinema*) Leinwand *f*; (*TV*) Bildschirm *m* ● *vt* schützen; (*conceal*) verdecken; vorführen (*film*); (*examine*) überprüfen; (*Med*) untersuchen

screw /skru:/ *n* Schraube *f* ● *vt* schrauben. ~ **up** *vt* festschrauben; (*crumple*) zusammenknüllen; zusammenkneifen (*eyes*); (*sl: bungle*) vermasseln

'screwdriver *n* Schraubenzieher *m*

scribble /'skrɪbl/ *n* Gekritzel *nt* ● *vt/i* kritzeln

script /skrɪpt/ *n* Schrift *f*; (*of speech, play*) Text *m*; (*Radio, TV*) Skript *nt*; (*of film*) Drehbuch *nt*

scroll /skrəʊl/ *n* Rolle *f* ● *vt* ~ **up/down** nach oben/unten rollen. ~ **bar** *n* Rollbalken *m*

scrounge /skraʊndʒ/ *vt/i* schnorren. ~**r** *n* Schnorrer *m*

scrub[1] /skrʌb/ *n* (*land*) Buschland *nt*, Gestrüpp *nt*

scrub[2] *vt/i* (*pt/pp* **scrubbed**) schrubben

scruff /skrʌf/ *n* **by the** ~ **of the neck** beim Genick

scruffy /'skrʌfɪ/ *adj* vergammelt

scrum /skrʌm/ *n* Gedränge *nt*

scruple /'skru:pl/ *n* Skrupel *m*

scrupulous /'skru:pjʊləs/ *adj* gewissenhaft

scuffle /'skʌfl/ *n* Handgemenge *nt*

sculpt|or /'skʌlptə(r)/ *n* Bildhauer(in) *m*(*f*). ~**ure** *n* Bildhauerei *f*; (*piece of work*) Skulptur *f*, Plastik *f*

scum /skʌm/ *n* Schmutzschicht *f*; (*people*) Abschaum *m*

scurry /'skʌrɪ/ *vi* (*pt/pp* **-ied**) huschen

scuttle[1] /'skʌtl/ *vt* versenken (*ship*)

scuttle[2] *vi* schnell krabbeln

sea /si:/ *n* Meer *nt*, See *f*; **at** ~ auf See; **by** ~ mit dem Schiff. ~**food** *n* Meeresfrüchte *pl*. ~**gull** *n* Möwe *f*

seal[1] /si:l/ *n* (*Zool*) Seehund *m*

seal[2] *n* Siegel *nt* ● *vt* versiegeln; (*fig*) besiegeln. ~ **off** *vt* abriegeln

'sea-level *n* Meeresspiegel *m*

seam /si:m/ *n* Naht *f*; (*of coal*) Flöz *nt*

'seaman *n* Seemann *m*; (*sailor*) Matrose *m*

seance /'seɪɑ:ns/ *n* spiritistische Sitzung *f*

search /sɜ:tʃ/ *n* Suche *f*; (*official*) Durchsuchung *f* ● *vt* durchsuchen; absuchen (*area*) ● *vi* suchen (**for** nach). ~ **engine** *n* Suchmaschine *f*. ~**ing** *adj* prüfend, forschend. ~**light** *n* [Such]scheinwerfer *m*. ~**-party** *n* Suchmannschaft *f*

sea: ~**sick** *adj* seekrank. ~**side** *n* **at/to the** ~**side** am/ans Meer

season /'si:zn/ *n* Jahreszeit *f*; (*social, tourist, sporting*) Saison *f* ● *vt* (*flavour*) würzen. ~**al** *adj* Saison-. ~**ing** *n* Gewürze *pl*

'season ticket *n* Dauerkarte *f*

seat /si:t/ *n* Sitz *m*; (*place*) Sitzplatz *m*; (*bottom*) Hintern *m*; **take a** ~ Platz nehmen ● *vt* setzen; (*have seats for*) Sitzplätze bieten (+ *dat*); **remain** ~**ed** sitzen bleiben. ~**-belt** *n* Sicherheitsgurt *m*; **fasten one's** ~**-belt** sich anschnallen

sea: ~**weed** *n* [See]tang *m*. ~**worthy** *adj* seetüchtig

seclu|ded /sɪ'klu:dɪd/ *adj* abgelegen. ~**sion** *n* Zurückgezogenheit *f*

second /'sekənd/ *adj* zweite(r,s); **on** ~ **thoughts** nach weiterer Überlegung ● *n* Sekunde *f*; (*Sport*) Sekundant *m*; ~**s** *pl* (*goods*) Waren zweiter Wahl ● *adv* (*in race*) an zweiter Stelle ● *vt* unterstützen (*proposal*)

secondary /'sekəndrɪ/ *adj* zweitrangig; (*Phys*) Sekundär-. ~ **school** *n* höhere Schule *f*

second: ~**-best** *adj* zweitbeste(r,s). ~ **'class** *adv* (*travel, send*) zweiter Klasse. **~-class** *adj* zweitklassig

'second hand *n* (*on clock*) Sekundenzeiger *m*

second-'hand *adj* gebraucht • *adv* aus zweiter Hand

secondly /'sekəndlɪ/ *adv* zweitens

second-'rate *adj* zweitklassig

secrecy /'si:krəsɪ/ *n* Heimlichkeit *f*

secret /'si:krɪt/ *adj* geheim; (*agent, police*) Geheim-; (*drinker, lover*) heimlich • *n* Geheimnis *nt*

secretarial /sekrə'teərɪəl/ *adj* Sekretärinnen-; (*work, staff*) Sekretariats-

secretary /'sekrətərɪ/ *n* Sekretär(in) *m*(*f*)

secretive /'si:krətɪv/ *adj* geheimtuerisch

secretly /'si:krɪtlɪ/ *adv* heimlich

sect /sekt/ *n* Sekte *f*

section /'sekʃn/ *n* Teil *m*; (*of text*) Abschnitt *m*; (*of firm*) Abteilung *f*; (*of organization*) Sektion *f*

sector /'sektə(r)/ *n* Sektor *m*

secular /'sekjʊlə(r)/ *adj* weltlich

secure /sɪ'kjʊə(r)/ *adj* sicher; (*firm*) fest; (*emotionally*) geborgen • *vt* sichern; (*fasten*) festmachen; (*obtain*) sich (*dat*) sichern

securit|y /sɪ'kjʊərətɪ/ *n* Sicherheit *f*; (*emotional*) Geborgenheit *f*; **~ies** *pl* Wertpapiere *pl*

sedan /sɪ'dæn/ *n* (*Amer*) Limousine *f*

sedate /sɪ'deɪt/ *adj* gesetzt

sedative /'sedətɪv/ *adj* beruhigend • *n* Beruhigungsmittel *nt*

sediment /'sedɪmənt/ *n* [Boden]satz *m*

seduce /sɪ'dju:s/ *vt* verführen

seduct|ion /sɪ'dʌkʃn/ *n* Verführung *f*. **~ive** *adj* verführerisch

see /si:/ *v* (*pt* **saw**, *pp* **seen**) • *vt* sehen; (*understand*) einsehen; (*imagine*) sich (*dat*) vorstellen; (*escort*) begleiten; **go and ~** nachsehen; (*visit*) besuchen; **~ you later!** bis nachher! **~ing that** da • *vi* sehen; (*check*) nachsehen; **~ about** sich kümmern um. **~ off** *vt* verabschieden; (*chase away*) vertreiben. **~ through** *vt* (*fig*) durchschauen (*person*)

seed /si:d/ *n* Samen *m*; (*of grape*) Kern *m*; (*fig*) Saat *f*; (*Tennis*) gesetzter Spieler *m*; **go to ~** Samen bilden; (*fig*) herunterkommen. **~ed** *adj* (*Tennis*) gesetzt

seedy /'si:dɪ/ *adj* schäbig; (*area*) heruntergekommen

seek /si:k/ *vt* (*pt*/*pp* **sought**) suchen

seem /si:m/ *vi* scheinen

seen /si:n/ *see* **see**[1]

seep /si:p/ *vi* sickern

seethe /si:ð/ *vi* **~ with anger** vor Wut schäumen

'see-through *adj* durchsichtig

segment /'segmənt/ *n* Teil *m*; (*of worm*) Segment *nt*; (*of orange*) Spalte *f*

segregat|e /'segrɪgeɪt/ *vt* trennen. **~ion** *n* Trennung *f*

seize /si:z/ *vt* ergreifen; (*Jur*) beschlagnahmen; **~ s.o. by the arm** jdn am Arm packen. **~ up** *vi* (*Techn*) sich festfressen

seldom /'seldəm/ *adv* selten

select /sɪ'lekt/ *adj* ausgewählt; (*exclusive*) exklusiv • *vt* auswählen; aufstellen (*team*). **~ion** *n* Auswahl *f*

self /self/ *n* (*pl* **selves**) Ich *nt*

self: ~-as'surance *n* Selbstsicherheit *f*. **~-as'sured** *adj* selbstsicher. **~-'catering** *n* Selbstversorgung *f*. **~-'centred** *adj* egozentrisch. **~-'confidence** *n* Selbstbewusstsein *nt*, Selbstvertrauen *nt*. **~-'confi-**

dent *adj* selbstbewusst. **~-'conscious** *adj* befangen. **~-con'tained** *adj* (*flat*) abgeschlossen. **~-con'trol** *n* Selbstbeherrschung *f*. **~-de'fence** *n* Selbstverteidigung *f*; (*Jur*) Notwehr *f*. **~-em'ployed** selbstständig. **~-e'steem** *n* Selbstachtung *f*. **~-'evident** *adj* offensichtlich. **~-in'dulgent** *adj* maßlos. **~-'interest** *n* Eigennutz *m*

self|ish /'selfɪʃ/ *adj* egoistisch, selbstsüchtig. **~less** *adj* selbstlos

self: ~-'pity *n* Selbstmitleid *nt*. **~-'portrait** *n* Selbstporträt *nt*. **~-re'spect** *n* Selbstachtung *f*. **~-'righteous** *adj* selbstgerecht. **~-'sacrifice** *n* Selbstaufopferung *f*. **~-'satisfied** *adj* selbstgefällig. **~-'service** *n* Selbstbedienung *f* ● *attrib* Selbstbedienungs-. **~-suf'ficient** *adj* selbstständig

sell /sel/ *v* (*pt/pp* **sold**) ● *vt* verkaufen; **be sold out** ausverkauft sein ● *vi* sich verkaufen. **~ off** *vt* verkaufen

seller /'selə(r)/ *n* Verkäufer *m*

Sellotape® /'seləʊ-/, *n* ≈ Tesafilm® *m*

'sell-out *n* **be a ~** ausverkauft sein; (🄵: *betrayal*) Verrat sein

selves /selvz/ *see* **self**

semester /sɪ'mestə(r)/ n Semester *nt*

semi|breve /'semɪbriːv/ *n* (*Mus*) ganze Note *f*. **~circle** *n* Halbkreis *m*. **~'circular** *adj* halbkreisförmig. **~'colon** *n* Semikolon *nt*. **~-de'tached** *adj* & *n* **~-detached [house]** Doppelhaushälfte *f*. **~-'final** *n* Halbfinale *nt*

seminar /'semɪnɑː(r)/ *n* Seminar *nt*

senat|e /'senət/ *n* Senat *m*. **~or** *n* Senator *m*

send /send/ *vt/i* (*pt/pp* **sent**) schicken; **~ for** kommen lassen (*person*); sich (*dat*) schicken lassen (*thing*). **~-er** *n* Absender *m*. **~-off** *n* Verabschiedung *f*

senil|e /'siːnaɪl/ *adj* senil

senior /'siːnɪə(r)/ *adj* älter; (*in rank*) höher ● *n* Ältere(r) *m/f*; (*in rank*) Vorgesetzte(r) *m/f*. **~ 'citizen** *n* Senior(in) *m(f)*

seniority /siːnɪ'ɒrətɪ/ *n* höheres Alter *nt*; (*in rank*) höherer Rang *m*

sensation /sen'seɪʃn/ *n* Sensation *f*; (*feeling*) Gefühl *nt*. **~al** *adj* sensationell

sense /sens/ *n* Sinn *m*; (*feeling*) Gefühl *nt*; (*common ~*) Verstand *m*; **make ~** Sinn ergeben ● *vt* spüren. **~less** *adj* sinnlos; (*unconscious*) bewusstlos

sensible /'sensəbl/ *adj*, **-bly** *adv* vernünftig; (*suitable*) zweckmäßig

sensitiv|e /'sensətɪv/ *adj* empfindlich; (*understanding*) einfühlsam. **~ity** *n* Empfindlichkeit *f*

sensual /'sensjʊəl/ *adj* sinnlich. **-ity** *n* Sinnlichkeit *f*

sensuous /'sensjʊəs/ *adj* sinnlich

sent /sent/ *see* **send**

sentence /'sentəns/ *n* Satz *m*; (*Jur*) Urteil *nt*; (*punishment*) Strafe *f* ● *vt* verurteilen

sentiment /'sentɪmənt/ *n* Gefühl *nt*; (*opinion*) Meinung *f*; (*sentimentality*) Sentimentalität *f* **~al** *adj* sentimental. **~ality** *n* Sentimentalität *f*

sentry /'sentrɪ/ *n* Wache *f*

separable /'sepərəbl/ *adj* trennbar

separate¹ /'sepərət/ *adj* getrennt, separat

separat|e² /'sepəreɪt/ *vt* trennen ● *vi* sich trennen. **~ion** *n* Trennung *f*

September /sep'tembə(r)/ *n* September *m*

septic /'septɪk/ *adj* vereitert

sequel /'si:kwl/ *n* Folge *f*; (*fig*) Nachspiel *nt*

sequence /'si:kwəns/ *n* Reihenfolge *f*

serenade /serə'neɪd/ *n* Ständchen *nt* ● *vt* ~ **s.o.** jdm ein Ständchen bringen

seren|e /sɪ'ri:n/ *adj* gelassen. **~ity** *n* Gelassenheit *f*

sergeant /'sɑ:dʒənt/ *n* (*Mil*) Feldwebel *m*; (*in police*) Polizeimeister *m*

serial /'sɪərɪəl/ *n* Fortsetzungsgeschichte *f*; (*Radio, TV*) Serie *f*. **~ize** *vt* in Fortsetzungen veröffentlichen/(*Radio, TV*) senden

series /'sɪəri:z/ *n inv* Serie *f*

serious /'sɪərɪəs/ *adj* ernst; (*illness, error*) schwer. **~ness** *n* Ernst *m*

sermon /'sɜ:mən/ *n* Predigt *f*

servant /'sɜ:vənt/ *n* Diener(in) *m*(*f*)

serve /sɜ:v/ *n* (*Tennis*) Aufschlag *m* ● *vt* dienen (+ *dat*); bedienen (*customer, guest*); servieren (*food*); verbüßen (*sentence*); **it ~s you right!** das geschieht dir recht! ● *vi* dienen; (*Tennis*) aufschlagen. **~r** *n* (*Computing*) Server *m*

service /'sɜ:vɪs/ *n* Dienst *m*; (*Relig*) Gottesdienst *m*; (*in shop, restaurant*) Bedienung *f*; (*transport*) Verbindung *f*; (*maintenance*) Wartung *f*; (*set of crockery*) Service *nt*; (*Tennis*) Aufschlag *m*; **~s** *pl* Dienstleistungen *pl*; (*on motorway*) Tankstelle und Raststätte *f*; **in the ~s** beim Militär; **out of/in ~** (*machine:*) außer/in Betrieb ● *vt* (*Techn*) warten

service: ~ area *n* Tankstelle und Raststätte *f*. **~ charge** *n* Bedienungszuschlag *m*. **~man** *n* Soldat *m*. **~ station** *n* Tankstelle *f*

serviette /sɜ:vɪ'et/ *n* Serviette *f*

servile /'sɜ:vaɪl/ *adj* unterwürfig

session /'seʃn/ *n* Sitzung *f*

set /set/ *n* Satz *m*; (*of crockery*) Service *nt*; (*of cutlery*) Garnitur *f*; (*TV, Radio*) Apparat *m*; (*Math*) Menge *f*; (*Theat*) Bühnenbild *nt*; (*Cinema*) Szenenaufbau *m*; (*of people*) Kreis *m* ● *adj* (*ready*) fertig, bereit; (*rigid*) fest; (*book*) vorgeschrieben; **be ~ on doing sth** entschlossen sein, etw zu tun ● *v* (*pt/pp* **set**, *pres p* **setting**) ● *vt* setzen; (*adjust*) einstellen; stellen (*task, alarm clock*); festsetzen, festlegen (*date, limit*); aufgeben (*homework*); zusammenstellen (*questions*); [ein]fassen (*gem*); einrichten (*bone*); legen (*hair*); decken (*table*) ● *vi* (*sun:*) untergehen; (*become hard*) fest werden. **~ back** *vt* zurücksetzen; (*hold up*) aufhalten; (🅸: *cost*) kosten. **~ off** *vi* losgehen; (*in vehicle*) losfahren ● *vt* auslösen (*alarm*); explodieren lassen (*bomb*). **~ out** *vi* losgehen; (*in vehicle*) losfahren ● *vt* auslegen; (*state*) darlegen. **~ up** *vt* aufbauen; (*fig*) gründen

settee /se'ti:/ *n* Sofa *nt*, Couch *f*

setting /'setɪŋ/ *n* Rahmen *m*; (*surroundings*) Umgebung *f*

settle /'setl/ *vt* (*decide*) entscheiden; (*agree*) regeln; (*fix*) festsetzen; (*calm*) beruhigen; (*pay*) bezahlen ● *vi* sich niederlassen; (*snow, dust:*) liegen bleiben; (*subside*) sich senken; (*sediment:*) sich absetzen. **~ down** *vi* sich beruhigen; (*permanently*) sesshaft werden. **~ up** *vi* abrechnen

settlement /'setlmənt/ *n* (*see* **settle**) Entscheidung *f*; Regelung *f*; Bezahlung *f*; (*Jur*) Vergleich *m*; (*colony*) Siedlung *f*

settler /'setlə(r)/ *n* Siedler *m*

'set-up *n* System *nt*

seven /'sevn/ *adj* sieben. **~'teen** *adj* siebzehn. **~'teenth** *adj* siebzehnte(r,s)

seventh /'sevnθ/ *adj* siebte(r,s)
seventieth /'sevntɪɪθ/ *adj* siebzigste(r,s)
seventy /'sevntɪ/ *adj* siebzig
several /'sevrl/ *adj & pron* mehrere, einige
sever|e /sɪ'vɪə(r)/ *adj* (**-r, -st,**) **-ly** *adv* streng; (*pain*) stark; (*illness*) schwer. **~ity** *n* Strenge *f*; Schwere *f*
sew /səʊ/ *vt/i* (*pt* **sewed**, *pp* **sewn** *or* **sewed**) nähen
sewage /'suːɪdʒ/ *n* Abwasser *nt*
sewer /'suːə(r)/ *n* Abwasserkanal *m*
sewing /'səʊɪŋ/ *n* Nähen *nt*; (*work*) Näharbeit *f*. **~ machine** *n* Nähmaschine *f*
sewn /səʊn/ *see* **sew**
sex /seks/ *n* Geschlecht *nt*; (*sexuality, intercourse*) Sex *m*. **~ist** *adj* sexistisch
sexual /'seksjʊəl/ *adj* sexuell. **~ 'intercourse** *n* Geschlechtsverkehr *m*
sexuality /seksjʊ'ælətɪ/ *n* Sexualität *f*
sexy /'seksɪ/ *adj* sexy
shabby /'ʃæbɪ/ *adj* , **-ily** *adv* schäbig
shack /ʃæk/ *n* Hütte *f*
shade /ʃeɪd/ *n* Schatten *m*; (*of colour*) [Farb]ton *m*; (*for lamp*) [Lampen]schirm *m*; (*Amer: window-blind*) Jalousie *f* ● *vt* beschatten
shadow /'ʃædəʊ/ *n* Schatten *m* ● *vt* (*follow*) beschatten
shady /'ʃeɪdɪ/ *adj* schattig; ([!]: *disreputable*) zwielichtig
shaft /ʃɑːft/ *n* Schaft *m*; (*Techn*) Welle *f*; (*of light*) Strahl *m*; (*of lift*) Schacht *m*
shaggy /'ʃægɪ/ *adj* zottig
shake /ʃeɪk/ *n* Schütteln *nt* ● *v* (*pt* **shook**, *pp* **shaken**) ● *vt* schütteln; (*shock*) erschüttern; **~ hands with s.o.** jdm die Hand geben ● *vi* wackeln; (*tremble*) zittern. **~ off** *vt* abschütteln
shaky /'ʃeɪkɪ/ *adj* wackelig; (*hand, voice*) zittrig
shall /ʃæl/ *v aux* **we ~ see** wir werden sehen; **what ~ I do?** was soll ich machen?
shallow /'ʃæləʊ/ *adj* (**-er, -est**) seicht; (*dish*) flach; (*fig*) oberflächlich
sham /ʃæm/ *adj* unecht ● *n* Heuchelei *f* ● *vt* (*pt/pp* **shammed**) vortäuschen
shambles /'ʃæmblz/ *n* Durcheinander *nt*
shame /ʃeɪm/ *n* Scham *f*; (*disgrace*) Schande *f*; **be a ~** schade sein; **what a ~!** wie schade!
shame|ful /'ʃeɪmfl/ *adj* schändlich. **~less** *adj* schamlos
shampoo /ʃæm'puː/ *n* Shampoo *nt* ● *vt* schamponieren
shan't /ʃɑːnt/ = **shall not**
shape /ʃeɪp/ *n* Form *f*; (*figure*) Gestalt *f* ● *vt* formen (**into** zu). **~less** *adj* formlos; (*clothing*) unförmig
share /ʃeə(r)/ *n* [An]teil *m*; (*Comm*) Aktie *f* ● *vt/i* teilen. **~holder** *n* Aktionär(in) *m*(*f*)
shark /ʃɑːk/ *n* Hai[fisch] *m*
sharp /ʃɑːp/ *adj* (**-er, -est**) scharf; (*pointed*) spitz; (*severe*) heftig; (*sudden*) steil; (*alert*) clever; (*unscrupulous*) gerissen ● *adv* scharf; (*Mus*) zu hoch; **at six o'clock ~** Punkt sechs Uhr ● *n* (*Mus*) Kreuz *nt*. **~en** *vt* schärfen; [an]spitzen (*pencil*)
shatter /'ʃætə(r)/ *vt* zertrümmern; (*fig*) zerstören; **~ed** (*person:*) erschüttert; ([!]: *exhausted*) kaputt ● *vi* zersplittern
shave /ʃeɪv/ *n* Rasur *f*; **have a ~** sich rasieren ● *vt* rasieren ● *vi* sich rasieren. **~r** *n* Rasierapparat *m*

S

shawl /ʃɔːl/ *n* Schultertuch *nt*
she /ʃiː/ *pron* sie
shears /ʃɪəz/ *npl* [große] Schere *f*
shed[1] /ʃed/ *n* Schuppen *m*
shed[2] *vt* (*pt/pp* **shed**, *pres p* **shedding**) verlieren; vergießen (*blood, tears*); ~ **light on** Licht bringen in (+ *acc*)
sheep /ʃiːp/ *n inv* Schaf *nt*. ~**-dog** *n* Hütehund *m*
sheepish /ˈʃiːpɪʃ/ *adj* verlegen
sheer /ʃɪə(r)/ *adj* rein; (*steep*) steil; (*transparent*) hauchdünn
sheet /ʃiːt/ *n* Laken *nt*, Betttuch *nt*; (*of paper*) Blatt *nt*; (*of glass, metal*) Platte *f*
shelf /ʃelf/ *n* (*pl* **shelves**) Brett *nt*, Bord *nt*; (*set of shelves*) Regal *nt*
shell /ʃel/ *n* Schale *f*; (*of snail*) Haus *nt*; (*of tortoise*) Panzer *m*; (*on beach*) Muschel *f*; (*Mil*) Granate *f* ● *vt* pellen; enthülsen (*peas*); (*Mil*) [mit Granaten] beschießen. ~ **out** *vi* [!] blechen
ˈ**shellfish** *n inv* Schalentiere *pl*; (*Culin*) Meeresfrüchte *pl*
shelter /ˈʃeltə(r)/ *n* Schutz *m*; (*air-raid* ~) Luftschutzraum *m* ● *vt* schützen (**from** vor + *dat*) ● *vi* sich unterstellen. ~**ed** *adj* geschützt; (*life*) behütet
shelve /ʃelv/ *vt* auf Eis legen; (*abandon*) aufgeben
shelving /ˈʃelvɪŋ/ *n* (*shelves*) Regale *pl*
shepherd /ˈʃepəd/ *n* Schäfer *m* ● *vt* führen
sherry /ˈʃerɪ/ *n* Sherry *m*
shield /ʃiːld/ *n* Schild *m*; (*for eyes*) Schirm *m*; (*Techn & fig*) Schutz *m* ● *vt* schützen (**from** vor + *dat*)
shift /ʃɪft/ *n* Verschiebung *f*; (*at work*) Schicht *f* ● *vt* rücken; (*take away*) wegnehmen; (*rearrange*) umstellen; schieben (*blame*) (**on to** auf + *acc*) ● *vi* sich verschieben; ([!]: *rush*) rasen
shifty /ˈʃɪftɪ/ *adj* (*pej*) verschlagen
shimmer /ˈʃɪmə(r)/ *n* Schimmer *m* ● *vi* schimmern
shin /ʃɪn/ *n* Schienbein *nt*
shine /ʃaɪn/ *n* Glanz *m* ● *v* (*pt/pp* **shone**) ● *vi* leuchten; (*reflect light*) glänzen; (*sun:*) scheinen ● *vt* ~ **a light on** beleuchten
shingle /ˈʃɪŋgl/ *n* (*pebbles*) Kiesel *pl*
shiny /ˈʃaɪnɪ/ *adj* glänzend
ship /ʃɪp/ *n* Schiff *nt* ● *vt* (*pt/pp* **shipped**) verschiffen
ship: ~**building** *n* Schiffbau *m*. ~**ment** *n* Sendung *f*. ~**per** *n* Spediteur *m*. ~**ping** *n* Versand *m*; (*traffic*) Schifffahrt *f*. ~**shape** *adj & adv* in Ordnung. ~**wreck** *n* Schiffbruch *m*. ~**wrecked** *adj* schiffbrüchig. ~**yard** *n* Werft *f*
shirt /ʃɜːt/ *n* [Ober]hemd *nt*; (*for woman*) Hemdbluse *f*
shit /ʃɪt/ *n* (*vulgar*) Scheiße *f* ● *vi* (*pt/pp* **shit**) (*vulgar*) scheißen
shiver /ˈʃɪvə(r)/ *n* Schauder *m* ● *vi* zittern
shoal /ʃəʊl/ *n* (*fish*) Schwarm *m*
shock /ʃɒk/ *n* Schock *m*; (*Electr*) Schlag *m*; (*impact*) Erschütterung *f* ● *vt* einen Schock versetzen (+ *dat*); (*scandalize*) schockieren. ~**ing** *adj* schockierend; ([!]: *bad*) fürchterlich
shoddy /ˈʃɒdɪ/ *adj* minderwertig
shoe /ʃuː/ *n* Schuh *m*; (*of horse*) Hufeisen *nt* ● *vt* (*pt/pp* **shod**, *pres p* **shoeing**) beschlagen (*horse*)
shoe: ~**horn** *n* Schuhanzieher *m*. ~**-lace** *n* Schnürsenkel *m*. ~**-string** *n* **on a** ~**-string** [!] mit ganz wenig Geld
shone /ʃɒn/ *see* **shine**
shoo /ʃuː/ *vt* scheuchen ● *int* sch!

shook /ʃʊk/ *see* **shake**

shoot /ʃuːt/ *n* (*Bot*) Trieb *m*; (*hunt*) Jagd *f* ●*v* (*pt/pp* **shot**) ●*vt* schießen; (*kill*) erschießen; drehen (*film*) ●*vi* schießen. ~ **down** *vt* abschießen. ~ **out** *vi* (*rush*) herausschießen. ~ **up** *vi* (*grow*) in die Höhe schießen/(*prices:*) schnellen

shop /ʃɒp/ *n* Laden *m*, Geschäft *nt*; (*workshop*) Werkstatt *f*; **talk** ~ [!] fachsimpeln ●*vi* (*pt/pp* **shopped**, *pres p* **shopping**) einkaufen; **go** ~**ping** einkaufen gehen

shop: ~ **assistant** *n* Verkäufer(in) *m*(*f*). ~**keeper** *n* Ladenbesitzer(in) *m*(*f*). ~**-lifter** *n* Ladendieb *m*. ~**-lifting** *n* Ladendiebstahl *m*

shopping /ˈʃɒpɪŋ/ *n* Einkaufen *nt*; (*articles*) Einkäufe *pl*; **do the** ~ einkaufen. ~ **bag** *n* Einkaufstasche *f*. ~ **centre** *n* Einkaufszentrum *nt*. ~ **trolley** *n* Einkaufswagen *m*

shop-ˈwindow *n* Schaufenster *nt*

shore /ʃɔː(r)/ *n* Strand *m*; (*of lake*) Ufer *nt*

short /ʃɔːt/ (**er, -est**) kurz; (*person*) klein; (*curt*) schroff; **a** ~ **time ago** vor kurzem; **be** ~ **of ...** zu wenig ... haben; **be in** ~ **supply** knapp sein ●*adv* kurz; (*abruptly*) plötzlich; (*curtly*) kurz angebunden; **in** ~ kurzum; ~ **of** (*except*) außer; **go** ~ Mangel leiden

shortage /ˈʃɔːtɪdʒ/ *n* Mangel *m* (**of** an + *dat*); (*scarcity*) Knappheit *f*

short: ~**bread** *n* ≈ Mürbekekse *pl*. ~ **ˈcircuit** *n* Kurzschluss *m*. ~**coming** *n* Fehler *m*. ~ **ˈcut** *n* Abkürzung *f*

shorten /ˈʃɔːtn/ *vt* [ab]kürzen; kürzer machen (*garment*)

short: ~**hand** *n* Kurzschrift *f*, Stenographie *f*. ~ **list** *n* engere Auswahl *f*

short|ly /ˈʃɔːtlɪ/ *adv* in Kürze; ~**ly before/after** kurz vorher/danach. ~**ness** *n* Kürze *f*; (*of person*) Kleinheit *f*

shorts /ʃɔːts/ *npl* Shorts *pl*

short: ~**-ˈsighted** *adj* kurzsichtig. ~**-sleeved** *adj* kurzärmelig. ~ **ˈstory** *n* Kurzgeschichte *f*. ~**-ˈtempered** *adj* aufbrausend. ~**-term** *adj* kurzfristig. ~ **wave** *n* Kurzwelle *f*

shot /ʃɒt/ *see* **shoot** ●*n* Schuss *m*; (*pellets*) Schrot *m*; (*person*) Schütze *m*; (*Phot*) Aufnahme *f*; (*injection*) Spritze *f*; ([!]: *attempt*) Versuch *m*; **like a** ~ [!] sofort. ~**gun** *n* Schrotflinte *f*. ~**-put** *n* (*Sport*) Kugelstoßen *nt*

should /ʃʊd/ *modal verb* **you** ~ **go** du solltest gehen; **I** ~ **have seen him** ich hätte ihn sehen sollen; **I** ~ **like** ich möchte; **this** ~ **be enough** das müsste eigentlich reichen; **if he** ~ **be there** falls er da sein sollte

shoulder /ˈʃəʊldə(r)/ *n* Schulter *f* ●*vt* schultern; (*fig*) auf sich (*acc*) nehmen. ~**-blade** *n* Schulterblatt *nt*

shout /ʃaʊt/ *n* Schrei *m* ●*vt/i* schreien. ~ **down** *vt* niederschreien

shouting /ˈʃaʊtɪŋ/ *n* Geschrei *nt*

shove /ʃʌv/ *n* Stoß *m* ●*vt* stoßen; ([!]: *put*) tun ●*vi* drängeln. ~ **off** *vi* [!] abhauen

shovel /ˈʃʌvl/ *n* Schaufel *f* ●*vt* (*pt/pp* **shovelled**) schaufeln

show /ʃəʊ/ *n* (*display*) Pracht *f*; (*exhibition*) Ausstellung *f*, Schau *f*; (*performance*) Vorstellung *f*; (*Theat, TV*) Show *f*; **on** ~ ausgestellt ●*v* (*pt* **showed**, *pp* **shown**) ●*vt* zeigen; (*put on display*) ausstellen; vorführen (*film*) ●*vi* sichtbar sein; (*film:*) gezeigt werden. ~ **in** *vt* hereinführen. ~ **off** *vi* [!] angeben ●*vt* vorführen; (*flaunt*) angeben mit. ~ **up** *vi* [deutlich] zu sehen sein; ([!]: *ar-*

S

rive) auftauchen ● *vt* deutlich zeigen; ([!]: *embarrass*) blamieren

shower /ˈʃaʊə(r)/ *n* Dusche *f*; (*of rain*) Schauer *m*; **have a ~** duschen ● *vt* **~ with** überschütten mit ● *vi* duschen

ˈshow-jumping *n* Springreiten *nt*

shown /ʃəʊn/ *see* **show**

show: ~-off *n* Angeber(in) *m*(*f*). **~room** *n* Ausstellungsraum *m*

showy /ˈʃəʊɪ/ *adj* protzig

shrank /ʃræŋk/ *see* **shrink**

shred /ʃred/ *n* Fetzen *m*; (*fig*) Spur *f* ● *vt* (*pt/pp* **shredded**) zerkleinern; (*Culin*) schnitzeln. **~der** *n* Reißwolf *m*; (*Culin*) Schnitzelwerk *nt*

shrewd /ʃru:d/ *adj* (**-er, -est**) klug. **~ness** *n* Klugheit *f*

shriek /ʃri:k/ *n* Schrei *m* ● *vt/i* schreien

shrill /ʃrɪl/ *adj*, **-y** *adv* schrill

shrimp /ʃrɪmp/ *n* Garnele *f*, Krabbe *f*

shrink /ʃrɪŋk/ *vi* (*pt* **shrank**, *pp* **shrunk**) schrumpfen; (*garment:*) einlaufen; (*draw back*) zurückschrecken (**from** vor + *dat*)

shrivel /ˈʃrɪvl/ *vi* (*pt/pp* **shrivelled**) verschrumpeln

S

Shrove /ʃrəʊv/ *n* **~ˈTuesday** Fastnachtsdienstag *m*

shrub /ʃrʌb/ *n* Strauch *m*

shrug /ʃrʌg/ *n* Achselzucken *nt* ● *vt/i* (*pt/pp* **shrugged**) **~ [one's shoulders]** die Achseln zucken

shrunk /ʃrʌŋk/ *see* **shrink**

shudder /ˈʃʌdə(r)/ *n* Schauder *m* ● *vi* schaudern; (*tremble*) zittern

shuffle /ˈʃʌfl/ *vi* schlurfen ● *vt* mischen (*cards*)

shun /ʃʌn/ *vt* (*pt/pp* **shunned**) meiden

shunt /ʃʌnt/ *vt* rangieren

shut /ʃʌt/ *v* (*pt/pp* **shut**, *pres p* **shutting**) ● *vt* zumachen, schließen ● *vi* sich schließen; (*shop:*) schließen, zumachen. **~ down** *vt* schließen; stilllegen (*factory*) ● *vi* schließen. **~ up** *vt* abschließen; (*lock in*) einsperren ● *vi* [!] den Mund halten

shutter /ˈʃʌtə(r)/ *n* [Fenster]laden *m*; (*Phot*) Verschluss *m*

shuttle /ˈʃʌtl/ *n* (*textiles*) Schiffchen *nt*

shuttle service *n* Pendelverkehr *m*

shy /ʃaɪ/ *adj* (**-er, -est**) schüchtern; (*timid*) scheu. **~ness** *n* Schüchternheit *f*

siblings /ˈsɪblɪŋz/ *npl* Geschwister *pl*

Sicily /ˈsɪsɪlɪ/ *n* Sizilien *nt*

sick /sɪk/ *adj* krank; (*humour*) makaber; **be ~** (*vomit*) sich übergeben; **be ~ of sth** [!] etw satt haben; **I feel ~** mir ist schlecht

sick|ly /ˈsɪklɪ/ *adj* kränklich. **~ness** *n* Krankheit *f*; (*vomiting*) Erbrechen *nt*

side /saɪd/ *n* Seite *f*; **on the ~** (*as sideline*) nebenbei; **~ by ~** nebeneinander; (*fig*) Seite an Seite; **take ~s** Partei ergreifen (**with** für) ● *attrib* Seiten- ● *vi* **~ with** Partei ergreifen für

side: ~board *n* Anrichte *f*. **~-effect** *n* Nebenwirkung *f*. **~lights** *npl* Standlicht *nt*. **~line** *n* Nebenbeschäftigung *f*. **~-show** *n* Nebenattraktion *f*. **~-step** *vt* ausweichen (+ *dat*). **~walk** *n* (*Amer*) Bürgersteig *m*. **~ways** *adv* seitwärts

siding /ˈsaɪdɪŋ/ *n* Abstellgleis *nt*

siege /si:dʒ/ *n* Belagerung *f*; (*by police*) Umstellung *f*

sieve /sɪv/ *n* Sieb *nt* ● *vt* sieben

sift /sɪft/ *vt* sieben; (*fig*) durchsehen

sigh /saɪ/ *n* Seufzer *m* ● *vi* seufzen

sight /saɪt/ *n* Sicht *f*; (*faculty*) Sehvermögen *nt*; (*spectacle*) Anblick *m*; (*on gun*) Visier *nt*; **~s** *pl* Sehenswürdigkeiten *pl*; **at first ~** auf den ersten Blick; **lose ~ of** aus dem Auge verlieren; **know by ~** vom Sehen kennen ● *vt* sichten

'sightseeing *n* **go ~** die Sehenswürdigkeiten besichtigen

sign /saɪn/ *n* Zeichen *nt*; (*notice*) Schild *nt* ● *vt/i* unterschreiben; (*author, artist:*) signieren. **~ on** *vi* (*as unemployed*) sich arbeitslos melden; (*Mil*) sich verpflichten

signal /'sɪgnl/ *n* Signal *nt* ● *vt/i* (*pt/pp* **signalled**) signalisieren; **~ to s.o.** jdm ein Signal geben

signature /'sɪgnətʃə(r)/ *n* Unterschrift *f*; (*of artist*) Signatur *f*

significan|ce /sɪg'nɪfɪkəns/ *n* Bedeutung *f*. **~t** *adj* (*important*) bedeutend

signify /'sɪgnɪfaɪ/ *vt* (*pt/pp* **-ied**) bedeuten

signpost /'saɪn-/ *n* Wegweiser *m*

silence /'saɪləns/ *n* Stille *f*; (*of person*) Schweigen *nt* ● *vt* zum Schweigen bringen. **~r** *n* (*on gun*) Schalldämpfer *m*; (*Auto*) Auspufftopf *m*

silent /'saɪlənt/ *adj* still; (*without speaking*) schweigend; **remain ~** schweigen

silhouette /sɪlu:'et/ *n* Silhouette *f*; (*picture*) Schattenriss *m* ● *vt* **be ~d** sich als Silhouette abheben

silicon /'sɪlɪkən/ *n* Silizium *nt*

silk /sɪlk/ *n* Seide *f* ● *attrib* Seiden-

silky /'sɪlkɪ/ *adj* seidig

sill /ʃɪl/ *n* Sims *m & nt*

silly /'ʃɪlɪ/ *adj* dumm, albern

silver /'sɪlvə(r)/ *adj* silbern; (*coin, paper*) Silber- ● *n* Silber *nt*

silver: ~-plated *adj* versilbert. **~ware** *n* Silber *nt*

SIM card *n* SIM-Karte *f*

similar /'sɪmɪlə(r)/ *adj* ähnlich. **~ity** *n* Ähnlichkeit *f*

simmer /'sɪmə(r)/ *vi* leise kochen, ziehen ● *vt* ziehen lassen

simple /'sɪmpl/ *adj* (**-r, -st**) einfach; (*person*) einfältig. **~-'minded** *adj* einfältig

simplicity /sɪm'plɪsətɪ/ *n* Einfachheit *f*

simpli|fication /sɪmplɪfɪ'keɪʃn/ *n* Vereinfachung *f*. **~fy** *vt* (*pt/pp* **-ied**) vereinfachen

simply /'sɪmplɪ/ *adv* einfach

simulat|e /'sɪmjʊleɪt/ *vt* vortäuschen; (*Techn*) simulieren

simultaneous /sɪml'teɪnɪəs/ *adj* gleichzeitig

sin /sɪn/ *n* Sünde *f* ● *vi* (*pt/pp* **sinned**) sündigen

since /sɪns/

● *preposition*

····➤ seit (+ *dat*). **he's been living here since 1991** er wohnt* seit 1991 hier. **I had been waiting since 8 o'clock** ich wartete* [schon] seit 8 Uhr. **since seeing you** seit ich dich gesehen habe. **how long is it since your interview?** wie lange ist es seit deinem Vorstellungsgespräch?

● *adverb*

····➤ seitdem. **I haven't spoken to her since** seitdem habe ich mit ihr nicht gesprochen. **the house has been empty ever since** das Haus steht seitdem leer. **he has since remarried** er hat danach wieder geheiratet. **long since** vor langer Zeit

● *conjunction*

····➤ seit. **since she has been living in Germany** seit sie in Deutschland wohnt*. **since they**

had been in London seit sie in London waren*. **how long is it since he left?** wie lange ist es her, dass er weggezogen ist? **it's a year since he left** es ist ein Jahr her, dass er weggezogen ist

····➤ (*because*) da. **since she was ill, I had to do it** da sie krank war, musste ich es tun

! *Note the different tenses in German

sincere /sɪn'sɪə(r)/ *adj* aufrichtig; (*heartfelt*) herzlich. **~ly** *adv* aufrichtig; **Yours ~ly** Mit freundlichen Grüßen

sincerity /sɪn'serətɪ/ *n* Aufrichtigkeit *f*

sinful /'sɪnfl/ *adj* sündhaft

sing /sɪŋ/ *vt/i* (*pt* **sang**, *pp* **sung**) singen

singe /sɪndʒ/ *vt* (*pres p* **singeing**) versengen

singer /'sɪŋə(r)/ *n* Sänger(in) *m(f)*

single /'sɪŋgl/ *adj* einzeln; (*one only*) einzig; (*unmarried*) ledig; (*ticket*) einfach; (*room, bed*) Einzel- ● *n* (*ticket*) einfache Fahrkarte *f*; (*record*) Single *f*; **~s** *pl* (*Tennis*) Einzel *nt* ● *vt* **~out** auswählen

S

single: ~-handed *adj & adv* allein. **~ 'parent** *n* Alleinerziehende(r) *m/f*

singly /'sɪŋglɪ/ *adv* einzeln

singular /'sɪŋgjʊlə(r)/ *adj* eigenartig; (*Gram*) im Singular ● *n* Singular *m*

sinister /'sɪnɪstə(r)/ *adj* finster

sink /sɪŋk/ *n* Spülbecken *nt* ● *v* (*pt* **sank**, *pp* **sunk**) ● *vi* sinken ● *vt* versenken (*ship*); senken (*shaft*). **~ in** *vi* einsinken; ([!]: *be understood*) kapiert werden

sinner /'sɪnə(r)/ *n* Sünder(in) *m(f)*

sip /sɪp/ *n* Schlückchen *nt* ● *vt* (*pt/pp* **sipped**) in kleinen Schlucken trinken

siphon /'saɪfn/ *n* (*bottle*) Siphon *m*. **~ off** *vt* mit einem Saugheber ablassen

sir /sɜː(r)/ *n* mein Herr; **S~** (*title*) Sir; **Dear S~s** Sehr geehrte Herren

siren /'saɪrən/ *n* Sirene *f*

sister /'sɪstə(r)/ *n* Schwester *f*; (*nurse*) Oberschwester *f*. **~-in-law** *n* Schwägerin *f*

sit /sɪt/ *v* (*pt/pp* **sat**, *pres p* **sitting**) ● *vi* sitzen; (*sit down*) sich setzen; (*committee:*) tagen ● *vt* setzen; machen (*exam*). **~ back** *vi* sich zurücklehnen. **~ down** *vi* sich setzen. **~ up** *vi* [aufrecht] sitzen; (*rise*) sich aufsetzen; (*not slouch*) gerade sitzen

site /saɪt/ *n* Gelände *nt*; (*for camping*) Platz *m*; (*Archaeology*) Stätte *f*

sitting /'sɪtɪŋ/ *n* Sitzung *f*; (*for meals*) Schub *m*

situat|e /'sɪtjʊeɪt/ *vt* legen; **be ~ed** liegen. **~ion** *n* Lage *f*; (*circumstances*) Situation *f*; (*job*) Stelle *f*

six /sɪks/ *adj* sechs. **~teen** *adj* sechzehn. **~teenth** *adj* sechzehnte(r,s)

sixth /sɪksθ/ *adj* sechste(r,s)

sixtieth /'sɪkstɪɪθ/ *adj* sechzigste(r,s)

sixty /'sɪkstɪ/ *adj* sechzig

size /saɪz/ *n* Größe *f*

sizzle /'sɪzl/ *vi* brutzeln

skate /skeɪt/ *n* Schlittschuh *m* ● *vi* Schlittschuh laufen. **~board** *n* Skateboard *nt* ● *vi* Skateboard fahren. **~boarding** *n* Skateboardfahren *nt*. **~r** *n* Eisläufer(in) *m(f)*

skating /'skeɪtɪŋ/ *n* Eislaufen *nt*. **~-rink** *n* Eisbahn *f*

skeleton /'skelɪtn/ *n* Skelett *nt*. **~ 'key** *n* Dietrich *m*

sketch /sketʃ/ *n* Skizze *f*; (*Theat*) Sketch *m* ● *vt* skizzieren
sketchy /ˈsketʃɪ/ *adj*, **-ily** *adv* skizzenhaft
ski /ski:/ *n* Ski *m* ● *vi* (*pt/pp* **skied**, *pres p* **skiing**) Ski fahren *or* laufen
skid /skɪd/ *n* Schleudern *nt* ● *vi* (*pt/pp* **skidded**) schleudern
skier /ˈski:ə(r)/ *n* Skiläufer(in) *m*(*f*)
skiing /ˈski:ɪŋ/ *n* Skilaufen *nt*
skilful /ˈskɪlfl/ *adj* geschickt
skill /skɪl/ *n* Geschick *nt*. **~ed** *adj* geschickt; (*trained*) ausgebildet
skim /skɪm/ *vt* (*pt/pp* **skimmed**) entrahmen (*milk*)
skimp /skɪmp/ *vt* sparen an (+ *dat*)
skimpy /ˈskɪmpɪ/ *adj* knapp
skin /skɪn/ *n* Haut *f*; (*on fruit*) Schale *f* ● *vt* (*pt/pp* **skinned**) häuten; schälen (*fruit*)
skin: ~-deep *adj* oberflächlich. **~-diving** *n* Sporttauchen *nt*
skinny /ˈskɪnɪ/ *adj* dünn
skip¹ /skɪp/ *n* Container *m*
skip² *n* Hüpfer *m* ● *v* (*pt/pp* **skipped**) *vi* hüpfen; (*with rope*) seilspringen ● *vt* überspringen
skipper /ˈskɪpə(r)/ *n* Kapitän *m*
ˈskipping-rope *n* Sprungseil *nt*
skirmish /ˈskɜ:mɪʃ/ *n* Gefecht *nt*
skirt /skɜ:t/ *n* Rock *m* ● *vt* herumgehen um
skittle /ˈskɪtl/ *n* Kegel *m*
skive /skaɪv/ *vi* 🄸 blaumachen
skull /skʌl/ *n* Schädel *m*
sky /skaɪ/ *n* Himmel *m*. **~light** *n* Dachluke *f*. **~ marshal** *n* bewaffneter Flugbegleiter *m*. **~scraper** *n* Wolkenkratzer *m*
slab /slæb/ *n* Platte *f*; (*slice*) Scheibe *f*; (*of chocolate*) Tafel *f*
slack /slæk/ *adj* (**-er, -est**) schlaff, locker; (*person*) nachlässig; (*Comm*) flau ● *vi* bummeln
slacken /ˈslækn/ *vi* sich lockern; (*diminish*) nachlassen ● *vt* lockern; (*diminish*) verringern
slain /sleɪn/ *see* **slay**
slam /slæm/ *v* (*pt/pp* **slammed**) ● *vt* zuschlagen; (*put*) knallen 🄸; (🄸: *criticize*) verreißen ● *vi* zuschlagen
slander /ˈslɑ:ndə(r)/ *n* Verleumdung *f* ● *vt* verleumden
slang /slæŋ/ *n* Slang *m*. **~y** *adj* salopp
slant /slɑ:nt/ Schräge *f*; **on the ~** schräg ● *vt* abschrägen; (*fig*) färben (*report*) ● *vi* sich neigen
slap /slæp/ *n* Schlag *m* ● *vt* (*pt/pp* **slapped**) schlagen; (*put*) knallen 🄸 ● *adv* direkt
slapdash *adj* 🄸 schludrig
slash /slæʃ/ *n* Schlitz *m* ● *vt* aufschlitzen; [drastisch] reduzieren (*prices*)
slat /slæt/ *n* Latte *f*
slate /sleɪt/ *n* Schiefer *m* ● *vt* 🄸 heruntermachen; verreißen (*performance*)
slaughter /ˈslɔ:tə(r)/ *n* Schlachten *nt*; (*massacre*) Gemetzel *nt* ● *vt* schlachten; abschlachten (*men*)
Slav /slɑ:v/ *adj* slawisch ● *n* Slawe *m*/ Slawin *f*
slave /sleɪv/ *n* Sklave *m*/ Sklavin *f* ● *vi* **~ [away]** schuften
slavery /ˈsleɪvərɪ/ *n* Sklaverei *f*
slay /sleɪ/ *vt* (*pt* **slew**, *pp* **slain**) ermorden
sledge /sledʒ/ *n* Schlitten *m*
sleek /sli:k/ *adj* (**-er, -est**) seidig; (*well-fed*) wohlgenährt
sleep /sli:p/ *n* Schlaf *m*; **go to ~** einschlafen; **put to ~** einschläfern ● *v* (*pt/pp* **slept**) ● *vi* schlafen ● *vt* (*accommodate*) Unterkunft bieten für. **~er** *n* Schläfer(in) *m*(*f*); (*Rail*) Schlafwagen *m*; (*on track*)

Schwelle *f*

sleeping: ~-bag *n* Schlafsack *m*. **~-pill** *n* Schlaftablette *f*

sleep: ~less *adj* schlaflos. **~-walking** *n* Schlafwandeln *nt*

sleepy /ˈsliːpɪ/ *adj* , **-ily** *adv* schläfrig

sleet /sliːt/ *n* Schneeregen *m*

sleeve /sliːv/ *n* Ärmel *m*; (*for record*) Hülle *f*. **~less** *adj* ärmellos

sleigh /sleɪ/ *n* [Pferde]schlitten *m*

slender /ˈslendə(r)/ *adj* schlank; (*fig*) gering

slept /slept/ *see* **sleep**

slew *see* **slay**

slice /slaɪs/ *n* Scheibe *f* ● *vt* in Scheiben schneiden

slick /slɪk/ *adj* clever

slid|e /slaɪd/ *n* Rutschbahn *f*; (*for hair*) Spange *f*; (*Phot*) Dia *nt* ● *v* (*pt*/*pp* **slid**) ● *vi* rutschen ● *vt* schieben. **~ing** *adj* gleitend; (*door, seat*) Schiebe-

slight /slaɪt/ *adj* (**-er, -est**) leicht; (*importance*) gering; (*acquaintance*) flüchtig; (*slender*) schlank; **not in the ~est** nicht im Geringsten; **~ly better** ein bisschen besser ● *vt* kränken, beleidigen ● *n* Beleidigung *f*

slim /slɪm/ *adj* (**slimmer, slimmest**) schlank; (*volume*) schmal; (*fig*) gering ● *vi* eine Schlankheitskur machen

slim|e /slaɪm/ *n* Schleim *m*. **~y** *adj* schleimig

sling /slɪŋ/ *n* (*Med*) Schlinge *f* ● *vt* (*pt*/*pp* **slung**) [T] schmeißen

slip /slɪp/ *n* (*mistake*) Fehler *m*, [T] Patzer *m*; (*petticoat*) Unterrock *m*; (*paper*) Zettel *m*; **give s.o. the ~** [T] jdm entwischen; **~ of the tongue** Versprecher *m* ● *v* (*pt*/*pp* **slipped**) ● *vi* rutschen; (*fall*) ausrutschen; (*go quickly*) schlüpfen ● *vt* schieben; **~ s.o.'s mind** jdm entfallen. **~ away** *vi* sich fortschleichen. **~ up** *vi* [T] einen Schnitzer machen

slipper /ˈslɪpə(r)/ *n* Hausschuh *m*

slippery /ˈslɪpərɪ/ *adj* glitschig; (*surface*) glatt

slipshod /ˈslɪpʃɒd/ *adj* schludrig

ˈslip-up *n* [T] Schnitzer *m*

slit /slɪt/ *n* Schlitz *m* ● *vt* (*pt*/*pp* slit) aufschlitzen

slither /ˈslɪðə(r)/ *vi* rutschen

slog /slɒg/ *n* **[hard] ~** Schinderei *f* ● *vi* (*pt*/*pp* **slogged**) schuften

slogan /ˈsləʊgən/ *n* Schlagwort *nt*; (*advertising*) Werbespruch *m*

slop|e /sləʊp/ *n* Hang *m*; (*inclination*) Neigung *f* ● *vi* sich neigen. **~ing** *adj* schräg

sloppy /ˈslɒpɪ/ *adj* schludrig; (*sentimental*) sentimental

slosh /slɒʃ/ *vi* [T] schwappen

slot /slɒt/ *n* Schlitz *m*; (*TV*) Sendezeit *f* ● *v* (*pt*/*pp* **slotted**) ● *vt* einfügen ● *vi* sich einfügen (**in** in + *acc*)

ˈslot-machine *n* Münzautomat *m*; (*for gambling*) Spielautomat *m*

slouch /slaʊtʃ/ *vi* sich schlecht halten

slovenly /ˈslʌvnlɪ/ *adj* schlampig

slow /sləʊ/ *adj* (**-er, -est**) langsam; **be ~** (*clock*:) nachgehen; **in ~ motion** in Zeitlupe ● *adv* langsam ● *vt* verlangsamen ● *vi* **~ down, ~ up** langsamer werden. **~ness** *n* Langsamkeit *f*

sludge /slʌdʒ/ *n* Schlamm *m*

slug /slʌg/ *n* Nacktschnecke *f*

sluggish /ˈslʌgɪʃ/ *adj* träge

sluice /sluːs/ *n* Schleuse *f*

slum /slʌm/ *n* Elendsviertel *nt*

slumber /ˈslʌmbə(r)/ *n* Schlummer *m* ● *vi* schlummern

slump /slʌmp/ *n* Sturz *m* ● *vi* fallen; (*crumple*) zusammensacken;

(*prices:*) stürzen; (*sales:*) zurückgehen
slung /slʌŋ/ *see* **sling**
slur /slɜ:(r)/ *vt* (*pt/pp* **slurred**) undeutlich sprechen
slurp /slɜ:p/ *vt/i* schlürfen
slush /slʌʃ/ *n* [Schnee]matsch *m*; (*fig*) Kitsch *m*
slut /slʌt/ *n* Schlampe *f* ⊡
sly /slaɪ/ *adj* (**-er, -est**) verschlagen ● *n* **on the ~** heimlich
smack /smæk/ *n* Schlag *m*, Klaps *m* ● *vt* schlagen ● *adv* ⊡ direkt
small /smɔ:l/ *adj* (**-er, -est**) klein ● *adv* **chop up ~** klein hacken ● *n* **~ of the back** Kreuz *nt*
small: ~ ads *npl* Kleinanzeigen *pl*. **~ 'change** *n* Kleingeld *nt*. **~pox** *n* Pocken *pl*. **~ talk** *n* leichte Konversation *f*
smart /smɑ:t/ *adj* (**-er, -est**) schick; (*clever*) schlau, clever; (*brisk*) flott; (*Amer, fam: cheeky*) frech ● *vi* brennen
smarten /'smɑ:tn/ *vt* **~ oneself up** mehr auf sein Äußeres achten
smash /smæʃ/ *n* Krach *m*; (*collision*) Zusammenstoß *m*; (*Tennis*) Schmetterball *m* ● *vt* zerschlagen; (*strike*) schlagen; (*Tennis*) schmettern ● *vi* zerschmettern; (*crash*) krachen (**into** gegen). **~ing** *adj* ⊡ toll
smear /smɪə(r)/ *n* verschmierter Fleck *m*; (*Med*) Abstrich *m*; (*fig*) Verleumdung *f* ● *vt* schmieren; (*coat*) beschmieren (**with** mit); (*fig*) verleumden ● *vi* schmieren
smell /smel/ *n* Geruch *m*; (*sense*) Geruchssinn *m* ● *v* (*pt/pp* **smelt** *or* **smelled**) ● *vt* riechen; (*sniff*) riechen an (+ *dat*) ● *vi* riechen (**of** nach)
smelly /'smelɪ/ *adj* übel riechend
smelt /smelt/ *see* **smell**
smile /smaɪl/ *n* Lächeln *nt* ● *vi* lächeln; **~ at** anlächeln
smirk /smɜ:k/ *vi* feixen
smith /smɪθ/ *n* Schmied *m*
smock /smɒk/ *n* Kittel *m*
smog /smɒg/ *n* Smog *m*
smoke /sməʊk/ *n* Rauch *m* ● *vt/i* rauchen; (*Culin*) räuchern. **~less** *adj* rauchfrei; (*fuel*) rauchlos
smoker /'sməʊkə(r)/ *n* Raucher *m*; (*Rail*) Raucherabteil *nt*
smoking /'sməʊkɪŋ/ *n* Rauchen *nt*; **'no ~'** 'Rauchen verboten'
smoky /'sməʊkɪ/ *adj* verraucht; (*taste*) rauchig
smooth /smu:ð/ *adj* (**-er, -est**) glatt ● *vt* glätten. **~ out** *vt* glatt streichen
smother /'smʌðə(r)/ *vt* ersticken; (*cover*) bedecken; (*suppress*) unterdrücken
smoulder /'sməʊldə(r)/ *vi* schwelen
smudge /smʌdʒ/ *n* Fleck *m* ● *vt* verwischen ● *vi* schmieren
smug /smʌg/ *adj* (**smugger, smuggest**) selbstgefällig
smuggl|e /'smʌgl/ *vt* schmuggeln. **~er** *n* Schmuggler *m*. **~ing** *n* Schmuggel *m*
snack /snæk/ *n* Imbiss *m*. **~-bar** *n* Imbissstube *f*
snag /snæg/ *n* Schwierigkeit *f*, ⊡ Haken *m*
snail /sneɪl/ *n* Schnecke *f*; **at a ~'s pace** im Schneckentempo
snake /sneɪk/ *n* Schlange *f*
snap /snæp/ *n* Knacken *nt*; (*photo*) Schnappschuss *m* ● *attrib* (*decision*) plötzlich ● *v* (*pt/pp* **snapped**) ● *vi* [entzwei]brechen; **~ at** (*bite*) schnappen nach; (*speak sharply*) [scharf] anfahren ● *vt* zerbrechen; (*say*) fauchen; (*Phot*) knipsen. **~ up** *vt* wegschnappen

snappy /ˈsnæpɪ/ *adj* (*smart*) flott; **make it ~!** ein bisschen schnell!
ˈ**snapshot** *n* Schnappschuss *m*
snare /sneə(r)/ *n* Schlinge *f*
snarl /snɑːl/ *vi* [mit gefletschten Zähnen] knurren
snatch /snætʃ/ *n* (*fragment*) Fetzen *pl* ● *vt* schnappen; (*steal*) klauen; entführen (*child*); **~ sth from s.o.** jdm etw entreißen
sneak /sniːk/ *n* 🅃 Petze *f* ● *vi* schleichen; (🅃: *tell tales*) petzen ● *vt* (*take*) mitgehen lassen ● *vi* **~ in/out** sich hinein-/hinausschleichen
sneakers /ˈsniːkəz/ *npl* (*Amer*) Turnschuhe *pl*
sneer /snɪə(r)/ *vi* höhnisch lächeln; (*mock*) spotten
sneeze /sniːz/ *n* Niesen *nt* ● *vi* niesen
snide /snaɪd/ *adj* 🅃 abfällig
sniff /snɪf/ *vi* schnüffeln ● *vt* schnüffeln an (+ *dat*)
snigger /ˈsnɪgə(r)/ *vi* [boshaft] kichern
snip /snɪp/ *n* Schnitt *m* ● *vt/i* **~ [at]** schnippeln an (+ *dat*)
snippet /ˈsnɪpɪt/ *n* Schnipsel *m*; (*of information*) Bruchstück *nt*
snivel /ˈsnɪvl/ *vi* (*pt/pp* **snivelled**) flennen
snob /snɒb/ *n* Snob *m*. **~bery** *n* Snobismus *m*. **~bish** *adj* snobistisch
snoop /snuːp/ *vi* 🅃 schnüffeln
snooty /ˈsnuːtɪ/ *adj* 🅃 hochnäsig
snooze /snuːz/ *n* Nickerchen *nt* ● *vi* dösen
snore /snɔː(r)/ *vi* schnarchen
snorkel /ˈsnɔːkl/ *n* Schnorchel *m*
snort /snɔːt/ *vi* schnauben
snout /snaʊt/ *n* Schnauze *f*
snow /snəʊ/ *n* Schnee *m* ● *vi* schneien; **~ed under with** (*fig*) überhäuft mit
snow: ~ball *n* Schneeball *m*. **~board** *n* Snowboard *nt*. **~-drift** *n* Schneewehe *f*. **~drop** *n* Schneeglöckchen *nt*. **~fall** *n* Schneefall *m*. **~flake** *n* Schneeflocke *f*. **~man** *n* Schneemann *m*. **~plough** *n* Schneepflug *m*
snub /snʌb/ *n* Abfuhr *f* ● *vt* (*pt/pp* **snubbed**) brüskieren
ˈ**snub-nosed** *adj* stupsnasig
snuffle /ˈsnʌfl/ *vi* schnüffeln
snug /snʌg/ *adj* (**snugger, snuggest**) behaglich, gemütlich
snuggle /ˈsnʌgl/ *vi* sich kuscheln (**up to** an + *acc*)
so /səʊ/ *adv* so; **so am I** ich auch; **so I see** das sehe ich; **that is so** das stimmt; **so much the better** umso besser; **if so** wenn ja; **so as to** um zu; **so long!** 🅃 tschüs! ● *pron* **I hope so** hoffentlich; **I think so** ich glaube schon; **I'm afraid so** leider ja; **so saying/doing, he/she ...** indem er/sie das sagte/tat, ... ● *conj* (*therefore*) also; **so that** damit; **so what!** na und! **so you see** wie du siehst
soak /səʊk/ *vt* nass machen; (*steep*) einweichen; (🅃: *fleece*) schröpfen ● *vi* weichen; (*liquid:*) sickern. **~ up** *vt* aufsaugen
soaking /ˈsəʊkɪŋ/ *adj & adv* **~ [wet]** patschnass 🅃
soap /səʊp/ *n* Seife *f*. **~ opera** *n* Seifenoper *f*. **~ powder** *n* Seifenpulver *nt*
soapy /ˈsəʊpɪ/ *adj* seifig
soar /sɔː(r)/ *vi* aufsteigen; (*prices:*) in die Höhe schnellen
sob /sɒb/ *n* Schluchzer *m* ● *vi* (*pt/pp* **sobbed**) schluchzen
sober /ˈsəʊbə(r)/ *adj* nüchtern; (*serious*) ernst; (*colour*) gedeckt. **~ up** *vi* nüchtern werden

'so-called *adj* sogenannt
soccer /'sɒkə(r)/ *n* [!] Fußball *m*
sociable /'səʊʃəbl/ *adj* gesellig
social /'səʊʃl/ *adj* gesellschaftlich; (*Admin, Pol, Zool*) sozial
socialis|m /'səʊʃəlɪzm/ *n* Sozialismus *m*. **~t** *adj* sozialistisch ● *n* Sozialist *m*
socialize /'səʊʃəlaɪz/ *vi* [gesellschaftlich] verkehren
socially /'səʊʃəlɪ/ *adv* gesellschaftlich; **know ~** privat kennen
social: ~ se'curity *n* Sozialhilfe *f*. **~ worker** *n* Sozialarbeiter(in) *m*(*f*)
society /sə'saɪətɪ/ *n* Gesellschaft *f*; (*club*) Verein *m*
sociolog|ist /səʊsɪ'ɒlədʒɪst/ *n* Soziologe *m*. **~y** *n* Soziologie *f*
sock /sɒk/ *n* Socke *f*; (*kneelength*) Kniestrumpf *m*
socket /'sɒkɪt/ *n* (*of eye*) Augenhöhle *f*; (*of joint*) Gelenkpfanne *f*; (*wall plug*) Steckdose *f*
soda /'səʊdə/ *n* Soda *nt*; (*Amer*) Limonade *f*. **~ water** *n* Sodawasser *nt*
sodden /'sɒdn/ *adj* durchnässt
sofa /'səʊfə/ *n* Sofa *nt*. **~ bed** *n* Schlafcouch *f*
soft /sɒft/ *adj* (**-er, -est**) weich; (*quiet*) leise; (*gentle*) sanft; ([!]: *silly*) dumm. **~ drink** *n* alkoholfreies Getränk *nt*
soften /'sɒfn/ *vt* weich machen; (*fig*) mildern ● *vi* weich werden
soft: ~ toy *n* Stofftier *nt*. **~ware** *n* Software *f*
soggy /'sɒgɪ/ *adj* aufgeweicht
soil¹ /sɔɪl/ *n* Erde *f*, Boden *m*
soil² *vt* verschmutzen
solar /'səʊlə(r)/ *adj* Sonnen-
sold /səʊld/ *see* **sell**
soldier /'səʊldʒə(r)/ *n* Soldat *m* ● *vi* **~ on** [unbeirrbar] weitermachen
sole¹ /səʊl/ *n* Sohle *f*
sole² *n* (*fish*) Seezunge *f*
sole³ *adj* einzig. **~ly** *adv* einzig und allein
solemn /'sɒləm/ *adj* feierlich; (*serious*) ernst
solicitor /sə'lɪsɪtə(r)/ *n* Rechtsanwalt *m*/-anwältin *f*
solid /'sɒlɪd/ *adj* fest; (*sturdy*) stabil; (*not hollow, of same substance*) massiv; (*unanimous*) einstimmig; (*complete*) ganz
solidarity /sɒlɪ'dærətɪ/ *n* Solidarität *f*
solidify /sə'lɪdɪfaɪ/ *vi* (*pt/pp* **-ied**) fest werden
solitary /'sɒlɪtərɪ/ *adj* einsam; (*sole*) einzig
solitude /'sɒlɪtju:d/ *n* Einsamkeit *f*
solo /'səʊləʊ/ *n* Solo *nt* ● *adj* Solo-; (*flight*) Allein- ● *adv* solo. **~ist** *n* Solist(in) *m*(*f*)
solstice /'sɒlstɪs/ *n* Sonnenwende *f*
soluble /'sɒljʊbl/ *adj* löslich
solution /sə'lu:ʃn/ *n* Lösung *f*
solvable /'sɒlvəbl/ *adj* lösbar
solve /sɒlv/ *vt* lösen
solvent /'sɒlvənt/ *n* Lösungsmittel *nt*
sombre /'sɒmbə(r)/ *adj* dunkel; (*mood*) düster
some /sʌm/ *adj & pron* etwas; (*a little*) ein bisschen; (*with pl noun*) einige; (*a few*) ein paar; (*certain*) manche(r,s); (*one or the other*) [irgend]ein; **~ day** eines Tages; **I want ~** ich möchte etwas/ (*pl*) welche; **will you have ~ wine?** möchten Sie Wein? **do ~ shopping** einkaufen
some: ~body /-bədɪ/ *pron & n* jemand; (*emphatic*) irgendjemand. **~how** *adv* irgendwie. **~one** *pron & n* = **somebody**

S

somersault /'sʌməsɔ:lt/ *n* Purzelbaum *m* ⓘ; (*Sport*) Salto *m*; **turn a ~** einen Purzelbaum schlagen/einen Salto springen

'something *pron & adv* etwas; (*emphatic*) irgendetwas; **~ different** etwas anderes; **~ like this** so etwas [wie das]

some: ~time *adv* irgendwann ● *adj* ehemalig. **~times** *adv* manchmal. **~what** *adv* ziemlich. **~where** *adv* irgendwo; (*go*) irgendwohin

son /sʌn/ *n* Sohn *m*

song /sɒŋ/ *n* Lied *nt*. **~bird** *n* Singvogel *m*

'son-in-law *n* (*pl* **~s-in-law**) Schwiegersohn *m*

soon /su:n/ *adv* (**-er, -est**) bald; (*quickly*) schnell; **too ~** zu früh; **as ~ as possible** so bald wie möglich; **~er or later** früher oder später; **no ~er had I arrived than ...** kaum war ich angekommen, da ...; **I would ~er stay** ich würde lieber bleiben

soot /sʊt/ *n* Ruß *m*

sooth|e /su:ð/ *vt* beruhigen; lindern (*pain*). **~ing** *adj* beruhigend; lindernd

sophisticated /sə'fɪstɪkeɪtɪd/ *adj* weltgewandt; (*complex*) hoch entwickelt

S

sopping /'sɒpɪŋ/ *adj & adv* **~[wet]** durchnässt

soppy /'sɒpɪ/ *adj* ⓘ rührselig

soprano /sə'prɑ:nəʊ/ *n* Sopran *m*; (*woman*) Sopranistin *f*

sordid /'sɔ:dɪd/ *adj* schmutzig

sore /sɔ:(r)/ *adj* (**-r, -st**) wund; (*painful*) schmerzhaft; **have a ~ throat** Halsschmerzen haben ● *n* wunde Stelle *f*. **~ly** *adv* sehr

sorrow /'sɒrəʊ/ *n* Kummer *m*

sorry /'sɒrɪ/ *adj* (*sad*) traurig; (*wretched*) erbärmlich; **I am ~** es tut mir Leid; **she is** *or* **feels ~ for him** er tut ihr Leid; **I am ~ to say** leider; **~!** Entschuldigung!

sort /sɔ:t/ *n* Art *f*; (*brand*) Sorte *f*; **he's a good ~** ⓘ er ist in Ordnung ● *vt* sortieren. **~ out** *vt* sortieren; (*fig*) klären

sought /sɔ:t/ *see* **seek**

soul /səʊl/ *n* Seele *f*

sound¹ /saʊnd/ *adj* (**-er, -est**) gesund; (*sensible*) vernünftig; (*secure*) solide; (*thorough*) gehörig ● *adv* **be ~ asleep** fest schlafen

sound² *n* (*strait*) Meerenge *f*

sound³ *n* Laut *m*; (*noise*) Geräusch *nt*; (*Phys*) Schall *m*; (*Radio, TV*) Ton *m*; (*of bells, music*) Klang *m*; **I don't like the ~ of it** ⓘ das hört sich nicht gut an ● *vi* [er]tönen; (*seem*) sich anhören ● *vt* (*pronounce*) aussprechen; schlagen (*alarm*); (*Med*) abhorchen (*chest*)

soundly /'saʊndlɪ/ *adv* solide; (*sleep*) fest; (*defeat*) vernichtend

'soundproof *adj* schalldicht

soup /su:p/ *n* Suppe *f*

sour /'saʊə(r)/ *adj* (**-er, -est**) sauer; (*bad-tempered*) griesgrämig, verdrießlich

source /sɔ:s/ *n* Quelle *f*

south /saʊθ/ *n* Süden *m*; **to the ~ of** südlich von ● *adj* Süd-, süd- ● *adv* nach Süden

south: S~ 'Africa *n* Südafrika *nt*. **S~ A'merica** *n* Südamerika *nt*. **~-'east** *n* Südosten *m*

southerly /'sʌðəlɪ/ *adj* südlich

southern /'sʌðən/ *adj* südlich

'southward[s] /-wəd[z]/ *adv* nach Süden

souvenir /su:və'nɪə(r)/ *n* Andenken *nt*, Souvenir *nt*

Soviet /'səʊvɪət/ *adj* (*History*) sowjetisch; **~ Union** Sowjetunion *f*

sow¹ /saʊ/ *n* Sau *f*

sow² /səʊ/ *vt* (*pt* **sowed**, *pp* **sown** *or* **sowed**) säen

soya /'sɔɪə/ *n* ~ **bean** Sojabohne *f*

spa /spɑ:/ *n* Heilbad *nt*

space /speɪs/ *n* Raum *m*; (*gap*) Platz *m*; (*Astronomy*) Weltraum *m* ●*vt* ~ **[out]** [in Abständen] verteilen

space: ~**craft** *n* Raumfahrzeug *nt*. ~**ship** *n* Raumschiff *nt*

spacious /'speɪʃəs/ *adj* geräumig

spade /speɪd/ *n* Spaten *m*; (*for child*) Schaufel *f*; ~**s** *pl* (*Cards*) Pik *nt*

Spain /speɪn/ *n* Spanien *nt*

span¹ /spæn/ *n* Spanne *f*; (*of arch*) Spannweite *f* ●*vt* (*pt/pp* **spanned**) überspannen; umspannen (*time*)

span² *see* **spick**

Span|iard /'spænjəd/ *n* Spanier(in) *m*(*f*). ~**ish** *adj* spanisch ●*n* (*Lang*) Spanisch *nt*; **the** ~**ish** *pl* die Spanier

spank /spæŋk/ *vt* verhauen

spanner /'spænə(r)/ *n* Schraubenschlüssel *m*

spare /speə(r)/ *adj* (*surplus*) übrig; (*additional*) zusätzlich; (*seat, time*) frei; (*room*) Gäste-; (*bed, cup*) Extra- ●*n* (*part*) Ersatzteil *nt* ●*vt* ersparen; (*not hurt*) verschonen; (*do without*) entbehren; (*afford to give*) erübrigen. ~ '**wheel** *n* Reserverad *nt*

sparing /'speərɪŋ/ *adj* sparsam

spark /spɑ:k/ *n* Funke *nt*. ~**[ing]-plug** *n* (*Auto*) Zündkerze *f*

sparkl|e /'spɑ:kl/ *n* Funkeln *nt* ●*vi* funkeln. ~**ing** *adj* funkelnd; (*wine*) Schaum-

sparrow /'spærəʊ/ *n* Spatz *m*

sparse /spɑ:s/ *adj* spärlich. ~**ly** *adv* spärlich; (*populated*) dünn

spasm /'spæzm/ *n* Anfall *m*; (*cramp*) Krampf *m*. ~**odic** *adj*, **-ally** *adv* sporadisch

spastic /'spæstɪk/ *adj* spastisch [gelähmt] ●*n* Spastiker(in) *m*(*f*)

spat /spæt/ *see* spit²

spatter /'spætə(r)/ *vt* spritzen; ~ **with** bespritzen mit

spawn /spɔ:n/ *n* Laich *m* ●*vt* (*fig*) hervorbringen

speak /spi:k/ *v* (*pt* **spoke**, *pp* **spoken**) ●*vi* sprechen (**to** mit) ~**ing!** (*Teleph*) am Apparat! ●*vt* sprechen; sagen (*truth*). ~ **up** *vi* lauter sprechen; ~ **up for oneself** seine Meinung äußern

speaker /spi:kə(r)/ *n* Sprecher(in) *m*(*f*); (*in public*) Redner(in) *m*(*f*); (*loudspeaker*) Lautsprecher *m*

spear /spɪə(r)/ *n* Speer *m* ●*vt* aufspießen

spec /spek/ *n* **on** ~ ⊡ auf gut Glück

special /'speʃl/ *adj* besondere(r,s), speziell. ~**ist** *n* Spezialist *m*; (*Med*) Facharzt *m*/-ärztin *f*. ~**ity** *n* Spezialität *f*

special|ize /'speʃəlaɪz/ *vi* sich spezialisieren (**in** auf + *acc*). ~**ly** *adv* speziell; (*particularly*) besonders

species /'spi:ʃi:z/ *n* Art *f*

specific /spə'sɪfɪk/ *adj* bestimmt; (*precise*) genau; (*Phys*) spezifisch. ~**ally** *adv* ausdrücklich

specification /spesɪfɪ'keɪʃn/ *n* (*also* ~**s**) *pl* genaue Angaben *pl*

specify /'spesɪfaɪ/ *vt* (*pt/pp* **-ied**) [genau] angeben

specimen /spesɪmən/ *n* Exemplar *nt*; (*sample*) Probe *f*; (*of urine*) Urinprobe *f*

speck /spek/ *n* Fleck *m*

speckled /'spekld/ *adj* gesprenkelt

spectacle /'spektəkl/ *n* (*show*) Schauspiel *nt*; (*sight*) Anblick *m*. ~**s** *npl* Brille *f*

S

spectacular /spek'tækjʊlə(r)/ *adj* spektakulär
spectator /spek'teɪtə(r)/ *n* Zuschauer(in) *m(f)*
speculat|e /'spekjʊleɪt/ *vi* spekulieren. **~ion** *n* Spekulation *f*. **~or** *n* Spekulant *m*
sped /sped/ *see* **speed**
speech /spiːtʃ/ *n* Sprache *f*; (*address*) Rede *f*. **~less** *adj* sprachlos
speed /spiːd/ *n* Geschwindigkeit *f*; (*rapidity*) Schnelligkeit *f* ● *vi* (*pt/pp* **sped**) schnell fahren ● (*pt/pp* **speeded**) (*go too fast*) zu schnell fahren. **~ up** (*pt/pp* **speeded up**) ● *vt/i* beschleunigen
speed: ~boat *n* Rennboot *nt*. **~ camera** *n* Geschwindigkeitsüberwachungskamera *f*. **~ dating** *n* Speeddating *nt*. **~ing** *n* Geschwindigkeitsüberschreitung *f*. **~ limit** *n* Geschwindigkeitsbeschränkung *f*
speedometer /spiː'dɒmɪtə(r)/ *n* Tachometer *m*
speedy /'spiːdɪ/ *adj* , **-ily** *adv* schnell
spell¹ /spel/ *n* Weile *f*; (*of weather*) Periode *f*
spell² *v* (*pt/pp* **spelled** or **spelt**) ● *vt* schreiben; (*aloud*) buchstabieren; (*fig: mean*) bedeuten ● *vi* richtig schreiben; (*aloud*) buchstabieren. **~ out** *vt* buchstabieren; (*fig*) genau erklären
spell³ *n* Zauber *m*; (*words*) Zauberspruch *m*. **~bound** *adj* wie verzaubert
'spell checker *n* Rechtschreibprogramm *nt*
spelling /'spelɪŋ/ *n* (*of a word*) Schreibweise *f*; (*orthography*) Rechtschreibung *f*
spelt /spelt/ *see* **spell²**
spend /spend/ *vt/i* (*pt/pp* **spent**) ausgeben; verbringen (*time*)
spent /spent/ *see* **spend**
sperm /spɜːm/ *n* Samen *m*
sphere /sfɪə(r)/ *n* Kugel *f*; (*fig*) Sphäre *f*
spice /spaɪs/ *n* Gewürz *nt*; (*fig*) Würze *f*
spicy /'spaɪsɪ/ *adj* würzig, pikant
spider /'spaɪdə(r)/ *n* Spinne *f*
spik|e /spaɪk/ *n* Spitze *f*; (*Bot, Zool*) Stachel *m*; (*on shoe*) Spike *m*. **~y** *adj* stachelig
spill /spɪl/ *v* (*pt/pp* **spilt** *or* **spilled**) ● *vt* verschütten ● *vi* überlaufen
spin /spɪn/ *v* (*pt/pp* **spun**, *pres p* **spinning**) ● *vt* drehen; spinnen (*wool*); schleudern (*washing*) ● *vi* sich drehen
spinach /'spɪnɪdʒ/ *n* Spinat *m*
spindl|e /'spɪndl/ *n* Spindel *f*. **~y** *adj* spindeldürr
spin-'drier *n* Wäscheschleuder *f*
spine /spaɪn/ *n* Rückgrat *nt*; (*of book*) [Buch]rücken *m*; (*Bot, Zool*) Stachel *m*. **~less** *adj* (*fig*) rückgratlos
'spin-off *n* Nebenprodukt *nt*
spinster /'spɪnstə(r)/ *n* ledige Frau *f*
spiral /'spaɪrl/ *adj* spiralig ● *n* Spirale *f* ● *vi* (*pt/pp* **spiralled**) sich hochwinden. **~ 'staircase** *n* Wendeltreppe *f*
spire /'spaɪə(r)/ *n* Turmspitze *f*
spirit /'spɪrɪt/ *n* Geist *m*; (*courage*) Mut *m*; **~s** *pl* (*alcohol*) Spirituosen *pl*; **in low ~s** niedergedrückt. **~ away** *vt* verschwinden lassen
spirited /'spɪrɪtɪd/ *adj* lebhaft; (*courageous*) beherzt
spiritual /'spɪrɪtjʊəl/ *adj* geistig; (*Relig*) geistlich
spit¹ /spɪt/ *n* (*for roasting*) [Brat]spieß *m*
spit² *n* Spucke *f* ● *vt/i* (*pt/pp* **spat**,

pres p **spitting**) spucken; (*cat:*) fauchen; (*fat:*) spritzen; **it's ~ting with rain** es tröpfelt

spite /spaɪt/ *n* Boshaftigkeit *f*; **in ~ of** trotz (+ *gen*) ● *vt* ärgern. **~ful** *adj* gehässig

splash /splæʃ/ *n* Platschen *nt*; ([!]: *drop*) Schuss *m*; **~ of colour** Farbfleck *m* ● *vt* spritzen; **~ s.o. with sth** jdn mit etw bespritzen ● *vi* spritzen. **~ about** *vi* planschen

splendid /ˈsplendɪd/ *adj* herrlich, großartig

splendour /ˈsplendə(r)/ *n* Pracht *f*

splint /splɪnt/ *n* (*Med*) Schiene *f*

splinter /ˈsplɪntə(r)/ *n* Splitter *m* ● *vi* zersplittern

split /splɪt/ *n* Spaltung *f*; (*Pol*) Bruch *m*; (*tear*) Riss *m* ● *v* (*pt/pp* **split**, *pres p* **splitting**) ● *vt* spalten; (*share*) teilen; (*tear*) zerreißen ● *vi* sich spalten; (*tear*) zerreißen; **~ on s.o.** [!] jdn verpfeifen. **~ up** *vt* aufteilen ● *vi* (*couple:*) sich trennen

splutter /ˈsplʌtə(r)/ *vi* prusten

spoil /spɔɪl/ *n* **~s** *pl* Beute *f* ● *v* (*pt/pp* **spoilt** *or* **spoiled**) ● *vt* verderben; verwöhnen (*person*) ● *vi* verderben. **~sport** *n* Spielverderber *m*

spoke¹ /spəʊk/ *n* Speiche *f*

spoke², **spoken** *see* **speak**

ˈspokesman *n* Sprecher *m*

sponge /spʌndʒ/ *n* Schwamm *m* ● *vt* abwaschen ● *vi* **~ on** schmarotzen bei. **~-bag** *n* Waschbeutel *m*. **~-cake** *n* Biskuitkuchen *m*

sponsor /ˈspɒnsə(r)/ *n* Sponsor *m*; (*godparent*) Pate *m*/Patin *f* ● *vt* sponsern

spontaneous /spɒnˈteɪnɪəs/ *adj* spontan

spoof /spuːf/ *n* [!] Parodie *f*

spooky /ˈspuːkɪ/ *adj* [!] gespenstisch

spool /spuːl/ *n* Spule *f*

spoon /spuːn/ *n* Löffel *m* ● *vt* löffeln. **~ful** *n* Löffel *m*

sporadic /spəˈrædɪk/ *adj*, **-ally** *adv* sporadisch

sport /spɔːt/ *n* Sport *m* ● *vt* [stolz] tragen. **~ing** *adj* sportlich

sports: ~car *n* Sportwagen *m*. **~ coat** *n*, **~ jacket** *n* Sakko *m*. **~man** *n* Sportler *m*. **~woman** *n* Sportlerin *f*

sporty /ˈspɔːtɪ/ *adj* sportlich

spot /spɒt/ *n* Fleck *m*; (*place*) Stelle *f* (*dot*) Punkt *m*; (*drop*) Tropfen *m*; (*pimple*) Pickel *m*; **~s** *pl* (*rash*) Ausschlag *m*; **on the ~** auf der Stelle ● *vt* (*pt/pp* **spotted**) entdecken

spot: ~ ˈcheck *n* Stichprobe *f*. **~less** *adj* makellos; ([!]: *very clean*) blitzsauber. **~light** *n* Scheinwerfer *m*; (*fig*) Rampenlicht *nt*

spotted /ˈspɒtɪd/ *adj* gepunktet

spouse /spaʊz/ *n* Gatte *m*/Gattin *f*

spout /spaʊt/ *n* Schnabel *m*, Tülle *f* ● *vi* schießen (**from** aus)

sprain /spreɪn/ *n* Verstauchung *f* ● *vt* verstauchen

sprang /spræŋ/ *see* **spring²**

sprawl /sprɔːl/ *vi* sich ausstrecken

spray¹ /spreɪ/ *n* (*of flowers*) Strauß *m*

spray² *n* Sprühnebel *m*; (*from sea*) Gischt *m*; (*device*) Spritze *f*; (*container*) Sprühdose *f*; (*preparation*) Spray *nt* ● *vt* spritzen; (*with aerosol*) sprühen

spread /spred/ *n* Verbreitung *f*; (*paste*) Aufstrich *m*; ([!]: *feast*) Festessen *nt* ● *v* (*pt/pp* **spread**) ● *vt* ausbreiten; streichen (*butter, jam*); bestreichen (*bread, surface*); streuen (*sand, manure*); verbreiten (*news, disease*); verteilen (*payments*) ● *vi* sich ausbreiten. **~ out** *vt* ausbreiten; (*space out*) verteilen ● *vi* sich verteilen

spree /spriː/ *n* [!] **go on a shopping ~** groß einkaufen gehen

sprightly /ˈspraɪtlɪ/ *adj* rüstig

spring[1] /sprɪŋ/ *n* Frühling *m* ● *attrib* Frühlings-

spring[2] *n* (*jump*) Sprung *m*; (*water*) Quelle *f*; (*device*) Feder *f*; (*elasticity*) Elastizität *f* ● *v* (*pt* **sprang**, *pp* **sprung**) ● *vi* springen; (*arise*) entspringen (**from** *dat*) ● *vt* **~ sth on s.o.** jdn mit etw überfallen

spring: **~-ˈcleaning** *n* Frühjahrsputz *m*. **~time** *n* Frühling *m*

sprinkl|e /ˈsprɪŋkl/ *vt* sprengen; (*scatter*) streuen; bestreuen (*surface*). **~ing** *n* dünne Schicht *f*

sprint /sprɪnt/ *n* Sprint *m* ● *vi* rennen; (*Sport*) sprinten. **~er** *n* Kurzstreckenläufer(in) *m*(*f*)

sprout /spraʊt/ *n* Trieb *m*; **[Brussels] ~s** *pl* Rosenkohl *m* ● *vi* sprießen

sprung /sprʌŋ/ *see* **spring**[2]

spud /spʌd/ *n* [!] Kartoffel *f*

spun /spʌn/ *see* **spin**

spur /spɜː(r)/ *n* Sporn *m*; (*stimulus*) Ansporn *m*; **on the ~ of the moment** ganz spontan ● *vt* (*pt/pp* **spurred**) **~ [on]** (*fig*) anspornen

spurn /spɜːn/ *vt* verschmähen

spurt /spɜːt/ *n* (*Sport*) Spurt *m*; **put on a ~** spurten ● *vi* spritzen

spy /spaɪ/ *n* Spion(in) *m*(*f*) ● *vi* spionieren; **~ on s.o.** jdm nachspionieren. ● *vt* ([!]: *see*) sehen

spying /ˈspaɪɪŋ/ *n* Spionage *f*

squabble /ˈskwɒbl/ *n* Zank *m* ● *vi* sich zanken

squad /skwɒd/ *n* Gruppe *f*; (*Sport*) Mannschaft *f*

squadron /ˈskwɒdrən/ *n* (*Mil*) Geschwader *nt*

squalid /ˈskwɒlɪd/ *adj* schmutzig

squall /skwɔːl/ *n* Bö *f* ● *vi* brüllen

squalor /ˈskwɒlə(r)/ *n* Schmutz *m*

squander /ˈskwɒndə(r)/ *vt* vergeuden

square /skweə(r)/ *adj* quadratisch; (*metre, mile*) Quadrat-; (*meal*) anständig; **all ~** [!] quitt ● *n* Quadrat *nt*; (*area*) Platz *m*; (*on chessboard*) Feld *nt* ● *vt* (*settle*) klären; (*Math*) quadrieren

squash /skwɒʃ/ *n* Gedränge *nt*; (*drink*) Fruchtsaftgetränk *nt*; (*Sport*) Squash *nt* ● *vt* zerquetschen; (*suppress*) niederschlagen. **~y** *adj* weich

squat /skwɒt/ *adj* gedrungen ● *vi* (*pt/pp* **squatted**) hocken; **~ in a house** ein Haus besetzen. **~ter** *n* Hausbesetzer *m*

squawk /skwɔːk/ *vi* krächzen

squeak /skwiːk/ *n* Quieken *nt*; (*of hinge, brakes*) Quietschen *nt* ● *vi* quieken; quietschen

squeal /skwiːl/ *n* Kreischen *nt* ● *vi* kreischen

squeamish /ˈskwiːmɪʃ/ *adj* empfindlich

squeeze /skwiːz/ *n* Druck *m*; (*crush*) Gedränge *nt* ● *vt* drücken; (*to get juice*) ausdrücken; (*force*) zwängen

squiggle /ˈskwɪgl/ *n* Schnörkel *m*

squint /skwɪnt/ *n* Schielen *nt* ● *vi* schielen

squirm /skwɜːm/ *vi* sich winden

squirrel /ˈskwɪrl/ *n* Eichhörnchen *nt*

squirt /skwɜːt/ *n* Spritzer *m* ● *vt/i* spritzen

St *abbr* (**Saint**) St.; (**Street**) Str.

stab /stæb/ *n* Stich *m*; ([!]: *attempt*) Versuch *m* ● *vt* (*pt/pp* **stabbed**) stechen; (*to death*) erstechen

stability /stəˈbɪlətɪ/ *n* Stabilität *f*

stable¹ /ˈsteɪbl/ *adj* (**-r, -st**) stabil
stable² *n* Stall *m*; (*establishment*) Reitstall *m*
stack /stæk/ *n* Stapel *m*; (*of chimney*) Schornstein *m* ● *vt* stapeln
stadium /ˈsteɪdɪəm/ *n* Stadion *nt*
staff /stɑːf/ *n* (*stick & Mil*) Stab *m* ● (*& pl*) (*employees*) Personal *nt*; (*Sch*) Lehrkräfte *pl* ● *vt* mit Personal besetzen. **~-room** *n* (*Sch*) Lehrerzimmer *nt*
stag /stæg/ *n* Hirsch *m*
stage /steɪdʒ/ *n* Bühne *f*; (*in journey*) Etappe *f*; (*in process*) Stadium *nt*; **by** *or* **in ~s** in Etappen ● *vt* aufführen; (*arrange*) veranstalten
stagger /ˈstægə(r)/ *vi* taumeln ● *vt* staffeln (*holidays*); versetzt anordnen (*seats*); **I was ~ed** es hat mir die Sprache verschlagen. **~ing** *adj* unglaublich
stagnant /ˈstægnənt/ *adj* stehend; (*fig*) stagnierend
stagnate /stægˈneɪt/ *vi* (*fig*) stagnieren
stain /steɪn/ *n* Fleck *m*; (*for wood*) Beize *f* ● *vt* färben; beizen (*wood*); **~ed glass** farbiges Glas *nt*. **~less** *adj* (*steel*) rostfrei
stair /steə(r)/ *n* Stufe *f*; **~s** *pl* Treppe *f*. **~case** *n* Treppe *f*
stake /steɪk/ *n* Pfahl *m*; (*wager*) Einsatz *m*; (*Comm*) Anteil *m*; **be at ~** auf dem Spiel stehen ● *vt* **~ a claim to sth** Anspruch auf etw (*acc*) erheben
stale /steɪl/ *adj* (**-r, -st**) alt; (*air*) verbraucht. **~mate** *n* Patt *nt*
stalk /stɔːk/ *n* Stiel *m*, Stängel *m*
stall /stɔːl/ *n* Stand *m*; **~s** *pl* (*Theat*) Parkett *nt* ● *vi* (*engine:*) stehen bleiben; (*fig*) ausweichen ● *vt* abwürgen (*engine*)
stalwart /ˈstɔːlwət/ *adj* treu ● *n* treuer Anhänger *m*
stamina /ˈstæmɪnə/ *n* Ausdauer *f*
stammer /ˈstæmə(r)/ *n* Stottern *nt* ● *vt/i* stottern
stamp /stæmp/ *n* Stempel *m*; (*postage ~*) [Brief]marke *f* ● *vt* stempeln; (*impress*) prägen; (*put postage on*) frankieren ● *vi* stampfen. **~ out** *vt* [aus]stanzen; (*fig*) ausmerzen
stampede /stæmˈpiːd/ *n* wilde Flucht *f* ● *vi* in Panik fliehen
stance /stɑːns/ *n* Haltung *f*
stand /stænd/ *n* Stand *m*; (*rack*) Ständer *m*; (*pedestal*) Sockel *m*; (*Sport*) Tribüne *f*; (*fig*) Einstellung *f* ● *v* (*pt/pp* **stood**) ● *vi* stehen; (*rise*) aufstehen; (*be candidate*) kandidieren; (*stay valid*) gültig bleiben; **~ still** stillstehen; **~ firm** (*fig*) festbleiben; **~ to reason** logisch sein; **~ in for** vertreten; **~ for** (*mean*) bedeuten ● *vt* stellen; (*withstand*) standhalten (+ *dat*); (*endure*) ertragen; vertragen (*climate*); (*put up with*) aushalten; haben (*chance*); **~ s.o. a beer** jdm ein Bier spendieren; **I can't ~ her** [!] ich kann sie nicht ausstehen. **~ by** *vi* daneben stehen; (*be ready*) sich bereithalten ● *vt* **~ by s.o.** (*fig*) zu jdm stehen. **~ down** *vi* (*retire*) zurücktreten. **~ out** *vi* hervorstehen; (*fig*) herausragen. **~ up** *vi* aufstehen; **~ up for** eintreten für; **~ up to** sich wehren gegen
standard /ˈstændəd/ *adj* Normal- ● *n* Maßstab *m*; (*Techn*) Norm *f*; (*level*) Niveau *nt*; (*flag*) Standarte *f*; **~s** *pl* (*morals*) Prinzipien *pl*. **~ize** *vt* standardisieren; (*Techn*) normen
ˈstand-in *n* Ersatz *m*
standing /ˈstændɪŋ/ *adj* (*erect*) stehend; (*permanent*) ständig ● *n* Rang *m*; (*duration*) Dauer *f*. **~-room** *n* Stehplätze *pl*
stand: ~-offish /stændˈɒfɪʃ/ *adj*

distanziert. **~point** *n* Standpunkt *m*. **~still** *n* Stillstand *m*; **come to a ~still** zum Stillstand kommen

stank /stæŋk/ *see* **stink**

staple¹ /'steɪpl/ *adj* Grund-

staple² *n* Heftklammer *f* ● *vt* heften. **~r** *n* Heftmaschine *f*

star /stɑ:(r)/ *n* Stern *m*; (*asterisk*) Sternchen *nt*; (*Theat, Sport*) Star *m* ● *vi* (*pt/pp* **starred**) die Hauptrolle spielen

starboard /'stɑ:bəd/ *n* Steuerbord *nt*

starch /stɑ:tʃ/ *n* Stärke *f* ● *vt* stärken. **~y** *adj* stärkehaltig; (*fig*) steif

stare /steə(r)/ *n* Starren *nt* ● *vt* starren; **~ at** anstarren

stark /stɑ:k/ *adj* (**-er, -est**) scharf; (*contrast*) krass

starling /'stɑ:lɪŋ/ *n* Star *m*

start /stɑ:t/ *n* Anfang *m*, Beginn *m*; (*departure*) Aufbruch *m*; (*Sport*) Start *m*; **from the ~** von Anfang an; **for a ~** erstens ● *vi* anfangen, beginnen; (*set out*) aufbrechen; (*engine:*) anspringen; (*Auto, Sport*) starten; (*jump*) aufschrecken; **to ~ with** zuerst ● *vt* anfangen, beginnen; (*cause*) verursachen; (*found*) gründen; starten (*car, race*); in Umlauf setzen (*rumour*). **~er** *n* (*Culin*) Vorspeise *f*; (*Auto, Sport*) Starter *m*. **~ing-point** *n* Ausgangspunkt *m*

startle /'stɑ:tl/ *vt* erschrecken

starvation /stɑ:'veɪʃn/ *n* Verhungern *nt*

starve /stɑ:v/ *vi* hungern; (*to death*) verhungern ● *vt* verhungern lassen

state /steɪt/ *n* Zustand *m*; (*Pol*) Staat *m*; **~ of play** Spielstand *m*; **be in a ~** (*person:*) aufgeregt sein ● *attrib* Staats-, staatlich ● *vt* erklären; (*specify*) angeben

stately /'steɪtlɪ/ *adj* stattlich. **~ 'home** *n* Schloss *nt*

statement /'steɪtmənt/ *n* Erklärung *f*; (*Jur*) Aussage *f*; (*Banking*) Auszug *m*

> **i** **state school** Eine direkt oder indirekt vom Staat finanzierte Schule in Großbritannien, die keine Schulgebühren verlangt. Der Besuch aller staatlichen Grundschulen und weiterführenden Schulen ist kostenlos. Die meisten Kinder in Großbritannien besuchen solche öffentlichen Schulen.

'statesman *n* Staatsmann *m*

static /'stætɪk/ *adj* statisch; **remain ~** unverändert bleiben

station /'steɪʃn/ *n* Bahnhof *m*; (*police*) Wache *f*; (*radio*) Sender *m*; (*space, weather*) Station *f*; (*Mil*) Posten *m*; (*status*) Rang *m* ● *vt* stationieren; (*post*) postieren. **~ary** *adj* stehend; **be ~ary** stehen

stationery /'steɪʃənrɪ/ *n* Briefpapier *nt*; (*writing materials*) Schreibwaren *pl*

'station-wagon *n* (*Amer*) Kombi[wagen] *n*

statistic /stə'tɪstɪk/ *n* statistische Tatsache *f*. **~al** *adj* statistisch. **~s** *n* & *pl* Statistik *f*

statue /'stætju:/ *n* Statue *f*

stature /'stætʃə(r)/ *n* Statur *f*; (*fig*) Format *nt*

status /'steɪtəs/ *n* Status *m*, Rang *m*

statut|e /'stætju:t/ *n* Statut *nt*. **~ory** *adj* gesetzlich

staunch /stɔ:ntʃ/ *adj* (**-er, -est**) treu

stave /steɪv/ *vt* **~ off** abwenden

stay /steɪ/ *n* Aufenthalt *m* ● *vi* bleiben; (*reside*) wohnen; **~ the night**

S

übernachten. ~ **behind** *vi* zurückbleiben. ~ **in** *vi* zu Hause bleiben; (*Sch*) nachsitzen. ~ **up** *vi* (*person:*) aufbleiben

steadily /'stedılı/ *adv* fest; (*continually*) stetig

steady /'stedı/ *adj* fest; (*not wobbly*) stabil; (*hand*) ruhig; (*regular*) regelmäßig; (*dependable*) zuverlässig

steak /steık/ *n* Steak *nt*

steal /sti:l/ *vt/i* (*pt* **stole**, *pp* **stolen**) stehlen (**from** *dat*). ~ **in/out** *vi* sich hinein-/hinausstehlen

stealthy /stelθı/ *adj* heimlich

steam /sti:m/ *n* Dampf *m* ● *vt* (*Culin*) dämpfen, dünsten ● *vi* dampfen. ~ **up** *vi* beschlagen

'steam engine *n* Dampfmaschine *f*; (*Rail*) Dampflokomotive *f*

steamer /'sti:mə(r)/ *n* Dampfer *m*

steamy /'sti:mı/ *adj* dampfig

steel /sti:l/ *n* Stahl *m*

steep /sti:p/ *adj* steil; (🅸: *exorbitant*) gesalzen

steeple /'sti:pl/ *n* Kirchturm *m*

steer /stıə(r)/ *vt/i* (*Auto*) lenken; (*Naut*) steuern; ~ **clear of s.o./sth** jdm/ etw aus dem Weg gehen. **~ing** *n* (*Auto*) Lenkung *f*. **~ing-wheel** *n* Lenkrad *nt*

stem¹ /stem/ *n* Stiel *m*; (*of word*) Stamm *m*

stem² *vt* (*pt/pp* **stemmed**) eindämmen; stillen (*bleeding*)

stench /stentʃ/ *n* Gestank *m*

stencil /'stensl/ *n* Schablone *f*

step /step/ *n* Schritt *m*; (*stair*) Stufe *f*; **~s** *pl* (*ladder*) Trittleiter *f*; **in** ~ im Schritt; ~ **by** ~ Schritt für Schritt; **take ~s** (*fig*) Schritte unternehmen ● *vi* (*pt/pp* **stepped**) treten; ~ **in** (*fig*) eingreifen. ~ **up** *vt* (*increase*) erhöhen, steigen; verstärken (*efforts*)

step: **~brother** *n* Stiefbruder *m*. **~child** *n* Stiefkind *nt*. **~daughter** *n* Stieftochter *f*. **~father** *n* Stiefvater *m*. **~-ladder** *n* Trittleiter *f*. **~mother** *n* Stiefmutter *f*. **~sister** *n* Stiefschwester *f*. **~son** *n* Stiefsohn *m*

stereo /'sterıəʊ/ *n* Stereo *nt*; (*equipment*) Stereoanlage *f*. **~phonic** *adj* stereophon

stereotype /'sterıətaıp/ *n* stereotype Figur *f*

steril|e /'steraıl/ *adj* steril. **~ize** *vt* sterilisieren

sterling /'stɜ:lıŋ/ *adj* Sterling-; (*fig*) gediegen ● *n* Sterling *m*

stern¹ /stɜ:n/ *adj* (**-er, -est**) streng

stern² *n* (*of boat*) Heck *nt*

stew /stju:/ *n* Eintopf *m*; **in a** ~ 🅸 aufgeregt ● *vt/i* schmoren; **~ed fruit** Kompott *nt*

steward /'stju:əd/ *n* Ordner *m*; (*on ship, aircraft*) Steward *m*. **~ess** *n* Stewardess *f*

stick¹ /stık/ *n* Stock *m*; (*of chalk*) Stück *nt*; (*of rhubarb*) Stange *f*; (*Sport*) Schläger *m*

stick² *v* (*pt/pp* **stuck**) ● *vt* stecken; (*stab*) stechen; (*glue*) kleben; (🅸: *put*) tun; (🅸: *endure*) aushalten ● *vi* stecken; (*adhere*) kleben, haften (**to** an + *dat*); (*jam*) klemmen; ~ **at it** 🅸 dranbleiben; ~ **up** for 🅸 eintreten für; **be stuck** nicht weiterkönnen; (*vehicle:*) festsitzen, festgefahren sein; (*drawer:*) klemmen; **be stuck with sth** 🅸 etw am Hals haben. ~ **out** *vi* abstehen; (*project*) vorstehen ● *vt* hinausstrecken; herausstrecken (*tongue*)

sticker /'stıkə(r)/ *n* Aufkleber *m*

'sticking plaster *n* Heftpflaster *nt*

sticky /'stıkı/ *adj* klebrig; (*adhesive*) Klebe-

stiff /stɪf/ *adj* (**-er, -est**) steif; (*brush*) hart; (*dough*) fest; (*difficult*) schwierig; (*penalty*) schwer; **be bored ~** 🄸 sich zu Tode langweilen. **~en** *vt* steif machen ● *vi* steif werden. **~ness** *n* Steifheit *f*

stifl|e /'staɪfl/ *vt* ersticken; (*fig*) unterdrücken. **~ing** *adj* **be ~ing** zum Ersticken sein

still /stɪl/ *adj* still; (*drink*) ohne Kohlensäure; **keep ~** stillhalten; **stand ~** stillstehen ● *adv* noch; (*emphatic*) immer noch; (*nevertheless*) trotzdem; **~ not** immer noch nicht

'stillborn *adj* tot geboren

still 'life *n* Stillleben *nt*

stilted /'stɪltɪd/ *adj* gestelzt, geschraubt

stimulant /'stɪmjʊlənt/ *n* Anregungsmittel *nt*

stimulat|e /'stɪmjʊleɪt/ *vt* anregen. **~ion** *n* Anregung *f*

stimulus /'stɪmjʊləs/ *n* (*pl* **-li** /-laɪ/) Reiz *m*

sting /stɪŋ/ *n* Stich *m*; (*from nettle, jellyfish*) Brennen *nt*; (*organ*) Stachel *m* ● *v* (*pt/pp* **stung**) ● *vt* stechen ● *vi* brennen; (*insect:*) stechen

stingy /'stɪndʒɪ/ *adj* geizig, 🄸 knauserig

stink /stɪŋk/ *n* Gestank *m* ● *vi* (*pt* **stank**, *pp* **stunk**) stinken (**of** nach)

stipulat|e /'stɪpjʊleɪt/ *vt* vorschreiben. **~ion** *n* Bedingung *f*

stir /stɜ:(r)/ *n* (*commotion*) Aufregung *f* ● *v* (*pt/pp* **stirred**) *vt* rühren ● *vi* sich rühren

stirrup /'stɪrəp/ *n* Steigbügel *m*

stitch /stɪtʃ/ *n* Stich *m*; (*Knitting*) Masche *f*; (*pain*) Seitenstechen *nt*; **be in ~es** 🄸 sich kaputtlachen ● *vt* nähen

stock /stɒk/ *n* Vorrat *m* (**of** an + *dat*); (*in shop*) [Waren]bestand *m*; (*livestock*) Vieh *nt*; (*lineage*) Abstammung *f*; (*Finance*) Wertpapiere *pl*; (*Culin*) Brühe *f*; (*plant*) Levkoje *f*; **in/out of ~** vorrätig/nicht vorrätig; **take ~** (*fig*) Bilanz ziehen ● *adj* Standard- ● *vt* (*shop:*) führen; auffüllen (*shelves*). **~ up** *vi* sich eindecken (**with** mit)

stock: ~broker *n* Börsenmakler *m*. **S~ Exchange** *n* Börse *f*

stocking /'stɒkɪŋ/ *n* Strumpf *m*

stock: ~market *n* Börse *f*. **~-taking** *n* (*Comm*) Inventur *f*

stocky /'stɒkɪ/ *adj* untersetzt

stodgy /'stɒdʒɪ/ *adj* pappig [und schwer verdaulich]

stoke /stəʊk/ *vt* heizen

stole /stəʊl/, **stolen** *see* **steal**

stomach /'stʌmək/ *n* Magen *m*. **~-ache** *n* Magenschmerzen *pl*

stone /stəʊn/ *n* Stein *m*; (*weight*) 6,35kg ● *adj* steinern; (*wall, Age*) Stein- ● *vt* mit Steinen bewerfen; entsteinen (*fruit*). **~-cold** *adj* eiskalt. **~-'deaf** *n* 🄸 stocktaub

stony /'stəʊnɪ/ *adj* steinig

stood /stʊd/ *see* stand

stool /stu:l/ *n* Hocker *m*

stoop /stu:p/ *n* **walk with a ~** gebeugt gehen ● *vi* sich bücken

stop /stɒp/ *n* Halt *m*; (*break*) Pause *f*; (*for bus*) Haltestelle *f*; (*for train*) Station *f*; (*Gram*) Punkt *m*; (*on organ*) Register *nt*; **come to a ~** stehen bleiben; **put a ~ to sth** etw unterbinden ● *v* (*pt/pp* **stopped**) ● *vt* anhalten, stoppen; (*switch off*) abstellen; (*plug, block*) zustopfen; (*prevent*) verhindern; **~ s.o. doing sth** jdn daran hindern, etw zu tun; **~ doing sth** aufhören, etw zu tun; **~ that!** hör auf damit! ● *vi* anhalten; (*cease*) aufhören; (*clock:*) stehen bleiben ● *int* halt!

stop: ~gap *n* Notlösung *f*. **~over** *n* (*Aviat*) Zwischenlandung *f*

S

stoppage /ˈstɒpɪdʒ/ *n* Unterbrechung *f*; (*strike*) Streik *m*

stopper /ˈstɒpə(r)/ *n* Stöpsel *m*

stop-watch *n* Stoppuhr *f*

storage /ˈstɔːrɪdʒ/ *n* Aufbewahrung *f*; (*in warehouse*) Lagerung *f*; (*Computing*) Speicherung *f*

store /stɔː(r)/ *n* (*stock*) Vorrat *m*; (*shop*) Laden *m*; (*department* ~) Kaufhaus *nt*; (*depot*) Lager *nt*; **in** ~ auf Lager; **be in ~ for s.o.** (*fig*) jdm bevorstehen ● *vt* aufbewahren; (*in warehouse*) lagern; (*Computing*) speichern. **~-room** *n* Lagerraum *m*

storey /ˈstɔːrɪ/ *n* Stockwerk *nt*

stork /stɔːk/ *n* Storch *m*

storm /stɔːm/ *n* Sturm *m*; (*with thunder*) Gewitter *nt* ● *vt/i* stürmen. **~y** *adj* stürmisch

story /ˈstɔːrɪ/ *n* Geschichte *f*; (*in newspaper*) Artikel *m*; ([!]: *lie*) Märchen *nt*

stout /staʊt/ *adj* (**-er, -est**) beleibt; (*strong*) fest

stove /stəʊv/ *n* Ofen *m*; (*for cooking*) Herd *m*

stow /stəʊ/ *vt* verstauen. **~away** *n* blinder Passagier *m*

straggl|e /ˈstræɡl/ *vi* hinterherhinken. **~er** *n* Nachzügler *m*. **~y** *adj* strähnig

straight /streɪt/ *adj* (**-er, -est**) gerade; (*direct*) direkt; (*clear*) klar; (*hair*) glatt; (*drink*); pur; **be** ~ (*tidy*) in Ordnung sein ● *adv* gerade; (*directly*) direkt, geradewegs; (*clearly*) klar; ~ **away** sofort; ~ **on** *or* **ahead** geradeaus; ~ **out** (*fig*) geradeheraus; **sit/stand up** ~ gerade sitzen/stehen

straighten /ˈstreɪtn/ *vt* gerade machen; (*put straight*) gerade richten ● *vi* gerade werden; ~ **[up]** (*person:*) sich aufrichten. ~ **out** *vt* gerade biegen

straightˈforward *adj* offen; (*simple*) einfach

strain /ˈstreɪn/ *n* Belastung *f*; **~s** *pl* (*of music*) Klänge *pl* ● *vt* belasten; (*overexert*) überanstrengen; (*injure*) zerren (*muscle*); (*Culin*) durchseihen; abgießen (*vegetables*). **~ed** *adj* (*relations*) gespannt. **~er** *n* Sieb *nt*

strait /streɪt/ *n* Meerenge *f*; **in dire ~s** in großen Nöten

strand[1] /strænd/ *n* (*of thread*) Faden *m*; (*of hair*) Strähne *f*

strand[2] *vt* **be ~ed** festsitzen

strange /streɪndʒ/ *adj* (**-r, -st**) fremd; (*odd*) seltsam, merkwürdig. **~ly** *adv* seltsam, merkwürdig; ~ **enough** seltsamerweise. **~r** *n* Fremde(r) *m/f*

strangle /ˈstræŋɡl/ *vt* erwürgen; (*fig*) unterdrücken

strap /stræp/ *n* Riemen *m*; (*for safety*) Gurt *m*; (*to grasp in vehicle*) Halteriemen *m*; (*of watch*) Armband *nt*; (*shoulder~*) Träger *m* ● *vt* (*pt/pp* **strapped**) schnallen

strapping /ˈstræpɪŋ/ *adj* stramm

strategic /strəˈtiːdʒɪk/ *adj*, **-ally** *adv* strategisch

strategy /ˈstrætədʒɪ/ *n* Strategie *f*

straw /strɔː/ *n* Stroh *nt*; (*single piece, drinking*) Strohhalm *m*; **that's the last** ~ jetzt reicht's aber

strawberry /ˈstrɔːbərɪ/ *n* Erdbeere *f*

stray /streɪ/ *adj* streunend ● *n* streunendes Tier *nt* ● *vi* sich verirren; (*deviate*) abweichen

streak /striːk/ *n* Streifen *m*; (*in hair*) Strähne *f*; (*fig: trait*) Zug *m*

stream /striːm/ *n* Bach *m*; (*flow*) Strom *m*; (*current*) Strömung *f*; (*Sch*) Parallelzug *m* ● *vi* strömen

ˈstreamline *vt* (*fig*) rationalisieren. **~d** *adj* stromlinienförmig

street /striːt/ *n* Straße *f*. **~car** *n*

S

(*Amer*) Straßenbahn *f*. **~lamp** *n* Straßenlaterne *f*

strength /streŋθ/ *n* Stärke *f*; (*power*) Kraft *f*; **on the ~ of** auf Grund (+ *gen*). **~en** *vt* stärken; (*reinforce*) verstärken

strenuous /'strenjʊəs/ *adj* anstrengend

stress /stres/ *n* (*emphasis*) Betonung *f*; (*strain*) Belastung *f*; (*mental*) Stress *m* ● *vt* betonen; (*put a strain on*) belasten. **~ful** *adj* stressig [!]

stretch /stretʃ/ *n* (*of road*) Strecke *f*; (*elasticity*) Elastizität *f*; **at a ~** ohne Unterbrechung; **have a ~** sich strecken ● *vt* strecken; (*widen*) dehnen; (*spread*) ausbreiten; fordern (*person*); **~ one's legs** sich (*dat*) die Beine vertreten ● *vt* sich erstrecken; (*become wider*) sich dehnen; (*person:*) sich strecken. **~er** *n* Tragbahre *f*

strict /strɪkt/ *adj* (**-er, -est**) streng; **~ly speaking** streng genommen

stride /straɪd/ *n* [großer] Schritt *m*; **take sth in one's ~** mit etw gut fertig werden ● *vi* (*pt* **strode**, *pp* **stridden**) [mit großen Schritten] gehen

strident /straɪdnt/ *adj* schrill; (*colour*) grell

strife /straɪf/ *n* Streit *m*

strike /straɪk/ *n* Streik *m*; (*Mil*) Angriff *m*; **be on ~** streiken ● *v* (*pt/pp* **struck**) ● *vt* schlagen; (*knock against, collide with*) treffen; anzünden (*match*); stoßen auf (+ *acc*) (*oil, gold*); abbrechen (*camp*); (*impress*) beeindrucken; (*occur to*) einfallen (+ *dat*); **~ s.o. a blow** jdm einen Schlag versetzen ● *vi* treffen; (*lightning:*) einschlagen; (*clock:*) schlagen; (*attack*) zuschlagen; (*workers:*) streiken

striker /'straɪkə(r)/ *n* Streikende(r) *m/f*

striking /'straɪkɪŋ/ *adj* auffallend

string /strɪŋ/ *n* Schnur *f*; (*thin*) Bindfaden *m*; (*of musical instrument, racket*) Saite *f*; (*of bow*) Sehne *f*; (*of pearls*) Kette *f*; **the ~s** (*Mus*) die Streicher *pl*; **pull ~s** [!] seine Beziehungen spielen lassen ● *vt* (*pt/pp* **strung**) (*thread*) aufziehen (*beads*)

stringent /'strɪndʒnt/ *adj* streng

strip /strɪp/ *n* Streifen *m* ● *v* (*pt/pp* **stripped**) ● *vt* ablösen; ausziehen (*person, clothes*); abziehen (*bed*); abbeizen (*wood, furniture*); auseinander nehmen (*machine*); (*deprive*) berauben (*of gen*); **~ sth off sth** etw von etw entfernen ● *vi* (*undress*) sich ausziehen

stripe /straɪp/ *n* Streifen *m*. **~d** *adj* gestreift

stripper /'strɪpə(r)/ *n* Stripperin *f*; (*male*) Stripper *m*

strive /straɪv/ *vi* (*pt* **strove**, *pp* **striven**) sich bemühen (**to** zu); **~ for** streben nach

strode /strəʊd/ *see* **stride**

stroke¹ /strəʊk/ *n* Schlag *m*; (*of pen*) Strich *m*; (*Swimming*) Zug *m*; (*style*) Stil *m*; (*Med*) Schlaganfall *m*; **~ of luck** Glücksfall *m*

stroke² ● *vt* streicheln

stroll /strəʊl/ *n* Bummel *m* [!] ● *vi* bummeln [!]. **~er** *n* (*Amer: pushchair*) [Kinder]sportwagen *m*

strong /strɒŋ/ *adj* (**-er** /-gə(r)/, **-est** /-gɪst/) stark; (*powerful, healthy*) kräftig; (*severe*) streng; (*sturdy*) stabil; (*convincing*) gut

strong: ~hold *n* Festung *f*; (*fig*) Hochburg *f*. **~-room** *n* Tresorraum *m*

strove /strəʊv/ *see* **strive**

struck /strʌk/ *see* **strike**

structural /'strʌktʃərl/ *adj* baulich

structure /'strʌktʃə(r)/ *n* Struktur

f; (*building*) Bau *m*

struggle /'strʌgl/ *n* Kampf *m*; **with a ~** mit Mühe ● *vt* kämpfen; **~ to do sth** sich abmühen, etw zutun

strum /strʌm/ *v* (*pt*/*pp* **strummed**) ● *vt* klimpern auf (+ *dat*) ● *vi* klimpern

strung /strʌŋ/ *see* **string**

strut[1] /strʌt/ *n* Strebe *f*

strut[2] *vi* (*pt*/*pp* **strutted**) stolzieren

stub /stʌb/ *n* Stummel *m*; (*counterfoil*) Abschnitt *m*. **~ out** *vt* (*pt*/*pp* **stubbed**) ausdrücken (*cigarette*)

stubble /'stʌbl/ *n* Stoppeln *pl*

stubborn /'stʌbən/ *adj* starrsinnig; (*refusal*) hartnäckig

stubby /'stʌbɪ/ *adj*, (**-ier, -iest**) kurz und dick

stuck /stʌk/ *see* **stick**[2]. **~-'up** *adj* 🅸 hochnäsig

stud /stʌd/ *n* Nagel *m*; (*on clothes*) Niete *f*; (*for collar*) Kragenknopf *m*; (*for ear*) Ohrstecker *m*

student /'stju:dnt/ *n* Student(in) *m*(*f*); (*Sch*) Schüler(in) *m*(*f*)

studio /'stju:dɪəʊ/ *n* Studio *nt*; (*for artist*) Atelier *nt*

studious /'stju:dɪəs/ *adj* lerneifrig; (*earnest*) ernsthaft

stud|y /'stʌdɪ/ *n* Studie *f*; (*room*) Arbeitszimmer *nt*; (*investigation*) Untersuchung *f*; **~ies** *pl* Studium *nt* ● *v* (*pt*/*pp* **studied**) ● *vt* studieren; (*examine*) untersuchen ● *vi* lernen; (*at university*) studieren

stuff /stʌf/ *n* Stoff *m*; (🅸*: things*) Zeug *nt* ● *vt* vollstopfen; (*with padding, Culin*) füllen; ausstopfen (*animal*); (*cram*) [hinein]stopfen. **~ing** *n* Füllung *f*

stuffy /'stʌfɪ/ *adj* stickig; (*old-fashioned*) spießig

stumbl|e /'stʌmbl/ *vi* stolpern; **~e across** zufällig stoßen auf (+ *acc*). **~ing-block** *n* Hindernis *nt*

stump /stʌmp/ *n* Stumpf *m* ● **~ up** *vt*/*i* 🅸 blechen. **~ed** *adj* 🅸 überfragt

stun /stʌn/ *vt* (*pt*/*pp* **stunned**) betäuben

stung /stʌŋ/ *see* **sting**

stunk /stʌŋk/ *see* **stink**

stunning /'stʌnɪŋ/ *adj* 🅸 toll

stunt /stʌnt/ *n* 🅸 Kunststück *nt*

stupendous /stju:'pendəs/ *adj* enorm

stupid /'stju:pɪd/ *adj* dumm. **~ity** *n* Dummheit *f*. **~ly** *adv* dumm; **~ly [enough]** dummerweise

sturdy /'stɜ:dɪ/ *adj* stämmig; (*furniture*) stabil; (*shoes*) fest

stutter /'stʌtə(r)/ *n* Stottern *nt* ● *vt*/*i* stottern

sty /staɪ/ *n* (*pl* **sties**) Schweinestall *m*

style /staɪl/ *n* Stil *m*; (*fashion*) Mode *f*; (*sort*) Art *f*; (*hair~*) Frisur *f*; **in ~** in großem Stil

stylish /'staɪlɪʃ/ *adj*, -ly *adv* stilvoll

stylist /'staɪlɪst/ *n* Friseur *m*/ Friseuse *f*. **~ic** *adj*, **-ally** *adv* stilistisch

suave /swɑ:v/ *adj* (*pej*) gewandt

sub'conscious /sʌb-/ *adj* unterbewusst ● *n* Unterbewusstsein *nt*

'subdivi|de *vt* unterteilen. **~sion** *n* Unterteilung *f*

S

subdue /səb'dju:/ *vt* unterwerfen. **~d** *adj* gedämpft; (*person*) still

subject[1] /'sʌbdʒɪkt/ *adj* **be ~ to sth** etw (*dat*) unterworfen sein ● *n* Staatsbürger(in) *m*(*f*); (*of ruler*) Untertan *m*; (*theme*) Thema *nt*; (*of investigation*) Gegenstand *m*; (*Sch*) Fach *nt*; (*Gram*) Subjekt *nt*

subject[2] /səb'dʒekt/ *vt* unterwerfen (**to** *dat*); (*expose*) aussetzen (**to** *dat*)

subjective /səb'dʒektɪv/ *adj*

subjektiv
subjunctive /səbˈdʒʌŋktɪv/ *n* Konjunktiv *m*
sublime /səˈblaɪm/ *adj* erhaben
submaˈrine *n* Unterseeboot *nt*
submerge /səbˈmɜːdʒ/ *vt* untertauchen; **be ~d** unter Wasser stehen ● *vi* tauchen
submission /səbˈmɪʃn/ *n* Unterwerfung *f*
submit /səbˈmɪt/ *v* (*pt/pp* **-mitted**, *pres p* **-mitting**) ● *vt* vorlegen (**to** *dat*); (*hand in*) einreichen ● *vi* sich unterwerfen (**to** *dat*)
subordinate¹ /səˈbɔːdɪnət/ *adj* untergeordnet ● *n* Untergebene(r) *m/f*
subordinate² /səˈbɔːdɪneɪt/ *vt* unterordnen (**to** *dat*)
subscribe /səbˈskraɪb/ *vi* spenden; **~ to** (*fig*); abonnieren (*newspaper*). **~r** *n* Spender *m*; Abonnent *m*
subscription /səbˈskrɪpʃn/ *n* (*to club*) [Mitglieds]beitrag *m*; (*to newspaper*) Abonnement *nt*; **by ~** mit Spenden; (*buy*) im Abonnement
subsequent /ˈsʌbsɪkwənt/ *adj* folgend; (*later*) später
subside /səbˈsaɪd/ *vi* sinken; (*ground:*) sich senken; (*storm:*) nachlassen
subsidiary /səbˈsɪdɪərɪ/ *adj* untergeordnet ● *n* Tochtergesellschaft *f*
subsid|ize /ˈsʌbsɪdaɪz/ *vt* subventionieren. **~y** *n* Subvention *f*
substance /ˈsʌbstəns/ *n* Substanz *f*
subˈstandard *adj* unzulänglich; (*goods*) minderwertig
substantial /səbˈstænʃl/ *adj* solide; (*meal*) reichhaltig; (*considerable*) beträchtlich. **~ly** *adv* solide; (*essentially*) im Wesentlichen
substitut|e /ˈsʌbstɪtjuːt/ *n* Ersatz *m*; (*Sport*) Ersatzspieler(in) *m(f)* ● *vt* **~e A for B** B durch A ersetzen ● *vi* **~e for s.o.** jdn vertreten. **~ion** *n* Ersetzung *f*
subterranean /sʌbtəˈreɪmɪən/ *adj* unterirdisch
ˈsubtitle *n* Untertitel *m*
subtle /ˈsʌtl/ *adj* (**-r, -st**), **-tly** *adv* fein; (*fig*) subtil
subtract /səbˈtrækt/ *vt* abziehen, subtrahieren. **~ion** *n* Subtraktion *f*
suburb /ˈsʌbɜːb/ *n* Vorort *m*. **~an** *adj* Vorort-. **~ia** *n* die Vororte *pl*
ˈsubway *n* Unterführung *f*; (*Amer: railway*) U-Bahn *f*
succeed /səkˈsiːd/ *vi* Erfolg haben; (*plan:*) gelingen; (*follow*) nachfolgen (+ *dat*); **I ~ed** es ist mir gelungen; **he ~ed in escaping** es gelang ihm zu entkommen ● *vt* folgen (+ *dat*)
success /səkˈses/ *n* Erfolg *m*. **~ful** *adj*,**-ly** *adv* erfolgreich
succession /səkˈseʃn/ *n* Folge *f*; (*series*) Serie *f*; (*to title, office*) Nachfolge *f*; (*to throne*) Thronfolge *f*; **in ~** hintereinander
successive /səkˈsesɪv/ *adj* aufeinander folgend
successor /səkˈsesə(r)/ *n* Nachfolger(in) *m(f)*
succumb /səˈkʌm/ *vi* erliegen (**to** *dat*)

such /sʌtʃ/
● *adjective*
····➤ (*of that kind*) solch. **such a book** ein solches Buch; so ein Buch [!]. **such a person** ein solcher Mensch; so ein Mensch [!]. **such people** solche Leute. **such a thing** so etwas. **no such example** kein solches Beispiel. **there is no such thing** so etwas gibt es nicht; das gibt es gar nicht. **there is no such person**

eine solche Person gibt es nicht. **such writers as Goethe and Schiller** Schriftsteller wie Goethe und Schiller

····➤ (*so great*) solch; derartig. **I've got such a headache!** ich habe solche Kopfschmerzen! **it was such fun!** das machte solchen Spaß! **I got such a fright that ...** ich bekam einen derartigen *od* [T] so einen Schrecken, dass ...

····➤ (*with adjective*) so. **such a big house** ein so großes Haus. **he has such lovely blue eyes** er hat so schöne blaue Augen. **such a long time** so lange

● *pronoun*

····➤ **as such** als solcher/solche/solches. **the thing as such** die Sache als solche. (*strictly speaking*) **this is not a promotion as such** dies ist im Grunde genommen keine Beförderung

····➤ **such is: such is life** so ist das Leben. **such is not the case** das ist nicht der Fall

····➤ **such as** wie [zum Beispiel]

suchlike /ˈsʌtʃlaɪk/ *pron* [T] dergleichen

suck /ʃʌk/ *vt/i* saugen; lutschen (*sweet*). ~ **up** *vt* aufsaugen ● *vi* ~ **up to s.o.** [T] sich bei jdm einschmeicheln

suction /ˈsʌkʃn/ *n* Saugwirkung *f*

sudden /ˈsʌdn/ *adj* plötzlich; (*abrupt*) jäh ● *n* **all of a** ~ auf einmal

sue /su:/ *vt* (*pres p* **suing**) verklagen (**for** auf + *acc*) ● *vi* klagen

suede /sweɪd/ *n* Wildleder *nt*

suet /ˈsu:ɪt/ *n* [Nieren]talg *m*

suffer /ˈsʌfə(r)/ *vi* leiden (**from** an + *dat*) ● *vt* erleiden; (*tolerate*) dulden

suffice /səˈfaɪs/ *vi* genügen

sufficient /səˈfɪʃnt/ *adj* genug, genügend; **be** ~ genügen

suffocat|e /ˈsʌfəkeɪt/ *vt/i* ersticken. ~**ion** *n* Ersticken *nt*

sugar /ˈʃʊgə(r)/ *n* Zucker *m* ● *vt* zuckern; (*fig*) versüßen. ~ **basin,** ~**-bowl** *n* Zuckerschale *f*. ~**y** *adj* süß; (*fig*) süßlich

suggest /səˈdʒest/ *vt* vorschlagen; (*indicate, insinuate*) andeuten. ~**ion** *n* Vorschlag *m*; Andeutung *f*; (*trace*) Spur *f*. ~**ive** *adj* anzüglich

suicidal /su:ɪˈsaɪdl/ *adj* selbstmörderisch

suicide /ˈsu:ɪsaɪd/ *n* Selbstmord *m*

suit /su:t/ *n* Anzug *m*; (*woman's*) Kostüm *nt*; (*Cards*) Farbe *f*; (*Jur*) Prozess *m* ● *vt* (*adapt*) anpassen (**to** *dat*); (*be convenient for*) passen (+ *dat*); (*go with*) passen zu; (*clothing:*) stehen (**s.o.** *jdm*); **be** ~**ed for** geeignet sein für; ~ **yourself!** wie du willst!

suit|able /ˈsu:təbl/ *adj* geeignet; (*convenient*) passend; (*appropriate*) angemessen; (*for weather, activity*) zweckmäßig. ~**ably** *adv* angemessen; zweckmäßig

ˈ**suitcase** *n* Koffer *m*

suite /swi:t/ *n* Suite *f*; (*of furniture*) Garnitur *f*

sulk /sʌlk/ *vi* schmollen. ~**y** *adj* schmollend

sullen /ˈsʌlən/ *adj* mürrisch

sultry /ˈsʌltrɪ/ *adj* (**-ier, -iest**) (*weather*) schwül

sum /sʌm/ *n* Summe *f*; (*Sch*) Rechenaufgabe *f* ● *vt/i* (*pt/pp* **summed**) ~ **up** zusammenfassen; (*assess*) einschätzen

summar|ize /ˈsʌməraɪz/ *vt* zusammenfassen. ~**y** *n* Zusammenfassung *f* ● *adj*, **-ily** *adv* summarisch; (*dismissal*) fristlos

summer /'sʌmə(r)/ *n* Sommer *m*. **~time** *n* Sommer *m*

summer camp Amerikanische Feriencamps haben eine lange Tradition. Sie bieten ein umfassendes Fitnessprogramm, und Schulkinder haben die Möglichkeit, alle erdenklichen Sportarten und Spiele in den Sommerferien auszuprobieren. Hier erhalten die Teilnehmer Survival-Training und lernen außerdem Unabhängigkeit und Führungseigenschaften. Tausende von Studenten arbeiten während der Sommermonate als Betreuer in den Feriencamps.

summery /'sʌmərɪ/ *adj* sommerlich

summit /'sʌmɪt/ *n* Gipfel *m*. **~ conference** *n* Gipfelkonferenz *f*

summon /'sʌmən/ *vt* rufen; holen (*help*); (*Jur*) vorladen

summons /'sʌmənz/ *n* (*Jur*) Vorladung *f* ● *vt* vorladen

sumptuous /'sʌmptjʊəs/ *adj* prunkvoll; (*meal*) üppig

sun /sʌn/ *n* Sonne *f* ● *vt* (*pt/pp* **sunned**) **~ oneself** sich sonnen

sun: ~bathe *vi* sich sonnen. **~-bed** *n* Sonnenbank *f*. **~burn** *n* Sonnenbrand *m*

Sunday /'sʌndeɪ/ *n* Sonntag *m*

'sunflower *n* Sonnenblume *f*

sung /sʌŋ/ *see* **sing**

'sunglasses *npl* Sonnenbrille *f*

sunk /sʌŋk/ *see* **sink**

sunny /'sʌnɪ/ *adj* (**-ier**, **-iest**) sonnig

sun: ~rise *n* Sonnenaufgang *m*. **~-roof** *n* (*Auto*) Schiebedach *nt*. **~set** *n* Sonnenuntergang *m*. **~shade** *n* Sonnenschirm *m*. **~shine** *n* Sonnenschein *m*. **~stroke** *n* Sonnenstich *m*. **~-tan** *n* [Sonnen]bräune *f*. **~-tanned** *adj* braun [gebrannt]. **~-tan oil** *n* Sonnenöl *nt*

super /'su:pə(r)/ *adj* [!] prima, toll

superb /sʊ'pɜ:b/ *adj* erstklassig

superficial /su:pə'fɪʃl/ a oberflächlich

superfluous /sʊ'pɜ:flʊəs/ *adj* überflüssig

superintendent /su:pərɪn'tendənt/ *n* (*of police*) Kommissar *m*

superior /su:'pɪərɪə(r)/ a überlegen; (*in rank*) höher ● *n* Vorgesetzte(r) *m/f*. **~ity** *n* Überlegenheit *f*

superlative /su:'pɜ:lətɪv/ a unübertrefflich ● *n* Superlativ *m*

'supermarket *n* Supermarkt *m*

super'natural *adj* übernatürlich

supersede /su:pə'si:d/ *vt* ersetzen

superstiti|on /su:pə'stɪʃn/ *n* Aberglaube *m*. **~ous** *adj* abergläubisch

supervis|e /'su:pəvaɪz/ *vt* beaufsichtigen; überwachen (*work*). **~ion** *n* Aufsicht *f*; Überwachung *f*. **~or** *n* Aufseher(in) *m*(*f*)

supper /'sʌpə(r)/ *n* Abendessen *nt*

supple /'sʌpl/ *adj* geschmeidig

supplement /'sʌplɪmənt/ *n* Ergänzung *f*; (*addition*) Zusatz *m*; (*to fare*) Zuschlag *m*; (*book*) Ergänzungsband *m*; (*to newspaper*) Beilage *f* ● *vt* ergänzen. **~ary** a zusätzlich

supplier /sə'plaɪə(r)/ *n* Lieferant *m*

supply /sə'plaɪ/ *n* Vorrat *m*; **supplies** *pl* (*Mil*) Nachschub *m* ● *vt* (*pt/pp* **-ied**) liefern; **~ s.o. with sth** jdn mit etw versorgen

support /sə'pɔ:t/ *n* Stütze *f*; (*fig*) Unterstützung *f* ● *vt* stützen; (*bear weight of*) tragen; (*keep*) ernähren; (*give money to*) unterstützen; (*speak* *in favour of*) befürworten; (*Sport*) Fan sein von. **~er** *n* Anhänger(in) *m*(*f*); (*Sport*) Fan *m*

suppose /sə'pəʊz/ *vt* annehmen; (*presume*) vermuten; (*imagine*) sich (*dat*) vorstellen; **be ~d to do sth** etw tun sollen; **not be ~d to** 🄸 nicht dürfen; **I ~ so** vermutlich. **~dly** *adv* angeblich

supposition /sʌpə'zɪʃn/ *n* Vermutung *f*

suppress /sə'pres/ *vt* unterdrücken. **~ion** *n* Unterdrückung *f*

supremacy /suː'preməsɪ/ *n* Vorherrschaft *f*

supreme /suː'priːm/ *adj* höchste(r,s); (*court*) oberste(r,s)

sure /ʃʊə(r)/ *adj* (**-r**, **-st**) sicher; **make ~** sich vergewissern (**of** *gen*); (*check*) nachprüfen ● *adv* (*Amer*, 🄸) klar; **~ enough** tatsächlich. **~ly** *adv* sicher; (*for emphasis*) doch; (*Amer: gladly*) gern

surf /'sɜːf/ *n* Brandung *f* ● *vi* surfen

surface /'sɜːfɪs/ *n* Oberfläche *f* ● *vi* (*emerge*) auftauchen

'surfboard *n* Surfbrett *nt*

surfing /'sɜːfɪŋ/ *n* Surfen *nt*

surge /sɜːdʒ/ *n* (*of sea*) Branden *nt*; (*fig*) Welle *f* ● *vi* branden; **~ forward** nach vorn drängen

surgeon /'sɜːdʒən/ *n* Chirurg(in) *m*(*f*)

surgery /'sɜːdʒərɪ/ *n* Chirurgie *f*; (*place*) Praxis *f*; (*room*) Sprechzimmer *nt*; (*hours*) Sprechstunde *f*; **have ~** operiert werden

surgical /'sɜːdʒɪkl/ *adj* chirurgisch

surly /'sɜːlɪ/ *adj* mürrisch

surname /'sɜːneɪm/ *n* Nachname *m*

surpass /sə'pɑːs/ *vt* übertreffen

surplus /'sɜːpləs/ *adj* überschüssig ● *n* Überschuss *m* (**of** an + *dat*)

surpris|e /sə'praɪz/ *n* Überraschung *f* ● *vt* überraschen; **be ~ed** sich wundern (**at** über + *acc*). **~ing** *adj* überraschend

surrender /sə'rendə(r)/ *n* Kapitulation *f* ● *vi* sich ergeben; (*Mil*) kapitulieren ● *vt* aufgeben

surround /sə'raʊnd/ *vt* umgeben; (*encircle*) umzingeln; **~ed by** umgeben von. **~ing** *adj* umliegend. **~ings** *npl* Umgebung *f*

surveillance /sə'veɪləns/ *n* Überwachung *f*; **be under ~** überwacht werden

survey[1] /'sɜːveɪ/ *n* Überblick *m*; (*poll*) Umfrage *f*; (*investigation*) Untersuchung *f*; (*of land*) Vermessung *f*; (*of house*) Gutachten *nt*

survey[2] /sə'veɪ/ *vt* betrachten; vermessen (*land*); begutachten (*building*). **~or** *n* Landvermesser *m*; Gutachter *m*

survival /sə'vaɪvl/ *n* Überleben *nt*; (*of tradition*) Fortbestand *m*

surviv|e /sə'vaɪv/ *vt* überleben ● *vi* überleben; (*tradition:*) erhalten bleiben. **~or** *n* Überlebende(r) *m*/*f*; **be a ~or** nicht unterzukriegen sein

susceptible /sə'septəbl/ *adj* empfänglich/ (*Med*) anfällig (**to** für)

suspect[1] /sə'spekt/ *vt* verdächtigen; (*assume*) vermuten; **he ~s nothing** er ahnt nichts

suspect[2] /'sʌspekt/ *adj* verdächtig ● *n* Verdächtige(r) *m*/*f*

suspend /sə'spend/ *vt* aufhängen; (*stop*) [vorläufig] einstellen; (*from duty*) vorläufig beurlauben. **~ders** *npl* (*Amer: braces*) Hosenträger *pl*

suspense /sə'spens/ *n* Spannung *f*

suspension /sə'spenʃn/ *n* (*Auto*) Federung *f*. **~ bridge** *n* Hängebrücke *f*

suspici|on /sə'spɪʃn/ *n* Verdacht *m*; (*mistrust*) Misstrauen *nt*; (*trace*)

Spur *f*. **~ous** *adj* misstrauisch; (*arousing suspicion*) verdächtig

sustain /sə'steɪn/ *vt* tragen; (*fig*) aufrechterhalten; erhalten (*life*); erleiden (*injury*)

sustenance /'sʌstɪnəns/ *n* Nahrung *f*

swagger /'swæɡə(r)/ *vi* stolzieren

swallow[1] /'swɒləʊ/ *vt/i* schlucken. **~ up** *vt* verschlucken; verschlingen (*resources*)

swallow[2] *n* (*bird*) Schwalbe *f*

swam /swæm/ *see* **swim**

swamp /swɒmp/ *n* Sumpf *m* ● *vt* überschwemmen

swan /swɒn/ *n* Schwan *m*

swank /swæŋk/ *vi* [T] angeben

swap /swɒp/ *n* [T] Tausch *m* ● *vt/i* (*pt/pp* **swapped**) [T] tauschen (**for** gegen)

swarm /swɔ:m/ *n* Schwarm *m* ● *vi* schwärmen; **be ~ing with** wimmeln von

swat /swɒt/ *vt* (*pt/pp* **swatted**) totschlagen

sway /sweɪ/ *vi* schwanken; (*gently*) sich wiegen ● *vt* (*influence*) beeinflussen

swear /sweə(r)/ *v* (*pt* **swore**, *pp* **sworn**) ● *vt* schwören ● *vi* schwören (**by** auf + *acc*); (*curse*) fluchen. **~-word** *n* Kraftausdruck *m*

sweat /swet/ *n* Schweiß *m* ● *vi* schwitzen

sweater /'swetə(r)/ *n* Pullover *m*

Swed|e *n* Schwede *m*/Schwedin *f*. **~en** *n* Schweden *nt*. **~ish** *adj* schwedisch

sweep /swi:p/ *n* Schornsteinfeger *m*; (*curve*) Bogen *m*; (*movement*) ausholende Bewegung *f* ● *v* (*pt/pp* **swept**) ● *vt* fegen, kehren ● *vi* (*go swiftly*) rauschen; (*wind:*) fegen

sweeping /'swi:pɪŋ/ *adj* ausholend; (*statement*) pauschal; (*changes*) weit reichend

sweet /swi:t/ *a* (**-er, -est**) süß; **have a ~ tooth** gern Süßes mögen ● *n* Bonbon *m & nt*; (*dessert*) Nachtisch *m*

sweeten /'swi:tn/ *vt* süßen

sweet: ~heart *n* Schatz *m*. **~ness** *n* Süße *f*. **~ 'pea** *n* Wicke *f*. **~-shop** *n* Süßwarenladen *m*

swell /swel/ *n* Dünung *f* ● *v* (*pt* **swelled**, *pp* **swollen** *or* **swelled**) ● *vi* [an]schwellen; (*wood:*) aufquellen ● *vt* anschwellen lassen; (*increase*) vergrößern. **~ing** *n* Schwellung *f*

swelter /'sweltə(r)/ *vi* schwitzen

swept /swept/ *see* **sweep**

swerve /swɜ:v/ *vi* einen Bogen machen

swift /swɪft/ *adj* (**-er, -est**) schnell

swig /swɪɡ/ *n* [T] Schluck *m*

swim /swɪm/ *n* **have a ~** schwimmen ● *vi* (**pt swam**, *pp* **swum**) schwimmen; **my head is ~ming** mir dreht sich der Kopf. **~mer** *n* Schwimmer(in) *m*(*f*)

swimming /'swɪmɪŋ/ *n* Schwimmen *nt*. **~-baths** *npl* Schwimmbad *nt*. **~-pool** *n* Schwimmbecken *nt*; (*private*) Swimmingpool *m*

'swimsuit *n* Badeanzug *m*

swindle /'swɪndl/ *n* Schwindel *m*, Betrug *m* ● *vt* betrügen. **~r** *n* Schwindler *m*

swine /swaɪn/ *n* (*pej*) Schwein *nt*

swing /swɪŋ/ *n* Schwung *m*; (*shift*) Schwenk *m*; (*seat*) Schaukel *f*; **in full ~** in vollem Gange ● (*pt/pp* **swung**) ● *vi* schwingen; (*on swing*) schaukeln; (*dangle*) baumeln; (*turn*) schwenken ● *vt* schwingen; (*influence*) beeinflussen

swipe /swaɪp/ *n* [T] Schlag *m* ● *vt* [T] knallen; (*steal*) klauen

swirl /swɜːl/ *n* Wirbel *m* ● *vt/i* wirbeln
Swiss /swɪs/ *adj* Schweizer-, schweizerisch ● *n* Schweizer(in) *m*(*f*); **the** ~ *pl* die Schweizer. ~ '**roll** *n* Biskuitrolle *f*
switch /swɪtʃ/ *n* Schalter *m*; (*change*) Wechsel *m*; (*Amer, Rail*) Weiche *f* ● *vt* wechseln; (*exchange*) tauschen ● *vi* wechseln; ~ **to** umstellen auf (+ *acc*). ~ **off** *vt* ausschalten; abschalten (*engine*). ~ **on** *vt* einschalten
switchboard *n* [Telefon]zentrale *f*
Switzerland /ˈswɪtsələnd/ *n* die Schweiz
swivel /ˈswɪvl/ *v* (*pt/pp* **swivelled**) ● *vt* drehen ● *vi* sich drehen
swollen /ˈswəʊlən/ *see* **swell**
swoop /swuːp/ *n* (*by police*) Razzia *f* ● *vi* ~ **down** herabstoßen
sword /sɔːd/ *n* Schwert *nt*
swore /swɔː(r)/ *see* **swear**
sworn /swɔːn/ *see* **swear**
swot /swɒt/ *n* [!] Streber *m* ● *vt* (*pt/pp* **swotted**) [!] büffeln
swum /swʌm/ *see* **swim**
swung /swʌŋ/ *see* **swing**
syllable /ˈsɪləbl/ *n* Silbe *f*
syllabus /ˈsɪləbəs/ *n* Lehrplan *m*; (*for exam*) Studienplan *m*
symbol /ˈsɪmbəl/ *n* Symbol *nt* (**of** für). ~**ic** *adj*, **-ally** *adv* symbolisch ~**ism** *n* Symbolik *f*. ~**ize** *vt* symbolisieren
symmetr|ical /sɪˈmetrɪkl/ *adj* symmetrisch. ~**y** *n* Symmetrie *f*
sympathetic /sɪmpəˈθetɪk/ *adj*, **-ally** *adv* mitfühlend; (*likeable*) sympathisch
sympathize /ˈsɪmpəθaɪz/ *vi* mitfühlen
sympathy /ˈsɪmpəθɪ/ *n* Mitgefühl *nt*; (*condolences*) Beileid *nt*
symphony /ˈsɪmfənɪ/ *n* Sinfonie *f*
symptom /ˈsɪmptəm/ *n* Symptom *nt*
synagogue /ˈsɪnəgɒg/ *n* Synagoge *f*
synchronize /ˈsɪŋkrənaɪz/ *vt* synchronisieren
synonym /ˈsɪnənɪm/ *n* Synonym *nt*. ~**ous** *adj* synonym
synthesis /ˈsɪnθəsɪs/ *n* (*pl* **-ses** /-siːz/) Synthese *f*
synthetic /sɪnˈθetɪk/ *adj* synthetisch
Syria /ˈsɪrɪə/ *n* Syrien *nt*
syringe /sɪˈrɪndʒ/ *n* Spritze *f*
syrup /ˈsɪrəp/ *n* Sirup *m*
system /ˈsɪstəm/ *n* System *nt*. ~**atic** *adj*, **-ally** *adv* systematisch

Tt

tab /tæb/ *n* (*projecting*) Zunge *f*; (*with name*) Namensschild *nt*; (*loop*) Aufhänger *m*; **pick up the** ~ [!] bezahlen
table /ˈteɪbl/ *n* Tisch *m*; (*list*) Tabelle *f*; **at [the]** ~ bei Tisch. ~**-cloth** *n* Tischdecke *f*. ~**spoon** *n* Servierlöffel *m*
tablet /ˈtæblɪt/ *n* Tablette *f*; (*of soap*) Stück *nt*
'**table tennis** *n* Tischtennis *nt*
tabloid /ˈtæblɔɪd/ *n* kleinformatige Zeitung *f*; (*pej*) Boulevardzeitung *f*
taciturn /ˈtæsɪtɜːn/ *adj* wortkarg
tack /tæk/ *n* (*nail*) Stift *m*; (*stitch*) Heftstich *m*; (*Naut & fig*) Kurs *m* ● *vt* festnageln; (*sew*) heften ● *vi* (*Naut*) kreuzen

tackle /ˈtækl/ *n* Ausrüstung *f* ● *vt* angehen (*problem*); (*Sport*) angreifen

tact /tækt/ *n* Takt *m*, Taktgefühl *nt*. **~ful** *adj* taktvoll

tactic|al /ˈtæktɪkl/ *adj* taktisch. **~s** *npl* Taktik *f*

tactless /ˈtæktlɪs/ *adj* taktlos. **~ness** *n* Taktlosigkeit *f*

tag /tæg/ *n* (*label*) Schild *nt* ● *vi* (*pt/pp* **tagged**) **~ along** mitkommen

tail /teɪl/ *n* Schwanz *m*; **~s** *pl* (*tailcoat*) Frack *m*; **heads or ~s?** Kopf oder Zahl? ● *vt* (🄸: *follow*) beschatten ● *vi* **~ off** zurückgehen

tail: ~back *n* Rückstau *m*. **~ light** *n* Rücklicht *nt*

tailor /ˈteɪlə(r)/ *n* Schneider *m*. **~-made** *adj* maßgeschneidert

taint /teɪnt/ *vt* verderben

take /teɪk/ *v* (*pt* **took**, *pp* **taken**) ● *vt* nehmen: (*with one*) mitnehmen; (*take to a place*) bringen; (*steal*) stehlen; (*win*) gewinnen; (*capture*) einnehmen; (*require*) brauchen; (*last*) dauern; (*teach*) geben; machen (*exam, subject, holiday, photograph*); messen (*pulse, temperature*); **~ sth to the cleaner's** etw in die Reinigung bringen; **be ~n ill** krank werden; **~ sth calmly** etw gelassen aufnehmen ● *vi* (*plant*:) angehen; **~ after s.o.** jdm nachschlagen; (*in looks*) jdm ähnlich sehen; **~ to** (*like*) mögen; (*as a habit*) sich (*dat*) angewöhnen. **~ away** *vt* wegbringen; (*remove*) wegnehmen; (*subtract*) abziehen; **'to ~ away'** 'zum Mitnehmen'. **~ back** *vt* zurücknehmen; (*return*) zurückbringen. **~ down** *vt* herunternehmen; (*remove*) abnehmen; (*write down*) aufschreiben. **~ in** *vt* hineinbringen; (*bring indoors*) hereinholen; (*to one's home*) aufnehmen; (*understand*) begreifen; (*deceive*) hereinlegen; (*make smaller*) enger machen. **~ off** *vt* abnehmen; ablegen (*coat*); sich (*dat*) ausziehen (*clothes*); (*deduct*) abziehen; (*mimic*) nachmachen ● *vi* (*Aviat*) starten. **~ on** *vt* annehmen; (*undertake*) übernehmen; (*engage*) einstellen; (*as opponent*) antreten gegen. **~ out** *vt* hinausbringen; (*for pleasure*) ausgehen mit; ausführen (*dog*); (*remove*) herausnehmen; (*withdraw*) abheben (*money*); (*from library*) ausleihen; **~ it out on s.o.** 🄸 seinen Ärger an jdm auslassen. **~ over** *vt* hinüberbringen; übernehmen (*firm, control*) ● *vi* **~ over from s.o.** jdn ablösen. **~ up** *vt* hinaufbringen; annehmen (*offer*); ergreifen (*profession*); sich (*dat*) zulegen (*hobby*); in Anspruch nehmen (*time*); einnehmen (*space*); aufreißen (*floorboards*); **~ sth up with s.o.** mit jdm über etw (*acc*) sprechen

take: ~-away *n* Essen *nt* zum Mitnehmen; (*restaurant*) Restaurant *nt* mit Straßenverkauf. **~-off** *n* (*Aviat*) Start *m*, Abflug *m*. **~-over** *n* Übernahme *f*

takings /ˈteɪkɪŋz/ *npl* Einnahmen *pl*

talcum /ˈtælkəm/ *n* **~ [powder]** Körperpuder *m*

tale /teɪl/ *n* Geschichte *f*

talent /ˈtælənt/ *n* Talent *nt*

talk /tɔːk/ *n* Gespräch *nt*; (*lecture*) Vortrag *m* ● *vi* reden, sprechen (**to/with** mit) ● *vt* reden; **~ s.o. into sth** jdn zu etw überreden. **~ over** *vt* besprechen

talkative /ˈtɔːkətɪv/ *adj* gesprächig

tall /tɔːl/ *adj* (**-er, -est**) groß; (*building, tree*) hoch. **~ 'story** *n* übertriebene Geschichte *f*

tally /ˈtælɪ/ *vi* übereinstimmen

t

tame /teɪm/ *adj* (**-r, -st**) zahm; (*dull*) lahm [!] ● *vt* zähmen. **~r** *n* Dompteur *m*

tamper /'tæmpə(r)/ *vi* **~ with** sich (*dat*) zu schaffen machen an (+ *dat*)

tampon /'tæmpɒn/ *n* Tampon *m*

tan /tæn/ *adj* gelbbraun ● *n* Gelbbraun *nt*; (*from sun*) Bräune *f* ● *v* (*pt/pp* **tanned**) ● *vt* gerben (*hide*) ● *vi* braun werden

tang /tæŋ/ *n* herber Geschmack *m*; (*smell*) herber Geruch *m*

tangible /'tændʒɪbl/ *adj* greifbar

tangle /'tæŋgl/ *n* Gewirr *nt*; (*in hair*) Verfilzung *f* ● *vt* **~ [up]** verheddern ● *vi* sich verheddern

tank /tæŋk/ *n* Tank *m*; (*Mil*) Panzer *m*

tanker /'tæŋkə(r)/ *n* Tanker *m*; (*lorry*) Tank[last]wagen *m*

tantrum /'tæntrəm/ *n* Wutanfall *m*

tap /tæp/ *n* Hahn *m*; (*knock*) Klopfen *nt*; **on ~** zur Verfügung ● *v* (*pt/pp* **tapped**) ● *vt* klopfen an (+ *acc*); anzapfen (*barrel, tree*); erschließen (*resources*); abhören (*telephone*) ● *vi* klopfen. **~-dance** *n* Stepp[tanz] *m* ● *vi* Stepp tanzen, steppen

tape /teɪp/ *n* Band *nt*; (*adhesive*) Klebstreifen *m*; (*for recording*) Tonband *nt* ● *vt* mit Klebstreifen zukleben; (*record*) auf Band aufnehmen

'tape-measure *n* Bandmaß *nt*

taper /'teɪpə(r)/ *vi* sich verjüngen

'tape recorder *n* Tonbandgerät *nt*

tar /tɑ:(r)/ *n* Teer *m* ● *vt* (*pt/pp* **tarred**) teeren

target /'tɑ:gɪt/ *n* Ziel *nt*; (*board*) [Ziel]scheibe *f*

tarnish /'tɑ:nɪʃ/ *vi* anlaufen

tarpaulin /tɑ:'pɔ:lɪn/ *n* Plane *f*

tart¹ /tɑ:t/ *adj* (**-er, -est**) sauer

tart² *n* ≈ Obstkuchen *m*; (*individual*) Törtchen *nt*; (*sl: prostitute*) Nutte *f* ● *vt* **~ oneself up** [!] sich auftakeln

tartan /'tɑ:tn/ *n* Schottenmuster *nt*; (*cloth*) Schottenstoff *m*

task /tɑ:sk/ *n* Aufgabe *f*; **take s.o. to ~** jdm Vorhaltungen machen. **~ force** *n* Sonderkommando *nt*

tassel /'tæsl/ *n* Quaste *f*

taste /teɪst/ *n* Geschmack *m*; (*sample*) Kostprobe *f* ● *vt* kosten, probieren; schmecken (*flavour*) ● *vi* schmecken (**of** nach). **~ful** *adj* (*fig*) geschmackvoll. **~less** *adj* geschmacklos

tasty /'teɪstɪ/ *adj* lecker

tat /tæt/ *see* **tit²**

tatters /'tætəz/ *npl* **in ~s** in Fetzen

tattoo /tə'tu:/ *n* Tätowierung *f* ● *vt* tätowieren

tatty /'tætɪ/ *adj* schäbig; (*book*) zerfleddert

taught /tɔ:t/ *see* **teach**

taunt /tɔ:nt/ *n* höhnische Bemerkung *f* ● *vt* verhöhnen

taut /tɔ:t/ *adj* straff

tawdry /'tɔ:drɪ/ *adj* billig und geschmacklos

tax /tæks/ *n* Steuer *f* ● *vt* besteuern; (*fig*) strapazieren. **~able** *adj* steuerpflichtig. **~ation** *n* Besteuerung *f*

taxi /'tæksɪ/ *n* Taxi *nt* ● *vi* (*pt/pp* **taxied**, *pres p* **taxiing**) (*aircraft:*) rollen. **~ driver** *n* Taxifahrer *m*. **~ rank** *n* Taxistand *m*

'taxpayer *n* Steuerzahler *m*

tea /ti:/ *n* Tee *m*. **~-bag** *n* Teebeutel *m*. **~-break** *n* Teepause *f*

teach /ti:tʃ/ *vt/i* (*pt/pp* **taught**) unterrichten; **~ s.o. sth** jdm etw beibringen. **~er** *n* Lehrer(in) *m*(*f*). **~ing** *n* Unterrichten *nt*

tea: ~-cloth *n* (*for drying*) Ge-

schirrtuch *nt*. **~cup** *n* Teetasse *f*
teak /tiːk/ *n* Teakholz *nt*
team /tiːm/ *n* Mannschaft *f*; (*fig*) Team *nt*; (*of animals*) Gespann *nt*
'teapot *n* Teekanne *f*
tear[1] /teə(r)/ *n* Riss *m* ● *v* (*pt* **tore**, *pp* **torn**) ● *vt* reißen; (*damage*) zerreißen; **~ oneself away** sich losreißen ● *vi* [zer]reißen; (*run*) rasen. **~ up** *vt* zerreißen
tear[2] /tɪə(r)/ *n* Träne *f*. **~ful** *adj* weinend. **~fully** *adv* unter Tränen. **~gas** *n* Tränengas *nt*
tease /tiːz/ *vt* necken
tea: ~-set *n* Teeservice *nt*. **~ shop** *n* Café *nt*. **~spoon** *n* Teelöffel *m*
teat /tiːt/ *n* Zitze *f*; (*on bottle*) Sauger *m*
'tea-towel *n* Geschirrtuch *nt*
technical /'teknɪkl/ *adj* technisch; (*specialized*) fachlich. **~ity** *n* technisches Detail *nt*; (*Jur*) Formfehler *m*. **~ly** *adv* technisch; (*strictly*) streng genommen. **~ term** *n* Fachausdruck *m*
technician /tek'nɪʃn/ *n* Techniker *m*
technique /tek'niːk/ *n* Technik *f*
technological /teknə'lɒdʒɪkl/ *adj* technologisch
technology /tek'nɒlədʒɪ/ *n* Technik *f*
teddy /'tedɪ/ *n* **~ [bear]** Teddybär *m*
tedious /'tiːdɪəs/ *adj* langweilig
tedium /'tiːdɪəm/ *n* Langeweile *f*
teenage /'tiːneɪdʒ/ *adj* Teenager-; **~ boy/girl** Junge *m*/Mädchen *nt* im Teenageralter. **~r** *n* Teenager *m*
teens /tiːnz/ *npl* **the ~** die Teenagerjahre *pl*
teeter /'tiːtə(r)/ *vi* schwanken
teeth /tiːθ/ *see* **tooth**
teeth|e /tiːð/ *vi* zahnen. **~ing troubles** *npl* (*fig*) Anfangsschwierigkeiten *pl*
teetotal /tiː'təʊtl/ *adj* abstinent. **~ler** *n* Abstinenzler *m*
telebanking /'telɪbæŋkɪŋ/ *n* Telebanking *nt*
telecommunications /telɪkəmjuːnɪ'keɪʃnz/ *npl* Fernmeldewesen *nt*
telegram /'telɪgræm/ *n* Telegramm *nt*
telegraph /'telɪgrɑːf/ **~ pole** *n* Telegrafenmast *m*
telephone /'telɪfəʊn/ *n* Telefon *nt*; **be on the ~** Telefon haben; (*be telephoning*) telefonieren ● *vt* anrufen ● *vi* telefonieren
telephone: ~ booth *n*, **~ box** *n* Telefonzelle *f*. **~ directory** *n* Telefonbuch *nt*. **~ number** *n* Telefonnummer *f*
tele'photo /telɪ-/ *adj* **~ lens** Teleobjektiv *nt*
telescop|e /'telɪskəʊp/ *n* Teleskop *nt*, Fernrohr *nt*. **~ic** *adj* (*collapsible*) ausziehbar
televise /'telɪvaɪz/ *vt* im Fernsehen übertragen
television /'telɪvɪʒn/ *n* Fernsehen *nt*; **watch ~** fernsehen; **~ [set]** Fernseher *m* [I]
teleworking /'telɪwɜːkɪŋ/ *n* Telearbeit *f*
tell /tel/ *vt/i* (*pt/pp* **told**) sagen (**s.o.** jdm); (*relate*) erzählen; (*know*) wissen; (*distinguish*) erkennen; **~ the time** die Uhr lesen; **time will ~** das wird man erst sehen; **his age is beginning to ~** sein Alter macht sich bemerkbar. **~ off** *vt* ausschimpfen
telly /'telɪ/ *n* [I] = **television**
temp /temp/ *n* [I] Aushilfssekretärin *f*
temper /'tempə(r)/ *n* (*disposition*)

Naturell *nt*; (*mood*) Laune *f*; (*anger*) Wut *f*; **lose one's ~** wütend werden ● *vt* (*fig*) mäßigen

temperament /ˈtemprəmənt/ *n* Temperament *nt*. **~al** *adj* temperamentvoll; (*moody*) launisch

temperate /ˈtempərət/ *adj* gemäßigt

temperature /ˈtemprətʃə(r)/ *n* Temperatur *f*; **have** *or* **run a ~** Fieber haben

temple¹ /ˈtempl/ *n* Tempel *m*

temple² *n* (*Anat*) Schläfe *f*

tempo /ˈtempəʊ/ *n* Tempo *nt*

temporary /ˈtempərərɪ/ *adj*, **-ily** *adv* vorübergehend; (*measure, building*) provisorisch

tempt /tempt/ *vt* verleiten; (*Relig*) versuchen; herausfordern (*fate*); (*entice*) [ver]locken; **be ~ed** versucht sein (**to** zu). **~ation** *n* Versuchung *f*. **~ing** *adj* verlockend

ten /ten/ *adj* zehn

tenaci|ous /tɪˈneɪʃəs/ *adj*, **-ly** *adv* hartnäckig. **~ty** *n* Hartnäckigkeit *f*

tenant /ˈtenənt/ *n* Mieter(in) *m*(*f*); (*Comm*) Pächter(in) *m*(*f*)

tend /tend/ *vi* **~ to do sth** dazu neigen, etw zu tun

tendency /ˈtendənsɪ/ *n* Tendenz *f*; (*inclination*) Neigung *f*

tender /ˈtendə(r)/ *adj* zart; (*loving*) zärtlich; (*painful*) empfindlich. **~ly** *adv* zärtlich. **~ness** *n* Zartheit *f*; Zärtlichkeit *f*

tendon /ˈtendən/ *n* Sehne *f*

tenner /ˈtenə(r)/ *n* [!] Zehnpfundschein *m*

tennis /ˈtenɪs/ *n* Tennis *nt*. **~-court** *n* Tennisplatz *m*

tenor /ˈtenə(r)/ *n* Tenor *m*

tense /tens/ *adj* (**-r, -st**) gespannt ● *vt* anspannen (*muscle*)

tension /ˈtenʃn/ *n* Spannung *f*

tent /tent/ *n* Zelt *nt*

tentative /ˈtentətɪv/ *adj*, **-ly** *adv* vorläufig; (*hesitant*) zaghaft

tenterhooks /ˈtentəhʊks/ *npl* **be on ~** wie auf glühenden Kohlen sitzen

tenth /tenθ/ *adj* zehnte(r,s) ● *n* Zehntel *nt*

tenuous /ˈtenjʊəs/ *adj* schwach

tepid /ˈtepɪd/ *adj* lauwarm

term /tɜːm/ *n* Zeitraum *m*; (*Sch*) ≈ Halbjahr *nt*; (*Univ*) ≈ Semester *nt*; (*expression*) Ausdruck *m*; **~s** *pl* (*conditions*) Bedingungen *pl*; **in the short/long ~** kurz-/langfristig; **be on good/bad ~s** gut/nicht gut miteinander auskommen

terminal /ˈtɜːmɪnl/ *adj* End-; (*Med*) unheilbar ● *n* (*Aviat*) Terminal *m*; (*of bus*) Endstation *f*; (*on battery*) Pol *m*; (*Computing*) Terminal *nt*

terminat|e /ˈtɜːmɪneɪt/ *vt* beenden; lösen (*contract*); unterbrechen (*pregnancy*) ● *vi* enden

terminology /tɜːmɪˈnɒlədʒɪ/ *n* Terminologie *f*

terminus /ˈtɜːmɪnəs/ *n* (*pl* **-ni** /-naɪ/) Endstation *f*

terrace /ˈterəs/ *n* Terrasse *f*; (*houses*) Häuserreihe *f*. **~d house** *n* Reihenhaus *nt*

terrain /teˈreɪn/ *n* Gelände *nt*

terrible /ˈterəbl/ *adj*, **-bly** *adv* schrecklich

terrific /təˈrɪfɪk/ *adj* [!] (*excellent*) sagenhaft; (*huge*) riesig

terri|fy /ˈterɪfaɪ/ *vt* (*pt/pp* **-ied**) Angst machen (+ *dat*); **be ~fied** Angst haben. **~fying** *adj* Furcht erregend

territorial /terɪˈtɔːrɪəl/ *adj* Territorial-

territory /ˈterɪtərɪ/ *n* Gebiet *nt*

terror /ˈterə(r)/ *n* [panische] Angst *f*; (*Pol*) Terror *m*. **~ism** *n* Terrorismus *m*. **~ist** *n* Terrorist(in) *m*(*f*).

~**ize** *vt* terrorisieren

terse /tɜːs/ *adj* kurz, knapp

test /test/ *n* Test *m*; (*Sch*) Klassenarbeit *f*; **put to the ~** auf die Probe stellen ● *vt* prüfen; (*examine*) untersuchen (**for** auf + *acc*)

testament /ˈtestəmənt/ *n* Testament *nt*

testify /ˈtestɪfaɪ/ *v* (*pt/pp* **-ied**) ● *vt* beweisen; ~ **that** bezeugen, dass ● *vi* aussagen

testimonial /testɪˈməʊnɪəl/ *n* Zeugnis *nt*

testimony /ˈtestɪmənɪ/ *n* Aussage *f*

ˈ**test-tube** *n* Reagenzglas *nt*

tether /ˈteðə(r)/ *n* **be at the end of one's ~** am Ende seiner Kraft sein ● *vt* anbinden

text /tekst/ *n* Text *m* ● *vt/i* texten. ~**book** *n* Lehrbuch *nt*

textile /ˈtekstaɪl/ *adj* Textil- ● *n* ~**s** *pl* Textilien *pl*

ˈ**text message** *n* SMS-Nachricht *f*

texture /ˈtekstʃə(r)/ *n* Beschaffenheit *f*; (*of cloth*) Struktur *f*

Thai /taɪ/ *adj* thailändisch. ~**land** *n* Thailand *nt*

Thames /temz/ *n* Themse *f*

than /ðən/, *betont* /ðæn/ *conj* als

thank /θæŋk/ *vt* danken (+ *dat*); ~ **you [very much]** danke [schön]. ~**ful** *adj* dankbar. ~**less** *adj* undankbar

thanks /θæŋks/ *npl* Dank *m*; ~! [!] danke! ~ **to** dank (+ *dat or gen*)

that /ðæt/

pl **those**

● *adjective*

····➤ der (*m*), die (*f*), das (*nt*), die (*pl*); (*just seen or experienced*) dieser (*m*), diese (*f*), dieses (*nt*), diese (*pl*). **I'll never forget that day** den Tag werde ich nie vergessen. **I liked that house** dieses Haus hat mir gut gefallen

● *pronoun*

····➤ der (*m*), die (*f*), das (*nt*), die (*pl*). **that is not true** das ist nicht wahr. **who is that in the garden?** wer ist das [da] im Garten? **I'll take that** ich nehme den/die/das. **I don't like those** die mag ich nicht. **is that you?** bist du es? **that is why** deshalb

····➤ **like that** so. **don't be like that!** sei doch nicht so! **a man like that** ein solcher Mann; so ein Mann [!]

····➤ (*after prepositions*) da .... **after that** danach. **with that** damit. **apart from that** außerdem

····➤ (*relative pronoun*) der (*m*), die (*f*), das (*nt*), die (*pl*). **the book that I'm reading** das Buch, das ich lese. **the people that you got it from** die Leute, von denen du es bekommen hast. **everyone that I know** jeder, den ich kenne. **that is all that I have** das ist alles, was ich habe

● *adverb*

····➤ so. **he's not ˈthat stupid** so blöd ist er [auch wieder] nicht. **it wasn't ˈthat bad** so schlecht war es auch nicht. **a nail about ˈthat long** ein etwa so langer Nagel

····➤ (*relative adverb*) der (*m*), die (*f*), das (*nt*), die (*pl*). **the day that I first met her** der Tag, an dem ich sie zum ersten Mal sah. **at the speed that he was going** bei der Geschwindigkeit,

t

die er hatte

● *conjunction*

····➤ dass. **I don't think that he'll come** ich denke nicht, dass er kommt. **we know that you're right** wir wissen, dass du Recht hast. **I'm so tired that I can hardly walk** ich bin so müde, dass ich kaum gehen kann

····➤ **so that** (*purpose*) damit; (*result*) sodass. **he came earlier so that they would have more time** er kam früher, damit sie mehr Zeit hatten. **it was late, so that I had to catch the bus** es war spät, sodass ich den Bus nehmen musste

thatch /θætʃ/ *n* Strohdach *nt*. **~ed** *adj* strohgedeckt

thaw /θɔ:/ *n* Tauwetter *nt* ● *vt/i* auftauen; **it's ~ing** es taut

the /ðə/, *vor einem Vokal* /ðɪ:/ *def art* der/die/das; (*pl*) die; **play ~ piano/violin** Klavier/Geige spielen ● *adv* **~ more ~ better** je mehr, desto besser; **all ~ better** umso besser

theatre /ˈθɪətə(r)/ *n* Theater *nt*; (*Med*) Operationssaal *m*

theatrical /θɪˈætrɪkl/ *adj* Theater-; (*showy*) theatralisch

theft /θeft/ *n* Diebstahl *m*

their /ðeə(r)/ *adj* ihr

theirs /ðeəz/ *poss pron* ihre(r), ihrs; **a friend of ~** ein Freund von ihnen; **those are ~** die gehören ihnen

them /ðem/ *pron* (*acc*) sie; (*dat*) ihnen

theme /θi:m/ *n* Thema *nt*. **~ park** *n* Themenpark *m*

them'selves *pron* selbst; (*reflexive*) sich; **by ~** allein

then /ðen/ *adv* dann; (*at that time in past*) damals; **by ~** bis dahin; **since ~** seitdem; **before ~** vorher; **from ~ on** von da an; **now and ~** dann und wann; **there and ~** auf der Stelle ● *adj* damalig

theology /θɪˈɒlədʒɪ/ *n* Theologie *f*

theoretical /θɪəˈretɪkl/ *adj* theoretisch

theory /ˈθɪərɪ/ *n* Theorie *f*; **in ~** theoretisch

therap|ist /ˈθerəpɪst/ *n* Therapeut(in) *m*(*f*). **~y** *n* Therapie *f*

there /ðeə(r)/ *adv* da; (*with movement*) dahin, dorthin; **down/up ~** da unten/oben; **~ is/are** da ist/sind; (*in existence*) es gibt ● *int* **~, ~!** nun, nun!

there: ~abouts *adv* da [in der Nähe]; **or ~abouts** (*roughly*) ungefähr. **~fore** /-fɔ:(r)/ *adv* deshalb, also

thermometer /θəˈmɒmɪtə(r)/ *n* Thermometer *nt*

Thermos ® /ˈθɜ:məs/ *n* **~ [flask]** Thermosflasche ® *f*

thermostat /ˈθɜ:məstæt/ *n* Thermostat *m*

these /ði:z/ *see* **this**

thesis /ˈθi:sɪs/ *n* (*pl* **-ses** /-si:z/) Dissertation *f*; (*proposition*) These *f*

they /ðeɪ/ *pron* sie; **~ say** (*generalizing*) man sagt

thick /θɪk/ *adj* (**-er, -est**) dick; (*dense*) dicht; (*liquid*) dickflüssig; (*[!]: stupid*) dumm ● *adv* dick ● *n* **in the ~ of** mitten in (+ *dat*). **~en** *vt* dicker machen; eindicken (*sauce*) ● *vi* dicker werden; (*fog:*) dichter werden; (*plot:*) kompliziert werden. **~ness** *n* Dicke *f*; Dichte *f*; Dickflüssigkeit *f*

thief /θi:f/ *n* (*pl* **thieves**) Dieb(in) *m*(*f*)

thigh /θaɪ/ *n* Oberschenkel *m*

thimble /ˈθɪmbl/ *n* Fingerhut *m*

thin /θɪn/ *adj* (**thinner, thinnest**) dünn ● *adv* dünn ● *v* (*pt/pp* **thinned**) ● *vt* verdünnen (*liquid*) ● *vi* sich lichten

thing /θɪŋ/ *n* Ding *nt*; (*subject, affair*) Sache *f*; **~s** *pl* (*belongings*) Sachen *pl*; **for one ~** erstens; **just the ~!** genau das Richtige! **how are ~s?** wie geht's? **the latest ~** [!] der letzte Schrei

think /θɪŋk/ *vt/i* (*pt/pp* **thought**) denken (**about/of** an + *acc*); (*believe*) meinen; (*consider*) nachdenken; (*regard as*) halten für; **I ~ so** ich glaube schon; **what do you ~ of it?** was halten Sie davon? **~ over** *vt* sich (*dat*) überlegen. **~ up** *vt* sich (*dat*) ausdenken

third /θɜːd/ *adj* dritte(r,s) ● *n* Drittel *nt*. **~ly** *adv* drittens. **~-rate** *adj* drittrangig

thirst /θɜːst/ *n* Durst *m*. **~y** *adj*, **-ily** *adv* durstig; **be ~y** Durst haben

thirteen /θɜːˈtiːn/ *adj* dreizehn. **~th** *adj* dreizehnte(r,s)

thirtieth /ˈθɜːtɪɪθ/ *adj* dreißigste(r,s)

thirty /ˈθɜːtɪ/ *adj* dreißig

this /ðɪs/ *adj* (*pl* **these**) diese(r,s); (*pl*) diese; **~ one** diese(r,s) da; **I'll take ~** ich nehme diesen/diese/dieses; **~ evening/morning** heute Abend/Morgen; **these days** heutzutage ● *pron* (*pl* **these**) das, dies[es]; (*pl*) die, diese; **~ and that** dies und das; **~ or that** dieses oder das da; **like ~** so; **~ is Peter** das ist Peter; (*Teleph*) hier [spricht] Peter; **who is ~?** wer ist das? (*Teleph, Amer*) wer ist am Apparat?

thistle /ˈθɪsl/ *n* Distel *f*

thorn /θɔːn/ *n* Dorn *m*

thorough /ˈθʌrə/ *adj* gründlich

thoroughbred *n* reinrassiges Tier *nt*; (*horse*) Rassepferd *nt*

thorough|ly /ˈθʌrəlɪ/ *adv* gründlich; (*completely*) völlig; (*extremely*) äußerst. **~ness** *n* Gründlichkeit *f*

those /ðəʊz/ *see* **that**

though /ðəʊ/ *conj* obgleich, obwohl; **as ~** als ob ● *adv* [!] doch

thought /θɔːt/ *see* **think** ● *n* Gedanke *m*; (*thinking*) Denken *nt*. **~ful** *adj* nachdenklich; (*considerate*) rücksichtsvoll. **~less** *adj* gedankenlos

thousand /ˈθaʊznd/ *adj* **one/a ~** [ein]tausend ● *n* Tausend *nt*. **~th** *adj* tausendste(r,s) ● *n* Tausendstel *nt*

thrash /θræʃ/ *vt* verprügeln; (*defeat*) [vernichtend] schlagen

thread /θred/ *n* Faden *m*; (*of screw*) Gewinde *nt* ● *vt* einfädeln; auffädeln (*beads*). **~bare** *adj* fadenscheinig

threat /θret/ *n* Drohung *f*; (*danger*) Bedrohung *f*

threaten /ˈθretn/ *vt* drohen (+ *dat*); (*with weapon*) bedrohen; **~ s.o. with sth** jdm etw androhen ● *vi* drohen. **~ing** *adj* drohend; (*ominous*) bedrohlich

three /θriː/ *adj* drei. **~fold** *adj & adv* dreifach

thresh /θreʃ/ *vt* dreschen

threshold /ˈθreʃəʊld/ *n* Schwelle *f*

threw /θruː/ *see* **throw**

thrift /θrɪft/ *n* Sparsamkeit *f*. **~y** *adj* sparsam

thrill /θrɪl/ *n* Erregung *f*; [!] Nervenkitzel *m* ● *vt* (*excite*) erregen; **be ~ed with** sich sehr freuen über (+ *acc*). **~er** *n* Thriller *m*. **~ing** *adj* erregend

thrive /θraɪv/ *vi* (*pt* **thrived** *or* **throve**, *pp* **thrived** *or* **thriven** /ˈθrɪvn/) gedeihen (**on** bei); (*business:*) florieren

throat /θrəʊt/ *n* Hals *m*; **cut s.o.'s ~** jdm die Kehle durchschneiden

throb /θrɒb/ *n* Pochen *nt* ● *vi* (*pt/pp* **throbbed**) pochen; (*vibrate*) vibrieren

throes /θrəʊz/ *npl* **in the ~ of** (*fig*) mitten in (+ *dat*)

throne /θrəʊn/ *n* Thron *m*

throttle /'θrɒtl/ *vt* erdrosseln

through /θru:/ *prep* durch (+ *acc*); (*during*) während (+ *gen*); (*Amer: up to & including*) bis einschließlich ● *adv* durch; **wet ~** durch und durch nass; **read sth ~** etw durchlesen ● *adj* (*train*) durchgehend; **be ~** (*finished*) fertig sein; (*Teleph*) durch sein

throughout /θru:'aʊt/ *prep* **~ the country** im ganzen Land; **~ the night** die Nacht durch ● *adv* ganz; (*time*) die ganze Zeit

throve /θrəʊv/ *see* **thrive**

throw /θrəʊ/ *n* Wurf *m* ● *vt* (*pt* **threw**, *pp* **thrown**) werfen; schütten (*liquid*); betätigen (*switch*); abwerfen (*rider*); (🄸: *disconcert*) aus der Fassung bringen; 🄸 geben (*party*); **~ sth to s.o.** jdm etw zuwerfen. **~ away** *vt* wegwerfen. **~ out** *vt* hinauswerfen; (**~** *away*) wegwerfen; verwerfen (*plan*). **~ up** *vt* hochwerfen ● *vi* sich übergeben

'throw-away *adj* Wegwerf-

thrush /θrʌʃ/ *n* Drossel *f*

thrust /θrʌst/ *n* Stoß *m*; (*Phys*) Schub *m* ● *vt* (*pt/pp* **thrust**) stoßen; (*insert*) stecken

thud /θʌd/ *n* dumpfer Schlag *m*

thug /θʌg/ *n* Schläger *m*

thumb /θʌm/ *n* Daumen *m* ● *vt* **~ a lift** 🄸 per Anhalter fahren. **~tack** *n* (*Amer*) Reißzwecke *f*

thump /θʌmp/ *n* Schlag *m*; (*noise*) dumpfer Schlag *m* ● *vt* schlagen ● *vi* hämmern; (*heart:*) pochen

thunder /'θʌndə(r)/ *n* Donner *m* ● *vi* donnern. **~clap** *n* Donnerschlag *m*. **~storm** *n* Gewitter *nt*. **~y** *adj* gewittrig

Thursday /'θɜ:zdeɪ/ *n* Donnerstag *m*

thus /ðʌs/ *adv* so

thwart /θwɔ:t/ *vt* vereiteln; **~ s.o.** jdm einen Strich durch die Rechnung machen

tick¹ /tɪk/ *n* **on ~** 🄸 auf Pump

tick² *n* (*sound*) Ticken *nt*; (*mark*) Häkchen *nt*; (🄸: *instant*) Sekunde *f* ● *vi* ticken ● *vt* abhaken. **~ off** *vt* abhaken; 🄸 rüffeln

ticket /'tɪkɪt/ *n* Karte *f*; (*for bus, train*) Fahrschein *m*; (*Aviat*) Flugschein *m*; (*for lottery*) Los *nt*; (*for article deposited*) Schein *m*; (*label*) Schild *nt*; (*for library*) Lesekarte *f*; (*fine*) Strafzettel *m*. **~ collector** *n* Fahrkartenkontrolleur *m*. **~ office** *n* Fahrkartenschalter *m*; (*for entry*) Kasse *f*

tick|le /'tɪkl/ *n* Kitzeln *nt* ● *vt/i* kitzeln. **~lish** *adj* kitzlig

tidal /'taɪdl/ *adj* **~ wave** Flutwelle *f*

tide /taɪd/ *n* Gezeiten *pl*; (*of events*) Strom *m*; **the ~ is in/out** es ist Flut/Ebbe ● *vt* **~ s.o. over** jdm über die Runden helfen

tidiness /'taɪdɪnɪs/ *n* Ordentlichkeit *f*

tidy /'taɪdɪ/ *adj* **, -ily** *adv* ordentlich ● *vt* **~ [up]** aufräumen

tie /taɪ/ *n* Krawatte *f*; Schlips *m*; (*cord*) Schnur *f*; (*fig: bond*) Band *nt*; (*restriction*) Bindung *f*; (*Sport*) Unentschieden *nt*; (*in competition*) Punktgleichheit *f* ● *v* (*pres p* **tying**) ● *vt* binden; machen (*knot*) ● *vi* (*Sport*) unentschieden spielen; (*have equal scores, votes*) punktgleich sein.

~ **up** *vt* festbinden; verschnüren (*parcel*); fesseln (*person*); **be ~d up** (*busy*) beschäftigt sein

tier /tɪə(r)/ *n* Stufe *f*; (*of cake*) Etage *f*; (*in stadium*) Rang *m*

tiger /ˈtaɪɡə(r)/ *n* Tiger *m*

tight /taɪt/ *adj* (**-er, -est**) fest; (*taut*) straff; (*clothes*) eng; (*control*) streng; ([!]: *drunk*) blau ● *adv* fest

tighten /ˈtaɪtn/ *vt* fester ziehen; straffen (*rope*); anziehen (*screw*); verschärfen (*control*) ● *vi* sich spannen

tightrope *n* Hochseil *nt*

tights /taɪts/ *npl* Strumpfhose *f*

tile /taɪl/ *n* Fliese *f*; (*on wall*) Kachel *f*; (*on roof*) [Dach]ziegel *m* ● *vt* mit Fliesen auslegen; kacheln (*wall*); decken (*roof*)

till¹ /tɪl/ *prep & conj* = **until**

till² *n* Kasse *f*

tilt /tɪlt/ *n* Neigung *f* ● *vt* kippen; [zur Seite] neigen (*head*) ● *vi* sich neigen

timber /ˈtɪmbə(r)/ *n* [Nutz]holz *nt*

time /taɪm/ *n* Zeit *f*; (*occasion*) Mal *nt*; (*rhythm*) Takt *m*; **~s** (*Math*) mal; **at ~s** manchmal; **~ and again** immer wieder; **two at a ~** zwei auf einmal; **on ~** pünktlich; **in ~** rechtzeitig; (*eventually*) mit der Zeit; **in no ~** im Handumdrehen; **in a year's ~** in einem Jahr; **behind ~** verspätet; **behind the ~s** rückständig; **for the ~ being** vorläufig; **what is the ~?** wie spät ist es? wie viel Uhr ist es? **did you have a nice ~?** hat es dir gut gefallen? ● *vt* stoppen (*race*); **be well ~d** gut abgepaßt sein

time: ~ bomb *n* Zeitbombe *f*. **~less** *adj* zeitlos. **~ly** *adj* rechtzeitig. **~-switch** *n* Zeitschalter *m*. **~-table** *n* Fahrplan *m*; (*Sch*) Stundenplan *m*

timid /ˈtɪmɪd/ *adj* scheu; (*hesitant*) zaghaft

timing /ˈtaɪmɪŋ/ *n* (*Sport, Techn*) Timing *nt*

tin /tɪn/ *n* Zinn *nt*; (*container*) Dose *f* ● *vt* (*pt/pp* **tinned**) in Dosen konservieren. **~ foil** *n* Stanniol *nt*; (*Culin*) Alufolie *f*

tinge /tɪndʒ/ *n* Hauch *m*

tingle /ˈtɪŋɡl/ *vi* kribbeln

tinker /ˈtɪŋkə(r)/ *vi* herumbasteln (**with** an + *dat*)

tinkle /ˈtɪŋkl/ *n* Klingeln *nt* ● *vi* klingeln

tinned /tɪnd/ *adj* Dosen-

ˈtin opener *n* Dosenöffner *m*

tinsel /ˈtɪnsl/ *n* Lametta *nt*

tint /tɪnt/ *n* Farbton *m* ● *vt* tönen

tiny /ˈtaɪnɪ/ *adj* winzig

tip¹ /tɪp/ *n* Spitze *f*

tip² *n* (*money*) Trinkgeld *nt*; (*advice*) Rat *m*, [!] Tipp *m*; (*for rubbish*) Müllhalde *f* ● *v* (*pt/pp* **tipped**) ● *vt* (*tilt*) kippen; (*reward*) Trinkgeld geben (**s.o.** jdm) ● *vi* kippen. **~ out** *vt* auskippen. **~ over** *vt/i* umkippen

tipped /tɪpt/ *adj* Filter-

tipsy /ˈtɪpsɪ/ *adj* [!] beschwipst

tiptoe /ˈtɪptəʊ/ *n* **on ~** auf Zehenspitzen

tiptop /tɪpˈtɒp/ *adj* [!] erstklassig

tire /ˈtaɪə(r)/ *vt/i* ermüden. **~d** *adj* müde; **be ~d of sth** etw satt haben; **~d out** [völlig] erschöpft. **~less** *adj* unermüdlich. **~some** *adj* lästig

tiring /ˈtaɪrɪŋ/ *adj* ermüdend

tissue /ˈtɪʃuː/ *n* Gewebe *nt*; (*handkerchief*) Papiertaschentuch *nt*

tit /tɪt/ *n* (*bird*) Meise *f*

ˈtitbit *n* Leckerbissen *m*

title /ˈtaɪtl/ *n* Titel *m*

to /tu:/, *unbetont* /tə/

● *preposition*

····➤ (*destinations: most cases*) zu (+ *dat*). **go to work/the station** zur Arbeit/zum Bahnhof gehen. **from house to house** von Haus zu Haus. **go/come to s.o.** zu jdm gehen/kommen

····➤ (*with name of place or points of compass*) nach. **to Paris/Germany** nach Paris/Deutschland. **to Switzerland** in die Schweiz. **from East to West** von Osten nach Westen. **I've never been to Berlin** ich war noch nie in Berlin

····➤ (*to cinema, theatre, bed*) in (+ *acc*). **to bed with you!** ins Bett mit dir!

····➤ (*to wedding, party, university, the toilet*) auf (+ *acc*).

····➤ (*up to*) bis zu (+ *dat*). **to the end** bis zum Schluss. **to this day** bis heute. **5 to 6 pounds** 5 bis 6 Pfund

····➤ (*give, say, write*) + *dat*. **give/say sth to s.o.** jdm etw geben/sagen. **she wrote to him/the firm** sie hat ihm/an die Firma geschrieben

····➤ (*address, send, fasten*) an (+ *acc*). **she sent it to her brother** sie schickte es an ihren Bruder

····➤ (*in telling the time*) vor. **five to eight** fünf vor acht. **a quarter to ten** Viertel vor zehn

● *before infinitive*

····➤ (*after modal verb*) (*not translated*). **I want to go** ich will gehen. **he is learning to swim** er lernt schwimmen. **you have to** du musst [es tun]

····➤ (*after adjective*) zu. **it is easy to forget** es ist leicht zu vergessen

····➤ (*expressing purpose, result*) um ... zu. **he did it to annoy me** er tat es, um mich zu ärgern. **she was too tired to go** sie war zu müde um zu gehen

● *adverb*

····➤ **be to** (*door, window*) angelehnt sein. **pull a door to** eine Tür anlehnen

····➤ **to and fro** hin und her

toad /təʊd/ *n* Kröte *f*

toast /təʊst/ *n* Toast *m* ● *vt* toasten (*bread*); (*drink a* ~ *to*) trinken auf (+ *acc*). **~er** *n* Toaster *m*

tobacco /təˈbækəʊ/ *n* Tabak *m*. **~nist's [shop]** *n* Tabakladen *m*

toboggan /təˈbɒɡən/ *n* Schlitten *m* ● *vi* Schlitten fahren

today /təˈdeɪ/ *n* & *adv* heute; ~ **week** heute in einer Woche

toddler /ˈtɒdlə(r)/ *n* Kleinkind *nt*

toe /təʊ/ *n* Zeh *m*; (*of footwear*) Spitze *f* ● *vt* ~ **the line** spuren. **~nail** *n* Zehennagel *m*

toffee /ˈtɒfɪ/ *n* Karamell *m* & *nt*

together /təˈɡeðə(r)/ *adv* zusammen; (*at the same time*) gleichzeitig

toilet /ˈtɔɪlɪt/ *n* Toilette *f*. ~ **bag** *n* Kulturbeutel *m*. ~ **paper** *n* Toilettenpapier *nt*

toiletries /ˈtɔɪlɪtrɪz/ *npl* Toilettenartikel *pl*

token /ˈtəʊkən/ *n* Zeichen *nt*; (*counter*) Marke *f*; (*voucher*) Gutschein *m* ● *attrib* symbolisch

told /təʊld/ *see* **tell** ● *adj* **all** ~ insgesamt

tolerable /ˈtɒlərəbl/ *adj*, **-bly** *adv* erträglich; (*not bad*) leidlich

toleran|ce /ˈtɒlərəns/ *n* Toleranz *f*. **~t** *adj* tolerant

tolerate /ˈtɒləreɪt/ *vt* dulden, tolerieren; (*bear*) ertragen

toll /təʊl/ *n* Gebühr *f*; (*for road*) Maut *f* (*Aust*); **death ~** Zahl *f* der Todesopfer

tomato /təˈmɑːtəʊ/ *n* (*pl* **-es**) Tomate *f*

tomb /tuːm/ *n* Grabmal *nt*

ˈtombstone *n* Grabstein *m*

ˈtom-cat *n* Kater *m*

tomorrow /təˈmɒrəʊ/ *n* & *adv* morgen; **~ morning** morgen früh; **the day after ~** übermorgen; **see you ~!** bis morgen!

ton /tʌn/ *n* Tonne *f*; **~s of** [!] jede Menge

tone /təʊn/ *n* Ton *m*; (*colour*) Farbton *m* ● *vt* **~ down** dämpfen; (*fig*) mäßigen. **~ up** *vt* kräftigen; straffen (*muscles*)

tongs /tɒŋz/ *npl* Zange *f*

tongue /tʌŋ/ *n* Zunge *f*; **~ in cheek** [!] nicht ernst

tonic /ˈtɒnɪk/ *n* Tonikum *nt*; (*for hair*) Haarwasser *nt*; (*fig*) Wohltat *f*; **~ [water]** Tonic *nt*

tonight /təˈnaɪt/ *n* & *adv* heute Nacht; (*evening*) heute Abend

tonne /tʌn/ *n* Tonne *f*

tonsil /ˈtɒnsl/ *n* (*Anat*) Mandel *f*. **~litis** *n* Mandelentzündung *f*

too /tuː/ *adv* zu; (*also*) auch; **~ much/little** zu viel/zu wenig

took /tʊk/ *see* **take**

tool /tuːl/ *n* Werkzeug *nt*; (*for gardening*) Gerät *nt*. **~bar** *n* Werkzeugleiste *f*

tooth /tuːθ/ *n* (*pl* **teeth**) Zahn *m*

tooth: ~ache *n* Zahnschmerzen *pl*. **~brush** *n* Zahnbürste *f*. **~less** *adj* zahnlos. **~paste** *n* Zahnpasta *f*. **~pick** *n* Zahnstocher *m*

top[1] /tɒp/ *n* (*toy*) Kreisel *m*

top[2] *n* oberer Teil *m*; (*apex*) Spitze *f*; (*summit*) Gipfel *m*; (*Sch*) Erste(r) *m/f*; (*top part or half*) Oberteil *nt*; (*head*) Kopfende *nt*; (*of road*) oberes Ende *nt*; (*upper surface*) Oberfläche *f*; (*lid*) Deckel *m*; (*of bottle*) Verschluss *m*; (*garment*) Top *nt*; **at the/on ~** oben; **on ~ of** oben auf (+ *dat/acc*); **on ~ of that** (*besides*) obendrein; **from ~ to bottom** von oben bis unten ● *adj* oberste(r,s); (*highest*) höchste(r,s); (*best*) beste(r,s) ● *vt* (*pt/pp* **topped**) an erster Stelle stehen auf (+ *dat*) (*list*); (*exceed*) übersteigen; (*remove the ~ of*) die Spitze abschneiden von. **~ up** *vt* nachfüllen, auffüllen

top: ~ ˈhat *n* Zylinder[hut] *m*. **~-heavy** *adj* kopflastig

topic /ˈtɒpɪk/ *n* Thema *nt*. **~al** *adj* aktuell

topple /ˈtɒpl/ *vt/i* umstürzen

torch /tɔːtʃ/ *n* Taschenlampe *f*; (*flaming*) Fackel *f*

tore /tɔː(r)/ *see* **tear[1]**

torment[1] /ˈtɔːment/ *n* Qual *f*

torment[2] /tɔːˈment/ *vt* quälen

torn /tɔːn/ *see* **tear[1]** ● *adj* zerrissen

torpedo /tɔːˈpiːdəʊ/ *n* (*pl* **-es**) Torpedo *m* ● *vt* torpedieren

torrent /ˈtɒrənt/ *n* reißender Strom *m*. **~ial** *adj* (*rain*) wolkenbruchartig

tortoise /ˈtɔːtəs/ *n* Schildkröte *f*. **~shell** *n* Schildpatt *nt*

tortuous /ˈtɔːtjʊəs/ *adj* verschlungen; (*fig*) umständlich

torture /ˈtɔːtʃə(r)/ *n* Folter *f*; (*fig*) Qual *f* ● *vt* foltern; (*fig*) quälen

toss /tɒs/ *vt* werfen; (*into the air*) hochwerfen; (*shake*) schütteln; (*unseat*) abwerfen; mischen (*salad*); wenden (*pancake*); **~ a coin** mit einer Münze losen ● *vi* **~ and turn** (*in bed*) sich [schlaflos] im Bett wälzen

tot[1] /tɒt/ *n* kleines Kind *nt*; ([!]: *of liquor*) Gläschen *nt*

tot² *vt* (*pt/pp* **totted**) ~ **up** [!] zusammenzählen

total /ˈtəʊtl/ *adj* gesamt; (*complete*) völlig, total ● *n* Gesamtzahl *f*; (*sum*) Gesamtsumme *f* ● *vt* (*pt/pp* **totalled**); (*amount to*) sich belaufen auf (+ *acc*)

totalitarian /təʊtælɪˈteərɪən/ *adj* totalitär

totally /ˈtəʊtəlɪ/ *adv* völlig, total

totter /ˈtɒtə(r)/ *vi* taumeln

touch /tʌtʃ/ *n* Berührung *f*; (*sense*) Tastsinn *m*; (*Mus*) Anschlag *m*; (*contact*) Kontakt *m*; (*trace*) Spur *f*; (*fig*) Anflug *m*; **get/be in** ~ sich in Verbindung setzen/in Verbindung stehen (**with** mit) ● *vt* berühren; (*get hold of*) anfassen; (*lightly*) tippen auf/an (+ *acc*); (*brush against*) streifen [gegen]; (*fig: move*) rühren; anrühren (*food, subject*); **don't** ~ **that!** fass das nicht an! ● *vi* sich berühren; ~ **on** (*fig*) berühren. ~ **down** *vi* (*Aviat*) landen. ~ **up** *vt* ausbessern

touch|ing /ˈtʌtʃɪŋ/ *adj* rührend. ~**y** *adj* empfindlich

tough /tʌf/ *adj* (**-er, -est**) zäh; (*severe, harsh*) hart; (*difficult*) schwierig; (*durable*) strapazierfähig

toughen /ˈtʌfn/ *vt* härten; ~ **up** abhärten

tour /tʊə(r)/ *n* Reise *f*, Tour *f*; (*of building, town*) Besichtigung *f*; (*Theat, Sport*) Tournee *f*; (*of duty*) Dienstzeit *f* ● *vt* fahren durch ● *vi* herumreisen

touris|m /ˈtʊərɪzm/ *n* Tourismus *m*, Fremdenverkehr *m*. ~**t** *n* Tourist(in) *m(f)* ● *attrib* Touristen-. ~**t office** *n* Fremdenverkehrsbüro *nt*

tournament /ˈtʊənəmənt/ *n* Turnier *nt*

ˈtour operator *n* Reiseveranstalter *m*

tousle /ˈtaʊzl/ *vt* zerzausen

tow /təʊ/ *n* **give s.o./a car a** ~ jdn/ein Auto abschleppen ● *vt* schleppen; ziehen (*trailer*)

toward[s] /təˈwɔːdz/ *prep* zu (+ *dat*); (*with time*) gegen (+ *acc*); (*with respect to*) gegenüber (+ *dat*)

towel /ˈtaʊəl/ *n* Handtuch *nt*. ~**ling** *n* (*cloth*) Frottee *nt*

tower /ˈtaʊə(r)/ *n* Turm *m* ● *vi* ~ **above** überragen. ~ **block** *n* Hochhaus *nt*. ~**ing** *adj* hoch aufragend

town /taʊn/ *n* Stadt *f*. ~ **ˈhall** *n* Rathaus *nt*

tow-rope *n* Abschleppseil *nt*

toxic /ˈtɒksɪk/ *adj* giftig

toy /tɔɪ/ *n* Spielzeug *nt* ● *vi* ~ **with** spielen mit; stochern in (+ *dat*) (*food*). ~**shop** *n* Spielwarengeschäft *nt*

trac|e /treɪs/ *n* Spur *f* ● *vt* folgen (+ *dat*); (*find*) finden; (*draw*) zeichnen; (*with tracing-paper*) durchpausen

track /træk/ *n* Spur *f*; (*path*) [unbefestigter] Weg *m*; (*Sport*) Bahn *f*; (*Rail*) Gleis *nt*; **keep** ~ **of** im Auge behalten ● *vt* verfolgen. ~ **down** *vt* aufspüren; (*find*) finden

ˈtracksuit *n* Trainingsanzug *m*

tractor /ˈtræktə(r)/ *n* Traktor *m*

trade /treɪd/ *n* Handel *m*; (*line of business*) Gewerbe *nt*; (*business*) Geschäft *nt*; (*craft*) Handwerk *nt*; **by** ~ von Beruf ● *vt* tauschen; ~ **in** (*give in part exchange*) in Zahlung geben ● *vi* handeln (**in** mit)

t

ˈtrade mark *n* Warenzeichen *nt*

trader /ˈtreɪdə(r)/ *n* Händler *m*

trade: ~ **ˈunion** *n* Gewerkschaft *f*. ~ **ˈunionist** *n* Gewerkschaftler(in) *m(f)*

trading /ˈtreɪdɪŋ/ *n* Handel *m*

tradition /trəˈdɪʃn/ *n* Tradition *f*. ~**al** *adj* traditionell

traffic /'træfɪk/ *n* Verkehr *m*; (*trading*) Handel *m*

traffic: ~ circle *n* (*Amer*) Kreisverkehr *m*. **~ jam** *n* [Verkehrs]stau *m*. **~ lights** *npl* [Verkehrs]ampel *f*. **~ warden** *n* ≈ Hilfspolizist *m*; (*woman*) Politesse *f*

tragedy /'trædʒədɪ/ *n* Tragödie *f*

tragic /'trædʒɪk/ *adj*, **-ally** *adv* tragisch

trail /treɪl/ *n* Spur *f*; (*path*) Weg *m*, Pfad *m* ● *vi* schleifen; (*plant:*) sich ranken ● *vt* verfolgen, folgen (+ *dat*); (*drag*) schleifen

trailer /'treɪlə(r)/ *n* (*Auto*) Anhänger *m*; (*Amer: caravan*) Wohnwagen *m*; (*film*) Vorschau *f*

train /treɪn/ *n* Zug *m*; (*of dress*) Schleppe *f* ● *vt* ausbilden; (*Sport*) trainieren; (*aim*) richten auf (+ *acc*); erziehen (*child*); abrichten/(*to do tricks*) dressieren (*animal*); ziehen (*plant*) ● *vi* eine Ausbildung machen; (*Sport*) trainieren. **~ed** *adj* ausgebildet

trainee /treɪ'ni:/ *n* Auszubildende(r) *m/f*; (*Techn*) Praktikant(in) *m*(*f*)

train|er /'treɪnə(r)/ *n* (*Sport*) Trainer *m*; (*in circus*) Dompteur *m*; **~ers** *pl* Trainingsschuhe *pl*. **~ing** *n* Ausbildung *f*; (*Sport*) Training *nt*; (*of animals*) Dressur *f*

trait /treɪt/ *n* Eigenschaft *f*

traitor /'treɪtə(r)/ *n* Verräter *m*

tram /træm/ *n* Straßenbahn *f*

tramp /træmp/ *n* Landstreicher *m* ● *vi* stapfen; (*walk*) marschieren

trample /'træmpl/ *vt/i* trampeln

trance /trɑ:ns/ *n* Trance *f*

tranquil /'træŋkwɪl/ *adj* ruhig. **~lity** *n* Ruhe *f*

tranquillizer /'træŋkwɪlaɪzə(r)/ *n* Beruhigungsmittel *nt*

transaction /træn'zækʃn/ *n* Transaktion *f*

transcend /træn'send/ *vt* übersteigen

transfer¹ /'trænsfɜ:(r)/ *n* (*see* **transfer²**) Übertragung *f*; Verlegung *f*; Versetzung *f*; Überweisung *f*; (*Sport*) Transfer *m*; (*design*) Abziehbild *nt*

transfer² /træns'fɜ:(r)/ *v* (*pt/pp* **transferred**) ● *vt* übertragen; verlegen (*firm, prisoners*); versetzen (*employee*); überweisen (*money*); (*Sport*) transferieren ● *vi* [über]wechseln; (*when travelling*) umsteigen

transform /træns'fɔ:m/ *vt* verwandeln. **~ation** *n* Verwandlung *f*. **~er** *n* Transformator *m*

transfusion /træns'fju:ʒn/ *n* Transfusion *f*

transistor /træn'zɪstə(r)/ *n* Transistor *m*

transit /'trænsɪt/ *n* Transit *m*; (*of goods*) Transport *m*; **in ~** (*goods*) auf dem Transport

transition /træn'sɪʒn/ *n* Übergang *m*. **~al** *adj* Übergangs-

translat|e /træns'leɪt/ *vt* übersetzen. **~ion** *n* Übersetzung *f*. **~or** *n* Übersetzer(in) *m*(*f*)

transmission /trænz'mɪʃn/ *n* Übertragung *f*

transmit /trænz'mɪt/ *vt* (*pt/pp* **transmitted**) übertragen. **~ter** *n* Sender *m*

transparen|cy /træns'pærənsɪ/ *n* (*Phot*) Dia *nt*. **~t** *adj* durchsichtig

transplant¹ /'trænsplɑ:nt/ *n* Verpflanzung *f*, Transplantation *f*

transplant² /træns'plɑ:nt/ *vt* umpflanzen; (*Med*) verpflanzen

transport¹ /'trænspɔ:t/ *n* Transport *m*

transport² /træn'spɔ:t/ *vt* transportieren. **~ation** *n* Transport *m*

transpose /træns'pəʊz/ *vt*

umstellen

trap /træp/ *n* Falle *f*; (▣: *mouth*) Klappe *f*; **pony and ~** Einspänner *m* ● *vt* (*pt/pp* **trapped**) [mit einer Falle] fangen; (*jam*) einklemmen; **be ~ped** festsitzen; (*shut in*) eingeschlossen sein. **~'door** *n* Falltür *f*

trash /træʃ/ *n* Schund *m*; (*rubbish*) Abfall *m*; (*nonsense*) Quatsch *m*. **~can** *n* (*Amer*) Mülleimer *m*. **~y** *adj* Schund-

trauma /'trɔ:mə/ *n* Trauma *nt*. **~tic** *adj* traumatisch

travel /'trævl/ *n* Reisen *nt* ● *v* (*pt/pp* **travelled**) ● *vi* reisen; (*go in vehicle*) fahren; (*light, sound:*) sich fortpflanzen; (*Techn*) sich bewegen ● *vt* bereisen; fahren (*distance*). **~ agency** *n* Reisebüro *nt*. **~ agent** *n* Reisebürokaufmann *m*

traveller /'trævələ(r)/ *n* Reisende(r) *m/f*; (*Comm*) Vertreter *m*; **~s** *pl* (*gypsies*) Zigeuner *pl*. **~'s cheque** *n* Reisescheck *m*

trawler /'trɔ:lə(r)/ *n* Fischdampfer *m*

tray /treɪ/ *n* Tablett *nt*; (*for baking*) [Back]blech *nt*; (*for documents*) Ablagekorb *m*

treacher|ous /'tretʃərəs/ *adj* treulos; (*dangerous, deceptive*) tückisch. **~y** *n* Verrat *m*

tread /tred/ *n* Schritt *m*; (*step*) Stufe *f*; (*of tyre*) Profil *nt* ● *v* (*pt* **trod**, *pp* **trodden**) ● *vi* (*walk*) gehen; **~ on/in** treten auf/ in (+ *acc*) ● *vt* treten

treason /'tri:zn/ *n* Verrat *m*

treasure /'treʒə(r)/ *n* Schatz *m* ● *vt* in Ehren halten. **~r** *n* Kassenwart *m*

treasury /'treʒərɪ/ *n* Schatzkammer *f*; **the T~** das Finanzministerium

treat /tri:t/ *n* [besonderes] Vergnügen *nt* ● *vt* behandeln; **~ s.o. to sth** jdm etw spendieren

treatment /'tri:tmənt/ *n* Behandlung *f*

treaty /'tri:tɪ/ *n* Vertrag *m*

treble /'trebl/ *adj* dreifach; **~ the amount** dreimal so viel ● *n* (*Mus*) Diskant *m*; (*voice*) Sopran *m* ● *vt* verdreifachen ● *vi* sich verdreifachen

tree /tri:/ *n* Baum *m*

trek /trek/ *n* Marsch *m* ● *vi* (*pt/pp* **trekked**) latschen

trellis /'trelɪs/ *n* Gitter *nt*

tremble /'trembl/ *vi* zittern

tremendous /trɪ'mendəs/ *adj* gewaltig; (▣: *excellent*) großartig

tremor /'tremə(r)/ *n* Zittern *nt*; **[earth] ~** Beben *nt*

trench /trentʃ/ *n* Graben *m*; (*Mil*) Schützengraben *m*

trend /trend/ *n* Tendenz *f*; (*fashion*) Trend *m*. **~y** *adj* ▣ modisch

trepidation /trepɪ'deɪʃn/ *n* Beklommenheit *f*

trespass /'trespəs/ *vi* **~ on** unerlaubt betreten

trial /'traɪəl/ *n* (*Jur*) [Gerichts]verfahren *nt*, Prozess *m*; (*test*) Probe *f*; (*ordeal*) Prüfung *f*; **be on ~** auf Probe sein; (*Jur*) angeklagt sein (**for** wegen); **by ~ and error** durch Probieren

triang|le /'traɪæŋgl/ *n* Dreieck *nt*; (*Mus*) Triangel *m*. **~ular** *adj* dreieckig

tribe /traɪb/ *n* Stamm *m*

tribunal /traɪ'bju:nl/ *n* Schiedsgericht *nt*

tributary /'trɪbjʊtərɪ/ *n* Nebenfluss *m*

tribute /'trɪbju:t/ *n* Tribut *m*; **pay ~** Tribut zollen (**to** *dat*)

trick /trɪk/ *n* Trick *m*; (*joke*) Streich *m*; (*Cards*) Stich *m*; (*feat of skill*)

Kunststück *nt* ● *vt* täuschen, [I] hereinlegen

trickle /ˈtrɪkl/ *vi* rinnen

trick|ster /ˈtrɪkstə(r)/ *n* Schwindler *m*. **~y** *adj adj* schwierig

tricycle /ˈtraɪsɪkl/ *n* Dreirad *nt*

tried /traɪd/ *see* **try**

trifl|e /ˈtraɪfl/ *n* Kleinigkeit *f*; (*Culin*) Trifle *nt*. **~ing** *adj* unbedeutend

trigger /ˈtrɪgə(r)/ *n* Abzug *m*; (*fig*) Auslöser *m* ● *vt* ~ **[off]** auslösen

trim /trɪm/ *adj* (**trimmer, trimmest**) gepflegt ● *n* (*cut*) Nachschneiden *nt*; (*decoration*) Verzierung *f*; (*condition*) Zustand *m* ● *vt* schneiden; (*decorate*) besetzen. **~ming** *n* Besatz *m*; **~mings** *pl* (*accessories*) Zubehör *nt*; (*decorations*) Verzierungen *pl*

trio /ˈtriːəʊ/ *n* Trio *nt*

trip /trɪp/ *n* Reise *f*; (*excursion*) Ausflug *m* ● *v* (*pt/pp* **tripped**) ● *vt* ~ **s.o. up** jdm ein Bein stellen ● *vi* stolpern (**on**/**over** über + *acc*)

tripe /traɪp/ *n* Kaldaunen *pl*; (*nonsense*) Quatsch *m*

triple /ˈtrɪpl/ *adj* dreifach ● *vt* verdreifachen ● *vi* sich verdreifachen

triplets /ˈtrɪplɪts/ *npl* Drillinge *pl*

triplicate /ˈtrɪplɪkət/ *n* **in** ~ in dreifacher Ausfertigung

tripod /ˈtraɪpɒd/ *n* Stativ *nt*

tripper /ˈtrɪpə(r)/ *n* Ausflügler *m*

trite /traɪt/ *adj* banal

triumph /ˈtraɪʌmf/ *n* Triumph *m* ● *vi* triumphieren (**over** über + *acc*). **~ant** *adj* triumphierend

trivial /ˈtrɪvɪəl/ *adj* belanglos. **~ity** *n* Belanglosigkeit *f*

trod, trodden *see* **tread**

trolley /ˈtrɒlɪ/ *n* (*for food*) Servierwagen *m*; (*for shopping*) Einkaufswagen *m*; (*for luggage*) Kofferkuli *m*; (*Amer: tram*) Straßenbahn *f*

trombone /trɒmˈbəʊn/ *n* Posaune *f*

troop /truːp/ *n* Schar *f*; **~s** *pl* Truppen *pl*

trophy /ˈtrəʊfɪ/ *n* Trophäe *f*; (*in competition*) ≈ Pokal *m*

tropics /ˈtrɒpɪks/ *npl* Tropen *pl*. **~al** *adj* tropisch; (*fruit*) Süd-

trot /trɒt/ *n* Trab *m* ● *vi* (*pt/pp* **trotted**) traben

trouble /ˈtrʌbl/ *n* Ärger *m*; (*difficulties*) Schwierigkeiten *pl*; (*inconvenience*) Mühe *f*; (*conflict*) Unruhe *f*; (*Med*) Beschwerden *pl*; (*Techn*) Probleme *pl*; **get into** ~ Ärger bekommen; **take** ~ sich (*dat*) Mühe geben ● *vt* (*disturb*) stören; (*worry*) beunruhigen ● *vi* sich bemühen. **~-maker** *n* Unruhestifter *m*. **~some** *adj* schwierig; (*flies, cough*) lästig

trough /trɒf/ *n* Trog *m*

troupe /truːp/ *n* Truppe *f*

trousers /ˈtraʊzəz/ *npl* Hose *f*

trousseau /ˈtruːsəʊ/ *n* Aussteuer *f*

trout /traʊt/ *n inv* Forelle *f*

trowel /ˈtraʊəl/ *n* Kelle *f*

truant /ˈtruːənt/ *n* **play** ~ die Schule schwänzen

truce /truːs/ *n* Waffenstillstand *m*

truck /trʌk/ *n* Last[kraft]wagen *m*; (*Rail*) Güterwagen *m*

trudge /trʌdʒ/ *vi* latschen

true /truː/ *adj* (**-r, -st**) wahr; (*loyal*) treu; (*genuine*) echt; **come** ~ in Erfüllung gehen; **is that ~?** stimmt das?

truly /ˈtruːlɪ/ *adv* wirklich; (*faithfully*) treu; **Yours** ~ mit freundlichen Grüßen

trump /trʌmp/ *n* (*Cards*) Trumpf *m* ● *vt* übertrumpfen

trumpet /ˈtrʌmpɪt/ *n* Trompete *f*. **~er** *n* Trompeter *m*

truncheon /ˈtrʌntʃn/ *n* Schlagstock *m*
trunk /trʌŋk/ *n* [Baum]stamm *m*; (*body*) Rumpf *m*; (*of elephant*) Rüssel *m*; (*for travelling*) [Übersee]koffer *m*; (*Amer: of car*) Kofferraum *m*; **~s** *pl* Badehose *f*
trust /trʌst/ *n* Vertrauen *nt*; (*group of companies*) Trust *m*; (*organization*) Treuhandgesellschaft *f*; (*charitable*) Stiftung *f* ● *vt* trauen (+ *dat*), vertrauen (+ *dat*); (*hope*) hoffen ● *vi* vertrauen (**in**/**to** auf + *acc*)
trustee /trʌsˈtiː/ *n* Treuhänder *m*
ˈ**trust|ful** /ˈtrʌstfl/ *adj*, **-ly** *adv*, **~ing** *adj* vertrauensvoll. **~worthy** *adj* vertrauenswürdig
truth /truːθ/ *n* (*pl* **-s** /truːðz/) Wahrheit *f*. **~ful** *adj* ehrlich
try /traɪ/ *n* Versuch *m* ● *v* (*pt*/*pp* **tried**) ● *vt* versuchen; (*sample, taste*) probieren; (*be a strain on*) anstrengen; (*Jur*) vor Gericht stellen; verhandeln (*case*) ● *vi* versuchen; (*make an effort*) sich bemühen. **~ on** *vt* anprobieren; aufprobieren (*hat*). **~ out** *vt* ausprobieren
trying /ˈtraɪɪŋ/ *adj* schwierig
T-shirt /ˈtiː-/ *n* T-Shirt *nt*
tub /tʌb/ *n* Kübel *m*; (*carton*) Becher *m*; (*bath*) Wanne *f*
tuba /ˈtjuːbə/ *n* (*Mus*) Tuba *f*
tubby /ˈtʌbɪ/ *adj* rundlich
tube /tjuːb/ *n* Röhre *f*; (*pipe*) Rohr *nt*; (*flexible*) Schlauch *m*; (*of toothpaste*) Tube *f*; (*Rail*, 🅸) U-Bahn *f*
tuberculosis /tjuːbɜːkjʊˈləʊsɪs/ *n* Tuberkulose *f*
tubular /ˈtjuːbjʊlə(r)/ *adj* röhrenförmig
tuck /tʌk/ *n* Saum *m*; (*decorative*) Biese *f* ● *vt* (*put*) stecken. **~ in** *vt* hineinstecken; **~ s.o. in** *or* **up** jdn zudecken ● *vi* (🅸: *eat*) zulangen
Tuesday /ˈtjuːzdeɪ/ *n* Dienstag *m*
tuft /tʌft/ *n* Büschel *nt*
tug /tʌg/ *n* Ruck *m*; (*Naut*) Schleppdampfer *m* ● *v* (*pt*/*pp* **tugged**) ● *vt* ziehen ● *vi* zerren (**at** an + *dat*)
tuition /tjuːˈɪʃn/ *n* Unterricht *m*
tulip /ˈtjuːlɪp/ *n* Tulpe *f*
tumble /ˈtʌmbl/ *n* Sturz *m* ● *vi* fallen. **~down** *adj* verfallen. **~-drier** *n* Wäschetrockner *m*
tumbler /ˈtʌmblə(r)/ *n* Glas *nt*
tummy /ˈtʌmɪ/ *n* 🅸 Bauch *m*
tumour /ˈtjuːmə(r)/ *n* Tumor *m*
tumult /ˈtjuːmʌlt/ *n* Tumult *m*
tuna /ˈtjuːnə/ *n* Thunfisch *m*
tune /tjuːn/ *n* Melodie *f*; **out of ~** (*instrument*) verstimmt ● *vt* stimmen; (*Techn*) einstellen. **~ in** *vt* einstellen: ● *vi* **~ in to a station** einen Sender einstellen. **~ up** *vi* (*Mus*) stimmen
tuneful /ˈtjuːnfl/ *adj* melodisch
Tunisia /tjuːˈnɪzɪə/ *n* Tunesien *nt*
tunnel /ˈtʌnl/ *n* Tunnel *m* ● *vi* (*pt*/*pp* **tunnelled**) einen Tunnel graben
turban /ˈtɜːbən/ *n* Turban *m*
turbine /ˈtɜːbaɪn/ *n* Turbine *f*
turbulen|ce /ˈtɜːbjʊləns/ *n* Turbulenz *f*. **~t** *adj* stürmisch
turf /tɜːf/ *n* Rasen *m*; (*segment*) Rasenstück *nt*
Turk /tɜːk/ *n* Türke *m*/Türkin *f*
turkey /ˈtɜːkɪ/ *n* Truthahn *m*
Turk|ey *n* die Türkei. **~ish** *adj* türkisch
turmoil /ˈtɜːmɔɪl/ *n* Aufruhr *m*; (*confusion*) Durcheinander *nt*
turn /tɜːn/ *n* (*rotation*) Drehung *f*; (*bend*) Kurve *f*; (*change of direction*) Wende *f*; (*Theat*) Nummer *f*; (🅸: *attack*) Anfall *m*; **do s.o. a good ~** jdm einen guten Dienst erweisen; **take ~s** sich abwechseln; **in ~** der Reihe nach; **out of ~** außer der Reihe; **it's your ~** du bist an der

Reihe ● *vt* drehen; (~ *over*) wenden; (*reverse*) umdrehen; (*Techn*) drechseln (*wood*); ~ **the page** umblättern; ~ **the corner** um die Ecke biegen ● *vi* sich drehen; (~ *round*) sich umdrehen; (*car:*) wenden; (*leaves:*) sich färben: (*weather:*) umschlagen; (*become*) werden; ~ **right/left** nach rechts/links abbiegen; ~ **to s.o.** sich an jdn wenden. ~ **away** *vt* abweisen ● *vi* sich abwenden. ~ **down** *vt* herunterschlagen (*collar*); herunterdrehen (*heat, gas*); leiser stellen (*sound*); (*reject*) ablehnen; abweisen (*person*). ~ **in** *vt* einschlagen (*edges*) ● *vi* (*car:*) einbiegen; (🅘: *go to bed*) ins Bett gehen. ~ **off** *vt* zudrehen (*tap*); ausschalten (*light, radio*); abstellen (*water, gas, engine, machine*) ● *vi* abbiegen. ~ **on** *vt* aufdrehen (*tap*); einschalten (*light, radio*); anstellen (*water, gas, engine, machine*). ~ **out** *vt* (*expel*) vertreiben, 🅘 hinauswerfen; ausschalten (*light*); abdrehen (*gas*); (*produce*) produzieren; (*empty*) ausleeren; [gründlich] aufräumen (*room, cupboard*) ● *vi* (*go out*) hinausgehen; (*transpire*) sich herausstellen. ~ **over** *vt* umdrehen. ~ **up** *vt* hochschlagen (*collar*); aufdrehen (*heat, gas*); lauter stellen (*sound, radio*) ● *vi* auftauchen

turning /ˈtɜːnɪŋ/ *n* Abzweigung *f*. ~**-point** *n* Wendepunkt *m*

turnip /ˈtɜːnɪp/ *n* weiße Rübe *f*

turn: ~**-out** *n* (*of people*) Beteiligung *f*. ~**over** *n* (*Comm*) Umsatz *m*; (*of staff*) Personalwechsel *m*. ~**pike** *n* (*Amer*) gebührenpflichtige Autobahn *f*. ~**table** *n* Drehscheibe *f*; (*on record player*) Plattenteller *m*. ~**-up** *n* [Hosen]aufschlag *m*

turquoise /ˈtɜːkwɔɪz/ *adj* türkis[farben] ● *n* (*gem*) Türkis *m*

turret /ˈtʌrɪt/ *n* Türmchen *nt*

turtle /ˈtɜːtl/ *n* Seeschildkröte *f*

tusk /tʌsk/ *n* Stoßzahn *m*

tutor /ˈtjuːtə(r)/ *n* [Privat]lehrer *m*

tuxedo /tʌkˈsiːdəʊ/ *n* (*Amer*) Smoking *m*

TV /tiːˈviː/ *abbr* **television**

tweed /twiːd/ *n* Tweed *m*

tweezers /ˈtwiːzəz/ *npl* Pinzette *f*

twelfth /twelfθ/ *adj* zwölfter(r,s)

twelve /twelv/ *adj* zwölf

twentieth /ˈtwentɪɪθ/ *adj* zwanzigste(r,s)

twenty /ˈtwentɪ/ *adj* zwanzig

twice /twaɪs/ *adv* zweimal

twig /twɪg/ *n* Zweig *m*

twilight /ˈtwaɪ-/ *n* Dämmerlicht *nt*

twin /twɪn/ *n* Zwilling *m* ● *attrib* Zwillings-

twine /twaɪn/ *n* Bindfaden *m*

twinge /twɪndʒ/ *n* Stechen *nt*; ~ **of conscience** Gewissensbisse *pl*

twinkle /ˈtwɪŋkl/ *n* Funkeln *nt* ● *vi* funkeln

twin 'town *n* Partnerstadt *f*

twirl /twɜːl/ *vt/i* herumwirbeln

twist /twɪst/ *n* Drehung *f*; (*curve*) Kurve *f*; (*unexpected occurrence*) überraschende Wendung *f* ● *vt* drehen; (*distort*) verdrehen; (🅘: *swindle*) beschummeln; ~ **one's ankle** sich (*dat*) den Knöchel verrenken ● *vi* sich drehen; (*road:*) sich winden. ~**er** *n* 🅘 Schwindler *m*

twit /twɪt/ *n* 🅘 Trottel *m*

twitch /twɪtʃ/ *n* Zucken *nt* ● *vi* zucken

twitter /ˈtwɪtə(r)/ *n* Zwitschern *nt* ● *vi* zwitschern

two /tuː/ *adj* zwei

two: ~**-faced** *adj* falsch. ~**-piece** *adj* zweiteilig. ~**-way** *adj* ~**-way traffic** Gegenverkehr *m*

tycoon /taɪˈkuːn/ *n* Magnat *m*

t

tying /'taɪɪŋ/ *see* **tie**

type /taɪp/ *n* Art *f*, Sorte *f*; (*person*) Typ *m*; (*printing*) Type *f* ● *vt* mit der Maschine schreiben, [!] tippen ● *vi* Maschine schreiben, [!] tippen. **~writer** *n* Schreibmaschine *f*. **~written** *adj* maschinegeschrieben

typical /'tɪpɪkl/ *adj* typisch (**of** für)

typify /'tɪpɪfaɪ/ *vt* (*pt*/*pp* **-ied**) typisch sein für

typing /'taɪpɪŋ/ *n* Maschineschreiben *nt*

typist /'taɪpɪst/ *n* Schreibkraft *f*

tyrannical /tɪ'rænɪkl/ *adj* tyrannisch

tyranny /'tɪrənɪ/ *n* Tyrannei *f*

tyrant /'taɪrənt/ *n* Tyrann *m*

tyre /'taɪə(r)/ *n* Reifen *m*

Uu

ugl|iness /'ʌglɪnɪs/ *n* Hässlichkeit *f*. **~y** *adj* hässlich; (*nasty*) übel

UK *abbr* **United Kingdom**

ulcer /'ʌlsə(r)/ *n* Geschwür *nt*

ultimate /'ʌltɪmət/ *adj* letzte(r,s); (*final*) endgültig; (*fundamental*) grundlegend, eigentlich. **~ly** *adv* schließlich

ultimatum /ʌltɪ'meɪtəm/ *n* Ultimatum *nt*

ultra'violet *adj* ultraviolett

umbrella /ʌm'brelə/ *n* [Regen-]schirm *m*

umpire /'ʌmpaɪə(r)/ *n* Schiedsrichter *m* ● *vt*/*i* Schiedsrichter sein (bei)

umpteen /ʌmp'ti:n/ *adj* [!] zig. **~th** *adj* [!] zigste(r,s)

un'able /ʌn-/ *adj* **be ~ to do sth** etw nicht tun können

una'bridged *adj* ungekürzt

unac'companied *adj* ohne Begleitung; (*luggage*) unbegleitet

unac'countable *adj* unerklärlich

unac'customed *adj* ungewohnt; **be ~ to sth** etw (*acc*) nicht gewohnt sein

un'aided *adj* ohne fremde Hilfe

unanimous /ju:'nænɪməs/ *adj* einmütig; (*vote, decision*) einstimmig

un'armed *adj* unbewaffnet

unas'suming *adj* bescheiden

unat'tended *adj* unbeaufsichtigt

un'authorized *adj* unbefugt

una'voidable *adj* unvermeidlich

una'ware *adj* **be ~ of sth** sich (*dat*) etw (*gen*) nicht bewusst sein. **~s** *adv* **catch s.o. ~s** jdn überraschen

un'bearable *adj*, **-bly** *adv* unerträglich

unbeat|able /ʌn'bi:təbl/ *adj* unschlagbar. **~en** *adj* ungeschlagen; (*record*) ungebrochen

unbe'lievable *adj* unglaublich

un'biased *adj* unvoreingenommen

un'block *vt* frei machen

un'bolt *vt* aufriegeln

un'breakable *adj* unzerbrechlich

un'button *vt* aufknöpfen

uncalled-for /ʌn'kɔ:ldfɔ:(r)/ *adj* unangebracht

un'canny *adj* unheimlich

un'ceasing *adj* unaufhörlich

un'certain *adj* (*doubtful*) ungewiss; (*origins*) unbestimmt; **be ~** nicht sicher sein. **~ty** *n* Ungewissheit *f*

un'changed *adj* unverändert

un'charitable *adj* lieblos

uncle /'ʌŋkl/ *n* Onkel *m*

Uncle Sam Eine Bezeichnung für die USA und ihre Einwohner. Meist dargestellt durch einen mit Frack und Zylinder in den Farben und mit den Sternen der Nationalflagge bekleideten hageren Mann mit weißen Haaren und Backenbart. Die Bezeichnung ist besonders durch das Poster von 1917 zur Rekrutierung von Soldaten "*I want you*" bekannnt geworden.

un'comforta|ble *adj*, **-bly** *adv* unbequem; **feel ~** (*fig*) sich nicht wohl fühlen

un'common *adj* ungewöhnlich

un'compromising *adj* kompromisslos

uncon'ditional *adj*, **~ly** *adv* bedingungslos

un'conscious *adj* bewusstlos; (*unintended*) unbewusst; **be ~ of sth** sich (*dat*) etw (*gen*) nicht bewusst sein. **~ly** *adv* unbewusst

uncon'ventional *adj* unkonventionell

unco'operative *adj* nicht hilfsbereit

un'cork *vt* entkorken

uncouth /ʌn'ku:θ/ *adj* ungehobelt

un'cover *vt* aufdecken

unde'cided *adj* unentschlossen; (*not settled*) nicht entschieden

undeniable /ʌndɪ'naɪəbl/ *adj*, **-bly** *adv* unbestreitbar

under /'ʌndə(r)/ *prep* unter (+ *dat*/*acc*); **~ it** darunter; **~ there** da drunter; **~ repair** in Reparatur; **~ construction** im Bau; **~ age** minderjährig ● *adv* darunter

'undercarriage *n* (*Aviat*) Fahrwerk *nt*, Fahrgestell *nt*

'underclothes *npl* Unterwäsche *f*

under'cover *adj* geheim

'undercurrent *n* Unterströmung *f*; (*fig*) Unterton *m*

'underdog *n* Unterlegene(r) *m*

under'done *adj* nicht gar; (*rare*) nicht durchgebraten

under'estimate *vt* unterschätzen

under'fed *adj* unterernährt

under'foot *adv* am Boden

under'go *vt* (*pt* **-went**, *pp* **-gone**) durchmachen; sich unterziehen (+ *dat*) (*operation, treatment*)

under'graduate *n* Student(in) *m*(*f*)

under'ground¹ *adv* unter der Erde; (*mining*) unter Tage

'underground² *adj* unterirdisch; (*secret*) Untergrund- ● *n* (*railway*) U-Bahn *f*. **~ car park** *n* Tiefgarage *f*

'undergrowth *n* Unterholz *nt*

'underhand *adj* hinterhältig

under'lie *vt* (*pt* **-lay**, *pp* **-lain**, *pres p* **-lying**) zugrunde liegen (+ *dat*)

under'line *vt* unterstreichen

under'lying *adj* eigentlich

under'mine *vt* (*fig*) unterminieren, untergraben

underneath /ʌndə'ni:θ/ *prep* unter (+ *dat*/*acc*) ● *adv* darunter

'underpants *npl* Unterhose *f*

'underpass *n* Unterführung *f*

under'privileged *adj* unterprivilegiert

under'rate *vt* unterschätzen

'undershirt *n* (*Amer*) Unterhemd *nt*

under'stand *vt*/*i* (*pt*/*pp* **-stood**) verstehen; **I ~ that ...** (*have heard*) ich habe gehört, dass ... **~able** *adj* verständlich. **~ably** *adv* verständlicherweise

under'standing *adj* verständnisvoll ● *n* Verständnis *nt*; (*agreement*)

Vereinbarung *f*; **reach an ~** sich verständigen

'understatement *n* Untertreibung *f*

under'take *vt* (*pt* **-took**, *pp* **-taken**) unternehmen; **~ to do sth** sich verpflichten, etw zu tun

'undertaker *n* Leichenbestatter *m*; [firm of] **~s** Bestattungsinstitut *n*

under'taking *n* Unternehmen *nt*; (*promise*) Versprechen *nt*

'undertone *n* (*fig*) Unterton *m*; **in an ~** mit gedämpfter Stimme

under'value *vt* unterbewerten

'underwater[1] *adj* Unterwasser-

under'water[2] *adv* unter Wasser

'underwear *n* Unterwäsche *f*

under'weight *adj* untergewichtig; **be ~** Untergewicht haben

'underworld *n* Unterwelt *f*

unde'sirable *adj* unerwünscht

un'dignified *adj* würdelos

un'do *vt* (*pt* **-did**, *pp* **-done**) aufmachen; (*fig*) ungeschehen machen

un'done *adj* offen; (*not accomplished*) unerledigt

un'doubted *adj* unzweifelhaft. **~ly** *adv* zweifellos

un'dress *vt* ausziehen; **get ~ed** sich ausziehen ● *vi* sich ausziehen

un'due *adj* übermäßig

und'uly *adv* übermäßig

un'earth *vt* ausgraben; (*fig*) zutage bringen. **~ly** *adj* unheimlich; **at an ~ly hour** [!] in aller Herrgottsfrühe

un'easy *adj* unbehaglich

uneco'nomic *adj*, **-ally** *adv* unwirtschaftlich

unem'ployed *adj* arbeitslos ● *npl* **the ~** die Arbeitslosen

unem'ployment *n* Arbeitslosigkeit *f*

un'ending *adj* endlos

un'equal *adj* unterschiedlich; (*struggle*) ungleich. **~ly** *adv* ungleichmäßig

unequivocal /ʌnɪ'kwɪvəkl/ *adj* eindeutig

un'ethical *adj* unmoralisch; **be ~** gegen das Berufsethos verstoßen

un'even *adj* uneben; (*unequal*) ungleich; (*not regular*) ungleichmäßig; (*number*) ungerade

unex'pected *adj* unerwartet

un'fair *adj* ungerecht, unfair. **~ness** *n* Ungerechtigkeit *f*

un'faithful *adj* untreu

unfa'miliar *adj* ungewohnt; (*unknown*) unbekannt

un'fasten *vt* aufmachen; (*detach*) losmachen

un'favourable *adj* ungünstig

un'feeling *adj* gefühllos

un'fit *adj* ungeeignet; (*incompetent*) unfähig; (*Sport*) nicht fit; **~ for work** arbeitsunfähig

un'fold *vt* auseinander falten, entfalten; (*spread out*) ausbreiten ● *vi* sich entfalten

unfore'seen *adj* unvorhergesehen

unforgettable /ʌnfə'getəbl/ *adj* unvergesslich

unforgivable /ʌnfə'gɪvəbl/ *adj* unverzeihlich

un'fortunate *adj* unglücklich; (*unfavourable*) ungünstig; (*regrettable*) bedauerlich; **be ~** (*person:*) Pech haben. **~ly** *adv* leider

un'founded *adj* unbegründet

unfurl /ʌn'fɜːl/ *vt* entrollen

un'furnished *adj* unmöbliert

ungainly /ʌn'geɪnlɪ/ *adj* unbeholfen

un'grateful *adj* undankbar

un'happiness *n* Kummer *m*

un'happy *adj* unglücklich; (*not*

content) unzufrieden
un'harmed *adj* unverletzt
un'healthy *adj* ungesund
un'hurt *adj* unverletzt
unification /ju:nɪfɪ'keɪʃn/ *n* Einigung *f*
uniform /'ju:nɪfɔ:m/ *adj* einheitlich ● *n* Uniform *f*
unify /'ju:nɪfaɪ/ *vt* (*pt/pp* **-ied**) einigen
uni'lateral /ju:nɪ-/ *adj* einseitig
uni'maginable *adj* unvorstellbar
unim'portant *adj* unwichtig
unin'habited *adj* unbewohnt
unin'tentional *adj* unabsichtlich
union /'ju:nɪən/ *n* Vereinigung *f*; (*Pol*) Union *f*; (*trade* ~) Gewerkschaft *f*
unique /ju:'ni:k/ *adj* einzigartig. **~ly** *adv* einmalig
unison /'ju:nɪsn/ *n* **in ~** einstimmig
unit /'ju:nɪt/ *n* Einheit *f*; (*Math*) Einer *m*; (*of furniture*) Teil *nt*, Element *nt*
unite /ju:'naɪt/ *vt* vereinigen ● *vi* sich vereinigen
united /ju:'naɪtɪd/ *adj* einig. **U~ 'Kingdom** *n* Vereinigtes Königreich *nt*. **U~ 'Nations** *n* Vereinte Nationen *pl*. **U~ States [of America]** *n* Vereinigte Staaten *pl* [von Amerika]
unity /'ju:nətɪ/ *n* Einheit *f*; (*harmony*) Einigkeit *f*
universal /ju:nɪ'vɜ:sl/ *adj* allgemein
universe /'ju:nɪvɜ:s/ *n* [Welt]all *nt*, Universum *nt*
university /ju:nɪ'vɜ:sətɪ/ *n* Universität *f* ● *attrib* Universitäts-
un'just *adj* ungerecht
un'kind *adj* unfreundlich; (*harsh*) hässlich
un'known *adj* unbekannt
un'lawful *adj* gesetzwidrig
unleaded /ʌn'ledɪd/ *adj* bleifrei
un'leash *vt* (*fig*) entfesseln
unless /ən'les/ *conj* wenn ... nicht; **~ I am mistaken** wenn ich mich nicht irre
un'like *prep* im Gegensatz zu (+ *dat*)
un'likely *adj* unwahrscheinlich
un'limited *adj* unbegrenzt
un'load *vt* entladen; ausladen (*luggage*)
un'lock *vt* aufschließen
un'lucky *adj* unglücklich; (*day, number*) Unglücks-; **be ~** Pech haben; (*thing:*) Unglück bringen
un'married *adj* unverheiratet. **~ 'mother** *n* ledige Mutter *f*
un'mask *vt* (*fig*) entlarven
unmistakable /ʌnmɪ'steɪkəbl/ *adj*, **-bly** *adv* unverkennbar
un'natural *adj* unnatürlich; (*not normal*) nicht normal
un'necessary *adj*, **-ily** *adv* unnötig
un'noticed *adj* unbemerkt
unob'tainable *adj* nicht erhältlich
unob'trusive *adj* unaufdringlich; (*thing*) unauffällig
unof'ficial *adj* inoffiziell
un'pack *vt/i* auspacken
un'paid *adj* unbezahlt
un'pleasant *adj* unangenehm
un'plug *vt* (*pt/pp* **-plugged**) den Stecker herausziehen von
un'popular *adj* unbeliebt
un'precedented *adj* beispiellos
unpre'dictable *adj* unberechenbar
unpre'pared *adj* nicht vorbereitet
unpre'tentious *adj* bescheiden
un'profitable *adj* unrentabel

un'qualified *adj* unqualifiziert; (*fig: absolute*) uneingeschränkt
un'questionable *adj* unbezweifelbar; (*right*) unbestreitbar
unravel /ʌn'rævl/ *vt* (*pt/pp* **-ravelled**) entwirren; (*Knitting*) aufziehen
un'real *adj* unwirklich
un'reasonable *adj* unvernünftig
unre'lated *adj* unzusammenhängend; **be ~** nicht verwandt sein; (*events:*) nicht miteinander zusammenhängen
unre'liable *adj* unzuverlässig
un'rest *n* Unruhen *pl*
un'rivalled *adj* unübertroffen
un'roll *vt* aufrollen ● *vi* sich aufrollen
unruly /ʌn'ru:lɪ/ *adj* ungebärdig
un'safe *adj* nicht sicher
unsatis'factory *adj* unbefriedigend
un'savoury *adj* unangenehm; (*fig*) unerfreulich
unscathed /ʌn'skeɪðd/ *adj* unversehrt
un'screw *vt* abschrauben
un'scrupulous *adj* skrupellos
un'seemly *adj* unschicklich
un'selfish *adj* selbstlos
un'settled *adj* ungeklärt; (*weather*) unbeständig; (*bill*) unbezahlt
unshakeable /ʌn'ʃeɪkəbl/ *adj* unerschütterlich
unshaven /ʌn'ʃeɪvn/ *adj* unrasiert
unsightly /ʌn'saɪtlɪ/ *adj* unansehnlich
un'skilled *adj* ungelernt; (*work*) unqualifiziert
un'sociable *adj* ungesellig
unso'phisticated *adj* einfach
un'sound *adj* krank, nicht gesund; (*building*) nicht sicher; (*advice*) unzuverlässig; (*reasoning*) nicht stichhaltig
un'stable *adj* nicht stabil; (*mentally*) labil
un'steady *adj*, **-ily** *adv* unsicher; (*wobbly*) wackelig
un'stuck *adj* **come ~** sich lösen; (🄸: *fail*) scheitern
unsuc'cessful *adj* erfolglos; **be ~** keinen Erfolg haben
un'suitable *adj* ungeeignet; (*inappropriate*) unpassend; (*for weather, activity*) unzweckmäßig
unthinkable /ʌn'θɪŋkəbl/ *adj* unvorstellbar
un'tidiness *n* Unordentlichkeit *f*
un'tidy *adj*, **-ily** *adv* unordentlich
un'tie *vt* aufbinden; losbinden (*person, boat, horse*)
until /ən'tɪl/ *prep* bis (+ *acc*); **not ~** erst; **~ the evening** bis zum Abend ● *conj* bis; **not ~** erst wenn; (*in past*) erst als
un'told *adj* unermesslich
un'true *adj* unwahr; **that's ~** das ist nicht wahr
unused[1] /ʌn'ju:zd/ *adj* unbenutzt; (*not utilized*) ungenutzt
unused[2] /ʌn'ju:st/ *adj* **be ~ to sth** etw nicht gewohnt sein
un'usual *adj* ungewöhnlich
un'veil *vt* enthüllen
un'wanted *adj* unerwünscht
un'welcome *adj* unwillkommen
un'well *adj* **be** *or* **feel ~** sich nicht wohl fühlen
unwieldy /ʌn'wi:ldɪ/ *adj* sperrig
un'willing *adj* widerwillig; **be ~ to do sth** etw nicht tun wollen
un'wind *v* (*pt/pp* **unwound**) ● *vt* abwickeln ● *vi* sich abwickeln; (🄸: *relax*) sich entspannen
un'wise *adj* unklug
un'worthy *adj* unwürdig
un'wrap *vt* (*pt/pp* **-wrapped**) aus-

wickeln; auspacken (*present*)
un'written *adj* ungeschrieben
up /ʌp/ *adv* oben; (*with movement*) nach oben; (*not in bed*) auf; (*road*) aufgerissen; (*price*) gestiegen; **be up for sale** zu verkaufen sein; **up there** da oben; **up to** (*as far as*) bis; **time's up** die Zeit ist um; **what's up?** 🅵 was ist los? **what's he up to?** 🅵 was hat er vor? **I don't feel up to it** ich fühle mich dem nicht gewachsen; **go up** hinaufgehen; **come up** heraufkommen ● *prep* **be up on sth** [oben] auf etw (*dat*) sein; **up the mountain** oben am Berg; (*movement*) den Berg hinauf; **be up the tree** oben im Baum sein; **up the road** die Straße entlang; **up the river** stromaufwärts; **go up the stairs** die Treppe hinaufgehen
'upbringing *n* Erziehung *f*
up'date *vt* auf den neuesten Stand bringen
up'grade *vt* aufstufen
upheaval /ʌp'hi:vl/ *n* Unruhe *f*; (*Pol*) Umbruch *m*
up'hill *adj* (*fig*) mühsam ● *adv* bergauf
up'hold *vt* (*pt/pp* **upheld**) unterstützen; bestätigen (*verdict*)
upholster /ʌp'həʊlstə(r)/ *vt* polstern. **~y** *n* Polsterung *f*
'upkeep *n* Unterhalt *m*
up'market *adj* anspruchsvoll
upon /ə'pɒn/ *prep* auf (+ *dat*/*acc*)
upper /'ʌpə(r)/ *adj* obere(r,s); (*deck, jaw, lip*) Ober-; **have the ~ hand** die Oberhand haben ● *n* (*of shoe*) Obermaterial *nt*
upper class *n* Oberschicht *f*
'upright *adj* aufrecht
'uprising *n* Aufstand *m*
'uproar *n* Aufruhr *m*
up'set¹ *vt* (*pt*/*pp* **upset**, *pres p* **upsetting**) umstoßen; (*spill*) verschütten; durcheinander bringen (*plan*); (*distress*) erschüttern; (*food:*) nicht bekommen (+ *dat*); **get ~ about sth** sich über etw (*acc*) aufregen
'upset² *n* Aufregung *f*; **have a stomach ~** einen verdorbenen Magen haben
'upshot *n* Ergebnis *nt*
upside 'down *adv* verkehrt herum; **turn ~** umdrehen
up'stairs¹ *adv* oben; (*go*) nach oben
'upstairs² *adj* im Obergeschoss
'upstart *n* Emporkömmling *m*
up'stream *adv* stromaufwärts
'uptake *n* **slow on the ~** schwer von Begriff; **be quick on the ~** schnell begreifen
'upturn *n* Aufschwung *m*
upward /'ʌpwəd/ *adj* nach oben; (*movement*) Aufwärts-; **~ slope** Steigung *f* ● *adv* **~[s]** aufwärts, nach oben
uranium /jʊ'reɪnɪəm/ *n* Uran *nt*
urban /'ɜ:bən/ *adj* städtisch
urge /ɜ:dʒ/ *n* Trieb *m*, Drang *m* ● *vt* drängen; **~ on** antreiben
urgen|cy /'ɜ:dʒənsɪ/ *n* Dringlichkeit *f*. **~t** *adj* dringend
urine /'jʊərɪn/ *n* Urin *m*, Harn *m*
us /ʌs/ *pron* uns; **it's us** wir sind es
US[A] *abbr* USA *pl*
usable /'ju:zəbl/ *adj* brauchbar
usage /'ju:sɪdʒ/ *n* Brauch *m*; (*of word*) [Sprach]gebrauch *m*
use¹ /ju:s/ *n* (*see* **use²**) Benutzung *f*; Verwendung *f*; Gebrauch *m*; **be (of) no ~** nichts nützen; **it is no ~** es hat keinen Zweck; **what's the ~?** wozu?
use² /ju:z/ *vt* benutzen (*implement, room, lift*); verwenden (*ingredient, method, book, money*); gebrauchen (*words, force, brains*); **~ [up]** aufbrauchen

used¹ /ju:zd/ *adj* gebraucht; (*towel*) benutzt; (*car*) Gebraucht-

used² /ju:st/ *pt* **be ~ to sth** an etw (*acc*) gewöhnt sein; **get ~ to** sich gewöhnen an (+ *acc*); **he ~ to say** er hat immer gesagt; **he ~ to live here** er hat früher hier gewohnt

useful /'ju:sfl/ *adj* nützlich. **~ness** *n* Nützlichkeit *f*

useless /'ju:slɪs/ *adj* nutzlos; (*not usable*) unbrauchbar; (*pointless*) zwecklos

user /'ju:zə(r)/ *n* Benutzer(in) *m*(*f*)

usher /'ʌʃə(r)/ *n* Platzanweiser *m*; (*in court*) Gerichtsdiener *m*

usherette /ʌʃə'ret/ *n* Platzanweiserin *f*

USSR *abbr* (*History*) UdSSR *f*

usual /'ju:ʒʊəl/ *adj* üblich. **~ly** *adv* gewöhnlich

utensil /ju:'tensl/ *n* Gerät *nt*

utility /ju:'tɪlətɪ/ *adj* Gebrauchs-

utilize /'ju:tɪlaɪz/ *vt* nutzen

utmost /'ʌtməʊst/ *adj* äußerste(r,s), größte(r,s) ● *n* **do one's ~** sein Möglichstes tun

utter¹ /'ʌtə(r)/ *adj* völlig

utter² *vt* von sich geben (*sigh, sound*); sagen (*word*)

U-turn /'ju:-/ *n* (*fig*) Kehrtwendung *f*; **'no ~s'** (*Auto*) 'Wenden verboten'

Vv

vacan|cy /'veɪkənsɪ/ *n* (*job*) freie Stelle *f*; (*room*) freies Zimmer *nt*; **'no ~cies'** 'belegt'. **~t** *adj* frei; (*look*) [gedanken]leer

vacate /və'keɪt/ *vt* räumen

vacation /və'keɪʃn/ *n* (*Univ & Amer*) Ferien *pl*

vaccinat|e /'væksɪneɪt/ *vt* impfen. **~ion** *n* Impfung *f*

vaccine /'væksi:n/ *n* Impfstoff *m*

vacuum /'vækjʊəm/ *n* Vakuum *nt*, luftleerer Raum *m* ● *vt* saugen. **~ cleaner** *n* Staubsauger *m*

vagina /və'dʒaɪnə/ *n* (*Anat*) Scheide *f*

vague /veɪg/ *adj* **(-r,-st)** vage; (*outline*) verschwommen

vain /veɪn/ *adj* **(-er,-est)** eitel; (*hope, attempt*) vergeblich; **in ~** vergeblich. **~ly** *adv* vergeblich

valiant /'vælɪənt/ *adj* tapfer

valid /'vælɪd/ *adj* gültig; (*claim*) berechtigt; (*argument*) stichhaltig; (*reason*) triftig. **~ity** *n* Gültigkeit *f*

valley /'vælɪ/ *n* Tal *nt*

valour /'vælə(r)/ *n* Tapferkeit *f*

valuable /'væljʊəbl/ *adj* wertvoll. **~s** *npl* Wertsachen *pl*

valuation /væljʊ'eɪʃn/ *n* Schätzung *f*

value /'vælju:/ *n* Wert *m*; (*usefulness*) Nutzen *m* ● *vt* schätzen. **~ 'added tax** *n* Mehrwertsteuer *f*

valve /vælv/ *n* Ventil *nt*; (*Anat*) Klappe *f*; (*Electr*) Röhre *f*

van /væn/ *n* Lieferwagen *m*

vandal /'vændl/ *n* Rowdy *m*. **~ism** *n* mutwillige Zerstörung *f*. **~ize** *vt* demolieren

vanilla /və'nɪlə/ *n* Vanille *f*

vanish /'vænɪʃ/ *vi* verschwinden

vanity /'vænətɪ/ *n* Eitelkeit *f*

vapour /'veɪpə(r)/ *n* Dampf *m*

variable /'veərɪəbl/ *adj* unbeständig; (*Math*) variabel; (*adjustable*) regulierbar

variant /'veərɪənt/ *n* Variante *f*

variation /veərɪ'eɪʃn/ *n* Variation *f*; (*difference*) Unterschied *m*

varied /ˈveərɪd/ *adj* vielseitig; (*diet:*) abwechslungsreich

variety /vəˈraɪətɪ/ *n* Abwechslung *f*; (*quantity*) Vielfalt *f*; (*Comm*) Auswahl *f*; (*type*) Art *f*; (*Bot*) Abart *f*; (*Theat*) Varieté *nt*

various /ˈveərɪəs/ *adj* verschieden. **~ly** *adv* unterschiedlich

varnish /ˈvɑːnɪʃ/ *n* Lack *m* ● *vt* lackieren

vary /ˈveərɪ/ *v* (*pt*/*pp* **-ied**) ● *vi* sich ändern; (*be different*) verschieden sein ● *vt* [ver]ändern; (*add variety to*) abwechslungsreicher gestalten

vase /vɑːz/ *n* Vase *f*

vast /vɑːst/ *adj* riesig; (*expanse*) weit. **~ly** *adv* gewaltig

vat /væt/ *n* Bottich *m*

VAT /viːeɪˈtiː, væt/ *abbr* (**value added tax**) Mehrwertsteuer *f*, MwSt.

vault[1] /vɔːlt/ *n* (*roof*) Gewölbe *nt*; (*in bank*) Tresor *m*; (*tomb*) Gruft *f*

vault[2] *n* Sprung *m* ● *vt*/*i* ~ **[over]** springen über (+ *acc*)

VDU *abbr* (**visual display unit**) Bildschirmgerät *nt*

veal /viːl/ *n* Kalbfleisch *nt* ● *attrib* Kalbs-

veer /vɪə(r)/ *vi* sich drehen; (*Auto*) ausscheren

vegetable /ˈvedʒtəbl/ *n* Gemüse *nt*; **~s** *pl* Gemüse *nt* ● *attrib* Gemüse-; (*oil, fat*) Pflanzen-

vegetarian /vedʒɪˈteərɪən/ *adj* vegetarisch ● *n* Vegetarier(in) *m*(*f*)

vegetation /vedʒɪˈteɪʃn/ *n* Vegetation *f*

vehement /ˈviːəmənt/ *adj* heftig

vehicle /ˈviːɪkl/ *n* Fahrzeug *nt*

veil /veɪl/ *n* Schleier *m* ● *vt* verschleiern

vein /veɪn/ *n* Ader *f*; (*mood*) Stimmung *f*; (*manner*) Art *f*

velocity /vɪˈlɒsətɪ/ *n* Geschwindigkeit *f*

velvet /ˈvelvɪt/ *n* Samt *m*

vending-machine /ˈvendɪŋ-/ *n* [Verkaufs]automat *m*

vendor /ˈvendə(r)/ *n* Verkäufer(in) *m*(*f*)

veneer /vəˈnɪə(r)/ *n* Furnier *nt*; (*fig*) Tünche *f*. **~ed** *adj* furniert

venerable /ˈvenərəbl/ *adj* ehrwürdig

Venetian /vəˈniːʃn/ *adj* venezianisch. **v~ blind** *n* Jalousie *f*

vengeance /ˈvendʒəns/ *n* Rache *f*; **with a ~** gewaltig

Venice /ˈvenɪs/ *n* Venedig *nt*

venison /ˈvenɪsn/ *n* (*Culin*) Reh(fleisch) *nt*

venom /ˈvenəm/ *n* Gift *nt*; (*fig*) Hass *m*. **~ous** *adj* giftig

vent /vent/ *n* Öffnung *f*

ventilat|e /ˈventɪleɪt/ *vt* belüften. **~ion** *n* Belüftung *f*; (*installation*) Lüftung *f*. **~or** *n* Lüftungsvorrichtung *f*; (*Med*) Beatmungsgerät *nt*

ventriloquist /venˈtrɪləkwɪst/ *n* Bauchredner *m*

venture /ˈventʃə(r)/ *n* Unternehmung *f* ● *vt* wagen ● *vi* sich wagen

venue /ˈvenjuː/ *n* (*for event*) Veranstaltungsort *m*

veranda /vəˈrændə/ *n* Veranda *f*

verb /vɜːb/ *n* Verb *nt*. **~al** *adj* mündlich; (*Gram*) verbal

verbose /vɜːˈbəʊs/ *adj* weitschweifig

verdict /ˈvɜːdɪkt/ *n* Urteil *nt*

verge /vɜːdʒ/ *n* Rand *m* ● *vi* ~ **on** (*fig*) grenzen an (+ *acc*)

verify /ˈverɪfaɪ/ *vt* (*pt*/*pp* **-ied**) überprüfen; (*confirm*) bestätigen

vermin /ˈvɜːmɪn/ *n* Ungeziefer *nt*

V

vermouth /ˈvɜːməθ/ *n* Wermut *m*

versatil|e /ˈvɜːsətaɪl/ *adj* vielseitig. **~ity** *n* Vielseitigkeit *f*

verse /vɜːs/ *n* Strophe *f*; (*of Bible*) Vers *m*; (*poetry*) Lyrik *f*

version /ˈvɜːʃn/ *n* Version *f*; (*translation*) Übersetzung *f*; (*model*) Modell *nt*

versus /ˈvɜːsəs/ *prep* gegen (+ *acc*)

vertical /ˈvɜːtɪkl/ *adj* senkrecht ● *n* Senkrechte *f*

vertigo /ˈvɜːtɪgəʊ/ *n* (*Med*) Schwindel *m*

verve /vɜːv/ *n* Schwung *m*

very /ˈverɪ/ *adv* sehr; **~ much** sehr; (*quantity*) sehr viel; **~ probably** höchstwahrscheinlich; **at the ~ most** allerhöchstens ● *adj* (*mere*) bloß; **the ~ first** der/die/das allererste; **the ~ thing** genau das Richtige; **at the ~ end/beginning** ganz am Ende/Anfang; **only a ~ little** nur ein ganz kleines bisschen

vessel /ˈvesl/ *n* Schiff *nt*; (*receptacle & Anat*) Gefäß *nt*

vest /vest/ *n* [Unter]hemd *nt*; (*Amer: waistcoat*) Weste *f*

vestige /ˈvestɪdʒ/ *n* Spur *f*

vestry /ˈvestrɪ/ *n* Sakristei *f*

vet /vet/ *n* Tierarzt *m* /-ärztin *f* ● *vt* (*pt/pp* **vetted**) überprüfen

veteran /ˈvetərən/ *n* Veteran *m*

veterinary /ˈvetərɪnərɪ/ *adj* tierärztlich. **~ surgeon** *n* Tierarzt *m* /-ärztin *f*

veto /ˈviːtəʊ/ *n* (*pl* **-es**) Veto *nt*

VHF *abbr* (**very high frequency**) UKW

via /ˈvaɪə/ *prep* über (+ *acc*)

viable /ˈvaɪəbl/ *adj* lebensfähig; (*fig*) realisierbar; (*firm*) rentabel

viaduct /ˈvaɪədʌkt/ *n* Viadukt *nt*

vibrat|e /vaɪˈbreɪt/ *vi* vibrieren. **~ion** *n* Vibrieren *nt*

vicar /ˈvɪkə(r)/ *n* Pfarrer *m*. **~age** *n* Pfarrhaus *nt*

vice[1] /vaɪs/ *n* Laster *nt*

vice[2] *n* (*Techn*) Schraubstock *m*

vice[3] *adj* Vize-; **~ ˈchairman** stellvertretender Vorsitzender *m*

vice versa /vaɪsɪˈvɜːsə/ *adv* umgekehrt

vicinity /vɪˈsɪnətɪ/ *n* Umgebung *f*; **in the ~ of** in der Nähe von

vicious /ˈvɪʃəs/ *adj* boshaft; (*animal*) bösartig

victim /ˈvɪktɪm/ *n* Opfer *nt*. **~ize** *vt* schikanieren

victor /ˈvɪktə(r)/ *n* Sieger *m*

victor|ious /vɪkˈtɔːrɪəs/ *adj* siegreich. **~y** *n* Sieg *m*

video /ˈvɪdɪəʊ/ *n* Video *nt*; (*recorder*) Videorecorder *m* ● *attrib* Video-

video: ~ casˈsette *n* Videokassette *f*. **~ game** *n* Videospiel *nt*. **~ recorder** *n* Videorecorder *m*

Vienn|a /vɪˈenə/ *n* Wien *nt*. **~ese** *adj* Wiener

view /vjuː/ *n* Sicht *f*; (*scene*) Aussicht *f*, Blick *m*; (*picture, opinion*) Ansicht *f*; **in my ~** meiner Ansicht nach; **in ~ of** angesichts (+ *gen*); **be on ~** besichtigt werden können ● *vt* sich (*dat*) ansehen; besichtigen (*house*); (*consider*) betrachten ● *vi* (*TV*) fernsehen. **~er** *n* (*TV*) Zuschauer(in) *m*(*f*)

view: ~finder *n* (*Phot*) Sucher *m*. **~point** *n* Standpunkt *m*

vigilan|ce /ˈvɪdʒɪləns/ *n* Wachsamkeit *f*. **~t** *adj* wachsam

vigorous /ˈvɪgərəs/ *adj* kräftig; (*fig*) heftig

vigour /ˈvɪgə(r)/ *n* Kraft *f*; (*fig*) Heftigkeit *f*

vile /vaɪl/ *adj* abscheulich

villa /ˈvɪlə/ *n* (*for holidays*) Ferienhaus *nt*

village /ˈvɪlɪdʒ/ *n* Dorf *nt*. **~r** *n* Dorfbewohner(in) *m*(*f*)

villain /ˈvɪlən/ *n* Schurke *m*; (*in story*) Bösewicht *m*

vindicat|e /ˈvɪndɪkeɪt/ *vt* rechtfertigen. **~ion** *n* Rechtfertigung *f*

vindictive /vɪnˈdɪktɪv/ *adj* nachtragend

vine /vaɪn/ *n* Weinrebe *f*

vinegar /ˈvɪnɪgə(r)/ *n* Essig *m*

vineyard /ˈvɪnjɑːd/ *n* Weinberg *m*

vintage /ˈvɪntɪdʒ/ *adj* erlesen ● *n* (*year*) Jahrgang *m*. **~ ˈcar** *n* Oldtimer *m*

viola /vɪˈəʊlə/ *n* (*Mus*) Bratsche *f*

violat|e /ˈvaɪəleɪt/ *vt* verletzen; (*break*) brechen; (*disturb*) stören; (*defile*) schänden. **~ion** *n* Verletzung *f*; Schändung *f*

violen|ce /ˈvaɪələns/ *n* Gewalt *f*; (*fig*) Heftigkeit *f*. **~t** *adj* gewalttätig; (*fig*) heftig. **~tly** *adv* brutal; (*fig*) heftig

violet /ˈvaɪələt/ *adj* violett ● *n* (*flower*) Veilchen *nt*

violin /vaɪəˈlɪn/ *n* Geige *f*, Violine *f*. **~ist** *n* Geiger(in) *m*(*f*)

VIP *abbr* (**very important person**) Prominente(r) *m*/*f*

viper /ˈvaɪpə(r)/ *n* Kreuzotter *f*

virgin /ˈvɜːdʒɪn/ *adj* unberührt ● *n* Jungfrau *f*. **~ity** *n* Unschuld *f*

viril|e /ˈvɪraɪl/ *adj* männlich. **~ity** *n* Männlichkeit *f*

virtual /ˈvɜːtjʊəl/ *adj* **a ~ ...** praktisch ein ... **~ly** *adv* praktisch

virtu|e /ˈvɜːtjuː/ *n* Tugend *f*; (*advantage*) Vorteil *m*; **by** *or* **in ~e of** auf Grund (+ *gen*)

virtuoso /vɜːtjʊˈəʊzəʊ/ *n* (*pl* **-si** /-ziː/) Virtuose *m*

virtuous /ˈvɜːtjʊəs/ *adj* tugendhaft

virus /ˈvaɪərəs/ *n* Virus *nt*

visa /ˈviːzə/ *n* Visum *nt*

visibility /vɪzəˈbɪlətɪ/ *n* Sichtbarkeit *f*; (*range*) Sichtweite *f*

visi|ble /ˈvɪzəbl/ *adj*, **-bly** *adv* sichtbar

vision /ˈvɪʒn/ *n* Vision *f*; (*sight*) Sehkraft *f*; (*foresight*) Weitblick *m*

visit /ˈvɪzɪt/ *n* Besuch *m* ● *vt* besuchen; besichtigen (*town, building*). **~or** *n* Besucher(in) *m*(*f*); (*in hotel*) Gast *m*; **have ~ors** Besuch haben

visor /ˈvaɪzə(r)/ *n* Schirm *m*; (*Auto*) [Sonnen]blende *f*

vista /ˈvɪstə/ *n* Aussicht *f*

visual /ˈvɪzjʊəl/ *adj* visuell. **~ disˈplay unit** *n* Bildschirmgerät *nt*

visualize /ˈvɪzjʊəlaɪz/ *vt* sich (*dat*) vorstellen

vital /ˈvaɪtl/ *adj* unbedingt notwendig; (*essential to life*) lebenswichtig. **~ity** *n* Vitalität *f*. **~ly** *adv* äußerst

vitamin /ˈvɪtəmɪn/ *n* Vitamin *nt*

vivaci|ous /vɪˈveɪʃəs/ *adj* lebhaft. **~ty** *n* Lebhaftigkeit *f*

vivid /ˈvɪvɪd/ *adj* lebhaft; (*description*) lebendig

vocabulary /vəˈkæbjʊlərɪ/ *n* Wortschatz *m*; (*list*) Vokabelverzeichnis *nt*; **learn ~** Vokabeln lernen

vocal /ˈvəʊkl/ *adj* stimmlich; (*vociferous*) lautstark

vocalist /ˈvəʊkəlɪst/ *n* Sänger(in) *m*(*f*)

vocation /vəˈkeɪʃn/ *n* Berufung *f*. **~al** *adj* Berufs-

vociferous /vəˈsɪfərəs/ *adj* lautstark

vodka /ˈvɒdkə/ *n* Wodka *m*

vogue /vəʊg/ *n* Mode *f*

voice /vɔɪs/ *n* Stimme *f* ● *vt* zum

Ausdruck bringen. ~ **mail** *n* Voicemail *f*

void /vɔɪd/ *adj* leer; (*not valid*) ungültig; ~ of ohne • *n* Leere *f*

volatile /ˈvɒlətaɪl/ *adj* flüchtig; (*person*) sprunghaft

volcanic /vɒlˈkænɪk/ *adj* vulkanisch

volcano /vɒlˈkeɪnəʊ/ *n* Vulkan *m*

volley /ˈvɒlɪ/ *n* (*of gunfire*) Salve *f*; (*Tennis*) Volley *m*

volt /vəult/ *n* Volt *nt*. **~age** *n* (*Electr*) Spannung *f*

voluble /ˈvɒljʊbl/ *adj*, **-bly** *adv* redselig; (*protest*) wortreich

volume /ˈvɒljuːm/ *n* (*book*) Band *m*; (*Geometry*) Rauminhalt *m*; (*amount*) Ausmaß *nt*; (*Radio, TV*) Lautstärke *f*

voluntary /ˈvɒləntərɪ/ *adj*, **-ily** *adv* freiwillig

volunteer /vɒlənˈtɪə(r)/ *n* Freiwillige(r) *m/f* • *vt* anbieten; geben (*information*) • *vi* sich freiwillig melden

vomit /ˈvɒmɪt/ *n* Erbrochene(s) *nt* • *vt* erbrechen • *vi* sich übergeben

voracious /vəˈreɪʃəs/ *adj* gefräßig; (*appetite*) unbändig

vot|e /vəʊt/ *n* Stimme *f*; (*ballot*) Abstimmung *f*; (*right*) Wahlrecht *nt* • *vi* abstimmen; (*in election*) wählen. **~er** *n* Wähler(in) *m*(*f*)

vouch /vaʊtʃ/ *vi* ~ **for** sich verbürgen für. **~er** *n* Gutschein *m*

vowel /ˈvaʊəl/ *n* Vokal *m*

voyage /ˈvɔɪɪdʒ/ *n* Seereise *f*; (*in space*) Reise *f*, Flug *m*

vulgar /ˈvʌlgə(r)/ *adj* vulgär, ordinär. **~ity** *n* Vulgarität *f*

vulnerable /ˈvʌlnərəbl/ *adj* verwundbar

vulture /ˈvʌltʃə(r)/ *n* Geier *m*

Ww

wad /wɒd/ *n* Bausch *m*; (*bundle*) Bündel *nt*. **~ding** *n* Wattierung *f*

waddle /ˈwɒdl/ *vi* watscheln

wade /weɪd/ *vi* waten

wafer /ˈweɪfə(r)/ *n* Waffel *f*

waffle[1] /ˈwɒfl/ *vi* [!] schwafeln

waffle[2] *n* (*Culin*) Waffel *f*

waft /wɒft/ *vt/i* wehen

wag /wæg/ *v* (*pt/pp* **wagged**) • *vt* wedeln mit • *vi* wedeln

wage /weɪdʒ/ *n* (*also* **~s**) *pl* Lohn *m*

wager /ˈweɪdʒə(r)/ *n* Wette *f*

wagon /ˈwægən/ *n* Wagen *m*; (*Rail*) Waggon *m*

wail /weɪl/ *n* [klagender] Schrei *m* • *vi* heulen; (*lament*) klagen

waist /weɪst/ *n* Taille *f*. **~coat** *n* Weste *f*. **~line** *n* Taille *f*

wait /weɪt/ *n* Wartezeit *f*; **lie in ~ for** auflauern (+ *dat*) • *vi* warten (**for** auf + *acc*); (*at table*) servieren; **~ on** bedienen • *vt* **~ one's turn** warten, bis man an der Reihe ist

waiter /ˈweɪtə(r)/ *n* Kellner *m*; **~!** Herr Ober!

waiting: ~-list *n* Warteliste *f*. **~-room** *n* Warteraum *m*; (*doctor's*) Wartezimmer *nt*

waitress /ˈweɪtrɪs/ *n* Kellnerin *f*

waive /weɪv/ *vt* verzichten auf (+ *acc*)

wake[1] /weɪk/ *n* Totenwache *f* • *v* (*pt* **woke**, *pp* **woken**) ~ **[up]** • *vt* [auf]wecken • *vi* aufwachen

wake[2] *n* (*Naut*) Kielwasser *nt*; **in the ~ of** im Gefolge (+ *gen*)

Wales /weɪlz/ *n* Wales *nt*

walk /wɔ:k/ *n* Spaziergang *m*; (*gait*) Gang *m*; (*path*) Weg *m*; **go for a ~** spazieren gehen ● *vi* gehen; (*not ride*) laufen, zu Fuß gehen; (*ramble*) wandern; **learn to ~** laufen lernen ● *vt* ausführen (*dog*). **~ out** *vi* hinausgehen (; *workers:*) in den Streik treten; **~ out on s.o.** jdn verlassen

walker /ˈwɔ:kə(r)/ *n* Spaziergänger(in) *m*(*f*); (*rambler*) Wanderer *m*/Wanderin *f*

walking /ˈwɔ:kɪŋ/ *n* Gehen *nt*; (*rambling*) Wandern *nt*. **~-stick** *n* Spazierstock *m*

wall /wɔ:l/ *n* Wand *f*; (*external*) Mauer *f*; **drive s.o. up the ~** [!] jdn auf die Palme bringen ● *vt* **~ up** zumauern

wallet /ˈwɒlɪt/ *n* Brieftasche *f*

ˈwallflower *n* Goldlack *m*

wallop /ˈwɒləp/ *vt* (*pt*/*pp* **walloped**) [!] schlagen

wallow /ˈwɒləʊ/ *vi* sich wälzen; (*fig*) schwelgen

ˈwallpaper *n* Tapete *f* ● *vt* tapezieren

walnut /ˈwɔ:lnʌt/ *n* Walnuss *f*

waltz /wɔ:lts/ *n* Walzer *m* ● *vi* Walzer tanzen

wander /ˈwɒndə(r)/ *vi* umherwandern, [!] bummeln; (*fig: digress*) abschweifen. **~ about** *vi* umherwandern

wangle /ˈwæŋgl/ *vt* [!] organisieren

want /wɒnt/ *n* Mangel *m* (**of** an + *dat*); (*hardship*) Not *f*; (*desire*) Bedürfnis *nt* ● *vt* wollen; (*need*) brauchen; **~ [to have] sth** etw haben wollen; **~ to do sth** etw tun wollen; **I ~ you to go** ich will, dass du gehst; **it ~s painting** es müsste gestrichen werden ● *vi* **he doesn't ~ for anything** ihm fehlt es an nichts. **~ed** *adj* (*criminal*) gesucht

war /wɔ:(r)/ *n* Krieg *m*; **be at ~** sich im Krieg befinden

ward /wɔ:d/ *n* [Kranken]saal *m*; (*unit*) Station *f*; (*of town*) Wahlbezirk *m*; (*child*) Mündel *nt* ● *vt* **~ off** abwehren

warden /ˈwɔ:dn/ *n* (*of hostel*) Heimleiter(in) *m*(*f*); (*of youth hostel*) Herbergsvater *m*; (*supervisor*) Aufseher(in) *m*(*f*)

warder /ˈwɔ:də(r)/ *n* Wärter(in) *m*(*f*)

wardrobe /ˈwɔ:drəʊb/ *n* Kleiderschrank *m*; (*clothes*) Garderobe *f*

warehouse /ˈweəhaʊs/ *n* Lager *nt*; (*building*) Lagerhaus *nt*

wares /weəz/ *npl* Waren *pl*

war: ~fare *n* Krieg *m*. **~like** *adj* kriegerisch

warm /wɔ:m/ *adj* (**-er, -est**) warm; (*welcome*) herzlich; **I am ~** mir ist warm ● *vt* wärmen. **~ up** *vt* aufwärmen ● *vi* warm werden; (*Sport*) sich aufwärmen. **~-hearted** *adj* warmherzig

warmth /wɔ:mθ/ *n* Wärme *f*

warn /wɔ:n/ *vt* warnen (**of** vor + *dat*). **~ing** *n* Warnung *f*; (*advance notice*) Vorwarnung *f*; (*caution*) Verwarnung *f*

warp /wɔ:p/ *vt* verbiegen ● *vi* sich verziehen

warrant /ˈwɒrənt/ *n* (*for arrest*) Haftbefehl *m*; (*for search*) Durchsuchungsbefehl *m* ● *vt* (*justify*) rechtfertigen; (*guarantee*) garantieren

warranty /ˈwɒrəntɪ/ *n* Garantie *f*

warrior /ˈwɒrɪə(r)/ *n* Krieger *m*

ˈwarship *n* Kriegsschiff *nt*

wart /wɔ:t/ *n* Warze *f*

ˈwartime *n* Kriegszeit *f*

war|y /ˈweərɪ/ *adj* , **-ily** *adv* vorsichtig; (*suspicious*) misstrauisch

was /wɒz/ *see* **be**

wash /wɒʃ/ *n* Wäsche *f*; (*Naut*) Wellen *pl*; **have a ~** sich waschen ● *vt* waschen; spülen (*dishes*); aufwischen (*floor*); **~ one's hands** sich (*dat*) die Hände waschen ● *vi* sich waschen. **~ out** *vt* auswaschen; ausspülen (*mouth*). **~ up** *vt/i* abwaschen, spülen ● *vi* (*Amer*) sich waschen

washable /ˈwɒʃəbl/ *adj* waschbar

wash-basin *n* Waschbecken *nt*

washer /ˈwɒʃə(r)/ *n* (*Techn*) Dichtungsring *m*; (*machine*) Waschmaschine *f*

washing /ˈwɒʃɪŋ/ *n* Wäsche *f*. **~-machine** *n* Waschmaschine *f*. **~-powder** *n* Waschpulver *nt*. **~-ˈup** *n* Abwasch *m*; **do the ~-up** abwaschen, spülen. **~-ˈup liquid** *n* Spülmittel *nt*

wasp /wɒsp/ *n* Wespe *f*

waste /weɪst/ *n* Verschwendung *f*; (*rubbish*) Abfall *m*; **~s** *pl* Öde *f* ● *adj* (*product*) Abfall- ● *vt* verschwenden ● *vi* **~ away** immer mehr abmagern

waste: ~ful *adj* verschwenderisch. **~ land** *n* Ödland *nt*. **~ ˈpaper** *n* Altpapier *nt*. **~-ˈpaper basket** *n* Papierkorb *m*

watch /wɒtʃ/ *n* Wache *f*; (*timepiece*) [Armband]uhr *f* ● *vt* beobachten; sich (*dat*) ansehen (*film, match*); (*keep an eye on*) achten auf (+ *acc*); **~ television** fernsehen ● *vi* zusehen. **~ out** *vi* Ausschau halten (**for** nach); (*be careful*) aufpassen

watch: ~-dog *n* Wachhund *m*. **~ful** *adj* wachsam. **~man** *n* Wachmann *m*

water /ˈwɔːtə(r)/ *n* Wasser *nt*; **~s** *pl* Gewässer *nt* ● *vt* gießen (*garden, plant*); (*dilute*) verdünnen ● *vi* (*eyes:*) tränen; **my mouth was ~ing** mir lief das Wasser im Munde zusammen. **~ down** *vt* verwässern

water: ~-colour *n* Wasserfarbe *f*; (*painting*) Aquarell *nt*. **~cress** *n* Brunnenkresse *f*. **~fall** *n* Wasserfall *m*

ˈwatering-can *n* Gießkanne *f*

water: ~-lily *n* Seerose *f*. **~logged** *adj* **be ~logged** (*ground:*) unter Wasser stehen. **~ polo** *n* Wasserball *m*. **~proof** *adj* wasserdicht. **~-skiing** *n* Wasserskilaufen *nt*. **~tight** *adj* wasserdicht. **~way** *n* Wasserstraße *f*

watery /ˈwɔːtərɪ/ *adj* wässrig

watt /wɒt/ *n* Watt *nt*

wave /weɪv/ *n* Welle *f*; (*gesture*) Handbewegung *f*; (*as greeting*) Winken *nt* ● *vt* winken mit; (*brandish*) schwingen; wellen (*hair*); **~ one's hand** winken ● *vi* winken (**to** *dat*); (*flag:*) wehen. **~length** *n* Wellenlänge *f*

waver /ˈweɪvə(r)/ *vi* schwanken

wavy /ˈweɪvɪ/ *adj* wellig

wax /wæks/ *n* Wachs *nt*; (*in ear*) Schmalz *nt* ● *vt* wachsen. **~works** *n* Wachsfigurenkabinett *nt*

way /weɪ/ *n* Weg *m*; (*direction*) Richtung *f*; (*respect*) Hinsicht *f*; (*manner*) Art *f*; (*method*) Art und Weise *f*; **~s** *pl* Gewohnheiten *pl*; **on the ~** auf dem Weg (**to** nach/zu); (*under way*) unterwegs; **a little/long ~** ein kleines/ganzes Stück; **a long ~ off** weit weg; **this ~** hierher; (*like this*) so; **which ~** in welche Richtung; (*how*) wie; **by the ~** übrigens; **in some ~s** in gewisser Hinsicht; **either ~** so oder so; **in this ~** auf diese Weise; **in a ~** in gewisser Weise; **lead the ~** vorausgehen; **make ~** Platz machen (**for** *dat*); **'give ~'** (*Auto*) 'Vorfahrt beachten'; **go out of one's ~** (*fig*) sich (*dat*) besondere Mühe geben (**to** zu); **get one's [own] ~** seinen Willen durchsetzen ● *adv* weit; ~ **behind** weit zurück. ~ **'in** *n* Eingang *m*

way 'out *n* Ausgang *m*; (*fig*) Ausweg *m*

WC *abbr* WC *nt*

we /wi:/ *pron* wir

weak /wi:k/ *adj* (**-er, -est**) schwach; (*liquid*) dünn. ~**en** *vt* schwächen ● *vi* schwächer werden. ~**ling** *n* Schwächling *m*. ~**ness** *n* Schwäche *f*

wealth /welθ/ *n* Reichtum *m*; (*fig*) Fülle *f* (**of** an + *dat*). ~**y** *adj* reich

weapon /'wepən/ *n* Waffe *f*; ~**s of mass destruction** Massenvernichtungswaffen *pl*

wear /weə(r)/ *n* (*clothing*) Kleidung *f*; ~ **and tear** Abnutzung *f*, Verschleiß *m* ● *v* (*pt* **wore**, *pp* **worn**) ● *vt* tragen; (*damage*) abnutzen; **what shall I** ~**?** was soll ich anziehen? ● *vi* sich abnutzen; (*last*) halten. ~ **off** *vi* abgehen; (*effect:*) nachlassen. ~ **out** *vt* abnutzen; (*exhaust*) erschöpfen ● *vi* sich abnutzen

weary /'wɪərɪ/ *adj* , **-ily** *adv* müde

weather /'weðə(r)/ *n* Wetter *nt*; **in this** ~ bei diesem Wetter; **under the** ~ 🄸 nicht ganz auf dem Posten ● *vt* abwettern (*storm*); (*fig*) überstehen

weather: ~**-beaten** *adj* verwittert; wettergegerbt (*face*). ~ **forecast** *n* Wettervorhersage *f*

weave[1] /wi:v/ *vi* (*pt*/*pp* **weaved**) sich schlängeln (**through** durch)

weave[2] *n* (*of cloth*) Bindung *f* ● *vt* (*pt* **wove**, *pp* **woven**) weben. ~**r** *n* Weber *m*

W

web /web/ *n* Netz *nt*; **the W**~ das Web. ~**master** *n* Webmaster *m*. ~ **page** *n* Webseite *f*. ~**site** *n* Website *f*

wed /wed/ *vt*/*i* (*pt*/*pp* **wedded**) heiraten. ~**ding** *n* Hochzeit *f*

wedding: ~ **day** *n* Hochzeitstag *m*. ~ **dress** *n* Hochzeitskleid *nt*. ~**-ring** *n* Ehering *m*, Trauring *m*

wedge /wedʒ/ *n* Keil *m* ● *vt* festklemmen

Wednesday /'wenzdeɪ/ *n* Mittwoch *m*

wee /wi:/ *adj* 🄸 klein ● *vi* Pipi machen

weed /wi:d/ *n* Unkraut *nt* ● *vt*/*i* jäten. ~ **out** *vt* (*fig*) aussieben

'weedkiller *n* Unkrautvertilgungsmittel *nt*

weedy /'wi:dɪ/ *adj* 🄸 spillerig

week /wi:k/ *n* Woche *f*. ~**day** *n* Wochentag *m*. ~**end** *n* Wochenende *nt*

weekly /'wi:klɪ/ *adj* & *adv* wöchentlich ● *n* Wochenzeitschrift *f*

weep /wi:p/ *vi* (*pt*/*pp* **wept**) weinen

weigh /weɪ/ *vt*/*i* wiegen. ~ **down** *vt* (*fig*) niederdrücken. ~ **up** *vt* (*fig*) abwägen

weight /weɪt/ *n* Gewicht *nt*; **put on**/**lose** ~ zunehmen/abnehmen

weight-lifting *n* Gewichtheben *nt*

weighty /'weɪtɪ/ *adj* schwer; (*important*) gewichtig

weir /wɪə(r)/ *n* Wehr *nt*.

weird /wɪəd/ *adj* (**-er, -est**) unheimlich; (*bizarre*) bizarr

welcome /'welkəm/ *adj* willkommen; **you're** ~**!** nichts zu danken! **you're** ~ **to (have) it** das können Sie gerne haben ● *n* Willkommen *nt* ● *vt* begrüßen

weld /weld/ *vt* schweißen. ~**er** *n* Schweißer *m*

welfare /'welfeə(r)/ *n* Wohl *nt*; (*Admin*) Fürsorge *f*. **W** ~ **State** *n* Wohlfahrtsstaat *m*

well[1] /wel/ *n* Brunnen *m*;

(*oil* ~) Quelle *f*

well² *adv* (**better, best**) gut; **as ~** auch; **as ~ as** (*in addition*) sowohl ... als auch; **~ done!** gut gemacht! ● *adj* gesund; **he is not ~** es geht ihm nicht gut; **get ~ soon!** gute Besserung! ● *int* nun, na

well: ~-behaved *adj* artig. **~-being** *n* Wohl *nt*

wellingtons /ˈwelɪŋtənz/ *npl* Gummistiefel *pl*

well: ~-known *adj* bekannt. **~-off** *adj* wohlhabend; **be ~-off** gut dransein. **~-to-do** *adj* wohlhabend

Welsh /welʃ/ *adj* walisisch ● *n* (*Lang*) Walisisch *nt*; **the ~** *pl* die Waliser. **~ man** *n* Waliser *m*

i

Welsh Assembly Das walisische Parlament, dessen Mitglieder in der Hauptstadt Cardiff zusammentreten. Es wurde 1999 (nach einer Volksabstimmung) eröffnet und verleiht Wales eine größere Autonomie gegenüber dem britischen Parlament in London. Das Parlament setzt sich aus 60 Mitgliedern zusammen, 40 sind direkt gewählt, die restlichen Abgeordneten von Regionallisten und nach dem Verhältniswahlrecht.

went /went/ *see* **go**

wept /wept/ *see* **weep**

were /wɜː(r)/ *see* **be**

west /west/ *n* Westen *m*; **to the ~ of** westlich von ● *adj* West-, west- ● *adv* nach Westen. **~erly** *adj* westlich. **~ern** *adj* westlich ● *n* Western *m*

West: ~ 'Germany *n* Westdeutschland *nt*. **~ 'Indian** *adj* westindisch ● *n* Westinder(in) *m*(*f*). **~ 'Indies** /-ˈɪndɪz/ *npl* Westindische Inseln *pl*

'westward[s] /-wəd[z]/ *adv* nach Westen

wet /wet/ *adj* (**wetter, wettest**) nass; (*fam: person*) weichlich, lasch; **'~ paint'** 'frisch gestrichen' ● *vt* (*pt/pp* **wet** or **wetted**) nass machen

whack /wæk/ *vt* [!] schlagen. **~ed** *adj* [!] kaputt

whale /weɪl/ *n* Wal *m*

wharf /wɔːf/ *n* Kai *m*

what /wɒt/

● *pronoun*

····➤ (*in questions*) was. **what is it?** was ist das? **what do you want?** was wollen Sie? **what is your name?** wie heißen Sie? **what?** ([!]: *say that again*) wie?; was? **what is the time?** wie spät ist es? (*indirect*) **I didn't know what to do** ich wusste nicht, was ich machen sollte

! The equivalent of a preposition with **what** in English is a special word in German beginning with *wo-* (*wor-* before a vowel): **for what? what for? =** wofür? wozu? **from what?** wovon? **on what?** worauf? worüber? **under what?** worunter? **with what?** womit? etc. **what do you want the money for?** wozu willst du das Geld? **what is he talking about?** wovon redet er?

····➤ (*relative pronoun*) was. **do what I tell you** tu, was ich dir sage. **give me what you can** gib mir, so viel du kannst. **what little I know** das bisschen, das ich weiß. **I don't agree with what you are**

saying ich stimme dem nicht zu, was Sie sagen

····➤ (*in phrases*) **what about me?** was ist mit mir? **what about a cup of coffee?** wie wäre es mit einer Tasse Kaffee? **what if she doesn't come?** was ist, wenn sie nicht kommt? **what of it?** was ist dabei?

● *adjective*

····➤ (*asking for selection*) welcher (*m*), welche (*f*), welches (*nt*), welche (*pl*). **what book do you want?** welches Buch willst du haben? **what colour are the walls?** welche Farbe haben die Wände? **I asked him what train to take** ich habe ihn gefragt, welchen Zug ich nehmen soll

····➤ (*asking how much/many*) **what money does he have?** wie viel Geld hat er? **what time is it?** wie spät ist es? **what time does it start?** um wie viel Uhr fängt es an?

····➤ **what kind of ...?** was für [ein(e)]? **what kind of man is he?** was für ein Mensch ist er?

····➤ (*in exclamations*) was für (+ *nom*). **what a fool you are!** was für ein Dummkopf du doch bist! **what cheek/luck!** was für eine Frechheit/ein Glück! **what a huge house!** was für ein riesiges Haus! **what a lot of people!** was für viele Leute!

what'ever *adj* [egal] welche(r,s) ● *pron* was ... auch; **~ is it?** was ist das bloß?; **~ he does** was er auch tut; **nothing ~** überhaupt nichts

whatso'ever *pron & adj* ≈ **whatever**

wheat /wi:t/ *n* Weizen *m*

wheel /wi:l/ *n* Rad *nt*; (*pottery*) Töpferscheibe *f*; (*steering* ~) Lenkrad *nt*; **at the ~** am Steuer ● *vt* (*push*) schieben ● *vi* kehrtmachen; (*circle*) kreisen

wheel: ~barrow *n* Schubkarre *f*. **~chair** *n* Rollstuhl *m*. **~-clamp** *n* Parkkralle *f*

when /wen/ *adv* wann; **the day ~** der Tag, an dem ● *conj* wenn; (*in the past*) als; (*although*) wo ... doch; **~ swimming/reading** beim Schwimmen/Lesen

when'ever *conj & adv* [immer] wenn; (*at whatever time*) wann immer; **~ did it happen?** wann ist das bloß passiert?

where /weə(r)/ *adv & conj* wo; **~ [to]** wohin; **~ [from]** woher

whereabouts[1] /weərə'baʊts/ *adv* wo

'whereabouts[2] *n* Verbleib *m*; (*of person*) Aufenthaltsort *m*

where'as *conj* während; (*in contrast*) wohingegen

whereu'pon *adv* worauf[hin]

wher'ever *conj & adv* wo immer; (*to whatever place*) wohin immer; (*from whatever place*) woher immer; (*everywhere*) überall wo; **~ possible** wenn irgend möglich

whether /'weðə(r)/ *conj* ob

which /wɪtʃ/

● *adjective*

····➤ (*in questions*) welcher (*m*), welche (*f*), welches (*nt*), welche (*pl*). **which book do you need?** welches Buch brauchst du? **which one?** welcher/welche/welches? **which ones?** welche? **which one of you did it?** wer von euch hat es getan? **which way?** (*which direction*) welche Richtung?; (*where*) wohin?; (*how*) wie?

····➤ (*relative*) **he always comes at**

one at which time I'm having lunch/by which time I've finished er kommt immer um ein Uhr; dann esse ich gerade zu Mittag/bis dahin bin ich schon fertig

● *pronoun*

····➤ (*in questions*) welcher (*m*), welche (*f*), welches (*nt*), welche (*pl*). **which is which?** welcher/welche/welches ist welcher/welche/welches? **which of you?** wer von euch?

····➤ (*relative*) der (*m*), die (*f*), das (*nt*), die (*pl*); (*genitive*) dessen (*m, nt*), deren (*f, pl*); (*dative*) dem (*m, nt*), der (*f*), denen (*pl*); (*referring to a clause*) was. **the book which I gave you** das Buch, das ich dir gab. **the trial, the result of which we are expecting** der Prozess, dessen Ergebnis wir erwarten. **the house of which I was speaking** das Haus, von dem *od* wovon ich redete. **after which** wonach; nach dem. **on which** worauf; auf dem. **the shop opposite which we parked** der Laden, gegenüber dem wir parkten. **everything which I tell you** alles, was ich dir sage

which'ever *adj & pron* [egal] welche(r,s); ~ **it is** was es auch ist

while /waɪl/ *n* Weile *f*; **a long** ~ lange; **be worth** ~ sich lohnen; **it's worth my** ~ es lohnt sich für mich ● *conj* während; (*as long as*) solange; (*although*) obgleich ● *vt* ~ **away** sich (*dat*) vertreiben

whilst /waɪlst/ *conj* während

whim /wɪm/ *n* Laune *f*

whimper /'wɪmpə(r)/ *vi* wimmern; (*dog:*) winseln

whine /waɪn/ *vi* winseln

whip /wɪp/ *n* Peitsche *f*; (*Pol*) Einpeitscher *m* ● *vt* (*pt/pp* **whipped**) peitschen; (*Culin*) schlagen. **~ped 'cream** *n* Schlagsahne *f*

whirl /wɜːl/ *vt/i* wirbeln. **~pool** *n* Strudel *m*. **~-wind** *n* Wirbelwind *m*

whirr /wɜː(r)/ *vi* surren

whisk /wɪsk/ *n* (*Culin*) Schneebesen *m* ● *vt* (*Culin*) schlagen

whisker /'wɪskə(r)/ *n* Schnurrhaar *nt*

whisky /'wɪskɪ/ *n* Whisky *m*

whisper /'wɪspə(r)/ *n* Flüstern *nt* ● *vt/i* flüstern

whistle /'wɪsl/ *n* Pfiff *m*; (*instrument*) Pfeife *f* ● *vt/i* pfeifen

white /waɪt/ *adj* (**-r, -st**) weiß ● *n* Weiß *nt*; (*of egg*) Eiweiß *nt*; (*person*) Weiße(r) *m/f*

white: ~ **'coffee** *n* Kaffee *m* mit Milch. **~-'collar worker** *n* Angestellte(r) *m*. ~ **'lie** *n* Notlüge *f*

whiten /'waɪtn/ *vt* weiß machen ● *vi* weiß werden

whiteness /'waɪtnɪs/ *n* Weiß *nt*

Whitsun /'wɪtsn/ *n* Pfingsten *nt*

whiz[z] /wɪz/ *vi* (*pt/pp* **whizzed**) zischen. **~-kid** *n* [!] Senkrechtstarter *m*

who /huː/ *pron* wer; (*acc*) wen; (*dat*) wem ● *rel pron* der/die/das, (*pl*) die

who'ever *pron* wer [immer]; ~ **he is** wer er auch ist; ~ **is it?** wer ist das bloß?

whole /həʊl/ *adj* ganz; (*truth*) voll ● *n* Ganze(s) *nt*; **as a** ~ als Ganzes; **on the** ~ im Großen und Ganzen; **the** ~ **of Germany** ganz Deutschland

whole: **~food** *n* Vollwertkost *f*. **~-'hearted** *adj* rückhaltlos. **~meal** *adj* Vollkorn-

'wholesale *adj* Großhandels- ● *adv* en gros; (*fig*) in Bausch und

Bogen. **~r** *n* Großhändler *m*

wholly /ˈhəʊlɪ/ *adv* völlig

whom /huːm/ *pron* wen; **to ~** wem ● *rel pron* den/die/das, (*pl*) die; (*dat*) dem/der/dem, (*pl*) denen

whopping /ˈwɒpɪŋ/ *adj* [T] Riesen-

whore /hɔː(r)/ *n* Hure *f*

whose /huːz/ *pron* wessen; **~ is that?** wem gehört das? ● *rel pron* dessen/deren/dessen, (*pl*) deren

why /waɪ/ *adv* warum; (*for what purpose*) wozu; **that's ~** darum

wick /wɪk/ *n* Docht *m*

wicked /ˈwɪkɪd/ *adj* böse; (*mischievous*) frech, boshaft

wicker /ˈwɪkə(r)/ *n* Korbgeflecht *nt* ● *attrib* Korb-

wide /waɪd/ *adj* (**-r,-st**) weit; (*broad*) breit; (*fig*) groß ● *adv* weit; (*off target*) daneben; **~ awake** hellwach; **far and ~** weit und breit. **~ly** *adv* weit; (*known, accepted*) weithin; (*differ*) stark

widen /ˈwaɪdn/ *vt* verbreitern; (*fig*) erweitern ● *vi* sich verbreitern

ˈ**widespread** *adj* weit verbreitet

widow /ˈwɪdəʊ/ *n* Witwe *f*. **~ed** *adj* verwitwet. **~er** *n* Witwer *m*

width /wɪdθ/ *n* Weite *f*; (*breadth*) Breite *f*

wield /wiːld/ *vt* schwingen; ausüben (*power*)

wife /waɪf/ *n* (*pl* **wives**) [Ehe]frau *f*

wig /wɪg/ *n* Perücke *f*

wiggle /ˈwɪgl/ *vi* wackeln ● *vt* wackeln mit

W

wild /waɪld/ *adj* (**-er, -est**) wild; (*animal*) wild lebend; (*flower*) wild wachsend; (*furious*) wütend ● *adv* wild; **run ~** frei herumlaufen ● *n* **in the ~** wild; **the ~s** *pl* die Wildnis *f*

wilderness /ˈwɪldənɪs/ *n* Wildnis *f*; (*desert*) Wüste *f*

wildlife *n* Tierwelt *f*

will[1] /wɪl/

● *modal verb*

past **would**

····▸ (*expressing the future*) werden. **she will arrive tomorrow** sie wird morgen ankommen. **he will be there by now** er wird jetzt schon da sein

····▸ (*expressing intention*) (*present tense*) **will you go?** gehst du? **I promise I won't do it again** ich verspreche, ich machs nicht noch mal

····▸ (*in requests*) **will/would you please tidy up?** würdest du bitte aufräumen? **will you be quiet!** willst du ruhig sein!

····▸ (*in invitations*) **will you have/would you like some wine?** wollen Sie/möchten Sie Wein?

····▸ (*negative: refuse to*) nicht wollen. **they won't help me** sie wollen mir nicht helfen. **the car won't start** das Auto will nicht anspringen

····▸ (*in tag questions*) nicht wahr. **you'll be back soon, won't you?** du kommst bald wieder, nicht wahr? **you will help her, won't you?** du hilfst ihr doch, nicht wahr?

····▸ (*in short answers*) **Will you be there? — Yes I will** Wirst du da sein? — Ja

will[2] *n* Wille *m*; (*document*) Testament *nt*

willing /ˈwɪlɪŋ/ *adj* willig; (*eager*) bereitwillig; **be ~** bereit sein. **~ly** *adv* bereitwillig; (*gladly*) gern. **~ness** *n* Bereitwilligkeit *f*

willow /ˈwɪləʊ/ *n* Weide *f*
ˈwill-power *n* Willenskraft *f*
wilt /wɪlt/ *vi* welk werden, welken
wily /ˈwaɪlɪ/ *adj* listig
win /wɪn/ *n* Sieg *m* ● *v* (*pt/pp* **won**; *pres p* **winning**) ● *vt* gewinnen; bekommen (*scholarship*) ● *vi* gewinnen; (*in battle*) siegen. **~ over** *vt* auf seine Seite bringen
wince /wɪns/ *vi* zusammenzucken
winch /wɪntʃ/ *n* Winde *f* ● *vt* **~ up** hochwinden
wind¹ /wɪnd/ *n* Wind *m*; ([!]: *flatulence*) Blähungen *pl* ● *vt* **~ s.o.** jdm den Atem nehmen
wind² /waɪnd/ *v* (*pt/pp* **wound**) ● *vt* (*wrap*) wickeln; (*move by turning*) kurbeln; aufziehen (*clock*) *vi* (*road:*) sich winden. **~ up** *vt* aufziehen (*clock*); schließen (*proceedings*)
wind: ~ farm *n* Windpark *m*. **~ instrument** *n* Blasinstrument *nt*. **~mill** *n* Windmühle *f*
window /ˈwɪndəʊ/ *n* Fenster *nt*; (*of shop*) Schaufenster *nt*
window: ~-box *n* Blumenkasten *m*. **~-cleaner** *n* Fensterputzer *m*. **~-pane** *n* Fensterscheibe *f*. **~-shopping** *n* Schaufensterbummel *m*. **~-sill** *n* Fensterbrett *nt*
ˈwindpipe *n* Luftröhre *f*
ˈwindscreen *n*, (*Amer*) **ˈwindshield** *n* Windschutzscheibe *f*. **~-wiper** *n* Scheibenwischer *m*
wind surfing *n* Windsurfen *nt*
windy /ˈwɪndɪ/ *adj* windig
wine /waɪn/ *n* Wein *m*
wine: ~-bar *n* Weinstube *f*. **~glass** *n* Weinglas *nt*. **~-list** *n* Weinkarte *f*
winery /ˈwaɪnərɪ/ *n* (*Amer*) Weingut *nt*
ˈwine-tasting *n* Weinprobe *f*
wing /wɪŋ/ *n* Flügel *m*; (*Auto*) Kotflügel *m*; **~s** *pl* (*Theat*) Kulissen *pl*
wink /wɪŋk/ *n* Zwinkern *nt*; **not sleep a ~** kein Auge zutun ● *vi* zwinkern; (*light:*) blinken
winner /ˈwɪnə(r)/ *n* Gewinner(in) *m*(*f*); (*Sport*) Sieger(in) *m*(*f*)
winning /ˈwɪnɪŋ/ *adj* siegreich; (*smile*) gewinnend. **~-post** *n* Zielpfosten *m*. **~s** *npl* Gewinn *m*
wint|er /ˈwɪntə(r)/ *n* Winter *m*. **~ry** *adj* winterlich
wipe /waɪp/ *n* **give sth a ~** etw abwischen ● *vt* abwischen; aufwischen (*floor*); (*dry*) abtrocknen. **~ out** *vt* (*cancel*) löschen; (*destroy*) ausrotten. **~ up** *vt* aufwischen
wire /ˈwaɪə(r)/ *n* Draht *m*
wiring /ˈwaɪərɪŋ/ *n* [elektrische] Leitungen *pl*
wisdom /ˈwɪzdəm/ *n* Weisheit *f*; (*prudence*) Klugheit *f*. **~ tooth** *n* Weisheitszahn *m*
wise /waɪz/ *adj* (**-r, -st**) weise; (*prudent*) klug
wish /wɪʃ/ *n* Wunsch *m* ● *vt* wünschen; **~ s.o. well** jdm alles Gute wünschen; **I ~ you could stay** ich wünschte, du könntest hier bleiben ● *vi* sich (*dat*) etwas wünschen. **~ful** *adj* **~ful thinking** Wunschdenken *nt*
wistful /ˈwɪstfl/ *adj* wehmütig
wit /wɪt/ *n* Geist *m*, Witz *m*; (*intelligence*) Verstand *m*; (*person*) geistreicher Mensch *m*; **be at one's ~s' end** sich (*dat*) keinen Rat mehr wissen
witch /wɪtʃ/ *n* Hexe *f*. **~craft** *n* Hexerei *f*
with /wɪð/ *prep* mit (+ *dat*); **~ fear/cold** vor Angst/Kälte; **~ it** damit; **I'm going ~ you** ich gehe mit; **take it ~ you** nimm es mit; **I haven't got it ~ me** ich habe es nicht bei mir

with'draw *v* (*pt* **-drew**, *pp* **-drawn**) ● *vt* zurückziehen; abheben (*money*) ● *vi* sich zurückziehen. **~al** *n* Zurückziehen *nt*; (*of money*) Abhebung *f*; (*from drugs*) Entzug *m*

wither /'wɪðə(r)/ *vi* [ver]welken

with'hold *vt* (*pt/pp* **-held**) vorenthalten (**from s.o.** jdm)

with'in *prep* innerhalb (+ *gen*) ● *adv* innen

with'out *prep* ohne (+ *acc*); **~ my noticing it** ohne dass ich es merkte

with'stand *vt* (*pt/pp* **-stood**) standhalten (+ *dat*)

witness /'wɪtnɪs/ *n* Zeuge *m*/ Zeugin *f* ● *vt* Zeuge/Zeugin sein (+ *gen*); bestätigen (*signature*)

witticism /'wɪtɪsɪzm/ *n* geistreicher Ausspruch *m*

witty /'wɪtɪ/ *adj* witzig, geistreich

wives /waɪvz/ *see* **wife**

wizard /'wɪzəd/ *n* Zauberer *m*

wizened /'wɪznd/ *adj* verhutzelt

wobb|le /'wɒbl/ *vi* wackeln. **~ly** *adj* wackelig

woke, woken /wəʊk, 'wəʊkn/ *see* **wake**[1]

wolf /wʊlf/ *n* (*pl* **wolves** /wʊlvz/) Wolf *m*

woman /'wʊmən/ *n* (*pl* **women**) Frau *f*. **~izer** *n* Schürzenjäger *m*

womb /wu:m/ *n* Gebärmutter *f*

women /'wɪmɪn/ *npl see* **woman**

won /wʌn/ *see* **win**

wonder /'wʌndə(r)/ *n* Wunder *nt*; (*surprise*) Staunen *nt* ● *vt/i* sich fragen; (*be surprised*) sich wundern; **I ~** da frage ich mich; **I ~ whether she is ill** ob sie wohl krank ist? **~ful** *adj* wunderbar

won't /wəʊnt/ = **will not**

wood /wʊd/ *n* Holz *nt*; (*forest*) Wald *m*; **touch ~!** unberufen!

wood: ~ed /-ɪd/ *adj* bewaldet. **~en** *adj* Holz-; (*fig*) hölzern. **~pecker** *n* Specht *m*. **~wind** *n* Holzbläser *pl*. **~work** *n* (*wooden parts*) Holzteile *pl*; (*craft*) Tischlerei *f*. **~worm** *n* Holzwurm *m*

wool /wʊl/ *n* Wolle *f* ● *attrib* Woll-. **~len** *adj* wollen

woolly /'wʊlɪ/ *adj* wollig; (*fig*) unklar

word /wɜ:d/ *n* Wort *nt*; (*news*) Nachricht *f*; **by ~ of mouth** mündlich; **have a ~ with** sprechen mit; **have ~s** einen Wortwechsel haben. **~ing** *n* Wortlaut *m*. **~ processor** *n* Textverarbeitungssystem *nt*

wore /wɔ:(r)/ *see* **wear**

work /wɜ:k/ *n* Arbeit *f*; (*Art, Literature*) Werk *nt*; **~s** *pl* (*factory, mechanism*) Werk *nt*; **at ~** bei der Arbeit; **out of ~** arbeitslos ● *vi* arbeiten; (*machine, system:*) funktionieren; (*have effect*) wirken; (*study*) lernen; **it won't ~** (*fig*) es klappt nicht ● *vt* arbeiten lassen; bedienen (*machine*); betätigen (*lever*). **~ off** *vt* abarbeiten. **~ out** *vt* ausrechnen; (*solve*) lösen ● *vi* gut gehen, [!] klappen. **~ up** *vt* aufbauen; sich (*dat*) holen (*appetite*); **get ~ed up** sich aufregen

workable /'wɜ:kəbl/ *adj* (*feasible*) durchführbar

worker /'wɜ:kə(r)/ *n* Arbeiter(in) *m*(*f*)

working /'wɜ:kɪŋ/ *adj* berufstätig; (*day, clothes*) Arbeits-; **be in ~ order** funktionieren. **~ class** *n* Arbeiterklasse *f*

work: ~man *n* Arbeiter *m*; (*craftsman*) Handwerker *m*. **~manship** *n* Arbeit *f*. **~shop** *n* Werkstatt *f*

world /wɜ:ld/ *n* Welt *f*; **in the ~** auf der Welt; **think the ~ of s.o.** große Stücke auf jdn halten. **~ly** *adj* weltlich; (*person*) weltlich gesinnt. **~-wide** *adj & adv* /-ˈ-/ weltweit

worm /wɜːm/ *n* Wurm *m*

worn /wɔːn/ *see* **wear** ● *adj* abgetragen. **~-out** *adj* abgetragen; (*carpet*) abgenutzt; (*person*) erschöpft

worried /ˈwʌrɪd/ *adj* besorgt

worry /ˈwʌrɪ/ *n* Sorge *f* ● *v* (*pt/pp* **worried**) ● *vt* beunruhigen; (*bother*) stören ● *vi* sich beunruhigen, sich (*dat*) Sorgen machen. **~ing** *adj* beunruhigend

worse /wɜːs/ *adj & adv* schlechter; (*more serious*) schlimmer ● *n* Schlechtere(s) *nt*; Schlimmere(s) *nt*

worsen /ˈwɜːsn/ *vt* verschlechtern ● *vi* sich verschlechtern

worship /ˈwɜːʃɪp/ *n* Anbetung *f*; (*service*) Gottesdienst *m* ● *vt* (*pt/pp* **-shipped**) anbeten

worst /wɜːst/ *adj* schlechteste(r,s); (*most serious*) schlimmste(r,s) ● *adv* am schlechtesten; am schlimmsten ● *n* **the ~** das Schlimmste

worth /wɜːθ/ *n* Wert *m*; **£10's ~ of petrol** Benzin für £10 ● *adj* **be ~ £5** £5 wert sein; **be ~ it** (*fig*) sich lohnen. **~less** *adj* wertlos. **~while** *adj* lohnend

worthy /ˈwɜːðɪ/ *adj* würdig

would /wʊd/ *modal verb* **I ~ do it** ich würde es tun, ich täte es; **~ you go?** würdest du gehen? **he said he ~n't** er sagte, er würde es nicht tun; **what ~ you like?** was möchten Sie?

wound¹ /wuːnd/ *n* Wunde *f* ● *vt* verwunden

wound² /waʊnd/ *see* **wind²**

wove, woven *see* **weave²**

wrangle /ˈræŋgl/ *n* Streit *m*

wrap /ræp/ *n* Umhang *m* ● *vt* (*pt/pp* **wrapped**) **~ [up]** wickeln; einpacken (*present*) ● *vi* **~ up warmly** sich warm einpacken. **~per** *n* Hülle *f*. **~ping** *n* Verpackung *f*

wrath /rɒθ/ *n* Zorn *m*

wreath /riːθ/ *n* (*pl* **~s** /-ðz/) Kranz *m*

wreck /rek/ *n* Wrack *nt* ● *vt* zerstören; zunichte machen (*plans*); zerrütten (*marriage*). **~age** *n* Wrackteile *pl*; (*fig*) Trümmer *pl*

wren /ren/ *n* Zaunkönig *m*

wrench /rentʃ/ *n* Ruck *m*; (*tool*) Schraubenschlüssel *m*; **be a ~** (*fig*) weh tun ● *vt* reißen; **~ sth from s.o.** jdm etw entreißen

wrestl|e /ˈresl/ *vi* ringen. **~er** *n* Ringer *m*. **~ing** *n* Ringen *nt*

wretch /retʃ/ *n* Kreatur *f*. **~ed** *adj* elend; (*very bad*) erbärmlich

wriggle /ˈrɪgl/ *n* Zappeln *nt* ● *vi* zappeln; (*move forward*) sich schlängeln; **~ out of sth** [!] sich vor etw (*dat*) drücken

wring /rɪŋ/ *vt* (*pt/pp* **wrung**) wringen; (**~** *out*) auswringen; umdrehen (*neck*); ringen (*hands*)

wrinkle /ˈrɪŋkl/ *n* Falte *f*; (*on skin*) Runzel *f* ● *vt* kräuseln ● *vi* sich kräuseln, sich falten. **~d** *adj* runzlig

wrist /rɪst/ *n* Handgelenk *nt*. **~-watch** *n* Armbanduhr *f*

write /raɪt/ *vt/i* (*pt* **wrote**, *pp* **written**, *pres p* **writing**) schreiben. **~ down** *vt* aufschreiben. **~ off**ˈ *vt* abschreiben; zu Schrott fahren (*car*)

ˈ**write-off** *n* ≈ Totalschaden *m*

writer /ˈraɪtə(r)/ *n* Schreiber(in) *m(f)*; (*author*) Schriftsteller(in) *m(f)*

writhe /raɪð/ *vi* sich winden

writing /ˈraɪtɪŋ/ *n* Schreiben *nt*; (*handwriting*) Schrift *f*; **in ~** schriftlich. **~-paper** *n* Schreibpapier *nt*

written /ˈrɪtn/ *see* **write**

wrong /rɒŋ/ *adj* falsch; (*morally*) unrecht; (*not just*) ungerecht; **be ~** nicht stimmen; (*person:*) Unrecht haben; **what's ~?** was ist los? ● *adv* falsch; **go ~** (*person:*) etwas falsch machen; (*machine:*) kaputtgehen; (*plan:*) schief gehen ● *n* Unrecht *nt* ● *vt* Unrecht tun (+ *dat*). **~ful** *adj* ungerechtfertigt. **~fully** *adv* (*accuse*) zu Unrecht

wrote /rəʊt/ *see* **write**

wrung /rʌŋ/ *see* **wring**

wry /raɪ/ *adj* (**-er, -est**) ironisch; (*humour*) trocken

Xmas /ˈkrɪsməs, ˈeksməs/ *n* [!] Weihnachten *nt*

X-ray /ˈeks-/ *n* (*picture*) Röntgenaufnahme *f*; **~s** *pl* Röntgenstrahlen *pl* ● *vt* röntgen; durchleuchten (*luggage*)

yacht /jɒt/ *n* Jacht *f*; (*for racing*) Segeljacht *f*. **~ing** *n* Segeln *nt*

yank /jæŋk/ *vt* [!] reißen

Yank *n* [!] Ami *m* [!]

yap /jæp/ *vi* (*pt/pp* **yapped**) (*dog:*) kläffen

yard[1] /jɑːd/ *n* Hof *m*; (*for storage*) Lager *nt*

yard[2] *n* Yard *nt* (= 0,91 *m*)

yarn /jɑːn/ *n* Garn *nt*; ([!]: *tale*) Geschichte *f*

yawn /jɔːn/ *n* Gähnen *nt* ● *vi* gähnen

year /jɪə(r)/ *n* Jahr *nt*; (*of wine*) Jahrgang *m*; **for ~s** jahrelang. **~ly** *adj & adv* jährlich

yearn /jɜːn/ *vi* sich sehnen (**for** nach). **~ing** *n* Sehnsucht *f*

yeast /jiːst/ *n* Hefe *f*

yell /jel/ *n* Schrei *m* ● *vi* schreien

yellow /ˈjeləʊ/ *adj* gelb ● *n* Gelb *nt*

yelp /jelp/ *vi* jaulen

yes /jes/ *adv* ja; (*contradicting*) doch ● *n* Ja *nt*

yesterday /ˈjestədeɪ/ *n & adv* gestern; **~'s paper** die gestrige Zeitung; **the day before ~** vorgestern

yet /jet/ *adv* noch; (*in question*) schon; (*nevertheless*) doch; **as ~** bisher; **not ~** noch nicht; **the best ~** das bisher beste ● *conj* doch

Yiddish /ˈjɪdɪʃ/ *n* Jiddisch *nt*

yield /jiːld/ *n* Ertrag *m* ● *vt* bringen; abwerfen (*profit*) ● *vi* nachgeben; (*Amer, Auto*) die Vorfahrt beachten

yoga /ˈjəʊgə/ *n* Yoga *m*

yoghurt /ˈjɒgət/ *n* Joghurt *m*

yoke /jəʊk/ *n* Joch *nt*; (*of garment*) Passe *f*

yolk /jəʊk/ *n* Dotter *m*, Eigelb *nt*

you /juː/ *pron* du; (*acc*) dich; (*dat*) dir; (*pl*) ihr; (*acc, dat*) euch; (*formal*) (*nom & acc, sg & pl*) Sie; (*dat, sg & pl*) Ihnen; (*one*) man; (*acc*) einen; (*dat*) einem; **all of ~** ihr/Sie alle; **I know ~** ich kenne dich/euch/Sie; **I'll give ~ the money** ich gebe dir/euch/Ihnen das Geld; **it does ~ good** es tut einem gut; **it's bad for ~** es ist ungesund

young /jʌŋ/ *adj* (**-er** /-gə(r)/, **-est** /-gɪst/) jung ● *npl* (*animals*) Junge *pl*; **the ~** die Jugend *f*. **~ster** *n* Jugendliche(r) *m/f*; (*child*) Kleine(r) *m/f*

your /jɔː(r)/ *adj* dein; (*pl*) euer; (*formal*) Ihr

yours /jɔːz/ *poss pron* deine(r), deins; (*pl*) eure(r), euers; (*formal, sg & pl*) Ihre(r), Ihr[e]s; **a friend of ~** ein Freund von dir/Ihnen/euch; **that is ~** das gehört dir/

w x y

Ihnen/euch
your'self *pron* (*pl* **-selves**) selbst; (*reflexive*) dich; (*dat*) dir; (*pl*) euch; (*formal*) sich; **by ~** allein
youth /ju:θ/ *n* (*pl* **youths** /-ð:z/) Jugend *f*; (*boy*) Jugendliche(r) *m*. **~ful** *adj* jugendlich. **~ hostel** *n* Jugendherberge *f*
Yugoslavia /ju:gə'slɑ:vɪə/ *n* Jugoslawien *nt*

Zz

zeal /zi:l/ *n* Eifer *m*
zealous /'zeləs/ *adj* eifrig
zebra /'zebrə/ *n* Zebra *nt*. **~ 'crossing** *n* Zebrastreifen *m*
zero /'zɪərəʊ/ *n* Null *f*
zest /zest/ *n* Begeisterung *f*
zigzag /'zɪgzæg/ *n* Zickzack *m* ● *vi* (*pt/pp* **-zagged**) im Zickzack laufen/ (*in vehicle*) fahren
zinc /zɪŋk/ *n* Zink *nt*
zip /zɪp/ *n* ~ **[fastener]** Reißverschluss *m* ● *vt* ~ **[up]** den Reißverschluss zuziehen an (+ *dat*)
'zip code *n* (*Amer*) Postleitzahl *f*
zipper /'zɪpə(r)/ *n* Reißverschluss *m*
zodiac /'zəʊdɪæk/ *n* Tierkreis *m*
zone /zəʊn/ *n* Zone *f*
zoo /zu:/ *n* Zoo *m*
zoological /zu:ə'lɒdʒɪkl/ *adj* zoologisch
zoolog|ist /zu:'ɒlədʒɪst/ *n* Zoologe *m*/-gin *f*. **~y** Zoologie *f*
zoom /zu:m/ *vi* sausen. **~ lens** *n* Zoomobjektiv *nt*

German irregular verbs

1st, 2nd, and 3rd person present are given after the infinitive, and past subjunctive after the past indicative, where there is a change of vowel or any other irregularity.

Compound verbs are only given if they do not take the same forms as the corresponding simple verb, e.g. *befehlen*, or if there is no corresponding simple verb, e.g. *bewegen*.

An asterisk (*) indicates a verb which is also conjugated regularly.

Infinitive	*Past tense*	*Past participle*
abwägen	wog (wöge) ab	abgewogen
ausbedingen	bedang (bedänge) aus	ausbedungen
backen (du bäckst, er bäckt)	backte (backte)	gebacken
befehlen (du befiehlst, er befiehlt)	befahl (befähle)	befohlen
beginnen	begann (begänne)	begonnen
beißen (du/er beißt)	biss (bisse)	gebissen
bergen (du birgst, er birgt)	barg (bärge)	geborgen
bewegen[2]	bewog (bewöge)	bewogen
biegen	bog (böge)	gebogen
bieten	bot (böte)	geboten
binden	band (bände)	gebunden
bitten	bat (bäte)	gebeten
blasen (du/er bläst)	blies	geblasen
bleiben	blieb	geblieben
braten (du brätst, er brät)	briet	gebraten
brechen (du brichst, er bricht)	brach (bräche)	gebrochen
brennen	brannte (brennte)	gebrannt
bringen	brachte (brächte)	gebracht
denken	dachte (dächte)	gedacht
dreschen (du drischst, er drischt)	drosch (drösche)	gedroschen
dringen	drang (dränge)	gedrungen
dürfen (ich/er darf, du darfst)	durfte (dürfte)	gedurft
empfehlen (du empfiehlst, er empfiehlt)	empfahl (empföhle)	empfohlen

Infinitive	*Past tense*	*Past participle*
erlöschen (du erlischst, er erlischt)	erlosch (erlösche)	erloschen
erschrecken* (du erschrickst, er erschrickt)	erschrak (erschäke)	erschrocken
erwägen	erwog (erwöge)	erwogen
essen (du/er isst)	aß (äße)	gegessen
fahren (du fährst, er fährt)	fuhr (führe)	gefahren
fallen (du fällst, er fällt)	fiel	gefallen
fangen (du fängst, er fängt)	fing	gefangen
fechten (du fichtst, er ficht)	focht (föchte)	gefochten
finden	fand (fände)	gefunden
flechten (du flichtst, er flicht)	flocht (flöchte)	geflochten
fliegen	flog (flöge)	geflogen
fliehen	floh (flöhe)	geflohen
fließen (du/er fließt)	floss (flösse)	geflossen
fressen (du/er frisst)	fraß (fräße)	gefressen
frieren	fror (fröre)	gefroren
gären*	gor (göre)	gegoren
gebären (du gebierst, sie gebiert)	gebar (gebäre)	geboren
geben (du gibst, er gibt)	gab (gäbe)	gegeben
gedeihen	gedieh	gediehen
gehen	ging	gegangen
gelingen	gelang (gelänge)	gelungen
gelten (du giltst, er gilt)	galt (gälte)	gegolten
genesen (du/er genest)	genas (genäse)	genesen
genießen (du/er genießt)	genoss (genösse)	genossen
geschehen (es geschieht)	geschah (geschähe)	geschehen
gewinnen	gewann (gewänne)	gewonnen
gießen (du/er gießt)	goss (gösse)	gegossen
gleichen	glich	geglichen
gleiten	glitt	geglitten
glimmen	glomm (glömme)	geglommen
graben (du gräbst, er gräbt)	grub (grübe)	gegraben
greifen	griff	gegriffen
haben (du hast, er hat)	hatte (hätte)	gehabt
halten (du hältst, er hält)	hielt	gehalten
hängen[2]	hing	gehangen
hauen	haute	gehauen
heben	hob (höbe)	gehoben
heißen (du/er heißt)	hieß	geheißen

Infinitive	*Past tense*	*Past participle*
helfen (du hilfst, er hilft)	half (hülfe)	geholfen
kennen	kannte (kennte)	gekannt
klingen	klang (klänge)	geklungen
kneifen	kniff	gekniffen
kommen	kam (käme)	gekommen
können (ich/er kann, du kannst)	konnte (könnte)	gekonnt
kriechen	kroch (kröche)	gekrochen
laden (du lädst, er lädt)	lud (lüde)	geladen
lassen (du/er lässt)	ließ	gelassen
laufen (du läufst, er läuft)	lief	gelaufen
leiden	litt	gelitten
leihen	lieh	geliehen
lesen (du/er liest)	las (läse)	gelesen
liegen	lag (läge)	gelegen
lügen	log (löge)	gelogen
mahlen	mahlte	gemahlen
meiden	mied	gemieden
melken	molk (mölke)	gemolken
messen (du/er misst)	maß (mäße)	gemessen
misslingen	misslang (misslänge)	misslungen
mögen (ich/er mag, du magst)	mochte (möchte)	gemocht
müssen (ich/er muss, du musst)	musste (müsste)	gemusst
nehmen (du nimmst, er nimmt)	nahm (nähme)	genommen
nennen	nannte (nennte)	genannt
pfeifen	pfiff	gepfiffen
preisen (du/er preist)	pries	gepriesen
raten (du rätst, er rät)	riet	geraten
reiben	rieb	gerieben
reißen (du/er reißt)	riss	gerissen
reiten	ritt	geritten
rennen	rannte (rennte)	gerannt
riechen	roch (röche)	gerochen
ringen	rang (ränge)	gerungen
rinnen	rann (ränne)	geronnen
rufen	rief	gerufen
salzen* (du/er salzt)	salzte	gesalzen
saufen (du säufst, er säuft)	soff (söffe)	gesoffen
saugen*	sog (söge)	gesogen
schaffen[1]	schuf (schüfe)	geschaffen
scheiden	schied	geschieden
scheinen	schien	geschienen

Infinitive	*Past tense*	*Past participle*
scheißen (du/er scheißt)	schiss	geschissen
schelten (du schiltst, er schilt)	schalt (schölte)	gescholten
scheren[1]	schor (schöre)	geschoren
schieben	schob (schöbe)	geschoben
schießen (du/er schießt)	schoss (schösse)	geschossen
schlafen (du schläfst, er schläft)	schlief	geschlafen
schlagen (du schlägst, er schlägt)	schlug (schlüge)	geschlagen
schleichen	schlich	geschlichen
schleifen[2]	schliff	geschliffen
schließen (du/er schießt)	schloss (schlösse)	geschlossen
schlingen	schlang (schlänge)	geschlungen
schmeißen (du/er schmeißt)	schmiss (schmisse)	geschmissen
schmelzen (du/er schmilzt)	schmolz (schmölze)	geschmolzen
schneiden	schnitt	geschnitten
schrecken* (du schrickst, er schrickt)	schrak (schräke)	geschreckt
schreiben	schrieb	geschrieben
schreien	schrie	geschrie[e]n
schreiten	schritt	geschritten
schweigen	schwieg	geschwiegen
schwellen (du schwillst, er schwillt)	schwoll (schwölle)	geschwollen
schwimmen	schwamm (schwömme)	geschwommen
schwinden	schwand (schwände)	geschwunden
schwingen	schwang (schwänge)	geschwungen
schwören	schwor (schwüre)	geschworen
sehen (du siehst, er sieht)	sah (sähe)	gesehen
sein (ich bin, du bist, er ist, wir sind, ihr seid, sie sind)	war (wäre)	gewesen
senden[1]	sandte (sendete)	gesandt
sieden	sott (sötte)	gesotten
singen	sang (sänge)	gesungen
sinken	sank (sänke)	gesunken
sitzen (du/er sitzt)	saß (säße)	gesessen
sollen (ich/er soll, du sollst)	sollte	gesollt
spalten*	spaltete	gespalten
spinnen	spann (spänne)	gesponnen
sprechen (du sprichst, er spricht)	sprach (spräche)	gesprochen
sprießen (du/er sprießt)	spross (sprösse)	gesprossen
springen	sprang (spränge)	gesprungen

Infinitive	*Past tense*	*Past participle*
stechen (du stichst, er sticht)	stach (stäche)	gestochen
stehen	stand (stünde, stände)	gestanden
stehlen (du stiehlst, er stiehlt)	stahl (stähle)	gestohlen
steigen	stieg	gestiegen
sterben (du stirbst, er stirbt)	starb (stürbe)	gestorben
stinken	stank (stänke)	gestunken
stoßen (du/er stößt)	stieß	gestoßen
streichen	strich	gestrichen
streiten	stritt	gestritten
tragen (du trägst, er trägt)	trug (trüge)	getragen
treffen (du triffst, er trifft)	traf (träfe)	getroffen
treiben	trieb	getrieben
treten (du trittst, er tritt)	trat (träte)	getreten
triefen*	troff (tröffe)	getroffen
trinken	trank (tränke)	getrunken
trügen	trog (tröge)	getrogen
tun (du tust, er tut)	tat (täte)	getan
verderben (du verdirbst, er verdirbt)	verdarb (verdürbe)	verdorben
vergessen (du/er vergisst)	vergaß (vergäße)	vergessen
verlieren	verlor (verlöre)	verloren
verzeihen	verzieh	verziehen
wachsen[1] (du/er wächst)	wuchs (wüchse)	gewachsen
waschen (du wäschst, er wäscht)	wusch (wüsche)	gewaschen
wenden[2]*	wandte (wendete)	gewandt
werben (du wirbst, er wirbt)	warb (würbe)	geworben
werden (du wirst, er wird)	wurde (würde)	geworden
werfen (du wirfst, er wirft)	warf (würfe)	geworfen
wiegen[1]	wog (wöge)	gewogen
winden	wand (wände)	gewunden
wissen (ich/er weiß, du weißt)	wusste (wüsste)	gewusst
wollen (ich/er will, du willst)	wollte	gewollt
wringen	wrang (wränge)	gewrungen
ziehen	zog (zöge)	gezogen
zwingen	zwang (zwänge)	gezwungen

Englische unregelmäßige Verben

Infinitiv	Präteritum	2. Partizip
be	was	been
bear	bore	borne
beat	beat	beaten
become	became	become
begin	began	begun
bend	bent	bent
bet	bet, betted	bet, betted
bid	bade, bid	bidden, bid
bind	bound	bound
bite	bit	bitten
bleed	bled	bled
blow	blew	blown
break	broke	broken
breed	bred	bred
bring	brought	brought
build	built	built
burn	burnt, burned	burnt, burned
burst	burst	burst
buy	bought	bought
catch	caught	caught
choose	chose	chosen
cling	clung	clung
come	came	come
cost	cost, costed (*vt*)	cost, costed
cut	cut	cut
deal	dealt	dealt
dig	dug	dug
do	did	done
draw	drew	drawn
dream	dreamt, dreamed	dreamt, dreamed
drink	drank	drunk

Infinitiv	Präteritum	2. Partizip
drive	drove	driven
eat	ate	eaten
fall	fell	fallen
feed	fed	fed
feel	felt	felt
fight	fought	fought
find	found	found
flee	fled	fled
fly	flew	flown
forecast	forecast, forecasted	forecast, forecasted
forget	forgot	forgotten, forgot *US*
freeze	froze	frozen
get	got	got, gotten *US*
give	gave	given
go	went	gone
grow	grew	grown
hang	hung, hanged	hung, hanged
have	had	had
hear	heard	heard
hide	hid	hidden
hit	hit	hit
hold	held	held
hurt	hurt	hurt
keep	kept	kept
kneel	knelt	knelt
know	knew	known
lay	laid	laid
lead	led	led
lean	leaned, leant	leaned, leant
leap	leaped, leapt	leaped, leapt

Infinitiv	*Präteritum*	*2. Partizip*
learn	learnt, learned	learnt, learned
leave	left	left
lend	lent	lent
let	let	let
lie	lay	lain
lose	lost	lost
make	made	made
mean	meant	meant
meet	met	met
pay	paid	paid
put	put	put
quit	quitted, quit	quitted, quit
read	read	read
ride	rode	ridden
ring	rang	rung
rise	rose	risen
run	ran	run
say	said	said
see	saw	seen
seek	sought	sought
sell	sold	sold
send	sent	sent
set	set	set
sew	sewed	sewn, sewed
shake	shook	shaken
shine	shone	shone
shoe	shod	shod
shoot	shot	shot
show	showed	shown
shut	shut	shut
sing	sang	sung
sink	sank	sunk
sit	sat	sat
sleep	slept	slept
sling	slung	slung

Infinitiv	*Präteritum*	*2. Partizip*
smell	smelt, smelled	smelt, smelled
speak	spoke	spoken
spell	spelled, spelt	spelled, spelt
spend	spent	spent
spit	spat	spat
spoil	spoilt, spoiled	spoilt, spoiled
spread	spread	spread
spring	sprang	sprung
stand	stood	stood
steal	stole	stolen
stick	stuck	stuck
sting	stung	stung
stride	strode	stridden
strike	struck	struck
swear	swore	sworn
sweep	swept	swept
swell	swelled	swollen, swelled
swim	swam	swum
swing	swung	swung
take	took	taken
teach	taught	taught
tear	tore	torn
tell	told	told
think	thought	thought
throw	threw	thrown
thrust	thrust	thrust
tread	trod	trodden
under-stand	under-stood	understood
wake	woke	woken
wear	wore	worn
win	won	won
write	wrote	written

Abbreviations/Abkürzungen

adjective	*adj*	Adjektiv
abbreviation	*abbr*	Abkürzung
accusative	*acc*	Akkusativ
Administration	*Admin*	Administration
adverb	*adv*	Adverb
American	*Amer*	amerikanisch
Anatomy	*Anat*	Anatomie
attributive	*attrib*	attributiv
Austrian	*Aust*	österreichisch
Motor vehicles	*Auto*	Automobil
Aviation	*Aviat*	Luftfahrt
Botany	*Bot*	Botanik
collective	*coll*	Kollektivum
Commerce	*Comm*	Handel
conjunction	*conj*	Konjunktion
Cookery	*Culin*	Kochkunst
dative	*dat*	Dativ
definite article	*def art*	bestimmter Artikel
demonstrative	*dem*	Demonstrativ-
Electricity	*Electr*	Elektrizität
something	*etw*	etwas
feminine	*f*	Femininum
figurative	*fig*	figurativ
genitive	*gen*	Genitiv
Geography	*Geog*	Geographie
Grammar	*Gram*	Grammatik
impersonal	*impers*	unpersönlich
inseparable	*insep*	untrennbar
interjection	*int*	Interjektion
invariable	*inv*	unveränderlich
someone	*jd*	jemand
someone (dat)	*jdm*	jemandem
someone (acc)	*jdn*	jemanden
someone's	*jds*	jemandes
Law	*Jur*	Jura
Language	*Lang*	Sprache
masculine	*m*	Maskulinum